NATURAL SCIENCES IN AMERICA

NATURAL SCIENCES IN AMERICA

Advisory Editor
KEIR B. STERLING

Editorial Board
EDWIN H. COLBERT
EDWARD GRUSON
ERNST MAYR
RICHARD G. VAN GELDER

CATALOGUE

OF THE

EDWARD E. AYER

ORNITHOLOGICAL LIBRARY

BY

JOHN TODD ZIMMER

ARNO PRESS
A New York Times Company
New York, N. Y. • 1974

Reprint Edition 1974 by Arno Press Inc.

Reprinted from a copy in the University
   of Illinois Library

NATURAL SCIENCES IN AMERICA
ISBN for complete set: 0-405-05700-8
See last pages of this volume for titles.

Manufactured in the United States of America

———◆———

Library of Congress Cataloging in Publication Data

Field Museum of Natural History, Chicago. Edward E.
   Ayer Ornithological Library.
   Catalogue of the Edward E. Ayer Ornithological
Library.

   (Natural sciences in America)
   Reprint of the 1926 ed. published by the Field
Museum of Natural History, Chicago as its Publication
239-240, zoological series, v. 16.
   1. Birds--Bibliography. 2. Birds--Bibliography--
Catalogs. 3. Field museum of natural history, Chicago.
Edward E. Ayer ornithological library. I. Zimmer,
John Todd, 1889-1957. II. Title. III. Series:
Field Museum of Natural History, Chicago. Publication
239-240.
Z5335.F45 1974   016.5982   73-17850
ISBN 0-405-05773-3

FIELD MUSEUM OF NATURAL HISTORY

PUBLICATION 239

ZOOLOGICAL SERIES   VOL. XVI

CATALOGUE

OF THE

EDWARD E. AYER

ORNITHOLOGICAL LIBRARY

PART I

BY

JOHN TODD ZIMMER

Assistant Curator of Birds

WILFRED H. OSGOOD
Curator, Department of Zoology
EDITOR

CHICAGO, U. S. A.

November, 1926

PRINTED IN THE UNITED STATES OF AMERICA
BY FIELD MUSEUM PRESS

HISTORICAL PREFACE

The ornithological library of the Field Museum of Natural History has been dedicated to Mr. Edward E. Ayer with more than usual reason. This library is not the result of any single gift of money nor of periodic gifts made perfunctorily as mere philanthropy. It is, rather, the culmination of a growth which began with a young boy's contact with raw nature in pioneer times, which was supported later by hard cash wrested from the opportunities of those times, and which was nurtured through many years by the personal devotion of a man of remarkable character. In fact, Mr. Ayer's interest in and relation to the library are bound up with the history of his life. The same might be said of other collections made by him, but no attempt at an account of any of them could be made without recognizing it.

Born at Kenosha, Wisconsin in 1841, Edward Ayer as a small boy went with his parents to a prairie farm in northern Illinois, a few miles from the present town of Harvard. His father, Elbridge Gerry Ayer, a native of Haverhill, Massachusetts, opened a small crossroads store there, and the place came to be known as "Ayer's Corners." Familiarity with the birds and other wild life of the region was naturally a part of the young boy's daily life and, like others of those times, he was privileged to have many experiences that are denied to the present generation. To this day, it is one of his delights to stand on the old ground and point out the spot where, as a stripling, he stood and witnessed one of the historic flights of the now extinct Passenger Pigeon, one of the really great flights in which the birds passed in clouds for hours and hours, literally darkening the sky. Such boyhood impressions doubtless assisted in kindling his interest in birds and in books about them during his later life. This interest was also fostered by a great, almost reverential sentiment toward things of the past which is one of his strongest characteristics. This sentiment, in its application to birds, takes the form of a sort of loyalty as to an old friend or neighbor.

In 1856, Mr. Ayer's father laid out the town of Harvard, Illinois and in 1860 he was the proprietor of a hotel there as well as being largely interested in nearby farming property. His eighteen-year-old son was serving as night clerk in the hotel and also carried such further responsibilities as rounding up strayed cattle when occasion demanded. While engaged in this latter occupation, in April 1860, he encountered a local party starting to cross the plains to California. His adventurous spirit was fired and, having obtained his parent's permission, he joined another train of wagons a few days later to make the long overland journey.

iii

Needless to say, he was close to nature all the way. There was much hard work combined with many interesting experiences, including several slight brushes with Indians, but owing to the season or to the nature of the route, no herds of buffalo were seen, this being a matter of great regret often expressed in later years by Mr. Ayer. He left the wagon train in Nevada and went to work shovelling quartz in a mine near Silver City. This provided money to take him to San Francisco where he found friends and obtained employment sawing wood with a buck-saw in a lumberyard.

It was only a short time after this that the Civil War broke out, and the first volunteer to be sworn in for California was Edward E. Ayer, this distinction being partly due to the initial letter of his name but also indicating that he lost no time in deciding where his duty lay. He was made a corporal at once and for the next three years was in service in southern California, Arizona, and New Mexico. During this time, while detailed in charge of a guard over a mine some sixty miles southwest of Tucson, Arizona, he spent some of the long hours reading a book which chance had thrown his way and which made a profound impression upon him. It was Prescott's "Conquest of Mexico" and, after reading it twice from cover to cover, the young corporal was filled with an enthusiasm for the romance and a respect for the deeds of early American history which have remained with him to the present day. In some privately circulated reminiscences, he said recently: "I want to reiterate that the finding of Prescott's 'Conquest of Mexico' in that mine in Arizona in '62 has been responsible and is to be credited as the principal force that has given me a vast amount of enjoyment in this world, and is absolutely responsible for the 'Ayer Library' now in the Newberry." After he had left the army and trekked back to his home in Harvard, Illinois, one of his first acts was the purchase in Chicago of Prescott's works on Mexico and Peru. The price was $17.50 and the dealer who offered it was so impressed with his character and sincerity that he allowed him to take it home for an initial payment of $3.50 and the promise of $3.50 monthly, the only terms possible for him at the time.

The four years of the western trip and the army service had been crowded with experiences that furnished the young man's main preparation for life. His college campus was the covered wagon trail and his fraternity brothers were the rough and ready pioneers of the far west. With this background, it would scarcely have been predicted that he would spend the latter half of his life as a patron of art and science, as a bibliophile, and as an ardent collector.

In his twenty-third year, Mr. Ayer began his business career, at first with his father in Harvard, but soon moving to Chicago where he developed a general railroad contracting business. During the next fifteen years his success was rapid and the foundation of an independent fortune was laid, principally through contracts with western railroads to which he furnished ties, telegraph poles, and lumber much of which came from a mill which he built and operated at Flagstaff, Arizona. In 1865, he was married to Emily Augusta Burbank of Lawrence, Massachusetts, who for sixty-one years has been his constant companion, sympathetic and inspiring in all his many activities.

Although Chicago was his headquarters, his business kept him in the west much of the time and there was much traveling connected with it, including long horseback trips in Mexico and in various western states. His contact with wild nature was close and almost constant. The birds and the beasts grew in his affections and he developed an especial interest in and sympathy for the American Indian. He was quick to see that primitive conditions were soon to pass, and in 1871 he began the formation of a collection of ethnological material illustrating the life and customs of the Indian. This was kept for some years in an outbuilding on his summer place at Lake Geneva, Wisconsin where it grew to an importance and value scarcely anticipated even by its owner. When the Field Museum was founded in 1893, this invaluable collection was presented to it, being perhaps the outstanding one of numerous gifts to the Museum by Mr. Ayer. Coincident with the Indian collection, he began his great library of Americana which is now in the Newberry Library of Chicago and on which he spent not less than forty thousand dollars per year for a long period, making it one of the finest, if not the very finest library of the kind in existence and having a present estimated value of over two million dollars.

In the early eighties, one of Mr. Ayer's recreations was duck shooting in the Mississippi Valley and no season passed without seeing him in the field, not only near home but elsewhere, from Minnesota to southern Illinois. This brought his attention to birds more especially than formerly and he began buying a few of the more important books about them. These included Audubon's "Birds of America" and other large illustrated works which were added to from time to time until he had in his own home a considerable collection of choice ornithological books. This, then, was the nucleus of the important library which afterward developed.

After the World's Columbian Exposition in 1893, Mr. Ayer was the leader of the small group of far-seeing men who took an active part in founding the Field Museum. In fact, he became the first president of its board of trustees and, although he retired from this heavily responsible office in 1899, he has continued to serve with unceasing interest in the welfare of the Museum, as a member of the board until the present time.

Among his first acts, after the organization of the Museum, was the presentation to it of his library of ornithological books. Thereafter he provided funds for additions to it, especially in the purchase of books sumptuously bound and profusely illustrated with colored plates. Probably the literature of no other branch of science includes so many such books as does that of ornithology, and their cost is usually prohibitive for all except the largest and finest libraries. It has been the unique history of this library, therefore, that the most expensive books have been the ones first acquired.

While housed in the old Fine Arts Building of the World's Fair, which was occupied by the Museum until 1920, the "Ayer Ornithological Library" was on public view in a room adjoining the general library which was also used as reading room. The richly bound volumes of folio size, which then formed a conspicuous part of it, will be recalled by many of the visitors to the Museum in those days. After removal to the Museum's present building, this library was merged with other ornithological books belonging to the Museum and the whole designated as the "Ayer Library." Meanwhile Mr. Ayer had presented the valuable Clarke collection of books on angling and ichthyology which occupied another section of the zoological library.

Since effort had been especially directed to the acquisition of books illustrated in color, the proportion of such books in the library was very large and it was found that the literature of ornithology was not comprehensively covered. With generous support from Mr. Ayer, this deficiency has been largely overcome during the past five years. The preparation of the catalogue has made it possible to prepare lists of desiderata and, in general, has greatly stimulated the growth of the library. Books have been added rapidly and continuously and, as the catalogue goes to press, it is evident that additions in the future will consist mainly of scarce items and of such new books on the subject as may appear. Mr. Ayer's interest and personal attention have never flagged. He has been a constant visitor to the library during its recent growth, consulting as to sources of purchase and examining accessions as received. At the age of eighty-five, his vigor and enthusiasm are the envy of many younger men, and it is to be hoped that years of activity may still be his. Born collector that he is, however, he thinks of his collections rather than himself and has provided a substantial bequest to the Museum for the continuance and growth of its library.

WILFRED H. OSGOOD

Curator of Zoology

AUTHOR'S PREFACE

Before entering into a discussion of the plan of the following catalogue, I wish to acknowledge the assistance of a number of people who have contributed, in one way and another, to the work. First, I wish to thank Mr. Edward E. Ayer for the opportunity of preparing the catalogue and for the invaluable privilege of adding any books to the library which were (and are) desirable and procurable. To Dr. Wilfred H. Osgood, Curator of Zoology, I am indebted for unlimited departmental facilities for pursuing the bibliographic investigations. To Dr. Charles E. Hellmayr, Associate Curator of Birds, I am grateful for generous freedom of access to manuscript notes and an unwritten fund of information respecting ornithological literature. From Drs. C. W. Richmond and H. C. Oberholser of Washington, D. C., Glover M. Allen of Boston, and A. Laubmann of Munich, I have received important notes respecting certain publications which are acknowledged in their places. Further acknowledgments are due to Mr. W. J. Gerhard, Associate Curator of Insects, and Miss Elsie Lippincott and Mrs. Emily M. Wilcoxson, Librarian and Assistant Librarian, respectively, for many courtesies and suggestions offered during the course of the work.

The catalogue makes no pretense of being a complete bibliography of ornithological works, nor does it contain a list of all the literature on the subject of birds which is available at Field Museum of Natural History. It includes the splendid collection of books dealing wholly or in part with birds which has been presented to Field Museum by Mr. Ayer, and all other works in the library of the museum which are entirely ornithological; general works not presented by Mr. Ayer are not included although they may contain more or less bird matter.

The catalogue is still further restricted (almost completely) to books and papers which stand apart so as to require citation by title, or which form parts of such publications, and omits numbered bulletins, circulars, reports, etc., and extracts from periodicals and serials; exceptions are made in the case of some of the more important papers dealing with the bird life of the entire United States or of the separate states within it. Author's reprints, sometimes repaged or retitled, which have been revised before reprinting (as have many of C. L. Bonaparte's writings, for example) are included as distinct works. A simple list of periodicals and dictionaries of natural history in the Edward E. Ayer Library is appended.

A departure from ordinary practices has been made with regard to the order of arrangement of titles. All the contributions of each author are listed in chronological sequence regardless of single or joint authorship. In cases of divided authorship, the book is discussed under the name of the senior author while cross-references are given under the various junior authors. Contributors, who have supplied chapters or sections of ornithological text in the works of other writers, are listed (in parentheses) under the senior author of the book in question, to which cross-references are given under the name of each contributor. Where possible, each cross-reference is filed under the dates of publication of the actual contribution, which may or may not be coextensive with the dates of the complete work.

Each title is transcribed line by line (with the various lines of the original title-pages separated by vertical dashes), except that long lists of publications or honorary titles have been curtailed and noted instead (in brackets) as, "[*etc., 7 lines.*]." Quotations, figures, vignettes, blazons, trade-marks, etc., are similarly noted. All such explanatory matter is printed in italics to distinguish it from lettering which is copied verbatim from the title-pages and which is printed in ordinary type. Horizontal, ruled lines are not transcribed or noted. Bold-faced type is used to segregate a distinctive "short title" from the mass of lettering in the transcriptions.

When the work under review occupies more than one volume, the first title is used as a standard. This is transcribed like the title of a single volume while the changes which occur from line to line in succeeding numbers are noted or transcribed (in brackets) with an indication (where necessary) of the volume in which the changes appear; the differentiae of the various volumes, where they occur within the same brackets, are separated by semicolons. For example: "With five [four (*Vol. II.*); three (*Vol. III.*)] colored plates. [*Line omitted* (*Vol. IV.*).]|."

If the transcription has been made from outside sources in the absence of an available original title-page, the entire title is enclosed in braces or brackets. If the book is without any published title, a descriptive one has been created. In the "Willughby Society" reprints, etc., the original title is placed in brackets following the title of the reissue. Occasionally, brackets have been transcribed intact from the title-pages, but these cases are usually recognizable.

The sign > (greater than), as used here, separates a title from a following subtitle. It is also used before a subtitle or subordinate title if the full title is not given, or before the full title if the volume quoted is not the first in a series to which it belongs.

The sign < (less than), separates the title of a contribution from the title of the complete work or periodical in which it appeared.

The sizes of the various books are calculated according to the actual number of folds made in the original sheets, modified as shown in the following scale quoted from The Century Dictionary:

Double elephant	27 x40	royal 4to	10 x13
elephant	22 x27	medium 4to	9 x12
antiquarian folio	26½x31	foliopost 4to	8½x11
double elephant folio	20 x27	demy 4to	8 x10½
columbier folio	17¼x24	cap 4to	7 x 8½
atlas folio	16½x26	imperial 8vo	8 x11½
elephant folio	14 x23	superroyal 8vo	7 x11
imperial folio	16 x22	royal 8vo	6½x10
superroyal folio	14 x22	8vo	6 x 9½
royal folio	12½x20	post 8vo	5½x 8½
medium folio	12 x19	demy 8vo	5¼x 8
demy folio	10½x16	crown 8vo	5 x 7½
crown folio	9½x15	cap 8vo	4¼x 7
flatcap folio	8½x14	12mo, about	5⅛x 7
foolscap folio	8 x12½	16mo, about	4½x 6
post folio	7½x12½	18mo	
imperial 4to	11 x14½	32mo	

For the sake of brevity, the titles of several important bibliographies have been omitted in numerous references throughout the following pages. These are as follows:

Carus and Engelmann = Bibliotheca Historico-Naturalis, Leipzig, 1846.

Coues = [Ornithological Bibliography]. Cf. infra, Coues, Elliott, 1878-80.

Engelmann = Bibliotheca Zoologica, Leipzig, 1861.

Mullens and Swann = A Bibliography of British Ornithology, London, 1916-17. Cf. infra.

Taschenberg = Bibliotheca Zoologica II, Leipzig, 1887-1899.

The following are the abbreviations and signs used in the catalogue:

Add.	addenda	corrig.	corrigenda
advt.	advertisement, or advertising matter	dat.	dated
ante, antea	before	ded.	dedication
cf. (confer)	compare	dir., direct.	directions
chromolith.	chromolithograph	ed.	editor, or editorial; also edition
circa	about	engr.	engraved
col.	colored	expl.	explanation
concl.	conclusion, or concluded	fig.	figure
conts.	contents, or list of contents	fold.	folded (or doubled)
		footn.	footnote
		frontisp.	frontispiece

half-tit.........	half-title
idem...........	the same
illum..........	illuminated
incl...........	included, or including
insert.........	inserted
introd.........	introduction, or introductory
l. (ll.)..........	leaf (leaves)
l.c. (locus citatus)......	place cited
Lief...........	Lieferung (Lieferungen)
livr...........	livraison
monochr........	monochrome
num...........	numbered
ornith.........	ornithological
p. (pp.)........	page (pages)
par............	paragraph
photogr.........	photograph
photograv......	photogravure
pl. (pll.)........	plate (plates)
portr..........	portrait
post...........	after
pr.l. (ll.).......	preliminary leaf (leaves)
pref...........	preface
pt.............	part
publ..........	published, or publisher
quot..........	quotation, or quoted
q.v. (quod vide)..	which see
rev............	reviewed, or reviewed in
sec............	section
ser............	series
sign..........	signature
sp. (spp.).......	species
subscrs.........	subscribers, or list of subscribers
subtit..........	subtitle
suppl..........	supplement, or supplementary
text-fig.........	text-figure
tit............	title, or title-page
unnum.........	unnumbered
vol............	volume

JOHN T. ZIMMER

Assistant Curator of Birds

FIELD MUSEUM OF NATURAL HISTORY
March 15, 1926

CATALOGUE

OF THE

EDWARD E. AYER

ORNITHOLOGICAL LIBRARY

PART I

Edward E. Ayer

CATALOGUE

OF THE

EDWARD E. AYER

ORNITHOLOGICAL LIBRARY

PART I

BY

JOHN T. ZIMMER

Abbott, Charles C.

1887. A naturalist's | rambles about home | by | Charles C. Abbott |
Second edition, revised | New York | D. Appleton and Company |
1887.

1 vol. crown 8vo, tit., pp. 1-485, 2 ll. (advt.). New York.

A series of popular essays on natural history based on the author's observations
in the vicinity of Trenton, New Jersey. Many of the chapters and notes relate
to birds and the portion of the appendix on pp. 451-475 contains an annotated
list of the birds of Mercer County, N. J. The original edition, published in
1884, was severely criticised in parts (Cf. Auk **2**, pp. 86-88, 1885) and in the
present edition some of its statements have been modified, although others
still remain open to question.

Adams, Andrew Leith.

1873. Field and Forest Rambles, | with notes and observations | on
the | natural history of eastern Canada. | By | A. Leith Adams,
M.A., M.B., F.R.S., F.G.S., | Staff Surgeon-Major. | Author of
[*etc., 2 lines.*] | [*Vignette.*] | The Ruby-throated Humming-bird. |
London: | Henry S. King & Co., | 65, Cornhill, & 12, Paternoster
Row. | 1873.

1 vol. post 8vo, pp. I-XVI, 1-333, 1 l.+pp. 1-32 (advt.), 4 pll. (1 fold.,
col.), 26 text-figs., tit.-vignette (by Gould). London.

Field studies and observations on the natural history, especially zoology and
geology, of New Brunswick, Canada. Aside from miscellaneous references elsewhere, ornithological matter is contained in Pt. II (pp. 117-195), Chapter XII
(pp. 285-294) and the appendix (pp. 296-302), comprising, respectively, special
chapters on bird life, a "Naturalist's Calendar" for the region, and a list of
the birds of New Brunswick. The only ornithological illustration is the title-
vignette by John Gould. Page 198 is wrongly numbered 174.

1

Adams, Henry B.

1874. See Adams, Henry Gardiner; and Adams, H B., **The Smaller British Birds.**

Adams, Henry Gardiner.

1853. See Bechstein, Johann Matthäus, **Cage and Chamber-Birds.**

Adams, Henry Gardiner. (Webber, C. W.)

1856. **Humming Birds** | Described and Illustrated | by H. G. Adams, | Author of "Nests and Eggs of Familiar Birds" [*etc.*, *2 lines.*] | with eight coloured plates. | London: | Groombridge and Sons, | 5, Paternoster Row.

1 vol. crown 8vo, 2 pr. ll. (tit. and index), pp. 1-144, pll. I-VIII (col.), figs. 1-6, 1 tailpiece. London.

A general, popular account of the family of Hummingbirds. On pp. 109-144 is found "My Humming Birds" by C. W. Webber; to this, all of the plates belong.

Adams, Henry Gardiner.

1871. **Nests and eggs** | of | familiar birds | Described and Illustrated | with an account of the | haunts and habits of the feathered architects, | and their times and modes of building. | By H. G. Adams, | author of [*etc.*, *2 lines.*] | illustrated with | sixteen coloured plates | London: | Groombridge and Sons, | 5, Paternoster Row. | 1871.

1 vol. crown 8vo, tit., pp. 1-238, pll. 1-16 (col.; 86 figs.). London.

Title self-explanatory. The book is intended for juvenile readers.

Adams, Henry Gardiner; and Adams, Henry B.

1874. **The** | **smaller** | **British Birds.** | With | descriptions of their nests, eggs, habits, | etc., etc., etc. | by | H. G. and H. B. Adams. | Illustrated with coloured plates of birds and eggs. | London: | George Bell and sons, York Street, Covent Garden. | M DCCC LXXIV.

1 vol. royal 8vo, pp. I-IV, 1-252, 32 pll. (col.). London.

A popular discussion of the appearance and habits of the smaller forms of British birds. Another edition was issued in 1894.

Adams, Henry Gardiner.

1900. See Bechstein, Johann Matthäus, **Cage and Chamber-Birds.**

Adams, William Henry Davenport.

1870. See Michelet, Jules, **The Bird.**

1874. Idem.

Adams, William Henry Davenport.

1885.   The bird world | Described with Pen and Pencil. | By | W. H. Davenport Adams, | author of "The Mediterranean Illustrated," "The Arctic World," etc. | and H. Giacomelli, | illustrator of "The Bird," by Michelet, "The Insect," etc. | [*Vignette.*] | London: Thomas Nelson and Sons. | Edinburgh and New York. | 1885.

1 vol. royal 8vo, pp. I-XII, 13-464, 51 pll. (on num. pp.), 99 text-figs.   Edinburgh and New York.

Sketches of bird-life whose "object is to gossip pleasantly about birds distinguished by the possession of some special character,—introducing, where appropriate, the descriptions of travellers, or the fancies of poets, or the associations of history and romance." The text is by Adams; the illustrations are by Giacomelli.

Albin, Eleazar.

1737.   A | **Natural History** | of | **English Song-Birds,** | And such of the Foreign as are usually | brought over and esteemed for their | Singing. | To which are added, | Figures of the Cock, Hen and Egg, of | each Species, exactly copied from Na- | ture; by Mr. Eleazar Albin: And cu- | riously Engraven on Copper. | London: | Printed and sold by A. Bettesworth and C. | Hitch in Pater-noster-Row; and S. Birt in | Ave-Mary-Lane, 1737.

1 vol. 12mo, 2 pr. ll. (tit. and pref.), pp. 1-97+3 pp. (index), frontisp., 23 pll.   London.

The original edition of this work, of which there were at least five editions and one anonymous piracy.

Albin, Eleazar.

1738.   A | **Natural History** | of | **Birds** | Illustrated | With Two Hundred and Five Copper Plates, | Curiously Engraven from the Life. | And exactly colour'd by the Author, | Eleazar Albin. | To which are added, | Notes and Observations by W. Derham, D.D. | Fellow of the Royal Society. | In two volumes. | Vol. I [II] | London: | Printed for W. Innys and R. Manby, Printers to the Royal Society, at the | West-End of St. Paul's.   M DCCXX XVIII.

2 vols. medium 4to, Vol. I, 4 pr.ll. (tit., list of subscrs., etc.) pp. 1-96+ 4 pp. (addenda, errata and index), pll. 1-101 (col.). Vol. II, 4 pr. ll. (tit., ded., pref. and list of subscrs.), pp 1-92+2 pp. (index), pll. 1-104 (col.).   London.

Descriptions of a variety of birds which are figured on the plates. A third volume was issued in 1740 as a supplement to this work under the title of "A Supplement to the Natural History of Birds" (q.v.).

Albin, Eleazar.

1740.   A | Supplement | to the | Natural History | of |Birds. |Illus-
trated | With a Hundred and One Copper Plates, | Curiously
Engraven from the Life; | And Exactly Colour'd by the Author, |
Eleazar Albin. | Being the Third and Last Volume. | London: |
Printed for W. Innys and R. Manby, Printers to the Royal Society,
at | the West-End of St. Paul's. | MDCCXL.

1 vol. medium 4to, 4 pr. ll. (tit., ded., etc.), pp. 1-95+1 (index), pll.
1-101 (col.). London.

Supplementary volume to the author's "A Natural History of Birds," 1738 (q.v.).

Alferakī, Serghyeī Nīkolaevīch.

See Alphéraky, Sergius.

Allen, Arthur A.

1922.   See Gault, Benjamin T., **Check List of the Birds of Illinois.**

Allen, Glover Morrill.

1901.   See Howe and Allen, **The Birds of Massachusetts.**

Allen, Glover Morrill.

1903.   A list of the birds | of | New Hampshire. | By | Glover M.
Allen. | From the Proceedings of the Manchester In- | stitute of
Arts and Sciences, | Vol. IV, 1902. | Manchester, N. H. | Nature
Study Press. | 1903.

1 vol. 8vo, tit., pp. 21-222. Manchester.

A catalogue of the birds recorded from New Hampshire, with notes on distribution,
records, dates of occurrence, etc. A bibliography and a general account of the
topography and faunal areas of the state are added.

Allen, Glover Morrill.

1925.   Birds and their | attributes | by | Glover Morrill Allen, Ph.D. |
[*Design.*] | Marshall Jones Company | Boston, Massachusetts.

1 vol. 8vo, pp. I-XIII+1, 1-338, frontisp. (col.; by F. W. Benson), 33
pll., text-figs. 1-5 and I-VI. Boston. 1925 (circa September).

"An introduction to a general survey of Birds, their structure, their habits and
their relations to ourselves." An excellent summary of the most recent information on the subject.

Allen, Joel Asaph.

1886.   A Revised List of the Birds of Massachusetts. <Bull. Amer.
Mus. Nat. Hist., 1, (Bull. 7), Art. XV, pp. 221-271, July 1886.

An annotated list of species recorded from the state, being a revision of the earlier
lists published in the Proc. Essex Inst., 4, No. 2, pp. 48-98, July 1864, and Bull.
Essex Inst., 10, pp. 3-37, 1878.

Allen, Joel Asaph.

1886. See American Ornithologists' Union, **The Code of Nomenclature and Check-List of North American Birds.**

Allen, Joel Asaph.

1889. See American Ornithologists' Union, **Check-List of North American Birds, Abridged Edition.**

Allen, Joel Asaph.

1889. See American Ornithologists' Union, **Supplement to the Code of Nomenclature and Check-list.**

Allen, Joel Asaph.

1891. **The American Ornithologists' Union | a seven years' retrospect** | An address delivered by the retiring | president at the Eighth Congress | of the Union, Nov. 19, 1890 | by | J. A. Allen | Published by order of the Union | New York | January, 1891.

1 vol. 8vo, tit., pp. 1-19, (orig. wrapper). New York. January 1891.

A general survey of the inception, growth and activities of the American Ornithologists' Union to date.

Allen, Joel Asaph.

1892. See American Ornithologists' Union, **The Code of Nomenclature.**

Allen, Joel Asaph.

1895. See American Ornithologists' Union, **Check-list of North American Birds, Second Edition.**

Allen, Joel Asaph.

1896. See Worlds Congress on Ornithology, **Papers presented to the—.**

Allen, Joel Asaph.

1910. See American Ornithologists' Union, **Check-list of North American Birds, Third Edition.**

Alphéraky, Sergius. [=Alferakī, Serghyeĭ Nīkolaevīch.]

1900. **Utkī Rosīī** | S. Alferakī | Pochetnagho chlena Russkagho Éntomologhicheskagho Obshchestra [etc., *3 lines*]. | S.-Peterburgh'. | Līto-Tīpoghrafiya A. É. Myunstera. Vas Ostr. Bol'sh. prosp. No. 63. | 1900.

2 pts. (in orig. covers) superroyal 8vo. Pt. I, 3 pr. ll. (half-tit., tit.

and ded.), pp. I-XXXIV, 1-64, 1. l. (subtit. to atlas), pll. I-VIII (col.). Pt. II, pp. 65-144, pll. IX-XVI (col.). St. Petersburg.

A monograph of the ducks of Russia. The work is incomplete, as represented here, reaching as far as *Nyroca nyroca* in the text and pl. XVI in the atlas, but I am unable to ascertain if it is complete as published. The only reference to it which I can find in literature is in the introduction to the author's "The Geese of Europe and Asia," 1905 (q.v.).

Alphéraky, Sergius [=Alferakī, Serghyeĭ Nĭkolaevĭch] (Göbel, C. F. Buturlin, Sergius Aleksandrovĭch).

1905. The Geese of Europe | and Asia | being the description of most of the old world species | by | Sergius Alphéraky | Corresponding Member [*etc.*, *3 lines.*] | with | twenty-four coloured plates by F. W. Frohawk | F.E.S., M.B.O.U. | and | frontispiece by Dr; P. P. Sushkin | London: Rowland Ward, Ltd. | "The Jungle," Piccadilly | MCMV.

1 vol. royal 4to, pp. I-X, 1-198, frontisp. (col.; by P. P. Sushkin), 24 pll. (col.; by Frohawk) London.

A monograph of Palaearctic geese. The work was published in Russian the preceding year. Appendix I, pp. 185-190, contains an account of the eggs of Russian geese by Göbel. Appendix II, pp. 191-195, is an extract from the diary of a visit to Kolguev in 1902 by Buturlin.

American Ornithologists' Union. (Allen, J. A.; Brewster, William; Coues, Elliott; Henshaw, Henry W.; Ridgway, Robert.)

1886. The code of nomenclature | and | check-list | of | North American Birds | Adopted by the American Ornithologists' Union | being the report of the committee of the | Union on classification and | nomenclature | Zoological Nomenclature is | a means, not an end, of Zoological Science | New York | American Ornithologists' Union | 1886.

1 vol. 8vo, pp. I-VIII, 1-392. New York.

A check-list of the species and subspecies of North American birds prepared by a committee of the American Ornithologists' Union appointed for the purpose. Original references are cited for generic, subgeneric, specific and subspecific names and for accepted combinations, and the types of the genera and subgenera are indicated. References are given (by number) to the check-lists of Baird—1858, Coues—1873, Ridgway—1880, and Coues—1882, and the geographical distribution of each form is noted. This check-list occupies pp. 72-367, being preceded by a code of nomenclature drawn up by the committee for their own guidance in the preparation of the check-list.

The "Code of Nomenclature" was reprinted separately in 1892 (q.v.), while the "Check-list" passed through several editions and is still in course of revision (Cf. "Abridged Ed.," 1889; "Second Ed.," 1895; "Third Ed.," 1910). The "Supplement" to the first edition was issued in book form 1889 (q.v.); later ones appeared in the pages of the Auk.

American Ornithologists' Union.

1887. **American Ornithologists' | Union | By-Laws and Rules | and | List of Members |** December, 1887 | New York | L. S. Foster, 35 Pine Street.

1 vol. 8vo, tit., pp. 1-20. New York. December 1887.

Title self-explanatory. Another edition was published in 1902 (q.v.).

American Ornithologists' Union. (Allen, J. A.; Brewster, William; Coues, Elliott; Merriam, C. Hart; Ridgway, Robert.).

1889. **Check-list | of | North American Birds |** According to the Canons of Nomenclature | of the | American Ornithologists' Union | **Abridged edition |** revised | Published by the American Ornithologists' Union | 1889.

1 vol. 8vo, pp. 1-4, 5-71 (on one side of paper, only). Washington.

A revised edition (but not the Second Edition, so called) of the A. O. U. Check-list of North American birds, embodying the changes which were indicated the same year in the Society's "Supplement to the Code of Nomenclature" (q.v.). The first edition was published in 1886 (q.v.) in combination with the Society's "Code of Nomenclature" which was republished separately in 1892 (q.v.). Second and third editions of the Check-list were published in 1895 and 1910 (q.v.). The present edition contains only the scientific and common names of the species with references, by number, to the check-lists of Baird—1858, Coues—1873, Ridgway—1880, and Coues—1882.

American Ornithologists' Union. (Allen, J. A.; Brewster, William; Coues, Elliott; Merriam, C. Hart; Ridgway, Robert.).

1889. **Supplement | to the | Code of Nomenclature and Check-list | of | North American Birds |** Adopted by the American Ornithologists' Union | prepared by | a committee of the Union | New York | American Ornithologists' Union | 1889.

1 vol. 8vo, pp. I-IV, 5-23. New York.

Additions, eliminations and changes of nomenclature affecting the first edition of the A. O. U. Check-list, 1886 (q.v.), as embodied in the "Abridged Edition" of the current year (q.v.).

American Ornithologists' Union. (Allen, J. A.; Brewster, William; Coues, Elliott; Henshaw, Henry W.; Ridgway, Robert.)

1892. **The | Code of Nomenclature | adopted by the | American Ornithologists' Union |** Zoölogical Nomenclature is a means, not an end, of Zoölogical Science | New York | American Ornithologists' Union | 1892.

1 vol. post 8vo, tit., pp. I-IV, 1 l. (conts.), pp. 1-72. New York.

Printed from the original electrotype plates of the original edition of 1886 (q.v.), with the addition of an index, pp. 71-72.

American Ornithologists' Union.   (Allen, J. A.; Brewster, William; Coues, Elliott; Merriam, C. Hart; Ridgway, Robert.).

1895. **Check-List | of | North American Birds** | prepared by a committee | of the | American Ornithologists' Union | **Second and revised edition** | Zoölogical Nomenclature is a means, not an end, of Zoölogical Science | New York | American Ornithologists' Union | 1895.

1 vol. 8vo, pp. I-XI+1, 1-372. New York.

The second edition of the Society's Check-list (Cf. ed. 1886.), embodying the changes in nomenclature and status of species which were made in the second to seventh supplements, published from time to time in the Auk following the issuance of the revised edition of the Check-list in 1889 (q.v.). A third edition appeared in 1910 (q.v.). The scope of the work is the same as that of the original edition.

American Ornithologists' Union.

1902. **American Ornithologists' | Union | By-Laws and rules** | November, 1902 | New York | American Ornothologists' Union.

1 vol. post 8vo, tit., pp. 1-10. New York, November 1902.

Title self-explanatory. (Cf. ed. 1887.)

American Ornithologists' Union.   (Allen, J. A.; Brewster, William; Dwight, Jonathan, Jr.; Merriam, C. Hart; Richmond, Charles W.; Ridgway, Robert; Stone, Witmer.)

1910. **Check-list | of | North American Birds** | prepared by a committee | of the | American Ornithologists' Union | **Third edition** (revised) | Zoölogical Nomenclature is a means, not an end, of Zoölogical Science | New York | American Ornithologists' Union | 1910.

1 vol. 8vo, pp. 1-430, 2 maps (fold.; 1 col.). New York.

The most recent edition of the present title (Cf. eds. 1886, 1889 and 1895.), embodying the changes published in various numbers of the Auk in the eighth to fifteenth supplements to the Check-list. The plan of the work follows that of the second edition, 1895, with a few alterations. References are given to the original designation of the various generic types and the mode of such designation is indicated, the citations of original references to accepted combinations of names are omitted, type localities are given for the species and subspecies, and serial numbers, prominent in former lists, are subordinated.

The sixteenth to eighteenth supplements, presenting adopted alterations to the present edition of the Check-list, have been published in the Auk, **29**, pp. 380-387, July 1912; idem, **37**, pp. 439-449, July 1920; and idem, **40**, pp. 513-525, July 1923. Proposed changes, not yet accepted by the Union, have been published by Oberholser in the Auk, **33**, pp. 425-431, Oct. 1916; idem, **34**, pp. 198-205, April 1917; idem, **35**, pp. 200-217, April 1918; idem, **36**, pp. 266-273, April 1919; idem, **37**, pp. 274-285, April 1920; idem, **38**, pp. 264-269, April 1921;

idem, **39**, pp. 243-249, April 1922; idem, **40**, pp. 677-682, Oct. 1923; and idem, **41**, pp. 590-595, Oct. 1924.

Amery, C. F.

1896. See World's Congress on Ornithology, **Papers presented to the—**.

Anderson, John.

1879. Anatomical and zoological researches: | comprising an account of the | zoölogical results of the two expeditions | to | **western Yunnan** | in | 1868 and 1875; | and | a monograph of the two Cetacean genera, Platanista and Orcella. | By | John Anderson, M.D., Edin., | Superintendent Indian Museum [*etc., 2 lines*]. | First Volume—Text. [Second Volume—Plates. | (84 Plates.)] | London: | Bernard Quaritch, 15, Piccadilly. | 1878.

2 vols. royal 8vo. Text, 2 pr. ll., pp. I-XXV, 1-985, 1 map (col., fold.), text-figs. 1-32. Plates, 3 pr. ll., pp. 1-29, pll. I-LXXX, XIIIA, XXVA, LXXVA and LXXVB (51 col.; XLV-LIV ornith., by Keulemans). London.

Title self-explanatory. Parts of the report are by other authors, but the ornithology is by Anderson. This occupies pp. 565-702 and pll. XLV-LIV, including the description of one new species of Sun-bird. The introduction is dated from Calcutta, December 21, 1878, which precludes the possibility of publication in London the same year. The Zoological Record for 1879 states definitely that the book was not in circulation until 1879.

Anderson, Randolph Martin.

1907. March, 1907. Vol. XI. Pages 125-417 | Proceedings | of the | Davenport Academy of Sciences | **The birds of Iowa** | by Rudolph M. Anderson | Davenport, Iowa, U. S. A. | Davenport Academy of Sciences | 1907. [*Cover-title.*].

1 vol. 8vo, cover-tit., pp. 125-417, 1 map. Davenport. March 1907.

An annotated list of species of birds known to occur in Iowa, giving an account of the local occurrence and distribution of each.

Andersson, Charles John. (Gurney, John Henry.)

1872. Notes | on | the birds of Damara Land | and the adjacent countries of | Southwest Africa. | By the late | Charles John Andersson. | Author of [*etc.*] | arranged and edited by | John Henry Gurney, | with some additional notes by the editor, and an introductory | chapter containing | a sketch of the author's life, abridged from the original published in Sweden. | London: | John Van Voorst, Paternoster Row. | MDCCCLXII.

1 vol. post. 8vo, pp. I-XLVIII, 1-394, frontisp. (map), 4 pll. London.

A descriptive, systematic account of the subject compiled by Gurney from Andersson's note book and a manuscript (partially completed at his death) of a projected work on the avifauna of south-western Africa. Numerous annotations are given by Gurney who studied Andersson's collections of birds.

André, Eugène.

1904.   A | Naturalist in the | Guianas | by Eugène André, F.R.G.S., F.Z.S., M.S.A. | with a preface by Dr. J. Scott Keltie | (Secretary of the Royal Geographical Society) | with thirty-four illustrations | and a map | London | Smith, Elder, & Co., 15 Waterloo Place | 1904.

1 vol. 8vo, pp. I-XIV, 1-310, frontisp., 33 pll. (2 col.), map. London.

The narrative of the author's experiences and observations on two collecting expeditions up the Orinoco and Caura rivers in 1897-98 and 1900-01. Considerable of the text relates to the birds of the region.

Annandale, Nelson; and Robinson, Herbert C. (Ogilvie-Grant, William Robert.)

1905. >Fasiculi Malayenses | Anthropological and zoological results of an expedition | to Perak and the Siamese Malay States, 1901-1902 | undertaken by | Nelson Annandale and Herbert C. Robinson | under the auspices of the University of Edinburgh and | the University of Liverpool | Report on the birds | by | W. R. Ogilvie-Grant | British Museum (Natural History), Cromwell Road, London | Price 10s. net | (Author's Advance Copy from Zoology— Part III) | July, 1905 | Published for | The University Press of Liverpool | by | Williams & Norgate | 14 Henrietta Street, Covent Garden, London | 1905.

1 vol. (pt.) demy 4to, 3 pr. ll. (tit., subtit. and introd.), pp. 65-123. Liverpool. July 1905.

The ornithological portion of Annandale and Robinson's 'Fasiculi Malayenses,' published in 4 parts in 1963-1907 Pt. III, which includes the present portion, is dated 1906 by the Zoological Record but was also distributed in sections as in the present instance; hence the report on the birds is to be quoted as of July 1905. The text consists of a catalogue of the specimens of 225 species of birds with notes on the colors of soft parts and an occasional discussion of other characteristics by Ogilvie-Grant, and with field notes by Robinson. *Pycnonotus robinsoni* and an unnamed species of *Chlorura* are newly described.

Anonymous.

1743.   Ornithologia nova: | Or, A New General | history | of | birds. | Extracted from the best Authorities in | various Languages, both Antient | and Modern. | With | Remarks and proper Observations upon | the different Species and Kinds throughout the | known World, from the most Curious Natural- | ists, Virtuoso's and

Travellers. | Containing, | A Description of a great Number of curious and un- | common birds, found in different parts of the | Universe. | Illustrated with about Four Hundred Figures, copied | from the best Originals. | In Two Volumes. | Vol. I [*II.* (?)]. | Birmingham: | Printed by T. Warren, Bookseller in the Bull- | Ring. M, DCC, XLIII. [*Title to Vol. II missing.*]

2 vols. in 1 vol., 16mo. Vol. I, pp. I-XII, 1 l., pp. 13-340, 171 wood-cuts (portrs. of birds) and numerous decorations. Vol. II, (no title-p.) pp. I-VIII, 3-314, 3 ll. (index, begun on p. 314), 182 woodcuts (portrs. of birds) and numerous decorations. Birmingham.

A curious work, describing the appearance and habits of numerous birds. Many of the accounts are based on travellers' tales; others are from more reliable sources. The woodcuts are extremely crude.

Anonymous.

1815. The | natural history | of | birds, | from the | works of the best authors, | antient & modern: | embellished with | numerous plates | Accurately Coloured from Nature. | In two volumes. | Vol. I [II]. | Bungay: | Printed and Published by Brightly & Childs. | Published also by T. Kinnersly. | 1815.

2 vols. 4to (5⅛ x 8¼). Vol. I, tit. pp. I-XXXV+1, 1-586, 69 pll. (col.). Vol. II, tit., pp. I-XV+1, 83 pll. (col.). Bungay.

A series of descriptions of birds from all countries, with notes on habits, under vernacular names, and arranged by so-called tribes. The plates are hand-colored, although hardly "accurately." There is a London edition of the same year, with slightly different title.

Anonymous.

1829. Catalogue | des oiseaux | composant le cabinet | de M. le Comte de Riocour, | a Aulnois, | Département de la Meurthe. | [*Vignette.*] | Nancy, | Imprimerie de Barbier, Rue Saint-Jean, No. 13. | 1829.

1 vol. post 8vo, tit., pp. 1-48, (orig. wrapper). Nancy.

A list of 1492 species of birds in the collection of Antoine Nicolas François, Comte de Riocour. The list is arranged in three columns giving serial number, vernacular name and Latin name of each species with the names of genera, families, tribes and orders centered above in their proper places. Vieillot described many new species from this collection, and it is possible that he was involved in the preparation of this catalogue, but the authorship is not given. The generic name *Averano* appears herein for the first time, with inclusion of "*A. caronculatus*" and "*nudi-collis.*" As neither of these species was included in that genus as proposed by Lesson in his "Traite d'Ornithologie," 1830-31, it becomes necessary to select a type species for the genus as here proposed, and accordingly I designate *A. caronculatus* [= *Procnias alba* (Hermann)] as such. The generic name *Eurilenus* is also proposed, based on *Eurilenus nasicus*. The latter appears to be the same as *Erolla nasica* [= *Cymbirhynchus macrorhynchus* (Gmelin)] described by Lesson in the "Traite d'Ornithologie" in 1830-31; both genus and species in the present catalogue are nomina nuda.

Another catalogue of this collection was published in 1889 by Boucard (q.v.).

Anonymous.

1832.   A | book | of | ornithology | for youth | [*Woodcut.*] | embracing descriptions of the most interesting and | remarkable birds in all countries, with | particular notices of | American birds. | Illustrated by numerous engravings. | Boston | William Hyde, and Co. | 1832 > Entered [*etc.*] by Samuel G. Goodrich [*etc.*].

1 vol. 12 mo., pp. I-XII[+?], 19-96, 101-104, 109-110, 119-134, 143-322. [many pages obviously missing], frontisp., 26 figs. [? missing]. Boston.

Popular descriptions of the habits and characteristics of various species of birds.

Anonymous.

1838-43.   See Jardine, William, **The Natural History of the Birds of Great Britain and Ireland.**

1844-64? Idem.

Anonymous.

Ornithological Illustrations. Série de 130 photographies des nids et des oeufs des oiseaux de mer des iles de St. Kilda, des Nlles Hébrides, etc du Sud de l'Afrique, et de ceux étudiés par Gätke à Helgoland.— 15 gr. col. originals. Réunies par Seebohm.]

1 vol. medium folio, 40 ll.

A collection of 129 photographs, 15 original water-color drawings (one signed by Keulemans and one by A. Smart) and two photostat copies of drawings, portions of which, at least, are by J. G. Millais. The collection is from the library of Henry Seebohm.

Anonymous.

[Chinese Drawings: Birds.]

2 vols. imperial folio 176 pll. (col.; 94, 127, 142 and 165 wanting).

These volumes consist of original paintings on paper, mounted on larger sheets and bound, 88 plates in each volume. A small signature in Chinese ideographs on each plate may be the name of the bird figured. The numbers are a later addition and the title is evidently supplied. The coloring is very rich but the figures appear to be somewhat fanciful as regards detail.

Anonymous.

[Chinese Drawings: Birds.]

1 vol. (13½ x 16), pll. 1-50

A series of fifty original watercolor drawings of birds, said to be by a native Chinese artist. The drawings are well executed but are not named.

Antinori, Orazio.

1864. Catalogo descrittivo | di | una collezione di uccelli | fatta da | Orazio Antinori | nell'interno dell'Affrica centrale nord | dal Maggio 1859 al Juglio 1861 | Milano | G. Daelli e Comp. | Editori del Politecnico | 1864.

1 vol. post 8vo, pp. I-XXIX+1, 1-117. Milan.

A descriptive catalogue of the birds collected in north-central Africa by the author in 1859-1861. Various species are described as new. A translation into German, with annotations, was published by R. Hartmann in the Journal für Ornithologie from 1865-69, but reached only as far as p. 62 of the original text.

Apgar, Austin C.

1898. Birds | **of the United States** | east of the Rocky Mountains | A manual for the identification of species | in hand or in the bush | By Austin C. Apgar | author of "Trees of the Northern United States," etc. | New York Cincinnati Chicago | American Book Company.

1 vol. crown 8vo, pp. 1-415, 70 text-cuts and numerous line-drawings of anatomical details, repeated where necessary. New York, Cincinnati and Chicago.

A students' and beginners' handbook with introductory chapters of a general nature, followed by keys for the determination of specimens, brief accounts of each of the species, keys for determination of the birds in the field, instructions for field work and collecting, and a glossary of technical terms. Line-drawings of anatomical details are used profusely to illustrate the keys and, occasionally, the text. The half-tone illustrations are mostly very poor; some of them are unrecognizable. The present copy is from the library of Winfred A. Stearns who has autographed the title-page, "suggested by W. A. Stearns."

Aplin, Oliver Vernon.

1889. The | **birds of Oxfordshire** | by | O. V. Aplin . | Member of the British Ornithologists' Union | With a Map. | [*Quot., 4 lines.*] | Oxford | At the Clarendon Press | 1889 | [All rights reserved].

1 vol. 8vo, pp. I-VII+1, 1-217, frontisp. (col.; by S. L. Mosley), 1 map (fold., col.), 1 text-fig. Oxford.

Notes on the habits and local distribution and occurrence of the various species of birds found in Oxfordshire, England, prefaced by a topographical and historical chapter.

Aplin, Oliver Vernon.

1898. See Butler, Arthur G., **British Birds,** 1896-98.

d'Arenberg, E.

1911-12. Les Oiseaux | Nuisibles | de France | et les modes de chasse ou de piégeage | propres à leur destruction | Suivi de quelques considérations sur les Buses et le Faucon cresserelle [*Omitted, Vol. II.*] | par le | Prince E. d'Arenberg | Livre premier [second] | Orléans | Imprimerie Henri Tessier | 56, Rue des Carmes, 56 | 1911 [1912].

2 vols. 12mo. Vol. I, pp. 1-109+1, 1 l. (conts.), 21 pll. (col.; by Malher). Vol. II, 2 pr. ll. (half-tit. and tit.), pp. 7-156, 27 pll. (col.). Orleans.

A discussion of the various birds of France considered as injurious, with short descriptions of each, accounts of their nidification and habits, reasons for adjudging them injurious, and methods for the destruction of the various species. Vol. I deals with the birds of prey; II, with the shrikes, jays, pigeons, fisheating birds, etc. The illustrations are not of a high order of merit.

Arévalo y Baca, José.

1887. Aves de España. | Memoria | premiada con accésit | por la | Real Academia de Ciencias | Exactas, Físicas y Naturales | en el concurso público de 1882 | escrita por | D. José Arévalo y Baca | Catedrático de la Universidad de Valencia. | [*Vignette.*] | Madrid.—1887 | Imprenta de los sres, viuda é hijo de Aguado | 8, Pontejos, 8.

1 vol. medium 4to, tit., pp. I-VI, 7-471. Madrid.

A catalogue of the birds of Spain, with scientific and vernacular names, brief characterizations, and short accounts of habits, food and distribution of each species.

Arngrimson, Frimann B.

1891. See Hagerup, Andreas T., **The Birds of Greenland.**

Arnold, Edward Carleton.

1907. A bird collector's | medley | by | E. C. Arnold, M. A. | With Twelve Coloured and Eight Collotype Plates from Drawings by the Author, | and various Illustrations in the Text | London | West, Newman & Co., 54, Hatton Garden | Simpkin, Marshall, Hamilton, Kent & Co. | 1907.

1 vol. demy 4to, 4 pr. ll., pp. 1-44, 20 pll. (12 col.; by the author), 20 cuts. London.

A popular account of some of the experiences of a bird collector in England.

Arnold, Edward Carleton.

1924.   British waders | illustrated in water-colour | with descriptive notes by | E. C. Arnold | [*Blazon.*] | Cambridge | at the University Press | MCMXXIV.

1 vol. medium 4 to, pp. I-VII+1, 1-102, pll. I-LI (col.; by the author). Cambridge.

A series of random notes on European and American shore-birds, with colored drawings of the various species discussed.

Arnold, Friedrich.

1897.   Die | **Vögel Europas.** | Ihre Naturgeschichte und Lebensweise in Freiheit und Gefangenschaft. | Nebst Anleitung | zur | Aufzucht, Eingewöhnung, Pflege, samt den Fang- und Jagdmethoden. | Von | Friedrich Arnold. | Mit 76 Textillustrationen und 48 Tafeln. | Stuttgart. | C. Hoffmann'sche Verlagsbuchhandlung. (A. Bleil). | 1897. [*Pasted slip reads*, Verlag für Naturkunde (Sprosser & Nägele).].

1 vol. imperial 8vo, tit., pp. 1-8, I-LXXX, 1-457, pll. 1-48, (col.), 76 text-figs. Stuttgart.

Descriptions and general account of the species of European birds. A popular work.

Arrigoni Degli Oddi, E.

1902.   Atlante Ornitologico | Uccelli Europei | con Notizie d'Indole Generale e Particolare | del | Dr. E. Arrigoni Degli Oddi | Professore [*etc., 3 lines.*]. | Con 50 tavole colorate | e duecentodieci disegni intercalati nel testo | [*Design.*] | Ulrico Hoepli | Editore-Libraio della Real Casa | Milano | 1902.

1 vol. medium 4to, 3 pr. ll. (half-tit., tit. and ded.), pp. IX-XIX+1, 1-165 (end of Pt. I), I-XXV+1, 1-566 (end of Pt. II), 1 l. (errata), pll. 1-50 (col.; by Aug. Specht and others?; 47 of birds, 3 of eggs.), text-figs. 1-210 (num. only in index). Milan.

An Italian manual of the birds of Europe with descriptions of each species and subspecies recognized by the author and with notes on distribution, variation, etc. Italian vernacular names are given with the scientific name and an occasional synonym. Part I contains a general discussion of avian structure, distribution, economic importance, migration, song, etc., and a bibliography of European ornithology. The plates are chromolithographs, mostly taken from "Die Vögel Europas" by Friedrich Arnold, 1897 (q.v.).

Arthur, Stanley Clisby.

1918.   State of Louisiana | Department of Conservation | M. L. Alexander, Commissioner | Bulletin 5 | **The birds of Louisiana** |

[*Seal.*] | Published by the | Department of Conservation | New Orleans Court Building | January, 1918.

  1 vol. 8vo, pp. 1-80, 7 pll. (on num. pp.), 4 text-figs. (maps.). New Orleans. January 1918.

An annotated list of the birds of the state.

Ashley, Edwin.

1917. See Mathews, Gregory M., **The Birds of Australia,** 1910-date.

Astley, Hubert Delaval.

1900. My birds | **in** | **freedom & captivity** | by the | Rev. Hubert D. Astley | Member of the British Ornithologists' Union, etc. | London | J. M. Dent & Co., Aldine House | 29 & 30 Bedford Street, W. C. | 1900.

  1 vol. 8vo, 3 pr. ll., pp. IX-XVI, 1-254, frontisp. 21 pll., 17 figs. London.

Notes on the author's experiences with, and impressions of, bird life in the field and aviary, illustrated with sketches by himself.

Astrolabe, Voyage de Découvertes de l' — ; Zoologie.

1830-35. See Dumont D'Urville.

Astrolabe et la Zélée, Voyage au Pole Sud et dans l'oceanie sur les corvettes l' — ; Zoologie.

1842-54. See Dumont Durville.

Atkinson, George E.

1907. See Mershon, W. B., **The Passenger Pigeon.**

Atkinson, John Christopher.

1861. British | **birds' eggs and nests,** | popularly described. | By | Rev. J. C. Atkinson, | author of [*etc.*, *2 lines.*]. | With coloured illustrations by W. S. Coleman. | London | Routledge, Warne, & Routledge, | Parringdon Street. | New York: 56, Walker Street. | 1861.

  1 vol. cap 8vo, pp. I-VIII, 1-182, 1 l. (advt.), 1 chart (fold., in pocket), pll. I-XII (col.). London.

A brief account of the habits and nidification of British birds. A folded chart gives a synoptical view of many of the species, with peculiarities of nesting site, materials of construction, number, color and marking of eggs, and remarks, in tabular form. The work is intended for the amateur egg-collector. Various later editions (Cf. ed. 1898.), have been issued.

Atkinson, John Christopher.

1898? British | birds' eggs and nests | popularly described | revised and re-edited | by | Rev. Canon Atkinson, D.C.L. | author [etc., 5 lines.]. | Illustrated by W. S. Coleman | London | George Routledge and Sons, Limited | New York: E. P. Dutton and Co.

1 vol. crown 8vo, pp. I-VII+1, 1-245, 1 chart (fold., in pocket), pll. I-XII. London.

A revised edition of the earlier work of the same title (q.v.). According to Mullens and Swann, this edition was issued in 1898 and 1904.

Audebert, Jean Baptiste; and Vieillot, Louis Jean Pierre.

1800-02. Oiseaux dorés | ou | a reflets métalliques | tome premier [second]. > [Reverse of title.] A Paris, | de l'imprimerie de Crape-let | An XI.

2 vols. superroyal folio. Vol. I, 2 pr. ll., pp. I-X, 1-128 (pref. and "Hist. Nat. des Colibris et des Oiseaux-Mouches"), 1-8 ("Jaca-mars"), 1-28 ("Promerops" and "Table Générale"), pll. 1-70 (col.; "Colibris et Oiseaux-Mouches"), 1-6 (col.; "Jacamars"), 1-9 (col.; "Promerops"). Vol. II, 2 pr. ll. (tit. and subtit.), pp. 1-88 ("Grim-pereaux"), 1-40 ("Oiseaux de Paradis" and "Table Générale"), pll. 1-88+26 (bis) (col.; "Grimpereaux"), 1-16 (col.; "Oiseaux de Paradis"). Paris.

Each volume of this work is also separately titled and divided into sections, some of which are separately paged (as noted above). The divisions are as follows.

(Vol. I.) >Histoire naturelle | et générale | des colibris, | oiseaux-mouches, | jacamars et promerops; | par J. B. Audebert et L. P. Vieillot. | A Paris, | chez Desray, libraire, Rue Hautefeuille, No 36. | An XI = 1802.

2 pr. ll. and pp. I-X: "Colibris," pp. 1-40, pll. 1-20; "Oiseaux-Mouches," pp. 41-118, pll. 21-64; supplement to "Colibris," pp. 119-128, pll. 65-70· "Jacamars" (by Vieillot), pp. 1-8, pll. 1-6: "Pro-merops" (by Vieillot), pp. 1-22, pll. 1-9; "Table Générale" (for Vol. I) pp. 23-28.

(Vol. II.) > Histoire naturelle | et générale | des grimpereaux | et | des oiseaux de paradis; | par J. B. Audebert et L. P. Vieillot. | A Paris, | chez Desray, libraire, Rue Hautefeuille, No. 36. | An XI = 1802.

2 pr. ll.: "Grimpereaux Souï-Mangas," pp. 1-68, pll. 1-40+26 (bis); "Grimpereaux Guit-guits," pp. 69-84, pll. 41-51; "Grimper-eaux Héoro-taires," pp. 85-106, pll. 52-71; "Grimpereaux," pp.

107-128, pll. 72-88: "Oiseaux de Paradis," pp. 1-34, pll. 1-16; "Table Générale" (for Vol. II), pp. 35-40.

Sherborn (Index Animalium, Sect. 2, Pt. 1, p. XIX, 1919) says that this work was issued in 32 parts over a period of 26 months. If the date on the title-page is correct, the work must have begun in 1800. The extent and separate dates of the individual parts is not known. The present copy is one of a probably limited number with the inscriptions on the plates lettered in gold.

Audouin, Jean Victor. (Newton, Alfred, *ed.*)

1883. The Willughby Society. | **Audoin's** | **Explication Sommaire** | **des Planches** | **d'Oiseaux de l'Égypte et de la Syriè** | publiées par | Jules-César Savigny. | [*Vignette*] | Edited by | Alfred Newton, M.A., F.R.S., etc. | London; MDCCCLXXXIII.

[> Explication sommaire | des | planches d'oixeaux | de l'Égypte et de la Syrie, | Publiées par Jules-César Savigny, | Membre de l'Institut; | offrant un exposé des caractères naturels des genres | avec la distinction des espèces, | par Victor Audouin.]

1 vol. post 8vo, pp. I-VII+1, "302-430" (=2-130), "450-456" (=132-138), 139. "Paris. 1828" London 1883.

Descriptions of, and notes on, the birds of Egypt and Syria, based on the 14 plates published by Savigny in 1810 (q.v.) in Vol. I, livraison 1, of the "Description de l'Égypte." The discussion of these plates was begun by Savigny in the text accompanying the plates (Livr. 1) under the title of "Système des Oiseaux de l'Égypte et de la Syrie" (q.v.). This discussion was never completed by him, and the entire subject was delegated by the French government to Audouin, whose contribution, here reprinted, was first published in about 1826; in Part 4 of the "Histoire Naturelle, Tome Premier," pp. 251-318 and 336-339, of the "Description". The above verbatim transcription, however, is taken from the Panckouke edition of 1820-30 where it occupies pp. 302-430 and 450-456 of Vol. XXIII, published in 1828. The differences between the two editions are not collated in the reprint, although the index (p. 139) contains references to both.

Audubon, John James.

1827-38. The | **Birds of America**; | from | original drawings | By | John James Audubon, | Fellow of the Royal Societies of London and Edinburgh [*etc. 4 lines.; 6 lines. (Vols. II-IIII.*)]. | London. | Published by the Author. | 1827-30. [Vol. II. | 1831-34.; Vol. III. | 1834-35.; Vol. IIII. 1835 to 38. | June 20.].

4 vols. double elephant. Vol. I, tit., pll. I-C (col.). Vol. II, tit., pll. CI-CC (col.). Vol. III, tit., pll. CCI-CCC (col.; pl. CCLIV wrongly num. CCLVI). Vol. IIII, tit., pll. CCCI-CCCCXXXV (col.). London. July 1827-June 20, 1838.

The original edition of Audubon's famous plates of North American birds. Issued without text (which followed in 1831-39 under the title of "Ornithological

Biography," q.v.) in 87 parts of 5 plates each. Scientific and common names are given on the plates and 47 specific names must date, therefore, from the present work and not from the subsequent text. The dates of the various parts are not clear. Many of the plates are dated, but some are not and the dates which are given do not always coincide with other available data. For example, pll. 286, 288 and 291-300 are dated 1836 but are included in Vol. III which bears the dates of 1834-35, and they were received at the Philadelphia Academy on October 2, 1835 (Cf. Stone, Auk, 23, pp. 301-302, 1906); Vol. IIII is dated 1835-38 but its plates are all dated 1836, 1837 or 1838. Other data are given by Stone (l.c.).

Pll. I-X were originally prepared by W. H. Lizars, Edinburgh, in 1826 and 1827, but difficulties regarding delivery and workmanship caused Audubon to transfer his project to other hands and the later plates were prepared by Robert Havell of London. Some of the earlier plates were retouched by the latter and bear a double imprint, while others bear only Havell's name and may have been entirely re-engraved, although there is some doubt about the latter point. In the copy at hand, pll. VIII and IX are marked as engraved by W. H. Lizars; I, II, VI, and VII, as engraved by W. H. Lizars and retouched by R. Havell, Junr., II and VII being dated 1829; III, IV, V, and X, as engraved, printed and coloured by R. Havell; XI et seq. are of the regular issue, by Havell. Stone (l.c., p. 300) records the copy in the library of the Philadelphia Academy as of the same composition. The 435 copper-plate engravings, colored by hand, contain 1065 life-sized figures of 489 supposedly distinct species. The only reissue of the plates in original dimensions was made in 1860, consisting of an incomplete series of lithograph copies, greatly inferior to the originals (Cf. ed. 1860-61). Other editions of the text, with the plates reduced to 8vo and inserted in the letterpress, were numerous, the first being by Audubon himself in 1840-44 (Cf. "Ornithological Biography," 1831-39).

Audubon, John James.

1831. **Ornithological biography,** | or an account of the habits of the | birds of the United States of America; | accompanied by descriptions of the objects represented | in the work entitled | The Birds of America, | and interspersed with delineations of Ameri-can | scenery and manners. | By John James Aubudon, F.R.SS. L. & E. | Fellow of the Linnean and Zoological Societies [etc., 6 lines.]. | Philadelphia: | Judah Dobson, Agent, 108 Chestnut Street; | and | H. H. Porter, Literary Rooms, 121 Chestnut Street, | MDCCCXXXI.

1 vol. royal 8vo, pp. I-XXIV, 1-512, 1-16 (advt.). Philadelphia.

A separate issue of Vol. I of the author's work (q.v., published in Edinburgh in 5 vols., 1831-39). It differs in some particulars from the Edinburgh edition. Some of the wording of the introduction is altered; that of the general text appears to be the same with minor changes in punctuation and the correction of at least one error (on p. 381, reference to pl. 85 in place of 75). In the table of contents, several more specific names are in lower-case type than in the Edinburgh copy. The letterpress is parallel, to a considerable degree, line for line, but there are many places where differences exist; page-references to species, however, remain the same. In the present copy, an unfriendly critic has made various marginal notes in pencil. The sixteen pages of advertising at the close of the volume consist of a prospectus of the folio, "Birds of America," with a list of the one hundred plates in Vol. I of that work and the year of publication of each plate. Extracts from reviews and a list of subscribers are added. This advertisement is not in the copy at hand of the Edinburgh edition. Another edition of Vol. I exists, published in 1835 by E. L. Carey and A. Hart, Philadelphia (Cf. W. C. Braislin, Auk. **35**, pp. 360-362, 1918.).

Audubon, John James.

1831. See Wilson, Alexander, and Bonaparte, **American Ornithology.**

Audubon, John James.

1831-39. Ornithological biography, | or an account of the habits of the | birds of the United States of America; [*comma instead of semicolon* (*Vols. III-V.*)] | accompanied by descriptions of the objects represented | in the work entitled | The Birds of America, | and interspersed with delineations of American | scenery and manners [together with an account of the digestive organs of many | of the species, illustrated by engravings on wood (*Vols. IV and V.*)]. | By John James Audubon, F.R.SS. L. & E. | Fellow of the Linnean and Zoological Societies [*etc. 3 lines.*; ? (*Vol. II.*); *7 lines.*(*Vol. III.*); *8 lines.* (*Vols. IV and V.*)]. [| ? (Vol. *II.*); Vol. III.; Vol. IV.; Vol. V.] | Edinburgh: | Adam Black. 55. North Bridge, Edinburgh [? (*Vol. II.*); Adam & Charles Black, Edinburgh (*Vols. III-V.*)]; | [*etc., 5 ll.*; *3 ll.* (*Vol. IV.*); *1 l.* (*Vol. V.*)]. | MDCCCXXXI [(MDCCCXXXV); MDCCCXXXV; MDCCCXXXVIII; MDCCCXXXIX (*Sic* = *MDCCC X X X I X.*)]

4 vols. (should be 5; (Vol. II of the present set belongs to Boston ed., 1835, q.v.) royal 8vo. Vol. I, pp. I-XXIV, 1-512. Vol. III, pp. I-XVI, 1-638, 9 text-cuts. Vol. IV, pp. I-XXVIII, 1-618, 39 text-cuts. Vol. V, pp. I-XL, 1-304, 14 text-cuts. Edinburgh.

The original text intended to accompany the author's "Birds of America" (1827-38, q.v.). Vol. I deals with the species figured on pll. I-C of that work; (II, pll. CI-CC); III, CCI-CCC; IV, pll. CCCI-CCCLXXXVII; V, pll. CCCLXXXVIII-CCCCXXXV. The last volume also contains "Descriptions of species found in North America but not figured in the 'Birds of America'," pp. 305-336; "Species seen within the limits of the United States, but not characterized," pp. 334-336; "Appendix; comprising additional observations on the habits, geographical distribution and anatomical structure of the birds described in this work; together with corrections of errors relative to the species," pp. 337-664. Five species of the "Birds of America" are suppressed in the text, eighteen new species are added, and eleven of those given in the early volumes are reduced to synonymy in the appendix, making 502 species treated in the whole work and 491 species recognized at its close. Two of the suppressed species have since been re-established. Of the total, 29 species date from this work. The introduction to Vol. I is dated March, 1831; II, December 1, 1834; III, December 1, 1835; IV, November 1, 1838; and V, May 1, 1839. In addition to this Edinburgh edition, Vol. I was published also in Philadelphia in 1831 and again in 1835 (Cf. 1831 ed.), and Vol. II was published in Boston in 1835 (q.v.).

In 1839, Audubon published his "A Synopsis of the Birds of North America" (q.v.), making considerable changes in nomenclature, arranging the species systematically, and forming an index to the present work and to the plates. In 1840-1844, text and plates (the latter reduced in size) were issued together under the original title of "The Birds of America" (q.v.). Other 8vo editions followed in 1856, 1859, 1860, 1861, 1863, 1865 and 1871 (Cf. eds. of 1859, 1860 and 1871.). In 1860, there commenced a reproduction of the plates in lithograph of the original size, accompanied by the text (Cf. ed. of 1860-61.), but the work was interrupted and never resumed. The text was also reissued in 1856 without plates. For complete bibliography, see Stone, Auk, **23**, pp. 298-312, 1906, and Herrick, Auk, **36**, pp. 372-380, 1919.

Audubon, John James.

1835.   Ornithological biography, | or an account of the habits of the | birds of the United States of America; | accompanied by descriptions of the objects represented | in the work entitled | The Birds of America, | and interspersed with delineations of American | scenery and manners. | By John James Audubon, F.R.SS. L. &. E. | [*etc., 8 lines.*] | Vol. II. | Boston: | Hilliard, Gray, and Company. | MDCCCXXXV.

1 vol. royal 8vo, pp. I-XXXII, 1-588. Boston.

Vol. II of the author's "Ornithological Biography" was published in Boston the year following the corresponding volume of the Edinburgh edition (q.v.), and is the only volume with a Boston imprint. The present copy is included in the Edinburgh set at hand, in place of the proper number which is missing. W. C. Braislin (Auk, **35**, pp. 361-362) says that this American edition of Vol. II differs on every page from the Edinburgh edition.

Audubon, John James.

1839.   A | **synopsis of the birds** | **of North America.** | By | John James Audubon, F.R.SS. L. & E. | Member of various scientific associations in | Europe and America. | Edinburgh: | Adam and Charles Black, Edinburgh, | [*etc., 2 lines.*] | MDCCCXXXIX.

1 vol. post 8vo, pp. I-XII, 1-359+1. Edinburgh.

This work consists of a systematic classification of the birds treated in the folio, "Birds of America," and "Ornithological Biography," with references to the plates and the text, respectively. Two species given in the "Biography" are suppressed and two others added making the total the same, 491 spp. The work is sometimes ascribed largely to Macgillivray, to whom acknowledgments are made by Audubon in the preface. Several new specific names date from this volume.

Audubon, John James.

1840-44. **The | birds of America, |** from | drawings made in the United States | and their territories. | By John James Audubon, F.R.SS. L. & E. | Fellow of the Linnean and Zoological Societies of London [*etc.*, 11 *lines*.] | Vol. I [-VII.]. | New York: [J. J. Audubon, (*Vols. VI and VII.*)] | published by J. J. Audubon. [77 William Street, New York, (*Vols. VI and VII.*)] | Philadelphia: [34 North Front Street, Philadelphia. (*Vols. VI and VII.*)] | J. B. Chevalier. [*Omitted* (*Vols. VI and VII.*)] | 1840 [1841; 1841; 1842; 1842; 1843; 1844].

7 vols. royal 8vo. Vol. I, pp. I-VIII, 9-256, pll. 1-70 (col.; 13 wrongly numbered 10), 2 text-cuts. Vol. II, pp. I-VII+1, 9-205, pll. 71-140 (col.), 4 text-cuts. Vol. III, pp. I-VIII, 9-233, 1 l. (list of subscrs.), pll. 141-210 (col.), 6 text-cuts. Vol. IV, pp. I-VIII, 9-321, 1 l. (list of subscrs.), pll. 211-280 (col.), 28 text-cuts. Vol. V, pp. I-VIII, 9-346, 1 l. (list of subscrs.), pll. 281-350 (col.), 14 text-cuts. Vol. VI, pp. I-VII+1, 9-457, 1 l. (list of subscrs.), pll. 351-420 (col.), 25 text-cuts. Vol. VII, pp. I-IX+1, 9-371, 1 l. (list of subscrs.), pll. 421-500 (col.), 18 text-cuts. New York and Philadelphia.

The original 8vo edition of this title. The purely ornithological text of Audubon's "Ornithological Biography," 1831-39 (q.v.), revised and rearranged by the author according to his "A Synopsis of the Birds of North America," 1839 (q.v.), with much additional matter but with the "Delineation of American Scenery and Manners" omitted. The plates are modified copies of those of the original folio, "The Birds of America," 1827-38 (q.v.), reduced by camera lucida and lithographed. Some of the backgrounds are entirely changed, others greatly modified, and the original composition is altered so that but one species is represented on a plate. In the case of four species, each occupies two plates, and in one case (pl. 88), the figures of two originals (pll. XXXV and XCV) have been combined on one plate. There are 7 species of the "Ornithological Biography" and "Synopsis" which are figured here for the first time and 17 new forms are added in an appendix. The plates are rearranged in accordance with the text and renumbered in sequence to correspond. In Vol. III the names on pll. 187 and 188 are transposed, and, curiously enough, this error is perpetuated throughout all the subsequent 8vo editions of the work. This edition, which is the only 8vo published by the author himself, was issued in 100 parts, 14 of which are found in each of Vols. I-VI, and 16 in Vol. VII.

Audubon, John James.

1859. >**The | birds of America, |** from | drawings made in the United States | and their territories. | By | John James Audubon,

F.R.S., &c., &c. | Vol. III | New York: | V. G. Audubon. | Roe Lockwood & Son, 411 Broadway. | 1859.

1 vol. (should be 7 vols.) royal 8vo. (Vols. I-II,?). Vol. III, tit., pp. V-VIII, 9-233, pll. 141-210 (col.), 6 text-cuts. (Vols. IV-VII, ?) New York.

Vol. III of the edition of 1859 which, apparently, is exactly similar, except for title-page, with that of 1860 (q.v.). The present copy is included in a set of the latter in place of the equivalent volume which is missing. There is no recorded difference in the editions except in the dates on the title-pages.

Audubon, John James.

1860. The | birds of America, | from | drawings made in the United States | and their territories. | By | John James Audubon, F.R.S., &c., &c. | Vol. I. [-VII. (*Vol. III missing, replaced by corresponding volume of 1859 ed., q. v.*)] | New York: | V. G. Audubon. | Roe Lockwood & Son, 411 Broadway. | 1860.

6 vols. (should be 7) royal 8vo. Vol. I, tit., pp. V-VIII, 11-246, pll. 1-70 (col.), 2 text-cuts. Vol. II, tit., pp. V-VII+1, 11-199, pll. 71-140 (col.), 4 text-cuts. (Vol. III?). Vol. IV, tit., pp. V-VIII, 9-321, pll. 211-280 (col.), 28 text-cuts. Vol. V, tit., pp. V-VIII, 9-346, pll. 281-350 (col.), 14 text-cuts. Vol. VI, tit., pp. V-VIII, 9-456, pll. 351-420 (col.), 25 text-cuts. Vol. VII, tit., pp. III-VIII, 9-372, pll. 421-500 (col.), 18 text-cuts. New York.

An early republication of the 8vo edition of Audubon, differing in various particulars from the original 8vo of 1840-44. Coues lists an 1856 edition, published like the present one by V. G. Audubon, which is said to have no regular publisher's imprint and to differ from the original 8vo only in the title-pages and in the pagination, while the plates remain the same, therefore with plain, uncolored backgrounds; but according to Herrick (Auk, **36**, p. 377, 1919), the plates of this edition had colored backgrounds, so they are probably the same as in the edition in hand. A reissue was published in 1859 and again the following year in the present form. Vol. III of the present set belongs to the 1859 edition (q.v.). The edition in hand differs from the original 8vo of 1840-44, in title-pages and in plates, while the pagination appears to approximate very closely that recorded by Coues for the 1856 edition. It is the same text, reset, without the appended lists of new subscribers, as presented in the original 8vo, and runs line for line and page for page with occasional departures. The plates, however, are distinctly different in one way or another. A universal change appears to be in the inscriptions which are in distinctly larger type. The plain backgrounds of the original 8vo are replaced by tinted ones; those which were tinted are altered in tone or some minor detail. Many of the elaborate scenic backgrounds of the original folio, which were modified or eliminated in the first 8vo, have been replaced and in some cases the size of the figures has been altered in consequence. The plates thus approximate those of the folio much more closely than do those of the first reduction but are inferior, in general execution, to the latter which were prepared under the supervision of the author himself. These plates were afterwards used in subsequent 8vo editions (Cf. ed. 1871.) where, however, they were accompanied by other changes, noticeably that of the increase in the number of volumes. The present edition bears the copyright of 1839 and was printed by R. Craighead.

Audubon, John James.

1860-61. **The | birds of America,** | from | drawings made in the United States | and their territories. | By | John James Audubon, F.R.S., &c., &c. | Re-issued by J. W. Audubon | Vol. I. [-VII. (*Final period omitted in Vol. VI.*)] | New York: | Roe Lockwood & Son, publishers. | 1861.

> The | birds of America; | from | original drawings | by | John James Audubon, | Fellow of the Royal Societies of London & Edinburgh [*etc.*, 7 ll.]. | Re-issued by J. W. Audubon. | Vol. I. | Roe Lockwood & Son, | Publishers. | New York | 1860. | Chromo-lithography by J. Bien, 180 Broadway.

8 vols.; 7 vols. (text) superroyal 8vo, 1 vol. (plates) double elephant. Vol. I, pp. I-VIII, 11-246, 2 text-cuts. Vol. II, pp. I-VII+1, 11-199, 4 text-cuts. Vol. III, pp. I-VIII, 9-233, 6 text-cuts. Vol. IV, pp. I-VIII, 9-321, 28 text-cuts. Vol. V, pp. I-VIII, 9-346, 14 text-cuts. Vol. VI, pp. I-VIII, 9-456, 25 text-cuts. Vol. VII, 2 pr. ll, (half-tit. and tit.), pp. III-VII+1,9-372, I-IV (index to atlas), 18 text-cuts. Atlas Vol. I (all published), 150 pll. (col.; variously numbered; on 105 sheets). New York.

The only edition of Audubon's work, subsequent to the first, 1827-38 (q.v.), with the plates in double elephant. Interrupted by the Civil War and never resumed. According to a prospectus of the work (Cf. Herrick, "Audubon the Naturalist" 2, pp. 389-390, 1917), the publication was scheduled to appear in 45 numbers, 44 of which were to contain 10 pll. on 7 sheets in each; the last number to comprise the 7 vols. of text but to be issued with the fifteenth number. Numbers 16-44 were never issued. The plates are all dated 1858, 1859 or 1860. They appeared without sequence but were numbered so as to make final arrangement more or less possible in accordance with the text. Each plate, therefore, carries the number of the part and series in the upper left hand corner thus, "1-1," "1-2," etc. to "15-10," and the final number in the upper right hand corner. This final number in most cases agrees with the numbering of the species (or plate) in the author's "Synopsis," 1839, or 8vo "Birds of America," 1840-44. Many of the sheets contain two plates, as advertised, and each of these is separately numbered. The following plates are included in the fifteen numbers:—3, 7, 14, 16, 18-22, 34, 43, 44-48 (47 wrongly num. 48), 53-58,[1] 62, 63, 70-76, 80, 82, 86, 88, 88, (bis, wrongly num.

---

[1] Audubon's original pl. CCCLIX, containing the Swallowtailed, Arkansaw and Say's Flycatchers, was divided into pll. 53, 54 and 59 in the 8vo edition; as reproduced here it is numbered 54. Pl. 53 of the present edition equals 52 of the 8vo edition, but is numbered 54 in error in the index.

89),[2] 89, 90, 95, 96, 101 (wrongly num. 71), 104, 108, 109, 113, 114, 116, 118-120, 123-125, 127, 128, 132, 133, 138, 141, 144, 146 (wrongly num. 144), 150, 151, 159, 163-165, 172-175, 177, 189, 191, 192, 195, 196, 199, 200, 204, 205, 216, 217, 219-222, 225, 226, 231, 239, 240, 243-246, 251-253, 255, 257, 273, 275, 278, 280, 287-289, 293, 296, 307, 308, 329, 331-333, 336, 337, 342-344, 346, 353, 357, 358, 363, 364, 367, 368, 371, 372, 375, 380, 385, 386, 388, 391, 395-398, 405, 414, 423, 428, 431 (wrongly num. 434), 434, 454, 465, 466, 479 (wrongly num. 389). Pll. 18, 82, 239, 240, 243, 253, 364, 395, 397 and 398, belonging to pt. 15, are not included in the index to plates. In addition to the errors of numbering catalogued above, there are numerous others in the inscriptions relating to the parts of issue, and others in the index. The lithographs are, of course, much inferior to the original engravings. The text presented herewith is that of the original 8vo and the 1859-60 reprint, but does not run page for page with either. It was printed by R. Craighead and carries the 1839 copyright, agreeing with the 1859-60 edition in these respects.

Audubon, John James. (Buchanan, Robert; Audubon, Lucy).

1869. The | **life and adventures** | of | **John James Audubon,** | the naturalist. | Edited, from materials supplied by his widow, | by Robert Buchanan. | **Third edition.** | [*Vignette = portr.*] Audubon at Green Bank, Liverpool (From a drawing by himself.) Sept. 1826. | London: | Sampson Low, Son, & Marston, | Crown Buildings, 188, Fleet Street. | 1869. | [The Right of Translation is reserved.].

1 vol. post 8vo, pp. I-VIII, 1-366, 1 l. (advt.). London.

In 1867, Lucy Audubon prepared a memoir of her husband, John James Audubon, which was accepted for publication by the London firm of publishers (above mentioned) and placed in the hands of Buchanan for editing. The work consisted principally of extracts from Audubon's diary. Buchanan deleted four-fifths of the work and added numerous (more or less unfriendly) comments in the form of a running narrative to bind the fragments together, and the present work is the result, appearing in the first edition in 1868. The publishers refused to return the original manuscript to Mrs. Audubon, and much unique material was thus lost. In 1869, Mrs. Audubon issued "The Life of John James Audubon, the Naturalist" (q.v., ed. 1890) which is substantially the same work as the present, with the omission of objectionable matter and the inclusion of some other passages (Cf. Francis H. Herrick, "Audubon the Naturalist" Vol. I, pp. 18-22, 1917).

Audubon, John James. (Lockwood, George R.)

1871? The | **birds of America,** | from | drawings made in the United States | and their territories. | By | John James Audubon,

---

[2]These two plates, both numbered 88 in the index but one wrongly inscribed 89, are copies of pll. XCV and XXXV of the original folio. They represent the Yellow Poll and Children's Warblers, respectively. Audubon considered these as distinct in his "Ornithological Biography," but united them in his "Synopsis" and his 8vo "Birds of America," and for the latter work combined parts of the two original plates to form a composite which was published as pl. 88 in the rearranged series. The present edition copies the original plates but uses the revised serial number; hence there are two plates, both correctly numbered 88.

F.R.S., &c., &c. | Vol. I [-VIII]. | New York: | George R. Lock-
wood, | late Roe Lockwood & Son, | 812 Broadway.

8 vols. royal 8vo. Vol. I, pp. I-VIII, I-XV, 11-246, pll. 1-70 (col.),
2 text-cuts. Vol. II, pp. I-VII+1, 11-199, pll. 71-140 (col.), 4 text-
cuts. Vol. III, pp. I-VIII, 9-233, pll. 141-210 (col.), 6 text-cuts.
Vol. IV, pp. I-VIII, 9-321, pll. 211-280 (col.), 28 text-cuts. Vol. V,
pp. I-VIII, 9-346, pll. 281-350 (col.), 14 text-cuts. Vol. VI, pp.
I-VII+1, 9-298, pll. 351-394 (col.), 19 text-cuts. Vol. VII, pp.
I-VII+1, 9-285, pll. 395-440 (col.), 12 text-cuts. Vol. VIII, pp.
I-VIII, 9-256, pll. 441-500 (col.), 12 text-cuts. New York.

The last, or a reprint of the last, complete edition of Audubon's work on the birds
of America. It is not dated and does not agree exactly with any recorded edition
which I can find, so I am not certain as to its date of issue. There is an edition
of 1865 in 8 vols. (said by Coues to be a later edition of J. W. Audubon's
reissue of 1861, but in 8 vols. instead of 7), which I have not seen; hence I can
not point out the differences between it and the present set. The edition of
1871 (without imprinted date), as recorded by Coues, agrees almost exactly
with that in hand, but Herrick (Audubon the Naturalist, **2**, p. 409, 1917),
referring to the same edition, says that the biography of Audubon (pp. I-XV
of Vol. I) is signed "G. R. L[ockwood]., 1870." In the copy at hand, this
biography is unsigned; hence the present edition may be a reprint of the 1871
edition, of later date. It bears the copyright of 1870. The plates are those of
the 1859-60 edition without changes other than those attributable to the use
of worn copperplates, on account of which they are inferior to the earlier issues.

Audubon, John James. (Audubon, Lucy, *ed.*)

1890. The | life | of | John James Audubon, | the naturalist. |
Edited by his Widow. | With an introduction by Jas. Grant
Wilson. | [*Woodcut.*] | New York: | G. P. Putnam's Sons, | 27
and 29 West 23d St. | 1890.

1 vol. 12mo, 1 l. (tit.), pp. I-X, 11-443, frontisp. (steel engr.) and 1
woodcut (on title-page). New York.

This edition is republished from the original of 1869, which is a copy, with some
additions and omissions, of "The Life and Adventures of John James Audubon,
the Naturalist" (Cf. third ed., 1869.), edited by Robert Buchanan from
Audubon's journals.

Audubon, John James. (Audubon, Maria R., *ed.*; Coues, Elliott.)

1897. Audubon and his | journals | by | Maria R. Audubon | with
zoölogical and other notes | by | Elliott Coues | [illustrated] |
Volume I [II] | New York | Charles Scribner's Sons | 1897.

2 vols. 8vo. Vol. I, pp. I-XIV, 1-532, 21 pll., 1 cut. Vol. II, pp.
I-VIII, 1-554+1, 23 pll., 1 cut. New York.

This work presents a detailed transcription of Audubon's journals, with many footnotes by Elliott Coues. The work is edited by Audubon's granddaughter who has supplied (pp. 5-77) an account of the life of the naturalist.

Audubon, John James.

1904. See Weed, Clarence Moores, **Bird Life Stories,** Book I.

Audubon, John James.

1907. See Mershon, W. B., **The Passenger Pigeon.**

Audubon, John Woodhouse.   (Hodder, Frank Heywood; Audubon Maria R.)

1906. Audubon's western | journal: 1849-1850 | Being the MS. record of a trip from New York to | Texas, and an overland journey through Mexico | and Arizona to the gold-fields of California | by | John W. Audubon | With biographical memoir by his daughter | Maria R. Audubon | Introduction, notes, and index by |, Frank Heywood Hodder | Professor of American History, University of Kansas | With folded map, portrait, and original drawings | [*Design.*] | Cleveland | The Arthur H. Clark Company | 1906.

1 vol. royal 8vo, 4 pr. ll. (half-tit., tit., conts. and illustrs.), pp. 11-249, 5 ll. (advt.), frontisp. (portr.), 5 pll. (by J. W. Audubon), 1 map (fold.). Cleveland.

A transcript of the journal of the younger son of John James Audubon on his western trip. Although mainly of historical interest, the book contains various observations on bird life as noted by the traveller.

Audubon, Lucy.

1869. See Audubon, John James, **The Life and Adventures of John James Audubon,** the Naturalist, edited by Robert Buchanan.

Audubon, Lucy.

1890. See Audubon, John James, **The Life of John James Audubon,** the Naturalist, edited by His Widow.

Audubon, Maria R.

1897. See Audubon, John James, **Audubon and his Journals.**

Audubon, Maria R.

1906. See Audubon, John Woodhouse, **Audubon's Western Journal: 1849-50.**

Azara, Felix de.   (Walckenaer, C. A.; Sonnini de Manoncour, Charles
N. Sigisb.)

1809.   **Voyages | dans | l'Amérique méridionale,** | par Don Félix de
Azara, | Commissaire et Commandant des limites Espagnoles dans
le Paraguay | depuis 1781 jusqu'en 1801; | Contenant la description
géographique, | politique, et civile du | Paraguay et de la rivière
de La Plata; l'histoire de la décou- | verte et de la conquête de ces
contrées; des détails nom- | breux sur leur histoire naturelle, et sur
les peuples sauvages | qui les habitent; le récit des moyens employés
par les | Jésuites pour assujétir et civiliser les indigènes, etc. |
Publiés d'apres les manuscrits de l'auteur, | avec une notice sur sa
vie et ses écrits, | par C. A. Walckenaer; | enrichis de notes par
G. Cuvier, | Secrétaire Perpétuel de la Classe des Sciences Phy-
siques de l'Institut, etc. | Suivis de l'histoire naturelle des Oiseaux
du Paraguay et de La Plata, par | le même auteur, traduite,
d'après l'original espagnol, et augmentée | d'un grand nombre de
notes, par M. Sonnini; | accompagnés d'un atlas de vingt-cinq
planches. | Tome premier [-quatrième]. | Paris, | Dentu, impri-
meur-libraire, | Rue du Pont-de-Lodi, No. 3. | 1809.

> Voyages | dans | l'Amerique méridionale, | par Don Félix de
Azara. | Collection de planches. | Paris, | Dentu, imprimeur-
libraire, | Rue du Pont-de-Lodi, No. 3. | 1809.

5 vols.; 4 vols. demy 8vo and 1 vol. demy folio.   Vol. I, pp. I-LX
(tit., pref. and biogr.), 1-389.   Vol. II, 2 pr. ll., pp. 1-562.   Vol. III,
2 pr. ll., pp. I-II, 1-479.   Vol. IV, 2 pr. ll., pp. 1-380.   Atlas, 2 pr. ll.,
pll. I-XXV (XI wrongly printed 'II') (8 fold.; XXII-XXV ornith.).
Paris.

Vols. I and II consist of a detailed account of the political and natural history of
Paraguay, from the manuscripts of Azara with notations by Walckenaer and,
in the case of certain remarks on mammals, by Cuvier (signed C. V.).   Pp.
383-388 of Vol. I contain notes on birds.   Vols. III and IV are devoted to a
translation, into French, of Azara's "Apuntamientos para la Historia Natural
de los Paxaros del Paraguay y Rio de la Plata," a rare ornithological work
published in Madrid in 1802-05.   This translation is by Sonnini who has supplied numerous footnotes.   On account of the rarity of the original work, the
present translation is often cited in its stead, as is Hartlaub's "Systematischer
Index to Don Felix de Azara's Apuntamientos," etc., 1847 (q.v.).

Babault, Guy.

1920.   **Mission Guy Babault | dans les provinces centrales | de
l'Inde** | dans la région occidentale de l'Himalaya et Ceylan |
1914 | Résultats scientifiques | **Oiseaux** | collectionnés au cours
de la mission | par G. Babault. | Membre Correspondant du

Muséum National d'Histoire Naturelle | Paris, 1920 | Tous droits de traduction et de reproduction réservés.

1 vol. medium 4to, tit., pp. 1-342, pll. I-VI (views), I-VI (col.; by A. Millot), 2 maps (fold.; col.). 1 text-fig. Paris.

The ornithology of the author's expedition to India, the western Himalayas and Ceylon. A separate section of the book is devoted to each of the three regions, with descriptions of the numerous collecting stations followed by the systematic discussion of the birds, including descriptions of new species. The colored plates of birds are not of especial merit.

Babault, Guy.

1923. See Ménégaux, Auguste, **Étude d'une Collection d'Oiseaux de l'Afrique Orientale Anglaise et de l'Ouganda.**

Baedeker, Fr. W. J. (Brehm, Christian Ludwig; and Paessler, Carl Wilhelm Gottfried.)

1855-63. **Die Eier | der | europaeischen Voegel** | nach der Natur gemalt | von | F. W. J. Baedeker. | Mit einer Beschreibung des Nestbaues | gemeinschaftlich bearbeitet mit | L. Brehm und W. Paessler. | Herausgegeben und verlegt von J. Baedeker. | Leipzig und Iserlohn. 1863. [*Line omitted.*].

1 vol. (or 2 vols. in 1 vol.) medium folio, 9 pr. ll. (2 tits., lith. tit., ded., index, introd. and pref.), 81 ll. (text), pll. 1-80 (col.). Leipzig and Iserlohn.

Plates by Baedeker; text by Brehm and Paessler. The work was issued in 10 parts of 8 pll., and corresponding text, each. A notice (in the Journ. für Orn. for May 1855) dated April 4, 1855, announces the appearance of the first part projected for the following week. Pt. 4 is reviewed in the Ibis for April, 1859. Carus & Engelmann quote Pts. 1-5 for 1855-59. Pt. 6 is noted in the Ibis for April 1861; Pt. 7 for July 1862; Pt. 8 for Oct. 1862. Taschenberg cites Pts. 4-10 as of 1859-65, but the Zoological Record for 1867 notes that the work was completed in 1863. The last reference is from a citation of a supplement to the present work consisting of 4 ll. (16 pp.), supposed to have been issued in 1866 by Paessler. This supplement, specially titled, is not in the present copy. The second title-page in the copy at hand, differing from the first title-page in the absence of date and publisher's imprint, may have been intended for use in dividing the work into two parts (letterpress and plates?); a bookseller's notation on a fly-leaf reads, "2 vols. in 1."

Bailey, Bert Heald. (Spencer, Clementina Sinclair.)

1918. Iowa | Geological Survey | Bulletin No. 6 | **The raptorial birds of Iowa.** | By Bert Heald Bailey, M.S., M.D. | [*Quot.*] | George F. Kay, Ph.D. State Geologist, | James H. Lees, Ph.D., Assitant State Geologist | [*Seal.*] | Des Moines | Published for the Iowa Geological Survey | 1918.

1 vol. 8vo, pp. 1-238, figs. 1-93 (40 maps). Des Moines.

A catalogue of the hawks and owls of Iowa, with field characters, brief description, measurements, range, list of stomach contents of Iowa specimens, local bibliography, and miscellaneous notes for each species. The work is posthumous, being edited by Clementina Spencer who has given also a biographical sketch of the author.

(Bailey), Florence Augusta Merriam.

1889. Birds | hrough an opera glass | by | Florence A. Merriam | [*Trade-mark.*] | Boston and New York | Houghton, Mifflin and Company | The Riverside Press, Cambridge | 1889.

1 vol. cap 8vo, pp. I-XIII+1, 1-223+1, 1 l. (advt.), 16 text-figs. Boston and New York.

A popular introduction to the study of New England birds, with descriptive accounts of seventy species. Issued as No. 3 of The Riverside Library for Young People. The illustrations are from Baird, Brewer and Ridgway, "A History of North American Birds," 1874 (q.v.).

(Bailey), Florence Augusta Merriam.

1896. A-birding on a bronco | by | Florence A. Merriam | [*Quot.*, *3 lines.*]. | Illustrated | [*Trade-mark.*] | Boston and New York | Houghton, Mifflin and Company | The Riverside Press, Cambridge | 1896.

1 vol. crown 8vo, pp. I-X, 1-226, 1 l. (index to illustrs.). 11 pll., 23 text-figs. Boston and New York.

A popular account of the author's ornithological observations in southern California.

(Bailey), Florence Augusta Merriam.

1898. Birds | of village and field | A Bird Book for Beginners | by | Florence A. Merriam | illustrated | [*Trade-mark.*] | Boston and New York | Houghton, Mifflin and Company | The Riverside Press, Cambridge | 1898.

1 vol. crown 8vo, pp. I-XLIX+1, 1-406, pll. I-XXVIII (by L. A. Fuertes, E. S. Thompson and J. L. Ridgway), text-figs. 1-220, 71 figs. (some duplicated). Boston and New·York.

An introductory hand-book of birds, with keys to the species (based on colors) short descriptions, remarks as to distribution, and accounts of habits and characteristics. An appendix contains migration and residence lists, an outline for field observations and a bibliography.

Bailey, Florence Augusta Merriam.

1918. See Bailey, Vernon; and Bailey, Florence M., Department of the Interior, **Wild Animals of Glacier National Park.**

Bailey, Florence Augusta Merriam.

1921. **Handbook of Birds** | **of the** | **Western United States** | including | the Great Plains, Great Basin, Pacific Slope, and Lower Rio Grande Valley | by | Florence Merriam Bailey | with thirty-three full-page plates by | Louis Agassiz Fuertes, and over six | hundred cuts in the text | **Revised edition** | Boston and New York | Houghton Mifflin Company | The Riverside Press Cambridge | 1921.

1 vol. 12mo, pp. I-LI+1, 1-590, 33 pll., 601 text-cuts. Boston and New York.

The original edition was published in November, 1902. The present edition is the fifth (eighth printing) with addenda [nomenclatorial changes and supplementary references] corrected to 1920. Clear descriptions, carefully arranged keys, brief pen-pictures and a wealth of illustrations combine to form a most useful "Handbook" which may be read, studied, or used as a work of reference.

Bailey, H. B.

1881. **"Forest and Stream"** | **bird notes.** | An index and summary | of all the | ornithological matter | contained in | "Forest and Stream." | Vols. I-XII. | Compiled by | H. B. Bailey. | New York: | Forest and Stream Publishing Co., | 39 Park Row. | 1881.

1 vol. 8vo, 2 pr. ll, (tit. and pref.), pp. 1-195. New York.

A useful index, arranged by authors, and by Latin and vernacular names of the species, and giving a short digest of each note under the reference to it.

Bailey, Harold H.

1913. **The Birds of Virginia.** | By | Harold H. Bailey | [*Vignette.*] | with fourteen full page colored plates | one map, and one hundred and eight | half-tones taken from nature | treating one hundred and eighty-five species and subspecies; | all the birds that breed within the state. | 1913 | J. P. Bell Company, Inc., | Publishers | Lynchburg, Va.

1 vol. post 8vo, pp. I-XXIII, 1-362, 14 pll. (col.), 185 halftones. Lynchburg.

A popular account of the species treated.

Bailey, Vernon; and Bailey, Florence Merriam.

1918. Department of the Interior | Franklin K. Lane, Secretary | National Park Service | Stephen T. Mather, Director | **Wild animals** | **of** | **Glacier National Park** | The mammals | With Notes on Physiography and Life Zones | By | Vernon Bailey | Chief Field Naturalist, Bureau of Biological Survey, Department of Agriculture | The birds | by | Florence Merriam Bailey |

Author of Handbook of Birds of the Western United States |
[*Seal.*] | Washington | Government Printing Office | 1918.

1 vol. 8vo, pp. 1-210, pll. I-XXXVII (XXXVII = map, fold., col.),
figs. 1-94. Washington.

A detailed report on the mammals and birds of Glacier National Park, Montana.
with many field-notes and other observations. The section relating to birds is
by Mrs. Bailey and occupies pp. 103-199, including pll. XXII-XXXVI and
figs. 19-94.

Baily, William L. (Cope, Edward Drinker, *ed.*)

1869. **Our own birds** | a familiar natural history | of the | birds |
of | the United States. | By | William L. Baily. | Revised and
edited by | Edward D. Cope, | Corresponding Secretary of the
Academy of Natural Sciences. | Philadelphia: | J. B. Lippincott
& Co. | 1869.

1 vol. 16mo, pp. I-X, 11-265, 10 pll. (on num. pp.), 50 text-figs.
Philadelphia.

A juvenile work, descriptive of a number of the birds of the United States (and
some extralimital forms). Most of the illustrations are after Audubon; some
are new.

Baird, Spencer Fullerton.

1858. **Catalogue** | of **North American birds,** | chiefly in the museum
of the | Smithsonian Institution. | By | Spencer F. Baird, |
Assistant Secretary of the Smithsonian Institution. | Washington: |
Smithsonian Institution. | October, 1858.

1 vol. 4to, pp. XVII-LVI. Washington. October 1858.

A reprint (supplied with a new title-page) of the same numbered pages of Vol.
IX of the U. S. Pacific Railroad Surveys "Reports of Explorations and Surveys,"
etc. (q.v.). In 1859, the list was reprinted in 8vo in greatly altered form and
issued in Vol. II (as Art. IV) of the Smithsonian Miscellaneous Collections.
In its new form it consisted of a simple list of names in Latin and English, with
serial numbers, and without any indication of the distribution of species as
given in the original; it was designed, according to the introduction, to facilitate
the labelling of specimens and to serve the purposes of a check-list. According
to Coues, some copies were issued, printed on but one side of the paper, for
further use in labelling specimens.

Baird, Spencer Fullerton.

1858. See U. S. Pacific Railroad Surveys, **Reports of Explorations
and Surveys—for a Railroad from the Mississippi River to the
Pacific Ocean, Birds, Vol. IX.**

1859. Idem, **Vol. X.**

Baird, Spencer Fullerton.

1859. See **United States and Mexican Boundary Survey, Birds.**

Baird, Spencer Fullerton, Cassin, John; and Lawrence, George Newbold.

1860. **The birds | of | North America; |** the descriptions of species based chiefly on the collections | in the | museum of the Smithsonian Institution. | By | Spencer F. Baird, | Assistant Secretary of the Smithsonian Institution, | with the co-operation of | John Cassin, | of the Academy of Natural Sciences of Philadelphia. | and | George N. Lawrence, | of the Lyceum of Natural History of New York. | With an Atlas of One Hundred Plates. | Text [Atlas]. |Philadelphia: J. B. Lippincott & Co. | 1860.

2 vols. medium 4to. Text, 2 pr. ll., pp. I-LVI, 1-1005. Atlas, tit., pp. I-XI, pll. I-XXXVIII, I (*bis*), 2, III-XXIV (*bis*), LXIII-C (= 100 pll., col.). Philadelphia.

The main body of text (pp. 1-1005) is identical with the same pages in Vol. IX of the U. S. Pacific Railroad Surveys, "Reports of Explorations," etc. (q.v.), and pp. I-VI represent pp. III-VII of the same, reset and dated "October 20, 1858" instead of October 20, 1853." Pp. VII-XV+1, containing the explanation of plates and systematic list of illustrations, are new. Three species, one of them (*Helminthophaga virginiae*) new and none of them mentioned in the original report, are discussed in footnotes to the list of illustrations without disturbing the original letterpress of the general text. Pp. III-XI of the Atlas are identical with VII-XV of the text. Pll. I-XIV, XVI-XXV, XXVII-XXXI, XXXIV and XXXVI-XXXVIII are from the Pacific Railroad Survey reports, some of them retouched or retitled; I (*bis*), 2, and III-XXIV (*bis*) are similarly from the U. S. and Mexican Boundary Survey report; the remainder are new or newly drawn.

Under the present title, the work was reissued in 1870 (q.v.) with some changes.

Baird, Spencer Fullerton, Cassin, John; and Lawrence, George Newbold.

1870. **The birds | of | North America; |** the descriptions of species based chiefly on the collections | in the | museum of the Smithsonian Institution. | By | Spencer F. Baird, | Assistant Secretary of the Smithsonian Institution, | with the co-operation of | John Cassin, | of the Academy of Natural Sciences of Philadelphia. | and | George N. Lawrence, | of the Lyceum of Natural History of New York. | With an Atlas of One Hundred Plates. | Text [Atlas.] |Philadelphia: J. B. Lippincott & Co. | 1860. | Salem: Naturalist's Book Agency. | 1870.

2 vols. medium 4to. Text, tit., pp. I-VII+1, XVI-LVI, 1-1005. Atlas, tit., pp. I-VII, pll. I-XXVIII, I (*bis*), XL-XLIII, VI (*bis*), XLV-XLVIII, XI-XII (*bis*), LI, XV-XVII (*bis*), LVI-C (= 100 pll., col.). Salem.

A later edition of the work of the same title published in 1860 (q.v.), with certain alterations. The title is changed as transcribed; the prefaces of text and atlas are reset and differently paged, with that of the text occupying fewer pages; the table of contents of the text is slightly altered to accord with the changes in pagination of the preface; the explanation of plates is reset on fewer pages and omitted from the volume of text, being found only in the atlas; the systematic list of illustrations is entirely omitted; most of the plates are retouched and renumbered or relettered, and in many cases are somewhat different in coloration from the originals. The general descriptive text appears to be the same in both editions.

Baird, Spencer Fullerton.

1873.   Smithsonian Miscellaneous Collections. | 181 | **Review** | of | **American birds,** | in the museum of the | Smithsonian Institution. | Part I. | By S. F. Baird. | [*Medallion.*] | Washington: | Smithsonian Institution. | 1864-1872.

1 vol. 8vo, (orig. wrapper), pp. I-VI, 1-478, 57 text-figs. Washington.

The final form of this paper. It was originally issued in sheets, as fast as it was printed, and distributed to various ornithologists for the purpose of eliciting criticisms and suggestions, but was not (according to a statement in the original edition) distributed to libraries or put in general circulation. These sheets are all signed with the date of issue (running from June 1864 to June 1866) and the numerous new names in the work must be quoted from the dates of the sheets on which they appeared. Pagination extended only to p. 450, and the title-page was slightly different from the present one. Later, for the present edition, the title-page was changed, the preliminary advertisement altered, an introduction written, the table of contents completed (to include the Vireonidae, Ampelidae and Laniidae), and a list of species and alphabetical index added on pp. 450-478, and the work was reissued in one volume. The final signature is dated January 1873, although the title-page cites 1864-72 only. Citation of "Smithsonian Miscellaneous Collections, 181" would seem to be correctly made only to the original issue, or to the present one when qualified as "Reissue."

Baird, Spencer Fullerton, Brewer, Thomas Mayo; and Ridgway, Robert.
(Coues, Elliott; Gill, Theodore Nicholas.)

1874.   A | **History** | of **North American Birds** | by | S. F. Baird, T. M. Brewer, and R. Ridgway | **Land Birds.** | Illustrated by 64 Chromo-Lithographic Plates and 593 Woodcuts. | Volume I [-III] | [*Vignette.*] | Boston | Little, Brown and Company | 1875.

3 vols. demy 4to. Vol. I, pp. I-XXVIII, 1-596, I-VI, 16 pll. (col.), pll. I-XXVI (col.), 189 woodcuts. Vol. II, 3 pr. ll., pp. 1-590, I-VI, 14 pll. (col.), pll. XXVII-LVI (col.), 170 woodcuts. Vol. III, 3 pr. ll., pp. 1-560, 1 l., pp. I-XXVIII, 9 pll. (col.), pll. LVII-LXIV (col.), 178 woodcuts. Boston.

A splendid work, authoritative and beautifully prepared. It deals with the life histories and habits as well as the classification of the birds of America north of Mexico, with a minimum of technicalities consistent with clearness. The coloring of the numbered plates is by chromo-lithograph; that of the unnumbered plates, by hand. The work was issued also with uncolored plates. A companion work by the same authors is the "Water Birds of North America," 1884 (q.v.), issued as "Memoirs of the Museum of Comparative Zoology at Harvard College," Vol. XII. Vols. I and II seem to have appeared by February, 1874 (Cf. Coues, Dept. Int., U. S. Geol. Surv. Terr., Misc. Publ. 3 "Birds of the Northwest," p. 96, footn.), while Vol. III appeared about December (Coues, Bibl., 1st Instalment, p. 700). Gill is responsible for the portion of the introduction (pp. XI-XIV, Vol. I) relating to birds as distinguished from other vertebrates. Coues prepared the tables of the orders and families (pp. XIV-XXVIII, Vol. I) and the glossary (pp. 535-560, Vol. III).

Baird, Spencer Fullerton.

1878. See Wilson, Alexander, and Bonaparte, **American Ornithology.**

Baird, Spencer Fullerton, Brewer, Thomas Mayo; and Ridgway, Robert.

1884. Memoirs of the Museum of Comparative Zoology | at Harvard College. | Vol. XII. | **The** | **Water Birds** | of | **North America.** | by | S. F. Baird, T. M. Brewer, | and R. Ridgway. | Issued in continuation of the | Publications of the Geological Survey of California. | J. D. Whitney, State Geologist. | Volume I [II]. | Boston: | Little, Brown, and Company. | 1884.

2 vols. demy 4to. Vol. I, pp. I-XI, 1-537, 211 text-cuts, (135 col.). Vol. II, 3 pr. ll., pp. 1-552, 282 text-cuts (201 col.). Boston.

The present work is, in reality, part of the same treatise as "A History of North American Birds—Land Birds," 1874 (q.v.), by the same authors, the two titles together forming the complete set. The volumes were to have been issued by the Geological Survey of California as a complement to the "Ornithology, Vol. I, Land Birds" by J. G. Cooper, 1870 (q.v.) in return for the use of the illustrations of Cooper's work for the volumes on the Land Birds by the present authors—hence the reference in the title quoted above. The colored illustrations are woodcuts, colored by hand. An edition was issued, also, with the cuts uncolored.

Bajon.

1777-78. **Memoires** | **pour servir** | **a l'histoire de Cayenne,** | **et** | **de la Guiane Françoise,** | Dans lesquels on fait connoître la nature du Climat | de cette contrée, les Maladies qui attaquent les Eu- | ropéens [les | Européens] nouvellement arrivés, & celles qui régnent | [qui | régnent] sur les Blancs & les Noirs; des Observa- | tions sur | [Observa- | tions sur] l'Histoire naturelle du pays, & sur la culture des | [sur la | culture des] Terres. | Avec des planches. | Par M. Bajon, ancien Chirurgien Major de l'Isle de Cayenne [*etc., 3 lines.*]. | Tome premier [second]. | Prix, 6 [5] liv. broché. | A Paris. | Chez { Grangé, Imprimeur-Libraire, rue de la Parcheminerie. | La Veuve Duchesne, Libraire, rue Saint-Jacques, au |

Saint-Jacques, | au] Temple du goût. | L'Esprit, Libraire, au Palais Royal, sous le Vestibule | du grand Escalier. | M.DCC.-LXXVII [M.DCC.LXXVIII].

2 vols. demy 8vo. Vol. I, 6 pr. ll., pp. I-XVJ, 1-462 (462 wrongly num. 162), 1 l. (errata), pll. 1-5 (of birds). Vol. II, 6 pr. ll., pp. 1-416, pll. 1-4 (2 of birds). Paris.

An account of Guiana, principally with reference to the human diseases current in the country, but with chapters on natural history. Pp. 374-405 of Vol. I and 245-286 of Vol. II are ornithological and describe the appearance, habits anatomy or other characteristics of a few birds of the region.

Baker, Edward Charles Stuart.

1913. Indian Pigeons | and | doves | by | E. C. Stuart Baker | F.Z.S., F.L.S., M.B.O.U. | Author of "Indian Ducks and their Allies." | With twenty-seven coloured plates from drawings by | H. Grönvold and G. E. Lodge. | Witherby & Co. | 326 High Holborn, London | 1913.

1 vol. superroyal folio, pp. I-XV, 1-260, frontisp. (col.), pll. 1-26 (col.). London.

A semi-popular treatment of the subject. Intended as a reference work for sportsmen as well as for specialists. It forms a sort of companion volume to the author's "Game-birds of India, Burma and Ceylon," 1921 (q.v.).

Baker, Edward Charles Stuart.

1921. The game-birds of India, | Burma and Ceylon. | Ducks and their allies [Snipe, bustards and sand-grouse] | (swans, geese and ducks). [Line omitted.] | Vol. I [II]. | By | E. C. Stuart Baker, O.B.E. [etc., 2 lines.] | With 30 [19] coloured plates | By H. Grönvold, G. E. Lodge and J. G. Keulemans. [By H. Grönvold]. | Second edition. [Two maps in colour and six black and white plates.] | Published by | The Bombay Natural History Society. | London: John Bale, Sons & Danielsson, Ltd., Oxford House, | 83-91, Great Titchfield Street W. I. | 1921.

> [Illustr. tit.] Indian Ducks [Indian] | and [Game Birds] | their allies [Snipe, Bustards, Sand Grouse,] | By | E. C. Stuart Baker. | Reprinted from the Bombay Natural History Society's journal; with corrections | & additions [corrections & | additions]. | 1921.

2 vols. superroyal 8vo. Vol. I, pp. I-XVI, 1-340, 1 illustr. tit., pll. I-XXX (col.), VIIA, VIIB and VIIc. Vol. II, pp. I-XVI, 1-328, 1 illustr. tit., pll. I-XIX (col.), A-F, maps (A and B col.). London.

A semi-popular account of the birds in the groups treated, intended for the use of the sportsman and general observer wishing to become acquainted with the species in the region. Additional volumes were planned but have not yet been published, although a similar work on "Indian Pigeons and Doves" (q.v.) was issued by the same author in 1913. Vol. I is entitled, "Second edition" since it represents a revision of the author's "Indian Ducks and their Allies," published in 1908. Both volumes are based on articles published in the Journal of the Bombay Natural History Society from 1896 onward.

Baker, Edward Charles Stuart.

1922-24. **The fauna of British India,** | including | Ceylon and Burma. | Published under the authority of the Secretary of | State for India in Council. | Edited by Sir Arthur E. Shipley, G.B.E., M.A. [*etc., 2 lines*; ScD. Cantab. *etc., 2 lines* (*Vol. II.*).].| **Birds.** Vol. I [II]. | (Second Edition.) | By | E. C. Stuart Baker, O.B.E., F.Z.S., Etc. | London: | Taylor and Francis, Red Lion Court, Fleet St. | Calcutta | Thacker, Spink & Co. | Bombay | Thacker & Co., Limited. | July, 1922. [April, 1924].

2 vols. 8vo. Vol. I, pp. I-XXIII+1, 1-479, frontisp. (col.), pll. I-VII (col.; by the author), text-figs. 1-93, 8 figs. (unnum.). Vol. II, pp. I-XXIII+1, 1-561, frontisp. (col.), pll. I-VII (col.), text-figs. 1-86. London.

A detailed monograph of the birds of British India to replace the antiquated and out-of-print volumes of the same title by Oates and Blanford, 1889-98 (q.v.). The general plan of the work is much the same as that of its predecessor but modern nomenclature is adopted with other changes necessary to bring the text up to date, and the result is an authoritative and concise account of all the birds inhabiting the region. The complete ornithological series is planned to occupy six volumes, of which two have been issued to date.

Baker, Max.

1924. See Kirkman, Frederick B., and Hutchinson, **British Sporting Birds.**

Baldamus, August Carl Eduard.

1860. See Naumann, Johann Friedrich, Johann Andreas Naumann's mehrerer gelehrten Gesellschaften Mitgliede, **Naturgeschichte der Vögel Deutschlands,** 1822-1860.

Baldamus, August Carl Eduard.

1892. **Das** | **Leben der europäischen Kuckucke.** | Nebst | Beiträgen zur Lebenskunde | der | übrigen parasitischen Kuckucke und Stärlinge. | Von | A. C. Eduard Baldamus, | Dr. phil. h. c. Mitgliede, [*etc., 2 lines.*]. | Mit 8 Farbendrucktafeln. | Berlin. | Verlag von Paul Parey. | Verlagshandlung für Landwirtschaft, Gartenbau und Forstwesen. | SW., 10 Hedemannstrasse. | 1892.

1 vol. royal 8vo, pp. I-VIII, 1-224, 1 l. (expl. of pll.), pll. I-VIII (col.; of eggs). Berlin.

A detailed study of the European Cuckoo and its parasitic habits, and of other parasitic birds.

Ball, Alice E.

1924.   Bird biographies | by | Alice E. Ball | Author of "A Year With the Birds" | illustrated by | Robert Bruce Horsfall | Painter of Backgrounds in Habitat Groups, American Museum | of Natural History, New York City | 56 colored plates | [*Design.*] | New York | Dodd, Mead and Company | 1924.

1 vol. royal 8vo, pp. I-XX, 1 l. (subtit.), pp. 1-295, 56 pll. (col.). New York.

"A guide-book for beginners"; "an introduction to 150 common land birds of the eastern United States." Descriptions of both sexes and the young are prefixed by a brief characterization of the "general appearance" and followed by remarks on note, song, habitat and range, forming the descriptive or diagnostic introduction to each species. The general text for each species follows, with notes on habits and economic importance, much of which is quoted from other sources. The species are arranged in three groups, winter birds, early spring birds and later spring birds, and lists are given under the first two headings.

Ball, Henry Lidgbird.

1789.   See Phillip, Arthur, **The Voyage of Governor Phillip to Botany Bay.**

Balston, Richard James; Shepherd, Charles William; and Bartlett, Edward.

1907.   Notes | on the | **birds of Kent** | by | R. J. Balston, D. L., J.P., F.Z.S., M.B.O.U., | Rev. C. W. Shepherd, M.A., F.Z.S., M.B.O.U. | and | E. Bartlett, F.Z.S. | with nine plates and a map | London | R. H. Porter | 7 Princes Street, Cavendish Square, W. | 1907.

1 vol. 8vo, pp. I-XIX, 1-465, frontisp., 8 pll. (col.), 1 map (col.). London.

A popular account of the habits of the various species treated.

Bancroft, Edward.

1769.   An | essay | on the | natural | history | of | Guiana, | In South America. | Containing | A Description of many Curious Productions | in the Animal and Vegetable Systems | of that Country. | Together with an Account of | The Religion, Manners, and Customs | of several tribes of its Indian Inhabitants. | Inter-

spersed with |A Variety of Literary and Medical Observations. |
In Several Letters | from | A Gentleman of the Medical Faculty, |
During his Residence in that Country. | [*Quot., 3 lines.*] | London, *t*|
Printed for T. Becket and P. A. De Hondt | in the Strand. |
MDCCLXIX.

1 vol. post 8vo, 2 pr. ll., pp. I-IV, 1-402, 3 ll., frontisp. London.

Title self-explanatory. The ornithological matter is contained on pp. 152-158.

Bannerman, David A.

1922. The Canary Islands | their history, natural history | and
scenery | An account of an ornithologist's | camping trips in the
archipelago | by | David A. Bannerman | M.B.E. [*etc.*] | with
illustrations and maps | Gurney and Jackson | London: 33 Pater-
noster Row | Edinburgh: Tweeddale Court | 1922.

1 vol. 8vo, pp. I-XV, 1-365, frontisp. (col., by Roland Green), 46
pll. (2 col., by Grönvold; 6 fold.), 4 maps (fold.).

A very thorough account of the subject, entertainingly written, with voluminous
notes on the natural history of the country, a large number of which are orhitho-
logical. Appendix B, pp. 328-350, is devoted to an annotated list of the birds
of the Islands.

Barbour, Thomas.

1923. Memoirs of the Nuttall Ornithological Club | No. VI | **The
Birds of Cuba** | By Thomas Barbour | With four plates | Cam-
bridge, Massachusetts | Published by the Club | June, 1923.

1 vol. imperial 8vo, pp. 1-141, pll. I-IV (photogravures). Cambridge.

An annotated list of species giving an account of their local status and distribution. The introductory chapters are historical and topographical.

Barboza du Bocage, José Vicente.

1877-81. Ornithologie | d'Angola | ouvrage publié sous les auspices
du | Ministère de la Marine et de Colonies | par | J. V. Barboza
du Bocage | Professeur de zoologie à l'Ecole Polytechnique, direc-
teur du Muséum nationale de Lisbonne | Lisbonne | Imprimerie
Nationale | 1881.

1 vol. superroyal 8vo, tit., pp. V-XXXII, 1-576, 1 l. (list of pll.), pll.
I-X (col.; by Keulemans). Lisbon.

An important monograph of the birds of Angola, giving, for each species, the
synonymy, reference to a published figure, the description, measurements and
habitat. Several new species are described. The work was issued in two parts.
Pt. I, containing pp. 1-256 and pll. I, III, IV and IX, was issued in 1877; Pt.
II, containing the introductory matter, pp. 257-276 and pll. II, V-VIII and X,
in 1881 (Zoological Record).

Barker, Edmond.

  1764. See Edwards, George, **Gleanings of Natural History, 1758-64.**
  1805-06. Idem.

Barrere, Pierre.

  1741. **Essai | sur | l'histoire naturelle | de la | France equinoxiale. |**
  Ou | de nombrement | Des Plantes, des Animaux, & des Miné- |
  raux, qui se trouvent dans l'Isle de Cayen- | ne, les Isles de Remire,
  sur les Côtes de | la Mer, & dans le Continent de la Guyane. | Avec |
  Leurs noms differens, Latins, François, & Indiens, | & quelques
  Observations sur leur usage dans | la Médecine & dans les Arts. |
  Par Pierre Barrere Corres- | pondant de l'Académie Royale des |
  Sciences de Paris, Docteur & Professeur | Royal en Médecine dans
  l'Université de | Perpignan, Médecin de l'Hôpital Mili- | taire de
  la même Ville, ci-devant Méde- | cin Botaniste du Roi dans l'Isle
  de | Cayenne. | A Paris, | Chez Piget, Quay des Augustins, à |
  l'Image S. Jacques. | M. DCC. XLI.

  1 vol. 16mo, pp. I-XXIV, 1-215+1, 4 ll. ("Privilege du Roi," etc.).
  Paris. 1741 (post June 15).

  Descriptions of the animals, plants and minerals of French Guiana. The birds
  occupy pp. 121-148 in the second part (pp. 121-215) devoted to animals and
  minerals. The species are grouped in genera arranged alphabetically. Since the
  book is pre-Linnean, none of the names are tenable, but the descriptions often
  form the basis for names afterwards applied by Linné. The work is rare. It is
  not mentioned by Coues. A certificate of the Académie Royale des Sciences
  at the close of the volume is dated June 15, 1741.

Barrington, Richard Manliffe.

  1900. **The | migration of birds |** as observed at | Irish lighthouses
  and lightships | including | the original reports | from 1888-97,
  now published for the first time, and | an analysis | of these and
  of the previously published reports from 1881-87. | Together with |
  an appendix | giving the measurements of about 1600 wings. | By |
  Richard M. Barrington, M.A., LL.B., F.L.S., | Member of the
  British Ornithologists' Union, [*etc.*, *3 lines.*] | London: | R. H.
  Porter, 7 Princes Street, Cavendish Square, W. | Dublin: |
  Edward Ponsonby, 116 Grafton Street.

  1 vol. 8vo, pp. I-XXV, 1-667, 1 map (fold.), 9 small maps in text.
  London.

  A most thorough report. Only 350 copies of the work were printed.

Barrows, Walter Bradford.

  1890. See Warren, Benjamin H, **Report on the Birds of Pennsylvania, Second Edition.**

E S S A I
S U R
L'HISTOIRE NATURELLE
D E L A
FRANCE EQUINOXIALE.
O U
DE'NOMBREMENT
Des Plantes, des Animaux, & des Miné-
raux, qui fe trouvent dans l'Ifle de Cayenne, les Ifles de Remire, fur les Côtes de
la Mer,& dans le Continent de la Guyane.

A V E C

Leurs noms differens, Latins, François, & Indiens,
& quelques Obfervations fur leur ufage dans
la Médecine & dans les Arts.

Par PIERRE BARRERE Coref-
pondant de l'Académie Royale des
Sciences de Paris, Docteur & Profeffeur
Royal en Médecine dans l'Univerficé de
Perpignan, Médecin de l'Hôpital Mili-
taire de la même Ville, ci-devant Méde-
cin Botanifte du Roi dans l'Ifle de
Cayenne.

A P A R I S,
Chez P I G E T, Quay des Auguftins, à
l'Image S. Jacques.

M. DCC. XLI.

TITLE-PAGE OF BARRERE'S "ESSAI."
See p. 40.

Barrows, Walter Bradford.

1912. Michigan Bird Life | A List of all the Bird Species known to occur in the State together with | an outline of their Classification and an account of the | Life History of Each Species, with special reference to its | Relation to Agriculture. With Seventy Full-page Plates | and One Hundred and Fifty-two Text Figures | By | Walter Bradford Barrows, S.B., | Professor of Zoology and Physiology and | Curator of the General Museum | Special Bulletin | of the | Department of Zoology and Physiology | of the | Michigan Agricultural College | Published by the Michigan Agricultural College | 1912.

1 vol. 16mo (6¼x9¼), pp. I-XIV, 1-822, pll. I-LXX, figs. 1-152. Lansing.

A complete descriptive catalogue of the birds of the state, with an account of the habits, distribution and migration of each species, tables for their determination and an introductory chapter with general notes and a bibliography.

Barthelémy-Lapommeraye.

1859-62. See Jaubert and Barthelémy-Lapommeraye, **Richesses Ornithologiques du Midi de la France.**

Bartlett, Edward.

1888-89. Part I [-V] February 29, 1888 [April. 1888; January. 1889; August. 1889; Nov. 30 1889]. | **A monograph** | **of the** | **weaver-birds,** | Ploceidæ, | **and** | arboreal and terrestrial | **finches,** | Fringillidæ, | by | Edward Bartlett, | Curator of the Maidstone Museum. | Contents. | Textor dinemelli [*etc., list of species in 2 columns*.]. | Maidstone: | published by the author. | 1888 [1889 (*Pts. III-V.*)]. | Printed by J. Burgiss-Brown, Week Street [Printed by Spottiswoode & Co., New-Street Square, London *Pts. III-V.*)].

5 pts. (in 1 vol.) demy 4to. Pt. I, (orig. wrapper), 16 ll. (variously paged), 6 pll. (col.; variously num.). Pt. II, (orig. wrapper), 26 ll., 6 pll. (col.), 1 text-fig. Pt. III, (orig. wrapper), 19 ll,. 7 pll. (col.). Pt. IV, (orig. wrapper), 18 ll., 6 pll. (col.). Pt. V, 22 ll., 4 pll. (should be 5; that of *Ploceus nigerrimus* and *P. albinucha* missing) (col.). London.

All published of a work which was planned to extend to between 90 and 95 parts and to embrace all the known species of Ploceidae and Fringillidae. In the fragmentary form in which the publication remains, the pagination and plate-numbering are incomplete, being distinct for each genus. Collation might be made as follows:

Cardinalis, pp. 1-13+1, 14-20+1, pll. I-II, 1 text-fig.; *Chrysomitris*, pp. 1-7+ 1, pll. I-II; *Coccothraustes*, pp. 1-8, pll. I-II; *Euplectes*, pp. 1-6, pl. I; *Malimbus*, pp. 1-10, pll. I-II; *Munia*, pp. 1-58, pll. I-VIII; *Paroaria*, pp. 1-11+1, pll. I-III; *Passer*, pp. 1-16, pl. I; *Phrygilus*, pp. 1-11+1, pll. I-II; *Ploceus*, pp. 1-12, pll. I-II (I missing); *Pyrrhula*, pp. 1-3+1, 4-11, pll. I-III; Textor, pp. 1-25+1, pll. I-IV.

As issued, Pt. I contained *Textor dinemelli*, *T. Boehmi*, *Chrysomitris atrata*, *Paroaria cucullata*, *Pyrrhula nipalensis* and *Munia oryzivora* (2 pll.); Pt. II, *Cardinalis virginianus*, *Chrysomitris uropygialis*, *Passer domesticus*, *Textor panicivora* (2 pll.) and *T. albirostris;* Pt. III, *Munia fuscata*, *M. malacca*, *Cardinalis igneus* (no plate issued), *Phrygilus fruticeti*, *Pyrrhula erithacus*, *Coccothraustes personatus*, *C. melanrus* and *Euplectes flammiceps;* Pr. IV, *Malimbus malimbicus*, *M. cristatus*, *Munia atricapilla*, *M. sumatrensis*, *Pyrrhula erythrocephala*, *Cardinalis phoeniceus* and *Phrygilus alaudinus;* Pt. V, *Ploceus nigerrimus*, *P. albinucha* (not mentioned on wrapper), *P. castaneofuscus*, *Paroaria dominicana*, *Munia minuta*, *M. brunneiceps*, *M. formosana*, *M. ferruginosa*, *M. maja*, *M. pallida*, *M. melaena*, *M. forbesi* and *M. spectabilis*.

Bartlett, Edward.

1907.   See Balston, Richard J., Shepherd and Bartlett, **Notes on the Birds of Kent.**

Barton, Benjamin Smith.   (Salvin, Osbert, *ed.*)

1883.   The Willughby Society. | **Barton's Fragments** | **of the** | **Natural History of Pennsylvania.** | [*Vignette.*] | Edited by | Osbert Salvin, M.A., F.R.S., &c. | London: MDCCCLXXXIII.

[Fragments | of the | natural history | of | Pennsylvania. | By Benjamin Smith Barton, M.D. | Part first. | Philadelphia: | printed, for the author, by Way & Groff, | and sold, in London, by Messrs. G. J. & J. Robinson, booksellers, | Pater-noster Row. | Price Four Shillings.]

> {Fragments | of the | natural history | of | Pennsylvania. | By Benjamin Smith Barton, M.D. | Correspondent-Member [*etc., 10 lines.*]. | Part first. | [*Quot., 4 lines.*]. | Philadelphia: | printed, for the author, by Way & Groff, | No. 48, North Third-Street. | 1799.}

1 vol. demy 4to, 2 pr. ll. (tit. and pref.), "3 pr. ll. (2 tits. and ded.), pp. V-XVIII (introd.), 1-24". "Philadelphia. 1799" London.

A miscellaneous assortment of ornithological observations and facts based on studies made in Pennsylvania. The introduction contains a series of essays on avian migration. This is followed by a "calendar" giving the dates of movement of birds of passage, the progress of vegetation and miscellaneous observations. Section III treats of the resident birds of Pennsylvania and an appendix contains various observations relating to the species mentioned in the preceding pages. Strict binomial nomenclature is used throughout, and, although thorough descriptions of the species are not given, a short characterization of certain peculiarities of some of the birds makes their recognition unquestionable. Many of the names and facts are taken from Bartram's "Travels through North and South Carolina," etc. of 1791. A detailed review of the work is given by Coues. The present copy is a reprint by The Willughby Society (q.v.). The editorial preface serves to introduce the volume.

Barton, Frank Townend.

1912. **Pheasants | In Covert and Aviary** | By | Frank Townend Barton, M.R.C.V.S. | Author of | Terriers [*etc., 2 lines.*] | With four coloured plates from life by H. Grönvold, | and thirty-seven other illustrations | London | John Long, Limited | Norris Street, Haymarket | MCMXII.

1 vol. demy 4to, pp. 1-288, frontisp. (col.), 24 pll. (3 col.), 9 text-figs. London.

A practical, non-technical manual on breeding and rearing pheasants.

Baskett, James Newton.

1896. See World's Congress on Ornithology, **Papers presented to the.**

Bassetiere, Gérard de la.

1913. **Essai sur le Chant | de | Quelques Oiseaux** | Préface de Gabriel Etoc | Illustrations d'Edouard Mérite et J. Péan de Saint-Gilles | [*Design.*] | Chez l'auteur | Huisseau-sur-Cosson (Loir-et-Cher) | 1913.

1 vol. royal 8vo, 3 pr. ll. (half-tit., tit. and ded.), pp. IX-XII, 1-180, frontisp. (col.), 6 text-figs. (full-p.). Huisseau-sur-Cosson.

A study of the songs of 63 species of birds, with onomatopoeic and musical notations, sometimes in considerable detail. The illustrations are poor.

Bates, Abraham H.

1896. See World's Congress on Ornithology, **Papers presented to the.**

Bates, Frank A.

1896. **The Game Birds | of North America** | A Descriptive Check-List | by | Frank A. Bates | President "Boston Scientific Society" [*etc., 2 lines.*]. | Illustrated | Boston | Bradlee Whidden | 1896.

1 vol. 12 mo, pp. 1-118, frontisp., 18 text-cuts. Boston.

A list of 124 species of North American birds "suitable for food and — — habitually pursued by man for sport, demanding skill and dexterity for — — capture." Brief descriptions and comments are given, with a key to the identification of various arbitrary groups. Intended for the sportsman.

Bau, Alexander.

1923. See Friderich, C. G., **Naturgeschichte der Vögel Europas.**

Beagle, Zoology of the Voyage of.

1838-44. See Darwin, Charles.

Bechstein, Johann Matthäus. (*Frisch, Johann Leonhard.*)

1789-95. Gemeinnützige | Naturgeschichte | Deutschlands | nach allen drey Reichen [*Period added* (*Vols. II-IV.*).] | Ein | Handbuch | zur deutlichern und vollständigern | Selbstbelehrung | besonders | für Forstmänner, Jugendlehrer und Oekonomen | von | J. M. Bechstein [*Period added* (*Vols. II-IV.*)] | Erster [—Vierter] Band [*Comma added* (*Vols. II-IV.*).] | welcher die nöthigen Vorkenntnisse und die Geschichte | der Säugethiere enthält [welcher die Einleitung in die Geschichte der Vögel | überhaupt, und die Geschichte der Raubvögel, Waldvögel, | und Wasservögel Deutschlands enthält (*Vol. II.*); welcher die Sumpf-und Hausvögel nebst einer | Untersuchung über die Frischischen Vögel enthält (*Vol. III.*); welcher die Singvögel, den Vögelkalender, einige Zusätze zu | den vorhergehenden Bänden und das Register uber die | drey Bände der Vögel Deutschlands enthält (*Vol. IV.*)] | Mit Kupfern [*Period added* (*Vols. II-IV.*).] Leipzig 1789 | bey Siegfried Lebrecht Crusius [Leipzig, | bey Siegfried Lebrecht Crusius. | 1791 (1793; 1795). (*Vols. II-IV.*)].

> Gemeinnützige | Naturgeschichte | der | Vögel Deutschlands | für aller Leser | vorzüglich | für Forstmänner, Jugendlehrer und Oekonomen | von Johann Matthäus Bechstein, | Gräflich Schaumburg-Lippischem Bergrath [*etc.*, 8 *lines.*]. | Dritter Band. | Mit Kupfern. | Leipzig, | bey Siegfried Lebrecht Crusius. | 1795.

4 vols. crown 8vo. Vol. I, 4 pr. ll. (tit., 3 ll. ded.), pp. I-XVI, 1-841+1 (errata), 3 ll. (advt.), 16 pll. (12 col.; num. I-XIII, XIIIb, XIIIc, XIVa-XIVd). Vol. II, pp. I-XVI, 1-840, frontisp., 18 pll. (num. IXXVI). Vol. III, pp. I-XX, 1 l. (half-tit.), pp. 1-800, frontisp., 12 pll. (num. I-XVII). Vol. IV, 1 l. (special title, quoted above), pp. I-XVIII, 1 l. (half-tit.), pp. 1-946, frontisp., 19 pll. (num. I-XXXI). Leipzig.

A natural history of the birds and mammals of Germany. Full descriptions and discussions are given, and a number of new species and genera are described. Vol. I, part of Appendix II of Vol. III and part of Appendix II of Vol. IV relate to mammals; the remainder of the work is ornithological.

The ornithological volumes, II-IV, are also considered as Vols. I-III of "Gemeinnützige Naturgeschichte der Vögel Deutschlands." Vol. IV of the present set bears an additional title-page thus lettered (cited above after the general title), and a half-title lettered in accordance, "Dritter Band." The half-title of the third volume of the set also reads, "Dritter Band," referring to the general series.

Supplement I of Vol. III (pp. 583-741) contains a review of the "Vorstellung der Vögel Deutschlands" by Johann Leonhard Frisch, 1733-63, (Cf. ed. 1817.), with the birds identified according to the nomenclature of Gmelin's edition of

Linnaeus. Supplement II (pp. 742-760) contains descriptions of species of mammals and birds not discussed in the preceding text of Vols. I-III. Supplement III (pp. 761-799) contains additional remarks on the birds of Vols. II and III. In Vol. IV, Supplement I (pp. 793-826) contains a calendar of birds. Supplement II (pp. 827-870) contains addenda to Vols. II-IV (I-III of the Ornithology). Supplement III (pp. 871-882) consists of a glossary of descriptive terms. Supplement IV (pp. 883-892) contains notes relative to a forestry school in which the author appears to have been interested. The last volume (pp. 893-946) contains a general index to the three volumes of birds.

A second edition of this work was issued in 1801-09 (q.v.).

Bechstein, Johann Matthaus.

1793-1812. See Latham, John, **Johann Lathams allgemeine Uebersicht der Vögel.**

Bechstein, Johann Matthäus.

1795. Naturgeschichte | **der** | **Stubenvögel** | oder | Anleitung | zur | Kenntniss und Wartung | derjenigen Vögel, | welche man in der Stube halten kann, | von | Johann Matthäus Bechstein. | Mit Kupfern. | Gotha, | bey Carl Wilhelm Ettinger. | 1795.

1 vol. cap 8vo, 3 pr. ll. (illum. tit., tit. and ded.), pp. V-X, 1 l. (expl. of pll.), pp. 1-488, 1 insert (fold.; table), 4 ll. (index), pll. I-IV (col.; on 2 ll.; fold.), col. fig. on illum. tit. Gotha.

A descriptive account of cage-birds, mostly European. Linnean nomenclature is usually adopted but in some cases the author uses names of his own. On p. 143 the name *Emberiza Elaeathorax* appears for the first time in nomenclature.

Bechstein, Johann Matthäus.

1801-09. Gemeinnützige | **Naturgeschichte** | **Deutschlands** | nach allen drey Reichen. | Ein | Handbuch | zur deutlichern und vollständigern | Selbstbelehrung | besonders | für Forstmänner, Jugendlehrer und Oekonomen | von | J. M. Bechstein [Johann Matthäus Bechstein (*Vols. III and IV.*)]. | Erster [—Vierter] Band [*Comma added* (*Vols. II and III.*); Vierter Band | in zwey Abtheilungen, (*Vol. IV.*).] | welcher die nöthigen Vorkenntnisse und die Geschichte | der Säugethiere enthält [welcher die Einleitung in die Naturgeschichte der Vö- | gel überhaupt, und die Geschichte der Raubvögel, | spechtartigen und krähenartigen Vögel Deutschlands | enthält (*Vol. II.*); welcher die sperlingsartigen, Sing- und schwalbenartigen Vögel, | die Tauben und hühnerartigen Vögel Deutschlands | enthält (*Vol. III.*); welche die Sumpf- und Schwimm-Vögel nebst dem Register | über die Vögel Deutschlands enthalten (*Vol. IV.*)]. | Mit 25 Kupfertafeln [Mit Kupfern (*Vols. II-IV.*)]. | **Zweyte vermehrte und verbesserte Ausgabe** [Auflage (*Vols.*

II-IV.)]. | Leipzig, [Leipzig 1809 (*Vol. IV.*)] | bey Siegfried
Lebrecht Crusius. [*No punctuation* (*Vol. II.*); *comma* (*Vol. III.*);
Bey Fr. Chr. Wilh. Vogel (*Vol. IV.*).] | 1801 [1805; 1807; *line
omitted in Vol. IV.*].

> Gemeinnützige | Naturgeschichte | der | Säugethiere Deutsch-
lands | für allerley Leser | vorzüglich | fur Forstmänner, Jugend-
lehrer und Oekonomen | von | J. M. Bechstein, | Mit Kupfern. |
Zweyte vermehrte und verbesserte Ausgabe. | Leipzig, | bey Sieg-
fried Lebrecht Crusius. | 1801 [*in Vol. I.*).

> Gemeinnützige | Naturgeschichte | der Vögel Deutschlands
[der | Vögel Deutschlands (*Vols. II and III* = *Vols. III and IV of
general title.*)] | für allerley Leser, [*No comma* (*Vols. II and III.*)]
| vorzüglich für [vorzüglich (*Vols. II and III.*)] Forstmänner,
Jugendlehrer und Oekonomen [für Forstmänner, *etc.* [*Vols. II and
III.*)] | von | J. M. Bechstein [Johann Matthäus Bechstein
(*Vols. II and III.*)]. | Erster Band [Zweyter Band (Vol. II.);
Dritter und letzter Band | in zwey Abtheilungen (Vol. III.)], |
welcher die Einleitung in die Naturgeschichte der Vö- | gel über-
haupt, und die Beschreibung der Raub-, specht- | artigen und
krähenartigen Vögel Deutschlands | enthält [welcher die sperlings-
artigen, Sing- und schwalbenartigen Vögel, | die Tauben und
hühnerartigen Vögel Deutschlands | enthält (*Vol. II.*); welche die
Sumpf- und Schwimm-Vögel Deutschlands nebst | dem Register
enthalten (*Vol. III.*)]. | Mit Kupfern. | Zweyte vermehrte und
verbesserte Ausgabe [Auflage (*Vols. II and III.*)]. | Leipzig,
[Leipzig 1809. (*Vol. III.*)] | bey Siegfried Lebrecht Crusius.
[*Comma* (*Vol. II.*); Bey Fr. Chr. Wilh. Vogel. (*Vol. III.*)] | 1805.
[1807. (*Vol. II.*); *line omitted* (*Vol. III.*).].

4 vols. crown 8vo. Vol. I, 1 l. (special tit.), pp. I-XXX, 1-1355+1,
frontisp., pll. I-XXIV (col.; by Capieux). Vol. II, 1 l. (special tit.),
pp. I-XXXIV, 1-1346, 2 ll. (errata), frontisp., 23 pll. (16 col., by
Capieux and Haussen; 1 fold.; num. I-VI, VIIa, VIIb, VIII-
XXXI). Vol. III, pp. I-XXX (incl. special tit.), 1-1486, frontisp.,
33 pll. (col.; num. I-IV, Va, Va (bis), Vb, VI-XLV). Vol. IV, pp.
I-XXXII (incl. special tit.), 1-1282, 1 l. (errata), frontisp., 32
pll. (col.; num. I-XXXVII). Leipzig.

A revised and enlarged edition of the author's previous work of the same title,
1789-95 (q.v.). A special title is given to the first volume, which deals entirely
with mammals, and one to the last three volumes, which deal with birds and
which are given also a new series of volume-numbers. The special titles are
quoted above; Vol. I of the ornithological series is Vol. II of the original work
etc. Vol. IV (of the original) is in two parts, the second of which begins on p.

529. Vol. IV, Supplement I (pp. 1163-1210) contains an ornithological calendar (revised from that of the first edition). Supplement II (pp. 1211-1220) contains material extracted from Lacépède and from Bertuch's "Tafeln der allgemeinen Naturgeschichte." A general index to the three volumes of birds is in Vol. IV, pp. 1221-1282. A supplement was begun by J. P. A. Leisler under the title of "Nachträge zu Bechsteins Naturgeschichte Deutschlands," in 1812 (q.v.).

Bechstein, Johann Matthäus.

1802-03. Ornithologisches | Taschenbuch | von und für | Deutschland | order | kurze Beschreibung | aller Vögel Deutschlands | für | Liebhaber dieses Theils der Naturgeschichte | von | Johan Matthäus Bechstein. | Erster [Zweyter] Theil. | Mit 19 [20] illuminirten Kupfern. | Leipzig, | bey Carl Friedrich Enoch Richter. | 1802 [1803].

2 vols. 12mo. Vol. I, 1 l. (notice), pp. I-XIV, 1-250, 19 pll. (col.). Vol. II, 2 ll. (tit. and subtit.), pp. XV-XXXIV+1, 251-550, 462a and 462b, 20 pll. (col.). Leipzig.

A condensed handbook of the birds of Germany, with brief descriptions, bibliographic references, vernacular names, accounts of distribution, nidification, etc., arranged by paragraphs. Several new species are described but are designated simply "mihi" as are the other species previously described elsewhere by Bechstein, making it necessary to check all such references to determine their novelty. Pages 463-484 of Vol. II contains a calendar in which are listed the birds which may be seen during each month, according to their status as migrants, residents, etc. Engelmann notes a third volume under date of 1812, issued also separately under the title, "Gattungskennzeichen der Vögel." This I have not seen, but Bechstein, on a preliminary leaf of Vol. I of the present work, says that Vol. II will contain "Zwey grossen Platten die Kennzeichen der Gattungen." These are not in Vol. II and perhaps may form the basis of the third volume issued much later. A second edition of the present work appeared in 1811-12.

Bechstein, Johann Matthäus.

1811-12. See Latham, John, **Kurze Uebersicht aller bekannten Vögel.**

Bechstein, Johann Matthäus. (Lehmann, Dr.)

1840. **Naturgeschichte** | der | **Stubenvögel** | oder | Anleitung | zur Kenntniss, Wartung, Zähnung, Fortpflanzung und | zum Fang derjenigen in- und ausländischen Vögel, | welche man in der Stube halten kann, | von | Dr. J. M. Bechstein. | Mit 6 sorgfältig illuminirten Kupfertafeln, enthaltend 50 naturgetreue Ab- | bildungen der beliebtesten Stubenvögel, und 1 | schwarzen Kupfertafel zur | Versinnlichung des Vogelfanges. | **Vierte vermehrte und verbesserte Auflage.** | Halle, 1840. | Verlag von Ed. Heynemann.

1 vol. post 8vo, pp. I-XXII, 1 l. (half-tit.), pp. 1-480, pll. I-VII (6 col.). Halle.

A fourth, revised edition of the author's work of the same title, the original edition of which was published in 1795 (q.v.). The present edition was edited and published, after the author's death, by Dr. Lehmann. The preface is dated April, 1840.

Bechstein, Johann Matthäus. (Adams, Henry Gardiner; Sweet, Robert.)

1853.   **Cage | and | Chamber-birds |** their natural history, habits, | food, diseases, management, and modes of capture. | Translated from the German by | J. M. Bechstein, M.D. | with considerable additions on | structure, migration, and economy, |compiled from various sources by H. G. Adams. | Incorporating the whole of | Sweet's British Warblers; | with numerous illustrations. | London: | H. G. Bohn, | York Street Covent Garden. | MDCCCLIII.

1 vol. cap 8vo, pp. I-XVI, 1-500, 31 pll. (9 col., not original), 15 woodcuts in text. London.

A translation of this classic, Bechstein's "Naturgeschichte der Stubenvögel," 1795 et seq. (q.v.), enlarged as noted in the title. A few of the plates are very crudely colored by hand, apparently by some former owner of the volume and not by the publishers, although a colored edition was issued the same year. Sweet's "British Warblers" incorporated in this edition, was originally published in 1823-29 (q.v.).

Bechstein, Johann Matthäus. (Adams, Henry Gardiner; Sweet, Robert.)

1900.   **Cage | and | chamber-birds |** their natural history, habits, food, | diseases, management, and modes of capture | translated from the German of | J. M. Bechstein, M.D. | with considerable additions on | structure, migration, and economy | compiled from various sources by H. G. Adams | incorporating the whole of | Sweet's British warblers | with numerous illustrations | London. | George Bell & Sons. | 1900.

1 vol. cap 8vo, pp. I-XVI, 1-500, 1-32 (advt.), 31 pll. (30 col.), 15 woodcuts. London.

Reprinted from the stereo plates of the earlier edition of 1853 (q.v.) with some alterations in the title but no changes in the text.

Beddard, Frank Evers.

1898.   **The | structure and classification | of | birds |** by | Frank E. Beddard, M.A., F.R.S. | Prosector and Vice-secretary of the Zoological Society of London | Longmans, Green, and Co. | 39 Paternoster Row, London | New York and Bombay | 1898 | All rights reserved.

1 vol. post 8vo, pp. I-XX, 1-548, 1-40 (advt.), text-figs. 1-252. London.

A thorough dissertation on the subject.

Beebe, Charles William. [Beebe, Mary Blair (=*Mrs.* C. W.).]

1905. Two bird-lovers in | Mexico | by | C. William Beebe | Curator of Ornithology [*etc., 3 lines.*] | Illustrated with photographs | from life taken by the author | [*Vignette.*] | Boston and New York | Houghton, Mifflin and Company | The Riverside Press, Cambridge | 1905.

1 vol. 8vo, pp. I-XIII+1, 1-407+1, 1 l. (imprint), 3 ll. (advt.), frontisp., 13 pll. (on num. pp.), 92 text-figs. Boston and New York.

Field studies of Mexican bird-life. Chapter XV, by Mrs. Beebe, gives an account of equipment, etc., used on the journey described in the book. An appendix gives a list of the birds and mammals observed.

Beebe, Charles William.

1906. American Nature Series | Group II. The Functions of Nature | **the bird | its form and function** | by | C. William Beebe | Curator of Ornithology [*etc., 4 lines.*] | with over three hundred and seventy illustrations | chiefly photographed from life | by the author | New York | Henry Holt and Company | 1906.

1 vol. 8vo, pp. I-XI, 1-496, 1 l. (advt.), frontisp. (col., by Walter King Stone), text-figs. 1-371 (33 full page). New York.

"An untechnical study of the bird in the abstract," of the morphological and physiological characteristics of birds in general with reference to their life and adaptations.

Beebe, Charles William.

1910. See Beebe, Mary Blair, and Beebe, C. William, **Our Search for a Wilderness.**

Beebe, Charles William.

1918-22. A monograph of the | pheasants | by | William Beebe | Curator of Birds [*etc., 6 lines.*]. | In four volumes | Volume I [-IV] | Published under the auspices of the | New York Zoological Society by | Witherby & Co. [H. F. & G. Witherby (*Vols. II-IV.*)] | 326 High Holborn, London, England | 1918 [1921; 1922; 1922].

4 vols. imperial 4to. (12 x 16). Vol. I, pp. I-XLIX, 1-198, pll. I-XIV and XVI-XX (=19, col.), 1-15+1a (photograv.), maps. I-V (col.). Vol. II, pp. I-XV, 1-269, pll. XXI-XLIV (col.), 16-39 (photograv.), maps VI-X (col.). Vol. III, pp. I-XVI, 1-204, pll. XLV-LXVIII (col.), 40-60 (photograv.), maps XI-XIV (col.).

Vol. IV, pp. I-XV, 1-242, pll. LXIX-XC+XV (col.), 61-87 (photograv.), maps XV-XX (col.). (Col. pll. by L. A. Fuertes, H. Grönvold, H. Jones, Chas. R. Knight, G. E. Lodge, E. Megargee and A. Thorburn.) London.

An elaborate, sumptuous work describing in detail, so far as known, the appearance and habits of all the species of pheasants. Special expeditions were made by the author to secure the materials on which much of this work is based. The illustrations, including portraits of birds and photographs of habitat and scenery in the ranges of the various species, add much to the beauty and value of the volumes.

Beebe, Mary Blair.
1905. See Beebe, C. William, **Two Bird-lovers in Mexico.**

Beebe, Mary Blair, and Beebe, Charles William.
1910. **Our search for a | wilderness | An account of two ornithological expeditions | to Venezuela and to British Guiana | by | Mary Blair, Beebe | and | C. William Beebe | Curator of Ornithology [etc., 5 lines.] | illustrated with photographs from life | taken by the authors | [Design.] | New York | Henry Holt and Company | 1910.

1 vol. 8vo, pp. I-XIX+1, 1-408, 1-4 (advt.), frontisp. (on num. p.), text-figs. 1-160. New York.

A narrative account of two observation-expeditions in northern South America. Many of the notes relate to birds, and Appendices A and B contain, respectively, a classified list of birds observed and local vernacular names of some of the species.

Beechey, Frederick William.
1831. **Narrative | of a | Voyage** to the Pacific | and | Beering's Strait, | to co-operate with | the polar expeditions: | performed in | His Majesty's ship Blossom, | under the command of | Captain F. W. Beechey, R.N. | F.R.S., F.R.A.S., and F.R.G.S. | in the years 1825, 26, 27, 28. | Published by authority of the Lords Commissioners of the Admiralty. | In two parts. | Part I [II]. | London: | Henry Colburn and Richard Bentley, | New Burlington Street. | MDCCCXXXI.

2 vols. foliopost 4to. Part I, pp. III-XX, 1 l., pp. 1-392, 14 pll., 3 (2) maps (1 missing = North-West Coast of America). Part II, pp. III-VII+1, 393-742, 1 l. (advt.), 9 pll. London.

Some notes are given on the birds and other animals of the various countries touched by the expedition. The full zoological report was published in 1839 in a separate volume entitled, "The Zoology of Captain Beechey's Voyage" (q.v.). The present volumes contain the bookplate of Frederick DuCane Godman.

Beechey, Frederick William. (Vigors, Nicholas Aylward.)

1839. The | zoology | of | Captain Beechey's voyage; | compiled from the | collections and notes made by Captain Beechey, | the officers and naturalist of the expedition, | during a voyage to the Pacific and Behring's Straits performed in | His Majesty's Ship Blossom, | under the command of | Captain F. W. Beechey, R.N., F.R.S., &c. &c. | in the years 1825, 26, 27, and 28, | by | J. Richardson, M.D., F.R.S., &c.; N. A. Vigors, Esq., A.M., F.R.S., &c.; G. T. Lay, Esq.; | E. T. Bennett, Esq., F.L.S., &c.; Richard Owen, Esq.; | John E. Gray, Esq., F.R.S., &c.; the Rev. W. Buckland, D.D., F.R.S., F.L.S., F.G.S., | &c., and G. B. Sowerby, Esq. | Illustrated with upwards of | fifty finely coloured plates by Sowerby. | Published under the authority of the Lords Commissioners of the Admiralty. | London: | Henry G. Bohn, 4 York Street, Covent Garden. | MDCCCXXXIX.

1 vol. medium 4to, pp. I-XII, 1-12, 9*13*+1, 13-180, pll. I-XLIV (44 col.), 1-3 (maps; 3 col.). London.

This comprehensive report contains sections relating to the various branches of zoology and one section relating to geology. The ornithological portion was written by N. A. Vigors and occupies pages 13-40 and plates III-XIV. Various new species are described.

Beetham, Bentley.

1910. The home-life | of the | spoonbill | the stork and some herons | photographed and described | by | Bentley Beetham, F.Z.S. | With thirty-two mounted plates | London | Witherby & Co. 326 High Holborn W.C. | MCMX.

1 vol. imperial 8vo, pp. I-VIII, 1-47, 1 l. (subtit.), pll. 1-32 (mounted on 16 ll.). London.

Essays on the Spoonbill, White Stork, Common Heron and Purple Heron of Great Britain, recounting the author's observations while securing the photographs which illustrate the volume.

Behn, Friedrich Daniel.

1760. See Klein, Jacob Theodor, **Vorbereitung zu einer vollständigen Vögelhistorie.**

Beilby, Ralph.

1797. See Bewick, Thomas, and Beilby, **History of British Birds,** 1797-1804.

Bekker, C. W.

1800-1811. See Borckhausen, Moritz B.; Lichthammer; Bekker; Lembcke and Bekker Jr., **Teutsche Ornithologie.**

Bekker Jr.

1800-1811. See Borckhausen, Moritz B.; Lichthammer; Bekker; Lembcke and Bekker Jr.; **Teutsche Ornithologie.**

Belding, Lyman.

1890. Land birds | of the | Pacific District | by | Lyman Belding. | San Francisco: | California Academy of Sciences, | September, 1890. < Occasional Papers | of the | California | Academy of Sciences. | II. | San Francisco, | 1890.

1 vol. 8vo, 2 pr. ll. (tits.), pp. 1-274. San Francisco. September 1890.

"This report, aims, mainly, to show the arrivals and departures of migrating species, as well as to give a catalogue of all the species known to occur in the district" which embraces California, Oregon, Washington and Nevada. The account discusses 295 species. It was prepared originally as a report submitted to the U. S. Department of Agriculture and consists of the author's own observations and those of other workers, each of whom is credited with his respective contributions under each species. The work forms a summary of the knowledge existing in 1890 of the occurrence and distribution of the land birds of the region.

Belding, Lyman.

1896. See World's Congress on Ornithology, **Papers presented to the—.**

Belon, Pierre.

1555. L'histoire de la natvre des | oyseavx, avec levrs | descriptions, & naïfs portraicts | retirez dv natvrel: | escrite en sept livres, | Par Pierre Belon du Mans | Av Roy. | [*Vignette.*] | A Paris, | On les vend en le grand salle du Palais, en la boutique de | Gilles Corrozet, pres la chambre des consultations. | 1555. | Auec priuilege du Roy.

1 vol. 4to (pt 6mo.?; 8½ x 13), 14 pr. ll., pp. 1-381+1 (149 wrongly num. 151; 230 wr. num. 236; 334 wr. num. 336), 139 woodcuts (illustrs.) and numerous decorations. Paris.

One of the earliest works dealing entirely with birds. The subject is discussed from a variety of aspects. Book 1 (pp. 1-80)is of a general nature and, among other things, presents a comparison between the skeletons of birds and men,— probably (according to Newton's "Dictionary of Birds") the first published account of this subject. Book 2 (pp. 81-148) discusses "la natvre des oyseavx vivants de rapine"; 3, "des oyseavx vivants le long des rivieres, ayants le pied plat"; 4, idem "qvi n'ont le pied plat"; 5, "des oyseavx de campagne, qvi sont leurs nids sur terre"; 6, "des oyseavx qui habitent indifferement"; and 7, "des oysillons, qvi hantent les hayes, buschettes, & buissons."

The fly-leaf of the present copy contains a manuscript bibliography of Belon (listing 6 titles) and a brief biographical note.

Bendire, Charles Emil.

1892-95. Smithsonian Institution. | United States National Museum. | Special Bulletin No. 1 [Special Bulletin]. | **Life histories** | **of** | **North American birds** [birds, | from the parrots to the grackles,] | with special reference to | their breeding habits and eggs, | with [*Line omitted.*] | twelve lithographic plates. [*Line omitted.*] | By | Charles Bendire, Captain, U.S. Army (Retired), [Captain and Brevet Major, U.S.A. (Retired).] Honorary Curator [*etc.,* *2 lines.*]. [| With | seven lithographic plates.] | Washington: | Government Printing Office. | 1892 [1895].

2 vols. 8vo (size of royal 4to). Special Bull. 1, pp. I-VIII, 1-446, pll. I-XII (col.; eggs). Special Bull. (3), pp. I-IX+1, 1-518, 7 ll. (expl. of pll.), pll. I-VII (col.; eggs). Washington.

All published of Bendire's monumental work, recently continued by A. C. Bent (q.v.). Detailed accounts of habits and nidification of the species, based on personal familiarity with them in the field as well as on notes and contributions supplied by correspondents and from other sources, rendered the work the most authoritative account of its subject to date.

The second volume, although not so indicated on the title-page, is Special Bulletin No. 3 of the U. S. National Museum; both volumes were published separately in the Smithsonian Contributions to Knowledge, Vols. 28 and 32, respectively, at the same dates as given above.

Bendire, Charles Emil.

1907. See Mershon, W. B., **The Passenger Pigeon.**

Bendire, Charles Emil.

1904. See Weed, Clarence Moores, **Bird Life Stories,** Book I.

Bennett, Edward Turner.

1831. The | gardens and menagerie | of the | Zoological Society | delineated. | Published, with the sanction of the Council, | under the superintendence of the | Secretary and Vice-secretary of the Society. | Vol. I. [*Line omitted (Vol. II.).*] | Quadrupeds [Birds]. | [*Vignette.*] | Chiswick: | Printed by Charles Whittingham. | Published by John Sharpe, Piccadilly, London. | M DCCC XXXI.

2 vols. 8vo. Vol. I, pp. I-XII, 1-308, 64 text-figs., 35 decorations, incl. tit.-vignette. Vol. II, pp. I-VIII, 1-328, 71 text-figs., 52 decorations, incl. tit.-vignette. Chiswick.

Accounts of the appearance and habits of various mammals and birds preserved in the menagerie of the Zoological Society, written without technicalities and confined to authenticated facts or statements which are substantiated by known anatomical peculiarities, to the exclusion of the marvellous. Vol. I is devoted to mammals; Vol. II to birds with at least one new name, *Crax yarrellii.*

Benoit, Luigi.

1840. **Ornitologia Siciliana** | o sia | catalogo ragionato | degli uccelli che si trovana in Sicilia | di | Luigi Benoit, | Socio corrispondente dell'Academia Giojenia | di scienze naturali di Catania. | Messina, | stamperia di Giuseppi Fiumara | 1840.

1 vol. post 8vo, pp. I-VIII, 1-231. Messina.

A descriptive catalogue of Sicilian birds.

Bent, Arthur Cleveland.

1919. Smithsonian Institution | United States National Museum | Bulletin 107 | **Life histories of North American** | **diving birds** | Order Pygopodes | By | Arthur Cleveland Bent | Of Taunton Massachusetts | [*Seal.*] | Washington | Government Printing Office | 1919.

1 vol. 8vo, pp. I-XIII+1, 1-245, pll. 1-55 (12 col.; 13 of eggs). Washington.

Begun as a continuation of Charles E. Bendire's uncompleted "Life Histories of North American Birds" (q.v.), but elaborated in scope and detail. Up to date, four parts have been issued, U. S. Nat. Mus. Bulls. 107, 113, 121 and 126 (q.v.), of which this is the first. The present volume embraces the Families Colymbidae, Gaviidae and Alcidae and contains an enormous amount of detailed information relative to the life-histories and habits of the birds in question. The illustrations consist of photographs of nests, nesting sites and birds, and of figures of the eggs of certain species, all but one in natural colors. The work is rendered more valuable by data contributed by a large corps of voluntary assistants in every part of the country.

Bent, Arthur Cleveland.

1921. Smithsonian Institution | U.S. National Museum | Bulletin 113 | **Life histories of North American** | **gulls and terns** | Order Longipennes | By | Arthur Cleveland Bent | Of Taunton Massachusetts | [*Seal.*] | Washington | Government Printing Office | 1921.

1 vol. 8vo, pp. I-X, 1-345, pll. 1-93 (17 col.; of eggs). Washington.

A continuation of U. S. Nat. Mus. Bull. 107, (q.v.), prepared in the same manner but devoted to the Families Stercoraridae, Laridae and Rynchopidae.

Bent, Arthur Cleveland.

1923. Smithsonian Institution | United States National Museum | Bulletin 126 | **Life histories of North American** | **wild fowl** | Order Anseres (Part) | By | Arthur Cleveland Bent | Of Taunton, Massachusetts | [*Seal.*] | Washington | Government Printing Office | 1923.

1 vol. 8vo, pp. I-IX+1, 1-250, pll. 1-46 (on 24 ll.). Washington.

A continuation, forming the fourth of the series, of the author's work on the life histories of North American birds (Cf. U. S. Nat. Mus. Bull. 107). The present volume discusses the Family Anatidae as far as the Genus *Perissonetta*. No figures of eggs are published in this number.

Beresford, William?

1789. See Dixon, George, **A Voyage Round the World;** but more particularly to the North-west Coast of America.

Berg, Bengt.

1921. Bengt Berg | **Swedish wild birds** | first series | [*Monogram.*] | Published by | Åhlén & Åkerlunds Förlags A.-B., | Stockholm.

1 vol. illum. cover, pp. 1-63+1, 25 pll. (on pp. 5-54), 1 tailpiece. Stockholm.

A series of photographs of bird-life with captions in Swedish and English, and with a few pages of descriptive text in English only. Designed for children.

Bergtold, W. H.

1917. A Study | of the | Incubation Periods | of | Birds | What determines their | lengths? | By | W. H. Bergtold, M.D., M.Sc. | Member of the American Ornithologists' Union | The Kendrick-Bellamy Co. | Denver, Colorado | 1917.

1 vol. 8vo, pp. 1-109, 1 insert-slip (errata). Denver.

A very interesting and detailed study of the factors governing the length of the incubation period in different species of birds. Reviewed in the Auk, **34,** pp. 488-489, Oct. 1917.

Berry, W.

1911. See [Grouse], **The Grouse in Health and Disease.**

Berthelot, Sabin.

1841. See Webb, Philip Barker, and Berthelot, [**Histoire Naturelle des Îles Canaries**] **Ornithologie Canarienne.**

Beseke, Johann Melchior Gottlieb.

1821. Beytrag | zur | Naturgeschichte | der | Vögel Kurlands | mit gemalten Kupfern. | Nebst | einem Anhange | über die | Augenkapseln der Vögel. | von | Joh. Melchior Gottlieb Beseke. | Neue Auflage | [*Erasure.*].

1 vol. cap 8vo, pp. 1-12 (tit. and pref.), 1-92, 8 pll. (6 col.; num. 1-9). Berlin.

A second "edition" of the original work published at Mitau in 1792. The original Mitau imprint is on p. 92 and the present "edition" appears to be nothing but the original supplied with a new title-page. The imprint has been erased from the bottom of the title-page and "1792 | Mitau" written in its stead, but the words "Neue Auflage" proclaim the edition to be the second and not the original. The work is a descriptive catalogue of the birds of Kurland, with descriptions of a number of new species, and a short essay (with two plates) on the avian eyeball.

Bettoni, Eugenio. (Sordelli, Ferdinando.)

1865-71. **Storia naturale | degli | uccelli che nidificano in Lombardia** | ad illustrazione della raccolta ornithologica dei fratelli | Ercole ed Ernesto Turati | scritta da Eugenio Bettoni | studente in medicina e chirurgia [Dottore in Scienze Naturali (*Vol. II.*)] | con tavole litografate e colorate prese dal vero | da | O. Dressler | membro corrispondente della Societa dei Naturalisti | nella Lusazia | Vol. I [II] | Milano ᛁ coi tipi del Pio Instituto del Patronato | 1865 [1868].

2 vols. in 3, superroyal folio and double elephant folio. Vol I, 3 pr, ll. (half-tit., tit. and pref.), pp. 1-16 (introd.), 68 ll.[1], illum. tit., pll. 2, 4, 6, 7, 9-14, 17, 19-26 (23 wrongly num. 25), 28, 29, 31-33, 35-37, 41-43, 45-47, 49-52, 54-56, 58, 62, 63, 66, 68, 70-73, 76, 77, 79, 88, 90, 95, 97, 100, 101, 105-107, 109, 110, 25a and 31a (col.). Vol. II, 2 pr. ll. (half-t. and tit., 66 ll.[1], pll. 1, 3, 5, 8, 15, 16, 18, 27, 30, 34, 38-40, 44, 48, 53, 57, 59-61, 64, 65, 67, 69, 74, 75, 78, 80-87, 89, 91-94, 96, 98, 99, 102-104, 108, 1a and I-VII (col.; I-VII of eggs). Milan.

The above collation of pages and plates is according to the arrangement proposed in the indices of the two volumes. The present copy, however, is bound in a different and rather curious manner. The text occupies one volume as follows. 3 pr. ll. of Vol. I, pp. 1-16 (introd.), 20 ll. (general description of the families belonging in Vol. I, arranged according to their serial number, and index to Vol. I), 2 pr. ll. of Vol. II, 33 ll. (families belonging in Vol. II, and index to Vol. II), 134 ll. (descrs. of species, arranged according to the numbering on the plates, including the two extra ll. for pll. 62 and 87). The plates are bound in two volumes. The double-sized plates, 31, 36, 39, 42, 55, 56, 74, 76, 85, 86, 101-103 and 107 are included in one volume (double elephant folio) without title. The remainder are arranged according to serial number and prefaced by the illuminated title which is properly the frontispiece to Vol. I of the text and plates combined.

The work was planned to be issued in parts of 1 or 2 pll. and 8 or 4 sheets of text each, according to a note in the Journ. für Orn., 1866 (pp. 43-46), a scheme which seems to have been carried out. The Journal reviews Pts. I-III with pll. 1-6, under date of Jan. 17, 1866. In the same periodical for 1867 (pp. 278-81, under

---

[1]There are two different texts for pl. 62, both describing the same species but differing slightly from each other. One is headed 'Pallenura sulphurea' and the other 'Budytes flava'. Pl. 62 is lettered 'Budytes flava' but there is a printed slip pasted on one side of the plate which bears the other name. Likewise (in Vol. II) there are two issues of text for Pl. 87, differing somewhat from each other. One is headed 'Lanius excubitur' and the other 'Lanius excubitor', while the corresponding plate carries the letter name only.

date of July, 1867) Pts. **I-XV** are reviewed with pll. 1-13, 15-24, and I-II. The Zool. Record for 1868 reviews Pts. **XVI-XXVI** (of Vol. I) and **I-IX** (of Vol. II) with pll. 25-37, 39-53, 55, 56 and III, under dates of 1867-68; under date of 1869, the same publication reviews Pts. **X-XXIII** (Vol. II) with pll. 54, 57-72, 74, 76 and IV. The Ibis for 1871 cites, under date of 1870, Pt. **XXIV** with pll. 78 and 79; **XXV**, 80 and 81; **XXVI**, 82 and 83; **XXVII**, 84 and V; **XXVIII**, 85; **XXIX**, 86; **XXX**, 87 and 88; **XXXI**, 89 and 90; **XXXII**, 91; **XXXIII**, 92 and 93; **XXXIV**, 94 and 95; **XXXV**, 96 and 97; **XXXVI**, 98 and VI; **XXXVII**, 100 and 104. The Zoological Record for 1871 cites pll. 99, 106, 108, 110 and VII, and says that the work is "finished by the publication of its forty-sixth part." Taschenburg says that the book appeared in 53 fasciculi, but this figure is less than the number accounted for by other sources of information.

The text appears to have been issued for each volume in some sort of order since the fasciculi are numbered separately for Vols. I and II. However, the plates, with a few omissions, appeared in numerical sequence, which is not the order of arrangement in the volumes. Apparently the text and plates in each fasciculus did not correspond or else the citation of fasciculi as quoted above for Vol. I and Vol. II is misleading.

On the obverse of the first page of text to *Phasianus colchicus* (Pl. 57) is a discussion of the "Fagiana acclimati in Lombardia" by F. Sordelli.

Beverly, Charles James.

1819. See Ross, John, **A Voyage of Discovery.**

Bewick, Thomas; and Beilby, Ralph.

1797-1804. History | of | British birds. | The figures engraved on wood by T. Bewick. | Vol. I [II]. | Containing the | history and description of land [water] birds. | [*Vignette.*] | Newcastle: | printed by Sol. Hodgson, for Beilby & Bewick: sold by them, [printed by Edward Walker, for T. Bewick: sold by him, and] and G. G. & J. Robinson, London [Longman and Rees, London]. | [Price 13s. (15s) in Boards.] | 1797 [1804].

2 vols. cap 4to (size of post 8vo). Vol. I, pp. I-XXX, 1-335+1, 206 woodcuts (119 ornithological). Vol. II, pp. I-XX, 1-400, 240 woodcuts (114 ornithological). Newcastle.

The rare first edition, including the first issue of Vol. I. A second edition of Vol. I is said by Newton (Dict. of Birds, introd. p. 20, footn. 1, 1893) to have been published probably the following year although it bears the same date, 1797, on the title-page. According to Newton (l.c.), the second issue is distinguished by having an inscription "Wycliffe, 1791" at the foot of the figure of the Sea Eagle on p. 11 and a misprint on p. 145 of *Sahæniclus* for *Schæniclus*. Mullens and Swann add the following distinguishing features of the first issue: p. 335, *third* (instead of *fourth*) edition of Bewick's Quadrupeds announced; figure of the magpie has a stump with two branches in the foreground.

The text of Vol. I was written by Beilby; Vol. II is wholly the work of Bewick. The work is usually cited as "Bewick's British Birds" in spite of the dula

authorship. The woodcuts are all the work of Bewick. The 233 cuts listed
as ornithological, include the specific bird portraits and the representations of
feathers and heads. Many of the smaller cuts also contain figures of birds but
these are mostly incidental and not of especial importance. It is for the woodcuts that the work is mostly valued; the text is largely a compilation of the
works of Pennant, Albin, Belon, and Willughby and Ray. The volumes
passed through eight editions of which the last two, in 1832 and 1847, were
issued after the death of Bewick (1828). A supplement to this work was
issued by Bewick in 1821 (q.v.)

Bewick, Thomas.

1821. A | supplement | to the | history | of | British birds. | The
figures engraved on wood by T. Bewick. | Part. I [II]. | Containing
the | history and description of land [water] birds. | [*Vignette.*] |
Newcastle: | printed by Edward Walker, Pilgrim Street, | for
T. Bewick: sold by him, and E. Charnley, Newcastle; | and
Longman and Co., London. | 1821.

1 vol. demy 4to.   Part I, pp. 1-50, 1 l., 43 woodcuts (21 ornithological). Part II, pp. 1-49+1, 40 woodcuts (21 ornithological). London.

The first edition of the supplements to Bewick. Only 42 of the 83 wood-cuts are
definitely illustrative of the subject matter.

Bexon, l'abbé.

1783-86.   See Buffon, **Histoire Naturelle des Oiseaux.**   1770-86.

Bickerton, William.

1912. The home-life | of the | terns | or | sea swallows | photo-
graphed and described | by | W. Bickerton, F.Z.S., M.B.O.U. |
Vice-President of the Hertfordshire Natural History Society and
Field Club. | With thirty-two mounted plates | London | Witherby
& Co. 326 High Holborn W.C. | MCMXII.

1 vol. 8vo (7½x10), pp. 1-88, 1 l. (subtit. to pll.), pll. 1-32 (mounted
on 16 ll.).   London.

Observations on the nesting habits of the five species of terns breeding in Great
Britain. Illustrated by photographs. The book is a companion volume to
"The Home-life of the Spoonbill", 1910, by Bentley Beetham (q.v.).

Birchley, Sumner W.

1919. British birds | for | Cages, Aviaries, and | Exhibition | by |
Sumner W. Birchley, | N.B.B. & M.C., L.P.O.S., &c., &c. | Vol. I
[II]. | London | Sherratt & Hughes | Manchester: 34 Cross
Street | 1909.

2 vols. royal 8vo. Vol. I, 3 pr. ll. (half-tit., tit. and ded.), pp. IX-XIV,
1 l. (subtit. of introd.), pp. 1-302, frontisp., 44 text-figs. (birds).
Vol. II, 2 pr. ll. (half-tit. and tit.), pp. VII-VIII, 1-234, 15 ll.

(figs.), 1 l.+pp. 1-38 (advt.), frontisp., 26 text-figs. (birds), 2 text-figs. (aviaries), figs. 1-23 (cages and accessories). London.

An account, for aviculturists, of the British birds useful for caging, and of the methods of catching and rearing them.

Bird, M. C. H.

1903. See Dutt, William Alfred, **The Norfolk Broads.**

Bishop, Louis Bennett.

1903. See Sanford, L. C., Bishop and Van Dyke, **The Water-fowl Family.**

Bishop, Louis Bennett.

1913. See Sage, Bishop and Bliss, State of Connecticut, Public Document No. 47, **The Birds of Connecticut.**

Blaauw, Frans Ernst.

1897. A | monograph | of | the Cranes | by | F. E. Blaauw, | Corresponding Member [*etc.*, *2 lines.*] | Illustrated by 22 Coloured Plates (the greater number drawn under the immediate superintendence of | the late Dr. G. F. Westerman) by Heinrich Leutemann and J. G. Keulemans. | Leiden and London: | E. J. Brill, R. H. Porter, | (Oude Rijn, 33a). (18, Princes Street, Cavendish Square, W.). | 1897.

1 vol. superroyal folio, pp. I-VIII, 1-64, 2 ll., pll. I-XVIII, VIIa, Xa, XIa, XVa, (=22; col.), 12 line cuts and 1 half-tone. Leyden and London.

An account of the family of Cranes, with full synonymies, descriptions of various plumages, and a discussion of habits and distribution. Only 170 copies were printed of which the present one is No. 94.

Black, Hortensia.

1896. See World's Congress on Ornithology, **Papers presented to the—.**

Blackburn, Mrs. Hugh.

1862. Birds | **Drawn from Nature** | By Mrs. Hugh Blackburn. | [*Illustr.*=*pl. XXIII.*] | Edmonston & Douglas, | Edinburgh, 1862.

1 vol. demy folio, lith. tit., pp. 1-6, 22 pll. Edinburgh.

A series of plates, drawn from living or freshly killed specimens, of various species of birds of Scotland. The text consists of a preface, index and more or less brief description of the subjects figured. The authoress explains that a number of projected plates were destroyed, thus decreasing the intended size of the work.   A second edition in 1868 contained 23 additional plates, probably (at least partly) those omitted from the original.   The plates were afterwards included in the series published in 1895 as "Birds from Moidart and Elsewhere" (q.v.).

Blackburn, Mrs. Hugh.

1895.   Birds from Moidart | and elsewhere | Drawn | from Nature | By JB. | Mrs. Hugh Blackburn. | [*Vignette.*] | Edinburgh, | David Douglas, | MDCCCXCV.

1 vol. royal 8vo, 3 pr. ll. (half-t., illustr. tit., and ded.), pp. V-VIII, 1-191, frontisp., 87 pll. (num. in text).   Edinburgh.

Uncolored lithographs of birds, mostly from Moidart, Inverness-shire, Scotland, accompanied by notes and anecdotes of the various species.   Some of the plates were published originally in the author's folio. 'Birds Drawn from Nature," 1862 (q.v.).

Blainville, Henri Marie Ducroytay de.

1841.   See Vaillant, **Voyage autour du Monde sur La Bonite,** 1841-52.

Blanchère, H. de la.

1876.   Les | **oiseaux gibier** | chasse—mœrs—acclimatation | par | H. de la Blanchère | avec quarante-cinq chromotypographies | et de nombreuses vignettes | [*Vignette.*] | Paris | J. Rothschild, éditeur | 13, rue des Saint-Pères, 13 | M DCCC LXXVI.

1 vol. imperial 4to, 2 pr. ll. (half-t. and tit.), pp. 1-140, pll. 1-45 (col.), 15 text-figs., numerous ornamental figs.   Paris.

A popular account of the game-birds of France, illustrated by colored plates of many of the species, and line-cuts of others.

Bland, Michael.

1838-43.   See Jardine, William, **The Natural History of the Birds of Great Britain and Ireland,** 1838-43.

1844-64?   Idem.

Blanford, William Thomas.

1870.   Observations| **on the** | **geology and zoology** | **of** | **Abyssinia,** | made during the progress of the British | expedition to that country in 1867-68. | By | W. T. Blanford, | Associate of the Royal School of Mines; [*etc., 3 lines.*] | late Geologist to the Abyssinian expedition. | With illustrations and geological map. | London: | Macmillan and Co. | 1870.

1 vol. post 8vo, pp. I-XII, 1-487, pll. (geol.) I-IV, (Zool.) I-VIII (8 col.) 1 pl. (col.), 1 map (col.), 9 text-cuts.   London.

A general work of which the introductory matter, pp. 1-39, 205-221, 285-443, and 479-487 and pll. (Zool.) II-VII are of ornithological interest. The book contains the bookplate of Henry Baker Tristram.

Blanford, William Thomas.

1895-98. See Oates and Blanford, **The Fauna of British India— Birds.** 1889-98.

Blasius, Johann Heinrich.

1860. See Naumann, Johann Friedrich, Johann Andreas Naumann's mehrerer gelehrten Gesellschaften Mitgliede, **Naturgeschichte der Vögel Deutschlands.** 1822-60.

Blasius, Johann Heinrich.

1862. A list | of the | birds of Europe: | by | Professor J. H. Blasius. | Reprinted from the German, | with the author's corrections. | Norwich: Matchett and Stevenson. London: Trübner and Co., | 60, Paternoster Row. | 1862. | [The right of publication is reserved.].

1 vol. 4to (size of post 8vo), pp. 1-24. Norwich and London.

A systematic list of European birds with their distribution briefly indicated, and with occasional British references added by the editor. Four new generic names are used, *Lithofalco, Schoenicola, Parnopia* and *Hylaespiza.* The paper purports to be an English translation of a corrected copy of a list privately printed in Germany by Blasius in 1861, supplied with the corrections by Blasius who is, therefore, the author of the work. The German original seems not to have been actually published; the present reprint is rare. The copy at hand is from the library of W. H. Mullens, originally from that of Edward Newman whose autograph appears on the cover.

Blasius, Rudolf.

1891. See Jäckel, Andreas Johannes, **Systematische Übersicht der Vögel Bayerns.**

Blasius, Wilhelm.

1893. **Museum Homeyerianum.** | Verzeichniss | der | ornithologischen Sammlungen | E. F. von Homeyer's. | Ausgestopfte Vögel, Bälge, Eier und Nester. | Braunschweig. | Druck von Albert Limbach. | 1893.

1 vol. post 8vo, pp. 1-35. Braunschweig. 1893 (circa June).

A catalogue of the Homeyer collection of 1785 stuffed birds, 5012 birdskins, 4950 eggs and 160 nests, representing 1086 species. Reference is given to Gray's "Hand-List".

Bliss, Walter Parks.

1913. See Sage, Bishop and Bliss, **The Birds of Connecticut.**

Blossom, Narrative of a Voyage to the Pacific and Beering's Strait—in His Majesty's Ship—.

1831. See Beechey, Frederick W.

Blossom, The Zoology of Captain Beechey's Voyage—in His Majesty's Ship—.

1839. See Beechey, Frederick W.

Blumenbach, Johann Friedrich.

1796-1810. Abbildungen | naturhistorischer Gegenstände | heraus-gegeben | von | Joh. Fried. Blumenbach. | Nro 1-100. | Göttingen | bey Heinrich Dieterich. | 1810.

> [*Idem, 5 lines.*] | Ites [-1otes] Heft [*Period added (Pts. 2-9.).* | Nro 1-10 [11-20; 21-30; 31-40; 41-50; 51-60; 61-70; 71-80; 81-90; 91-100]. ;| Göttingen | bey Johann Christian [Heinrich (*Pts.* 6-10.)] Dieterich [*Period added (Pts. 6-8.).*] | 1796 [1797; 1798; 1799; 1800; 1802; 1804; 1805; 1809; 1810].

1 vol. (10 pts.) demy 8vo, 119 ll., pll. 1-100 (11 col.; 19 of birds, 9 col.). Göttingen.

A series of plates illustrating various objects of natural history, each of which is described on an accompanying leaf of text. A general review of the plates is given at the beginning of the volume. The work was issued in 10 parts under titles as quoted (in second par.) above; the covering title was issued at the close of the work.

Blyth, Edward.

1840. See Cuvier, **Cuvier's Animal Kingdom.**

Blyth, Edward.

(1849?)-1852. Catalogue | of the | birds | in the | museum Asiatic Society. | By | Edward Blyth. | Published by order of the Society. | Calcutta: | printed by J. Thomas, Baptist Mission Press. | 1849.

1 vol. 4to (size of post 8vo), tit., pp. I-XXXIV, 1-403. Calcutta. (1849?)-1852 (post. Sept. 1).

A catalogue of the ornithological collection of the Society, which embraced speci-mens from all parts of the world. Synonymy and distribution and a list of the specimens of each species are given. A number of new names are used, some with descriptions, some without. Owing to delay in printing, the author found it necessary to add appendices 1-6, addenda to appendices 1-5 and "Further addenda to appendix, No. 1." at the close of the general text, and addenda to appendices 1-5, another appendix 6, still further addenda to appen-dices 1-3 and a special index, in the preface. The title-page is dated 1849 but the preface is dated June 20, 1852. Proof sheets of various parts were sent by Blyth in 1849 to certain of his correspondents who used the new names in their own papers, and the same sheets were exhibited at a meeting of the

Asiatic Society of Bengal in August of that year. These sheets include pp. 1-311. This may be considered as constituting publication, in which case pp. 1-311 will date 1849. The appendices were prepared from time to time and the whole work was completed and placed on sale in 1852. (Cf. Mathews, Birds of Australia, Suppl. No. 4, p. 10, 1925.)

Blyth, Edward, and Tegetmeier, William Bernhard.

1881. The | natural history | of the | Cranes. | A monograph by | the late Edward Blyth, C.M.Z.S. | Greatly enlarged and reprinted, with numerous illustrations, | by | W. B. Tegetmeier, F.Z.S., | Member of the British Ornithologists' Union; [etc.]. | [Monogram.] | Published for the author by | Horace Cox, 346, Strand, W.C. | and R. H. Porter, 6, Tenterden Street, W. | 1881.

1 vol. demy 4to (6½x10), tit., pp. V-VI, 1 l. (conts. and illustrs.), 1 insert slip (errata), pp. 1-91+1, frontisp. (col.), pll. I and II, 4 pll. (1 col., 1 fold.), 20 text-figs. London.

A monograph based on articles by Blyth published in "The Field" in 1873, and with many additions by Tegetmeier who prepared the work in its present form.

Boddaert, Pieter.

1767-70. See Pallas, Peter Simon, **Dierkundig Mengelwerk.**

Boddaert, Pieter. (Tegetmeier, William Bernhard, *ed.*)

1874. Reprint | of | Boddaert's Table | des | Planches Enlumineez d'Histoire | Naturelle. | Edited by | W. B. Tegetmeier, F.Z.S., | Member of the British Ornithologists' Union, &c. | London: | published (for the editor) at the Field office, | 346, Strand, W.C.

1 vol. royal 8vo, 2 pr. ll. (tit. and ed. pref.), pp. I-XV+1, 1-58. London.

A verbatim reprint, with all typographical and other errors, of Boddaert's exceedingly rare work of 1783. Boddaert, on p. IX, observes that he prepared the original for his own use but decided to print 50 copies for distribution; of these, a very few copies are known to be extant. The work is a list of Daubenton's "Planches Enluminées" (Cf. Buffon, Histoire Naturelle des Oiseaux, 1870-86.), 1008 plates of which 973 are of birds, with their titles or legends and with the names, Latin or vernacular, applied to the same species by Buffon, Brisson, Latham, Linnaeus, Edwards and others. To this list of synonyms is sometimes added a new name by the author, frequently identified as new by the term "mihi", often recognizable only by a species number "o" in the quoted reference, and in many cases without expressed authorship. The work abounds in typographical errors, some of which involve the orthography of names, but, fortunately, many of the errors can be proved such. The importance of the work lies in the priority of many of Boddaert's generic and specific names over later accepted terms, but the inconsistences of the book and its errors present numerous problems which have yet to be solved. A discussion of some of the problems is given by G. M. Mathews and T. Iredale in The Austral Avian

Record, **3**, No. 2, pp. 31-51, Nov. 19, 1915. The exact date of publication is unknown, but the dedication is dated Dec. 1, 1783.

Bogdanow, Modesto.

1884. Perechen' Ptītz' Rossiĭkoĭ Imperiĭ. | Modesta Bogdanova, | Dokt. ĭ Prof. Zoologhiĭ prĭ Ī. S.-Peterb. Univers. | Khanĭt. Zoologh. Muzeya Ī. Akad.   Nauk'. | Izdanie Imperatorskoĭ Akademiĭ Nauk'. | Vuipusk' I. | **Conspectus avium Imperii Rossici.** | Auctore | Modesto Bogdanow, | Zool. Doct. Univ. Caes. Petropol. Prof., Musei Zoologici Acad. Caes. Petrop. Custodi. | Fasciculus I. | S.-Peterburgh 1884.—St.-Pétersbourg, 1884. | Commissionnaires de l'Académie Impériale des Sciences: |

à St.-Pétersbourg: | à Riga: |
MM. Eggers & Cie et J. Glasounof; | M. N. Kymmel; |
à Leipzig |
Voss' Sortiment (G. Haessel). | Prix: 1 Rbl. = 3 Mark.

1 vol. foliopost 4to, 2 pr. ll. (tit. and pref.), pp. 1-122. St. Petersburg. 1884 (circa January).

Livraison I (all published) of a monograph of the birds of Russia. The Orders Columbae, Heteroclitae, Gallinae, Hydrogallinae and Grallae are treated in this number, which contains bibliographic references (including published figures) and local distribution, with more or less detailed notes and descriptions of numerous new forms. Published under the auspices of the Imperial Academy of Sciences in January, 1884.

Bolton, James.

1845. Harmonia ruralis; | or, | an essay | towards | a natural history | of British song birds: | illustrated with figures, the size of life, of the birds, male and female, in their most natural attitudes; | their nests and eggs, &c. | By | James Bolton. | Vol. I [II]. | A **new edition,** revised and augmented. | [*Vignette.*] | London: | Henry G. Bohn, York Street, Covent Garden. | MDCCCXLV.

2 vols. in 1 vol., royal 4to. Vol. I, pp. I-XXIV, 2 ll., pp. 1-66, frontisp. (col.; bird), pll. 1-40 (col.; 20 of birds, 17 of nests and eggs, 3 mixed). Vol. II, 1 pr. l., pp. 1-96, pll. 1-80 (col.; 21 of birds, 19 of nests and eggs, 1 mixed). London.

Popular descriptions of some British birds with accounts of their habits and nidification.

Bonaparte, Charles Lucien Jules Laurent.

1825-33. American | **ornithology;** | or | the natural history | of | birds inhabiting the United States, | not given by Wilson. | With figures drawn, engraved, and coloured from nature. | By | Charles Lucian Bonaparte. | Vol. I [-IV]. | Philadelphia: | Carey, Lea & Carey—Chesnut Street [Carey & Lea, Chesnut Street (*Vol. IV.*)]. | London: John Miller, 40 Pall Mall. | William Brown, Printer. | 1825 [1828; 1828; 1833].

4 vols. medium folio (12x15½). Vol. I, pp. I-VI, 1 l., pp. 1-105, pll. I-IX (col.). Vol. II, pp. I-VII, 1 l., pp. 1-95, pll. X-XV (col.). Vol. III, 2 pr. ll., pp. 1-60, pll. XVI-XXI (col.). Vol. IV, 2 pr. ll., pp. 1-142, pll. XXII-XXVII (col.). Philadelphia.

The plates are mostly by Titian R. Peale (T. Peal), and A. Rider, with part of one plate by Audubon; engraved by Alex Lawson and colored by hand. Originally planned to occupy only three volumes; possibly Vol. II was expanded beyond its contemplated limits so as to necessitate its division into two parts (Cf. Rhoads, Auk, XL, p. 341, 1923.). This work forms a sort of supplement to Alexander Wilson's "American Ornithology", 1808-14 (q.v.), and is included in Jardine's later edition of that work (1832, q.v.) as a "Continuation of Wilson's American Ornithology by Charles Lucian Bonaparte". It is included, also, in the Jameson edition of 1831 (q.v.) and the "Popular Edition" of 1864 (q.v.), but under the proper title of "Bonaparte's American Ornithology". In all of these, however, Bonaparte's name is joined with Wilson's on the title-pages.

Bonaparte, Charles Lucien Jules Laurent.

1826. Observations | on the | nomenclature | of | Wilson's Ornithology. | By Charles Lucian Bonaparte. | Philadelphia: | Published by Anthony Finley. | 1826.

1 vol. 8vo, 125 ll. (unpaged). Philadelphia.

An unpaged reprint of a series of articles published in the Journal of the Academy of Natural Sciences of Philadelphia in 1824 and 1825, with additional matter not in the original. The work consists of a critical review of the species of birds in Wilson's "American Ornithology", 1808-14 (q.v.), with various proposed changes in nomenclature. The original series of articles discussed only species Nos. 1-227 of Wilson's work; the present volume completes the series of 278 species. New names, accordingly, date from the "Journal Acad. Nat. Sci. Phil." when they occur among spp. 1-227, or from the present work for spp. 228-278. The dates of publication of the respective numbers of the "Journal" are given by Coues as follows. Vol. III, Pt. 2, pp. 340-352 (Nos. 1-22), April 5, 1824; pp. 353-371 (Nos. 23-58), April 27, 1824: Vol. IV, Pt. 1, pp. 25-32 (Nos. 59-69), July 1824; pp. 33-66 (Nos. 70-112), August 1824; pp. 163-200 (Nos. 113-167), December 1824: Vol. IV, Pt. 2, pp. 251-277 (Nos. 168-184 and review of various species previously treated), February 1825: Vol. V, Pt. 1, pp. 57-64 (Nos. 185-194), July 1825; pp. 65-106 (Nos. 195-227), August 1825.

Bonaparte, Charles Lucien Jules Laurent.

1827. Specchio | comparativo | delle ornitologie | di Roma e di Filadelfia | di | C. L. Bonaparte | Principe di Musignano | socio di diverse accademie | di Europa e di America. | Estratto dal No. XXXIII. | Del Nuovo Giornale de' Letterati | Pisa | dalla tipografia Nistri | MDCCCXXVII.

I vol. post 8vo, pp. I-XVI, 17-80. Pisa.

A list, in parallel columns, of 247 species of birds of Rome and 281 of Philadelphia, arranged under their respective genera and families, and intended to show the relationship of the two avifaunas. Local vernacular names and brief annotations are given for each species, together with the scientific name. Analytical tables of the genera and higher groups precede the catalogue. The work appears to be a reprint, probably repaged, from the "Nuovo Giornale de' Letterati". A supplement (q.v.) was published in 1832, a copy of which is bound with the present title in the volume at hand.

Bonaparte, Charles Lucien Jules Laurent.

1831. See Wilson, Alexander, and Bonaparte, **American Ornithology.**
1832. Idem.

Bonaparte, Charles Lucien Jules Laurent.

1832. **Supplemento | allo | specchio comparativo | delle ornitologie |** **di Roma e Filadelfia** | di | Carlo Luciano Bonaparte | Principe di Musignano | Estratto dal No. 64 del Nuovo Giornale | de' Letterati | Pisa | Tipografia Nistri E Cc. | 1832.

I vol. post 8vo, pp. 1-15. Pisa.

A volume of addenda and corrigenda to the author's "Specchio Comparativo" of 1827 (q.v.). Like that work, the present seems to be a repaged reprint of a contribution to the "Nuovo Giornale de' Letterati". Both are bound together in the copy at hand.

Bonaparte, Charles Lucien Jules Laurent.

1832-41. **Iconografia | della | fauna Italica** | per le quattro classi | degli | animali vertebrati | di | Carlo L. Principe Bonaparte | Principe di Canino e Musignano | socio delle principali accademie scientifiche | di Europa e di America | Tomo I [-III]. | Mammiferi e uccelli [Amfibi; Pesci] | Roma | dalla tipografia Salviucci | 1832-1841.

3 vols. demy folio. Vol. I, 7 pr. ll., 67 ll. (mammals), 67 ll. (birds), 24 pll. (col.; màmals), 24 pll. (col.; birds; by Petrus Quattrocchi and Carolus Ruspi). Vol. II, 5 pr. ll., 128 ll., 54 pll. (col.). Vol. III, 12 pr. ll., 266 ll., 78 pll. (col.). Rome.

Published in 30 parts the dates of which are given in the introductory pages of Vol. I while the distributive index in the front of each volume lists the species included in the volume with (among other things) the number of the part in which each species appeared. The dates for each species can thus be ascertained from the work itself. However, Salvadori (Ibis, 1888, pp. 320-325) has catalogued the species of birds with their respective dates. Salvadori gives the date of the "Introduzione" to the birds (which includes the citation of the new genus *Chettusia*) as 1841, after Pt. 30 (Dec. 21).

Bonaparte, Charles Lucien Jules Laurent.

1838. A | geographical and comparative | list of the | birds | of | Europe and North America. | By | Charles Lucian Bonaparte, | Prince of Musignano. | London: | John Van Voorst, 1, Paternoster-Row. | 1838.

1 vol. cap 4to, pp. I-VII, 1-67, 2 ll. (advt.) London.

A list of species of European and North American birds arranged in parallel columns with a few annotations. Various new names appear in this work. Mathews (Birds of Australia, VII, p. 446) gives the date of publication of this work as January 1838; in the same book (Suppl. 4, p. 11) the date is cited as April 14, 1838. The volume is reviewed in the Mag. Nat. Hist., New Ser., **2**, No. 16, p. 237, April 1838 and in the Ann. Mag. Nat. Hist., **1**, p. 318, June 1838.

Bonaparte, Charles Lucien Jules Laurent.

1840. Systema ornithologiæ | Caroli Luciani Bonaparte | Muxiniani Principis.

1 vol. post 8vo, pp. 1-25. Bologna.

The systematic arrangement of the subclasses, orders, families and subfamilies of birds, with diagnostic characters of each. The paper was originally printed in the Nuov. Annale delle Scienze Naturale di Bologna, Anno 2, Vol. **3**, pp. 440-455; **4**, pp. 24-33, 1844. What changes, if any, have been made (aside from alterations in pagination), I do not know.

Bonaparte, Charles Lucien Jules Laurent.

1850. Notice | sur | les travaux zoologiques | de | M. Charles-Lucien Bonaparte, | Membre correspondant [*etc. 4 lines.*], | Paris, | Bachelier, Imprimeur-Libraire | de l'École Polytechnique et du Bureau des Longitudes, | Quai des Grands-Augustins, no 55. | 1850.

1 vol. medium 4to, pp. 1-35. Paris.

The author's list of his own zoological publications to date, with short reviews of many of them. Eighty-seven publications are listed. One of a bound collection of Bonaparte's papers.

Bonaparte, Charles Lucien Jules Laurent; and Schlegel, Hermann.

1850. Monographie | des | Loxiens | par | Ch. L. Bonaparte | et | H. Schlegel. | Ouvrage | accompagné de 54 planches coloriées, | lithographiées | d'après les dessins | de | M. Bädeker | et autres naruralistes (*sic*). | Leiden et Düsseldorf, | chez | Arnz & Comp. | 1850.

1 vol. medium 4to, 3 pr. ll., pp. I-XVII, 1-55, pll. 1-54 (col.). Leyden and Düsseldorf. 1850 (antea Nov. 11).

A monograph of the subfamily *Loxiaceae* of the family *Fringillidae*, including the genera *Loxia, Corythus, Uragus, Carpodacus, Pyrrha, Erythrospiza, Chauno-proctus* and *Haematospiza*. Several new species are described, most of which are signed with Bonaparte's initials, solely. The plates are excellent. Six of them (23, 25, 29, 32, 34 and 35) are relabeled, to agree with the text, by slips pasted over the original divergent lettering. The introduction gives a general review of the entire family. The work dates before November 11 since it is mentioned in an extract of that date published in the Rev. et Mag. de Zool., 1850, p. 618.

Bonaparte, Charles Lucien Jules Laurent.

1850.   Revue | critique | de l'ornithologie | Européenne | de M. le Docteur Degland (de Lille) | par | Charles Lucien Bonaparte | Lettre | a M. De Selys Longchamps | [*Quot., 5 lines.*] | Bruxelles | Imprimerie et Librairie de Ve Wouters | 57, rue du Champ-de-Mars, et 13, rue d'Or | 1850.

1 vol. 12 mo, pp. 1-206. Brussels.

A critical review of Degland's "Ornithologie Européenne", 1849 (q.v.), in which Bonaparte finds much to criticise. *Oidemia deglandi*, described but not named by Degland, is named herein by Bonaparte. Following the review, there is (pp. 115-125) a "Conspectus Systematis Ornithologiae" consisting of a summary of all the known subfamilies and higher groups of birds with their distribution and the number of species in each. This is followed (pp. 127-206) by a "Conspectus Avium Europaearum" in which 530 species of European birds are listed under their genera, families, etc. with some synonymy and a statement as to the range of each.

Bonaparte, Charles Lucien Jules Laurent.

1850-57.   Conspectus | generum avium. | Auctore | Carolo Luciano Bonaparte. | Tom. I [II]. | Lugduni Batavorum, | apud | E. J. Brill, | Academiae Typographum. | 1850 [1857].

2 vols. in 1 vol., 4to (size of 8vo). Vol. I, 3 pr. ll., pp. 1-543. Vol. II, title, insert-slip (notice by publisher), pp. 1-232. Leyden.

A synoptic list of the genera of birds, with, except in the Psittaci, a complete list of species of each genus, the synonymy of each species and, usually, a brief description. Published in three parts, of which part 1 included pp. 1-272; part 2, pp. 273-543 (end of Vol. I); part 3 (all published of Vol. II), pp. 1-232. Dr. Richmond (Proc. U. S. Nat. Mus. 53, p. 579, footn., 1917) surmised that part 2 began with p. 273. Further evidence to this effect is at hand in the present copy which was received by the Field Museum library in three parts, as apportioned above, and catalogued under three numbers, the second of which is stamped on p. 273. There is also a manuscript index to Vol. I in the copy, prepared by an earlier (contemporary?) owner, in which the division of parts 1 and 2 is made at pp. 272-273. Part 1 was presented to the Paris Academy on June 24, 1850 (Cf. Rev. et Mag. 1850, p. 338.), although Bonaparte (Comptes Rendus Vol. XXXVII, p. 423, Sept. 1850) quotes March, ostensibly as date of publication. Part 2 may not have been published until 1851, but it is included in a review of the work (to date) by Lafresnaye, in the Rev. et Mag. for January, 1851 (publ. in Febr. but probably written in Jan.), from a copy which he had received from Bonaparte while in Holland *some time previously* (Rev. et Mag. 1851, pp. 56-59). In Bonaparte's "Notice sur les Travaux Zoologiques de M. Charles-Lucien Bonaparte—Paris—1850", the work is included under date of 1850 as being more than two-thirds published and as including the Passeres,—a characterization which applies only to parts 1 and 2 together. The last signature of part 2 was printed on Nov. 10, 1850, and the title-page to Vol. I (parts 1 and 2) which was issued in 1857, bears the date, 1850. I believe that the assumption is justified that part 2 appeared in 1850 near the close of the year.

Vol. II presents other difficulties. It would seem to have been issued in one part according to an insert-slip attached to p. 1 of the present copy. This slip reads as follows. "AVIS DE L'EDITEUR. La publication du second volume du Conspectus Generum Avium, ne devrait avoir lieu qu'après que l'ouvrage serait entièrement terminé.—La maladie de l'illustre auteur a retardé l'impression, quoiqu'il s'en occupait encore sur son lit de mort; cette mort prématurée l'ayant interrompu définitivement, je publie tout ce qu'il y a d'imprimé, jusqu'ou le manuscrit me manque. Un titre du Tom. I (complet en 543 pages) est joint à ce volume. Leide 1 Octobre 1857. E.J.B." The title-page of Vol. II is dated, in accordance, 1857.

However, Bonaparte undoubtedly distributed a number of copies of the various sheets of Vol. II, either as they were printed or in small groups of signatures, and these were noted and collated by some of the recipients at the time of receipt. Cabanis, in the "Journ. für Orn." for Jan. 1855 (p. 96) notes pp. 1-24; for March 1855 (p. 192), pp. 25-56; for May 1855 (p. 272), pp. 57-120; for July 1855 (p. 350), pp. 121-144; for Sept. 1855 (p. 448), pp. 145-159; for March 1857 (p. 144), pp. 161-208; for Jan. 1858 (p. 96), pp. 209-232. Each of these lots contains several signatures, variously dated. Certain parts are also noted in the "Naumannia", 5, p. 116, 1855; and 7, pt. 2, p. 100, 1857. G. R. Gray, "List of the Specimens of Birds in the British Museum", Pt. IV, 1856, quotes voluminously from this volume of Bonaparte's work and cites many genera and species (the former under date of 1854) which will have to date from Gray's work if Bonaparte is considered as not actually published until 1857. The genus *Uropelia* will serve as an example.

That the author believed his work to be published when the parts were sent out, is indicated by his paper in the Comptes Rendus for Nov. 24, 1856, p. 990, which he entitles as follows. "Additions et Corrections aux Tableaux paralléliques de l'Ordre des Herons et des Pélagiens ou Gavies, et a la partie correspondante, déjà publiée, du Conspectus Avium", etc. This paper makes corrections and additions to pp. 161-206 of Vol. II of the "Conspectus", the last of which pages is contained in a signature dated Febr. 1, 1856. In the same periodical for Nov. 3, 1856, p. 833, a more direct reference is made. The paper there begun presents additions and corrections to the author's "Coup d'oeil sur l'Ordre des Pigeons" and corresponding portions of the "Conspectus", and says, in part, "On lit à la page 9 du second volume de mon Conspectus Avium", etc.; "placé page 13 de mon Conspectus", etc.

Bonaparte, Charles Lucien Jules Laurent.

1852. [Unpaged sheet without title.]

A rare tract of which almost nothing is known. It contains a table of the orders of birds, a list of the families and subfamilies of the Longipennes, and a 'Conspectus Larinarum' with the names, distribution and number of included species in each of the genera of the Larinae. Finally, three new species of birds are described,—*Thalassidroma tethys, Chelidoptera albipennis* and *Cyanocitta Jolyaea.* Reference is made to the twenty-ninth "Versammlung deutscher Naturforscher und Aerzte in Wiesbaden," and the leaflet may bear some connection with that publication. The present copy was folded, sealed and addressed to "Baron Dubus Directeur du Musée de Bruxelles," and bears, on the reverse, two date-stamps, one of "Frankfurt, 26 Sep 1852" and the other of "Bruxelles 27 Sept 1852". Its date of publication is fixed, therefore, at about Sept. 26, 1852. It was reviewed by Cabanis in the "Journal für Ornithologie", Vol. I, p. 46, 1853 and has always been cited as dating from that republication. The discovery of the present copy of the original paper assists in placing the date more nearly where it belongs. Bound with other papers by Bonaparte.

Bonaparte, Charles Lucien Jules Laurent.

1853. Institut de France. | Académie des Sciences. | Extrait des Comptes rendus des séances de l'Academie des Sciences, tome XXXVII, | séance du 31 octobre 1853. | **Classification ornithologique par séries** | de S. A. Charles-Lucien Prince Bonaparte.

1 vol. medium 4to, pp. 1-6. Paris.

A repaged reprint of a paper published by the author in the "Comptes Rendus" for 1853, Vol. XXXVII, pp. 641-647. Most of the text is occupied by a list of the families and subfamilies of birds arranged in tabular order. The reprint is somewhat rearranged. P. 1 contains 9 ll. (of general text) from p. 641 of the original and 13 ll. of p. 642. P. 2 completes p. 642 of the original to which has been added the "Resume" from p. 647. Pp. 3-6 are reprints of pp. 643-646, with the matter occasionally spaced differently in the columns and with at least one misprint on p. 6, "Spheniscid" for "Spheniscidae". This reprint is bound with a collection of separates and reprints of Bonaparte's papers.

Bonaparte, Charles Lucien Jules Laurent.

1854. Notes | ornithologiques | sur les | collections rapportées en 1853 | Par M. A. Delattre, | et | classification parallélique des passereaux chanteurs; | Par Charles-Lucien Prince Bonaparte. | Paris, | Mallet-Bachelier, imprimeur-libraire | du Bureau des Longitudes, de l'École Polytechnique, | Rue du Jardinet, 12. | 1854.

1 vol. foliopost 4to, tit., pp. 1-95. Paris. April 1854.

A reprint, with many alterations, of the author's paper published originally in the "Comptes Rendus," Vol. XXXVII, pp. 806-810 (for Nov. 28, 1853), 827-835 (for Dec. 5, 1853) and 913-925 (for Dec. 19, 1853), and in Vol. XXXVIII,

Carl Lucian. *Prinz Bonaparte* setzt seine Ideen über die Eintheilung der Wirbelthiere in parallelen Serien, oder, wie er sagt, in Orgelröhren (*tuyaux d'orgue*) auseinander und er gibt die folgende Tafel seiner von ihm nach den neuen *Data* der Anatomie und Physiologie modificirten Classification dieser Vögel.

Aves.

Sectio I. **Insessores.** (*Altrix.*)

Ordo I. Psittaci.
II. Accipitres.
III. Passeres.
   1. *Volucres.*
   2. *Oscines.*
IV. Columbæ.
   1. *Inertes.*
   2. *Gyrantes.*
V. Gaviæ.
   1. *Longipennes.*
   2. *Totipalmi.*
VI. Herodii.

Sectio II. **Grallatores.** (*Præcoces.*)

VII. Grallæ.
   1. *Struthionaceæ*
   2. *Gallinaceæ*
VIII. Struthiones.
IX. Gallinæ.
X. Anseres.
   1. *Lamellirostres*
   2. *Urinatores.*

Der Prinz gibt hiernach eine vollkommene *Liste* der Arten von Larinæ, welche er in natürlichen Gattungen auf die folgende Weise eintheilt:

Gaviæ.

Tribus I. **Longipennes.**

Fam. I. Procellariidæ

Fam. II. Laridæ

Sub-fam. 1. *Diomedeinæ*
2. *Procellarinæ*
3. *Lestridinæ*
4. *Larinæ*
5. *Rhyncopinæ*
6. *Sterninæ*

Conspectus Larinarum.

		Species numeri.				Species numeri.
I. Gabianus. Bp.	M. Antarct.	1	VI. Leucophaeus. Bp.	Asia or. Am. m. occ.	2
II. Larus L.			VII. Blasipus. Bp.	Am. m.	2
Lari: majores	Cosmop.	15	VIII. Adelarus. Bp.	Afr. s. Am. m.	3
Gaviæ: minores	Cosmop.	4	IX. Xema. Bp.		
III. Gelastes Bp.	Cosm. Afr. s. Austral.	5	Chroicocephalus. Eyton.	Cosmop	18
IV. Rhodostetia. Macgill.	Arctic.	1	Xema. Leach.	Arctic	2
V. Pagophila. Kaup.	Arctic.	2	X. Rissa. Leach.	Arctic.	3
		28			38

Endlich benutzt der Prinz diese Gelegenheit um einige neue Arten von Vögeln bekannt zu machen und bespricht besonders die *Cyanocitta Jolyaea*, welche er dem Herrn Professor N. Joly gewidmet hat, als ein Andenken ihres Zusammentreffens in der neunundzwanzigsten Versammlung deutscher Naturforscher und Aerzte in Wiesbaden.

Diese neun Arten sind die folgenden:

1. *Thalassidroma tethys*, Bp. (noch minder als die *pelagica* ex Insulis Gallapagoes.)

2. *Chelidoptera albipennis*, Bp. ex Cumana. Kleiner und schwärzer als die einzige bekannte Art der Gattung. *Abdomine intense castaneo; tectricibus alarum inferioribus caudidis; remigibus primariis basi, seccundariis apice, latissime albis.*

3. *Cyanocitta Jolyaea*, ex Amer. m. *Similis C. viridi-cyanea, sed colore caeruleo splendidiore; fronte genisque late nigris; vertice et torque angusto jugulari albo-caeruleis; gula caerulea sub-cinerascente (nec nigra).*

A RARE TRACT BY C. L. BONAPARTE. 1852. [UNPAGED SHEET WITHOUT TITLE.]

See p. 70.

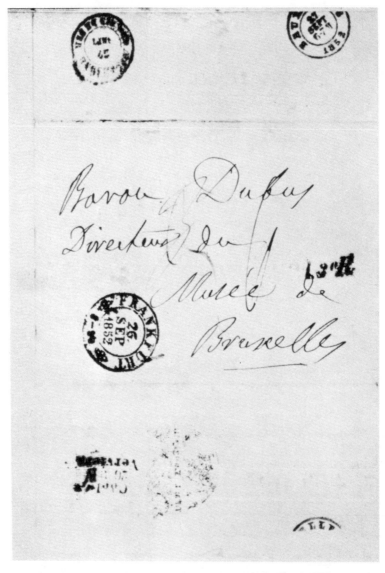

REVERSE OF TRACT BY C. L. BONAPARTE SHOWING DATE OF ISSUE.
See Pl. III, p. 70.

pp. 1-11 (for Jan. 2, 1854), 53-66 (for Jan. 16, 1854), 258-266 (for Febr. 6, 1854), 378-389 (for Febr. 27, 1854), 533-542 (for March 20, 1854) and 650-665 (for April 3, 1854). In the "Comptes Rendus" for May 1, 1854 (Vol. XXXVIII, pp. 800-801), it is announced that Bonaparte presents to the Academy a copy of the reprint which he has published; this fixes the date as some time in April of that year.

The paper is based on a collection of birds made by Delattre in California and Nicaragua, but extends to considerably wider limits and embraces a more or less general classification of the avian class. Many new genera and species were described in the original and still others in the reprint. I have noticed the following alterations in the reissue. P. 2; "*Micractur dynastes* Verr." is described: 8; Amydrus *ruppelli* and *morio* are mentioned; the genus *Nabouroupus* is established for *fulvipennis* Sw.: 12; *Xanthornus flavaxilla* Hahn is removed from identity with *Thilius cayennensis* and said only to resemble a *Thilius*: 19; *Schanicola* is changed to *Schaenicola*: 24; "*Callirhynchus peruvianus* Less.?" is newly described and said to be distinct from *C. drovoni* Verr. (it was later described as *masesus* in the "Comptes Rendus," XLII, p. 822, 1856): 35; *Chaetornis* Sw. and *Chlorepota* Smith are mentioned: 36; *Ixonotus* Verr. is mentioned; *Laedorusa* is emended to *Loedorusa*: 41; *Laedorusa* again is emended to *Loedorusa*: 49; *Alauda moreatica* emended to *A. moreotica*: 52; Myzomelinae and Melithreptinae in reversed order: 61; Leiotriciens emended to Leiothriciens: 66; *Chaunonotus* transferred to the Malaconotinae; *Timixos* Blyth and *Rhynchastatus* Bp. mentioned: 67; *Galbulus* Bp., *Broderipus* Bp., *Barruffius* Bp., *Xanthonotus* Bp., *Balicassius* Bp., *Dicranostreptus* Reichb., *Drongo* Reichb., *Musicus* Reichb. and *Buchanga* Hodgs. are included in the tables: 68; *Pomarea* Bp., *Charidhylas* Bp., *Tchitrea* Less., *Muscipeta* Duv., *Megabias* Verr. and *Todopsis* Bp., are listed; *Muscylvia* Less. emended to *Muscisylvia;* numerous species of Muscicapinae and Myiagrinae interchanged: 69; *Iridisornis* emended to *Irisornis:* 70; *Lanius chloris* Cuv. is said not to be an *Ixonotus* (as given in the original paper) but is suggested as the type of the genus *Meristes* Reichb. which Bonaparte withdraws from the synonymy of *Archolestes* Cab. for the purpose; *Cheptia* is emended to *Chaptia:* 76; *Ceblepyris caesia* (*cana* Cuv. and *capensis* auct.) are mentioned: 77; *Turdus phoeniceus* is placed in the genus *Lanicterus* with *Campephaga* (= *Cyrtes* Reichb.) *flava* Temm. as a synonym: 78; *Lanicterus swainsoni* Less. is said to be a synonym of *xanthornoides* (= *atrata* Swains, and *ater* Less.): 84; among the Ramphastidae, *Ramphomelus* (for *nigrirostris*), *Ramphoxanthus* (for *prasinus* and *albivitta*) and *Piperivorus* (for *piperivorus, viridis, bailloni, inscriptus,* etc.) are duly proposed and must date from this place and not from the author's "Conspectus Vol. Zygodactylorum" published in the Ateneo Italiano for May 1854, whence they are usually quoted; *Beauharnesius* is proposed but is a nomen nudum; "*Aulacorhamphus castaneirostris* Gould" is described from "Santa Martha" (probably intended for *A. castaneorhynchus* Gould); "*Piperivorus humboldti* Bp. ex Wagler" is described: 85; *Dryotomus verrauxi* from Santa Martha, *D. odoardus* from Mexico and *D. delattrii* from California are all described as new species: 86; *D. scapularis* is removed to a footnote where it is compared to *erythrops:* 87; *Milvulus tyrannus* is emended to *Despotes tyrannus; Xenops genibarbis* is included (by mistake?) in the Tyrannidae: 89; the number of genera and species cited for the subfamilies of hummingbirds is altered; *Heliomastes* is altered to

Heliomaster; Chrysuronia elicia is altered to *eliciae* and *Saucerottia sophia* to *sophiae:* 91; there is a footnote regarding *Ibis religiosa:* 92; *Halyplana* is emended to *Haliplana.* The title-page, also, is entirely new.

Bonaparte, Charles Lucien Jules Laurent.

1855. **Coup d'oeil | sur | l'ordre des pigeons, | par | S. A. Mon-seigneur le Prince Charles-Lucien Bonaparte. | Extrait des Comptes rendus des séances de l'Académie des Sciences, tomes XXXIX et XL. | Années 1854-1855. | Paris, | imprimerie de Mallet-Bachelier, gendre et successeur de Bachelier, | Rue du Jardinet, 12. | 1855.**

1 vol. medium 4to, tit., pp. 1-59. Paris. (1854?)-1855.

A repaged, revised reprint of a paper which was issued in parts in the "Comptes Rendus" in 1854 and 1855, Vol. XXXIX, pp. 869-880, 1072-1078 and 1102-1112, and Vol. XL, pp. 15-24, 96-102 and 205-215. A title-page is supplied for this reprint, and minor changes are made in the text here and there, but the general account follows the original with fair regularity except in the case of the discussion of the "Zénaïdiens." In the original (Vol. XL, pp. 20-24 and 96-102), the author divides this group into two series; in the reprint (pp. 33-43) he recognizes four series and rearranges the genera and species in a totally different manner. I have not discovered any newly described genera or species in the reprint, although some names are cited which are not in the original paper. Additions and corrections to the original of this work were published in the "Comptes Rendus" XLIII, pp. 833-841 and 942-949, 1856. A reprint thereof was published the same year (q.v.).

The date of publication of the present reprint is not entirely certain. Traces of original wrappers adhering to pp. 9, 17 and 41 indicate that the work appeared in at least four parts and, if so, the early pages may have been issued in 1855, the date of the originals of those pages. The present copy is bound with a number of other papers by Bonaparte.

Bonaparte, Charles Lucien Jules Laurent. (Gray, George Robert.)

1855. **Institut Impérial de France. | Académie des Sciences. | Extrait des Comptes rendus des séances de l'Académie des Sciences, tome XLI, | séance du 22 octobre 1855. | Catalogue | des | genres et sous-genres d'oiseaux contenus dans le Muséum Britannique, | Par M. Georges-R. Gray, | Conservateur du Musée Britannique.**

1 vol. medium 4to, pp. 1-12. Paris.

A reprint of a paper published in the "Comptes Rendus" for Oct. 22, 1855, Vol. XLI, pp. 649-661. Ostensibly a review of G. R. Gray's "Genera and Sub-genera of Birds", 1855 (q.v.), the paper expands into a discussion of "les principales espèces nouvelles qu'il vient d'observer en Écosse et en Angleterre," in which many new names appear (in the original). Some alterations occur in the reprint, mostly corrections of errors. *Spiziopteryx, Microglaux lieua, Somateria v. nigrum, Mantifringilla, Malacocichla deyas,* etc., are changed to *Spiziopteryx, M. licua, S. v.-nigrum, Montifringilla* and *M. dryas.* Various comments are emended and some material is added but I find no new names in the reissue. The title transcribed above is found only in this edition where, however, it is not on a separate title-page.

Bonaparte, Charles Lucien Jules Laurent. (Moquin-Tandon.)

1855. Institut Impérial de France. | Académie des Sciences. | Extrait des Comptes rendus des séances de l'Académie des Sciences, tome XLI. | **Note** | **sur** | **les oiseaux des Iles Marquises,** | et particulièrement sur le genre nouveau Serresius, | Par S. A. Monseigneur le Prince Bonaparte. **Note** | **sur** | **les Salanganes et sur leurs nids,** | Par S. A. Monseigneur le Prince Bonaparte.

1 vol. medium 4to, pp. 1-8. Paris.

A repaged reprint of the author's papers in the "Comptes Rendus" for 1855, Vol. XLI, pp. 1109-1113 and 976-979, with arrangement mixed. Pp. 1109-1113 (pt.) are given first, followed by pp. 976-979, an extract from p. 1157 by Moquin-Tandon (relative to *Eugenia imperatrix* Gould and having no connection with the present papers) and concluding with the final paragraph of p. 1113. This final paragraph refers to an appended "Conspectus Gaviarum systematicus" which follows on pp. 1114 and 1115 of the original but is omitted from the present reprint although it was republished in 1856 in a collection of papers. {Cf. [Miscellaneous reprints], 1856.}.

Bonaparte, Charles Lucien Jules Laurent.

1855. Institut Impérial de France. | Académie des Sciences. | Extrait des Comptes rendus des séances de l'Académie des Sciences, tome XL, | séance du 2 avril 1855. | **Tableaux synoptiques** | **de** | **l'ordre des Hérons,** | par | S. A. Monseigneur Charles-Lucien Bonaparte.

1 vol. medium 4to, pp. 1-8. Paris.

A repaged reprint of an article published in the "Comptes Rendus" for April 2, 1855, Vol. XL, pp. 718-725. A number of changes are made in this issue. The numbering of Subfamilies 8 to 12 and 14 to 18 are corrected to 7 to 11 and 12 to 16, respectively; genera 58 and 59 are transposed; three species are removed from the genus *Calherodias* and placed in *Nycticorax;* species 48 (*Ardea*) *pharaonis* is emended to *pharaonica;* species 70, (*Egretta*) *egrettoides,* synonym "*nivea ?* Cuv." is changed to "*nivea ?* Cuv. nec Auct."; the geographical table on p. 719 is placed before the systematic tables instead of at the close of the paper, and there may be other changes. The present copy is bound with other of Bonaparte's papers in a composite volume.

Bonaparte, Charles Lucien Jules Laurent.

1856. Institut Impérial de France. | Académie des Sciences. | Extrait des Comptes rendus des séances de l'Académie des Sciences, tome XLIII, | séances de 27 octobre et novembre 1856. | **Ornithologie fossile** servant d'introduction au Tableau comparatif | des Ineptes et des Autruches; | Par S. A. Monseigneur le Prince Ch.

Bonaparte. >Additions et Corrections au Coup d'oeil sur l'Ordre des Pigeons, | et à la partie correspondante du Conspectus Avium de S. A. | Monseigneur le Prince Ch. Bonaparte. > **Additions et Corrections aux Tableaux paralléliques** de l'Ordre | des Hérons et des Pélagiens ou Gavies, et à la partie | correspondante du Conspectus Avium. | (Séance du 24 novembre 1856.).

1 vol. medium 4to, pp. 1-46. Paris.

Reprints of three articles which appeared in the "Comptes Rendus" for 1856, Vol. XLIII, pp. 775-783 (for Oct. 27), 833-841 (for Nov. 3), 942-949 (for Nov. 17), 990-997 (for Nov. 24) and 1017-1027 (for Dec. 1). Like in other of Bonaparte's reprints, new matter and new arrangements are introduced into the present issue. The "Conspectus Ineptorum" (pp. 840-841 of the original) is placed before the reprint of p. 833. *Hemiphaga forsteri* is emended to *H. forsteni; Trocaza bouvryi* is emended to *T. buvryi;* a footnote is added to the discussion of *Leptoptila brasiliensis;* the names *Bartramia longicauda* and *Actiturus rufescens* are introduced; *Rallus subplumbeus* Sclater is described in detail; the order Palmipedes is altered to Anseres; footnotes are added giving discussions of *Anser caerulescens, A. parvipes, A. rufescens* and *A. melanopterus;* a paragraph on *Chloephaga* is added and one on a hybrid of *Rhynchaspis clypeata* and *Dafila acuta* omitted; several other paragraphs on Anseres have been re-arranged.

The present copy forms one of a collection of Bonaparte's papers bound in one volume, from the library of Henry Baker Tristram.

Bonaparte, Charles Lucien Jules Laurent.

1856. Institut Impérial de France. | Académie des Sciences. | Extrait des Comptes rendus des séances de l'Académie des Sciences, tome XLIII, | séance du 2 août 1856 [séances des 15 et 22 septembre 1856]. | **Excursions | dans les divers musées d'Allemagne, de Hollande et de Belgique,** | et | **tableaux paralléliques** | de | **l'ordre des Echassiers,** | Par S. A. Monseigneur le Prince Ch. Bonaparte.

2 pts. medium 4to. Pt. I, pp. 1-14. Pt. II, pp. 1-27. Paris.

Ostensibly a reprint of a paper which appeared in parts in the "Comptes Rendus" for 1856, Vol. XLIII, pp. 410-421 (for Aug. 25), 571-579 (for Sept. 15), 593-601 (for Sept. 22) and 643-652 (for Sept. 29). However, the author followed his usual custom and there are many deviations from the original.

The reprint is separately paged in two sections of which Pt. I contains pp. 410-421 of the original and Pt. II the remainder. The text is differently arranged in Pt. II in the following sequence of original pagination: pp. 571-578, 593-595, 643-646, 579, 596-601, 648-652 and 647. (The present copy is rearranged to bring all the systematic tables together). Various changes occur in the systematic tables, among which may be mentioned the following. Four species of the genus *Gambetta*, grouped under No. 242, are here left without a number; *Rhynchophilus glareoloides* is put into synonymy; *Numenius major* is likewise submerged; *N. femoralis* is given a number, No. 278, and many of the species of the same genus are rearranged; *N. taitensis* is emended to *N. tahitiensis; N. minor* is submerged; *Aramus* and its species, *A. scolopaceus,* are included for the first time; *Rallus setosus* is elevated from synonymy; *Porzana notata* is placed in the genus *Ortygometra; O. chilensis* and *O. notata* are omitted; *Porphyrio samoensis* is elevated; *Brachyptirallus* and its species, *B. ralloides,* are recognized; *Mareca capensis* is dropped; species *anatorius* (synonym of *Mergellus albellus*) is emended to *anatarius;* the figures in the geographical table of the Grallae are altered.

The general text also contains some changes. The typography of certain names is altered; the footnote on p. 577 is rearranged; *Podoa josephina* Bp. occurs (p. 9 of Pt. 2 of reprint) as a nomen nudum (described later in the author's "Conspectus Avium,", **2,** p. 182, post Nov. 1, 1855); *Leucus islandicus,* not mentioned in original text, is declared to be invalid; the reference to *Podiceps longirostris* is omitted. There are probably other changes not noticed in a hasty glance through the paper.

The date "2 août" in the title of Pt. I is an error for "25 août," the figure on the original number of the periodical. The original mailing wrapper of Pt. II is bound with the copy and bears a date stamp, "Paris, 16 Oct. 56," being addressed to Bernard Dubus of the Brussells Museum.

Numerous new species are described in the original paper from which they must be dated.

Bonaparte, Charles Lucien Jules Laurent.

1856.   [Miscellaneous reprints.]

1 vol. (pt.) medium 4to, pp. 9-30+1 l. Paris. 1856 (circa May 23).

A collection of papers by Bonaparte, revised, rearranged, retitled and repaged from the originals which appeared in different volumes of the "Comptes Rendus," as follows. The first three are not ornithological.

"Remarques," etc., "sur une nouvelle espèce d'Equide," p. 9, appeared in the magazine for Dec. 31, 1855, Vol. XLI, pp. 1219-1220.

"Paroles," etc., "sur les Observatoires projetés pour l'Algérie," pp. 10-11, appeared in the magazine for Dec. 24, 1855, Vol. XLI, pp. 1147-48.

"Communication," etc., "en présentant une nouvelle publication de M. Gray" (on Chelonia), pp. 11-12, appeared in the "Comptes Rendus" for March 17, 1856, Vol. XLII, pp. 513-514.

"Extrait d'une Lettre - á M. Geoffroy-Saint-Hilaire," p. 12, is the "Sur les Perdrix d'Europe" of the "Comptes Rendus" for March 17, 1856, Vol. XLII, p. 509.

"Espèces nouvelles d'Oiseaux d'Asie et d'Amérique, et tableaux paralléliques des Pélagiens ou Gaviae," pp. 13-15, 19, and 22-30, was published in the "Comptes Rendus" for April 28, 1856, Vol. XLII, pp. 764-776.

"Observations sur la zoologie géographique de l'Afrique, et Description d'un nouveau genre et de nouvelles espèces d'Oiseaux," pp. 16-19, is from the "Comptes Rendus" for May 5, 1856, Vol. XLII, pp. 819-822.

"Conspectus Gaviarum systematicus," pp. 20-21, is joined to the "Tableaux paralléliques des Pélagiens ou Gaviae" but appeared the previous year in the "Comptes Rendus" for Dec. 24, 1855, Vol. XLI, pp. 1114-1115 as part of a "Note sur les oiseaux des Iles Marquises" (q.v.).

The present copy, bound with a miscellaneous collection of Bonaparte's papers is preceded by its original mailing jacket addressed to "M. le Vicomte Bernard Dubus, Directeur du Musée de Bruxelles, Belgique" and is postmarked, "Paris 23 Mai 56." The dating stamp has left a more or less legible impression in duplicate on the blank leaf at the close of the paper and on one or two leaves preceding it. The date of publication of this paper is thus fixed with reasonable accuracy.

The incomplete pagination of this assortment of reprints makes it appear very probable that it is in continuation of the reprints of the "Note sur les oiseaux des Iles Marquises," etc., paged 1-8 and issued slightly in advance of the present lot. That it is intended as a continuation of something is further evidenced by the signature which is numbered "2". This brings to mind the fact that Bonaparte's revised reprints of papers from the "Comptes Rendus" are often recognizable by their signatures which distinguish them from mere extracts from that journal when the original pagination is not known for comparison. The original separates bear the letters "C.R." with volume numbers, etc.; the revised reprints are lettered "B."

Bonaparte, Charles Lucien Jules Laurent.

1856.   Tableaux paralléliques | de | l'ordre des Gallinacés. 1 vol. medium 4to, pp. 1-20. Paris.

Based on two papers and a note published by Bonaparte in the "Comptes Rendus" for 1856, Vol. XLII, pp. 874-884 (for May 12) and 952-957 (for May 19) but separately paged and with certain matter not in the original articles. The second part of the paper as here published (pp. 14-20) bears a subtitle, "Note sur les tableaux des Gallinacés". In addition to the matter indicated in that title, which includes descriptions of new species, there are discussions and descriptions of numerous non-gallinaceous birds from the Mexican collections of Auguste Sallé. Among the many changes from the original may be cited the following. In the "Tableaux" proper: *fronticornis* added to the synonymy of *Oreophasis derbyanus; albiventer* Wagler is removed from *Ortalida* and placed in *Penelopsis; P. albiventer* Less. is placed in the synonymy of *leucogaster* which, in turn, is elevated; *Rhynchotis perdix* is placed as a synonym of *R perdicarius*, the relationship being reversed; *Nothocercus bourcieri* is dropped; *N. scolopax* is added (here a nomen nudum); *N. strigulolus* Temm. is added, as are *Nothura punctulata* Goy and *Hepburnia concentrica* J. Gr.; the subgenus *Scleroptera*, gen. *Chaetops*, is rearranged with several species transferred from subgen. *Clamator;* some of the figures in the "Conspectus Gallinarum Geographicus" are altered; the short original diagnosis of *Tinamus weddelli* is omitted.

In the "Note sur les Tableaux" other changes occur. The note regarding *Francolinus concentricus* is omitted as is the mention of the Scleropterae and of *St. thoracica, charltoni* and *scutata. Tinamus weddelli* is described in detail and an exact locality given, in place of the brief diagnosis omitted from the "Tableaux"; *Crypturus adspersus* and *vermiculatus, Trogon capistratus, Nothocercus bourcieri* and *julius, Crypturus sovi* and *Rhynchotes perdicarius* are mentioned or discussed; a male of *Trogon xalappensis* Dubus is described in detail; and *Nothocercus scolopax* is described as new.

The present copy is bound with other reprints of Bonaparte's papers sent to Dubus.

Bonaparte, Charles Lucien Jules Laurent.

1856. **Tableaux paralléliques | des ordres Linnéens** | Anseres, Grallæ et Gallinæ. | Ineptes, Hérons, Pélagiens, Nullipennes. | Des | Altrices ou Sitistes, | et | Præcoces ou Autophages. | (Gallinacés, Échassiers, Palmipèdes et Rudipennes.) | Avec notes et descriptions d'espèces nouvelles | de | Perroquets, Rapaces, Passereaux et Pigeons; | par | Charles-Lucien Bonaparte. | Paris, | Mallet-Bachelier, Imprimeur-Libraire | de l'Ecole Impériale Polytechnique, du Bureau des Longitudes, | Quai des Augustins, 55. | 1856.

Title-page only, medium 4to. Paris.

This title-page appears to have been issued as a covering title for various reprints of articles published in the "Comptes Rendus" up to the date of this page. Included in a bound set of Bonaparte's papers.

Bonaparte, Charles Lucien Jules Laurent.

1857. **Remarques | A propos des Observations de M. Émile Blanchard** sur les Carac- | tères ostéologiques chez les Oiseaux de la famille des **Psittacides,** | et Tableau des genres de Perroquets disposés en séries pa- | rallèles; | Par S. A. Monseigneur le Prince C.-L. Bonaparte.

1 vol. medium 4to, tit., pp. 1-9. Paris.

A repaged reprint, with additions, of two articles published by the author in the "Comptes Rendus" for March 16 and 23, 1857, Vol. XLIX, pp. 534-539 and 595-597. Important additions are made in the reprint as follows. In the descriptive account, forming the first paper, the number of subfamilies is given as sixteen while in the synoptic tables, forming the second paper, eighteen are listed; in the reprint, eighteen are mentioned in both places. In the reprint of the descriptive text the names of the Psittaculidae and Plyctolophidae are emended to Araidae and Cacatuidae, agreeing with the original edition of the synoptic tables; the "Nestoriens" and "Nasiterniens" are mentioned in the descriptive text, having been in the original tables under Latin names. The following genera are mentioned for the first time in the text although, with the exception of *Ararauna*, they are in the original tables as nomina nuda: *Ararauna; Ara* (with type *Ps. macao* Linn.); *Sittace* with 3 species) *Arara* (with type *spixi*); *Primolius* (new genus with three species); *Psittacara* with two species); *Ognorhynchus* (new genus with type *icterotis* Massena); *Evopsitta* and *E. brasiliensis; Bolborhynchus* (new genus for *Myopsitta tigrina* and *catharina* of the original text); *Conurus astec* (emendation of *Conurus asteco*); *Ptilosclera* (new genus with type *versicolor* Vig.). In the synoptic table as reprinted, the genus *Ararauna* is mentioned and *Dasyptilus* is transferred from the Eclectinae to the Nestorinae.

The present reprint is bound with some other copies of Bonaparte's paper presented to Dubus by the author.

Bonaparte, Charles Lucien Jules Laurent. (Moquin-Tandon, A., *ed.*)

1857-58. **Iconographie | des pigeons |** non figurés par Mme Knip (Mlle Pauline Decourcelles) | dans les deux volumes de MM. Temminck et Florent Prevost | par | Charles-Lucien Bonaparte | Ouvrage servant d'illustration a son | Histoire Naturelle des Pigeons | Paris | P. Bertrand, Libraire-Éditeur | Rue de l'Arbresec, 22 | 1857.

1 vol. superroyal folio, 5 pr. ll. (half-tit., tit., conts. and dedicatory pref.), 62 ll. (gen. text), 1 l. (ed. notices), 55 pll. (col.; by Oudart, F. Willy and E. Blanchard; num. 1-9, 11-19, 25=20, 21-24, 20=25, 26, 28, 29, 31-36, 38-40, 42, 45, 51, 57, 58, 61, 62, 69, 70, 75, 102, 116, 119, 121, 125, 126, 133, 134 and 140).

A supplement to "Les Pigeons" by Temminck and Prévost (Cf. Knip 1809-11), intended to figure and describe those species of pigeons not treated in the earlier work.   The original plan embraced 30 livraisons of 150 plates but the author died immediately after the publication of livr. 4, leaving incomplete manuscript and plates for part of the remainder.   The publishers obtained the services of Moquin-Tandon to edit the manuscript and 8 more livraisons were published with 35 plates (20 had appeared in livrs. 1-4), reserving 7 plates for which there were no descriptions and 4 descriptions without plates.   Livr. 12 contained, with editorial notice and list of contents, 7 descriptions whose plates had appeared previously.   The list of contents gives the livraison-number for each plate and description; they were not always synchronous.   Plate 20 is numbered 25 in error and plate 25 is numbered 20 in the text as well as on the plate.   Plates 27, 29 and 124 (wrongly numbered 121 in text but corrected in the list of contents) were not issued, although their descriptions are given.   Exact dates are not available.   Livrs. 1-4 appeared in 1857, before Bonaparte's death in July; the publishers note that they have published the remainder of the work in the space of ten months, and date the notice, which appeared in the last part, July 1, 1858; thus livr. 5 seems to have appeared in Sept. 1857, and 12 in July 1858.   Intervening dates and the date of the first part are unobtainable.   The work appears to be rather rare and some copies are incomplete; the present one is complete, so far as published.   The hand-colored plates are very fine.

Bonaparte, Charles Lucien Jules Laurent.

1876.   See Wilson, Alexander, and Bonaparte, **American Ornithology.**
1877.   Idem.
1878.   Idem.

Bonhote, John Lewis.

1907.   **Birds of Britain |** by | J. Lewis Bonhote | M.A., F.L.S., F.Z.S. | Member of the British Ornithologists' Union | with | 100 illustrations in colour | selected by | H. E. Dresser | from his 'Birds of Europe' | London | Adam and Charles Black | 1907.

1 vol. cap 4to, pp. I-X, 1 l. pp. 1-405, 4 ll. (advt.), 100 pll. (col.), 1 fig. London.

A popular account of the habits of the species discussed.

Bonhote, John Lewis.

1910-13. See Kirkman, Frederick Bernuf Bever, **The British Bird Book.**

Bonite, La. Voyage autour du monde—sur—.

1841-52. See Vaillant.

Bonnaterre (l'Abbé); and Vieillot, Louis Jean Pierre.

1790-1823.   > Tableau | encyclopédique | et méthodique | des trois règnes de la nature. | Ornithologie. | Par l'Abbé Bonnaterre, [Par M. l'Abbe Bonnaterre. (*Atlas.*)] |
et continuée
Par L. P. Vieillot. [*Quot., 2 lines (Atlas.*).] |Premiere [Seconde; Troisième; (*Atlas not indicated.*)] partie. | [*Vignette.*] | A Paris, | Chez Mme veuve Agasse, Imprimeur-Libraire, rue des Poitevins, No 6 [Chez Panckoucke, Libraire, Hôtel de Thou, rue des Poitevins (*Atlas.*)]. | 1823 [M.DCC.XC (*Atlas*)] . [| Avec Approbation et Privilége due Roi. (*Atlas.*)].

4 vols. medium 4to. Vol. I, 2 pr. ll. (half-tit. and tit.), pp. III-XCVIJ+1, 1-402. Vol. II, 2 pr. ll. (half-tit. and tit.) pp. 403-902. Vol. III, 2 pr. ll. (half-tit. and tit.), pp. 903-1460. Atlas, tit., pll. 1-240 (2 fold.), 1-7 (7 fold.). Paris.

Part of a second edition of the "Encyclopédie Méthodique" (of which the birds were discussed by Mauduyt) but in reality entirely distinct from the original edition. The present portion was begun by Bonnaterre who published the plates, preface, introduction and the text up to p. 320, before his death, after which the ornithology was completed by Vieillot. The entire work, in both editions, is collated by Sherborn in the Annals and Magazine of Natural History, Ser. 7, Vol. **17**, pp. 577-582, 1906, from which I extract the following information relative to the ornithology. The work appeared in parts. Livr. **37** included "Ornithologie," pll. 1-77, 1790; livr. **38**, pll. 78- 177, 1790; livr. **40**, pp. I-LXXX, pll. 178-239 (240?), 1-7, 1790; livr. **47**, pp. LXXXI-XCVII, 1-192, 1791; livr. **51**, pp. 193-320, (1792); livr. **89**, (pp. 321-528), 1820; livr. **91**, pp. 529-848, 1822; livr. **93**, (pp. 849-1460), 1823. The plates of the second series, 1-7, are anatomical and bear reference to Vol. I, Pt. I of the original "Encyclopédie." The text contains a systematic review of the birds of the world, with detailed descriptions and many new names. It is strictly binomial.

Booth, Edward Thomas.

1881-87.   Rough notes | on the | birds observed | during twenty-five years' shooting and collecting | in the British Islands | by | E. T.

Booth. | With plates from drawings by E. Neale, | taken from specimens in the author's possession. | Volume I [-III] | London: | published by R. H. Porter, 6 Tenterden Street, W., | and | Messrs. Dulau & Co., Soho Square, W. | 1881-1887.

3 vols. superroyal folio (13x16½). Vol. I, pp. I-VII, 119 ll., 35 pll. (col.), 2 text-cuts. Vol. II, pp. I-V, 133 ll., 31 pll. (col.), 1 map (col.). Vol. III, pp. I-V, 113 ll., 48 pll. (col.), 1 map (col.), 1 text-cut (2 figs.). London.

A series of well written field notes accompanied by good plates. The work was issued in fifteen parts during the years 1881-1887, with discontinuous pagination to be bound in a prescribed order regardless of sequence of issue. The collation given is of the bound work. The contents and dates of the various parts are as follows, according to current reviews in the Ibis and Zoological Record.

Pt. 1, 1881; *Aquila chrysaetos, Haliaetus albicilla, Milvus regalis* and *Pandion haliaetus*, all figured. Pt. 2, 1882; *Circus cyaneus, Accipiter nisus, Buteo vulgaris, Falco peregrinus* and *Falco aesalon*, imm., all figured. Pt. 3, 1883; (contents not given). Pt. 4, 1883; Raven, Crossbill, Gray-headed Wagtail, Yellow Wagtail, Scandinavian Rock Pipit, Black Redstart, Wheatear and Willow Wren, figured. Pt. 5, 1883; Red-breasted Merganser (2 pll.), Gannet (6 pll.). Pt. 6, 1884; Ptarmigan (3 pll.), Arctic Skua (4 pll.); for text see Pt. 8. Pt. 7, 1884; Eider (3 pll.), Goosander (2 pll.), Pomatorhine Skua (1 pl.); for text see Pt. 8. Pt. 8, 1884; Montagu's Harrier (2 pll.), Woodcock (2 pll.), Whooper, Pochard, Goldeneye and Long-tailed Skua (1 pl. each); text for Pts. 6-8, Starling, Dipper, Fieldfare, Thrush, Blackbird, Blackcap, Ptarmigan, Peewit, Redshank, Purple Sandpiper, Coot, Arctic Skua, Rook, Tree Sparrow, Redwing, Golden-crested Wren, Whimbrel, Eider, Goosander, Common Gull, Herring Gull, Pomatorhine Skua, Montagu's Harrier, Greenfinch, Twite, Missel Thrush, Quail, Woodcock, Jack Snipe, Land Rail, Spotted Crake, Brent Goose, Whooper, Pochard, Golden Eye and Long-tailed Skua. Pt. 9, 1885; Shoveller (3 pll.), Dotterel, Black-tailed Godwit, Great Crested Grebe, Great Black-backed Gull and Fulmar, (1 pl. each); text on species mentioned and Cuckoo, Lark, Hedge Sparrow, Dartford Warbler, Wood Pigeon and Turtle Dove. Pt. 10, 1886; House Sparrow (2 pll.), Black Grouse, Red Grouse, Spoonbill, Grey-lag Goose, Scoter and immature Smew (1 pl. each); text on species figured and on Bullfinch, Redbreast, White-fronted Goose, Sclavonian Grebe and Little Grebe. Pt. 11, 1886; Rock Dove, Snipe, Curlew Sandpiper, Knot, Puffin, Roseate Gull and Little Gull (1 pl. each); also map of Breydon mudflats; text on species figured and on Ring Ouzel, White Stork, Turnstone, Spotted Redshank, Scaup, Razorbill, Cormorant and Arctic Tern. Pt. 12, 1886; Siskin, Common Sandpiper, Little Stint, Temminck's Stint and Sandwich Tern, (1 pl. each and map of Hickling Broad; text on these species and on Linnet, Lesser Redpoll, Mealy Redpoll, Stock Dove, Ringed Plover, Kentish Plover, Sanderling, Oyster-Catcher, Greenshank, Bar-tailed Godwit, Bean Goose, Mute Swan, Velvet Scoter, Eared Grebe, Black-throated Diver, Black Guillemot and Manx Shearwater. Pt. 13, 1886; Cuckoo, Hoopoe, Golden Oriole, Capercaillie, Stone Curlew, Heron, Gadwall (immature), (1 pl. each) and Red-necked Grebe (2 pll.); text on these species and on Green Sandpiper, Pheasant, Common Partridge, Red-legged Partridge, Wood Sandpiper, Pin-

tail Duck, Garganey and Common Teal. Pt. 12, 1887; Grey Phalarope
Kittiwake, Glaucous Gull and Stormy Petrel, (1 pl. each), Black-headed Gull
and Common Guillemot, (2 pll. each); text on these species and on Goldfinch,
Hawfinch, Shag, Bewick's Swan, Tufted Duck, Golden Plover, Grey Plover,
Lesser Tern, White-winged Black Tern, Black Tern and Great Northern Diver
Pt. 15, 1887; Ruff (pl.); text on this and on Snow Bunting, Bittern, Common
Sheld-Duck, Wigeon, Mallard, Dunlin and Common Tern; also title-pages,
contents, lists of plates, etc.

Boraston, John Maclair.

1905. Birds by | land & sea | The record of a year's work | with
field-glass and camera | by John Maclair Boraston | illustrated by
photographs | taken direct from nature | by the author | John
Lane: The Bodley Head | London & New York, MDCCCCV.

1 vol. 8vo, pp. I-VI, IX-XIV, 1 l. (half-tit.), pp. 1-281+1, 3 ll.
(advt.), 52 pll. London and New York.

A popular record of ornithological observations in the neighborhood of Stratford,
England, from September 1902 until September 1903.   Mullens and Swann
catalogue a London edition of 1904.

Borckhausen, Moritz Balthasar; Lichthammer, J. W.; Bekker, C. W.; Lembcke, Georg; Bekker *Jr.*

1800-11. Teutsche | Ornithologie | oder | Naturgeschichte | aller |
Vögel Teutschlands | in naturgetreuen | Abbildungen und Be-
schreibungen. | Herausgegeben | von | Borckhausen, Lichthammer,
C. W. Bekker, Lembcke, und Bekker Junior. | In XXI Hefte. |
Darmstadt, | im Verlage der Herausgeber.

1 vol. medium folio, 2 pr. ll. (tit. and list of subscrs.), 83 ll., 125 pll.
(col.; by H. Curtmann, T. C. Susemihl, E. F. Lichthammer, T.
Susemihl Jun., and Susemihl Bros.). Darmstadt.

Detailed descriptions and accounts of habits, distribution, etc., of German birds.
Engelmann cites 126 pll. but the present copy contains only 125.   The title-
page, which is at hand, is said to be missing from many copies.   The work
appeared in 21 parts under the above dates, according to a copy in the original
wrappers catalogued by the Library of the British Museum (Natural History).
A second edition was issued in 1837-41.

Borggreve, Bernard.

1869. Die | Vogel-Fauna von Norddeutschland. | Eine kritische
Musterung | der | europäischen Vogel-Arten | nach dem Gesichts-
punkte | ihrer Verbreitung über das nördliche Deutschland. |
Unter Benutzung der einschlägigen Literatur und nach eigenen
Beobachtungen | bearbeitet | von | Dr. Bernard Borggreve, |
Königl. Preuss. Oberförster und Docent an der Forstacademie zu
Münden. | Berlin. | Verlag von Julius Springer. | 1869.

1 vol. post 8vo, pp. I-XVI, 1-156+1 l., 2 ll. (advt.). Berlin.

The general part of the work, pp. 1-52, consists of studies of various phases of the distribution of birds in northern Germany, with a list of species classified according to distribution and seasonal occurrence. The special section, pp. 53-147, contains a systematic list of European species, with notes on distribution and bibliographic references. Pp. 149-156 contain a hand-list of 340 species recorded from northern Germany. A bibliogrpahy is given on pp. XV and XVI.

Borrer, William.

1891.   The | birds of Sussex | by | William Borrer, M.A., F.L.S., | Member of the British Ornithologists' Union | London: | R. H. Porter, 18 Princes Street, Cavendish Square | 1891.

1 vol. post 8vo, pp. I-XVIII, 1-385, 2 ll. (list of subscribers), 4 ll. (advt.), 6 pll. (col.; by J. G. Keulemans), 1 map (col.). London.

The book consists mainly of field notes without descriptions. The present copy formerly belonged to R. J. Balston (author of "Notes on the Birds of Kent"), and has many marginal notes by him.

Boucard, Adolphe.

1876.   Catalogus avium | hucusque descriptorum. | Auctor | Adolphus Boucard. | Londini, MDCCCLXXVI. | For sale at | 55, Great Russell Street, London, W.C. | and at all booksellers.

1 vol. post 8vo, pp. I-XIV, 1-352. London.

A hand-list of 11,031 species of birds arranged under 2456 genera, with the general distribution of each species briefly noted. The arrangement of genera, families and orders follows the author's own peculiar conception and has not been accepted generally. The inclusion of the Hirundinidae among the Macrochires is one of the striking irregularities. The preface is dated March 1, 1876. Another edition (q.v.) has the prefatory matter in French in place of the English of the present edition.

Boucard, Adolphe.

1876.   Catalogus avium | hucusque descriptorum. | Auctor | Adolphus Boucard. | Londini, MDCCCLXXVI. | En vente | 55, Great Russell Street, London, W.C. | et chez tous les libraires.

1 vol. post 8vo, pp. I-XIV, 1-352. London.

Identical with another edition (q.v.) of the same year except for the imprint, notice and preface which are in French instead of English. The general text is printed from the same plates.

Boucard, Adolphe.

1877.   See Rowley, George D., Ornithological Miscellany, 1875-78.

Boucard, Adolphe.

1889. Catalogue | des | oiseaux | de la | collection Riocour | Par A. Boucard | Paris 1889 | Tours | Imprimerie Paul Bousrez | 1889. 1 vol. demy 8vo, pp. 1-24. Tours.

A list of 1763 species of mounted birds in the collection of Antoine Nicolas François, Comte de Riocour. An anonymous catalogue of the same collection was published in 1829 (Cf. Anon., Catalogue des Oiseaux, etc., 1829.).

Boucard, Adolphe.

1892-95. Genera | of | humming birds. | Being also | A Complete Monograph of these Birds. | By | Mr. Adolphe Boucard, | Corresponding Member [etc., 9 lines.] | London, 1893-1895. 1 vol. post 8vo, pp. I-XIV, 1-412. London.

A descriptive catalogue of the humming birds, including various new genera and species. The work was issued in parts as a supplement to the author's periodical, "The Humming Bird," Vols. II-V, forming nearly the whole of the last volume of that work. The following dates of publication (supplied by Dr. C. E. Hellmayr) are from a copy in the State Museum at Münich. Pp. 1-56 (54), 1892; 55-106[1], 1893; 107-202, 1894; 203-266, March 1895; 267-282, June 1895; 283-330, June 1895; 331-394, end of August 1895; 395-402, October 1895 or later but before Christmas. The book contains some curious passages.

Bougainville, Louis Antoine, Baron de. (Lesson, René Primevère.)

1837. Journal | de la navigation | autour du globe | de | la Frégate la Thétis et de la Corvette l'Esperance | pendant les années 1824, 1825 et 1826 | publié par ordre du Roi | sous les auspices du Département de la Marine | par M. le Baron de Bougainville | Capitaine de vaisseau | Chevalier de Saint-Louis et de l'Ordre des Cincinnati, Commandant de la Légion d'Honneur | Chef de l'Expedition. | Tome premier [Tome second; Atlas]. | [Vignette.] | Paris | Arthus Bertrand, Libraire-Éditeur [Éditeur | Libraire de la Societé de Géographie, Rue Hautefeuille, 23 (Atlas.)]. | M DCCC XXXVII. 3 vols. medium 4to and superroyal folio. Vol. I, 2 pr. ll. (half-tit. and tit., pp. VIJ-VIIJ, 1-742, 18 text-cuts. Vol. II, pp. I-XVI, 1-351+1, 1-165+1 (meteorology and index), 1 l. (errata), 5 text-cuts. Atlas, 2 pr. ll. (tit. and table of pll.), pll. 1-56 (13 col.; by Prêtre and P. Bessa; 3 ornithological; 10 fold.). Paris.

The report of the circumnavigation of the globe in the Thétis and the Esperance during 1824-26. The ornithology of the voyage is discussed in Vol. II, pp. 311-331 by Lesson, although the new species there described were previously treated by Lesson in "L'Institut" No. 72, 1834. Pll. 39-41, by Bessa, are hand-colored portraits of birds, representing 4 species.

---

[1]Pp. 55-56, containing the text of *Chrysolampis moschitus* and *Eustephanus galeritus*, were issued in 1892 but were cancelled by pp. 55-56 containing *Abeillia* and a reprint of the account of *Chrysolampis moschitus*, issued in 1893.

Bourjot Saint-Hilaire, Alexandre.

1837-38. Histoire naturelle | des perroquets, | troisième volume | (supplémentaire), | pour faire suite aux deux volumes de Levaillant, | contenant les espèces laissées inédites par cet auteur ou récemment découvertes. | Ouvrage destiné | a compléter une monographie figurée de la famille des Psittacidés, le texte renfermant la | classification, la synonymie et la description de chaque espèce; | suivi d'un index général des espèces décrites dans tout l'ouvrage; | par le Docteur | Al. Bourjot Saint-Hilaire, | Professeur de Zoologie au Collége Royal de Bourbon. | Les figures lithographiées et coloriées avec soin | par | M. Werner, | peintre attaché au Muséum d'Histoire Naturelle. | Paris, | Chez F. G. Levrault, Libraire-Éditeur, Rue de la Harpe, No. 81. | Strasbourg, | même maison, Rue des Juifs, No. 33. | 1837-1838.

1 vol. superroyal folio, pp. I-XL, 1 l. (list of authors cited), 110 ll. (unpaged), 111 pll. (col.; by M. Werner), text-figs. 1-6. Paris and Strasbourg. (1835?-39?) 1837-38.

A supplement to Levaillant's "Histoire Naturelle des Perroquets" (q.v.), forming a third volume of that work as sometimes catalogued. There seems to be little doubt that this work is identical with the "Collection de Perroquets," etc., published by Bourjot Saint-Hilaire in 29 livraisons, from 1835-39. The imprint, secondary portions of title and number of plates correspond with that work as catalogued by Engelmann and Agassiz, both of whom catalog, also, the present title without cross-references, specifying but 105 plates for the latter in disagreement with the copy at hand. The "Mag. of Zool. and Bot.," 1, 1837, p. 282 (March? 1837) announces the "Collections" as about to be commenced in monthly livraisons of 4 pll. each, but Mathews (Austr. Av. Rec. IV, p. 13) quotes the "Athenaeum" of Jan. 23, 1836, p. 73, to the effect that part 1 was issued by that date. Mathews also quotes Wiegmann's "Archiv" in citing the dates of livrs. I-IV and XII-XXIV as 1835. The preface of the work at hand is dated February 28, 1838, the introduction, December 1, 1838. The order of plates in the work is, evidently, not that of their issue. The index of species calls for 115 pll., the number collated by the Cat. Libr. Brit. Mus. (Nat. Hist.), but only 111 seem to have been issued. They are lithographed and hand-colored. A fourth volume of the series was added in 1857-58 by Charles de Souancé under the title of "Iconographie des Perroquets," etc. (q.v.).

Bourns, Frank S.

1909-10. See McGregor, Richard C., **A Manual of Philippine Birds.**

Bouteille, Hippolyte, and Labatie, M. de.

1843-44. Ornithologie | du Dauphiné | ou | description des oiseaux | observes | dans les Départements de L'Isere, de La Drome, des Hautes-Alpes | et les contrées voisines, | par | Hippolyte Bouteille, pharmacien, | Membre du Jury médical [*etc., 3 lines.*]. | Avec la

collaboration de M. de Labatie, | Membre de la Société de Statis-
tique de L'Isere. | Ouvrage contenant 300 sujets dessinés d'apres
nature, | Par M. V. Cassien. | Tome premier [deuxième]. | Gre-
noble. | Hip. Bouteille, pharmacien, Grand 'Rue. | Et les princi-
paux libraires de la ville. | 1843.

2 vols. royal 8vo. Vol. I, pp. 1-416, pll. 1-37. Vol. II, pp. 1-358,
1 chart (fold.), pll. 38-72. Grenoble.

A descriptive, systematic account of the avifauna of the Province of Dauphiné
(as delimited in 1843). According to a note in the introduction of Vol. I,
Bouteille is the author of the text relating to the "Rapaces" (Vol. I, pp. 53-106)
and of the "Échassiers," "Pinnatipèdes," and "Palmipèdes" (Vol. II, pp.
77-322) while the author of the introduction (not named but probably Labatie)
is responsible for the remainder of the work.

Vol. II is dated on the title-page, 1843, but on p. 327 there is given a reference to
an occurrence in the spring of 1844, thus advancing the possible date of publication to that period or beyond it.

Bowles, John Hooper.

1896. See World's Congress on Ornithology, **Papers presented to
the—.**

Bowles, John Hooper.

1909. See Dawson and Bowles, **The Birds of Washington.**

Boyson, V. F. (Vallentin, Rupert.)

1924. The | Falkland | Islands | by | V. F. Boyson | With Notes
on the Natural History | by | Rupert Vallentin | Oxford | at the
Clarendon Press | 1924.

1 vol. post 8vo, pp. I-XII, 2 ll. (poem and subtit.), pp. 13-414, 24
pll. (on 22 ll.), 1 map (fold.). Oxford.

Most of the book is devoted to a historical, descriptive and statistical account of
the country. Pt. IV, by Rupert Vallentin, contains notes on the natural history
of the region with pp. 285-335 devoted to birds. On p. 308, *Haematopus quoyi*
is ostensibly proposed as a new name for *H. ater* Sharpe [misquoted "(Sharp)"],
but the name was proposed in 1912 by Brabourne and Chubb from whom the
compiler has evidently quoted the citation in its entirety. Three of the plates
are of ornithological subjects.

Brabourne, Lord [=Wyndham Wentworth Knatchbull-Hugessen, 3rd
Baron Brabourne], and Chubb, Charles.

1913. The birds | of | South America. | By | Lord Brabourne,
F.Z.S., M.B.O.U., | and | Charles Chubb, F.Z.S., M.B.O.U. |
(Zoological Department, British Museum). | Vol. I. | London: |
R. H. Porter, 7 Princes Street, Cavendish Square, W. | John
Wheldon & Co., 38 Great Queen Street, W. C. | Taylor & Francis,

Red Lion Court, Fleet Street, E. C. > A list | of the | Birds of South America.————.

1 vol. imperial 8vo, pp. I-XIX+1, 1-504, 1 map (col.). London.

As projected, this work was to have comprised 16 volumes with 400 plates, but the death of the senior author terminated the publication after the issue of the present volume, containing only the list of species. A series of 38 of the plates intended for this work was issued subsequently, under separate authorship and title, as "Illustrations of the Game Birds and Waterfowl of South America," by H. Grönvold, 1917 (q.v.).

Bradford, Mary Fluker.

1897. Audubon | by | Mary Fluker Bradford | New Orleans | 1897.
1 vol. demy 8vo, pp. 1-82, frontisp., 12 text-figs. New Orleans.

A biographical sketch of the life of Audubon. A presentation copy to Dr. J. A. Allen, with a letter from the author enclosed.

Brandt, Johann Frederick.

1839. Spicilegia | ornithologica exotica | auctore | Joanne Friderico Brandt, | Potentissimi Rossorum Imperatoris a Consiliis Status, [etc., 5 lines.]. | Fasciculus I | ex Actorum (Memoires VI. Série sciences nat. Tom. V.P.II.) | separatim impressus. | Petropoli | apud Graeff, Lipsiae apud Leop. Voss. | MDCCCXXXIX.
1 vol. demy 4to, 2 pr. ll. (tit. and pref.), pp. 1-37 (239-275 orig.), pll. I-IV (4 col.; by W. Pape). St. Petersburg.

A separately paged imprint, with special covering title, of the author's "Tentamen Monographiae Zoologicae Generis Phaëthon," belonging to the Mémoires de l'Académie Impériale de Sciences de St.-Pétersbourg, Ser. VI, Vol. V, Pt. 2 (Sci. Nat. Vol. III), pp. 239-275, Oct. 1840 (Cf. Ricker, Proc. Biol. Soc. Washington, 21, pp. 11-18, Jan. 23, 1908.). The present imprint appears to antedate the corresponding portion of the journal. The special title, marked "Fasciculus I," seems to have been intended as a covering title for a series of separate imprints of papers on exotic ornithology to be published in the "Mémoires," but no "Fasciculus II" appears to exist. The copy at hand is bound with the author's "Fuligulam (Lampronettam) fischeri," 1847 (q.v.). A number of new species are described herein.

Brandt, Johann Frederick.

1847. Fuligulam (Lampronettam) Fischeri | novam avium Rossicarum speciem | praemissis observationibus | ad | fuligularum generis sectionum | et | subgenerum quorundam | characteres et affinitates | spectantibus | descripsit | Joannes Fridericus Brandt | Academicus Petropolitanus. | Petropoli, | Typis Academiae Caesareae Scientiarum.
1 vol. demy 4to, pp. 1-19, 1 pl. (col.; by F. Prüss). St. Petersburg.

A separate, specially paged imprint of the author's paper of the same title, occupying pp. 1-16 of the Mémoires de l'Académie Impériale de Sciences de St.-Pétersbourg, Ser. VI, Vol. VIII Pt. 2, (Sci. Nat. Vol. VI), Febr. 1848 (Cf. Ricker, Proc. Biol. Soc. Washington, **21**, pp. 11-18, Jan. 23, 1908, where Pt. 2 of Vol. VIII is given the special number, 'Science Naturelle, Vol. 8' instead of 'Science Naturelle, Vol. 6' as in Carus and Engelmann.). It was published in this separate form in advance of the journal. New generic and specific names occur in the paper.

Brasil, Louis.

1913-14. See Wytsman, Paul, **Genera Avium**, 1905-14.

Brasil, Louis.

1914. Louis Brasil | Professeur adjoint de Zoologie à la Faculté des Sciences | de l'Université de Caen. | **Les oiseaux** | **d'eau, de rivage et de marais** | de France, de Belgique & des Iles Britanniques | Méthode pratique pour déterminer rapidement | et facilement, sans connaissances spéciales, tous les oiseaux | fréquentant la mer, | les eaux douces et leur voisinage. | Avec 142 figures | [*Monogram.*] | Paris | Librairie J.-B. Baillière et Fils | 19, Rue Hautefeuille, 19 | 1914.

1 vol. crown 8vo, pp. 1-338, 1 l. (conts.), text-figs. 1-142. Paris.

A sportsman's manual of 223 shore and water birds of France, Belgium and Great Britain. Tables for the determination of species with brief descriptions and notes on habits, etc., are supplemented by many line-cuts and excellent halftones by W. Kuhnert from Perriere and Salmon's "La Vie des Oiseaux illustrée."

Bree, Charles Robert.

1859-63 (-67). A | history | of the | birds of Europe, | not observed in the British Isles. | By C. R. Bree, Esq., M.D., F.L.S., | Author of [*etc., 2 lines.*] | Vol. I [-IV]. | [*Quot., 4 lines; omitted (Vols. II-IV.).*] | London: | Groombridge and Sons, Paternoster Row. | M DCCC LXVI [M DCCC LXIII; M DCCC LXIV; M DCCC LXIII].

4 vols. 4to (size of royal 8vo). Vol. I, tit., pp. I-XV+1, 1-207, 60 pll. (col.; by Fawcett). Vol. II, pp. I-IV, 1-203+117*, 60 pll. (col.). Vol. III, pp. I-IV, 1-247, 60 pll. (col.). Vol. IV, tit., pp. V-VI, 1-250, 58 pll. (col.), 2 text-figs. London.

Principally on account of the habits of non-British European birds, with brief descriptions and synonymy, forming a sort of sequel to Morris's "History of British Birds," 1870 (q.v.). The early numbers are reviewed in detail in the Ibis, 1859, pp. 81-99. Considerable confusion exists in the dates of publication as recorded for this work. Carus and Engelmann record Vol. I under 1859 and II under 1860. The Catalogue of the Library of the British Museum (Natural History) quotes Vol. I, 1863 and II-IV, 1867. Taschenberg gives Vol. I as of

1866; II, 1867; III, 1864; IV, 1863. A copy in the Tweeddale Library has
Vol. I, 1866. One in the Frederic Gallatin Jr. Library is catalogued as 1863-4.
Actually, the work appears to have been issued in 59 (or more) parts, of which
the 1st appeared early in 1859 and the 58th (which completed the work except
for the appendix, pp. 185 *et seq.*) in July 1863. Volume I (15 parts) was completed by October 1859, together with Pt. 16 of Vol. II; Pt. 24 by July 1860;
27 by Oct. 1860; Pt. 30 (completing Vol. II) by Jan. 1861; Pt. 43 on March 1,
1862; Pt. 58 on July 1, 1863 (Cf. Ibis 1, pp. 101, 198, 321 and 455; **2**, pp. 297
and 419; **3**, p. 106; **4**, p. 180; **5**, p. 463). A second edition (q.v.) was issued in
1875-76.

Bree, Charles Robert.

1875-76. A history | of the | birds of Europe, | not observed in the
British Isles. | By | Charles Robert Bree, M.D., F.Z.S., | Senior
Physician [*etc., 3 lines.*] | **Second edition,** enlarged. | Vol. I [-V]. |
[*Quot., 4 lines.*] | London: | George Bell and Sons, York Street,
Covent Garden. | M DCCC LXXV [M DCCC LXXVI (*Vol. V.*)].

5 vols. 4to (size of superroyal 8vo). Vol. I, pp. I-IX+1, 1 l. (conts.),
pp. 1-150, 54 pll. (53 col.). Vol. II, pp. I-IV, 1-171, 53 pll. (col.),
1 text-fig. Vol. III, pp. I-IV, 1-176, 50 pll. (col.). Vol. IV, pp.
I-IV, 1-180, 51 pll. (col.), 1 text-fig. Vol. V, 2 ll. (tit. and conts.),
pp. 1-175, 45 pll. (col.), 2 text-figs. London.

A second edition, with additions and omissions, of the author's earlier work of
the same title, 1859-63 (q.v.).

Brehm, Alfred Edmund.

1861. Das Leben der Vögel. | Dargestellt | für Haus und Familie. |
Von | Dr. A. C. Brehm, | Mitglied [*etc., 3 lines.*]. | Prachtausgabe |
mit 24 Abbildungen und drei Tafeln in Farbendruck. | Glogau, |
Verlag von C. Flemming. | 1861.

1 vol. 8vo, pp. I-XX, 1-707+1, pll. 1-3 [col.; eggs), 21 pll. (tinted).
Glogau.

A popular work consisting of essays on general ornithology, followed by sketches
of a number of individual species. There is a later edition of 1878 and various
translations also exist.

Brehm, Alfred Edmund. (Jones, Thomas Rymer.)

1869-73. Cassell's | book of birds. | From the text of Dr. Brehm. |
By | Thomas Rymer Jones, F.R.S., | Professor of Natural History
and Comparative Anatomy in King's College, London. | With
upwards of | Four Hundred Engravings, and a Series of Coloured
Plates. | In four volumes. | Vol. I [-IV]. | London: [*Line blank
(Vol. IV.*).] | Cassell, Petter, and Galpin; | and New York
[London, Paris, and New York (*Vol. IV.*)].

4 vols. in 2, demy 4to. Vol. I, pp. I-VIII, 1-312, pll. 1-10 (col.),
text-figs. 1-15, 111 text-figs. Vol. II, pp. I-VIII, 1-320, pll. 11-20
(col.), 112 text-figs. Vol. III, pp. I-VIII, 1-312, pll. 21-30 (col.),
112 text-figs. Vol. IV, pp. I-VIII, 1-312, pll. 31-40 (col.), 85 text-
figs. London, Paris and New York.

A general account of the birds of the world, mostly translated from Brehm's
"Illustrirte Thierleben," 1864-69, Vols. III-IV.

Brehm, Alfred Edmund. (Finsch, Otto.)

1870-76. Gefangene Vögel. | Ein Hand- und Lehrbuch | für |
Liebhaber und Pfleger einheimischer und fremdländischer Käfig-
vögel | von | A. E. Brehm, [| unter Mithilfe von O. Finsch |
und] | in Verbindung mit Baldamus, Bodinus, Bolle, Cabanis,
Cronan, Fiedler, Finsch, ['*Finsch*' omitted.] | von Freyberg, Girtan-
ner, von Gizicki, Herklotz, Alexander von Homeyer, [|] Köppen, |
[*No division.*] Liebe, Adolf und Karl Müller, Rey, Schlegel,
Schmidt, Stolker [|] und anderen bewährten | [*No division.*]
Vogelwirten des In- und Auslandes. | Erster Teil. | Erster Band:
Pfleger und Pfleglinge, Sittiche und Körnerfresser [Zweiter Band:
Weichfresser]. | Mit 4 Tafeln. [*Line omitted.*] | Leipzig und
Heidelberg. | C. F. Winter'sche Verlagshandlung. | 1872 [1876].

2 vols. royal 8vo. Vol. I, pp. I-VIII, 1-626, 1 l. (expl. of pll.), pll. 1-4
(1 col.). Vol. II, pp. I-IV, 1-827. Leipzig and Heidelberg.

Ostensibly a treatise on cage-birds, but in reality including most of the known
species of the groups treated. The various species, 1960 in number, are briefly
described or characterized and their distribution given, with a general account
of each group and sometimes of the individual forms. Pages 1-132 of Vol. I
comprise a treatise on the handling of caged birds. The work appeared in 24
livraisons, 1-11 constituting Vol. I and 1-13, Vol. II. The extent of each livraison
is uncertain but the numbers are noted in the Journal für Ornithologie as follows, the dates being the months for which the Journal was intended, not the
dates of actual issue. **Vol. I, Livr. 1,** Sept. 1870; **2-3,** Jan. 1871; **4,** March 1871;
5, May 1871; **6,** Sept. 1871; **7-11** (dated 1872), March 1873: **Vol. II, Livr. 1,**
Oct. 1873; **2,** Jan. 1874; **3-6** (?); **7,** July 1874; **8-9,** April 1875; **10-11** (dated
1875), July 1875; **12-13,** April 1876. The author apparently intended to
publish further volumes, since these two are marked, "Erster Teil," but no
more appeared.

Brehm, Christian Ludwig, and Schilling, Wilhelm.

1820-22. Beiträge | zur | Vögelkunde | in | vollständigen Be-
schreibungen | mehrerer | neu entdeckter und vieler seltener, oder
nicht gehörig | beobachteter | deutscher Vögel | mit fünf Kupfer-
tafeln [drei Abbildungen (*Vols. II and III.*)] | von | Christian
Ludwig Brehm | Pfarrer zu Renthendorf [*etc., 2 lines (Vols. I*

and II.); 5 *lines* | und | Wilhelm Schilling | Conservator am königlich preussichen Museum *etc.*, *2 lines. (Vol. III.).* | Erster [-Dritter] Band. | Neustadt an der Orla [*Comma added (Vols. II and III.*).] | Gedruckt und verlegt von J.K.G. Wagner. | 1820 [1822; 1822].

3 vols. crown 8vo. Vol. I, pp. I-XV+1, 1-967, 1 l., pll. I-V. Vol. II, pp. I-XIII+1, 1 l., pp. 1-768, pll. I-II (3 figs.). Vol. III, pp. I-XI+1, 1-920, 2 ll., pll. III-V. Neustadt.

A detailed natural history of the birds of Germany. Vols. I and II are by Brehm alone; Vol. III is by Brehm and Schilling.

Brehm, Christian Ludwig.

1823-24. Lehrbuch | der | Naturgeschichte | aller | europäischen Vögel, | von | Christian Ludwig Brehm, | Pfarrer zu Renthendorf [*etc.*, 7 *lines*; 10 *lines (Pt. 2.).*] | Erster [Zweiter] Theil. | Mit einem Kupfer [*Line omitted (Pt. 2.).*]. | Jena, | bei August Schmid. | 1823 [1824].

1 vol. (2 pts.) cap 8vo. Pt. 1, pp. I-XII, 1 l., pp. 1-416, 1 pl. (col.). Pt. 2, pp. I-VIII, 417-1047. Jena.

A handbook, of European ornithology. Numerous new species are described. The copy at hand has been trimmed from a larger size.

Brehm, Christian Ludwig.

1825-30. See Thienemann, Friedrich August Ludwig, **Systematische Darstellung der Fortpflanzung der Vögel Europa's,** 1825-1838.

Brehm, Christian Ludwig.

1831. Handbuch der Naturgeschichte | aller | **Vögel Deutschlands,** | worin | nach den sorgfältigsten Untersuchungen und den ge- | nauesten Beobachtungen mehr als 900 einheimische | Vögel-Gattung en zur Begründung einer ganz neuen | Ansicht und Behandlung ihrer Naturgeschichte voll- | ständig beschrieben sind. | Von | Christian Ludwig Brehm, | Pfarrer zu Renthendorf [*etc.*, *10 lines.*]. | Mit 47 ganz treu und sorgfältig nach der Natur gezeichneten | illuminirten Kupfertafeln. | Ilmenau, | 1831. | Druck und Verlag von Bernh. Friedr. Voigt.

1831. 1 vol. crown 8vo, pp. I-XXIV, 1-1085+3, frontisp. (col.), pll. I-XLVI (col.; by Bädeker and Goetz). Ilmenau.

Detailed descriptions and accounts of German birds. Many new names occur in this work.

Brehm, Christian Ludwig.

1832. **Handbuch** | **für den Liebenhaber** | der | Stuben-, Haus- | und aller der Zähmung werthen Vögel, | enthaltend | die genauesten Beschreibungen von 200 europäischen | Vögelarten und eine gründliche, auf vielen neuen | Beobachtungen beruhende Anweisung, die in- und | ausländischen Vögel zu fangen, einzugewöhnen, zu | füttern, zu warten, fortzupflanzen, vor Krankheiten | zu bewahren und von denselben zu heilen. | Unter Mitwirkung des | Herrn Felix Grafen von Gourcy-Droitaumont | herausgegeben | von | Ch. B. Brehm, | Pfarrer zu Renthendorf [*etc., 10 lines.*]. | Mit 8 ganz treu und sorgfältig nach der Natur gezeichneten illumi- | nirten Kupfertafeln. | Ilmenau, 1832. | Druck und Verlag von Bernh. Friedr. Voigt.

1 vol. demy 8vo pp. I-XXXVI, 1-410, 1 l. (errata), pll. 1-8 (col.; by Götz and Bädeker), 1 pl. (uncol.). Ilmenau. 1832 (post May).

A treatise on the birds (mostly European) capable of being caged or domesticated, including prefatory notes on breeding, rearing and caring for them in captivity. Many varieties, individual and otherwise, are described under binomial names and many new generic and specific names are proposed, although some of them were discussed in the author's work of the previous year, "Handbuch der Naturgeschichte aller Vögel Deutschlands" (q.v.). The preface is dated May, 1832.

Brehm, Christian Ludwig.

1855. **Der** | **vollständige Vogelfang.** | Eine gründliche Anleitung, | alle europäischen Vögel | auf dem Drossel-, Staaren-, Ortolan-, Regenpfeifer-, Strand- | läufer-und Entenheerde, mit Tag-, Nacht- und Zugnetzen, in | Steck-, Klebe-, Hänge-, | Glocken- und Deckgarnen, in Huhnerstei- | gen, Nachtigall- und andern Gärnchen, auf dem Tränkheerde, der | Krähen-, Heher- und Meisenhütte, in Raubvögelfallen und Ha- | bichtkörben, Teller- eisen und Schwanenhälsen, auf den Milanschei- | ben und Salz- lecken, in Erd- und Meisenkasten, Sprenkeln und | Aufschlägen, Dohnen, Lauf- und Fussschlingen, mit Leimruthen | und Leim- halmen, in Rohrfängen u. zu fangen. | Mit besonderer Berücksich- tigung der Vogelstellerei der | Franzosen und Afrikaner. | Nebst einer Uebersicht und kurzen Beschreibung aller europäischen Vögel, | unter denen sich viele neue Arten befinden | von | Christian Ludwig Brehm, | Pfarrer zu Renthendorf [*etc., 2 lines.*]. | Mit 2 lithographirten Tafeln. | Weimar, 1855. | Verlag, Druck und Lithographie von Bernh. Friedr. Voigt.

1 vol. demy 8vo, pp. I-XXVIII, 1-416, 2 ll. (advt.), pll. I and II. Weimar.

A descriptive catalogue of European birds in which many new names appear. Notes on the methods of capturing the various types or forms of birds are given in greater or lesser detail throughout the text. The work is more important to the systematist than its short-title would indicate.

Brehm, Christian Ludwig.

1855-63.   See Baedeker, Fr. W. J., **Die Eier der Europaeischen Voegel.**

Brenchley, Julius Lucius.   (Gray, George Robert.)

⌐1873.   **Jottings | during the | cruise of H. M. S. Curaçoa | among |** the south sea islands | in | 1865 | by | Julius L. Brenchley, M. A., F. R. G. S. | With numerous illustrations and natural history notices | [*Vignette.*] | London | Longmans, Green, and Co. | 1873. | All rights reserved.

1 vol. superroyal 8vo, pp. I-XXVIII, 1-487, 61 pll. (39 col.), 36 text-figs, 1 map (col.). London.

The birds were treated by G. R. Gray and the section dealing with them occupies pp. 353-394 and pll. 1-10 (col.; by J. Smit). Only the rarer species, or those of which the types were secured on the voyage, are discussed. The original descriptions of the latter were published, previously, in various places.

Brewer, Thomas Mayo.

1840.   See Wilson, Alexander, **American Ornithology.**

1853.   Idem.

Brewer, Thomas Mayo.

1857.   Smithsonian Contributions to Knowledge. | **North American |** **Oölogy;** | being an account of the habits and geographical distribution of the birds of North | America during their breeding season; with figures and | descriptions of their eggs. | By | Thomas M. Brewer, M. D. | Part I. | Washington City. | Published by the Smithsonian Institution: | 1857 | New York: D. Appleton & Co. > Smithsonian Contributions to Knowledge | North American | Oölogy. | By | Thomas M. Brewer, M. D. | Part I.—Raptores and Fissirostres | [Accepted for publication, February, 1856.].

1 vol. royal 4to, 1 pr. l., pp. I-VIII, 1-132, pll. I-V (74 figs., col.; by Otto Knisch, lithographed by L. H. Bradford & Co., Boston). Washington, New York.

Published June 1857, separately, as above. Later it was reprinted and published with identical pagination, but with the second title, only, in Vol. XI. of the Contributions, dated 1859. The plates in the latter are plain, not colored, and were lithographed separately by Bowen & Co., Philadelphia. There are several errors in the names of certain eggs figured, which have been noted by Coues in the Bibliographical Appendix to his Birds of the Colorado Valley, 1878 (q.v.), pp. 646-647. The work was never completed.

Brewer, Thomas Mayo.

1874. See Baird, Spencer F., Brewer, and Ridgway, **A History of North American Birds, Land Birds.**

1884. Idem, The **Water Birds of North America.**

Brewster, William.

1886. See American Ornithologists' Union, **The Code of Nomenclature and Check-list of North American Birds.**

1889. Idem. **Check-list of North American Birds, Abridged Edition.**

1889. Idem, **Supplement to the Code of Nomenclature and Check-list.**

1892. Idem, **The Code of Nomenclature.**

1895. Idem, **Check-list of North American Birds, Second Edition.**

Brewster, William.

1895. See Minot, Henry Davis, **The Land-birds and Game-birds of New England.**

Brewster, William.

1906. Memoirs of the Nuttall Ornithological Club. | No. IV. | **The birds | of the | Cambridge region | of | Massachusetts.** | By William Brewster. | With four plates and three maps. | Cambridge, Mass. | Published by the Club, | July, 1906.

1 vol. imperial 8vo, pp. 1-426, pll. I-VII (1 col., by Fuertes; include 3 maps). Cambridge. July 1906.

A thorough essay on the birds of the region without details of description or synonomy; embracing distribution, habits, seasonal occurrence, and much historical data.

Brewster, William.

1907. See Mershon, W. B., **The Passenger Pigeon.**

Brewster, William.

1910. See American Ornithologists' Union, **Check-list of North American Birds, Third Edition.**

Brimley, C. S.

1919. See Pearson, Brimley and Brimley, North Carolina Geological and Economic Survey, Vol. IV, **Birds of North Carolina.**

Brimley, H. H.

1919. See Pearson, Brimley and Brimley, North Carolina Geological and Economic Survey, Vol. IV, **Birds of North Carolina.**

Brisson, Mathurin Jacques.

1760. **Ornithologia | sive | synopsis methodica |** sistens avium divisionem in ordines | Sectiones, | Genera, Species | ipsarumque Varietates. | Cum accurata cujusque speciei | descriptione, Citationibus Auctorum de iis tractantium, | Nominibus eis ab ipsis E Nationibus impositis, Nomi- | nibusque vulgaribus. | A. D. Brisson, Regiæ Scientiarum Academiæ Socio. | Opus Figuris æneis adornatum. | Volumen I [-VI]. | [*Design.*] | Parisiis, | Ad Ripam Augustinorum, | Apud Cl. Joannem-Baptistam Bauche, Bibliopolam, | ad Insigne Stæ. Genovefæ, 6 Sti. Joannis in Deserto. | M. DCC. LX. | Cum approbatione, et privelegio regis. > [*Title also in French.*].

> **Supplementum** | ornithologiæ | sive | citationes, descriptionibusque | antea omissæ. & species de novo adjectæ, | ad suaquaque genera redactæ. | A. D. Brisson, Regiæ Scientiarum Academiæ Socio, | necnon Censore Regio. | [*Title also in French, 9 lines.*].

6 vols. and supplement in 6 vols., foliopost 4to. Vol. I, pp. J-XXIV, 1-526, J-LXIIJ (index and errata), 1 l. (notice), pll. I-XXXVII (fold.; by Martinet). Vol. II, 2 pr. ll. (half-tit. and tit.), pp. 1-516, J-LXVIJ+1, pll. I-XLVI (fold.). ·Vol. III, 2 pr. ll., pp. 1-734, J-XCJ+1, pll. I-XXXVII (fold.). Vol. IV, 2 pr. ll., pp. 1-576, J-LIV+1 l., pll. I-XLVI (fold.). Vol. V, 2 pr. ll., pp. 1-544, J-LV+1, pll. I-XLII (fold.). Vol. VI, 2 pr. ll., pp. 1-543+1, J-LXV+1+1 l., pll. I-XLVII (fold.). Suppl. tit., pp. 1-146, J-XXIJ+1 l., pll. I-VI (fold.). Paris.

One of the early systematic treatises on birds by a contemporary of Linné. Detailed descriptions are given of genera and species of a large number of birds. While the author is not consistently binomial and frequently uses a descriptive phrase in place of a specific name, many of his generic names are proposed in strict accordance with the modern canons of nomenclature and are tenable as has been set forth in Opinion 37 of the International Commission of Zoological Nomenclature. These generic names, according to the text of the Opinion 37, are in genitive or adjectival form when used as captions to generic diagnoses but are in the nominative form in the introductory tables of classification, in the tables of contents and always as the introductory word of the Latin diagnoses of species.

The titles of this work are in both Latin and French and the general text is also in both languages, in parallel columns except for the brief diagnoses and the synonymy which are given only in Latin. The long descriptions are very minute. The appendix is separately paged and titled but, at least in the present copy, is bound with Vol. VI. Vols. I-VI are dated 1760 and seem to have come out together. The appendix is not dated but is considered as of equal date with the remainder of the work; if so it must have appeared in the latter part of the year since it quotes Vol. II of Edward's "Gleanings of Natural History" (q.v.) which is also dated 1860.

Allen (Bull. Am. Mus. Nat. Hist., **28**, Art. 27, pp. 317-335, Nov. 11, 1910) has published an important "Collation of Brisson's Genera of Birds with those of Linnaeus."

British Museum. (Gadow, Hans; Hargitt, Edward; Hartert, Ernst; Ogilvie-Grant, William Robert; Savadori, Tommaso; Salvin, Osbert; Saunders, Howard; Sclater, Philip Lutley; Seebohm, Henry; Sharpe, Richard Bowdler; Shelley, George Ernest.

1874-98. Catalogue | of the | birds | in the | British Museum. | Volume I [-XXVII]. | London: | printed by order of the Trustees. | 1874 [*Mut. mut.*-1898].

27 vols. 8vo. Vol. I, pp. I-XIII+1, 1-479+1, pll. I-XIV (col.; by Keulemans), 60 text-cuts. Vol. II, pp. I-XI+1, 1-325+1, pll. I-XIV (col.; by Keulemans; I, II and IX missing), 34 text-cuts. Vol. III, pp. I-XIII+1, 1-343+1, pll. I-XIV (col.; by Keulemans), 56 text-cuts. Vol. IV, pp. I-XVI, 1-494, 1 l., pll. I-XIV (col.; by Keulemans), 63 text-cuts. Vol. V, pp. I-XVI, 1 l. (errata), pp. 1-426, 1 l., pll. I-XVIII (col.; by Keulemans and J. Smit), 15 text-cuts. Vol. VI, pp. I-XIII+1, 1-420, 1 l., pll. I-XVIII (col.; by Keulemans), 57 text-cuts. Vol. VII, pp. I-XVI, 1-698, 1 l., pll. I-XV (col.; by J. Smit), 45 text-cuts. Vol. VIII, pp. I-XIII+1, 1-385+1, pll. I-IX (col.; by J. Smit), 22 text-cuts. Vol. IX, pp. I-XII, 1-310, 1 l., pll. I-VII (col.; by J. Smit), 23 text-cuts. Vol. X, pp. I-XIII+1, 1-682, pll. I-XII (col.; by Keulemans), 68 text-cuts. Vol. XI, pp. I-XVII+1, 1-431, pll. I-XVIII (col.; by J. Smit), 33 text-cuts. Vol. XII, pp. I-XV+1, 1-871+1, pll. I-XVI (col.; by Keulemans and W. Hart). 54 text-cuts. Vol. XIII, pp. I-XVI, 1-701+1, 1-8 (advt.), pll. I-XV (col.; by J. Smit and Peter Smit), 48 text-cuts. Vol. XIV, pp. I-XIX+1 (I and II missing), 1 insert-slip, pp. 1-494, 1 l., pll. I-XXVI (col.; by J. Smit), 32 text-cuts. Vol. XV, pp. I-XVII+1, 1-371+1, 1-8 (advt.), pll. I-XX (col.; by J. Smit), 29 text-cuts. Vol. XVI, pp. I-XVI, 1-703+1, pll. I-XIV (col.; by Keulemans), 9 text-cuts. Vol. XVII, pp. I-XI+1, 1-522+1, pll. I-XVII (col.; by Keulemans and J. Smit), 1 text-cut. Vol. XVIII, pp. I-XV+1, 1-579+1, 1-8 (advt.), pll. I-XV (col.; by Peter Smit), 26 text-cuts. Vol. XIX, pp. I-XII, 1-484, 1 l., pp. 1-17 (advt.), pll. I-XIII (col.; by Keulemans and J. Smit), 1 text-cut. Vol. XX, pp. I-XVII+1, 1-658, 1 l., pp. 1-17 (advt.), pll. I-XVIII (col.; by Keulemans), 1 text-cut. Vol. XXI, pp. I-VII+1, 1 l., pp. 1-676, 1-17 (advt.), pll. I-XV

(col.; by Keulemans). Vol. XXII, pp. I-XVI, 1-585, 1 l., pll. I-VIII (col.; by Keulemans and J. Smit), 1 text-cut. Vol. XXIII, pp. I-XIII+1, 1-353+1, 1-17 (advt.), pll. I-IX (col.; by Keulemans). Vol. XXIV, pp. I-XII, 1-794, 1 l., pp. 1-19 (advt.), pll. I-VII (col.; by Keulemans), text-figs. 1-15, 5 text-cuts. Vol. XXV, pp. I-XV+1, 1-475+1, 1-19 (advt.), pll. I-VIII (col.; by J. Smit), 20 text-cuts. Vol. XXVI, pp. I-XVII+1, 1-687+1, 1-20 (advt.), pll. I-VIII, 1 A, 1 B, II A, V A and V B (=13 pll., col.; by Keulemans and J. Smit), text-figs. 1-9 and 1-2. Vol. XXVII, pp. I-XV+1, 1-636, 1 l., pp. 1-19 (advt.), pll. I-XIX (col.; by Keulemans and J. Smit). Lc don.

Unquestionably the most important work on systematic ornithology that has ever been published. According to the preface of Vol. XXVI (the last published, although not the last numerically), "the Catalogue is based, not only upon the immense collection of birds in the Museum, but also upon all other available material contained in public or private collections, or described in zoological literature. It therefore professes to be a complete list of every bird known at the time of the publication of the volume treating of the group to which it belongs." The general plan of treatment involves the full description of each species with a copious synonymy, citation of distribution and catalogue of specimens of each in the British Museum, giving for each specimen the locality and source of receipt. Genera and higher groups are defined and tables given for determination of these and of the species. It was originally intended that Sharpe would prepare the entire work, but other specialists in various groups were called to write certain volumes after the magnitude of the project became apparent. As a result, the accuracy and completeness of the different sections of the work are not uniform.

The composition, authorship and apparent date of the various volumes are as follows.

Vol. I.   Accipitres. Sharpe. Publ. June 1874 (Vol. XXVI, p. V).

II.   Striges. Sharpe. Pref. dated Dec. 1875; Mathews (Birds of Austr., Suppl. 4, p. 25) cites date of publ. as Dec. 14, 1875.

III.   Corvidae, Paradiseidae, Oriolidae, Dicruridae and Prionopidae. Sharpe. Introd. dated June 6, 1877; Mathews (l.c.) cites July 24, 1877.

IV.   Campophagidae and Muscicapidae. Sharpe. Pref. dated March 1879; Mathews (l.c.) cites March 26, 1879; rev. Ibis, July 1879.

V.   Turdidae (Warblers and Thrushes). Seebohm. Pref. dated Jan. 14, 1881; rev. Ibis, July 1881.

VI.   Timeliidae (Pt. 1). Sharpe. Introd. dated Dec. 26, 1881.

VII.   Timeliidae (Concl.). Sharpe. Pref. dated July 1, 1883; rev. Ibis, Oct. 1883.

VIII.   Paridae, Laniidae and Certhiidae. Gadow. Pref. dated June 28, 1883; rev. Ibis Oct. 1883.

IX.   Nectariniidae and Meliphagidae. Gadow. Pref. dated Febr. 11, 1884; rev. Ibis, July 1884.

X.   Dicaeidae, Hirundinidae, Ampelidae, Mniotiltidae and Motacillidae. Sharpe. Pref. dated March 9, 1885; rev. Ibis July 1885.

XI.   Coerebidae, Tanagridae and Icteridae. Sclater. Pref. dated May 7, 1886; rev. Ibis, July 1886.

XII.   Fringillidae. Sharpe. Publ. Febr. 25, 1888 (Ibis, April 1888).

XIII.   Artamidae, Sturnidae, Ploceidae, Alaudidae, Atrichiidae and Menuridae. Sharpe. Pref. dated May 14, 1890; rev. Ibis, Dec. 1890.

XIV.   Tyrannidae, Oxyrhamphidae, Pipridae, Cotingidae, Phytotomidae, Philepittidae, Pittidae, Xenicidae and Eurylaemidae. Sclater. Publ. June 28, 1888 (Ibis, Dec. 1888).

XV.   Dendrocolaptidae, Formicariidae, Conopophagidae and Pteroptochidae. Sclater. Pref. dated March 7, 1890; rev. Ibis, July 1890.

XVI.   Upupae and Trochili. Salvin.
Cypselidae, Caprimulgidae, Podargidae and Steatornithidae. Hartert.
Pref. dated June 12, 1892; rev. Ibis, Oct. 1892.

XVII.   Leptosomatidae, Coraciidae, Meropidae, Alcedinidae, Momotidae, Todidae and Coliidae. Sharpe.
Bucerotes and Trogones. Ogilvie-Grant.
Pref. dated June 1, 1892; rev. Ibis, Oct. 1892.

XVIII.   Picidae. Hargitt. Pref. dated June 9, 1890; rev. Ibis, Oct. 1890.

XIX.   Rhamphastidae, Galbulidae and Bucconidae. Sclater.
Indicatoridae, Capitonidae, Cuculidae and Musophagidae. Shelley.
Pref. dated March 28, 1891; rev. Ibis, July 1891.

XX.   Psittaci. Salvadori. "It was completed in December last, and is dated 1891, though it was not actually accessible to the public until the middle of last March" (Ibis, July 1892).

XXI.   Columbae. Salvadori. Pref. dated June 30, 1893; rev. Ibis, Oct. 1893.

XXII.   Pterocletes, Gallinae, Opisthocomi and Hemipodii. Ogilvie-Grant. Pref. dated Nov. 17, 1893; incl. in Zool. Rec. for 1893.

XXIII.   Rallidae, Heliornithidae, Aramidae, Eurypygidae, Mesitidae, Rhinochetidae, Gruidae, Psophiidae and Otididae. Sharpe. Pref. dated Febr. 28, 1894; rev. Ibis, July 1894.

XXIV.   Limicolae. Sharpe. Pref. dated July 10, 1896; noted at meeting of Brit. Orn. Club on Oct. 21, 1896.

XXV.   Gaviae. Saunders.
Tubinares. Salvin.
Pref. dated Dec. 16, 1895 but title-p. dated 1896.

XXVI.   Plataleae and Herodiones. Sharpe.
Steganopodes, Alcae and Impennes. Ogilvie-Grant.
Pref. dated Oct. 6, 1898; copy laid on table at meeting of Brit. Orn. Club on Oct. 19, 1898.

XXVII.   Chenomorphae, Crypturi and Ratitae. Salvadori. Pref. dated Sept. 6, 1895.

Full citations of the subtitle-pages of each volume (giving contents) are given under the various authors (q.v.).

Sharpe's "Hand-list of the Genera and Species of Birds," 1899-1909 (q.v.), gives page-references to all the species, genera and other groups treated in the present work. In addition, Vol. IX of the Bull. Brit. Orn. Club, April 1899, is devoted to an "Alphabetical Index to the Generic Names Adopted," etc., in the Catalogue.

British Museum. (Oates, Eugene William; Ogilvie-Grant, William Robert; Reid, Philip Savile Grey.)

1901-12. Catalogue | of the | collection | of | birds' eggs | in the | British Museum. | Volume I [-V]. | London: | printed by order of the Trustees. | 1901 [1902; 1903; 1905; 1912]. | (All rights reserved.).

> Catalogue | of the | collection | of | birds' eggs | in the | British Museum | (Natural History). | Volume I [-V]. | Ratitæ. Carinatæ (Tinamiformes - Lariformes) [Carinatæ (Charadriiformes - Strigiformes) (*Vol. II.*); Carinatæ (Psittaciformes - Passeriformes) (*Vol. III.*); Carinatæ (Passeriformes continued) (*Vol. IV.*); Carinatæ (Passeriformes completed) (*Vol. V.*)]. | By | Eugene W. Oates [W. R. Ogilvie-Grant (*Vol. V.*)]. [| Assisted by | Capt. Savile G. Reid. (*Vols. III and IV.*)] | London: | printed by order of the Trustees. | Sold by | Longmans & Co. [Longmans, Green & Co. (*Vol. V.*)], 39 Paternoster Row, E.C.; | B. Quaritch, 15 Piccadilly, W.; Dulau & Co., 37 Soho Square, W. [B. Quaritch, 11 Grafton Street, New Bond Street, W. (*Vol. V.*)]; | Kegan Paul, Trench, Trübner & Co., Charing Cross Road, W.C. [Kegan Paul & Co., 43 Gerrard Street, W. (*Vols. III and IV.*); Dulau & Co., Ltd., 37 Soho Square, W. (*Vol. V.*)]; | and at the | British Museum (natural history), Cromwell Road, S.W. | 1901 | [1902; 1903; 1905; 1912].

5 vols. 8vo. Vol. I, pp. I-XXIII+1, 1-252, 1-23 (advt.), pll. I-XVIII (col.; of eggs; by Grönvold). Vol. II, pp. I-XX, 1-400, 1-24 (advt.), pll. I-XV (col.; of eggs; by Grönvold). Vol. III, pp. I-XXIII+1, 1-349, 1-24 (advt.), pll. I-X (col.; of eggs; by Grönvold). Vol. IV, pp. I-XVIII, 1-352, 1-25 (advt.), pll. I-XIV (col.; of eggs; by Grönvold). Vol. V, pp. I-XXIII+1, 1-547, 1-30 (advt.), pll. I-XXII (col.; of eggs; by Grönvold). London.

Prepared somewhat after the plan of the British Museum's "Catalogue of the Birds," 1874-98 (q.v.), but following, with slight variations, the nomenclature of Sharpe's "Hand-list of the Genera and Species of Birds," 1899-1909 (q.v.), with which it corresponds in content of species, volume for volume. Under each species (subspecies are treated binomially) are given a list of bibliographic references, a description of the eggs, and a list of the specimens of the same in the British Museum with their sources.

The work was originally entrusted to Oates who prepared the manuscript for most of it. Owing to ill health he was obliged to give up the work after the second volume was completed, and Vols. III and IV were revised and issued by Reid. Various interruptions delayed the appearance of the final volume and in the meantime many additions were made to the collection, in consequence of which it was found necessary to rewrite most of the original manuscript. This was done by Ogilvie-Grant who appears as author of Vol. V.

The preface to Vol. I is dated Febr. 25, 1901 but the Museum's list of current publications (given in the advertising pages at the back) is dated March 5; the preface to Vol. II is dated Febr. 1, 1902; that of Vol. II is dated July 7, 1903; that of Vol. IV is dated Febr. 22 but the advertising pages are dated April 1; the preface of Vol. V is dated Sept. 13, 1912.

British Museum. (Wilson, Edward Adrian; Pycraft, William Plane.)

1907. > **National Antarctic expedition** | 1901-1904 | Natural history | Vol. II. | **Zoology** | (Vertebrata: Mollusca: Crustacea) | [*Blazon.*] | London: | printed by order of the Trustees of | the British Museum. | 1907 | (All Rights Reserved).

1 vol. 8vo (size of medium 4to), pp. I-XIV, 1-69 (Pt. I), 1-121 (Pt. II), 1-28 (Pt. III), 1-5 (Pt. IV). 1-67, 1-2, 1-12, 1, 1-28, 1-7, 1-2, 1-7, 1-6, pll. I (col.), I-IV (2 col.), I-XIII (col., by E. A Wilson; birds), 1-2, I-II, 3-7 (2 col.), 1-3, 3 pll. (unnum.; 1 of birds), 18 pll. (figs. 1-34), 23 pll. (figs. 1-46; birds), text-figs. 1-8 (birds,.. 1-17, 1 (unnum.), 1-30, 1-4, 1-4, 1 map (col.; fold.; in pocket)) London.

The second volume of the natural history report of the British National Antarctic Expedition of the S.S. 'Discovery' under Captain R. F. Scott. The present volume contains all the ornithology of the report. This is covered by Sections II and III, which comprise, respectively, a general report on "Aves" by Edward A. Wilson, and "On Some Points in the Anatomy of the Emperor and Adélie Penguins" by W. P. Pycraft. The complete Natural History occupies Vols. I-VI, 1907-12.

British Ornithologists' Union.

1883. **A list** | **of** | **British birds** | compiled by a committee | of the | British Ornithologists' Union. | [*Vignette.*] | [*Quot.*] | London: | John Van Voorst, 1 Paternoster Row. | 1883.

1 vol. 8vo, pp. I-XXXI+1, 1-229. London.

An annotated list of all the birds "of which even a single specimen has been obtained in an undoubtedly wild state within the confines of the British Islands." The official list of the British Ornithologists' Union, now superseded by the second edition (q.v.), 1915.

British Ornithologists' Union.

1915. **A list** | **of** | **British birds** | compiled by a committee | of the | British Ornithologists' Union. | [*Vignette.*] | [*Quot.*] | **Second and revised edition.** | Published by the | British Ornithologists' Union | and sold by | William Wesley & Son, 28 Essex Street, Strand. | London, W.C. | 1915.

1 vol. 8vo, pp. I-XXII, 1-430. London.

A revised and more fully annotated edition of the official list of British birds
(Cf. ed. 1, 1883.). Appendix I contains a hypothetical list, including species,
the records of whose occurrences are not considered satisfactory. Appendix II
contains "Nomina Conservanda." Appendix III is devoted to nomenclatorial
problems and changes.

British Ornithologists' Union. (Ogilvie-Grant, William Robert; Wollaston, A.F.R.)

1916.   Reports on the collections | made by the | British Ornithologists' Union Expedition | and the Wollaston Expedition | **in** | **Dutch New Guinea,** 1910-13. | Vol. I [II]. | London: | Francis Edwards, 83 High Street, Marylebone, W. | 1916.

2 vols. royal 4to. Vol. I, 2 pr. ll. (tit. and conts.), pp. I-V+1 (pref.,
by W. R. Ogilvie-Grant), 1-22, (introd., by A. F. R. Wollaston),
264 ll. (by various authors and variously paged), 20 pll. (9 col.),
40 text-figs., Maps A. and B. Vol. II, 2 pr. ll. (tit. and conts.),
236 ll., 21 pll. (4 col.), 36 text-figs. London.

The work consists, largely, of articles previously published in various places,
assembled and reprinted with both original and new pagination. Volume I
contains articles I-X; Vol. II, articles XI-XX. The ornithological matter is
contained in the preface, introduction and Part III of Volume I. The sub-title
of Part III is "[From the Ibis, Jubilee Supplement 2, 1915] | III | Report on
the Birds collected by the British Ornithologists' Union Expedition and | the
Wollaston Expedition in Dutch New Guinea. By W. R. Ogilvie-Grant, |
Assistant-Keeper, Zoological Department, British Museum (Natural History).";
pp. 1-240, pll. I-VIII (col.), text-figs. 1-3. The plates of birds are by H.
Grönvold.

Brodrick, William.

1855. See Salvin, Francis Henry; and Brodrick, **Falconry in the British Isles.**

1873. Idem, **Falconry in the British Isles, Second Edition.**

Broinowski, Gracius J.

1887-91.   The | birds of Australia, | comprising | three hundred full-page illustrations, | with | a descriptive account of the life and characteristic habits | of | over seven hundred species, | by | Gracius J. Broinowski. | Vol. I [-VI]. | Published by Charles Stuart & Co. [Published by the Proprietor (*Vol. III.*)], | Melbourne, Sydney, Adelaide, Brisbane, New Zealand, and Tasmania [Sydney, Melbourne, Adelaide, and Brisbane (*Vol. III.*)]. |[All rights reserved.] {1887. (*Vol. III.*)} | 1890. {*No date* (*Vol. II.*); [All rights reserved.] (*Vol. III.*); 1890 (*Vol. IV.*); 1891 (*Vols. V and VI.*)}.

6 vols. in 3, demy folio. Vol. I, 58 ll., pll. I-LII (col.). Vol. II, 74 ll., pll. I-LVIII (col.). Vol. III, 63 ll., pll. I-XLVII (col.; 1-25 and 27-29 num. in Arabic.) Vol. IV, 57 ll., pll. I-XLVIII (col.). Vol. V, 66 ll., pll. I-L (col.). Vol. VI, 50 ll., pp. I-XXX (index), 1 l. errata), pll. I-XLVII (col.). Melbourne, Sydney, Adelaide and Brisbane.

A series of non-technical descriptions of the appearance and habits of numerous Australian birds, illustrated by chromo-lithographs, the work of the author. Vol. III is dated earlier than Vol. I and contains some plates (those numbered in Arabic) which differ slightly in style from the remainder, giving the volume the appearance of having been prepared at different times. I can find no contemporary review to elucidate matters. The volume is usually quoted as dated.

Brook, Arthur.

1924. See Gilbert, H. A.; and Brook, **Secrets of Bird Life.**

Brooks, Allan.

1909. See Dawson, William Leon; and Bowles, **The Birds of Washington.**

Brown, D. G.

1884. The | **American bird fancier;** | or, | how to breed, rear, and care for | song and domestic birds; | with their | diseases and remedies. | By | D. G. Browne, | author of "The Silva Americana," "American Poultry Yard," etc. | **New edition,** revised and enlarged. | By Fuller Walker, M.D. | With numerous illustrations. | New York: | Orange Judd Company, | 751 Broadway. | 1884.

1 vol. cap 8vo, pp. 1-116, 25 woodcuts (named figures) and various miscellaneous tail and head-pieces. New York.

A book of little scientific value, being purely a manual for the cage-bird breeder.

Brown, Peter.

1776. **Nouvelles** | **illustrations** | **de** | **zoologie,** | contenant | cinquante planches enluminées | d'oiseaux curieux, | et qui non etés jamais descrits, | et quelques de quadrupedes, | de reptiles et d'insectes, | avec de courtes descriptions systematiques. | Par Pierre Brown. | A Londres: | Imprimé pour B. White, dans Fleet Street. | M. DCC. LXXVI. > [*Title also in English.*] New | illustrations | of | zoology, | [*etc.*].

1 vol. folio (size of folio-post 4to), 4 pr. ll., pp. 1-136, pll. I-L (col.; by the author). London.

A series of colored figures of various animals, accompanied by descriptions in English and French, on separate pages. The title, also, is in both languages.

Although the book was published in London, the French text and title is given precedence over the English, for which reason I have quoted the title in the former language. Pp. 1-104 and pll. I-XLII are ornithological. The preface is dated May 9, 1776.

Brown, Thomas, Captain.

1834. Illustrations | of the | game birds | of | North America | Chiefly the size of Nature | by | Captain Thomas Brown | F.L.S. M.W.S. M.K.S. M.P.S. | Late President of the Royal Physical Society, | &c. &c. &c. | Edinburgh | Frazer & Co. 54 North Bridge; | Wm. Curry Junr. & Co. Dublin; | John Smith & Son Glasgow; | & Smith Elder & Co. 65 Cornhill. | London. | MDCCCXXXIV | Designed & Engraved by James Turvey.

1 vol. columbier folio, 1 l. (engr. tit.), 16 pll. (col.). London.

A series of hand-colored engravings, some original, others copied from the plates of Alexander Wilson's "American Ornithology," 1808-14 (q.v.), Bonaparte's "American Ornithology," 1825-33 (q.v.), and possibly other works. The copies are often much altered in engraving, with entirely different backgrounds and coloring from those of the originals. The work is extremely rare and the latest references to it that I can find are in two articles by Walter Faxon in the Auk, **20**, pp. 236-241, 1903, where a full collation is given, and l.c. **36**, p. 626, 1919. It is advertised for sale by Fraser & Co on (advertising) p. 14 of Jardine's Naturalist's Library, Vol. XIX (Ornithology Vol. V), 1835. The plates are not numbered and in Faxon's copy appear to be arranged in slightly different order than in the copy at hand. According to Faxon they represent pll. 69-83 and 102 of Brown's "Illustrations of the American Ornithology of Alexander Wilson and Charles Lucian Bonaparte," etc., published in 1831-35 as a companion to Jameson's edition of Wilson, 1831 (q.v.). In Faxon's copy the backgrounds are said to be uncolored, but in the copy at hand they are fully colored; likewise his plates are watermarked 1835 while those at hand are watermarked from 1830 to 1834. The fly-leaf of the present copy bears an autographic inscription "To Robert Mann Esqr. with the sincere regards of his friend Thos. Brown. Manchester, 28th July, 1838.

Bruner, Lawrence.

1896. Some Notes | on | Nebraska Birds. | A List of the Species and Subspecies Found in the State, with Notes | on Their Distribution, Food-Habits, Etc. | Corrected to April 22d, 1896 | By Lawrence Bruner, | Professor of Entomology and Ornithology, University of Nebraska. | [Reprint from the Report of the Nebraska State Horticultural Society for the Year 1896.] | Lincoln, Neb.: | State Journal Company, Printers. | 1896.

1 vol. post 8vo, 1 p. (tit.), pp. 48-178, figs. 1-51. Lincoln.

Reprinted, with the addition of a title-page, without alteration of pagination. According to Palmer (Circ. 17, U. S. Dept. Agr., Biol. Surv., 1896), the paper appeared in May. Rev. Auk, July 1896. Complimentary copy from the author.

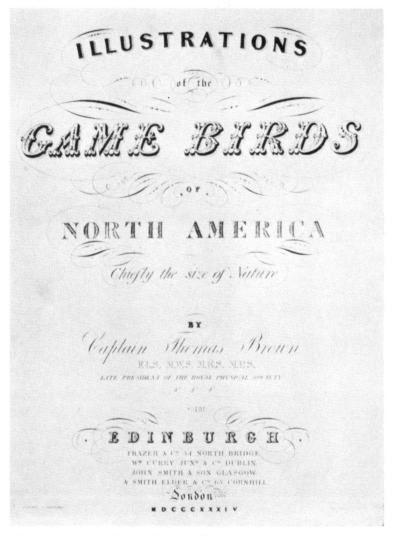

TITLE-PAGE OF CAPT. THOMAS BROWN'S "ILLUSTRATIONS OF THE GAME BIRDS OF
NORTH AMERICA."
See p. 102.

Bruner, Lawrence; Wolcott, Robert Henry; and Swenk, Myron Harmon.

1904. A | Preliminary Review | of the | Birds of Nebraska | with synopses | by | Lawrence Bruner Robert H. Wolcott | Myron H. Swenk.

1 vol. 8vo (5¾x8¼), pp. 1-116, 5 ll. (index), 9 text-figs. Omaha.

An annotated list of species with keys for their determination and for the separation of families and orders. Annotations give the local distribution and status of each species as a Nebraska bird. Originally published, with some differences, in the "Annual Report, Nebraska State Board of Agriculture for the Year 1903," 1904. A presentation copy from the junior author.

Brünnich, Marten Thrane.

1764. M. Th. Brünnichii | **ornithologia** | **borealis,** | Sistens | Collectionem Avium | Ex omnibus, Imperio Danico subjectis, | provinciis, insulisque borealibus | Hafniæ factam, | Cum | Descriptionibus Novarum, | Nominibus Incolarum, | Locis Natalium | et | Icone. | Imprimatur, J. C. Kall. | Hafniæ, MDCCLXIV.

1 vol. crown 8vo, 4 pr. ll. (tit., ded. and pref.), pp. 1-80, 1 pl. (fold.). Copenhagen.

A discussion of the birds of Denmark and Danish territory, with bibliographic references, vernacular (as well as binomial Latin) names, accounts of local distribution, and descriptions of many forms, a number of which are new. Various species occurring in North America are newly described herein.

Bryan, William Alanson.

1901. A | key | to the | birds of the Hawaiian group. | By | William Alanson Bryan, | Curator of Ornithology in the Museum. | Honolulu, H. I.: | Bishop Museum Press. | 1901.

1 vol. imperial 8vo, pp. I-IV, 5-76, pll. XVI-XXX, text-figs. 1-17. Honolulu.

A series of tables for the determination of Hawaiian birds, illustrated by photographs of skins. The work was published first in the Memoirs of the Bishop Museum, Vol. I, pp. (257) 259-332. The present copy is inscribed "To Dr. D. G. Elliot, With the Author's Compliments."

Bryant, Harold Child.

1918. See Grinnell, Joseph; Bryant; and Storer, **The Game Birds of California.**

Buchanan, Robert.

1869. See Audubon, John James, **The Life and Adventures of John James Audubon,** the Naturalist, edited by Robert Buchanan.

Buckley, Thomas Edward.

1895. See Harvie-Brown; and Buckley, **A Fauna of the Moray Basin.**

Bucknill, John Alexander Strachey.

1900. The | birds of Surrey | by | John A. Bucknill, M.A. | With illustrations and a map | London | R. H. Porter, 7 Princes Street, Cavendish Square | 1900.

1 vol. post 8vo, pp. I-LVI, 1-374, 6 pll. (photogravures), 13 text-cuts (by Mrs. Bell and H. W. Murray), 1 map (tinted). London.

A popular account of local birds, with notes on habits and distribution.

Buffon, George Louis Leclerc. (Montbeillard, Philib. Guenau de Bexon, l'abbé; Daubenton, Edme Louis.)

1770-86. Histoire | naturelle | des oiseaux. | Tome Premier [-Dixième]. | [*Blazon.*] | A Paris, [| Suivant la Copie (*Vols. VI-X.*)] | de l'imprimerie royale. | M.DCCLXX [M.DCCLXXII M.DCCLXXIV; M.DCCLXXVII; M.DCCLXXVIII; M.DCC-LXXIII; M.DCCLXXIII; M.DCCLXXXIII; M.DCC.LXXXIV; M.DCCLXXXVI].

10 vols. in 20 (plates in separate volumes), crown folio. Vol. I, 3 pr. ll. (tit. and conts.), pp. J-XXIJ (pref.), 1 l. (subtit.), pp. 1-313+1, 1 l. (pll. and errata), 75 pll. (col.; by Martinet). Vol. II, 3 pr. ll., pp. 1-488, 1 l. (pll. and errata), 53 pll. (col.). Vol. III, 4 pr. ll., pp. 1-282, 1 l. (pll. and errata), 98 pll. (col.). Vol. IV, 6 pr. ll., pp. 1-405+1, 1 l. (pll. and errata), 97 pll. (col.). Vol. V, pp. J-XJ+1, 1-363+1, 1 l. (pll. and errata), 98 pll. (col.) Vol. VI, pp. J-XIJ, 1-582, 1 l. (pll. and errata), 102 pll. (col.). Vol. VII, tit., 1 l. (pll. and errata), pp. J-XIJ, 1-435, 142 pll. (col.). Vol. VIII, tit., 1 l. (pll. and errata), pp. J-VIIJ, 1-412, 140 pll. (col.). Vol. IX, pp. J-VIIJ, 1-423+1, 1 l. (pll. and errata), 109 pll. (col.). Vol. X, pp. J-IV, 1-562, 1 l. (pll. and errata), 94 pll. (col.; 35 not ornithological). Paris. 1770 (1771?)-86.

One of the early and important landmarks in the history of ornithology. It is based on the nine volumes of "Oiseaux" in Buffon's "Histoire Naturelle Générale." first edition, with some changes in the text. Many species of birds are described under vernacular names, and general discussions are given of habits, relationships, etc. Some of the species were later given Latin names by Hermann in his "Tabula Affinitatum Animalium" (q.v.) of 1783 (reviewed in part by Stresemann in the Novit. Zool. **27**, pp. 327-332, June 1920), although the references are not to the present edition but to the original work. Boddaert, the same year as Hermann, or later, named many of Buffon's species (apparently from Daubenton's illustrations, as mentioned below), but where his names clash with those of Hermann, the latter have priority (Cf. Richmond,

Auk, **17**, p. 179, 1900.). Gmelin, in the 13th edition of the "Systema Naturae" of Linnaeus, 1788, also named many of Buffon's birds, but his references are to the original nine volumes of the "Oiseaux" of the "Hist. Nat. Générale," which he quotes under their sectional title of "Histoire Naturelle des Oiseaux" to the resultant confusion with the present edition. The early history of the first editions of Buffon is somewhat as follows.

Buffon, in 1749, began the publication of his "Histoire Naturelle Générale," completed in 1804 (after his death), in 44 quarto volumes. Of these, the nine volumes of birds (Vols. 23-31) appeared from 1770 to 1783.[1] A separate edition of the same work in 71 volumes, 12mo, was begun in 1752 and completed in 1805, of which the ornithology occupied 18 volumes (Vols. 47-64). [2] In 1765, Daubenton the younger (whose father was collaborator with Buffon in the "Hist. Nat. Générale"), instigated by Buffon, commenced the publication of a series of 1008 colored plates, 973 of which are of birds, drawn by Martinet. These were issued without text other than the vernacular names (often from Brisson) on their legends. They appeared in promiscuous order in 42 cahiers, from 1765 to 1780 or a little later [3] in both large and small folio, and appear to lack any definite title or title-page, although the collection seems always to have been known as "Daubenton's Planches Enluminées."

Daubenton's work seems to have been intended originally to illustrate the volumes of "Oiseaux" of Buffon's "Hist. Nat. Générale," even though the latter did not commence until the plates were in course of publication. Buffon (Hist. Nat. des Oiseaux, I, pp. VJ-IX and VII, p. IJ) and Boddaert (Table, p. VIII) both credit the enterprise with that definite purpose. However, in view of the limited edition of the colored plates,—insufficient to provide a set for each copy of the "Hist. Nat. Générale,"—a new set of 262 back-and-white plates was prepared for the ornithological volumes of that work (Cf. Buffon, Hist. Nat. des Oiseaux, I, p. IX.). At the same time Buffon produced, in ten volumes, a special edition of the ornithology (in both large and small folio) under the title transcribed above, designed expressly to accompany Daubenton's plates. Each volume contains a list of these plates with the order of arrangement and references to the pages where they are to be inserted in the volume, and the text refers to them simply as "les planches enluminées No.—." No reference is made in the text to 35 non-ornithological plates which accompany the present set (and other recorded sets) of the work, except as they are included in the total number of plates mentioned in Vol. VII, p. IJ.

Boddaert, on p. 28 of his "Table," identifies pl. 476 of Daubenton as the "Ecorcheur des Philippines" and the "Piegriesche de la Louisanie" (*sic*), figs. 1 and 2, and nowhere mentions a "Tinamou de Cayenne." In Buffon's illustrations, pl. 476 represents the "Tinamou de Cayenne," while the two shrikes are not figured on any plate. In Vol. I of the text, pp. 237 and 242, Buffon discusses the two shrikes and refers to figs. 1 and 2 of pl. 476, but on a leaf of errata at the close of the volume he deletes these plate-references. Pl. 476 with the figure of the Tinamou, is placed in Vol. II opposite p. 414 where there is a slight accompanying reference to the species, while on p. 223 of Vol. V

---

[1]This is the edition quoted by Gmelin and by Hermann.

[2]This edition is quoted by Boddaert in his "Table des Planches Enluminées de M. D'Aubenton" (Cf. Boddaert, "Reprint of Boddaert's Table," 1874.), where it is cited simply as "Buffon."

[3]Boddaert gives 1781 as the date of completion and Newton (Dict. Birds, Introd. p. 10), assigns one year earlier. Buffon, in the Hist. Nat. des Oiseaux, (collated herewith), VII, p. IJ, 1783, says that the 42nd and last cahier of Daubenton's plates has just been published.

there is a full discussion with a proper reference to the plate by number. Sonnini, in his edition of Buffon, 1800-05 (q.v.), Vol. 39, p. 358, footn., calls attention to the error but not to the correction. The question arises as to whether or not a plate of the shrikes was ever issued by Daubenton and cancelled by Buffon. Dr. Hellmayr advises me that in a copy of Daubenton's plates examined by him (preserved as an atlas of plates without accompanying text), pl. 476 represented the Tinamou. It seems most probable that Boddaert never saw the plate of the shrikes to which he refers, nor the errata by which Buffon cancelled all references to such a plate, but that he prepared his remarks from Buffon's descriptions (including the plate-number); his discussion adds nothing to Buffon's account. In such case, "Daubenton's Planches Enluminées" and the illustrations of the present work are strictly identical.

A virtual supplement to Buffon's "Oiseaux" is found in the "Nouveau Recueil de Planches Coloriées" of Temminck and Laugier, 1820-39 (q.v.), and another supplement to both of these in the "Iconographie Ornithologique" of Des Murs, 1845-49 (q.v.), both series being issued in uniform style and size to agree with their predecessor. Temminck and Laugier's work contains a composite list of Buffon's (Daubenton's?) plates and their own, arranged in systematic order. A considerable part of the early volumes of the "Histoire Naturelle des Oiseaux" was written by Montbeillard whose contributions are published over his own name in Vols. III-VII. In Vol. VII, Buffon announces the retirement of Montbeillard from the ornithological field and acknowledges the services of Bexon in his place thenceforth, although nothing seems to be published over the latter's name. The contributions of Montbeillard are as follows. Vol. III, entire volume; IV, pp. 1-204 and 250-405; V. pp. 53-131, 163-183 and 294-363; VI, pp. 1-30, 197-207, 228-372, 389-477 and 491-582; VII, pp. 230-350.

Buffon, George Louis Leclerc.

1785-87. > Histoire | Naturelle | générale | et particuliere, | Par M. le Comte de Buffon, Inten- | dant [Buffon, | Intendant (*Vols. X-XVIII.*)] du jardin du Roi, de l'Acadé- | mie [de | l'Académie (*Vols. X-XVIII.*)] Françoise et de celle des Scien- | ces [des | Sciences (*Vols. X-XVIII.*)], &c. | Oiseaux, Tome I[-XVIII]. | Aux **Deux-Ponts,** | Chez Sanson & Compagnie. | M. DCC. LXXXV [M. DCC. LXXXV (*Vols. II-VI.*); M. DCC. LXXXVI (*Vol. VII.*); ? (*Vol. VIII missing.*); M. DCC. LXXXVII (*Vols. IX-XVIII.*)].

17 (should be 18) vols. cap 8vo. Vol. I, pp. J-XXXIV, 1 l. (notice), pp. 1-258, pll. 1-12 (col.). Vol. II, pp. 1-264, pll. 1-11 (col.; 3, 8 and 9 missing). Vol. III, pp. 1-303, pll. I-VI (col.; III-IV missing). Vol. IV, pp. 1-299, pll. I-III and 4-8 (col.). Vol. V, pp. 1-372, pll. 1-7 (col.). Vol. VI, pp. 1-199+1, J-CXLIX+1, 150-154, pll. 4, 3, 2 and 1 (col.; renumbered by hand, 1, 2, 3 and 4). Vol. VII, pp. 1-336, pll. 1-3 (col.). Vol. VIII missing. Vol. IX, pp. 1-377+1, 1-5, pll. 1-6 (col.). Vol. X, pp. 1-246, J-XLIX+1, 1-4, pll. 1-3 (col.). Vol. XI, pp. 1-400, 1-8, pll. 1-6 (col.). Vol. XII, pp.

1-391+1, 1-6, pll. 1-4 (col.). Vol. XIII, pp. 1-370, 1-6, pll. 1-6 (col.). Vol. XIV, pp. 1-299+1, J-XVIIJ, 1-6, pll. 1-5 (col.). Vol. XV, pp. 1-349, 1-6, pll. 1-7 (col.). Vol. XVI, pp. 1-258, 1-3+1, pll. 1-7 (col.). Vol. XVII, pp. 1-385+1, 1-3, pll. 1-10 (col.). Vol. XVIII, pp. 1-110, J-CXLIX+1, 1 l., pll. 1, 2, III and IV (col.). Deux-Ponts (=Zweibrücken). 1785-87 (-91).

The ornithological volumes of the "Deux-Ponts Edition" of Buffon's work. This edition (according to Oberholser, Bull. 86, U. S. Nat. Mus., p. 94, footn., 1914) is the one quoted by Suckow in his "Anfangsgründe der theoret. und angewandten Naturgesch. der Thiere, 1797-1801. The complete series, published from 1785 to 1791, includes 54 volumes. In the present copy of the ornithological portion, a former owner has added Latin names to the plates.

Buffon, George Louis Leclerc. (Sonnini de Manoncour, Charles Nicolas Sigisbert; Virey, Jules Joseph.)

1800-05. > **Histoire naturelle, | générale et particuliere, |** par Leclerc de Buffon; | Nouvelle Edition, accompagnée de Notes, et dans laquelle | les Supplémens sont insérés dans le premier texte, à la | place qui leur convient. | L'on y a ajouté l'histoire | naturelle des Quadrupèdes et des Oiseaux découvertes | depuis la mort de Buffon, | celles des Reptiles, des Poissons, | des Insectes et des Vers; enfin, l'histoire des Plantes dont | ce grand Naturaliste n'a pas en le tems de s'occuper. | Ouvrage formant un Cours complet d'Histoire Naturelle; | par [redige par (*Vols. 43, 49, 50, 53-57, 63 and 64.*)] **C. S. Sonnini, |** membre de plusieurs sociétés savantes | Tome trente-neuvième [*mut. mut.* (*Vols.* 39, 40, 43, 49, 50, 53-57, 63 *and* 64.*);]. | [*Monogram.*] | A Paris, | de l'imprimerie de F. Dufart. | An IX [*mut. mut.*].

> Histoire naturelle | des oiseaux, | par Leclerc de Buffon; | Augmentée de Notes, d'Additions considérables, et mise | au courant des connoissances actuelles; avec un grand | nombre de Figures des Oiseaux les plus connus, gravées | d'après les Dessins de De Sève. | Ouvrage formant une Ornithologie complette. | Rédigé par [Par (*Vols.* 58-60.)] C. S. Sonnini, | membre de plusieurs sociétés savantes [| et littéraires (*Vols.* 45-48, 51, 52 *and* 58.)]. | Tome premier [*mut. mut.* (*Vols.* 37, 38, 41, 42, 44-48, 51, 52, *and* 58-62.).]. | [*Monogram.*] | A Paris, | de l'imprimerie de F. Dufart. | An XI [*mut. mut.*].

85 (88) vols. crown 8vo; Ornithology in 13 vols. as follows.[1] Vol. 37 (*1*), 'An XI'; pp. 1-381, pll. I-IV (col.). Vol. 38 (*2*), 'An XI'; pp. 1-333, pll. V-XVI (col.; XIII wrongly num. XV; VI and VII

---

[1]The figure in italics and parenthesis is the number of the volume in the ornithological series. The 'An—' is the date on the respective volume *in the present set.*

missing). Vol. 39 (3), 'An IX'; pp. 1-397, pll. XVII-XXIV (col.).
Vol. 40 (4), 'An XI'; pp. 1-360, pll. XXV-XXXIII (col.). Vol. 41
(5), 'An XI'; 2 pr. ll., pp. 1-399, pll. XXXIV-XLI (col.). Vol. 42
(6), 'An XI'; pp. 1-368, pll. XLII-LII+1 pl. (unnum.) (col.).
Vol. 43 (7), 'An XI'; pp. 1-333, pll. LIII-LXX (col.). Vol. 44
(8), 'An XII'; pp. I-X, 11-381, pll. LXXI-LXXXIV (col.). Vol. 45
(9), 'An XII'; pp. 1-378+1, pll. LXXXV-XCII (col.). Vol. 46
(10), 'An XII'; pp. 1-390, pll. XCIII-CII (col.). Vol. 47 (11),
'An XII'; pp. 1-410, pll. CIII-CIX (col.). Vol. 48 (12), 'An XII';
pp. 1-399, pll. CX-CXVIII (col.). Vol. 49 (13), 'An XII'; pp. 1-381,
pll. CXIX-CXXVIII (col.; CXXVII and CXXVIII, respectively
wrongly num. CXXII and CXXIII). Vol. 50 (14), 'An XII';
pp. 1-392, pll. CXXIX-CXXXVII (col.). Vol. 51 (15), 'An XII';
pp. 1-397, pll. CXXXVIII-CXLV (col.). Vol. 52 (16), 'An XII';
pp. 1-395, pll. CXLVI-CLIV (col.). Vol. 53 (17), 'An XIII';
pp. 1-429, pll. CLV-CLX (col.). Vol. 54 (18), 'An XII'; pp. 1-420,
pll. CLXI-CLXVII (col.; CLXVIII listed in index but included in
following vol. where it is also listed in the index). Vol. 55, (19),
'An XII'; pp. 1-142, pll. CLXVIII-CLXXVII (col.). Vol. 56 (20),
'An XII'; pp. 1-396, pll. CLXXVIII-CLXXXIII (col.; CLXXX
wrongly num. CLXXXI). Vol. 57 (21), 'An X'; pp. 1-400, pll.
CLXXXIV-CXCV (col.). Vol. 58 (22), 'An XII'; pp. 1-383, pll.
CXCVI-CCVI (col.; CCII missing). Vol. 59 (23), 'An XI'; pp.
1-416, pll. CCVII-CCXVIII (col.). Vol. 60 (24), 'An XI'; pp.
1-389, pll. CCXIX-XXCCVI (col.). Vol. 61 (25), 'An XIII';
pp. 1-413, pll. CCXXVII-CCXXXII (col.). Vol. 62 (26), 'An
XIII'; pp. 1-468, pll. CCXXXIII-CCXLV (col.; CCXXXVII
wrongly num. CCXXXVIII). Vol. 63 (27), 'An X'; pp. I-XX,
21-396, pll. CCXLVI-CCLIII (col.; CCXLVII wrongly num.
CCXLVIII). Vol. 64 (28), 'An X'; pp. 1-390, pll. CCLIV-CCLVI
(col.).; [257 col. pll. (3 missing) by Barraband (Vols. 37-42) and
De Sève (43-64).]. Paris.

The ornithological volumes of the "Sonnini Edition" of Buffon, containing Buffon's original text augmented by numerous footnotes signed by Sonnini and by
Virey. Many binomial names are cited in these footnotes, being quoted from
previous authors, especially from Daudin whose "Traité élémentaire et complet
d'Ornithologie," 1799-1800, had just appeared. Several reissues of the present
edition seem to have appeared and, judging by the mixed dates on the title-
pages of the present set, several of them are represented here although no volume bears a date later than that of the completion of the entire work (excepting the index.) In Vol. I, pp. 19 and 20 are on an inserted leaf which appears
to be a replacement for a cancelled leaf; p. 19 has the signature "B 2*". Three
styles of title-page (with variations) are given, one with the title and numeration

of the entire series, one with title and numeration for the ornithological series, and one with the general title and the special numeration. In addition, Vol. 43 has the title-page of the general series and the preliminary half-title page of the ornithological series.

According to the title-page of the "Tables Analytiques" or index to this edition of Buffon (by Sue, 1808, q.v.), the entire set (excluding the three volumes of index) is composed of 124 volumes; Engelmann cites 129 (including the "Tables") but his detailed list totals only 124, 64 of which compose the annotated reissue of Buffon's original text, 61 the new "Suites à Buffon" by various authors, and 3 the "Tables Analytiques." The first 64 vols. are numbered in sequence (as well as separately by subjects); the "Suites" are numbered only by subjects.

Of the entire edition, the present set includes the following. *Ouvrage de Buffon.* Vols. 22-34, ' Quadrupèdes,' (266 pll., 203 col.; Vol. 25 lacks 1 pl.; Vol. 33 belongs to uncolored issue). Vols. 35-36, 'Singes,' (79 col. pll.). Vols. 37-64 'Oiseaux,' (collated in detail above). *Suite à Buffon.* Vols. 1-14, 'Crustacés et Insectes' by Latreille, (113 col. pll.). Vols. 1-13, 'Poissons' by Sonnini, (80 pll., 79 col.). 1 Vol., 'Cetacées' by Sonnini, (5 col. pll.). Vols. 1-8, 'Reptiles' by Daudin, (100 pll., 94 col.). Vol. 1-6, 'Mollusques' by Denys-Montfort, (72 pll., 53 col.; Vol. 2 belongs to uncolored issue). Vols. 1-3, 'Tables Analytiques' by Sue (catalogued separately; q.v.).

Buffon, George Louis Leclerc. (Lacepède, Bernard Germain Étienne de la Ville.)

1818. > Œuvres | complètes | de Buffon, | Mises en ordre, précédées d'une Notice sur la vie de l'Auteur, et | suivies d'un Discours intitulé: Vue générale des progrès de | plusieurs branches des sciences naturelles depuis le milieu | du dernier siècle; | Par M. le Comte de **Lacepède.** | Nouvelle édition, | ornée de nouvelles et superbes figures. | Tome neuvième. | Paris, | Rapet et Cie, Rue Saint-André-des-Arcs, No. 41. | 1818.

4 vols. in 5 (complete work 17 vols.), post 8vo. Vol. IX, 2 pr. ll. (half-tit. and tit.), pp. 1-608, (*pll. 1-30*). Vol. X, 2 pr. ll., pp. 1-620, (*pll. 31-63*). Vol. XI, 2 pr. ll., pp. 1-582, (*pll. 64-94*). Vol. XII, 2 pr. ll., pp. 1-603, [2 pr. ll., pp. 1-112 (= "Vue Générale des Progrès—des Sciences Naturelles)], (*pll. 95-126*). Atlas, 3 orig. wrappers, pll. 1-126 (col.; by Prêtre). Paris.

The ornithological volumes of one of Lacépède's editions of Buffon's "Histoire Naturelle" (Cf. Buffon, "Histoire Naturelle des Oiseaux," 1770-86.). Buffon's original text is followed closely and only vernacular names are used for the species discussed. Vol. XII closes with a separately paged and titled copy of Lacépède's "Vue Générale des Progrès de Plusieurs Branches des Sciences Naturelles" including a possibly altered reprint of the same author's "Tableaux Méthodiques des Mammifères et des Oiseaux" (Cf. Lacepède, "Vue Générale," etc., 1819). The entire edition, of which the present set is a part, occupies 17 volumes; the last five were written by Lacepède and included by the publishers in the set as a sort of supplement. Vol. XII, therefore, closes Buffon's portion of the text. In the present copy, all the plates are withdrawn from their respective volumes and bound together in a separate volume with three of the original wrappers. These wrappers are lettered 4th, 5th and 6th livraisons and contain the plates for the 9th, 10th and 11th volumes of text, but are undated. Engelmann gives the dates for the entire work (17 vols.) as 1817-19.

Buffon, George Louis Leclerc; and Daubenton, Louis Jean Marie. (Desmarest, Anselme-Gaëtan; Lamouroux.)

1824-31. Oeuvres | complètes | de Buffon, | avec les descriptions anatomiques | de Daubenton, | son collaborateur. | Nouvelle édition, | dirigée par M. Lamouroux [commencée par feu M. **Lamouroux,** Professeur d'Histoire (*Vols. VI-XV, XX-XXIX, XXXIII-XL.*)] | Professeur d'histoire Naturelle. [Naturelle; | et continuée par M. A. G. Desmarest, | Membre titulaire de l'Académie royale de Médécine, *etc.*, *2 lines* (*Vols. VI-XV, XX-XXIX, XXXIII-XL.*).] | Théorie de la terre.-Tome Ier [*Idem*, II (-XI) (*Vols. II-XI.*); Histoire générale des animaux (*Vol. XII.*); Histoire naturelle de l'homme.-Tome I (-III) (*Vols. XIII-XV.*); Mammifères.-Tome I (-XIV) (*Vols. XVI-XXIX.*); Oiseaux.-Tome I (-XI) (*Vols. XXX-XL.*)]. | A Paris, | chez Verdière et Ladrange, | libraires, Quai des Augustins. | 1824 [(*Vols. I-V, XVI-XIX, XXX-XXXII.*); 1825 (*Vols. VI-VII, XX-XXI.*); 1826 (*Vols. VIII-IX, XXII-XXIII, XXXIII-XXXV.*); 1827 (*Vols. X, XXIV-XXVI, XXXVI.*); 1828 (*Vols. XI-XIV, XXVII, XXXVII.*); 1829 (*Vols. XV, XXVIII, XXXVIII.*); 1830 (*Vols. XXXIX-XL.*); 1831 (*Vol. XXIX.*)]. > Oeuvres | complètes | de Buffon. | Tome Ier [-XL].

26 vols. post 8vo; Ornithology in 11 vols. as follows. Vol. XXX, 2 pr. ll. (subtit. and tit.), pp. J-XXVJ, 1-469, pll. 1-16, 1 (bis), 2 bis, 3(bis), 4(bis), 5(bis), 7 bis, 9(bis), 11 bis, 11(ter) (col.). Vol. XXXI, 2 pr. ll., pp. 1-458, pll. 17-23, 16(bis), 16 ter, 22(bis) (col.). Vol. XXXII, 2 pr. ll., pp. 1-500, pll. 24-36, 42, 23(bis), 23 ter, 24(bis), 28(bis), 29 *bis*, 30 bis, 34(bis), 36(bis), 36 ter. (col.). Vol. XXXIII, 2 pr. ll., pp. 1-486, pll. 37-41, 44-55, 38(bis), 41(bis), 43(bis), 48(bis), 51(bis), 54(bis) (col.). Vol. XXXIV, 2 pr. ll., pp. 1-490, pll. 56-66, 56(bis), 57(bis), 57(ter), 58(bis), 58 ter, 59(bis), 60(bis), 60(ter), 62(bis), 65(bis) (col.). Vol. XXXV, 2 pr. ll., pp. 1-548, pll. 67-84, 77(bis), 78(bis), 81(bis) (col.). Vol. XXXVI, 2 pr. ll., pp. 1-496, pll. 90-116, 97 *bis*, 114(bis), 115(bis) (col.). Vol. XXXVII, 2 pr. ll., pp. 1-546, pll. 117-131, 122(bis), 124(bis), 125(bis), 130(bis) (col.). Vol. XXXVIII, 2 pr.

ll., pp. 1-473, pll. 85-89, 132-143, 132(bis), 136(bis), 136(ter), 137(bis), 140(bis), 143(bis) (col.). Vol. XXXIX, 2 pr. ll., pp. 1-570, pll. 144-167, 155(bis), 156(bis) (col.). Vol. XL, 2 pr. ll., pp. 1-486, I-XXVIII (table of figs.), 1-12 (table of pll.), pll. 168-190, 169 bis. Paris.

The "Lamouroux Edition" of Buffon's work, not including the supplementary volumes of "Suite à Buffon" which are absent from the set at hand. This edition was commenced by Lamouroux whose initials appear at the close of certain footnotes in the earlier volumes. The work was completed by Desmarest who annotated the remainder. Engelmann cites inclusive dates of 1824-32, although the last volume bears the date 1831. The plates, by P. Oudart, are unusually fine. A reprint of this edition was published in Brussels in 1828-33 (q.v.).

Buffon, George Louis Leclerc.   (Cuvier, Georges Léopold C.F.D.; Richard, A.)

1825-28. Oeuvres | complètes | de Buffon | mises en ordre et précédes d'une notice historique | par **M. A. Richard,** | Professeur agrégé a la faculté de médecine a Paris; | suivies de deux volumes | sur les progrès des sciences physiques et naturelles | depuis la mort de Buffon, | par | M. le Baron Cuvier, | Secrétaire Perpétuel de l'Académie Royale des Sciences. | [*Design.*] | A Paris | chez Baudouin frères, éditeurs [Delangle frères (*Vols. XX-XXVIII.*)], | rue de Vaugirard, No. 17 [éditeurs-libraires (*Vols. XX-XX-VIII.*)], | et chez N. Delangle, éditeur, [*Line omitted (Vols. XX-XXVIII.*).] | rue du Battoir, No 19 [rue du Battoir-Saint-André-des-Arcs, No 19 (*Vols. XX-XXVIII.*)]. | M.DCCC.-XXVII [(*Vols. I-XIII.*); M.DCCC XXV (*Vol. XIV.*); M.DCCC-XXVI (*Vols. XV-XIX.*); M.DCCC.XXVI (*Vols. XX-XXIII.*); M.DCCC.XXVII (*Vols. XXIV and XXVI.*); M.DCCC.XXVIII (*Vols. XXV, XXVII-XXVIII.*)]: > Oeuvres | complètes | de Buffon. | Tome premier [II-XXVIII]. [*Two vols. atlas without title-pages.*].

> Histoire | des progres | des sciences naturelles, | depuis 1789 jusqu'a ce jour, | par | M. le Baron Cuvier, | Conseiller d'état, | Secrétaire Perpétuel [*etc., 3 lines.*] | [*Design.*] | A Paris | chez Baudouin frères, éditeurs, [*etc., 4 lines (Compl. I.*); Delangle frères, *etc. 3 lines (Compl. II-IV.*).] | M.DCCC XXVI [M.DCCC.-XXVIII (*Compl. II-IV.*)]. > Oeuvres | complètes | de Buffon. | Complément. | Tome I [-IV].

34 vols. 8vo; Ornithology in 10 vols. as follows. Vol. XX, 2 pr. ll. (half-tit. and tit.), pp. 1-448. Vol. XXI, 2 pr. ll., pp. 1-430. Vol. XXII, 2 pr. ll., pp. 1-438. Vol. XXIII, 2 pr. ll., pp. 1-455. Vol.

XXIV, 2 pr. ll., pp. 1-464. Vol. XXV, 2 pr. ll., pp. 1-504. Vol.
XXVI, 2 pr. ll., pp. 1-441. Vol. XXVII, 2 pr. ll., pp. 1-501. Vol.
XXVIII, 2 pr. ll., pp. 1-483 (incl. general index to Vols. I-XXVIII).
Atlas ;(ornithological volume), pll. 1-110, 3 bis, 12 bis, 12 ter,
17 bis, 30 bis, 31 bis, 33 bis, 81 bis (col.; by Vauthier). Paris.

One of the numerous editions of Buffon. Various footnotes throughout the work
are signed "A. R." (=A. Richard). The supplementary volumes do not appear
to contain any ornithological matter. A note in the last volume of "Complément" announces that title-pages will be supplied for the two volumes of plates,
but those volumes are without titles in the present set.

Buffon, George Louis Leclerc; and Daubenton, Louis Jean Marie.
(Desmarest, Anselme-Gaëtan; Lamouroux.)

1828-33. **Oeuvres | complètes | de Buffon, |** suivies de ses con-
tinuateurs | Daubenton, Lacépède, Cuvier, Duméril, Poiret, |
Lesson et Geoffroy-St-Hilaire. | Buffon et Daubenton. | Théorie de
la terre [(*4 vols.*); Histoire naturelle de l'homme (*1 vol.*); Mam-
mifères (*5 vols.*); Oiseaux (*4 vols.*); Planches (*6 vols.*)]. | Tome I
[-IV (*Théorie, etc.*); *Line ommitted* (*Homme.*); I-V (*Mammi-
fères.*); I-IV (*Oiseaux.*); I. | Théorie de la terre et histoire des
minéraux, 34 Pl. | Histoire naturelle de l'homme, 27 Pl. (*Plan-
ches. I.*); II | Mammifères.-Nos 1 a 152 (*Planches, II.*); III. |
Mammifères.-Nos 153 a 303 (*Planches, III.*); IV. | Mammifères.-
Nos 304 a 467 (*Planches, IV.*); V. | Oiseaux.-Nos 1 a 80 (*Plan-
ches, V.*); VI. | Oiseaux.-Nos 81 a 190 (*Planches, VI.*)]. | Seule
édition complète, | avec figures coloriées. | A **Bruxelles,** | chez
Th. Lejeune, libraire-éditeur,| Rue des Éperonniers, Sn 8, No 397.|
1828 [1829 (*Théorie, etc., II and III*; *Homme*; *Mammifères, III*;
Oiseaux, III.): 1830 (*Théorie, etc., IV*; *Mammifères, IV and V*;
Oiseaux, IV.); 1833 (*Planches, I-VI.*)].

> Oeuvres | complètes | de Buffon | et de ses continuateurs. |
Tome I [-XIV; Planches. | Tome I (-VI)]. [*Half-title*].

20 vols. 4to (size of royal 8vo).[1] Théorie de la Terre, I (I), pp.
1-484. Théorie, etc., II (II), 2 pr. ll., pp. 1-483. Théorie, etc.,
III (III), 2 pr. ll., pp. 1-503. Théorie, etc., IV (IV), 2 pr. ll., pp.
1-501. Hist. Nat. de l'Homme, (V), 2 pr. ll., pp. 1-440. Mammifères, I (VI), 4 pr. ll., pp. 1-470. Mammifères, II (VII), pp.
1-492. Mammifères, III (VIII), 2 pr. ll., pp. 1-490. Mammifères,
IV (IX), 2 pr. ll., pp. 1-396. Mammifères V (X), 2 pr. ll., pp.
1-339+1. Oiseaux, I (XI), 2 pr. ll., pp. 1-470. Oiseaux, II (XII),
pp. 1-476. Oiseaux, III (XIII), 2 pr. ll., pp. 1-408. Oiseaux, IV

[1]Number in parenthesis indicates serial number on half-title page.

(XIV), pp. 1-415. Planches, I, 4 pr. ll., 4 pll. (2 portrs.), 2 maps. (fold.), pll. 1-6 (Théorie de la Terre), 1-16 (Minereaux), 1-7 (Générale des Animaux), 1 pl.+pll. 1-26 (10 col.; Homme). Planches, II, 2 pr. ll., pll. 1-152 (55 col.; 84 wrongly num. 24; Mammifères), 1 chart (fold.). Planches, III, 2 pr. ll., pll. 153-303, 167 bis and 167 ter (85 col.; Mammifères). Planches, IV, 2 pr. ll., pll. 304-467 (88 col.; 324 wrongly num. 323, 338 wrongly num. 332, 333 and 334 with numbers transposed; Mammifères). Planches, V, 2 pr. ll., pll. 1-80, 1(bis), 2 bis, 4(bis), 5 bis, 7 bis, 9 bis, 11 bis, 11(ter), 16(bis), 16(ter), 22(bis), 23 bis, 23 ter, 24 bis, 28 bis, 29(*bis*), 43(bis), 56(bis) and 57(bis) (=99 pll., col.; 23 wrongly num. 25; Oiseaux). Planches, VI, 2 pr. ll., pll. 81-190, 97 (*bis*) (=91 pll. col.; Oiseaux). Brussels.

A Belgian edition of Buffon's work. Very little information is available concerning this issue, but a comparison with the "Lamouroux Edition" of 1824-31 (q.v.), shows that the text of the two editions is the same, including the annotations by Lamouroux and Desmarest, although the entire work is reset; typography, pagination and lineation are all different. The plates are the same except that those of the present work are lithographic copies of the original engravings; the lettering on them is somewhat different from that of the originals. The plates are bound separately with special title-pages provided for them (the originals are inserted in the text); some of the plates appear to be missing as may be ascertained by comparison with the list of plates at the close of Vol. XL of the "Lamouroux Edition" of (for the birds) by comparison with the collation given under the other work.

Vols. I of Mammifères and I of Oiseaux possess an extra set of half-titles and title-pages. This half-title differs from the regular one (possessed in common with all other volumes of the set) in presenting the names of Buffon and Daubenton above the volume number which is a special number for the subject and not for the entire series. The full title omits the names of Buffon and Daubenton, immediately preceding the subject and volume number; in the case of Vol. I of Mammifères, it also omits the name of Lesson from the list of "continuateurs," and bears the date 1827 in place of that of 1828 given on the regular title-page. As noted in the transcription of title, the regular half-title carries a serial number for the entire series, not borne by the full title-page.

Daubenton's name is associated with that of Buffon because he was the actual author of many (if not most) of the painstaking and detailed descriptions in Buffon's original volumes, although he was not given full credit for his work during Buffon's lifetime. This is Daubenton the elder, father of the Daubenton who issued the "planches enluminées" to accompany Buffon's special edition of his "Histoire Naturelle des Oiseaux" 1770-86 (q.v.).

Buffon, George Louis Leclerc. (Comte, Achille; Clarke, Benjamin.)

1841. The | book of birds: | edited and abridged | from the text of Buffon. | By | M. Achille Comte, | Professor of Natural History [*etc., 3 lines.*]. | Illustrated by One Hundred and Fifty Designs, | by

Victor Adam. | Translated from the original | By Benjamin Clarke, | Author of the "Zoological Gardens," etc. etc. | London: | R. Tyas, 8, Paternoster Row. | 1841.

1 vol. 4to (size of royal 8vo), 3 pr. ll. (illustr. tit., tit. and conts.), pp. V-XXXIII+1, 1-292, pll. 1-38 (col.; by V. Adam). London.

An English translation, apparently slightly abridged, of Comte's "Description des Oiseaux," itself an abridged edition of the ornithological portions of Buffon's "Histoire Naturelle" (q.v.). The illustrated title-page is headed "Le Comte's Book of Birds". The present copy is from the library of W. H. Mullens.

Buffon, Henri Nadault de.

1863. See Humbert-Bazile, **Buffon sa Famille, ses Collaborateurs et ses Familiers.**

Buhle, Christian, Adm. Adolph.

1818-28. See Naumann, Johann Friedrich; and Buhle, **Die Eier der Vögel Deutschlands.**

Buhle, Christian Adm. Adolph.

1835. > Die | **Naturgeschichte** | in | getreuen Abbildungen | und mit | ausführlicher Beschreibung | derselben. | Vögel. | Leipzig 1835, | bei Eduard Eisenach. | Zeitz, bei Im. Webel.

1 vol. 4to (size of royal 8vo), 3 pr. ll. (tit. and index), pp. 1-354, engr. tit. (=pl. 1 ?), pll. 2-21, 20 (bis) and 21 (bis), 24-85, 67 (bis=86), 68 (bis=87), 88, 71 (bis=89), 90, 75 (bis=91), 74 (bis=92), 93-119, 119 (bis), 120-155, 156a, 156b, 157-183 (=185 pll.). Leipzig.

The ornithological volume of a general natural history published from 1829 to 1843. The present portion is said by Engelmann to have appeared in 27 parts, and also with colored plates. Representative species of birds from various countries are described and figured.

Buller, Walter Lawry.

1872-73. **A history | of the | birds of New Zealand.** | By | Walter Lawry Buller, Sc.D. | (Resident Magistrate of Wanganui, N.Z.), | Fellow of the Linnean Society, [etc., 4 lines.] | London: | John Van Voorst, 1 Paternoster Row. | 1873.

1 vol. royal 4to (cut to 9½x13), pp. I-XXIII, 2 ll. (reviews), pp. 1-384, 1 l. (notice; between p. 288 and p. 289), 36 pll. (35 col.; by J. G. Keulemans), 1 text-fig. London.

A monograph of the subject, with synonymy, native name, description, and account of habits and characteristics of each of 145 species. Only 500 copies of this edition were issued. The plates are hand-colored lithographs. The

work was published in 5 parts, the dates of publication of which are given by
Mathews (Birds of Australia, VII, p. 447), quoted below. The extent of each
part is ascertainable from the Zool. Record (systematic list), and is corrobo-
rated in the present copy by particles of the original wrappers which adhere
to the butts of the exterior leaves of most of the parts. Publication was as
follows. Pt. 1, pp. III-X (prospectus and list of subscribers), 1-72, March
1872; Pt. 2, pp. 73-148, June 1872; Pts. 3 and 4, pp. 149-180 and 181-288+1.
(notice of proposed suppl.), Dec. 1872; Pt. 5, pp. 289-384, I-II (title), XI-
XXIII (pref. and introd.), 2 ll. (reviews), April 1873.

A second edition was issued in 1887-88 (q.v.), and a supplement thereto in
1905-06.

Buller, Walter Lawry. (Hutton, Frederick Wollaston.)

1882. Colonial Museum and Geological Survey Department. | James
Hector, C.M.G., M.D., F.R.S., | Director. | **Manual | of the |
birds of New Zealand.** | By | Walter L. Buller, C.M.G., Sc.D.,
F.R.S., | author of "A History of the Birds of New Zealand." |
Published by command. | New Zealand: | by authority: George
Didsbury, Government Printer, Wellington. | 1882.

1 vol. 8vo, pp. I-XII, 1-107, 1 p. (advt.), frontisp. (by Buller), pll.
I-III, (IV not publ.), V-XXXVII, 1A, XIVA and XXIA (by
Keulemans and others), 24 text-cuts. Wellington.

A descriptive list of the birds of New Zealand. Descriptions and classification
are adopted from Hutton's "Catalogue of the Birds of New Zealand," 1871,
the predecessor of the present volume, with changes when absolutely necessary.
Sketches of the life histories of the species are taken from the author's "A
History of the Birds of New Zealand" (1st edition, 1872-73, q.v.), and all but
four of the plates are photo-lithographic reductions of Keulemans's colored
plates in that work.

Buller, Walter Lawry.

1887-88. A history | of the | birds of New Zealand. | By | Sir
Walter Lawry Buller, K.C.M.G., | D.Sc., F.R.S., | F.L.S., [etc.,
8 lines.]. | **Second edition.** | Volume I [II]. | London: | Published
(for the subscribers) by | the author, | 8 Victoria Chambers,
Victoria Street, Westminster, S.W. | 1888.

2 vols. imperial 4to. Vol. I, pp. I-LXXXIV, 1-250, 3 ll., pll. I-XXIV
(col.; by J. G. Keulemans), 83 text-figs. Vol. II, pp. I-XVI,
1-359, pll. XXV-XLIX (=25 pll., 24 col.; by J. G. Keulemans),
18 text-figs. London.

This edition is much enlarged and revised from the first one, published in 1872-
73 (q. v.). The plates are new and in the present copy are represented by two
specimens of each. One of these is the regular plate as issued with the work,
and the second, without legends of any kind, appears to be a special proof-
sheet (retouched by hand), more delicately executed than the regular issue,
and usually slightly different in color and softer in tone. The work was issued
in 13 parts, the dates and content of which I copy from Mathews (Birds of

Australia,VII, p. 447). Pt. 1, pp. 1-32, 4 pll., July 1887; Pt. 2, pp. 33-72, 4 pll., Oct. 1887; Pt. 3. pp. 73-120, 4 pll., Jan. 1888; Pts. 4-6, pp. 121-236, 12 pll., March 1888; Pt. 7 pp. 237-250 and I-LXXXIV, May 1888 (end of Vol. I); Pts. 8 and 9, pp. 1-104, 9 pll., Aug. 1888; Pts. 10 and 11, pp. 105-224, 7 pll., Nov. 1888; Pts. 12 and 13, pp. 225-359 and I-XV, 10 pll., Dec. 1888. According to a note in Vol. II, the edition consisted of 1000 copies. A supplement was issued in 1905-06.

Buller, Walter Lawry.

1888. A classified list ⌐ of | **Mr. S. William Silver's collection** | of | **New-Zealand birds** | (at the manor-house, Letcomb Regis), | with short descriptive notes | by | Sir Walter L. Buller, K.C.M.G., | D.Sc., F.R.S. | London: | E. A. Petherick and Co., 33 Paternoster Row. | 1888.

1 vol. royal 8vo, pp. 1-96, 42 text-cuts. London. 1888 (post. May).

An annotated catalogue of the species contained in Silver's collection, part of which won a diploma and medal at the Colonial and Indian Exhibition, 1886. Short notes on habits are given for many of the species, along with the distribution of each. A reference list of the exhibition cases containing the collection and the contents of each, follows. One species is described as new, *Ocydromus assimilis*, but this name was dropped later, without comment, when the author found *O. earli* Gray to be an earlier name for the same species and changed *O. earli* auctorum to *O. greyi* Buller. (Cf. Buller, A History of the Birds of New Zealand, Second Edition, 2, p. 115, 1887-88; Nov. 1888.)

Bullmore, William King.

1867. **Cornish fauna,** | a short account of all the | Animals Found in the County, | with descriptions and remarks | on the habits of many | of the | rarer birds, fishes, &c., | procured during the last six years. | By W. K. Bullmore, M.D., &c. | Truro: | printed by Heard and Sons, Boscawen Street. | 1867.

1 vol. post 8vo, cover tit., pp. 1-64. Truro.

An annotated list of the species of the vertebrates of Cornwall. The article was originally published in the Royal Cornwall Polytechnic Society's Thirty fourth Ann. Rept., pp. 1-64, 1866 (Sept.), and was reprinted and issued in the present form the following year. The subtitle at the head of p. 1 contains a transcript of the wording of the cover title, followed by "Part one.—Vertebrata." The ornithology is included in pp. 7-45.

Burbach, Otto.

1891. See Lentz, Harald Othmar, **Gemeinnützige Naturgeschichte.**

Burg, Gustav von.

1889-1923?. See Studer, Th.; and Fatio, **Katalog der Schweizerischen Vögel.**

Burmeister, Hermann.

1840. See Nitzsch, Christian Ludwig, **System der Pterylographie.**

Burmeister, Hermann.

1855-56. > Systematische Uebersicht | der | Thiere Brasiliens, | welche | während einer Reise durch die Provinzen von Rio de | Janeiro und Minas geraës | gesammelt oder beobachtet | wurden | von | Dr. Hermann Burmeister, | o. ö. Prof. d. Zoologie und Direct. d. zool. Mus. der Universität zu Halle. | Zweiter [Dritter] Theil. | **Vögel** (Aves). | Erste [Zweite] Hälfte. | Berlin, 1856. | Druck und Verlag von Georg Reimer.

2 vols. (should be 3; Vol. I not ornithological) post 8vo. Vol. II, pp. I-X, 1-526+1+426 (*bis*). Vol. III, pp. I-XIV, 1-466. Berlin.

A systematic, descriptive account of the birds collected and observed by the author in Brazil. A similar account of the mammals, published in 1854, constitutes Vol. I, not included in the present set. Vol. II (Aves Pt. I) was published in three parts, the first of which (including pp. 1-160 according to Carus and Engelmann is noted in the Journ. für Orn., May, 1855; the second (pp. 161-320, Carus and Engelmann) is noted in the same periodical for Jan. 1856, being cited as of 1855; the third (pp. 321-426, Carus and Engelmann, but probably 321-526+1+426 *bis*) is given by Carus and Engelmann as of date 1856. Vol. III (Aves Pt. II) is cited entire by Carus and Engelmann under date of 1856 but is not mentioned in the Journ. für Orn. until March 1857; its preface is dated September 3, 1856 and it probably appeared late in that year.

The present copy is from the library of Tschusi zu Schmidhoffen and contains a manuscript index to the genera of birds treated in the two volumes.

Burmeister, Hermann.

1856. **Anatomie** | der | **Coracina scutata.** | Von | Professor H. Burmeister. | Mit 1 Tafel. | Halle, | Druck und Verlag von H. W. Schmidt. | 1856.

1 vol. foliopost 4to, tit., pp. 1-22, pl. VIII. Halle.

A separately paged reprint of Burmeister's paper of the same title, first published in the Abhandl. Naturf. Ges. Halle, Bd. 3, Jahrg. 1855, pp. 191-212, 1856. The work is bound with Müllers' "Über die bisher unbekannten typischen Verschiedenheiten der Stimmorgane der Passerinen" and two papers on Mammalia; the volume bears the autograph of P. L. Sclater.

Burnell, Elizabeth F.

1925. See Wyman, Luther E.; and Burnell, **Field Book of Birds of the Southwestern United States.**

Burns, Franklin Lorenzo.

1919. **The Ornithology of** | **Chester County,** | **Pennsylvania** | by |

Franklin Lorenzo Burns | in co-operation with local ornithologists | [*Quot.*, 5 *lines.*] | Boston | Richard G. Badger | The Gorham Press.

1 vol. demy 8vo, pp. 1-122, 21 pll. Boston.

Part I is devoted to a discussion of physical features, habitats, biographical notes and reviews of faunal lists. Part II is an annotated list of 247 species and subspecies, with a hypothetical list of 16 forms.

Burroughs, John.

1877. Birds and Poets | with other papers | by | John Burroughs, | author of "Wake-Robin" and "Winter Sunshine" | New York | Published by Hurd and Houghton | Cambridge: | The Riverside Press | 1877.

1 vol. cap 8vo (4⅝x6½), pp. I-IV, 5-263. Cambridge.

A literary essay, with many observations on bird life and ways. The first edition.

Bushman, An Old.

See Wheelwright, Horace William.

Butler, Amos W.

1891. A | catalogue | of the | birds of Indiana. | By | Amos W. Butler.

> The | Birds of Indiana, | with | illustrations | of many of the species. | Prepared for the | Indiana Horticultural Society, | and | Originally Published in its Transactions for 1890. | By | Amos W. Butler, | of | Brookville. | Wm. B. Burford, printer and binder.

1 vol. 8vo, tit., pp. 5-135, wrapper, 97 text-cuts. Indiana.

An annotated list of species, giving the local distribution and records of occurrence for each. Originally published as Appendix C, pp. 1-135, of the Transactions of the Indiana Horticultural Society for 1890 (1891) and reissued in a limited number of copies in the present form. The second title, quoted above, is from the original wrapper. The present copy is from the library of C. Hart Merriam,—a presentation by the author. A more complete, descriptive catalogue was issued by the author in 1898 as "The Birds of Indiana" (q.v.).

Butler, Amos W.

1896. See World's Congress on Ornithology, **Papers presented to the—**.

Butler, Amos W.

1898. > The | birds of Indiana. | A descriptive catalogue of the birds that have | been observed within the state, with an | account of their habits. | By Amos W. Butler. < Twenty-second Annual Report (for 1897) of the Department of Geology and Natural Resources of Indiana. Indianapolis. 1898.

1 vol. 8vo, pp. 515-1187, pll. XXI-XXV, 112 text cuts.   Indian-
apolis.

A manual of the birds of the state, discussing 321 species and subspecies, 81 hypothetical forms and 2 probably erroneous records.   Descriptions, migration
data, distribution, nidification and notes on habits are given, with keys for
determination of the species and higher groups, adapted from the works of
Ridgway, Coues and Jordan.   The work was issued both in separate form and
in the original inclusive report of the State Geologist.

Butler, Arthur Gardiner.

1886.   **British birds' eggs:** | a handbook | of | British oölogy. |
By | Arthur Gardiner Butler, F.L.S., F.Z.S., &c. | Illustrated by
the Author, in Chromo-lithography. | London: | E. W. Janson,
35, Little Russell Street.

1 vol. post 8vo, pp. I-VIII, 1-219, frontisp. (col.), pll. I-XXXVII
(col.).   London.

Short accounts of the nidification of British birds, accompanied by chromo-
lithographs of the eggs, the latter sometimes shown in several varieties.   A
check-list of species breeding in Great Britain is added.   On p. 208 is given a
table of the dates of publication of the six parts in which the work was issued.
These dates are from June to November, 1886; Mullens and Swann quote
1885-86.

Butler, Arthur Gardiner.   (Aplin, Oliver Vernon; Cordeaux, John;
Forbes, Henry Ogg; Macpherson, Hugh Alexander; Mathew,
Murray Alexander; Slater, Henry Horrocks; Tegetmeier, William
Bernhard.)

1896-98.   **British birds | with their | Nests and Eggs |** in six vol-
umes | Order Passeres [*mut. mut.*] | (First Part) [*mut. mut.*] | By
Arthur G. Butler, Ph. D. [*etc., 5 lines; mut. mut.*] | Illustrated by |
F. W. Frohawk, M.B.O.U., F.E.S. | Volume I [-VI] | Brumby &
Clarke, Limited, | Baker Street, Hull, and 5, Farringdon Avenue,
London, E. C.

Mutanda.

(*Vol. I.*) *As above.*

(*Vol. II.*) Order Passeres | (Second Part) | *etc.*

(*Vol. III.*) Order Picariæ. | By Arthur G. Butler, Ph.D., [*etc.*], |
Orders Striges and Accipitres. | By Rev. Murray A. Mathew,
M.A., [*etc., 2 lines.*]. | Order Steganopodes. | By Henry O. Forbes,
LL.D. [*etc., 2 lines.*] | *etc.*

(*Vol. IV.*) Orders Herodiones and Odontoglossæ. | By Henry O.
Forbes, LL.D. [*etc., 2 lines.*] | Order Anseres. | By John Cordeaux,
F.R.G.S., [*etc., 3 lines.*]. | Orders Columbæ and Pterocletes. | By
W. B. Tegetmeier, | M.B.O.U., [*etc., 2 lines.*]. | *etc.*

(*Vol. V.*) Orders Gallinæ, Fulicariæ and Alectorides. | By W. B. Tegetmeier, M.B.O.U., [*etc., 2 lines.*]. | | Order Limicolæ. | By Rev. Henry H. Slater, M.A., [*etc.*], | *etc.*

(*Vol. VI.*) Order Gaviæ. | By Henry O. Forbes, LL.D. [*etc., 2 lines.*]. | Order Pygopodes. | By O. V. Aplin, F.L.S. [*etc., 2 lines.*]. | Order Tubinares. | By Rev. H. A. Macpherson, M.A. [*etc., 2 lines.*]. | *etc.*

6 vols. royal 4to. Vol. I, 2 pr. ll., pp. 1-208, pll. I-III (col.; eggs), 56 pll. (birds). Vol. II, 2 pr. ll., pp. 1-192, pll. IV-VII (col.; eggs), 51 pll. (birds), 2 text-figs. Vol. III, 2 pr. ll., pp. 1-175, pll. VIII-XIII (col.; eggs), 45 pll. (birds). Vol. IV, 2 pr. ll., pp. 1-218+1, pll. XIV and XV (col.; eggs), 55 pll. (birds), 6 text-figs. Vol. V, 2 pr. ll., pp. 1-178, pll. XVI-XVIII (col.; eggs), 62 pll. (birds), 2 text-figs. Vol. VI, 2 pr. ll., pp. 1-252, pll. XIX-XXIV (col.; eggs), 49 pll. (birds). London.

A very good account of the subject, including discussions of numerous casual visitors not fully recognized as British birds. Vol. I was published in 1896, II in 1896-97, III and IV in 1897, and V and VI in 1898. Vols. I and II were republished by Butler in 1907-08, with additional colored plates, as "Birds of Great Britain and Ireland" (q.v.).

Butler, Arthur Gardiner.

1899. **Foreign Finches | in captivity | Second edition.** | By | Arthur G. Butler, Ph.D., [*etc.*] | Corresponding Member of Various Foreign Societies | Author of "British Birds Eggs" [*etc., 3 lines.*] | Illustrated by F. W. Frohawk, M.B.O.U., F.E.S. | Delineator of the series of plates issued with "British Birds, with their Nests and Eggs," &c. | Brumby and Clarke, Limited, | Hull and London. | 1899.

1 vol. large superroyal 8vo, 3 pr. ll., pp. I-VIII, 1-317, 60 pll. (col.). Hull and London.

Rather wider in scope than its title signifies since it deals with a number of birds not truly finches. Eighty foreign (non-British) cage birds are discussed with regard to their songs and activities in captivity, their food, and occasionally their wild existence.

Butler, Arthur Gardiner.

1907-08. **Birds | of | Great Britain and Ireland** | Order Passeres, complete in two volumes. | By Arthur G. Butler, M.B.O.U., [*etc., 5 lines.*]. | Illustrated by | H. Grönvold and F. W. Frohawk, M.B.O.U., F.E.S. | Volume I [II]. | Caxton Publishing Co., [London, W.C.:] | Clun House, Surrey Street, Strand, London, W.C. [Caxton Publishing Company, Clun House, Surrey Street, Strand].

2 vols. crown folio (9x11½). Vol. I, 3 pr. ll., pp. 1-210, pll. I-IV (col.; eggs), 1-56 (col.; birds). Vol. II, 3 pr. ll., pp. 1-216, pll. V-VII and VII A (col.; eggs), 57-107 (col.; birds), 2 text-figs. London.

A reprint of Vols. I and II of the author's (and others') " British Birds with their Nests and Eggs," 1896-98 (q.v.), with some additions but with certain typographical errors of the original left unaltered. The text includes discussions of 26 species not in the earlier volumes, 18 of which occupy an appendix. The plates of the eggs are likewise copied (with altered backgrounds); the plates of the birds appear to be new. No references are given to the original work.

Butler, Edward Arthur.

1880. A catalogue | of the | birds of the southern portion of the | Bombay Presidency. | By | Captain E. A. Butler, H. M.'s 83rd regiment. | Contributed to the Bombay Gazetteer. | Bombay: | Printed at the Government Central Press. | 1880.

1 vol. 8vo, pp. 1-113+insert (Addenda), 1 map (tinted). Bombay.

The work consists of annotated lists of 426 species of birds from the region and 97 extralimital forms.

Buturlin, Sergius Aleksandrovich.

1905. See Alphéraky, Sergius, **The Geese of Europe and Asia.**

Byron, H. S. D.

1907. See Davis, William J., **The Birds of Kent.**

Cabanis, Jean Louis; and Heine, Ferdinand.

1850-63. Museum Heineanum. | Verzeichniss | der | ornithologischen Sammlung | des | Oberamtmann | Ferdinand Heine, [*No comma (Pts. II-IV.*).] | auf | Gut St. Burchard | vor | Halberstadt. | Mit kritischen Anmerkungen und Beschreibung der [fast (*Pts. II-IV.*)] | neuen Arten, systematisch bearbeitet [*No comma (Pts. II and III.*); sämmtlicher Arten systematisch bearbeitet (*Pt. IV, Secs. 1 and 2.*)] | von | Dr. Jean Cabanis, | erstem Custos der Königlichen zoologischen Sammlung zu [in (*Pt. IV, Secs. 1 and 2.*)] Berlin [| und | Ferdinand Heine, | Stud. philos. (*Pts. II-IV.*)]. | I [-IV]. Theil, | die | Singvögel [Schreivögel (*Pt. II.*); Schrillvögel | und die Zusammenstellung der Gattungen und Arten des 1-3. Theils (*Pt. III.*); Klettervögel (*Pt. IV, Secs. 1 and 2.*)] | enthaltend. [| Heft I: Kuckuke und Faulvögel. (*Pt. IV, Sec. 1*); Heft 2: Spechte. (*Pt. IV, Sec. 2.*)] | Halberstadt, 1850-1851 [1859-1860 (*Pt. II.*); 1860 (*Pt. III.*); 1862-63 (*Pt. IV, Sec. 1.*); 1863 (*Pt. IV, Sec. 2.*)]. | In Commission bei

R. Frantz [In Commission der Frantz'schen Buchhandlung (G. Loose) (*Pt. IV, Secs.* 1 *and* 2.)].

5 pts. in 2 vols. 4to (size of post 8vo). Pt. I, 2 pr. ll. (half-tit. and tit.), pp. III-VIII, 1-233+1. Pt. II, 3 pr. ll. (tit., pref. and half-tit.), pp. 3-175+1. Pt. III, 2 pr. ll., pp. 3-220 (102-220=index, pts. I-III), 1 l. (errata). Pt. IV, Sec. 1, 3 pr. ll. (half-tit. pt. IV, tit. pt. IV, Sec. 1, half-tit. pt. IV Sec. 1), pp. 3-229. Pt. IV, Sec. 2, 2 pr. ll., pp. 3-179+1. Halberstadt.

A catalogue of the ornithological collection of Ferdinand Heine, with detailed synonymy and numerous references and notes, including descriptions of new species. Part I is from the pen of Cabanis, alone; the remainder of the work is by Cabanis and Heine (the younger, son of the founder of the collection). The various signatures of the work are dated, but the dates are those of printing, not necessarily of publication. The final signatures of each part are dated as follows. Pt. **I,** October 23, 1851; **II,** January 20, 1860; **III,** November 1, 1860; **IV,** Sec. 1, April 21, 1863; **IV,** Sec. 2, December 30, 1863. There is evidence that certain portions of the work were distributed in advance of the complete parts. Sclater, on p. VIII of his "Monograph of the Tanagrine Genus Calliste," 1857-58 (q.v.), says, "I am informed that the sheets of his work (=*pp. 1-32 of Pt. I*) containing the Tanagers—though not in England—were in circulation in Germany in the latter part of the year 1850," and he sinks certain of his own names in favor of those of Cabanis. The Ibis for January 1861 (p. 108) reviews, from an "early copy," pp. 1-81 of Pt. III; in the October number, the remainder of the work, as far as a "portion of the Index," is reviewed, also from an "early copy." Besides these published accounts there is evidence at hand in the form of a separate copy of Vol. III, tit. and pp. 1-82, only, enclosed in a wrapper which is inscribed, "M. Verreaux à Paris. F. Heine."

Cairns, John S.

1896. See World's Congress on Ornithology, **Papers presented to the—.**

Caius, John.

See Kay, John.

Cairns, Douglas.

1924. See Kirkman, Frederick B.; and Hutchinson, **British Sporting Birds.**

Calwer, C. G.

1854. **Recensio avium** | in | academici | liberi Baronis de Mueller | ornithologico museo | Stuttgardiano | collectarum. | Colligit | Dr. C. G. Calwer. | Stuttgardiæ MDCCCLIV. | Ex typis officinae regiae.

1 vol. 8vo, tit., pp. 1-77+1, (orig. wrapper). Stuttgart.

A systematic catalogue of the collection of birds beloning to Baron Müller. The synonymy of the genera and species is given in great detail but there are no descriptions; consequently the few apparently new names (accredited to Müller but never published by him) are nomina nuda.

Campbell, Archibald James.

1901. **Nests and eggs | of | Australian birds** | including the | geographical distribution of the species | and | popular observations thereon | by | Archibald James Campbell | Melbourne | With Map, 28 Coloured Plates and 131 Photographic Illustrations | [Part II. |] Printed for the Author | by | Pawson & Brailsford, Sheffield| 1901. | (All rights reserved).

2 vols. royal 8vo. Vol. I, pp. I-XL, 1-524, frontisp. (portr.), 69 pll. (1 col., by C. C. Brittlebank), 1 map. Vol. II, tit. pp. 525-1102, frontisp. (portr.), pll. 1-27 (col.; eggs), 47 pll. Sheffield.

An excellent account of the nidification of 765 Australian birds, with copious notes from the field and numerous photographs of nests and nesting sites. Colored figures are given of the eggs of a number of species, and there is one colored plate of the Rose-breasted Robins and nest.

?Canivet.

1846. **Catalogue | de la | magnifique collection d'oiseaux | de M. le prince d'Essling**, Duc de Rivoli, | dont la vente aura lieu aux enchères publiques | dans sa galerie, rue de Lille, 98, | le 8 Juin 1846 | jusqu'au 25 du même mois et jours suivants, s'il y a lieu, | a midi précis, | par le ministère de M. Maciet, | Commissaire-Priseur a Paris, cité Trévise, 10. | Exposition publique, du dimanche 31 mai jusqu'au 7 Juin, de midi à 4 heures. | Les acquéreurs payeront, en sus du prix d'adjudication, 5 cent. par franc, applicable aux frais de vente. | Le catalogue se distribue chez MM. Canivet, rue Saint-Thomas-du-Louvre, 24; et Parzudaki, rue du Bouloi, 2, qui se chargeront des commissions des personnes qui ne pourraient pas | assister à la vente. | S'adresser, pour renseignements préalables, a M. Canivet. | Paris, | imprimerie Schneider et Langrand, | rue d'Erfurth, 1.

1 vol. royal 8vo, tit., pp. 1-41, 1 pl. (col.). Paris. 1846 (ante June).

A sale-catalogue of the collection of birds belonging to Prince Masséna d'Essling which was purchased in June 1846 by Thomas B. Wilson and placed in the Academy of Natural Sciences of Philadelphia where it still rests. The catalogue contains an alphabetical list of the species of each genus with the number of specimens and the habitat, with the genera arranged alphabetically under their respective orders. No parrots are listed although the collection, as purchased by Wilson, contained a number of them, including several new species which were described by Masséna and Souancé in the Revue et Magasin de Zoologie, 1854, pp. 71-74. The plate, which is not mentioned in the text of the catalogue, may not properly belong here.

The collection of parrots described by Souancé in the Revue et Magasin de Zoologie, 1856, pp. 54-64, 152-158 and 208-226 is one assembled by Prince Masséna d'Essling after the disposal of the present assortment (Cf. Stone, Proc. Acad. Nat. Sci. Phil. 1899, pp. 52-54, 1900).

Capen, Elwin A.

1886. Oölogy of New England: | a description of the | eggs, nests, and breeding habits | of the | birds known to breed in New England, | with | Colored Illustrations of their Eggs. | By | Elwin A. Capen. | Boston: | Alfred Mudge & Son, Printers, | 24 Franklin Street. | 1886.

1 vol. demy folio, pp. 1-116, pll. I-XXV (col.). Boston.

Colored figures of typical examples of the eggs of New England birds accompanied by brief descriptions of the eggs, nests and nesting habits of the species.

Cara, Gaetano.

1842. Elenco | degli uccelli | che trovansi nell'Isola di Sardegna | od | ornitologia Sarda | di | Gaetano Cara | incaritato della direzione del R. Museo | di Storia Naturale e d'antichita' | dell'Universita' di Cagliari | Membro corrispondente di varie Società Scientifiche | Dedicata | a | S. A. R. Vittorio Emanuele | Duca di Savoia | [*Vignette.*] | Torino, | presso i fratelli Reycend e Ca. | Librai di S.S.R.M. | 1842.

1 vol. post 8vo, pp. I-XII, 1-207+1, 1 l. (errata). Torino.

A descriptive catalogue of the birds of Sardinia.

Cassin, John.

1853-56. Illustrations | of the | Birds | of | California, Texas, Oregon, British and | Russian America. | Intended to contain descriptions and figures | of all | North American Birds | not given by former American authors, | and a | general synopsis of North American Ornithology. | By | John Cassin, | Member of the Academy of Natural Sciences of Philadelphia; [*etc.*, 5 *lines.*] | 1853 to 1855. | Philadelphia: | J. B. Lippincott & Co. | 1856.

1 vol. demy 4to, pp. I-VIII, 1-298, pll. 1-50 (col.; 1-20 by George G. White). Philadelphia.

This work was issued in ten parts from 1853 to 1855. In 1856 the preface, contents and index were added. The perface mentions proposed later volumes of the same series, but they were never published. Fifty species are fully described and figured and many more treated more briefly in the synopsis. Three species are described as new.

In the Proc. Bost. Soc. Nat. Hist., Vol. IV, various parts are recorded in the accessions to the library during the quarters preceding the various dates given below. Pts. 1-2 were received during the quarter ending March 31, 1854; 2-5 (2 and 3 also previously recorded), June 30, 1854; 7, Dec. 31, 1854; 8, March 31,

1855. A publication of the same title, but ascribed to Cassin and Stephens and called Pt. 1, is recorded for the quarter ending June 30, 1852. This may be the trial or specimen number which was cancelled as unsatisfactory, according to Coues who lists it under date of 1853.

Cassin, John.

1858. See U. S. Pacific Railroad Surveys, **Reports of Explorations and Surveys—for a Railroad from the Mississippi River to the Pacific Ocean, Birds. Vol. IX.**

Cassin, John.

1858. See Wilkes, Charles, **U. S. Exploring Expedition,** Vol. VIII.

Cassin, John.

1859. See Page, Thomas J., **La Plata, the Argentine Confederation, and Paraguay.**

Cassin, John.

1860. See Baird, Spencer F.; Cassin; and Lawrence, **The Birds of North America.**

1870. Idem.

Castelnau, Francis L. de Laporte de.   (Des Murs, Marc Athanese Parfait Oeillet.)

1856.   > **Expédition | dans les parties centrales | de | l'Amérique du Sud,** | de Rio de Janeiro a Lima, et de Lima au Para; | exécutée | par ordre du gouvernement Français pendant les années 1843 a 1847, | sous la direction du Comte | Francis de Castelnau. | Ouvrage qui a obtenu une médaille hors ligne de la Société de Géographie. | Zoologie. | Oiseaux. | Paris, | Chez P. Bertrand, Libraire-Éditeur, | rue de l'Arbre-Sec, 22 | 1855. > **Animaux nouveaux ou rares | recueillis pendant l'expédition** | dans les parties centrales | de | l'Amerique du Sud, | de Rio de Janeiro a Lima, et de Lima au Para; | exécutée | par ordre du gouvernement Français pendant les années 1843 a 1847, | sous la direction du Comte | Francis de Castelnau. | Ouvrage qui a obtenu une médaille [etc.]. | **Oiseaux** | par M. O. Des Murs, | Membre de plusieurs sociétés savantes. | Paris, | Chez P. Bertrand, Libraire-Éditeur, | rue de l'Arbre-Sec, 22 | 1855.

1 vol. medium 4to, 2 pr. ll., pp. 1-98, 1 l., (original wrappers), pll. 1-20 (col.). Paris.

The zoology of Castelnau's expedition, in three volumes, forms Pt. 7 of the complete work (contained in 14 vols. in 13, published from 1850-59). The third portion of Vol. I of Pt. 7 (here collated) relates to the birds and was written by Des Murs after the death of Deville who was charged originally with the preparation of that section of the work. The general title (in the first part of the above transcription) is from the original wrapper but does not occur in the complete issue of Vol. I. The title of Vol. I is very similar, reading, "Expedition . . . Géographie. | Septième partie. | Zoologie. | Paris . . . 1855." A second title in the complete volume reads, "Animaux nouveaux . . . Géographie. | Tome premier. | Paris . . . 1855." The subtitle of the section on Ornithology follows in its place.

Although dated 1855 on both wrapper and title-page, Des Murs's report appears to have been published a year later. According to the "Comptes Rendus" for Dec. 17, 1855, Vol. 41, p. 1094, the Académie des Sciences received Livrs. 12-14 of the Zoology on that date; the same publication for June 30, 1856, Vol. 42, p. 1275, notes that the Académie des Sciences received Livrs. 15-18 on that date; the same publication for Dec. 15, 1856, Vol. 43, p. 1134, records the receipt of Livrs. 19-20 (Sherborn and Woodward, Ann. Mag. Nat. Hist. (7) 8, p. 164, 1901, erroneously give the date as Dec. 8 and the page reference as 1133). These livraisons include all of the systematic ornithology, which is distributed as follows, according to a "Table et classification des matières contenues dans le premier volume." The "Table" is given on certain preliminary pages of Vol. I of Pt. 7 but is not included in the several sections of that volume issued separately as in the present instance. Livr. 14 contained the ornithological title; Livr. 16, pll. 1-5; Livr. 17, feuilles 1-5 (=pp. 1-40), pll. 6-10; Livr. 18, feuilles 6-10 (=pp. 41-80), pll. 11-14; Livr. 19, feuilles 11-13 (=pp. 81-98+1 l.), pll. 15-16; Livr. 20, pll. 17-20.

In the first section of Vol. I of Pt. 7 (Anatomie par M. Paul Gervais), pp. 65-92 and pll. 14-16 are devoted to the "Deuxième Memoire. Description osteologique de l'hoazin, du kamichi, du cariama et du savacou, suivi de remarques sur les affinites naturelles des oiseaux, par M. Paul Gervais." This ornithological matter is distinct from Des Murs's report and the two are not found together except in the complete volume.

Catesby, Mark.

1772-81. See Edwards, George; and Catesby, **Verzameling van Uitlandsche en Zeldzaame Vogelen.**

Cecil, M. W. (Lady William).

1904. **Bird notes from | the Nile** | by | Lady William Cecil. | [*Quot., 3 lines.*] | Westminster: | Archibald Constable & Co., Ltd., | 2, Whitehall Gardens. | 1904.

1 vol. cap 8vo., pp. I-XII, 1-113+1, 1 l. (advt.), frontisp. (col.), 12 pll., 9 text-figs. London.

Popular notes on Egyptian ornithology, ancient and modern.

Chamberlain, Montague.

1887. **A catalogue | of | Canadian birds,** | with | Notes on the Distribution of the Species. | By | Montague Chamberlain. | Saint John, N.B. | J. and A. McMillan, 98 Prince William Street. | 1887.

1 vol. cap 4to (6½x8¾), 1 pr. 1. (title), pp. I-V, 1 l., pp. 1-143. Saint John.

An annotated list of species, with scientific and common names and a statement of their known distribution in Canada. A presentation copy to C. B. Cory from the author.

Chamberlain, Montague.

1888.   A Systematic Table | of | Canadian Birds. | By | Montague Chamberlain. | Saint John, N.B. | Published for the Author. | 1888.

1 vol., medium folio (cut to 12x13), 1 pr. l., pp. I-III, 1-14 (printed only on one side of the paper). Saint John.

"The species of the *Table* are identical with those of the *Catalogue* of 1887 (q.v.), except for a few additions and eliminations which will be found noted in the Appendices." The species are arranged in tabular form without annotations except in the appendix.

Chamberlain, Montague.

1891.   See Hagerup, Andreas T., The Birds of Greenland.

Chamberlain, Montague.

1891.   See Nuttall, Thomas, A Popular Handbook of the Ornithology of the United States and Canada.

Chapman, Abel.

1889.   Bird-life of the borders | Records of | wild sport and natural history | on moorland and sea | By | Abel Chapman | London: | Gurney and Jackson, 1, Paternoster Row | (Successors to Mr. Van Voorst) | 1889.

1 vol. 8vo, pp. I-XII, 1-286, 1 l. (advt.), 15 pll., 39 text-cuts (1 full page). London.

A popular account of experiences and observations in the hunting field.

Chapman, Abel.

1924.   The | borders and beyond | Arctic . . . Cheviot . . . Tropic | [*Quot., 2 lines.*]. | By | Abel Chapman, M.A. | Author of [*etc., 3 lines.*] | with nineteen coloured plates by W. H. Riddell. and 170 sketches by the author | maps, diagrams, etc. | Gurney and Jackson | London: 33 Paternoster Row | Edinburgh: Tweeddale Court | 1924.

1 vol. 8vo, pp. I-XXI+1, 1-489, 1p.+1 l. (advt.), 35 pll. (14 col.), 190 text-figs., 2 maps (fold.). London.

Notes and observations on natural history subjects, taken from personal observations of a lifetime, mostly on the borders of England and Scotland. A considerable part of the subject matter relates to birds.

Chapman, Frank Michler.

1896. See World's Congress on Ornithology, **Papers presented to the—**.

Chapman, Frank Michler.

1900. **Handbook of birds | of eastern North America** | with keys to the species | and descriptions of their plumages, nests, and eggs | their distribution and migrations | and a brief account of their haunts and habits | with introductory chapters on the | study of ornithology, how to identify birds | and how to collect and preserve birds | their nests, and eggs | by | Frank M. Chapman | Assistant Curator [*etc., 3 lines.*]. | With full-page plates in colors and black and white | and upward of one hundred and fifty cuts | in the text | **Sixth edition** | New York | D. Appleton and Company | 1900.

1 vol. crown 8vo, 1 l. (advt.), pp. I-XIV, 1-431, pll. I and II (col.), 18 pll., text-figs. 1-115+1 (on inside of cover=fig. 4). New York.

A condensed manual of the birds of eastern North America,—scientific with a minimum of technicalities. The first edition was issued in 1895. See also ed. 1912.

Chapman, Frank Michler. (Cooke, Wells W.; Forbush, Edward Howe.)

1907. **The warblers | of | North America** | by | Frank M. Chapman | with the coöperation of other ornithologists | with twenty-four full-page colored plates, illustrating | every species, from drawings by Louis Agassiz Fuertes | and Bruce Horsfall, and half-tones | of nests and eggs | New York | D. Appleton & Company | 1907.

1 vol. royal 8vo, 3 pr. ll. (half-tit., tit. and pref.), pp. V-IX+1, 1-306, pll. I-XXIV (124 figs.; col.; by Fuertes and Horsfall), 8 pll. (8 figs., nests; 120 figs, eggs). New York.

An excellent discussion of 74 varieties of North American warblers, with full descriptions and with the range, migration, habits, song, nest and eggs of each variety thoroughly discussed. Considerable of the text is from published accounts by other authors or from manuscript contributions by numerous correspondents, to each of whom full credit is given for every quotation. In addition, a chapter on the migration of warblers (pp. 14-20) is accredited to Cooke (who also supplied the migration tables and much of the accounts of distribution throughout the work) and one on the food of warblers (pp. 23-32) is by Forbush. The book is very well illustrated.

Chapman, Frank Michler.

1908. **Camps and cruises | of an | ornithologist** | By | Frank M. Chapman | Curator of Ornithology [*etc., 5 lines.*]. | With 250 photographs from nature by the author | New York | D. Appleton and Company | 1908.

1 vol. 8vo, pp. I-XVI, 1-432, frontisp. (col.), 1 pl. (col.), 259 text-figs. New York.

A popular account of the author's experiences in search of material for the "habitat groups" of birds in the American Museum of Natural History, New York City.

Chapman, Frank Michler.

1912. Color key to | North American Birds | With Bibliographical Appendix | By | Frank M. Chapman | Curator of Ornithology | in the American Museum of Natural History | Author of [*etc., 2 lines.*] | With Upward of 800 Drawings | by | Chester A. Reed, B.S. | **Revised Edition** | New York | D. Appleton & Company | 1912.

1 vol. 8vo, pp. I-X, 1-356, 884 figs. New York.

The birds are arranged according to orders, the lower groups then according to families, and the Passeres primarily according to colors, forming a convenient and efficient guide to the beginner for field identifications. The illustrations consist of 725 full figures of birds, colored or tinted except where plumage is gray or black and white, 4 tinted figures of details of bird structure, 29 plain figures of structural details in key to species, 127 full size black and white figures of such details in synopsis of orders and families, and 1 full page figure of bird topography. The first edition was issued in 1903 by Doubleday, Page & Co.

Chapman, Frank Michler.

1912. Handbook of birds | of eastern North America | with introductory chapters on | the study of birds in nature | by | Frank M. Chapman | Curator of Ornithology [*etc., 3 lines.*]. | With full-page plates in colors and black and white | by Louis Agassiz Fuertes | and text-cuts by Tappan-Adney and Ernest Thompson Seton | **Revised edition** | New York and London | D. Appleton and Company | 1912.

1 vol. crown 8vo, pp. I-XXIX+1, 1-530, pll. I-XXIV (8 col.), 1 chart (col.; fold.), text-figs. 1-136. New York and London. May 1912.

A revised edition of the author's work of the same title published in 1895 (Cf. sixth ed., 1900.) The work is brought up to date and much material added.

Chapman, Frank Michler.

1914. Bird studies | with a camera | with introductory chapters | on the outfit and methods | of the bird photographer | By Frank M. Chapman | Assistant Curator [*etc., 4 lines.*] | [*Fig.*] | With

over one hundred photographs | from nature, by the author |
New York and London | D. Appleton and Company | 1914.

1 vol. crown 8vo, pp. I-XIV, 1-218, frontisp. (=fig. 1), figs. 2-110,
13 initials and tailpieces. New York and London.

Studies of various species of birds in the field, illustrated with photographs taken
by the author, whose experiences in securing them form an interesting portion
of the text. The first two chapters of the book are descriptive of outfit and
method in photographing birds. The original edition was published in 1900.

Chapman, Frank Michler.

1920. **What bird is that?** | A pocket museum | of the land birds
of | the eastern United States | arranged according to season | by |
Frank M. Chapman | Curator of Birds [*etc.*, *2 lines.*] | with 301
birds in color | by | Edmund J. Sawyer | D. Appleton and Com-
pany | New York   London | 1920.

1 vol. crown 8vo, pp. I-XXVI, 1-144, 8 p ll. (on the backs of pp.
XVII-XXIV;=301 figs.; col.), 9 text-figs. New York.

A popular guide to the eastern land-birds with a brief discussion of the various
species treated. In the plates, the birds are first arranged according to residence (permanent or transient), and the spring migrants according to dates
of arrival at New York City.

Chapman, Frank Michler.

1922. Popular edition in colors | **Bird-life** | A guide to the study
of | our common birds | By | Frank M. Chapman | Curator of
Ornithology [*etc.*, *5 lines.*] | with seventy-five full-page colored
plates | after drawings by Ernest Thompson Seton | New York
and London | D. Appleton and Company | 1922.

1 vol. demy 8vo, pp. I-VIII, 1-88, pll. I-LXXV (col.), text-figs.
1-25. New York and London.

A popular account of the commoner birds of eastern North America, prefaced by
a general discussion of bird forms, habits and relationships. The first edition
was published in 1897.

Cheney, John Vance.

1892. See Cheney, Simeon Pease, **Wood Notes Wild.**

Cheney, Simeon Pease. (Cheney, John Vance.)

1892. **Wood Notes Wild** | notations of bird music | by | Simeon
Pease Cheney | Author of the "American Singing-Book" | Col-
lected and arranged with appendix, notes, | bibliography, and
general index | By | John Vance Cheney | Author of the "Golden
Guess" [*etc.*, *2 lines.*]. | Boston | Lee and Shepard Publishers | 10
Milk St. next "The Old South Meeting House" | 1892.

1 vol. demy 8vo, pp. I-XIV, 1-261, frontisp. (portr.). Boston.

An effort to write the songs of numerous New England birds in musical notation, with bits of biographies and other observations interspersed with the descriptions. The latter half of the book consists of an appendix containing supplementary notes (with references) drawn from various sources, and relating to other sounds in nature beside the songs of birds. This appendix is compiled by John Vance Cheney, editor of the work.

Chenu, Jean Charles. (Des Murs, Marc Athanese Parfait Oeillet.)

1852-54. > **Encyclopédie | d'histoire naturelle |** ou **|** traité complet de cette science **|** d'après **|** les travaux des naturalistes les plus éminents de tous le pays et de toutes les époques **|** Buffon, Daubenton, Lacépède, **|** G. Cuvier, F. Cuvier, Geoffroy Saint-Hilaire, Latreille, de Jussieu, **|** Brogniart, etc., etc. **|** Ouvrage resumant les Observations des Auteurs anciens et comprenant toutes les Découvertes modernes **|** jusqu'a nos jours [*Period added Vols. II and IV-VI.*).] **|** Par le Dr. Chenu **|** Chirurgien-Major [*etc.*]. **| Oiseaux |** Avec le collaboration de M. Des Murs, **|** membre de plusieurs Sociétés savantes. [**|** Deuxième (-Sixième) partie (*Period added, Vol. II.*)] **|** [*Vignette.*] **|** Paris **|** Chez Maresq et Compagnie Chez Gustave Havard, **|** éditeurs de l'encyclopédie, libraire. **|** 5, Rue du Pont-de-Lodi (Près le Pont Neuf). 15 Rue Guénégaud (Près la Monnaie).

6 vols. demy 4to. Vol. I, 2 pr. ll., pp. 1-312, 2 ll., pll. 1-40 (20 wrongly num. 23), text-figs. 1-405, 1 decoration, tit.-vignette (=fig. 166). Vol. II, 4 pr. ll., pp. 1-311, pll. 1-40, text-figs. 1-222, 1 decoration, tit.-vignette (=fig. 55). Vol. III, 4 pr. ll., pp. 1-312, pll. 1-40, text-figs. 1-333, 1 decoration, tit.-vignette (=pl. 7, fig. 1). Vol. IV, (orig. wrapper), 4 pr. ll., pp. 1-312, pll. 1-40, text-figs. 1-398, 1 decoration, tit.-vignette (=fig. 223). Vol. V, (orig. wrapper), 4 pr. ll., pp. 1-312, pll. 1-40, text-figs. 1-371, 1 decoration, tit.-vignette (=fig. 139). Vol. VI, (orig. wrapper), 4 pr. ll., pp. 1-312, pll. 1-40, text-figs. 1-352, 1 decoration, tit.-vignette (=pl. 31, fig. 3). Paris.

The above six volumes form the ornithological part of a set of 22 volumes, to which may be added 9 volumes of "Tables alphabétiques," one to each section of the work, published later than the general text. The volume of the "Tables" on ornithology (by Desmarest) is not included in the present set. This set contains the original wrappers to Vols. IV-VI, dated, respectively, 1853, 1853 and 1854. Waterhouse indirectly gives the date of Vols. II and III as 1852 (*Galbuloides* and *Sylviorthorhynchus*), and Gray (Cat. Gen. and Subgen. Birds, 1855) assigns the date 1852 to Vol. I (*Strigymnhemipus*).

The work is rare and important as it contains a number of new names. Des Murs is probably the author of most of the ornithological text although he is given slight mention on the title-pages and none on the original wrappers.

Christy, Robert Miller.

1890. Essex Field Club Special Memoirs.-Vol. II. | **The** | **Birds of Essex:** | A Contribution | to the | natural history of the county. | By | Miller Christy, F.L.S. | With 162 woodcut illustrations, two plans, and | a frontispiece. | Chelmsford: | Edmund Durant & Co., 90, High Street. | Buckhurst Hill: | The Essex Field Club. | London: | Simpkin, Marshall, Hamilton, Kent, & Co., Ltd. | 1890.

1 vol. demy 8vo, pp. I-VIII, 1-302, 3 ll. (advt.), frontisp. (monochr.), pll. I-II (col.; plans), 162 text-figs. Chelmsford and London.

A catalogue of the species of birds recorded from Essex County, England, giving quotations from early accounts and more recent records of occurrence. Preliminary chapters give biographical notices of the principal Essex ornithologists, notices of the chief Essex bird collections, migration tables, and accounts of hawks and hawking and of wild fowl decoys. The illustrations are accredited to various sources.

Chubb, Charles.

1913. See Brabourne and Chubb, **The Birds of South America.**

Chubb, Charles. (McConnell, Helen Mackenzie; Quelch, John J.)

1916-21. **The birds** | **of** | **British Guiana,** | based on the collection of | Frederick Vavasour McConnell, | Camfield Place, Hatfield, Herts. | By | Charles Chubb, F.Z.S., M.B.O.U., | Zoological Department, British Museum. | With | A Preface by Mrs. F. V. McConnell. | Vol. I [II]. | London: | Bernard Quaritch, 11 Grafton Street, W. | 1916 [1921].

2 vols. royal 8vo, Vol. I, pp. I-LIII, 1-528, frontisp. (portr.), 16 pll. (photogr.), 1 map (tinted), pll. I-X (col.), text-figs. 1-95. Vol. II, pp. I-XCVI, 1-615, 8 pll. (photogr.), pll. I-X (col.), text-figs. 1-214. London.

An account of the birds of British Guiana, with descriptions, etc. Volume I, p. 3 contains a preface by Mrs. McConnell, and on pp. V-XXXV is a description of McConnell's first Roraima expedition, apparently also from her pen. Volume II, pp. V-LXXVIII, contains a description of the second Roraima expedition, written by John J. Quelch.

Clark, Edward B.

1901. **Birds of lakeside** | **and prairie** | by | Edward B. Clark | with sixteen illustrations in color | A. W. Mumford, Publisher | Chicago New York.

1 vol. 8vo (5¾x7½), 6 pr. ll. (half-tit., tit., ded., pref., conts. and list of illustrs.), pp. 9-150, 16 pll. (col.). Chicago and New York.

Popular essays on bird life in Chicago and the prairies of Illinois and Indiana. The illustrations are from the periodical, "Birds and Nature."

Clarke, Benjamin.

1841. See Buffon, G. L. L., **The Book of Birds.**

Clarke, William Eagle.

1912. Studies | in | Bird Migration | by | William Eagle Clarke | Keeper of the Natural History Department, the Royal Scottish Museum | with maps, weather charts, and other illustrations | Volume I [II]. | London | Gurney and Jackson | Edinburgh: Oliver and Boyd | 1912.

2 vols. 8vo. Vol. I, pp. I-XVI, 1-323, pll. I-IX, (1 map, 6 charts), 1 text-cut. Vol. II, pp. I-VII, 1-346, pll. X-XXV, 1 text-cut (map). London.

A very detailed series of studies of the various aspects of the migration of birds, with special attention to the British and Irish coasts. Some of the chapters are general and others relate to certain species or certain localities. The relationship between migrational and meteorological phenomena is given some prominence.

Clubb, Joseph A.

1914. Handbook and guide | to the | British birds | on exhibition in | The Lord Derby Natural History | Museum, Liverpool. | Illustrated by twelve plates and plan of arrangement. | [*Blazon.*] | Liverpool: | C. Tinling & Co., Ltd., 53, Victoria Street. | 1914.

1 vol. post 8vo, 4 pr. ll., pp. V-IX+1, 1-69, 12 pll., 1 chart (floor-plan; fold.). Liverpool.

A catalogue of 32 exhibition cases in the Liverpool Museum, with a short discussion of the species exhibited in each. The plates are photographs of some of the groups on display.

Cobbett, L.

1911. See [Grouse], **The Grouse in Health and Disease.**

Collett, Robert; and Nansen, Fridtjof.

1899. See Nansen, **The Norwegian North Polar Expedition** 1893-1896, IV. An Account of the **Birds.**

Collin, Jonas.

1879. See Kjaerbolling, Niels, **To Nye Tavler** til Dr. Kjaerbölling's **Skandinaviens Fugle.**

Comte, Achille.

1841. See Buffon, G. L. L., **The Book of Birds.**

Cook, A. J.

1893. Bulletin 94. April, 1893. | Michigan | Agricultural Experiment Station | State Agricultural College. | Zoölogical Department. | **Birds of Michigan** | Illustrated | By A. J. Cook. | [*Notice, 3 lines.*].

1 vol. 8vo, tit., pp. 1-148, 11 text-cuts. Lansing.

An annotated list of the species of birds occurring in Michigan, prefaced by a local bibliography.

Cook, Sullivan.

1907. See Mershon, W. B., **The Passenger Pigeon.**

Cooke, Wells W.

1897. The State Agricultural College | The Agricultural Experiment Station | Bulletin No. 37 | Technical Series No. 2 | **The** | **Birds of Colorado** | by | W. W. Cooke | Approved by the Station Council | Alston Ellis, President | Fort Collins, Colorado | March, 1897 | The Smith-Brooks Printing Company | Denver.

1 vol. post 8vo, pp. 1-143. Fort Collins. March 1897.

An annotated list of the birds of the state, based on all records obtainable. A detailed bibliography is given. Supplements to this list were published later as Bulletins 44 and 56 of the Station, "Further Notes on the Birds of Colorado," 1898 and "A Second Appendix," 1900 (q.v.), with which the present copy is bound.

Cooke, Wells W.

1898. The State Agricultural College | The Agricultural Experiment Station | Bulletin No. 44 | Technical Series No. 4 | **Further Notes** | **on the** | **Birds of Colorado** | An Appendix to Bulletin No. 37, on the | Birds of Colorado | By | W. W. Cooke | Approved by the Station Council | Alston Ellis, President | Fort Collins, Colorado | March, 1898 | The Smith-Brooks Printing Company | Denver.

1 vol. post 8vo, pp. 145-176. March 1898.

Supplementary notes and additions to the original paper on "The Birds of Colorado," 1897 (q.v.), published as Bulletin 37 of the Station. A second supplement was issued as Bulletin 56, "A Second Appendix," 1900 (q.v.). The present copy is bound with the other two papers (and some others) by the same author.

Cooke, Wells W.

1900. Bulletin 56. (Technical Series No. 5.) May, 1900. | The Agricultural Experiment Station | of the | Agricultural College of

Colorado. | **The** | **Birds of Colorado** | **A Second Appendix** to Bulletin | No. 37 | By | W. W. Cooke | Published by the Experiment Station | Fort Collins, Colorado. | 1900.

1 vol. post 8vo, pp. 177-239. Fort Collins. May 1900.

A second appendix to Bulletin 37 of the Station, "The Birds of Colorado," 1897 (q.v.), bringing the subject-matter up to date. The present copy is bound with the original paper and the first supplement, Bull. 44, "Further Notes," etc. (q.v.).

Cooke, Wells W.

1907. See Chapman, Frank M., **The Warblers of North America.**

Coombs, Frank B.

1896. See World's Congress on Ornithology, **Papers presented to the—.**

Cooper, James Fenimore.

1907. See Mershon, W. B., **The Passenger Pigeon.**

Cooper, James Graham. (Baird, Spencer Fullerton.)

1870. Geological Survey of California. | J. D. Whitney, State Geologist. | Ornithology. | Volume I. | **Land Birds.** | Edited by S. F. Baird, | from the manuscript and notes of | J. G. Cooper. | Published by authority of the Legislature. | 1870.

1 vol. demy 4to, pp. I-XI+1, 1-592, 663 woodcuts. Cambridge.

A report on the birds of California prepared by Cooper from his own observations and field work, and submitted to Baird for revision and publication. Baird added considerable matter, which appears over his signature, in addition to the technical descriptions which were taken, principally, from Baird, Cassin and Lawrence's "The Birds of North America," 1860 (q.v.). The general accounts, except where signed otherwise, are from the pen of Cooper. Volume II was to have comprised a similar volume on the water birds, but was replaced by the two volumes of Baird, Brewer and Ridgway on "The Water Birds of North America," 1884 (q.v.), issued, eventually, in the Memoirs of the Museum of Comparative Zoology at Harvard College, Vol. XII.

Cooper, J. W.

1869?. **Game Fowls,** | their origin and history, | with a | description of the breeds, strains and crosses. | The American and English | modes of feeding, training, and | heeling; | how to breed and cross, | improving quality and preserving feather, | together with a | description and treatment | of all diseases incident to game fowls. | By J. W. Cooper, M.D. | Standard edition. | Published and sold by the author—price $5.00. | Address by mail Dr. J. W. Cooper, West Chester, Pa.

1 vol. post 8vo, pp. 1-304, 2 pll. (col.). Philadelphia.

Title self-explanatory. The work was "entered according to Act of Congress in the year 1869."

Cooper, Susan Fenimore.

1851. Rural hours. | By | a lady. | [*Quot., 4 lines.*]. With Illustrations. | **Fourth edition.** | New-York: | George P. Putnam, 155 Broadway. | MDCCCLI.

1 vol. 8vo. pp. I-VI, (7)-521, illum. tit., 20 pll. (col.; 15 ornith.). New York.

This work, by the daughter of James Fenimore Cooper, contains, "in a journal form, the simple record of those little events which make up the course of the seasons in rural life," including numerous references to New England bird life. The first edition appeared in 1850.

Cope, Edward Drinker.

1869. See Baily, William L., **Our Own Birds.**

Coquille, Voyage autour du Monde, Sur La Corvette, La—; Zoologie.

1826-30. See Duperrey, L. I.

Coquille, Voyage autour du Monde, sur La Corvette, La—; (Narrative).

1839. See Lesson, Réne Primèvere.

Cordeaux, John.

1897. See Butler, Arthur G., **British Birds,** 1896-98.

Cordeaux, John.

1899. A list | **of** | **British birds** | **Belonging to the Humber District** | (having a special reference to their migrations). | Revised to April, 1899. | By | John Cordeaux, J. P., F.R.G.S., M.B.O.U., | Ex-President Yorkshire Naturalists' Union [*etc., 7 lines.*]. | London: | R. H. Porter, 7, Princes Street, Cavendish Square, W. | 1899.

1 vol. 8vo, pp. I-VIII, 1-40. London.

A list "of all species of birds, now included in the British List, which have occurred in the Humber District in the last half century," with notes on occurrence, migration and nesting.

Cordier, A. H.

1923. Birds | **Their Photographs and Home Life** | by | A. H. Cordier, M.D. | Former Professor [*etc., 8 lines.*] | With 145 Illustrations from Photographs of Wild Birds, | by the Author | Publishers Dorrance Philadelphia.

1 vol. 8vo, 3 pr. ll., pp. 1-247, 73 pll. (figs. 1-144).   Philadelphia. September 1923.

A popular account of the habits of 85 species of birds, prefaced by chapters on materials for, and methods of, bird photography. Illustrated from photographs.

Cornalia, Emilio.

1850.   See Osculati, Gaetano, **Esplorazione delle Regioni Equatoriali.**

Corwin, Cruise of the Revenue Marine Steamer,—.

1887.   See Healy, Michael A.

Cory, Charles Barney.

1878.   A naturalist | in the | Magdalen Islands; | giving | a des-cription of the islands and list of the birds taken | there, with other ornithological notes. | By | Charles B. Cory. | Illustrated from sketches by the author. | Boston. | 1878.

1 vol. (small) cap 4to, pp. I-IV, 5-93, 2 pll., 1 text-cut.   Boston.

Pages 7-29 embrace a short account of the islands and the author's experiences there.   Pages 31-78 contain a catalogue of the birds taken or observed in the region.   A hypothetical list of species forms an appendix on pages 79-83.

Cory, Charles Barney.

1879.   Description of a new species | of the | Family Ardeidae, from the Bahama Islands. | By Charles B. Cory. | . . . | Boston, October 8, 1879.

1 loose leaf (5¼x8¼).   Boston.   October 8, 1879.

The original description of a supposedly new *Ardea cyanirostris.*   The complete publication consists of this isolated leaf.

Cory, Charles Barney.

1880.   Birds | of the | Bahama Islands; | containing | many birds new to the islands, and a number of undescribed | winter plumages of North American species. | By | Charles B. Cory, | Author of "A Naturalist in the Magdalen Islands," etc. | Illustrated. | Boston: | Published by the author, | 8 Arlington Street. | 1880.

1 vol. demy 4to, pp. 1-250, 8 pll. (hand-col.).   Boston.

A popular account of one hundred and forty-nine species of Bahama birds with descriptions and notes and a hypothetical list of thirty-six additional forms. Reissued, enlarged, in an edition of 1890 (q.v.).

Cory, Charles Barney.

1880-83.   The | beautiful and curious | Birds of the World. | By | Charles B. Cory, | Fellow of the Linnean Society of London; [*etc., 4 lines.*] | Author of "Birds of the Bahama Islands," etc. |

Boston, U. S. A. | 1883. | Published by the Author for the sub-scribers.

1 vol. double-elephant folio, 23 ll., pll. 1-20 (numbered only in index) (hand-col.; 8 by J. Smit). Boston.

Issued in seven parts, in an edition of two hundred copies. It consists of hand-colored plates interleaved with pages of descriptive matter not arranged according to classification. Part I is reviewed in the Bull. Nuttall Orn. Club, **5,** p. 236, Oct. 1880; II (issued Febr. 1881), in 6, p. 111, April, 1881; III in **6,** p. 240, Oct. 1881; IV and V, in **8,** p. 55, Jan. 1883; VII in Auk, **1,** p. 81, Jan. 1884. The plate of the Great Auk, issued in Pt. II is the original of the pic-ture of that bird which, for many years, adorned the cover of "The Auk." A second copy of the work contains several of the plates in duplicate, uncolored

Cory, Charles Barney.

1884-5. The | birds | of | Haiti and San Domingo. | By | Charles B. Cory, | Fellow of the Linnæan Society of London; [*etc., 8 lines.*] | Estes and Lauriat, | Boston, U. S. A. | 1885.

1 vol. folio post 4to, 1 pr. l., pp. 6-198, pll. 1-23 (numbered only in index; 22 hand-colored), 2 text-cuts (10 figs.); 4 wrappers bound in the back of the volume. Boston.

Issued in four parts, according to the wrappers, Parts I-III dated 1884, and Part IV, 1885. A monograph of the birds of the islands mentioned in the title, with synonymy, description and notes for each of the species.

Cory, Charles Barney.

1885. A | list of the birds | of the | West Indies, | including the | Bahama Islands and the Greater and Lesser Antilles, excepting | the islands of Tobago and Trinidad. | By | Charles B. Cory. | Estes & Lauriat, | Boston, U. S. A. | 1885.

1 vol. post folio, pp. 1-33. Boston.

A list of 482 species, numbered and arranged systematically, without annotations. This impression was cancelled because printed on both sides of the paper, and a corrected impression published the same year. A second edition (q.v.) was issued the following year.

Cory, Charles Barney.

1886. A | list of the birds | of the | West Indies, | including the | Bahama Islands and the Greater and Lesser Antilles, excepting | the islands of Tobago and Trinidad. | By | Charles B. Cory. | **Revised edition.** | Estes & Lauriat, | Boston, U. S. A. | 1886.

1 vol. post folio, 2 pr. ll. (tit. and index), ll. 5-34+1 (printed on one side only). Boston.

Similar to the author's work of the same title, dated the previous year (q.v.), but with some changes and additions. The species are not numbered in this edi-tion and the list is printed on but one side of the paper. Dr. Oberholser advises me that almost all of the present issue was destroyed by fire.

Cory, Charles Barney.

1889.   The | birds of the West Indies. | Including | all species known
to occur in the Bahama Islands, the Greater | Antilles, the Cay-
mans, and the Lesser Antilles, excepting | the islands of Tobago
and Trinidad. | By | Charles B. Cory, | Curator of Birds in the
Boston Society [*etc.*, *6 lines.*] Author of | "The Beautiful and
Curious Birds of the World," [*etc.*, *4 lines.*] | Illustrated. | Estes &
Lauriat, | Boston, U. S. A. | 1889.

1 vol. superroyal 8vo, 1 pr. l., pp. 1-324, 2 pll. (maps), 19 text-figs.
Boston.

A manual of the birds of the West Indies with an extended bibliography of West
Indian ornithology and descriptions of the species of birds other than well
known North American forms. Much of the text was originally published by
the author in "The Auk," 1886-1888, and some of the drawings are taken from
the same source.

Cory, Charles Barney.

1890.   The birds | of the | Bahama Islands | containing | Many
birds new to the Islands, and a number of undescribed | winter
plumages of North American birds. | By Charles B. Cory, | Curator
of Birds in the Boston Society [*etc.*, *6 lines.*]. | Author of | The
Beautiful and Curious Birds of the World, [*etc.*, *4 lines.*]. | **Revised
edition.** | Estes & Lauriat, | Boston, U. S. A. | 1890.

1 vol. demy 4to, pp. 1-8, 8 ll. (bibliography and list of birds described
since 1880), pp. 9-250, 8 pll. Boston.

Identical with the edition of 1880 (q.v.) with the exception of 16 pages of additional text and a new title-page. The new text contains an ornithological bibliography of the Bahama Islands and a discussion of the species and subspecies
of birds described since the earlier edition was published. This edition was
made up from the unsold copies of the original work altered as mentioned
above. The plates are uncolored. Author's copy.

Cory, Charles Barney.

1892.   Catalogue | of West Indian birds, | containing a list of all
species known to occur in the Bahama Islands, the | Greater
Antilles, the Caymans, and the Lesser Antilles, excepting | the
islands of Tobago and Trinidad, | by | Charles B. Cory, | Fellow
of the Linnæan and Zoölogical Societies of London [*etc.*, *4 lines.*]. |
Author of | "The Beautiful and Curious Birds of the World,"
[*etc.*, *3 lines.*]. | Published by the author. | Boston, U. S. A. | 1892.

1 vol. imperial 8vo, pp. 1-163, 1 map. Boston.

A list of species with their distribution noted, with remarks on certain forms, and
with a complete bibliography of ornithological publications relating to the
West Indies.

Cory, Charles Barney.

1896. **Hunting and fishing** | **in** | **Florida,** | including a | key to the water birds | known to occur in the state. | By | Charles B. Cory. | Curator of the Department of Ornithology [*etc.*, *4 lines.*] | Author of | "The Beautiful and Curious Birds of the World," [*etc.*, *4 lines.*]. | For sale by | Estes & Lauriat, | Boston, Mass. | 1896.

1 vol. 8vo (7x9), 1 pr. 1., pp. 1-304, frontisp., 1 pl., 320 text-figs. (248 of birds by Edward Knobel). Boston.

Pages 133-304 comprise a "Key to the water birds of Florida" with 248 illustrations, which is more than a key since it includes an annotated list with succinct descriptions and notes on distribution.

Cory, Charles Barney.

1896. **A** | **list of the birds** | **of** | **eastern North America** | by | Charles B. Cory | For sale by | Bradley Whidden | 18 Arch St., Boston | Boston | 1896.

1 vol. 8vo, cover-tit., pp. 1-42. Boston.

A check-list of 570 species and varieties of birds occurring in North America east of the ninetieth meridian. Scientific and common names, 'A.O.U. number', and an indication of occurrence in New England, Illinois or Florida, are given for each species. This list was embodied, with an occasional note on other distribution, with some alterations, in the author's "The Birds of Eastern North America," 1899 (q.v.). The present copy is bound with several other small papers by the same author.

Cory, Charles Barney.

1896. **A list** | **of the** | **birds of Florida** | by | Charles B. Cory | For sale by | Bradley Whidden | 18 Arch St., Boston | Boston | 1896.

1 vol. 8vo, cover-tit., pp. 1-24. Boston.

A simple list of 352 species and subspecies, with scientific and vernacular names.

Cory, Charles Barney.

1897. **How to know** | **the** | **Ducks, Geese and Swans** | **of** | North America | all the species being grouped according to size and color | By | Charles B. Cory | Curator of the Department of Ornithology [*etc.*, *4 lines.*]. | Author of (*etc.*, *5 lines.*]. | For sale by | Little, Brown & Co. | Boston. | 1897.

1 vol. demy 4to, pp. 1-95, frontisp., 138 text-figs. Boston.

A manual for the determination of North American ducks, geese and swans. Arranged on the same principle as the author's "How to Know the Shore Birds," 1897 (q.v.). The present copy is included in one volume with several other papers by the same author.

Cory, Charles Barney.

1897. How to know | the | shore birds | (Limicolæ) | of | North America | (south of Greenland and Alaska) | all the species being grouped according to size and color | By | Charles B. Cory | Curator of the Department of Ornithology in the Field Columbian Museum, Chicago; [*etc.*, *4 lines.*]. | Author of [*etc.*, *5 lines.*]. | For sale by | Little, Brown & Co. | Boston | 1897.

1 vol. demy 4to, pp. 1-89, frontisp., 178 figs. Boston.

A compact manual for sportsmen and others, to aid in the identification of the North American species of shore birds. Brief, illustrated keys to the species (which are arranged according to size), are followed by a descriptive list arranged in systematic order. The form of the keys was original with the author and are simple and efficient, being designed for persons without technical knowledge. Uniform in size and style with the "How to Know the Ducks, Geese and Swans of North America," 1897 (q.v.). The present copy is bound with several other papers by the same author.

Cory, Charles Barney.

1899. The birds | of | Eastern North America | known to occur east of the ninetieth meridian | Water birds [Part II] | Part I [Land birds] | Key to the families and species | By | Charles B. Cory | Curator of the Department of Ornithology [*etc.*, *4 lines.*]. | Author of [*etc.*, *6 lines.*]. | Special edition printed for the | Field Columbian Museum, Chicago, Ill.

2 vols. in 1 vol., superroyal 8vo (7x9). Vol. I, 2 pr. ll. (prelim. key and tit.), pp. III-VIII+1, 1-142, 532 text-figs. Vol. II, pp. I-IX+1, 131-387, frontisp., 722 text-figs. Chicago.

A special edition of the author's work of the same title published in Boston the same year, and differing only in the title-pages. The plan of the work is that successfully followed by the author in his earlier works, "How to Know the Shore Birds" and "How to Know the Ducks, Geese and Swans," 1897 (q.v.). Appended is a check-list of species, based on the author's previous "A List of the Birds of Eastern North America," 1896 (q.v.) but with the addition of several species and subspecies and annotations relative to distribution, habitat, etc.

Costa, Oronzio Gabriele.

1857. > Fauna | del | Regno di Napoli | ossia | enumerazione di tutti gli animali | che abitano le diverse regioni di questo regno | e le acque che le bagnano | contenente | la descrizione de nuovi o poco esttamente conosciuti | con figure ricavate da originali viventi e dipinte al naturale | di | Oronzio-Gabriele Costa | Professore di Zoologia | Dottore in Medicina [*etc.*, *4 lines.*]. | Uccelli | Napoli | Tipografia di Gaetano Sautto | Vico Cinquesanti, num. 29. | 1857.

1 vol. foliopost 4to, 2 pr. ll. (subtit. and tit.), pp. I-V+1, 7-88 (end
of Pt. I), 1-66, 1 l. (conts.), pll. I-XV (col.; by Salv. Calyó).
Naples.

The ornithological portion of the author's elaborate work on the fauna of the
Province of Naples, Italy. Part I contains a systematic catalogue of species;
II, detailed descriptions of certain noteworthy species. The work was published over a period of years from 1829-1860 (Engelmann, and Carus and Engelmann) or later [Cat. Library British Museum (Natural History)]. The preface
to the present portion is dated 1839 and the title-page, 1857. The preface to
Pt. II mentions the intended publication of a third part, to which I can find
no other reference.

Cotton, John. (Tyas, Robert, *ed.*)

1854-56?. **Beautiful birds** | described | Edited from the Manuscript
of John Cotton, F.Z.S. | by the | Rev. Robert Tyas, B.A. | Author
of | "Flowers from the Holy Land," etc., etc. | With thirty-six
illustrations | by James Andrews, F.R.H.S. | Vol. I [II.; III.]. |
London | Madgwick, Houlston & Co., Ltd [*Period added (Vols.
II and III*.).] | 7 Paternoster Buildings, E.C.

3 vols. cap 8vo. Vol. I, pp. I-XX, 1-92 (Birds of Prey), 1-16 (Thrushes),
1-16 (Warblers), 1-15+1 (Nightingale and other Warblers), 1-16
(Goldcrests and Titmice), 1-16 (Shrikes), 1-16 (Chatterers and
Flycatchers), 12 pll. (by James Andrews), 46 text-figs. Vol. II,
pp. I-X, 1 l. (list of pll.), pp. 1-15+1 (Bee-eaters and Swallows),
1-16 (Nightjars and Kingfishers), 1-16 (Cuckoos), 1-16 (Wood-
peckers), 1-16 (Wrynecks, Creepers, Honey-eaters and Nectar
Birds), 1-16 (Hummingbirds), 113-192, 12 pll., 70 text-figs. Vol.
III, pp. I-VIII, 1 l. (list of pll.), pp. 1-198, 12 pll., 75 text-figs.
London (n.d.).

A popular outline of ornithology, based largely on the classification of Swainson,
following a modified "quinary system." The work originally appeared in thirty-
six monthly parts with colored plates, in 1854-6; the present reissue, with some
alterations on the title-page and with uncolored plates, is without date and I
am unable to trace its appearance.

Coues, Elliott.

1868. {A List | of the | **Birds of New England.** | By Elliott Coues, |
Assistant Surgeon, U.S.A. | - | [Reprinted from the Proceedings of
the Essex Institute, Vol. V.] | - | Salem, Mass. | Essex Institute
Press. | 1868.} > Catalogue of the Birds of North America con-
tained in the | Museum of the Essex Institute; - with which is in- |
corporated A List of the Birds of New England. | With brief
Critical and Field Notes. | By Dr. Elliott Coues, U. S. A.

1 vol. 8vo, (Title-p. missing.), pp. 1-71. Salem.

A repaged copy of the author's "Catalogue of the Birds of North America contained in the Museum," etc., published in the Communications of the Essex Institute, 5, Art. 12, pp. 249-314, May 1868, with the addition of a title-page (missing) and an index (pp. 67-71). The subtitle is differently divided, also, in the two issues. Coues (Ornith. Bibliogr., 1st Instalment, from which the title-page is quoted as above) says that the reprint gives the faunal list precedence over the museum catalogue, but this is true only as regards the title, —the general text is unaltered. Coues adds, of the reprint, "Only 50 copies extant." The present copy is inscribed, "C from C" (Cory from Coues?). An extract of this paper from the original periodical is among the pamphlets in this library.

Coues, Elliott.

1872. **Key** | to | **North American birds** | containing a concise account of every species of | living and fossil bird | at present known from the continent north of the Mexican | and United States boundary. | Illustrated by 6 steel plates, and upwards of 250 woodcuts. | By | Elliott Coues, | Assistant Surgeon United States Army. | Salem: Naturalists' Agency. | New York: Dodd and Mead. | Boston: Estes and Lauriat. | 1872.

1 vol. demy 4to., 4 pr. ll., pp. 1-361, 3 pp. (advt.), pll. 1-6, text-figs. 1-238. Boston.

The first edition of a justly popular work which has appeared in five editions. Written in an easy style with scientific accuracy the book soon became a standard work of reference, useful alike to the scientist and to the layman. Cf. eds. 1887 and 1903.

Coues, Elliott.

1873-74. **A** | **check list** | **of** | **North American Birds.** | By | Elliott Coues. | Salem. | Naturalists' Agency. | 1873.

1 vol. 8vo., pp. 1-137+1, 1-3 (advt.). Salem.

A list of species and subspecies recognized by the author, arranged and numbered consecutively, with an appendix on pages 123-137. The list was printed and a few copies distributed in 1873, without the appendix which delayed the final publication until the following year. The list thus may be quoted as of 1873 and the appendix 1874. In the latter year the same list appeared as part of a volume by the author entitled, "Field Ornithology" (q.v.), the general text of which, later, was incorporated into the "Key to North American Birds," (editions 2 et seq.; cf. ed. 1887) while the "Check List" passed through a second edition, without extraneous matter, in 1882 (q.v.).

Coues, Elliott.

1874. Department of the Interior. | United States Geological Survey of the Territories. | F. V. Hayden, U. S. Geologist-in-Charge. | Miscellaneous publications—No. 3. | **Birds of the northwest:** | a hand-book | of | the ornithology | of the | region drained by the Missouri River | and its tributaries. | By Elliott Coues, | Captain and Assistant Surgeon U. S. Army. | Washington: | Government Printing Office. | 1874.

1 vol. 8vo, pp. I-XI+1, 1-791. Washington.

A thorough treatment of the subject. Extensive synonymies, distribution of species, specimens secured on United States government expeditions, field notes on habits, and descriptions of new species and genera, with occasional analytical keys have made an authoritative and readable book. Estes and Lauriat, in 1877, rebound and reissued 214 copies of the book, with a new title-page but otherwise unchanged, as "Birds of the Northwest. The work was issued in December, 1874 (Coues, Bibl., 1st Instalment, p. 702), presumably after the publication of Vol. III of Baird Brewer and Ridgway's History of North American Birds, Land Birds (q.v., 1874) which is quoted in the present work, although both appeared about the same time.

Coues, Elliott.

1874. Field | ornithology. | Comprising a | manual of instruction | for | procuring, preparing and preserving birds | and a | Check List of North American Birds. | By | Dr. Elliott Coues, U. S. A. | [*Monogram.*] | Salem: | Naturalists' Agency. | Boston: Estes & Lauriat. | New York: Dodd & Mead. | 1874.

1 vol. 8vo, pp. I-IV, 1-116, 1-137+1, 1-3 (advt.), 1 text-fig. Salem.

The first portion of the volume (pp. 5-116) contains thorough instructions for the bird-collector. This was originally intended for inclusion in the author's "Key to North American Birds," 1872 (q.v.), was omitted from the first edition of that work on account of want of space, but was inserted in the second (1884) and subsequent editions, and was later (1890) embodied in the author's "Handbook of Field and General Ornithology" (q.v.). The second part of the present volume comprises the author's "A Check List of North American Birds" with supplement, —identical in all respects with that work (q.v., 1873-74) which is simply another form of the same publication.

Coues, Elliott.

1874. See Baird, Spencer F.; Brewer; and Ridgway, **A History of North American Birds, Land Birds.**

Coues, Elliott.

1878. Department of the Interior | United States Geological Survey of the Territories | F. V. Hayden, U. S. Geologist-in-Charge | Miscellaneous publications—No. 11 | **Birds of the Colorado Valley** | A repository of | scientific and popular information | concerning | North American ornithology | By Elliott Coues | [*Quot.*] | Part first | Passeres to Laniidæ | Bibliographical Appendix | Seventy Illustrations | Washington | Government Printing Office | 1878.

1 vol. 8vo, pp. I-XVI, 1-807, 2 vignettes, text-figs. 1-66. Washington.

The general text up to page 565 comprises the first part of a work which was never completed. The bird life of the Colorado Basin is analyzed in detail with short

characterizations in Latin and complete descriptions in English of each species, with detailed synonymies, and long discussions of habits and distribution.
The genera and higher groups are discussed critically, with reference to habits
as well as taxonomy.

The Bibliographical Appendix, occupying pages 567-784 marked the beginning of a work of which four parts were published at various times and in
various places. The present instalment is subtitled "List of faunal publications
relating to North American ornithology." Further details of the entire work as
published are given below under the present author's "Ornithological Bibliography, 1878-80" (q.v.).

Coues, Elliott.

1878-80. [Ornithological Bibliography.]

1 vol. 8vo, 979 pp. (variously paged), 7 ll. (extraneous matter).
Washington.

Part I. Faunal publications relating to North America. Misc.
Publ. U. S. Geol. Surv. Terr. **11**, 567-784, 1878. (Cf. Birds of the
Colorado Valley.).

Part II. Faunal publications relating to the rest of America. Bull.
U. S. Geol. Geog. Surv. Terr. **5**, (2), 239-330, 1879 (Cf. Second
Instalment Amer. Ornith. Bibliography).

Part III. Systematic publications relating to American species,
arranged according to families. Bull. U. S. Geol. Geog. Surv.
Terr. **5,** (4), 521-1072, 1880 (Cf. Third Instalment, etc.).

Part IV. Faunal publications relating to British birds. Proc. U. S.
Nat. Mus. **2** (1879), 359-482, 1880 (Cf. Fourth Instalment, etc.).

The four parts given above are all that were ever published. The author's intention was to complete an entire ornithological bibliography, but, in order to
make available to other workers such portions of the whole as were in a more
or less finished condition as well as to invite criticism for the betterment of the
entire project, the several instalments were published from time to time. So
far as perfected, the bibliography is very complete and there are but few omissions, but various departments of the subject are not treated, even in the
American sections. The collation of each part is given separately under the
respective heading.

Copies of Parts I-IV have been extracted from their original covers and bound
together in one volume which is collated above. The volume was never issued
in this form.

Coues, Elliott.

1879. [Department of the Interior. | Bulletin | of | the United
States | Geological and Geographical Survey | of | the Territories. |
F. V. Hayden, | U. S. Geologist-in-Charge. | 1879-'80. | Volume
V. | Washington: | Government Printing Office. | 1880.] > Volume
V. 1879. Number 2. > Art. XVII.-**Second Instalment of American**

Orni- | thological Bibliography. | By Dr. Elliott Coues, U. S. A.
1 vol. (pt.) 8vo, pp. 153-330. Washington. September 6, 1879.

The bibliography occupies pages 239-330 and gives the titles of faunal publications
relating to the ornithology of America other than North America. Together
with the first instalment it gives a nearly complete faunal bibliography of the
ornithology of the entire continent. The various other instalments are grouped
with this one under the present author's "Ornithological Bibliography," 1878-
80 (q.v.), and in the copy at hand, are bound together in one volume.

Coues, Elliott.

1880. [Department of the Interior. | Bulletin | of | the United
States | Geological and Geographical Survey | of | the Territories. |
F. V. Hayden, | U. S. Geologist-in-Charge. | 1879-'80. | Volume
V. | Washington: | Government Printing Office. | 1880.] > De-
partment of the Interior. | United States Geological and Geographi-
cal Survey. | F. V. Hayden, U. S. Geologist-in-charge. | Bulletin |
of | the United States | Geological and Geographical Survey | of |
the Territories. | Volume V. . , . Number 4. | Washington: |
Government Printing Office. | September 30, 1880. > Volume V.
1879. Number 4. | Art. XXVI.-**Third Instalment of American
Orni- | thological Bibliography.** | By Dr. Elliott Coues, U. S. A.
1 vol. (pt.) 8vo, pp. I-VII, 521-1072. Washington. Sept. 30, 1880.

The bibliography occupies pages 521-1066 and contains the titles of all publications treating of particular species, genera or families of birds arranged by
families, dates, and author's names, and relating only to American species.
It thus supplements the first and second instalments of the work, and together
with them was calculated to form a nearly complete bibliography of American
ornithology. A fourth part, relating to British ornithology, was published the
same year as the present contribution. The four parts are listed jointly under
the present author as "Ornithological Bibliography," 1878-80 (q.v.), and are
bound together in one volume in the copy at hand. Date is from the original
wrapper of this number.

Coues, Elliott.

1880. [Department of the Interior: | U. S. National Museum. |
-19- | Proceedings | of the | United States National Museum. |
Vol. II. | 1879. | Published under the direction of the Smithsonian
Institution. | Washington: | Government Printing Office. | 1880.]
> **Fourth instalment of Ornithological Bibliography:** | being a list
of faunal publications relating to British birds. | By Dr. Elliott
Coues, U. S. A.
1 vol. 8vo, pp. I-IV, 1-499. Washington.

The bibliography occupies pages 359-482 and gives the titles of faunal publications relating purely to British birds in Great Britain, whether or not they occur
more or less regularly elsewhere. The various instalments of the "Bibli-

ography" are grouped together under the above author's "Ornithological Bibliography," 1878-80 (q.v.), and, in the present set, are bound together in one volume.

Coues, Elliott.

1881-83.   See Stearns, Winfred A.; and Coues, **New England Bird Life.**

Coues, Elliott.

1882.   The | Coues **check list** | of | **North American Birds.** | **Second edition,** | Revised to Date, and entirely Rewritten, under Direction of the Author, | with a dictionary of the | etymology, orthography, and orthoepy | of the | scientific names | the concordance of previous lists, and a catalogue of his | ornithological publications. | [*Monogram.*] | Boston: | Estes and Lauriat. | 1882.

1 vol. demy 4to (6¾x9¾), pp. 1-165, 1 l. (advt.). Boston.

The "Check List" of 1873-4 (q.v.) brought up to date and enlarged as indicated in the title.

Coues, Elliott; and Prentiss, Daniel Webster.

1883.   Department of the Interior: | U. S. National Museum. | -32- | Bulletin | of the | United States National Museum. | No. 26. | Published under the direction of the Smithsonian Institution. | Washington: | Government Printing Office. | 1883.

[*Second title.*] **Avifauna Columbiana:** | being a | list of birds | ascertained to inhabit the | District of Columbia, | with the times of arrival and departure | of such as are non-residents, and | brief notices of habits, etc. | The **second edition,** | revised to date, and entirely rewritten. | By | Elliott Coues, M.D., Ph.D., | Professor of Anatomy in the National Medical College, etc., | and | D. Webster Prentiss, A.M., M.D., | Professor of Materia Medica and Therapeutics in the National Medical College, etc. | Washington: | Government Printing Office. | 1883.

1 vol. 8vo, pp. 1-133, 1 l. (expl. of pl.), frontisp., 1 pl., 4 maps (fold.; 3 col.), text-figs. 1-100. Washington.

Based on a paper by the same authors entitled, "Natural History. List of birds" (etc. as above) published on pages 399-421 of the Annual Report of the Board of Regents of the Smithsonian Institution . . . for the year 1861, Washington, 1862, the present contribution brings the subject matter up to date and adds information obtained since the publication of the first article. The list is annotated and treats of two hundred and forty-eight species of birds observed in the District of Columbia.

Coues, Elliott.

1886. See American Ornithologists' Union, **The Code of Nomenclature and Check-list of North American Birds.**

Coues, Elliott.

1887. **Key | to | North American Birds.** | Containing a concise account of every species of living and fossil | bird at present known from the continent north of the | Mexican and United States boundary, inclusive | of Greenland and Lower California, | with which are incorporated | general ornithology: | an outline of the structure and classification of birds; | and | field ornithology, | a manual of collecting, preparing, and preserving birds. | The **Third Edition,** | exhibiting the nomenclature of the American Ornithologists' Union, and | including descriptions of additional species, etc. | By Elliott Coues, A.M., M.D., Ph.D., | Late Captain and Assistant Surgeon U. S. Army [*etc.,* 6 *lines.*]. | Profusely illustrated. | [*Monogram.*] | Boston: | Estes and Lauriat. | 1887.

1 vol. royal 8vo., pp. I-X, I-IV, XI-XXX, 1-895, frontisp. (col.; by R. W. Shufeldt), text-figs. 1-561. Boston.

Printed from the same plates as the second edition (1884) with the addition of an appendix on pages 865-985 in which are included discoveries and nomenclatorial changes made since the earlier work. Since the "Check List" of the American Ornithologists' Union was published in the interim (1886 q.v.), comparisons between it and the systematic arrangement used in the "Key" are made by means of parallel columns. The second edition, used as the basis for the present one, was an entirely rewritten work although bearing the same general title as the first edition, its predecessor(q.v., 1872). Among the innovations, on pages 1-227, are extended chapters on field ornithology and general ornithology which were published later as a separate work (Cf. Coues, Handbook of Field and General Ornithology, 1890). The chapter on field ornithology was originally published in conjunction with the "Check List" in 1874 as a separate work under the title, "Field Ornithology" (q.v.).

Coues, Elliott.

1889. See American Ornithologists' Union, **Check-list of North American Birds, Abridged Edition.**

Coues, Elliott.

1889. See American Ornithologists' Union, **Supplement to the Code of Nomenclature and Check-list.**

Coues, Elliott.

1890. **Handbook | of | field and general | ornithology** | a manual of the structure and | classification of birds | with instructions for | collecting and preserving specimens | by | Professor Elliott Coues,

M.A., M.D., etc. | Vice-president American Ornithologists' Union; [*etc.*, *2 lines.*] | Illustrated | London | Macmillan and Co. | 1890 | All rights reserved.

1 vol. 8vo, 4 pr. ll., pp. 1-343, text-figs. 1-112. London.

Extracted from Coues's "Key" (editions after the first; Cf. ed. 1887.) and published separately as being of interest to European readers apart from the discussion of American species contained in the main body of the original work. The nature of the text is explained in the title, to which it is desirable to add the remark that for thoroughness of treatment (considering the scope of the subject) this work has not yet been excelled.

Coues, Elliott.

1892. See American Ornithologists' Union, **The Code of Nomenclature.**

Coues, Elliott.

1895. See American Ornithologists' Union, **Check-list of North American Birds, Second Edition.**

Coues, Elliott.

1896. See World's Congress on Ornithology, **Papers presented to the—.**

Coues, Elliott.

1897. See Audubon, John James, **Audubon and His Journals.**

Coues, Elliott. (Elliot, Daniel Giraud; Farley, J. A.)

1903. **Key** | to | **North American Birds.** | Containing a concise account of every species of living and fossil | bird at present known from the continent north of the | Mexican and United States boundary, inclusive | of Greenland and Lower California, | with which are incorporated | general ornithology: | an outline of the structure and classification of birds; | and | field ornithology, | a manual of collecting, preparing, and preserving birds. | The **Fifth Edition,** | (entirely revised) | exhibiting the nomenclature of the American Ornithologists' Union, and including | descriptions of additional species | in two volumes. | Volume I [II]. | By Elliott Coues, A.M., M.D., Ph.D., | Late Captain and Assistant Surgeon U. S. Army [*etc.*, *5 lines.*]. | Profusely Illustrated. | [*Monogram.*] | Boston: | The Page Company | Publishers.

2 vols. royal 8vo. Vol. I, 1 pr. l., pp. I-XLI+1, 1-535, 2 pll. (1 col.; by L. A. Fuertes), figs. 1-353. Vol. II, pp. I-VI, 537-1152, 1 pl. (col.; by L. A. Fuertes), figs. 354-747. Boston.

The last and most complete edition of the famous "Key" (Cf. ed. 1872.), published after the death of the author, from manuscript left by him, and with a short appendix listing the species recognized by the American Ornithologists' Union after the completion of the manuscript. This appendix is presumably by J. A. Farley who edited the manuscript of the work. The plan of the work is similar to that of previous editions but the accounts are much more comprehensive and contain in the general text some matter previously relegated to an appendix. Many additional illustrations, including two colored plates, are a further improvement to the work. This edition is copyrighted by Dana Estes and Co. and some copies bear the imprint of that firm. The publisher's preface is dated October, 1903. Pp. XXXV-XLI contain a necrology of Coues by Elliot.

Couper, William.

1883. See Samuels, Edward Augustus, **The Birds of New England and Adjacent States.**

1869. See Samuels, Edward Augustus, **Ornithology and Oölogy of New England.**

1883. See Samuels, Edward Augustus, **Our Northern and Eastern Birds.**

Courcelles, Pauline de.

See Knip, Madame.

Coward, Thomas Alfred. (Oldham, Charles; Dockray, John A.)

1910. The | vertebrate fauna | of | Cheshire | and Liverpool Bay | edited by | T. A. Coward, F.Z.S. | author of "Picturesque Cheshire." | In two volumes | Volume I [II]. | The mammals and birds of Cheshire [The Dee as a wildfowl resort] | by | T. A. Coward and C. Oldham, F.Z.S., M.B.O.U. [John A. Dockray] | authors of "The birds of Cheshire" [The reptiles and amphibians of Cheshire | by | T. A. Coward and C. Oldham, F.Z.S., M.B.O.U. | Authors of "The Birds of Cheshire" | - | The fishes of Cheshire and Liverpool Bay | by | James Johnstone, B.Sc. (Lond.) | Author of "British Fisheries" and "Conditions of Life in the Sea"] | With illustrations from photographs by | Thomas Baddeley | Witherby & Co. | 326 High Holborn London | 1910.

2 vols. 8vo. Vol. I, pp. I-XXXII (introd.), 1-472, 34 pll. Vol. II, pp. I-XL, 1-204, 14 pll., 1 map (col.; fold.), 7 text-figs. London.

Accounts of the local occurrence, distribution and habits of the vertebrates of the County of Cheshire and Liverpool Bay, England; scientific and vernacular names are given but descriptions are omitted. The ornithological portion comprises "The Birds of Cheshire," Vol. I, pp. 91-459, and "The Dee as a Wildfowl resort," Vol. II, pp. XXI-XL. There are no plates of birds and the illustrations are mostly of local scenery. An earlier work on the birds of Cheshire was published by Coward and Oldham in 1900.

Coward, Thomas Alfred.

1910-13. See Kirkman, Frederick Bernuf Bever, The **British Bird Book.**

Coward, Thomas Alfred.

1920. The birds | of the British Isles | and their eggs | by | T. A. Coward, F.Z.S., F.E.S. [M.B.O.U. | F.Z.S., F.E.S.] | Author of [*etc., 3 lines.*] | First [Second] series | comprising | Families Corvidæ to Sulidæ [Anatidæ to Tetraonidæ] | with | 242 [213] accurately coloured illustrations | by Archibald Thorburn and others | reproduced from Lord Lilford's work | "Coloured Figures of the Birds of the British Islands" | and 65 [69] photographic illustrations | by Richard Kearton [by E. L. Turner, R. Kearton] | and others | Second impression [*Impression not noted*] | London | Frederick Warne & Co. Ltd. | and New York | (All rights reserved) [1920].

2 vols. cap 8vo (4½x6¼). Vol. I, pp. I-VII+1, 1-376, pll. 1-159 (96 col.; by A. Thorburn, J. G. Keulemans and J. Smit). Vol. II, pp. I-VII+1, 1-376, pll. 1-159 (96 col.; by A. Thorburn and J. G. Keulemans). London.

A popular account of the habits and distribution of British birds, well illustrated with colored portraits of the birds and their eggs, and photographs of the birds and their nests in life.

Coxe, R. C.

1815-22. See Hunt, John, **British Ornithology.**

Crane, E. H.

1896. See World's Congress on Ornithology, **Papers presented to the—.**

Crawshay, Richard.

1907. The | birds | of | Tierra del Fuego | by | Richard Crawshay | Captain | Reserve of Officers: late Inniskilling Dragoons | London | Bernard Quaritch | 1907.

1 vol. foliopost 4to, pp. I-XL, 1-158, 44 pll. (21 col.; by J. G. Keulemans), 1 map (col.), 1 text-cut. London.

An account of the species of birds observed and collected in Tierra del Fuego by the author, with quotations from the works of other investigators and with some synonymies, notes on habitat and descriptions of the colors of the soft parts of the specimens taken. The book is well illustrated with colored figures of the species and photogravures of scenery.

Crichton, Andrew.

1834. See Jardine, William, **The Natural History of Gallinaceous Birds.**

1835. See Selby, Prideaux John, [**The Natural History of Pigeons**].

1837. See Swainson, William, **The Natural History of the Birds of Western Africa.**

1844-64? See Swainson, William, **The Natural History of the Birds of Western Africa.**

1844-64? See Jardine, William, **The Natural History of Gallinaceous Birds.**

1844-64? See Selby, Prideaux John, **The Natural History of Pigeons**

Cunningham, Robert Oliver.

1871. Notes on | the natural history | of the | Strait of Magellan | and west coast of Patagonia | made during the voyage of H.M.S. "Nassau" | in the years 1866, 67, 68, & 69 | by | Robert O. Cunningham, | M.D., F.L.S., etc. | naturalist to the expedition | with map and illustrations | Edinburgh | Edmonston and Douglas | 1871 | All rights reserved.

1 vol. post 8vo., pp. I-XVI, 1 l., pp. 1-517, 21 pll. (5 tinted), 1 map. Edinburgh.

A narrative of a voyage of nearly three years' duration with special reference to the natural history of the regions visited. Many of the observations and three of the plates are of ornithological interest.

Curaçoa, Jottings during the Cruise of—.

1873. See Brenchley, Julius L.

Cuvier, Georges Léopold Chrétien Frédéric Dagobert. (Schinz, Heinrich Rudolph.)

1821-25. **Das Thierreich** | eingetheilt | nach dem Bau der Thiere | als | Grundlage ihrer Naturgeschichte | und der vergleichenden | Anatomie | von | dem Herrn Ritter von Cuvier | Staatsrath von Frankreich | und | beständiger Secretär der Academie der Wissenschaften U.S.W. | Aus dem Französischen frey übersetzt | und mit vielen Zusätzen versehen | von | H. R. Schinz, med. Dr. | Secretär [Mitglied (*Vol. IV.*)] der naturforschenden Gesellschaft [*etc., 2 lines.*]. | Erster [-Vierter] Band. | Säugethiere und Vögel [Reptilien, Fische, Weichthiere, | Ringelwürmer (*Vol. II.*); Krebse, Spinnen, Insekten (*Vol. III.*); Zoophyten (*Vol. IV.*)]. | Stuttgart und Tübingen, | in der J. G. Cotta'schen Buchhandlung. | 1821 [1822; 1823; 1825].

4 vols. crown 8vo. Vol. I, pp. I-XXXVIII, 1-894. Vol. II, pp. I-XVI, 1-835. Vol. III, pp. I-XVIII, 1-932, 1 l. (errata). Vol. IV, pp. I-XIII+1, 1-793. Stuttgart.

A German translation of Cuvier's "Règne Animal" (Cf. ed. 1829-30.), edited by Schinz with numerous annotations by the editor. The general discussion of the birds occupies pp. 438-868 and 889 of Vol. I. In Vol. IV, pp. 512-555, Schinz adds descriptions and comments on various species and genera, as an appendix to the earlier text. In Vol. V, also, pp. 562-570, is the ornithological portion of a comparative table showing the genera of Linné (1788) and the present work; a bibliography occupies pp. 635-767 of which 635-658 are strictly ornithological.

In at least one instance, Schinz presents a new name in ornithology. On p. 782 of Vol. I, *Tringa pygmaea* is described and accredited to Brehm. Brehm, however, did not publish his description until the following year (Beiträge zur Vogelkunde, **3**, p. 355, 1822) when he named it *schinzii*, as pointed out by Schinz in the present work (Vol. IV, pl. 529.)

Cuvier, Georges Léopold Chrétien Frédéric Dagobert.

1825-28. See Buffon, George Louis Leclerc, **Oeuvres Completes de Buffon**, Richard ed.

Cuvier, Georges Léopold Chrétien Frédéric Dagobert. (Griffith, Edward; Pidgeon, Edward; Gray, John Edward; Swainson, William.)

1827-35. The | **animal kingdom** | arranged in conformity with its | organization, | by the Baron Cuvier, | Member of the Institute of France, &c. &c. &c. | with | additional descriptions [supplementary additions to each order, (*Vols. X and XII-XV.*)] | of [*Line omitted (Vols. X and XII-XV.*).] | all the species hitherto named, and of [*Line omitted (Vols. X and XII-XV.*).] | many not before noticed, [*Line omitted (Vols. X and XII-XV.*).] | by | **Edward Griffith**, F.L.S., A.S., &c. [A.S., | Corresponding Member etc., *2 lines (Vols. VI-X and XII-XV.*); A.S., &c. | Corresponding Member etc. *1 line (Vol. XI.*)] | and others. | Volume the first [-tenth *and* twelfth-fifteenth; Supplementary volume on the fossils (*Vol. XI.*)]. | London: | printed for Geo. B. Whittaker [Whittaker, Treacher, and Co. (*Vols. VI-IX, XI and XIII-XV.*); Whittaker and Co. (*Vols. X and XI.*)]. | Ave-Maria-Lane. | MDCCCXXVII [MDCCCXXIX (*Vols. VI-VIII.*); MDCCCXXX (*Vol. XI.*); MDCCCXXXI (*Vol. IX.*); MD-CCCXXXII (*Vols. XIV-XV.*); MDCCCXXXIII (*Vol. XIII.*); MDCCCXXXIV (*Vols. X and XII.*)].

> The | Class Aves | arranged by the Baron Cuvier, | with | specific descriptions | by | Edward Griffith, F.L.S., A.S., &c. | and | Edward Pidgeon, Esq. | the additional species inserted in the text of Cuvier | by | John Edward Gray, Esq., F.G.S., &c. | Volume the first [second; third]. | London: | printed for Whittaker, Treacher, and Co. | Ave-Maria-Lane. | MDCCCXXXIX

A Classified | index and synopsis | of the | animal kingdom | arranged in conformity with its | organization, | by the Baron Cuvier, |Member of the Institute of France, &c. &c. &c. | with supplementary additions to each order, | by | Edward Griffith, F.R.S. S.A. &c. | and others. | London: | printed for Whittaker and Co. | Ave-Maria-Lane. | MDCCCXXXV.

16 vols. demy 4to. (Only the ornithological volumes and index collated here.) Vol. VI (Aves I), 4 pr. ll., pp. 1-548, 32 pll., 1 text-fig. Vol. VII (Aves II), 4 pr. ll., pp. 1-586, 60 pll. Vol. III (Aves III), 3 pr. ll., pp. 1-690, 168 pll. Index and Synopsis (=Vol. XVI?), 1 pr. l., pp. I-CXIX+1, 1-328. London.

This entire work is a translation into English of Cuvier's "Règne Animal" (Cf. ed. 2, 1829-30.), with supplementary additions and changes necessary to bring the subject matter up to date. The ornithological text is arranged in systematic sequence with the account of each order divided into two parts. The first part of each account consists of a careful translation of Cuvier's text supplemented by detailed descriptions of species which Cuvier mentioned only by name or not at all. These interpolations are indented on the page and are printed in small type to distinguish them from Cuvier's text, and appear to be the work of John Edward Gray.[1] The second part of the account of each order consists of a voluminous account of habits and peculiarities of numerous species, genera and larger groups of the order in question, and it appears probable that Pidgeon is responsible for this portion of the text.[2] New names occur on several of the plates to which reference is made in Pidgeon's text but not in Gray's [Cf. *Phytotoma bloxami*, pl. at p. 319, and *Regulus byronensis*, pl. at p. 42, both in Vol. VII (Aves II).]. The authorship of these names has been credited to Gray but perhaps should belong to Pidgeon. New names also occur in the systematic lists undoubtedly written by Gray.

At the close of Vol. VIII (Aves III), pp. 677-690, occurs "Observations on several of the genera and species of the order Passeres of Cuvier, by William Swainson," with page-references to the preceding volumes.

The index-volume presents first "A Tabular View of the Classification of Animals adopted by the Baron Cuvier; with specific examples." 'The ornithology of this synopsis occupies pp. XIII-XXV but is without evidence of authorship. Many of the vernacular generic names adopted by Cuvier are here given in Latin and a species (not necessarily the type) is cited for each. A bibliography closes the volume.

Sherborn (Index Animalium, Sect. 2, Pt. 1, p. XLI, 1922) states that the work was issued in parts (3 to each vol.) and that it was said to be a quarterly. Mathews (Birds of Australia, **7**, p. 475, 1919) gives a few dates supplied by Richmond, as follows. Pt. **14** (Aves I), advertised on Dec. 1, 1827; **15**, advertised on March 29, 1828 as to be published on March 31; (**16** including 18 pll.) publ.

---

[1] A statement on pp. 675 and 676 of Vol. VIII (Aves III) speaks of the systematic portions of the foregoing accounts as having been entrusted to a certain gentleman who was in possession of unusual opportunities for practical information on the subject. The first of the systematic accounts, that of the Accipitres in Vol. VI (Aves I), has a footnote on p. 86 signed by Gray who assumes authorship of the entire preceding list.

[2] All footnotes in this section of the text are signed by "E. P(idgeon)." if signed at all, and reference is sometimes made to J. E. Gray as to another person.

Aug. 6, 1828 (rev. Athenaeum); 19, publ. May 21, 1829 (rev. Athenaeum); 20 (including 16 pll.), advt. on Aug. 15, 1829; 21 (including 21 pll.), advertised on Oct. 31, 1829; the three volumes listed in Lit. Gazette for Jan. 23, 1830. The division of the volumes into parts is uncertain.

Titles transcribed above are the full title for the general work, the subtitle (or sectional title) for the birds, and the separate title for the index volume which does not carry the general title.

Cuvier, Georges Léopold Chrétien Frédéric Dagobert; and Latreille, Pierre André.

1829-30. **Le** | **règne animal** | distribué d'après son organisation, | pour servir de base | a l'histoire naturelle des animaux | et d'introduction a l'anatomie comparée. | Par M. le baron Cuvier, | Grand Officier de la Légion-d'Honneur, [*etc., 5 lines.*] | Avec figures dessinées d'après nature. | **Nouvelle édition,** revue et augmentée. | Tome I [-V.] [| Crustacés, arachnides et partie des insectes. | Par M. Latreille, | Chevalier de la Legion-d'Honneur *etc., 2 lines.* (*Vol. IV*); Suite et fin des insectes. | Par M. Latreille, | Chevalier *etc., 2 lines* (*Vol. V.*)] | Paris, | chez Déterville, libraire, | Rue Hautefeuille, No. 8; | et chez Crochard, libraire, | Cloître Saint-Benoit, No. 16. | 1829 [1829; 1830; 1829; 1829].

5 vols. demy 8vo. Vol. I, pp. J-XXXVJ, XXIX-XXXVIIJ, 1-584. Vol. II, pp. J-XV+1, 1-406. Vol. III, pp. J-XVJ, 1-504. Vol. IV, pp. J-XXVIJ+1, 1-584. Vol. V, pp. J-XXIV, 1-556, pll. I-XX (by Laurillard; III and IV of birds). Paris.

The second edition of Cuvier's work, succeeding the first edition of Dec. 7, 1816. (For this date cf. Mathews, Novit. Zool. **18**, p. 18, 1911.) Vols. IV and V (not ornithological) were prepared by Latreille at Cuvier's request. The ornithological matter is found in Vol. I, pp. 301-584, and on pll. III and IV in Vol. V. Mathews (Birds of Australia, Suppl. 4, p. 31, 1925) says that Vols. I, II, IV and V appeared before April 11, 1829, and Vol. III not until March 27, 1830; no data given.

Cuvier, Georges Léopold Chrétien Frédéric Dagobert (Voigt, Friedrich Siegfried.)

1831-43. **Das** | **Thierreich,** | geordnet nach seiner Organisation. | Als | Grundlage der Naturgeschichte der Thiere und Ein- | leitung in die vergleichende Anatomie. | Vom | Baron von Cuvier, | Grossofficier der Ehrenlegion [*etc., 6 lines.*]. | Nach der zweiten, vermehrten Ausgabe übersetzt und | durch Zusätze erweitert | von | F. S. Voigt, Hofrath [*etc., 5 lines* (*Vols. I-III.*); Geheimen Hofrath *etc., 5 lines* (*Vols. IV-VI.*).] | Erster [-Sechster] Band, | die Säugethiere und Vögel [die Reptilien und Fische (*Vol. II.*); die Mollusken (*Vol. III.*); die Anneliden, Crustaceen, Arachniden und

| die ungeflügelten Insekten (*Vol. IV.*); die eigentlichen Insekten (*Vol. V.*); die Zoophyten (*Vol. VI.*)] enthaltend. | Leipzig: | F. A. Brockhaus. | 1831 [1832; 1834; 1836; 1839; 1843].

6 vols. 8vo. Vol. I, pp. I-XLVIII, 1-975. Vol. II, pp. I-XVI, 1-539. Vol. III, pp. I-XVIII, 1-621. Vol. IV, pp. I-XIV, 1 l. (subtit.), pp. 1-516. Vol. V, pp. I-XXVII+1, 1-686, 1 l. (errata). Vol. VI, pp. I-XVI, 1-579. Leipzig.

Cuvier's "Règne Animal," second edition of 1829-30 (q.v.), translated into German by Voigt and published with notes and additions by the editor. The ornithological matter is contained in Vol. I, pp. 344-958 and 960-961. An annotated bibliography is given at the close of Vol. VI. New names occur in this edition which must be credited to Voigt.

Cuvier, Georges Léopold Chrétien Frédéric Dagobert. [D'Orbigny, Alcide.]

1838-43. Le | **règne animal** | distribué | d'après son organisation, | pour servir de base a l'histoire naturelle des animaux, | et d'introduction a l'anatomie comparée, | par | Georges Cuvier. | Edition | accompagnée de planches gravées, | représentant | les types de tous les genres, | les caractères distinctifs des divers groupes et les modifications de structure | sur lesquelles repose cette classification; | par | une réunion **de disciples** de Cuvier, | MM. Audouin, Deshayes, Alcide D'Orbigny, Doyère, Dugès, Duvernoy, Laurillard, | Milne Edwards, Roulin et Valenciennes. | Paris | Fortin, Masson et Cie, Libraires, | Successeurs de Crochard, | Place de l'École-de-Médecine, N. 1. | Imprimé chez Paul Renouard, | Rue Garancière, n. 5. > Les oiseaux. | avec un atlas, | par M. Alcide D'Orbigny. | Texte [Atlas.].

2 vols. demy 4to (7x10-½). Text, 2 pr. ll., pp. I-V+1, 1-370, 1 pl. (engr. tit.). Atlas, 2 pr. ll., 102 ll., pll. 1, 2, and 1-100 (=102 pll., 95 col.; by Verner, D'Orbigny and E. Travies). Paris.

These two volumes represent the ornithological portion of the "Disciples Edition" of Cuvier, published in 22 vols. from 1838-49. The volume of text appears to be a verbatim reprint of the ornithological part of Vol. I of the second edition of the "Règne Animal" (q.v., 1829-30). The "Atlas" with its explanatory descriptions of the plates contained therein, is probably to be accredited entirely to D'Orbigny. The plates are very fine for the period.

According to Engelmann, the ornithology of this series occupied 27 livraisons. Sherborn [Ann. Mag. Nat. Hist. (9), **10**, p. 555, 1922] records the exact dates on which the various parts were received at the British Museum. The dates may be summarized as follows. Pp. 1-66, 1838; 67-82, 1839; 83-90, 1844; ("obviously an imperfection supplied later"); 91-106, 1840; 107-114, 1841; 115-122, 1842 ("obviously an imperfection supplied later"); 123-138, 1841; 139-258, 1842; 259-370, 1843. ("As neither plates nor explanation to plates are dated, I presume they accompanied the text,"—Sherborn).

Cuvier, Georges Léopold Chrétien Frédéric Dagobert. (Blyth, Edward.)

1840.   Cuvier's | Animal Kingdom, | Arranged according to its Organization; | forming the basis for | a natural history of animals, | and | an introduction to comparative anatomy. |

Mammalia, birds, and reptiles,	The Molluscous animals,
by Edward Blyth.	by George Johnston, M.D.
The fishes and Radiata,	The articulated animals,
by Robert Mudie.	by J. O. Westwood, F.L.S.

Illustrated by three hundred engravings on wood. | London: | Wm. S. Orr and Co., Amen Corner, Paternoster Row. | MDCCCXL.

1 vol. 8vo, pp. I-VII+1, 1-670, text-figs. 1-209 (67-132 of birds), 1-142. London.

An English translation of the second edition of Cuvier's "Règne Animal," 1829-30 (q.v.), with additions supplied by various editors entrusted with the different sections.   Blyth is responsible for the ornithology which occupies pp. 154-267 and 67-132.   Oberholser (Proc. Biol. Soc. Wash., **35**, p. 79, 1922) cites the genus *Habia* from this edition.

Cuvier, Georges L. C. F. D.

1844-64?   See Selby, Prideaux John, [**The Natural History of Parrots**], reissue.

Dam, D. C. van.

1868.   See Pollen and Dam, **Recherches sur le Faune de Madagascar.**

Danford, C. G.

1889.   See Rudolf Franz Carl Josef, Crown Prince of Austria, **Notes on Sport and Ornithology.**

Darwin, Charles. (Gould, John; Eyton, Thomas Campbell; Gray, George Robert.)

1838-44.   The | zoology | of | the voyage of H.M.S. Beagle, | under the command of Captain Fitzroy, R.N., | during the years | 1832 to 1836. | Published with the approval of | The Lords Commissioners of Her Majesty's Treasury. | Edited and Superintended by | Charles Darwin, Esq. M.A. F.R.S. Sec. G.S. | Naturalist to the expedition. | Part I [-V]. | Fossil Mammalia: [Mammalia *(Pt. II.)*; Birds, *(Pt. III.)*; Fish. *(Pt. IV.)*; Reptiles, *(Pt. V.)*] | by | Richard Owen, Esq. F.R.S. [*etc., 2 lines. (Pt. I.)*; George R. Waterhouse, Esq. *etc., 2 lines (Pt. II.)*; John Gould, Esq. F.L.S. *(Pt. III.)*; the Rev. Leonard Jenyns, M.A., F.L.S., &c. *(Pt. IV.)*; Thomas Bell, Esq., F.R.S., F.L.S. *etc., 2 lines. (Pt. V.)*] | Lon-

don:|published by Smith, Elder and Co. 65, Cornhill.|MDCCCXL
[MDCCCXXXIX;MDCCCXLI;MDCCCXLII;MDCCCXLIII].

> [*Pt. III.*] Birds, | Described by | John Gould, Esq. F.L.S. |
with | a notice of their habits and ranges, | by Charles Darwin,
Esq. M.A. F.R.S. Sec. Geolog. Soc. | and with an anatomical ap-
pendix, | by T. C. Eyton, Esq, F.L.S. | Illustrated by numerous
coloured engravings.

5 pts. in 3 vols, medium 4to. Pt. I, tit., pp. I-IV (pref.), I-IV (conts.
and pll.), 1-111, pll. I-XXXII (3 fold.). Pt. II, 2 pr. ll., (subtit.
and tit.), pp. I-IX+1, 1-97+1, 1 l. (index), pll. 1-35 (32 col.),
4 text-figs. Pt. III, 4 pr. ll. (subtit., tit., list of pll. and errata),
pp. I-II, 1-156, 4 ll. [index], pll. 1-50 (col.; by J. Gould). Pt. IV,
pp. I-XV+1, 1-172, pll. 1-29. Pt. V, pp. I-VI, 1 l. (list of spp. and
pll.), 1-51, pll. 1-20. London.

The report on the zoological collections obtained by the members of the Beagle
expedition. As indicated above, Pt. III is devoted to the birds. The "descriptions of the new species and names of those already known" were supplied
by Gould, but owing to the incompleteness of his manuscript, Darwin was
obliged to emend and enlarge certain portions of this part of the text. Darwin
acknowledges the assistance of Gray in the matter of synonymy and general
arrangement, and gives frequent references to him in places where his assistance has been used. He also states ("Advertisement," pp. I and II) that Gould
is to be credited with all new descriptions of genera and species and he (Darwin)
with all accounts of habits and ranges, although he has not indicated the division of text throughout the work. The case proves to be not so simple as it
seems.

The generic names of some of the new species have been altered to accord with
generic changes proposed herein by Gray, as, for example, *Myiobius magnirostris*, p. 48, pl. VIII. Gould's manuscript name, *Tyrannula magnirostris*, is
cited in synonymy but appears on the plate, while the new combination is
given without authority other than that it follows Gray's proposal of *Myiobius*
for *Tyrannula* of Swainson. In this case, the authorship of the species may
remain with Gould since the plate has priority over the text (see below), but
Darwin appears to be properly the author of the new combination of names.
In the case of *Myiobius parvirostris*, described on the same page but not figured,
Darwin also becomes the author of the species.

In other cases, generic names have been altered in similar manner but the new
names are used, likewise, on the plates whence they cannot be quoted as of
Gould, since Gould never used the combination of terms, even in manuscript.
Such cases, including *Pachyramphus albescens*, p. 50, pl. XIV, must bear Darwin's name as author. In still other cases, as that of *Opetiorhynchus nigro-
fumosus*, p. 68, Gould's manuscript specific name is subordinated owing to
supposed synonymy, but it had already appeared on the plate (Pl. XX in
the example given) whence it may still be quoted as of Gould. Most of the
new species, fortunately, are described and accredited properly without
discrepancy.

Among other material and matter ascribed to Gray is a page of "Corrigenda" (on a leaf following the list of plates). This is easily overlooked but important since it contains several new names which may have priority over Gray's "List of the Genera of Birds," second edition, 1841 (q.v.), from which they are usually quoted. Eyton's anatomical "Appendix" occupies pp. 147-156. The entire report was issued in parts, of which the ornithology comprised Nos. 3, 6, 9, 11 and 15. The dates and contents of each were obtained by Sherborn from the publishers and given by him (Ann. Mag. Nat. Hist., (6) **20**, p. 483, 1897) as follows. Pt. 3, pp. 1-16, July 1838; Pt. 6, pp. 17-32, Jan. 1839; Pt. 9, pp. 33-56, July 1839; Pt. II, pp. 57-96, Nov. 1839; Pt. **15**, pp. 97-164, March 1841. Each part contained 10 plates, presumably issued in numerical sequence; a review of the first three numbers on birds (given in the Rev. Zool. for Nov. 1839, pp. 338-339) cites pll. 1-30. Sherborn does not cite the allocation of title-pages and other preliminary matter (including the page with Gray's "Corrigenda"); it is presumed that they appeared with Pt. 15.

Daubenton, (le jeune), Edme Louis.

1765-80. [Planches enluminées d'histoire naturelle].

See Buffon, George L.L., Histoire Naturelle des Oiseaux, 1770-86.

Daubenton, Louis Jean Marie.

1824-31. See Buffon, George L. L.; and Daubenton, **Oeuvres complètes de Buffon.**

1828-33. Idem.

David, Armand; and Oustalet, Emile.

1877. Les | oiseaux de la Chine | par | M. L'Abbe Armand David, M.C. | ancien missionnaire en Chine, | Correspondant de l'Institut, du Muséum d'Histoire Naturelle, etc. | et | M. E. Oustalet | Docteur ès Sciencés, Aide-Naturaliste au Muséum, | Membre Correspondant de la Société Zoologique de Londres | Avec un Atlas de 124 Planches, dessinées et lithographiées | par M. Arnoul et coloriées au pinceau [Atlas] | Paris | G. Masson, éditeur | Libraire de l'Académie de Médecine | Boulevard Saint-Germain, en face de l'École de Médecine | M DCCC LXXVII.

2 vols. royal 8vo. Text, 2 pr. ll., pp. I-VII+1, 1-573. Atlas, pp. I-VI+1 l., pll. 1-124 (col.). Paris.

A catalogue of the birds of China so far as known to the date of publication, with synonymies, descriptions and notes on distribution, variation and other relative matter. The plates are clear and well drawn.

Davie, Oliver.

1885. An | egg check list | of | North American birds | giving accurate descriptions of the color and size of the eggs, | and locations of the nests of the land and water | birds of North America. |

By Oliver Davie. | **First edition.** | Columbus, O. | Hann & Adair, | 1885.

1 vol. 8vo, pp. 1-77. Columbus.

The original edition of the book afterwards issued, in several editions, under the title of "Nests and Eggs of North American Birds" (Cf. ed. 4, 1889, and ed. 5, 1898). Pages 5-54 are occupied by the check list of species, classified according to Ridgway's "Nomenclature of North American Birds" (q.v., 1881) with both scientific and vernacular names and with brief descriptions of the eggs, position of the nests, and the distribution of the species. Pages 55-73 contain more or less detailed "Notes" on some of the species. The remainder of the book consists of "Brief Directions for Collecting and Preserving Birds' Eggs and Nests." The book is printed throughout on light cardboard, yellow in color.

Davie, Oliver.

1889. Nests and eggs | of | North American birds | by | Oliver Davie | The **fourth edition** | Introduction by J. Parker Norris. | Illustrations | by | Theodore Jasper, A.M., M.D. and W. Otto Emerson | Columbus | Hann & Adair | 1889.

1 vol. 8vo, 5 pr. ll., pp. 1-455+1, I-XII, pll. I-XIII. Columbus.

One of the earliest "classics" on North American oology, containing descriptions of the nests, eggs, and nesting habits of the birds of the country. The original edition (1885) was published under a slightly different title, " An Egg Check List of North American Birds" (q.v.), and in a much more abbreviated form. A fifth edition was issued in 1898 (q.v.).

Davie, Oliver.

1898. Nests and eggs | of | North American Birds | by | Oliver Davie | Author of "Methods in the Art of Taxidermy," Etc. | **The fifth edition** | Revised, augmented and illustrated | Part II. | Ornithological and oölogical collecting | (The preparation of skins, nests and eggs for the cabinet.) | Columbus: | The Landon Press. | 1898.

1 vol. 8vo, 4 pr. ll. (half-tit., tit., ded. and pref.), pp. 1-509+1, 1-18 (Pt. II), I-XXI (index), 7 ll. (advt.), frontisp. (by Fuertes, from The Osprey), 168 text-figs., pll. 1-5 (on num. pp.). Columbus.

A revised edition of the earlier work of the same title, 1889 (q.v.), brought up to date and illustrated by a profusion of figures of varying degrees of excellence or imperfection. These figures are numbered according to the "A. O. U. Check-List" number of the species which they represent.

There is a second impression of the fifth edition, published in Philadelphia by David Mackay, 1900(?). It differs in the title-page and possibly other slight particulars.

Davies, Hugh.

1790. See Pennant, Thomas, **Indian Zoology.**

1795. See Latham and Davies, **Faunula Indica.**

Davis, William J. (Byron, H. S. D.)

1907.   The | birds of Kent. | By | William J. Davis, | Author of
"Birds of the Dartford District," etc. | [*Vignette.*] | Dartford: |
Printed and Published by J. and W. Davis, | 31 & 33, Hythe
Street. | 1907. | London: | Elliot Stock, Paternoster Row. | [All
rights reserved.].

1 vol. crown 8vo, 5 pr. ll. (advt., half-tit., tit. and pref.), pp. 1-304,
1 l. (insert), 2 ll. (advt.), frontisp., 1 map (fold.), 1 text-fig. (decoration). Dartford and London.

An annotated list of the birds of the county with descriptions of the eggs and
nests of the various species and accounts of the local records and distribution
of each. Pp. 261-270 contain " A list of the birds observed in East Kent during
the past twenty years by Mr. H. S. D. Byron, St. Peter's, Thanet." The
unpaged leaf at pp. 260-261 contains " Appendix II." Pp. 299-304 are headed
"Memorandum" and are left blank.

Dawson, William Leon; and Jones, Lynds.

1903.   The birds of Ohio | A complete, scientific and | popular
description of the 320 species of birds | found in the state | by |
William Leon Dawson, A.M., B.D. | with introduction and analyt-
ical keys by | Lynds Jones, M.Sc. | Instructor in zoology in Ober-
lin College. | Illustrated by 80 plates in color-photography, and
more than 200 | original half-tones, showing the favorite haunts of
the | birds, flocking, feeding, nesting, etc., from photo- | graphs
taken by the author and others. | Sold only by subscription |
Columbus | The Wheaton Publishing Co. | 1903 | All rights
reserved.

2 vols. imperial 8vo. Vol. I., pp. I-XLVII+1, 1-368, pll. 1-41 (col.),
155 half-tones. Vol. II, 2 pr. ll., pp. 369-671, pll. 42-80 (col.), 57
half-tones. Columbus.

A popular account of the birds of the state, illustrated with photographs and colored plates from the "Birds and Nature" series.

Dawson, William Leon; and Bowles, John Hooper. (Jones, Lynds;
Brooks, Allan.)

1909.   The birds of Washington | A complete scientific and | popular
account of the 372 species of birds | found in the state | by | William
Leon Dawson, A.M., B.D., of Seattle | author of "The Birds of
Ohio" | assisted by | John Hooper Bowles, of Tacoma | Illustrated
by more than 300 original half-tones of birds in life, nests, | eggs,
and favorite haunts, from photographs by the | author and others. |
Together with 40 drawings in the text and a series of | full-page
color-plates. | By Allan Brooks | Original edition | printed only for

advance subscribers. | Volume I [II] | Seattle | The Occidental
Publishing Co. | 1909 | All rights reserved.

2 vols. imperial 8vo. Vol. I, 3 pr. ll., pp. I-XVI+3, 1-458, 8 pll.
(col.; by Allan Brooks), 168 half-tones. Vol. II, 3 pr. ll., pp.
I-III+3, 459-997, 4 pll. (col.; by Allan Brooks), 193 half-tones.
Seattle.

A popular account of the birds of the state of Washington, with descriptions,
scientific and common names, recognition marks, nesting data and copious
notes on habits. A supplementary chapter on "Analytical Keys" is by Lynds
Jones, and a "British Columbia Supplement with annotations by Allan Brooks"
follows. The present set forms copy No. 242 of the "Original Edition" of 350
copies. Many of the paragraphs are copied verbatim from the senior author's
"Birds of Ohio", 1903 (q.v.).

Dawson, William Leon.

1923. The Birds of California | A Complete, Scientific and | Popular
Account of the 580 Species and Subspecies of Birds | Found in the
State | By | William Leon Dawson | of Santa Barbara | Director
of the International Museum of Comparative Oölogy, Author of
"The Birds of Ohio" | and (with Mr. Bowles) of "The Birds of
Washington" | Illustrated by 30 Photogravures, 120 Full-page
Duotone Plates and More Than | 1100 Half-tone Cuts of Birds in
Life, Nests, Eggs, and | Favorite Haunts, from Photographs |
Chiefly by | Donald R. Dickey, Wright M. Pierce, Wm. L. Finley |
and the Author | Together with 44 Drawings in the Text and a
Series of | 110 Full-page Color Plates | Chiefly by | Major Allan
Brooks | Format De Luxe | Large Paper Edition | Complete in
Four Volumes | Volume One [-Four] | South Moulton Company|
San Diego, Los Angeles, San Francisco | 1923 | Sold Only by
Subscription. All Rights Reserved.

4 vols. royal 4to. Vol. I, 3 pr. ll., pp. I-XVII+1, 1-522, 62 pll. (39
col.,-37 by Allan Brooks, 1 by George Miksch Sutton and 1 photograph; 15 duotones and 8 photogravures), 252 text-figs. (halftones).
Vol. II, pp. I-XII, 1 l., pp. 523-1034, 73 pll. (34 col. by Brooks;
34 duotones and 5 photogravures), 284 text-figs. (halftones). Vol.
III, pp. I-XIV, 1 l., pp. 1035-1548, 62 pll. (15 col. by Brooks; 38
duotones and 9 photogravures), 340 text-figs. (halftones). Vol. IV,
pp. I-XIV, 1 l., pp. 1549-2121, 63 pll. (22 col.,-20 by Brooks, 1 by
Louis Agassiz Fuertes and 1 photograph; 33 duotones and 8 photogravures), 272 text-figs. (halftones). Los Angeles.

A popular description of the birds of California and their habits, copiously illustrated with many fine color-plates and photographs from life. Published in a
variety of editions. The present copy is number sixty-seven of the "Large
Paper Edition, De Luxe," autographed by the author.

Deane, Ruthven.

1907. See Mershon, W. B., **The Passenger Pigeon.**

Dearborn, Ned.

1898. A | preliminary list | of the | birds | of | Belknap and Merrimack Counties | **New Hampshire** | with notes | by | Ned Dearborn | Presented to the faculty of the New Hampshire College | of Agriculture and the Mechanic Arts as a thesis | for the degree of Master of Science, | June, 1898 | Durham | New Hampshire College | 1898.

1 vol. post 8vo, pp. 1-34. Durham.

An annotated list of species based on personal observations and records by other observers. The paper is bound with several other contributions by the same author.

Dearborn, Ned.

1903. See Weed, Clarence M.; and Dearborn, **Birds in their Relations to Man.**

Decken, Carl Claus von der. (Finsch, Otto; Hartlaub, Gustav.)

1870. > Baron Carl Claus von der Decken's | **Reisen in Ost-Afrika** | in den Jahren 1859-1865. | Herausgegeben im Auftrage der Mutter des Reisenden, | Fürstin Adelheid von Pless. | Wissenschaftlicher Theil. | Vierter Band. | **Die Vögel Ost-Afrikas.** | Leipzig und Heidelberg. | C. F. Winter'sche Verlagshandlung. | 1870. > Baron Carl Claus von der Decken's | Reisen in Ost-Afrika. | Vierter Band: | Die Vögel Ost-Afrikas | von | Dr. O. Finsch und Dr. G. Hartlaub. | Mit 11 Tafeln in Buntdruck. N. d. Natur gez. von O. Finsch. | Leipzig und Heidelberg. | C. F. Winter'sche Verlagshandlung. | 1870.

1 vol. superroyal 8vo, pp. I-VIII, 1 l., pp. 1-897+1, frontisp. (col.), pll. I-X (col.; by O. Finsch), 1 pl. (metric and inch scale). Leipzig and Heidelberg.

This work forms the fourth and last volume of the complete work (4 volumes in 6) and comprises a monograph of all of the birds of East Africa by Finsch and Hartlaub. A report discussing only those birds collected by Baron von der Decken was published the year previously in Section 1 of Volume III of the same work, under the authorship of J. Cabanis. The present account is considerably more comprehensive. The illustrations are lithographed in colors.

Degland, Come Daguet.

1849. Ornithologie | Européenne, | ou | catalogue analytique et raisonné | des | oiseaux observés en Europe, | Par C.-D. Degland, | Docteur en médecine [*etc.*, *4 lines.*]. | Tome premier [deuxième]. |

Se trouve: | A Paris, A Lille, | Libraire Encyclopédique de Roret, chez L. Danel, imprimeur, | Rue Hautefeuille, 10. Grande-Place. | MDCCCXLIX.

2 vols. post 8vo. Vol. I, 4 pr. ll., pp. 1-632. Vol. II, 1 pr. l., pp. 1-540. Paris and Lille.

Diagnoses and descriptions of the apecies and higher groups of the birds of Europe with synonymies and various pertinent observations. The work is full of errors and was criticised in detail by Bonaparte in his "Revue Critique de de l'Ornithologie Européenne de M. le Docteur Degland (de Lille)," 1850 (q.v.). A second edition was published by Z. Gerbe after the death of Degland (Cf. Degland and Gerbe, 1867.). The present copy is from the library of H. B. Tristram.

Degland, Come Daguet; and Gerbe, Z.

1867. Ornithologie | Européenne | ou | catalogue descriptif, analy- tique et raisonné | des | oiseaux observés en Europe | Deuxième edition, entièrement refondue | par | C. D. Degland Z. Gerbe | Membre de la Société impériale des Sciences, [*etc., 3 lines.*] Pré-parateur du Cours d'Embryogénie comparée [*etc., 3 lines.*]. | Tome I [II] | Paris | J. B. Baillière et Fils, | Libraires de l'Académie Impériale de Médecine, | 19, rue Hautefeuille, pres le boulevard Saint-Germain | Londres Madrid New-York | Hippolyte Baillière C. Bailly-Baillière Baillière Brothers | 1867 | Tous droits résérves.

2 vols. post 8vo. Vol. I, pp. I-XXX (I and II missing), 1-610. Vol. II, pp. I-XV+1, 1-637. Paris.

M. Degland, at the time of his death, was preparing a supplement to his earlier work of the same title (q.v., 1849). The manuscript was edited by Gerbe who combined it with the earlier work and published it in the form of a new edition of the complete treatise, under joint authorship, although his own rôle was principally that of editor. Some of the errors of the first edition are corrected but others are unnoticed. A so-called supplement was published in 1912 by E. L. Trouessart, under the title of "Catalogue des Oiseaux d'Europe" (q.v.).

DeKay, James Ellsworth.

1844. > Zoology | of | **New-York,** | or the | New-York fauna; | comprising detailed descriptions of all the animals hitherto ob-served within the | state of New-York, with brief notices of those occasionally found near | its borders, and accompanied by appro-priate illustrations. | By James E. De Kay. | Part II. **Birds.** | Albany: | Printed by Carroll and Cook, printers to the Assembly. | 1844.

1 vol. in 2 vols., medium 4to, engr. title-p., pp. III-XII, 1-380, 1 l., pll. 1-141 (col.; by J. W. Hill). Albany.

A systematic account of the birds of the region, with descriptions, synonymies and annotations of the species, and diagnoses of the genera and higher groups. The Natural History of the State of New York was published in 20 volumes, of which the five volumes of Zoology were written by DeKay. The present work forms Part II of the zoological series. Only 300 copies were issued with the plates colored. The Edward E. Ayer Library also contains a set of original paintings by J. W. Hill including 76 of the illustrations of the above volume. See Hill, J. W., [Illustrations for DeKays' "Zoology of New York"].

Delacour, Jean; and Jabouille, Pierre.

1925. Archives d'histoire naturelle | publiées par la | Société Nationale d'Acclimatation de France | I | **Recherches ornithologiques** | **dans la Province de Quangtri** | (Centre Annam) | et quelques autres régions de l'Indochine Française | par | Jean Delacour | Président de la Section d'Ornithologie de la Société Nationale d'Acclimation [*etc., 7 lines.*] | et | Pierre Jabouille | Administrateur de 1 re classe des Services Civils de l'Indochine [*etc., 4 lines.*] | Paris | Au Siège de la Société: 198, Boulevard Saint-Germain (VIIe) | 1925.

1 vol. royal 8vo, 2 pr. ll. (half-tit. and tit.), pp. I-XII, 1-197, pll. I-XXVII+XI bis (17 of birds; 9 col.; by Delacour, Grönvold, A. Millot, etc.), 1 text-fig. (reduction of Pl. XVI). Paris.

A detailed report on the birds collected in the Province of Quangtri, Central Annam, French Indo China, by the authors. The new species (although noted herein as "sp. nov.," etc.) were described previously in the Bull. Brit. Orn. Club, XLV, pp. 28-35, 1924. An account of the collection was also published in the Ibis, January 1925, pp. 209-260, pll. VI and VII (=XI bis and XXVI of the present work), and text-figs. 8 and 9 (=pll. II and III of the present work).

The brochure appears to be the first number of a projected series of papers. As the style and extent of the remainder are uncertain, I have catalogued this one under the individual, instead of collective, title.

Delamarre de Monchaux, Le Comte.

1923. Encyclopédie pratique | du | naturaliste | IX. | > Les oiseaux | **Les oiseaux** | **chanteurs** | principales espèces d'Europe | par | Le Comte Delamarre de Monchaux | Correspondant de l'Académie d'Agriculture [*etc., 4 lines.*] | 96 planches [*Design.*] 174 figures | coloriées noires | Paul Lechevalier | éditeur | 12. Rue de Tournon | Paris Vie | 1923.

1 vol. 16mo, pp. I-LXIII+1, 1 p. (unnum.)+pp. 1-106+1, pll. 1-96 (col.; by Walter Heubach; on 48 ll.), pll. (=text-cuts) I-XIX, 1 text-fig. (unnum.). Paris.

An introduction to the principal song-birds of Europe, with general introductory chapters and an account of each species opposite a colored plate of the same.

Fourteen volumes of the "Encyclopédie" are listed on p. II, of which two are zoological, the remainder botanical; the present is the only volume on birds.

Denne, David.

1896. See Wintle, Ernest D., **The Birds of Montreal.**

Denton, Sherman F.

1889. Incidents | of a | collector's rambles | in | Australia, New Zealand, and | New Guinea | by | Sherman F. Denton | Artist to the U. S. Fish Commission, Washington, D. C. | With Illustrations by the Author | Boston 1889 | Lee and Shepard publishers | 10 Milk Street next "The Old South Meeting House" | New York Chas. T. Dillingham | 718 and 720 Broadway.

1 vol. post 8vo, pp. I-IX+1, 1-272, frontisp., 14 pll. (on num. pp.), 40 text-figs. Boston.

A popular narrative of the author's experiences on a collecting trip to Australia and neighboring countries in 1881 and 1882. Notes on the habits of some of the birds encountered are included in the account and 10 of the illustrations are of birds.

Descourtilz, J. Théodore.

1854-56? **Ornithologie brésilienne** | ou | histoire des oiseaux du Brésil, | remarquables par leur plumage, leur chant ou leurs habitudes. | Par | le Dr. J. T. Descourtilz, | Membre de la Société Linnéenne de Paris et de la Société Auxiliare de l'Industrie | de Rio de Janeiro. | [*Blazon.*] | Rio de Janeiro: | Éditeur, Thomas Reeves.

1 vol. columbier folio, pp. 1-42, pll. 1-48 (col.). Rio de Janeiro.

This work contains descriptions and figures of 164 species of Brazilian birds, including 15 new species and a new genus. According to Carus and Engelmann, and Coues, it was issued in four parts under dates of 1854-56, but the reverse of the title-page is lettered, "Londres:| de l'imprimerie de Joseph Masters et Cie., | Rue d'Aldersgate, 1852." This title-page appeared in Pt. I. A separate copy of Pt. I is at hand, bound in original wrappers (boards) containing pp. 1-14 and pll. 1-12; the cover-title agrees with the title transcribed above to which is added the dedication (also on p. 3) and the words, "Part I." The examination of the complete work, with respect to slight peculiarities of typography and arrangement, reveals rather conclusively that Pt. II probably contained pp. 15-22 and pll. 13-24; Pt. III, pp. 23-32 and pll. 25-36; Pt. IV, pp. 33-42 and pll. 37-48, but no dates are available for any part. Carus and Engelmann also cite an edition in English, without date.

Desfontaines, René Louiche. (Newton, Alfred, *ed.*)

1880. The Willughby Society. | Desfontaines's | **Mémoire** | sur | **quelques nouvelles espèces d'oiseaux** | **des côtes de Barbarie.** |

[*Vignette.*] | Edited by | Alfred Newton, M.A., F.R.S., etc. | London: MDCCCLXXX.

1 vol. demy 4to, pp. I-IV, "tit. (of periodical), pp. 496-505+1, pll. X-XVI (by Fossier)" 2 ll. (advt.). London.

A facsimile reprint of the pages of the "Histoire del'Académie Royale des Sciences" for 1789, in which appeared Desfontaines's "Mémoire," and of the plates accompanying the same. The reprint was issued by the Willughby Society (q.v.).

Deslongchamps, Eugene.

See Eudes-Deslongchamps.

Desmarest, Anselme-Gaëtan.

1805-(1807). Histoire naturelle | des | tangaras, | des manakins et des todiers, | par Anselme-Gaëtan Desmarest; | Avec figures imprimées en couleur, d'après les dessins de Mademoiselle | Pauline de Courcelles, élève de Barraband. | Paris, | Garnery, rue de Seine; | Delachaussée, rue du Temple, No. 37 | XIII.=1805.

1 vol. superroyal folio, 3 pr. ll., pp. 1-8, 34 ll., pp. 1-12, 24 ll., 72 pll. (col.). Paris.

The work was published in 12 livraisons, the contents of which may be ascertained from the "Avis servant de table" which gives the final arrangement of plates in the volume and the livraisons in which plates and text appeared. Sherborn (Index Animalium, Sect. 2, Pt. 1, p. XLIII, 1922) cites Livrs. 1-4, 1805; 5-10, 1806 and 11-12, 1807. The present copy, bound in boards, has on the front cover the date "XIV.=1805" with other slight alterations in the wording of the title. This cover may have been one of the wrappers of the work as issued. Englemann's citation quotes two volumes, 1805, (49 and 23 plates, duplicated—colored and uncolored), with a portrait of the author. I can find no other reference to the portrait in any bibliographies.

The present copy seems to have belonged to Lorenz von Oken whose surname is inscribed on the inside of the cover. A second copy differs in having the index to the plates bound as a fourth preliminary leaf instead of at the close of the volume.

Desmarest, Anselme-Gaëtan.

1825-31. See Buffon, George L. L.; and Daubenton, **Oeuvres complètes de Buffon,** 1824-31.

1828-33. Idem, 1828-33.

Des Murs, Marc Athanese Parfait Oeillet.

1842. Ova | avium plurimarum | ab O. Des Murs, | e Societate Cuvieriana, Parisiis, collecta.

1 vol. post 8vo, pp. 1-24. Paris.

A simple list of avian species under Latin names, with the general distribution indicated for most of them. The date is given on p. 3. It appears to be a catalogue of the species represented in an oological collection of the author's, but there is no explanatory text of any kind. The title is listed by Engelmann.

Des Murs, Marc Athanese Parfait Oeillet.

1845-49. Iconographie ornithologique | Nouveau recueil général | de planches peintes | d'oiseaux, | Pour servir de Suite et de Complément aux Planches Enluminées de Buffon, | Éditions in-folio et in-4to de l'Imprimerie Royale, 1770, | et aux planches coloriées | de MM. Temminck et Laugier de Chartrouse, | mêmes formats, | accompagné d'un texte raisonné, critique et descriptif, | publié | par O. Des Murs, | membre de plusieurs sociétés savantes. | Figures dessinées et peintes par Oudard, Peintre attaché au Muséum d'Histoire naturelle de Paris. | Première partie. | A Paris, | chez Friedrich Klincksieck, libraire, rue de Lille, No 11; | et a l'étranger, | A Londres, chez Williams et Norgate. A Vienne, chez Braumüller, Seidel, libraires de la Cour I. et R. | A Berlin, chez A. Hirschwald. A Saint-Pétersbourg, chez Bellizard et Cie. | 1849.

1 vol. demy folio, 2 pr. ll., pp. 1-11+1, 146 ll., pll. 1-72 (col.; 1-24 by Alphonse Prévost, 25-72 by Oudart). Paris.

Published in 12 livraisons of 6 plates each with corresponding text. The text of each species is separately dated but as these dates are not consecutive throughout they probably represent the completion of the manuscript and not the dates of issue. Sherborn (Index Animaliam, Sect. 2, Pt. 1, p. XLIII, 1922) gives the following dates. Livr. 1, post Aug. 1845; 2, Febr. 1846; 3, July 1846; 4-6, Febr. 1847; 7, post Jan. 1847; 8, post March 1847; 9, post July 1847; 10 post Sept. 1847; 11, post Febr. 1848, 12, post Dec. 1848 = 1849.

The plates are very finely executed. Errors in the numbering are as follows; 51 is num. 53; 53,-51; 69,-70; 70,-71; 71,-68; The work forms a supplement to Buffon's "Histoire Naturelle des Oiseaux," 1770-86 (q. v.), and the "Nouveau Recueil de Planches Coloriées" of Temminck and Laugier, 1820-38 (q.v.).

Des Murs, Marc Athanese Parfait Oeillet.

1846-49. See Petit-Thouars, **Voyage Autour du Monde sur le Frégate La Vénus,** 1846-55.

Des Murs, Marc Athanese Parfait Oeillet.

1847-54. See Gay, Claudio, **Historia Fisica y Politica de Chile,** Zoologia, 1844-54.

Des Murs, Marc Athanese Parfait Oeillet.

1852-54. See Chenu, Jean Charles, **Encyclopédie d'Histoire Naturelle.**

Des Murs, Marc Athanese Parfait Oeillet.

1856. See Castelnau, Francis de, **Expédition dans la Parties Centrales de l'Amérique du Sud.**

Des Murs, Marc Athanese Parfait Oeillet.

1886. Musée ornithologique | illustré | Description | des oiseaux
d'Europe | leurs œufs et de leurs nids | Tome premier [deuxième;
troisième | 1re Partie: Texte, pages 1 à 200.-Planches 1 à 94;
troisième | 2e Partie: Texte, pages 201 à fin.-Planches 95 à 150;
quatrième] | Les Oiseaux d'Eau ou Palmipèdes [de Rivage et les
Coureurs (*Vol. II.*); des Champs et des Bois ou Passereaux (*Vol.
III, Pts. 1 and 2.*); de Proie ou Rapaces (*Vol. IV.*)] | [*Vig-
nette.*] | Paris | J. Rothschild, Éditeur | 13, Rue des Saints-Pères,
13 | Droits réservés.

> Les oiseaux d'eau [Les oiseaux (*Vols. II-IV.*) | de rivage et de
terre (*Vol. II.*); des champs et des bois (*Vol. III.*); de proie
(*Vol. IV.*)] | Classification-Synonymie-Description [Classification-
Synonymie-Description-Mœurs (*Vols. II-III.*)] Mœurs [(*Vols. I
and IV.*); *line omitted* (*Vols. II-III.*)] | Iconographie | et |
Histoire Naturelle des Palmipèdes [Échassiers (*Vol. II.*); Pas-
sereaux (*Vol. III.*); Rapaces (*Vol. IV.*)] | par | O. Des Murs |
Membre de la Société royale [*etc., 3 lines.*)] Avec 80 [65; 150;
50] chromotypographies | [*Design and monogram.*] | Paris | J.
Rothschild. Éditeur | 13, Rue des Saints-Pères, 13 | 1886 [1887
(*Vols. III and IV.*)].

4 vols. in 5, demy 4to. Vol. I, pp. I-XII, 1-200, pll. 1-80 (col.).
Vol. II, pp. I-XI+1, 1-176, pll. 1-65 (col.). Vol. III, Pt. 1, pp.
I-XV+1, 1-200, pll. 1-94 (col.). Vol. III, Pt. 2, 2 pr. ll. (tit. and
subtit.), pp. 201-315, pll. 95-150 (col.). Vol. IV, pp. I-VIII,
1-214, pll. 1-50 (col.). Paris.

A descriptive catalogue of the birds of Europe, of which the reviewer in the Ibis,
1886, p. 193, had little to say in commendation. The colored plates of birds,
nests and eggs are largely from F. O. Morris's "A History of British Birds,"
1870 (q.v.) and "A Natural History of the Nests and Eggs of British Birds,"
1866-67 (q.v.), and from Bree's "A history of the Birds of Europe not observed
in the British Isles," 1859-63 (q.v.).

Despott, Giuseppi.

1915. A list | of the | birds of Malta | compiled for the | University
Museum of Natural History | by | Gius. Despott, | Curator of the
Museum. | Malta | Government Printing Office. | 1915.

1 vol. post 8vo, 2 pr. ll. (tit., pref.), pp. 1-39. Malta.

An annotated list of 340 species, giving, for each, the English, Italian and Maltese
vernacular names, the status of the species as a Maltese bird and an indication
if specimens are present in the University Museum. The present copy is
bound with several other papers on the same subject by Despott.

Dewar, Douglas.

1909. Birds of | the plains | by Douglas Dewar, F.Z.S., I.C.S. | with sixteen illustrations | from photographs of living birds | by Captain F. D. S. Fayrer, I.M.S. | London: John Lane The Bodley Head | New York: John Lane Company MCMIX.

1 vol. 8vo, pp. I-VIII, 2 ll. (list of illustrs. and half-tit.), pp. 1-257, 11 ll. (advt.), 16 pll. London.

Accounts of a number of the birds of the plains of India, written in popular form. An appendix contains a list of British birds found in India and a glossary of Indian words used in the text.

Dewar, Douglas.

1915. Birds of the | Indian hills | by Douglas Dewar | A companion volume to | the bird volumes of "The Fauna of British India" | London: John Lane, The Bodley Head | New York: John Lane Company | Toronto: Bell & Cockburn MCMXV.

1 vol. crown 8vo, pp. 1-263+1. London.

A popular introduction to the common birds of the Himalayas, the Nilgiris and the Palni Hills of India. Some of the matter is reprinted from various periodicals and newspapers. The bird volumes of "The Fauna of British India" to which reference is made in the title, are those by Oates and Blanford, 1889-98 (q. v.).

Dewar, Douglas.

1923. Indian birds | being a key to the common | birds of the plains of India | by Douglas Dewar | A companion volume to | the bird volumes of "The | Fauna of British India" & | Jerdon's "Birds of India" | London | John Lane The Bodley Head Limited.

1 vol. crown 8vo, pp. 1-230, 1 l. (advt.). London.

A popular work for the identification, in the field, of common birds of the plains of India, exclusive of the game birds. Pages 23-85 contain a series of keys in which the birds are classified according to structural peculiarities, color and habits. A list of Hindustani names of various species is prefixed. The remainder of the book contains a descriptive list with references to other publications which discuss each of the species in question. The first edition was issued in 1910; the revised edition, of which this is a later reprint, in 1920.

Dewar, John M.

1924. The bird as a diver | a contribution to the natural | history of diving birds | by | John M. Dewar, M.D. | London | H. F. & G. Witherby | 326 High Holborn, W.C. | 1924.

1 vol. post 8vo, pp. I-XII, 1-173. London.

A detailed study of the various factors influencing and accompanying the diving habit in birds which practise this action. Twenty-three species of diving birds and nearly six thousand dives were studied in the course of the investigation.

Diener, Carl. (Lambrecht, Koloman.)

1921. > **Fossilium Catalogus** | 1: Animalia. | Editus a | C. Diener.|
Pars 12: | K. Lambrecht | **Aves.** | [*Design.*] | W. Junk | Berlin
W. 15. | 1921.

1 vol. superroyal 8vo, 2 pr. ll. (tit. and pref.), pp. 1-104. Berlin.
March 25, 1921.

A catalogue of all fossil birds, giving bibliographic references and synonyms and
noting the specimens on which the various species were based. It is marked
as Pt. 12 of Section 1 of the complete work which, apparently, is planned to
embrace all fossils. The explicit date is from the original wrapper.

Dietrich, Friedrich.

1912. **Die Vogelwelt** | **in der Umgebung von** | **Hamburg** | Eine
Anleitung zu ornithologischen Beobachtungen | von | Dr. Fr.
Dietrich | [*Trade-mark.*] | Hamburg 1912 | Verlag von C. Boysen.

1 vol. crown 8vo, pp. I-V+1, 1 l., pp. 1-116. Hamburg.

A series of essays on the bird-life of the neighborhood of Hamburg, written in the
form of narratives of field-journeys. At the close of the foregoing, are given
a check-list of the 130 species of birds treated in the essays, several tables for
the determination of some of the species according to appearance, song and
nidification, a migration-table, a breeding calendar and a short bibliography.

Diggles, Silvester.

1877. **Companion** | **to** | **Gould's Handbook;** | or, | synopsis | of
the | birds of Australia. | Containing | nearly one-third of the
whole, or about 220 examples, | for the most part | From the
Original Drawings. | By Silvester Diggles. | Vol. I [II]. | In this
volume the following genera are treated of - | eagles, falcons, and
hawks, | owls, goat-suckers, and swallows, | kingfishers and
shrikes, | fly-catchers, robins, and wrens, | larks, finches, and
thrushes, | bower birds, and crows, | honey-eaters, cuckoos, and
creepers, | etc., etc. [parrots, | pigeons and quails, | mound
builders, | waders, | swimmers, | etc., etc.] | Brisbane: | Printed
by Thorne & Greenwell, Edward Street. | MDCCCLXXVII.

2 vols. imperial 4to. Vol. I, pp. I-IX+1, 61 ll., 60 pll. (col.). Vol. II,
pp. I-VI, 65 ll., 63 pll. (col.). Brisbane. (1866-77.)

Originally published in parts under the title, "The Ornithology of Australia,"
from 1866-70, with 126 plates. Later, after the work was brought to a close,
the matter was indexed, the title changed, and the book issued as collated
above. Three plates were omitted from the later issue and noted in the indices, "description only," although they had been published in the original.
This may have been due to the necessity for redrawing the first six parts during
the course of publishing the original, in order to permit an increase in the circulation. The missing plates and errors in the indices of plates are as follows,—

11A not republished; 43A not distinguished from 43; 75A listed as 75 and not republished, while 75 is not listed; 96A listed and republished but not numbered; 106 not republished. The original dates and numbers are given by Mathews, Austral Avian Record 3, pp. 102-108, 1915.

Dillwyn, Lewis Llewellyn.

1855. See Motley, James; and Dillwyn, **Contributions to the Natural History of Labuan.**

Dionne, Charles Eusebe.

1883. Les | oiseaux du Canada | par | C.-E. Dionne | Curateur du Musée Zoologique de l'Université Laval | [*Vignette.*] | Québec | Imprimerie de P.-G. Delisle | 1883.

1 vol. 12mo, pp. I-XLIII+1, 1-284+1 l., text-figs. 1-35. Quebec.

An annotated list of the birds of Canada with keys to the genera and short descriptions of the species and families. The fly-leaf bears, "Elliott Coues from the author, June 1883", and the letter which accompanied the presentation is attached to the reverse. The original wrapper is bound with the volume. It bears the same title, a different vignette and the substitution of the word "typographie" for "imprimerie."

Dionne, Charles Eusebe.

1889. Catalogue | des | oiseaux | de la Province de Quebec | avec des notes sur leur distribution geographique | par | C.-E. Dionne | [*Vignette.*] | Québec | Des presses à vapeur de J. Dussault, 1 Port Dauphin | 1889.

1 vol. 8vo, pp. 1-119+1. Quebec.

A list of species with some synonymies and notes on distribution.

Dionne, Charles Eusebe.

1906. Les | oiseaux | de la | Province de Quebec | par | C.-E. Dionne | Maître-ès-Arts, [*etc.*, 6 *lines.*]. | [*Vignette.*] | Québec | Dussault & Proulx | 1906.

1 vol. 8vo, pp. I-VIII, 1-414, 1 l. (errata), (orig. wrappers), pll. I-VIII (after various artists), text-figs. 1-21, various decorations. Quebec.

A descriptive catalogue of the birds of the province. The preface is dated September, 1906.

Dixon, Charles.

1883. See Seebohm, Henry, **A History of British Birds,** 1882-85.

Dixon, Charles.

1888. Our rarer birds | being | studies in ornithology & oology | by | Charles Dixon | author of | 'Rural Bird-Life,' [*etc.*, 2 *lines.*] | with twenty illustrations by Charles Whymper | and a frontispiece by

J. G. Keulemans | [*Seal.*] | London | Richard Bentley & Son, New Burlington Street | Publishers in Ordinary to Her Majesty the Queen | 1888.

1 vol. post 8vo, pp. I-XIV, 1 l., pp. 1-373+1, 1 l. (advt.), frontisp., 20 text-cuts.

A popular account of the habits of some of the rarer British birds.

Dixon, Charles.

1893. **Jottings about birds** | By Charles Dixon | With Coloured Frontispiece by J. Smit | London: Chapman and Hall, Ld. | 1893 | [All rights reserved].

1 vol. demy 8vo, pp. I-VI, 1 l., pp. 1-239, frontisp. (col.). London.

Miscellaneous notes about birds. Pages 1-78 contain an annotated list of the birds of Algeria, and pages, 170-179, a similar list for St. Kilda.

Dixon, Charles.

1897. **Curiosities of bird life** | an account of the sexual adornments, wonderful | displays, strange sounds, sweet songs, curious | nests, protective and recognitory colours, | and extraordinary habits of birds | by | Charles Dixon | author of | "The Migration of British Birds," [*etc., 2 lines.*]. | London | George Redway | Hart Street, Bloomsbury | 1897.

1 vol. demy 8vo, pp. I-XII, 1-322. Bloomsbury.

A popular account of peculiarities in form, color and habits of birds.

Dixon, Charles.

1900. **Among the birds** | in | **northern shires** | by | Charles Dixon | Author of "Rural Bird-Life" [*etc., 3 lines.*] | with coloured frontispiece and forty other illustrations | by Charles Whymper | Blackie and Son Limited | London Glasgow and Dublin | 1900.

1 vol. post 8vo, pp. I-X, 1-303, 1 pl. (col.), 40 text-figs. London.

A popular account of bird-life in the northern parts of the British Isles.

Dixon, Charles.

1900. **The Game Birds and Wild Fowl** | of | **The British Islands.** | By Charles Dixon, | Author of | "Rural Bird-Life," [*etc., 5 lines.*]. | **Second Edition,** enlarged, improved and thoroughly revised by the Author. | With | 41 coloured plates, representing 56 coloured illustrations drawn specially | for this Edition | By Charles Whymper. | Sheffield: | Pawson & Brailsford, Publishers, High Street and Mulberry Street. | 1900.

1 vol. imperial 8vo, pp. I-XXVIII, 1-476, pll. I, II, IIa, III-XI, XIa, XII-XXXIV (XXXV not issued), XXXVI-XL (=41 pll., col.). Sheffield.

An account of the habits of British game birds, with notes on distribution, relationships and classification, and with synonymy and a paragraph of diagnostic characters of each species. Originally issued in 1893 in smaller form
without plates, and reissued in 1895 with minor changes. The present edition
is cited by Mullens and Swann in 4to, and folio. The present copy is imperial
8vo, as collated above.

Dixon, Charles.

1909. **The bird-life of** | **London** | by | Charles Dixon | with illus-
trations in | colour and black and white | [*Vignette.*] | London |
William Heinemann | 1909.

1 vol. 8vo, pp. I-XII, 1-335, 24 pll. (8 col.; by John Duncan). London.

A popular discussion of the birds known to have been found within a fifteen mile
radius of St. Paul's, London.

Dixon, George. (Beresford, William?)

1789. **A** | **voyage round the world;** | but more particularly to the |
north-west coast of America: | performed in 1785, 1786, 1787, and
1788, | in | the King George and Queen Charlotte, | Captains
Portlock and Dixon. | Dedicated, by permission, to | Sir Joseph
Banks, Bart. | By Captain George Dixon. | London: | Published
by Geo. Goulding, | Haydn's Head, No. 6, James Street, Covent
Garden. | 1789.

1 vol. flatcap folio, pp. (I, II missing), III-XXIX+1, 1 l., pp. 1-360,
1-47, 17 pll., 5 charts. London.

A narrative of the voyage, with occasional notes about birds. On pages 356-360
are descriptions of four birds accompanied by as many plates by W. Lewin.
The narrative consists of a series of letters written by one of the officers on
board the Queen Charlotte to a friend in London, and afterwards edited by
Captain Dixon who added the detailed notes in the appendix. The letters
are signed "W. B.," which, from the list of ship's officers given by Portlock in
his work of the same title and date as the present one (q.v.), seems to point to
William Beresford, Assistant Trader. The official account of the voyage is
given by Captain Portlock, Commander of the Expedition, in his book.

Dockray, John A.

1910. See Coward, Thomas A., **The Vertebrate Fauna of Cheshire
and Liverpool Bay.**

Dombrowski, Robert Ritter von. (Tschusi zu Schmidhoffen, Victor
Ritter von.)

1912. **Ornis Romaniæ** | Die Vogelwelt rumänien's | systematisch
und biologisch-geographisch beschrieben | von | Robert Ritter von
Dombrowski | Bukarest. | Staatsdruckerei. | 1912.

1 vol. imperial 8vo, pp. 1-872, I-LIV (index), 2 text-figs. Bucharest.

A monograph of the birds of Roumania with descriptions of new races, at least one of which is credited to Tschusi and Dombrowski. The book is reviewed in the Ornithologische Jahrbuch for May-August, 1912, pp. 152-154.

Donovan, Edward.

1794-1819. The | natural history | of | British birds; | or a | selec-tion of the most rare, beautiful, and interesting | birds | which inhabit this country: | the descriptions from the | Systema Na-turæ | of Linnæus; | with | general observations, | either original, or collected from the latest | and most esteemed | English orni-thologists; | and embellished with | figures, | drawn, engraved, and coloured from the original specimens. [| Vol. II (-X; *III and V missing.*).] | By E. Donovan. | London: | Printed for the author; and for F. and C. [F. C. and J. (*Vols. VI-X.*)] Rivington, | No. 62, St. Paul's Church-yard [Rivington, No. 62, | St. Paul's Church-yard, and No. 3 Waterloo-Place, | Pall Mall [*Vol. X*).]. 1794 [*1795*; (*1796, Vol. III.*); 1797; (*1798, Vol. V.*); 1809; 1816; 1817. 1818; 1819].

10 vols. (incl. 2 vols. of third ed.) in 5, cap 4to (5½x9). Vol. I, 57 ll., pll. 1-24 (col.). Vol. II, 40 ll., pll. 25-48 (col.). Vol. III (missing); Vol. IV, 51 ll., pll. 73-100 (col.). Vol. V (missing). Vol. VI, 30 ll., pll. 125-148 (col.). Vol. VII, 50 ll., pll. 149-172 (col.). Vol. VIII, 37 ll., pll. 173-196 (col.). Vol. IX, 34 ll., pll. 197-220 (col.). Vol. X, 56 ll., pll. 221-244 (col.). London.

Title self-explanatory. The plates are not well drawn and are often inaccurate, but the hand-coloring is delicate and gives the book an artistic, if not scientific, importance. According to Mullens and Swann the work seems to have been issued in 50 monthly parts, each consisting of 2 plates and the accompanying text. The first five volumes were reissued in 1799 and the entire work in 1815-20. The present set contains Vols. III and V of the last edition in place of the corresponding numbers of the first edition to which the remaining volumes belong. These two volumes are collated separately below under their own dates, 1815-20 (q.v.).

Donovan, Edward.

1815-20. > The | natural history | of | British birds; | or a | selec-tion of the most rare, beautiful, and interesting | birds | which inhabit this country: | the descriptions from the | Systema Natu-ræ | of Linnæus; | with | general observations, either original, or collected from the latest | and most esteemed | English ornitholo-gists; | and embellished with | figures, drawn, engraved, and coloured from the original specimens. | Vol. III. | By E. Donovan. | A new edition. | London: | Printed for the author; and for F. C. and J. Rivington, | No. 62, St. Paul's Church-yard. 1815.

> The | natural history | of | British birds; | or, a selection of the | most rare, beautiful, and interesting | birds | which inhabit this country. | The descriptions from the Systema Naturæ of Linnæus | with | general observations, | either original, or collected from the | latest and most esteemed | English ornithologists: | and embellished with | figures, | drawn, engraved, and coloured from the original specimens. | By E. Donovan, F.L.S. W.S. | Author of the Natural Histories of British Fishes, Insects, Shells, Quadrupeds, &c. | In ten volumes, | Vol. V. | London: | Printed for the author; | and for F. C. and J. Rivington, 62, St. Paul's Church-yard, | and 3, Waterloo-Place, Pall-Mall; | By R. Gilbert, St. John's-Square Clerkenwell. | 1820.

2 vols. (should be 10; included in set of 1st ed.) cap 4to (5½x9). Vol. III, 37 ll., pll. 49-72 (col.). Vol. V, 49 ll., pll. 101-124 (col.). London.

The third edition of these two volumes. The present copies are bound with a set of the original edition, 1794-1819 (q.v.), to replace the corresponding original numbers which are missing.

Donovan, Edward.

1834. The | naturalist's repository, | or | miscellany | of | exotic natural history, | exhibiting | rare and beautiful specimens | of | foreign birds, insects, shells, | quadrupeds, fishes, and marine productions; | more especially such | new subjects | as have not hitherto been figured, or correctly described; | forming a | compendium of the most interesting modern discoveries | in zoology. | By | E. Donovan, F.L.S. W.S., &c. | Author of the Natural Histories of British Birds, Insects, Fishes, Shells, and Quadrupeds; | Insects of China, India, and New Holland. | In five volumes, | with one hundred and eighty coloured plates. | Vol. I [-V]. | London: | Printed for the author, and Simpkin & Marshall. | MDCCCXXXIV.

5 vols. 4to (size of 8vo). Vol. I, 104 ll., pll. 1-36 (col.). Vol. II, 119 ll., pll. 37-72 (col.). Vol. III, 53 ll., pll. 73-108 (col.). Vol. IV, 59 ll., pll. 109-144 (col.). Vol. V, 50 ll., pll. 145-180 (col.). London.

The ornithological matter is contained on 52 leaves and 28 plates in the first four volumes, thus; Vol. I, 23, ll., pll. 2, 5, 7, 10, 14, 17, 20, 23, 25, 30, 33; Vol. II, 18 ll., pll. 39, 42, 45, 48, 63, 64, 68, 72; Vol. III, 6 ll., pll. 74, 80, 92, 96, 98; Vol. IV, 5 ll., pl. 112, 117, 128, 137. Errors in numbering of plates, aside from those mentioned in prefatory footnotes, are 20 and 19 transposed and 81 wrongly numbered 84. Among those noted in the footnotes, 25 is wrongly numbered 27.

This work was published originally in parts. Engelmann cites inclusive dates of 1823-27 as does Hagen (Bibliotheca Entomologica, 1, p. 177), but Agassiz cites 1821 et. seq. The preface to Vol. I is dated March 1, 1823, and as this came out with the twelfth and last part of that volume as indicated therein, it is fairly certain that the first part was issued early in 1822. The first plates of Vol. I are dated April 1822 and the last, April 1, 1823; the last in Vol. II, March 1, 1824; Vol. III, April 1, 1825; Vol. IV, March 1, 1826; Vol. V, Dec. 1, 1826. The present set is supplied with new title-pages dated, as transcribed above, 1834; but the body of the work is identical with the original. That this format is nothing but the old letterpress and plates with new titles is indicated by the fact that the watermarks on the plates of Vol I are dated 1821 and those of Vol. V, 1824, a circumstance hardly likely if the work had been reprinted. Hagen (loc. cit.) records a "Neue Titel-Ausgabe. 1834."

D'Orbigny, Alcide Dessalines.

1838-43. See Cuvier, G.L.C.F.D., **Le Règne Animal.**

d'Orbigny, Alcide Dessalines.

1839-40. See Sagra, Ramon de la, **Histoire Physique, Politique et Naturelle de l'Ile de Cuba.**

D'Oyly, C.

1829. See Smith, C.W.; and D'Oyly, **Oriental Ornithology.**

Dresser, Henry Eeles. (Sharpe, Richard Bowdler; Walden, Viscount = Hay, Arthur.)

1871-82. A history | of | the birds of Europe, | including all the species inhabiting the | western palæarctic region. | By | H. E. Dresser, F.L.S., F.Z.S., etc. | Volume I [-VIII]. | London: | published by the author, | 6 Tenterden Street, Hanover Square, W. | 1871-1881.

8 vols. royal 4to. Vol. I, pp. I-II (illustr. tit. and ded.), pp. IX-XIII+1 (list of subscribers), III-XLVI, 1-102 (prefatory matter and indices). Vol. II, illustr. tit., pp. I-VIII, 322 ll., 95 pll. (col.), 2 text-figs. Vol. III, illustr. tit., pp. I-VIII, 310 ll., 86 pll. (col.), 1 text-fig. Vol. IV, illustr. tit., pp. I-VIII, 318 ll., 92 pll. (90 col.), 4 text-figs. Vol. V, illustr. tit., pp. I-VIII, 334 ll., 90 pll. (col.), 6 text-figs. Vol. VI, illustr. title, pp. I-VIII, 354 ll., 92 pll. (col.), 8 text-figs. Vol. VII, illustr. titl., pp. I-VIII, 330 ll., 89 pll. (88 col.), 4 text-figs. Vol. VIII, illustr. tit., pp. I-VIII, 333 ll., 89 pll. (col.), 2 text-figs. (Vol. IV of the present set lacks plate No. 259; Vol. V and VI each contain a duplicate plate belonging to Vol. VII.) London.

A very thorough manual of the subject, beautifully illustrated by J. G. Keulemans, Joseph Wolf, E. Neale and others. Unfortunately for the reader, neither pages nor plates are numbered, except in the indices. The work was issued in 84 parts without regard to sequence of subject matter, and reference to the tables is necessary to determine the date of publication of any subject. Volume

I appeared last, in December, 1881, according to the original wrapper which is bound with that volume in the set at hand, but Mullens and Swann give 1882 as the final date. The author gives credit to R. B. Sharpe for certain parts of the earlier numbers (I-XII), 1871, and to A. Walden (Marquis of Tweeddale) for other contributions. A "Supplement" (q.v.) was issued in 1895-96.

Dresser, Henry Eeles.

1876. See Eversmann, Edward, **Reprint of Eversmann's Addenda ad Celeberrimi Pallasii Zoographiam Rosso-Asiaticam.**

Dresser, Henry Eeles.

1876. See Rowley, George D., **Ornithological Miscellany,** 1875-78.

Dresser, Henry Eeles.

1884-86. A monograph | of the | **Meropidæ,** | or | family of the bee-eaters. | By | H. E. Dresser, F.L.S., F.Z.S., &c., | Member of the British Ornithologists' Union, [*etc., 4 lines.*] | [*Vignette.*] [*Quotation.*] | London: | Published by the author at 6 Tenterden Street, W. | 1884-1886.

1 vol. imperial 4to, pp. I-XX, 1-144, 34 pll. (col.; by J. G. Keulemans). London.

A thorough discussion of the group. The hand-colored plates are very fine. Issued in parts, the actual dates of publication of which are given at the close of the volume.

Dresser, Henry Eeles.

1893. A monograph | of the | **Coraciidæ,** | or | family of the rollers. | By | H. E. Dresser, F.L.S., F.Z.S., &c., | Ex-President of the Yorkshire Naturalists' Union, [*etc., 4 lines.*] | [*Vignette*] | [*Quotation.*] |Published by the author at Topcylffe Grange, | Farnborough, R. S. O., Kent. | 1893.

1 vol. imperial 4to, pp. I-XX, 1-111, 27 pll. (col.; by J. G. Keulemans). Farnborough.

A thoroughly detailed study of the group, with excellent hand-colored plates.

Dresser, Henry Eeles.

1895-96. Supplement | to | **a history** | of | **the birds of Europe,** | including all the species inhabiting the | Western Palaearctic Region, | forming | volume IX. | By | H. E. Dresser, F.L.S., F.Z.S., &c | London: | published by the author (by special permission), | at the office of | The Zoological Society of London, | 3 Hanover Square, W., | and at | Topclyffe Grange, Farnborough, R.S.O., Kent. | 1895-1896.

1 vol. royal 4to, illustr. tit., pp. I-XXV+1, 1-441, pll. 634-722 (col.; by Keulemans, J. Wolf and Thorburn). London.

The present volume may be considered as Vol. IX of the author's "History of the Birds of Europe," 1871-82 (q.v.). It was intended to treat only of species not included in the original work, but offers occasional corrections to the original letterpress, also. This "Supplement" appeared in nine parts, the dates of which are given in a synopsis of the letterpress, on pp. V-VIII. For the most part the plates accompanied their respective descriptions, but occasionally substitutions were made which are noted on the wrappers but not in the letterpress. The distribution of the plates among the nine parts is as follows. Pt. I, pll. 634-644; Pt. II, pll. 645-650, 652-654 and 657; Pt. III, pll. 651, 655-663 and 665; Pt. IV, pll. 664 and 666-674; Pt. V, pll. 675-684; Pt. VI, pll. 685-693 and 696; Pt. VII, pll. 695, 697-700, 704, 706, 708, 711 and 713; Pt. VIII, pll. 694, 701, 702, 705, 709, 714-716 and 719; Pt. IX, pll. 703, 707, 710, 712, 717, 718 and 720-722. The descriptions are indexed on pp. V-VIII where, however, they are numbered in a sequence of species which does not correspond with the numbers on the plates. Errors in the names of *Melizohpilus deserticola, Parus cinereus* and *Bucanetes obsoletus* (called *M. deserticolus, Parus atriceps* and *Erythrospiza absoleta* on the plates) are corrected on the wrappers, in the lists of plates.

Dresser, Henry Eeles.

1905-10.   Eggs | of | the birds of Europe | including all the species inhabiting the | western palæarctic area | by | H. E. Dresser, F.L.S., F.Z.S., &c. | Member of the British Ornithologists' Union, [*etc., 4 lines.*] | [*Vignette.*] | Vol. I.- Letter-press [II. -Plates] | London | Published by the author (by special permission) | at the office of | The Royal Society for the Protection of Birds | 23 Queen-Anne's Gate, W. | 1910.

2 vols. royal 4to. Vol. I. pp. I-XX, 1-837, 167 figs. Vol. II, 79 ll., 106 pll. (col.). London.

Originally published in 24 parts. Pages 1-505 are arranged in apparently miscellaneous order due to an alteration in the proposed sequence. A table, showing the original and revised numeration of pages and plates and the numbers of the parts in which each appeared, is given in the prefatory matter of Vol. I, pp. IX-XX. The parts were issued as follows, according to the current numbers of the Ibis. Pt. I, 1905, (rev. Ibis, Jan. 1906); II, Dec. 1905; III-IV, Jan.-April 1906; V-VI, Nov. 1906; VII-VIII, May 1907; IX-X, Oct. 1907; XI-XIII, 1908 (rev. Ibis, April 1908); XIII-XIV, 1909 (Zool. Record; rev. Ibis, April 1909). XVII-XVIII, April 1909; XIX-XX, Sept. 1909; XXI-XXII, Febr. 1910; XXIII-XXIV, Nov. 1910. The book presents a detailed discussion of the nesting habits and breeding ranges of European birds with halftones of nests and nesting sites and colored figures of the eggs.

Dresser, Henry Eeles.

1902-03.   A manual of | Palæarctic birds | by | H. E. Dresser, F.L.S., F.Z.S., &c. | author of "The Birds of Europe," etc., etc. |

[*Vignette.*] | Part I [II] | London | Published by the author at 3 Hanover Square, W. | 1902 [1903] | All rights reserved.

2 vols. 8vo. Vol. I, pp. I-VII+1, 4 ll., pp. 1-498, frontisp. (by J. Wolf). Vol. II, 4 pr. ll., pp. 499-922, frontisp. (col.; by J. Wolf). London.

A list of 1219 species and subspecies of Palaearctic birds, with synonymies, short descriptions, and brief notes on distribution and habits. Subspecies are treated binomially.

Droste-Hülshoff, Ferdinand.

1869. Die Vogelwelt | der | Nordseeinsel Borkum. | Nebst | einer vergleichenden übersicht | der | in den südlichen Nordseeländern | vorkommenden Vögel | von | Ferd. Baron Droste-Hülshoff, | Geschaftsführer der Deutschen Ornithologen-Gesellschaft [*etc., 3 lines.*]. | Nebst einer lithographirten Tafel und einer Karte. | Münster, | Selbstverlag des Verfassers. | In Commission bei W. Niemann. | 1869.

1 vol. post 8vo, pp. I-XIX+1, 1-389+1, 1-16 (suppl.), 2 pll. (fold.; 1 monochr.). Münster.

An account of the birds of the island of Borkum, with descriptions of the various species and notes on habits, migrations, etc. The supplement contains a comparative review of the birds of the southern coasts of the North and East Seas, with the species arranged in various lists according to habitat, occurrence, etc.

Dubois, Alphonse.

1861-72. See Dubois, Charles Frederic; and Dubois, Alphonse, Les Oiseaux de l'Europe et leurs Oeufs.

Dubois, Alphonse.

1866. See Dubois, Charles Frédéric, Catalogue Systématique des Oiseaux de l'Europe.

Dubois, Alphonse.

1871. Conspectus | systematicus & geographicus | avium Europæarum, | auctore | Alph. Dubois, | Doctore Scient. Nat.; [*etc., 2 lines.*]. | Bruxellis, | Apud C. Muquardt, H. Merzbach, Succrs, | MDCCCLXXI. | Depositum.

1 vol. imperial 8vo, pp. 1-35. Brussels.

A check-list of European birds, giving the names of 253 genera and 575 species, (in addition to numerous "varietates climactericae") with the general distribution of the various forms.

Dubois, Alphonse.

1902-04. Synopsis avium | nouveau | manuel d'ornithologie | par | Alphonse Dubois | Docteur en Sciences Naturelles, [*etc., 6 lines.*] |

Première [Deuxième] partie | (1899-1902) [(1902-1904)] | Brux-
elles | H. Lamertin, éditeur | 20, Rue du March-Au-Bois | 1902
[1904].
2 vols. foliopost 4to. Vol. I, pp. I-XV+1, 1-729+1, pll. I-XII (col.;
by the author). Vol. II, pp. I-IX+1, 731-1339, pll. XIII-XVI
(col.; by the author). Brussels.

A synonymic list of species, with marginal notations regarding the distribution
of each. The work was issued in 17 parts of which 1-10 comprise Vol. I, and
11-17, Vol. II. Mathews (Birds of Australia, Suppl. 4, pp. 37-38, 1925) has
recorded (erroneously under the authorship of Charles Frédéric Dubois) the
dates of receipt of the various parts at the British Museum, together with the
pagination of the contents of each part; the plate-numbers are from a copy in
the U. S. National Museum examined by Dr. Hellmayr. The dates of receipt
at the British Museum, etc., are as follows. Pt. **1**, pp. 1-80, pl. 1, recd. Oct.
21, 1899; **2**, pp. 81-160, pl. 2, Febr. 17, 1900; **3**, pp. 161-224, pll. 3-4, May 9,
1900; **4**, pp. 225-288, pll. 5-6, Aug. 21, 1900; **5**, pp. 289-368, pl. 7, Jan. 22, 1901;
6, pp. 369-448, pl. 8, May 4, 1901; **7**, pp. 449-528, pl. 9, Aug. 3, 1901; **8**, pp.
529-608, pl. 10, Nov. 2, 1901; **9**, pp. 609-688, pl. 11, (dat. 1901), Febr. 11, 1902;
10, pp. 689-729, I-XV, pl. 12 (no pl. recorded by Mathews), (dat. March 1902),
May 8, 1902; **11**, pp. 731-834, pl. 13, Oct. 18, 1902; **12**, pp. 835-914, pl. 14, Jan.
3, 1903; **13**, pp. 915-994, pl. 15, June 13, 1903; **14**, pp. 995-1074, pl. 16, Aug.
29, 1903; **15**, pp. 1075-1169, no pl., Febr. 6, 1904 (recorded in Zool. Record for
1903); **16** and **17**, pp. 1171-1339, I-X, (dat. July 1904), Aug. 27, 1904.
Plate IV is wrongly numbered VI.

Dubois, Alphonse.

1907-13. See Wytsman, Paul, **Genera Avium**, 1905-14.

Dubois, Charles Frédéric.

1854-60. **Planches coloriées** | des | oiseaux de la Belgique | et | de
leurs œufs; | par Ch. F. Dubois, | Membre [Membre Honoraire
(*Vol. III.*)] | de plusieurs sociétés savantes. | Tome Ier [II;
III]. | Avec 120 [140; 152] planches. | Bruxelles - Leipzig - Gand. |
C. Muquardt. | 1854 [1857; 1860].
3 vols. royal 8vo. Vol. I, 2 pr. ll., pp. I-CLV+1, 108 ll., pll. 1-89,
1a, 9a, 54a, 55a, 55b, 56a, 56b, 72a, 76a, 77a, 77b, 78a, 79a, 79b,
I-XVII (=120 pll., col.; by the author; Roman numerals, eggs).
Vol. II, 1 pr. l., 114 ll., pll. 90-190, 93a, 94a, 95a, 96a, 101a, 101b,
123a, 144a, 151a, 161a, 166a, 172a, 179a, 180a, 185a, 190a, XVIII-
XXXVI, XXXVIA (=157 pll., col.; by the author; Roman numerals, eggs). Vol. III, 1 pr. l., pp. CLVII-CLX, 149 ll., pll. 191-300,
191a, 203a, 294a, 295a, XXXVII-LXXIV (=152 pll., col.; by the
author; Roman numerals, eggs). Brussels.

A series of 429 hand-colored plates of Belgian birds, with appended synonymies,
brief discussions of habits, and descriptions of the genera and higher groups.

There are numerous errors in the numbering of the plates and pages (or leaves), which are numbered to correspond. The following errors have been noted. P. 2 is wrongly numbered 4; p. and pl. 13,-12; p. 14,-13; pl. 17,- 16; p. and pl. 22,-23; p. 38,-37; p. and pl. 44,-43; pl. 75,-90; p. 75,-89; pl. 77b,-67b; p. and pl. 114,-115; p. and pl. 119,-118; pl. 160,-15?; pl. 161,-15?; pl. 183,-185; p. 214,-114; pl. 254,-154; pl. 260,-246; p. and pl. 270,-242; pl. XLII,-XXXIX. There are no pages for pll. 1a, 9a, 17, 151a, 158, 160, 161a, 180a; Nos. 104 and 105 are on one page of text.

The work was published in 141 livraisons concerning which not much information is available. The "Revue et Magasin" records Livrs. 116-130 as of 1860, in the periodical for December of that year; in the number for October 1861, Livrs. 131-141 are recorded as of 1859-60. An advertisement on p. IV of Vol. I of Dubois and Dubois's "Les Oiseaux de l'Europe," 1861-72 (q.v.), the present work is advertised as having been published in 1854-60 although in the preface to Vol. II of the same work, Alphonse Dubois remarks that the book was commenced (not necessarily published) in 1851.

The present series was continued by the "Les Oiseaux de l'Europe" which treats of the birds of Europe not found in Belgium; the two works together constitute an illustrated review of the birds of all Europe.

Dubois, Charles Frédéric; and Dubois, Alphonse.

1861-72. Les | oiseaux de l'Europe | et | leurs œufs, | décrits et dessinés d'après nature | par | Ch.-F. Dubois, | membre honoraire de plusieurs sociétés savantes, | et | Alph. Dubois fils, | Docteur en Sciences Naturelles [*etc., 2 lines*; *etc., 3 lines* (*Vol. II.*).] | Deuxième série, | espèces non observées en Belgique. | Tome premier. [second] | Avec 167 [avec 152] planches coloriées. | Bruxelles - Leipzig - Gand, | chez C. Muquardt [Chez C. Muquardt, H. Merzbach, Succr.]. | 1868 [1872.] | Tous droits réservés.

2 vols. superroyal 8vo. Vol. I, pp. I-XLVI, 139 ll. (complete?), pll. 1-106, 1a, 2a, 2b, 2c, 5a, 5b, 5c, 5e, 19a, 20a, 22a, 23a, 23b, 27a, 29a, 32a, 34a, 35a, 35b, 36a, 38a, 41a, 41b, 43a, 44a, 50a, 50b, 55a, 72a, 74a, 75a, 82a, 83a, 88a, 99a, 105b, 106a, I-XVIII, XIVA, XVA, XVIA, XVIIA, XVIIIA. (col.; Roman numerals, eggs). Vol. II, pp. XLVII-CXXII, 132 ll. (complete?), frontisp. (portr.), pll. 107-202 (131, 169, 185, 189 and 191 missing), 111a, 114a, 116a, 118a, 119a, 119b, 124a, 127a, 131a, 131b, 134a, 135a, 137b, 139a, 140a, 144a, 145a, 149a, 149b, 152a, 155a, 155b, 157a, 158a, 160a, 160b, 163a, 163b, 163c, 164(*bis*), 164a, 174a, 174b, 175b, 175c, 177(*bis*),177a, 180a, 199b, XIX-XXXVII (col.; Roman numerals, eggs.) Brussels.

A continuation of the senior author's "Planches Coloriées des Oiseaux de la Belgique," 1854-60 (q.v.). The earlier series discussed the birds of Belgium; the present volumes relate to European species not found in Belgium. The above enumeration of plates is as given in the lists of contents of the two volumes, with the exception of pll. 164 (*bis*) and 177 (*bis*) which are not listed.

Actually, many of the plates are differently numbered (with the leaves usually numbered to correspond). The following mistakes have been noted. Vol. I: (page and plate) 2c, wrongly numbered 2b; 5b,-5a; 32a,-33a; 52,-59; 59,-52; 82a,-83a, 105b,-105a.   Vol. II: (page and plate) 114a, wrongly numbered 114; 119,-118b;119a,-119; 119b,-119a; 127,-125a; 127a,-127; 131,-134; 141,-142, 142,-141; 144-145 (only on page); 152a,-152b; 158,-158a; 169, -168a; 173,-174; 174b,-174a; 175b,-175a; 181,-182; 183,-181b; 184,-182; 185,-183; 186,-184(only on plate); 189,-183; 191,-192.   There are no pages of text for pll. 2a, 2c, 5a, 5c, 41a, 116, 131b, 155a, 157a, 164 (*bis*), 177 (*bis*), and 184, but this may be due to imperfection in the copy.

This work, like its predecessor, appeared in livraisons with (according to the Ibis, Oct. 1864, p. 396) three plates and accompanying text to each part. The various parts were so mixed in contents that it is impossible to fix the dates of most of the plates with even approximate accuracy.   Livrs. 1-10 are reviewed in the Revue et Magasin for July, 1862, p. 280, as having appeared in 1861; 11-25 in the same periodical for April, 1864, p. 118, as of 1861-62; 26-40 in the same for Sept. 1866, p. 351, as of 1863-64; 78-98 in the same for Jan. 1870, p. 34, as of 1866-69.   In the same journal for Jan. 1870, p. 351, it is stated that Livrs. 182-218, complete series (=41-77, present series), had been delayed but would be issued shortly.   The contents of a few assortments of livraisons are given in the references cited.   Livrs. 1-10 are said to contain the text to pll. 10, 80, 87, 88, 90, 93, 94 and 118; 26-40 are said to contain pll. 13, 15, 16, 21, 22, 47, 70, 83, 102, 103, 116, 118, 136, 140 and VI; 78-98 are said to contain the following species (named in the review but here given by number), -1a, 27a, 32a, 35b, 36a, 43a, 44a, 46, 47, 48, 49, 50a, 50b, 60, 66 and 88a, together with (in Livrs. 89-91) the title-page, preface, descriptions of genera and list of contents (pp. I-XLVI) of Vol. I. This preface bears the date of April 1868; that of Vol. II, December 1871.   Vol. I is autographed by "Dr. Gustav Flor, Dorpat, 1868," and Vol. II, the same "1872" so the dates on the title-pages are probably correct.

The present work appears to contain an occasional new name such as, for example, *Phylloscopus pallasii*, proposed on p. 83 of Vol. I although relegated to the synonymy of *Reguloides superciliosus* on p. CIX of Vol. II.

C. F. Dubois died in 1867 leaving his son, Alphonse Dubois, the junior author, to complete the work. The preface to Vol. I is signed by Alphonse who speaks of certain alterations which he intends to make in the plan of the work.

The present copy has bound with it the authors' "Catalogue Systématique des Oiseaux de l'Europe," 1866 (q.v.). The present copy is from the library of "Othmar Reiser, Sarajevo. 1888."

Dubois, Charles Frédéric; and Dubois, Alphonse,

1866.   [Catalogue systématique des Oiseaux de l'Europe.]

1 vol. superroyal 8vo, pp. 1-16. Brussels.

A check-list of 570 species of European birds, giving the scientific and vernacular names of each and marking those species not known from Belgium and those not yet figured in the authors' current "Les Oiseaux de l'Europe," 1861-72 (q.v.). The preface, signed May 1865, is an appeal addressed to ornithologists to supply data needed to complete the larger work, the particular need of which the present list may serve to indicate.   This paper, in the present copy, is without title-page and is bound with Vol. I of the "Les Oiseaux de l'Europe" but it is reviewed in the "Revue et Magasin" for Sept. 1866, p. 351, as a separate publication. The title given above is from the heading of p. 3.

Duges, Alfred.

1896. See World's Congress on Ornithology, **Papers presented to the—.**

Dugmore, A. Radclyffe.

1920. **Bird homes.** The nests | eggs and breeding habits of | the land birds breeding in the | eastern United States; with | hints on the rearing and pho- | tographing of young birds | by | A. Radclyffe Dugmore | Illustrated with photographs | from nature by the author | Garden City New York | Doubleday, Page & Company | 1920.

1 vol. superroyal 8vo, pp. I-XVI, 1-183, 48 pll. (16 col.), 11 text-cuts. Garden City and New York.

A popular discussion of the subject, with short descriptions of the species and of their nests and eggs.   The species are arranged according to the situations in which their nests are built.   The first edition of the work was published in 1900.

Dumont D'Urville, Jules Sébastien César. (Quoy, Jean René Const.; and Gaimard, Jean Paul.)

1830-35. > **Voyage | dé découvertes | de l'Astrolabe** | Exécuté par ordre du Roi, | pendant les années 1826-1827-1828-1829, | sous le commandement | de M. J. Dumont D'Urville. | Zoologie | par | MM. Quoy et Gaimard. | Tome premier [second]. | Paris [*Comma added.*] | J. Tastu, éditeur-imprimeur, | No 36, Rue de Vaugirard. | 1830 [1832. (*Vol. II, Pt.* 1.); 1833. (*Vol. II, Pt.* 2.)].

> Voyage | de la corvette | l'Astrolabe | exécuté | pendant les années 1826-1827-1828-1829 | sous le commandement | de | M. Jules Dumont D'Urville | Capitaine de Vaisseau. | Atlas. | [*Vignette.*] | Paris | Publié par J. Tastu, Editeur. | MDCCCXXXIII. | L'écriture gravée sur acier par Hacq.

4 vols. 8vo and superroyal folio. Vol. I, 2 pr. ll. (half-tit. and tit.), pp. I-L, 1 l. (subtit.), pp. 5-268. Vol. II, (Pt. 1), tit., pp. 1-320; (Pt. 2), 2 ll. (half-tit. and tit.), pp. 321-686. Atlas (in 2 vols.); Mammals, Pll. 1-28 (23 col.); Birds, 1-31, (col.; by Prêtre, Prévost and Oudart); Fishes, 1, 5(=2), 3, 4, 7, 10-12, 14, 15, 19, 20, (col.); Mollusks, 1-66, 65(bis=67), 68-93, 45 bis, 66 bis, (col.); Zoophytes, 1-26, (col.); Insects, 1-12, (col.).   Paris.

Part of the zoological report (by Quoy and Gaimard) from the complete report on the voyage of the Astrolabe.   The text, in the present copy, is incomplete but contains all the ornithological matter, which is in Vol. I. The Zoology (excluding Entomology) forms the 3rd division of the complete report and is advertised in each of the volumes at hand as comprising 5 volumes while the Entomology forms the 4th division in 1 volume. However, only 4 vols. of the 3rd division appear to have been issued. Furthermore, the indices of Vol. I (pp. 261 and 265) refer to the preceding pages as constituting only a first part of that volume, so a second part, evidently, was in contemplation (probably to discuss the fishes and reptiles, which are not elsewhere treated). Vol. II was issued in two parts, as indicated in the collation. The concluding portion of the text relating to the Mollusks, the text for the Zoophytes and that for the Insects are missing although the plates are all present. The plates, in the copy at hand, are bound in two volumes with duplicate title-pages, all up to Mollusk Pl. 25 being contained in the first volume and the remainder in the second.

Details as to dates of publication are very meager but are summarized by Sherborn and Woodward in the Ann. and Mag. Nat. Hist. ser. 7, **8**, p. 333, 1901. The dates given on the title-pages of Vols. I and II (Pts. 1 and 2) appear to be accurate. Fortunately the plates bear only vernacular names and their dates are, therefore, unimportant. The entomological plates issued in 1835, extend the full date of the present copy to that year.

The ornithological matter occupies pp. 153-259 and respective portions of the errata and indices of Vol. I. It consists almost entirely of descriptions of new species of birds from New Guinea, New Zealand, Celebes, Australia and other points reached on the voyage, with occasional descriptions of imperfectly known or unfigured birds previously described by former workers.

Dumont d'Urville, Jules Sébastien César. (Hombron; Jacquinot, Honoré; Pucheran, Jacques.)

1842-54. > Voyage | au Pole Sud | et dans l'océanie [et | dans l'océanie (*Atlas.*)] | sur les corvettes | l'Astrolabe et la Zélée; [*No semicolon (Atlas.*).] | exécuté par ordre du Roi [*Line omitted (Atlas.*).] | pendant les années 1837-1838-1839-1840, [*No comma (Atlas.*).] | sous le commandement | de M.J. [M. (*Atlas.*)] Dumont-d'Urville, [*No comma (Atlas.*).] | Capitaine de vaisseau; [*Comma (Vol. II.); no punctuation (Atlas.*).] | publié par ordonnance de sa Majesté, [publié par ordre du gouvernement, (*Vols III-V.); same, without comma (Atlas.*).] | sous la direction supérieure | de M. Jacquinot, Capitaine de vaisseau, Commandant de la Zélée. [et sous la direction supérieure de M. Jacquinot, Capitaine de vaisseau, Commandant de la Zélée (*Atlas.*)] | Zoologie, [*No comma (Atlas.*).] | par MM. Hombron et Jacquinot. [*Line omitted (Atlas.*).] | Tome premier. [-quatrième.; *line omitted (Atlas.*).] | Paris, [*No comma (Atlas.*).] | Gide et Cie [et J. Baudry (*Vols. III-V and Atlas.*)], éditeurs, [*No comma (Atlas.*).] | Rue des Petits-Augustins [Rue Bonaparte (*Vols. III-V.*)], 5. [*No period*

(Atlas.).] | 1846 [1853 *(Vols. III and IV.)*; 1854 *(Vol. V.)*; 1842 a 1853 (Atlas.)].

7 vols. in 6, 8vo and superroyal folio. Vol. I, 3 pr. ll. (half-tit., tit. and subtit.), pp. 1-404. Vol. II, 3 pr. ll., pp. 1-384. Vol. III, pp. 1-166 (Mammals and Birds), 1 l. (subtit.), pp. 1-56, 1 l. (subtit.), pp. 1-107. Vol. IV, 3 pr. ll., pp. 1-422. Vol. V, pp. I-VIII, 1-132. Atlas (Pt. 1), 3 pr. ll. (half-tit., tit. and index to all zool. pll.), pll. 1-6, 9-10, 13-24, 2A, 2B, 4 bis, 10A, 17A, 20A-20D (26 col.; mammals); 1-33, 12 bis, 24 bis, 25 bis, and 31 bis (36 col.; by Oudart, Werner and A Prévost; birds). Atlas (Pt. 2), 2 pr. ll. (half-tit. and tit.), pll. 1-7+2 bis; 1, 2, 6 (=3); 1; 1-5; 1-19; 1-3; 1-3; 1-9; 3-12, 14, 16, 17, 19, 21-29; (col.). Paris.

The zoological portion of the complete report on the voyage of the Astrolabe and Zélée. Vol. III contains all the text relating to birds. This is found in Part 1 of the volume, pp. 6-166 under the subtitle "Zoologie, Mammifères et Oiseaux par M. Honoré Jacquinot et M. le Dr. Pucheran," of which pp. 47-158 and 164-166 are ornithological. Although Jacquinot's name appears on the subtitle-page, a statement in the introduction (obviously by Pucheran although un-signed) announces that neither Hombron nor Jacquinot is to be held respons-ible for errors in the nomenclature adopted in the succeeding text for which he (Pucheran) is alone to blame. It is evident that Pucheran must be quoted as author of the ornithology and mammalogy. (Mathews (Birds of Australia 7, p. 461) states that he possesses a copy of this portion with Pucheran's name alone on the subtitle-page. However, on pp. 128-152 is an article credited to Jacquinot, entitled, "Remarques sur quelques points de l'Anatomie et de la Physiologie des Procellarides, et Essai d'une nouvelle Classification de ces Oiseaux." This appears to be the paper by Hombron and Jacquinot published in the "Comptes Rendus" XVIII, pp. 353-358, number for March 4, 1844 (publ. March 11?). Vol. III is correctly dated 1853 according to Sherborn (Ann. and Mag. Nat. Hist. ser. 7, 7, p. 390). The plates of birds appeared at various dates from May 1842 to July 1846, as tabulated on p. 16 of Vol. III, and all of these antedate the text. However, all of the plates except Pl. 32 contain only vernacular names. Pl. 32 (published in April 1844) is illustrative of Jacquinot's article on the Procellariidae and contains several generic and specific names which are antedated by the number of the "Comptes Rendus" mentioned above. Illustrations are given of the bill of *Priocella garnotii* which is a nomen nudum in the text under the spelling, *"Prioc. Garnotti."* Some of the species figured by Hombron and Jacquinot in the Atlas were described by Gray (Genera of Birds) and Bonaparte (Conspectus Avium) before Pucheran's text appeared. These references are quoted by Pucheran.

Duperrey, Louis Isidore. (Lesson, René Primèvere; Garnot, Prosper.)

1826-30. > Voyage | autour du monde, | Exécuté par Ordre du Roi, | Sur la Corvette de Sa Majesté, **La Coquille,** pendant | les années 1822, 1823, 1824 et 1825, | sous le Ministère et conformé-ment aux instructions de S.E.M. le Marquis | de Clermont-Tonnerre, Ministre de la Marine; | Et publié sous les auspices | de Son Excellence Mgr le Cte de Chabrol, | Ministre de la Marine et des Colonies, | par M.L.I. Duperrey, | Capitaine de Frégate, Chevalier de Saint-Louis et Membre de la Légion d'Honneur, | Commandant de l'Expédition. | **Zoologie,** | par MM. Lesson et Garnot [par M. Lesson (*Vol. II, Pts.* 1, 2.)]. | Tome Premier [Second]. = 1 re [2 e] Partie. | [*Vignette.*] | Paris. | Arthus Bertrand, libraire-éditeur, | Rue Hautefeuille, No 23. | 1826 [1828; 1830; 1830].

> Voyage | autour du monde, | Exécuté par Ordre du Roi, | sur | La Corvette de Sa Majesté, | La Coquille, | Pendant les années | 1822, 1823, 1824 et 1825, | Sous le Ministère de S.E.M. le Marquis de Clermont-Tonnerre, | et publié | Sous les Auspices de Son Excellence M. Le Cte. De Chabrol, Ministre de la Marine et des Colonies; | par | L. I. Duperrey, | Chevalier de St. Louis et de la Légion d'Honneur, Capitaine de Frégate, | Commandant de l'Expédition. | Histoire naturelle, Zoologie. | Atlas. | Paris, | Arthus Bertrand, libraire-éditeur, | Rue Hautefeuille No. 23. | 1826. | Ecrit par C. F. Ermeler. De l'Imprimerie de Rémond. Gravé par Abel Malo.

2 vols. (4 pts.) and Atlas, in 5 vols. Vol. I, Pt. 1, 2 pr. ll. (half-tit. and tit.), pp. I-IV, 1-360. Vol. I, Pt. 2, 2 pr. ll., pp. 361-743. Vol. II, Pt. 1, 2 pr. ll., pp. 1-471. Vol. II, Pt. 2, 2 pr. ll., pp. I-XIJ, 9-319[1], 1 l. (subtit. "Deuxième Division"), pp. 1-155. Atlas, tit., 4 ll. (expl. of pll.), pll. 1-50, 21 bis, 31 bis, 35 bis (mammals and birds; 49 col.; 10-50 of birds by Prêtre and Prévost); 1-7 (reptiles; col.); 1-38 (fishes; col.); 1-16 (mollusks; col.); 1-5 (crustaceans; col.); 1-21, 14 bis (insects; col.); 1-16 (zoophytes; col.). Paris.

The zoological portion of Duperrey's report on the voyage of La Coquille. This portion is by Lesson and Garnot, each of whom supplied certain sections of the text as indicated in the headings of the chapters. The ornithological matter is all contained in Vol. I, Pts. 1 and 2. The complete zoology appeared in 28 livraisons, the dates of which have been recorded by Sherborn and Woodward in the Annals and Mag. of Nat. Hist., (7), **7**, pp. 391-392, 1901, from records in the 'Bilbiographie de la France.' Mathews discovered the allocation of the ornithological plates in current numbers of Férussac's "Bull. de Sciences Naturelles," and has republished the figures in the Austral Avian Record, **2**, Nos. 3 and 4, pp. 49-54, 1913. The combined data are as follows for the text and for the plates of birds.

Vol. I: Livr. 1, pp. 1-48, pll. 13, 20 and 28, Nov. 1, 1826; 2, pp. 49-88, pll. 11, 34, 36 and 43, Jan. 17, 1827; 3, pp. 89-128, pll. 12, 19, 26, 32 and 47, April 18, 1827; 4, pp. 129-168, pll. 31, 37, 40, 41, 42 and 50, July 25, 1827; 5, pp. 169-216, pll. 18, 22, 25, 35, and 45, Oct. 17, 1827; 6, pp. 217-256, pll. 21, 21 bis, 27,

[1] Pp. 1-8 were not published, being reserved for the preface which, however, required more space than was originally intended and actually appeared on pp. I-XIJ.

33 and 39, March 22, 1828; **7**, pp. 257-296, pll. 10, 17, 30, 44 and 48, June 21, 1828; **8**, pp. 287-352, pll. 15, 24, 38, 46 and 49, Nov. 29, 1828; **9**, pp. 353-408, pll. 14 and 16, Febr. 28, 1829; **10**, pp. 409-456, pll. 23, 29 and 35 bis, April 4, 1829; **11**, pp. 457-504, pl. 31 bis, May 30, 1829; **12**, pp. 505-560, July 4, 1829; **13**, pp. 561-600, Nov. 21, 1829; **14**, pp. 601-648, Jan. 9, 1830; **15**, pp. 649-696, April 3, 1830; **16**, pp. 697-743, May 1, 1830. Vol. **II**, Pt. 1: Livr. "16" (=17), pp. 1-24, June 12, 1830; **18**, pp. (25-471), ?-1830; **19**, ? (plates only ?) Dec. 11, 1830; **20**, ?, April 30, 1831; **21**, ?, June 11, 1831; **22**, ?, July 2, 1831; **23**, ?, Aug. 6, 1831; **24**, ?, Sept. 17, 1831. Vol. **II**, Pt. 2, Sect. 1: Livr. **25**, pp. 1 (=9?)-216, Nov. 12, 1831; **26** (pt.), pp. 217-319, Dec. 10, 1831. Vol. **II**, Pt. 2, Sect. 2: Livr. 26 (pt.), pp. 1-182, Dec. 10, 1831; **27** pp. 129-135, Jan. 28, 1832; **28**, pp. 136-155, ?-1832.

The plates of the birds antedate the corresponding descriptions in the text and hence must be cited, under Lesson and Garnot together, for certain names. Some of the species were first described elsewhere (Annales des Sciences Naturelles, Lesson's 'Manuel d'Ornithologie,' etc.) by Lesson or Garnot, although this is not always indicated in the present work where these species are again described, ostensibly as new. Furthermore, Lesson and Garnot do not always agree as to the nomenclature of some of the birds and sometimes discuss the same species under different names. The authors' general remarks in early chapters occasionally contain a characterization of a species which has priority over the detailed description in a later chapter. Thus the hummingbird, *Thaumastura cora*, is treated as follows. *Orthorynchus Cora* Lesson and Garnot, Voy. Coquille, Zool., pl. 31, fig. 4 (livr. 4), July 25, 1827; *orthorynchus Cora* Lesson, Voy. Coquille, Zool., Vol. I, Pt. 1, p. 252 (livr. 6), March 22, 1828; *Ornismya Cora* Lesson, Manuel d'Orn., **2**, p. 82, June 1828; *Ornismya Cora* Lesson, Hist. Nat. Ois.-Mouches, pp. XXI, 52, pl. VI, 1829; *Orthorynchus Cora* Lesson, Voy. Coquille, Zool. 1. p. 682 (livr. 15), April 3, 1830.

A narrative of the voyage, with occasional notes on zoology and with a number of colored plates of birds and mammals, was published by R. P. Lesson in 1839 (q.v.).

Dupetit-Thouars, Abel Aubert.

See Petit-Thouars, Abel Aubert du.

Du Plessis, J.

1758-60. See Edwards, George, **Gleanings of Natural History,** 1758-64.

1805. Idem, 1805-06.

Durand, David.

1745-51. See Edwards, George, **Histoire Naturelle d'Oiseaux peu Communs.**

D'Urban, William Stewart Mitchell; and Mathew, Murray Alexander.

1892. The | birds of Devon. | By | W. S. M. D'Urban, F.L.S., F.E.S., | formerly Curator of the Albert Memorial | Museum, Exeter, | and | The Rev. Murray A. Mathew, M.A., F.L.S., |

Member of the British Ornithologists' Union, | Vicar of Buckland
Dinham, Somerset. | With an introduction and some remarks on
the | migration of Devonshire birds. | Illustrated by Coloured
Plates, Photographs, and Maps. | London: | R. H. Porter, 18
Princes Street, Cavendish Square. | 1892. | [All Rights reserved.].

1 vol. post 8vo, pp. I-LXXXVII+1, 1-459+1, 1-7+1, frontisp.
(col.), pll. I-IV (col.; by J. G. Keulemans), 4 pll., 3 maps. London.

An account of the distribution and habits of the various species, with notes on
local records of occurrence. This is the first edition. In 1895 a supplement
seems to have been issued, and also a second edition of the whole work including
the supplement; a copy of the second edition is collated below.

D'Urban, William Stewart Mitchell; and Mathew, Murray Alexander.

1895.   The | birds of Devon. | By | W. S. M. D'Urban, F.L.S., |
formerly Curator of the Albert Memorial | Museum, Exeter, |
and | The Rev. Murray A. Mathew, M.A., F.L.S., | Member of
the British Ornithologists' Union, | Vicar of Buckland Dinham,
Somerset. | With an introduction and some remarks on the |
migrations of Devonshire birds. | Illustrated by Coloured Plates,
Photographs, and Maps. | **Second edition,** with supplement. |
London: | R. H. Porter, 18 Princes Street, Cavendish Square. |
1895. | [All Rights reserved.].

1 vol. post 8vo, pp. I-LXXXVII+1, 1-459+1, 1-7+1, 1-31, frontisp.
(col.), pll. I-IV (col.; by J. G. Keulemans), 4 pll., 4 maps. London.

Printed from the same plates as the first edition (q.v., 1892), with a slightly altered
title-page and the addition of a 31-page supplement containing matter acquired
after the date of publication of the first edition. This supplement is said to
have been issued separately the same year as the present edition.

Dutt, William Alfred.   (Patterson, Arthur; Bird, M. C. H.; Everitt,
Nicholas.)

1903.   The | Norfolk Broads | by | William A. Dutt | assisted by
numerous contributors | with forty-eight coloured and twenty-nine
uncoloured | illustrations by Frank Southgate | Methuen & Co. | 36
Essex Street W.C. | London | 1903.

1 vol. 8vo, pp. I-VIII, 1-379, 73 pll. (48 col.), 4 full-page cuts, 1 map.
London.

An interesting account of the marshlands of eastern Norfolk, beautifully illustrated. There are many ornithological notes scattered through the book, and
certain sections are devoted to the natural history of the region. Principal
among these latter are, Chapter XIII, "Wild Life on Breydon," by Arthur
Patterson; Chapter XIV, "Bird Life," by the Rev. M. C. H. Bird; Chapter
XXII, "Wild-fowling," by Nicholas Everitt; and Appendix II, "A List of the
Birds, Mammals, Reptiles, Amphibians, and Fishes of Broadland" (pp. 348-

360 "Birds") by the author. Eight colored and thirteen uncolored plates are illustrations of birds or relate to bird-shooting.

Dutton, F. G.

1883-88. See Greene, William Thomas, **Parrots in Captivity.**

Dwight, Jonathan, Jr.

1910. See American Ornithologists' Union, **Check-list of North American Birds, Third Edition.**

Dzieduszycki, Wladimir, Graf.

1880. Grfl. Dzieduszycki'sches | Museum | in | Lemberg. | Lemberg. | I Vereins-Buchdruckerei. | 1880.

> **Grfl. Dzieduszycki'sches | Museum | in Lemberg.** | I Abtheilung. | **Zoologie** | Wirbelthiere. | II. | **Vögel** | gesammelt, bestimmt und verzeichnet | von | Wladimir Graf Dzieduszycki. | Lemberg. | I Vereins-Buchdruckerei. | 1880.

1 vol. post 8vo, pp. I-XLI+1, 1-204, 1-20, 3 pll. (plans; 2 fold.). Lemberg.

An annotated catalogue of the collection of birds belonging to the author. Pp. I-XXIV contains a general account of the author's museum and collections with floor plans of the building. The remainder of the volume is entirely ornithological, paged continuously with the first part but with a second title (as above). Judging from the arrangement of the volume, the first part was intended to be prefixed to each of whatever separate reports were issued on the various departments of the museum. In series, the present volume would be Part II of Section I of a complete report.

Eaton, Elon Howard.

1910-14. New York State Education Department [The University of the State of New York] | New York State Museum | John M. Clarke, Director | Memoir 12 | **Birds of New York** | by | Elon Howard Eaton | Part 1 [2] | Introductory chapters; water birds and game birds [general chapters; land birds] | [*Contents, 8 lines, double column (Pt. 1.); 6 lines, double column (Pt. 2.)*] | Albany | University [The University] of the State of New York | 1910 [1914].

2 vols. medium 4to. Vol. (Pt.) 1, pp. 1-501, 3 ll. (fold.; migration tables), 75 ll. (fold.: Sect. 1, pts. 1-15; 2, pts. 1-18; 3, pts. 1-21; 4, pts. 1-21:-local lists), 42 printed guard-sheets, pll. 1-42 (col.; by Fuertes), 1 map (insert, fold., col.), 22 text-maps. (col.), 79 text-cuts. Vol. (Pt.) 2, pp. 1-719, 64 printed guard-sheets, pll. 43-106 (col.; by Fuertes), 65 text-cuts. Albany.

An excellent and comprehensive report on the birds of the state. Descriptions of each species are followed by detailed discussions of distribution, haunts and habits, and special chapters are devoted to general subjects. Photographs and drawings are scattered through the text and a series of fine colored plates by Fuertes illustrates the various species accurately and artistically.

Eaton, John Matthews. (Moore, John.)

1858. Dedicated | to the young and inexperienced fancier. | **A** | **treatise** | **on the art of** | **breeding and managing** | **tame, domes-ticated, foreign,** | **and** | **fancy pigeons,** | carefully compiled from the best authors, with observations and reflections, | containing all that is necessary to be known of tame, domesticated, foreign | and fancy pigeons, in health, disease, and their cures. | By | John Matthews Eaton. | [*Quot., 3 lines.*] | Published for, and to be obtained of, the author, | 81 Upper Street, Islington Green, London, N. | 1858.

1 vol. post 8vo, pp. I-XIX, 20-200, 18 pll. (col.; by D. Wolstenholme). London.

A curious volume on pigeon-breeding, illustrated by hand-colored engravings. The fore part of the book (pp. VII-109, is composed of an earlier work by John Moore (1735) entitled, "Columbarium: or the Pigeon-House," with footnotes by the present author, new or extracted from other works to which due credit is given. Much of the remainder of the work consists of similar extracts.

Eckeberg, Carl Gustav.

1765. See Osbeck, Peter, **Reise nach Ostindien und China.**

Eckstorm, Fannie Hardy.

1901. **The woodpeckers** | by | Fannie Hardy Eckstorm | with illustrations | [*Design.*] | Boston and New York. Houghton, Mifflin and Company | The Riverside Press, Cambridge | 1901.

1 vol. post 8vo, 4 pr. ll. (tit., ded., conts. and list of illustrs.), pp. 1-131, 5 printed guard-sheets, 5 pll. (col.; by L. A. Fuertes), 21 text-cuts. Boston and New York.

A popular account of the habits and peculiarities of woodpeckers in general and several North American species in particular. The book is intended for juvenile consumption and contains considerable reliable information, pleasantly written.

Eder, Robert.

1908. **Die Vögel Niederösterreichs** | von | Robert Eder. | [*Design.*] | 1908. | Mödling bei Wien. | Selbstverlag des Verfassers. | Druck J. Pasternak, Mödling.

1 vol. crown 8vo, tit., pp. I-III+1, 1-108. Mödling.

A contribution to the ornithology of the southern portion of the Province of Lower Austria.

Edwards, Alphonse Milne.
See Milne Edwards, Alphonse.

Edwards, George.
1743-51. A | natural history | of | Uncommon birds, | and of | Some
other Rare and Undescribed animals, | Quadrupedes, | ⎱ | Fishes,
Reptiles, | ⎰ | Insects, &c. |
Exhibited in Two Hundred and Ten Copper-Plates, | From Designs
copied immediately from Nature, and curiously coloured after
Life. | With a full and accurate Description of each figure. | To
which is added, | A brief and General Idea of Drawing and Paint-
ing in Water-Colours; with Instructions | for Etching on Copper
with Aqua Fortis: Likewise some Thoughts on the Passage of |
Birds; and Additions to many of the Subjects described in this
Work. | In Four parts. | By George Edwards, | Library-Keeper
to the Royal-College of physicians. | [*Vignette.*] | London: | Printed
for the Author, at the College of Physicians, in Warwick-Lane.
> [*Pt. I.*] A | natural history | of | birds. | Most of which have
not been figur'd or describ'd, and | others very little known from ob-
scure or too brief | Descriptions without Figures, or from Figures
very ill | design'd. | Containing | The Figures of Sixty Birds and
Two Quadrupedes, engrav'd | on Fifty-two Copper Plates, after
curious Original Drawings from | Life, and exactly Colour'd. | With
full and accurate Descriptions. | By George Edwards. | Natura
semper eadem, sed Artes sunt variæ. | London: | Printed for the
Author, at the College of Physicians in Warwick-Lane. | M.DCC.-
XLIII.
> [*Pt. II.*] A | natural history | of | birds, | Most of which have
not been figured or described, and | others very little known, from
obscure or too brief | Descriptions without Figures, or from Figures
very ill | designed: | containing | The Figures of Sixty-One Birds
and Two Quadrupedes, engrav'd | on Fifty-Three Copper Plates,
afrer (*sic*) curious Original Drawings from | Life, and exactly
Colour'd. With full and accurate Descriptions. | To which is
added, | An appendix, by Way of Illustration. | Part II. | By
George Edwards. | London: | Printed for the Author, at the College
of Physicians in Warwick-Lane. | M.DCC.XLVII.
> [*Pt. III.*] A | natural history | of birds, | The most of which
have not hitherto been figured or | described, and the rest, by
Reason of obscure, or too | brief Descriptions, without Figures, or
of Figures very | ill design'd, are hitherto but little known. | This
part exhibits | The Representations of Fifty-Nine Birds, engraven

the great pied Mountain Finch or Bramlin. 1788.

Edwards' first Essay towards Etching a Bird

UNPUBLISHED DRAWING BY GEORGE EDWARDS, FROM THOMAS PENNANT'S COPY OF
EDWARDS ''A NATURAL HISTORY OF UNCOMMON BIRDS.''
See pp. 192-194.

on Fifty-Two | Copper Plates, and coloured in their natural and proper Colours, | after curious Original Paintings, design'd from the Life: With a | full and accurate Description of each Bird. | Part III. | By George Edwards, Library-Keeper to the | Royal College of Physicians. | London: | Printed for the Author, at the College of Physicians in Warwick-Lane. | M. DCC. L.

> [*Pt. IV.*] A | natural history | of | birds. | The most of which have not hitherto been either figured or described, | and the Rest, by Reason of Obscure, or too brief Descriptions with- | out Figures, or of Figures very ill designed, are hitherto but little | known. | Containing | The Representations of thirty-nine Birds, engraven on thirty-seven Copper-Plates, | after curious Original Drawings from Life; together with a full and accurate | Description of each. | To which are added, by way of Appendix, | Sixteen Copper-Plates, representing the Figures of many curious and undescribed | Animals, such as Quadrupedes (both Land and Amphibious) | Serpents, Fishes and Insects: | The whole Containing | Fifty-three Copper- Plates, which is the full Number given in each of the foregoing Parts of | this Work.   Every Bird, Beast, &c. is colour'd from the Original Painting, ac- | cording to Nature. | Part IV. and Last. | By George Edwards, | Library-Keeper to the Royal College of Physicians. | London: | Printed for the Author, at the College of Physicians, in Warwick-Lane. | M.DCC.LI.

2 vols. (4 pts.) crown folio (9x11½). Pt. I, 2 pr. ll. (tit. and introd.), pp. I-XXIV, 1-52, frontisp. (col.), pll. 1-52 (col.), 1 pl. (extra). Pt. II, pp. I VIII, 53-128, pll. 53-105 (col.), 1 pl. (uncol.). Pt. III, 2 pr. ll. (tit. and ded.), pp. 106-157, pll. 106-157 (col.; 130 and 156 not numbered). Pt. IV, 4 pr. ll. (subtit., ded., pref. and list of subscrs.), pp. 158-248, pll. 158-210 (col.). London.

A series of colored plates (190 of birds) accompanied by detailed descriptions and accounts of the animals and other objects depicted. Parts I and II compose Vol. I, and III and IV, Vol. II. The author seems to have intended each volume to be the last one, but extended the work to four parts and continued it under the title of "Gleanings of Natural History" (q.v.) to seven parts. The work was issued under the subtitles; the full title, with the introduction, was added at the completion of the fourth part. The four parts of the present title were translated into French and issued, mostly, subsequent to their respective originals (Cf. "Histoire Naturelle d'Oiseaux," 1745-51.). Another English edition, differing from the present one in various ways, was published with the same dates on the title-pages but may have been of later issue (Cf. following title.). A larger (medium folio) edition (q.v.) appeared about 1805, after the author's death. Edwards's work, with Catesby's "Natural History of Caro- lina," was translated into German by Huth and published in 1768-76, and this combined work was retranslated into Dutch by Houttuyn and published in 1772-81 as the "Verzameling van Uitlandsche en Zeldzaame Vogelen" (q.v.).

Edwards uses vernacular names in the general text, following these by Latin and English names in the catalogues placed at the close of Pts. II and IV; but these Latin names, even if binomial, are pre-Linnean and untenable. Linné later named many of the species in his "Systema Naturae" and further, in 1776, published a "Catalogue of the Birds, Beasts, Fishes, Insects, Plants, &c. contained in Edwards's Natural History," (q.v.), sometimes considered as part of Edwards's volumes. See also, "Some Memoirs of the Life and Works of George Edwards," 1776.

The present copy is of unusual interest since it, together with the accompanying volumes of the "Gleanings," belonged to Thomas Pennant and contains numerous personalia. The Latin name of each species of bird, according to Latham's "Index Ornithblogicus" (q.v.), is written at the bottom of the respective plate in Pennant's handwriting and a manuscript index of these names (in the "Nat. Hist." and the "Gleanings") with references to Edwards and Latham, is enclosed in an envelope fastened in the front of Vol. I. At the end of Pt. II is placed the beginning of a manuscript list of North American birds figured by Edwards, also by Pennant. In addition, there is an uncolored plate of "The great pied Mountain Finch or Bramlin. 1739" (the last two figures being engraved backwards), below which is written by Pennant, "Edwards' first Essay towards Etching a Bird" (See frontispiece, Pt. II.). Other personalia are in the corresponding volumes of the "Gleanings" (q.v.).

Edwards, George.

1743-51?. **A | natural history | of | uncommon birds, |** and of | Some other Rare and Undescribed animals, $\left|\begin{array}{l}\text{Quadrupedes,}\\\text{Reptiles,}\end{array}\right\}\left\{\begin{array}{l}\text{Fishes,}\\\text{Insects, &c.}\end{array}\right|$ Exhibited in Two Hundred and Ten Copper-Plates, | From Designs copied immediately from Nature, and curiously coloured after Life. | With a full and accurate Description of each figure. | To which is added, | A brief and General Idea of Drawing and Painting in Water-Colours; with Instructions for | Etching on Copper with Aqua Fortis: Likewise some Thoughts on the Passage of Birds; | and Additions to many of the Subjects described in this Work. | In Four parts. | By George Edwards, | Library-Keeper to the Royal College of physicians. | [*Vignette.*] | London: | Printed for the Author, at the College of Physicians, in Warwick-Lane.

> [*Pt. II*] A | natural history | of | birds, | Most of which have not been figur'd or describ'd, and | others very little known from obscure or too brief | Descriptions without Figures, or from Figures very ill | design'd. | Containing | The Figures of Sixty Birds and Two Quadrupedes, en- | grav'd on Fifty-two Copper Plates, after curious Original | Drawings from Life, and exactly colour'd. | With full and | accurate Descriptions. | By George Edwards. | Natura

semper eadem, sed Artes sunt variæ. | London: | Printed for the Author, at the College of Physicians, in Warwick-Lane. | M DCC XLIII.

> [*Pt. II.*] A | natural history | of | birds, | Most of which have not been figured or described, and | others very little known, from obscure or too brief | Descriptions without Figures, or from Figures very ill designed: | containing | The Figures of Sixty-One Birds and Two Quadrupedes, engrav'd | on Fifty-Three Copper Plates afrer (*sic*) curious Drawings from | Life, and exactly Colour'd. With full and accurate Descriptions. | To which is added, | An Appendix, by Way of Illustration. | Part II. | By George Edwards. | London: | Printed for the Author, at the College of Physicians in Warwick-Lane. | M.DCC.XLVII.

> [*Pt. III.*] A | natural history | of | birds, | The most of which have not hitherto been figured or | described, and the rest, by Reason of obscure, or too | brief Descriptions, without Figures, or of Figures very | ill design'd, are hitherto but little known. | This part exhibits | The Representations of Fifty-Nine Birds, engraven on Fifty-Two | Copper Plates, and coloured in their natural and proper Colours, | after curious Original Paintings, design'd from the Life: With a | full and accurate Description of each Bird. | Part III. | By George Edwards, Library-Keeper to the | Royal College of Physicians. | London: | Printed for the Author, at the College of Physicians in Warwick-Lane. | M.DCC.L.

> [*Pt. IV.*] A | natural history | of | birds. | The most of which have not hitherto been either figured or described, | and the Rest, by Reason of Obscure, or too brief Descriptions with- | out Figures, or of Figures very ill designed, are hitherto but little | known. | Containing | The Representations of thirty-nine Birds, engraven on thirty-seven Copper-Plates, | after curious Original Drawings from Life; together with a full and accurate | Description of each. | To which are added, by way of Appendix, | Sixteen Copper-Plates, representing the Figures of many curious and undescribed | Animals, such as Quadrupedes (both Land and Amphibious) | Serpents, Fishes and Insects: | The whole Containing | Fifty-three Copper-Plates, which is the full Number given in each of the fore-going Parts of | this Work. Every Bird, Beast, &c. is colour'd from the Original Painting, ac- | cording to Nature. | Part IV. and Last. | By George Edwards, | Library-Keeper to the Royal College of Physicians. | London: | Printed for the Author, at the College of Physicians, in Warwick-Lane. | M.DCC.LI.

2 vols. (4 pts.) in 4, crown folio (9x11). Part I, 2 pr. ll. (full tit. and introd.), pp. I-XIX+1, 1-52, (pll. 1-52; col.). Pt. II, pp. I-VIII, 53-128[1], (pll. 54-104+1; col.). Pt. III, 2 pr. ll. (subtit. and ded.), pp. 106-157, (pll. 106-157; col.). Pt. IV, 4 pr. ll. (subtit., ded., pref. and list of subscrs.), pp. 158-248, (pll. 158-210; col.).) London.

A second edition of Edwards's work of the same title (Cf. foregoing), with the same dates on the title-pages but with numerous alterations. The whole of Pt. I is reset (including the full title and introduction which, in the original edition, were published after, or with, Pt. IV); the dedication and preface are repaged and the list of subscribers is omitted; the resetting of the general text has altered the style of typography but not the pagination except that the last paragraphs on pp. 19 and 20 have been interchanged. In Pt. II the subtitle-page appears to be unaltered, and the text the same, except in the appendix (pp. 107-214). The matter on pp. 121-124 and at the bottom of p. 120 (auto-biographical details) has been deleted, but to avoid changes in the pagination of pp. 125-128, the missing page-numbers have been crowded onto pp. 119 and 120, as indicated in the collation. Pts. III and IV appear to be unchanged. The original illustrations (if any were published with this edition) are missing, being replaced by water-colored copies made by an unknown artist. Pl. 105 is missing, but the portrait of a Samoyed, p. 118, is numbered 105 and is colored; it is uncolored and unnumbered in the original edition. Each part is bound separately, with the French edition (q.v.) of each part added at the close. The title-page, only, of "Some Memoirs of the Life and Works of George Edwards" (Cf. Robson, J., 1776) is included in Pt. I.

There is no indication of the actual dates of publication of this edition. It is evidently subsequent to that which I have interpreted as the original edition, since an accounting is made for the eliminated pages. The French translation, which certainly dates after the original in Pts. I-III, retains the matter which is eliminated in the present edition, and this suggests that the present edition may have followed the French one.

Edwards, George. (Durand, David.)

1745-51. Histoire naturelle | d'oiseaux peu communs: | et d'autres | Animaux rares & qui n'ont pas été Decrits, | Consistant en | Quadrupedes, } { Poissons, | Représentés sur Cent Dix | Reptiles, } { Insectes, &c. | Planches en Taille douce, | Avec une ample & exacte Description de chaque Figure. | A laquelle on a ajouté | Quelques Reflexions sur les Oiseaux de Passage; & un Supplément à plusieurs | des Sujets qui sont décrits dans cet Ouvrage. | En quatre parties. | Par George Edwards, | Bibliothécaire du Collége-Royal des Mede-cins. | [*Vignette*.] | à Londres: | Imprimé pour l'Autour au Collége-Royal des Médecins. MDCCLI.

---

[1]Pp. 119, 120 and 121 and pp. 122, 123 and 124 occupy opposite sides of one leaf!

> [*Pts. I-II.*] Histoire naturelle | de | divers oiseaux, | Qui n'avoient
point encore été figurez ni décrits, | ou qui n'étoient que peu connus
d'après des | descriptions obscures ou abrégées sans figures, | ou
d'après des figures mal dessinées: | contenant | Les figures de LX
[LXI (*Pt. II.*)]. Oiseaux & de deux Quadrupedes, gravez | sur
LII [LIII (*Pt. II.*)]. Planches sur les desseins Originaux, d'après
le Naturel vivant, | & fidellement coloriez; avec des descriptions
pleines & éxactes. [| A quoi on a joint, | Par voye d'Appendice,
quelques Eclaircissemens sur l'Histoire Naturelle des Oiseaux. |
II. Partie.] | Par George Edwards. | Traduit de l'Anglois par
M.D. de la S.R. | Natura semper eadem; sed Artes variæ. [*Line
omitted* (*Pt. II.*).] | A Londres, | Imprimé pour l'Auteur: au
Collége des Medecins in [en (*Pt. II.*)] Warwick-Lane. | M DCC
XLV [M DCC XLVIII (*Pt. II.*)].

> [*Pts. III-IV.*] Histoire naturelle | de | divers oiseaux. | Qui
n'avoient point encore été figures ni décrits, ou qui n'étoient | que
peu connus d'après des descriptions obscures ou abrégées | sans
figures, ou d'après des figures mal dessinées. | Contenant | Les
figures de LIX [XXXIX (*Pt. IV.*)] Oiseaux, gravées sur LII
[XXXVII (*Pt. IV.*)] Planches sur les desseins | originaux;
d'après le Naturel vivant, & fidellement coloriées; [avec des des-
criptions pleines & exactes. (*Pt. IV.*)] | avec des descriptions
pleines & exactes. [*Line missing* (*Pt. IV.*).] | [*Design* (*Pt. III.*);
A quoi on a joint par voye d'Appendix, | Seize Planches qui
représentant les figures de plusieurs Animaux rares & qui n'ont |
pas encore été décrits, comme de Quadrupedes (Terrestres &
Amphibies,) | de Serpens, de Poissons, & d'Insectes: | Le tout
compris | Dans LIII Planches, ce qui fait un nombre égal à celui
de chacune des Parties | précédentes. Chaque Animal est colorié
sur le dessein original, qui a été fait | immédiatement d'après
Nature. (*Pt. IV.*)] | III [IV]. Partie. | Par George Edwards, |
Bibliothécaire du Collége Royal des Medecins. | A Londres: |
Imprimé pour l'Auteur: au Collége Royale des Médecins en |
Warwick-Lane. M DCC LI.

2 vols. (4 pts.) in 4, crown folio. Pt. I, 5 pr. ll. (full tit., introd.,
subtit., ded.), pp. I-XXI, I-LII+1. Pt. II, 2 pr. ll. (subtit. and
ded.), 1 p. (blank), pp. LIII-CV, 1-26. Pt. III, 2 pr. ll. (subtit.
and ded.), 1 p. (half-tit.), pp. CVI-CLVII. Pt. IV, subtit., 1 p.
(ded.), pp. CLVIII-CCX, 211-236. London.

The French translation (by David Durand) of Edwards's "A Natural History of
Uncommon Birds," 1743-51 (q.v.), with some alterations. The French descrip-

tions are arranged in the same sequence as the English accounts, but the first description is on a right-hand page and the second one on the opposite side of the leaf, while the first English account is on a left-hand page with No. 2 on the following leaf. Thus when the two editions are combined and interleaved, the English and French descriptions of each plate are on opposite pages, between which the plate may be conveniently inserted. Some copies are bound in this manner but the set at hand has the French text of each part collected separately at the end of the volumes. The dates, as shown above, differ from those of the English edition. Further evidence that the translation was published subsequent to the original English edition is found on p. 105 of Pt. II, where it is stated that "there is a French Translation of this Work design'd." The French text is continued by the French portions of the author's "Gleanings of Natural History," 1758-64 (q.v.). The translator of the present work has added, at the bottom of p. XXVII, Pt. I, an original observation on the migration of birds. This was quoted by Edwards in Pt. II of the English edition, p. 116 and again on p. 10 of Part II of the present translation.

The present copy is bound with what appears to be a second edition of the English text of 1743-51 (q.v.); there is no French text in the copy of the original issue of the same years, also collated above.

Edwards, George. (Du Plessis, J.; Barker, Edmond.)

1758-64. Gleanings | of | natural history, | exhibiting figures of | quadrupeds, birds, insects, plants, &c. [quadrupeds, birds, fishes, insects, &c. (*Pt. II.*)] | Most of which have not, till now, been either Figured or Described. | With | descriptions of seventy [one hundred (*Pt. II.*); Eighty-five (*Pt. III.*)] different Subjects, | Designed, Engraved, and Coloured after Nature, | On fifty [fifty-two (*Pt. III.*)] copper-plate prints. [| Part II.; Part III.] | By | George Edwards, | Fellow of the Royal Society, and of the Society of | Antiquaries, London. | London: | Printed for the author, at the Royal College of Physicians, | in Warwick-Lane. | M DCC LVIII [M DCC LX; M DCC LXIV]. [*Title also in French-*, "Glanures d'histoire naturelle," *or* "Glanures de l'histoire naturelle" (*Pt. III.*), *etc.*].

3 parts in 3 vols., crown folio (9 x 11½). Pt. I, 4 pr. ll. (Engl. tit French tit., half-tit. and ded.), pp. 1-108, frontisp. (portr.), 50 pll. (col.; num. 211-260 in text; only 8 num. on pll.), 2 pll. (col.; extras), 1 text-fig. Pt. II, 6 pr. ll. (tits., ded. and list of subscrs.), pp. I-XXXV+1, 109-220, 50 pll. (col.; num. 261-310 in text; only 9 num. on pll.). Pt. III, 4 pr. ll. (tits., ded. and list of subscrs.), pp. I-VII+1, 221-347, 52 pll. (col.; num. 311-362 in text; only 8 num. on pll.). London.

The continuation of the author's "A Natural History of Uncommon Birds," 1743-51 (q.v.), with separate pagination but with the plates, 128 of which are ornithological, numbered in sequence following those of the earlier work.

Usually, as in the present case, both works are bound uniformly and considered as Pts. I-VII of one work. The present volumes are somewhat differently arranged than those of the "Natural History." Separate titles in English and French are given, and the text is in both languages, in parallel columns. The translation of Pts. I and II is by Du Plessis; that of Pt. III, by Barker.

As with "A Natural History of Uncommon Birds," a second edition was issued with the same dates on the title-pages, but with some differences in the text (Cf. following title.), and another edition in medium folio in 1805 (q.v.). It is likewise incorporated into the "Verzameling van Uitlandsche en Zeldzaame Vogelen," 1772-81 (q.v.).

The present set, with that of the "Natural History," belonged to Thomas Pennant and contains various evidences of his ownership. The Latin names of the birds, following Latham, are written at the foot of the respective plates in Pennant's handwriting, with an occasional critical note. The back cover of Pt. III contains a manuscript letter to Pennant signed by George Edwards, respecting a painting which Edwards was presenting to Pennant, and on the opposite page is a brief notation by Pennant regarding the disposition made of the gift. A loose sheet contains an uncolored print of the figures of the "Black Linnet" and "Olive-coloured Linnet" from Pl. 362, trimmed to the shape of the birds and mounted on the sheet on which are written the names of the species. The volume is further augmented by the addition of uncolored copies of 11 plates from Albin's "Supplement to the Natural History of Birds," 1740 (q.v.), 1 from his "History of Esculent Fish," 1794 and 1, ornithological, from an unknown source but resembling Albin's plates and possibly an unpublished example of his work. Pt. I is enriched by the addition of two unpublished plates by Edwards representing two species of Quadrumana, one of which is further figured on Pl. 218.

On p. IX of Pt. II, Edwards notes several plates which were not drawn by himself.

Edwards, George. (Du Plessis, J.; Barker, Edmond.)

1758-64?. Gleanings | of | natural history, | exhibiting figures of | quadrupeds, birds, insects, plants, &c. [quadrupeds, birds, fishes, insects, &c. (*Pt. II.*)] | Most of which have not, till now, been either Figured or Described. | With | descriptions of seventy [one hundred (*Pt. II.*); Eighty-five (*Pt. III.*)] different Subjects, | Designed, Engraved, and Coloured after Nature, | On fifty [fifty-two (*Pt. III.*)] copper-plate prints. [| Part II.; Part III.] | By | George Edwards, | Fellow of the Royal Society, and of the Society of Antiquaries, London. | London: | Printed for the author, at the Royal College of Physicians, | in Warwick-Lane. | M DCC LVIII [M DCC LX; M DCC LXIV]. [*Title also in French,*-"Glanures d'histoire naturelle," *or* "Glanures de l'histoire naturelle" (*Pt. III.*), etc.].

3 parts in 3 vols., crown folio (9 x 11). Pt. I, 4 pr. ll. (half-tit., ded., Engl. tit. and French tit.), pp. 1-108, (pll. 211-260; col.), 1 text-fig.

Pt. II, 6 pr. ll. (tits. ded. and list of subscrs.), pp. I-XXXV+1[1], 1-220, (pll. 261-310; col.). Pt. III, 4 pr. ll. (tits. ded. and list of subscrs.), pp. I-VII+1, 221-347, (pll. 311-362; col.). London.

A second edition of the work of the same title and date (q.v.) and continuing the second edition of the "Natural History of Uncommon Birds," 1743-51(q.v.). The edition differs from the original in several particulars. The preface is shortened by the omission of certain matter (which is not strictly ornithological) on pp. II-VIII and XX-XXIV and the numbers of the missing pages are grouped together on four adjoining pages, as indicated in the footnote to the collation. The title-pages and general text appear to be unaltered but the original plates (if any in this edition) are missing, being replaced by copies in water-colors by unknown artists.

At the end of Pt. III is bound a copy of Linné's "Catalogue of the Birds," etc., 1776 (q.v.).

Edwards, George; and Catesby, Mark. (Houttuyn, Martinus; Huth, George Leonhard; Seligmann, Johann Mich.)

1772-81. Verzameling | van | uitlandsche en zeldzaame | vogelen,| benevens eenige vreemde | dieren en plantgewassen: | in 't Engelsch naauwkeurig beschreeven en naar | 't Leven met Kleuren afge-beeld, | door | G. Edwards en M. Catesby: | Verfolgens, ten opzigt van de Plaaten merkelyk | verbeterd, in 't Hoogduitsch uitgegeven | door | J. M. Seligmann: | Thans in 't Nederduitsch vertaald en met | aanhaalingen van andere Autheuren | verrykt, door | M. Houttuyn, Medic. Doctor. | Eerste [-Vyfde] band, | behelzende | Het eerste en tweede [derde en vierde (*Vol. II.*); vyfde en zesde (*Vol. III.*); zeevende en achste (*Vol. IV.*); negende (*Vol. V.*)] deel. | Te Amsterdam, | By Jan Christian Sepp, Boek-verkooper. | MDCCLXXII [MDCCLXXVI (*Vols. II-IV.*); MDCCLXXXI (*Vol. V.*)].

5 vols. in 4, royal folio. Vol. I, 2 pr. ll. (tit. and ded.), pp. I-XVI, 1-84, pll. I-CII (col.; 100 of birds). Vol. II, 2 pr. ll., pp. 1-108, 2 ll. (list of pll. in Vol. II), pll. I-CXIV (col.; 109 of birds; LIV wrongly num. IV). Vol. III, 2 pr. ll., pp. 1-118, pll. I-CV (col.; 89 of birds). Vol. IV, 2 pr. ll., pp. 1-56 (Pt. 7.), 1-56 (Pt. 8 and conts.), pll. I-C (col.; 77 of birds). Vol. V, tit., pp. 1-90, 1 l. (conts. of Vol. V), 3 ll. (index to Vols. I-V), pll. I-LII (col.; 50 of birds). Amsterdam.

In 1749-76, there was published in Nuremberg a German translation, by G. L. Huth, of Edwards's "A Natural History of Uncommon Birds" and "Gleanings of Natural History" (q.v.) and Catesby's "Natural History of Carolina, Florida and the Bahama Islands," combined into one work under the title of "Samm-lung verschiedenen ausländischer und seltener Vögel." This was published in

---

1 pp. I-IV and V-VIII occupy opposite sides of a single leaf, as do pp. XIX-XXI and XXII-XXIV

nine parts. The plates of Edwards and Catesby were re-engraved by Seligmann and some of those by Edwards further embellished by the addition of figures of plants not in the originals. The present work is a translation of the German work, into Dutch, by Houttuyn with Seligmann's plates. The text appears to follow Edwards and Catesby closely, with the addition of descriptions of the new botanical subjects; the plates are rather good copies of the originals (with the additions mentioned), differing from them somewhat in coloration. The nine parts of the German book are embraced by the five volumes, each of which was published with two parts of the translation except Vol. V which closed the work with Part 9. In Vols. I-III the pagination is continuous for each volume, through both parts contained therein; in Vol. IV each part (Pts. 7 and 8) is paged separately. In the present copy, Vols. IV and V are bound in one volume.

Edwards, George.

1776. See Robson, J., **Some Memoirs of the Life and Works of George Edwards.**

Edwards, George.

1805?. **A | natural history | of | birds. |** Most of which have not been figured or described, and others very | little known, from obscure or too brief descriptions without | figures, or from figures very ill designed. | Containing the figures of | Sixty Birds and Two Quadrupedes, | engraved on fifty-two copper-plates, | after curious original drawings from life, and exactly coloured. | With full and accurate Descriptions. | By George Edwards. | Natura semper eadem, sed artes sunt variæ. | London: | Published by Will. Gardiner, No. 98, Pall-Mall, and Messrs. | Robinsons, Paternoster-Row. | M.DCCC.II. | T. Rickaby, Printer, Peterborough-court, Fleet-street.

> [*Idem, 7 lines.*] | Containing the figures of | Sixty-one Birds and Two Quadrupedes, | engraved on fifty-three copper-plates, | after curious original drawings from life, and exactly coloured, | With full and accurate Descriptions. | To which is added, | an appendix, by way of illustration. | Part. II. | By George Edwards. | London: [*etc.*].

> A | natural history | of | birds. | the most of which have not hitherto been figured or described, and | the rest, by reason of obscure or too brief descriptions, | without figures, or of figures very ill designed, | are hitherto but little known. | This part exhibits the representations of | Fifty-Nine Birds, | engraven on fifty-two copper-plates, | and coloured in their natural and proper colours, | after curious original paintings, designed from the life: |

With a full and accurate Description of each Bird. | Part III. | By George Edwards. | London: [etc.].

> A | natural history | of birds, | most of which have not hitherto been either figured or described, and | the rest, by reason of obscure, or too brief descriptions without | figures, or of figures very ill designed, are hitherto | but little known, | containing the representations of | Thirty-nine Birds, | engraved on thirty-seven copper-plates, | With full and accurate Descriptions. | To which are added, by way of appendix, | sixteen copper-plates, representing the figures of many curious and | undescribed animals, such as quadrupedes (both land and | amphibious), serpents, fishes, and insects: | the whole containing | fifty-three copper-plates, which is the full number given in each of the foregoing | parts of this work. | Part IV. | By George Edwards. | London: | Published by Will. Gardiner, No. 48, Pall-Mall, and Messrs. | Robinsons, Paternoster-Row. | M.DCCC.III. | C. Rickaby, Printer, Peterborough-court, Fleet-street.

2 vols. (4 parts), medium folio. Part I, 1 pr. l., pp. V-XXIII+1,1-52 pll. 1-52 (col.). Part II, pp. I-IV, 53-126, pll. 53-105 (col.). Part III, 2 pr. ll., pp. 106-157, pll. 106-157 (col.). Part IV, 1 pr. l., pp. 158-210+1, 218-249, pll. 158-210 (col.). London.

A posthumous edition of Edwards's "A Natural History of Uncommon Birds," 1743-51 (q.v.), with minor alterations in the text and with all the plates but Nos. 134 and 179 in reverse (backwards), lettering and numbering included. They appear as though they had been transferred from drawings or printed sheets and not printed from the copper plates. Pll. 134 and 179 are in natural position and show the impression of the edges of the copper-plates, which the remainder do not. All the plates are exceptionally finely colored and of softer finish than those of the original edition. The general title-page is omitted. Although 1802 and 1803 are given on the subtitles of each part, there are plates in each part which are watermarked 1803 and 1805, from which it would appear that the reissue (including that of the "Gleanings of Natural History" continuing the present work) appeared entire, in 1805 or 1806. According to Mullens and Swann, a large-paper edition, 1802-1805, to which this apparently belongs, was issued in an edition of twenty-five copies only. The changes in the text are principally those of wording, certain antiquated terms being replaced by more modern ones, but the typography is entirely different. Parts I and II form the first volume; III and IV, the second. As in the original edition, the work was continued by "Gleanings of Natural History" (q.v.).

Edwards, George. (Du Plessis, J.; Barker, Edmond.).

1805-06. Gleanings | of | natural history, | exhibiting figures of | quadrupeds, birds, insects, plants, &c. | most of which have not, till now, been either figured or described. | With | descriptions of seventy different subjects, designed, engraved, and | coloured after nature, | on | Fifty Copper-plate Prints. | Volume V. | By George Edwards. | London: | Published by Will. Gardiner, No. 98, Pall-Mall, and Messrs. | Robinsons, Paternoster-Row. | M.DCCC.V. | C. Rickaby, Printer, Peterborough-court, | Fleet-street. > [*Title also in French*, "Glanures | d'histoire naturelle," *etc.*].

> Gleanings | of | natural history, | exhibiting figures of | quadrupeds, birds, fishes, insects, &c. | Most of which have not, till now, been either figured or described; | with | Descriptions of one hundred different Subjects, | designed, engraved, and coloured after Nature, | on fifty copper-plate prints. | Part II. | By | George Edwards, | Fellow of the Royal Society, and of the Society of Antiquaries, London. | London: | Printed by George Sidney, Northumberland Street, Strand. | 1806. > [*Title also in French*].

> Gleanings | of | natural history, | containing figures of | quadrupeds, birds, insects, plants, &c. | Most of which have not, till now, been either figured or described: | with | Descriptions of eighty-five different Subjects, | designed, engraved, and coloured after Nature, | on fifty-two copper-plate prints. | Part III. | By | George Edwards, | Fellow of the Royal Society, and of the Society of Antiquaries, London. | London: | Printed by George Sidney, Northumberland Street, Strand. | 1806. > [*Title also in French*].

2 vols. (3 parts), medium folio. Part I, 2 pr. ll., pp. I-XXXV+1, 1-138, pll. 211-276 (col.). Part II, 4 pr. ll., pp. 139-215+1, pll. 277-310 (col.). Part III, 3 pr. ll., pp. I-VII+1, 217-347, pll. 311-362 (col.). London.

The continuation of the posthumous edition of Edwards's "Natural History of Birds" (q.v.) and similar to it in all respects. As in the original edition, 1758-64 (q.v.), French and English versions are given in parallel columns and a French title-page is supplied. Translations are by Du Plessis and Barker as in the original edition. Plates 232, 278, 298, 316, 317 and 337 are in natural position; the remainder are reversed. Some plates in each part are watermarked 1803 and 1805 and the latter date, consequently, is the earliest one possible for any part. Part I comprises the first volume; Pts. II and III, the second. The work is uniform with the reissue of the "Natural History of Birds" and probably came out with it, all parts together.

Edwards, John.

1819. See Ross, John, **A Voyage of Discovery.**

Ehrenberg, Christian Gottfried. (Hemprich, Friedrich Wilhelm.)

1828-33. {Symbolae physicae | seu | icones et descriptiones | corporum | naturalium novorum aut minus cognitorum. quae ex itin eribus | per | Libyam Aegyptum Nubiam Dongolam | Syriam Arabiam et Habessiniam | publico institutis sumptu | Friderici Guilelmi Hemprich | et | Christiani Godofredi Ehrenberg | Medicinae et Chirurgiae Doctorum | studio | annis MDCCCXX-MDCCCXXV | redierunt. | Regis iussu et impensis | publico usui obtulit | superstes | Dr. C. G. Ehrenberg, | Eques Ordinis Aquilae Rubrae [*etc.*, *2 lines*] | Pars zoologica I. | Berolini ex officina Academica. | Venditur a Mittlero. | MDCCCXXVIII}[1].

> [Symbolae physicae | seu | icones et descriptiones | avium | quae ex itinere | per | Africam borealem et Asiam | occidentalum | Friderici Guilelmi Hemprich | et | Christiani Godofredi Ehrenberg | Medicinae et Chirurgiae Doctorum | studio | novae aut illustratae redierunt. Percensuit | et | regis iussu et impensis | editit | Dr. C. G. Ehrenberg. | Decas prima. | Berolini ex officina Academica. | Venditur a Mittlero. | MDCCCXXVIII].

> **Avium decas I.** | Continuata explicatio. | Observatae collectaeque 133 avium species africanae et asiaticae | denuo et scrupulose | collatis exuviis, percensentur, multae primum adumbrantur.
1 vol. superroyal folio, (tit. missing), subtit., 32 ll. (signs. a-i, k-u, x-z and aa-gg), pll. I-X (col.; by Müller). Berlin.

The ornithological portion of Ehrenberg's report on the collections made by himself and Hemprich (who died in the field) on their expedition to northern Africa and western Asia in 1820-25. Numerous new species are described, all of which must be credited to Ehrenberg although most of them are initialed "H. et E." in the text. The work is often quoted as "Hemprich & Ehrenberg, Symbolae Physicae," etc. According to the Catalogue of the Library of the British Museum (Natural History), signatures a and b (4 ll.) and all the plates were issued in 1828; the remaining signatures (1 leaf each) appeared in 1833. These later signatures are dated December 1832, January 1833 and February 1833.

A review of the types of the new species of birds, described herein, is given by Dresser and Blanford in the Ibis, 1874, pp. 335-343. Certain plates were left unpublished by Ehrenberg, and these were later discussed and described by various specialists in a "Symbolae physicae seu icones adhuc ineditae," etc., published in 1899-1900. The ornithology of this supplement consists of a single plate (Pl. XI) of skeletal features of *Ciconia abdimii*, named but not otherwise discussed in the text in Vol. (I) Zoologica, 1899.

Eliot, Willard Ayres.

1923. **Birds of** | **the Pacific coast** | including a brief account of the distribution | and habitat of one hundred and eighteen | birds that are more or less common to | the Pacific Coast states and British | Columbia, many of which are | found eastward to the Rocky |

---

[1]From copy in the John Crerar Library, Chicago.

[2]From wrapper of copy in the library of the Bavarian State Museum at Münich; transcribed by Dr. C. E. Hellmayr. No title-page in this copy.

Mountains and beyond | By | Willard Ayres Eliot | with fifty-six color plates by | R. Bruce Horsfall | G. P. Putnam's Sons | The Knickerbocker Press | New York and London | 1923.

1 vol. cap 8vo, pp. I-XVII+1, 1-211, 56 pll. (col.; by R. Bruce Horsfall). New York.

A popular account of a number of birds of the western coast of the United States. The illustrations are badly reproduced, being carelessly printed and inaccurate as to color in many cases.

Elliot, Daniel Giraud.

1864-65. A | monograph of the Tetraoninae, | or family of the grouse. | By | Daniel Giraud Elliot, | Fellow of the Zoological Society of London [*etc., 4 lines.*] | New York: | Published by the author, No. 27 West Thirty-third Street. | 1865.

1 vol. double-elephant folio (18½ x 23), 26 ll., 27 pll. (col.; by D. G. Elliot, J. Wolf and Wm. S. Morgan). New York.

Published in five parts; Pts. I-II, 1864; III-V. 1865 (according to Coues). Subject matter is distributed as follows according to the index number in the list of plates. Pt. I—numbers 2, 7, 10, 13, 14, 23; II—3, 4, 9, 12, 15, 18; III—5, 8, 16, 17, 19; IV and V (published together)—1, 6, 11, 20, 21, 22, 1 (eggs) and 2 (eggs).

Elliot, Daniel Giraud.

1866-69. The | new and heretofore unfigured species of | the birds | of | North America. | By | Daniel Giraud Elliot, | Chevalier de l'Ordre Italien [*etc., 5 lines.*] | Vol. I [II]. | New York: | Published by the author. | 1869.

2 vols. double-elephant folio (18½ x 23). Vol. I, 45 ll., 29 pll. (col.; by D. G. Elliot, J. Wolf and Edw. Sheppard), 18 text-figs. Vol. II, 46 ll., 43 pll. (col.; by D. G. Elliot, J. Wolf and Edwin Sheppard), 5 text-figs. New York.

Published in fifteen parts; Pts. I and II, 1866; III-VIII, 1867; IX-XII, 1868; XIII-XV, 1869 (according to Coues and the Ibis). More explicit dates are suggested by the review of Pt. I in the Ibis for Oct. 1866; that of Pt. IV in Oct. 1867; that of IX in July 1868. The subject matter is arranged as follows, according to the index numbers. Numbers 1 to 40 are in Vol. I, and 41 to 114 in Vol. II. Pt. I—numbers 8, 26, 48, 95, 108; II—36, 49, 52, 58, 62; III— 17, 22, 61, 97, 104; IV—25, 27, 78, 84, 107; V—7, 30, 53, 63, 81; VI—24, 37, 47, 106, 109; VII—28, 50, 56, 66, 69, 70; VIII—10, 12, 13, 14, 15, 46, 88, 89, 111; IX—5, 29, 35, 60, 93, 94; X—3, 16, 20, 51, 85, 86; XI—9, 18, 32, 43, 75, 76; XII—21, 31, 40, 41, 71, 72; XIII—33, 38, 39, 42, 80; XIV and XV— (issued together)—59, 65, 67, 68, 77, 99, 101, introductory matter and title-pages. The introduction treats of thirty-two species not given in the general text. These are listed in the indices of both volumes in their proper relations to the other forms, with references to the introduction. Some of them are figured in the text-cuts,—their index numbers are 1, 4, 6, 11, 19, 23, 34, 44, 45, 54, 55, 57, 64, 73, 74, 79, 82, 83, 87, 90, 91, 92, 96, 98, 100, 102, 103, 105, 110, 112, 113 and 114.

The genus *Exanthemops* is new.

Elliot, Daniel Giraud.

1867. A | monograph | of | the Pittidae, | or, | Family of Ant Thrushes. | By | Daniel Giraud Elliot, | Fellow of the Zoological Society of London [*etc., 2 lines.*]. | New York: | D. Appleton & Company, 443 & 445 Broadway. | 1867.

1 vol. imperial folio, pp. 1-102, 31 pll. (I-XXXI in index; col.; by the author and P. Oudart). New York.

A reprint of the author's original work of the same title which was published in 6 parts in the years 1861-63. The plates are hand-colored lithographs from drawings mostly by Elliot. Whether they are from the original stock or are reprinted, I am uncertain. The original edition appeared with title-page dated 1863. Apparently there are no important changes (if any) in the text, although the pagination is continuous throughout the volume instead of separate for each species as in the original printing. Except for the alteration in the date, the title-page is unchanged. A later edition, revised and much enlarged, was issued in 1893-95 (q.v.).

Elliot, Daniel Giraud.

1870-72. A | monograph | of the | Phasianidæ | or | family of the pheasants. | By | Daniel Giraud Elliot, | Knight of the Royal Portuguese Order [*etc., 7 lines.*] | Volume I [II]. | 1872: | Published by the author, 27 west thirty-third street, | New York.

2 vols. double-elephant folio. Vol. I, 2 pr. ll., pp. I-XXX, 44 ll., 33 pll. (31 col.; by J. Wolf and J. Smit). Vol. II, 57 ll., 48 pll. (col.; by J. Wolf and J. Smit). New York.

Issued in six parts irrespective of sequence of pages; Pt. **I**, June 1870 (rev. Ibis, Oct. 1870); **II—V**, 1871 (rev. Ibis, Oct. 1872); **VI**, Oct. 1872 (dat. March, but issued in Oct.; rev. Ibis, Jan. 1873). The subject matter of each part is distributed as follows, according to the number of the volume and the index-number as given in the list of plates. Part **I** —(Vol. I.), numbers 4, 8, 12, 15, 20, 27, 28, (Vol. II.), 12, 14, 18, 21, 24, 32, 41, 44; Part **II**—(Vol. I.), 5, 6, 10, 19, 25, 30, (Vol. II.), 1, 11, 25, 26, 31, 34, 37, 39, 47; Part **III**—(Vol. I.), 7, 11, 22, 23, 33, (Vol. II.), 3, 8, 9, 15, 23, 27, 28, 36, 38, 40; Part **IV**—(Vol. I.), 9, 17, 21, 26, 31, (Vol. II.), 2, 4, 6, 10, 29, 30, 35, 42, 43; Part **V**—(Vol. I.), 3, 13, 14, 16, 18, 24, 29, 32, (Vol. II.), 5, 7, 16, 19, 22, 33, 45, 46; Part **VI**—(Vol. I.), 1, 2, 30 bis, (Vol. II.), 13, 13 bis, 17, and introductory text which is placed in Vol. I.

Considered by many to be the finest of Elliot's monographs. The hand-colored plates are excellent.

Elliot, Daniel Giraud.

1873. A | monograph of the Paradiseidæ | or | birds of paradise. | By | Daniel Giraud Elliot, | Commander of the Royal Order [*etc., 11 lines.*] | 1873: | Printed for the subscribers, by the author.

1 vol. double-elephant folio (18½ x 23), pp. I-XXXII, 45 ll., 37 pll. (36 col.; by J. Wolf and J. Smit). London.

Issued in seven parts. The work contains full descriptions, synonymies and discussions of the species, with fine hand-colored plates.

Elliot, Daniel Giraud.

1877-82. A | monograph | of the | Bucerotidæ, | or | family of the hornbills. | By | Daniel Giraud Elliot, | Commander of the Royal Orders of [*etc., 10 lines.*] | Author of [*etc., 4 lines.*] | Published for the subscribers by the author. | 1882.

1 vol. demy folio, pp. I-XXXII, 75 ll., 60 pll. (57 col. by J. G. Keulemans; 3 plain by J. Smit), 7 text-figs. London.

A comprehensive treatment of the entire family of hornbills. The work was issued in ten parts with the subject matter distributed as follows, according to the number of the species (not plate) as given in the list of plates in the volume. Pt. I—species No. 10, 18, 24, 29, 40, 54; II—1, 7, 13, 16, 35, 39, 52; III—4, 15, 26, 47, 53; IV—3, 11, 21, 41, 55, 56; V—20, 32, 37, 45, 48, 50, 51; VI—2, 14, 23, 36, 46, 57; VII—8, 12, 19, 31, 42, 49; VIII—3, 17, 27, 38, 43, 60; IX—5, 22, 33, 58, 59; X—9, 25, 28, 30, 44 (plate XLIV not issued). The introductory matter appears to have been issued in Part X; possibly the two plates (and accompanying text) of generic characters were also issued in that part.

The dates of publication are slightly confused. The Catalogue of the Library of the British Museum (Natural History) cites 1876-82, but Pt. I is reviewed as of 1877 in the Ibis for July of that year and is cited in the Zoological Record for 1877. The Catalogue of a Collection of Books on Ornithology in the Library of Frederic Gallatin, Jr. cites two formats (both designated as "Original Edition"), an imperial folio dated 1876-82 and an imperial 4to dated 1877-82, both with original wrappers. Pts. II-IV are cited in the Zool. Rec. for 1877 and given as of that date in the Ibis for Oct. 1878. Pt. V is cited by the Zool. Rec. for 1878 but is given as of 1877 in the Ibis for Oct. 1878. Pt. VI is cited by the Zool. Rec. for 1879 but dated 1878 in the Ibis for Jan. 1880. Pts. VII and VIII are given as of 1880 by the Zool. Rec. and the Ibis for Jan. 1881. Pt. IX is given as of 1881 and X as of 1882 in the Zool. Rec. of 1882 and the Ibis of Jan. 1883. Both the Zool. Rec. and the Ibis quote a "small folio" but they may refer to different formats.

Elliot, Daniel Giraud.

1878-79. Smithsonian contributions to knowledge. | 317 | **A** | **classification** | **and** | **synopsis of the Trochilidæ.** | By | Daniel Giraud Elliot, F.R.S.E., Etc. | (Accepted for publication, January, 1878.].

1 vol. royal 4to, pp. I-XII, 1-277, text-figs. 1-127. Washington.

A thorough monograph of this interesting family of birds, with keys to the genera and species. The various signatures are dated April, 1878 to March 1879, but the entire work was published in April 1879, according to a statement on p. XIV of the table of contents of Vol. XXIII of the Smithsonian "Contributions," of which the present paper forms Article V.

Elliot, Daniel Giraud.

1893-95. A | monograph of the Pittidæ, | or. family of ant-thrushes. | By | Daniel Giraud Elliot, | Commander of the Royal Orders [*etc., 12 lines.*] | London: | Bernard Quaritch, 15 Piccadilly, W. | 1893-1895.

1 vol. elephant folio, pp. I-XXXIII+1, 55 ll., 51 pll. (col.; by D. G. Elliot, W. Hart, P. Oudart and Maubert). London.

Published in five parts: Pt. I, April 1893 (rev. Auk., Jan. 1894); II, Jan. 1894 (dat. Dec. 1893 but apparently not issued until Jan. 1894; rev. Ibis, April 1894); III, 1894 (dat. Febr.; rev. Auk., July, 1894); IV, 1894 (dat. Sept.; rev. Auk, Jan. 1895); V, 1895 (dat. Jan. 1895; rev. Auk, Jan. 1896; rev. Ibis, July 1895). The subject matter is distributed as follows, according to the index number of the species. Part I—numbers 2, 7, 12, 17, 18, 22, 36, 40, 45, 47; II—1, 4, 9, 13, 19, 25, 35, 41, 46; III—5, 10, 23, 29, 31, 32, 34, 43; IV—3, 14, 20, 21, 24, 28, 38, 39, 42, 44; V—6, 8, 11, 15, 16, 25A, 26, 27, 30, 33, 37.

An enlarged and revised edition of the author's earlier work of the same title (Cf. ed. 1867.). A few of the plates of this work are taken from the earlier one but most of them are new, while the text is entirely rewritten.

Elliot, Daniel Giraud.

1895. North American Shore Birds | A history of the | snipes, sand-pipers, plovers and their allies | inhabiting the beaches and marshes of the | Atlantic and Pacific coasts, the prairies, | and the shores of the inland lakes and | rivers of the North American continent; | their popular and scientific names, together with a full | description of their mode of life, nesting, migration and | dispersions, with descriptions of the summer and | winter plumages of adults and young, so that | each species may·be readily identified. | A Reference Book for the Naturalist, Sportsman and Lover of Birds | by | Daniel Giraud Elliot, F.R.S.E., Etc. | Ex-president American Ornithologists' Union | Curator of Zoölogy in the Field Columbian Museum, Chicago; Author of "Birds of | North America," Illustrated Monographs of Ant Thrushes, Grouse, | Pheasants, Birds of Paradise, Hornbills, Cats, Etc. | With seventy-four plates | New York | Francis P. Harper | 1895.

1 vol. demy 4to, pp. I-XVI, 17-268, 72 pll. (by Edwin Sheppard), 2 text-figs. New York.

A popular and scientific account of the habits and distribution of the shore birds of North America, illustrated in black-and-white, with an appendix containing analytical keys for the determination of the various families, genera and species. The present copy is number 12 of a large paper edition of which only 100 copies were issued, autographed by the author. It is also a presentation copy to Mr. Edward E. Ayer from Mr. Elliott. Reviewed in detail by Coues in the Auk, **13**, pp. 64-67, 1896, where it is given a publication-date of Sept. 26. A second edition appeared in 1897.

Elliot, Daniel Giraud.

1897. **The | gallinaceous | game birds | of | North America |** in- cluding the partridges, grouse, ptarmigan, and wild turkeys; with accounts of their dis- | person, habits, nesting, etc., and full descrip- | tions of the plumage of both adult and young, to- | gether with their popular and scientific names | A book written both for those who love to seek these birds afield with | dog and gun, as well as those who may only desire to learn the | ways of such attractive creatures in their haunts | by | Daniel Giraud Elliot, F.R.S.E., etc. | Ex-President of the American Ornithologists' Union | Author of [*etc.*, *4 lines*.]. | With forty-six plates | **Second edition** | New York | Francis P. Harper | 1897.

1 vol. demy 8vo, pp. I-XVIII, 19-220, 1 l., 1 l. (advt.), pll. 1-46 (by Edwin Sheppard), color charts on inside back cover. New York.

A companion volume to the author's "North American Shore Birds," 1895 (q.v.), with which it agrees in manner of treatment. Reviewed by Coues in the Auk, **15**, pp. 63-65, 1898. This second edition appeared in November, a month after the first edition was published.

Elliot, Daniel Giraud.

1898. **The | wild fowl | of the | United States | and | British possessions |** or the | swan, geese, ducks, and mergansers | of | North America | with accounts of their habits, nesting, migra- | tions, and dispersions, together with descrip- | tions of the adults and young, and keys | for the ready identification of the species | A book for the Sportsman, and for those desirous of knowing how to | distinguish these web-footed birds and to learn | their ways in their native wilds | By | Daniel Giraud Elliot, F.R.S.E., etc. | Ex- President of the American Ornithologists' Union | Author of the New and Heretofore Unfigured Birds [*etc.*, *7 lines*.] | With sixty- three plates | New York | Francis P. Harper | 1898.

1 vol. demy 8vo, pp. I-XXII, 19-316, frontisp., pll. 1-63 (by Edwin Sheppard, D. G. Elliot, and J. Wolf). New York.

A companion volume to "North American Shore Birds" and "The Gallinaceous Game Birds of North America," 1895 and 1897, by the same author. A popular account of the species and their habits, with keys for their determination. A presentation copy from the author to Dr. S. E. Meek.

Elliot, Daniel Giraud.

1903. See Coues, Elliott, **Key to North American Birds, Fifth Edition.**

Erebus and Terror, The Zoology of the Voyage of H.M.S.—.

1844-75. See Richardson, John; and Gray.

Eschscholz, Friedrich. (Rathke, Martin Heinrich.)

1829-33. **Zoologischer Atlas,** | enthaltend | Abbildungen und Beschreibungen neuer Thierarten, | während des | Flottcapitains von Kotzebue | zweiter Reise um die Welt, | auf der Russisch-Kaiserlichen Kriegsschlupp Predpriaetië in den Jahren 1823-1825 | beobachtet | von | Dr. Friedr. Eschscholz, | Professor und Director des zoologischen Museums an der Universität zu Dorpat [*etc.*, *2 lines*; weiland Professor [*etc.*, *2 lines., Pt. V.*)]. | Erstes Heft. [-Viertes Heft.; Fünftes Heft, | herausgegeben | von | D. Martin Heinrich Rathke, | Hofrath und Professor zu Dorpat. | Mit dem Bildnisse des Dr. Eschscholz.] | Berlin, 1829 [1829; 1829; 1831; 1833]. | Gedruckt und verlegt | bei G. Reimer.

1 vol. (5 pts.) crown folio. Pt. I, pp. I-IV, 1-17, pll. I-V (col.; 1 of birds). Pt. II, tit., pp. 1-13, pll. VI-X (col.). Pt. III, tit., pp. 1-18, pll. XI-XV (col.; 1 of birds). Pt. IV, tit., pp. 1-19, pll. XVI-XX (col.; 1 of birds). Pt. V, pp. I-VIII, 1-28, pll. XXI-XXV (col.), 1 pl. (frontisp. to vol.; portr.). Berlin.

A series of descriptions of zoological material collected on Kotzebue's second voyage around the world, 1823-26, with colored plates by the author and E. Bommer. Three plates relate to birds,—pll. II, XII and XVII. Of the species and genera described, *Thinocorus rumicivorus* retains validity in both names; the others are synonyms. Pt. V was edited and issued by Rathke after the death of Eschscholz. The preface to Pt. I is dated May 1829. The present copy is from the library of F. D. Godman.

Eudes-Deslongchamps, Eugene.

1880? Catalogue descriptif | des | Trochilidés | ou | oiseaux-mouches aujourd'hui connus | Revue d'après les exemplaires du Musée de Caen | par | M. Eug. Eudes-Deslongchamps | Professeur de Zoologie a la faculté des sciences de Caen | Ier fascicule avec planches | Prix: 15 francs | Caen.-F. Le Blanc-Hardel, imprimeur | Rue Froid, 2 et 4 |

Paris {Savy, Libraire-éditeur, 77, Boulevard St-Germain
Deyrolles, Naturaliste, 23, Rue de la Monnaie

1 vol. 8vo, 2 pr. ll. (half-tit. and tit.), pp. 1-489, pll. II-VI (by the author). Caen.

The first part (all published) of a proposed monograph of the humming-birds, with special reference to the collections of the Museum of Caen. The original publication appeared in the Annuaire Mus. Hist. Nat. Caen, 1 pp. 59-534, pll. II-VI, 1880. What changes aside from those of pagination, exist in the present reprint, I do not know. The copy at hand was autographed by the author in presentation to Professor Owen. The genus *Melanotrochilus* is proposed as new.

Evans, Arthur Humble.

1890-99. See Wilson, Scott B.; and Evans, A. H., **Aves Hawaiienses.**

Evans, Arthur Humble.

1903. See Turner, W., **Turner on Birds.**

Evans, Arthur Humble.

1909. > The | **Cambridge natural history** | edited by | S. F. Harmer, Sc.D., F.R.S. [*etc., 2 lines.*] | and | A. E. Shipley, M.A., Fellow of Christ's College, Cambridge [*etc., 2 lines.*] | Volume IX > **Birds** | By A. H. Evans, M.A., Clare College, Cambridge | Macmillan and Co., Limited | St. Martin's Street, London | 1909.
1 vol. 8vo, pp. I-XVI, 1-635, 2 ll. (advt.), 1 map (fold., col.), text-figs. 1-144. London.

A general review of the birds of the world, comprising " a short description of the majority of the forms in many of the Families, and of the most typical or important of the innumerable species included in the large Passerine Order. Prefixed to each group is a brief summary of the Structure and Habits; a few further particulars of the same nature being subsequently added where necessary, with a statement of the main Fossil forms as yet recorded." An enormous amount of information is compressed into a small space in this excellent volume. The first impression was in 1899.

Evans, Arthur Humble.

1911. See [Grouse], **The Grouse in Health and Disease.**

Evans, Arthur Humble.

1916. **The Birds of Britain** | their distribution | and habits | by | A. H. Evans, M.A., F.Z.S., M.B.O.U. | Cambridge: | at the University Press | 1916.
1 vol. post 8vo, pp. I-XII, 1-275, 94 text-figs. Cambridge.

A popular introduction to the orders, suborders and families of British birds, with accounts of the habits and characteristics of the commoner species. A list of occasional visitors is added at the close of the volume. The book is primarily intended for schools and is accurate and instructive. The illustrations are almost all from photographs, mostly from life, and show birds and nests.

Evans, William Edward.

1888. The | **songs of the birds;** | or, | analogies of animal and | spiritual life. | By the late | Rev. W. E. Evans, M.A. | formerly

Canon of Hereford, and author of | "Family Prayers." | [*Quot.*, *5 lines.*] | **New edition** with numerous illustrations | Sampson Low, Marston, Searle & Rivington, Ltd. | St. Dunstan's House, Fetter Lane, Fleet Street. | 1888.

1 vol. crown 8vo, pp. I-VI, 1-282, 47 text-figs. London.

A juvenile work in which the habits of a number of British (chiefly of Hereford-shire) birds are described, with moral reflections and conclusions drawn there-from. The first and second editions were published in 1845 and 1851.

Everitt, Nicholas.

1903. See Dutt, W. A., **The Norfolk Broads.**

Eversmann, Eduard. (Lichtenstein, Anton August Heinrich.)

1823. Reise | von | Orenburg nach Buchara | von | Eduard Eversmann | Dr. der Medezin and Philos. Mitgliede der naturforschenden Gesellschaft zu Moskau, | nebst einem | Wortverzeichniss aus der Afgahnischen Sprache | begleitet | von einem naturhistorischen Anhange und einer Vorrede | von | H. Lichtenstein Dr. | Mitgliede der Königl. Akademie der Wissenschaften [*etc., 2 lines.*]. | Mit zwei Kupfern und dem Plane von Buchara. | Berlin, 1823. | Im Verlage von E. H. G. Christiani.

1 vol. foliopost 4to, pp. I-VIII, 1-35, 2 pll., 1 map. Berlin.

Eversmann's narrative of his journey from Orenburg to Bokhara, with occasional notes on the animal life of the region traversed. An appendix contains a de-tailed report by Lichtenstein on the zoological collections of the expedition, in which the birds are treated on pp. 125-139. Various new species are des-cribed. The plates are not ornithological. Further notes on some of the species were given by Eversmann in his "Addenda ad Celeberrimi Pallasii Zoographiam Rosso-Asiaticam," 1835-1842 (Cf. reprint, 1876.).

Eversmann, Edward. (Dresser, Henry E.)

1876. Reprint | of | Eversmann's Addenda | ad | Celeberrimi Pallasii | Zoographiam Rosso-Asiaticam. | Edited by | H. E. Dresser, F.Z.S., &c. | London: | published by the editor, | 6 Ten-terden Street, Hanover Square, W. | 1876.

{ Addenda | ad celeberrimi Pallasii zoographiam [ad | celeberrimi Pallasii [*Fasc. II.*); ad | celeberrimi Pallasii [*Fasc. III.*)] | Rosso-Asiaticam [soographiam Rosso-Asiaticam (*Fasc. II.*); zoographiam Rosso-Asiaticam (*Fasc. III.*)]. | Aves [Fasciculus II; Fasciculus III]. | Auctore [Auctore | (*Fasc. II and III.*)] Dre. Eduardo Eversmann. | [*Design.*] | Kasani [Casani (*Fasc. II and III.*)]. | In officina Universitatis Typographica [Ex Universitatis officina typographica (*Fasc. II and III.*)]. | 1835 [1841; 1842]. }

1 vol. post 8vo, tit., pp. I-II, "1-32, 1-16, 1-19." London.

Facsimile reprints of the three facsiculi of Eversmann's " Addenda," published originally at Kasani in 1835, 1841 and 1842. The originals are extremely rare owing to a fire in the publishing house which destroyed the stock on hand. The preface of the reprint is dated Sept. 11, 1875.

The papers contain descriptions and accounts of birds and other animals of Orenburg Province and adjacent portions of former Asiatic Russia. The material was obtained from various sources including the author's own collection made on the journey which he describes in his "Reise von Orenburg nach Buchara," 1823 (q.v.). Some of the species are new. The only relation which the work bears to Pallas's "Zoographia Rosso-Asiatica," 1811-14, is that it treats of the same region and supplies discussions which supplement those in the earlier work.

Eydoux, Fortuné.

1839. See Laplace, Cyrille Pierre Théodore, **Voyage autour du Monde, executé sur "La Favorite,"** . . . **Zoologie.**

Eydoux, Fortuné.

1841. See Vaillant, **Voyage autour du Monde, sur La Bonite,** 1841-52.

Eyton, Thomas Campbell.

1836. **A history | of the | rarer British birds.** | By T. C. Eyton, esq. | [*Vignette.*] | Illustrated with Woodcuts. | London: | Longman, Rees, Orme, Brown, Green, and Longman; | and Houlston and Son, Paternoster-Row. | MDCCCXXXVI. > A | catalogue | of | British Birds. | By T. C. Eyton, esq. | London: | [*Imprint and date as on general title page.*]

1 vol. cap 4to, pp. I-VI, 1 l. (corrigenda), pp. 1-101+1, 80 woodcuts; pp. I-VI, 1 l. (erratum), pp. 1-67. London.

The first part of this work was intended by the author as a supplement to Bewick and Beilby's "History of British Birds" 1797-1804 (q.v.). The second part, separately paged, titled and prefaced (also, according to Coues, separately issued), is listed in the table of contents of the first part; hence both parts evidently are to be considered under the single title as given above. As in Bewick, many of the vignettes are not of ornithological interest.

Eyton, Thomas Campbell.

1841. See Darwin, Charles, **The Zoology of the Voyage of H. M. S. Beagle,** 1838-43.

Eyton, Thomas Campbell.

1867. **Osteologia avium; | or, | a sketch of the osteology | of birds. |** By | T. C. Eyton, Esq., F.G.S., F.L.S., | And Corresponding Member of Institute of Philadelphia. [| Plates.] | To be had of Mr. Prince, at Mr. J. Gould's, Charlotte Street, | Bedford Square, London. | Published by R. Hobson, Wellington, Salop. | 1867.

2 vols. foliopost 4to. (Text), pp. I-VI (tit., pref. and bibliogr.), I-X (introd.), 1-229+1, I-VII (index). Plates, tit., pp. I-IV (list of pll.), pll. (Introduction) 1-4; (Skeletons) 1A-4A, 1A bis, 2A bis, 1B-8B, 1C, 1D, 1E-5E, 1F-3F, (4F not publ.), 5F-13F, 1G, 1H-4H, 1I, 1J, 1K-15K, 1L-12L; (Details) 1-17, 17 (*bis*), 18, 19.1 (=19), 20-28, 28 (*bis*), 29-35, 35 (*ter*), 35 bis, 36-40, ?(=41; erased and rewritten by hand). Wellington.

This work contains descriptions of the complete osteology of many species of birds and of the distinctive features in the skeletons of others. The plates are careful drawings of skeletons entire and in detail, by Erxleben. A supplement (q.v.) was published in 1869.

Eyton, Thomas Campbell.

1869. Supplement to | osteologia avium; | or, a sketch. of the osteology | of birds. | By | T. C. Eyton, Esq., F.G.S., F.Z.S, | And Corresponding Member of Institute of Philadelphia. | To be had of Mr. Prince, at Mr. J. Gould's, Charlotte Street, | Bedford Square, London. | Published by R. Hobson, Wellington, Salop. | 1869.

1 vol. foliopost 4to, 2 pr. ll. (tit., pref. and index), 18 pll. (by G. Scharf). Wellington.

A series of plates illustrating the osteology of ducks, geese and swans (with the sterna of an *Alca*, *Phalacrocorax* and *Podiceps*) not included in the original "Osteologia Avium," 1867 (q.v.). Five of the plates are new; the remainder are from the author's "A Monograph of the Anatidae."

Eyton, Thomas Campbell.

1869. A | synopsis | on | the Anatidæ, | or | duck tribe. | By | T. C. Eyton, esq., F.G.S., F.Z.S., | And Corresponding Member of the Natural History Society of | Philadelphia. | Wellington, Salop: | printed by R. Hobson, Market Square. | MDCCCLXIX.

1 vol. cap 4to, 3 pr. ll., pp. 1-141. Wellington.

A second edition of the "Monograph of the Anatidae or Duck Tribe" of 1838, without the plates. It contains condensed descriptions (in Latin and English) of the species, genera, and higher groups of the ducks of the world.

Faber, Friedrich.

1825-26. Ueber | das Leben | der | hochnordischen Vögel. | Von | Friedrich Faber, | Königl. Dänischem Regimensquartermeister und Auditeur [etc., *4 lines.*]. | [*Monogram.*] | Mit vier Tabellen. | Leipzig: | Ernst Fleischer. | 1826.

1 vol. 8vo, pp. I-XVI, 1-321+1, 1 l. (advt.), tables (I)-IV (fold.), 1 insert (fold; num. 321 B). Leipzig.

A study of the life of birds, with references to boreal species. The book was issued in two parts and contains two subtitle-pages, the first, dated 1825, at the beginning of the work, and the second, dated 1826, occupying pp. 159-160. The present copy is from the F. D. Godman library.

Fabricius, Otho.

1780. Favna | Groenlandica, | systematice sistens | animalia Groen- landiae occiden- | talis hactenvs indagata, qvoad nomen | speci- ficvm, triviale, vernacvlvmqve; synonyma avcto- | rvm plvrivm, descriptionem, locvm, victvm, genera- | tionem, mores, vsvm, captvramqve singvli, provt | detegendi occasio fvit, maximaqve parte secvn- | dvm proprias observationes | Othonis Fabricii | ministri evangelii, qvondam Groen- | landis ad Coloniam Fri- derichshaab, posthaac Norvagis | Drangedaliae, nvnc vero Danis Hopvnti ivtiae, mem- | bri societatis scientarvm qvae est Hafniae. | [*Vignette.*] | Hafniae et Lipsiae, | Impensis Ioannis Gottlob Rothe, | avlae atqve vnivers. reg. bibliopolae. | MDCCLXXX.

1 vol. crown 8vo, pp. I-XVI, 1-452, 1 pl. (fold.). Copenhagen and Leipzig.

Descriptions of the animals of Greenland. The birds are discussed on pp. 53- 124, including Nos. 33, 34, 34b and 35-85 and forming Pt. II of the text.

Fantham, H. B.

1911. See [Grouse], **The Grouse in Health and Disease.**

Farley, J. A.

1903. See Coues, Elliott, **Key to North American Birds, Fifth Edition.**

Farren, William.

1910-13. See Kirkman, Frederick Bernuf Bever, **The British Bird Book.**

Farren, William.

1924. See Kirkman, Frederick B.; and Hutchinson, **British Sporting Birds.**

Farwell, Ellen Drummond.

1919. Bird Observations | Near | Chicago | by | Ellen Drummond Farwell | Introduction by | Mary Drummond | With Illustrations | Privately Printed.

1 vol. crown 8vo, pp. 1-192, 10 pll. Chicago.

Jottings and notes on birds made by the author for her own information and amusement.

Fatio, Victor.

1869-1904. Faune | des | vertébrés | de | la Suisse | par | Victor Fatio, Dr. Phil. | Volume I [-V] | Histoire naturelle | des | mammifères [oiseaux | Ire partie | rapaces, grimpeurs, percheurs, bailleurs | et passereaux (*Vol. II, Pt. I.*); oiseaux | IIme partie | gyrateurs, sarcleurs, échassiers, hérodions, | lamellirostres, totipalmes, longipennes et uropodes (*Vol. II, Pt. II.*); reptiles et des batraciens (*Vol. III.*); poissons | Ire partie | I. Anarthroptérygiens | II. Physostomes | cyprinidés (*Vol. IV.*); poissons | IIme partie | Physostomes (suite et fin) | anacanthiens, chondrostéens | cyclostomes (*Vol. V.*)] | Avec 8 planches dont 5 coloriées [Avec 3 planches hors texte, dont 2 en couleurs, 1 carte géographique coloriée, | 135 figures dans le texte, dont 127 originales, et 26 tableaux. (*Vol. II, Pt. I.*); Avec 1 planche en couleurs, hors texte, | 120 figures originales, dans le texte, 23 tableaux et une 2e appendice | à la première partie. (*Vol. II, Pt. II.*); Avec 5 planches dont 3 coloriées (*Vol. III.*); Avec 5 planches, dont 2 en couleur, comprenant 178 figures originales. (*Vol. IV.*); Avec 4 planches, dont 1 en couleur, comprenant 84 figures originales. (*Vol. V.*)]| Genève et Bale | H. Georg, libraire-éditeur [Georg & Co, libraires-éditeurs (*Vol. II, Pts. I and II.*); H. Georg, libraireéditeur | Paris, J. B. Baillière et fils (*Vol. III.*)] | 1869 [1899; 1904; 1872; 1882; 1890] [| Tous droits réservés. (*Vols. II-IV.*)]. 5 vols. in 6, 8vo. Vol. I, 2 pr. ll., pp. 1-410, 1 l. (errata), pll. I-VIII (5 col.). Vol. II, Pt. I, 2 pr. ll., pp. VII-X, 1 l. (expl. of map), pp. 1-840, 1 insert-slip (dir. to binder), pl. I, 1 map. (col.), text-figs. 1-135. Vol. II, Pt. II, 2 pr. ll., pp. I-II, 841-1743, I-XXXVI (introd. to Vol. II), 1 insert-slip (dir. to binder), 3 print. guard-sheets, pll. II-IV (col.; by Hainard), text-figs. 1-120. Vol. III, 2 pr. ll., pp. I-XII, 1-603, pll. I-V (3 col.). Vol. IV, pp. I-XIV, 1-786, 1 l., pp. I-VI, pll. I-V (2 col.). Vol. V, 2 pr. ll., pp. I-LXXX, 1-576, 1 l. (subtit.), pp. 1-13+1, 1-13, pll. I-IV (1 col.). Geneva and Basel.

Detailed monographs on the vertebrate fauna of Switzerland. The ornithology comprises Vol. II, Pts. I and II which appeared out of order at the end of the series. This portion of the work consists of a very thorough manual of the birds of Switzerland.

Fatio, Victor.

1889-1901. See Studer, Theophil; and Fatio, **Katalog der Schweizerischen Vögel.** 1889-date.

Favorite, La, Voyage autour du monde . . . sur la corvette—.

1839. See Laplace, M.

Fehringer, Otto.

1922. Die Singvögel | mitteleuropas | von | Professor Dr. Otto Fehringer | Heidelberg. | Mit 96 farbigen Tafeln nach Aquarellen von Kunstmaler | Walter Heubach und 17 Textabbildungen | [*Blazon.*] | Heidelberg | Carl Winters Universitätsbuchhandlung.

1 vol. crown 8vo, pp. I-VIII, 1-107, pll. 1-96 (col.; by Heubach; on 48 ll)., text-figs. 1-17. Heidelberg.

A popular work on the song-birds of central Europe. Following a general discussion of especial interest to cage-bird fanciers, a list is given of the various species in question and of related forms. The general text describes the appearance, habits and song of representative species of each arbitrary group, with a colored plate opposite to the text of each. Two copies are at hand, one bound in cloth, the other in boards, half cloth.

Filippi, Filippo de.

1865. Note | di un viaggio | in | Persia | nel 1862 | di | F. de Filippi | Professore di Zoologia [*etc., 4 lines.*]. | Volume unico | Milano | G. Daelli & C. editori | 1865.

1 vol. 8vo, pp. I-VIII, 2 ll. (index and subtit.), pp. 1-396, 1 l. (errata), text-figs. 1-7 (non-ornithological). Milan.

A narrative of the author's travels in Persia in 1862, with voluminous notes on the natural history of the country. Chapter XX, pp. 340-363, is devoted to a discussion and list of the animals of western Persia, containing the ornithological matter on pp. 344-352. Descriptions of various species and subspecies discovered by Filippi are given here but they seem to have been published elsewhere previously. In the general text, on p. 162, *Curruca cinerea* var *persica* is described for the first time.

Finley, William Lovell.

1907. American Birds | studied and photographed | from life | ·by | William Lovell Finley | illustrated from photographs by | Herman T. Bohlman | and the author | Charles Scribner's Sons | New York 1907.

1 vol. 8vo, pp. I-XVI, 1-256, 47 pll. New York.

Observations on the habits of a number of North American birds, illustrated by photographs of the birds in question. Entertainingly written and with a great deal of first hand information. The photographs are excellent.

Finn, Frank.

1900. A | guide | to the | zoological collections | exhibited in the | bird gallery | of the | Indian Museum. | By | F. Finn, B.A., F.Z.S., | Deputy Superintendent. | [*Blazon.*] | Calcutta: | Printed by Order of the Trustees of the Indian Museum. | 1900. | Price Twelve annas.

1 vol. 8vo, 3 pr. ll. (tit., pref. and errata), pp. 1-131. Calcutta.

A descriptive catalogue of the collection of birds exhibited in the Indian Museum. Structural differences of the higher groups are mentioned but the author has "devoted considerably more space to peculiarities of habit, and the economic importance of the several groups." Introductory chapters relate to general anatomy, geographical distribution, etc. The collection is not restricted to Indian birds.

Finn, Frank.

1907. **Ornithological | & other oddities** | by Frank Finn, B.A., F.Z.S. | Late Deputy Superintendent of | the Indian Museum, Calcutta | With fifty-six illustrations | reproduced from photographs | London: John Lane, The Bodley Head | New York: John Lane Company MCMVII.

1 vol. post 8vo, pp. I-XVI, 1 l., pp. 1-295, 32 pll. (27 ornithological). London.

Mainly devoted to birds and to a discussion of unusual habits or other peculiarities of numerous forms. Several chapters are of a general nature and one or two relate only to mammals. The illustrations are mostly from photographs of living animals.

Finn, Frank.

1915. **Indian sporting birds** | by | Frank Finn, B.A., F.Z.S. | Late Deputy Superintendent, Indian Museum, Calcutta | Author of "The Waterfowl of India and Asia" [etc., *2 lines.*] | With over 100 Illustrations from Hume and Marshall's | "Game-Birds of India, Burma and Ceylon" | London | Francis Edwards | 83A High Street, Marylebone, W. | 1915.

1 vol. royal 8vo, pp. I-XI+1, 1-280, 103 pll. (col.; by W. Foster, M. Herbert, S. Herbert, E. Neale, C. Davenport and A. W. Strutt). London.

A popular account of the habits and distribution of the game birds of India, illustrated with chromo-lithographs taken from Hume and Marshall's "The Game Birds of India, Burmah and Ceylon," 1879-81 (q.v.).

Finn, Frank; and Robinson, E. Kay.

1922-23. **Birds of Country** | Their Eggs, Nests, Life, Haunts and our

Identification | By | Frank Finn, B.A., F.Z.S. | and | E. Kay Robinson, F.Z.S. | Vol. I [II] | About | 800 | Illustrations | and | 30 beautiful | Coloured | Plates | | [*Cut.*] | | Arranged | in | Alphabetical | Order | from most | Up-to-Date | Knowledge | London: Hutchinson & Co., Paternoster Row.

2 vols. foliopost 4to. Vol. I, 2 pr. ll. (tit., conts. and list of illustrs.), pp. 1-480, 18 pll. (col.), 573 text-figs. Vol. II, 2 pr. ll., pp. 481-960, 4 ll. (index), 12 pll. (col.), 592 text-figs. London.

The greater part of the book is devoted to a popular account of the birds of Great Britain, identified under their vernacular names which are arranged alphabetically. A part of Vol. II (pp. 720-884) contains an account of "Birds of the Empire" in which characteristic, interesting species from world-wide British territories are briefly described and discussed under their common names. These are arranged geographically under Asia, Africa, America and Australia. Vol. II closes with a general chapter on the classification of birds. The book is profusely illustrated with half-tones of which at least one occurs on every page. Many of these are photographs of living birds; the remainder are photographs of mounted specimens or reproductions of drawings. The work appears to have been published in parts, the first of which, including pp. 1-40, is reviewed in the Ibis for July, 1922.

Finsch, Otto.

1865. Index | ad | Caroli Luciani Bonaparte | Conspectus Generum Avium. | Auctore | O. Finsch. | Lugduni Batavorum, | apud | E. J. Brill. | 1865.

1 vol. 4to (size of 8vo), pp. 1-23. Leyden.

An index to the genera in Bonaparte's "Conspectus Generum Avium," 1850-57 (q.v.). The present copy is in the original wrapper which is lettered the same as the title-page.

Finsch, Otto; and Hartlaub, Gustav.

1867. Beitrag | zur | Fauna Centralpolynesiens. | Ornithologie | der | Viti-, Samoa- und Tonga-Inseln | von | O. Finsch und G. Hartlaub. | Mit 14 nach der Natur lithographirten und colorirten Kupfertafeln. | Halle, Druck und Verlag von H. W. Schmidt. | 1867.

1 vol. royal 8vo, pp. I-XL, 1-290, pll. I-XIV (col.; by O. Finsch). Halle.

A detailed treatise on the birds of the region mentioned, with full synonymies, descriptions and notes. The illustrations are hand-colored. The present copy is from the F. D. Godman library.

Finsch, Otto.

1867-68. Die Papageien, | Monographisch bearbeitet | von | Otto Finsch [Dr. Otto Finsch], | Conservator der zoologischen Sammlung [Sammlungen] der Gesellschaft "Museum" zu Bremen [*etc., 3 lines. (Vol. II, Pts. 1 and 2.)*] | Erster Band [Zweiter Band. | Erste (Zweite) Haelfte]. | Mit einer Karte und einer lithographirten Tafel [Mit 5 nach der Natur lithographirten und colorirten Tafeln und | Uebersichts-Tabellen zur geographischen Verbreitung. (*Vol.*

II, Pt. 1.); *line omitted* (*Vol. II, Pt. 2.*).]. | Leiden, E. J. Brill. [*Vol. II, Pt. 2 has this line obliterated by a pasted slip on which is printed,* "Rotterdam, | Van Baalen & Söhne (van Hengel & Eeltjes)."] | 1867 [1868].

2 vols. in 3, 8vo. Vol. I, pp. I-XII, 1-561+1, 1 l. (errata), pl 1 (by O. Finsch), 1 map (col.). Vol. II, Pt. 1, pp. I-VII+1, 11 ll., pp. 1-498. Vol. II, Pt. 2, 1 pr. l., pp. 499-996, 2 ll., pll. 2-6 (col.; by O. Finsch). Leiden.

A very thorough monograph of the parrots and their allies, with a bibliography, a detailed discussion of distribution, anatomy, classification, etc., and a diagnostic treatment of each species.

Finsch, Otto.

1869-75. See Heuglin, Martin Theodor von, **Ornithologie Nordost Afrika's.**

Finsch, Otto; and Hartlaub, Gustav.

1870. See Decken, Carl Claus van der, **Reisen in Ost-Afrika in den Jahren 1859-1865.**

Finsch, Otto.

1870-76. See Brehm, Alfred Edmund, **Gefangene Vögel.**

Finsch, Otto.

1876. See Rowley, George D., **Ornithological Miscellany,** 1875-78.

Finsch, Otto.

1881. See Thomson, C. Wyville, **Reports on the Scientific Results of the Voyage of H. M. S. Challenger; Report on the Birds.**

Finsch, Otto.

1899. O. Finsch: | **Systematische Uebersicht | der | Ergebnisse seiner Reisen** | und schriftstellerischen Thätigkeit | (1859-1899). | Mit Anmerkungen und Anhang: Auszeichnungen. | Berlin. | Verlag von R. Friedländer & Sohn. | 1899.

1 vol. 8vo, pp. 1-153. Berlin.

An annotated catalogue of the author's voyages, publications, exhibited collections, membership in organizations, decorations, geographical namesakes, published biographies and portraits and new species and genera named by or for him.

Finsch, Otto.

1901. Das Tierreich. | Eine Zusammenstellung und Kennzeichnung der | rezenten Tierformen. | In Verbindung mit der | Deutschen

Zoologischen Gesellschaft | herausgegeben von der | Königlich Preussischen Akademie der Wissenschaften zu Berlin. | General-redakteur: Franz Eilhard Schulze. | [*Quot.*] | **15. Lieferung.** | **Aves.** | Redakteur A. Reichenow. | **Zosteropidae** | bearbeitet von | Dr. Otto Finsch, | Abteilungs-Vorstand am Reichs-Museum für Naturgeschichte in Leiden. | Mit 32 Abbildungen. | Berlin. | Verlag von R. Friedländer und Sohn. | Ausgegeben im März 1901.

1 vol. (pt.) superroyal 8vo, pp. I-XIV, 1-54, 1 l. ("Nomenclator generum et subgenerum."), 1 fig. (topography of bird), text-figs. 1-31. Berlin. March. 1901.

A monograph of the family of White-eyes, with brief descriptions, synonymies, notes on distribution and keys to genera and species. A bibliography is included. See also under "Tierreich."

Fischer, Jacob Benjamin. (Hagen, Karl Gottfried.)

1791. Versuch | einer | Naturgeschichte | von | Livland, | entworfen | von | J. B. Fischer. | Zwote vermehrte und verbesserte Auflage. | Mit Kupfern. | Königsberg, | bey Friedrich Nicolovius. | 1791.

1 vol. demy 8vo, pp. I-XXIV, 1-826, pll. I-IV (3 fold.). Königsberg.

The second edition of Fischer's work (the first edition of which was published in 1778) revised and edited by Hagen. The work is a general natural history of animals, plants and minerals of Livland. Pp. 1-132 relate to the geography and meteorology of the region; pp. 163-236 discuss the birds. The preface is dated Jan. 5, 1791.

Fischer, Wilhelm Johannes.

1914. Über die Vogelfauna | Württembergs. | Inaugural-Dissertation | zur | Erlangung der Doktorwürde | der | hohen naturwissenschaftlichen Fakultät | der Eberhard-Karls-Universität in Tübingen | vorgelegt von | Wilhelm Johannes Fischer | aus Winnenden. | Verlag des Bundes für Vogelschutz e. V. | Stuttgart 1914.

1 vol. royal 8vo, 2 pr. ll. (tit. and conts.), pp. 1-309. Stuttgart.

A study of the avifauna of Württemburg with reference to the local occurrence and distribution of the species.

Fisher, Albert Kenrick.

1890. See Warren, Benjamin H., **Report on the Birds of Pennsylvania, Second Edition.**

Fisher, Albert Kenrick.

1893. U. S. Department of Agriculture | Division of Ornithology and Mammalogy | Bulletin No. 3 | **The | hawks and owls | of**

the | **United States** | in their relation to agriculture | Prepared under the direction of | Dr. C. Hart Merriam, Ornithologist | by A. K. Fisher, M.D. | Assistant Ornithologist | Published by authority of the Secretary of Agriculture | Washington | Government Printing Office | 1893.

1 vol. 8vo, pp. 1-210, pll. 1-26 (col.; by J. L. and R. Ridgway). Washington.

A thorough discussion of the economic value of American hawks and owls. Each species is treated in detail with appended descriptions and tables based on the examination of the birds' stomachs. The plates are lithographed in colors.

Fitz Gerald, Edward Arthur; and Vines, Stuart. (Gosse, Philip.)

1899. The | **highest Andes** | A record of the first ascent | of Aconcagua and Tupungato in | Argentina, and the exploration | of the surrounding valleys | by | E. A. Fitz Gerald | author of "Climbs in the New Zealand Alps" | with chapters by | Stuart Vines, M.A., F.R.G.S. | and contributions by | Professor Bonney, D.Sc., LL.D., F.R.S., G. C. Crick, F.G.S. | R. I. Pocock, G. A. Boulenger, F.R.S. | I. H. Burkill, Philip Gosse | with two maps by A. E. Lightbody, A.M.I.C.E., F.R.G.S., | fifty-one illustrations, and a panorama | Methuen & Co. | 36 Essex Street, W.C. | London | 1899.

1 vol. royal 8vo, pp. I-XVI, 1-390, 46 pll. (1 fold.), 2 maps (col.; fold.), 6 text-cuts. London.

A narrative of exploration in the Andes of Argentina; mostly geographical, but with zoological observations scattered through the text and with more detailed discussions of animal life in the appendices. Appendix C, Pt. II, pp. 342-352, by Philip Gosse, relates exclusively to birds which are treated under two headings, "Birds of the Aconcagua Valleys" and "Birds Collected at Lujan, Fifteen Miles South of Mendoza." None of the illustrations are ornithological.

Fitzsimons, F. W.

1923. The natural history | of South Africa | by | F. W. Fitzsimons, F.Z.S., F.R.M.S., etc. | Director, Port Elizabeth Museum | Birds | in two volumes | Vol. I [II]. | With 10 coloured plates and numerous | illustrations from photographs, etc. | Longmans, Green and Co. | 39 Paternoster Row, London, E.C. 4 | New York, Toronto | Bombay, Calcutta and Madras | 1923.

2 vols. demy 8vo. Vol. I, pp. I-XVI, 1-288, pll. I-V (col.; by O. G. Finch-Dawes and J. G. Keulemans), 1 pl., 189 text-figs. Vol. II, pp. I-VII+1, 1-323, pll. VI-X (col.; by J. G. Keulemans), 93 text-figs. London.

A popular account of the birds of South Africa. Volume I consists of a general account of the economic importance of birds. Volume II contains a list of

South African birds with notes on their diet, a discussion of the description, distribution and habits of the birds illustrated in both volumes, and a systematic list of the species. The colored plates are from other publications as acknowledged in the preface.

Flagg, Wilson.

1875. The | birds and seasons | of | New England. | By Wilson Flagg, | author of "The Woods and By-ways of New England." | With Illustrations. | [*Quot., 2 lines.*] | [*Monogram.*] | Boston: | James R. Osgood and Company, | Late Ticknor & Fields, and Fields, Osgood, & Co. | 1875.

1 vol. demy 8vo, pp. I-VI, 1-457, 5 pll. (photograv.; scenery; should be 12 pll.). Boston.

A series of pleasing essays on nature in New England, in which birds occupy a large share of the discussions. The author shows considerable familiarity with his subject and writes in an easy, entertaining manner. Coues lists 12 plates in the copy examined by him but the present example has only 5, although it does not appear to have been mutilated.

Fleming, John.

1822. The | philosophy | of | zoology; | or | a general view of the | structure, functions, and classification | of animals. | By John Fleming, D.D. | minister of Flisk, Fifeshire, | Fellow of the Royal Society of Edinburgh, of the Wernerian | Natural History Society, &c. | In two volumes. | With engravings. | Vol. I [II]. | Edinburgh: | printed for Archibald Constable & Co. Edinburgh: | and Hurst, Robinson & Co. London. | 1822.

2 vols. post 8vo. Vol. I, tit., pp. V-LII, 1-432, pll. I-V (by M. F.; 1 of birds). Vol. II, tit., pp. 1-618. Edinburgh.

Vol. I contains detailed observations which "relate to what may be termed the Motive, the Sentient, the Nutritive, and Reproductive Functions of Animals. The various Organs of the animal frame have been described, their actions investigated, and the important purposes of life, to which they are subservient, have at the same time been pointed out." Vol. II, Pt. I, discusses distribution, migration, hibernation, etc. and Pt. II relates to classification. Under the latter head, the birds are treated in detail on pp. 218-265 with a descriptive list of 227 genera and the citation of one or more species under each. This list is the portion of the work of principal ornithological interest; it contains new generic names. Mathews (Birds of Australia, **7**, p. 451, cites a review in Froriep's "Notizen," No. 43, July, 1822.

Fleming, John.

1828. A | history | of | British animals, | exhibiting the | descriptive characters and systematical | arrangement | of | the genera and species of quadrupeds, birds, | reptiles, fishes, mollusca, and radiata | of the United Kingdom; | including | the indigenous, extirpated, and extinct | kinds, together with periodical | and occasional visitants. | By | John Fleming, D.D. F.R.S.E. M.W.S. &c. | minister of Flisk, Fifeshire; | and author of the "Philosophy of Zoology." | Edinburgh: | printed for Bell & Bradfute, Edinburgh; | and James Duncan, London. | MDCCCXXVIII.

1 vol. 8vo, pp. I-XXIII+1, 1-565, 1 l. (errata). Edinburgh.

Sufficiently explained by the title. The birds are on pp. 41-146. Synoptic tables are given for the various genera. Mathews (Birds of Australia, 7, p. 451) notes a review of this work in the Edinburgh New Philos. Zool. Journal for Jan.-March, 1828, p. 412, dated April 1.

Floericke, Kurt.

1892-93. Versuch einer | Avifauna der Provinz Schlesien. | Von | Dr. Curt Floericke, | Assistenten am zoologischen Institut der Universität Marburg. | I [II]. Lieferung. | Marburg. | Universitäts-Buchdruckerei (C. L. Pfeil). | 1892 [1893].

1 vol. (2 pts.) 8vo. Pt. 1, pp. 1-157, pl. I. Pt. II, tit., pp. 163-321, pl. II (col., fold.). Marburg.

A descriptive and biographical review of the birds of Silesia. Historical notes and a bibliography are given in the prefatory chapters. The present copy is in the original wrappers.

Floericke, Kurt.

1922. Dr. Kurt Floerickes | **Vogelbuch** | Gemeinverständliche Naturgeschichte | der mitteleuropäischen Vogelwelt | für | Forst- und Landwirte, Jäger, Naturfreunde und | Vogelliebhaber, Lehrer und die reifere Jugend | und für alle Gebildeten des deutschen Volkes | Mit 50 Tafeln in Buntdruck nach Original-Aquarellen | von Kark Neunzig | **Zweite,** bedeutend vermehrte, gänzlich | umgearbeitete und neu illustrierte **Auflage** | [*Design.*]
| Stuttgart 1922 Wiesbaden
| Franckh'sche Verlagshandlung Pestalozzi-Verlagsanstalt.

1 vol. superroyal 8vo, pp. 1-496, frontisp. (portr.), pll. I-LIV (53 col.; 50 birds, 3 eggs, 1 stomach-contents and pellets), col. fig. (on cover), text-figs. 1-99. Stuttgart and Wiesbaden.

A popular work on the birds of central Europe, illustrated by colored plates of the species. The author has discarded the rule of priority wherever it excites his abhorrence of tautonymous names, either binomial or trinomial, and as a result he has accepted synonyms or supplied new names for species and subspecies in a great number of cases. Among the noticeable innovations is the inclusion of *Cisticola*, *Troglodytes* and *Cinclus* in the Timeliidae. The first edition of this work was published in 1907 or 1908.

Flourens, Marie Jean Pierre.

1860. Des manuscrits | de **Buffon** | avec | des fac-simile de Buffon et de ses collaborateurs | par | P. Flourens | membre de l'Académie Française [*etc., 8 lines.*]. | Paris | Garnier frères, libraires-éditeurs | 6, Rue des Saints-Pères et Palais-Royal, 215 | 1860.

1 vol. 12mo, 3 pr. ll. (half-tit., tit. and notice), pp. I-XCV+1, 1-298, frontisp. (portr.), 8 inserts (fold.; facsimiles). Paris.

A study of the life of Buffon and of his manuscripts, with voluminous notes on the parts played by his collaborators in the production of his "Histoire Naturelle Générale," 1749-1804 (Cf. Hist. Nat. des Oiseaux, 1770-86.).

Forbes, Henry Ogg.

1885. A naturalist's wanderings | in the | **Eastern Archipelago** | a narrative of travel and exploration | From 1878 to 1883 | by | Henry O. Forbes, F.R.G.S., | Member of the Scottish Geographical Society [*etc., 3 lines.*] | with numerous illustrations from the author's sketches | and descriptions by Mr. John B. Gibbs | [*Vignette.*] | **Second edition** | London | Sampson Low, Marston, Searle & Rivington | Crown Buildings. 188, Fleet Street | 1885.

1 vol. 8vo, pp. I-XIX+1, 1-536, frontisp. (col.), 14 pll., 4 insert-maps (col.; 3 fold.), 87 text-figs, London.

The narrative of the author's travels in the East Indies, to the Cocos-Keeling Islands, Java, Sumatra, Timor-Laut, the Moluccas, Buru and Timor. Many ornithological notes are scattered through the text and special reports on birds are found in the appendices to several parts, on pp. 44, 268-274, 355-368 and 409-410. The colored frontispiece, one plate and two figures are ornithological. The first edition is also dated 1885.

Forbes, Henry Ogg.

1897-98. See Butler, Arthur G., **British Birds.** 1896-98.

Forbes, Stephen Alfred.

1889-95. See (Illinois) State Laboratory of Natural History, Natural History Survey of Illinois, **The Ornithology of Illinois.**

Forbes, William Alexander.

1881. See Thomson, C. Wyville, **Reports on the Scientific Results of the Voyage of H. M. S. Challenger; Report on the Birds.**

Forbes, William Alexander.

1885. In memoriam. | **The collected** | **scientific papers** | **of the late** | **William Alexander Forbes,** M.A., | Fellow of St. John's College, Cambridge; Lecturer on comparative anatomy at | Charing Cross Hospital; Prosector to the Zoological Society of London. | Edited |

by | F. E. Beddard, M.A., | Prosector to the Zoological Society of London. | With a preface | by | P. L. Sclater, M.A., Ph.D., F.R.S., | Secretary to the Zoological Society of London. | London: | R. H. Porter: 6 Tenterden Street, W. | 1885.

1 vol. royal 8vo, pp. I-XIII+1, 1 l., pp. 1-496, frontisp. (etched portr.), pll. I-XXV (15 col.), 141 text-figs. London.

A collection of the scientific papers of Mr. Forbes, 68 in number (43 relating to ornithology), with marginal references to original publications. Of the plates, 18 are ornithological (9 col.), and of the text-figures 102 relate to birds. The book was published as a memorial by the Zoological Club of which Forbes had been a member.

Forbush, Edward Howe.

1907. See Chapman, Frank M., **The Warblers of North America.**

Forbush, Edward Howe.

1913. Useful birds | and their protection. | Containing | brief descriptions of the more common and useful species of | Massachusetts, with accounts of their food habits, | and a chapter on the means of attract- | ing 'and protecting birds. | By | Edward Howe Forbush, | Ornithologist to the Massachusetts State Board of | Agriculture. | Illustrated by the author, | C. Allan Lyford, Chester A. Reed, and others. | **Fourth Edition.** | Published under Direction of | The Massachusetts State Board of Agriculture, | By Authority of the Legislature. | 1913.

1 vol. royal 8vo, 1 pr. 1., pp. I-XX, 1-451, frontisp. (col.; by L. A. Fuertes), 52 pll. (pll I-LX, numbered by cuts), text-figs. 1-171. Boston.

A very thorough discussion of the economic ornithology of Massachusetts, including the descriptions of the various species, accounts of their habits and food, and various chapters of a more general nature. The first edition was issued in 1907.

Forbush, Edward Howe.

1916. A history of the | **Game Birds, Wild-Fowl | and Shore Birds |** of | **Massachusetts** and Adjacent States | Including those used for food which have disappeared since the | settlement of the country, and those which are now hunted | for food or sport, with observations on their | former abundance and recent decrease | in numbers; also the means for | conserving those still | in existence | By Edward Howe Forbush | State Ornithologist of Massachusetts | **Second Edition,** 1916 | Issued by the | Massachusetts State Board of Agriculture | By Authority of the Legislature of 1912.

1 vol. 8vo, pp. I-XVIII, 1 pr. l., pp. 1-636, frontisp. (col.; by L. A. Fuertes), 30 pll. (pll. I-XXXVI, numbered by cuts), 108 text-figs. Boston.

An account of the game birds of New England, with special reference to their economic importance and abundance, with descriptions and figures of the species, notes on food habits, causes of decrease in numbers and other interesting facts. The first edition of this work was issued in 1912. The present edition is largely a reprint of the first with the addition of appendices embodying certain necessary changes and additions and with alterations of certain figures.

Forrest, Herbert Edward.

1919.   A handbook | to the | vertebrate fauna | of | North Wales | by | H. E. Forrest, | author of "The Vertebrate Fauna of North Wales"; | "Fauna of Shropshire," | etc. | Witherby & Co | 326 High Holborn London | 1919.

1 vol. post 8vo, 3 pr. ll. (tit., introd. and conts.), pp. 1-106. London.

A resumé of the species of vertebrates of present or former occurrence in North Wales, giving the status and distribution of each species. Addenda and corrigenda given to the author's "The Vertebrate Fauna of North Wales," 1907, are making the present work a sort of appendix to the larger, descriptive volume.

Forskål, Petrus.

1775.   Descriptiones | animalium | avium, amphibiorum, | piscium, insectorum, vermium; | quæ | in itinere orientali | observavit | Petrus Forskål. | Prof. Haun. | Post mortem auctoris | edidit | Carsten Niebuhr. | Adjuncta est | materia medica kahirina | atque | tabula maris rubri geographica. | Hauniæ, 1775. | Ex officina Mölleri, aulæ Typographi. | Apud Heineck et Faber.

1 vol. cap 4to, pp. 1-20, I-XXXIV, 1 l., pp. 1-164, frontisp. (map). Copenhagen.

A posthumous work on the animal life of the Arabian Peninsula, with descriptions of numerous species, local names, etc. The ornithological portion is found on pages VI-VIII and 1-12. Figures of some of the animals (including one bird) were published the following year under the title, "Icones Rerum Naturalium" (q.v.).

Forskål, Petrus.

1776.   Icones | rerum | naturalium, | quas | in itinere orientali | depingi curavit | Petrus Forskål, | Prof. Haun. | Post mortem auctoris | ad regis mandatum | æri incisas editit | Carsten Niebuhr. | Hauniæ, | Ex officina Mölleri, aulæ Typographi. | MDCCLXXVI.

1 vol. demy 4to, pp. 1-15, pll. I-XLIII (8 fold.; 1 of birds). Copenhagen.

Illustrations of some of the species of plants and animals described in the author's "Flora Aegyptiaco-Arabica" and his "Descriptiones Animalium," 1775 (q.v.) with page and number references to the earlier works. Pl. XXI is ornithological. A posthumous work.

Forster, John Reinhold.

1788. Enchiridion | historiae | naturali | inserviens, | quo | termini at delineationes | ad | avium, piscium, | insectorum et plantarum | adumbrationes | intelligendas et concinnandas, | secundum | methodum systematis Linneani | continentur, | editore | Io. Reinholdo Forster, | LL. Med. et Philos. D. et LL. AA. M. | In tenui labor. | Virgil. | Halae, | prostat apud Hemmerde et Schwetschke. | MDCCLXXXVIII.

1 vol. post 8vo, 8 pr. ll. (tit., ded., pref.), pp. 1-224. Halle.

Largely a glossary of technical terms in ornithology, ichthyology, entomology and botany (separately treated), with the characters of orders and genera listed at the close of each section. Pages 1-38 contain the "Fundamenta et termini ornithologiae secundum metodum et ad ductum celeberrimi equitis Caroli a Linné." Most of the characters given for the birds are not decisive enough for determination *per se*, since no specific names are quoted, but at least one genus, *Gavia*, dates from this work. The book is quite rare. The present copy is from the library of W. A. Stearns. Mathews (Birds of Australia, **7**, p. 451) states that the work was noticed in the Göttinger Anzeiger for March 27, 1788, p. 489.

Forster, John Reinhold.

1790. See Pennant, Thomas, **Indian Zoology.**

Forster, John Reinhold.

1795. See Latham, John; and Davies, **Faunula Indica.**

Forster, John Reinhold. (Lichtenstein, Anton August Heinrich.)

1844. Descriptiones | animalium | quae | in itinere ad maris australis terras | per annos 1772 1773 et 1774 suscepto | collegit observavit et delineavit | Ioannes Reinoldus Forster | regiae societatis scientiarum Londinensis sodalis | nunc demum editae auctoritate et impensis | academiae litterarum regiae Berolinae | curante | Henrico Lichtenstein | academiae socio. | Berolini ex officina academica | MDCCCXLIV. | Vendit Duemmleri libraria.

1 vol. post 8vo, pp. I-XIII+1, 1-424, 1 l. Berlin.

Descriptions of 305 species of animals collected by Forster in 1772-75 during a journey to S. Africa, Australia, New Zealand, etc. The book was published posthumously by Lichtenstein who added many annotations. The preface is dated January 1844. Some of the species are antedated by Wagler in his "Systema Avium" and in Heft. 5 of the Isis, 1829, where the names are accredited to Forster's (unpublished) manuscript. The present copy contains the bookplate of Frederick DuCane Godman.

Forster, John Reinhold. (Sclater, Philip Lutley, *ed.*)

1882. The Willughby Society. | **Forster's** | **Catalogue of the Animals of North America,** | or | **Faunula Americana.** | [*Vignette.*] | Edited by | Philip Lutley Sclater, M.A., Ph.D., F.R.S. | London: | 1882.

{A | catalogue | of the | animals | of | North America. | Containing, | An Enumeration of the known Quadrupeds, Birds, | Reptiles, Fish, Insects, Crustaceous and | Testaceous Animals; many of which are New, and | never described before. | To which are added, | short directions | for | Collecting, Preserving, and Transporting, | all Kinds of | natural history curiosities. | By John Reinhold Forster, F.A.S. | [*Quot., 3 lines.*]. | London: | Sold by B. White, at Horace's Head, in Fleet Street. | M.DCC.LXXI.}

1 vol. 8vo, pp. I-IV, "1-43, 1 pl. (by M. Griffith)," 2 ll. (advt.). London. "1771." 1882.

Pages 6-34 contain a list of North American animals, with the birds on pp. 8-17. A large number of binomial names are used, some of them for the first time, but since there are no descriptions, the names are here nomina nuda. The copy is a reprint issued by The Willughby Society (q.v.). The preface by the editor contains a short account of the author.

Forster, John Reinhold. (Sclater, Philip Lutley, *ed.*)

1882. The Willughby Society. | **Forster's** | **Animals of Hudson's Bay.** | [*Vignette.*] | Edited by | Philip Lutley Sclater, M.A., Ph. D., F. R. S. | London: | 1882.

1 vol. 8vo, pp. I-IV, "382-433," 2 ll. (advt.). London. "1772." 1882.

Miscellaneous accounts of a number of birds from Hudson's Bay, followed by detailed descriptions of eight supposed new species. The paper is entitled, "An Account of the Birds sent from Hudson's Bay; with Observations relative to their Natural History; and Latin Descriptions of some of the most uncommon"; it was published originally in the Philosophical Transactions of London, 1772, Art. XXIX, pp. 382-433. A copy of the original, also, is in the collection of pamphlets in the Ayer Library. The present copy is reprinted by The Willughby Society (q.v.). The editorial preface gives some account of the origin of the work.

Forster, Thomas Ignatius Maria. (Forster, Edward, Jr.)

1817. **Observations** | **of the** | **natural history** | **of** | **swallows;** | with a | collateral statement of facts | relative to their | migration, and to their brumal torpidity: | and | a table of reference to authors. | Illustrated with | figures of five species, | engraved on wood, by Willis. | To which is added, | a general catalogue of

British birds, | With the Provincial Names for each, &c. &c. &c. |
By Thomas Forster, F.L.S. | Corresp. Memb. Acad. Nat. Sciences
at Philadelphia, &c. &c. &c. | **Sixth edition,** enlarged. | London: |
Printed for T. and G. Underwood, 32, Fleet Street; Baldwin, |
Cradock, and Joy, Paternoster Row; and Treuttel and | Würtz,
at Paris and Strasbourg. | 1817.

1 vol. post 8vo, pp. I (?)-XIV, 1 l., pp. 1-97, 5 pll. London.

The first edition of this work was issued in 1808 under the title of "Observations
on the Brumal Retreat of the Swallow," etc. There are two sixth editions of
1817, differing, it is said, in the titles, that of the other edition reading "the
swallow tribe" instead of "swallows" (l. 5) and with the "sixth edition enlarged"
omitted. The "Catalogvs avium | in | insulis Britannicis habitantivm. |
Cvra et stvdio | Edvardi Forsteri, Ivnioris." occupies pages 65-97 and is the
same as issued separately by Edward Forster under his own name in the same
year. The "Extract of a Journal of Natural History, - - during several
Years, at Clapton, near London" on pages 55-63, is also ascribed to the authorship of Edward Forster by Mullens and Swann.

Fraser, Louis.

1846-48. Zoologia typica, | or | figures of new and rare mammals |
and birds | described in the Proceedings, or exhibited in the col-
lections | of the | Zoological Society of London. | By | Louis
Fraser, | (late Curator to the Society;) | Naturalist to the Niger
Expedition, 1841-2. | London:-Published by the author. | 1849. | To
be had of Messrs. Hyde & Co., 61, Fleet Street.

1 vol. demy folio, 1 pr. l. (tit.), pp. I-VIII, 70 ll., illum. tit., 70 pll.
(col.; by H. M. Turner, Jr., and Charles Couzens). London.

A series of seventy colored plates illustrating new and rare mammals and birds
not before figured (a large proportion of which had been described by the
author), with a page of notes accompanying each plate. The work was issued
in an edition of 250 copies, and was originally planned as a more extended
publication. Of the plates, 42 relate to birds, figuring 46 species.

The dates are little known. Sherborn (Index Animalium, Sect. 2, Pt. 1, p.
LVI, 1922) notes that "Ten parts had appeared by the end of 1846; 2 parts of
Birds are recorded as 1847 in Arch. f. Nat. 1848 (2), 3; and the whole was
finished by 1848 (*ibid.* 1849) (2), 1." Carus and Engelmann cite 20 parts
and 100 plates under dates of 1848-49.

Frauenfeld, Georg Ritter von.

1868. Neu aufgefundene Abbildung | **des** | **Dronte** | und eines
zweiten kurzflügeligen Vogels, wahrscheinlich des | poule rouge au
bec de bécasse | der Maskarenen | in der Privatbibliothek S. M.
des verstorbenen Kaisers Franz. | Erläutert von | Georg Ritter
von Frauenfeld. | Mit 4 Tafeln. | Herausgegeben von der K. K.

Zoologisch-Botanischen Gesellschaft. | Wien. | C. Ueberreuter'sche Buchdruckerei (M. Salzer). | 1868.

1 vol. superroyal folio, 3 pr. ll., pp. 1-16, 1 l., pll. 1-4 (2 col.). Vienna.

A discussion of various references to, and figures of, the dodo and other extinct birds.

Freycinet, Louis de. (Quoy, Jean René Const.; and Gaimard, Jean Paul.)

1824-26. > **Voyage | autour du monde,** | Enterpris par Ordre du Roi, | sous le Ministère et conformément aux instructions de S. Exc. M. le Vicomte du Bouchage, | Secrétaire d'État au Département de la Marine, | Éxecuté **sur les corvettes de S. M. l'Uranie et la Physicienne,** | pendant les années 1817, 1818, 1819 et 1820; | Publié sous les Auspices | de S. E. M. le Comte Corbière, Secrétaire d'État de la Marine et des Colonies, | Pour la partie Nautique; | par M. Louis de Freycinet, | Capitaine de vaisseau, Chevalier de Saint-Louis et de la Légion d'honneur, Correspondant de | l'Académie royale des sciences de l'Institut de France, &c.; Commandant de l'expédition. | **Zoologie,** | par MM. Quoy et Gaimard, médecins de l'expédition. | [*Vignette.*] | Paris, | chez Pillet Aîné, imprimeur-libraire, Rue Christine, No 5. | 1824.

> Voyage | autour du monde | Fait par ordre du Roi, | sur les corvettes de S. M: l'Uranie et la Physicienne, | pendant les années 1817, 1818, 1819 et 1820. | Histoire naturelle: Zoologie. | Planches. | Paris, | imprimerie en taille-douce de Langlois. | 1824.

2 vols. medium 4to and superroyal folio. Text, 4 pr. ll. (half-tit., tit. and pref.), pp. 1-712. Atlas, tit., pp. 1-15 (expl. of pll.), pll. 1-96 (71 col.; 27 of birds, col., by P. Oudart and Prêtre). Paris.

The zoological portion, by Quoy and Gaimard, of Freycinet's report on the voyage of the Uranie and Physicienne. The ornithological matter is contained in Chapters V and VI, ("Description des Oiseaux," pp. 90-141, and "Remarques sur les Oiseaux pélagiens et sur quelques autres Palmipèdes," pp. 142-169,) and in a general discussion of mammals and birds in Chapter II, pp. 12-50. Pll. 13-39 are ornithological. The zoology of the voyage appeared in 16 livraisons, the dates of which are given by Sherborn and Woodward (Ann. and Mag. of Nat. Hist., (7), **7**, p. 392, 1901) as follows. Livr. **1**, pp. 1-40, June 26, 1824; **2**, pp. 41-88, July 31, 1824; **3**, pp. 89-128, Aug. 28, 1824; **4**, pp. 129-184, Sept. 18, 1824; **5**, pp. 185-232, Oct. 9, 1824; **6**, pp. 233-280, Nov. 20, 1824; **7**, pp. 281-328, Dec. 18, 1824; **8**, pp. 329-? (6 sheets), Jan. 29, 1925; **9**, pp. ?-424 (6 sheets), March 26, 1925; **10**, pp. 425-?, May 7, 1825; **11**, pp. ?-496, May 7, 1825; **12**, pp. 497-? (5 sheets), August 6, 1825; **13**, pp. ? (5 sheets), Oct. 1, 1825; **14**, pp. ?-616, Dec. 17, 1825; **15**, pp. 617-? (6 sheets), April 26, 1826; **16**, pp. ?-712 (6 sheets), June 14, 1826. Probably the plates appeared with the corresponding text.

Fric, Antonin Jan [=Fritsch, Ant.].

1877. The | **birds of Europe** | by | Ant. Fritsch, M.D. | London |
Trübner & Co., Ludgate Hill | Prague: the author | 1877.
1 vol. royal folio, 1 pr. l., 6 ll., pll. 1-61 (col.). London.

The plates of the present work are the same as those of the author's "Naturgeschichte die Vögel Europa's" published in Prague, 1853-70,[1] which included
a second volume of text. There was also issued an edition in the Czech language which was not completed so far as I can learn. The spelling of the English names in the present edition leaves room for doubt that this was actually
published in London. It may be a reissue of certain pages of the original
edition with an English title page. The text of this issue consists of a list of
species with references to the plates and to several published works of Johns,
Bree, and Degland and Gerbe, and with the names in Latin, German, English
and French.

Friderich, C. G. (Bau, Alexander.)

1923. Friderich | **Naturgeschichte** | der | **Vögel europas** | **Sechste,** |
dem gegenwärtigen Stand der ornithologischen Wissenschaft |
entsprechend vermehrte und verbesserte **Auflage** | Neu bearbeitet
von | Alexander Bau | Mit 551 naturtreuen Farbendruckbildern
auf 50 Tafeln, | 35 Textbildern, 1 Tafel mit Darstellungen der
Raubvogelflugbilder | und 3 Tafeln mit 116 Abbildungen von
Vogeleiern | [*Blazon.*] | Stuttgart 1923 | E. Schweizerbart'sche
Verlagsbuchhandlung | (Erwin Nägele) / G.m.b.H.

1 vol. imperial 8vo, 4 pr. ll. (half-tit., tit., pref. and conts.;=pp.
A-H?), pp. J-N+1, 1 l. (subtit.), pp. I-LXXVII+1, 1 l. (subtit.),
pp. 1-884, 1 l. (advt.), pll. 1-53 (col.; 3 of eggs; by Aug. Specht),
1 pl. (uncol.), 34 text-figs. Stuttgart.

Sixth edition of C. G. Friderich's "Naturgeschichte aller deutschen Zimmer-,
Haus-, und Jagdvögel," etc., first published in 1847 [2]; revised by Bau. The
work consists of a popular natural history of the birds of Europe, illustrated by
chromolithographs. Originally, as indicated by the title of the first edition,
the scope was less extended.

Frisch, Jodocus Leopold.

1817. See Frisch, Johann Leonhard, **Vorstellung der Vögel Deutschlands.**

Frisch, Johann Leonhard.

1795. See Bechstein, Johann Matthäus, **Gemeinnützige Naturgeschichte Deutschlands,** 1789-95.

---

[1]A copy of Lief. 1 was presented to the Deutschen Ornithologen-Gesellschaft at a meeting held
July 13, 1853. Cf. Journ. für Orn., Extra Heft (Errinnerungsschrift), I Jahrg., p. 9, 1853.

[2]Carus and Engelmann and others quote 1849; a preface to the present work gives 1847.

Frisch, Johann Leonhard. (Frisch, Jodocus Leopold; Zorn von Plobsheim, Friedrich August.

1817. **Vorstellung** | der | **Vögel Deutschlandes** | und | beyläufig auch einiger | Fremden; | nach ihren Eigenschaften beschrieben | von | Johann Leonhard Frisch | Rector des Gymnasii zum grauen Kloster in Berlin und Mitgliede der Königl. | Akademie der Wissenschaften, | in Kupfer gebracht, | und nach ihren natürlichen Farben dargestellt | von | Ferdinand Helfreich Frisch | Kupferstecher in Berlin. [| Supplementheft zu den XII Klassen, aus XI Blatt.] | Berlin, | gedruckt bey Friedr. Wilhelm Birnstiel, Königl. privil. Buchdrucker, 1763. | Jetzt Verlag der Nicolaischen Buchhandlung seit 1817.

1 vol. in 2 vols., crown folio, 104 ll. (incl. 25 tits. and subtits.), frontisp., pll. 1-241, ad 31, 114B, ad No. 212, Suppls. 28, 31, 33, 106, 107, 109, 152, 157, 165, 185A and 185B (col.; 102-104 of bats). Berlin.

A later edition of the author's "Vorstellung der Vögel Deutschlands," originally published in 1733-63 in 14 parts and a supplement. Johann Leonhard Frisch, according to a prefatory note, died at the completion of the fourth part of his work, from which point it was taken up by his son, Jodocus Leopold Frisch. The supplement, including Latin and vernacular indices to the plates, was written by Baron von Zorn, Most of the plates were prepared by a third son, Ferdinand Helfreich Frisch who died after twenty-two years of work upon them, and the remainder, after various difficulties, were completed by his son, Johann Christoph Frisch. The text is not voluminous.

According to Schalow (Beiträge zur Vogelfauna der Mark Brandenburg, pp. 63-64, 1919), the present issue was produced by the Nicolaischen Verlagsbuchhandlung (legal successors of Birnstiel, publisher of the original edition) from a stock of old plates supplied with new title-pages. Schalow says that he knows of no copy of the reprint with text or with the full set of 255 plates, but the copy at hand seems to be complete in every detail. The full number of plates, all colored, are in the atlas, accompanied by the general title-page (transcribed above) which is new. The reprinted title-pages for the various parts of the atlas are bound with the text in a separate volume. These titles are thirteen in number instead of fourteen as in the original, owing to certain changes. The original Pts. 1-3, embracing Class I of the author's divisions, were issued separately with three distinct title-pages; in the present reprint there is only one inclusive title-page for all three parts, to which is added the (presumably) original leaf of preface. Also, there is a title-page for the supplementary plates, similar to the general title-page of the work but differing as transcribed (in brackets) above; no such title-page occurred in the original, according to Schalow's collation (l.c., pp. 51-61).

The text is of composite construction. That of Classes I and II (issued in Pts. 3 and 4 of the original) is new and is supplied with new subtitle-pages, dated 1817. The subject matter in this may be revised since that of each Class occupies (including the respective subtitle-pages) 13 pages instead of

11 of the original as collated by Schalow. The letterpress and subtitles of Classes III-XII (Pts. 4-14 of the original edition) and the text of the supplement (without title here or in the original) appear to belong to the first edition intact. There are minor differences between the subtitles and the transcriptions of the originals as presented by Schalow, but they are such as might be due to printer's errors in the copy. The number of pages is unaltered and the paper is unquestionably old and different from that used in the undoubtedly reprinted portions of the work.

It seems probable, therefore, that in making up the new edition of this work, the publishers may have utilized a stock of old plates and most of the letterpress but reprinted such portions as were needed to make complete copies of the stock on hand.

Schalow (l.c.) has given voluminous notes regarding the details of composition and publication of the original work. A review of the species was given by Johann Leonhard Frisch in Suppl. I of Vol. III of J. M. Bechstein's "Gemeinnützige Naturgeschichte Deutschlands," 1789-95 (q.v.).

Frivaldszky, Joannes.

1891. **Aves Hungariæ.** | Enumeratio systematica avium Hungariæ cum notis | brevibus biologicis, locis inventionis virorumque | a quibus oriuntur. | E mandato commissionis Hungaricae secundi ornithologorum | universalis congressus | conscripsit | Joannes Frivaldszky | Consiliaris Regius [*etc., 2 lines.*]. | [*Vignette.*] | Budapestini. 1891. Typis Societatis Franklinianæ.

1 vol. 8vo, pp. I-IX+1, 1-197, 1 pl. (col.), 12 text-figs. Budapest.

An annotated list of 325 species of Hungarian birds.

Fürbringer, Max.

1888. **Untersuchungen** | zur | **Morphologie und Systematik** | der | **Vögel** | zugleich ein Beitrag zur Anatomie der Stütz- und Bewegungsorgane | von | Max Fürbringer | o.ö Professor der Anatomie [*etc., 2 lines.*] | Mit 30 Tafeln | [*Quot., 2 lines.*] | I. Specieller [II. Allgemeiner] Theil | Brust, Schulter und proximale Flügelregion der Vögel [Resultate und Reflexionen auf morphologischem Gebiete | Systematische Ergebnisse und Folgerungen] | Amsterdam | Verlag von Tj. Van Holkema | 1888.

2 vols. imperial 4to. Vol. I, 3 pr. ll. (half-tit., tit. and ded.), pp. III-XLIX+1, 1-834. Vol. II, 2 pr. ll. (half-tit. and tit.), pp. 835-1751, pll. I-XXVIII, XXIXa, XXIXb, XXX (col.; 3 fold.; by author). Amsterdam.

A detailed treatise on the anatomy and classification of birds. Volume I deals particularly with the osteology, neurology and myology of the shoulder-girdle; Volume II, with exceedingly detailed studies of the classification of birds based on their complete anatomy. An extended bibliography. is appended

Führer, Ludwig von.

1894-1905. See Reiser and Führer, **Materialen zu Einer Ornis Balcanica.**

Gadow, Hans.

1883. Catalogue | of the | **Passeriformes,** | or | perching birds, | in the | collection | of the | British Museum. | **Cichlomorphæ: Part V.** | Containing the families | Paridæ and Laniidæ | (Titmice and Shrikes), | and | **Certhiomorphæ** | (Creepers and Nuthatches). | By | Hans Gadow, Ph.D. | London: | printed by order of the Trustees. | 1883.

See British Museum, **Catalogue of the Birds,** 1874-98, Vol. VIII.

Gadow, Hans.

1884. Catalogue | of the | **Passeriformes,** | or | perching birds, | in the | collection | of the | British Museum. | **Cinnyriomorphæ:** | containing the families | Nectariniidæ and Meliphagidæ | (Sunbirds and Honey-eaters). | By | Hans Gadow, M.A., Ph.D. | London: | printed by order of the Trustees. | 1884.

See British Museum, **Catalogue of the Birds,** 1874-98, Vol. IX.

Gadow, Hans.

1899. See Wilson, Scott B.; and Evans, A. H., **Aves Hawaiienses,** 1890-99.

Gadow, Hans.

1893-96. See Newton, Alfred, **A Dictionary of Birds.**

Gaimard, Jean Paul.

1824-26. See Freycinet, **Voyage Autour du Monde . . . sur les corvettes . . . l'Uranie et la Physicienne.**

Gaimard, Jean Paul.

1830-35. See Dumont D'Urville, Jules, **Voyage de Découvertes de l'Astrolabe.**

[Gallatin, Frederic, Jr.]

1908. Catalogue | of a collection of | books on ornithology | in the library of | Frederic Gallatin, Jr. | [*Vignette.*] | New York | Privately printed | MCMVIII.

1 vol. 8vo, pp. 1-177+1, 3 printed guard-sheets, 3 pll. (2 portrs., 1 bird). New York.

An annotated catalogue of the ornithological books in the library of Frederic Gallatin, Jr., compiled by The Knickerbocker Book Shop.

Gardiner, Edward Gardiner.

1884. Beiträge | zur | Kenntniss des Epitrichiums | und der | Bildung des Vogelschnabels. | Inaugural-Dissertation | zur | Erlangung der philosophischen Doctorwürde | der | hohen philosophischen Facultät der Universität Leipzig | vorgelegt von | Edward G. Gardiner | aus Boston, U. S. of A. | Leipzig 1884.

1 vol. royal 8vo, tit., pp. 1-50, 1 l., pll. I-II (fold.). Leipzig.

A study of the embryonic development of the avian bill, especially with reference to the epitrichial layer.

Gardiner, Linda.

1923. See Hudson, William Henry, **Rare Vanishing & Lost British Birds.**

Garnot, Prosper.

1826-30. See Duperrey, L. I., **Voyage autour du Monde, sur la Corvette, La Coquille.**

Garrod, Alfred Henry.

1881. See Thomson, C. Wyville, **Reports on the Scientific Results of the Voyage of H. M. S. Challenger; Report on the Birds.**

Gätke, Heinrich.

1891. **Die Vogelwarte Helgoland.** | Von | Heinrich Gätke, | Ehrenmitglied des Britischen Ornithologen-Vereins [*etc.*, *5 lines.*] | Herausgegeben | von | Professor Dr. Rudolf Blasius. | Braunschweig | Joh. Heinr. Meyer. | 1891.

1 vol. 8vo, 7 pr. ll., pp. 1-609, frontisp. Braunschweig.

An important contribution to the study of bird-migration, based on the observations of fifty years in a region unusually favorable for that subject of investigation. There is a second edition of the work in German as well as a translation into English, "Heligoland as an Ornithological Observatory," 1895 (q.v.).

Gätke, Heinrich. (Rosenstock, Rudolph, *transl.*)

1895. **Heligoland | as an | ornithological observatory** | the result of fifty years' experience | by | Heinrich Gätke | Corresponding Member of the Zoological Society of London [*etc.*, *5 lines.*] | Translated by | Rudolph Rosenstock, M. A. Oxon. | [*Vignette.*] | [*Quot.*, *2 lines.*] | Edinburgh: David Douglas, 10 Castle Street | 1895 | [All rights reserved].

1 vol. 8vo, pp. I-X, 1 l., pp. 1-599, frontisp., 1 pl., 13 text-figs. Edinburgh.

A translation of the author's " Die Vogelwarte Helgoland," 1891 (q.v.), with corrections and additions supplied by the author.

Gault, Benjamin True. (Ridgway, Robert; Allen, Arthur A.)

1922.   Check list | of the | birds of Illinois | Together with a short |
list of 200 commoner | birds and Allen's | Key to Birds Nests |
Published by the | Illinois Audubon Society | 10 South La Salle
Street, Chicago | 1922.

1 vol. (pamphlet, 4½x7½), pp. 1-80, 1 text-map (col.). Chicago.

Most of the book (pp. 30-80) is occupied by a check-list of all birds recorded
from Illinois, with notes on status and distribution. A shorter list of the
commoner species is prefixed. Ridgway contributes an introductory chapter
giving an account of the zonal distribution of species, especially as regards the
species breeding in the Lower Austral, and those breeding in the Transition,
Zones, with list of Illinois trees similarly restricted. Allen's "Key to Birds'
Nests", from Bird-Lore **22**, pp. 369-373, is reprinted by permission.

Gay, Claudio. (Des Murs, Marc Athanese Parfait Oeillet.)

1844-54?   > Historia | fisica y politica | de Chile | segun documen-
tos adquiridos en esta republica | durante doce años de residencia
en ella | y publicada | bajo los auspicios del supremo gobierno | por
Claudio Gay | ciudadano Chileno, | individuo de varias sociedades
cientificos nacionales y estrangeras, | Caballero de la Legion de
Honor. | Zoologia. | [*Line omitted.*] | Tomo primero [Laminas]. |
[Blazon.] | Paris | en casa del autor. | Chile | en el Museo de
Historia Natural de Santiago. | MDCCCXLVII [MDCCCXLVIII].

2 vols., demy 8vo and demy folio. Text, pp. 1-496. Atlas, cover-tit.,
25 pll. (21 col.; by Werner, A. Prévost, P. Oudart and Cl. Gay;
14 ornith., 13 col.). Paris.

The complete work of the above title comprises 23 volumes of text and 2 volumes
of plates. Of the text, 8 volumes relate to zoology, the first of which (collated
above) contains the mammals and birds. The ornithology occupies pp. 183-496
and was written by Des Murs (according to statements on pp. 11 and 183)
while Gay contributed only field notes. In spite of this fact, several of the
new names on the plates are followed by Gay's name. Vol. 8 of the zoological
series, treating of Mollusks and Zoophytes and published in 1854, contains
some ornithological matter as follows. P. 474 contains descriptions of *Fulica
chilensis* (new) and *Rhynchops nigra*; p. 477, errata and corrigenda; p. 478, an
index to the plates of birds (and mammals); pp. 479-486, a concordance of
common and scientific names, including those of birds; pp. 487-499, a general
index to the orders, families and genera of the entire work. (A typewritten
copy of the ornithological portions of pp. 474 and 477 has been inserted in the
present volume.)

Authorities appear to agree as to the date of publication of the volume of
text in the present copy. The date of the plates is open to question. All
the zoological plates occur, in the complete work, in Vol. II of the atlas, but
they were issued at widely different times. Those in the present set (comprising all of the mammals and birds) are accompanied by an original wrapper
dated 1848. This wrapper is lettered very like the title-page of text and is

transcribed above in lieu of the title-page of Vol. II of the atlas. There is nothing to show, however, that it appeared with any of the plates which are now associated with it; its printed date agrees with the date of publication of Vol. II of the zoological text which had nothing to do with birds or mammals.

Des Murs, in his "Iconographie Ornithologique," 1845-49 (q.v.), gives very good evidence that some of the plates preceded the text. In Livr. 1, in the discussion of the genus *Merganetta* (pp. 2 and 3 of the unpaged text relating to that genus), he says, "Dès la même année (=1844), M. Gay . . . l'a également fait figurer dans l'Atlas de son immense Ouvrage sur le Chili. . . et lui a donné le nom de *Raphipterus*." In Livr. 8 of the "Iconographie," in the discussion of the genus *Sylviorthorhynchus* (in the last paragraph), he says, "Nous avons établi ce Genre particulier . .sur une jolie Espèce qu'a découverte M. Gay, et que ce savant Voyageur nous avoit confiée pour en joindre la description á la figure qu'il en a publiée dans son Grand Ouvrage sur le Chili." In the text to pll. 5 and 45, *Raphypterus chilensis* Gay and *Sylviorthorhynchus desmurii* are quoted from Gay's "Historia fisica y politica de Chile," 1844.

Fulica chilensis, described by Des Murs in Vol. VIII, 1854, is mentioned by Bonaparte in the "Comptes Rendus" for Dec. 19, 1853, p. 925. Hartlaub also cites it in the Journal für Ornithologie, 1, Extra-Heft, 1853, publ. 1854. Bonaparte quotes Gay as the authority for the name without giving the reference; Hartlaub quotes the "Historia fisica" and says that Des Murs is about to publish, or has published, a figure of the species in that work, but that he has not seen a copy of it. Neither citation thus supplies any definite information as to whether the name had been published on a plate or in the text at the time of writing.

An uncolored plate of osteological details is headed, "Ornitologia" (without number). The first two colored plates of birds are marked, "Ornitologia No. 1" and " Ornitologia No. 2." The plate of *Raphipterus chilensis* is lettered, "Zoologia No." (blank) and all the remaining plates of birds are labeled, "Ornitologia No." (blank). Dr. Richmond, who has supplied me with various references on this work, remarks (in litt.) that the earliest plates to be published appear to be those marked, "Zoologia No."

Gengler, J.

1906. Die | Vögel des Regnitztales | und seiner Nebentäler | von Fürth bis Bamberg | mit Einschluss von | Nürnberg und Umgebung | von | Dr. J. Gengler | Mitglied der Deutschen Ornithologischen Gesellschaft [*etc.*, *4 lines*.]. | Mit 12 vom Verfasser gemalten Tafeln. | 1906 | Druck und Verlag von U. E. Sebald | Nürnberg.

1 vol. post 8vo, pp. I-IV, 1-191+1, V-XIII+1, 1 l. (errata), 12 pll. (11 col.; by Gengler). Nuremberg.

An annotated list of 283 species of birds found in the lower valley of the Regnitz River, Germany. Diagnostic markings, bibliographic references, distribution and other notes are given.

Gengler, J.

1920. Balkanvögel. | Ein ornithologisches Tagebuch | von | Dr. J. Gengler. | Mit 15 Abbildungen. | 1920 | Verlagsbuchhandlung H. A. Pierer | Altenburg S.-A. und Leipzig.

1 vol. 8 vo, pp. 1-210, 1 l. (advt.), pll. I-VI (figs. 1-15). Altenburg and Leipzig.

An account of the birds observed and collected by (and for) the author during the German military operations in the Balkan Peninsula, 1916-1918. An itinerary is followed by a systematic list of 261 species and subspecies, a bibliography, and a detailed discussion of the birds included in the list.

Gentry, Thomas George.

1876-77. Life-histories | of the | birds of eastern Pennsylvania | by | Thomas G. Gentry, | Member of the Academy of Natural Sciences of Philadelphia, [*etc., 2 lines.*] | In two volumes. Vol. I. | Philadelphia: | published by the author. | 1876.

> Life-histories | of the | birds | of eastern Pennsylvania, | by | Thomas G. Gentry, | Member of [*etc., 3 lines.*] | Volume II. | Salem, Mass. | The Naturalists' Agency. | 1877.

2 vols. crown 8vo. Vol. I, 4 pr. ll., pp. XI-XIV, 1 l., pp. 1-399. Vol. II, 4 pr. ll., pp. 1-336. Philadelphia. 1876. Salem. 1877.

A popular account of the birds of eastern Pennsylvania, chiefly valuable for its notes on the food-habits of the various species, based on analyses of stomach-contents. Originally projected as a work to be complete in two volumes, it was later found to exceed the proposed limits and the subject matter beginning with the wading-birds was reserved for a third volume which was never published. The present copy is from the library of Elliott Coues to whom it was presented by the author. A manuscript letter from the author to Dr. Coues is inserted in Volume I.

Gentry, Thomas George.

1878. The | house sparrow | at | home and abroad, | with some | concluding remarks upon its usefulness, | and | copious references to the literature of the subject. | By | Thomas G. Gentry, | author of Life-Histories of Birds of Eastern Pennsylvania, | Member of the Philadelphia Academy [*etc., 4 lines.*]. | Philadelphia: | Claxton, Remsen, and Haffelfinger. | 1878.

1 vol. 8 vo, 1 pr. l., pp. V-VI, 7-128, frontisp. (col.; by Edwin Sheppard). Philadelphia.

The first American work dealing entirely with the English Sparrow. The question of the bird's usefulness or undesirablility is fully discussed with conclusions which agree with most of the modern opinions based on longer familiarity with the species. A bibliography is appended. A presentation copy to C. B. Cory from the author.

Gentry, Thomas George.

1880-82. **Nests and eggs | of | birds of the United States.** | Illustrated. | [*Fig. of Chipping Sparrow.*] | By Thomas G. Gentry, | Author of [*etc., 10 lines, in 2 columns*] | Philadelphia. | Published by J. A. Wagenseller. | 1882.

1 vol. crown folio, 1 pr. l., pp. V-X, 1-300, frontisp. (portr.), illum. title-p., 54 pll. (col.; by Edwin Sheppard). Philadelphia.

> Published in 25 parts. A popular account of the nesting habits of fifty species of North American birds with chromolithographic illustrations of the species and of their nests and eggs. One of the plates is duplicated in the present copy. The illuminated title page is the only complete one. The text is not always reliable. A critical review of the work is given in the Bull. Nuttall Orn. Club, 1882, pp. 246-249.

Geoffroy Saint-Hilaire, Isidore. (Jacquemont, Victor.)

1842(?)-43. **Description | des | collections | de Victor Jacquemont. | Mammifères et Oiseaux,** | par | M. Isidore Geoffroy Saint-Hilaire, | Membre de l'Institut [*etc., 3 lines.*]. | 1842-1843. | Paris.- Typographie de Firmin Didot frères, rue Jacob, 56.

1 vol. imperial 4to, pp. 1-90, 1 l. (index), pll. 1-8 (7 col.; by Werner and A Prévost; 2 ornithological). Paris.

> An author's (advance?) copy of the ornithological and mammalogical portion of Jacquemont's "Voyage dans l'Inde." In the complete work, the text is found in Vol. IV and the plates in Atlas, Vol. II, both under date of 1844 although the letterpress for the mammals and birds appears to have been published in 1843. Geoffroy presented a copy of this section of the work to the Académie Royale des Sciences de Paris on May 8, 1843 (recorded in the Revue Zoologique, 1843, p. 151), but it is impossible to say whether it was an author's separate (as collated above) or the regular number of the "Voyage." The copy at hand is enclosed in an original wrapper of the "Voyage" on which the livraison-number is not marked, but which is dated 1843[1]. It is probable, therefore, that the date 1842-1843 on the title-page is misleading. This title-page is not found in the complete work, being replaced by one lettered simply, "Description | des | collections. | Zoologie. | IV. | I"[2]. The ornithology occupies pp. 81-89 and pll. 7-8. One new species of bird, *Ardea brag*, is described and figured.

Georgi, Johann Gottlieb.

1765. See Osbeck, Peter, **Reise nach Ostindien und China.**

---

[1]Voyage | Dans l'Inde, | par | Victor Jacquemont, | Pendant les Années 1828 à 1832. | Publié sous les auspices | De M. Guizot, | Ministre de l'Instruction Publique, | Livraison. | Paris, | Typographie de Firmin Didot Frères, Libraires, | Imprimeurs de l'Institut de France, | Rue Jacob, No. 56. | 1843 [*Figured Border.*].

[2]Copy in John Crerar Library, Chicago.

[Gerini, Giovanni.]

1767-76. [Storia Naturale degli Uccelli.]

5 vols. in 1, superroyal folio (14x18), pll. I-CVIII (col.; by Viol. Vanni, Lor. Lorenzi and S. Manetti; XVIII, LXXXV and ? missing). Florence.

A series of execrable drawings, hand-colored, of various birds from various countries. Above each of them is inscribed a vernacular Italian name with a Latin equivalent, sometimes binary, sometimes not. Below, each plate bears a dedication to some personage or other. There is no title-page and the back of the cover is inscribed simply "Volatili." The above title is taken from the "Atlante Ornitologico" of Arrigoni degli Oddi, 1902 (q.v.), pp. 122-123, 1902. Gerini's names have not been accepted, except occasionally as with *Falco merillus* (Pll. XVIII and XIX) cited by Sharpe (Hand List 1, p. 275, No. 34, 1899) and Madarász (Magyarország Madarai, Pt. VI, p. 234, 1901). According to Paolo Savi (Ornithologica Toscana, 1, pp. V-VI, 1827-31), Gerini, having died in 1751, is not responsible for any of the above work other than for the assembling of the collection of birds which forms the basis of the drawings; the publication is ascribed to certain unnamed individuals without a knowledge of ornithology.

Buffon (Histoire Naturelle des Oiseaux, 1, p. VJ, footn., 1770) mentions this work as being noticeable for the inferiority of its plates and the unscientific nature of its nomenclature, which, he says, renders the natural history of birds more confused rather than simplified.

Gervais, Paul.

1839. See Laplace, Cyrille Pierre Théodore, **Voyage autour du Monde executé sur La Favorite, . . . Zoologie.**

Giacomelli, F.

1881. See Watkins, Morgan George, **Pictures of Bird Life in Pen and Pencil.**

Giacomelli, H.

1885. See Adams, William Henry Davenport, **The Bird World Described with Pen and Pencil.**

Gibbs, Morris.

1879. Article XXIV.-**Annotated List of the Birds of | Michigan. |** By Dr. Morris Gibbs. > Bulletin. U. S. Geol. and Geogr. Survey of the Territories, **5,** No. 3, pp. 481-497, Nov. 30, 1879.

1 pamphlet, 8vo, pp. 481-497. Washington, Nov. 30, 1879.

An annotated list of 310 species and subspecies, with brief annotations giving distribution and status of each, and with occasional references to special records. Extracted from the Bulletin in which it appeared.

Gibbs, Morris.

1907. See Mershon, W. B., **The Passenger Pigeon.**

Giebel, Christoph.Gottfried Andreas.

1872-77. Thesaurus | ornithologiae. | Repertorium | der gesammten ornithologischen Literatur | und | Nomenclator | sämmtlicher Gattungen und Arten der Vögel | nebst Synonymen und geographischer Verbreitung. | Von | Dr. C. G. Giebel, | Professor der Zoologie und Director des zoologischen Museums | der Universität in Halle. | Erster [-Dritter] Band. | Leipzig: | F. A. Brockhaus. | 1872 [1875; 1877].

3 vols. 8vo. Vol. I, pp. I-VIII, 3 ll., pp. 1-868. Vol. II, pp. I-VI, 1-787. Vol. III, pp. I-VI, 1-861. Leipzig.

Issued in 8 half-volumes. The work is divided into two general sections, the first of which is devoted to an ornithological bibliography (Vol. I., pp. 1-252), and the second to a "nomenclator ornithologicus" (Vol. I, pp. 253-868; Vol. II and III, complete). The bibliography is arranged in a very heterogeneous manner and is almost useless, while the "nomenclator" is not entirely reliable.

Giglioli, Enrico Hillyer.

1886. Ministero di Agricoltura, Industria e Commercio. | Direzione Generale dell' Agricoltura. | Ufficio Ornitologico. | **Avifauna Italica** | Elenco delle specie di uccelli | stazionarie o di passaggio in Italia | collo loro sinonimia volgare | e con notizie piu specialmente intorno alle migrazioni ed alla nidificazione | compilato dal Dottore | Enrico Hillyer Giglioli | Professore [*etc.*, *3 lines.*] | Per servire alla inchiesta ornitologica. | [*Blazon.*] | Firenze. | Coi tipi dei successori Le Monnier. | 1886.

1 vol. 8vo, pp. I-VII+1, 1-623, 1 l. Florence.

An annotated list of species of the birds of Italy, with a compilation of the common names used for them in various districts and an account of their distribution.

Giglioli, Enrico Hillyer.

1889-91. Ministero di Agricoltura, Industria e Commercio. | Direzione Generale dell' Agricoltura. | Ufficio Ornitologico. | **Primo resoconto | dei resultati della inchiesta ornitologica in Italia.** | Parte prima [seconda; terza ed ultima] | Avifauna Italica [Avifaune locali.; Notizie d'indole generale]⌐| Elenco sistematico delle specie di uccelli [Risultati della inchiesta ornitologica (*Pt. II.*); Migrazioni, nidificazione, alimentazione, ecc. (*Pt. III.*)] | stazionarie o di passagio in Italia [nelle singole provincie (*Pt. II.*); *Line omitted* (*Pt. III.*).] | con nuovi nomi volgari e colle notizie sin qui fornite dai collaboratori | nella inchiesta ornitologica [*2 lines omitted* (*Pts. II and III.*).] | compilato dal Dottore | Enrico Hillyer Giglioli | Professore [*etc.*, *3 lines.*]. | Con una carta delle stazioni ornitologiche in Italia. [*Line omitted* (*Pts. II and III.*).] | [*Blazon.*] | Firenze. | Coi tipi dei successori Le Monnier. | 1889 [1890; 1891].

3 vols. 8vo. Vol. I, pp. I-VII+1, 1-706, 1 map. Vol. II, pp. I-VIII, 1-693, 2 ll. (errata and addenda). Vol. III, pp. I-VII+1, 1-518. Florence.

An elaboration and revision of the author's "Avifauna Italica" of 1886 (q.v.). In Vol. I the species are treated in systematic order, with a list of vernacular names and notes on distribution arranged by districts, provinces and specific localities. In Vol. II a list of species is given for each province, with a description of the physical characteristics of each region. Vol. III contains general remarks and notes on migration, nidification, alimentation, etc., arranged by provinces. No species are described.

Giglioli, Enrico Hillyer.

1907. Ministero di Agricoltura, Industria e Commercio | Direzione Generale dell' Agricoltura | Ufficio Ornitologico | **Secondo resoconto | dei risultati della inchiesta ornitologica in Italia** | Avifauna Italica | Nuovo elenco sistematico delle specie di uccelli | stazionarie, di passagio o di accidentale comparsa in Italia; | coi nomi volgari, colla loro distribuzione geografica, | con notizie intorno alla loro biologia, ed un esame critico delle variazioni | e delle cosidette sottospecie | compilato dal Dottore | Enrico Hillyer Giglioli | Professore ordinario di Zoologia e Anatomia dei Vertebrati | nel R. Istituto di Studi Superiori in Firenze, Membro del Comitato ornitologico internazionale | e Direttore dell' Ufficio ornitologico | [*Blazon.*] | Firenze | coi tipi dello stab. tipografico S. Giuseppe | 1907.

1 vol. superroyal 8vo (6¾ x 9¾), pp. I-XXIV, 1-784. Florence.

A second edition of Pt. I of the author's "Primo Resoconto," etc., 1889 (q.v.). No descriptions are given and the text consists almost entirely of lists of vernacular names of the species and accounts of the distribution of each. No subspecies are recognized. Dultz & Co., Munich, in their "Antiquariats-Katalog 19," 1916, announce their purchase of the full stock of this book which they quote under publication date of 1911, but the work was reviewed in the Journal für Ornithologie in January 1908 and in the Auk in April of the same year, and, no doubt, was actually published in 1907 as given on the title-page.

Gilbert, H. A.; and Brook, Arthur.

1924. **Secrets | of bird life** | by | H. A. Gilbert | and | Arthur Brook | with forty-one photographs | Arrowsmith::London::W.C.1.

1 vol. 8vo, pp. 1-203, 32 pll. London.

An account of the authors' experiences in photographing British birds. The narrative appears to be by the senior author, while the junior author is responsible for the photographs which form the excellent illustrations.

Gill, Theodore Nicholas.

1874. See Baird, Spencer F.; Brewer; and Ridgway, **A History of North American Birds, Land Birds.**

Giraud, Jacob P., Jr.

1844. The | birds of Long Island. | By J. P. Giraud, Jr., | Member of the Lyceum of Natural History, New-York, Corresponding | Member of the Academy of Natural Sciences, Philadelphia, &c. | New-York: | Published by Wiley & Putnam, 161 Broadway. | Tobitt's Print, 9 Spruce st. | 1844.

1 vol. 4to (5½ x 8⅞) pp. I-XXI+1, 1 l., pp. 1-397, 1 pl. New York.

A general account of the habits of the birds found on Long Island, with descriptions and some synonymy.

Girton, Daniel. (Thompson, W.)

1805. The new and complete | pigeon-fancier; | or. | modern treatise | on | domestic pigeons: | containing | The most valuable Information concerning the Nature, Pro- | perties, and Management of all their various Species, | under the following heads: | 1. An useful, comprehensive and entertaining Natural History of | Pigeons. -2. Full and ample Directions for building a Pigeon-House, or Dove-Cote. -3. Plain and necessary Instructions for stocking and | managing the Pigeon-House, or Dove-Cote, with a particular Account | of those Pigeons which are most advantageous for that Purpose; and | an Abstract of the Laws now in Force relating to Pigeons. -4. Ac- | count of the best Methods now in Practice, for preventing Pigeons | from leaving their Habitations. -5. An accurate and clear Descrip- | tion of all the valuable Species of Fancy-Birds and Toys now bred in | England, France, and Holland. -6. Rules necessary to be observed in | distinguishing the Sexes of young Pigeons. -7. Useful Particulars re- | lative to coupling or matching of Pigeons. -8. The most eligible Me- | thods of erecting and furnishing a Loft for Pigeons. -9. Remarks | and Observations on the Diet proper for Pigeons. -10. The Diseases | of Pigeons, with the best Remedies for each Distemper, as prac- | ticed | by the most experienced Fanciers. -11. General Remarks on Pigeon- | Fanciers and Pigeon-Keepers; with Advice highly worthy the At- | tention of both. | The whole | Being an useful, instructive, and sure Guide to Pigeon-Fanciers | in every Sphere of Life, comprehending all that is necessary | to be known in the whole delightful Fancy of Pigeons. | By Daniel Girton, Esq. | of the County of Bucks. | A **new Edition,** revised and improved by Mr. W. Thomp-

Das

Abändern der Vögel

durch

Einfluſs des Klima's.

———

Nach

zoologischen, zunächst von den europäischen Landvögeln
entnommenen Beobachtungen dargestellt, mit den entsprechenden
Erfahrungen bei den europäischen Säugthieren verglichen,

und

durch Thatsachen aus dem Gebiete der Physiologie, der Physik
und der physischen Geographie erlautert.

Von

Dr. CONSTANTIN LAMBERT GLOGER

zu Breslau,

Mitgliede der kaiserl. Leopoldinisch - Carolinischen Akademie der Naturforscher, der schlesischen
Gesellschaft für vaterländische Cultur, und der naturforschenden Gesellschaften zu Halle
und Görlitz.

--»›‹•◊•◊•◊‹«--

62581

Breslau 1833.

In Commission bei August Schulz und Comp.

———

Gedruckt in der Akademischen Buchdruckerei zu Berlin.

TITLE-PAGE OF GLOGER'S "DAS ABÄNDERN DER VÖGEL."

See p. 245.

son, | Author of the New and Complete Bird-Fancier and | the Gardener's Calendar. | Embellished with correct Portraits of Twelve of the most choice | Pigeons, drawn from the Life. | London: | Printed by S. Couchman, Throgmorton-Street; | For Alex. Hogg & Co. at the King's-Arms, | No. 16, Paternoster-Row. | [Price only One Shilling and Sixpence.].

1 vol. 12mo, pp. 1-63+1 (advt.), frontisp. London.

The first edition of this curious little book was published in 1799.

Gladstone, Hugh Steuart.

1923. Notes on the birds | of | Dumfriesshire | a continuation of | The Birds of Dumfriesshire | by | Hugh S. Gladstone | M.A., F.R.S.E., F.Z.S., M.B.O.U., F.S.A. (Scot.) | Dumfries | Published by the Council of the Dumfriesshire and Galloway Natural History | and Antiquarian Society, Dumfries and Maxwelltown Ewart Public Library. | 1923.

1 vol. 8vo, pp. 1-112, 2 ll. frontisp., 3 pll. Dumfries.

Intended as a continuation of the same author's "The Birds of Dumfriesshire," published in 1910, bringing the subject matter up to date. Edition limited to 250 copies of which this is copy No. 8.

Gloger, Constantin Wilhelm Lambert.

1833. Das | Abändern der Vögel | durch | Einfluss des Klima's. | Nach | zoologischen, zunächst von den europäischen Landvögeln | entnommenen Beobachtungen dargestellt, mit den entsprechen- | den | Erfahrungen bei den europäischen Säugethieren vergleichen, | und | durch Thatsachen aus dem Gebiete der Physiologie, der Physik | und der physischen Geographie erläutert. | Von | Dr. Constantin Lambert Gloger | zu Breslau, | Mitgliede [etc., 3 lines.]. | Breslau 1833. | In Commission bei August Schulz und Com. | Gedruckt in der Akademischen Buchdruckerei zu Berlin.

1 vol. demy 8vo, pp. I-XXIX+1+1 l., 1-159. Breslau.

A very detailed study of climatic variation of birds. The paper closes with a "Systematisches Verzeichniss der klimatischen Varietäten der europäischen Landvögel und der auf sie gegründeten Nominal-Species." The present copy is bound with the author's "Schlesiens Wirbelthier-Fauna," and a previous owner has added to the volume a photograph of the author. The preface is dated Dec. 1832.

Gloger, Constantin Wilhelm Lambert.

1833. Schlesiens | Wirbelthier-Fauna. | Ein | systematischer Ueber- | blick | der | in dieser Provinz vorkommenden | Säugethiere, Vögel, Amphibien | und Fische; | mit Rücksicht auf | den allgemeinen

Character des Landes, so wie auf das locale | und quantitative
Vorkommen seiner Thiere, namentlich mit | Angabe ihres Anstei-
gens auf Berghöhen und ihrer wichtigsten | Abänderungen. | Von |
Dr. Constantin Lambert Gloger, Mitgliede [*etc., 5 lines.*]. | Breslau,
1833. | Druck und Verlag von Grass, Barth und Comp.

1 vol. demy 8vo, pp. I-XIV, 1-78. Breslau. 1833 (after Sept. 17).

An annotated list of the vertebrate fauna of Silesia. The birds are treated on pp.
15-64, where 282 species are listed. Vernacular and Latin names are used,
the latter emended to conform to the author's puristic views. The copy is
bound with the author's "Das Abändern der Vögel," with a photograph of
Gloger supplied by a former owner of the volume. The preface of the present
work is dated Sept. 17, 1833. The classification adopted by Gloger is somewhat advanced for his time.

Gloger, Constantin Wilhelm Lambert.

**1834. Vollständiges Handbuch | der | Naturgeschichte der Vögel |
Europa's, | mit besonderer Rücksicht auf Deutschland. | Von | Dr.
Constantin Lambert Gloger, | Mitgliede der Kaiserlichen Leo-
poldinisch-Carolinischen Akademie [*etc., 5 lines.*]. | Erster Theil, |
die deutschen Landvögel enthaltend. | Breslau 1834, | bei August
Schulz und Comp. | Gedruckt bei Grass, Barth und Comp.**

1 vol. post 8vo, pp. I-LVI, 1-600. Breslau. 1834 (post Nov. 15).

An incomplete work on the birds of Europe, especially of Germany. Although
the present volume is noted as "Erster Theil," it is the only portion of the work
published and treats of the land birds. Some new names are used in the nomenclature, but these are largely emendations, so far as species are concerned.
The work marks an important advance in other particulars of classification,
and Gloger herein is the first ornithologist to divide his Passerine group into
two suborders based on the presence or absence of song-muscles[1]. The volume,
according to Engelmann, appeared in 6 sections but the single date is quoted
for all. The preface is dated November 15, 1834.

Gloger, Constantin Wilhelm Lambert.

**1841-42. Gemeinnütziges | Hand- und Hilfsbuch | der | Naturge-
schichte. | Für gebildete Leser aller Stände, | besonders | für die
reifere Jugend und ihre Lehrer. | Von | Dr. C. W. L. Gloger, | Mit-
gliede der Kaiserlichen Leopoldinisch-Carolinischen Akademie der
Naturforscher [*etc., 5 lines.*]. | Erster Band, | enthaltend | die
erste Hälfte der Naturgeschichte der Thiere, | nebst | erfahrungs-
mässigen Andeutungen | über | den gegenwärtigen Zustand und
Erfolg des Unterrichts in dieser Wissenschaft, nament- | lich auf
Gymnasien, und Vorschlägen über fernere Einrichtung desselben im**

---

[1]Newton, Dictionary of Birds, Introd., p. 57, 1893.

Ver- | hältnisse zu seinem wirklichen Zwecke. | Breslau, 1842. | Verlag von Aug. Schulz & Comp.

1 vol. 8vo, pp. I-XXXXIV, 1-495+1. Breslau.

Intended as the first volume of a general work on natural history, but actually all that was published. It treats only of mammals and birds, the latter on pp. 175-476 and 477. New generic names, many of them valid, are used. The index purports to show the new names used in the work by showing them printed in italics, but not all of the names so printed are new and there are many omissions.

The work seems to have appeared in 7 parts. Engelmann cites 7 parts and there are 7 original wrappers bound in at the close of the volume at hand, the last one being marked "Heft. 7 (schluss),'' the figure and last word being hand-written. Some of these wrappers are stained and the mark has been transferred to the pages which, apparently, were originally enclosed therein; one wrapper is shorter than the pages of text and the first and last pages of its original contents show a correspondingly broad grimy margin; and at 6 places in the book the butts of the leaves show traces of the original green wrappers adhering to the sheets. From this evidence it seems fairly certain that Heft 1 contained pp. 1-80; 2, pp. 81-160; 3, pp. 161-240; 4, pp. 241-320; 5, pp. 321-400; 6, pp. 401-448; 7, pp. 449-496+1 and I-XXXXIV. Pp. 477-480 are alone in doubt. They comprise the last page of text and the first pages of the index and consist of a single folded sheet which is not part of signature 30 (pp. 465-476) nor of signature 32 (pp. 481-496+1). Two leaves are missing from signature 30 (whose final 3 pp. may have been blank), and p. 477 has a note printed at the foot cancelling a (former?) p. 477[1], so it is apparent that an original p. 477 has been suppressed and replaced by that one which contains the first page of the index on its reverse. There is no evidence, however, to show that this reissue was not published in Heft 7. The original wrappers for Pts. 1-5 are undated; those of 6 and 7 are dated 1842. These figures agree with those of Sherborn (Index Animalium, Sect. 2, Pt. 1, p. LX, 1922) who, from other sources, cites pp. 1-400 as of 1841 and 401-496 and I-XXXXIV as of 1842. Thomas (Ann. and Mag. Nat. Hist, (6), **15**, p. 189, 1895) quotes a reference to pp. 1-160 dated May, 1841, which gives an approximate date for the first two parts of this rare work.

Gmelin, Johann Friedrich.

1802.   See Linné, Karl von, **A General System of Nature.**

Göbel, C. F.

1905.   See Alphéraky, Sergius, **The Geese of Europe and Asia.**

Godman, Frederick DuCane.

1879-1904.   See Salvin, Osbert; and Godman, **Biologia Centrali-Americana, Aves.**

Godman, Frederick Du Cane.

1882.   See Lichtenstein, Anton August Heinrich, **Catalogus Rerum Naturalium Rarissimarum,** The Willughby Society.

---

[1]"Carton für Seite 477 etc."

Godman, Frederick Du Cane. (Pycraft, William Plane.)

1907-1910. A | monograph | of the | petrels | (order Tubinares) |
by | Frederick Du Cane Godman | D.C.L. F.R.S. | President of
the British Ornithologists' Union | with hand-coloured plates | by
J. G. Keulemans | Witherby & Co. | 326 High Holborn London |
1907-1910.

1 vol. royal 4to, pp. I-LV+1, 1-381, pll. 1-103, 5A, 98A and 102A
(106 pll, col.; by J. G. Keulemans). London.

Published in five parts which are reviewed in the Zoological Record and current
numbers of the Auk and the Ibis. The accounts in the Zoological Record and
the Auk do not agree as to the pagination and plate-numbers included in the
various parts; that in the Auk appears to be more probably incorrect since it
is not consistent in itself. The following arrangement seems to be correct.
Pt. I, dated Dec. 1907, pp. 1-68, pll. 1-19 +5A; II, March 1908, pp. 69-152, pll.
20-39; III, Sept. 1908, pp. 153-232, pll. 40-66; IV, April 1909, pp. 233-296,
pll. 67-84; V, May 1910, pp. 297-381, I-LV, pll. 85-103 +98A and 102A.

According to the reviewer in the Auk, 27, pp. 350-351, July 1910, Salvin
originated the idea of publishing the present work and had some of the plates
prepared at the time of his death. Godman took over the project and, with
the acknowledged assistance of R. B. Sharpe, published the work as it exists.
Pp. XIV-XX contain an essay by Pycraft "On the Systematic Position of the
Petrels."

The present copy is No. 122 of the edition, which was limited to 225 copies.

Goeldi, Emilio Augusto.

1894-1900. As | aves do Brasil | por | Emilio Augusto Goeldi | Dr.
Ph.; Director do Museu Paraense | Primeira [Segunda?] parte |
Livraria Classica de Alves & C. | Rio de Janeiro | 46, Rua Gon-
calves Dias, 46 S. Paulo | 9, Rua de Quitanda, 9 | 1894 [1900?]

1 vol. cap 8vo, 2 pr. ll., pp. 1-664, 1-82 (index). Rio de Janeiro.

Published in two parts, of which the first part, issued in 1894, embraced pp. 1-311,
and the second part, issued in 1900, pp. 311 (reprinted?)-664 and 1-82 (index).
The present copy lacks the 1894 issue of p. 311 and the title page of the second
part which may be, *mut. mut.*, the same as that of the first part. Pt. II is
reviewed in the Ibis for 1901, p. 501, as of date 1900. The book contains a
running account of the distribution and occurrence of the birds of Brazil,
without descriptions. In the years 1900-1906, there was published, as an
illustrative supplement to this work, the "Album de Aves Amazonicas" (q.v.).
A preliminary half-title of the present work reads, "Monographias Brasileiras
| II," the first number of the series being the author's "Os Mammiferos do
Brasil" published in 1893.

Goeldi, Emilio Augusto.

1900-06. Museu Goeldi | (Museu Paraense) | de historia natural
e ethnographia | Album de aves Amazonicas | organisado pelo
Professor | Dr Emilio A. Goeldi. | Director do mesmo Museu |

Publicaçao iniciada por ordem de S. Excia o Sñr Dr José Paes de
Carvalho, | Ex-Governador | e continuada dob o governo de S.
Excia o Sñr Dr Augusto Montenegro | Desenhos do Sñr. Ernesto
Lohse, desenhista-lithographo do museu Goeldi | Supplemento
illustrativo a'obra "Aves do Brazil" | pelo Dr Emilio A. Goeldi |
Livraria classica de Alves & Cie, Rio de Janeiro, 1894-1900 (2
volumes) | 1900-1906. [*Illustr. border.*]

1 vol. medium 4to (in original fascicles). Fasc. I, pll. 1-12. Fasc. II,
pll. 13-24. Fasc. III, title, pp. 1-46+1 l., 12 ll. (9 printed), pll.
25-48. Plates lithographed in colors; by Ernesto Lohse.) Belem
(Para).

A collection of 48 plates in color illustrating Goeldi's "Aves do Brasil," (q.v.).
Reference to that work is made on the plates and in the index.   Fasc. I is
dated 1900; II, 1902; III,1906.

Goffin, A.

1862.   See Rijksmuseum van Naturlijke Historie, **Muséum d'Histoire
Naturelle des Pays-Bas,** 1862-81 (-1907).

Gordon, William John.

1892?.   Our country's birds | and how to know them. | A guide to
all the birds of Great Britain. | By | W. J. Gordon. | With an
illustration in colour of every species | and many original diagrams
by | G. Willis and R. E. Holding. | Nineteenth thousand. | Lon-
don: | Simpkin, Marshall, Hamilton, Kent & Co., Limited.

1 vol. demy 8vo, pp. I-VII+1, 1-152, pll. I-XXXIII (col.), 38 text-
cuts. London.

A popular handbook for the identification of British birds.   The plates are
lithographed and mostly inaccurate as to color.   The original impression appears to have been issued in 1892.

Goss, Nathaniel Stickney.

1883.   A catalogue | of the | **birds of Kansas.** | By | N. S. Goss. |
Published under the direction of the Executive Council. | Topeka,
Kansas: | Kansas Publishing House. | 1883.

1 vol. 8vo, pp. I-IV, 5-34+insert-slip (errata). Topeka.

An annotated list of the species of birds known to occur in Kansas.   A revised
edition was published in 1886 (q.v.).

Goss, Nathaniel Stickney.

1886.   A revised catalogue | of the | **birds of Kansas** | with descrip-
tive notes of the nests and eggs of the | birds known to breed in
the state. | By N. S. Goss. | Published under the direction of the

Executive Council. | May, 1886. | Topeka: | Kansas Publishing House: T. D. Thacher, State Printer. | 1886.

1 vol. 8vo, pp. I-IV, 1 l., pp. 1-76. Topeka. May 1886.

The author's "A Catalogue of the Birds of Kansas," 1883 (q.v.), revised and somewhat elaborated, with the addition of species not recorded in the first work.

Goss, Nathaniel Stickney.

1891. History | of the | birds of Kansas | By N. S. Goss. | Illustrating 529 birds. | Topeka, Kansas: | Geo. W. Crane & Co., printers and binders. | 1891.

1 vol. superroyal 8vo, pp. 1-692, 1 l. (index to pll.), pll. I-XXXV, 1 text-fig. Topeka.

A manual of the birds of the state, with complete descriptions and accounts of habits and nidification. The illustrations are from photographs of mounted birds in the author's collection and show most of the species although many of them are of little use for purposes of identification. The general descriptions are quoted from Baird, Brewer and Ridgway, Ridgway, and Coues, but there are many original notes on the colors of soft parts, habits, songs, etc., which are useful and important.

Gosse, Philip Henry. (Hill, Richard.)

1847. The | birds of Jamaica. | By | Philip Henry Gosse; | assisted by Richard Hill, Esq., of Spanish-Town. | London: | John Van Voorst, Paternoster Row. | M.DCCC.XLVII.

1 vol. 12mo, 1 l. (advt.), 1 pr. l., pp. I-X, 1-447+insert-slip (errata). London.

An account of the habits of the birds of Jamaica, a large proportion of which appears to have been compiled from the notes of Richard Hill. A number of new species are described by the author. A volume of 52 colored plates was published in 1849 by the same author under the title of "Illustrations of the Birds of Jamaica," (q.v.).

Gosse, Philip Henry.

1849. Illustrations | of the | birds of Jamaica. | By | Philip Henry Gosse. | London: | John Van Voorst, 1, Paternoster Row. | 1849.

1 vol. folio (7 x 10½), 2 pr. ll. (tit., advt. and conts.), pll. II, IV, VI-X, XII, XIV, XVI-XXIV, XXVIII, XXXII, XXXIV, XXXVII, XXXVIII, XL-XLII, XLIV, XLV, LII, LIII, LVI, LVIII-LXII, LXIV-LXVII, LXXIV, LXXXIV, LXXXV, XC, XCIII, CII, CIV, CVIII, CX, CXI, CXIII, CXX (=52 pll.; col.; by the author). London.

A series of colored plates intended to illustrate the author's "Birds of Jamaica," 1847 (q.v.), to which page-references are given on the plates. The original plan was to give a figure of each species described in the earlier work, but this was modified "by omitting such species as had been well figured before, in works easily available to the British public." Two species are figured (on pl. XXII and XLV) which are not mentioned in the text. The present volume has inscribed on the fly leaf, "The late W. Yarrell's copy," and bears, also, the bookplate of Henry Wemyss Feilden.

Gosse, Philip.

1899. See Fitz Gerald, Edward A.; and Vines, Stuart, **The Highest Andes.**

Gould, John. (Vigors, N. A.)

1831-32. A | century of birds | from | the Himalaya Mountains. | By | John Gould, A.L.S. | London: | 1832.

1 vol. imperial folio, 6 pr. ll., 72 ll., 80 pll. (col.; by E. Gould). London.

This work appeared in two forms, one with the backgrounds of the plates uncolored, the other with them colored. The present copy belongs to the latter series. Although no actual dates of publication appear to be available, a remark by Vigors in an early number of the Proceedings of the Committee of Science and Correspondence of the Zoological Society of London, Vol. I. pp. 170 and 176, (meeting for Dec. 27, 1831) indicates that the work was being, or had been, issued in regular monthly parts. This would tend to show that publication was commenced in 1831 or earlier. Some of the plates were exhibited to the Society at a meeting held on Nov. 23, 1830; see Proceedings, Vol. I, p. 6. The plates were executed by Mrs. (E.) Gould from Gould's sketches and the scientific descriptions, with most, if not all, of the remaining letterpress, were written by Vigors to whom Gould makes acknowledgment in the "Advertisement" on a preliminary leaf. Whether or not the nomenclature of the various species should be quoted from this folio or from the Proc. Comm. Sci. Corr. Zool. Soc. Lond., Vol. I, in which the descriptions were published somewhat contemporaneously, depends on the actual dates of publication of the two works, but the authorship, in any case, is that of Vigors, not of Gould. The descriptions in the "Proceedings" were issued as follows, quoting the pagination of Vol. I. Pp. 7-9, Jan. 6, 1831; 22-23, Febr. 1, 1831; 35, March 2, 1831; 41-44, April 6, 1831; 54-55, May 6, 1831; 170-176, March 2, 1832. The 80 hand-colored plates contain 102 figures of birds, of which 2 represent species (and sexes) figured twice; the remaining 100 figures form the basis for the title of "Century." This was the first of Gould's famous folios.

Gould, John.

1832-37. The | birds of Europe. | By | John Gould, F.L.S., &c. | In five volumes. | Vol. I [-V]. | Raptores [Insessores; Insessores; Rasores.Grallatores; Natatores]. | London: | Printed by Richard and John E. Taylor, Red Lion Court, Fleet Street. | Published by the author, 20 Broad Street, Golden Square. | 1837.

5 vols. imperial folio. Vol. I, pp. I-XII, 1 l., pp. 1-4, 51 ll., 50 pll. (col.). Vol. II, 101 ll., 99 pll. (col.; nos. 51-149). Vol. III, 95 ll.,

93 pll. (col.; nos. 150-242). Vol. IV, 105 ll., 103 pll. (col.; nos. 243-345). Vol. V, 105 ll., 103 pll. (col.; nos. 346-449; 447 and 448 on one plate). London.

Issued in 22 parts, the first of which appeared June 1, 1832. The remainder were planned to appear on the first of each third month thereafter. The preface was written on August 1, 1837, which would have been in time for the issuance of Pt. XXII on September 1 in accordance with the program, but whether the program was followed throughout I am unable to determine. The plates in the bound volumes are in accordance with a "General List of Plates," widely differing from the order of publication. As to the plates in each number, I am able to allocate but a few. Pt. I apparently contained, among others, plates 23, 27, 61, 216, 233, 260 and 379; Pts. II and III included pll. 19, 53, 59, 97, 120, 148, 160, 204, 217, 246, 258 and 289; Pt. X contained pll. 28, 159, 282 and 314: Pt. XI included pl. 297. The plates, drawn by Gould and E. Lear, were hand-colored by Mrs. Gould.

Gould, John. (Owen, Richard.)

1833-35. A | monograph | of | the Ramphastidæ, | or | family of toucans. | By | John Gould, F.L.S. | London: | published by the author, 20, Broad Street, Golden Square. | 1834.

> {A | Monograph | of the | Family of Ramphastidae [Ramphastidae (*Pt. III.*)] | or Toucans; [or | Family of Toucans. (*Pt. III.*)] | By | J. Gould, | F.L.S. | Pt. 1. ["1" *crossed out and replaced by* "2" (*Pt. II.*); *line omitted, but* "Pt. 3" *added by hand* (*Pt. III.*).] | To be completed in Two Parts. [Price £ 2-0 (*Pt. III.*)] | London. | Published by the Author, 20, Broad Street, Golden Square. | 1833 [1835 (*Pt. III.*)]. | Printed by C. Hullmandel.}

1 vol. imperial folio, 47 ll., 34 pll. (33 col.; by J. and E. Gould and E. Lear). London.

Published in three parts. Through the kindness of Dr. C. E. Hellmayr and of Dr. A. Laubmann of the Bavarian State Museum at Münich, I am enabled to transcribe the titles and give the contents of the several parts, from a copy in the library of the Münich Museum. They are as follows.

Pt. I contained text and plates of *Pteroglossus bitorquatus*, *Ramphastos carinatus*, *Pter. ulocomus*, *R.. culminatus*, *Pter. maculirostris*, *Pter. hypoglaucus*, *R. discolorus*, *Pter. prasinus*, *Pter. regalis*, *R. swainsonii*, *Pter. sulcatus*, and *Pter. bailloni*. Pt. II contained the title-page (dated 1834), the preface, introduction, etc., descriptions of the generic characters of the genera *Ramphastos* and *Pteroglossus* and the text and plates of *Pter. azarae*, *Pter. inscriptus*, *R. toco*, *Pter. castanotis*, *R. cuvieri*, *R. ariel* (*tucanus* Linne?), *Pter. culik*, *R. erythrorhynchus*, *Pter. aracari*, *R. vitellinus*, *Pter. viridis*, a new description of *R. culminatus*, and Owen's paper and plate of "Observations on the Anatomy of the Toucan." An insert-slip is attached to the cover, entitled "To the binder," giving the sequence to be followed in arranging the letterpress and plates, and closing with the statement, "The description of *Ramphastos culminatus*, given in Part I, to be cancelled, and the one in Part II inserted in its stead." Pt. III contained text and plates of *R. citreopygus, R. osculans, Pter. pluricinctus, Pter. humboldtii, Pter. langsdorffiii, Pter. nattererii, Pter. reinwardtii, Pter. derbianus, Pter. haematopygus* and *Pter. pavoninus.* There is another insert-slip in this part addressed "To the binder," giving a new order of arrangement for the contents of the work at the close of which is placed Owen's contribution; then follows the same note as in Pt. II regarding the cancellation of the original text of *R. culminatus* and the statement, "The Synopsis Specierum given in Part II to be cancelled, and the one in Part III inserted in its stead. N.B. The directions to the Binder in Part II to be disregarded." The present copy lacks the original text of *Ramphastos culminatus.*

In the Proc. Zool. Soc. London, 1834, p. 79, in a paper read July 8, 1834, (publ. Nov. 25, 1834) there is a statement to the effect that Gould's monograph of the Ramphastidae " is just completed"; this statement presumably refers to the completion of the two parts mentioned on the original wrappers of Pts. I and II and fixes the approximate date for Pt. II.

In 1852-54, Gould issued a new edition of the work (q.v.) under the same title as the present, and in 1855 published his "Supplement to the First Edition" (q.v.), giving the text and plates of the species included in the revised, but not the original, edition.

Gould, John.

1836-38. A | monograph | of | the Trogonidæ, | or | family of trogons. | By | John Gould, F.L.S., &c. | London: | Printed by Richard and John E. Taylor, Red Lion Court, Fleet Street. | Published by the author, 20 Broad Street, Golden Square. | 1838.

1 vol. imperial folio, 2 pr. ll., pp. I-VII+1, 39 ll., 36 pll. (col.). London.

Published in 3 parts. Part I is mentioned by Swainson in Vol. I of his "On the Natural History and Classification of Birds" in "The Cabinet Cyclopaedia" of Dionysius Lardner (q.v.), and therefore must date 1836 or earlier. I do not know what species were included in this part. In Vol. II (pp. 337 and 338), Swainson cites *Trogon elegans, T. ambiguus, T. melanocephala, Harpactes malabaricus, M. erythrocephalus,* and *Calurus resplendens* from Gould's work, so that these species were undoubtedly included in Part I or in Parts I and II if both were in print before July, 1837. A second edition, quite different from the first, was published in 1858-75 under the same title (q.v.).

Gould, John.

1837-38. The | birds of Australia, | and the adjacent islands. | By John Gould, F.L.S., &c. | Part I [II]. | [*List of contents.*] | London: | Printed by Richard and John E. Taylor, Red Lion Court, Fleet Street. | Published by the author, 20, Broad Street, Golden Square. | August, 1837 [February, 1838].

2 parts (all published) in 1 vol. imperial folio. Part I, cover-tit., 10 ll., 10 pll. (col.). Part II, cover-tit., 10 ll., insert-slip (notice to subscribers), 10 pll. (col.). London.

After the commencement of the present book, Gould found himself so handi-
capped by lack of specimens that he cancelled the work and set out for Australia to procure more and better material. After his return he began the publication of "The Birds of Australia" (q.v., 1840-48). Of the plates in the present
work, Nos. 6, 7, 9 and 10 of Pt. I, and 3, 4, 8, 9 and 10 of Pt. II were reprinted
in the later work with occasional minor alterations in colors; the remainder
were redrawn. This unfinished folio is said to be the rarest of Gould's works.

Gould, John.

**1837-38. A synopsis | of the | birds of Australia, | and the adja-
cent islands. | By | John Gould, F.L.S., &c. | Author of various
works [*etc., 3 lines.*] | London: | Published by the author, 20
Broad Street, Golden Square. | 1837-38.**

1 vol. imperial 8vo, 77 ll., pp. 1-8, 73 pll. (col.). London.

Issued in 4 parts: Pt. **I** (19 pll.), January, 1837; Pt. **II** (18 pll.), January, 1837;
Pt. **III** (18 pll.), April, 1838; Pt. **IV** (18 pll.), April 1838. The work consists
chiefly of diagnoses, descriptions, and synonymies of the species figured on the
plates. Pages 1-8 at the conclusion of Pt. IV contain original descriptions of
several new genera and 36 new species which were read before the London
Zoological Society in December, 1837 but not published by that body until
December 5, 1838 (P. Z. S. Lond. 1837, pp. 138-157), after the appearance of
the present volume.

Gould, John.

**1837-38. [Price £1 15s. (*Pt. II.*)] | Icones avium, | or | figures and
descriptions | of | new and interesting species of birds | from various
parts of the world. | By | John Gould, F.L.S., &c. | forming a
supplement | to his previous works. | Part I. [Part II] | [*List of
species, 5 lines in double column (Pt. I.*).; Monograph of the Capri-
mulgidæ, | part I. | *List of species, 4 lines, in double column (Pt.
II.*) | London: | Printed by Richard and John E. Taylor, Red Lion
Court, Fleet Street. | Published by the author, 20, Broad Street,
Golden Square. | August, 1837 [August, 1838].**

2 parts (all published), imperial folio. Part I, cover-tit., 10 ll., 10 pll.
(col.). Part II, (cover-tit.), 8 ll., 8 pll. (col.).

This work was interrupted by Gould's departure for Australia in search of material
for his work on the birds of that region, and was never resumed. Certain of
the species were described in papers read in advance before the Zoological
Society of London, but in most cases these descriptions were never published
in the "Proceedings" of that body. Four species in Pt. I (Nos. 2, 3, 4 and 5
of the subjoined list), ascribed to "Proc. of Zool. Soc. Part. V., 1837", without
pagination, were not so published and must date from the present work; two
species (Nos. 7 and 9) were published but are antedated by the folio. In Pt.
II, five species (Nos. 2, 3, 4, 6 and 8), ascribed to "Proc. of Zool. Soc. Part VI
1838," without pagination, did not appear except in the present book.

The two parts contained the following species as listed on the wrappers. Pt. I:-*Eurylaimus (Crossodera) Dalhousieae, Todus multicolor, Ianthocincla phœnicea, Calliope pectoralis, Microura squamata, Paradoxornis flavirostris, Pteroglossus (Selenidera) Gouldii, Numida vulturina, Ortyx plumifera, Cursorius rufus.* Pt. II:-*Amblypterus anomalus, Nyctidromus Derbyanus, Semeïophorus (Macrodipteryx?) vexillarius, Lyncornis cerviniceps, Lyncornis macrotis,* [*Lyncornis*] *Temminckii, Batrachostomus auritus, Nyctibius pectoralis.*

Gould, John.

1838-41. See Darwin, Charles, **The Zoology of the Voyage of H. M. S. Beagle,** 1838-43.

Gould, John.

1840-48. The | birds of Australia. | By | John Gould, F.R.S., | F.Z.S., [*etc., 5 lines.*] | In seven volumes. | Vol. I [-VII]. | London: | Printed by Richard and John E. Taylor, Red Lion Court, Fleet Street. | Published by the author, 20, Broad Street, Golden Square. | 1848.

7 vols. imperial folio. Vol. I, 9 ll., pp. V-CII, 1-13+1, 37 ll., 36 pll. (col.), text-figs. 1-3. Vol. II, 106 ll., 104 pll. (col.). Vol. III, 99 ll., 97 pll. (col.). Vol. IV, 106 ll., 104 pll. (col.; 2 fold.). Vol. V, 94 ll., 92 pll. (col.). Vol. VI, 84 ll., 82 pll. (col.). Vol. VII, 87 ll., 85 pll. (col.). London.

This sumptuous work was issued in 36 parts, of which Pt. I appeared in 1840, Pts. II-V in 1841, VI-IX in 1842, X-XIII in 1843, XIV-XVII in 1844, XVIII-XXI in 1845, XXII-XXV in 1846, XXVI-XXIX in 1847 and XXX-XXXVI in 1848. According to Mathews (Birds of Australia, Suppl. 4, p. 48, 1925, the first part was dated December 1, 1840, and Pts. II-XXXII appeared regularly on March 1, June 1, September 1 and December 1 thereafter, except that Pts. XXXIII-XXXVI were all dated and(appeared on) December 1, 1848. The final arrangement in the completed volumes is irrespective of the sequence of issue. The actual year of publication of each plate may be ascertained from F. H. Waterhouse's "The Dates of Publication of Some of the Zoological Works of the late John Gould," 1885 (q.v.).

Owing to delay in the publication of the various sheets of the Proceedings of the Zoological Society of London, to which Gould submitted the descriptions of his new species for early publication, many of the new names must date from the present work.

This work forms a thorough treatise on the birds of the Australian region (including an occasional species from outlying territory) with 600 hand-colored plates executed from drawings by the author and Mrs. (E.) Gould. Three years after the completion of this work the author commenced a supplement (q.v.) which was completed in 1869. On August 1, 1848, the introductory matter of the present work (pp. V-CII and 1-13) was issued under the title of "Introduction to the Birds of Australia" (q.v.), preceding the folio containing the same material by four months. In 1865 the text of the entire work, including the supplement and even further enlarged to bring the subject matter to date, was issued without plates as a "Handbook to the Birds of Australia" (q.v.). Prior to the present folio, the author issued his "A Synopsis of the Birds of Australia," 1837-38 (q.v.), and two parts of a folio entitled "The Birds of Australia and the Adjacent Islands," 1837-38 (q.v.). The latter work was cancelled, due to the insufficiency of specimens for study, and the author proceeded to Australia for the collection of more ample material, incorporating the results of his investigations in the present issue of the work.

Gould, John. (Sturm, Johann Heinrich Christian Friedrich; Sturm, Johann Wilhelm; Owen, Richard; Wagner, Rudolf.)

1841-47. J. Gould's | monographie | der | Ramphastiden | oder | Tukanartigen Voegel. | Aus dem Englischen Übersetzt, | mit Zusætzen und neuen Arten vermehrt | von | Johann Heinrich Christian Friedrich Sturm, | der kaiserl. naturforschenden Gesellschaft [*etc., 2 lines.*] | und | Johann Wilhelm Sturm, | der königl. bayer. botan. Gesellschaft [*etc., 3 lines.*] | Erstes [-Viertes] Heft | [*List of contents, 5 lines in double column, (Pts. I-III.); 3 lines double column and 4 lines full width, (Pt. IV.).*] | Nürnberg, 1841 [1841; 1842; 1847]. | Gedruckt auf Kosten der Herausgeber. | (Panierstrasse S. Nr. 709.).

1 vol. crown folio, 42 ll., 38 pll. (36 col., by J. Gould and Friedrich Sturm; 2 plain, by G. Scharf and A. Köppel). Nürnberg.

Issued in four parts, with dates as given above. Pts. I-III contained 10 plates and 10 leaves of text, each; Pt. IV contained 6 colored plates and the accompanying text, and a translation of Owen's article on the anatomy of the toucan with its plate, to which is added a second plate and further remarks by Rudolf Wagner. The principal part of the general text is based on Gould's Monograph of the Ramphastidae," 1833-35 (q.v.), of which it is, in places, a literal translation; but considerable of the matter is rewritten or revised and there are additional species described herein for the first time. The plates are sometimes redrawn and reduced from Gould, but frequently altered or designed afresh, while the illustrations of the new species are entirely new. There is no title-page, since the work was never carried to completion, and the title as quoted above, is taken from the wrapper of Pt. IV, bound with the present copy, and from facsimiles of the wrappers of Pts. I, II and III, obtained from copies in the Zoological Museum at Munich.

The contents of the four parts, as indicated on the wrappers, is as follows. I-*Ramphastos culminatus, R. Cuvieri, Pteroglossus melanorhynchus, P. Azarae, P. bitorquatus, P. prasinus, P. maculirostris, P. Gouldii, P. Nattereri* and *P. Reinwardtii.* II-*Pteroglossus castanotis, P. torquatus, P. pluricinctus, P. Humboldti, P. Langsdorfii, P. Wagleri, P. albivitta, P. atrogularis, P. Lichtensteinii* and *P. haematopygus.* III-*Ramphastos Toco, R. carinatus, R. vitellinus, R. Temminckii, R. dicolorus, Pteroglossus hypoglaucus, P. Sturmii, P. Humboldti* (foemina), *P. inscriptus* and *P. Derbianus.* IV-*Ramphastos Swainsonii, Pteroglossus Beuharnaisii, P. Azarae, P. Bailloni, P. piperivorus* and *P. sulcatus;* also the text to *Pteroglossus flavirostris* and *P. Wiedii* and the anatomical article by Owen and Wagner.

Gould, John.

1843-44. See Hinds, R. B., **The Zoology of the Voyage of H. M. S. Sulphur, Birds.**

Gould, John.

1844-50. **A monograph | of | the Odontophorinæ, | or | partridges** of America. | By | John Gould, F.R.S., | F.L.S., [*etc., 6 lines.*] | London: | Printed by Richard and John E. Taylor, Red Lion Court, Fleet Street. | Published by the author, 20, Broad Street, Golden Square. | 1850.

1 vol. imperial folio, 4 pr. ll., pp. 11-23+1, 33 ll., 32 pll. (col.). London.

Published in 3 parts, of which Pt. I appeared in 1844, II in 1846 and III in 1850, the first two parts with 10 plates each and the last with 12 plates. The dates and allocation of these plates is given by Waterhouse in his "The Dates of Publication of Some of the Zoological Works of the late John Gould," 1885 (q.v.), pp. 56 and 57. Pt. I was received by the Boston Society of Natural History on February 26, 1845, and Pt. II on June 20, 1846, according to information kindly furnished me by Dr. Glover M. Allen of that institution.

Gould, John.

1848. **Introduction | to the | birds of Australia.** | By | John Gould, F.R.S., | F.L.S., [*etc., 9 lines.*] | London: | Printed for the author, by Richard and John E. Taylor, Red Lion Court, Fleet Street. | 1848.

1 vol. post 8vo, pp. I-VIII, 1-134, text-figs. 1-3. London. August 1, 1848.

This little work consists of the preface and introduction to the author's folio work, "The Birds of Australia," 1840-48 (q.v.), Vol. I, pp. V-CII and 1-13, December 1, 1848. These according to the author, were set up in small type for facility of correction and issued in a limited edition in that form prior to the issue of the larger work. Sherborn (Index Animalium, Sect. 2, Pt. 1, p. LXI, 1922) appears to reject this volume and refers to the introductory "Notice" for a statement that "these are but proofsheets" and the folio the authoritative text. However, the "Notice" is worded somewhat differently and says that readers "must . . . still regard it more as a proof-sheet than otherwise, inasmuch as it contains many imperfections, most of which have been corrected in the folio edition." As issued in the folio, the matter is entirely reset and does not affect the validity of anything contained in the present issue which was "printed in an octavo form, for distribution among my scientific friends and others, to whom I trust it will be at once useful and acceptable." Various new names must be quoted from this 8vo edition and not from the folio. Mathews (Austral Av. Rec. 4, No. 1, p. 9, 1920) gives the date of publication as August 1, 1848; source of information not cited.

The present copy contains the bookplate of Frederick DuCane Godman, and was a presentation copy from the author.

Gould, John.

1849–61. A monograph | of | the Trochilidæ, | or | family of hum-ming-birds. | By | John Gould, F.R.S., | F.L.S., [etc., 8 lines.] | In five volumes. | Vol. I [-V]. | London: | Printed by Taylor and Francis, Red Lion Court, Fleet Street. | Published by the author, 26 Charlotte Street, Bedford Square. | 1861. | [The author reserves to himself the right of translation.].

5 vols. imperial folio. Vol. I, 4 pr. ll., pp. V-CXXVII+1, 42 ll., 41 pll. (col.; nos. 1-41). Vol. II, 77 ll., 75 pll. (col.; nos. 42-116). Vol. III, 90 ll., 87 pll. (col.; nos. 117-203). Vol. IV, 82 ll., 80 pll. (col.; nos. 204-283). Vol. V, 79 ll., 77 pll. (col.; nos. 284-360). London.

Published in 25 parts of which Pt. I was issued in 1849, II in 1851, III and IV in 1852, V and VI in 1853, VII and VIII in 1854, IX and X in 1855, XI and XII in 1856, XIII and XIV in 1857, XV and XVI in 1858 (May 1 and September 1), XVII and XVIII in 1859, XIX and XX in 1860 and XXI-XXV in 1861. The last part contained only the introductory matter, title-pages and lists of contents for each of the projected volumes. In the introduction, the nomenclature is revised and a brief review given of the various species of the group, including some not figured in the general work. The introduction was republished in 8vo form the year of appearance of the last part, 1861, under the title, "An Introduction to the Trochiliæ (q.v.). The allocation of the various plates to their respective parts is given by Waterhouse in his "The Dates of Publication of Some of the Zoological Works of the late John Gould," 1885 (q.v.), pp. 45-55. A supplementary volume was issued during the years 1880-87 (being completed by R. B. Sharpe after Gould's death) under the title, "A Monograph . . . Supplement" (q.v.).

Gould, John. (Sharpe, Richard Bowdler.)

1850–83. The | birds of Asia. | By | John Gould, F.R.S., | F.L.S., [etc., 8 lines.] | Dedicated to the Honourable East India Company. | In seven volumes. | Volume I [-VII]. | London: | Printed by Taylor and Francis, Red Lion Court, Fleet Street. | Published by the author, 26 Charlotte Street, Bedford Square. | 1850-1883.

7 vols. imperial folio. Vol. I, 4 pr. ll., pp. 1-9+1, 77 ll., 76 pll. (col.). Vol. II, 77 ll., 75 pll. (col.). Vol. III, 80 ll., 78 pll. (col.). Vol. IV, 74 ll., 72 pll. (col.). Vol. V, 85 ll., 83 pll. (col.). Vol. VI, 77 ll., 75 pll. (col.). Vol. VII, 73 ll., 71 pll. (col.). London.

Published in 35 parts, of which Pts. I and II appeared in 1850, III-XXVIII at the rate of one each year from 1851 to 1866, Pts. XXIX and XXX in 1877, XXXI in 1879, XXXII in 1880, XXXIII in 1882 and XXXIV and XXXV in 1883. The last three numbers were issued after the death of Gould (1881) by R. B. Sharpe who wrote the introduction and whose initials appear after many of the dis-cussions of the various species in the posthumous parts. The year of appear-ance of each plate is given in the index to the volume in which the plate was finally placed, and a general index in Vol. I assigns each species to its proper volume. The following further dates are available for certain parts, from current reviews in the Ibis: XVII, April, 1865; XVIII, April 1, 1866; XIX, May 1, 1867; XX, April 1, 1868; XXI, April 1, 1869; XXII, March 1, 1870; XXVI, August 1, 1874; XXVII, March 1875; XXVIII, July 1, 1876; XXIX, April 1, 1877; XXX, October 1, 1877; XXI July 1, 1879; XXXII, July 1, 1880. The 530 plates are hand-colored, most of them being drawn by Gould but a few being the work of J. Wolf.

Gould, John.

1851-69. The | birds of Australia. | By | John Gould, F.R.S., | F.L.S. [etc., *13 lines.*] | Supplement. | London: | Printed by Taylor and Francis, Red Lion Court, Fleet Street. | Published by the author, 26, Charlotte Street, Bedford Square. | 1869.

1 vol. imperial folio, pp. I-IV, 79 ll., 81 pll. (col.; 1 fold.). London.

Issued in five parts, of which Pt. I appeared on March 15, 1851, **II** on September 1, 1855, **III** on September 1, 1859, **IV** on December 1, 1867 and **V** on August 1, 1869, according to Mathews, Birds of Australia, Suppl. 4, p. 48, 1925.

The final arrangement of plates in the volume is different from that of their issue. The latter may be ascertained from the list of plates in the volume and from F. H. Waterhouse's "The Dates of Publication of Some of the Zoological Works of the Late John Gould," 1885 (q.v.). The present work is intended to treat of the species discovered after the publication of the folio to which this volume forms a supplement, "The Birds of Australia," 1840-48 (q.v.).

Among the species included in Pt. I, several were also discussed in a paper by Gould on the "Researches in Natural History of John McGillivray, Esq." published in Jardine's Contributions to Ornithology for 1850, pp. 92-106+105*, which will hold priority for the new names unless a more exact and subsequent date can be proved for Jardine's magazine. The species in question are those numbered 5, 6, 12, 16 and 45 in the list of plates; Nos. 36 (Pt. III.) and 67 (Pt. II.) have undoubted priority in Jardine's "Contributions." Nos. 5 and 6 were also published in the Proc. Zool. Soc. Lond., 1850, p. 200 (publ. Febr. 28, 1851) which likewise antedates Pt. I of the folio.

Gould, John. (Owen, Richard.)

1852-54. A monograph | of | the Ramphastidæ, | or | family of toucans. | By | John Gould, F.R.S., | F.L.S. [etc., *7 lines.*] | London: | Printed by Taylor and Francis, Red Lion Court, Fleet Street. | Published by the author, 20, Broad Street, Golden Square. | 1854.

1 vol. imperial folio, 4 ll., pp. 9-26, 2 ll., 52 pll. (51 col.). London.

A revised edition of Gould's earlier work of the same title, 1833-35 (q.v.), with new plates and with discussions of various species not formerly treated. The uncolored plate of anatomical details and its accompanying text, from the pen of Richard Owen, are unchanged. The text and plates of the species newly discussed in this edition were republished the following year, 1855 (q.v.), as a supplement to the first edition.

Carus and Engelmann cite this edition as having appeared in 3 parts. Pt. I is reviewed under date of 1852 in the Naumannia, 1853, pp. 237-240. It is said to contain text and plates of *Pteroglossus bitorquatus, Pter. flavirostris, Pter. Azarae, Pter. castanotis, Pter. viridis, Selenidera piperivora, Ramphastos Cuvieri, R. carinatus, R. erythrorhynchus, R. Ariel, Andigena hypoglaucus, A. nigrirostris, A. laminirostris* and *A. cuculeatus.* The preface, which probably appeared with the last part, is dated May 1, 1854.

Gould, John.

1855. **Supplement | to | the first edition of | a | monograph | of | the Ramphastidæ, |** or | family of toucans. | By | John Gould, F.R.S., | F.L.S. [*etc., 7 lines.*] | London: | Printed by Taylor and Francis, Red Lion Court, Fleet Street. | Published by the author, 20, Broad Street, Golden Square. | 1855.

> Supplement | To The | First Edition | of a | Monograph | of the | Ramphastidae, | or | Toucans. | By | John Gould, F.R.S., &c. [| Part II.] | Contents. | [*Pt. I, 7 lines., double column,-*] Ramphastos Inca. | " brevicarinatus. | " ambiguus. | " citreolae-mus. | Pteroglossus erythropygius. | " Mariae. | Andigena nig-rirostris. | Andigena cucullatus. | " laminirostris. | Selenidera Gouldi. | Aulacoramphus castaneorhynchus. | " albivitta. | " atrogularis. | " caeruleicinctus. [*Pt. II, 3 lines in double column and 1 line single column*;-Pteroglossus Azarae. | "flavirostris. | " Sturmi. | Pteroglossus poecilorostris. | " Wiedi. | Aulacoramphus caeruleogularis. | Title.-Introduction.-List of Plates.] | London: | Published by the Author, 20, Broad Street, Golden Square. | January 1st, 1855. | [Price Three Guineas (Price Two Guineas).]. 1 vol. imperial folio, 2 pr. ll., pp. 9-26, 20 pll. (col.). London.

The present work consists of the plates and accompanying text relating to the species discussed by Gould in the second edition of his "Monograph of the Ramphastidae," 1852-54 (q.v.) but not included in the first edition, 1833-35 (q.v.). It seems to have been designed to add to the first edition to make it equivalent to the second edition, but as there are various alterations made in the species included in the first edition, of which changes no mention is made in the supplement, the equality is not maintained. The introduction, re-printed from the second edition, gives the classification as adopted in the complete work. The present copy is united with the volume to which it forms the supplement. There is, in addition, a copy of pl. 7 and its accompanying text, from Pt. I of Gould's "Icones Avium," 1837-38 (q.v.), inserted in the volume.

This supplement was issued in two parts, the cover-titles and contents of which are as given above, from a copy in the Bavarian State Museum, kindly examined by Dr. Q. Laubmann of that institution.

Gould, John.

1858-75. A monograph | of | the Trogonidæ, | or | family of trogons. | By | John Gould, F.R.S. &c. | London: | Printed by Taylor and Francis, Red Lion Court, Fleet Street. | Published by the author, 26 Charlotte Street, Bedford Square. | 1875.

1 vol. imperial folio, 2 pr. ll., pp. V-XX, 49 ll., 47 pll. (col.). London.

Published in 4 parts, of which Pt. I appeared in 1858, II in 1869, III in June 1875 and IV in September 1875. The allocation of plates is given by Waterhouse in his "The Dates of Publication of Some of the Zoological Works of the late John Gould," 1885 (q.v.), pp. 58 and 59. This is a second edition of the same author's work of 1838 (q.v.), but is entirely rewritten and is illustrated by new plates.

Gould, John.

1861. An | introduction | to | the Trochilidæ, | or | family of humming-birds. | By | John Gould, F.R.S., &c. &c. | London: | Printed for the author, by Taylor and Francis, Red Lion Court, Fleet Street. | 1861. | [The Author reserves to himself the right of Translation.].

1 vol. post 8vo, 4 pr. ll., pp. I-IV, 1-212. London.

This volume consists of the introductory matter of Gould's folio "Monograph of the Trochilidae," 1849-61 (q.v.), pp. V-CXXXVII, with an explanatory "Notice." The indices, at the close of the introduction, are improved by page-references, and the volume forms a handy reference book to the folio while giving a brief review of the classification of this group of birds. The present copy is one presented to P. L. Sclater by Gould, and contains numerous annotations by the former.

Gould, John.

1862-73. The | birds | of | Great Britain. | By | John Gould, F.R.S., &c. | In five volumes. | Volume I [-V]. | London: | Printed by Taylor and Francis, Red Lion Court, Fleet Street. | Published by the author, 26, Charlotte Street, Bedford Square. | 1873.

5 vols. imperial folio. Vol. I, 6 pr. ll., pp. I-CXL, 35 ll., 37 pll. (col.), 1 text-fig. Vol. II, 78 ll., 78 pll. (col.), text-figs. 1 and 2. Vol. III, 71 ll., 76 pll. (col.). Vol. IV, 87 ll., 90 pll. (col.). Vol. V, 88 ll., 86 pll. (col.). London.

Published in 25 parts. Pts. I and II appeared on October 1, 1862; thereafter two parts appeared annually (on August 1 and September 1 in 1866 to 1872 and probably also in the other years), and the last part, containing title-pages and indices for all the volumes, the preface and introduction, and certain plates, was issued in December, 1873. The allocation of the plates to their respective parts as issued has been made by Waterhouse in his "The Dates of Publication of Some of the Zoological Works of the Late John Gould," 1885 (q.v.), pp. 6-14. The 367 hand-colored plates are mostly by Gould; a few are by J. Wolf.

Gould, John.

1865. **Handbook | to the | birds of Australia.** | By | John Gould, F.R.S., etc. | Author of [*etc., 5 lines.*] | In two volumes. | Vol. I [II]. | London: | Published by the author, | 26 Charlotte Street Bedford Square. | 1865. | [The right of Translation is reserved.].

2 vols. 8vo. Vol. I, pp. I-VIII, 1-636, 1 insert-slip (advt.). Vol. II, 3 pr. ll., pp. 1-629, figs. 1-3. London. 1865 (September 1 and December 2?).

A reprint of the text (without the introductory matter) of the author's "The Birds of Australia," 1840-48 (q.v.), and the three published parts of the "Supplement," 1851-69 (q.v.), with such additions, corrections and alterations as were thought necessary. On pages 523-583 of Vol. II, the species treated by the author in his larger work which are not strictly Australian in distribution are collected and discussed separately. The dates of publication have been taken from an insert-slip by the publishers offering Vol. I as published "this day," September 1, and promising Vol. II for December 2. Both volumes are reviewed in the Ibis for Jan. 1866, pp. 111-113, as of completion in 1865.

Gould, John.

1873. **An | introduction | to the | birds of Great Britain.** | By | John Gould, F.R.S., &c., &c. | London: | Printed for the author, | by Taylor and Francis, Red Lion Court, Fleet Street. | 1873. | [Price Five Shillings and Sixpence.] | [The Author reserves to himself the right of Translation.].

1 vol. post 8vo, 2 pr. ll., pp. I-IV, 1-135+1, 1-14 (list of subscribers), 1-4 (advt.), 1 text-fig. London.

This volume contains the lengthy introductory matter of the author's "The Birds of Great Britain," 1862-73 (q.v.), printed in 8vo form for ease of correction and issued as such. The date of issue may be later than that of Pt. XXV of the folio which contained the same matter (4 pr. ll. and pp. I-CXL), although the pages of advertising at the end of the present volume are dated August, 1873, and the preface (as in the folio) is dated November 1, the same year.

Gould, John; and Sharpe, Richard Bowdler.

1875-88. **The | birds of New Guinea** | and the | adjacent Papuan islands, | including many | new species recently discovered | in Australia. | By | John Gould, F.R.S. | Completed after the author's death | by | R. Bowdler Sharpe, F.L.S. &c., | Zoological Department, British Museum. | Volume I [-V]. | London: | Henry Sotheran & Co., 36 Piccadilly. | 1875-1888. | [All rights reserved.].

5 vols. imperial folio. Vol. I, 2 pr. ll., pp. I-III+1, 56 ll., 56 pll. (col.). Vol. II, 60 ll., 58 pll. (col.). Vol. III, 74 ll., 72 pll. (col.). Vol. IV, 61 ll., 59 pll. (col.). Vol. V, 77 ll., 75 pll. (col.). London.

Published in 25 parts, of which Pt. **I** was issued on Dec. 1, 1875; **II**, Jan. 1, 1876; **III**, May 1, 1876; **IV**, Jan. 1, 1877; **V**, June 1, 1877; **VI**, Febr. 1, 1878; **VII**, June 1, 1878; **VIII**, Oct. 1, 1878; **IX**, March 1, 1879; **X**, Sept. 1, 1879; **XI**, Febr. 1, 1880; **XII** in 1881; **XIII** in 1882; **XIV** and **XV** in 1883; **XVI-XVIII** in 1884; **XIX** and **XX** in 1885; **XXI** and **XXII** in 1886; **XXIII** in 1887; and **XXIV** and **XXV** in 1888. The distribution of the plates among their respective parts is given in the indices to the various volumes, which, with the introductory matter and title-pages, appeared with Pt. XXV. Gould's death in 1881 transferred the responsibility of the monograph to R. B. Sharpe who completed the work and to whom must be ascribed the subject-matter appearing in Pts. XIII-XXV. The 320 hand-colored plates are by Gould and W. Hart. The work was brought to a close long before the subject was exhausted.

Gould, John. (Sharpe, Richard Bowdler.)

1880-?. Monograph | of the | Pittidæ. | [*Vignette.*] **| By | John Gould, F.R.S. &c. | Part I. | Contents. | Pitta bengalensis. Eucichla ellioti. | Eucichla cyanura. Leucopitta maxima. | - boschii. Cyanopitta steerii. | - schwaneri. Phœnicocichla arquata. | - gurneyi. Melampitta lugubris. | London: | published by the author, 26, Charlotte Street, Bedford Square, W.C. | October 1st, 1880. |** [N. B. The Illustrations are principally taken from the Author's works on the 'Birds of Asia,' 'Australia,' and 'New Guinea.'] **|** [Price Three Guineas.].

1 vol. imperial folio, 10 ll. 10 pll. (col.), [10 ll.]. London. October 1, 1880 (-?).

All published of the author's projected work which was interrupted by his death. There appears to be some uncertainty as to the actual publication of the final 10 sheets without plates. These were written by Gould but edited by Sharpe, whose initials appear at the foot of each. Sharpe, himself, in "An Analytical Index to the works of the late John Gould," p. XXIII, 1893, says that a single part was published. The title, quoted above, is from the original wrapper (or board cover) where the first part alone is mentioned. The remaining pages may have been sold by the printer without authority.

Gould, John; and Sharpe, Richard Bowdler.

1880-87. A | monograph | of | the Trochilidæ, | or | family of humming-birds. | By | John Gould, F.R.S. | Completed after the author's death | by | R. Bowdler Sharpe, F.L.S. &c., | Zoological Department, British Museum. | Supplement. | London: | Henry Sotheran & Co., 36 Piccadilly. | 1887. | [The right of translation is reserved.].

1 vol. imperial folio, 104 ll., 58 pll. (col.; by Gould and Hart). London.

Published in 5 parts, of which Pt. **I** appeared in 1880, **II** in 1881, **III** in 1883, **IV** in 1885 and **V** in 1887. Gould died after the first part had been issued, but Pt. **II** appeared shortly thereafter in the form which he had planned. The completion of the work was then undertaken by the publishers who obtained the services of Sharpe to write the remaining text, Hart to prepare the plates, and Salvin to supervise the whole. Gould had planned to complete the work in four parts for which he had already prepared a large number of the plates. It was found that he had underestimated the probable extent of the project and that there were many species yet to be included if the work were to be a complete exposition of all the hummingbirds discovered since the publication of the original monograph (q.v.) in 1849-61. The resulting increase in the text and illustrations required an extra part.

The allocation of the plates of Pts. I-IV is given by Waterhouse in his "Dates of Publication of Some of the Zoological Works of the late John Gould," 1885 (q.v.), pp. 45-55; the remaining plates and the introductory matter appeared in Pt. V.

Gould, John.

1885. See Waterhouse, F. H., **The Dates of Publication of Some of the Zoological Works of the late John Gould,** F.R.S.

Gould, John.

1893. See Sharpe, R. B., **An Analytical Index to the Works of the late John Gould,** F.R.S.

Graham-Smith, G. S.

1911. See [Grouse], **The Grouse in Health and Disease.**

Grandidier, Alfred.

1874. See Milne Edwards, Alphonse, **Recherches sur le Faune Ornithologique Éteinte des Iles Mascareignes et de Madagascar.**

Grandidier, Alfred. (Milne-Edwards, Alphonse.)

1876-85. > Histoire | physique, naturelle et politique | de | Madagascar | publiée | par Alfred Grandidier [*Period added (Vols. XIV and XV.).*] | Volume XII [-XV]. | Histoire naturelle des oiseaux | par | MM. Alph. Milne Edwards et Alf. Grandidier. | Tome I [-IV]. Texte [Atlas.-I; Atlas.-II; Atlas.-III]. | [*Blazon.*] | Paris. | Imprimé par autorisation de M. le Garde des Sceaux [*Comma added (Vols. XIV and XV.).*] | à l'Imprimerie Nationale. | M DCCC LXXIX [M DCCC LXXVI; M DCC LXXIX; M DCCC LXXXI].

4 vols. royal 4to. Vol. XII, 3 pr. ll. (half-tit., tit. and pref.), pp. 1-779. Vol. XIII, 2 pr. ll. pll. 1-104, 1A, 9A, 9A bis, 9B, 9C, 12A, 13A, 14A, 16A, 19A, 24A, 26A, 29A, 29B, 29C, 30A, 32A, 36A, 36B, 36C, 36D, 38A, 39A, 40A, 41A, 41B, 41C, 66A, 66B, 84A, 89A, 103A, 104A, 104B, 104C (61 col., by Keulemans, Huet and

Faguet). Vol. XIII, 2 pr. ll., pll. 105-207, 106A, 107A, 107B, 108A, 111A, 113A, 113B, 117A, 121A, 121B, 121C, 123A, 123B, 125A, 126A, 126B, 128A, 131A, 131A (*bis* = *131B*), 138A, 140A, 141A, 144A, 145A, 146A, 154A, 156A, 160A, 164A, 170A, 170b, 172A, 177A, 190A, 200A, 201A (63 col.). Vol. XV, 2 pr. ll., pll. 208-308, 214A, 225A, 227A, 227B, 227C, 227D, 229A, 230A, 233A, 233B, 241A, 247A, 249A, 268A, 268B, 271A, 275A, 281A, 290A, 290B (40 col., 8 of eggs). Paris.

A thorough monograph of the birds of Madagascar, forming part of a general work on the island, as indicated in the above title, begun in 1876(75?) but still incomplete. The present portions, complete for the ornithology, were issued in parts at various times. The following information is collected from the Zoological Record. The text was issued in three parts as follows: Pp. 1-176, 1879; 177-376, 1882 (Febr. 15 or after); 377-779, 1885. The plates appeared in four installments. Some of them were incorrect in certain particulars and were replaced by others issued later. The reissued numbers are indicated below. Most of the reissues are designated as such in the Zoological Record, but others are recognizable only by the duplication of numbers and there may be others which were overlooked. In 1876 appeared Pt. I of Vol. I of the atlas (= Vol. XIII of the entire work, pt.), containing pll. 1-70, 9A, 9B, 12A, 13A, 14A, 26A, 38A, 39A, 40A, 41A. In 1878 were issued pll. 71-104, 9A bis, 30A, 36A, 36B, 36C. In 1879 appeared pll. 105-144, 107A, 108A and (131A =) 131B. The remainder of the plates and the reissues of some of the earlier ones came out under covers dated 1879 and 1881 but the Zoological Record for 1881 states that they were accompanied by a circular which proved that they could not have been issued prior to February 15, 1882 and, "in fact, were not issued until much later," being received in May 1882. These include pll. 145-303, 1A, 9C, 16A, 19A, 24A, 29A, 29B, 29C, 32A, 36D, 41B, 41C, 66A, 66B, 84A, 89A, 103A, 104A, 104B, 104C, 106A, 107B, 111A, 113A, 113B, 117A, 121A, 121B, 121C, 123A, 123B, 125A, 126A, 126B, 128A, 131A, 138A, 140A, 141A, 144A, 145A, 146A, 154A, 156A, 160A, 164A, 170A, 170b, 172A, 177A, 190A, 200A, 201A, 214A, 225A, 227A, 227B, 227C, 227D, 229A, 230A, 230B, 233A, 233B, 241A, 247A, 249A, 268A, 268B, 271A, 275A, 281A, 290A, 290B, and the following reissues, 1, 2, 9, 10, 12, 13, 15, 16, 19, 22, 24, 27, 28, 31, 32, 35, 37-40, 42-45, 47, 48, 50, 51, 53, 54, 57, 58, 66-68, 90, 13A, 30A.

Grant, John B.

1894. Our common birds | and how to know them | by | John B. Grant | with sixty-four plates. | **Fourth edition** | New York | Charles Scribner's Sons | 1894.

1 vol. ½ imperial 8vo (oblong), pp. 1-224, 64 text-cuts (full-page; numbered Plates I-LXIV). New York.

A popular book, with non-technical descriptions of a number of species and brief notes on distribution, habits, etc., illustrated by photographs of mounted specimens. The first edition appears to have been issued in 1891.

Grässner, Fürchtegott.

1860. Die Vögel Deutschlands und ihre Eier | von | Fürchtegott Grässner, | Oberlehrer an den Franckeschen Stiftungen zu Halle. | Eine vollständige Naturgeschichte sämmtlicher Vögel Deutschlands | und der benachbarten Länder | mit besonderer Berücksichtigung ihrer Fortpflanzung. | Zweite sehr vermehrte und gänzlich umgearbeitet Auflage | des früher erschienenen Werkes: | Die Eier der Vögel Deutschlands von Naumann und Buhle. | Mit zehn Kupfertafeln. | Halle, | C. G. Knapp's Verlags-Buchhandlung. | 1860.

1 vol. royal 4to, pp. I-VIII, 1-215, pll. I-X (col.; by Fr. Naumann; eggs). Halle.

General ornithology is discussed on pp. 1-50. Orders, families and species are discussed in the remainder of the work, with descriptions of birds, nests and eggs and accounts of habits and nidification. Although designated as a second edition of J. F. Naumann and C. A. Buhle's "Die Eier der Vögel Deutschland," 1818-1828 (q.v.), the present work is all newly written and distinct from its predecessor except for the illustrations, and even the latter, although printed from the same plates, are differently colored.

Graves, George.

1816. Ovarium Britannicum; | being | a correct delineation | of | the eggs | of such | birds | as are natives of, or domesticated in | Great Britain. | By | George Graves, F.L.S. | Author of British Ornithology, &c. | London: | printed for the author, and sold by Sherwood, | Neely, & Jones, Paternoster-Row, and | J. Harding, St. James's-Street. | 1816.

1 vol. 8vo, pp. I-VI, 15 pll. (col.; mostly unnum.; by Graves). London.

The first part (all published) of a projected work explained by the above title. The preface bears the date of January 1, 1816. The present copy is bound with the third volume of the author's "British Ornithology," 1821 (q.v.). It bears the bookplate of W. H. Mullens.

Graves, George.

1821. British ornithology: | being | The History, | with a coloured representation, | of | every kown [*sic*; known (*Vols. II and III.*)] species | of | British birds. | By George Graves, | Fellow of the Linnean Society; | Author of the Naturalist's Pocket Book, Ovarium Brittanicum, Editor of the | New Edition of Curtis's Flora Londinensis, &c. | **Second edition.** [*Line omitted (Vol. III.*).] | Vol. I [II; III]. | London: | Printed for the author, | by W. and S. Graves, Sherborne Lane, Lombard Street; | and sold by | Sherwood, Neely, and Jones, Paternoster Row. | 1821.

3 vols. in 1 vol. 8vo. Vol. I, 64 ll., 48 pll. (col.). Vol. II, 64 ll., 48 pll. (col.). Vol. III, 60 ll., 48 pll. (col.). London.

This work is a second edition of the author's book of the same title issued in 1811-21, the same third volume being used for both editions. The hand-colored plates are not of a high order of merit. The second edition is said to have been issued also with uncolored plates.

Another copy is at hand in 3 vols., showing considerable variation in the coloring of the plates. With Vol. III is bound a copy of the author's "Ovarium Britannicum," 1816 (q.v.). This copy is from the library of W. H. Mullens.

Gray, George Robert.

1840. A list | of the | genera of birds, | with | an indication of the typical species of each genus. | Compiled from various sources | by | George Robert Gray, | Ornithological Assistant [*etc., 3 lines.*] | Printed by Richard and John E. Taylor, | Red Lion Court, Fleet Street. | 1840.

1 vol. post 8vo, pp. I-VIII, 1-80. London. 1840 (ante April).

A catalogue of the known genera of birds (under their respective families, etc.) with their synonyms and with the name of the type species of each and its synonyms. New names are supplied by the author where any generic name and all of its synonyms are untenable, including terms which have prior usage in botany. The work is extremely important in view of the new names as well as for the type-designations. A second edition was published in 1841 (q.v.). Mathews (Birds of Australia, **7**, pp. 453) notes that the work was reviewed in the Isis for April 1840. The preface is dated October 1839. (See also Selby, Prideaux John, A Catalogue of the Generic and Sub-generic Types of the Class Aves, 1840.)

Gray, George Robert.

1841. A list | of the | genera of birds, | with their synonyma, | and | an indication of the typical species of each genus. | By | George Robert Gray. | **Second edition,** | revised, augmented, and accompanied with an index. | London: | printed and sold by Richard and John E. Taylor, | Red Lion Court, Fleet Street. | 1841.

1 vol. post 8vo, pp. I-XII, 1-115. London.

A revised edition of the author's work of the same title (q.v.) published the previous year, with many changes and additions. Although recognizing that the foundation of the binomial system of nomenclature was laid by Linné in 1758 (Cf. p. VIII.), the author cites Linnean names from the first edition of the "Systema Naturae," 1735, in order to credit Linné with generic names used by him in 1835 and by later authors, but not found in the tenth edition of Linné's work. The present edition of Gray contains new names not in the first edition, supplied by the author when no others were available. An appendix (q.v.) was issued in 1842. Sherborn (Index Animalium, Sect. 2, Pt. 1, p. LXII, 1922) gives October 1841 as the date of publication. Mathews (Birds of Australia, **7**, p. 453) gives the date as September, quoting from the covers of the Annals and Magazine of Natural History for Sept.-Oct., 1841. What is virtually a further revised edition is found in Gray's "Catalogue of the Genera and Subgenera of Birds contained in the British Museum," 1855 (q.v.).

Gray, George Robert.

1842. Appendix | to | a list | of | the genera of birds. | By | George Robert Gray. | London: | printed and sold by Richard and John E. Taylor, Red Lion Court, Fleet Street. | 1842.

1 vol. post 8vo, pp. I-IV, 5-16. London. 1842 (ante April).

Additions to, and corrections of, the second edition of the author's "A List of the Genera of Birds," 1841 (q.v.). The date is from Sherborn, Index Animalium, Sect. 2, Pt. 1, p. LXII, 1922. Mathews (Birds of Australia, **7**, p. 453) notes the work as "on sale April 1, 1842."

Gray, George Robert.

1844-49. The | genera of birds: | comprising | their generic charac- ters, | a notice of the habits of each genus, | and | an extensive list of species | referred to their several genera. | By | George Robert Gray, F.L.S. | Senior Assistant of the Natural History Department in the British Museum; | Corresponding Member [*etc., 6 lines.*]. | Illustrated by | David William Mitchell, B.A. F.L.S. | Secretary to the Zoological Society of London; | Honorary Member [*etc., 2 lines.*]. | In three volumes. | Vol. I [II; III]. | 1844-1849. | London: | Longman, Brown, Green, and Longmans, | Paternoster- Row. | 1849.

3 vols. imperial 4to. Vol. I, title, pp. V-XVI, 150 ll. (pp. 1-300), pll. I-LXXII (col.), 57 pll. (uncol.; 11 double-page). Vol. II, pp. I-IV, 91 ll. (pp. 301-483), pll. LXXIII-CXX+CXXa (=49 col.), 42 pll. (uncol.; 7 double-page). Vol. III, title, pp. III-IV, 93 ll. (pp. 484-669), pp. 1-117, pll. CXXI-CXXXIX, CXLI- CLXXXV (=64 col.), 151 pll. (uncol.; 8 double-page). London.

Issued in 50 parts without respect to the final arrangement. The text relating to each group is dated, on the final page, with the month and year of publication and I have noted 48 different dates of this sort which agree well with other data at hand. Through the kindness of Dr. Glover M. Allen of the Boston Society of Natural History, I have been put in possession of the dates of receipt of the various parts, as recorded in the Society's books. With a few excep- tions, the dates of receipt in Boston agree with the month and year as printed at the foot of the various pages, and indicate that publication must have been very early in the months indicated. The dates of receipt and other notes are as follows.

Pt. 1, May 22, 1844; **2,** July 19, 1844 (evidently the pages signed "May 1844"); **3,** July 19, 1844; **4,** Sept. 8, 1844 (evidently the pages signed "August 1844"); **5,** Sept. 22, 1844; **6,** Oct. 24, 1844; **7,** Nov. 27, 1844; **8,** Dec. 24, 1844; **9,** Jan. 27, 1845; **10,** Febr. 20, 1845; **11,** Mar. 22, 1845; **12,** Apr. 23, 1845; **13,** May 22, 1845; **14,** June 22, 1845; **15,** July 22, 1845; **16,** Aug. 20, 1845; **17,** Sept. 29, 1845; **18,** Nov. 5, 1845; (evidently the pages signed "October 1845"); **19,** Nov. 21, 1845; **20,** Dec. 24, 1845; **21,** Jan. 26, 1846; **22,** Febr. 21, 1846; **23,** March 22, 1846; **24,** Apr. 24, 1846; **25,** May 25, 1846; **26,** June 20, 1846; **27,** July 21, 1846; **28,** Aug. 22, 1846; **29,** Sept. 19, 1846; **30,** Oct. 22, 1846; **31,** Nov. 19, 1846; **32,** Dec. 18, 1846; **33,** Jan. 27, 1847; **34,** Febr. 26, 1847; **35,** Mar. 27, 1847; **36** Apr. 23, 1847; **37,** May 18, 1847; **38,** June 19, 1847; **39,** July 31, 1847; **40** Sept. 22, 1847; **41,** Oct. 23, 1847; **42,** Dec. 28, 1847; **43,** Mar. 10, 1848; **44** June 16, 1848 (marked "no. for June"); **45,** Aug. 28, 1848; **46,** Dec. 19, 1848; **47,** Apr. 12, 1849 (marked "for March"); **48,** May 18, 1849 (I can find no signatures dated between March and June, 1849. The Proc. Bost. Soc. Nat. Hist. for June 30, 1849 notes that Pt. 48 included the appendix.); **49,** June 25, 1849; **50,** Nov. 1, 1849 (probably title-pages, etc.; I can find no signatures dated after June 1849).

The discussion of the Struthiones is dated "March 1844"; the signature, "4 I," indicates that this is in error for "March 1846" as given on other signatures in the work with adjacent numbers. The original discussions of the Accipitrinae, Buteoninae and Ploceinae were suppressed and replaced by substitute parts published in June, June, and March, respectively, 1849. Footnotes in the tables of contents indicate such a substitution. Certain new names which occur on these pages must, therefore, be quoted from the earlier suppressed sheets (Cf. Richmond, Proc. U. S. Nat. Mus., **53,** p. 596, footn. 1, 1917.). The original pages of the Ploceinae were published in Pt. 1.

Gray, George Robert.

1844-68. List | of the | specimens of birds | in | the collection | of the | British Museum. [| By G. R. Gray [*etc., mut. mut.*) (*Pt. III, Sect. II-Pt. V.*)] | Part I.-Accipitres [Part II. Section I. | Fissirostres; Part III. | Gallinæ, Grallæ, and Anseres; Part III. Section I. | Ramphastidæ; Part III. Section II. | Psittacidæ; Part III. Sections III. & IV. | Capitonidæ and Picidæ; Part IV. | Columbæ; Part V. | Gallinæ]. | Printed by order of the Trustees. | London: 1844 [1848 (*Pt. II. Sect. I.*); 1844 (*Pt. III.*); 1855 (*Pt. III, Sect. I.*); 1859 (*Pt. III, Sect. II.*); 1868 (*Pt. III, Sects. III and IV.*); 1856 (*Pt. IV.*); 1867 (*Pt. V.*)].

8 vols. (should be 9) cap 8vo. Pt. I, pp. I-VIII, 1-54. Pt. II, Sect. I, tit., pp. 1-80. Pt. III, tit., pp. 1-209. Pt. III, Sect. I, 2 pr. ll., pp. 1-16, 1-4 (advt.). Pt. III, Sect. II, 2 pr. ll. (tit. and pref.), pp. 1-110. Pt. III, Sects. III and IV, 2 pr. ll., pp. 1-137. Pt. IV, 2 pr. ll., pp. 1-73+1, 1-4 (advt.). Pt. V, 2 pr. ll., pp. 1-120. London.

A systematic catalogue of the specimens of birds in the British Museum, with supplementary lists of desiderata, forming a complete catalogue of known species, so far as the respective groups are discussed. Numerous new species are described. Full synonymy is given for each species in the collection and the source of each specimen is added. Exact dates for the parts are not available, but the years, as given on the title-pages, are probably correct. Pt. I is reviewed in the Revue Zoologique for July, 1844. Pt. III (Sect. II) has the preface dated March 1, 1859 and is reviewed in the Ibis for July of that year. Pt. III (Sects. III and IV) has the preface dated January 1868. Pt. IV has the preface dated April 12, 1856 and was quoted by Bonaparte in a paper read before the Académie des Sciences de Paris on Nov. 3 of that year. Pt. V, dated 1867, was reviewed in the Ibis for January 1868, the date being given as on the title-page. Pt. I was revised and republished in 1848, but this revision is missing from the present set. Pts. IV and V are revisions of parts of Pt. III; the three orders contained in the latter volume were afterwards subdivided. The series was never completed, being superseded by the "Catalogue of Birds in the British Museum" of varied authorship (Cf. British Museum 1874-98.).

Gray, George Robert.

1855. Catalogue | of the | genera and subgenera | of | birds | contained in the | British Museum. | London: | printed by order of the Trustees. | 1855.

1 vol. 12mo, 2 pr. ll. (tit. and introd.), pp. 1-192, 1-4 (advt.). London.

A "complete List of the Genera and Subgenera of Birds, with their chief Synonyma and Types." Species not contained in the British Museum are marked with a dagger. The type-designations form the chief value of the work at the present time. Many changes in nomenclature appear between the present work and the author's earlier "A List of the Genera of Birds," eds. 1840 and 1841 (q.v.), of which this may be considered as a revision. Bonaparte presented a copy of the work to the Academy of Science of Paris at a meeting held October 22, 1855; noted in the "Comptes Rendus," 41, pp. 649 and 674, 1855; this is the earliest definite record I can find. Cabanis notes the work in the Journal für Ornithologie for July 1855, but the date of that periodical is itself uncertain. The preface of Gray's work is dated April 6, 1855.

Gray, George Robert.

1855. See Bonaparte, Charles Lucien, Institut Impérial de France., Catalogue des genres et sous-genres d'oiseaux contenus dans le Muséum Britannique.

Gray, George Robert.

1859. Catalogue | of the | birds | of the | tropical islands of the Pacific Ocean, | in the collection of the | British Museum. | By | George Robert Gray, F.L.S., F.Z.S., etc. | London: | printed by order of the Trustees. | 1859.

1 vol. post 8vo, 2 pr. ll., pp. 1-72, 1-8 (advt.). London 1859 (post Oct. 1).

An annotated list of all the species of birds found in the various islands of the tropical Pacific Ocean, with detailed synonymies, including some native names, and with descriptions of new species. The present copy was presented to John Gould by the author. The preface is dated October 1, 1859.

Gray, George Robert.

1859. See Gray, John Edward; and Gray, G. R., **Catalogue of the Mammalia and Birds of New Guinea.**

Gray, George Robert.

1869-71. **Hand-list | of | genera and species | of | birds, |** distinguishing those contained | in the | British Museum. | By | G. R. Gray [George Robert Gray (*Vols. II and III.*)], F.R.S. etc., | Assistant Keeper of the Zoological Collections. | Part I [-III]. | Accipitres, Fissirostres, Tenuirostres, [Conirostres, Scansores, Columbæ, and (*Vol. II.*); Struthiones, Grallæ, and Anseres, (*Vol. III.*)] | and Dentirostres [Gallinæ (*Vol. II.*); with indices of generic and specific names (*Vol. III.*)]. | London: | printed by order of the Trustees. | 1869 [1870; 1871].

3 vols. post 8vo. Vol. I, pp. I-XX, 1-404. Vol. II, pp. I-XV+1, 1-278. Vol. III, pp. I-XI+1, 1-350. London.

"The object of this Hand-List is to give a complete List of all the Genera with their Subdivisions; and also a comprehensive List of the species of Birds under the respective divisions to which they are supposed to belong." The work catalogues 2915 genera and subgenera and 11,162 species with numerous synonyms of each and with bibliographic references to published illustrations. The range of each species is noted and a table of genera and subgenera is given in each volume. Vol. III contains indices to the genera and subgenera and to the species of the entire work, with certain synonymic and other notes incorporated into them which are not in the general text. This book was superseded by Sharpe's "A Hand-List of the Genera and Species of Birds," 1899-1909 (q.v.). The preface of Vol. I is dated May 10, 1869; the volume is reviewed in the Ibis for January 1870 as just having been issued, being cited, however, under date of 1869. Vol. II has its preface dated November 9, 1870, and Vol. III, July 8, 1871; these are said by Mathews (Birds of Australia, Suppl. 4, p. 60, 1925) to have appeared before Nov. 23, 1870 and Aug. 18, 1871, respectively.

Gray, George Robert.

1871. **A fasciculus | of | the birds of China. |** By | G. R. Gray, F.R.S., F.L.S., etc.

1 vol. crown folio, pp. 1-8, 12 pll. (col.; by W. Swainson). London.
A series of hand-colored plates, originally designed for another publication, with a short account of each species. Plate VI is missing from the present copy.

Gray, George Robert.

1871? [Privately printed.] | **From the prefaces | to the | 'List of the Genera of Birds,' | and to the | 'Genera of Birds,' | with some additional remarks.**

1 vol. (pamphlet, size of post 8vo), pp. 1-10. London. (Post) 1871.

A resumé of the purpose and plan of the author's published works on avian genera. Reference is made to the index of the author's "Hand-List of Genera and Species of Birds," 1869-71 (q.v.), which fixes the date, approximately, as after 1871.

Gray, George Robert.

1873. See Brenchley, Julius L., **Jottings during the Cruise of H. M. S. Curaçoa.**

Gray, George Robert.

1875. See Richardson, John; and Gray, John Edward, **The Zoology of the Voyage of H. M. S. Erebus & Terror,** 1844-75.

Gray, John Edward.

1829. See Cuvier, G.L.C.F.D., **The Animal Kingdom,** 1827-35.

Gray, John Edward. (Hardwicke, Thomas.)

1830-35. **Illustrations | of | Indian zoology;** | chiefly selected from the collection | of | Major-General Hardwicke, F.R.S., | L.S , M.R.A.S., M.R.I.A., &c., &c. | By | John Edward Gray, F.R.S., | F.G.S., [etc., 4 lines.] | Vol. I [II]. | London: | Published by Treuttel, Wurz, Treuttel, Jun. and Richter, Soho Square; 17, Rue Bourbon, Paris; and Grande | Rue, Strasburg; also by Parbury, Allen and Co., 7, Leadenhall Street [Published by Adolphus Richter and Co., Soho Square, and Parbury, Allen and Co., 7, Leadenhall Street]. | MDCCCXXX - MDCCCXXXII [MDCCCXXXIII - MDCCCXXXIV].

2 vols. in 1 vol., superroyal folio. Vol. I, 4 pr. ll. (tit., ded., suscrs. and list of pll.), frontisp. (portr.), 100 pll. (col.; 58 of birds). Vol. II, 2 pr. ll. (tit. and list of pll.), 102 pll. (col.; 32 of birds). London.

A series of plates of animals, not all from India, largely from specimens and drawings collected by Hardwicke,—some from other sources. A text seems to have been planned but it was never published. The work was issued in 20 parts of which the lists of plates in the volumes announce that I-X compose Vol. I and XI-XX, Vol. II. Kinnear (Ibis, 1925, pp. 484-489) has given a careful account of the work and a list of dates on which the various parts were received by the Linnean Society and the Hon. East India Company. He further supplies the contents of each part from a copy in original wrappers. Kinnear's data are as follows, using the numbering of the ornithological plates as given in the lists (the plates are unnumbered).

Vol. I: Pt. I, pll. 20 and 40, recd. Jan. 6, 1830 (H. E. I. Co.); II, pll. 35, 39, 54, 64, Mar. 30, 1830 (H. E. I. Co.); III, pll. 26 and 42, July 15, 1830 (Lin. Soc.); IV, pll. 25, 34, 52, 57, 68, Oct. 6, 1830 (H. E. I. Co.); V, pll. 23, 24, 29, 41, 63, 66, 69, Jan. 25, 1831 (H. E. I. Co.); VI, pll. 22, 28, 30, 31, 58, 70, April 7, 1831 (H. E. I. Co.); VII, pll. 32, 33, 37, 53, 56, July 27, 1831 (H. E. I. Co.);

VIII, pll. 15, 18, 19, 38, 47, 49, 55, 60, Oct. 19, 1831 (Lin. Soc.); IX, pll. 14, 16, 17, 44, 45, 46, 50, 51, 59, 61, Dec. 2, 1831 (Lin. Soc.); X, pll. 21, 27, 36, 43, 48, 62, 65, 67, 71, April 14, 1832 (H. E. I. Co.). Vol. II, Pt. XI, pll. 28, 29, 40, 46, July 11, 1832 (Lin. Soc.); XII, pll. 31, 34, 47, 49, Oct. 8, 1832 (H. E. I. Co.); XIII-XIV, pll. 26, 38, 44, 55, Mar. 12, 1834 (H. E. I. Co.); XV-XVI, pll. 25, 27, 30[1], 33, 39, 41, 42, 43, 48, 50[2], 53, 54, April 10, 1834 (H. E. I. Co.); XVII-XVIII, pll. 32, 37, 45[3], 52, 56, Oct. 1, 1834 (Lin. Soc.); XIX-XX, pll. 35, 36, 51, Febr. 20, 1835 (H. E. I. Co.).

Gray, John Edward.

1844-45. See Richardson, John; and Gray, **The Zoology of the Voyage of H. M. S. Erebus & Terror.**

Gray, John Edward.

1846-50. Gleanings | from | the menagerie | and | aviary | at | **Knowsley Hall.** [| Hoofed quadrupeds.] | Knowsley: | 1846 [1850].

1 vol. (2 pts.) imperial folio. (First part), 2 pr. ll. (tit. and pref.), 5 ll., pll. 1-15+2 pll. (unnum. = 16 and 17) (col.; by E. Lear). (Hoofed quadrupeds), 2 pr. ll., pp. 1-76, 62 pll. (53 col.; by B. Waterhouse Hawkins; = pll. I-XLVII, XLIX-LIX and XIa of index and 3 pll. not mentioned in the text; pl. XLVIII missing). Knowsley.

A series of colored plates of animals and birds, drawn from live examples in the Knowsley menagerie and aviary and accompanied by descriptions and other notes on the species. Pll. 8-16 of the first part are of birds, including the figure of a new species, *Rollulus superciliosus*, described in the accompanying text. The preface of this part is dated August 1, 1846; that of the later part, August 1, 1850. The three extra plates in the second part (all mammals) are of *Cephalophus rufilatus*, *Coassus superciliaris* and *C. rufus*. The book is rare. The present copy is in exceptionally fine condition.

Gray, John Edward; and Gray, George Robert.

1859. Catalogue | of the | mammalia and birds | of | **New Guinea,** | in the collection of the | British Museum. | By | John Edward Gray, Ph.D., F.R.S., | and | George Robert Gray, F.L.S., etc | London: | printed by order of the Trustees. | 1859.

1 vol. post 8vo, 2 pr. ll. (tit. and pref.), pp. 1-63, 1-8 (advt.), text-figs. 1-9. London.

An annotated catalogue giving the synonymy and habitat of the various species in the collection, with descriptions of a number of the species (previously characterized by the junior author in the Proceedings of the Zoological Society

---

[1] Name altered on cover to *Lanius keroula.*
[2] Name altered on cover to *Charadrius ventralis.*
[3] Names altered on cover to *Cryptonyx ferrugineus* (for *oculea*) and *C. longirostris* (for *Francolinus magnirostris*).

of London) and occasional notes on other forms. A supplementary table lists the names and localities, only, of desiderata from New Guinea. The ornithology of the catalogue occupies pp. 16-63. The preface is dated "1 Dec. 1858" and the title-page, "1859."

Gray, Robert.

1871. The | birds of the west of Scotland | including | the Outer Hebrides | with occasional records of the occurrence of the rarer | species throughout Scotland generally. | By | Robert Gray | late Secretary to the Natural History Society of Glasgow; | Member of [*etc., 3 lines.*] | [*Blazon.*] | Glasgow: Thomas Murray & Son | MDCCCLXXI.

1 vol. post 8vo, pp. I-X, 1 l., pp. 1-520, 15 pll. Glasgow.

An account of the habits of the various birds known to have been found in western Scotland. The present copy is from the library of Lieut.-Colonel L. Howard Irby and contains a few annotations in his handwriting.

Greene, William Thomas. (Dutton, F. G.)

1883-87(-88). Parrots | in captivity. | By | W. T. Greene, M.A., M.D., F.Z.S., Etc., | Author of "The Amateur's Aviary of Foreign Birds," &c. | With notes on several species by the Hon. and Rev. F. G. Dutton. | Vol. I [II; III]. | Illustrated with coloured plates. | London: | George Bell and Sons, York Street, Covent Garden. | MDCCCLXXXIV [MDCCCLXXXIV, MDCCCLXXXVII].

3 vols. superroyal 8vo. Vol. I, pp. I-X, 1-144, 27 pll. (col.). Vol. II, pp. I-XIV, 1-114, 27 pll. (col.). Vol. III, pp. I-VIII, 1-144, 27 pll. (col.). London.

An account of the habits of 81 varieties of parrots (including cockatoos, macaws, parrakeets, etc.) with special reference to their behavior in cage or aviary. Supplementary remarks on many of the forms are credited to F. G. Dutton. The first two volumes were issued in 18 parts, of which Pts. 1-6 (Vol. I, pp. 1-97?) appeared in 1883, the remainder in 1884. Volume III appeared entire in 1887. A fourth volume, which I have not seen, was begun in 1888 and carried through 2 parts with 9 col. pll. and corresponding text.

Grieve, Symington.

1885. The great auk, or garefowl | (Alca impennis, Linn.) | Its History, Archæology, and Remains | by | Symington Grieve | Edinburgh | London | Thomas C. Jack, 45 Ludgate Hill | Edinburgh: Grange Publishing Works | 1885.

1 vol. foliopost 4to, pp. III-XI+1, pp. 1-141+1, 1 l., pp. 1-58, frontisp., 3 pll. (2 col.), 1 map (col.), 6 text-cuts. London and Edinburgh.

A discussion of the available records and information relative to the extinct Great Auk. The appendix contains, among other matters, translations from several papers on the subject by foreign authors.

Griffith, Edward.

1827-35. See Cuvier, G.L.C.F.D., **The Animal Kingdom.**

Grimshaw, Percy H.

1911. See [Grouse], **The Grouse in Health and Disease.**

Grinnell, George Bird.

1901. American | duck | shooting | By | George Bird Grinnell | Author of Pawnee Hero Stories | and Folk-Tales, Blackfoot | Lodge Tales, The Story of the | Indian, | The Indians of Today, etc. | With Fifty-eight Portraits of North | American Swans, Geese and Ducks by | Edwin Sheppard | and numerous Vignettes in the text by | Wilmot Townsend | [*Fig.*] | New York | Forest and Stream Publishing Company.

1 vol. 8vo, 1 pr. l., pp. 1-623+1, 1-10 (advt.), 11 pll. (on 10 ll.), 132 text-cuts (58 bird portr., 19 named figs., 55 vignettes), 7 half-tones. New York.

Part I contains a discussion of the various species of North American ducks, geese and swans with an illustration of each. Part II relates to the art of hunting these birds.

Grinnell, Joseph.

1912. Cooper Ornithological Club | **Pacific Coast Avifauna | Number 8 | A systematic list of the | birds of California** | by | Joseph Grinnell | Contribution from the Museum of Vertebrate Zoology | of the University of California | [*Seal.*] | Hollywood, California | Published by the Club | August 30, 1912.

1 vol. superroyal 8vo, pp. 1-23. Hollywood. August 30, 1912.

A list of 530 species and subspecies of birds recorded from California.

Grinnell, Joseph; Bryant, Harold Child; and Storer, Tracy Irwin.

1918. The game birds of California | Contribution from the University of California | Museum of Vertebrate Zoology | by | Joseph Grinnell | Harold Child Bryant | and | Tracy Irwin Storer | University of California Press | Berkeley | 1918.

1 vol. superroyal 8vo, 1 pr. l., pp. I-X, 1-642, pll. 1-16 (col.; by L. A. Fuertes and Allan Brooks), text-figs. 1-94, 1 insert (table 7). Berkeley. Dec. 28, 1918.

A detailed discussion of the game birds of California, with descriptions and notes on habits, distribution, field marks, song, nidification and economic importance.

Grinnell, Joseph; and Storer, Tracy Irwin.

1924. Animal life in the | Yosemite | an account of the mammals, birds, | reptiles, and amphibians in | a cross-section of the | Sierra Nevada | by | Joseph Grinnell | and | Tracy Storer | Contribution from the Museum of Vertebrate Zoology | University of California | [*Design.*] | University of California Press | Berkeley, California | 1924.

1 vol. 6¾ x 10, pp. I-XVIII, 1-752, pll. 1-62 (12 col., by Allan Brooks, 9 of birds; 48 on num. pp.; 1 chart, fold,. col.; 1 map, fold., col.), text-figs. 1-65, 7 tables (col.). Berkeley. April 17, 1924.

The report on a natural history survey of the Yosemite Valley, with regard to the occurrence and local distribution of vertebrate forms, their food relations, breeding habits and behavior. Field characters are given for each species and a detailed account follows. Photographs, colored plates and line-drawings are used as illustrations. The work constitutes a valuable handbook of information on the vertebrate life of the region.

Griscom, Ludlow.

1923. Birds of the | New York City region | by | Ludlow Griscom | Assistant Curator of Ornithology | With the cooperation of the | Linnæan Society of New York | [*Vignette.*] | The American Museum of Natural History | Handbook series, No. 9 | New York. Published by the Museum | 1923.

1 vol. post 8vo, pp. 1-400, pll. I-VI (col.; by L. A. Fuertes), figs. 1-30, 1 map. New York.

An annotated list of the species of birds recorded from, or observed within, a defined area in the vicinity of New York City; including notes on distribution, recognition in the field, bibliographic references, etc.

Grönvold, Henrik. (Swann, Harry Kirke.)

1915-17. Illustrations | of the | game birds and water fowl | of | South America. | By | H. Grönvold. | London: | John Wheldon & Co., | 38, Great Queen Street, Kingsway, W.C. | 1917.

1 vol. royal 4to, pp. 1-11, pll. 1-38 (col.). London.

A series of 38 plates by Grönvold, originally intended to serve as a portion of the illustrations of Brabourne and Chubb's "The Birds of South America," 1913 (q.v.). The death of Lord Brabourne ended that work when only one volume had been issued and before any of the plates had appeared, although some of these were completed and others were in course of preparation. Later, these plates were issued separately under the present title, with short explanatory notes by H. Kirke Swann. A half-title with the work reads, "The birds | of | South America. | Vol. II (Plates.)," but the two publications are, in reality distinct. A first series of 19 plates appears to have been issued in 1915; the remainder, with the short text, appeared in 1917.

[**Grouse.**] Berry, W.; Cobbett, L.; Evans, Arthur Humble; Fantham, H. B.; Graham-Smith, G. S.; Grimshaw, Percy H.; Leiper, R. T.; Leslie, A. S.; Lovat, Lord; Rastall, R. H.; Shipley, A. E.; Smith, H. Hammond; Wilson, Edward A.

1911. The grouse | in health and disease | being the final report of the | committee of inquiry on grouse disease | Volume I [II | Appendices] | With 59 full-page plates, mostly in colour [With 41 maps] | and 31 illustrations in the text [*Line omitted.*] | London | Smith, Elder & Co., 15 Waterloo Place | 1911 | [All rights reserved].

2 vols. 8vo (8¾ x 11). Vol. I, pp. I-XXIII+1, 1-512, frontisp. (col.), pll. I-LVIII+XXVIIa (39 col.), figs. 1-30, 1-2, 1 text-cut (9 figs., unnum.). Vol. II, pp. I-VII+1, 1-150, pl. LXX (map., col.), 40 text-maps. London.

A study of *Lagopus scoticus* of Great Britain, made by a committee appointed as a Departmental Committee of the Board of Agriculture and Fisheries to investigate the so-called "Grouse Disease." The report as here presented gives, in Vol. I, the details of life-history, changes of plumage, anatomy, physiology and systematic position of the species, a series of detailed studies on parasites and diseases of grouse, and a section on the management and economics of grouse moors. Vol. II contains financial accounts, studies of crops and gizzards meteorological tables, etc.

Gruvel.

1789. See Molina, Essai sur l'Histoire Naturelle du Chili.

Guillemard, Francis Henry Hill.

1886. The | cruise of the Marchesa | to | Kamschatka & New Guinea | with notices of Formosa, Liu-Kiu, and various | islands of the Malay Archipelago | By F. H. H. Guillemard | M.A., M.D. (Cantab.) | Fellow of the Linnean Society; [*etc., 2 lines.*]. | With Maps and numerous Woodcuts | drawn by J. Keulemans, C. Whymper, and others | and engraved by Edward Whymper | [*Quot., 3 lines.*] | In two volumes - Vol. I [II]. | London | John Murray, Albemarle Street | 1886.

2 vols. royal 8vo. Vol. I, pp. I-XVII+1, 1 l., pp. 1-284, 11 pll. (1 col.), 42 text-figs, 5 maps. Vol. II, 20 pll. (1 col.), 69 text-figs., 9 maps. London.

A general account of the voyage, with numerous notes on natural history scattered through the volumes. Many of these notes relate to birds. In addition, in Appendix II of Vol. I (pp. 274-278) and Appendix I of Vol. II (pp. 361-371), there are lists of the species of birds collected or observed in the different localities. In Vol. I, the colored frontispiece and 3 figs. and in Vol. II, the colored frontispiece, 6 plain plates and 5 figs. are of birds. The technical report on the ornithology of the voyage was published by the author in various numbers of the Proceedings of the Zoological Society of London for the year 1885.

Gundlach, Johannes.

1873-76. Contribucion | á la | ornitologia Cubana, | por el | Dr. Juan Gundlach, | socio de merito [*etc., 5 lines.*]. | Habana. | Imp. "La Antilla," de N. Cacho-Negrette, | Calle de Cuba Numero 51. | 1876.
1 vol. 4to (size of royal 8vo), 2 pr. ll., pp. 1-364. Havana.

An annotated list of the species of birds recorded from Cuba, with miscellaneous notes. A first appendix contains rather detailed synonymies of the various species, and some corrections of the text. A second supplement adds more corrections and emendations and presents the general indices, concluding with a long list of errata. The work, as here collated, was published in Havana and issued in sheets with the "Anales de la Real Academia de Ciencias," Vols. IX-XII, in the years 1873 (?)—1876. It also appeared in German, without the appendices, in the Journal für Ornithologie, during the years 1871-75. Taschenberg ascribes the work to "Habana. Don S. de Uhagon, Madrid. 1876," an imprint which does not appear on the copy at hand and which, possibly, refers to a third edition. The German transcript, only, is quoted by the Zoological Record. The copy here collated is autographed by the author in presentation to Don Simon de Cardenas, his friend and early protector, for whose relief when subsequently impoverished, Gundlach sold his Cuban collections.

Gurney, John Henry.

1864. A | descriptive catalogue | of | the raptorial birds | in the | Norfolk and Norwich Museum, | compiled and arranged | by | John Henry Gurney. | Part one: | containing | Serpentariidæ, Polyboridæ, Vulturidæ. | London: John Van Voorst, Paternoster Row. | Norwich: Matchett and Stevenson, Market-Place. | 1864.
1 vol. demy 4to, pp. I-VI, 7-90. London and Norwich.

The first portion of a work which was never completed. It contains short descriptions and accounts of the habits of the various species of hawks and owls with a list of the specimens of each contained in the Norfolk and Norwich Museum.

Gurney, John Henry.

1872. See Andersson, Charles John, **Notes on the Birds of Damara Land** and the Adjacent Countries of South-west Africa.

Gurney, John Henry.

1884. A list | of the | diurnal birds of prey, | with | references and annotations; | also | a record of specimens | preserved in the | Norfolk and Norwich Museum. | By | John Henry Gurney. |

London: | John Van Voorst, 1 Paternoster Row, E.C. | MDCCC-LXXXIV.

1 vol. 4to (size of post 8vo), pp. I-XVI+1, 1-187. London.

A tabular list of species, giving references to published notes by the author and others and recording the number of specimens of each species in the museum. Copious footnotes are supplied throughout the list and the work closes with fifteen appendices (discussing certain species in detail) and an index. The copy was presented to C. B. Cory by the author.

Gurney, John Henry (Jun.).

1876. Rambles of a Naturalist | in | Egypt and other countries. | With an analysis of | the claims of certain foreign birds | to be considered British, | and other ornithological notes. | By | J. H. Gurney, Jun., F.Z.S. | London: | Jarrold and Sons, 3, Paternoster Buildings.

1 vol. post 8vo, pp. I-VI, 1 l., pp. 1-307. London.

A miscellaneous collection of general notes and observations.

Gurney, John Henry, (Jun.)

1877. See Rowley, George D., **Ornithological Miscellany,** 1875-78.

Gurney, John Henry (Jun.).

1894. Catalogue | of the | **birds of prey** | (Accipitres and Striges), | with the | number of specimens in Norwich Museum. | By | J. H. Gurney, F.Z.S. | London: | R. H. Porter, 18 Princes Street, Cavendish Square, W. | 1894.

1 vol. 8vo, 1 pr. l., pp. 1-56, frontisp., 2 charts (double-page), 1 text-fig. (full-page). London.

A check-list of species, with the regional distribution of each and a note as to the number of specimens of each in the Norwich Museum.

Gurney, John Henry (Jun.).

1913. The gannet | a bird with a history | by | J. H. Gurney, F.Z.S. | Author of [etc., 2 lines.]. | Illustrated with numerous photographs, maps and | drawings, and one coloured plate by Joseph Wolf | Witherby & Co. | 326 High Holborn, London | 1913.

1 vol. 8vo, pp. I-LI+1, 1-567, frontisp. (chart), 5 pll. (2 col.; by J. Wolf and E. Wilson), 136 text-figs. London.

A detailed account of a single species (*Sula bassana*), with discussions of its early history, distribution, habits, utility, anatomy, physiology and other interesting details.

Gurney, John Henry (Jun.).

1921. Early annals | of ornithology | by | J. H. Gurney, F.Z.S. | Author of [*etc.*, *2 lines.*]. | With illustrations from photographs and old prints | H. F. & G. Witherby | 326 High Holborn, London | 1921.

1 vol. post 8vo, 4 pr. ll. (half-tit., tit., pref. and conts.), pp. 1-240, 2 pll. (fold.), 34 text-cuts. London.

An attempt "to collect all the ancient passages about birds, of any special interest, but more particularly those which concerned British Birds" with the subject matter arranged in order of date. Folk-lore and legend together with more reliable chronicles are given in great detail with bibliographic references. A mass of information is thus presented which is very scattered in its original sources.

Hachisuka, Masa U.

1925. **A comparative hand list | of | the birds of | Japan and the British Isles** | by | Masa U. Hachisuka, F.Z.S. | Member of the Ornithological Society of Japan, Member of the British Ornithologists' Union | Cambridge | at the University Press | 1925.

1 vol. demy 4to, 4 pr. ll. (half-tit., tit., ded. and foreword), pp. 1-107. Cambridge.

Sufficiently explained by the title. Japan, as considered herein, is strictly construed, including only Tanegashima and Yakushima, in addition to the central islands. Original descriptions are cited, with English vernacular names for all species and Japanese names for the Japanese forms. Breeding species, exceptional visitors and rare visitors are indicated.

Hagelberg, W.

? > W. Hagelberg's | **Zoologischer Hand-Atlas.** | Naturgetreue Darstellung des Thierreichs | in | seinen Hauptformen. | B. | **Vögel.** Aves. | 285 Abbildungen auf 24 Tafeln. | Berlin, | Ferd. Dümmlers Verlagsbuchhandlung | Harrwitz & Goszmann.

1 vol. superroyal 8vo, 30 ll., pll. 21-44 (col.; on pp. opposite text). Berlin. (Date ?)

A curious book, apparently the second volume of a set including other zoological subjects. The illustrations consist of small, embossed, lithographed cards, with portraits of different birds, mounted 12 or, in one case, 9 to the page and described on the opposite page of text. Both common and Latin names are given. The work is of no scientific importance.

Hagen, Karl Gottfried.

1791. See Fischer, Jacob Benjamin, **Versuch einer Naturgeschichte von Livland.**

Hahn, Carl Wilhelm; and Küster, Heinrich Carl.

1818-36. [**Vögel aus Asien, Africa, America und Neuholland,** in Abbildungen nach der Natur mit Beschreibungen.] 1 vol. (19 pts.) demy 4to, 1 l. (prospectus), 49 ll., 2 insert-slips (in Pts. III and XVII), 114 pll. (col.; numbered, Liefs. I-XIX, pll. 1-6 each). Nuremberg.

A series or rather crude hand-colored plates with accompanying descriptions. The work was originally planned to occupy 48 parts of 6 pll. each. It was begun by Hahn, alone, and carried by him to Pt. XVII; the remaining numbers were prepared and issued by Küster. In 1850 the original 19 numbers appear to have been reissued, together with a new part (XX) which contained title-page, index, etc. The original parts carry no title-page. I have quoted the above title from a leaf of prospectus which is bound with the work and which refers to it under that name; the new title is more complete and is dated 1850.

Pts. I-V contain a separate leaf of text for each plate; VI, XI and XIII-XV, each have but 2 ll. text (or text and pref.) for all their respective plates; the remaining parts each have but 1 l. text. Sherborn (Index Animalium, Sect. 2, Pt. 1, p. LXIV, 1922) gives the dates of publication as follows. Pts. I-II, 1818; III-V, 1819; VI-VIII, 1820; IX-X, 1821; XI-XII, 1822; XIII-XIV, 1823; XV, 1826; XVI, 1829; XVII, 1831; XVIII, 1834; XIX, 1836. Dr. Laubmann (in litt. to Dr. Hellmayr) notes that the wrapper of Pt. XIII bears the date, 1822, at variance with Sherborn's conclusions; the preface of this part is dated September 1822. Some approximate dates are available from the prefaces, insert-slips, etc. accompanying certain parts, as follows. Pt. III, insert-slip dated June 1819; VI, note dated Febr. 1820; XI, note dated April (no year); XIII, preface dated Sept. 1822; XVII, insert-slip dated August 1831; XIX, text dated Febr. 1836. Engelmann cites a revised edition of Pts. I-XII, dated 1823.

Hahn, Carl Wilhelm.

1830-35. See Reider, Jakob Ernst von; and Hahn, **Fauna Boica - Deutschlands Vögel.**

Hahn, Carl Wilhelm; and Küster, Heinrich Carl.

1834-41. **Ornithologischer | Atlas |** oder naturgetreue | Abbildung und Beschreibung | der | aussereuropäischen Vögel | von | Dr. C. W. Hahn. | Erste Abtheilung. | Papageien. | (Psittacus, Linn.) | Mit fein colorirten Tafeln. | Nürnberg, | C. H. Zeh'sche Buchhandlung. | 1834.

> Ornithologischer | Atlas | der | aussereuropäischen Vögel [| (Fortsetzung von Dr. C. W. Hahn's Werk)] | von | Dr. C. W. Hahn [H. C. Küster]. | Erste Abtheilung [Siebzehntes Heft]. | Die Papageien [Bucconidae. | I]. | Erstes Heft. [*Line omitted.*] | Mit acht fein colorirten Tafeln. | Nürnberg, | C. H. Zeh'sche Buchhandlung. | 1834 [1841]. [*Decorated border.*] [*Cover-titles.*] 1 vol. post 8vo, 1 l. (prospectus; insert.; fold.), pp. 1-100 (*Psittacus*;

incl. subtit., Pt. I, and pref., Pt. 7), 1-6 (*Nectarinia*), 1-4 (*Cinnyris*), 1-2 (*Diglossa*), 1-2 (*Scaphorhynchus*).

1 vol. post 8vo, 1 l. (prospectus; insert.; fold.); pp. 1-100, pll. 1-79+57 (*bis*) (*Psittacus*; incl. subtit. Pt. 1 and pref. Pt. 7), pp. 1-6, pll. 1-4 (*Nectarinia*); pp. 1-4, pll. 1-2, 3a and 3b (*Cinnyris*); pp. 1-2, pll. 1-2 (*Diglossa*); pp. 1-2, pl. 1 (*Scaphorhynchus*); pp. 1-2, pll. 1-2 (*Ocypterus*); pp. 1-4, pll. 1-3 (*Thamnophilus*); pp. 1-2, pl. 1 (*Coracina*); pp. 1-2, pll. 1-2 (*Procnias*); pp. 1-2, pl. 1 (*Cephalopterus*); pp. 1-8, pll. 1-8 (*Pipra*); pp. 1-4, pll. 1-3 (*Crotophaga*); pp. 1-2, pl. 1 (*Scythrops*); pp. 1-15, pll. 1-15 (*Picus*); pl. 1, (*Picumnus*); pp. 1-6, pll. 1-5 (*Bucco*); pp. 1-2, pll. 1-2 (*Pogonias*); pp. 1-2, pl. 1 (*Monasa*).; 3 ll. (manuscript index), 2 orig. wrappers (Pts. 1 and 17). Nuremberg.

The above 85 ll. of text and 136 colored plates are descriptive and illustrative of various birds not found in Europe. The work was issued in 17 parts, of which only the first 6 were completed by Hahn. After Hahn's death the remaining parts were written and published by Küster. The contents of Pts. 1 and 17 are noted on the final wrapper of those parts (included in the present copy) and many of the pages and plates in the other parts are recognizable from their signature-numbers. A careful examination of these and other marks makes the following arrangement seem fairly certain. Pt. **1**, *Psittacus*, pp. 1-20, pll. 1-8; **2**, pp. 21-32, pll. 9-16; **3**, pp. 33-40, pll. 17-24; **4**, pp. 41-48, pll. 25-33 (text to pl. 25 in Pt. 3); **5**, pp. 49-56, pll. 34-40; **6**, pp. 57-64, pll. 41-48; **7**, pp. 65-76, pll. 49-56; **8**, *Nectarinia* and *Cinnyris;* **9**, *Psittacus*, pp. 77-84, pll. 57-63 +57 (*bis*); **10**, *Picus*, pp. 1-12, pll. 1-7, and *Picumnus;* **11**, *Psittacus*, pp. 85-92, pll. 64-71; **12**, *Diglossa, Scaphorhynchus, Ocypterus* and *Thamnophilus;* **13**, *Coracina, Procnias, Cephalopterus* and *Pipra*, pp. 1-4, pll. 1-4; **14**, *Picus*, pp. 13-15, pll. 8-15; **15**, *Pipra*, pp. 5-8, pll. 5-8; **16**, *Psittacus*, pp. 93-100, pll. 72-79; **17**, *Bucco, Pogonias* and *Monasa*.

Sherborn (Index Animalium, Sect. 2, Pt. 1, p. LXIV, 1922) gives the dates of publication as follows. Pts. **1-3**, 1834; **4**, 1834 or 1835; **5-9**, 1836; **10-13**, 1837; **14-15**, 1838; **16**, 1840; **17**, 1849. The last figure appears to be an error for 1841. The cover of that part is dated 1841 and a note on the back cover is dated March 1841, while Engelmann (whose work dates 1846) gives the final date for the whole work (Pts. 1-17) as 1841.

Attached to the plate of *Picumnus minutissimus* is a clipping from the original wrapper in which it appeared, reading, "Der Text zu diesem Vogel folgt in einem der nächsten Hefte, mit der übrigen Arten von Picumnus." Beneath, some one has written, "nicht erschienen." Some errors exist in the numbering of the plates of *Psittacus*. Pl. 12 should be 9, 9-11, 11-12, 18-17, 17, 18; 30, 29; and 29, 30. The present copy is from the library of F. D. Godman and contains his bookplate.

Haines, Charles Reginald.

1907. Notes | on the | birds of Rutland | by | C. Reginald Haines, M.A., F.S.A., F. R. Hist. S. | Sometime Member of the British

Ornithologists' Union | [*Quot., 5 lines.*]. | London: | R. H. Porter | 7, Princes Street, Cavendish Square, W. | 1907 | [All rights reserved].

1 vol. crown 8vo, pp. I-XLVII+1, 1-175, frontisp. (col.; by E. F. T. Bennett), 6 pll., 1 text-fig., 1 map. London.

A list of the species of birds recorded from the county of Rutland, England, with a discussion of the habits and local occurrence of each. Apparently published by subscription.

Hales, Henry.

1896. See World's Congress on Ornithology, **Papers presented to the—.**

Hall, Robert.

**1899. A key | to the | Birds of Australia | and | Tasmania | with their | geographical distribution | in Australia | By Robert Hall | Melbourne | Melville, Mullen and Slade, Collins Street | London | Dulau and Co., 37 Soho Square | [Copyright].

1 vol. post 8vo, pp. I-X, 1 l., pp. 1-116, frontisp. (p. II), 1 fig. (chart). Melbourne and London.

A systematic list of species, with short descriptions of each.

Hall, Robert.

**1900. The | insectivorous birds | of | Victoria | with chapters on birds more or less useful | by | Robert Hall | Author of "A Key to the Birds of Australia and Tasmania" | Melbourne | Published by the author at 312 Flinders-St | 1900 | [Copyright].

1 vol. crown 8vo, pp. I-VIII, 1-257+1, 1 l. (advt.), frontisp. (p. II), 2 text-figs. (unnum.), figs. 1-55. Melbourne.

A popular account of a considerable number of birds of Victoria, arranged according to their food-habits, with a short description of each species and of its nest and eggs, its scientific name and the derivation, and a general discussion of habits. About half of the illustrations are reduced in black and white (half-tones) from Gould's "Birds of Australia."

Hammer, Friedrich Ludwig.

1804. See Hermann, Johann, **Observationes Zoologicae.**

Hamonville, Jean Charles Louis Tardif d'.

**1876. Catalogue | des | oiseaux d'Europe | ou | énumération des espèces et races d'oiseaux | dont le présence, soit habituelle, soit fortuite, a été dument | constatée dans les limites géographiques de l'Europe | par | J. C. L. T. d'Hamonville | Conseiller Général, [*etc.*, *3 lines.*] | Paris London W.C. | J. B. Bailliere et Fils B. Quaritch, Bookseller | 19, Rue Hautefeuille 15, Piccadilly Street | 1876.

1 vol. royal 8vo, 2 pr. ll. (half-tit. and tit.), pp. 1-73. Paris and London. 1876 (post March 20).

A tabular list of the genera and species of European birds, giving their Latin and vernacular names and general distribution. Several new names occur in the column of Latin terms. The "Avertissement" is dated March 20, 1876.

Hancock, John.

1874. Natural history transactions | of | Northumberland and Durham; | being papers read at the | meetings of the Natural History Society | of | Northumberland, Durham, and Newcastle-upon-Tyne, | and the | Tyneside Naturalists' Field Club, | 1873. | Vol. VI. | [*Vignette.*] | London: | Williams & Norgate, 14, Henrietta Street, Covent Garden; | and 20, South Frederick Street, Edinburgh. | Newcastle-upon-Tyne: F. & W. Dodsworth. | 1874. | [All rights reserved.] > **A catalogue** | **of** | **the birds** | **of** | **Northumberland and Durham.** | By John Hancock. | With fourteen photographic copper-plates, from | drawings by the author.

1 vol. 8vo, pp. I-XXV+1, 1-174, 2 ll. (appendix and errata), frontisp., pll. 1-13 (by Hancock). London.

An annotated "local list."

Haniel, Curt B. (Hellmayr, Charles Edward).

1914. > **Zoologie von Timor** | Ergebnisse der unter Leitung | von Joh. Wanner im Jahre 1911 | ausgeführten Timor-Expedition | nach eigenen Sammlungen unter | Mitwirkung von Fachgenossen | herausgegeben | von | C. B. Haniel | I. Lieferung | Stuttgart 1914 | Im Kommissionverlag der E. Schweizerbartschen Verlags- | buchhandlung, Nägele und Dr. Sproesser in Stuttgart > Zoologie von Timor. I. Lieferung | I. **Die Avifauna** | **von Timor** | von | C. E. Hellmayr | mit einer Farbentafel | (Tafel I) | Ausgegeben am 10. Januar 1914 | Stuttgart 1914 | Im Kommissionsverlag [*etc.*, *2 lines.*].

1 vol. medium 4to, pp. I-VI, 1-112, 1 l. (expl. of pl.), pl. I (col.; by Grönvold). Stuttgart. January 10, 1914.

An annotated review of the birds of the island of Timor by Hellmayr, based primarily on the collections of the Wanner Expedition of 1911. Several new subspecies are described. The brochure forms Lieferung I of a projected report on the zoology of the island, under editorship of Haniel, but is all published to date. A supplement was published by Hellmayr in the Novitates Zoologica, **23,** pp. 96-111, April, 1916.

Hantzsch, Bernhard.

1905. Beitrag zur Kenntnis | der | Vogelwelt Islands | Von | Bernhard Hantzsch | Mit 26 Abbildungen und 1 Karte | [*Vignette.*] | Berlin | Verlag von R. Friedländer & Sohn | 1905.

1 vol. royal 8vo, pp. I-IV, 1 l., pp. 1-341, Berlin.

A detailed, annotated list of the birds of Iceland, with a preliminary discussion of the topography of the country.

Hardwicke, Thomas.

1830-35. See Gray, John Edward, **Illustrations of Indian Zoology.**

Hardy, Manly.

1896. See World's Congress on Ornithology, **Papers presented to the—.**

Hargitt, Edward.

1890. Catalogue | of the | Picariæ | in the | collection | of the | British Museum. | Scansores, | containing the family | Picidæ. | By | Edward Hargitt. | London: | printed by order of the Trustees. | Sold by | Longmans & Co., 39 Paternoster Row; [*etc.,* *3 lines.*]; | and at the | British Museum (Natural History), Cromwell Road, S.W. | 1890.

See British Museum, **Catalogue of the Birds,** 1874-98, Vol. XVIII.

Harley, James.

1840. See MacGillivray, William, **A History of British Birds,** 1837-40.

Harris, Henry E.

1901. Essays and photographs. | **Some birds** | of the | **Canary Islands and South Africa.** | By | Henry E. Harris. | 92 illustrations | London | R. H. Porter, 7, Princes Street, Cavendish Square. | 1901.

1 vol. 8vo, pp. I-XIV, 1 l., pp. 1-212, frontisp., pll. I-LV. London.

A popular, running account of observations made by the author while on visits to the Canary Islands and South Africa; illustrated with photographic reproductions, most of which are ornithological.

Hartert, Ernst.

1892. See Salvin, Osbert; and Hartert, **Catalogue of the Picariae in the Collection of the British Museum,** 1892.

Also, British Museum, **Catalogue of the Birds,** 1874-98, Vol. XVI.

Hartert, Ernst.

1897. **Das Tierreich.** | Eine Zusammenstellung und Kennzeichnung der | rezenten Tierformen. | Herausgegeben | von der | Deutschen Zoologischen Gesellschaft. | Generalredakteur: Franz Eilhard Schulze. | 1. **Lieferung.** | Aves. | Redakteur: A. Reichenow. | **Podargidae, Caprimulgidae** | und | **Macropterygidae** | bearbeitet von | Ernst Hartert, | Direktor des Zoologisches Museums in Tring (England). | Mit 16 Abbildungen im Texte. | Berlin. | Verlag von R. Friedländer und Sohn. | 1897.

1 vol. (pt.) superroyal 8vo, pp. I-VIII, 1-98, I-IV ("Beiblatt zur 1. Lieferung."), text-figs. 1-13, 1 text-fig. (unnum., in "Beiblatt"). Berlin.

A monograph of the families of Frogmouths, Goatsuckers and Swifts (as arranged by the author), with tables to the species, genera and higher groups, short descriptions of each, and brief synonymy, and with the distribution of the species added. The supplementary pages contain a diagram (with explanation) of the topography of a bird. The work is reviewed in the Ornithologische Monatsberichte for May, 1897 and must have appeared not later than April. See also under "Tierreich."

Hartert, Ernst.

1900. **Das Tierreich.** | Eine Zusammenstellung und Kennzeichnung der | rezenten Tierformen. | Herausgegeben | von der | Deutschen Zoologischen Gesellschaft. | Generalredakteur: Franz Eilhard Schulze. | 9. **Lieferung.** | Aves. | Redakteur: A. Reichenow. | **Trochilidae** | bearbeitet von | Ernst Hartert, | Direktor des Zoologischen Museums in Tring (England). | Mit 34 Abbildungen im Texte. | Berlin. | Verlag von R. Friedländer und Sohn. | Ausgegeben im Februar 1900.

1 vol. (pt.) superroyal 8vo, 2 pr. ll, (tit. and 2nd tit.), pp. I-IX+1, 1-254, text-figs. 1-34. Berlin. Febr. 1900.

A monograph of the Hummingbirds with brief diagnoses and synonymy and with tables for the determination of genera and species. See also under "Tierreich." A second copy, separately bound is in the collection.

Hartert, Ernst.

1903-22. **Die Vögel** | **der paläarktischen Fauna.** | Systematische Übersicht | der | in Europa, Nord-Asien und der Mittelmeerregion | vorkommenden Vögel. | Von | Dr. Ernst Hartert. | Band I [II; III]. | Mit 134; [122; 12] Abbildungen. | Berlin 1910 [1912-21; 1921-22]. | Verlag von R. Friedländer und [& (*Vols. II and III.*)] Sohn. | Agents in London: Witherby & Co. [H. F. & G. Witherby (*Vols. II and III.*)], 326 High Holborn.

3 vols. royal 8vo. Vol. I, pp. I-XLIX+1, 1-832, text-figs. 1-134.
Vol. II, pp. I-XXIV, 833-1764, text-figs. 135-256. Vol. III, pp.
I-XII, 1-2328, text-figs. 257-268. Berlin.

Published in 19 parts, the contents and dates of publication of which are given
in Vol. I, p. XIII; Vol. II, p. XXIV; and Vol. III, p. XII. Pp. XIII-XLIX
of Vol. I belong to Pt. 6 of that volume, issued in June, 1910, although omitted
from the list of dates of publication. The work is a thorough monograph of
the birds of the Palaearctic Region, indispensable to the ornithological study
of that portion of the world. Supplementary contributions are in progress,
the first of which has been published under the above title, "Nachtrag I,"
1923 (q.v.).

Hartert, Ernst.

1905. See Wytsman, Paul, **Genera Avium,** 1905-14.

Hartert, Ernst.

1910-13. See Kirkman, Frederick Bernuf Bever, **The British Bird
Book.**

Hartert, Ernst; Jourdain, Francis Charles Robert; Ticehurst, Norman
Frederick; and Witherby, Harry Forbes.

1912. A hand-list of | British birds | with an account of the distribu-
tion of each | species in the British Isles and abroad. | By Ernst
Hartert | F. C. R. Jourdain | N. F. Ticehurst | and | H. F.
Witherby. | Witherby & Co. | 326 High Holborn London.
W.C. | 1912.

1 vol. post 8vo, pp. I-XII, 1-237. London.

A distributional list of species with brief synonymies and with trinomial nomenclature according to the International Code.

Hartert, Ernst.

1919-24. See Witherby, Harry Forbes, **A Practical Handbook of
British Birds.**

Hartert, Ernst.

1923. Die Vögel | der paläarktischen Fauna. | Systematische Über-
sicht | der | in Europa, Nord-Asien und der Mittelmeerregion | vor-
kommenden Vögel. | Von | Dr. Ernst Hartert. | **Nachtrag I** | (bis
Januar 1923). | Berlin 1923. | Verlag von R. Friedländer & Sohn.

1 vol. royal 8vo, 1 pr. l., pp. 1-92. Berlin.

A supplement to the author's work of the same title, 1903-22 (q.v.), containing
changes and additions to that work from October, 1921 to January, 1923.

Harting, James Edmund.

1866. The | birds of Middlesex. | A contribution | to | The Natural History of the County. | By | James Edmund Harting, F.Z.S. | London: | John Van Voorst, 1, Paternoster Row. | M.DCCC.-LXVI.

1 vol. 12mo, pp. I-XVI, 1-284, frontisp. (monochr.), 1 text-fig. London.

A popular account of the birds of Middlesex County, England, with notes on habits, songs, nidification, distribution and local occurrences.

Harting, James Edmund.

1871. The | birds | of | Shakespeare. | Critically examined, explained, and illustrated. | By | James Edmund Harting, F.L.S., F.Z.S., | Member of the British Ornithologists' Union, | Author of "The Birds of Middlesex," | etc., etc. | [*Blazon.*] | London: | John Van Voorst, Paternoster Row. | MDCCCLXXI.

1 vol. post 8vo, 2 pr. ll., pp. VII-XXII, 1 l., pp. 1-321, frontisp., 33 text-figs. London.

An interesting analysis of the allusions to birds made by Shakespeare, with explanations of obscure and obsolete terms and comments on the ornithological accuracy of the quotations.

Harting, James Edmund.

1877. Our summer migrants. | An account of | the migratory birds | which pass the summer in | the British Islands. | By J. E. Harting, F.L.S., F.Z.S. | Author of [*etc., 3 lines.*] | Illustrated from designs by Thomas Bewick. | Second edition. | [*Vignette.*] | London: | Bickers and Son, | 1, Leicester Square. | 1877.

1 vol. crown 8vo, pp. I-X, 1-336, 37 text-figs. London.

A popular account. First edition issued in 1875; later editions in 1889 and 1901.

Harting, James Edmund.

1880. See Rodd, Edward Hearle, **The Birds of Cornwall and the Scilly Islands.**

Harting, James Edmund.

1883. Essays on sport | and | natural history. | By | James Edmund Harting, | Author of | "Extinct British Animals," "A Handbook of British Birds," "Rambles in Search | of Shells," etc. etc. | With illustrations. | London: | Horace Cox, "The Field" Office, | 1883.

1 vol. post 8vo, pp. I-X, 1-485, 1-32 (advt.), frontisp., 32 text-figs. London.

A collection of miscellaneous essays, many of which are of ornithological interest.

Harting, James Edmund.

1891. **Bibliotheca Accipitraria** | A | catalogue of books | ancient and modern | relating to | falconry | with notes, glossary, and vocabulary | by | James Edmund Harting | Librarian to the Linnean Society of London | [*Vignette.*] | London | Bernard Quaritch, 15 Piccadilly | 1891.

1 vol. 8vo, pp. I-XXVIII, 1-289, frontisp. (col.), 25 pll., 4 text-figs. (incl. title-vignette). London.

A bibliography of books on falconry, with numerous quotations and reproductions of illustrations from the works cited and from other sources.

Harting, James Edmund.

1901. **A handbook** | of | **British birds** | showing the distribution of the resident | and migratory species in the | British Islands | with | an index to the records of the rarer visitants | by | J. E. Harting, F.L.S., F.Z.S. | Member of the British Ornithologists' Union | **New and revised edition** | with thirty-five coloured plates, carefully | reproduced from original drawings | by the late Professor Schlegel | London | John C. Nimmo | 14 King William Street, Strand | MDCCCCI.

1 vol. 8vo, pp. I-XXXI+1, 1-520, pll. 1-35 (col.; by Schlegel). London.

An annotated list of species, with a detailed bibliography of the records for rare and accidental visitants to which a separate section of the book is devoted. The colored plates are composed of figures of the heads and feet of the various species. The first edition of this work (which I have not seen) was published in 1872.

Hagerup, Andreas T. (Chamberlain, Montague.)

1891. **The** | **Birds of Greenland.** | By Andreas T. Hagerup. | Translated from the Danish | by | Frimann B. Arngrimson. | Edited by Montague Chamberlain. | Boston: | Little, Brown, and Company. | 1891.

1 vol. 8vo, pp. I-VII, 9-62. Boston.

In the Auk, 6, pp. 211-218 and 291-297, 1889, under editorship of Chamberlain, appeared an account of the birds of southern Greenland from the manuscript of Hagerup. The present work, to p. 39, is a revised and enlarged discussion of the same subject,—a discussion of the habits and occurrence of the birds of Ivigtut, Greenland. Pp. 41-62 comprise a catalogue of 139 species of birds of the whole of Greenland, with annotations on local occurrence and distribution. Chamberlain has added numerous notes throughout the work.

Hartlaub, Carl Johann Gustav.

1846. Erster Nachtrag | zum | Verzeichniss | der | Vögelsamm-
lung | des | Museum's. | Bremen. | Druck von F. C. Dubbers. |
1846.

1 vol. cap 8vo, pp. I-IV, 5-21, (orig. wrappers). Bremen. 1846 (post
Sept.).

A supplement to the author's "Systematisches Verzeichniss der Naturhistorischen
Sammlung des Gesellschaft Museum, Abt. 1, Vögel, Bremen, 1844." The
present work consists of a list of 240 species of birds, with the citation of a
locality (sometimes very general) and a reference to the original description
or a published figure. A number of the species are new and one genus, *Neornis*,
(based on an undescribed species) also is new. However, there are no descriptions and the new names are all nomina nuda. The book, as well as its predecessor, is rare. The preface is dated September.

Hartlaub, Carl Johann Gustav.

1847. Systematischer Index | zu | Don Felix de Azara's | Apun-
tamientos para la historia natural | de los páxaros | del | Paraguay
y Rio de la Plata. | Von | Dr. G. Hartlaub. | Bremen, | Druck von
C. Schünemann. | 1847.

1 vol. demy 4to, pp. I-VI, 1-29. Bremen.

A tabular list of the 448 species of birds given by Azara in his "Apuntamientos"
(Cf. Azara, Voyages dens l'Amerique Meridionale, 1809.) with parallel columns
showing the page-references to two editions of Azara and the nomenclature
according to various authors. The work is extremely useful to the systematist
since it is considerably less rare than the original treatise to which it forms an
index. The present copy has many marginal annotations in the handwriting
of Count Berlepsch.

This work is noted as just published, in the Revue Zoologique for July 1847.

Hartlaub, Carl Johann Gustav.

1857. System | der | Ornithologie Westafrica's | von | Dr. G.
Hartlaub, | auswärtigem Mitgliede [*etc.*, 7 *lines.*] | Bremen, 1857. |
Druck and Verlag von C. Schünemann. | Paris: London: | A.
Franck, Williams & Norgate, | rue Richelieu, 67. 14 Henrietta
Street, Coventgarden.

1 vol. post 8vo, pp. I-LXVI, 1 l., pp. 1-280, 1 l. (insert-folder).
Bremen.

A monograph of the birds of West Africa, with Latin diagnoses, remarks on distribution, synonymies and miscellaneous notes. The preface is dated April 1.

Hartlaub, Carl Johann Gustav.

1861. Ornithologischer Beitrag | zur | Fauna Madagascar's. | Mit
Berücksichtigung der | Inseln Mayotta, Nossi-Bé und St. Marie,
sowie der | Mascarenen und Seychellen. | Von | Dr. G. Hart-

laub, | Mitgliede der [*etc.*, *5 lines.*] | (Mit zahlreichen Berichtigungen und Zusätzen aus Cabanis Journal für Ornithologie | von 1860 besonders abgedruckt.) | Bremen, 1861. | Druck und Verlag von C. Schunemann. | Paris: London: | A. Franck, Williams & Norgate, | rue Richelieu, 67   14, Henrietta Street, Conventgarden (*sic*).

1 vol. post 8vo, pp. I-XII, 1-87. Bremen.

A treatise on the birds of Madagascar, revised and emended from the author's "Systematische Uebersicht der Vögel Madagascars" published in the Journal für Ornithologie, Nos. 43-45, January-May, 1860. The preface is dated Febr. 1, 1861. The present copy is interleaved.

Hartlaub, Carl Johann Gustav.

1867. See Finsch, Otto; and Hartlaub, Gustav, **Beitrag zur Fauna Centralpolynesiens.**

Hartlaub, Carl Johann Gustav.

1870. See Decken, Carl Claus van der, **Baron Carl Claus van der Decken's Reisen in Ost-Afrika** in den Jahren 1859-1865.

Hartlaub, Carl Johann Gustav.

1875. See Mommsen, August, **Griechische Jahreszeiten.**

Hartlaub, Carl Johann Gustav.

1877. Die Vögel | **Madagascars** | und | der benachbarten Inselgruppen. | Ein Beitrag | zur | Zoologie der äthiopischen Region. | Von | G. Hartlaub. | Mit einer kürzlich entdeckten Original-Abbildung der Dronte | von R. Savry. | Halle, | Druck und Verlag von H. W. Schmidt. | 1877.

1 vol. 8vo, pp. I-XLII, 1-425+1, 1 pl. (frontisp.). Halle.

A monograph of the birds of Madagascar and the neighboring islands, with descriptions, synonymies and detailed notes. The present copy was a presentation one and contains a manuscript letter by the author, without address but apparently to E. Perceval Wright, judging by the context.

Hartlaub, Carl Johann Gustav.

1888. See James, F. L., **The Unknown Horn of Africa.**

Harvie-Brown, John Alexander.

1879. The | **capercaillie in Scotland** | By J. A. Harvie-Brown, F.Z.S. | Member of the British Ornithologists' Union, | etc. | [*Vignette.*] | [*Quot.*, *5 lines.*] | Edinburgh: David Douglas | MDCCCLXXIX | [All rights reserved.].

1 vol. 8vo, pp. I-XV+1, 1 l. (subtit.), pp. 1-155, 2 pll., 1 map (col.; fold.). Edinburgh.

A general account of the subject, with studies of the derivation of the name, the history of the species in Scotland and the causes of its former extinction, its reintroduction and subsequent dispersal, and its economic status.

Harvie-Brown, John Alexander; and Buckley, Thomas Edward.

1895. A fauna | of the Moray Basin | by | J. A. Harvie-Brown, | and | Thomas E. Buckley. | Vol. I [II] | David Douglas, Edinburgh, 1895 O.A.J.L. [*Title on illustr. background.*].

2 vols. royal 8vo. Vol. I, pp. I-XXII, 1 l., pp. 1-306, 1 l. (erratum), illum. tit., 13 pll. (1 fold.), 3 text-figs. Vol. II, 4 pr. ll., pp. 1-309, illum. tit., 7 pll. (1 col.), pll. I-IX (3 fold.), 1 map (col.; fold.), 11 text-figs. Edinburgh.

A detailed discussion of the vertebrate fauna of the Moray Basin of Scotland, with chapters on the physical features of the region. A large portion of the work relates to birds. A half-title page reads, "A Vertebrate Fauna | of | the Moray Basin," etc., often quoted as the title. The work forms one of a series of titles published on "The Vertebrate Fauna of Scotland" (Cf. Harvie-Brown and Macpherson, A Fauna of the North-west Highlands & Skye, 1904.). The present copy bears a presentation inscription from Elliott Coues to Mrs. Coues.

Harvie-Brown, John Alexander; and Macpherson, Hugh Alexander. (Macpherson, A. Holte.)

1904. A fauna | of the | north-west highlands | & Skye | by| J. A. Harvie-Brown | and | Rev. H. A. Macpherson. | Edinburgh, David Douglas, 1904. O.A.J.L. [*Title on illustr. background.*].

1 vol. royal 8vo, pp. I-CIV, 1 l., pp. 1-378, 1 l., 8 ll. (advt.), illustr. tit., 18 pll., 3 maps (1 fold., col.), 30 text-figs. Edinburgh.

Historical, topographical and general discussions of the region under consideration are given, with biographical sketches of Thomas Edward Buckley and the junior author (the latter by A. Holte Macpherson), on pp. XXI-CIV; the remainder of the book is zoological. The birds occupy pp. 49-361 and 372. The volume is one of a series on "A Vertebrate Fauna of Scotland" which title appears on a subtitle-page (Cf. Harvie-Brown and Buckley, A Fauna of the Moray Basin, 1895.).

Harvie-Brown, John Alexander.

1905. Travels of a Naturalist | in Northern Europe | Norway, 1871 | Archangel, 1872 | Petchora, 1875 | by | J. A. Harvie-Brown, F.R.S.E., F.Z.S. | Member [*etc., 6 lines.*] | With coloured plates and other illustrations | and 4 maps | Vol. I [II] | London: T. Fisher Unwin | Paternoster Square. MCMV.

2 vols. royal 8vo. Vol. I, pp. I-XIV, 1-260, frontisp., 14 pll., 4 text-

figs., 2 maps. Vol. II, pp. I-VIII, 261-541, frontisp., 9 pll. (2 col.),
3 ll. (expl. of pll.), 31 text-figs., 2 maps. London.

An account, mostly ornithological, of three journeys in northern Europe.

Hasselt, J. C. van.

1820.   See Kuhl, Heinrich, **Beiträge zur Zoologie und vergleichenden Anatomie.**

Hatch, P. L.

1892.   See Nachtrieb, Henry F., The Geological and Natural History Survey of **Minnesota. First Report of the State Zoölogist,** accompanied with **Notes on the Birds of Minnesota.**

Hay, Arthur. [= Walden, Viscount.]

1871.   See Dresser, H. E., **A History of the Birds of Europe,** 1871-82.

Hay, Arthur [= Tweeddale, Marquis of.]

1878.   See Rowley, George D., **Ornithological Miscellany,** 1875-78.

Hay, Arthur [= Tweeddale, Marquis of.]

1881.   See Thomson, C. Wyville, **Reports on the Scientific Results of the Voyage of H. M. S. Challenger; Report on the Birds.**

Hay, Arthur. [= Tweeddale, Arthur, Ninth Marquis of.]   (Ramsay, Robert G. Wardlaw; and Russell, William Howard.)

1881.   The | ornithological works | of | **Arthur, Ninth Marquis of Tweeddale,** | Fellow [*etc., 3 lines.*]. | Reprinted from the originals, | by the desire of his widow. | Edited and revised by his nephew, | Robert C. Wardlaw Ramsay, F.L.S., F.Z.S., M.B.O.U., | Captain 74th Highlanders (late 67th regiment). | Together with a | biographical sketch of the author | by | William Howard Russell, LL.D. | For private circulation. | London: | printed by Taylor and Francis, Red Lion Court, Fleet Street. | 1881.

1 vol. royal 4to, 3 pr. ll. (half-tit., tit. and ded.), pp. III-LXIV, 1-760, frontisp. (portr.), text-figs. 1-8, 1-2 and 1-4. London.

A reprint of Tweeddale's ornithological writings which the editor has altered only in case of "obvious misprints, orthographical errors, or where I (Ramsay) have found corrections in the Author's handwriting." In Appendix I, pp. 653-660, the editor has presented a revised list of Philippine birds, showing details of distribution,—his own work. A lengthy biographical sketch by Russell occupies pp. XIII-LXII.

Hayes, William.

1771-75.   A | natural history | of | British birds | &c. | with their | portraits, | Accurately drawn, and beautifully coloured from

Nature, | By Mr. Hayes. | London: | Printed for S. Hooper, No 25, Ludgate-Hill, | M.DCC.LXXV.

1 vol. imperial folio, title, pp. 1-24, 40 pll. (col.; 2 fold.). London.

A series of hand-colored plates with explanatory text, neither of which is of scientific value. Several introduced species are included in the number. Only 5 pll. have a printed title; the remainder are labeled by hand; none are numbered except in the text. The arrangement of the plates is indescribably mixed in the binding of the present copy.

Hayes, William.

[1771-79?]. [Miscellaneous plates of birds.]

1 vol. superroyal folio, 16 pll. (col.).

An assortment of 16 hand-colored plates, 9 of which are taken from the author's "A Natural History of British Birds," 1771-75 (q.v.). Of these, all are more or less altered in color and rather more finely executed, several have the printed date changed (by hand) from "1771" to "1778," and others have slightly different titles. The remaining 7 plates are dated 1779; 5 of these are of subjects illustrated in the author's "Portraits of Rare and Curious Birds," 1749-79 (q.v.), mostly similar in style but not identical. There is no text or title.

Hayes, William; and family.

1794-99. Portraits | of | rare and curious birds, | with their | descriptions, | from the menagery of Osterly Park, | in the county of Middlesex. | By W. Hayes, and family. | London: | Printed by W. Bulmer and Co. | Shakespeare Printing Office: | and published for the author by R. Faulder, | New Bond-Street. | 1794.

"Idem. Vol. II. London: [etc.] 1799. . . . second vol. has 'Vol. II' on title" (Mullens & Swann).

2 vols. in 1 vol., 4to (text, medium 4to; pll., imperial 4to). Vol. I, 3 pr. ll., pp. 1-50, [frontisp. (col.)], 50 pll. (col.). Vol. II, [2 pr. ll.], pp. 51-101, 50 pll. (col.). London.

A collection of hand-colored etchings, drawn by Hayes and members of his family and accompanied by a short discussion of each subject. The work is rather crude. The present copy is bound in a single volume and lacks the colored frontispiece of Vol. I and the title and preliminary matter of Vol. II, references to which I have quoted from Mullens and Swann.

Hayward, Jane Mary.

1895. Bird notes | by the late | Jane Mary Hayward | edited by Emma Hubbard | with fifteen illustrations from drawings by G. E. Lodge | and frontispiece | London | Longmans, Green, and Co. | and New York: 15 East 16th Street | 1895 | All rights reserved.

1 vol. crown 8vo, pp. I-XVII+1, 1 l., pp. 1-181, 1-24 (advt.), frontisp. (scenic), 15 text-figs. London and New York.

Notes on the bird-life of an English garden; frequently protracted observations on the same individual birds. Entirely popular but showing evidence of close and sympathetic observation.

Headley, Frederick Webb.

1895. The structure | and | life of birds | by | F. W. Headley, M.A., F.Z.S. | Assistant Master at Haileybury College | with seventy-eight illustrations | London | Macmillan and Co. | and New York | 1895 | The Right of Translation and Reproduction is Reserved.

1 vol. demy 8vo, 3 pr. ll., pp. IX-XX, 1-412, frontisp., text-figs. 1-77. London.

A discussion of the origin, anatomy, physiology, development, habits and many other phenomena of bird existence, treated in a non-technical manner.

Headley, Frederick Webb.

1912. The | flight of birds | By F. W. Headley, M.B.O.U. | Author of "The Structure and Life of Birds" | "Life and Evolution" &c. | With sixteen plates | and many text-figures | Witherby & Co. | 326 High Holborn London | 1912.

1 vol. crown 8vo, pp. I-X, 1-163, pll. I-XVI, text-figs. 1-27. London.

A thorough discussion of the flight of birds, the mechanics underlying it and the physiological and anatomical adaptations developed for it.

Healy, Michael A. (McLenegan, S. B.; Townsend, Charles H.)

1887. Report | of the | cruise of the Revenue Marine Steamer | Corwin | in the | Arctic Ocean | in | the year 1885 | by |Capt. M. A. Healy, U.S.R.M., | Commander. | Washington: | Government Printing Office. | 1887.

1 vol. imperial 8vo, pp. 1-102, 42 pll. (4 col.; 1 of birds, by J. L. Ridgway), 2 maps, 3 text-cuts. Washington.

Pp. 1-20 contain the general report by Healy; 21-52, a narrative of the exploration of the Kowak River, Alaska, by John C. Cantwell; 53-80, McLenegan's account of the exploration of the Noätak River, Alaska, with an annotated list of 48 species of birds on pp. 76-80; and 81-102 "Notes on the Natural History and Ethnology of Northern Alaska" by Townsend, of which pp. 98-101 are ornithological, containing an annotated list of 49 species of birds.

Hecla and Fury, Journal of a Third Voyage for the Discovery of a North-west Passage, in the—.

1826. See Parry, William Edward.

Heermann, Adolphus L.
1859. See U. S. Pacific Railroad Surveys, **Reports of Explorations and Surveys . . . for a Railroad from the Mississippi River to the Pacific Ocean, Vol. X.**

Heidecke, Ernst.
1897. **Ueber den Schnabelwulst | des jugendlichen Sperlings. |** Inaugural-Dissertation | zur | Erlangung der Doktorwürde | der | Hohen philosophischen Fakultät | der | Universität Leipzig | vorgelegt von | Ernst Heidecke | appr. Zahnarzt | aus Breitenworbis. | Leipzig | 1897.
1 vol. 8vo, pp. 1-50, 1 l., 1 pl. (fold.). Leipzig.
A detailed study of certain structures in the bills of young sparrows.

Heine, Ferdinand.
1860-63. See Cabanis, Jean Louis; and Heine, **Museum Heineanum,** 1851-63.

Heine, Ferdinand; and Reichenow, Anton.
1890. **Nomenclator | Musei Heineani Ornithologici. |** Verzeichniss der Vogel-Sammlung | des | Königlichen Oberamtmanns Ferdinand Heine | auf Klostergut St. Burchard vor Halberstadt, | herausgegeben
von | Ferdinand Heine und Anton Reichenow |
auf Kloster Hadmersleben in Berlin. |
Berlin. | R. Friedländer & Sohn. | 1882 bis 1890.
1 vol. superoyal 8vo, pp. I-VI, 1-373, frontisp. (portr.). Berlin.
A catalogue of the birds in the collection of Ferdinand Heine, arranged in systematic order. Type specimens are indicated by an asterisk. Many new names are employed, a large number of which are synonyms. The work was printed from 1882 to 1890 as indicated in the dated signatures, but the work was not issued until 1890, the preface being dated in September of that year. The senior author was the son of the founder of the collection.

Hellmayr, Charles Edward.
1903. **Das Tierreich. |** Eine Zusammenstellung und Kennzeichnung der | rezenten Tierformen. | Begrundet von der Deutschen Zoologischen Gesellschaft. | Im Auftrage der | Königl. Preuss. Akademie der Wissenschaften zu Berlin | herausgegeben von | Franz Eilhard Schulze. | [*Quot.*] | **18. Lieferung. |** Aves. | Beirat: A. Reichenow. | **Paridae, Sittidae und Certhiidae |** bearbeitet von | C. E. Hellmayr | in München. | Mit 76 Abbildungen. | Berlin. | Verlag von R. Friedländer und Sohn. | Ausgegeben im März 1903.

1 vol. (pt.) superroyal 8vo, pp. I-XXXI+1, 1-255, 1 text-fig. (topography of bird), text-figs. 1-75. March 1903.

A monograph of the families of Titmice, Nuthatches and Tree-creepers, with more or less detailed descriptions and synonymies, tables to the subfamiles, genera and species, a bibliography and a "Nomenclator generum et subgenerum." See also under "Tierreich."

Hellmayr, Charles Edward.

1906. See Ménégaux, Auguste; and Hellmayr, **Etude des especes critiques et des types du groupe Passereaux Tracheophones de l'Amerique tropicale.**

Hellmayr, Charles Edward.

1910-13. See Wytsman, Paul, **Genera Avium,** 1905-14.

Hellmayr, Charles Edward.

1914. See Haniel, C. B., **Zoologie von Timor.**

Hellmayr, Charles Edward; and Laubmann, Alfred.

1916. Nomenclator der Vögel Bayerns. | Von | C. E. Hellmayr und A. Laubmann. | Im Auftrage der | Ornithologischen Gesellschaft in Bayern | herausgegeben | von | C. E. Hellmayr | Kustos der Ornithologischen Abteilung [*etc., 2 lines.*] | Ausgegeben am 30. Mai 1916. | München 1916 | Im Buchhandel zu beziehen durch die Verlagsbuchhandlung | Gustav Fischer in Jena.

1 vol. 8vo, pp. I-VIII, 1-68. Munich. May 30, 1916.

A critical review of the nomenclature of Bavarian birds. Pt. I (pp. 1-33) contains a check-list of species, giving for each the accepted Latin name (binomial or trinomial), the preferred vernacular name, the reference to the original description, the quotation of original name and type locality as given by the describer, and the type locality as defined at present. Pt. II (pp. 33-35) contains a similar list for species the records of whose local occurrence are questionable. Pt. III (pp. 35-55) is devoted to a list of genera with original references and type-designations. A first supplement was published by Laubmann in the Verh. Orn. Ges. Bayerns, **15**, Heft 2, pp. 187-246, **1922.**

Hemprich, Friedrich Wilhelm.

1828-33. See Ehrenberg, **Symbolae Physicae.**

Henderson, George; and Hume, Allan Octavian.

1873. Lahore to Yarkand. | Incidents of the route | and | Natural History | of the | countries traversed | by | the expedition of 1870, | under | T. D. Forsyth, Esq., C.B. | By | George Henderson, M.D., F.L.S., F.R.G.S. | Medical Officer to the Expedition, Officiating Superintendent | of the Botanic Gardens, Calcutta; |

and | Allan O. Hume, Esq., C.B., F.Z.S. | Secretary to the Government of India, for the Department | of Agriculture, Revenue and Commerce. | London: | L. Reeve & Co., 5, Henrietta St., Covent Garden. | 1873.

1 vol. royal 8vo, pp. I-XIV, 1 l. (subtit.), pp. 1-370, 1 l.+pp. 1-16 (advt.), pll. I-XXXII (col.; of birds; by Keulemans), 25 pll. (unnum.; 8 col.), 1 map (col.; fold.), 26 text-figs. (17 of birds). London. 1873 (antea July).

Part I, pp. 1-150, contains Henderson's narrative of the expedition, including various casual notes on birds. Part II, pp. 151-346, is devoted to natural history and the major part, pp. 153-304 with pll. I-XXXII and 17 text-figs. consists of the ornithological results of the expedition discussed by Hume. The entomological report appears to be by H. W. Bates and the botanical one by Henderson and J. D. Hooker. Part III and the Appendix are meteorological. The ornithological report contains descriptions of several new species and detailed discussions of others, including field-notes by Henderson. The work is reviewed in the Ibis for July, 1873.

Henshaw, Henry Wetherbee.

1874. See Yarrow, H. C.; and Henshaw, Engineer Department, U. S. Army, **Report upon Ornithological Specimens collected in the Years 1871, 1872, and 1873.**

Henshaw, Henry Wetherbee.

1875. See Wheeler, George Montague, **Report on United States Geographical Surveys west of the one hundredth meridian,** Vol. V, Chap. III, Report on the Ornithological Collections made in Portions of Nevada, Utah, etc.

Henshaw, Henry Wetherbee.

1886. See American Ornithologists' Union, **The Code of Nomenclature and Check-list of North American Birds.**

Henshaw, Henry Wetherbee.

1892. See American Ornithologists' Union, **The Code of Nomenclature.**

Hepburn, Archibald.

1840. See Macgillivray, William, **A History of British Birds,** 1847-40.

Herman, Otto.

1905. Magyar Ornithologiai Központ | Hungarian Central Office of Ornithology | **Recensio critica** | **automatica** | of the | **doctrine of bird-migration** | by | Otto Herman | late Member of the Hun-

TABULA
AFFINITATUM
ANIMALIUM

OLIM ACADEMICO SPECIMINE EDITA

NUNC

UBERIORE COMMENTARIO

ILLUSTRATA

CUM ANNOTATIONIBUS

AD HISTORIAM NATURALEM ANIMALIUM

AUGENDAM FACIENTIBUS.

AUCTORE

JOHANNE HERMANN

M. D. ET PROF.

ARGENTORATI 1783.

Impenfis JOH. GEORGII TREUTTEL , Bibliopolæ.

TITLE-PAGE OF HERMANN'S "TABULA AFFINITATUM ANIMALIUM."
See p. 299.

garian Parliament, [etc., 16 lines.]. | With one map. | Budapest | Printed by order of the Royal Hungarian Ministry of | Agriculture | 1905.

1 vol. medium 4to, pp. I-IX+1, 1-74, 1 map. Budapest.

An essay on bird-migration with analyses of published articles on the subject, a classification of the various problems involved and bibliographic references to each, and recommendations for further study.

Hermann, Johann.

1783. **Tabula** | **affinitatum** | **animalium** | olim academico specimine edita | nunc | uberiore commentario | illustrata | cum annotationibus | ad historiam naturalem animalium | augendam facientibus. | Auctore | Johanne Hermann | M.D. et Prof. | Argentorati 1783. | Impensis Joh. Georgii Treuttel, Bibliopolæ.

1 vol. demy 4to, 2 pr. ll. (tit. and ded.), pp. 1-370, 1 l., 3 inserts (fold.; tables), various decorations. Strasburg.

A detailed study of the classification of the vertebrates, in which the birds are discussed on pp. 131-235 and the first insert. The work is very important because binomial names are given for the first time to many species previously described or figured under vernacular names in Buffon's "Histoire Naturelle Générale; Oiseaux," 1749, and Daubenton's accompanying plates (Cf. Buffon, Hist. Nat. des Oiseaux, 1770-86). A review of the new names in Hermann is given by Stresemann in the Novit. Zool. **27**, pp. 327-332, 1920. The actual date of publication is unknown but is supposed to be prior to Boddaert's "Table de Planches Enluminées" (Cf. Reprint, 1874.) which also proposes names for species described in Buffon. The book is quite rare.

Hermann, Johann. (Hammer, Friedrich Ludwig.)

1804. Johannis Hermann | Phil. et Med. Doct., [etc., 4 lines.] | **observationes** | **zoologicae** | qubus novae complures, aliaeque | animalium species | describuntur et illustrantur | opus posthumim | editit | Fridericus Ludovicus Hammer | Hist. natur. Prof. Societ. Agric. Scient. et Artium Argentor. sodalis | pars prior | observationum quatuor centurias continens | Argentorati | apud Amandum Koenig, bibliopolam | Parisiis | apud eundem, a ripam Augustinorum No 31 | XII (1804).

1 vol. demy 4to, pp. I-VIII, 1-332, frontisp. (portr.). Strasburg and Paris.

Previously unpublished notes and descriptions by Hermann, edited and published by Hammer with occasional notes added by the latter. Some of the descriptions which, apparently, were not in Latin in the manuscript, have been translated into Latin to agree with the remainder of the text, but these translations are so marked and all editorial notes are specified and enclosed in parentheses or brackets. There would appear to be no occasion to quote Hammer as the author of any of the new names as has been done by some recent workers. There are numerous new species and genera described in the work, not all of which have been identified in recent years.

The volume, although called "pars prior," is the only portion of the work published, and contains descriptions of vertebrates, only. The birds occupy pp. 93-215. Later portions were planned to deal with insects, worms, zoophytes, etc., and illustrations were in course of preparation, but these were never issued.

Herrick, Francis Hobart.

1902. The Home Life | of Wild Birds | [*Fig.*] | A New Method of | the Study and | Photography of Birds | by | Francis Hobart Herrick | With 141 Original Illustrations from Nature | by the Author | G. P. Putnam's Sons | The Knickerbocker Press | New York and London | 1902.

1 vol. 8vo (size of demy 4to), pp. I-XIX+1, 1-148, 1 l. (advt.), 1 printed guard-sheet, frontisp. (photograv.), text-figs. 1-130, 8 text-figs. (unnum.). New York and London.

The discussion of a method of bird-photography advocated by the author,-that of moving the nest, when necessary, to situations most favorable to the photographer, rather than attempting to secure the picture under trying conditions. Detailed studies of a number of species are given, illustrated with photographs taken by the proposed method.

Herrick, Francis Hobart.

1917. Audubon | the | naturalist | a history of his life and time | by | Francis Hobart Herrick, Ph.D., Sc.D. | Professor of Biology in Western Reserve University; | Author of "The Home Life of Wild Birds," etc. | In two volumes | illustrated | [*Blazon.*] | Volume I [II] | D. Appleton and Company | New York London | 1917.

2 vols. post 8vo. Vol. I, pp. I-XL, 1 l., pp. 1-451, 34 pll. (1 col., after Audubon; on 31 ll.) 22 text-figs. (facsimiles). Vol. II, pp. I-XIII+1, 1 l., pp. 1-494, 23 pll. (3 col.; after Audubon), 12 text-figs. (facsimiles, etc.). Medallion (portr.) on covers of both volumes. New York and London.

A detailed, sympathetic account of the life of Audubon, with facsimiles and transcripts of numerous documents, copies of portraits of the naturalist, his family and contemporaries, photographs of scenes of particular interest, and reproductions of many paintings and drawings (four of them in colors). A bibliography of articles by, and relating to, Audubon is included.

Hervieux de Chanteloup, J. C.

1718. A | New treatise | of | Canary-Birds. | Containing | The manner of Breeding and | Coupling them, that they may | have Beautiful Young Ones. | With | Curious Remarks relating to the | Signs and Causes of their Distem- | pers, and the Method of

Curing them. | Written in French by Mr. Hervieux, | and Translated into English. | London: | Printed for Bernard Lintot, at the | Cross-Keys between the Temple-Gates: | And Benjamin Barker, and Charles King | in Westminster-Hall, 1718.

1 vol. 12mo, 4 pr. ll., pp. 1-163, 5 pp. (advt.), 2 pll. London.

A curious little volume, the original edition of which (in French) was published in 1705.

Hetherington, W. H.

1831. See Wilson, Alexander; and Bonaparte, **American Ornithology**

Heuglin, Martin Theodor von. (Finsch, Otto.)

1869-75. Ornithologie Nordost-Afrika's | der | Nilquellen- und Küsten-Gebiete | des | Rothen Meeres und des nördlichen Somal-Landes | von | M. Th. von Heuglin. | In vier Theilen. | Mit 51 Tafeln Abbildungen (nach der Natur gezeichnet vom | Verfasser) und mit einer zoo-geographischen Karte. | Cassel. | Verlag von Theodor Fischer. | 1869-1874.

2 vols. royal 8vo. Vol. I, tit., pp. (I-IV) (subtit. Vol. I, Pt. 1 and dedication), A-H (table of contents), 1 l. (corrections), pp. V-CVIII (introd.), 1 l. (note by author), 1-416 (synopsis of species, partim), pll. I, II, III, IV, VI, VII (*Atticora*), VII (*Cisticola*), VIIIa, VIIIb, IX, X, XI, XIIa, XIIb, XIII and XIV; 2 ll. (subtit. Vol. I, Pt. 2, 1 l. (notice to subscribers), pp. 417-851+1 (continuation of text), pll. XV, XVI, XVII, XX, XXI, XIXa, XVIII, XIX. (Hyphantornis), XIX (Ortygospiza, etc.), XXIa, XXIII, XXIIIb, XXIV, XXVb, XXVI, XXVII and XXVIII. Vol. II, 1 l. (subtit. Vol. II, Pt. 1), pp. 853-1261+1 (continuation of text), pll. XXIX, XXX, XXXI, XXXII, XXXIII, XXXIV and XXXV; subtit. (Vol. II, Pt. 2), pp. 1263-1512 (continuation of text), pll. XXXVI, XXXVII, XXXVIII, XXXIX, XL, XLIII, XLII, XLVIII, IL, L and LI, 1 map; subtit. ("Nachträge und Berichtigungen"), 1 l. (foreword), pp. I-CCCXXV (appendix and indices). Cassel.

A technical account of the birds of north-east Africa, with Latin diagnoses and detailed synonymies. The work was published in 57 parts of which the actual dates of publication appear to be indeterminable. From the Zoological Record and the Journal für Ornithologie, it would seem that the double part, Nos. **1-2,** pp. 1-64, pll. I, II, XXV and XXVI was issued before March, 1869; Nos. **3-4** and **5-6,** pp. 65-142, pll. IX, XIII, XV, XXX, VI, XVI, XVII and XIX, before Sept. 1869; Nos. **7-11,** pp. 143-416, pll. ?, before Dec. 31, 1869; Nos. **12-15,** pp. ?, pll. XXIXa, XXIII, X and XI, before July, 1870; Nos. **16-17,** pp. ? -656, pll. VII and XXVb, before Oct. 3, 1870; Nos. **18-19** and **20-21,** before March, 1871 and **22-23,** before Sept. 1871 (Nos. **18-23** with pp. 657-852, pll. XVIII, XXX, and XIV); Nos. **24-27,** pp. I-XLVIII (Nachträge) and 853-916, pll.

II (?), II, XLII and XLIII, in 1872; Nos. **28-43**, pp. 917-1512, pll. XXXVII, XL, XIIb, XXI, XXXVIII, XXXIX, VIIIa and VIIIb, 1873; Nos. **44-57**, pp. ?, pll. ?, in 1874 or 1875?. There is only one general title-page,—at the beginning of the first volume. There are five subtitles,—one each for Vol. I, Pt. 1; Vol. I, Pt. 2; Vol. II, Pt. 1; Vol. II, Pt. 2; and the "Nachträge und Berichtigungen. . . Mit Beitragen von Dr. O. Finsch," included in Vol. II. The last consists of additions and corrections to the text of the main work, with annotations by Finsch, and, at first sight, appears to be a separate work, with distinct title and signatures. It is, however, part of the main work, issued in parts from time to time with the general series, and is included in the general table of contents. The 51 plates and the map are given new numbers in the table of contents.

Heuglin, Martin Theodor von.

1877. **Reise in Nordost-Afrika.** | Schilderungen | aus dem | Gebiete der Beni Amer und Habab | nebst zoologischen Skizzen | und einem Führer für Jagdreisende | von | M. Th. v. Heuglin. | Zwei Bände. | Erster [Zweiter] Band. | Mit einer Karte [drei colorirten Tafeln] und sieben [drei] Illustrationen. | Braunschweig, | Druck und Verlag von George Westermann. | 1877.

2 vols. in 1 vol., post 8vo. Vol. I, pp. I-XIV, 1 l., pp. 1-285, 7 pll. (1 ornithological), 1 map (col.; fold.). Vol. II, pp. I-VI, 1 l., pp. 1-304, 6 pll. (3 col.; 2 ornithological). Braunschweig.

An account of the author's travels in northeastern Africa in 1875. Vol. I contains the narrative with occasional ornithological notes and 1 bird-plate; Vol. II consists of a report on the mammals and birds of which pp. 141-270, 279-286 and 291-293 and 2 colored plates are ornithological.

Hewitson, William Chapman.

1831-42. **British oology;** | being | illustrations | of the | eggs of British birds, | with figures of each species, | as far as practicable, | drawn and coloured from nature: | accompanied by | descriptions of the materials and situation of their nests, | number of eggs, &c. | By William C. Hewitson | Vol. I [II; (III)]- | [*Quot.*, 11 *lines*; 7 *lines.* (*Vol. II.*).] | Newcastle upon Tyne: | Published for the author, | by Charles Empson [Currie and Bowman], 32, Collingwood Street.

> [Idem. Supplement, issued without title.]

3 (4) vols. in 3, 8vo. Vol. I, 2 pr. ll., pp. 1-15+1 (introd.), (1 l., insert, index to English names, issued with Supplement), pp. 1-4 (index), 81 ll., 72 pll. (col.). Vol. II, 2 pr. ll., (1 l., insert, index to English names, issued with Supplement), pp. 5-8 (index), 91 ll., 83 pll. (col.). Newcastle. 1831-38.

Supplement, 15 ll. (+2 ll. transferred to Vols. I and II, q.v.), 14 pll. (col.). London. October 1, 1842.

The book consists of an account of the breeding habits of the various species of British birds, with colored plates of their eggs. It was issued in 37 parts, not including the supplement, from April 1, 1831, to June 1, 1838. With Pt. XXXVII was issued a title-page to Vol. III with, however, a recommendation to subscribers to have the work bound in two volumes, as was done with the present copy. The third title-page is missing from this copy. The plates are hand-colored and are not arranged in numerical sequence. Two later editions were issued under a slightly different title, as "Coloured Illustrations of the Eggs of British Birds," etc., 1842-46 and 1853-56 (q.v.). The present work was, of necessity, printed at various times and in various places, according to a statement by the author in the third edition of the work, and a complete collation would be unwieldy even if it were available.

Hewitson, William Chapman.

1842-46. Coloured illustrations | of the | eggs of British birds, | accompanied with descriptions | of the | eggs, nests, etc. | By | William C. Hewitson. | In two volumes. | Vol. I [II]. | London: | John Van Voorst, Paternoster Row. | M.DCCC.XLVI.

2 vols. post 8vo. Vol. I, pp. I-XVI, 1-223+1, 34*+1, 89*-90*, 140* +1, pll. I-LIX, XII*, XXV*, XXXVII* (=62 pll., col.). Vol. II, 2 pr. ll., pp. 225-470, 247*-248, 283*+1, 368*+1, 430*+1, pll. LX-CXXXI, LXVII*, LXXVIII*, CI*, CXX* (=76 pll., col.). London.

Said to have been issued in monthly parts from 1842 to 1846. The work is something more than a new edition of the earlier "British Oology," 1831-42 (q.v.), since the text is rewritten and enlarged and the plates are different. Plate LXV is wrongly numbered LXI. There are several printed corrections interleaved in the copy, the source of which I do not know; they are probably cut from a page of emendations. There is a third edition, 1853-56, under the same short title as the present one (q.v.).

Hewitson, William Chapman.

1853-56. Coloured illustrations | of the | eggs of British birds, | with descriptions of | their nests and nidification. | By | William C. Hewitson. | **Third edition.** | In two volumes. | Vol. I [II]. | London: | John Van Voorst, Paternoster Row. | M.DCCC.LVI.

2 vols. post 8vo. Vol. I, pp. I-XVI, 1-289+1, 178*+1, 202*+1, 210*+1, pll. I-LXXIV, XLV*, LI*, LIII* (=77 pll., col.). Vol. II, 2 pr. ll., pp. 290-532, 290*, 334*+1, pll. LXXV-CXLV, XC* (=72 pll., col.). London.

Said to have been issued in 38 parts from May 1853, to June 1856. This edition is enlarged further than the second, 1842-46 (q.v.), and is partly rewritten and supplied with different plates.

Hilgert, Carl.

1908. Katalog | der | Collection von Erlanger | in | Nieder-Ingel-heim a.Rh. | von | Carl Hilgert. | Berlin 1908. | Verlag von R. Friedländer & Sohn.

1 vol. 8vo, pp. I-VII+1, 1-527, frontisp. Berlin.

A catalogue of 12,589 birskins and 1,140 sets of birds' eggs in the collection of Carlo von Erlanger, the majority of which appear to be from portions of Africa.

Hill, J. W.

[1844.] [Illustrations for DeKay's "Zoology of New York."]

1 vol. (8½x11 in.). Not published.

A series of 94 original water-color drawings, 76 of birds and 18 of insects, the originals of the corresponding plates in DeKay's "Zoology of New York," 1844 (q.v.). The drawings are trimmed to approximately 4¼x6½ in., and are mounted on cardboard.

Hill, Richard.

1847. See Gosse, Philip Henry, **The Birds of Jamaica.**

Hinds, Richard Brinsley. (Gould, John.)

1843-44. No. III (IV).] [Price 10s. | **The** | **zoology** | **of** | **the voyage of H. M. S. Sulphur,** | under the command of | Captain Sir Edward Belcher, R.N., C.B., F.R.G.S., etc. | during the years 1836-42. | Published under the authority of | the Lords Commissioners of the Admiralty. | Edited and Superintended by | Richard Brinsley Hinds, Esq., Surgeon, R.N. | attached to the expedition. | Birds, | by | John Gould, Esq., F.R.S., etc. | London: | published by Smith, Elder and Co. 65, Cornhill. | MDCCCXLIII [MDCCC-XLIV]. | **Birds.-Part I [II].** October, 1843 [January, 1844]. | Stewart and Murray, Old Bailey. [*Cover titles.*].

2 parts, royal 4to. No. III (Birds,-Pt. I.), pp. 37-44, pll. 19-26 (col.; by Gould and Waterhouse Hawkins). No. IV (Birds.-Pt. II.), pp. 45-50, pll. 27-34 (col.; by Gould). Copy in original wrappers. London.

The ornithology of the voyage (by Gould) forming Pts. III and IV of the complete zoological report, issued in 12 parts from 1843-45. A number of new species of birds described herein are cited as having been previously diagnosed by the author in the Proceedings of the Zoological Society of London for 1843. Those which occur in Pt. IV (Birds.-II) may be quoted from the Proceedings; those in Pt. III (Birds,-I) must be quoted from the present paper since the pages of the Proceedings on which they occur were not issued until December, 1843, two months after the date of this part of the present work (as shown by the covers).

Hodder, Frank Heywood.

1906. See Audubon, John Woodhouse, **Audubon's Western Journal: 1849-50.**

Hoffman, Ralph.

1904. **A guide to the | birds of New England | and | eastern New York** | containing a key for each season and short | descriptions of over two hundred and | fifty species with particular refer- | ence to their appearance | in the field | by | Ralph Hoffman | Member of the American Ornithologists' Union | with four full-page plates by Louis | Agassiz Fuertes and nearly | one hundred cuts in | the text | [*Trade-mark.*] | Boston and New York | Houghton, Mifflin and Company | The Riverside Press, Cambridge.

1 vol. crown 8vo, pp. I-XIII+1, 1-357+1, 2 ll. (advt.), 4 pll. (by Fuertes), 95 text-cuts, 1 text-map. Boston and New York. April 1904.

A manual of the birds of eastern New York, northern New Jersey and New England, in which "every effort has been made to emphasize the aspect of birds as seen out of doors, to describe their general or most prominent colors rather than any mark difficult to see on the living bird, and to call attention to their characteristic habits and haunts." This purpose the author has accomplished with signal success and his characterizations are concise and decisive. Keys, based on these sorts of characters, are given for March, April and May and for summer, autumn and winter. Local lists of breeding birds, arranged by life-zones, and a list of reference works are appended.

Hoffman, W. J.

1881. **Annotated List of the Birds of Nevada.** < Bull. U. S. Geol. Geog. Surv. Terr., **6**, No. 2, pp. 203-256, 2 pll., 1 map, 1881.

An annotated list of species, preceded by "remarks on the distribution of vegetation in Nevada as affecting that of the avi-fauna."

Holböll, Carl. (Paulsen, J. H.)

1846. **Ornithologischer Beitrag | zur | Fauna Groenlands | von |** Carl Holböll. | Uebersetzt und mit einem Anhang versehen | von | J. H. Paulsen, | Dr. Med. | [*Monogram.*] | Leipzig, | Ernst Fleisch-er. | 1846.

1 vol. 8vo, pp. I-X, 1-102 (interleaved), frontisp. (col.; by Fr. Nau-mann). Leipzig.

A study of the birds of Greenland. Originally published by Holböll under the title of "Ornithologiske Bidrag til den grønlandiske Fauna," in Krøyer's Natur-historisk Tidskrift, **4** (4), pp. 361-457, 1843, whence are dated the new species described herein. Translated by Paulsen and supplemented by an 'Anhang,' pp. 85-102, for issue in the present form, and again reissued in 1854.

Holmer, M. R. N.

1923. **Indian bird-life** | by | M. R. N. Holmer | [*Blazon.*] |Humphrey Milford | Oxford University Press | London Bombay Calcutta Madras | 1923.

1 vol. crown 8vo, pp. I-IX+1, 1 l., pp. 1-100, frontisp. (fold.; col.), (vignette on wrapper). London, Bombay, Calcutta, Madras.

A popular guide to the study of the birds of India in the field.

Holub, Emil; and Pelzeln, August von.

1882. **Beiträge | zur | Ornithologie Südafrikas.** | Mit besonderer Berücksichtigung | der von Dr. Holub auf seinen südafrikanischen Reisen gesammelten | und im Pavillon des Amateurs zu Wien ausgestellten Arten. | Von | Dr. Emil Holub und Aug. von Pelzeln. | Mit 2 Tafeln in Farbendruck, Holzschnitten und 32 Zinkographien [Mit 3 Tafeln in Farbendruck, einer Karte und 94 Holzschnitten]. | Wien. | Alfred Hölder, k. k. Hof- und Universitäts-Buchhändler. | 1882.

1 vol. (royal 8vo, pp. I-VIII, 9-384, 1 l. (errata), pll. I-III (col.; by J. Sommer), I-II (figs. 1-32; on pp. 363 and 365), 57 text-figs., 1 map (col.). Vienna.

A discussion, in systematic order, of the birds secured or observed in southern Africa by Emil Holub. The various paragraphs are initialed by the authors; those by Holub consisting of field-notes and observations, those by Pelzeln being of a more technical nature. Two species are described as new. The title on the wrapper differs from that on the title-page only in the number of illustrations cited; that on the wrapper is the more accurate, although not perfectly correct. The variations are given in brackets in the above citation. The reasons for the alteration are given by the author on p. 359.

Holub, Emil.

1896. See World's Congress on Ornithology, **Papers presented to the —.**

Hölting, Heinrich.

1912. **Über den mikroskopischen Bau | der Speicheldrüsen einiger Vögel** | (Gallus domesticus, Perdix cinerea, | Anser domesticus, Anas, Picus viridis, | Garrulus glandarius, Lanius excubitor, | Corvus frugilegus, Fringilla coelebs) | Inagural-Dissertation | zur | Erlangung der veterinär-medizinischen Doktorwürde | der | vereinigten medizinischen Fakultät | der Grossherzoglich Hessischen Ludwigs-Universität | zu Giessen | vorgelegt von | Heinrich Hölting | Tierarzt | Hannover | M. & H. Schaper | 1912.

1 vol. 8vo, pp. 1-38, 1 l., (orig. wrappers), pll. 1-6 (5 col.). Hannover.

An anatomical study of the salivary glands in certain birds.

Hombron; and Jacquinot, Honoré.

1842-54. See Dumont d'Urville, J., **Voyage au Pole Sud et dans l'Océanie sur les Corvettes l'Astrolabe et la Zélée, Zoologie.**

Homeyer, Eugen Ferdinand von.

1881. Ornithologische Briefe. | Blätter der Erinnerung | an | seine Freunde | gesammelt von | E. F. von Homeyer. | Berlin. | Verlag von Theobald Grieben. | 1881.

1 vol. post 8vo, pp. I-VI, 1-340, 5 text-figs. Berlin.

Portions of the author's correspondence (from about 1832 to date) with various ornithologists, including Gätke, Radde, Bädeker, Meyer, Landbeck, Kjär-bölling, Wied, Gloger, Thienemann, Brehm, J. F. Naumann, Tschusi, and others. In addition to biographical details of interest, the work contains a quantity of ornithological matter that probably never found its way into print under its own titles.

Hornaday, William Temple.

1913. Our vanishing | wild life | its | extermination and preservation | by | William T. Hornaday, Sc.D. | Director of the New York Zoological Park [*etc., 3 lines.*] | with maps and illustrations | [*Quot., 2 lines.*] | New York | New York Zoological Society | 1913.

1 vol. 8vo, pp. I-XV+1, 1-411, 1 p. (advt.), 95 text-cuts. New York.

A stirring appeal for the preservation of wild life, giving a comprehensive survey of the situation to date and recommendations for the future. Birds occupy a large portion of the discussion.

Horsbrugh, Boyd.

1912. The | game-birds & water-fowl | of | South Africa | by Major Boyd Horsbrugh | Member of the British Ornithologists' Union [*etc., 2 lines.*] | with coloured plates | By Sergeant C. G. Davies (Cape Mounted Riflemen), M.B.O.U., M.S.A.O.U. | London: | Witherby & Co. 326 High Holborn | 1912.

1 vol. demy 4to, pp. I-XII, 1-159, pll. 1-45, 46a, 46B, 46c, 47-65 (=67 pll., col.). London.

An account of the various species of game-birds and water-fowl of South Africa, with brief synonymies, local names, short descriptions, remarks on distribution and interesting notes on habits, etc. The illustrations are excellent.

Horsfield, Thomas; and Moore, Frederic.

1854-58. A catalogue | of | the birds | in | The Museum | of | the Hon. East India Company. | By | Thomas Horsfield, M. & Ph.D., F.R.S., [Keeper of the Company's Museum, | and | Frederic Moore, | Assistant. | Vol. I [II]. | Printed by Order of the Court of Directors. | [*Blazon.*] | London: | Wm. H. Allen and Co. |

Booksellers to the Hon. East-India Company, | 7, Leadenhall Street. | 1856-8.

2 vols. in 1 vol., 4to (size of post 8vo). Vol. I, 2 pr. ll. (half-tit. and tit.), pp. III-XXX, 1-451+1. Vol. II, tit., pp. 453-752, I-V+1 (index to native names in Vol. II), I-IV (index to generic names, Vol. II), I-IX (index to specific names, Vol. II). London.

A catalogue of the species of birds in the collection of the East India Company, with synonymy, native names, lists of specimens and numerous discussions or descriptions, often quoted from other authors. Various species are renamed or described as new by the junior author although many of the new species are accredited to Moore in reference to papers published by him in the Proc. Zool. Society of London, 1854 and 1855. These names, likewise, have been quoted from the Proc. Zool. Soc. London by recent authors, although some of them should date from the present work.

Vol. I of the "Catalogue" was published late in 1854, in spite of the date (1856-8) on the title-page. The Appendix No. II (pp. 414-423) containing some errata for the volume, is signed "August 19th, 1854" and the preface, presumably written when the rest of the volume was already printed, is dated Sept. 15. Furthermore, Hartlaub, in the following year (Journ. für Orn., 3, pp. 317-320), reviews the work as having been published in 1854. On the other hand, the Proc. Zool. Soc. London for 1854 was all published in 1855 except pp. 1-32 (containing some descriptions of five new species of the genus *Ruticilla* by Moore) and these came out on Dec. 30, 1854. With the very improbable exception of the new species of *Ruticilla*, therefore, all the new species in Vol. I must date from the "Catalogue." The new names in Vol. II, accredited to the Proc. Zool. Soc. London for 1855 date from the journal in question. Vol. II was received by the Boston Society of Natural History during the quarter ending Dec. 31, 1858.

Horvath, Geza.

1901. See Zichy, Jenö, **Dritte Asiatische Forschungsreise.**

Houttuyn, Martinus.

1772-81. See Edwards, George; and Catesby, **Verzameling van Uitlandsche en Zeldzaame Vogelen.**

Houttuyn, Martinus.

1797-1829. See Nozeman, Cornelius, **Nederlandsche Vogelen,** 1770-1829.

Howard, Henry Eliot.

1907-15. The | **British warblers** | a history with problems | of | their lives | by | H. Eliot Howard, F.Z.S., M.B.O.U. | Illustrated by Henrik Grönvold | Vol. I [II] | With 17 [18] Coloured and 30 [21] Photogravure Plates and 4 [8] Maps | London | R. H. Porter | 7, Princes Street, Cavendish Square, W. | 1907-1914.

2 vols. in 10 parts, imperial 8vo. Vol. I, pp. I-XV+1, 1-203+1, pll. 1-51 (17 col.). Vol. II, pp. I-X, 1-260, pll. 1-47 (18 col.). [Numbering of pp. and pll. as given in indices.]. London.

Issued in 10 parts, of which Pt. 1 appeared in February 1907; 2 in March 1908; 3 in February 1909; 4 in December 1909; 5 in November 1910; 6 in December 1911; 7 in November 1913; 8 in December 1913; 9 in October 1914; and 9* in June 1915. As issued, the plates are unnumbered and the text is variously paged, and both appeared without regard to the final arrangement. On p. XI of Vol. I and p. VII of Vol. II, lists are given showing the various species included in the volume, the number of the part in which each was issued and its date, the original pagination and the final pagination. Plates accompanied the corresponding text except in the following cases, which are here noted under the plate-numbers as given on pp. XIII and XIV of Vol. I and pp. IX and X of Vol. II. Vol. I:-pl. 2 appeared in Pt. 5; 3 in 6; 5, 6 or 7 in 5 (exact numbering in doubt); 11 in 9*; 21 in 7; 26 and 27 in 3; 29 in 7; 30 in 8; 37 and 40 in 3; 50 and 51 in 9. Vol. II:-pll. 12 and 13 appeared in Pt. 7; 18, 19 and 20 in 5; 23 in 2; 27 in 5; 28, 29 and 32 in 2; 43, 44 and 45 in 1; 46 in 4; 47 in 9*. Pt. 4 contained a temporary title-page and list of contents of Pts. 1-4 (2 ll.). Pt. 8 contained a reissue of pp. 25-26 on the Marsh Warbler (=pp. 97-98 of Vol. II), to replace the original pages issued with Pt. 7 which were thereby cancelled. Pt. 9* contained a reissue of pp. 11-12 and 21-22 of the "General Summary and Concluding Remarks (=pp. 203-204 and 213-214 of Vol. II), to replace the original pages issued with Pt. 9 and thereby cancelled. In addition to the matter collated, Pts. 1-9 and 9* each contained a subtitle and list of contents (2 ll.). The list of contents for Pt. 2 includes a reference to the figure of the female Chiff Chaff (pl. 40 of Vol. I) which was not issued until Pt. 3, as noted above. The present copy is complete except for the original pages 11-12 and 21-22 of the "General Summary and Concluding Remarks" which have been replaced by the reissues. The work presents a detailed study of the life-histories of British Warblers, with a philosophical discussion of the instincts and habits of the various species. The illustrations are very fine.

Howard, Henry Eliot.

1920. **Territory in | bird life** | by H. Eliot Howard | with illustrations by | G. E. Lodge and H. Grönvold | London | John Murray, Albemarle Street, W. | 1920.

1 vol. post 8vo, pp. I-XIII+1, 1-308, 1 l. (advt.), 1 insert-slip (corrigenda, p. 238), 11 pll., 2 charts. London.

A study of bird-behavior with respect to assumed dominion over local, restricted breeding territory, and the relation of this to reproduction and other activities.

Howe, Reginald Heber, Jr.; and Sturtevant, Edward.

1899. **The | birds of Rhode Island.** | By | Reginald Heber Howe, Jr., | Member of the Nuttall Ornithological Club, | and | Edward Sturtevant, S.B., | Instructor of Natural Sciences at Saint George's School, Newport. | Members of the American Ornithologists' Union. | Illustrated. | 1899.

1 vol. 8vo, pp. I-III, 6 pll. (Rhode Island?). October 1899.

An annotated list of the species of birds known to have occurred in Rhode Island, with a bibliography, notes on migratory and breeding species and a discussion of Cormorant Rock and its avian visitors. A supplement (q.v.) was published in 1903. The supplement supplies the date of publication of the present work.

Howe, Reginald Heber, Jr.

1899. On the | birds' highway | by | Reginald Heber Howe, Jr. | With Photographic Illustrations by the Author and a | Frontispiece in Color from a Painting by | Louis Agassiz Fuèrtes | [Blazon.] | Boston | Small, Maynard & Company | 1899.

1 vol. crown 8vo, 5 pr. ll., pp. XIII-XV+1, 1-175, frontisp. (col.; by L. A. Fuertes), 58 text-figs. (11 full-page). Boston.

A popular account of local observations on bird-life, with an appendix containing several lists of species observed at different localities; dates not given.

Howe, Reginald Heber, Jr.; and Allen, Glover Morrill.

1901. The | birds of Massachusetts | by | Reginald Heber Howe, Junior, | and | Glover Morrill Allen, | Members of the Nuttall Ornithological Club | and | Associate Members of the American Ornithologists' Union | Published by subscription | Cambridge, Massachusetts | 1901.

1 vol. 8vo, pp. 1-154. Cambridge.

An annotated list of the birds known from Massachusetts, with a discussion of the faunal areas of the state and a bibliography. The edition was limited to 500 copies, of which the present copy is No. 401.

Howe, Reginald Heber, Jr.; and Sturtevant, Edward.

1903. A | supplement | to | The Birds of Rhode Island | by | Reginald Heber Howe, Junior | and | Edward Sturtevant | Middletown | Rhode Island | 1903.

1 vol. 8vo, pp. 1-24. Middletown.

Additional notes supplementing the authors' original paper of October 1899 (q.v.). The complete list of species is reprinted (without annotations other than the newly added notes), thus giving an up to date check-list of the birds of the state as well as a supplement to the earlier volume.

Howell, Arthur H.

1911. Issued October 12, 1911. | U. S. Department of Agriculture | Biological Survey - Bulletin No. 38 | Henry W. Henshaw, Chief | **Birds of Arkansas** | by | Arthur H. Howell | Assistant Biologist, Biological Survey | [Seal.] | Washington | Government Printing Office | 1911.

1 vol. 8vo, pp. 1-100, pll. I-VII (1 map, col., fold.), text-figs. 1-4. Washington. Oct. 12, 1911.

An annotated list of the birds of the state, giving the local status of each, with notes on habits, food, dates of occurrence, etc. The introduction discusses the physical features, life zones game restrictions, etc., of Arkansas.

Howell, Arthur H.

1924. Birds of Alabama | by | Arthur H. Howell | Assistant Biologist, Bureau of Biological Survey, | United States Department of Agriculture | Issued in co-operation with the | United States Department of Agriculture | Bureau of Biological Survey | Edward W. Nelson, Chief of Bureau | by the | Department of Game and Fisheries of Alabama | I. T. Quinn, Commissioner | [*Seal.*] | Brown Printing Company | State Printers and Binders | Montgomery, Ala. | 1924.

1 vol. 16mo (6½x9½), pp. 1-384, pll. I-VII (on 5 ll.), text-figs. 1-31 (full-page). Montgomery.

An annotated list of the birds of Alabama, with detailed accounts of state records general habits of the species (including song and nidification) and food habits A bibliography is appended.

Hübner, Ernst.

1908. Ernst Hübner | **Avifauna** | **von Vorpommern** | **und Rügen** | [*Monogram.*] | Verlag von | Theodor Oswald Weigel, Leipzig | 1908.

1 vol. superroyal 8vo, pp. I-XIX+1, 1-155+1. Leipzig.

An annotated catalogue of 318 species and subspecies of birds of Vorpommern and Rügen, with supplementary chapters on migration, winter flocking, changes in fauna, etc.

Hudson, William Henry.

1888-89. See Sclater, Philip Lutley; and Hudson, **Argentine Ornithology.**

Hudson, William Henry.

1920. Adventures | **among birds** | by | W. H. Hudson | author of [*etc., 2 lines.*] | [*Vignette.*] | New York | E. P. Dutton & Company | 681 Fifth Avenue | 1920.

1 vol. demy 8vo, pp. I-X, 1 l., pp. 1-319, 61 text-figs. (after Bewick). New York.

A series of essays dealing with the author's observations on, and experiences with, birds. The illustrations are taken from Bewick's "History of British Birds,"- twenty-seven being named bird-portraits. The first edition of the book appeared in 1913.

Hudson, William Henry.

1920. **Birds in town | & village** | by | W. H. Hudson, | F.Z.S.| Author of [*etc.*, *2 lines.*] | [*Design.*] | With pictures in colour | by | E. J. Detmold | New York | E. P. Dutton & Company | 681 Fifth Avenue.

1 vol. post 8vo, pp. I-IX+1+1 l., 1-323, 8 pll. (col.), numerous decorations (some repeated). New York.

Most of the volume consists of the author's "Birds in a Village" (1893) revised and reprinted. The conclusion of the volume, pp. 265-323, "Birds in a Cornish Village," is new, being substituted for the original conclusion which is omitted. The book consists of essays in which bird-life forms the principal topic. The plates illustrate several British species.

Hudson, William Henry.

1920. **Birds | of La Plata** | by | W. H. Hudson | [*Vignette.*] | with twenty-two coloured | illustrations by | H. Gronvold | Volume one [two] | 1920 | London & Toronto | J. M. Dent & Sons Ltd. | New York: E. P. Dutton & Co.

2 vols. superroyal 8vo (7 x 9½). Vol. I, pp. I-XVII+1, 1-244, 11 pll. (col.). Vol. II, pp. I-IX+1, 1-240, 11 pll. (col.). London and Toronto.

An account of the habits of the birds of the La Plata region of Argentina, with brief descriptions. The whole is taken, with slight modifications, from Sclater and Hudson's "Argentine Ornithology," 1888-89 (q.v.), without being brought up to date. The plates, however, are new.

Hudson, William Henry. (Gardiner, Linda.)

1923. **Rare | vanishing & lost | British birds** | compiled from notes by | W. H. Hudson | by | Linda Gardiner | [*Vignette.*] | With 25 coloured plates by | H. Gronvold | MCMXXIII | London and Toronto | J. M. Dent & Sons Ltd. | New York: E. P. Dutton & Co.

1 vol. 8vo, pp. I-XIX+1, 1-120, 25 pll. (col.; by Grönvold). London and Toronto.

Based on the author's "Lost British Birds," published in 1894 (Society for the Protection of Birds, No. 14), and manuscript notes made with the intention of publishing a revised, enlarged edition. After Hudson's death, this material was edited by Linda Gardiner and published in the form presented herewith. Twenty-five species of birds, extinct or nearing extinction as British birds (thirteen were included in the first edition), are discussed as to former occurrence, reasons for reduction in numbers, etc. The plates illustrate the various species.

Humbert-Bazile. (Buffon, Henri Nadault de.)

1863. **Buffon | sa famille, ses collaborateurs | et ses familiers** | Mémoires par M. Humbert-Bazile | son secrétaire | mis en ordre,

annotés et augmentés de documents inédits | par | M. Henri
Nadault de Buffon | son arrière-petit-neveu | avec cinq portraits
sur acier | [*Blazon.*] | Paris | Ve Jules Renouard, libraire-éditeur |
6, Rue de Tournon | 1863 | Droits réservés.

1 vol. post 8vo, pp. I-XV+1, 1-430, 1 l. (list of portrs. and errata),
6 pll. Paris.

The biography and family history of Buffon, with notes on his principal collaborators; from the memoirs of his secretary, edited by his nephew.

Hume, Allan Octavian.

1869-70. My scrap book: | or | rough notes | on | Indian oology
and ornithology. | Edited by Allan Hume. | Calcutta: | Printed
by C. B. Lewis, Baptist Mission Press. | 1869.

1 vol. 8vo, pp. I-X, 1-237+1, I-IV (subtit. and pref. to Pt. I, No. 2),
239-422. Calcutta.

Intended to be continued at greater length, this work was terminated with the
second number and includes only the raptorial birds. According to a statement
by the author in his periodical, "Stray Feathers," Vol. V, page 125, the dates of
publication are uncertain, but No. 1 (to p. 237) was issued "either at the end
of February 1869, or during the first few days of March" while No. 2 "was not
issued until quite the end of March," 1870.

Hume, Allan Octavian.

1873. See Henderson, George; and Hume, **Lahore to Yarkand.**

Hume, Allan Octavian.

1873-75. Nests and eggs | of | **Indian birds.** | By | Allan Hume. |
Rough draft. | Part I. | Calcutta: | Office of Superintendent of
Government Printing. | 1873. [*Title-pages of Pts. II and III
missing.*].

1 vol. royal 8vo, 2 pr. ll. (tit. and ded.), pp. 1-2, 1-3+1, 1-662. Calcutta.

A presentation of all the information in the author's hands relative to the nidification of Indian birds; published as a rough draft with the idea of indicating
where more information was desirable and with a request for contributions on
the subject. With these contributions in hand, a second edition was published
in 1889-90 under title of "The Nests and Eggs of Indian Birds" (q.v.). The
present work was issued in three parts; pp. 1-236 in 1873, 237-489+1 in 1874
and 491-662 in 1875, according to reviews in the Ibis.

Hume, Allan Octavian.

1879. List | of | **the birds of India.** | Reference edition. | By Allan
Hume. | Corrected to 1st March 1879. | Calcutta: | Published by
A. Acton, Calcutta Central Press Co., Ld. | 1879.

1 vol. 8vo, (cover-tit.), pp. 1-78. Calcutta.

A reprint, with slightly altered title and separate pagination, of the author's "A Rough Tentative List of the Birds of India" published in "Stray Feathers," Vol. VIII, No. 1, pp. 73-150, April, 1879.

Hume, Allan Octavian; and Marshall, Charles Henry Tilson.

1879-81. The | Game Birds | of | India, Burmah, and Ceylon. | Hume and Marshall. | Volume I [II; III]. [Calcutta: | Published by A. O. Hume and C. H. T. Marshall, | 8 Hastings' Street. | 1881 (*Vol. III only.*). [*Titles illustrated.*] > Calcutta: | Published by A. O. Hume and C. H. T. Marshall, | 8, Hastings' Street, | 1879 [1880; 1881 (*On title-page in Vol. III.*)].

3 vols. 4to (6x10). Vol. I, illustr. tit. insert-slip (imprint), pp. 1-2, insert-slip (notice to reader), 1 l. (suppl. preface), pp. I-II, 1-259, 5 insert-slips (emend. at pp. 114, 152, 176, 202 and 248), 45 pll. (col.; by C. Davenport, E. Neale, M. Herbert, Stanley Wilson, W. Foster and A. W. Strutt). Vol. II, illustr. tit., insert-slip (imprint), pp. I-II, 1-264, 44 pll. (col.). Vol. III, illustr. tit., pp. I-II, 1-438, I-VI (index), 51 pll. (col.), pll. I-IV (col.; eggs). Calcutta. 1879, 1880, 1881.

A general account of the habits, distribution and variability of the game birds of the region treated, illustrated by rather poor lithographs. Hume appears to have written the text, while Marshall gave his attention to the preparation of the plates. The dates 1878, 1879 and 1880, respectively, are printed on the backs of the volumes but these antedate the publisher's imprint and, in the case of Vol. I, antedate the author's preface which is dated July 1, 1879.

Hume, Allan Octavian. (Oates, Eugene William.)

1889-90. The | nests and eggs | of | Indian birds. | By | Allen O. Hume, C.B. | **Second edition.** | Edited by | Eugene William Oates, | Author of 'A Handbook to the Birds of British Burmah', and of | the birds [the Passeres] in 'The Fauna of British India.' | Vol. I [II; III]. | With four portraits. | London: | R. H. Porter, | 18 Princes Street, Cavendish Square, W. | 1889 [1890; 1890].

3 vols. 8vo. Vol. I, pp. I-X, 1 l. (errata), pp. 1-397, frontisp. (pl. I; col.), 4 pll. (portrs.). Vol. II, pp. I-IX+1, 1-420, frontisp. (pl. II; col.), 4 pll. (portrs.). Vol. III., pp. I-IX+1, 1-461, frontisp. (pl. III; col.), 4 pll. (portrs.). London.

A second edition of Hume's "Nests and Eggs of Indian Birds, Rough Draft," 1873-1875 (q.v.). The materials and notes for the present edition were transmitted by Hume to Oates who edited and produced the present work, adding many footnotes and altering the nomenclature and arrangement according to his own ideas. Oates, therefore, must be quoted for at least the nomenclatorial portion of the work. At the time of editing this book, Oates was writing his volumes on "The Fauna of British India," 1889-98 (q.v.), in which various new names are used that appear also in the present work. The evidence tends to show, however, that the "Nests and Eggs" appeared before the "Fauna," volume for volume. The prefaces of the present book antedate those of the "Fauna" and the latter work regularly quotes this one with page-references. If this surmise is correct, the new names should be quoted from the present volumes, "Oates in Hume."

Hunt, John. (?Coxe, R. C.)

1815-22. British | ornithology ; | Containing portraits of all the | British Birds, | including those of Foreign Origin, | which have become domesticated; | drawn, engraved and coloured | after Nature, | by | J. Hunt, | with descriptions compiled from the | works of the most | Esteemed Naturalists, | & arranged according to the | Linnæan Classification. | Vol. I. [-III] | Inscribed by Permission | To Sir J. E. Smith, M.D. F.R.S. | and President of the Linnæan Society. | Norwich; 1815 [1822 (*Vol. III.*)] Printed by Bacon & Co. | for the Proprietor & may be had of the Booksellers. [*Line omitted or trimmed off (Vol. III.).*].

3 vols. post 8vo. Vol. I, tit., pp. 1-183, 34 pll. (col.). Vol. II, tit., pp. 1-365, pll. I-IV (uncol.; anatomical), 55 pll. (52 col.). Vol. III, tit., pp. 1-138, 99 pll. (94 col.). Norwich.

A rare work on British ornithology. The text, according to Newton (Dictionary of Birds, Pt. I, Introd., p. 42, footn.) may have been written by R. C. Coxe, but this is doubted by Mullens and Swann. The work was never completed; page 138 of Vol. III ends in the middle of a sentence, and there are 78 plates (77 col.) in that volume for which no text exists. The book appeared in 15 parts with 12 colored plates in each part (according to Engelmann). The number of plates appears to be variable in different copies. The present set (from the library of W. H. Mullens) is one of the most complete.

Huntington, Dwight W.

1904. Our feathered game | a handbook of the North American game birds | by | Dwight W. Huntington | with eight full-page shooting scenes in color | and one hundred and thirty-five bird portraits | Charles Scribner's Sons | New York 1904.

1 vol. demy 8vo, pp. I-XII, 1 l., pp. 1-396, 1 l., 8 pll. (col.; by author) pll. I-XXIX (on 15 ll.). New York.

A popular book on hunting, with an appendix containing descriptive notes on the various species of game birds of North America.

Hurdis, H. J.

1897. See Hurdis, John L., Rough Notes and Memoranda relating to the Natural History of the Bermudas.

Hurdis, John L. (Hurdis, H. J.)

1897. **Rough Notes and Memoranda | relating to the | Natural History of the Bermudas |** by the late | John L. Hurdis | formerly | Controller of Customs and Navigation Laws in those Islands | Edited by his daughter | H. J. Hurdis | London: | R. H. Porter | 7, Princes Street, Cavendish Square, W. | 1897.

1 vol. 8vo, pp. I-VI, 1 l. (conts. and errata), pp. 1-408. London.

Voluminous notes and records made by the author between 1840 and 1855 and published, after his death, by his daughter who has supplied (pp. 1-3) "Preliminary remarks on the peculiar and highly interesting character of the ornithology of the Bermudas." Most of the notes relate to birds. Pp. 303-314 contain a systematic list of the birds of Bermuda with a supplement thereto.

Husen, Ebba, von.

1913. **Zur Kenntnis des | Pectens im Vogelauge. |** Inaugural-Dissertation | zur Erlangung der Doktorwürde | einer hohen naturwissenschaftlichen Fakultät | der Eberhard-Karls-Universität in Tübingen | eingereicht von | Ebba von Husen | aus Reval. | Tübingen 1913.

1 vol. 8vo, tit., pp. 1-56, (orig. wrapper), pll. 1-4 (double). Tübingen.

A detailed study of the pecten of the avian eye.

Hutchinson, Horace. G.

1924. See Kirkman, Frederick B.; and Hutchinson, **British Sporting Birds.**

Huth, George Leonhard.

1772-81. See Edwards, George; and Catesby, **Verzameling van Uitlandsche en Zeldzaame Vogelen.**

Hutton, Frederick Wollaston.

1882. See Buller, Walter Lawry, **Manual of the Birds of New Zealand.**

Ihering, Hermann von.

1899. **As Aves do Estado do Rio | Grande do Sul |** por | H. von Jhering, Dr. med. et phil. | Director do Museu Paulista. | (Impresão em separado das paginas 113 a 154 do | Annuario do Estado do Rio Grande do Sul | para o anno de 1900.) | Porto Alegre | Editores: Gundlach & Krake, Livreiros | 497 Rua dos Andradas 501 | 1899.

1 vol. (pamphlet) demy 8vo, cover-tit., pp. 1-42. Porto Alegre.

An annotated catalogue of 363 species of birds of the state of Rio Grande do Sul, Brazil. Scientific and vernacular names are given. References are given to the author's account of the birds of São Paulo published in Vol. III of the Revista do Museu Paulista. As indicated in the title, the present form of the work is a separately paged impression of pp. 113-154 of the Yearbook of the State of Rio Grande do Sul for 1900.

Ihering, Hermann von.

1907. See Museu Paulista, **Catalogos da Fauna Brazileira,** Vol. I.

Ihering, Rodolpho von.

1907. See Museu Paulista, **Catalogos da Fauna Brazileira,** Vol. I.

Illiger, Johann Karl Wilhelm.

1811. Caroli Illigeri D. | Acad. reg. scient. berolinens. et bavaricae sod. | Museo zoologico berolin. praefecti, | professoris extraord. | **Prodromus | systematis | mammalium et avium** | additis | terminis zoographicis utriusque classis, | eorumque | versione germanica. | [*Quot., 3 lines.*] | Berolini | Sumptibus C. Salfeld | 1811.

1 vol. crown 8vo, pp. I-XVIII, 1-301+1. Berlin.

A list of the genera of mammals and birds, with synoptic tables to the orders and families, descriptions of the same and of the genera, and a list of species of each genus. A glossary of technical terms, in Latin and German, precedes each section. The section on birds occupies pages 145-286 and part of pages 287-301+1 (index to glossaries and errata). The present copy is from the library of Dr. C. G. A. Giebel.

(Illinois) State Laboratory of Natural History.   (Ridgway, Robert; Forbes, Stephen A.)

1889-95. Natural history survey of Illinois, | State Laboratory of Natural History, | S. A. Forbes Director. | **The | ornithology | of Illinois.** | Part I, descriptive catalogue, | By Robert Ridgway. | Part II, economic ornithology [*Vol. I only.*]. | By S. A. Forbes [*Vol. I only.*]. | Volume I [Volume II. | Part I]. | Published by Authority of the State Legislature. | Springfield, Ill.: | H. W. Rokker, Printer and Binder. | 1889 [1895].

2 vols. superroyal 8vo. Vol. I, pp. I-VIII, 1-520, frontisp. (col.; by R. Ridgway), pll. I-XXXII. Vol. II, 2 pr. ll., pp. 1-282, pll. I-XXXIII. Springfield.

A monograph of the birds of the state of Illinois, including popular and scientific synonymy, habitat, full descriptions, and general notes on the habits of each species, and with many synoptic keys. Part II, on economic ornithology, by S. A. Forbes was not published.

Ingersoll, Ernest.

1878. See Pope, A., **Upland Game Birds and Water Fowl of the United States.**

Ingersoll, Ernest.

1879-82 (-?). [Nests and eggs of American birds.]

1 vol. 4to (7x9), (no tit.), pp. 1-112, pll. I-X (col.). Salem.

Descriptions of the nests and eggs and accounts of the nesting habits of North American birds. The work appeared in parts. Pt. **I,** pp. 1-24 and pll. I and II was issued in March 1879. Pt. **II,** pp. 25-48 and pll. III and IV was published in August 1879. Pt. **III,** pp. 49-72 and pll. V and VI appeared in October, 1879. Pt. **VI** and **VII** are noticed in "The Ornithologist and Oologist" VI, No. 12, Febr. 1882, p. 96. I am unable to determine if the book was ever completed or not. The first three parts are reviewed in the Auk and in Taschenberg.

Ingersoll, Ernest (ed.). (Dawson, William Leon; Townsend, Charles Haskins; Nelson, Edward W.; Bent, Arthur Cleveland; Grinnell, Joseph.)

1914. Alaskan bird-life | as | Depicted by Many Writers | Edited by | Ernest Ingersoll | Seven Plates in Colors and Other Illustrations. | Published by the | National Association of Audubon Societies | New York, 1914.

1 vol. 8vo, pp. 1-72, 13 pll. (7 col.; 6 dupl., outlines, for coloring; by Bruce Horsfall and Allan Brooks), 6 text-figs. New York.

A popular description of the bird-life of Alaska, by the editor and various other contributors.

Ingraham, D. P.

1896. See World's Congress on Ornithology, **Papers presented to the—.**

Irby, Leonard Howard Lloyd.

1875. The | ornithology | of the | Straits of Gibraltar. | By | Lieut.-Colonel L. Howard L. Irby, F.Z.S., | H.-P. Late Seventy-fourth Highlanders, | Member of the British Ornithologists' Union. | [*Quot.*]. | London: | Published by R. H. Porter, | 6 Tenderden Street, Hanover Square. | 1875.

1 vol. post 8vo, 2 pr. ll., pp. 1-236, 2 maps (fold.). London.

An account of the habits of the birds of the regions bordering the Straits of Gibraltar, mostly from field notes by the author, with an annotated list of the species not seen by him but recorded by others, and an introduction on the topography and zoological characteristics of the area. A second edition (q.v.) was issued twenty years later. The present copy is from the library of J. Lewis Bonhote and contains his bookplate.

Irby, Leonard Howard Lloyd.

1895. The | ornithology | of the | Straits of Gibraltar. | By | Lieut.-Colonel L. Howard L. Irby, F.L.S., | Late Seventy-fourth Highlanders. | **Second edition,** | revised and enlarged. | With an

appendix | containing a list of the Lepidoptera of the neighbor-
hood. | Flumina amo sylvasque inglorius. | London: | R. H.
Porter, | 18 Princes Street, Cavendish Square. | 1895.

1 vol. imperial 8vo, 4 pr. ll., pp. 1-326, 14 pll. (8 col., by A. Thorburn;
6 half-tone, by J. Smit), 21 text-figs., 2 maps (fold.). London.

The text of this edition is much the same as that of the first, 1875 (q.v.), but with
the species arranged in a different order and with alterations and additions based
on further observations by the author. The colored plates of birds are very
attractive.

Iredale, Tom.

1921. See Mathews, Gregory M.; and Iredale, **A Manual of the
Birds of Australia.**

Isabella and Alexander, A Voyage of Discovery in His Majesty's
Ships—.

1819. See Ross, John.

Ives, Charles.

1880. **The isles of summer;** | or | Nassau and the Bahamas. |
[*Quot., 3 lines.*]. | Illustrated Edition. | By Charles Ives, M.A. | a
member of the New Haven bar. | New Haven, Conn.: | published
by the author. | 1880.

1 vol. crown 8vo, pp. 1-356, 7 printed guard-sheets, 26 pll. (1 ornith.).
New Haven.

A descriptive account of the Bahama Islands and of the author's experiences in
the region. Chapter XV, pp. 247-264, relates entirely to birds.

Jabouille, Pierre.

1925. See Delacour, Jean; and Jabouille, **Recherches Ornithologiques dans la Province de Quangtri.**

Jäckel, Andreas Johannes. (Blasius, Rudolf, *ed.*)

1891. **Systematische Übersicht** | der | **Vögel Bayerns** | mit Rück-
sicht | auf das örtliche und quantitative Vorkommen der Vögel, |
ihre Lebensweise, ihren Zug und ihre Abänderungen. | Von |
Andreas Johannes Jäckel, | weiland k. Pfarrer in Windsheim [*etc.*,
2 lines.]. | Herausgegeben | von | Prof. Dr. Rudolf Blasius. |
München und Leipzig. | Kommissionsverlag von R. Oldenbourg. |
1891.

1 vol. royal 8vo, pp. I-XXIV, 1-392, frontisp. (portr.). Munich and
Leipzig.

A posthumous work on the birds of Bavaria, with special reference to migration
and local distribution. The editor, Rudolf Blasius, has supplied numerous
supplementary notes and a biographical preface.

Jackson, Annie C.

1919-24. See Witherby, Harry Forbes, **A Practical Handbook of British Birds.**

Jacob, Nellie D.

1881-86. See Jones, Howard E.; and Jones, Mrs. N. E., **Illustrations of the Nests and Eggs of Birds of Ohio,** 1879-86.

Jacquemont, Victor.

1842 (?)-43. [Voyage dans l'Inde] *etc.*
See Geoffroy Saint-Hilaire, Isidore, **Description des Collections de Victor Jacquemont.**

Jacquin, Joseph Franz Edlen von.

1784. Beyträge | zur | Geschichte der Vögel. | Herausgegeben | von | Joseph Franz Edlen von Jacquin, | der physisch-medizini- schen Gesellschaft zu Basel| Mitgliede.| Mit ausgemahlten Kupfer- tafeln. | Wien, | gedruckt und verlegt bey Christian Friederich Wappler. | 1784.

1 vol. foliopost 4to, 4 pr. ll., pp. 1-45+1, 1 l., pll. 1-19 (col.). Vienna.

Descriptions of thirty-two American birds, with figures of nineteen species. Sev- eral new species are described. The plates are excellent for the period.

Jacquinot, Honoré.

1842-53. See Dumont d'Urville, J., **Voyage au Pole Sud et dans l'Océanie sur les Corvettes l'Astrolabe et la Zélée,** Zoologie. 1842-54.

James, Frank Linsley. (Thrupp, J. Godfrey; Shelley, George Ernest; Hartlaub, Carl Johann Gustav.)

1888. The | unknown horn of Africa. | An exploration from Ber- bera | to the Leopard River. | By | F. L. James, M.A., F.R.G.S. | Author of "Wild Tribes of the Soudan." | With additions by J. Godfrey Thrupp, M.R.C.S. | The map by W. D. James and Percy Aylmer. | The narrative illustrations by Rose Hake, and the drawings | of the fauna by K. Keuleman, from specimens chiefly | collected by E. Lort-Phillips. | London: | George Philip & Son, 32 Fleet Street. | 1888.

1 vol. 8vo, pp. I-XIV, 1-344, pll. I-IX (1 monochr.; 5 of birds), 1-4 (plants), 1 pl. (insects), 9 pll. (monochr.), 20 text-figs. 1 map (col.; fold.; in pocket). London.

The narrative of an expedition through Somaliland, with occasional notes on the birds of the region traversed. The appendix contains (pp. 276-308) a reprint of Shelley's report on the collection of birds secured by the expedition, first published in the Ibis, 1885, pp. 389-418. Pp. 309-317 contain a reprint of Hartlaub's report on a new species of barbet of the genus *Trachyphonus* secured by the expedition, first published in the Ibis, 1886, pp. 105-112. The illustrations of birds (5 pll. by J. G. Keulemans) are from these articles in the Ibis and from Seebohm's "The Geographical Distribution of the Family Charadriidae," 1887 (q.v.).

James, Harry Berkeley. (Sclater, Philip Lutley.)

1892. **A new list | of | Chilian birds** | compiled by the late | Harry Berkeley James, F.L.S., F.Z.S., F.R.G.S. | with a preface | by | P. L. Sclater, M.A., Ph.D., F.R.S. | Printed for private use. | London: | Printed by Taylor and Francis, | Red Lion Court, Fleet Street. | 1892.

1 vol. royal 8vo, pp. I-VII+1, 1-15. London. 1892 (post Nov. 1).

A synoptic list of the species of birds found in Chile from Chiloe Island to the province of Tarapacá, with their status as migrants or residents and with the local names. The preface by Sclater, giving a summary of James's life and works, is dated November 1, 1892.

Jameson, James Sligo. (Sharpe, Richard Bowdler.)

1890? **The story of | the rear column** | of the | Emin Pasha | Relief Expedition | by the late | James S. Jameson | Naturalist to the Expedition | Edited by | Mrs. James S. Jameson | Illustrated by C. Whymper from the author's original | sketches | With new map and facsimile letter from Tippu Tib | Natural history appendix: | Birds, by R. R. Bowdler Sharpe, F.Z.S. | Coleoptera, by H. W. Bates, F.R.S. | Lepidoptera, Rhopalocera and Heterocera | by Osbert Salvin, F.R.S., F. DuCane Godman, F.R.S., | H. Druce, F.L.S. | Authorized Edition | New York | United States Book Company | Successors to | John W. Lovell Company | 150 Worth St., Cor. Mission Place.

1 vol. 8vo, pp. I-XXXII, 1-455, frontisp. (portr.), 1 map (2 pts.; fold., col.), 2 facsimiles (fold.), 98 text-figs. New York.

Extracts from the diary and correspondence of J. S. Jameson, written while a member of the Emin Pasha Relief Expedition. The book was published (posthumously) to vindicate the writer against charges which had been preferred against him by the leader of the expedition, H. M. Stanley, in his book, "In Darkest Africa," and in later writings. The natural history appendix contains, on pp. 392-422, an account of Jameson's ornithological work by Sharpe, and extracts from Jameson's diaries giving notes on various species of birds collected or observed. Jameson's collection of birds was discussed by Shelley in the Ibis, 1890, pp. 156-170. The original edition of the present work was published in London in 1890; the present edition is undated.

Jameson, Robert.

1831.   See Wilson, Alexander; and Bonaparte, **American Ornithology.**

[Japanese Drawings.]

1 vol. 12mo, 12 pll. (col.; fold.).

1 vol. 12mo, 18 pll. (col.; 16 fold.).

Two small volumes of colored pictures of Japanese birds, without text other than the inscriptions on the plates.

Jardine, William; and Selby, Prideaux John.

1826-43.   Illustrations | of | ornithology | by | Sir William Jardine Bart. F.R.S.E. F.L.S. M.W.S. &c. | and | Prideaux John Selby Esq: F.R.S.E. F.L.S. M.W.S. &c. | With the co-operation of | J. E. Bicheno Esq. Sec. L.S. &c. | J. G. Children Esq. F.R.S. [etc.] | Major-General T. Hardwicke F.R.S. [etc.] | T. Horsfield M.D. [etc.] | R. Jameson Esq. F.R.S.E. [etc.] | Sir T. Stamford Raffles L.L.D. [etc.] | N. A. Vigors Esq. M.A. [etc.] [Preceding 8 lines omitted from vol. of New Series.] | Vol. I [II; III; (New Series without vol. no.)] | Edinburgh, | published by W. H. Lizars, 3 St. James Square: | Longman, Rees, Orme, Brown & Green; and S. Highley, London: | W. Curry Junr. & Co. Dublin [Preceding 4 lines replaced in New Series by "Edinburgh; | published by W. H. Lizars, 3 St. James Square; S. Highley 32. Fleet Street London, | and W. Curry Junr. & Co. 9. Upper Sackville Street Dublin"].

4 vols. medium 4to. Vol. I, engr. tit., 64 ll. (signs. A-L and A-G), pll. 1-50 (col.), 1-50 (plain), 2 ll., index to Vols. I and II; belong in Vol. II.). Vol. II, engr. tit., 59 ll. [signs H-Q4, A-F3 and C4-D3 (Addenda, issued with Pt. 7)], pll. 51-100 (col.), 51-100 (plain). Vol. III, engr. tit., 60 ll. [signs. A-C3, A-E, insert-slip (erratum), A-D4 and 16 ll. without sign.], pll. 101-110, 106 (bis)-110 (bis), 111-136 and 139-151 (col.), pll. 101-110, 106 (bis)-110 (bis), 111-136 and 139-151 (plain). New Series, engr. tit., 62 ll. (without sign.), pll. I-LIII N.S. (col.; 1 double), 18 text-figs. Edinburgh.

A series of hand-colored plates (by Jardine, Selby, E. Lear, Thompson, James Stewart, A. F. Rolfe, Gould and R. Mitford), with detailed text, including descriptions of many new species and new genera. The first three volumes have a duplicate of each plate in black and white; these are lacking in the volume of the New Series. Plate 93 is wrongly labeled 94; 135 and 136 are wrongly labeled 138 and 137, respectively, both the latter numbers being omitted from the series. In Vol. III, at the end of the text to Pl. 121, there is visible, on a blank portion of the page, a reverse impression apparently transferred from a missing insert-slip. This insert-slip is important since it emends the spelling of the specific name on pl. 82, establishing it as *"Catila* instead of *Calita"* (= *Psittaca Calita*).

The work was issued in 19 parts, the dates of publication of which are obscure. Sherborn (Ibis, 1894, p. 326; idem 1899, p. 483) has given the dates on which Pts. 1-10 (Vols. I-III) were received by Longmans from Lizars, and the dates of publication of Pts. 1-9 (New Series) as given on the original wrappers, with the contents of each part. As his list does not consider the duplicated numbers [pll. 106 (*bis*)-110 (*bis*)] or the Addenda and Index to Vol. I and II. I append an emended list.

Part 1 Signs. A-F4 Pll. 1-16 Recd. by Longmans Febr., 1827.[1]

2	G-L	17-32	June, 1827.
3	A-G	33-50	April, 1828; end of Vol. I.
4	H-L2	51-65	Nov., 1828.
5	M-Q4	66-81	July, 1829.
6	A-F3	82-100	Aug., 1830; end of Vol. II[2]
7	A-D3 (incl. Addenda) +2 ll. (index to Vols. I and II)		
		101-110	Dec., 1830.
8	A-E +Insert-slip (errata)		
		106(*bis*)-110(*bis*), 112-120	Oct., 1831.
9	A-D4	111[3], 121-135	Febr., 1833.
10	(16 ll.)[4]	136, 139-151	Dec., 1835; end of Vol. III.

New Series.

Part 1	7 ll.	Pll. 1-6	Dated on wrapper 1837. Noted *Athenaeum*, Febr. 11, 1837.[5]
2	8	7-12	1837. May 27, 1837.
3	5	13-17	1837. Published Dec. 1, 1837.
4	6	18-23	1838. Noted *Athenaeum*, June 30, 1838.
5	8	24-29	1839. Mch. 23, 1839.
6	8	30-35	1839. Febr. 22, 1840.
7	6	36-41	1840. July 25, 1840.
8	6	42-47	1842.
9	8 (incl. Contents)		
		48-53	1843. Adv. as ready *Publ. Circular*, June 15, 1843.

In certain advertising pages accompanying Jardine's "The Natural History of Hummingbirds" (1840), there is the announcement of Pts. 1-7, Second Series, with six plates in each. If this is strictly accurate, the above table will need

---

[1]The authors, in the text to pl. 100, refer to their "1st Number, published in 1826."

[2]The following number, 7, was originally intended as part of Vol. II, since it is included in the index to Vols. I and II, but it is also included in the index to Vol. III where it is accompanied by a note regarding the duplication of numbers in it and the succeeding part. I have collated the work as represented in the present copy.

[3]"Damaged and delayed" (Sherborn).

[4]Including the index to Vol. III (1 l.), which I am not certain appeared with this part.

[5] Mathews, in his Birds of Australia, Vol. VII, p. 475, quotes Richmond (in MS) or the dates given in this last column.

further emending. Likewise, in Vol. I, Ornithological Series (1st ed.) of Jardine's "The Naturalist's Library" (1833), Pt. 9 of the First Series is announced with seventeen plates; an examination of pl. 136 (wrongly numbered 137) and its accompanying text shows that it agrees closely with pl. 135 (wrongly numbered 138) and its letterpress, while pl. 139 differs in being dated "(1835)" while its text shows a change in type. It is possible, therefore, that Pt. 9 contained pl. 136.

Jardine, William.

1832. See Wilson, Alexander; and Bonaparte, **American Ornithology.**

Jardine, William.

1833. The | **natural history** | of | **humming-birds.** | Illustrated by thirty-five [thirty-one] plates, coloured, [*Semicolon (Vol. II.).*] | and numerous wood-cuts; with [with portrait and memoir of Pennant.] | memoir of Linnaeus. [*Line omitted (Vol. II.).*] | By Sir William Jardine, Bart. | F.R.S.E., F.L.S., &c. &c. | Vol. I [II]. Edinburgh: | W. H. Lizars, and Stirling and Kenney; | Longman, Rees, Orme, Brown, Green, and | Longman, London; | and W. Curry Jun, and Co. Dublin. | 1833.

2 vols., cap 8vo. Vol. I, 1 l.+pp. 1-6 (advt.), 3 pr. ll. (subtit., illum. tit., and serial tit.) pp. I-III+1, 5-147, 1-31+1+1-8 (advt.), frontisp., pll. 1-34 (col.), 11 text-figs. Vol. II, 5 pr. ll. (subtit., illum. tit., serial tit., and subject titles for Vols. I and II), pp. I-IV, 1-3+1, 1-166, 1-34+1-8+1-4 (advt.), pll. 1-30, 5 text-figs. Edinburgh.

Vols. I and II of the Ornithological Series (1st ed.) of Jardine's "The Naturalist's Library," 1833-43 (q.v.). The work presents a condensed monograph of the Humming Birds with synonymy and a short account of each species, and with brief descriptions of those not figured. At the close of the second volume is given a synopsis of all the forms, with descriptions of all of them. Somewhat detailed biographies of Linnaeus and Pennant are given in the front of the volumes. The colored plates are without backgrounds other than the twigs (uncolored on which the birds are represented as perching. In this respect the two volumes differ from all the remainder of the ornithological series of "The Naturalist's Library," original edition. Latin names, only, are on the plates. Both of the above quoted title-pages are in the second volume; the serial and general titles are given under Jardine, "The Naturalist's Library," 1833-43 (q.v.). A special edition was issued by Lizars in 1840 under the present title (q.v.). Later editions (q.v., 1844-64) were published of the entire series in which the present books form Vols. VI and VII of the Ornithology. The preface of Vol. II (1st ed.) is dated November 1833.

Jardine, William. (Selby, Prideaux John; Swainson, William.)

1833-43. The | **naturalist's library.** [| Conducted by | Sir William Jardine, Bart. | F.R.S.E., F.L.S., &c. &c. (*Vols. V-VIII and X.*)] |

Ornithology. | Vol. I [-XIV (*XI wrongly num. X.*)]. | Humming-birds [*mut. mut., 1-4 lines.*]. | By | Sir William Jardine, Bart. [*mut. mut.*] | F.R.S.E. F.L.S. &c. &c. [*mut. mut., 1-2 lines.*] | Edin-burgh: | W. H. Lizars, and Stirling and Kenney; [W. H. Lizars, 3, St. James' Square; (*Vols. V, VII-XI and XIV.*); *idem with comma instead of semicolon* (*Vols. XII and* XIII.); W. H. Lizars, 3 James's Square (*Vol. VI.*)] | Longman, Rees, Orme, Brown, Green, and [Samuel Highley, London; (*Vol. IV.*): S. Highley, 32 (*Comma added, Vols. VII, VIII, X and XII-XIV.*) Fleet Street, London; and (*Vols. V-XIV.*)] | Longman, London; [*Line omitted* (*Vols. IV-XIV.*).] | and [*Omitted* (*Vols. V-XIV.*).] W. Curry, [*Comma omitted* (*Vols. II-VI.*).] Jun. & Co. Dublin. | 1833 [-1843] [*Similar titles for Mammalia, Ichthyology and Entomology.*].

40 vols. cap 8vo. (Collation of ornithological volumes given under various authors and titles.) Edinburgh.

A series of separate works on Mammalogy, Ornithology, Ichthyology and Entomo-logy, written by various authors, edited by Jardine, and published in the present uniform style. According to an editorial note in the last volume, the series contains more than 1280 plates including more than 4000 figures. In addition to the general subject matter, each of the volumes contains a portrait and memoir of some noted naturalist (See below.). As the books appeared, they were tabulated in a list printed in the front of the volumes and given a serial number in the order of their appearance. These numbers (1-40) are often quoted by the editor in referring to the various volumes, but they do not appear on any title-page. The original title (quoted above) gives each volume a serial number with reference to its subject matter (Mammalia, I-XIII; Orni-thology, I-XIV; Ichthyology, I-IV; Entomology, I-VII). At the close of the work (Orn., Vol. XIV), a set of new title-pages was issued in which the order was changed and the entire series numbered from I-XL, although still grouped by subjects (Cf. Jardine, The Naturalist's Library, Vols. I-XL, 1843.). In addition, each volume contains still another title-page with full title and author-ship for the text, but with no reference to the general title of "The Naturalist's Library." Later editions of the series (by Bohn, Chatto and Windus, and Lizars) have another altered arrangement for the volumes whose numbering does not correspond to that of the present edition (Cf. Jardine,"The Naturalist's Library," reissues, 1844-64.). For convenience, the various volumes on or-nithology are collated separately under their respective authors and titles. The comparative list given on next page will show the relationship between the various numbers, title-pages, etc. Column *a* gives the number of the volume in the ornithological series; *b*, the serial number as issued; *c*, the number of the volume in the whole set, as later arranged; *d*, the number of the volume in the ornithological series of later editions; *e*, the author; and *f*, the title and original date. For further data, see the separate titles.

a	b	c	d	e	f
I	1	XIV	VI	Jardine	Humming-Birds (I), 1833.
II	3	XV	VII	"	" " (II), 1833.
III	5	XX	XIV	"	Gallinaceous Birds, 1834.
IV	6	XXI	VIII	"	Game Birds, 1834.
V	9	XIX	IX	Selby	Pigeons, 1835.
VI	15	XVIII	X	"	Parrots, 1836.
VII	17	XXII	XI	Swainson	Birds of West Africa (I), 1837.
VIII	19	XXIII	XII	"	" " " " (II), 1837.
IX	20	XXIV	I	Jardine	Birds, Gt. Britain & Ireland (I), 1838.
X	21	XVII	XIII	Swainson	Flycatchers, 1838.
XI	24	XXV	II	Jardine	Birds, Gr. Britain & Ireland (II), 1839.
XII	34	XXVI	III	"	" " " " " (III), 1842.
XIII	36	XVI	V	"	Sunbirds, 1843.
XIV	40	XXVII	IV	"	Birds, Gt. Britain & Ireland (IV), 1843.

Below are given the names of the naturalists whose biographies are included in the various volumes of the entire work, according to the serial numbers of the volumes (Column II.).

No. 1, Linnaeus; 2, Buffon; 3, Pennant; 4, Cuvier; 5, Aristotle; 6, Sir Thomas Stamford Raffles; 7, Sir Joseph Banks; 8, Ray; 9, Pliny; 10, Werner; 11, Camper; 12, John Hunter; 13, Sir Hans Sloane; 14, Madame Merian; 15, Bewick; 16, Lacépède; 17, Bruce; 18, Lamarck; 19, Le Vaillant; 20, Sir Robert Sibbald; 21, Baron Haller; 22, Aldrovandus; 23, Francis Peron; 24, William Smellie; 25, Pallas; 26, Huber; 27, Salviani; 28, Azara; 29, Swammerdamm and De Geer; 30, Dr. Barclay; 31, Gesner; 32, Schomburgk; 33, Latreille; 34, John Walker; 35, Dru Drury; 36, Francis Willughby; 37, Rondelet; 38, Burckhardt; 39, Humboldt; 40, Alexander Wilson. A chronological list of these naturalists is given by Michael Bland in No. 40 (q.v.).

According to the Catalogue of the Library of the British Museum (Natural History), the work was republished in 1845-46 and reissued by Bohn in 1848. Mullens and Swann cite a reprint by Bohn in 1852-55 and another by W. H. Allen without date. A set is at hand composed of several editions combined, including volumes issued by Chatto and Windus, by Lizars, by Lizars and Bohn, and by Bohn (Cf. Reissues, 1844-64?).

Jardine, William. (Selby, Prideaux John; Swainson, William.)

1833-43. The | naturalist's library. | Edited by | Sir William Jardine, Bart., | F.R.S.E., F.L.S., etc., etc. | Vol. I [-XL]. | Mammalia [(*Vols.* I-XIII.); Ornithology (*Vols. XIV-XXVII.*); Ichthyology (*Vols. XXVIII-XXXIII.*); Entomology (*Vols. XXXIV-XL.*)]. |Introduction to Mammalia. [*mut. mut., 1-5 lines.*]. | By Lieut.-Col. Charles Hamilton Smith [*etc. 3 lines; mut. mut., 0-3 lines.*]. | Edinburgh: | W. H. Lizars, 3, St. James' Square; | S. Highley, 32. Fleet Street, London; and | W. Curry, Jun. and Co., Dublin. | 1843.

40 vols. cap 8vo. Edinburgh.

The above lettering appears on a set of title-pages for the entire work issued with Vol. XL, all bearing the date 1843 regardless of the actual date of publication of each volume. As is noted, the subjects are grouped and the volumes numbered consecutively from I to XL, at variance with the original title which begins a new series for each branch of the subject (Cf. Jardine, The Naturalist's Library, Ornithology, Vols. I-XIV, 1833-43). The present serial numbers are not to be confused with those (1-40) of the list of volumes in the order of publication, given with most of the volumes and frequently quoted by the editor in prefatory remarks as "the Sixth Volume of the Naturalist's Library," etc. The relations between the present system of numbering and that of the original titles of the volumes dealing with birds, "Ornithology, Vols. I-XIV," together with the subjects and authors of each volume are given under the original title (q.v.).

Jardine, William. (Crichton, Andrew.)

1834. The | natural history | of | gallinaceous birds. | Vol. I. | Illustrated by thirty-two plates, coloured. | By | Sir William Jardine, Bart. | F.R.S.E. [etc.]. | With memoir of Aristotle by | Andrew Crichton, | Author of "The History of Arabia," &c. &c. | Edinburgh: | W. H. Lizars, and Stirling and Kenney; | Longman, Rees, Orme, Brown, Green, and | Longman, London; | and W. Curry Jun. and Co. Dublin. | 1834.

1 vol. cap 8vo, 5 pr. ll. (various tits., 1 illum.), pp. 9-232, 1-32 (advt.), 1 insert-slip (between pp. 34 and 35), frontisp. (portr.), pll. 1-29 +18* (col.; some numbered in Roman), 2 text-figs. Edinburgh.

Vol. III of the Ornithological Series (1st ed.) of Jardine's "The Naturalist's Library," 1833-43 (q.v.). In later editions, 1844-64 (q.v.) it became Vol. XIV. The work consists of a descriptive account of the turkeys, peacocks, pheasants etc. The second and third parts of the "Gallinaceous Birds" are indicated as such on their serial title-pages ("Ornithology" Vols. IV and V), but their subject titles refer simply to "Game-Birds," 1834, and "Pigeons," 1835 (by P. J. Selby, q.v.). The memoir of Aristotle, by Crichton, occupies pp. 17-112. Scientific names, only, appear on the plates, some of which are copied from Gould and Audubon while others are new, by Stewart.

Jardine, William.

1834. The | natural history | of | game-birds. | Illustrated by thirty-one plates, coloured; | with memoir and portrait of | Sir T. Stamford Raffles. | By | Sir William Jardine, Bart. | F.R.S.E. [etc.]. | Edinburgh: | W. H. Lizars, and Stirling and Kenney; | Samuel Highley, London; | W. Curry Jun. and Co. Dublin. | 1834.

1 vol. cap 8vo, 4 pr. ll. (various tits.; 1 illum.), pp. VII-XI+1, 17-175 +1, 1-45+1+4 ll. (advt.), frontisp. (portr.), pll. 1-30 (col.; some num. in Roman). Edinburgh.

Vol. IV of the Ornithological Series (1st ed.) of Jardine's "The Naturalist's Library," 1833-43 (q.v.); on the serial title-page it is also called "Gallinaceous-birds, part II". In later editions it remained Vol. IV, Ornithological Series. The book is descriptive of the grouse, partridges and tinamous. The plates contain only Latin names, at variance with later editions. The memoir of Raffles occupies pp. 17-66 (Cf. later edition, 1844). The preface is dated December 1844.

Jardine, William. (Anonymous; Bland, Michael.)

1838-43. The | natural history | of the | birds of Great Britain | and Ireland. | Part I [-IV]. | Birds of Prey [Incessores (*Pt. II.*); Rasores and Grallatores (*Pt. III.*); Natatores (*Pt. IV.*). | Illustrated by thirty-six plates, with memoir and [thirty-two plates, with memoir and (*Pt. II.*); thirty-four coloured plates, with (*Pt. III.*); thirty-three coloured plates, (*Pt. IV.*)]. | portrait of Sir Robert Sibbald, Bart. M.D. [portrait of William Smellie (*Pt. II.*); portrait and memoir of John Walker, D.D. (*Pt. III.*); with portrait and memoir of Wilson (*Pt. IV.*)]. | By | Sir William Jardine, Bart. | F.R.S.E. [*etc.*]. | Edinburgh: | W. H. Lizars, 3 [*Comma, (Pts. III and IV.)*] St. James' Square; | S. Highley, 32 [*Comma, (Pts. III and IV.)*.] Fleet Street, London; and | W. Curry, Jun. and Co. [*Comma added (Pt. IV.)*.] Dublin. | 1838 [1839; 1842; 1843].

4 vols. cap 8vo. Pt. I, 1 l. (list of vols. in set), 5 pr. ll. (various tits. and pref.; 1 tit. engr.), pp. XI-XIV, 17-315, frontisp. (portr.), pll. 1-5, (6 missing), 7-32, (30 dupl.), (col.; by Stewart; 4 of eggs), 48 text-figs. Pt. II, 1 l. (list of vols.), 4 pr. ll. (tits.; 1 illum.), pp. VII-XII, 17-409, frontisp. (portr.), pll. 1-30 (col.; by Stewart; 3 of eggs), 41 text-figs. Pt. III, 2 ll. (list of vols.), 3 pr. ll. (tits.; 1 illum.), pp. IX-XVI, 17-349, frontisp. (portr.), pll. 1-34 (col.; by Stewart), 9 text-figs. Pt. IV, 2 ll. (list of vols.), 3 pr. ll. tits. (1 engr.), pp. IX-XVI, 17-313+1, 1 l. (dir. to binder), 40 ll. substitute title-pages for entire set), frontisp. (portr.), pll. 1-30+2* (col.; by Stewart), 18 text-figs. Edinburgh.

Vols. IX, XI, XII and XIV Ornithological Series (1st ed.) of Jardine's "The Naturalist's Library," 1833-43 (q.v.), becoming Vols. I-IV in later editions of the same, 1844-64 (q.v.). English names and scenic backgrounds appear on the plates. The serial title of Vol. XI is inscribed "Vol. X", but the correct number is placed on the binding. The memoir of Sir Robert Sibbald in Pt. I (Vol. IX) is by the pen of an anonymous friend of Jardine. The substitute title-pages at the close of the fourth volume (the last of the entire series) are intended to supplant the serial titles under which the work was issued.

A chronological table of the naturalists whose memoirs appear in the 40 vols. of "The Naturalist's Library" is given on pp. 51-53 of Pt. IV, over the initials of Michael Bland. The prefaces are dated, respectively, December 1837, September 1839, March 1842, and July 1843.

Jardine, William.

1839(?).   Sir William Jardine's | **Illustrations of the** | **duck tribe.** | [*Design.*] | Privately printed at the expense of the author, | Jardine Hall, Lockerby, Dumfries, N.B.

1 vol. (size of) medium 4to, 2 pr. ll. (tit. and list of pll.), 9 pll. (num. 1-9 in list), (orig. wrapper). Dumfries. (Date?)

A set of pll. 62, 95, 137, 138, 146 and 147 (Original Series), and XXIII and XXIX, New Series, of Jardine and Selby's "Illustrations of Ornithology," 1826-43 (q.v.), uncolored and accompanied by a title-page and list of plates. The latter contains the names copied from the plates including an error on No. 3 (orig. No. 147). No date is available for this collection, except that of the original publication of the last plate. The original wrapper is lettered the same as the title-page.

Jardine, William.

1840.   The | natural history | of | **humming-birds.** | Vol. I [II]. | By | Sir William Jardine, Bart. | F.R.S.E., F.L.S., &c. &c. | Illustrated by thirty-four [thirty-one] coloured plates, numerous | woodcuts, with portrait and | memoir of Linnæus [Pennant]. | Edinburgh: | W. H. Lizars, 3, St. James' Square; | S. Highley, 32, Fleet Street, London; | and | W. Curry, Jun. and Co. Dublin. | 1840.

2 vols. post 8vo. Vol. I, pp. 1-14 (advt.), illum. tit., tit., pp. XI-XV+1, 25-191, frontisp. (portr.), pll. 1-34 (col.), 11 text-figs. Vol. II, pp. 1-14 (advt.), illum. tit., tit., pp. III-VIII, 1-192, frontisp. (portr.), pll. 1-30, 5 text-figs. Edinburgh.

A special edition of the work first published in 1833 (q.v.), with some changes. The title-pages are new; the text is reset with altered pagination and is printed on larger paper with wide margins further distinguished by the addition of double-ruled borders; and the memoirs of Linnaeus and Pennant are considerably enlarged. The plates have been retouched and newly colored, and have colored scenic backgrounds added, while English, instead of Latin, names are on the legends.

Jardine, William.

1840.   See Wilson, Alexander, **American Ornithology.**

Jardine, William.

1843.   The | natural history | of the | **Nectariniadæ,** | or | sunbirds. | Illustrated by thirty-two coloured plates, with | portrait and memoir of | Willoughby. (*sic*) | By | Sir William Jardine, Bart. | F.R.S.E. [*etc.*]. | Edinburgh: | W. H. Lizars, 3, St. James' Square; | S. Highley, 32, Fleet Street, London; and | W. Curry, Jun. and Co. Dublin. | 1843.

1 vol. cap 8vo, 2 ll. (list of vols.), 3 pr. ll. (tits.; 1 illum.), pp. IX-XV+1, 17-277, frontisp. (portr.), pll. 1-24, 26 (=25), 27 (=26),

27 (*bis* = 27), 29 (= 28), 29 (*bis* = 29), 30 (col.; by Stewart), 17 text-figs. Edinburgh.

Vol. XIII, Ornithological Series (1st ed.), of Jardine's "The Naturalist's Library," 1833-43 (q.v.), reprinted as Vol. V in later editions, 1844-64 (q.v.). The plates bear only Latin names. The back is incorrectly inscribed Vol. XIV. The errors in the numbering of pll. 25-29 are not perpetuated in the text; they are corrected in later editions.

Jardine, William.

1844. The | natural history | of | game-birds. | Illustrated by thirty-one plates, coloured; | with memoir and portrait of | Sir T. Stamford Raffles. | By | Sir William Jardine, Bart. | F.R.S.E. [*etc.*]. | Edinburgh: | W. H. Lizars, 3, St. James' Square; | S. Highley, 32, Fleet Street, London; and | W. Curry, Jun., and Co., Dublin. | 1844.

1 vol. cap 8vo, 4 pr. ll. (illum. tit., tit., and conts.), pp. 17-197, frontisp. (portr.), pll. 1-30 (col.; some num. in Roman). Edinburgh.

A reprint of Vol. IV of the Ornithological Series (1st ed.) of Jardine's "The Naturalist's Library, 1833-43 (q.v.) with the addition of further memoirs of Raffles on pp. 66-88 and a consequent repagination of the remainder of the volume. The plates are less carefully colored than in the first edition and bear, in addition to the Latin names, English names and localities. The only full title-page is as transcribed above; the illuminated title-page, alone, is inscribed "The Naturalist's Library. Ornithology. Vol. IV." Cf. Jardine, "The Naturalist's Library" reissues, 1844-64.

Jardine, William. (Selby, Prideaux John; Swainson, William.)
1844-64? [The Naturalist's Library, reissues.]

14 vols. cap 8vo. London and Edinburgh. (1844; 1845-46; 1848; 1852-55; 1864; etc.)

A set of the 14 ornithological volumes of Jardine's "The Naturalist's Library," composed of copies from various editions (after the first), bound more or less uniformly but varying so erratically in title-pages, etc. that the detailed transcription of the titles under one heading is inconvenient. The volumes bear the imprint of Bohn, Lizars and Bohn, Lizars, or Chatto and Windus, sometimes differing on the engraved and regular title-pages, and with or without a reference to "The Naturalist's Library." The numbering of the volumes appears to agree in the various editions so combined. In the citation of the original edition, 1833-43 (q.v.), are given the titles and contents of each volume in the present series (as well as the original) and the collation of each volume will be found under its particular author and title. The reprint of Jardine's "Natural History of the Nectariniadae" is dated 1864 and is catalogued under that date; the remaining reprints are undated and are catalogued under the inclusive date, "1844-64?". The original edition is bound in brown; the later ones are in red.

Jardine, Wilnam. (Anonymous; Bland, Michael.)

1844-64? [The Natural History of the Birds of Great Britain and Ireland.]

> The | naturalist's library. | Edited by | Sir William Jardine, Bart., | F.R.S.E. [etc.]. | Vol. I. | Ornithology. | Birds of Great Britain and Ireland, Part I. | By the editor. | London: | Henry G. Bohn, York St., Covent Garden.

> [*Idem, 5 lines.*] | Vol. II. | Ornithology. | Birds of Great Britain and Ireland.- Part II. | By the editor. | Edinburgh: | W. H. Lizars, 3, St. James' Square. | London: S. Highley, Fleet Street; | T. Nelson, Paternoster Row. Dublin: W. Curry, Jun., & Co. | Manchester: J. Ainsworth, 93, Piccadilly. | and all booksellers.

> [*Idem, 5 lines.*] | Vol. III [IV]. | [*Design.*] | Ornithology. | Birds of Great Britain and Ireland, Part III [IV]. | By the editor. | London: | Chatto & Windus, Piccadilly.

4 vols. cap 8vo. Vol. I, 5 pr. ll. (engr. tit., tit., conts. and subtit.), pp. 17-315, frontisp. (portr.), pll. 1-32 (col.; by Stewart; 4 of eggs), 48 text-figs. Vol. II, 5 pr. ll. (illum. tit., tit., conts. and subtit.), pp. 17-409, frontisp. (portr.), pll. 1-30 (col.; by Stewart; 3 of eggs), 41 text-figs. Vol. III, 5 pr. ll. (illum. tit., tit., conts. and subtit.), pp. 17-349, frontisp. (portr.), pll. 1-34 (col.; by Stewart), 9 text-figs. Vol. IV, 4 pr. ll. (engr. tit., tit. and conts.), pp. 17-313, frontisp. (portr.), pll. 1-30+2* (col.; by Stewart). Edinburgh and London. (Dates?).

Reprints of Vols. IX, XI, XII and XIV Ornithological Series (1st ed.) of Jardine's "The Naturalist's Library," 1833-43 (q.v.). The plates are altered in coloration and have had a portion of the backgrounds removed. Several editions appear to be represented in the set here collated. Vol. II by Lizars has Bohn's imprint on the illuminated title-page and differs from all the other volumes in having the price (4s, 6d) printed on the binding; the tooling on the back is also slightly different in pattern from that of the others. Cf. Jardine, "The Naturalist's Library,"reissues, 1844-64.

Jardine, William. (Crichton, Andrew.)

1844-64? [The Natural History of Gallinaceous Birds.]

The | naturalist's library. | Edited by | Sir William Jardine, Bart., | F.R.S.E. [etc.]. | Vol. XIV. | Ornithology. | Gallinaceous birds. | By the editor. | Edinburgh: | W. H. Lizars, 3, St. James' Square. | London: | Henry G. Bohn, York St., Covent Garden.

1 vol. cap 8vo, 5 pr. ll. (illum. tit., tit., conts. and subtit.), pp. 17-255, frontisp. (portr.), pll. 1-17 (18 missing), 18*-29 (col.; some numbered in Roman), 2 text-figs. Edinburgh and London. (Date ?).

A reprint, partly reset, of Vol. III, Ornithological Series (1st ed.) of Jardine's "The Naturalist's Library," 1833-43 (q.v.), with some alterations. At the close of the volume, pp. 133-255 have been added, containing observations on poultry. The plates are imperfectly colored and sometimes contain English names and localities, as well as Latin names. The illuminated title-page contains the imprint of Bohn, not of Lizars and Bohn. Cf. Jardine, "The Naturalist's Library," reissues, 1844-64.

Jardine, William.

1844-64? [The Natural History of Humming-Birds.]

> The | naturalist's library | edited by | Sir William Jardine, Bart. | F.R.S.E. [etc.] | Vol. VI. | [Design.] | Ornithology. | Humming Birds, Part I, | By the editor. | London: | Chatto & Windus, Piccadilly.

> The | naturalist's library. | Edited by | Sir William Jardine, Bart., | F.R.S.E. [etc.] | Vol. VII. | Ornithology. | Humming Birds.-Part II. | By the editor. | London: | Henry G. Bohn, York Street., Covent Garden.

2 vols. cap 8vo. Pt. I, 5 pr. ll. (illum. tit., tit., conts. and subtit.), pp. I-XXXI+1, 25-191, frontisp. (portr.), pll. 1-34 (col.), 11 text-figs. Pt. II, 5 pr. ll., pp. 1-192, pll. 1-30 (col.), 4 text-figs. London. (Date ?)

Late editions of the two volumes which first appeared as Vols. I and II of the Ornithology (1st ed.) of Jardine's "The Naturalist's Library," 1833-43 (q.v.), and afterwards in a special edition under their subject-title (q.v., 1840). The typography of the present issue is that of the special edition, without the double ruled border to the pages, and the plates likewise show the elaborated backgrounds of that edition (here uncolored), while the figures of the birds show considerable variation in color from either previous issue. Latin and English names and the country of origin are given on the plates. The memoir of Pennant in Pt. II agrees with that of the special editon, while that of Linnaeus in Pt. I is further enlarged by "Anecdotes of Linnaeus," a "List of the Works of Linnaeus" and a list of "Supplements written by Linnaeus himself." The copies here collated are evidently representatives of two distinct reissues of uncertain dates. The imprints on the illuminated title-pages agree with those on the respective full title-pages,—not the case in some other volumes of the same set. Cf. Jardine, "The Naturalist's Library," reissues, 1844-64.

Jardine, William.

1853. See Wilson, Alexander, **American Ornithology.**

Jardine, William.

1855. See Strickland, Hugh E., **Ornithological Synonyms.**

Jardine, William.

1864. The | natural history | of the | Nectariniadæ, | or sun-birds. | Illustrated by thirty-two coloured plates, | with portrait and memoir of | Willoughby. (*sic*) | By | Sir William Jardine, Bart. | F.R.S.E. [*etc.*]. | London: | Henry G. Bohn, York Street, Covent Garden. | 1864.

1 vol. cap 8vo, 4 pr. ll. (illum. tit., tit. and conts.), pp. 17-277, frontisp. (portr.), pll. 1-30 (28 unnum.), (col.; by Stewart), 17 text-figs. London.

A reprint of Vol. XIII, Ornithological Series (1st ed.), of Jardine's "The Naturalists' Library," 1833-43 (q.v.). The plates differ from those of the original issue in coloration, in the addition of the habitat, in the re-lettering of the plate-numbers (including the correction of errors in pll. 25-29), and in a slight loss of some of the backgrounds. Cf. Jardine, "The Naturalist's Library," re-issues, 1844-64.

Jardine, William.

1876. See Wilson, Alexander; and Bonaparte, **American Ornithology.**

1877. Idem.

Jasper, Theodore.

1874-78. Ornithology; | or, the | science of birds. | From the text of Dr. Brehm. | With two hundred and twelve illustrations | by | Theodore Jasper, A.M., M.D. | Columbus, Ohio: | Jacob H. Studer & Co. | 1878.

1 vol. folio (11½x14½), 3 pr. ll. (title, contents, list of illustrs.), pp. 1-156, pll. A-D, 1-37 (monochr.). Columbus.

A popular discussion of general ornithology and the classification of birds. Issued in 40 parts in conjunction with "Studer's popular Ornithology. The Birds of North America" (q.v.) by the same author.

Jasper, Theodore. (Studer, Jacob H., *publ.*)

1874-78. Studer's popular ornithology. | **The | birds of North America:** | drawn and colored from life by | Theodore Jasper, A.M., M.D. | One hundred and nineteen colored plates, | representing upwards of seven hundred different species and | varieties of North American birds, including a popular | account of their habits and characteristics. | Columbus, Ohio: | published by Jacob H. Studer & Co., | 1878. | Copyright, 1876, by Jacob H. Studer. All rights reserved.

1 vol. folio (11½x14½), 8 pr. ll. (title, publ. card and indices), pp. 1-182, pll. I-CXIX (col.). Columbus.

Published in 40 parts in combination with the same author's "Ornithology, or the Science of Birds" (q.v.). Each part, except the last ones, contained 4 ll. of text (3 ll., of the present work and 1 l. of the "Ornithology") and 4 pll. (3 col. of the present work and 1 monochr. of the "Ornithology"). The dates of issue of the various parts are given by Coues as follows. Pts. I-V, Jan. 29, 1874; **VI,** Apr. 8, 1874; **VII,** June 9, 1874; **VIII,** July 16, 1874; **IX,** Aug. 18,

1874; **X**, Sept. 23, 1874; **XI**, Oct. 22, 1874; **XII**, Mar. 2, 1875; **XIII**, Mar. 24, 1875; **XIV-XV**, June 29, 1875; **XVI-XVII**, Sept. 18, 1875; **XVIII-XIX**, Jan. 26, 1876; **XX-XXI**, Apr. 20, 1876; **XXII-XXIII**, July 26, 1876; **XXIV-XXV**, Oct. 7, 1876; **XXVI-XXVII**, Jan. 3, 1877; **XXVIII-XXIX**, May 12, 1877; **XXX-XXXI**, Aug. 6, 1877; **XXXII-XXXIII**, Nov. 5, 1877; **XXXIV-XXXV**, Mar. 8, 1878; **XXXVI-XXXVII**, June 8, 1878; **XXXVIII-XXXIX**, Sept. 23, 1878; **XL** announced for Oct. 1878. Coues mentions five impressions of the work under the same date. There is, also, at least one other edition (q.v., 1881). The book consists of a popular account of North American birds, largely compiled from a variety of sources and illustrated by chromolithographs. It is not of high scientific value and contains numerous errors. The nomenclature of the indices does not agree, in detail, with that of the text, being more in accordance with the text of the later edition.

Jasper, Theodore. (Studer, Jacob H., publ.)

1881? Studer's popular Ornithology. | **The** | **birds** | **of** | **North America** | Upwards of seven hundred different species and varieties, comprising all that are | known to exist on this Continent, are represented on the one hundred and nineteen | crayon plates, artistically drawn and colored from Nature by | Theodore Jasper, A.M.M.D. | including a letter press devoted to giving a popular account | of their habits and characteristics, based on standard authorities, and the most eminent writers on ornithology of the day. | Edited and published by | Jacob H. Studer & Co. | Copyright 1881, by | Jacob H. Studer. | All rights reserved. | Tribune Building, New York City & Columbus, Ohio. | Lith. Letter-Press & Binding by Courier Co. Buffalo, N. Y.

1 vol. folio (11½x14½), 4 ll. (indices), 1 l. (engr. title), pp. 1-182, pll. I-CXIX (col.). New York and Columbus.

A revised edition of the earlier work of the same title, 1874-78 (q.v.). Much of the text is printed from the same plates as the former edition, but some of the matter is rewritten and reset and there are corrections and alterations in the nomenclature. The illustrations, for the most part, are from the same plates as the original, retouched, but pll. I-XIII are radically altered, with changed backgrounds, different figures introduced, attitudes varied, etc. and sometimes with the entire plate printed backwards. The coloration of most of the plates is different from that of the original series. There is no date on the title-page other than that of the copyright, 1881. In Ward's Natural Science Bulletin, 2; No. 1, p. 12, Jan. 1, 1883, the fourth edition of the work is reviewed as of 1882, and said to be published by Jacob H. Studer & Co., Tribune Building, New York. The copy at hand may belong to this fourth edition and hence date 1882.

Jaubert, Jean Baptiste; and Barthélemy-Lapommeraye.

1859-62. Richesses ornithologiques | du | midi de la France, | ou | description méthodique de tous les oiseaux observés en Provence | et dans les départements circonvoisins, | par MM. | J.-B. Jaubert,

Docteur en Médecine [etc., 2 lines.] | et | Barthélemy-Lapommeraye, Directeur du Museum [etc., 2 lines.] | Marseille. | Typ. et Lith. Barlatier-Feissat et Demonchy, | Place Royale, 7A. | 1859. 1 vol. royal 4to, pp. 1-547, 20 pll. (col.; by J. Susini). Marseilles.

A detailed account of the birds of southern France. The work was issued in 7 livraisons of which the first is reviewed in the Ibis for April, 1859, the second and third (under dates of 1859 and 1860) in the Revue et Magasin for Febr. 1860, the fifth in the Rev. et Mag. for September 1861, and the completed work (livrs. not numbered) in the same publication for Oct. 1862; the Ibis 1864, p. 396, acknowledges the receipt of the 6th and 7th livraisons, completing the work. Pt. 1 included pp. 1-72 and 3 pll. Of the remainder I can not ascertain the contents with certainty, but the following division is suggested for future confirmation. Pt. 2, pp. 73-144?; Pt. 3, pp. 145?-216; Pt. 4, pp. 217-288?; Pt. 5, pp. 289?-368?; Pts. 6 and 7, pp. 368?-concl. The present copy contains the bookplate of Charles Robert Bree.

Jentink, F. A.

1881. See Rijksmuseum van Naturlijke Historie, **Muséum d'Histoire Naturelle des Pays-Bas,** 1862-81 (-1907).

Jenyns, Leonard. (Yarrell, William.)

1835. A | manual | of | British vertebrate animals: | or | descriptions | of | all the animals belonging to the classes, | Mammalia, Aves, Reptilia, Amphibia, | and Pisces, | which have been | hitherto observed in the British Islands: | including the | domesticated, naturalized, and extirpated species: | the whole systematically arranged. | By the | Rev. Leonard Jenyns, M.A. | Fellow of the Linnean, Zoological, and Entomological Societies | of London; and of the Cambridge Philosophical Society. | Cambridge: | printed at the Pitt Press, by John Smith, | Printer to the University. | Sold by J. & J. J. Deighton; and T. Stevenson, Cambridge; | and Longman & Co., London. | M.DCCC.XXXV. 1 vol. 8vo, pp. I-XXXII, 1-559. London. 1835 (post Oct. 24).

A descriptive catalogue of British vertebrates. The birds, of which 312 species and 26 doubtful (or doubtfully recorded) species are discussed, occupy pp. 49-286. To Yarrell are accredited the descriptions of the eggs which are embodied in the general text. A bibliography is included, on pp. XXV-XXXII. The preface is dated Oct. 24, 1835.

Jerdon, Thomas Claverhill.

1843-47. Illustrations | of | Indian ornithology, | containing | fifty figures | of | new, unfigured and interesting species of birds, | chiefly from the south of India. | By T. C. Jerdon, Esq. | Madras Medical Establishment. | Madras: | Printed by P. R. Hunt, American Mission Press. | 1847.

1 vol. 4to (6x9), 3 pr. ll., pp. I-II, 80 ll., pll. I-L (col.; by native East Indian artists). Madras.

A collection of notes and descriptions of Indian birds, illustrated by hand-colored drawings. The work was issued in parts, of which Pt. 1, published in 1843 (after Nov. 3, the date of the preface), contained 24 ll. and pll. I-XII. Sherborn (Index Animalium, Sect. 2, Pt. 1, p. LXXI) adds the following dates. Pt. 2, pll. 13-25, Mar. 1845; 3, pll. 26-40, Apr. 1846; 4, pll. 41-50, Aug. 1847. According to the author pll. I-VI and XII exist in two (or possibly three) forms. In the original form, the backgrounds of these plates were incomplete as compared with the later types. The additional backgrounds were added to 30 copies printed subsequently, and some of the earlier prints were retouched by the colorists to correspond to the later form while others were left as originally issued. The present set were retouched. Sherborn (l. c.) notes that there was also an edition in 8vo.

Jerdon, Thomas Claverhill.

1862-64. The | birds of India [*Colon added* (*Vols. II and III.*).] | being | a natural history | of all | the birds known to inhabit continental India: [*Semicolon* (*Vol. III.*).] | with | Descriptions of the Species, Genera, Families, Tribes, and Orders, and a | Brief [Orders, | and a Brief (*Vol. III.*)] Notice of such Families as are not found in India, | making it a | manual of ornithology | specially adapted for India, | by | T. C. Jerdon, | Surgeon Major, Madras Army, | Author of "Illustrations of Indian Ornithology." | In Two [Three (*Vol. III.*)] Volumes. | Vol. I [II.-part I; III]. | Calcutta: | Printed for the author by the Military Orphan Press. [*Comma in place of period* (*Vol. II.*); George Wyman and Co., Publishers, (*Vol. III.*)] | 6, Bankshall Street [1A, Hare Street, Calcutta (*Vol. III.*)]. | 1862 [1863; 1864].

3 vols. 4to (size of 8vo). 9 pr. ll., pp. I-XLV+1, 1-535. Vol. II, Part I (see Vol. III), 4 pr. ll., pp. 1-439+1. Vol. III (called "Vol. II, Part II" everywhere but on title), 4 pr. ll., pp. I-IV, 2 ll. (contents), pp. 441-876, I-XXXII (index to complete work). Calcutta.

A thorough work on the birds of India, with descriptions, some synonymy (including native names) and voluminous notes on habits and distribution.

Job, Herbert Keightley.

1903. Among the water- | fowl Observation, adventure, | photography. A popular narra- | tive account of the water-fowl | as found in the northern and | middle states and lower Canada, | east of the Rocky Mountains | by | Herbert K. Job | profusely illustrated by photographs from nature, | mostly by the author | [*Trade-mark.*] | New York | Doubleday, Page & Co. | 1903.

1 vol. 8vo (6⅛ x 8⅜), pp. I-XXI+1, 1-224, cover-fig., frontisp., 96 text-figs. New York.

An account of the author's experiences in bird-study, especially in photographing and studying water birds. Illustrated with excellent photographs.

Job, Herbert Keightley.

1905. Wild wings | Adventures of a Camera-Hunter among the larger | Wild Birds of North America on Sea and Land | by | Herbert Keightley Job | Author of "Among the Water-Fowl," | Member of The American Ornithologists' Union. etc. | with an introductory letter | by Theodore Roosevelt | with one hundred and sixty illus- | trations after photographs from life | by the author | [*Vignette.*] | Houghton Mifflin & Company | Boston and New York. The | Riverside Press Cambridge.

1 vol. 8vo, pp. I-XXIV, 2 ll., pp. 1-341, frontisp., 18 pll. (on numbered pp.), 144 text-cuts (half-tone; incl. those on title and half-titles). Boston and New York. May 1905.

A popular account of the author's journeys in search of photographs of birds, illustrated with many of the photographs secured on these excursions.

Job, Herbert Keightley.

1910. How to study birds | a practical guide for amateur | bird-lovers and camera-hunters | by | Herbert Keightley Job | author of [*etc., 3 lines.*] | Illustrated with photographs | from life by the author | New York | A. L. Burt Company | publishers.

1 vol. post 8vo, tit., pp. V-IX+1, 2 ll. (list of illustrs.), pp. 15-272, 32 pll. New York.

A "handbook of method" which aims "to give, simply, clearly, and thoroughly, every possible suggestion and bit of practical information which may be useful to those who are beginning the fascinating study of birds in their native haunts." Chapters on equipment, identifying birds, where to find birds, camera hunting, and numerous other topics, form a useful book of reference for beginners. The illustrations are from photographs by the author.

Job, Herbert Keightley.

1923. Propagation | of wild birds | A Manual of Applied Ornithol- | ogy | treating of practical methods of propa- | gation of quails, grouse, wild turkey, | pheasants, partridges, pigeons and | doves, and waterfowl, in Amer- | ica, and of attracting and | increasing wild birds in | general, including | song-birds | By Herbert K. Job | Economic Ornithologist [*etc., 4 lines.*]. | [*Trade-mark.*] | Illustrated from photographs | Mostly by the Author | Garden City New York | Doubleday, Page & Company | 1923.

1 vol. 8vo, pp. I-XXI+1, 1-308, frontisp., 61 pll. (on 31 ll.). Garden City and New York.

An excellent treatise on the subject applied to North America. The first edition of the book appeared in 1915, from which the present edition is revised and enlarged by the addition of matter inserted in the appendix. Some of the original text appeared also in Bulls. 2 and 3 of the National Association of Audubon Societies, April and May, 1915.

Johns, Charles Alexander.

1862. **British birds | in their haunts.** | By the | Rev. C. A. Johns, B.A. F.L.S. | Author of [*etc., 2 lines.*] | With illustrations on wood, | drawn by Wolf, engraved by Whymper. | Published under the direction of the | Committee of General Literature and Education, appointed by | the Society for Promoting Christian Knowledge. | London: | Society for Promoting Christian Knowledge; | sold at the depositories: | 77, Great Queen Street, Lincoln's Inn Fields; | 4, Royal Exchange; 48, Piccadilly; | and by all booksellers. | 1862. 1 vol. demy 8vo, pp. I-XXXII, 1-626, 190 text-figs. London.

A popular account of the habits of British birds, with a short description of each species and a synoptic list of genera, with descriptions of each, under their respective families and orders. The woodcuts are excellent. This is the first of the editions, of which there were at least a dozen, including several abridgements (Cf. ed. 1922.). Mullens and Swann list the 12th edition published in 1911. A note in the present copy indicates that it is from the library of Robert Gray.

Johns, Charles Alexander. (Owen, Jean A. = Mrs. Owen Visger.)

1922. **British birds in | their haunts** | By the late | Rev. C. A. Johns, F.L.S. | Author of Flowers of the Field | Edited, Revised, and Annotated by | J. A. Owen | Author of Birds in their Seasons, etc | Collaborator in all Books by a 'Son of the Marshes' | Illustrated with 64 Coloured Plates (256 Figures) by | William Foster, M.B.O.U. | with a glossary of common and provincial names and | of technical terms | **Seventh edition** | [*Trade-mark.*] | London | George Routledge & Sons Limited | New York: E. P. Dutton & Co. 1 vol. post 8vo, pp. I-XXV+1, 1-326, 64 pll. (col.; by Foster; on 32 ll.). London.

A revised edition of the original work of the same title, 1862 (q.v.), edited and revised by J. A. Owen (Mrs. Owen Visger). The alterations are in the arrangement, nomenclature and characterizations and in the substitution of colored plates for the original woodcuts.

Johnston, I. H.

1923. **Birds of West Virginia** | [*Col. fig.*] | Their Economic Value | and Aesthetic Beauty | 1923 | I. H. Johnston, State Ornithologist |

Compiled and Published by | State Department of Agriculture | Charleston | J. H. Stewart, Commissioner.

1 vol. 8vo, pp. 1-138, 2 pll. (on 1 l.), 62 figs. (43 col., incl. fig. on title-p.; by L. A. Fuertes). Charleston.

A popular account of some of the birds of West Virginia, with a check list of the species recorded from the state and miscellaneous sections on bird protection, bird banding, migration and other allied topics.

Jones, Genevieve Estelle.

1879. See Jones, Howard E; and Jones, Mrs. N. E., **Illustrations of the Nests and Eggs of Birds of Ohio,** 1879-86.

Jones, Howard E.; and Jones Mrs. N. E. [= Virginia E.]. (Jones, Genevieve Estelle; Shulze, Eliza J.; McMullin, S. H.; Jacob, Nellie D.)

Illustrations | of the | nests and eggs | of | birds of Ohio | with text | Illustrations by Text by | Circleville, | Mrs. N. E. Jones Howard Jones, A.M., M.D. | Ohio, U. S. A. | 1886.

1 vol. in 3 vols., folio (15¼x17), pp. I-XXXVIII, XXXVIIIa-d, 1 l., pp. 41-319, pll. I-LXVIII (col.; by Genevieve E. Jones, Eliza J. Shulze and Virginia E. Jones). Circleville. 1879-86.

A beautiful work illustrating the nests and eggs of birds of Ohio in handcolored lithographs, accompanied by a letterpress with detailed descriptions of the eggs and of the position, construction and characteristics of the nests, and with notes on habits of the species. The introduction contains variously arranged lists of the species recorded from Ohio and keys for the determination of the eggs. On pp. 315-319 is an etymological key by S. H. McMullin; otherwise the text is entirely by Howard E. Jones. The plates were begun by Genevieve E. Jones and Eliza J. Shulze and continued by Virginia E. Jones and (in part) by Nellie D. Jacob. An explanation of the varied authorship is given on pp. V-VI. The work was issued in 23 parts as follows (Cf. Coues, Auk 4, p. 150, 1887.). Part 1, pp. 41-46, pll. I-III, July 1879 (A few copies issued as prospectus in Dec. '78 and reviewed in Bull. Nuttall Orn. Club 4, No. 1, p. 52, Jan. 1879.); 2, pp. 47-54, pll. IV-VI, Oct. '79; 3, pp. 55-58, pll. VII-IX, Jan. '80; 4, pp. 59-66, pll. X-XII, Apr. '80; 5, pp. 67-70, pll. XIII-XV, July '80; 6, pp. 71-82, pll. XVI-XVIII, Oct. '80; 7, pp. 83-90, pll. XIX-XXI, Jan. '81; 8, pp. 91-98, pll. XXII-XXIV, Apr. '81; 9, pp. 99-106, pll. XXV-XXVII, July '81; 10 and 11, pp. 107-118, pll. XXVIII-XXXIII, ("Oct. '81"-) Jan. '82; 12, pp. 119-122, pll. XXXIV-XXXVI, Apr. '82; 13, pp. 123-138, pll. XXXVII-XXXIX, July '82; 14 and 15, pp. 139-154, pll. XL-XLV, ("Oct. '82"-) Jan. '83[1]; 16, pp. 155-166, pll. XLVI-XLVIII, Apr. '83; 17 and 18, pp. 167-190, pll. XLIX-LIV ("July"-) Oct. '83; 19, pp. 191-206, pll. LV-LVII, Jan. '84; 20, pp. 207-234, pll. LVIII-LX, Apr. '84; 21 and 22, pp. 235-286, pll. LXI-

[1]Issued about Jan. 1, 1883. Cf. Coues, Bull. Nuttall Orn. Club, 8, p. 112, 1883.

LXVI, ("July"-) Oct. '84[1]; **23**, pp. 287-319, I-XXXVIII, XXXVIIIa-d, pll. LXVII-LXVIII, Dec. '86. Plate LV is wrongly numbered LVI.

For accuracy and beauty in the delineation of nests, this work has never been excelled.

Jones, Lynds.

1903. Ohio State Academy of Science | Special Papers No. 6 | **The birds of Ohio** | a revised catalogue | by | Lynds Jones, M. Sc. | Oberlin College | Published by the Academy of Science with the | Emerson McMillin Research Fund | Publication Committee: | J. H. Schaffner, L. H. McFadden, Gerard Fowke | October 15, 1903.

1 vol. post 8vo, title, pp. 1-241, frontisp. (map., fold.). Columbus. Oct. 15, 1903.

An annotated list of species, prepared as a revision of Wheaton's "Report on the Birds of Ohio," 1882 (q.v.).

Jones, Lynds.

1909. See Dawson, William Leon; and Bowles, **The Birds of Washington.**

Jones, Mrs. N. E. [= Virginia E.].

1881-86. See Jones, Howard E.; and Jones, Mrs. N. E., **Illustrations of the Nests and Eggs of Birds of Ohio,** 1879-86.

Jones, Thomas Rymer.

1869-73. See Brehm, Alfred Edmund. **Cassell's Book of Birds.**

Jones, Thomas Rymer.

1872? The | **natural history** | of | **birds:** | A Popular Introduction to Ornithology. | By | Thomas Rymer Jones, F.R.S., | Professor of Natural History [*etc., 3 lines.*] | With two hundred and twenty illustrations. | [*Seal.*] | London: | Frederick Warne and Co., | Bedford Street, Covent Garden | New York: Scribner, Welford, and Armstrong.

1 vol. 8vo (5¼x7¼), 4 pr. ll., pp. XI-XX, 1-452, 4 ll. (advt.), frontisp., figs. 1-59, 61-216, 84*, 101*, 180*, 7 text-figs. (unnum.). London.

A general popular account of the families and subfamilies of the birds of the world. There are at least three other editions dated 1867, 1871 and 1880. Regarding the present edition, I can find no information except the date of the preface, June 16, 1872.

Jones, Virginia E.

See Jones, Mrs. N. E.

---

[1]Reviewed in Auk, **3**, No. 3, p. 400, July, 1886.

Jonston, Johannes.

1657 (-65?) (1) **Historiæ naturalis** | de quadrupedibus | libri I, [de insectis | libri III, | de serpentibus | et draconibus | libri II,; de avibus | libri VI.] | Cum æneis figuris, [*No comma (Book VI.).*] | Johannes Jonstonus [Joh. Jonstonvs (*Books III and II.*).], | Medicinæ Doctor [Med. Doctor (*Books III and II.*)], | concinnavit. | Amstelodami, | Apud Ioannem Iacobi Fil. Schipper. MDCLVII. [*Title to "de Piscibus, libri V" missing.*]

(2) Historiæ | naturalis | de | serpentibus, | libri II. | Joannes Jonstonus | Medicinæ Doctor Concinnavit. | [*Col. fig.*] | Amstelodami, | Apud Joannem Jacobi Fil. Schipper. | Anno M DC. LXV.

(3) Historiæ naturalis | de exanguibus | aquaticis | libri IV. | Cum figuris Æneis. | Joannes Jonstonus | Med. D. Concinnavit. | [*Col. fig.*] | Amstelodami, | Sumptibus. | Joahnnis Jacobi Schipperi, | M DC. LXV.

1 vol. flatcap folio, (no general title); 1 l. (illum. tit. to Libr. I), pp. 3-6 (ded. and pref.), 1-164, 1 l. (index), pll. I-LXXV (col.; V, VII and LXX missing); 1 l. (illum. tit. to Libr. II, as transcr. in par. 2; ded. on reverse), pp. 3-38, pll. I-XII (col.); 1 l. (illum. tit. to Librs. III and II, as transcr. in par. 1), 3 ll. (ded., pref. and addenda), pp. 1-148 (text to "Insectis" only), pll. I-XXVIII (col.; of "Insectis" only; V, VI and VII missing); 1 l. (illum. tit. to Libr. IV, as transcr. in par. 3), pp. 3-58, 1 l. (index), pll. I-XX (col.; II, IX and XI missing); (illum. tit. to Libr. V missing), pp. 3-7 (pref. and index), 1-160, pll. I-XLVIII (col.; XVII, XVIII, XXXI and XXXII missing); 1 l. (illum. tit. to Libr. VI), 5 ll. (ded., pref. and index), pp. 1-160, pll. I-LXII (col.; XII, XIV, XV, XXII, XXIII, XXX-XXXII, XLII and LXII missing). Amsterdam.

This apparently is the second edition of the work of the same title, published in Frankfort in 1650 (-62?). The present edition differs, in certain particulars, from the first, according to the Catalogue of the Library of the British Museum (Natural History). The plates are said to be reversed, as are the title-pages. The present copy, as may be noted, has two general styles of title-page, the first of which (cf. par. 1 above) is almost entirely occupied by a large decorative drawing, and bears the date 1657. The second style (pars. 2 and 3) has the wording printed in large characters and the design reduced to a small plate, while it bears the date 1665. I am not certain that the coloring of the plates is original. The drawings are said to be the work of Mattheus (jun.) and Caspar Merian[1]. The work is valuable chiefly on account of the curious illustrations, although the first edition is of more importance, being quoted largely by Linnaeus. The portion on ornithology (Libr. VI) comprises title, 5 leaves

[1]Henry Sotheran & Co's "Price Current of Literature," No. 789, 1924.

of preliminary matter and 160 pages of text, and 62 plates of birds, including various monstrosities and such fabulous creatures as the harpy, griffon, and phoenix. See also a late edition of Book VI under the title of Theatrum Universale de Avibus, 1756.

The present copy is bound in irregular order, as follows; Libr. I, Libr. V, Libr. IV, Libr. VI, Libr. III (with II mentioned on the title), and Libr. II.

Jonston, Johannes.

1756. Ioannis Ionstoni | **theatrvm** | **vniversale** | **de avibvs** | tabvlis dvabvs et sexaginta | ab illo celeberrimo | Mathia Meriano | aeri incisis ornatvm | ex scriptoribvs tam antiqvis, qvam | recentioribvs, Theophrasto, Dioscoride, Aeliano, | Oppiano, Plinio, Gesnero, Aldrovando, Wottonio, Tvernero, | Movffeto, Agricola, Boetio, Baccio, Rvveo, Schonfeldio, | Freygio, Mathiolo, Tabernamontano, Bavhino, | Ximene, Bvstamantio, Rondeletio, Bellonio, | Citesio, Theveto, Marggravio, | Pisone | et aliis maxima cvra conlectvm | et | ob raritatem denvo inprimendvm | suscepit | [*Vignette*-Favente- Iehova- Excrescam.] | Franciscvs Iosephvs Eckebrecht | Bibliopola Heilbrvnnensis | Typis Christiani de Lannoy. | MDCC-LVI.

> [Historiæ Naturalis | de aubibvs | Libri VI. | Cum æneis figuris | Iohannes Ionstonus | Med. Doctor | Concinnauit. | Francofvrti ad Moenvm | Impensa | Matthæi Meriani | M.D.C.L.]

1 vol. 4to (8½x14), title, 2 pr. ll. (pref.), pp. 1-238, 5 ll. (indices), pll. I-XXIX, 30-62, (col.) (title to 1st ed. and portr., "Ioannes Maria | Vicecomes.", added.). Heilbronn.

A late edition of the "Libri VI" of Jonston's "Historiae Naturalis," of 1650 (Cf. 1657-65.), with the same general text, slightly altered, and with the same plates. The pages are headed, "Historia Natvralis de Gvibus." in spite of the altered title. The present copy is composed solely of the portion (or book) on ornithology, the sectional title of which is quoted in the absence of the entire work. The title quoted in brackets is on what appears to be a copy of the title-page of the original edition. The portrait of "Ioannes Maria Vicecomes" is of uncertain origin.

[Jordan, David Starr.] (Palmer, William.)

1899. **[The Fur Seals and Fur Seal Islands of the North Pacific Ocean** by David Starr Jordan (*etc.*).] > **The avifauna** | **of** | **the Pribilof Islands.** | By | William Palmer. | (Extracted from the Fur Seals and Fur-Seal Islands of the North Pacific Ocean, | Part III, pp. 355-431, Plates XXXVIII-XLI.) | Washington: | Government Printing Office. | 1899.

1 pamphlet, superroyal 8vo, cover-tit., pp. 355-431, pll. XXXVIII-XLI. Washington.

Article XVII, occurring in Vol. III of the report of the U. S. Fur Seal Commission, extracted and supplied with an individual wrapper, separately titled. The article is an important contribution, with detailed descriptions, keys and synonymies and voluminous notes from the author's personal observations as well as from other sources. One plate is of scenic views, one is of eggs, and two are of feather structure.

Jordan, Denham. [" = A Son of the Marshes."]

1895. The | Wild-Fowl and Sea-Fowl | of | Great Britain | by | a son of the marshes | author of "On Surrey Hills," "Woodland, Moor, and Stream" | edited by J. A. Owen | with illustrations by Bryan Hook | London: Chapman and Hall, Ld. | 1895 | [All rights reserved].

1 vol. 8vo, 4 pr. ll., pp. 1-326, frontisp., 11 pll. London.

Popular sketches of bird-life in Great Britain.

Jourdain, Francis Charles Robert.

1906-09. Subscriptions for the complete work only received. Part I. | The eggs | of | European Birds, | by the | Rev. Francis C. R. Jourdain, | M.A., M.B.O.U. | To be completed in about 10 parts, | containing about 140 coloured plates | by A. Reichert and the author. | Price 10/6 net. | London. | R. H. Porter. 7 Princes St. Cavendish Square W. | Gera-Untermhaus. | Fr. Eugen Köhler. | 1906. [No final title issued?]

1 vol. (not complete), royal 8vo, 1 l. (title, Pt. I), pp. III-IV, 1-320, pll. 1-25, 27-33, 35-40, 44, 52, 68, 69, 72, 87, 88, 90, 92, 94, 105, 113, 121 and 122 (col.), (4 front covers inserted at end of vol.). London.

The first four parts (all published) of a work on the oology of Europe. Under each species or subspecies, a short account is given of distribution, nidification, breeding season, number of eggs laid and measurements of eggs (averaged from series), and other information. The illustrations show, where possible, several varieties of the eggs of each species or race. Pt. I included a subtitle, pp. III-IV, 1-80, pll. 1-14, dated 1906 (rev. in Ibis, Oct. 1906; II included pp. 81-160, pll. 16-20, 24, 25, 39, 40, 52, 113, 121, 122, dated 1906 altered by hand to 1907 (rev. in Ibis, July, 1907); Pt. III included pp. 161-240, pll. 15, 21, 22, 28, 29, 68, 69, 72, 87, 88, 90, 92, 94, 105, dated 1909 (rev. Ibis, July 1909); Pt. IV included pp. 241-320, pll. 23, 27, 30-33, 35, 38, dated 1909 (rev. in Ibis, April 1911, under date of 1910; rev. in Zoological Record, 1910, under date of 1909). The work has never been completed. The author supplied many measurements of eggs to H. E. Dresser for his work on "Eggs of the Birds of Europe," 1905-10 (q.v.), which was partially contemporaneous and of the same scope, and possibly allowed his own work to lapse in favor of the larger book.

Jourdain, Francis Charles Robert.

1910-13.   See Kirkman, Frederick Bernuf Bever, **The British Bird Book.**

Jourdain, Francis Charles Robert.

1912.   See Hartert, Ernst; Jourdain; Ticehurst; and Witherby, **A Hand-List of British Birds.**

Jourdain, Francis Charles Robert.

1919-20.   See Mullens, W. H.; Swann; and Jourdain, **A Geographical Bibliography of British Ornithology.**

Jourdain, Francis Charles Robert.

1919-24.   See Witherby, Harry Forbes, **A Practical Handbook of British Birds.**

Jourdain, Francis Charles Robert.

1924.   See Kirkman, Frederick B.; and Hutchinson, **British Sporting Birds.**

Judd, Wilbur Webster.

1907.   **The Birds | of | Albany County |** a catalogue of the species | recorded in this vicinity, with | notes on their lives and | habits, and brief field-marks | for aid in identification | by | Wilbur Webster Judd | Containing One Plate from a Water-color by William | S. Barkentin; Ten Plates from Pen and Ink | Drawings by George Louis Richard, and Eleven Half-tones from | Photographs | Albany, New York | Nineteen Hundred and Seven.

1 vol. royal 8vo, 3 pr. ll. (half-tit., tit. and ded.), pp. 9-178, pll. I-XXI (1 col.).   Albany.   December 1907.

Short, popular accounts of the birds found in Albany County, New York. The copy is autographed and numbered '215' of the first edition of three hundred copies.

Kaup, Johann Jacob.

1844.   **Classification | der | Säugethiere und Vögel |** von | J. J. Kaup. | [*Quot., 3 lines.*] | Darmstadt. | Druck und Verlag von C. W. Leske. | 1844.

1 vol. post 8vo, pp. I-X, 1-144, 2 ll. (expl. of pll.), 2 pll. (fold.). Darmstadt.

A detailed exposition of the author's views on the classification of birds and mammals, following a modification of the "Quinary System" and its accompanying errors. A number of separate papers occupy pp. 96-144, the most important of which is a "Skizze einer Classification der Falken" (pp. 96-128) containing a considerable number of new generic names. Of the plates, the second is ornithological. Mathews (Austr. Av. Rec. **4**, No. 1, p. 12, 1920) cites the date of publication as March 15, 1844 but does not give the basis for this assumption. A supplement to this work was issued the same year (Cf. Nachträge zur Classification der Säugethiere und Vögel.).

Kaup, Johann Jacob.

1844. Nachträge | zur | Classification der Säugethiere | und | Vögel | von | J. J. Kaup. | Darmstadt. | Druck und Verlag von C. W. Leske. | 1844.

1 vol. demy 8vo, pp. I-VI, 1-14. Darmstadt.

Additional and revisory notes to the author's "Classification der Säugethiere und Vögel" (q.v.) published earlier the same year.

Kaup, Johann Jacob.

1849. Erste | Zoologische Vorlesung. | Ueber | Classification der Vögel | von | Dr. Kaup. | Darmstadt, 1849. | Druck der Hofbuchdruckerei von Ernst Bekker.

1 vol. post 8vo, pp. 1-4 (tit. and pref.), I-X (introd.), 1-40. Darmstadt. 1849 (post April).

An essay on the classification of birds and the characters on which classification is based. The present copy is from the library of Jules Verreaux. The preface is dated April, 1849.

Kay, John. [=Caius, John.]

1903. See Turner, William, **Turner on Birds.**

Kearton, Cherry.

1924. Photographing | wild life | across the world | by | Cherry Kearton | with eighty-four photographs | [*Design.*] | J. W. Arrowsmith (London) Ltd. | 6 Upper Bedford Place, Russell Square, London.

1 vol. 8vo, pp. 1-319, 56 pll. (photos.; 9 of birds). London.

Narratives of the author's experiences in photographing animal life in various countries; illustrated by some of the photographs taken on the journeys. According to the publishers' note, the volume includes about two thirds of an earlier work, "Wild Life Across the World" (1913) with eleven of the illustrations of that book, and considerable new material. Many of the incidents (and 9, or parts of 9, plates) relate to birds.

Kearton, Richard.

1883-(88?). See Swaysland, Walter, **Familiar Wild Birds.**

Kearton, Richard.

1898. Wild Life at Home | how to study and photograph it | by | R. Kearton, F.Z.S. | Author of [*etc., 2 lines.*] | Fully illustrated by

photographs taken | direct from nature by C. Kearton | Cassell
and Company, Limited | London, Paris, New York & Melbourne |
1898 | All rights reserved.

1 vol. crown 8vo (5¼x7½), 2 pr. ll. (tit., ded.), pp. VII-XV+1, 1-188,
frontisp. (monochr.), 97 text-figs. London.

An account of experiences in photographing animal life and of methods used, illustrated by numbers of the photographs. Chapters III and IV, pp. 46-112,
relate to birds.

Kearton, Richard.

1906. Our bird friends | a book for all boys and girls | by | Richard
Kearton, F.Z.S. | Author of [*etc., 3 lines.*] | With one hundred
original illustrations from | photographs by | C. Kearton | Cassell
and Company, Limited | London, Paris, New York & Melbourne.
MCMVI | All rights reserved.

1 vol. crown 8vo (5¼x7½), pp. I-XVI, 1-215, frontisp. (monochr.),
100 text-figs. London.

A book about birds for children. First printed October 1900.

Kearton, Richard.

1924. See White, Gilbert, **Natural History of Selborne.**

Keeler, Charles A.

1893. Evolution of the colors | of | **North American land birds** | by |
Charles A. Keeler. | San Francisco: | California Academy of
Sciences, | January, 1893.

1 vol. 8vo, tit., pp. V-XII, 1-361, pll. I-XIX (col.; 5 fold.), 1 text-
cut, 2 diagrams. San Francisco. January 1893.

A detailed essay on the subject, with some fact and considerable theory. Reviewed at length in the Auk, **10,** pp. 189-196 and 373-380, 1893 (including the
author's rejoinder to the earlier criticism and a reply thereto). Issued as
Occasional Papers of the California Academy of Sciences, III. The copy at
hand was presented to D. G. Elliot by the author.

Keeler, Charles A.

1907. Bird notes afield | Essays on the birds | of the Pacific Coast
with a | field check list | by | Charles Keeler | Illustrated with |
reproductions | of photographs | [*Vignette.*] | Paul Elder and
Company | San Francisco and New York.

1 vol. post 8vo, pp. I-IX+1, 1-226, 16 pll. (monochr.). San Francisco
and New York.

A popular account of local bird-life. The appendix contains "a descriptive list
of California land birds with key." The present copy is of the second edition;
the first edition was first issued October 1899.

Kelsall, John Edward; and Munn, Philip Winchester.

1905. **The | birds of Hampshire | and the | Isle of Wight. | By |** The Revd. J. E. Kelsall, M.A., | Member of the British Ornithologists' Union, | and | Philip W. Munn, | Fellow of the Zoological Society; Member of the British Ornithologists' Union. | London: | Witherby & Co., 326, High Holborn, W.C | 1905.

1 vol. post 8vo, pp. I-XLIV, 1-371, 16 pll., 1 map (fold.; col.). London.

An annotated list of species, with notes on the local distribution of the various forms and the records of occurrences.

Kennedy, Alexander William Maxwell Clark.

1868. The | birds of Berkshire | and | Buckinghamshire: | a contribution to the | natural history of the two counties. | By | Alexander W. M. Clark Kennedy, | "An Eton Boy," | Member of the High Wycombe Natural History Society. | Eton | Ingalton and Drake. | London: | Simpkin, Marshall, and Company. | 1868.

1 vol. crown 8vo, pp. I-XIV, 1 l. (conts.), pp. 1-232, 4 pll. (col.), 1 text-fig. Eton.

A catalogue of 225 species of birds recorded from the two counties in question, with notes on local occurrence, habits, etc. Published by the author at the age of sixteen.

Kennerly, C. B. R.

1859. See U. S. Pacific Railroad Surveys, **Reports of Explorations and Surveys . . . . . . for a Railroad from the Mississippi River to the Pacific Ocean,** Vol. X.

Kermode, Francis.

1904. Provincial Museum, Victoria, B.C. | **Catalogue | of | British Columbia Birds.** | Victoria B.C.: | Printed by Richard Wolfenden, I.S.O., V.D., Printer to the King's Most Excellent Majesty. | 1904.

1 vol. 8vo, tit. cover, pp. 1-69. Victoria.

An annotated list of 363 species of birds known to occur in British Columbia.

Keulemans, John Gerrard.

1869-76. **Onze Vogels | in huis en tuin, |** beschreven en afgebeeld | door | J. G. Keulemans, | Adsistent aan 's Rijks Museum van Natuurlijke Historie. | Deel I [-III]. | [*Fig.*] | Leyden [Leiden (*Vols. II and III.*)], 1869 [1873; 1876]. P. W. M. Trap.

3 vols. post folio. Vol. I, tit., 2 ll. (conts.), 131 ll., 70 pll. (col.; by the author). Vol. II, tit., 2 ll. (conts.), 133 ll., 70 pll. (col.). Vol. III, tit., 2 ll. (conts.), 110 ll., 60 pll. (col.). Leyden.

Popular accounts of the habits of miscellaneous birds from various parts of the world, illustrated by excellent hand-colored plates of all the species.

Keyser, Leander S.

1896. See World's Congress on Ornithology, **Papers presented to the—**.

Keyser, Leander S.

1897. **In bird land** | by | Leander S. Keyser | [*Quot., 9 lines.*] | **Fourth edition** | [*Trade-mark.*] | Chicago | A. C. McClurg and Company | 1897.

1 vol. crown 8vo, pp. 1-269, 1 l. (advt.). Chicago.

A series of essays, reprinted from various periodicals, on bird life as observed by the author, mostly in the vicinity of Springfield, Ohio. The first edition was published in 1894.

Keyser, Leander S.

1898. Appleton's home reading books | **News from the** | **birds** | by | Leander S. Keyser | [*Vignette.*] | New York | D. Appleton and Company | 1898.

1 vol. crown 8vo, pp. I-XXII, 1-229+1, 1 l. (advt.), frontisp., 21 text-figs. New York.

A collection of original observations on bird life, popularly treated for juvenile and school usage.

Keyser, Leander S.

1902. **Birds of the Rockies** | By Leander S. Keyser | author of "In Bird Land," etc. | With Eight Full-page Plates (four in color) | by Louis Agassiz Fuertes; Many Illustra- | tions in the text by Bruce Horsfall, and | Eight Views of Localities from Pho- | tographs | with a complete check- | list of Colorado birds | [*Trade-mark.*] | Chicago. A. C. McClurg and Co. | Nineteen hundred and two.

1 vol. royal 8vo (6½x8½), 4 pr. ll. (half-tit., tit., ded. and conts.), pp. VII-XIV, 15-355, pll. I-VIII (4 col.; by Fuertes), 39 text-figs. (8 full-page). Chicago.

A popular account of various ornithological jaunts and observations made by the author in the Rocky Mountain region. Pleasantly written and containing many interesting notes. The book closes with an annotated check list of Colorado birds, based on Wells W. Cooke's "The Birds of Colorado," 1897 (q.v.).

Keyser, Leander S.

1907. **Our bird** | **comrades** | By | Leander S. Keyser | Author of [*etc., 2 lines.*] | [*Fig.*] | Rand, McNally & Company | Chicago New York London.

1 vol. 8vo (6x7½), 3 pr. ll. (half-tit., tit. and ded.), pp. 5-197, 15 (should be 16) pll. (col.). Chicago.

A series of popular essays on birds and bird-life. The illustrations (color-photographs) are of poor quality; one is missing.

Kinberg, Johan Gustav Hjalmar.

1881-87?. See Sundevall, Carl J.; and Kinberg, **Svenska Foglarna,** 1856-87?.

King, Clarence. (Ridgway, Robert.)

1877. [*Blazon.*] | Professional papers of the Engineer Department, U. S. Army. | No. 18. | **Report** | of the | **geological exploration of the fortieth parallel,** | made | by order of the Secretary of War according to acts of | Congress of March 2, 1867, | and March 3, 1869, | under the direction of | Brig. and Bvt. Major General A. A. Humphreys, | Chief of Engineers | by | Clarence King, | U. S. Geologist. | [*Vignette.*] | I-II > Volume IV. > United States Geological Exploration of the Fortieth Parallel. | Clarence King, Geologist-in-charge. | Part I. | Palæontology. | By | F. B. Meek. | Part II. | Palæontology. | By | James Hall and R. P. Whitfield. | Part III. | **Ornithology.** | By | Robert Ridgway. | Submitted to the Chief of Engineers and published by order of the Secretary of | War under authority of Congress. | Illustrated by XXIV plates. | Washington: | Government Printing Office. | 1877. V-VI.

1 vol. medium 4to, pp. I-XII, 1-197+1, 17 ll. (expl. of pll.), pll. I-XVII, 1 l. (subtit. Pt. II), 1 insert-slip (errata), pp. 199-302, 7 ll. (expl. of pll.), pll. I-VII, pp. 303-669. Washington.

Pt. III (pp. 303-669) consists of Ridgway's report on the avifauna of the region lying between Sacramento, California and the vicinity of Salt-Lake City, Utah, as investigated during a period from June 1867 to August 1869. Detailed field notes are a feature of the work which also includes descriptions of the localities visited, local faunal lists and other important matter. On p. 392 is a note to the effect that a report on the same subject was prepared much earlier and stereotyped in 1870,[1] and that various quotations were made by authors from time to time from the proof sheets. This original report was so long delayed that it became out of date and was suppressed and the plates were destroyed without being published. The present report was then prepared, differing considerably from the original, and published in 1877. Separate issues of Part III are also in existence.

---

[1]Coues states 1871-72, not 1870.

King, W. Ross.

1866. **The sportsman | and | naturalist in Canada,** | Or Notes | on | the natural history of the game, game birds | and fish of that country. | By | Major W. Ross King, | Unattached. | F.R.G.S., F.S.A.S. | Author of | "Campaigning in Kaffirland." | Illustrated with coloured plates and woodcuts. | London: | Hurst and Blackett, publishers, | 13, Great Marlborough Street. | 1866. | The right of Translation is reserved.

1 vol. superroyal 8vo, pp. I-XV+1, insert-slip (errata), 1 l. (list of illustrs.), pp. 1-334, 6 pll. (col.; by W. L. Walton), 13 text-figs. London.

A popular transcript of observations on the animal life of Canada made during three years of residence in the region. Many of the notes relate to birds and three of the colored plates and one woodcut are also ornithological. A manuscript note is inclosed recording errata not mentioned in the book or on the insert-slip which this note seems to have accompanied. According to this note, on p. 293, line 5, the sign, "$" appears to have been omitted from certain copies, thus indicating that there may have been two impressions of the volume. The present copy contains the "$".

King George and Queen Charlotte, A Voyage round the World in the—

1789. See Dixon, George.
1789. See Portlock, Nathaniel.

Kirkman, Frederick Bernuf Bever. (Bonhote, John Lewis; Coward, Thomas Alfred; Farren, William; Hartert, Ernst; Jourdain, Francis Charles Robert; Pycraft, William Plane; Selous, Edmund; Thomson, Arthur Landsborough; Turner, Emma Louisa; Wells, Thomas.)

1910-13. **The | British Bird | book** | an account of all the birds, nests | and eggs found in the British Isles | edited by | F B Kirkman B A Oxon | illustrated by two hundred coloured | drawings and numerous photographs | volume I [II; III; IV] | T C & E C Jack | 16 Henrietta Street London W C | and Edinburgh | 1911 [1911; 1912; 1913].

4 vols. royal 4to. Vol. I, 2 pr. ll. (half-tit. and tit.), pp.V-XII (conts. and list of pll.), 3 insert-slips (notice; errata in Sect. I. errata in Sect. II), pp. III-XVIII (pref.; various lists, etc.), pp. 1-449, pll. 1-46+18a (col.), I-XVII, 1 map, text-figs. 1-7 (preface), 1-4, 1 text-fig. (unnum.). Vol. II, 2 pr. ll. (half-tit. and tit.), pp. V-XII, 1-540, pll. 47-93+Egg Plate E (col.), XVIII-XXXVII, +Egg Plate E*, text-figs. 1-6, 4 text-figs. (unnum.). Vol. III; 2 pr. ll. (half-tit. and tit.) pp. V-XII, 1-609, pll. 94-135 (col.),

XXXIX-LVIII, text-figs. 1-4, 1-2, 1-3, 3 text-figs. (unnum.).
Vol. IV, 2 pr. ll. (half-tit. and tit.), pp. V-XII, 1-692, pll. 136-178
(col.), Egg Pll. A-D, F-R, V, W (col.), LIX-LXXIX, U, Egg Pll.
S and T, text-figs. 1-9, 1-2, 5 text-figs. (unnum.; maps). (Col.
pll. by Winifred Austen, G. E. Collins, H. Grönvold, H. Goodchild,
G. E. Lodge, Alfred Priest, A. W. Seaby and H. Wormald.) London
and Edinburgh.

A detailed, popular account of British birds, primarily of their habits but with
additional information for the identification of the forms treated; excellently
prepared and illustrated, although many of the colored plates are picturesque
rather than instructive. The photographs of nests and eggs are very good.
The work was issued in 12 parts, of which Pt. I appeared May 24, 1910; **II,**
Oct. 14, 1910; **III,** Jan. 23, 1911; **IV,** April 4, 1911; **V,** June 14, 1911; **VI,** Nov.
8, 1911; **VII,** Jan. 30; 1912, **VIII,** April 16, 1912; **IX,** June 28, 1912; **X,** Dec. 18,
1912; **XI,** June 1913; **XII,** Nov. 1913. Pts. I-III compose Vol. I; IV-VI, Vol.
II; VII-IX, Vol. III; X-XII, Vol. IV. The work is a symposium.

Kirkman, Frederick Bernuf Bever; and Hutchinson, Horace G. (Baker,
Max; Cairns, Douglas; Farren, William; Jourdain, Francis
Charles Robert; Malden, W. J.; Pollard, Hugh B. C.; Pycraft,
William Plane; Thomson, Arthur Landsborough; Wyatt, John H.)

1924. British | sporting birds | edited by | F. B. Kirkman and
Horace G. Hutchinson | the chapters on the natural history of |
each bird and the plates illustrating the | book drawn from The
British Bird Book | [Cut] | Contributors | Sporting Natural His-
tory | the Hon. Douglas Cairns W. P. Pycroft | Max Baker Rev.
F. C. R. Jourdain | W. J. Malden William Fanen | John H. Wyatt
A. L. Thompson | Hugh B. C. Pollard | London: T. C. & E. C.
Jack, Ltd. | 35 & 36 Paternoster Row, E.C. | and Edinburgh | 1924.
1 vol. foliopost 4to, pp. I-XII, 1-428, pll. I-XLIII (31 col.; by Winifred Austin, G. E. Collins, H. Grönvold, G. E. Lodge and W. A.
Seaby, and from photos.), text-figs. 1-3, 5 text-figs. (unnum.).
London and Edinburgh.

Chapters on the natural history of British game birds, taken, with the illustrations,
from Kirkman's "The British Bird Book," 1910-13 (q.v.) and supplemented
by new chapters on the shooting of the various sorts of game described.

Kittlitz, Friedrich Heinrich von.

1832-33. [Kupfertafeln zur Naturgeschichte der Vögel.]
1 vol. demy 8vo, (tit. missing), pp. I-II, 3-28, pll. 1-36 (col.). Frankfort am Main.

A series of hand-colored copper-plates of birds, accompanied by a short text which
includes the original descriptions of several species. The work was of ambi-
tious intent but was terminated the year following its inception. Three parts

appeared as follows. Part I, pp. I-II, 3-8, pll. 1-12, 1832; **XX**, pp. 9-20, pll. 13-24, 1832? (date quoted by Gadow, Cat. Birds Brit. Mus. 10, p. 474 under *Motacilla lugens* Kittl.; III, pp. 21-28, pll. 25-36, 1833.

Kjaerbölling, Niels.

1851-52. Danmarks Fugle, | beskrevn | af | N. Kjaerbølling. | Hertil et Billedvaerk med 304 naturtroe, colorerede Afbildninger; | udgivet med offentlig Understöttelse. | Kjøbenhavn. | Forfatterens Forlag. | Trykt i Sally B. Salomons Bogtrykkeri. | 1852.

> Ornithologia Danica. | Danmarks Fugle | i | 304 Afbildninger | af | de gamle Hanner, | med særskilt Text | af | N. Kjærbölling. | Kjøbenhavn. | Forfatterens Forlag (Gyldendalske Boghandling). | 1851. | Trykt hos Sally B. Salomon, Brünnichs Efterfølger.

2 vols. crown 8vo and crown folio. Text, 3 pr. ll. (tit. and pref.), pp. I-XXXIV (introd.), 1-422, I-IX+1+1 l. (index and errata). Atlas, tit., pll. I-XXI, XXIIa, XXIIb, XXIII-XXVII, XXVIIIa-XXVIIIc, XXIX-XXXII, XXXIIIa, XXXIIIb, XXXIV-XXXIX, XLa, XLb, XLI-L, LIa, LIb, LII-LV (col.; by the author), Copenhagen.

A handbook of Danish ornithology, illustrated by colored figures of the species. Judging by the complete agreement between plates and text, this constitutes the original work as issued. In 1854, 35 additional plates were issued as a supplement under the same short title (q.v.) as the atlas collated above. In 1856 (?) a second supplement appeared under the (sub) title of "De i det øvrige Scandinavien: . . forekommende Fuglearter" (q.v.) and, in the same year, a covering title of "Icones Ornithologiae Scandinavicae" (q.v.) was issued to embrace all three parts of the work. Jonas Collin, who issued a revised edition of the entire work in 1875-77, published two supplementary plates to his edition under the title of "To Nye Tavler til Dr. Kjaerbølling's Skandinaviens Fugle," (Cf. Kkaerbölling, 1879.). In the present copies the plates of these four works (or four portions of the same work) are bound in one volume; the original text, in 8vo, is separately bound.

Kjaerbölling, Niels.

1854. Ornithologia Danica. | Danmarks Fugle | i 252 Afbildninger af de dragtskiftende gamle Hanner, | samt de fra Hannerne væsentligt afvigende Hunner og unge Fugle. | Af | N. Kjærbölling. | 1854. 1 vol. crown folio, tit., pll. "Suppl." 1-"Suppl." 35 (other serial numbers also given) (col.). Copenhagen.

A series of colored plates of Danish birds intended to supplement those offered with the author's "Danmarks Fugle" of 1851-52 (q.v.).

Kjaerbölling, Niels.

1856. > De i det øvrige Scandinavien: | Sverrig, Norge, Paa Island og Færøerne | **forekommende** | **Fuglearter,** | der ei ere bemærkede i Danmark. | 45 colorerede Afbildninger. | Af | N. Kjærbølling.

1 vol. crown folio, (sub)title, pll. 2 "det Suppl." 1-2 "det Suppl." 8 (col.). Copenhagen. 1856(?).

Additional plates forming a second supplement to those presented in the author's "Danmarks Fugle" of 1851-52 (q.v.), and bound with them in the present copy. A title-page covering the original work and both supplements, and lettered "Icones Ornithologiae Scandinavicae" (q.v., 1856), may have appeared with this second supplement.

Kjaerbölling, Niels.

1856. Icones | ornithologiæ Scandinavicæ. | Scandinaviens: | Danmarks, Sverrigs, Norges, Islands of Færøernes | Fugle | i 600 colorerede Afbildninger | med særskilt Text | af | N. Kjærbølling. | Kjobenhavn. | Forfatterens Forlag. | 1856.

1 l., crown folio, (title-p. only). Copenhagen.

Title page covering the author's original "Danmarks Fugle" (with its atlas entitled, "Ornithologia Danica," etc.), the first supplement thereto entitled, "Ornithologia Danica," etc., and the second supplement with (sub)title of, "De i det øvrige Scandinavien . . Fuglearter," all of which are bound together in the present copy (Cf. Danmarks Fugle, 1852.). This covering title may have been issued with the second supplement.

Kjaerbölling, Niels. (Collin, Jonas.)

1879. To nye Tavler | til | Dr. Kjærbølling's | Skandinaviens Fugle. | Tegnede og lithographerede af C. Cordts. Kollorerede af Froken Hallesen. | Udgivet | Af | Jonas Collin. | [*Monogram.*] | Kjøbenhavn. | L. A. Jørgensens Forlag. | 1879. | O. C. Olsen & Co.

1 vol. crown folio, (cover-)tit., 2 pll. (col.; by C. Cordts). Copenhagen.

Two plates supplementary to Collin's "Skandinaviens Fugle" which is a revised edition of Kjaerbölling's "Icones Ornithologiae Scandinavicae" (q.v.), issued in 1875-77. The present copy is bound with the first edition of the latter work, 1852 (q.v.).

Klein, Jacob Theodor.

1750. Iacobi Theodori Klein | Secr. Civ. Ged. | Soc. Reg. Lond. et Acad. Scient. Bonon. Sodalis | historiae avivm | prodromvs | cvm praefatione | de | ordine animalivm in genere. | Accessit | historia mvris alpini | et | vetvs vocabvlarivm animalivm | msc. | cvm figvris. | [*Cut.*] | Lvbecae | apvd Ionam Schmidt. | MDCCL.

1 vol. demy 4to, 8 pr. ll., pp. 1-238, 7 pll. (4 fold.). Lübeck.

A general treatise on systematic ornithology with chapters on bird-migration, the hibernation of swallows and storks, and the life-history of the Alpine marmot, and a comparative list of zoological names in Latin (reprinted from "Georgii Agricolae de Animantibus subterraneis; 16 apud Froben. 1549") with their

German equivalents. The work was translated into German and published in 1760 as the "Vorbereitung zu einer vollständigen Vögelhistorie" (q.v.).

Klein, Jacob Theodor.

1759. Iac. Theod. Klein | Imperial. Academ. Scientt. Petropol. | Regiae Societat. Londinens. | et Academ. Bononiens. | membri | **stemmata** | **avivm** | qvadraginta tabvlis aeneis | ornata; | accedvnt | nomenclatores: | Polono-Latinvs | et | Latino-Polonvs. | Geschlechtstafeln | der Vögel, | mit vierzig Kupfern erläutert. | Lipsiae | Apvd Adam. Henr. Holle. | 1759.

1 vol. medium 4to, tit., 7 ll., pp. 1-48, pll. I-XL (fold.). Leipzig.

A study of the feet, heads and tongues of birds, as exhibited by various species or groups in the classification adopted by the author. The present copy contains the bookplate of Frederick DuCane Godman.

Klein, Jacob Theodor. (Behn, Friedrich Daniel.)

1760. Jak. Theodor Kleins, | Secret. der Stadt Danzig, der königl. Societ. in London | und der bologn. Akad. der Wissensch. Mitgliedes, | **Vorbereitung** | **zu einer vollständigen** | **Vögelhistorie,** | nebst einer Vorrede | von der Ordnung der Thiere Überhaupt, | und einem Zusatz | der Historie des Murmelthieres, | wie auch | eines alten Wörterbuchs der Thiere. | Aus dem Lateinischen übersetzt | durch | D. H. B. | [*Vignette.*] | Leipzig und Lübeck, | bey Jonas Schmidt 1760.

1 vol. post 8vo, 12 pr. ll., pp. 1-427, 6 pll. (fold.), 1 table of classif. (fold.). Leipzig and Lübeck.

A translation, into German, of Klein's "Historiae Avium Prodromus," 1750 (q.v.), with the same plates, two of which have been combined. The translation is the work of the editor, Friedrich Daniel Behn. There is also a revised edition, published in 1760 by Gottfried Teyger, which I have not seen.

Klein, Jacob Theodor.

1766. Jacobi Theodori Klein | Imperial. Academ. Scient. Petropol. Reg. Soc. Londin. Academ. Bonon. Aliarumque, | dum viveret, societatum membri ! **ova avium** | **plurimarum** | ad naturalem magnitudinem | delineata | et genuinis coloribus picta | J. T. Klein | Sammlung | verschiedener | Vögel Eyer | in natürlicher Grösse | und mit lebendigen Farben | geschildert und beschrieben. | Leipzig, Königsberg und Mietau, | bey Johann Jacob Kanter 1766.

1 vol. demy 4to, pp. 1-36, pll. I-XXI (col.; eggs), 3 decorations. Leipzig, Königsberg and Mitau.

Descriptions of the eggs of various species of birds from unrecorded localities over the world. Poorly colored figures of 145 eggs are given. The text is in both Latin and German.

Kleinschmidt, O.

1913. **Die Singvögel** | **der Heimat** | 86 farbige Tafeln | mit systematisch-biologischem Text | nebst Abbildung der wichtigsten Eier- und Nestertypen | letztere meist nach Naturaufnahmen in Schwarzdruck | von | O. Kleinschmidt [*Monogram.*] | 1913 | Verlag von Quelle & Meyer in Leipzig.

1 vol. 8vo, pp. I-X, 1 p. (contents), pp. 1-107 (2-100 on reverse of pll.), 1 l. (index and advt.), 8 ll. (advt.), pll. 1-100 (86 col.; by Kleinschmidt), 9 text-figs. Leipzig.

A popular account of the song-birds of Germany illustrated by excellent plates.

Knatchbull-Hugessen, Wyndham Wentworth, 3rd Baron Brabourne.

See Brabourne, Lord.

Knight, Charles William Robert.

1922. **Wild life** | **in the tree tops** | By | Capt. C. W. R. Knight | M.C., F.R.P.S., M.B.O.U. | [*Trade-mark.*] | Fifty-three illustrations from | photographs taken by the author | George H. Doran Co., New York | Thornton Butterworth Limited | 15 Bedford Street, London, W.C. 2.

1 vol. demy 4to, pp. 1-144, 32 pll. (photogrs.). New York and London.

An account of the author's "observations and experiences whilst studying those birds - and mammals - whose habit it is to frequent the upper branches" of trees in the British Islands. Most of the narratives, and of the excellent photographs which illustrate the work, relate to birds. The first impression of the book was made in 1921.

Knight, Ora Willis.

1897. Bulletin No. 3. | The University of Maine | Department of Natural History. | **A list of the** | **birds of Maine** | Showing their Distribution by Counties | And their Status in Each County. | Prepared under the auspices of the United Ornithologists of Maine | by | Ora W. Knight, B.S., | Assistant in Natural History. | Augusta | Kennebec Journal Print | 1897.

1 vol. 8vo, pp. 1-184. Augusta.

An annotated list of species, with notes on occurrence, distribution and habits. C. Hart Merriam's copy, presented by the author.

Knight, Ora Willis.

1908. **The birds of Maine** | with key to and description of the various | species known to occur or to have occurred | in the state,

an account of their distribu- | tion and migration, showing their
relative | abundance in the various counties of the | state as well
as other regions, and con- | tributions to their life histories | by |
Ora Willis Knight, M.S. | Member of Maine Ornithological So-
ciety [*etc., 2 lines.*] | Bangor, Maine | 1908.

1 vol. royal 8vo, pp. I-XVII+1, 19-693, 1 map, 27 pll., [38 photogrs.
(36 col.) added]. Bangor.

The title is self-explanatory. The present copy is No. 27 of the Subscription
Edition of three hundred signed copies (the regular edition was of two hundred
copies). In addition to the colored and plain photographs mentioned in the
collation, it contains two letters from O. W. Knight to John Lewis Childs and
(as a loose insert) a copy of "The Warbler," Vol. II, No. 1, pp. 1-8, pl. I, 1906,
in which is an article by Knight respecting the Yellow Palm Warbler, the
subject of the letters.

Knight, Wilbur Clinton.

1902. University of Wyoming. | Agricultural College Department. |
Wyoming Experiment Station, | Laramie, Wyoming. | Bulletin
No. 55. | September, 1902. | [*Vignette.*] Rocky Mountain Jay |
"Camp Robber". | **The Birds of Wyoming.** | By Wilbur C.
Knight. | Bulletins will be sent free upon request. Address:
Director Experiment | Station, Laramie, Wyo.

1 vol. 8vo, tit., pp. 1-174, 48 pll. (on 24 ll.; by Frank Bond), 55 text-
figs. Laramie. Sept. 1902.

An annotated list of the birds of Wyoming. Copy presented to Field Museum by
the author.

Knip, Madame. (Temminck, Coenraad Jacob.)

1809-11. Les pigeons, | par Madame Knip, | née Pauline de
Courcelles, | premier peintre d'histoire naturelle | se S. M. l'Im-
pératrice Reine Marie-Louise. | Le texte par C. J. Themminck
(*sic*), | Directeur de l'Académie des Sciences et des Arts de Harlem,
etc. | [*Monogram.*] | A Paris, | Chez { Mme Knip, Auteur et
Garnery, Libraire, Rue
Éditeur, Rue de Sorbonne, Musée des Artistes | de l'Imprimerie
de Seine, Hotel Mirabeau, No. 6 |
de Mame. | M.DCCC XI.

1 vol. superroyal folio, 2 pr. ll. (half-tit. and tit.), pp. 1-13+1 (discourse on pigeons), 2 ll. (unnum.;=pp. 23-26), pp. 27-34, 129-134
(=35-40), 133 (=41; end of Des Columbars), 1 p. (blank), pp.
1-128 (Les Colombes), 1-30 (Les Colombi-Gallines), I-III (contents), pll. 1-11 (Les Columbars), 1-18 (Les Colombes), 1-25, 25
(bis), 26-53, 34 (=54), 55-59 (end of Les Colombi-Gallines)
(=87 pll.; col.). Paris.

A noted work, stolen from Temminck, the original author, by Madame Knip, the artist, who suppressed the titles and introductory matter and substituted others of her own (cited above). A history of the transaction is given by Coues (Bull. U. S. Geol. Geog. Surv. Terr. **5**, (1), pp. 794-6, 1878. The general text is by Temminck. The work was issued in 15 livraisons, each, apparently (except for the last one), with 6 plates. Stone (Proc. Acad. Nat. Sci., Philad., **57**, p. 756, footn.), records dates from a copy in original covers, from which the following arrangement may be deduced. Livrs. **1-5**, pp. 23-41 (Les Columbars) and 1-49 (Les Colombes), pll. 1-11 (Les Columbars) and 1-18 (Les Colombes) all appeared in 1809; livrs. **6-8**, pp. 50-80, pll. 19-36 (Les Colombes) appeared in 1810; livrs. **9-15**, pp. 81-128 (Les Colombes) and 1-30 (Les Colombi-Gallines), 1-13+1 (discourse on pigeons), half-tit. and tit., pll. 37-59 (Les Colombes) and 1-16 (Les Colombi-Gallines) were issued in 1811. In the present copy, errors in pagination have been corrected (with a pen) as indicated above in the collation. In addition three lines of text are omitted from the bottom of p. 26 (unnum.; Les Colombars) and plates 33 and 47 are cited in the text as "XXXI" and "LXVII," respectively. In the second edition of this volume (1838, q.v.), some of the errors of the present edition are corrected. The lacuna between pp. 14 of the preliminary discourse and 23 of the general text, due in reality to the omission of some of Temminck's work, is explained by Madame Knip (reverse of half-tit.) on the ground of typographical error! Pages 23-41 (originally 129-134 and 133 bis) seem to have been transferred from a place in the volume beyond pp. 1-128 although they refer to pll. 1-11 (or I-XI) which are in proper position at the beginning of the text. In 1813-15 Temminck republished the text of the work in 8vo, 3 vols., including the gallinaceous birds, under the title "Histoire Naturelle Générale des Pigeons et des Gallinacés" (q.v.), and on pp. 640-644 of Vol. III presents his case with reference to the dispute with Madame Knip. According to the statement given there, Temminck was preparing to publish an illustrated folio on the gallinaceous birds, as a continuation of that on the pigeons, when the interruption occurred, but the work was abandoned and never resumed. The 8vo "Histoire Naturelle," in a measure, took the place of the larger projected work. Since the arrangement of species and groups is the same as that in the present work, it seems probable that the alteration in sequence and consequent re-pagination, as quoted above, was authorized by Temminck and cannot be ascribed to the machinations of Madame Knip. Of the original folio of Temminck, entitled, "Histoire Naturelle Générale des Pigeons," only twelve copies were seen and approved by Temminck, eight of which he retained himself.

Knip, Madame. (Temminck, Coenraad Jacob; Prévost, Florent.)

1838-43? Les pigeons, | par Madame Knip, | née Pauline de Courcelles, | le texte par C. J. Themminck (*sic*) [le texte par Florent Prévost], | Directeur de l'Académie des Sciences et des Arts de Harlem, etc., [Aide Naturaliste et Chef des Travaux Zoologique au Muséum] | et des Musées Royaux de Hollande [d'Histoire Naturelle]. | Tome premier [second]. | Deuxième édition. [*Line omitted.*] | [*Monogram.*] | A Paris, | Chez { Mme Knip, Auteur des / Bellizard, Dufour et

dessins, et Éditeur, Rue du Bac, No 77 [Bac, Passage Ste-Marie, 3].
Cie, Libraires, Rue de Verneuil, 1 bis
Typographie de Firmin Didot Frères, Rue Jacob, 56 [Paris.-
Typographie (*etc.*).].

2 vols. superroyal folio. Vol. I, 2 pr. ll. (half-tit. and tit.), pp. 1-13+1,
1-34, 129-134 (=35-38; 133-134 not altered), 133 (not altered),
1 p. (blank), pp. 1-128, 1-30, I-III, 87 pll. (col.; unnum.; in text
as in 1st ed., 1809-11, q.v.). Vol. II, 2 pr. ll. (half-tit. and tit.),
pp. 1-68, 67-68 (bis), 69-90, 93-114, 1 l. (contents), 60 pll. (col.;
unnum.; I-LX in text). Paris.

The first volume is a reprint, with alterations, of the same work of 1809 (q.v.)
The second volume, with text by Prévost, is new. Among the changes in the
first volume are the following. The title-page is altered; the missing 3 ll. at
the bottom of p. 26 are supplied; pp. 24-28 are numbered; p. 25 bears signature
"7"; pp. 23-26 have their headings altered to agree with the headings of the
rest of the work (they are different in the 1st ed.); the plate numbers are suppressed throughout, being barely visible although not inked; pp. 133-134 and
134 (*bis*) are left with the pagination unaltered, although on pp. 129-132 the
corrections have been made as in the copy of the 1st ed. (q.v.). Pll. XXXIII
and XLVII are wrongly given in the text as "XXXI" and "LXVII," as in
ed. 1. Vol. II contains less errors, but the reference to pl. VI is given as "XI,"
and pll. VII and VIII (with the accounts referring to them) are transposed in
sequence.

An illustrated supplement, by Charles Lucien Bonaparte, appeared in 1857-58
under the title, "Iconographie des Pigeons" (q.v.).

The inclusive dates are from Coues, after Engelmann.

Knobel, Edward.

1899. Field key | to the | land birds | illustrated | by | Edward
Knobel | Boston | Bradlee Whidden | 1899.

1 vol. crown 8vo, 3 pr. ll., pp. 1-55, pll. I-IX (col.), 35 text-figs.
Boston.

A popular handbook for the identification of birds in the field in eastern North
America. The colored plates contain figures of the species arranged according
to size, with reference numbers which, in the text, accompany short descriptions
that supplement the plates.

Knowlton, Frank Hall. (Lucas, Frederic A.)

1909. American Nature Series | Group 1. Natural History | **Birds
of the World** | a popular account | by | Frank H. Knowlton,
Ph.D. | United States National Museum | Member of the American
Ornithologists' Union [*etc.*, *2 lines.*] | with a chapter on the anatomy
of birds | by | Frederic A. Lucas | Curator-in-Chief, Brooklyn
Institute of Arts and Sciences | the whole edited by | Robert
Ridgway | Curator of Birds, United States National Museum |

with 16 colored plates and 236 illustrations | [*Blazon.*] | New York | Henry Holt and Company | 1909.

1 vol. imperial 8vo (trimmed), pp. I-XIII+1, 1-873, 16 pll. (col.; by Mary Mason Mitchell), figs. 1-233, 19a, 32a and 103a. New York.

A comprehensive, general survey of the entire class of birds, with descriptions of characteristic species and with introductory chapters on anatomy, distribution, migration and classification. Chapter II, pp. 13-25, on "The Anatomy of Birds," is by Frederic A. Lucas.

Knox, Arthur Edward.

1850.   Ornithological rambles | in | Sussex; | with | a systematic catalogue | of | the birds of that county, | and | remarks on their local distribution. | By A. E. Knox, M.A., F.L.S., &c. | Second edition. | London: | John Van Voorst, Paternoster Row. | M.-DCCC.L.

1 vol. crown 8vo, pp. I-X, 1-254, 4 pll. (monochr.; by Knox). London.

A popular account of general observations on birds in Sussex, England. The "systematic catalogue" (pp. 181-254) is an annotated list of the species of Sussex birds. The work appeared in three editions, of which this is the second. The first was published in 1849.

Koenig, Alexander. (le Roi, Otto.)

1911.   Avifauna Spitzbergensis. | Forschungsreisen nach der Bären-Insel | und dem Spitzbergen-Archipel, mit ihren | faunistischen und floristischen Ergebnissen. | Herausgegeben und verfasst | von | Alexander Koenig. | Mit 74 Textbildern, 26 Heliogravüren, 34 Farbentafeln und einer Karte. | Bonn 1911.

1 vol. imperial 4to (trimmed), 2 pr. ll. (tit. and ded.), pp. VII-X, 1 l. (subtit.), pp. 1-294, frontisp. (col.; by A. Thorburn), pll. I-XXXIII (col.; by J. G. Keulemans, H. Schultze and G. Krause), 26 pll. (heliogravure), text-figs. 1-5, 1-4, and 1, 63 text-figs. (unnum.), 1 map (fold.). Bonn.

An account of three ornithological expeditions to Spitzbergen with a detailed discussion of the avifauna of the region. The general portions are by Koenig, the detailed ornithological sections by le Roi. A report on the Arthropoda collected by the expeditions, the work of various authors, is appended.

Kohts, Alexander Erich.

1910.   See Lorenz, Theodor, Die Birkhuhner Russlands.

Kollibay, Paul.

1906.   Die Vögel | der Preussischen Provinz | Schlesien | Von | Paul Kollibay | Vorsitzendem des Vereins schlesischer Ornithologen

[*etc.*, *3 lines.*] | [*Trade-mark.*] | Breslau 1906 | Verlag von Wilh. Gottl. Korn.

1 vol. 8vo, pp. 1-370, frontisp. (portrs.), 3 text-figs. Breslau.

Accounts of the occurrence and distribution in Silesia of some 317 forms of birds, with concise characterizations of each; said to be the first comprehensive treatment of the subject since Gloger's "Schlesiens Wirbelthier-Fauna" of 1833 (q.v.). With the copy are bound a supplement (from Orn. Jahrb., 20 Jahrg., Heft 5-6, pp. 192-202, 1909) and a copy of the "Mitteilungen der Schlesischen Komitees für Naturdenkmalpflege," Nos. 2 and 3, May 1911.

Koningsberger, Jacob Christian.

1909. > Mededeelingen | uitgaande van het | Departement van Landbouw | No. 7. | **De Vogels van Java** | en | hunne oeconomische beteekenis | door | Dr. J. C. Koningsberger. | Deel II | (met 52 platen). | Batavia | G. Kolff & Co. | 1909.

1 vol. superroyal 8vo (7¼x10¼), 4 pr. ll., pp. 1-87, 52 pll. (=figs. 1-52). Batavia.

The second part of a work on the economic ornithology of Java. Part 1 was issued about seven years previously.

Krause, Georg.

1901. Die | **Columella der Vögel** | (Columella auris avium) | ihr Bau und dessen Einfluss auf | die Feinhörigkeit | neue Untersuchungen und Beiträge | zur | comparativen Anatomie des Gehörorganes | von | Georg Krause | Mit 4 Tafeln in Lichtdruck und 2 Textillustrationen | Berlin | R. Friedländer & Sohn | 1901.

1 vol. crown folio, pp. I-VII+1, 1-26, pll. I-IV, 2 text-figs. Berlin.

A detailed, comparative study of the columella, or sound-transmitting bone, of the avian ear.

Krause, Georg.

1905-13. Georg Krause. | **Oologia** | **universalis** | **palaearctica** | [*Blazon.*] | Stuttgart | Fritz Lehmann, Verlag. | 1906.

78 parts, (size of) medium 4to, tit., index, 18 subtits., 158 ll. (text), 157 pll. (should be 158) (col.; by Krause). Stuttgart.

A series of large, beautifully drawn and colored plates of the eggs of Palaearctic birds, showing series and variations in greater or less number. The text, in German and English, gives name and synonymy, and details of nidification in concise form for each species, with full data for each egg or clutch shown. The work was interrupted in 1913 and has never been resumed. It was issued in 78 livraisons, each of which, after the first, contained 2 pll.,-the first one, 4 pll. As these plates are not numbered, it is necessary to list them by subjects. For convenience, the dates will be given first, as ascertained from the Journal für Ornithologie and the Zoological Record. Livr. 1 noted (as sample copy) J.f.O. Oct. 1905; **2-3**, J.f.O. Oct. 1906; **4-11**, 1906, noted J.f.O. Jan. 1907; **12-21**,

J.f.O. July 1907; **22-23**, 1907; **24-34**, 1907, noted J.f.O. Jan. 1908; **35-40**, 1908; **41-47**, 1908; noted J.f.O. Jan. 1909; **48-49**, J.f.O. April 1909; **50-51**, J.f.O. Oct. 1910; **52-53**, 1910, noted J.f.O. Jan. 1911; **54-61**, J.f.O. July 1911; **62-64**, 1911; **65-71**, J.f.O. Oct. 1911; **72**, 1911; 1911; **73-77**, 1912; **78**, J.f.O. July 1913. Contents of livraisons are as follows. **1**, *Coturnix coturnix, Corvus corax, Turdus musicus, Aquila chrysaëtus* I, subtit. Accipitres; **2**, *Uria troile* I and II, tit. and index; **3**, *Pyrrhula europaea, Coccothraustes coccothraustes*, subtit. Passeres; **4**, *Gyps fulvus, Aquila orientalis*, subtit. Pygopodes; **5**, *Lanius collurio, Vultur monachus*, subtit. Pterocletes; **6**, *Cettia cetti, Anser fabalis*, subtit. Gallinae; **7**, *Tetrao urogallus, Cisticola cisticola*, subtit. Alcae; **8**, *Lyrurus tetrix, Colymbus glacialis*, subtit. Chenomorphae; **9**, *Nisaëtus fasciatus, Ardeola ralloides*, subtit. Limicolae; **10**, *Nycticorax nycticorax, Phoyx purpurea*, subtit. Herodiones; **11**, *Garzetta garzetta, Cygnus musicus*, subtit. Gaviae; **12**, *Lagopus mutus, Larus marinus*, subtit. Plataleae; **13**, *Milvus ictinus, Procellaria pelagica;* **14**, *Fringilla coelebs, Uria rhingvia;* **15**, *Oriolus galbula, Colymbus septentrionalis;* **16**, *Tetrastes bonasia, Gypaetus barbatus;* **17**, *Graculus graculus, Neophron percnopterus* I; **18**, *Larus gelastes, Sterna cantiaca;* **19**, *Panurus biarmicus, Parus cristatus;* **20**, *Otis tarda* I, *Aegialitis alexandrina;* **21**, *Aquila chrysaëtus* II, *Alca torda;* **22**, *Turdus viscivorus, Monticola saxatilis;* **23**, *Sturnus vulgaris, Sturnus unicolor;* **24**, *Pastor roseus, Alle alle;* **25**, *Caprimulgus ruficollis, Platalea leucorodia*, subtit. Fulicariae; **26**, *Cerchneis naumanni, Falco subbuteo*, subtit. Picariae; **27**, *Cerchneis vespertina, Pernis apivorus*, subtit. Columbae; **28**, *Buteo vulgaris* I and II, subtit. Tubinares; **29**, *Accipiter nisus* I and II, subtit. Steganopodes; **30**, *Hierofalco gyrfalco, Falco regulus*, subtit. Alectorides; **31**, *Falco communis* I and II, subtit. Hemipodii; **32**, *Cerchneis tinnuncula* I and II; **33**, *Caprimulgus europaeus, Cygnus olor;* **34**, *Neophron percnopterus* II, *Pandion haliaëtus* I; **35**, *Pica pica, Anser ferus;* **36**, *Garrulus glandarius, Aquila maculata* I; **37**, *Lanius excubitor, Lanius minor;* **38**, *Hierofalco candicans, Hierofalco islandus;* **39**, *Grus grus* I and II; **40**, *Anthropoides virgo, Uria grylle;* **41**, *Pandion haliaëtus* II, *Larus cachinnans;* **42**, *Charadrius pluvialis, Larus minutus;* **43**, *Otis tarda* II, *Hierofalco saker;* **44**, *Aquila melanaëtus* I and II; **45**, *Pteroclurus alchata, Falco eleanorae;* **46**, *Circus pygargus, Harelda glacialis;* **47**, *Circus aeruginosus, Branta bernicla;* **48**, *Pterocles arenarius, Cygnus bewicki;* **49**, *Rhodostethia rosea, Clangula islandica;* **50**, *Asio otus, Syrnium aluco;* **51**, *Scops giu, Asio accipitrinus;* **52**, *Hypolais polyglotta, Sitta syriaca;* **53**, *Crex crex, Hydrochelidon nigra;* **54**, *Eudromias morinellus, Aquila clanga;* **55**, *Cuculus canorus* I, *Aquila maculata* II; **56**, *Cuculus canorus* II and III; **57**, *Cuculus canorus* IV, *Gallinula chloropus;* **58**, *Turnix sylvatica, Regulus ignicapillus;* **59**, *Cuculus canorus* V, *Nucifraga caryocatactes;* **60**, *Hirundo rustica, Gelochelidon anglica;* **61**, *Pyrrhocorax alpinus, Sitta caesia;* **62**, *Cuculus canorus* VI, *Acrocephalus aquaticus;* **63**, *Falco feldeggii, Plegadis falcinellus;* **64**, *Astur palumbarius, Anser albifrons;* **65**, *Perdix perdix, Nyctea scandiaca;* **66**, *Saxicola deserti, Circaëtus gallicus;* **67**, *Haliaëtus albicillus, Ardea cinerea;* **68**, *Oedicnemus oedicnemus, Buteo ferox* I; **69**, *Recurvirostra avocetta, Buteo desertorum;* **70**, *Houbara undulata, Nisaetus pennatus;* **71**, *Aegialitis dubia, Circus cyaneus;* **72**, *Milvus korschun* I and II; **73**, *Trypanocorax frugilegus* I and II; **74**, *Zapornis parva, Circus macrurus;* **75**, *Buteo cirtensis, Megalestris catarrhactes;* **76**, *Aegialitis hiaticula, Scolopax rusticola;* **77**, *Syrrhaptes paradoxus, Vanellus vanellus;* **78**, *Buteo ferox* II, *Aquila adalberti.*

The present copy is in the original wrappers. Text and plates, with one or two exceptions, are printed on cardboard.

Krider, John.

1879. Forty years notes | of a | field ornithologist, | by John Krider, | Member of the Philadelphia Academy of Natural Sciences, | and Author of Krider's Sporting Anecdotes, | Philadelphia. | Giving a description of all birds killed and | prepared by him. | Philadelphia: | Press of Joseph H. Weston, 438 Walnut Street. | 1879.

1 vol. post 8vo, 2 pr. ll. (tit. and pref.), pp. I-XI+1, 1-84, (orig. wrapper with cut of Bald Eagle on back). Philadelphia.

An annotated list of the species of birds collected by the author during the preceding forty years. The annotations consist of extremely brief remarks concerning the abundance, distribution, or habits of the various species, usually without definite dates of occurrence or capture, even for the rarer forms whose records would be especially valuable.

Krohn, H.

1925. Die Vogelwelt | Schleswig-Holsteins | und ihre | Erforschung im Verlauf | von fünf Jahrhunderten von 1483 | bis zur gegenwart | von | H. Krohn | Hamburg | Im Sonnenschein-Verlag | Hamburg 33.

1 vol. demy 8vo, pp. 1-494, 1 pl. (fold.; maps). Hamburg.

A review of the ornis of Schleswig-Holstein as recorded in literature and represented in collections. A rather unfavorable critique of the book is given by H. Hildebrandt in the Ornithologische Monatsberichte, **33**, No. 5, pp. 159-161, Sept. 1925.

Krüper, Theobald.

1875. See Mommsen, August, **Griechische Jahreszeiten.**

Kuhl, Heinrich. (Hasselt, J. C. van.)

1820. Beiträge | zur | Zoologie | und | vergleichenden Anatomie | von | Heinrich Kuhl, | Doctor der Philosophie und vieler gelehrten Gesellschaften des In- und Auslandes | Mitgliede. | Mit Abbildungen, gezeichnet vom Verfasser. | Frankfurt am Main, | Verlag der Hermannschen Buchhandlung. | 1820.

1 vol. (2 pts.) demy 4to, 5 pr. ll. (tit., ded., pref. and subtit. of Pt. I), pp. 1-151+1, 2 ll. (subtit. and pref. of Pt. II), pp. 1-212, 1 l. (errata), pll. I, II and III (on 1 p.), IV and V (on 1 p.), VI, "VI+", "VI++", VII-XI (= 11 pll.; fold.) Frankfurt am Main. 1820 (post April 9).

Miscellaneous papers which the author wished to get into print before a projected journey to India. Part I is entitled, "Beiträge zur Zoologie," and contains (pp. 133-151) a section on ornithology consisting of "Beiträge zur Kenntniss der Procellarien," with descriptions of several new species. Part II is entitled, "Beiträge zur vergleichenden Anatomie" and is accredited to van Hasselt and Kuhl, with "Abbildungen und Beschreibungen von Dr. H. Kuhl." Section III of Pt. II comprises "Beiträge zur Zergliederung der Vögel in den Jahren 1817, 1818 and 1819," occupying pp. 71-104. The preface to the entire work is dated April 9, 1820.

Kuhl, Heinrich.

1820.   H. Kuhl, Ph. Dr. Ac. C. L. C. N. C. S. | **Conspectus Psittacorum.** | Cum specierum definitionibus, novarum descriptionibus, | synonymis et circa patriam singularum naturalem | adversariis, adjecto indice museorum, ubi earum | artificiosae exuviae servantur. | Cum Tabulis III. aeneis pictis.

1 vol. foliopost 4to, pp. 1-104, pll. I-III (col.; by Huard and A. Prévost). Bonn.

A monograph of the parrots, containing descriptions of many new species.

Kumlien, Ludwig.

1879.   Department of the Interior: | U. S. National Museum. | -15- | Bulletin | of the | United States National Museum. | No. 15. | Published under the direction of the Smithsonian Institution | Washington: | Government Printing Office. | 1879. > **Contributions | to the | natural history | of | Arctic America,** | made in connection with | the Howgate polar expedition, 1877-78, | by | Ludwig Kumlien, | Naturalist of the expedition. | Washington: | Government Printing Office. | 1879.

1 vol. 8vo, pp. 1-179. Washington.

The report on the natural history of a polar exploration. Kumlien is responsible for the introduction and the reports on ethnology, mammalogy and ornithology, while various authors contributed the remainder. The ornithological portion occupies pp. 69-105.

Kumlien, Ludwig; and Hollister, Ned.

1903.   Vol. 2 [*corrected to* "*3*"]. (New Series) January, April, July, 1903. Nos. 1, 2 and 3 | Bulletin | of the | Wisconsin | Natural History | Society | **The birds of Wisconsin** | By L. Kumlien and N. Hollister· | Published with the co-operation | of the | Board of Trustees | of the | Milwaukee Public Museum. | Milwaukee, Wisconsin.

1 vol. 8vo, pp. I-IV, 1-143, 8 pll. Milwaukee.

An annotated list of the birds of Wisconsin.

Kuroda, Nagamichi.

1913. **Geese and swans | of | the world** | by | N. Kuroda | The Ornithological Society | of Japan | 1913.

1 vol. 8vo (7½x10), 4 ll., pp. 1-118, 1-2 (bibl.), 5 ll. (blank), pp. 1-4 (index), 1 l., 9 pll. (4 col.). Tokyo.

Text in Japanese except for the scientific nomenclature, bibliography and various notes and tabulations.

Kuser, John Dryden.

1917. **The | Way to Study Birds** | By | John Dryden Kuser | With 9 Illustrations in Color | G. P. Putnam's Sons | New York and London | The Knickerbocker Press | 1917.

1 vol. cap 8vo, 3 pr. ll. (half-tit., tit. and ded.), pp V-XI+1,1-85, 9 pll. (col.; by L. A. Fuertes). New York and London.

A beginner's guide to the study of birds in the vicinity of New York City, with a discussion of methods of study and record.

Küster, Heinrich Carl.

1834-36. See Hahn, Carl Wilhelm; and Kuster, **Voegel aus Asien, Afrika, Amerika und Neuholland,** 1818-1836.

Küster, Heinrich Carl.

1836-41. See Hahn, Carl Wilhelm, **Ornithologischer Atlas,** 1834-41.

CATALOGUE

OF THE

EDWARD E. AYER
ORNITHOLOGICAL LIBRARY

PART II

UNPUBLISHED DRAWING BY C. L. LANDBECK FROM HIS PERSONAL COPY OF HIS
"SYSTEMATISCHE AUFZÄHLUNG DER VÖGEL WÜRTEMBERGS."

See p. 367.

FIELD MUSEUM OF NATURAL HISTORY

PUBLICATION 240

ZOOLOGICAL SERIES   VOL. XVI

CATALOGUE

OF THE

EDWARD E. AYER

ORNITHOLOGICAL LIBRARY

PART II

BY

JOHN TODD ZIMMER

Assistant Curator of Birds

WILFRED H. OSGOOD
Curator, Department of Zoology
EDITOR

CHICAGO, U. S. A.

November, 1926

PRINTED IN THE UNITED STATES OF AMERICA
BY FIELD MUSEUM PRESS

CATALOGUE

OF THE

EDWARD E. AYER

ORNITHOLOGICAL LIBRARY

PART II

BY

JOHN T. ZIMMER

Labatie, M. de.

1844. See Bouteille, Hipp.; and Labatie, **Ornithologie du Dauphiné,** 1843-44.

Lacépède, Bernard Germain Étienne de la Ville.

1818. See Buffon, George L. L., **Oeuvres Complètes.**

Lacépède, Bernard Germain Étienne de la Ville.

1819. Vue générale | des progrès | de plusieurs branches | des sciences naturelles, | depuis la mort de Buffon, | Pour faire suite aux Œuvres complètes | de ce grand naturaliste; | Par M. le Comte de Lacepède. | Paris, | Rapet et Cie, Rue Saint-André-Des-Arcs, No. 41, | Éditeurs des Œuvres complètes de Buffon, en douze | volumes in -8o., avec cinq volumes de supplément, par M. le Comte de Lacepède. | 1818.

1 vol. post 8vo, 2 pr. ll. (half-tit. and tit.), pp. 1-112. Paris.

A general essay on the (then) recent progress in natural science. On. pp. 74-89 and 92-112 are a "Tableau des Sous-Classes, Divisions, Sous-Divisions, Ordres et Genres des Oiseaux" and a "Table Méthodique de la Classe des Mammifères." These appear to be the "Tableaux Méthodiques des Mammifères et des Oiseaux" first published in 1799 in the author's "Discours d'Ouverture et de Clôture du Cours d'Histoire Naturelle," etc. (Cf. Richmond, Auk, **16,** pp. 325-329, 1899 and l.c. **17,** pp. 166-167, 1900.). On pp. 72-73 and 90-91 are supplements to the "Tableau" and "Table," containing references to various authors whose recent works may be consulted for additions to the lists of genera and subgenera here published. The arrangement of the new genera of birds in these lists is the same as copied by Richmond (l.c., **17,** p. 167) from Lacépède's original Tableaux and it appears probable, therefore, that the tables have not been altered here, but I am unable to state this definitely in the absence of the original work. Although the title-page bears the date, 1818, the general text (p. 71) is dated December 12, 1818, and Engelmann quotes the work under date of the following year, which is probably correct. The present copy is bound with Vol. XII of Lacépède's "Oeuvres Completes de Buffon, Nouvelle (Rapet) Ed.," 1817-19 (Cf. Buffon, 1818.). It forms a sort of appendix or supplement to this work and was originally intended to be issued with Vol. XII; a note by the publishers on p. 566 of that volume announces that it will form a separate volume which will be issued separately a month later and supplied free to subscribers. It therefore may be considered to form a distinct publication under its own title.

Lacroix, Adrien.

1873-75. Catalogue raisonné | des oiseaux | observés | dans les Pyrénées Françaises | et les régions limitrophes | comprenant | les départements de la Haute-Garonne, de l'Aude, de l'Ariège, du Gers, | de l'Hérault, des Hautes-Pyrénées, | du Tarn, du Tarn-et-Garonne et des Pyrénées-Orientales | suivi de deux tables alphabétiques des espèces et de leurs synonymes | en patois de Toulouse | avec huit planches coloriées | par | Adrien Lacroix | Membre Fondateur de la Société d'Histoire Naturelle de Toulouse | Toulouse Paris | Édouard Privat   J.-B. Baillière et Fils, | Libraire-Éditeur,   Libraire de l'Académie nationale de Médecine | Rue des Tourneurs, 45   Rue Hautefeuille, 19 | 1873-1875.

1 vol. 8vo, pp. 1-299, pll. 1-8 (col.; by Lacroix). Toulouse and Paris.

A synonymic, distributional catalogue, without descriptions. I can find no information relative to its manner of publication except that much the same subject matter was covered by the author in articles published in the Bulletin de la Société d'Histoire Naturelle de Toulouse, 1872-75. The present work may be a compilation of these, published in 1875. The preface, dated April 9, 1873, begins on a page whose heading is the title of one of the articles, not of the complete work,-reading, "Catalogue raisonné des Oiseaux Observés sur le versant Français des Pyrénées," etc.

The copy has the name of Lacroix in manuscript on the title-page and contains the bookplate of F. D. Godman.

Lafresnaye, Frédéric de.

1838. Essai | d'une nouvelle manière de grouper les genres | et les espèces | De l'Ordre | des Passereaux | (Passeres L.) | d'après leurs rapports de mœurs et d'habitation, | Par F. de La Fresnaye. | Falaise, | Brée l'aîné, imprimeur-libraire. | Paris; Meilhac, libraire, Cloître Saint-Benoît, 10. | 1838.

1 vol. post 8vo, tit., pp. 1-25. Falaise.

A rare paper on the general classification of Passerine birds, including the descriptions of two new species, *"Turdus nivei-capillus"* (p. 16) and *"Argya luctuosa"* (p. 22). It appears to be a separate work but Bangs and Penard (Bull. Mus. Comp. Zool., **63**, No. 2, p. 31, June 1919) cite it as having some connection with the Memoires de la Société académique des Sciences, Arts et Belles-Lettres de Falaise. Engelmann cites the title under date of 1841 which is evidently an error.

Laimbeer, Richard Harper.

1923. Birds I have known | by | Richard Harper Laimbeer | illustrated with 50 colored plates, | and with 48 snapshots from life | by the author | G. P. Putnam's Sons | New York & London | The Knickerbocker Press | 1923.

1 vol. post 8vo, pp. I-XVIII, 1-401, 50 pll. (col.; by Allan Brooks, L. A. Fuertes, Bruce Horsfall and L. Sawyer), 49 text-figs. (full p.). New York and London.

A popular account of observations on bird-life on Long Island, U. S. A. The colored plates are from the leaflets of the National Association of Audubon Societies.

Laing, Hamilton M.

1913. Out with | the birds | by | Hamilton M. Laing | Illustrated with Photographs | [*Design.*] | New York | Outing Publishing Company | MCMXIII.

1 vol. post 8vo, pp. 1-249, 24 pll. New York.

Miscellaneous popular essays on bird-life and on the author's experiences afield.

Laishley, Richard.

1858. A | popular history | of | British birds' eggs. | By | Richard Laishley. | London: | Lovell Reeve, Henrietta Street, Covent Garden. | 1858.

1 vol. crown 8vo (4¾x6¼), pp. I-XI+1, 1-313, pll. I-XX (col.). London.

A popular account of the nests and eggs of British birds, illustrated with very poor colored plates.

Lambrecht, Koloman.

1921. See Diener, C., **Fossilium Catalogus, Aves.**

Lamouroux.

1824. See Buffon, George L. L.; and Daubenton, **Oeuvres completes de Buffon,** 1824-31.

1828. Idem, 1828-33.

Landbeck, Christian Ludwig.

1834. Systematische Aufzählung | der | Vögel Würtembergs, | mit | Angabe ihrer Aufenthaltsörter und ihrer Strichzeit. | Aus Auftrag | der Central-Stelle des landwirtschaftlichen Vereins in Würtemberg | entworfen | von | Christian Ludwig Landbek. |

Grundherrl. von Gemmingen-Steinegg'schem Rent-Beamten. | Besonders abgedrukt aus dem Correspondenzblatt des landwirtschaftlichen | Vereins. | Stuttgart und Tübingen, | in der J. G. Cotta-'schen Verlagshandlung. | 1834.

1 vol. post 8vo, (orig. cover), pp. I-XII, 1-84, [103-107 (altered to 85-89)+1, 333-336, 64 ll. (manuscript), 13 pll. (col.; 2 fold.)]. Stuttgart and Tübingen. 1834 [-?].

A detailed account of the birds of Wurtemberg. This is the author's own copy with marginal annotations and 64 ll. of manuscript notes. Some of these notes were published subsequently by the author in various places. The illustrations are all extras and comprise 13 plates, two of which are original drawings, 2 apparently unpublished lithographs, 8 lithographs prepared for publication as pll. I-V, VIII, IX and XI of the author's "Naturgeschichte und Abbildungen sämmtlicher Vögel Europa's" (which never appeared), and 1 etching of uncertain origin. There are also appended two supplements which appear to have been published in the "Correspondenzblatt des landwirtschaftlichen Vereins" where the present work made its first appearance; I am unable to fix any dates for them. A reference in each of the supplements indicates that the general work appeared in the "Corr. Bl. des landw. Vereins, Jahrgang 1835, Bd. I, H(eft) 1, S. 17," a year later than the date on the title-page of the separate reprint. A manuscript note by Homeyer on the inside of the front cover explains the origin of the present copy.

Langdon, Frank W.

1877. A catalogue | of the | Birds of the Vicinity of Cincinnati, | with notes. | By | Frank W. Langdon. | Salem, Mass.: | The Naturalist's Agency. | 1877.

1 vol. 8vo, pp. 1-18. Salem. April 1877.

An annotated check-list of 282 species and subspecies. A revised list (q.v.) was published in 1879. The copy at hand was presented to Ernest Ingersoll by the author; the letter accompanying the gift is attached. The date, as quoted, is given by the author in his revised list.

Langdon, Frank W.

1879. A revised list | of | Cincinnati birds, | by | Frank W. Langdon. | 1879. | Printed by James Barclay, 269 Vine Street, Cincinnati, O.

1 vol. 8vo, cover-tit., pp. 1-27. Cincinnati.

A separately paged reprint of the author's paper published in the Journal of the Cincinnati Society of Natural History, 1, No. 4, pp. 167-193, Jan. 1879. The original list, "A Catalogue of the Birds of the Vicinity of Cincinnati" (q.v.), was published in 1877. The title transcribed above is from the original wrapper.

Langville, J. Hibbert.

1884. Our birds | in | their haunts: | a popular treatise on the birds of | eastern North America. | By | Rev. J. Hibbert Langille,

M.A. | [*Quot., 9 lines.*] | Boston: | S. E. Cassino & Company. |
1884.

1 vol. 8vo, pp. 1-624, 2 pll., 24 text-figs. (3 full-p.). Boston.

An extensive series of essays on bird-life, based on personal observations, arranged
by species (not in systematic order) and illustrated by woodcuts. Of a distinctly
popular nature, the book contains a mass of information presented in literary
form.

Laplace, Cyrille Pierre Théodore. (Eydoux, Fortune; Gervais, Paul.).

1839. > **Voyage** | **atour du monde** | par les mers de l'Inde et de
Chine | exécuté **sur la corvette** de l'état | **La Favorite** | pendent
les années 1830. 1831 et 1832 | sous le commandement | de M. La-
place | Capitaine de frégate; | publié | par ordre de M. le Vice-
Amiral Comte de Rigny | Ministre de la Marine et des Colonies. |
Tome V. | [*Vignette.*] | Paris. | Arthus Bertrand, Éditeur, |
Libraire de la Société de Géographie de Paris | et de la Société
Royale des Antiquaires du Nord, Rue Hautefeuille, 23. | M DCCC
XXXIX. > **Zoologie** | par | M. Fortuné Eydoux, Cirurgien [*etc.*,
5 lines.]. > 2e partie. | Zoologie, | par | MM. Fortuné Eydoux
et Paul Gervais.

1 vol. 8vo, pp. J-VIIJ, 2 ll. (subtit. and tit. of Pt. I), pp. 1-195+1,
1-64 (incl. tit. of Pt. II), 64 bis-64 quater., 65-200, I-IV (incl. tit.
of Suppl.), 5-30, 1-2 (index to Suppl.), pll. 1-60 (51 col.; 1 fold.;
16 ornith., 15 col.), Suppl. pll. 1-10 (col.). Paris.

The report on the zoology of the voyage of La Favorite. This forms the fifth
volume of text of the complete report of 1833-39, which embraces 5 vols. text
and 2 vols. plates (not including the plates in the present volume). It consists
of a reprint of various papers which appeared in the "Magasin de Zoologie"
during the years 1836-39. The ornithological portion, which occupies pp. 29-64
quater. of Pt. II and pll. 10-25, appeared in the "Magasin" as follows. Pp. 29-64
and pll. 10-24 appeared in 1836 as pp. 3-37 (pagination separate) and pll.
62-76, one leaf (pp. 1-2) being occupied by a title-page, not reprinted; pp. 64
bis-64 quater. and pl. 25 appeared in 1838 as pp. 1-3 (pagination separate) and
pl. 86. The text of the reprint is practically identical with its original, although
there are minor alterations; pl. 18 (70 in the original) is labeled *Passerina
montana* instead of *P. guttata*, an error which is corrected on p. 49, footn.
There are some differences, also, in the coloration of the plates. The ornithological text is the work of Eydoux and Gervais; the plates are by E. Traviés,
G. Prêtre and A. Prévost.

Lardner, Dionysius. (Swainson, William.)

1836-37. > [**The cabinet cyclopaedia** . . . **On the natural history
and classification of birds** (*etc.*).]

> The | cabinet | of | natural history. | Conducted by the | Rev.
Dionysius Lardner, LL.D. [*etc.*, *2 lines.*] | assisted by | eminent

scientific men. | On | the natural history and classification | of | birds. | By | William Swainson, Esq. A.C.G. [(*etc.*, *4 lines.*; William Swainson. A.C.G. (*etc.*, *2 lines*)]. | Vol. I [II]. | London: | printed for | Longman, Rees, Orme, Brown, Green & Longman, | Paternoster-Row; | and John Taylor, | Upper Gower Street. | 1836 [1837].

2 vols. cap 8vo. Vol. I, 2 pr. ll.[1], pp. V-VIII, 1-365, vignette (on engr. tit.), text-figs. 1-113. Vol. II, 2 pr. ll. (see last footnote), pp. V-VI, 1 l. (note), pp. 1-398, vignette (on engr. tit.), text-figs. 114-338. London.

A little work of considerable scope in which the author reviews the entire class, Aves. Pt. I relates to the "structure and natural history of birds in general"; Pt. II, to the "bibliography, nomenclature and preservation" (=taxidermy) "of birds"; Pt. III, to the "natural history and relations of the different orders, tribes, and families of birds"; Pt. IV contains a "synopsis of a natural arrangement of birds" in which families and genera are described (some of the genera being new) and characteristic species are listed. Pt. V, intended for this work and containing descriptions of numerous species, was issued in 1837 as Pt. III of "Animals in Menageries" (q.v.), another volume of the present series of "The Cabinet Cyclopaedia." Some new species are named in the present work in various parts of the text. Vol. I contains Pts. I, II and a portion of III; Vol. II completes the work. The numerous text-figures are mostly illustrative of morphological details and are of excellent quality, being drawn by the author. The text is not entirely reliable since many of the author's statements are strained to accord with the "Quinary System" of classification, adopted throughout. Sherborn (Index Animalium, Sect. 2, Pt. 1, p. CXXI, 1922) cites Vol. I under date of Oct. 1836 and II, under date of June 1837; Richmond (Auk, **17**, p. 179, 1900) quotes Vol. II under date of July, 1837.

In the present copy, the original title-pages bearing the words, "The Cabinet Cyclopaedia," have been replaced by the substitute title-pages reading, "The Cabinet of Natural History." These substitute title-pages appear to have been issued with certain volumes to permit all the works relating to natural history to be segregated, if desired, under their own special heading.

Lardner, Dionysius. (Swainson, William.)

1837. > The | cabinet cyclopædia. | Conducted by the | Rev. Dionysius Lardner, LL.D. [*etc.*, *2 lines.*] | assisted by | eminent literary and scientific men. | Natural History. | **Animals in menageries.** | By | William Swainson, A.C.G. F.R.S. L.S. | Vice-President of the Ornithological Society, etc. | London: | printed for | Longman, Orme, Brown, Green, & Longmans, | Paternoster-Row; | and John Taylor, | Upper Gower Street. | 1838.

---

[1]Engraved title and second title-page which is evidently an insert, the original title-page of "The cabinet cyclopaedia" having been removed. Both title-pages appear to have been supplied with the natural history volumes of this series.

> The | cabinet | of | natural history. | Conducted by the | Rev. Dionysius Lardner, [*etc.*, *2 lines.*] | assisted by | eminent scientific men. | Animals in menageries. [*etc.*, *as above*].

1 vol. cap 8vo, 3 pr. ll. (half-tit., tit. and engr. tit.; latter not quoted), pp. V-VI, 1-373+1, 2 ll. (advt. by author, and second tit. quoted), Vignette (on engr. tit.), figs. 1-71. London.

Accounts of the habits and peculiarities of mammals and birds found in menageries and aviaries or suitable for preservation therein; compiled from various sources. This was the original content of the work (Pts. I and II), but a third part was added to include matter which had been omitted, through necessity, from a former work, "On the Natural History and Classification of Birds," 1836-37 (q.v.), in the same series as the present volume. This added matter was originally intended to form Pt. V. (Vol. II) of that treatise and is cited as such in the text of the volume, itself, as well as in the author's "Birds of Western Africa," 1837 (q.v.). A note on the unpaged leaf in Vol. II of the "Nat. Hist. and Classif. of Birds" and a footnote on p. 244 of Vol. II of the "Birds of Western Africa" explain the necessity for omitting the paper from its indicated position (owing to the bulk of the volume) and state the plan to publish it in connection with a later volume of the series, as was done herewith. The note in the "Birds of Western Africa" further states that "proof sheets have been forwarded to our most distinguished ornithologists," a circumstance which may constitute a prior publication of the subject matter, dating between June and September, 1837. The paper is important since it consists of descriptions and notes on the habitat of 229 species, 1 genus and 1 subgenus of birds, most of which are new.

The present volume bears the date 1838 but Sherborn (Index Animalium, Sect. 2, Pt. 1, p. CXXXI, 1922) gives the date of publication as December 1837. The work forms Vol. 98 of "The Cabinet Cyclopaedia."

Latham, John.

1781-85. A | General Synopsis | of | Birds. | Vol. I. Pt. 1st. [I. Pt. 2d. (*altered by pen from* "*II*"); II. Part 1st.; II pt. 2nd.; III. pt. 1st.; III. pt. 2nd.] | [*Vignette (col. and named in Vol. I, Pts. 1 and 2, only.).*] | London: | Printed for Benj. White [Prnited (*sic*) for Leigh & Sotheby (*Vol. II Pt. 1.*); Printed for Leigh & Sotheby (*Vol. II Pt. 2, Vol. III Pts. 1 and 2.*). | York Street, Covent Garden. (*Vol. II Pts. 1 and 2, Vol. III Pts. 1 and 2.*)] | MDCC-LXXXI [MDCCLXXXII (*Vol. I Pt. 2.*); MDCCLXXXIII (*Vol. II pts. 1 and 2.*); MDCCLXXXV (*Vol. III Pts. 1 and 2.*).].

3 vols. in 6, demy 4to. Vol. I Pt. 1, illum. tit., pp. I-VI (pref.), 1 l. (subtit.), pp. 1-416, pll. 1-5, VI-XVI (*col.*). Vol. I Pt. 2, illum. tit. pp. 417-788, 1 l. (direct. for pll.), 16 ll. (index and errata), pll. XVII-XXXV (*col.*). Vol. II Pt. 1, illum. tit., pp. I-II (pref.), pp. 1-366, pll. XXXVI-L (*col.*). Vol. II Pt. 2, illum. tit., pp. 367-808, 1 l. (direct for pll.), 18 ll. (index and errata), pll. LI-LXIX (*col.*). Vol. III Pt. 1, illum. tit., pp. I-III+1 (pref.), pp. 1-328,

pll. LXXXCV (*col.*). Vol. III Pt. 2, illum. tit., pp. 329-628, 1 l. (direct. for pll.), 3 ll. (generic catal.), 6 ll. (bibliogr. and errata), 12 ll. (index), pll. XCVI-CVI (col.). London.

A series of descriptions and colored plates of birds of the world, arranged under vernacular names but with a list of synonyms under each, including Linnaean binomials. At the completion of the work, the author prepared an "Index Ornithologicus," 1790 (q.v.), in which a scientific nomenclature is adopted for the species. He also issued a "Supplement," 1787, and a "Supplement II," 1801 (q.v.), to the present work, and after the completion of the second supplement issued a "Supplementum Indicis Ornithologici," 1801 (q.v.), to establish the nomenclature of the forms therein. Considerably later, a new edition of the work was issued under the title of "A General History of Birds," 1821-28 (q.v.). An edition in German, revised and supplemented by Bechstein, appeared in 1793-1812 (Cf. Latham, Johann Lathams Allgemeine Uebersicht der Vögel.). Of the present series of works, the edition was 500 copies except of "Supplement II" which Latham states (Gen. Hist. Bds. 1, p. VI) was published by his booksellers and not by himself and limited to 250 copies. The preface to Vol. I Pt. 1 is dated Jan. 1, 1781; of II Pt. 1, Dec. 1, 1783; of III Pt. 1, May 2, 1785. The plates are by the author.

Latham, John.

1787. **Supplement | to the | General Synopsis | of | Birds. |** [*Vignette (col.*).] | London: | Printed for Leigh & Sotheby, | York Street, Covent Garden. | MDCCLXXXVII.

1 vol. demy 4to, illum. tit., pp. I-III+1, 1-298, 8 ll. (direct. for pll., bibliogr., errata and index), pll. CVII-CXIX (col.). London.

This volume contains revisory notes on some of the species of birds treated by the author in his "General Synopsis," 1781-85 (q.v.), with additional species discussed in full as in the earlier work. Species and plates are numbered in continuance of the series in the "General Synopsis" and are included, likewise, in the "Index Ornithologicus," 1790 (q.v.). A detailed "List of the Birds of Great Britain" occupies pp. 281-298. The preface of this supplement is dated May 1, 1787. A second supplement followed in 1801 (q.v.).

Latham, John.

1789. See Phillip, Arthur, **The Voyage of Governor Phillip to Botany Bay.**

Latham, John.

1790. **Index ornithologicus, | sive | systema ornithologiæ; | complectens | avium divisionem | in classes, ordines, genera, species, | ipsarumque varietates: | adjectis | synonymis, locis, descriptionibus, &c. | Studio et opera | Joannis Latham, S.R.S. | Volumen I [II]. | Londini, | sumptibus authoris: | prostant venales apud Leigh et Sotheby, | York-Street, Covent-Garden. | M.DCC.XC.**

2 vols. demy 4to. Vol. I, pp. I-XVIII, 1-466. Vol. II, tit., pp. 467-920. London.

A systematic catalogue of the birds of the world, based on the author's "General Synopsis of Birds," 1781-85 (q.v.), and the first "Supplement" thereto, 1787 (q.v.). It contains Latin diagnoses of the species, genera and higher groups and assigns binomial names to the species which, in the earlier works, were discussed under vernacular names. Synonymy, habitat and diagnostic notes, aside from the descriptions, are given for each species. Mathews (Birds of Australia, Suppl. 4, p. 75, 1925) states that it was acknowledged by the Philos. Soc., London, on Dec. 9. A "Supplementum Indicis Ornithologici" (q.v.) followed the present work in 1801 and supplied the same details for the "Supplement II," 1801 (q.v.), as are given herein for the original work and first "Supplement."

Latham, John.

1790. See Pennant, Thomas, **Indian Zoology.**

Latham, John (Bechstein, Johann Matthäus.)

1793-1812. Johann Lathams | allgemeine Uebersicht | der Vögel. | Aus dem Englischen übersetzt | und | mit Anmerkungen und Zusätzen versehen | von | Johann Matthäus Bechstein [Dr. Johann Matthäus Bechstein (*Vol. IV.*)], | Gräflich Schaumburg [*etc.*, *4 lines* (*Vol. I.*); *5 lines* (*Vol. II.*); *6 lines* (*Vol. III.*); Herzoglich Sachsen, *etc. 9 lines* (*Vol. IV.*).]. | Ersten [-Vierten] Bandes erster [zweyter] Theil. [, | welcher | die Vögel nach ihren Kennzeichen der Art | nebst | den Zusätzen zu obigem Werke | enthält (*Vol. IV.*)] | Mit zwanzig [neunzehn (*Vol. I, Pt. II.*); funfzehn (*Vol. II, Pt. I.*); drey und zwanzig (*Vol. II, Pt. II.*); acht und dreyzig (*Vol. III, Pt. I.*); vier und zwanzig (*Vol. III, Pt. II.*); 44 (*Vol. IV, Pt. I.*); (*no number, Vol. IV, Pt. II.*)] ausgemahlten Kupfertafeln [Kupfern (*Vol. IV.*)]. | Nürnberg, | in der Kaiserlich privilegirten Kunst- und Buchhandlung A. C. Weigels und Schneiders [bey C. Weigel und Schneider (*Vol. I, Pt. II.*); in der kaiserl. königl. privilegirten Kunst- und Buchhandlung A. C. Weigels und Schneiders (*Vol. II.*); *idem* - A. C. Schneider und Weigel (*Vol. III, Pt. I.*); *idem* - A. C. Schneiders und Weigels (*Vol. III, Pt. II.*); bey Adam Gottlieb Schneider und Weigel (*Vol. IV.*)]. | 1793 [1793; 1794; 1795; 1796; 1798; 1811; 1812].

> Anhang | zum ersten Bande | von | Lathams allgemeiner Uebersicht | der Vögel, | welcher | Zusätze, Bermerkungen und Berichtigungen | der deutschen Benennungen enthält | von | Johann Matthäus Bechstein. | Mit zwey Kupfertafeln. | Nürnberg, | in der Kaiserlich privilegirten Kunst- und Buchhandlung A. C. Weigels und Schneiders. | 1793.

>4 vols. (8 parts) demy 4to. Vol. I, Pt. I; 7 pr. ll. (tit., illum. tit., translator's note, pref. and conts.), pp. 1-346, 1 l. (errata), pll. 1-19 (col.). Vol. I, Pt. II; 7 pr. ll., pp. 347-649+1, pll. 20-37 (col.; 33 and 34 wrongly numbered 35 and 36, respectively). Vol. I, Suppl.; tit., pp. 651-738, pll. Zus. I and II (col.). Vol. II, Pt. I; 7 pr. ll., pp. 1-366, 1 l. (errata), pll. 38-51 (col.). Vol. II, Pt. II; 6 pr. ll., pp. 369-775+1, pll. 52-73 (col.; 53 num. by hand; 57 with figures cut out and mounted on new sheet, hand-lettered and numbered). Vol. III, Pt. I; 6 pr. ll., pp. 1-275+1, pll. 74-100, 79b, 80a, 80b (=81a), 83b, 83c, 84b, 88b, 89b, 92a and 92b (col.). Vol. III, Pt. II; 5 pr. ll., pp. 277-548, pll. 101-123 (col.). Vol. IV, Pt. I; 5 pr. ll. (including separate title-p.), pp. I-IV, 1-320, pll. 1-41+1 (unnum.) (col.; 1 fold.). Vol. IV, Pt. II; 4 pr. ll. (including separate title-p.), pp. 321-576, pl. 42 (col.). Nuremberg.

An edition, in German, of Latham's, "A General Synopsis of Birds," 1781-85, and the first "Supplement" thereto, 1787 (q.v.) (comprising Vols. I-III) and of the "Index Ornithologicus," 1790 (q.v.) (comprising Vol. IV). Much additional matter is added by the translator and editor, Bechstein. A large part of the addenda to Vol. I is added at the close of the volume (pp. 651-738 and pll. "Zus." 1 and 2) under the separate title-page, "Anhang zum ersten Bande," etc.; the additions to the other volumes are scattered through the text. The plates, for the most part, are reproductions of those in Latham's original work. Pts. I and II of Vol. IV contain additional title-pages lettered, "Kurze Uebersicht aller bekannten Vögel," etc., which, for convenience, are transcribed under that title (q.v., 1811-12). Engelmann cites a complete index to Bechstein's edition by Joh. Gtfr. von Rademacher, published in 1813.

Latham, John; and Davies, Hugh. (Forster, Johann Reinhold.)

1795. **Faunula Indica** | id est | catalogus animalium | Indiae orientalis | quae hactenus | naturae curiosis | innotuerunt; | concinnatus | a | Joanne Latham, | Chirurgo Dartfordiae Cantii, | et | Hugone Davies, | Pastore in Aber | Provinciae Caernarvon. | Secundis curis editus, correctus et auctus | a | Joanne Reinholdo Forster, | LL. Med. et Phil. D. et LL. AA.M. Med. Philos. et Imprimis Hist. Nat. | et Rei Metallicae. Prof. P. O. in Universitate | Literraria Halensi. | Halae ad Salam, | impensis Joannis Jacobi Gebauri. |ΦⱣCCLXXXXV.

1 vol. medium folio, tit., 1 l. (pref.), pp. 1-38. Halle.

A systematic list of oriental or near-oriental animals with their Latin binomial names, mostly copied from the second edition of Pennant's "Indian Zoology," 1791 (q.v.), and published here as an extract (with additional title-page) from Forster's "Indische Zoologie . . . Zweite Auflage," 1795. The history of the publication is as follows. In 1769 Pennant published (in English and French) his "Indian Zoology," which was left more or less incomplete. His materials were turned over to Forster who, in 1781, published his "Zoologia Indica" or

"Indische Zoologie" (in Latin and German),-a translation of Pennant's work with the addition of three more plates (supplied by Pennant), the descriptions of the three birds and two fishes figured thereon, and other matter left unfinished or not supplied by Pennant, including a brief 'faunula' or list of Indian animals. In 1791, Pennant issued a second edition of his own work, consisting of a reprint of his first edition and an English translation (not strictly literal as regards descriptions of species) of the additions made by Forster, and with the further addition of "The Indian Faunula" entirely rewritten and enlarged by Latham and Davies (Davies being the author of the ornithology in it). In 1795, Forster published a reprint of his first translation, to which he added "The Indian Faunula" of Latham and Davies with certain additions of his own, and, the same year, issued this portion separately, with added title-page, as collated above. The original list published in Pennant's work (1791), contained English names for the mammals and birds but Latin names for the rest of the animals. The revised list in Forster (1795) contains Latin names throughout but is credited by Forster to Latham and Davies except for the additional species which he credits to himself. Presumably the ornithological portion remains the work of Davies in so far as it retains the species of the old list. The ornithological additions by Forster are not always easily discernible, but in most cases Davies's names may be recognized as the Latin forms of the English terms used in Pennant, and, by elimination, the new names may be recognized. (Cf. Allen, Bull. Am. Mus. Nat. Hist. **24,** Art. 5, pp. 111-116, Febr. 7, 1908.)

Latham, John.

1801?. **Supplement. II. | to the | General Synopsis | of | Birds. |** [*Vignette. (col.)*] | London. | Printed for Leigh, Sotheby & Son, | York Street, Covent Garden. | MDCCCI.

1 vol. demy 4to, illum. tit., pp. 1-376, 271*-272*, 10 ll. (index and direct. for pll.), pll. CXX-CXL, CXXXVI* and CXXXVIII* (col.). London.

A second supplement to the author's "General Synopsis," 1781-85 (q.v.), listing all the species treated in the original work, in the first "Supplement" and in the present work, revising the former discussions where necessary, and adding some new species. Consecutive numbering of species and plates follows that of the earlier volumes. The "Supplementum Indicis Ornithologici," 1801 (q.v.), including the species in this volume only, is bound with the present volume and may have been issued with it. The date of the present volume is somewhat in doubt. The present copy is dated "MDCCCI" as quoted above, but Engelmann cites "1802," while Mullens & Swann note "MDCCCII," adding that the last numeral appears to have been added after the work was printed. All the plates in the "Supplement II" bear the legend, "Published as the Act directs May 30, 1801, by Leigh, Sotheby & Son, York Street, Covent Garden." This volume was issued directly by the publishers to whom Latham disposed of his manuscript, whereas in the earlier volumes the author retained ownership until just prior to the publication of the present work (Cf. Latham, General History of Birds" 1, p. VI.). The impression of the present volume was reduced to 250 copies.

Latham, John.

1801?. Supplementum | indicis ornithologici, | sive | systematis ornithologiæ. | Studio et opera | Joannis Latham, M.D. S.R.S. | Londini: | prostat apud G. Leigh, J. et S. Sotheby, | York-Street, Covent-Garden. | M,DCCC,I.

1 vol. demy 4to, tit., pp. I-LXXIV. London.

A supplement to the "Index Ornithologicus," 1790 (q.v.), presenting a similar index for the "Supplement II to the General Synopsis," 1801 (q.v.). The date of publication is given on the title as "M,DCCC,I," quoted above, but Engelmann gives "1802" and Mullens and Swann include it with the "Supplement II" under date of "MDCCCII," with a notation as to apparent alteration of figures after printing (Cf. antea, Latham, Supplement II, 1801.).

Latham, John. (Bechstein, Johann Matthäus.)

1811-12. Kurze Uebersicht | aller bekannten Vögel [der Vögel] | oder | ihre Kennzeichen der Art | nach | Lathams General Synopsis of Birds | und | seinem Index ornithologicus | entworfen | von | Dr | Johann Matthäus Bechstein, | Herzoglich Sachsen [etc., 9 lines; Zweyter Theil nebst Register (Pt. II.)]. | Mit 44 [No number (Pt. II.).] ausgemahlten Kupfern, auch ohne dieselben. | Nürnberg, | bey Adam Gottlieb Schneider und Weigel. | 1811 [1812]. 1 vol. (2 parts) demy 4to, (collation given elsewhere). Nuremberg.

The two parts constituting Vol. IV, Pts. I and II, of Bechstein's edition of Latham's "General Synopsis of Birds" (Cf. Latham, Johann Lathams allgemeine Uebersicht der Vögel, 1793-1812.) and issued also under the present title. Both titles are given in this volume which is collated under the general work.

Latham, John.

1821-28. A | general history | of | birds. | By John Latham, M.D. | F.R.S. A.S. and L.S. | Acad. Cæs. Nat. Curios. Reg. Holm. et Soc. Nat. Scrut. Berolin. Soc. &c. &c. | Vol. I [-X]. | Winchester: | Printed by Jacob and Johnson, for the author:-sold in London by | G. and W. B. Whittaker, Ave-Maria-Lane; John Warren, Bond-Street, [Semicolon (Vols. IV, V and X.).] | W. Wood, 428, Strand; and J. Mawman, 39, Ludgate-Street. | 1821 [1822] (Vols. II-V.); 1823 (Vols. VI-VIII.); 1824 (Vols. IX-X.)].

> Index | to the | general history | of | birds. | By John Latham, M.D. | F.R.S. [etc., 2 lines.] | Winchester: | printed and published by Jacob and Johnson, for the author. | May be had in London of Messrs. Whittaker, Ave-Maria-Lane; and W. Wood, | 428, Strand. | 1828.

11 vols. in 10, foliopost 4to. Vol. I, pp. I-XXXII, 1-375+1 (direct.

for pll.), pll. I-XVII (col.). Vol. II, tit., pp. 1-345+1 (direct. for
pll.), pll. XVIII-XXXVII (col.). Vol. III, tit., 1 l. (direct. for pll.),
pp. 1-416, pll. XXXIX-LIX (col.). Vol. IV, tit., pp. 1-362, 1 l.
(direct. for pll. and errata), pll. LX-LXXVIII+LXVII* (col.).
Vol. V, tit., pp. 1-350, 1 l. (direct. for pll.), pll. LXXIX-XCII,
LXXXV* and LXXXVII* (col.). Vol. VI, tit., 1 l. (direct. for
pll.), pp. 1-336, pll. XCIII-CIV, XCVIII* and CIV (*bis*=CIV*)
(col.). Vol. X, tit., 1 l. (list of add. subscrs. and direct. for pll.),
CXVI, CIV**, CVII* and CXII* (col.). Vol. VIII, tit., pp. 1-391-
+1 (direct. for pll.), pll. CXVII-CXXXIX+CXXIV* (col.). Vol.
IX, tit., pp. 1-433+1 (direct. for pll.), pll. CXL-CLXII (CXLVIII
missing; CXLIX duplicated; CLVII wrongly numbered CLIII)
(col.). Vol. X, tit., 1 l. (list of add. subscrs. and direct. for pll.),
pp. 1-456, pll. CLXIII-CLXXXIV (col.). Index, tit., pp. 3-4
(orders and genera), 5-7+1 (list of pll.), 9-16+1 l. (Vol. I.), 6 ll.
(Vol. II.), 8 ll. (Vol. III.), 7 ll. (Vol. IV.), 7 ll. (Vol. V.), 7 ll.
(Vol. VI.), 8 ll. (Vol. VII.), 7 ll. (Vol. VIII.), 8 ll. (Vol. IX.), 8 ll.
(Vol. X.), 1 l. (author's note). Winchester.

A new edition of the author's "General Synopsis of Birds," 1781-85 (q.v.), rewritten and enlarged to include the species treated in the two supplements to that
work as well as forms discovered since their publication. The nomenclature is
vernacular except for the scientific names mentioned in the synonymy, and
the new species described in the work were left for later authors to name.
Most of the plates present the same figures of birds as are given in the earlier
work; some of them are new. The "Index," in the present copy is bound in,
intact, at the close of Vol. X, but it was issued in such form as to be divided
into sections, if so desired, with the index to each volume attached to its own
letterpress.

Latreille, Pierre André.
1829-30. See Cuvier, G.L.C.F.D.; and Latreille, **La Règne Animal.**

Laubmann, Alfred.
1916. See Hellmayr, Charles Edward; and Laubmann, **Nomenclator
der Vögel Bayerns.**

Laugier de Chartrouse, Meiffren.
1820-39. See Temminck, Coenraad Jacob; and Laugier, **Nouveau
Recueil de Planches Coloriées d'Oiseaux.**

Lawrence, George Newbold.
1858. See U. S. Pacific Railroad Surveys, **Reports of Explorations
and Surveys . . . for a Railroad from the Mississippi River to
the Pacific Ocean, Vol. IX, Birds.**

Lawrence, George Newbold.

1860. See Baird, Spencer F.; Cassin; and Lawrence, **The Birds of North America.**

1870. Idem.

Lawrence, George Newbold.

1899. See Ober, Frederick A., **Camps in the Caribbees.**

Layard, Edgar Leopold.

1867. The | **birds of South Africa.** | A descriptive catalogue | of | all the known species occurring south of the | 28th parallel of south latitude. | By | Edgar Leopold Layard, | Fellow of the Zoological Society, Member of the Entomological | Society, and of various foreign societies. | Cape Town : | J. C. Juta, Wale-Street. | London: | Longman, Green, & Co., 39, Paternoster Row. | 1867.

1 vol. post 8vo, pp. I-XVI, 1-192, (193-196 omitted through wrong numbering), 197-382, I-II (glossary), I-XXI (index), 1 insert (expl. of error in pagination), frontisp. Cape Town.

Descriptions of 702 species of birds found by the author or recorded (erroneously or not) by other writers as occurring in South Africa; with original and compiled notes on habits, etc. A number of new species are described. A revised edition of the work was published under the same short title in 1875-84 (q.v.). P. L. Sclater's copy, presented by the author.

Layard, Edgar Leopold. (Sharpe, Richard Bowdler.)

1875-84. The | **birds** | of | **South Africa,** | by Edgar Leopold Layard, | C.M.G., F.Z.S., M.B.O.U., | H.B.M. Consul at Noumea, New Caledonia. | **New edition.** | Thoroughly revised and augmented | by | R. Bowdler Sharpe, | Senior Assistant, Department of Zoology, British Museum, | F.L.S. [*etc., 3 lines.*], | London: | Bernard Quaritch, 15 Piccadilly, W. | 1875-1884.

1 vol. 8vo, pp. I-XV+1 (tit., pref., introd. and bibliogr.), IX-XVII+1 (systematic list and errata), 1 l. (list of pll.), pp. 1-890, pll. I-XII (col.; by J. G. Keulemans). London.

A revised edition of Layard's "Birds of South Africa," published in Cape Town in 1867 (q.v.). The revised work eliminates the descriptions of genera and higher groups and the more detailed references included in the original work and consists of descriptions of the species with accounts of the habits and distribution of each. The work appeared in 6 parts as follows (from current reviews in the Ibis). Part I, pp. 1-80, pll. II and IX, May 1875; II, pp. 81-160, pll. XI and XII, Oct. 1875; III, pp. 161-240, pll. V, VII and X, Aug. 1876; IV, pp. 241-336, pl. VI, Apr. 1877; V, pp. 337-528, pll. III and VIII, Apr. 1882; VI, pp. 529-890 (I-XV+1, IX-XVII+1 and 1 l. list uf pll.)[1], Apr. 1884. The sys-

---

[1] This preliminary matter, judging from its context, must have appeared at the close of the work with Pt. VI, although I cannot find a contemporary reference to it.

tematic list of species does not agree in all the details of nomenclature with the general text. The latter contains numerous descriptions of new species and genera. These are to be accredited to Sharpe who, as editor of the new edition, rewrote many parts of it and added much new matter.

Leach, William Elford.

1814-17. The | **zoological miscellany;** being | descriptions of new, or interesting | animals. | By | William Elford Leach, M.D. F.L.S. & W.S. &c. | Illustrated with | coloured figures, drawn from nature, | by R. P. Nodder, | animal painter, and draftsman in natural history. | London: | printed by B. McMillan, Bow-Street; | for E. Nodder & Son, 34, Tavistock-Street, | Covent-Garden; and sold by all booksellers. | 1814.

> The | zoological miscellany; | being | descriptions of new, or interesting | animals, | by William Elford Leach, M.D. F.L.S. & W.S. [M.D. F.R.S. & L.S. (*Vol. III.*)] | Fellow of the Royal College of Physicians of Edinburgh [*etc., 3 lines; 5 lines. (Vol. III.*).] | Illustrated with | coloured figures, drawn from nature [Coloured figures, engraved from | original drawings (Vol. III.)], | by R. P. Nodder, | animal painter, and draftsman [engraver (*Vol. III.*)] in natural history. | Vol. I [-III]. | London: | Printed by B. McMillan, Bow-Street [by R. and A. Taylor, Shoe-Lane (*Vol. III.*)], | for E. Nodder & Son [For R. P. Nodder (*Vol. III.*)], 34, Tavistock-Street, Covent-Garden; | and sold by all booksellers. | 1814 [1815; 1817].

3 vols. 4to (size of 8vo). Vol. I, tit., pp. 1-144, pll. 1-60 (col.). Vol. II, pp. 1-154, 4 ll. (indices, advt. and errata), pll. 61-120 (col.). Vol. III, pp. I-V+1, 1-151+1, pll. 121-149+135B (col.). London.

A series of descriptions of new or noteworthy species and genera of animals, accompanied by hand-colored plates. The work is a continuation of Shaw and Nodder's "Naturalist's Miscellany." Vols. I and II were issued in parts, according to a statement in an advertisement at the close of Vol. III; Vol. III appears to have been issued entire. An examination of the signatures in Vols. I and II shows various places where there are less than four leaves to a signature, and, as these occur at more or less regular intervals, it seems probable that they mark the ends of the various parts. According to these marks, the following arrangement of parts is suggested. Vol. I; pp. 1-18, 19-28, 29-38, 39-48, 49-58, 59-70, 71-80, 81-92, 93-102, 103-114, 115-126, 127-138, 139-144 (indices and advt.). Vol. II; pp. 1-12, 13-28 (27-28 are blank), 29-44?, 45-60, 61-76?, 77-88, 89-100, 101-112, 113-124, 125-134, 135-144, 145-154, 4 ll. (indices, etc.). In Vol. II, pl. 80 was issued with the part containing p. 59 where there is a statement that the explanation of this plate will appear with the following number; it occurs on p. 61. It seems that five plates, in serial order, accompanied the first 12 parts of each volume. Pll. 1-4 (of Vol. I) are dated "Jany. 1814," 6-8, "Feby. 1814," 14, "March 1814." The final part of these first two volumes

probably came out the years after the dates on the respective subtitle-pages;
in Vol. I, p. 144 is an advertisement of a work said to have been published on
Jan. 1, 1815, and on the last page of Vol. II is a similar advertisement for a
work which "was published" Jan. 1, 1815. Vol. III was planned to appear
Jan. 1, 1817, according to a statement at the close of Vol. II.

There is only one full title-page for all three volumes.

Leach, William Elford.

1819. See Ross, John, **A Voyage of Discovery.**

Leach, William Elford. (Salvin, Osbert, *ed.*)

1882. The Willughby Society. | **Leach's** | **Systematic Catalogue** | of
the | **Specimens of the Indigenous Mammalia** | **and Birds in the**
British Museum. | [*Vignette.*] | Edited by | Osbert Salvin, M.A.,
F.R.S., &c. | London, MDCCCLXXXII.

[Systematic catalogue | of the specimens of | the indigenous mam-
malia and birds | that are preserved in | The British Museum: |
with their localities and authorities, | To which is added | a list |
of | the described species that are wanting | to complete the collec-
tion of | British mammalia and birds | London: | printed by
Richard and Arthur Taylor, Shoe-Lane. | 1816.]

1 vol. royal 8vo, pp. I-IV, "1-42, 1 l." London. "1816," 1882.

A catalogue of specimens giving the Latin and English names, sex, locality and
donor. The matter is arranged as if on specimen labels, which fact, coupled
with the exceeding rarity of the original book, has led to the belief that the work
was printed for the express purpose of being cut into actual labels but that it was
never published. For a long time, only one copy (that in the British Museum)
was known, but another copy has come to light in the Academy of Natural
Sciences of Philadelphia. This, together with the fact that the preface contains
a statement to the effect that species not enumerated in the list are desiderata
and will be acceptable (followed by a list of species not represented in the
collection), seems to prove that the paper was actually published and distributed. There are no descriptions and the new specific names, used in the
paper, are nomina nuda, but the generic names are tenable although some of
them are antedated by Koch's "System der Baierischen Zoologie," published
before July the same year (Cf. Richmond, Proc. U. S. Nat. Mus., **35**, No.
1656, Dec. 16, 1908, p. 621, footn. a.). Leach's preface is dated August 30,
1816. The present copy is a reprint published by The Willughby Society (q.v.).
A preface by Salvin gives a short review of the work.

Lear, Edward.

1830-32. **Illustrations** | of | **the family of Psittacidæ,** | or | par-
rots: | the greater part of them | species hitherto unfigured, | con-
taining | forty-two lithographic plates, | drawn from life, and on
stone, | By Edward Lear, A.L.S. | London: | published by E. Lear,
61 Albany Street, Regent's Park. | 1832.

1 vol. superroyal folio, 4 pr. ll. (tit., ded., list. subscrs., list of pll.), 42 pll. (col.). London.

A series of hand-colored lithographs, beautifully executed, without descriptive text. The work is noted for its artistic value combined with accuracy of portrayal. The work was issued in 12 parts, the contents of all, and the dates of some, of which Mathews (Austr. Av. Record 1, pp. 23-24, 1912) has recorded from the original wrappers, as follows. The numbers (used for brevity to replace the names) are according to the list of plates on the last leaf of text in the volume. Part I, pll. 23 or 24, 33 and 31, Nov. 1, 1830; II, pll. 1, 42, 4 and 21 or 22, Nov. 1, 1830; III, pll. 26, 9 and 30, Jan. 1, 1831; IV, pll. 20, 10, 2 and 25, Febr. 1, 1831; V, pll. 18, 15 or 14 and 12, May 1, 1831; VI, pll. 17, 13, 5 and 38, Aug. 1, 1831; VII, pll. 37, 36 and 11, Sept. 1, 1831; VIII, pll. 27, 29 and 34, Oct. 1, 1831; IX, pll. 7, 40, 3 and 41, no date; X, pll. 35, 16, 39 and 14 or 15, no date; XI, pll. 8, 24 or 23 and 32, no date; XII, pll. 19, 6, 28 and 22 or 21, with title-page (and probably remainder of text?), no date except date on title-page, "1832." Dubious numbers in the above list are due to separate plates of the same species, not segregated by Mathews.

Lechner, A. A. van Pelt.
See Van Pelt Lechner, A. A.

Lee, Oswin A. J.
1896-99. Among | British birds | in | their nesting haunts | Vol. I [Vol. II; *Line omitted (Vol. III.)*; Vol. IV] | Illustrated by the camera | by Oswin A. J. Lee [Vol. III. By Oswin A. J. Lee]. | Edinburgh. David Douglas. 1897 [1899 *(Vol. IV.)*]. [*Title on illustr. background, signed "O.A.J.L."*].

4 vols. medium folio. Vol. I, pp. I-VI, 1 l. (introd.), pp. 1-159, 40 pll., 21 text-figs. Vol. II, pp. I-VI, 1-145, 40 pll., 15 text-figs. Vol. III, pp. I-VI, 1-155, 40 pll., 14 text-figs. Vol. IV, pp. I-VI, 1-167, 40 pll., 16 text-figs. Edinburgh.

A series of splendid, full-page photogravures showing the nests and nesting sites of some 122 species of British birds. The text consists of a general discussion of the habits of each species with descriptions of the subjects of each plate and the circumstances under which the photograph was taken. The book was issued in 16 parts of 10 plates each, -Pt. I in 1896, II-VII in 1897, VIII-XII in 1898, and XIII-XVI in 1899. The author's ill health prevented the completion of the work.

Lefèvre, Auguste.
1844-45? An | atlas | of the | eggs | of the | birds of Europe. | By Auguste Lefèvre. | Part 1 [-17 *(Numerals hand-written.)*] | Paris: | Auguste Lefèvre, Rue Dauphine, 24. | London: | J. E. Warwick, Naturalist, | 23, New Street, Kennington. | 1844.

1 vol. superroyal 8vo, (15 orig. wrappers), 136 pll. (col.). Paris and London.

A series of hand-colored lithographs (numbered 1-136 by hand), without text other than the legends which contain the common and scientific names of the species quoted from Temminck, Gould, Naumann and Bonaparte. One plate is devoted to each species and several varieties of coloration are often figured. Some of the plates are moderately good but others are very poorly executed. Seventeen parts, of eight plates each, are present and appear to comprise all published. There is no title except that on the original wrappers as transcribed above. The cover of Pt. 1 is placed in the front of the volume in lieu of a title-page; the remaining covers are bound together at the close. These wrappers are identical except for the hand-written number and are dated 1844. One wrapper is numbered "4-6" and one, "8-10"; the remainder each bear a single number. The third page of each contains a statement to the effect that the work was supposed to appear monthly. The Zool. Soc., London, catalogues a copy with a French title, dated 1848; I can find no other references.

Leffingwell, William Bruce.

1890. **Wild fowl shooting.** | Containing | scientific and practical descriptions | of | Wild Fowl: Their Resorts, Habits, Flights | and the most | successful method of hunting them. | Treating of the selection of guns for wild fowl shooting; how to | load, to aim, and to use them successfully; decoys, and the | proper manner of using them; blinds, how and where | to construct them; boats, how to build and use | them scientifically; retrievers, their | characteristics, how to select, | and how to train them. | By William Bruce Leffingwell. | Chicago: | Rand, McNally & Co. | 1890.

1 vol. post 8vo, 2 pr. ll. (tit. and ded.), pp. 1-373, 1 p. (reverse of p. 373)+9 ll. +1 p. (lining of rear cover) (advt.), frontisp., 5 pll., 8 text-figs. Chicago.

A book on hunting and hunting experiences.

Legge, William Vincent.

1878-80. **A history | of the | birds of Ceylon.** | By | Captain W. Vincent Legge, R.A., | Fellow of the Linnean Society [*etc.*, 5 lines.]. | London: | published by the author. | 1880.

1 vol. in 2 vols., royal 4to, pp. I-XLVI, 1-2 (list of orig. subscrs.), 1-4 (subscr. list), 1-345+1, 345 (*bis*)-1237, frontisp. (col. map), 1 pl. (uncol.), 34 pll. (col.; by J. G. Keulemans; numbered I-XXXIV in list of pll.), 11 woodcuts (32 figs.). London.

A complete monograph of the birds of Ceylon. Issued in 3 parts as follows, according to a list on pp. XLV and XLVI of the work. Part **I**, pp. 1-345, 10 pll. (I, II, IV-VII, X-XII, XIV), November 1878; **II**, pp. 345 (*bis*)-730, 10 pll. (III, VIII, IX, XIII, XV, XVII-XIX, XXI, XXII), September 1879; **III**, pp. 731-1237, introd. pp. (except orig. list. of subscrs.?), 14 pll. (XX, XXIII-XXXIV, frontisp., uncol. pl.), September 1880. Page 345 (*bis*) contains a reprint of the 13 lines of text on p. 345 and the continuation from that point.

The hand-colored plates are very fine. The present copy is bound in two volumes, the first of which contains introductory matter and pp. 1-692, frontisp., uncol. pl. and 29 col. pll.; the second volume completes the work.

Leiper, R. T.

1911. See [Grouse], **The Grouse in Health and Disease.**

Leisler, Johann Philipp Achilles.

1812-13. **Nachträge | zu | Bechsteins | Naturgeschichte Deutschlands | von | Dr. J. P. A. Leisler, | Grosherzoglich Frankfurtischem Obermedezinalrathe [*etc., 4 lines; 7 lines* (*Vol. II.*).] | Erstes [Zweites] Heft. | Mit einem illuminirten Kupfer. | Hanau 1812 [1813]. | Bei Johann Gerhard Scharneck.**

1 vol. (2 pts.) demy 8vo, 3 pr. ll. (subtit., ded. and pref.), pp. I-XII, 1-99+1, 1 pl. (col.; by C. Westermayr), subtit. (Pt. II.), pp. I-IV, 107-200, pl. II (col.; by Westermayr). Hanau.

Critical notes on some of the birds discussed by Johann Matthäus Bechstein in his "Gemeinnützige Naturgeschichte Deutschlands; Zweyte Ausgabe," 1801-1809 (q.v.), and related species. Several new species are described. The work was planned to be considerably more comprehensive, with four parts to constitute each volume, but only the two parts here collated were issued.

Lemaire, C. L.

1836. **Bibliothèque | zoologique. > Histoire naturelle | des oiseaux | exotiques | Par C. L. Lemaire, | Docteur en Médecine [*etc., 2 lines*.]. | Ouvrage orné de figures | peintes d'après nature. | Par Pauquet. | Et gravées sur acier. | Paris. | Pauquet, éditeur, Debure, libraire, | rue des Grands-Augustins, 17. rue du Battoir, 19. | 1836.**

1 vol. 4to (size of 8vo), 2 pr. ll. (half-tit. and subtit.), pp. 1-156, 1 l. (illum. subtit. of pll.), pll. 1-80 (col.; by Pauquet). Paris.

Brief descriptions of a number of representative species of non-European birds, illustrated by hand-colored engravings. Latin names are given to most of the species treated. The work forms the second volume of the first edition of the "Bibliothèque Zoologique," of which the second edition appeared in 1846. A third edition, by Prévost and Lemaire was published in 1863. A companion volume, in all three editions, is entitled, "Hist. Nat. des Ois. d'Europe" (q.v., under Prévost and Lemaire, 1864).

Lemaire, C. L.

1864. See Prévost, Florent; and Lemaire, **Histoire Naturelle des Oiseaux d'Europe.**

Le Maout, Emmanuel.

1853. Les | trois règnes | de la nature | Règne animal > **Histoire naturelle | des | Oiseaux** | suivant la classification | de | M. Isidore Geoffroy-Saint-Hilaire | avec l'indication de leurs mœrs | et de leurs rapports avec les arts, le commerce et l'agriculture | par | M.Emm. Le Maout | Docteur en Médecine. | [*Blazon.*] | Paris | L. Curmer | Rue Richelieu, 47 (au premier). | M DCCC LIII.

1 vol. demy 4to, 2 pr. ll. (cov.-tit. and tit.), pp. I-XLVIII (introd.), 1-425+1, 1 l. (errata and list of pll.), frontisp. (monochr.), pll. 1-14 (col.), 20 pll. (17 monochr., 2 col. monochr., 2 steel engr.), 501 text-figs. Paris.

A general treatise on the birds of the world, with tables for the determination of genera and higher groups and descriptions of typical species. The covering title, "Les Trois Règnes de la Nature" includes at least one other work by the same author,-a treatise on botany dated 1851; the third section of the subject would, presumably, be geological, but I can find no trace of its publication.

Lembeye, Juan.

1850. Aves | de la Isla de Cuba, | por | Juan Lembeye. | [*Flourish.*] | Habana. | Imprenta del Tiempo, | Calle de Aguiar Num. 45. | 1850.

1 vol. 4to (6¾x10), pp. 1-136, 2 ll. (index and list of subscrs.), pll. 1-20 (18 col.; after Audubon). Havana.

A descriptive account of the species of the birds of Cuba, with synonymies and notes on habits, distribution, etc. A catalogue of the species known from Cuba is given on pp. 127-136. As this list is brought to date of October 1850, the work must have been published during, or after, October of that year. It is considered a great rarity. Many of the descriptions were supplied by Juan Gundlach (Cf. Gundlach, Contr. Orn. Cubana, p. 15, 1876.). The copy at hand was presented by the author to Srta. Bina Heffenone.

Lembcke, Georg.

1800-11. See Borckhausen, Moritz B.; Lichthammer; Bekker; Lembcke; and Bekker Jr., **Teutsche Ornithologie.**

Lemée, Carlos.

1909. Los | pájaros insectivoros | bajo | el punto de vista agricola | por | Carlos Lemée | La Plata | Talleres Gráficos de Joaquín Sesé, Editor | Calle 47, esquina 9 | 1909.

1 vol. 8vo, pp. 1-125, 6 pll. (on numbered pp.). La Plata.

A general discussion of economic ornithology, followed by an examination of certain birds of Argentina with regard to their economic importance.

Lenz, Harald Othmar. (Burbach, Otto.)

1891. Gemeinnützige | **Naturgeschichte** | von | Prof. Dr. Harald Othmar Lenz. | Fünfte Auflage | (zweiter Abdruck) | bearbeitet von O. Burbach. | Zweiter Band: | **Die Vögel.** | Mit 12 Tafeln

Abbildungen. | Gotha. | Verlag von E. F. Thienemanns Hof-
buchhandlung. | 1891.

1 vol. post 8vo, pp. I-VIII, 1-638, 1 l. (list of illustrs., advt.), pll.
I-XII (col.). Gotha.

The fifth edition of Vol. 5 of Lenz's "Gemeinnützige Naturgeschichte," first
published in 5 vols. in 1851-59 (Vol. 2, 1851). The present volume contains a
very general treatment of the birds of the world, popularly described. The
edition is edited by O. Burbach.

Léotaud, Antoine.

1866. **Oiseaux | de | l'Isle de la Trinidad,** | (Antilles), | par | A.
Léotaud, | Docteur en Médecine [*etc., 2 lines.*]. | Ouvrage publié
par souscription nationale | Port d'Espagne: | Chronicle Publish-
ing Office | 1866.

1 vol. royal 8vo, 2 pr. ll. (half-tit. and tit.), pp. I-XX, 1 l. (subtit.),
pp. 1-560, 1 l. (subtit.), pp. I-VIII (scientific index), I-IV (vernacular index). Port of Spain.

A descriptive catalogue of the birds of Trinidad. The first comprehensive faunal
paper on the ornithology of the region in question.

Le Roi, Otto.

1911. See Koenig, Alexander, **Avifauna Spitzbergensis.**

Leslie, A. S.

1911. See [Grouse], **The Grouse in Health and Disease.**

LeSouëf, William Henry Dudley.

1904. [*Cover-tit.*] **Collection | of | Australian Birds' | Eggs and
Nests** | in the possession of | D. Le Souëf, | Director, Zoological
Gardens, | Melbourne. | Rae Bros., Printers, | Elizabeth St. N.,
Melbourne. [*Decorated border.*].

1 vol. demy 4to, cover-tit., pp. 1-23+1, 1 l. Melbourne.

A systematic list of the Australian species represented in the author's collection
of nests and eggs, giving Latin and vernacular names, the number of clutches
in the collection and occasional remarks. The final 3 pp. (unnumbered) are
headed "Appendix" and are left blank for manuscript insertions. This list
contains the first use of the name "*Dromaeus diemenensis,*" here a nomen
nudum but later described by Le Souëf in the Bull. Brit. Orn. Club, **21**, p. 13,
1907.

LeSouëf, William Henry Dudley.

1911. See Lucas, A. H. S.; and LeSouëf, **The Birds of Australia.**

Lesson, René Primevère.

1826-30. See Duperrey, L. I., **Voyage autour du Monde, Sur la Corvette, La Coquille.**

Lesson, René Primevère.

1828. **Manuel** | **d'ornithologie,** | ou | description | des genres et des | principales espèces d'oiseaux; | par R. P. Lesson. | [*Quot.,* *2 lines.*]. | Tome premier [second]. | Paris, | Roret, Libraire, Rue Hautefeuille, | au coin de celle du battoir. | 1828.

2 vols. 18mo (3½x5¾). Vol. I, 3 ll. (advt.), pp. I-IV, 1-421. Vol. II, pp. 13-32 (advt.), 2 ll. (half-tit. and tit.), pp. 1-448, 1 l. (advt.). Paris.

Brief characterizations of the genera and higher groups of birds and the principal species of each genus, prefaced by a resumé of the systems of classification adopted by a number of antecedent authors. The work formed one of a large series of manuals issued by the publishers. An atlas containing 129 plates was issued, uniform with the present volumes. Mathews (Birds of Austr., **7**, p. 456) states that the work was acknowledged by the "B.F." (=Bibliographie de la France) as received June 28, 1828. A review of the genotypes in this work was given by Laubmann in the Archiv für Naturgeschichte, 85 Jahrg., 1919, Abt. A., **4**, pp. 137-168, Aug. 1920.

Lesson, René Primevère.

1829-30. **Histoire naturelle** | **des** | **Oiseaux-Mouches,** | ouvrage orné de planches | dessinées et gravées par les meilleurs artistes, | et dédié | A S.A.R. Mademoiselle; | par R. P. Lesson, | Officier de Santé [*etc., 8 lines.*] | [*Quot., 2 lines*] | Paris. | Arthus Bertrand, Libraire, | éditeur du voyage autour du monde du Capitaine Duper-rey, | Rue Hautefeuille, No 23.

1 vol. in 2 vols. (pt.) 8vo, pp. J-XLVJ, 1 l. (blank), pp. 1-223, pll. 1-85+48 bis (col.; by Bessa, Bévalet, Mlle. Zoë Dumont, Mme. Lesson, Prêtre and Vauthier). Paris.

The first of a series of three volumes dealing with the hummingbirds. The present volume was succeeded by the "Histoire Naturelles des Colibris," 1830-32 (q.v.), and "Les Trochilidées," 1832-33 (q.v.). The date of publication of the present volume is somewhat in doubt. Coues asserts that the work began in January 1829 and ended in September 1829, but Giebel, Engelmann, Agassiz, the Zoological Society of London, the Library of the British Museum (Natural History), and others, cite 1829-30. Cuvier in the second edition of "Le Règne Animal," Vol. III, p. 385, 1830 (preface to volume dated March 1830), remarks that the work in question was then in course of publication. The Catalogue of the Library of the British Museum (Natural History), quoting the "Bibliographie de la France" assigns livrs. 1-10 to the year 1829 and the remainder of the volume to 1830. Sherborn (Index Animalium, Sect. 2, Pt. 1, p. LXXX, 1922) says, "pp. 1-144, pls. I-XL, 1829; 145-224, XLI-XLVI, 1830."

The work was issued in 17 livraisons and the signatures are as follows. Preliminary matter, 4 ll. (without sign.), the preface dated Jan. 10, 1829; signs. "b" and "c", table of species, dated May 1829; sign. "d," completion of table and a supplement thereto which is dated September 1829; signs. 1-12, general text; 2 ll. (without sign.), index. In the present copy, this volume and the one on "Des Colibris" are divided and bound with the text to both in one volume and the plates in a second volume. A third volume in uniform binding consists of the author's "Histoire Naturelle des Oiseaux de Paradis et des Epimaques," 1834-35, (q.v.), text and plates. The volume of plates in the present copy is prefaced by the front wrapper of Livraison 17 of the present title, which bears the following inscription surrounded by a broad, figured border. "Histoire naturelle | des | Oiseaux-Mouches, | par R. P. Lesson, | auteur | de la zoologie du voyage autour du monde, etc.; | dédiée | A S.A.R. Mademoiselle. | 17 Livraison. | et Derniere | [*Monogram.*] | Paris. | Arthus Bertrand, Libraire-Éditeur, | Rue Hautefeuille, No. 23. | Imprimerie de Rignoux, Rue des Francs-Bourgeois-S-Michel, No. 8. | 1829." The figures and words "17e" and "et Derniere" are written by hand, which suggests that the same wrappers were used throughout the publication, with numbers added as required, in which case the date printed below would not present conclusive evidence as to date of publication.

Lesson, René Primevère.

1830-31. Traité | d'ornithologie, | ou | tableau méthodique | des ordres, sous-ordres, familles, tribus, | genres, sous-genres et races d'oiseaux. | Ouvrage entièrement neuf, | formant le catalogue le plus complet des espèces réunies dans les | collections publiques de la France. | Par R. P. Lesson, | Professeur d'histoire naturelle [*etc., 6 lines.*]. | [*Monogram (Vol. I.*); Planches. (*Vol. II.*)], Paris, | Chez F. G. Levrault, rue de la Harpe, no. 81, | Strasbourg, même Maison, rue des Juifs, no. 33; | Bruxelles, Libraire parisienne, rue de la Magdeleine, no. 438. | 1831.

2 vols. 8vo. Vol. (I), pp. J-XXXIJ, 1-659. Vol. (II), pp. J-XIJ, pll. 1-119 (col.; by Prêtre). Paris.

A descriptive catalogue of birds, with a synoptic list of genera and higher groups and with diagnoses and synonymies following in the main text; illustrated by hand-colored plates. The work was published in 8 livraisons, regarding whose dates of publication there is considerable doubt. Mathews (Novit. Zool. **18**, p. 14, 1911) quotes, from the "Bibliothèque Française," (=Bibliographie de la France) the dates of receipt of the various livraisons as follows. Livr. **1**, Feb. 13, 1830; **2**, May 8, 1830; **3**, July 10, 1830; **4**, Sept. 25, 1830; **5**, ?; **6**, about March 1, 1831; **7**, April 9, 1831; **8**, June 11, 1831. Livrs. 1-4 and 7-8 are accredited with 5 sheets of text each, livr. **1** with no plates, **2** with 30 pll., 3-4 and 7-8 with 15 pll. each, but this arrangement does not account for all the letterpress and allows one plate over the number published (assuming that livrs. 5 and 6 were similar to the adjacent numbers). In the "Revue Zoologique," 1848, pp. 39-48, Lafresnaye refers a number of times to the "Traité d'Ornithologie" which he says was published in 8 livraisons from November 1828 to November

1830, but this statement is not supported by any other reference I can find. Mathews (l.c.) assigns certain pages to the various parts, but he does not account for the prefatory matter (pp. I-XXXIJ) which includes the title dated 1831 and the preface dated November 1830. Furthermore, since the Bibliographie de la France apparently omits all mention of Livr. 5, the contents of this and the succeeding parts are uncertain.

Lesson, René Primevère.

1830-32. Histoire naturelle | des Colibris, | suivie | d'un supplement | a l'histoire naturelle | des | Oiseaux-Mouches; | ouvrage orné de planches | dessinées et gravées par les meilleurs artistes, | et dédié | A M. le Baron Cuvier. | Par R. P. Lesson. | [*Quot., 9 lines.*] | Paris. | Arthus Bertrand, Libraire, | éditeur du voyage du monde du Capitaine Duperrey, | Rue Hautefeuille, No 23.

1 vol. in 2 vols. (pt.) 8vo, pp. I-X, 1-196, pll. 1-25, 12 bis and 13 bis (Colibr.), 1-39 (Suppl. Ois.-Mouches) (=66 pll.; col.; by Prêtre and Bévalet). Paris.

A continuation of the author's "Hist. Nat. des Oiseaux-Mouches," 1829-30 (q.v.), with a supplement to the earlier volume. The pagination is continuous in this volume but the plates are numbered separately for the Colibris and for the Suppl. Ois.-Mouch. There is a question as to the dates of publication. Most authors and bibliographers quote 1830-31, both dates appearing in the text, and a notice by the editor on p. II of "Les Trochilidées," 1832-33 (q.v.), states that the present work completed its publication in December 1831. The Catalogue of the Library of the British Museum (Natural History), quoting the "Bibliographie de la France," assigns Livrs. **1-3** to 1830; **4-12**, 1831; and **13**, 1832; with plates issued in the first 12 parts only. The signatures are as follows. Titles and ded., 3 ll. (no sign.); 2 ll. preface (no sign.); signs. 1-12, text; 2 ll. (no sign.), index[1]. This title was followed by the work entitled "Les Trochilidées," 1832-33 (q.v.), and was reissued in 1847. A second copy in the Ayer Ornithological Library is bound in one volume.

Lesson, René Primevère.

1832-33. Les | Trochilidées | ou | les Colibris | et | les Oiseaux-Mouches, | suivis d'un | Index Général, | dans lequel sont décrites et classées méthodiquement toutes les races | et espèces du genre Trochilus. | Ouvrage orné de planches | dessinées et gravées par les meilleurs artistes, | par R. P. Lesson. | [*Quot., 2 lines.*] | Paris. | Arthus Bertrand, Libraire, | éditeur du voyage autour du monde par le Capitaine Duperrey, | Rue Hautefeuille, No 23.

1 vol. 8vo, 2 pr. ll. (half-tit. and tit.), pp. I-IV (notice by editor and pref.), 1-171+1, J-XLIIJ ("Index Général," etc.), pll. 1-66 (col.; by Prêtre and Bévalet). Paris.

---

[1]The index and the preface are on the same quality of paper; the 3 pr. ll. (titles and ded.) are on a different quality, indicating that these may have been issued at different times.

The concluding volume of the series relating to the hummingbirds (Cf. "Histoire Naturelle des Oiseux-Mouches," 1829-30, and "Hist. Nat. des Colibris," 1830-32.). The general text is of the same nature as that of the preceding volumes. Following it, on pp. J-XLIIJ, is given a general synoptic index to all the hummingbirds, with short diagnoses and some synonymy of the species and higher groups. This is separately titled, as follows. "Index | général et synoptique | des oiseaux | du | genre Trochilus, | Par R. P. Lesson. | Paris. | Arthus Bertrand, Libraire, | éditeur du voyage autour du monde par le Capitaine Duperrey, | Rue Hautefeuille, No. 23. | M DCCC XXXII." There is a difference of authorities as to dates of publication. The work was issued in 14 livraisons. Engelmann gives 1832-33 as dates of issue; Coues cites only 1832; the Library of the British Museum (Natural History), quoting from the "Bibliographie de la France," assigns Livrs. 1-7 to 1832 and the rest of the book to 1833; the title-page of the "Index" in the work in question bears the date 1832 (probably in the 11th or 12th livr.), while the author's preface is dated December 1831. The signatures are as follows. Half-tit. and tit. (2 ll.), no sign.; sign. "a" (2 ll.), ed. notice and pref.; signs. 1-11 (4), text; 2 ll., no sign., table; signs. "a"-"f" (2) (4 ll. to each sign. except in "f"), "Index." Sherborn (Index Animalium, Sect. 2, Pt. 1, p. LXXX, 1922) says "Pp. 1-112, 1832; 113-172, & pls. I-XLIII, 1833."

Lesson, René Primevère.

1832-35. Illustrations | de zoologie, | ou | recueil de figures d'animaux | peintes d'après nature; | par | R.-P. Lesson, | Membre correspondant de l'Institut [etc., 5 lines.]. | Ouvrage orné de planches | dessinées et gravées par les meilleurs artistes, | et | servant de complément aux traités généraux ou spéciaux publiés sur | l'histoire naturelle et a les tenir au courant des nouvelles | découvertes et des progrès de la science. | Paris, | Arthus Bertrand, Libraire-Éditeur, | Rue Hautefeuille, No 23.

1 vol. royal 8vo, 4 pr. ll. (half-tit., tit. and pref.), 103 ll., pll. 1-60 (col.; by Prêtre, Bessa, Bévalet and Lesson; 40 of birds). Paris.

Descriptive accounts and colored plates of new genera and species of animals, Pll. 1, 4, 5, 9, 11, 13, 16, 18, 20, 23, 25, 28, 29, 31, 45, 46, 49, 50, 52 and 60 are of birds. The work was issued in 20 livraisons of 3 pll. each. Many of the contributions are dated, but the dates are those of preparation, not of publication. Mathews (Novit. Zool., 18, p. 12, 1911) quotes the following dates from the "Bibliotheque Française" (=Bibliographie de la France). Livr. 1, July 14, 1832; 2, Sept. 1, 1832; 3, Oct. 13, 1832; 4, Nov. 3, 1832; 5, Dec. 1, 1832; 6, Febr. 23, 1833; 7, April 13, 1833; 8, Aug. 10, 1833; 9, Aug. 24, 1833; 10, Oct. 19, 1833; 11, Dec. 21, 1833; 12, March 22, 1834; 13, May 17, 1834; 14, Aug. 2, 1834; 15, Jan. 17, 1835. Livrs. 17 and 20, according to Mathews (l. c.), are cited in the Comptes Rendus for Dec. 1835, p. 517; therefore, Livrs. 16-20 will date 1835. Sherborn (Index Animalium, Sect. 2, Pt. 1, p. LXXX, 1922) says, "pls. 1-15, 1832; 16-33, 1833; 34-42, 1834; 43-60, 1835."

Lesson, René Primevère.

1834-35. **Histoire naturelle | des | Oiseaux de Paradis | et | des Épimaques;** | ouvrage orné de planches, dessinées et gravées par les meilleurs artistes; | par R.-P. Lesson, | Correspondant de l'Académie [*etc., 6 lines.*]. | Paris. | Arthus Bertrand, Libraire, | éditeur du voyage autour du monde de Capitaine Duperrey, | Rue Hautefeuille, No 23.

1 vol. 8vo, pp. J-VIJ+1 (half-tit., tit. and pref.), 1-34 ("Synopsis"), 1 l. (subtit.), pp. 1-248, pll. 1-40, 11 bis, 25 bis and 25 ter (col.: 3 fold.; by Prêtre and Oudart). Paris.

A monograph of the Birds of Paradise. The work is divided into several sections,— a synopsis of species with scientific descriptions and synonymies, (pp. 1-34), introduction (pp. 1-7), a description of New Guinea and its inhabitants (pp. 9-107), the general treatment of each of the species (pp. 109-237), synonymic index (pp. 239-244), tables of plates and subject matter (pp. 245-248). The work was issued in livraisons and is usually cited as published entirely in 1835[1], but the Catalogue of the Library of the British Museum (Natural History), quoting the "Bibliographie de la France" states that Livrs. 1-4, embracing 4 sheets (8 ll.) of text and 16 pll., appeared in 1834. Sherborn (Index Animalium, Sect. 2, Pt. 1, p. LXXX, 1922) adds, "Prob. in 16 pts. of which 1-4, pp. 1-64, 1834; 5-7, 65-112, 1835."

Lesson, Renè Primevère.

1837. See Bougainville, **Journal de la Navigation autour du Globe de la Fregate La Thétis et de la Corvette L'Espérance.**

Lesson, René Primevère.

1839. **Voyage | autour | du monde** | enterpris par ordre du gouvernement | **sur la corvette La Coquille;** | par P. Lesson, | Membre correspondant de l'Institut. | [*Vignette.*] | Paris. | P. Pourrat frères, éditeurs, | rue des Petits-Augustins, 5, | Et chez les Libraires et aux Dépôts de Pittoresques de la France | et dé l'étranger. | 1839. >Voyage | autour | du monde. | Tome Premier [Second].

2 vols. 8vo. Vol. I, 2 pr. ll. (subtit. and tit., pp. 1-510, 1 l. (conts. and errata), 18 pll. (4 col.; 1 fold.; 2 ornith., col.), (tit.-vignette). Vol. II, 2 pr. ll., pp. 1-547, 1 l. (errata), 24 pll. (15 col.; 1 fold; 8 ornith., col.), (tit.-vignette). Paris.

A narrative of the voyage of La Coquille during the years, 1822-25. Numerous notes on natural history are scattered through the text and colored plates of some of the birds and mammals are given together with other illustrations. The official report was published some years earlier by Louis I. Duperrey, the ornithology being supplied by Lesson and Garnot (Cf. Duperrey, Voyage autour du monde—sur—La Coquille, 1826-30.).

---

[1]The preface is dated April 10, 1835.

Lesson, René Primevère. (Ménégaux, Auguste.)

1913. Articles | d'ornithologie | de | R.-P. Lesson | Médecin, Pharmacien en chef de la Marine, | Professeur a l'École de Médecine Navale de Rochefort | Parus dans l'Echo du Monde Savant | de 1842 à 1845. | Réimpression faite par les soins | de | A. Menegaux | Professeur [*etc., 3 lines.*] | Paris | Edition de la Revue Française d'Ornithologie | 55, rue de Buffon, 55 | En vente à Munich | chez MM. Dultz et Co, Libraires | 6, Landwehrstrasse, 6 | 1913.

1 vol. 12mo (variable; size of 16mo), pp. 1-280 frontisp. (portr.). Paris.

A reprint of Lesson's ornithological writings from the "Echo du Monde Savant" of 1842 and 1845, with original pagination noted in place; edited by A. Ménégaux. The work is important owing to the rarity of the originals.

Levaillant, François.

1796-1812. Histoire naturelle | des | oiseaux d'Afrique, | par Fran-çois Levaillant. | Tome premier [-sixième]. | [*Blazon.*] | Paris, | Delachaussée, Rue du Temple, No. 73 [37 (*Vols. II-IV.*); 40 (*Vols. V-VI.*)]. | XIII.-1805 [XIV.-1806 (*Vol. V.*); M.DCCC.VIII (*Vol. VI.*)].

6 vols. superroyal folio. Vol. I, pp. J-XIJ, 1-129, [frontisp. (orig. water-color drawing; extra)], pll. 1-49 (col.). Vol. II, pp. 1-151, pll. 50-97 (col.). Vol. III, 2 pr. ll., pp. 1-147, pll. 98-150 (col.). Vol. IV, pp. 1-104, pll. 151-199 (col.). Vol. V, pp. 1-124, pll. 200-247 (col.). Vol. VI, pp. 1-132, pll. 248-300 (col.). Paris.

An account of the birds of Africa (not always strictly defined), classified under vernacular names. The plates are engravings, printed in colors and afterwards retouched by hand. The first edition, in 4to, was issued in 51 livraisons from 1796 to 1812 and the present edition is ascribed to the same period by the "Catalogue of the Library of the British Museum (Natural History)," although the title-pages present only the dates 1805 to 1808 as in the above transcription. Aside from the change from 4to to folio, I do not know what differences exist in the two editions. A continuation of the work was contemplated by Levaillant [Cf. Cat. Libr. Brit. Mus. (Nat. Hist.).] but was not produced. Ostensibly based on the author's personal observations and collections in southern Africa, the book is a monument of deception. An infinity of detail is given of the habits of the various species and of the circumstances under which the specimens described or figured were secured by the author in Africa, but many of these species do not inhabit any part of that continent. Some of the specimens thus claimed to have been taken personally, have proved to be artifacts. Errors of previous authors have been perpetuated, with an added element of personality given by Levaillant who cites exact data for his supposed specimens. A careful review of the work is given by Sundeevall in the second part of his "Kritisk

Framställning af Fogelarterna uti Äldre Ornithologiska Arbeten" published in the Kon. Vet. Akad. Hand., Bd. 2, No. 3, 1857.

Levaillant, François.

1801-02. **Histoire naturelle | d'une partie | d'oiseaux nouveaux | et rares | de l'Amérique et des Indes,** | Par François Levaillant: | Ouvrage destine par l'Auteur à faire partie de son Ornithologie | d'Afrique. | Tome premier. | A Paris, | Chez J. E. Gabriel Dufour, libraire rue de Tournon, | No. 1126. | Et à Amsterdam, chez le même libraire. | De l'imprimerie de Didot jeune, Quai des Augustins, No. 22. | An IX (1801).

1 vol. superroyal folio, 2 pr. ll. (half-tit. and tit.), pp. J-IIJ+1 (pref.), 1-112, pll. 1-49 (col.), 1-49 (uncol.; dupls. of col. pll.). Paris.

A work intended to supplement the "Hist. Nat. des Oiseaux d'Afrique" (q.v.) by describing and figuring birds not properly included in that work. One volume, only, was published which consists of monographs of the Bucerotidae and the Cotingidae, with 49 of the proposed 240 plates. The work was continued under a separate title (Cf. Levaillant, Histoire Naturelle des Oiseaux de Paradis, etc.). The present volume was issued in 8 parts of which 1-4 appeared in 1801 and 5-8 in 1802 (Cat. Libr. Brit. Mus. [Nat. Hist.)], but I am uncertain as to the division of parts. The Bucerotidae are treated on pp. 1-51 and pll. 1-24, and the Cotingidae on pp. 53-110 and pll. 25-49, an arrangement which divides the volume into two nearly equal parts. The plates are duplicated, one of each being colored and one plain. The former are printed in colors and retouched by hand. No scientific nomenclature is used in the text.

Levaillant, François.

1801-05. **Histoire naturelle | des perroquets,** | par | François Levaillant. | Tome premier [second]. | [*Monogram.*] | A Paris, | Chez Levrault, Schoell et Ce., Rue de Seine S.G. | Strasbourg, de l'imprimerie de Levrault. | An XII (1804) [An XIII (1805)].

2 vols. superroyal folio. Vol. I, 4 pr. ll. (half-tit., tit., ded. and pref.), pp. 1-135+1, 1 l. (table), pll. 1-71+2 (bis) (=72 col). Vol. II, 2 pr. ll. (half-tit., and tit.), pp. 1-112, 1 l. (table), pll. 72-139, 95 (bis), 98 (bis), 107 (bis), 108 (bis), and 110 (bis) (=73 col.; by Barraband). Paris.

A monograph of the parrots, illustrated by engraved plates printed in colors and retouched by hand. The work was issued in 24 livraisons for which the following dates are given by the Cat. Libr. Brit. Mus. (Nat. Hist.), without information concerning the extent of each livraison. Livrs. **1-2**, 1801; **4-8**, 1802; **10-16**, 1803; **17-20**, 1804; **22-24**, 1805. A supplementary volume was issued by Bourjot Saint-Hilaire in 1837-38 under the same title as above, "troisième volume" (q.v.), and in 1857-58, Charles de Souancé added an additional volume under the title of "Iconographie des Perroquets" (q.v.). No scientific nomenclature is used in the present work.

Levaillant, François.

1801-06. > Histoire naturelle | des Oiseaux de Paradis | et des Rolliers, | suivie | de celle des Toucans et des Barbus, | par | François Levaillant. | Tome premier [second]. | [*Monogram.*] | Paris, |

Chez { Denné le jeune, Libraire de S.A.I. le Prince Joseph, rue Vivienne, no. 10.   Perlet, Libraire, rue de Tournon.   1806.

2 vols. superroyal folio. Vol. I, 2 pr. ll. (half-tit. and tit.), pp. 1-153 +1, J-IJ (table), pll. 1-13, 16 (=14), 15-56 (col.; 2 fold.; by Barraband), 56 pll. (uncol.; without legend; dupls. of col. pll.). Vol. II, 2 pr. ll. (half-tit. and tit.), pp. 1-34, 41-48 (=35-42), 43-106, 109-111+1 (=107-110), 111-133+1, J-IJ (table), 1 l. (errata), pll. 1-18, 18 (*bis*; =19), 20-37, A, 38-57 (col.; by Barraband) 58 pll. (uncol.; without legend; dupls. of col. pll.). Paris.

A work which may be considered as a continuation of the author's "Hist. Nat. d'une partie d'Oiseaux Nouveaux," etc., 1801-02 (q.v.). It consists of a similar series of monographs on groups not always coinciding with modern ones, as follows. Vol. I:-Introd., pp. 1-7; Ois. de Paradis, pp. 9-68, pll. 1-24; Rolliers, pp. 69-115, pll. 25-39; Geais, pp. 117-153, pll. 40-56. Vol. II:-Introd. pp. 1-6; Toucans, pp. 7-46, pll. 1-18; Barbus, pp. 47-89, pll. 18 (*bis*, =19),20-38; Barbus Tamatias, pp. 91-100, pll. 39-43; Barbacous, pp. 101-106, pll. 44-46; Jacamars, pp. 109 (=107), 108-126, pll. 47-54; suppl. to Barbus, pp. 127-133, pll. 55-57. A third volume in two parts, each with separate pagination and numbering of plates, and with title altered to "Hist. Nat. des Promerops et des Guépiers," including a supplement to the two volumes here collated, was issued in sequence after the present numbers, forming livraisons 20-33. This portion is lacking from the set examined. An indication of this work may be found on p. 1 of Vol. I of the present set, where a half-title includes "des Promerops" among the subjects mentioned. A covering title is said [Cat. Libr. Brit. Mus. (Nat. Hist.)] to have been issued for the three volumes. The same authority quotes the following dates of publication for Livrs. 1-14, without assigning pagination for them. Livrs. 1 and 2, 1801; 3-5, 1802; 6-12, 1803; 13-14, 1804; 15-19, not cited. The dates are not important since only vernacular names are used in the text. The plates are printed in colors and retouched by hand.

Leverkuhn, Paul.

1891. Fremde Eier im Nest. | Ein Beitrag zue Biologie der Vögel | von | Paul Leverkühn. | Nebst einer bibliographischen Notiz über Lottinger. | [*Quot., 4 lines.*] | 1891. | Berlin. London. | R. Friedländer und Sohn, Karlstrasse 11. Gurney and Jackson, 1 Paternoster Row. | Wien. Paris. | E. Soeding, Wallnerstrasse 13. P. Klincksieck, 52 Rue des Écoles. | Leiden. New York. | E. Brill, Oude Rijn 38. A. E. Pettit, 15 Cortlandt Street.

1 vol. 8vo, pp. I-X, 1 l. (conts.), pp. 1-212, 2 ll. (list of author's papers). Berlin.

An interesting study of the parasitic instinct among birds, including the occasional, as well as the habitual, offenders against both their own and other species. The information is based on voluminous data compiled from all possible sources.

Leverkuhn, Paul.

1896. See World's Congress on Ornithology, **Papers presented to the—**

Levick, G. Murray.

1914. Antarctic | penguins | a study of their social habits | by | Dr. G. Murray Levick, R.N. | Zoologist to the British Antarctic Expedition | [1910-1913] | New York | McBride, Nast & Company | 1914.

1 vol. post 8vo, pp. I-X, 1-139, frontisp., 55 pll. (figs. 1-74). New York.

A thorough, detailed study of the habits of the Adélie Penguin, copiously illustrated with photographs taken in the haunts of the species.

Lewin, John William.

1822. A | natural history | of the | birds of New South Wales, | collected, engraved, and faithfully painted after nature, | by | John William Lewin, A.L.S. | late of Paramatta, New South Wales. | Illustrated with twenty-six plates. | London: | printed for J. H. Bohte, foreign bookseller to His Majesty, | 4 York-Street, Covent-Garden; | by G. Schulze, 13, Poland Street. | 1822.

1 vol. medium folio (11x15), 2 pr. ll. (tit. and conts.), pp. 1-26, pll. I-XXVI (by Lewin). London.

A collection of etched drawings of birds of New South Wales, accompanied by a brief description of each species, without scientific nomenclature. The work constitutes a third edition of the "Birds of New Holland," etc., published in 1808, with the addition of 8 new plates (pll. VII and XIX-XXV). The second edition, published in Sydney in 1813, was entitled "Birds of New South Wales." A "new and improved edition" (q.v.), under the same title as the present one, was issued in 1838. The present edition exists, also, with colored plates [Cf. Cat. Libr. Brit. Mus. (Nat. Hist.).].

Lewin, John William.

1838. A | natural history | of the | birds of New South Wales, | collected, engraved, and faithfully painted after nature, | by | John William Lewin, A.L.S. | late of Paramatta, New South Wales. | New and improved edition, | to which is added | a list of the synonymes of each species, | incorporating the labours of T. Gould,

Esq., N. A. Vigors, Esq., T. Horsfield, M.D., and W. Swainson, Esq. | London: | Henry G. Bohn, 4, York Street, Covent Garden. | MDCCCXXXVIII.

1 vol. demy folio, 3 pr. ll. (tit., synonymic index and list of contents), pp. 1-26, pll. I-XXVI (col.; by Lewin). London.

The fourth edition of Lewin's "Birds of New Holland." The text and plates (except for the coloring of the latter) are the same as those in the earlier edition catalogued above under the present general title, 1822 (q.v.), with the addition, in the present work, of a list of synonyms (scientific and vernacular) for each species.

Lewin, William.

1795-1801. The | birds | of | Great Britain, | systematically arranged, accurately engraved, | and painted from nature; | with descriptions, including | the natural history of each bird : | From Observations the Result of more than Twenty Years Application to the | Subject, in the Field of Nature; in which the distinguishing Character of each | Species is fully explained, and its Manner of Life truly described. | The figures engraved from the subjects themselves [*Comma added (Vols. II-VIII.*).] by the author, | W. Lewin, | Fellow of the Linnæan Society, | and painted under his immediate direction. | In eight volumes. | Vol. I [-VIII]. | London: | printed for J. Johnson, in St. Paul's Church-yard. | 1795 [1796; 1796; 1797; 1797; 1800; 1800; 1801]. [| T. Bensley, Printer, Bolt Court, Fleet Street. (Vols. II-VIII.)].

8 vols. in 2, medium 4to. Vol. I, 11 ll. (unnum.), pp. 21-75+1, 2 ll. (index), frontisp. (col.), pll. 1-31, *18, *19, 27 (bis) (birds; col.), 1-7 (eggs; col.). Vol. II, pp. 1-75+1, 2 ll. (index), pll. 32-66 (birds; col.), 8-14 (eggs; col.). Vol. III, pp. 1-75+1, 2 ll. (index), pll. 67-97, 66 (bis), 81*, 84*, 94* (birds; col.), 16-22 (eggs; col.). Vol. IV. pp. 1-75+1, 2 ll. (index), pll. 98-131, 100* (birds; col.), 23-29 (eggs; col.). Vol. V, pp. 1-75+1, 2 ll. (index), pll. 132-166 (birds; col.), 30-36 (eggs; col.). Vol. VI, pp. 1-77+1, 2 ll. (index), pll. 167-202 (birds; col.), 37-42 (eggs; col.). Vol. VII, pp. 1-73+1, 2 ll. (index), pll. (203)-236 (birds; col.), 43-50 (eggs; col.). Vol. VIII, pp. 1-71+1, 2 ll. (index), pll. 237-267, 245 (bis), 251 (bis) (birds; col.), 51-58 (eggs; col.). London.

The second edition of the work first published in 1789-94. The text, in both English and French, embraces a short description of each species and an account of its habits. The plates are rather poor. Pl. 15 seems not to have been published. As bound, Vols. I-IV are in one volume; V-VIII in the second.

Lewis, Elisha Joseph. (Burges, Arnold.)

1885. The | American Sportsman: | containing | hints to sports-
men, notes on shooting, | and the habits of the | Game Birds and
Wild Fowl of America. | By | Elisha J. Lewis, M.D., | Member
of the American Philosophical Society [*etc.*, *2 lines*.]. | A new edi-
tion, thoroughly revised, | containing new chapters on the origin,
breeding, and science of breaking dogs, | and full information on
breech-loading and hammerless | guns, etc., etc. | By Arnold
Burges. | Profusely illustrated. | Philadelphia: | J. B. Lippin-
cott & Co. | 1885.

1 vol. post 8vo, pp. 1-553 (11-12 missing), 1 pl., 48 text-figs. and
various pictorial initials. Philadelphia.

A volume primarily of interest to the sportsman, containing accounts of many
species of North American game birds. This is the fourth edition of the work,
the first having been published in 1855.

Lichtenstein, Anton August Heinrich.

1823. See Eversmann, Eduard, **Reise von Orenburg nach Buchara.**

Lichtenstein, Anton August Heinrich.

1844. See Forster, Johann Reinhold, **Descriptiones Animalium.**

Lichtenstein, Anton August Heinrich. (Tegetmeier, William Bernhard,
ed.)

1882. The Willughby Society. | **Lichtenstein's** | **Catalogus** | **Rerum**
Naturalium Rarissimarum. | [*Vignette.*] | Edited by | W. B. Teget-
meier, F.Z.S. | London: MDCCCLXXXII.

{Catalogus | Rerum naturalium rarissimarum | Hamburgi, d
XXI Octobr. 1793. | Auctionis lege distrahendrarum. | Sectio
Prima | Continens mammalia & Aves | Verzeichniss | [V] on
hochsteltenem, aus allen Welttheilen mit vieler Mühe und kosten |
zusammen gebrachten, auch aus unterschiedlichen Cabinettern |
Samlungen und Auctionem ausgehobenen | Naturalien | welche
von einem Liebhaber, als Mitglied der Batavischen und | verschie-
dener anderer Naturforschenden Gesellschaften | gesamlet worden |
Erster Abschnitt | bestehend | in wohlconditionarten, mehren-
theils ausländischen, nach dem Leben | augestellten | Säugethieren
und Vögeln | theils los, theils in sauberen Kastchen mit Glas ver-
sehen; nebst den | dazu gehorigen Schranken von Mahogoni-Holz
verfertiget | welche am | Montag den 21sten Octobr. 1793 | und
den folgenden Tagen | auf dem Eimbeckschen Hause | offentlich
verkauft werden sollen | durch den Mackler | Johann Hinrich

Schöen | Dieses Cabinett ist drey Wochen vorher am Verkauss-
Orte ausgestellet | und vom 7ten October bis zum Verkauf, taglich
offentlich | an besehen. | Hamburg. | gedrukt bey Gottl. Fried.
Schniebes.}

1 vol. 4to (size of royal 8vo), pp. I-IV, "6 pr. ll. (tit., notice and pref.
in Latin and German), pp. 1-60," 2 ll. (advt.). "Hamburg. 1793."
London. 1882.

A catalogue of a collection of mammals and birds to be sold by auction at Hamburg, with descriptions of many new species (some of which have not since
been identified) and notes on all of them. The preface, signed by Lichtenstein, is dated Sept. 1, 1793. The present copy is a reprint (in increased size)
of the original, published by The Willughby Society (q.v.). The preface by
the editor contains a brief notice regarding the author.

Another reprint of this paper, edited by F. D. Godman, was issued by the
Willughby Society the same year (q.v.).

Lichtenstein, Anton August Heinrich. (Godman, Frederick Du Cane.)
1882. The Willughby Society. | **Lichtenstein's Catalogus Rerum
Naturalium Rarissimarum.** | [*Vignette.*] | Edited by | F. Du Cane
Godman, F.R.S. &c. | London: MDCCCLXXXII.

{Catalogus | Rerum naturalium rarissimarum | Hamburgi, d
XXI Octobr. 1793. | Auctionis lege distrahendarum. | Sectio
Prima | Continens mammalia & Aves | Verzeichniss | von höchst-
seltenen, aus allen Welttheilen mit vieler Mühe und Kosten |
zusammen gebrachten, auch aus unterschiedlichen Cabinettern, |
Sammlungen und Auctionen ausgehobenen | Naturlien | welche
von einem Liebhaber, als Mitglied der Batavischen und | ver-
schiedener anderer Naturforschenden Gesellschaften | gesammlet
worden. | Erster Abschnitt, | bestehend | in wohlconditionirten,
mehrentheils ausländischen, nach dem Leben | aufgestellten |
Säugethieren und Vögeln, | theils los, theils in sauberen Kästchen
mit Glas versehen, nebst den | dazu gehörigen Schränken von
Mahagoni-Holz verfertiget | welche am | Montag den 21sten
Octobr. 1793 | und den folgenden Tagen | auf dem Eimbeckschen
Hause | öffentlich verkauft werden sollen | durch den Mackler |
Johann Hinrich Schöen | Dieses Cabinett ist drey Wochen vorher
am Verkauss-Orte aufgestellet | und vom 7ten October bis zum
Verkauf, täglich öffentlich | zu besehen. | Hamburg. | gedruckt
bey Gottl. Fried. Schniebes.}

1 vol. 4to (size of royal 8vo), pp. I-IV, "6 pr. ll. (tit., notice and pref.
in Latin and German), pp. 1-60," 2 ll. (advt.). "Hamburg. 1793."
London. 1882.

The nature of the work is identical with that of the same title, edited by W. B. Tegetmeier, published the same year also by the Willughby Society (q.v.). The details of the two reprints are not identical, as will be shown hereunder.

The prefaces of the two editions vary in the details given of the life of Lichtenstein and differ noticeably in their summaries of the new species contained in the succeeding pages. Tegetmeier lists but 36 new species; Godman gives the number as 38, including, properly, No. 362 (*Columba assimilis*) and No. 500 (*Turdus macrourus*) which are not mentioned by Tegetmeier.

Tegetmeier calls his edition "a literal reprint (the orthographical and typographical errors being intentionally reproduced)" "line for line and letter for letter" from the copy in the Banksian Library, British Museum; Godman says his edition is "reproduced *literatim et verbatim*" from the copy in the Library of the British Museum. In spite of this fact, differences occur throughout, beginning with the reprinted title-page, lines 4, 8, 9, 10, 14, 15, 17, 18, 19, 20, 21, 26, 29, 30 and 31. A common source of difference in the later pages is in the diphthongs 'æ' and 'œ' which are interpreted in one form by Tegetmeier and exactly the opposite by Godman. The other differences are too numerous to mention. However, it is obviously impossible that both editions can be exact reprints of the same copy.

There is no published evidence which I can find to explain the reason for the two editions. Godman's issue was printed by Taylor and Francis, and Tegetmeier's by Horace Cox, but since both firms were employed in the printing of other of the Willughby reprints, no light is thrown on the possible unauthenticity of either edition. The Catalogue of the Library of the British Museum (Natural History), The Zoological Record for 1882, and the Catalogue of the Library of the Zoological Society of London mention only Godman's reprint. There is no current review in the Ibis. The advertising pages at the close of each copy list that particular edition among the regular publications of the Society but say nothing of another edition. A possible solution of the puzzle is suggested by the advertising pages of the reprint of "Wagler's six ornithological memoirs from the Isis," 1884 (q.v.). In these there appears a statement, signed by Godman as Secretary of the Society, that there had been considerable delay in the publication of some of the numbers, on account of which the Committee had made a change in regard to editorial supervision which it was hoped would obviate further difficulties of this nature. The present paper was among those which had been delayed since it was due in 1880, and Tegetmeier was Director of the Society!

Lichtenstein, Martin Heinrich Karl.

1854. Nomenclator | avium | Musei Zoologici Berolinensis. | Namenverzeichniss | der | in der zoologischen Sammlung der Königlichen | Universität zu Berlin | aufgestellten Arten von | Vögeln | nach den in der neueren Systematik am meisten | zur Geltung gekommenen | Namen der Gattungen | und | ihrer Unterabtheilungen. | Berlin. | Gedruckt in der Buchdruckerei der Königlichen Akademie | der Wissenschaften. | 1854.

1 vol. 8vo, pp. I-VIII, 1-123. Berlin.

A hand-list of the specimens of birds in the Berlin Museum, giving the distribution of each species, the number of specimens at hand and, in some cases, the price at which duplicates will be sold. The list seems to have been published by Lichtenstein whose name is signed to the preface although acknowledgments are made (p. *VI*) for a certain amount of assistance rendered by Cabanis. Some confusion exists in the fact that Lichtenstein quotes his own genera as "Licht." and those of Cabanis as "Nob." but the arrangement of species is not entirely that followed by Cabanis, and the latter author, in his "Museum Heineanum," 1850-63 (q.v.), cites the present work as of Lichtenstein, so Cabanis, probably, is not to be quoted under the present title. Many of the names used elsewhere by Cabanis, and first published by him, were taken from specimens in the Berlin Museum labelled in the first place by Lichtenstein, so the names characterized as "Nob" in the "Nomenclator" may have been originated by Lichtenstein, although published first by Cabanis. The "Nomenclator" is useful, principally, for the definite localities given for the species, many of which were described elsewhere, without such exact information, from the specimens listed herein.

Lichthammer, J. W.

1800-1811. See Borckhausen, Moritz B.; Lichthammer; Bekker; Lembcke and Bekker Jr., **Teutsche Ornithologie.**

Lilford, Lord [= Thomas Littleton Powys, fourth Baron Lilford]. (Salvin, Osbert.)

1891-98.   Coloured figures | of the | birds of the British Islands. | Issued by | Lord Lilford, F.Z.S., etc., | President of the British Ornithologists' Union. | **Second edition.** | Volume I [-VII]. | London: | R. H. Porter, 7 Princes Street, Cavendish Square, W. | 1891-1897.

7 vols. in 8. Vol. I, pp. I-XXXV (XXXII wrongly numbered XXXI), 61 ll., frontisp. (portr.), 51 pll. (col.). Vol. II, pp. I-IX+1, 60 ll., 54 pll. (col.). Vol. III, pp. I-IX+1, 65 ll., 66 pl. (col.). Vol. IV, pp. I-IX+1, 78 ll., 65 pll. (col.). Vol. V, pp. I-IX+1, 69 ll., 59 pll. (col.). Vol. VI, pp. I-IX+1, 75 ll., 65 pll. (col.). Vol. VII, pp. I-IX+1, 72 ll. pp. 145-170 (appendix and index), 61 pll. (col.). [Extra volume contains title (without vol. no.), duplicate index (pp. 149-170 of Vol. VII), and original wrappers of Pts. I-XXXVI.] London.

A short account of each of the British birds and its habits, preceded by a brief synonymy and illustrated by colored plates (chromolith.). Most of the plates are by Thorburn and Keulemans; a few are by G. E. Lodge and W. Foster. The first edition was begun in Oct. 1885 and issued in parts. The second edition, also in parts, commenced in April 1891 (at the time Pt. XVIII, first ed., appeared) and overtook the first edition in Sept. 1894 with the issue of Pt. XXVIII, after which the same parts of both editions appeared simultaneously until the completion of the work. The editions are said to be identical except in Pts. VII-XVII in which various improvements were made in the second issue. The work was incomplete at the time of Lord Lilford's death and was then taken in hand by Osbert Salvin (as explained in a note on pp. XXIII-XXIV of Vol. I) who produced Pts. XXXIV-XXXVI. The original wrappers of the second edition bear the following dates. Pts. **I-IV**, April 1891; **V-VI**, June 1891; **VII**, July 1891; **VIII**, Aug. 1891; **IX**, Oct. 1891; **X**, Dec. 1891; **XI**, Febr. 1892; **XII**, May 1892; **XIII**, June 1892; **XIV**, July 1892; **XV**, Aug. 1892; **XVI-XVII**, Nov. 1892; **XVIII**, Dec. 1892; **XIX**, Feb. 1893; **XX**, March 1893; **XXI**, May 1893; **XXII**, June 1893; **XXIII**, July 1893; **XXIV**, Oct. 1893; **XXV**, Nov. 1893; **XXVI**, Dec. 1893; **XXVII**, Aug. 1894; **XXVIII**, Sept. 1894; **XXIX**, Nov. 1894; **XXX**, Febr. 1895; **XXXI**, June 1895; **XXXII**, April 1896; **XXXIII**, Nov. 1896; **XXXIV**, April 1897; **XXXV**, Nov. 1897; **XXXVI**, [N.d.,; Jan. 1898 (Mullens & Swann).] The concluding part appears to have contained the full text for the complete work, the frontispiece, the title-pages and all prefatory matter for each volume, and the general index.

Collations of both editions, showing the various species and the number and date of the part in which the plate of each appeared, are given in Vol I, pp. XXV-XXVI, Vol. II, pp. V-VI and Vol. III, pp. V-VI.

Lilford, Lord [= Thomas Littleton Powys, fourth Baron Lilford].

1895. Notes | on the | birds of Northamptonshire | and neighborhood. | By | Lord Lilford, | President of the British Ornithologists' Union [*etc.*, *2 lines.*]. | Vol. I [II]. | Illustrated | by | Messrs. A. Thorburn and G. E. Lodge. | And a map. | London: | R. H. Porter, 18 Princes Street, Cavendish Square, W. | 1895.

2 vols. royal 8vo. Vol. I, pp. I-XVI, 1-352, frontisp., 16 pll. (by A. Thorburn), 31 text-figs. (by G. E. Lodge). Vol. II, pp. I-VIII, I-VIII 1 l. (list of illustrs.), pp. 1-315, 7 pll., 13 text-figs., 1 map. London.

A detailed account of the author's personal observations on the habits of a large number of birds of Northamptonshire, England, and outlying regions. Many of the notes are reprinted from the "Journal of the Northamptonshire Natural History Society," according to a statement by the author in his preface. A large paper edition of 100 copies was issued the same year.

Lilford, Lord [= Thomas Littleton Powys, fourth Baron Lilford]. (Trevor-Battye, Aubyn, *ed.*)

1903. Lord Lilford | on |birds | being a collection of informal and | unpublished writings by the late | President of the British Ornithologists' | Union. With contributed papers upon | falconry and otter hunting, his | favourite sports. Edited by | Aubyn Trevor-Battye | M.A., F.L.S., etc. | Member of the British Ornithologists' Union | and illustrated by | Archibald Thorburn | London: Hutchinson & Co. | Paternoster Row 1903.

1 vol. 8vo (7½x9¾), pp. I-XVII+1, 1-312, frontisp. (portr.), 12 pll. (by A. Thorburn), 1 text-fig. London.

A posthumous publication, containing transcriptions from certain of Lord Lilford's journals and correspondence, and his record of occurrences in his aviary.
The editor has supplied notes and introductory remarks throughout the volume.

Linné, Karl von.

1746. Caroli Linnæi | Medic. & Botan. Prof. Upsal; Horti Acade-
mici Præfect; Acad. Imperial. | Monspeliens: Stockholm: Upsal:
Soc; Hujusque Secretar. | **Fauna** | **Svecica** | Sistens | Animalia
Sveciæ Regni: | quadrupedia, aves, amphibia, | pisces, insecta,
vermes, | Distributa | Per | classes & ordines, | genera & species. |
Cum | Differentiis Specierum, | Synonymis Autorum, | Nomini-
bus Incolarum, | Locis Habitationum, | Descriptionibus Insec-
torum. | Stockholmiæ | Sumtu & literis Laurentii Salvii | 1746.

1 vol. crown 8vo, 14 pr. ll., pp. 1-411, frontisp., pll. I-II (fold.; by
I. Leche). Stockholm.

The first edition of Linné's work on the zoology of Sweden, with detailed descriptions of most of the species. The occasional binary terms are not accepted
binomials since the work precedes the 10th edition of the author's 'Systema
Naturae.' The second edition of the present work (q.v.) published in 1761,
made use of binomials. In the present edition the birds occupy pp. 16-93.

Linné, Karl von.

1761. Caroli Linnæi, | Equit. aur. de Stella Polari; | Archiatr.
Reg. Med. & Botan. Profess. Upsal. &c. | **Fauna** | **Svecica** | Sis-
tens | Animalia Sveciæ Regni: | mammalia, aves, amphibia, |
pisces, insecta, vermes. | Distributa | Per | classes & ordines, |
genera & species, | Cum | Differentiis Specierum, | Synonymis
Auctorum, | Nominibus Incolarum, | Locis Natalium, | Descrip-
tionibus Insectorum. | **Editio Altera,** Auctior. | Cum Privilegio
S.R.M. 'tis Sveciæ & S.R.M. 'tis Poloniæ ac Electoris Saxon. |
Stockholmiæ, | Sumtu & Literis Direct. Laurentii Salvii, | 1761.

1 vol. in 2 vols., 24 pr. ll., pp. 1-578 (interleaved), frontisp., pll. I-
II (fold.; by I. Leche). Stockholm.

A revised and enlarged edition of the author's work of the same title of 1746
(q.v.). Various species are added and the binomial nomenclature, consistently
introduced by the author in the meanwhile, is here adopted. The birds are
discussed on pp. 19-100. The margins and interpolated leaves are filled with
manuscript annotations by a former owner of the copy. A third edition was
issued in 1800.

Linné, Karl von.

1776. A | catalogue | of the | birds, beasts, fishes, insects, plants,
&c. | contained in | Edwards's natural history, | in seven volumes, |
with their Latin names | By Sir. C. Linnæus, | Medical and

Botanical Professor of the Royal Academy | at Upsal, &c. | London: | printed for J. Robson, bookseller, New Bond Street. | MDCCLXXVI.

1 vol. crown folio, pp. 1-15, 1 p. (advt.). London.

A list of the species figured in the "Natural History of Uncommon Birds" and "Gleanings of Natural History" (q.v.) by Edwards, with Latin binomials applied by Linné. This work was prepared by Linné after Edwards's death and appears to have been published by Robson for inclusion in copies of Edwards's work since a notice on p. 15 gives directions for its insertion in copies of the latter. The paper on "Some Memoirs of the Life and Works of George Edwards" (probably by Robson, q.v.) was issued the same year as the present brochure, and in the copy at hand is included in the same wrapper. A second copy of this catalogue is bound with Pt. III of the second edition of Edwards's "Gleanings."

Linné, Karl von. (Gmelin, Johann Friedrich; Turton, William.)

1802. **A general | system of nature,** | through the | three grand kingdoms | of | Animals, Vegetables, and Minerals; | systematically divided | into their several | classes, orders, genera, species, and varieties, | with their | habitations, manners, economy, structure, | and peculiarities. | Translated from Gmelin's last Edition of the celebrated | Systema Naturæ, | by Sir Charles Linné: [*Period instead of colon* (*Vols. II and III.*).] | Amended and enlarged by the improvements and | discoveries of later naturalists and societies, | With appropriate Copper-plates, | by William Turton, M.D. | author of The Medical Glossary. | Vol. I [-IV]. | [*Quot., 4 lines.*]. | London: | printed for Lackington, Allen and Co. Temple of the | Muses, Finsbury-Square; | sold also by Mr. Cooke, and Messrs. Hanwell and Parker, | Oxford; Mr. Deighton, Cambridge; Mr. Archer, Dublin; and Messrs. Mundell and Son, Edinburgh. | 1802.

4 vols. post 8vo. Vol. I, pp. I-VII+1, 1-943+1, 2 pll. (1 of birds). Vol. II, pp. 1-717+1+1 l., 1 pl. Vol. III, pp. 1-784. Vol. IV, pp. 1-727. London. (1800?-) 1802.

Turton's translation of the 13th edition of Linné's "Systema Naturae" which was published by Gmelin in 1788-93. The ornithology occupies pp. 131-637 of Vol. I, and one plate. Vol. I was printed in 1800 and III in 1801, according to a statement in the colophon of each, but actual publication, judging by the date on the title-pages, appears to have been reserved until completion of the four volumes. These four volumes are complete for zoology but embrace only that subject. Three additional volumes on the remaining subjects of natural history were published subsequently with a reissue of the present four which were then supplied with new title-pages, making the complete set of seven volumes. The present set, however, is to be quoted separately. Engelmann confuses the two editions and cites colored plates.

Linné, Karl von.

1907. See Lönnberg, Einar, **Caroli Linnæi . . . Methodus Avium Sveticarum.**

Littler, Frank Mervyn.

1910.   A handbook | of the | Birds of Tasmania | and its dependencies | by | Frank Mervyn Littler, F.E.S. | (Member of the Australasian Ornithologists' Union). | Launceston, Tasmania: | published by the author. | 1910. | [All Rights Reserved.].

1 vol. 8vo, 2 pr. ll. (half-tit. and tit.), pp. III-XVIII, 1-242, 42 pll. Launceston.

An account of the birds of Tasmania and dependencies, with descriptions of the various plumages and of the nest and eggs, a statement of the breeding season and geographical distribution, and a paragraph of observations on each species.

Lloyd, Llewellyn.

1867.   The | game birds and wild fowl | of | Sweden and Norway; | with | an account of the seals and salt-water fishes | of those countries. | By L. Lloyd, | author of [*etc., 2 lines.*]. | Second edition, | With Map, Woodcuts, and Chromo Illustrations. | London: | Frederick Warne and Co. | Bedford Street, Covent Garden. | 1867. | [All rights reserved.].

1 vol. superroyal 8vo, pp. I-XX, 1-599, 52 pll. (48 col.; by M. Körner; W. von Wright and J. Wolf), 61 text-cuts (74 figs.), 1 map (fold.). London.

A popular treatment of the subject, including voluminous notes on methods of hunting and capturing the animals discussed. Most of the book is ornithological. Pages 1-371, 36 plates (33 col. and 3 plain) and 47 text-cuts (58 figs.) relate to birds. The colored plates are chromo-lithographs; those by Körner are said (by the Zool Record) to be copied from Nilsson's "Skandanaviska Foglar." The first edition was issued earlier but in the same year as the present one. It is probably that which is catalogued by Taschenberg as published by Day & Son, London, 1867.

Loche.

1858.   Catalogue | des mammifères | et | des oiseaux | observés en Algérie | par le Capitaine Loche | (du 45e de ligne) | Chevalier de la Légion [*etc., 2 lines.*], | et Conservateur de l'Exposition Permanente | des Produits de l'Algérie | rédigé d'après la classification | de S. A. le Prince Charles-Lucien Bonaparte | Paris | Libraire d'Arthur Bertrand | Rue Hautefeuille, 21 | Droit de traduction et de reproduction réservé.

1 vol. demy 8vo, pp. J-XJ+1, 1-158. Paris.

A catalogue of the mammals and birds observed in Algeria by the author, with synonymy (scientific and local vernacular) and distribution of each species, and with references to specimens in the collection of the "Exposition." Supplementary lists record the species known from the region but not found by the author. The ornithology occupies pp. 33-158. No date is given on the title-page, but the preface is dated March 1, 1858. The present copy was autographed (on the wrapper) by the author in presentation to Louis Reichenbach, Dresden.

Lockwood, George R.

1871. See Audubon, John James, **The Birds of America.**

Lodge, Reginald Badham.

1903. **Pictures of | bird life |** on | woodland, meadow, mountain | and marsh | by | R. B. Lodge | medallist Royal Photographic Society | with | numerous colour and half-tone illustrations | from photographs from life by the author |
S. B. Bousefield & Co., Ltd. London 1903
Norfolk House
Norfolk Street
W.C.
1 vol. 8vo (7x9¾), pp. 1-376, 8 pll. (col.), 231 text-figs. London.

An account of the experiences of the author in hunting birds with the camera, illustrated with photographs, and with chapters on methods and equipment employed in bird-photography.

Lönnberg, Einar. (Linné, Karl von.)

1907. Uppsala Universitets Årsskrift 1907. | Linnéfest-Skrifter. 5. | **Caroli Linnæi** | Med., Botan. & Zoolog. Cult. | **Methodus | avium Sveticarum** | utgifven | af | Einer Lönnberg > Caroli Linnæi [*etc., 7 lines.*] | Uppsala 1907 | Almqvist & Wiksells Boktryckeri-A.-B.
1 vol. royal 8vo, 2 pr. ll., pp. 1-96, 1 pl. (fold.). Upsala.

A transcript of an unpublished manuscript by Linné on the birds of Sweden, entitled, "Methodus Avium Sveticarum," with notes by Lönnberg. The original manuscript is said to have been in the form of a pocket notebook, interleaved with loose sheets containing additional matter of questionable date; the notebook carried a title-page bearing the date January 1, 1731.

Lord, John Keast.

1866. **The naturalist | in | Vancouver Island and | British Columbia.** | By | John Keast Lord, F.Z.S. | Naturalist to the British North American Boundary Commission. | [*Vignette.*] The 'Kettle' Falls: a salmon leap on the upper Columbia [Syniakwateen (The

Crossing)]. | In two volumes—Vol. I [II]. | London: | Richard
Bentley, New Burlington Street, | publisher in ordinary to Her
Majesty. | 1866.

2 vols. demy 8vo. Vol. I, tit., pp. V-XIV, 1 l. (list of illustrs. and
errata), pp. 1-358, frontisp., 6 pll. (2 of birds). Vol. II, tit., pp.
V-VII+1, 1 l. (illustrs. and errata), pp. 1-375, frontisp., 3 pll.
London.

A description of the author's travels and observations as naturalist of the commission which was sent to mark the boundary between Canada and the United
States from the Pacific coast to the eastern slope of the Rocky Mountains. In
addition to numerous ornithological notes scattered through the text, a list of
the birds observed by the author is given in the appendix to Vol. II, on pp.
291-301.

Lorenz, Ludwig von.

1887. See Pelzeln, August von; and Madarász, **Monographie der
Piridae.**

Lorenz, Theodor.

1887. Beitrag | zur Kenntnis | der | ornithologischen Fauna | an
der Nordseite des | Kaukasus. | Von | Th. Lorenz. | Moskau. |
[*Medallion.*] Buchdruckerei von E. Leissner & J. Romahn, Arbat,
Haus Platonow. [*Medallion.*] | 1887.

1 vol. imperial 4to, pp. I-XII, 1-62, pll. I-V (col.), 2 text-figs. Moscow.

A report on a collection of birds made by the author in northern Caucasia. The
plates appear to be hand-colored photogravures of mounted specimens supplied with additional backgrounds and accessories. They are signed by Lorenz.

Lorenz, Theodor. (Kohts, Alexander Erich.)

1910—? Theodor Lorenz. | **Die Birkhühner Russlands** | deren Bas-
tarde, Ausartungen und Varietäten. | Fragmente einer künstler-
isch-wissenschaftlichen Monographie. | Mit 50 Textillustrationen
und 24 kolorierten Foliotafeln. | Nach dem Tode des Verfassers
bearbeitet und herausgegeben | von | Alexander Erich Kohts |
Assistent am Zoologischen Institut der Frauenhochschule in Mos-
kau. | [*Vignette.*] | Wien, 1910-1911. | Verlag der Moskauer Firma
Theodor Lorenz' Nachfolger.

1 vol. atlas folio. 2 pr. ll. (tit. and ded.), pp. 1-9+1, 2 ll. (advt.),
pll. I-XIX, Xb, XIIb, XIIIb, XIIIc, XIVB (col.), text-figs. 1-3.
Vienna.

A study of the Russian Black Cock, *Tetrao tetrix*, illustrated by large, hand-colored
photogravures; published posthumously. I am unable to ascertain the degree
of completeness of the present copy. The advertising sheets, noted in the

collation, announce that half of the 24 projected plates are presented with Lieferung I and that the remainder will appear in II and III, while a No. IV will be published if necessary to complete the work. The 24 plates are all present, but only Pt. I of the text, with 3 text-figures, is included while the prospectus calls for 4 parts of text and 50 figures. The set at hand is enclosed in an original wrapper of Lief. I, dated 1910.

Lovat, Lord.

1911. See [Grouse], **The Grouse in Health and Disease.**

Low, George.

1813. Fauna Orcadensis: | or, | the natural history | of the | quadrupeds, birds, reptiles, and fishes, | of | Orkney and Shetland. | By | the Rev. George Low, | Minister of Birsa and Haray. | From a Manuscript in the possession of Wm. Elford Leach, M.D. F.L.S. &c. | Edinburgh: | printed by George Ramsay and Company, | for Archibald Constable and Company, Edinburgh; and for Longman, | Hurst, Rees, Orme, and Brown, —and White, Cochrane, and Co. | London. | 1813.

1 vol. demy 4to, pp. I-XX, 1-230. Edinburgh.

Accounts of the habits and the local distribution and occurrence of the vertebrates of the Orkney and Shetland islands. The preface notes that the work was prepared by Low under the encouragement of Thomas Pennant but that it remained unpublished at the author's death in 1795. It states also that many of the notes were plagiarized by Rev. George Barry in his "History of Orkney," 1805, from the manuscript which was then in his possession. This manuscript, coming afterwards into Leach's hands, was edited and published as presented herewith.

Low, George C.

1924. The literature of | **the Charadriiformes** | from 1894-1924 | with a classification of the order, and | lists of the genera, species and subspecies | by | George C. Low, M.A., M.D., | M.R.C.P., F.Z.S., M.B.O.U. | H. F. & G. Witherby | 326 High Holborn, W.C.1 | 1924.

1 vol. post 8vo, pp. I-XI+1, 1-220. London.

A thorough bibliography of the group Charadriiformes, prefaced by a discussion of several systems of classification of the group. The literature is tabulated under authors which are arranged by years under generic names, and the genera are placed in their respective families according to a scheme of classification given at the head of the family in question. Each of the families occupies a chapter. A list of general references and one of general literature on the group are placed in chapters I and II. The work is planned to carry the literature from the point where it was left by R. B. Sharpe in 1896, Vol. XXIV of the Catalogue of Birds in the British Museum (q.v.).

Lucanus, Friedrich von.

1922. Die | Rätsel des Vogelzuges. | Ihre Lösung auf experimentel-
lem Wege durch | Aeronautik, Aviatik und Vogelberingung. | Von |
Friedrich von Lucanus, | Oberstleutnant a. D. [*etc., 2 lines.*]. |
Mit vier Textabbildungen und einer Tafel. | [*Blazon.*] | Langen-
salza | Hermann Beyer & Söhne | (Beyer & Mann) | Herzogl.
Sächs. Hofbuchhändler. | 1922.

1 vol. 8vo, pp. I-VIII, 1-226, 1 pl., 4 text-maps. Langensalza.

A detailed study of bird-migration and its problems. A second edition (q.v.)
appeared the following year.

Lucanus, Friedrich von.

1923. Die | Rätsel des Vogelzuges. | Ihre Lösung auf experimentel-
lem Wege | durch Luftfahrt und Vogelberingung. | Von | Fried-
rich von Lucanus, | Oberstleutnant a.D. [*etc., 2 lines.*]. | **Zweite,**
vermehrte und verbesserte **Auflage.** | [*Blazon.*] | Mit 4 Textabbil-
dungen und 1 Tafel. | Langensalza | Hermann Beyer & Sonne |
(Beyer & Mann) | Herzogl. Sächs. Hofbuchhändler | 1923.

1 vol. 8vo, pp. I-XI+1, 1-243, 1 pl., 4 text-maps. Langensalza.

A second edition of the author's work of the same title (q.v.) published the preceding year, with added notes.

Lucanus, Friedrich von.

1925. Das Leben der Vögel | von | Friedrich von Lucanus | [*De-
sign.*] | Mit 19 farbigen Tafeln | und 136 Textabbildungen | August
Scherl G. m. b. H. Berlin SW 68.

1 vol. 8vo, pp. 1-428+1, 3 pp. (advt.), pll. 1-19 (col.; 3 of eggs),
136 text-figs. Berlin.

A general study of the life of birds, their structure and development, their breeding, song, flight and distribution. The colored plates of birds are by Erich
Schröder; those of eggs are from photographs.

Lucas, A. H. S.; and LeSouëf, W. H. Dudley.

1911. The Birds of Australia | by | A. H. S. Lucas, M.A. (Oxon.
and Melb.), B.Sc. (Lond.) | Ex-President of the Linnean Society
of New South Wales [*etc., 3 lines.*], | and | W. H. Dudley Le Souëf,
C.M.Z.S., M.B.O.U., &c., | Director Zoological Gardens, Mel-
bourne; | Author of "Wild Life in Australia." | Joint Authors of
"The Animals of Australia." | [*Blazon.*] | Little Collins Street,
Melbourne; | Christchurch, Wellington and Dunedin, N.Z.; |
Addle Hill, Carter Lane, London: | Whitcombe and Tombs Lim-
ited. | 1911.

1 vol. post 8vo, pp. I-XI+1, 1-489, frontisp. and 5 pll. (col.; by Mrs.

Ellis Rowan), 186 text-figs. Melbourne, Christchurch, Wellington, Dunedin and London.

An accurate, popular account of the birds of Australia, with descriptions of many species and notes on nidification and general habits.

Lucas, Frederic A.

1909. See Knowlton, Frank Hall, **Birds of the World.**

Lucas, John.

1887. The pleasures | of a | pigeon-fancier. | By the | Rev. J. Lucas. | New York : | O. Judd Co., David W. Judd, Pres't, | 751 Broadway. | 1887.

1 vol. crown 8vo, 4 pr. ll., pp. 1-119+1, 2 ll. insert (facsim. letter), 8 pll. (3 col.), 7 text-figs. New York.

A series of essays on pigeon-fancying,—rambling in nature but with a general intent to offer instructive suggestions based on personal experiences. The colored plates, and some of the other illustrations, represent various breeds of pigeons.

Lydekker, Richard.

1893-96. See Newton, Alfred, **A Dictionary of Birds.**

Lydekker, Richard.

1916. Wild life of the world | a descriptive survey of the | geographical distribution| of animals | by R. Lydekker, F.R.S. | illustrated with | over six hundred engravings from original drawings | and | one hundred and twenty studies in colour | [*Vignette.*] | Vol. I [-III]. | London | Frederick Warne and Co. | and New York [*Add* 1916 (*Vols. II and III.*).].

3 vols. (12 parts) imperial 8vo. Vol. I, pp. I-XIV, 1-472, 40 pll. (col.; by W. Kuhnert), 246 text-figs. Vol. II, pp. I-XII, 1-440, 39 pll. (col.; by Kuhnert and Weczorzicky), 205 text-figs. Vol. III, pp. I-XI+1, 1-457, 41 pll. (col.), 144 text-figs. London and New York.

A popular work descriptive of animal life (vertebrate and invertebrate), arranged according to geographical distribution. Of the colored plates, 42 relate to birds; of the text-figures, 222 are ornithological. The present copy is in the original 12 parts.

Maclaud, Ch.

1906. Gouvernement Général l'Afrique Occidentale Française | **Notes | sur les | mammifères et les oiseaux | de l'Afrique Occidentale** | Casamance, Fouta-Dialon, Guinées Française & Portugaise | par | Le Docteur Ch. Maclaud | Administrateur des Col-

onies, | Chargé de Mission, | Correspondant du Muséum d'Histoire naturelle de Paris. | Préface de M. Edmond Perrier, | Directeur du Museum d'Histoire naturelle de Paris | Membre de l'Institut. | Paris-Vendome | imprimerie G. Vilette | 1906.
1 vol. cap 8vo, pp. I-XIV, 1 l. (subtit.), pp. 1-352, (orig. covers), pll. ("Figs.") 1-8 and 10-16, fig. 9 (in text), 1 map (fold.). Paris.

This little volume presents brief descriptions of 78 mammals and 256 birds of western Africa, with a few notes on habits, etc., and photographs of some mounted specimens. Pp. 79-306, pll. ("Figs.") 10-16, and (text-) fig. 9 are ornithological. The original wrapper bears the imprint of "Augustin Challamel, Editeur" and a vignette of the head of a chimpanzee.

McClymont, James R.

1920. Essays | on | early ornithology | and kindred subjects | by | James R. McClymont | M.A., author of [etc., 2 lines.] | with three plates | London | Bernard Quaritch Ltd. | 11 Grafton Street, New Bond Street | 1920.
1 vol. cap 4to, 4 pr. ll., pp. 1-35, 3 pll. London.

A series of small essays relating to early chronicles which contain references to birds and to some other subjects.

McConnell, Helen Mackenzie.

1916. See Chubb, Charles, **The Birds of British Guiana,** 1916-1921.

MacGillivray, William.

1836. Descriptions | of the | rapacious birds | of | Great Britain. | By | William MacGillivray, A.M. | Conservator of the Museum of the Royal College of Surgeons [etc., 6 lines.]. | Maclachlan & Stewart, Edinburgh: | Baldwin & Cradock, London; and | Hodges & Smith, Dublin. | MDCCCXXXVI.
1 vol. cap 8vo, pp. I-VII+1, 1-482, pll. I-II, 21 text-figs. Edinburgh.

A detailed discussion of the British birds of prey, with full descriptions of each species and of their respective genera and families, and with accounts of their habits.

Macgillivray, William. (Harley, James; Hepburn, Archibald.)

1837-40. A | history of | British birds, etc., Vols. I-III.
3 vols. post 8vo. Collation the same as given below for the first three volumes in the complete set, 1837-52 (q.v.), except that a half-title occupies a leaf in each volume preceding the title, and Vol. II contains pp. 1-24 (advt.) at the close.

MacGillivray, William. (Harley, James; Hepburn, Archibald.)

1837-1852. A | history | of | British birds, | indigenous and migratory: | including | their organization, habits and relations; | remarks on classification and nomenclature; | an account of the principal organs of birds, and | observations relative to practical | ornithology. | Illustrated by | numerous engravings. | By William MacGillivray, A.M., [etc., *5 lines*.; *mut. mut.*, *7 lines* (*Vol. II.*); *mut. mut.*, *6 lines* (*Vol. III.*); *mut. mut.*, *6 lines*. (*Vols. IV and V.*).] | Vol. I [-V]. | Rasores, scrapers, or gallinaceous birds; [Cantatores, songsters. (*Vol. II.*); Reptatores, creepers; Scansores, climbers; Cuculinæ (*Vol. III.*); Cursores, or runners. (*Vol. IV.*); Cribratores, or sifters. (*Vol. V.*)] | Gemitores, cooers, or pigeons; [*Line omitted* (*Vol. II.*).; Raptores, plunderers, or rapacious birds; (*Vol. III.*); Tentatores, or probers. (*Vol. IV.*); Urinatores, or divers (*Vol. V.*)] | Deglubitores, huskers, or conirostral birds; [*Line omitted* (*Vol. II.*); Excursores, snatchers; volitatores, gliders; (*Vol. III.*); Aucupatores, or stalkers. (*Vol. IV.*); Mersatores, or plungers. (*Vol. V.*)] | Vagatores, wanderers, or crows and allied genera [*Line omitted* (*Vols. II and V.*); Jaculatores, darters (*Vol. III.*); Latitores, or skulkers (*Vol. IV.*)] | London: | printed for Scott, Webster, and Geary [William S. Orr and Co., Amen Corner (*Vols. IV and V.*)], | 36, Charterhouse Square [Paternoster Row (*Vols. IV and V.*)]. | 1837. [1839.; 1840.; 1852; 1852.].

5 vols. post 8vo. Vol. I, tit., pp. I-XV+1, 1-631, pll. I-IX, text-figs. 1-95. Vol. II, tit., pp. I-XII, 1-503, pll. X-XIII, text-figs 96-185. Vol. III, tit., pp. I-XII, 1-768, pll. XIV-XXII, text-figs. 186-278. Vol. IV, 2 pr. ll. (tit. and ded.), pp. VII-XXVIII, 1-700, pll. XXIII-XXVI, text-figs. 1-59. Vol. V, 2 pr. ll. (tit. and ded.), pp. VII-XX, I-688, pll. XXVII-XXIX, text-figs. 60-100. London.

A complete natural history of the birds of Great Britain, written in great detail and containing a mass of information on the particulars of avian anatomy, as well as full accounts of the habits and characteristics of each of the species and a great deal of information of a general nature. The system of classification adopted by the author is unusual, but the general discussions and the anatomical descriptions are authoritative. Some of the remarks are attributed to notes presented by various correspondents and Vol. III contains two contributions definitely accredited to other authors. These are a "Catalogue of Land Birds of Leicestershire" by James Harley (pp. 646-664) and "Obesrvations on the Song of Birds" by Archibald Hepburn (pp. 741-744).

MacGillivray, William.

1840-42. A | manual | of | British ornithology: | being a short description of the | birds of Great Britain and Ireland, | including the essential characters of the species, | genera, families, and orders. | By | William MacGillivray, A.M., M.W.S., &c. | Conservator of the Museum [*etc.*, *4 lines*.); Professor of Natural History *etc., 3 lines.*]. | Part I. The land birds [Part II. The water birds]. | London: | printed for Scott, Webster, and Geary, | Charterhouse Square. | 1840 [1842].

2 vols. cap 8vo. Vol. I, pp. 1-248, 1-12 (advt.), text-figs. 1-31. Vol. II, pp. 1-272. London.

A compact handbook of British birds, containing descriptions of all the species, genera and higher groups in the classification adopted by the author, with synonymy and a brief general discussion of each. A second edition in one volume was published in 1846.

McGregor, Richard C. (Bourns, Frank S.; Worcester, Dean C.)

1909-10. A manual | of | Philippine birds | by | Richard C. McGregor | Part I [II] | Galliformes to Eurylæmiformes [Passeriformes] | [*Seal.*] | Manila | Bureau of Printing | 1909 | 77719 [83286] > Department of the Interior, | Bureau of Science, | Manila. | Publication No. 2, Part I [II]. | (Actual date of publication, April 15, 1909.) [(Actual date of publication, January 31, 1910.)].

1 vol. (2 parts), 8vo. Part I, pp. I-X, 1-412. Part. II, 1 l. (tit.; missing), pp. XI-XVI, 413-769. Manila.

A monograph of the birds of the Philippine Islands, containing full descriptions of the various plumages of each species, synoptic tables, synonymies (including native names) distribution of species by islands, notes on habits, and other related matter. Where available material was inadequate for complete original description, the author has quoted from other sources. Included in the text are manuscript notes by Bourns and Worcester, originally prepared for publication elsewhere but here published for the first time.

McGregor, Richard C.

1920. Index to the genera | of birds | by | Richard C. McGregor | [*Seal.*] | Manila | Bureau of Printing | 1920 | 161464 > Department of Agriculture and Natural Resources | Bureau of Science | Manila | Publication No. 14 | (Actual date of publication, March 31, 1920.).

1 vol. royal 8vo, pp. 1-185. Manila. March 31, 1920.

A useful index to the generic and subgeneric names of birds as found in the following works. Bonaparte, Charles L., Conspectus Generum Avium, 1850-57; Gray, George R., Hand-list of Genera and Species of Birds, 1869-71; British Museum, Catalogue of the Birds in —, 1874-98; Sharpe, R. B., A Hand-list of the Genera and Species of Birds, 1899-1909; Dubois, Alphonse, Synopsis Avium, 1902-04; and three lists by Chas. W. Richmond in the Proc. U. S. Nat. Mus., **24**, pp. 663-729, 1902; l.c., **35**, pp. 583-655, 1909; l.c., **53**, pp. 565-636, 1917. A total of 8,839 names are listed in this index.

McIlhenny, Edward A. (Shufeldt, Robert Wilson.)

1914. The wild turkey | and its hunting | by | Edward A. McIlhenny | [*Trade-mark.*] | Illustrated from Photographs | Garden City New York | Doubleday, Page & Company | 1914.

1 vol. post 8vo, pp. I-XI+1, 1-245, pll. I-VII, 13 pll. (unnum.), 1 text-fig. Garden City and New York.

A detailed account of the Wild Turkey and its habits, based on the author's personal observations. Chapters III and IV on "The Turkey Prehistoric" and "The Turkey Historic" are by Shufeldt.

McIlwraith, Thomas.

1894. The | birds of Ontario | being a concise account of every species of bird | known to have been found in Ontario | with a | description of their nests and eggs | and instructions for collecting birds and preparing | and preserving skins, also directions how | to form a collection of eggs | By Thomas McIlwraith | Member of the American Ornithologists' Union | **Second edition**—enlarged and revised to date | with illustrations | Toronto | William Briggs, Wesley Buildings | Montreal: C. W. Coates Halifax: S. F. Huestis | MDCCCXCIV.

1 vol. post 8vo, pp. I-IX+1, 11-426, frontisp. (portr.), 40 text-figs. Toronto.

An annotated list of species, with descriptions of plumages, nests and eggs of each and some account of habits, distribution and other characteristics. The book is a revised and enlarged edition of the work which appeared under the same title in 1886.

McLenegan, S. B.

1887. See Healy, Michael A., **Report of the Cruise of the Revenue Marine Steamer, Corwin.**

Macoun, James M.

1909. See Macoun, John; and Macoun, **Catalogue of Canadian Birds.**

Macoun, John.

1900-04. Geological Survey of Canada. | George M. Dawson. C.M.G., LL.D., F.R.S., Director [Robert Bell, M.D., Sc.D., (Cantab.), LL.D., F.R.S. (*Pts. II and III.*)] | **Catalogue | of | Canadian birds.** | Part I [-III]. | Water birds, gallinaceous birds, and [Birds of prey, woodpeckers, fly-catchers, (*Pt. II.*); Sparrows, swallows, vireos, warblers, (*Pt. III.*)] | pigeons [crows, jays and blackbirds (*Pt. II.*); wrens, titmice and thrushes (*Pt. III.*)]. | Including the following orders [order (*Pt. III.*)]: | Pygopodes,

Longipennes, Tubinares, Steganopodes, [Raptores, Coccyges, Pici, Macrochires, and part (*Pt. II.*); Passeres after the Icteridæ (*Pt. III.*)] | Anseres, Herodiones, Paludicolæ, Limi- [of the Passeres (*Pt. II.*); *Line omitted* (*Pt. III.*).] | colæ, Gallinæ, and Colum- bæ. [*Line omitted* (*Pts. II and III.*).] | By | John Macoun, M.A., F.R.S.C. | Naturalist to the Geological Survey of Canada | [*Bla- zon.*] | Ottawa: | printed by S. E. Dawson, printer to the Queen's [King's (*Pts. II and III.*)] most | Excellent Majesty. | 1900 [1903; 1904]. | No. 692 [*Line omitted* (*Pts. II and III.*).].

1 vol. (3 pts.) royal 8vo, pp. I-VIII+1, 1-218 (Pt. I.); I-IV, 1 l., pp. 219-413+1 (Pt. II.); I-IV, 415-733+1, I-XXIII (index) (Pt. III.). Ottawa.

An account of the species of Canadian birds, giving the various records of local occurrence and breeding and lists of the museum specimens at hand.

Macoun, John; and Macoun, James M.

1909. Canada | Department of Mines | Geological Survey Branch | Hon. W. Templeman, Minister: A. P. Low, Deputy Minister; R. W. Brock, Director. | **Catalogue** | of | **Canadian birds** | by | John Macoun | Naturalist to the Geological Survey, Canada. | and | James M. Macoun, | Assistant Naturalist to the Geological Survey, Canada. | [*Blazon.*] | Ottawa: | Government Printing Bureau | 1909. | [No. 973.].

1 vol. royal 8vo, pp. I-VIII, 1-761+1, I-XVIII (index). Ottawa.

An enlarged and revised edition of the senior author's work of the same title published in 1900-04 (q.v.).

McMullin, S. H.

1879-86. See Jones, Howard E.; and Jones, Mrs. N. E., **Illustrations of the Nests and Eggs of Birds of Ohio.**

Macpherson, A. Holte.

1904. See Harvie-Brown, John Alexander; and Macpherson, Hugh Alexander, **A Fauna of the North-west Highlands and Skye.**

Macpherson, Hugh Alexander.

1898. See Butler, Arthur G., **British Birds, 1896-98.**

Macpherson, Hugh Alexander.

1904. See Harvie-Brown, John Alexander; and Macpherson, **A Fauna of the North-west Highlands & Skye.**

Macpherson, H. B.

1910. The home-life | of a | Golden Eagle | photographed and described | by | H. B. Macpherson | with thirty-two mounted plates | **Second revised edition** | London | Witherby & Co. 326 High Holborn W. C. | MCMX.

1 vol. superroyal 8vo. (7½x10), pp. 1-45+1, 1 l., pll. 1-32 (mounted on 16 ll.). London.

A detailed account of periodical observations on the nesting habits of a pair of Golden Eagles in the Grampian Mountains of Scotland. The first edition was published in 1909.

Madarász, Gyula [= Madarász, Julius von].

1887. See Pelzeln, August von; and Madarász, **Monographie der Pipridae.**

Madarász, Gyula (= Madarász, Julius von).

1899-1903. A Magyar Nemezeti Muzeum Kiadvanya. | **Magyarorszag** | **madarai** | a hazai madárvilág megismerésének | verézfonala | 170 eredeti szövegrajzzal és 9 mümelléklettel | irts | Dr. Madarász Gyula | M.N. Muzeumi Igazgató-ör | [*Vignette.*] | Anhang: Die Vögel Ungarns | auszug in deutscher sprache. | Budapest, 1899-1903.

1 vol. (15 pts.) imperial 8vo, pp. I-XXXIII+1, 1 l., pp. 1-666, 2 insert-slips (errata), pll. I-IX (6 col.), 171 text-figs. Budapest.

A monograph of the birds of Hungary. The introductory matter and text to p. 450 is in Magyar, as is the vernacular index; the remainder of the text to p. 630 is occupied by a resumé, in German, of the preceding account. An index to the scientific names is appended. The work was issued in 15 parts (I-XV) which, in the present copy, are in the original wrappers. The matter is arranged as follows. I, pp. 1-44, 1899; II, pp. 45-88, pll. I and II, 1899; III, pp. 89-120, pl. III, 1900; IV, pp. 121-166, pl. IV, 1900; V, pp. 167-212, 1900; VI, pp. 213-266+1 insert-slip, pl. V, 1901; VII, pp. 267-308, 1901; VIII-IX (double no.), pp. 309-378+1 insert-slip, pl. VI, 1902; X, pp. 379-412, pll. VI-VIII, 1902; XI, pp. 413-450, 1903; XII, pp. 451-498, 1903; XIII, pp. 499-546, 1903; XIV, pp. 547-630, 1903; XV, pp. I-XXXIII+1+1 l., pp. 631-666, 1903.

Madarász, Gyula [= Madarász, Julius von].

1901. See Zichy, Jenö, **Dritte Asiatische Forschungsreise.**

Malden, W. J.

1924. See Kirkman, Frederick B.; and Hutchinson, **British Sporting Birds.**

Malherbe, Alfred.

1859-62. **Monographie** | des | **Picidées** | ou histoire naturelle | des Picidés, Picumninés, Yuncinés ou Torcols | comprenant | dans la première partie | L'origine mythologique, les mœurs, les migrations, l'anatomie, la physiologie, la répartition géographique, | les divers systèmes de classification de ces oiseaux grimpeurs zygodactyles, ainsi qu'un | dictionnaire alphcbétique des auteurs et des ouvrages cités par abréviation; | dans la deuxième partie, | La synonymie, la description en latin et en français, l'histoire de chaque espèce, ainsi qu'un | dictionnaire alphabétique et synonymique latin de toutes les espèces; | par | Alf. Malherbe | Conseiller a la Cour Impériale de Metz [*etc.*, *6 lines.*] | Texte - Vol. I [Texte - Vol. XI; Planches - Vol. III; Planches - Vol. IV] | Metz - 1861 [1862; 1861; 1862] | Typographie de Jules Verronais, Imprimeur de la Société | d'Histoire naturelle de la Moselle.

4 vols. superroyal folio. Vol. I, tit., pp. I-LXX, (Pt. I.), 1-214 (Pt. II.), text-figs. a-g (eggs), 18 text-figs. (various numbering). Vol. II, tit., pp. 1-315+1 (Pt. II.), 5 ll. (bibliogr.). Vol. III, tit., pp. 1-8, pll. I-LXI+XLIII bix (col.; by Delahaye, Mesnel and P. Oudart). Vol. IV, tit., pp. 1-6, pll. LXII-CXXI+LXXXVII bix (altered from ?). (col.) Metz.

A thorough monographic revision of the woodpeckers, illustrated with colored plates. The work was issued in 24 parts from 1859 to 1862 in an edition of 100 copies, printed at the author's expense. Pt. 1 is noticed in the Ibis for Oct. 1859, Pts. 2 and 3 (including *Hemilophus validus* and *Megapicus sclateri*) in the number for April 1860, and the 6th part in the number for Oct. 1860, but the extent of each part I am unable to ascertain. The plates, occypying Vols. III and IV, seem to have been issued along with the text in Vols. I and II. The work was reviewed and revised by Sundevall in 1866 in his "Conspectus Avium Picinarum" (q.v.).

Malm, August Wilhelm.

1877. **Göteborgs och Bohusläns** | **fauna** | ryggradsdjuren; | af | A. W. Malm. | Med nio taflor, af hvilka fyra I färgtryck; samt fem | i texten tryckta träsnitt. | Utgifven af författaren, med understöd af | Staten. | Göteborg. | Göteborgs Handelstidnings Aktiebolags Tryckeri. | 1877.

i vol. (2 pts.) royal 8vo, 5 pr. ll., pp. 1-370, duplicate tit., subtit. (Pt. II.), pp. 371-674, pll. I-IX (4 col.; 2 fold.; none of birds), 5 text-figs. Göteborg.

A manual of the vertebrate fauna of the provinces Göteborgs and Bohusläns, Sweden. The ornithological matter is contained principally on pp. 24-49 (essays on vernacular names and migrations of birds), 60-93 (tables for determination), 161-364 (general discussion) and 645-647 (addenda). The author's dislike of tautonymic names has led to the renaming of 28 species (of birds and many other animals), all of which are called *"Linnéi."* The book was issued in two parts, as indicated in the collation above, and is designated as a memorial of the one hundredth anniversary of the death of Linné on Jan. 10, 1778.

Marchesa, Cruise of the—to Kamschatka and New Guinea.

1886. See Guillemard, Francis Henry Hill.

Marriner, George R.

1909. The kea: | a New Zealand problem | including | a full description of this very interesting bird, its habitat | and ways, together with a discussion of the | theories advanced to explain its | sheep-killing propensities. | By | George R. Marriner, F.R.M.S. | Member of the Australian Ornithological Union | Curator, Public Museum, Wanganui, New Zealand. | Late Assistant [*etc.*] | [*Blazon.*] | Williams and Norgate, | 14, Henrietta Street, Covent Garden, London, W.C. | 1909.

1 vol. post 8vo, pp. 1-151, frontisp. (on p. 8), 44 text-figs., 1 map. London.

A general account of the subject, based on the personal experiences of the author and of numerous other observers.

Marshall, Charles Henry Tillson; and Marshall, George Frederick Leycester.

1870-71. A monograph | of | **the Capitonidæ,** | or | scansorial barbets. | By | C. H. T. Marshall, F.Z.S., | Bengal Staff Corps. | and | G. F. L. Marshall, F.Z.S., | Royal Bengal Engineers. | London: | published by the authors. | 1871. > [*Idem, 11 lines.*] | The plates drawn and lithographed by J. G. Keulemans. | London: | published by the authors, | 11 Hanover Square. | 1870-71.

1 vol. royal 4to, 6 pr. ll. (2 titles, ded., list of subscrs., conts., list of pll.), pp. I-XLI+1 (pref., introd., gen. acct.), 91 ll. (text), 4 ll. (index), 73 pll. (numbered I-LXXIII in text; col.; by Keulemans). London.

Issued in 9 parts, of which Pts. I-V appeared in 1870 and VI-IX in 1871. According to the data in the Zoological Record, the plates (as numbered in the text) appeared in the following manner, presumably accompanied by the corresponding text. Pt. **I,** pll. XVI, XXII, XXXI, LXXII, III, LVII, LXI, LXII; Pt. **II,** pll. IV, II, XLVI, LVI, LXVI, XXXVII, XXXVI, XXX; Pt. **III,** pll. XL, XXXIX, XXVI, XXV, XXXII, XLIV, LXXIII, VIII; Pt. **IV,** pll. XXXV, XXIX, XXVII, XLI, LIX, LX, LVIII, LII; Pt. **V,** pll. XVIII, XLII, LXX, LIII, LXXI, IX, X, VI; Pt. **VI,** pll. V, XIV, XV, XXXVIII, LV, XLV, L, LXVIII; Pt. **VII,** pll. XLIII, XX, XIX, XXI, XXIV, I, LIV, XLVII; Pt. **VIII,** pll. XXVIII, XVII, XXIII, XI, XII, LXIX, LXIII, LXIV; Pt. **IX,** pll. VII, XIII, LI, XLVIII, XLIX, LXVII, LXV, XXXIV, XXXIII. The introductory matter is said to have appeared in Pt. V (Cf. Zool. Rec. **7**, p. 42.). In the present copy, two title-pages are given, differing slightly as cited above. Plates I, XIX, XLIII and XLV are excellent watercolor copies, —not the printed plates as issued.

Marshall, Charles Henry Tillson.

1879-81. See Hume, Allan O.; and Marshall, **The Game Birds of India, Burmah and Ceylon.**

Marshall, George Frederick Leycester.

1870-71. See Marshall, Charles H. T.; and Marshall, **A Monograph of the Capitonidae.**

Martens, Eduard Karl von.

1867-76. Die | preussische expedition | nach | Ost-Asien. | Nach amtlichen Quellen. | **Zoologischer Theil. |** Erster [Zweiter] Band. Allgemeines und Wirbelthiere [Die Landschnecken]. | Mit XV Tafeln [Mit XXII Illustrationen]. | Bearbeitet von Prof. [*"Prof."* omitted (*Vol. II.*).] Dr. Eduard v. Martens. | [*Blazon.*] | Berlin MDCCCLXXVI [Berlin MDCCCLXVII]. | Verlag der Königlichen Geheimen Ober-Hofbuchdruckerei | (R. v. Decker).

2 vols. imperial 8vo. Vol. I, pp. I-XII, 1-412, pll. 1-15 (12 col.; 2 of birds, 1 col.). Vol. II, pp. I-XII, 1-447, pll. 1-22 (12 col.; none of birds). Berlin.

The zoology of the Prussian expedition to eastern Asia. More or less detailed notes are given (in Vol. I) on the ornithology (and general zoology) of Madeira, Rio Janeiro, Japan, China, Philippine Islands, Siam, Singapore and the Indian Archipelago. Vol. II relates entirely to Mollusca. The botany and the general account appear to have been issued separately.

Martin, E. T.

1907. See Mershon, W. B., **The Passenger Pigeon.**

Martin, R.; and Rollinat, R.

1914. Description et moeurs | des mammifères, oiseaux | reptiles, batraciens et poissons | de la | France centrale | par | R. Martin et R. Rollinat | [*Fig.*] | Paul Lechevalier | 12, Rue de Tournon | Paris (VIe) | 1914.

1 vol. royal 8vo, pp. I-VI, 1-464, 1 l. (conts. and advt.). Paris.

A handbook of the vertebrates of central France, giving short descriptions of classes, orders, families, genera and species, and notes on distribution and local occurrence. No trinomials are used. The birds (272 species) occupy pp. 73-263 and 441-451.

Martin, William Charles Linnaeus.

1852. A | general history | of | humming-birds, | or the | Trochili- dæ: | with especial reference to the | collection of J. Gould, F.R.S. &c. | now exhibiting in the | gardens of the Zoological Society of London. | By | W. C. L. Martin, | late one of the scientific officers of the Zoological | Society of London. | London: | H. G. Bohn, York Street, Covent Garden. | 1852.

1 vol. cap 8vo, pp. I-VII+1, 1 l. (list of pll.), pp. 1-232, frontisp. (col.), pll. 1-14+"3(*)" (col.). London.

A little work supplementing Jardine's "Natural History of Humming-birds," 1833 (q.v.) in the Naturalist's Library. According to Coues, the present work was issued as a later volume of that series. The volume is composed of a gen- eral discussion of hummingbirds and their habits (occupying rather more than half of the text) and descriptions of a considerable number of species not (with one exception) treated by Jardine. The plates are engravings, with the figures of the birds colored by hand but with the backgrounds uncolored. A curious error occurs on plates 4 and 8 on which the remiges and rectrices of the birds are shown imbricated in reverse order, the outer ones overlapping the inner!

Martorelli, Giacinto.

1884. Osservazioni | sui | mammiferi ed uccelli | fatte in Sar- degna | dal | Dott. Giacinto Martorelli | con tavole litografiche colorate dell' autore | Pistoia | Tip Cino dei Fratelli Bracali | 1884.

1 vol. crown folio, pp. 1-54, 1 l. (errata), pll. I-IV (3 col.; by the author; 2 of birds, 1 of a bird nest). Pistoia. 1884 (post Febr. 29).

Observations on the mammals and birds of Sardinia, noted by the author in 1882 and 1883. Most of the work (pp. 11-54 and pll. II-IV) is ornithological.

Martorelli, Giacinto.

1895. Monografia illustrata | degli | uccelli di rapina | in Italia | del | Dott. Giacinto Martorelli | Direttore della Raccolta Ornito- logica Turati nel Museo Civico di Milano. | Con 45 fotoiniscioni e 4 tavole sincromiche | su disegni e tavole colorite originali dell' autore | [Monogram.] | Ulrico Hoepli | Editore-librajo della Real Casa | Milano | 1895.

1 vol. royal 4to, 4 pr. ll., pp. 1-215, pll. I-IV (col.), 46 text-figs. Milan. A monograph of the Italian birds of prey.

Massachusetts. (Peabody, William B. O.)

1839. Reports | on the | fishes, reptiles and birds | of | Massachu- setts. | Published agreeably to an order of | the legislature, | by the commissioners on the zoological and botanical | survey of the state. | Boston: | Dutton and Wentworth, State Printers. | 1839.

> A | report | on the | ornithology of Massachusetts. | By | William B. O. Peabody.

1 vol. 8vo, pp. I-XII, 2 ll. (conts. and subtit.), 1-426, pll. I-IV. Boston.

A set of three reports on the zoology of Massachusetts. The ornithological portion, written by Peabody, occupies pp. 255-404 (no pll.). The introduction is dated August 13, 1839 and is signed by G. B. E., =George B. Emerson, Chairman of the Commissioners who prepared the complete volume. The book is somewhat rare. The present copy contains the illuminated bookplate of John Lewis Childs.

Matheson, Darley.

1914. British Game Birds | By | Darley Matheson | Illustrated | London: | Francis Griffiths | 34 Maiden Lane, Strand, W.C. | 1914.

1 vol. 8vo, pp. 1-173, frontisp. (col.), 31 pll. (9 col.). London.

A popular account of some of the more important game birds of Great Britain, including introduced species, with special attention to their rearing and domestication.

Mathew, Murray Alexander.

1892. See D'Urban, W. S. M.; and Mathew, M. A., **The Birds of Devon.**

Mathew, Murray Alexander.

1894. The | birds of Pembrokeshire | and its islands. | By | The Rev. Murray A. Mathew, M.A., F.L.S., | Member [*etc., 3 lines.*]. | [*Vignette.*] | [*Quot.*] | London: | R. H. Porter, | 18, Princes Street, Cavendish Square. | 1894. | [All Rights Reserved.].

1 vol. medium 4to, pp. I-LIII, 1-131, frontisp. (= 1st pl., enlarged), 3 pll., 2 maps (fold.; col.), 1 text-fig. (key to frontisp.). London.

An account of the birds of Pembrokeshire, Wales, mostly with reference to local occurrences of the species. An edition in 8vo was issued the same year. The present copy contains the bookplate of W. H. Mullens.

Mathew, Murray Alexander.

1895. See D'Urban, W. S. M.; and Mathew, M. A., **The Birds of Devon, Second edition.**

Mathew, Murray Alexander.

1897. See Butler, Arthur G., **British Birds,** 1896-98.

Mathews, Gregory M. (Ashley, Edwin.)

1910 - date. The | birds | of | Australia | by | Gregory M. Mathews | F.R.S.E. | Member [*etc., 3 lines.*] | with hand-coloured plates | Volume I [-XI; *XII?, tit.-. not yet publ.*]. | Witherby &

Co. [H. F. & G. Witherby (*Vols. III, et seq.*)] | 326 High Holborn London | 1910-1911 [*mut. mut.*].

> Supplement No. 1 [-3]. | The | birds | of | Australia | Check list | of the | birds of Australia | part 1 [-3]. | Orders Casuariformes to Menuriformes [Order Passeriformes (Part) (*Pt. 2.*); Order Passeriformes (Concluding Part) (*Pt. 3.*)]. | Showing under each genus and species every synonym at present known to the Author, with | references to coloured plates in this work and in Gould's folio Birds of Australia. | By | Gregory M. Mathews | F.R.S.E., Etc. | Witherby & Co. [H. F. & G. Witherby (*Pts. 2 and 3.*)] | 326 High Holborn London | 1920 [1923; 1924]

> The | birds | of | Australia | bibliography | of the | birds of Australia | books used in the preparation of this work with a few | biographical details of authors and collectors. | By | Gregory M. Mathews | F.R.S.E., Etc. | H. F. & G. Witherby | 326 High Holborn London | 1925 [*Suppls. 4 and 5.*].

12 vols. (Vol. XII not yet complete) and 5 suppls., imperial 4to (10x14). Vol. I, pp. I-XIV, 1-301, 183*-184* (183-184 cancelled and missing), 67 pll. (col.; num. 1-67 in text), 6 text-figs. Vol. II, pp. I-XIV, 1-527, 57 pll. (col.; 68-124 in text), 36 text-figs. Vol. III, pp. I-XVII+1, 1-512, 75 pll. (col.; 125-199 in text), 23 text-figs. Vol. IV, pp. I-XII, 1-334, 34 pll. (col.; 200-233 in text), 4 text-figs. Vol. V, pp. I-XI+1, 1-440, 41 pll. (col.; 234-274 in text), 6 text-figs. Vol. VI, pp. I-XIX+1, 1-516, 50 pll. (col.; 275-324 in text), 14 text-figs. Vol. VII, pp. I-XII, 1-499, 46 pll. (col.; 325-370 in text). Vol. VIII, pp. I-X, 1-316, 29 pll. (col.; 371-399 in text) (Suppl. 1 bound with this vol.). Vol. IX, pp. I-XIV 1-518, 54 pll. (col.; 400-453 in text). Vol. X, pp. I-XI+1, 1-451, 37 pll. (col.; 454-490 in text) (Suppl. 2 bound with this vol.). Vol. XI, pp. I-XIII+1, 1-593, 51 pll. (col.; num. 491-541 in text). Vol. XII (incomplete; Pts. 1-5), pp. 1-224, 29 pll. (col.; num. 542-570 in text). Check List (Suppls. 1-3), pp. I-IV, 1-116, I-XVI, 117-156, 2 ll. (half-tit. and tit. of Pt. 3), pp. VII-VIII, 157-244. Bibliography (Suppls. 4 and 5), pp. I-VIII, 1-96, frontisp. (portrs.) (Pt. 1), pp. 97-149 (Pt. 2.). London.

A monograph of Australian birds, with detailed accounts of every species and group and a mass of information of a bibliographic nature scattered through the work. The book is being issued in parts and is not yet complete although the last volume is now in progress. The dates and details of publication of Vols. I-VII, Pt. 4 are given in Vol. VII, pp. 458-459; the remainder up to Vol. XI, Pt. 7 may be ascertained, by species, in the Check List and it is assumed that a complete collation will be given with the concluding number when it appears. The Check List is separately paged and titled but forms an integral part of the general work. It contains alterations and additions to the general text as made necessary by researches since the publication of the parts of the work concerned (except for portions of Pt. 3 which antedate the yet unpublished conclusion of Vol. XII). It also gives a resumé of the forms treated in the work, with references to original descriptions and to plates in Gould and the present work, and with notes on the distribution of the species. The Bibliography is explained by its title.

The colored plates are by J. G. Keulemans, H. Grönvold, H. Goodchild, G. E. Lodge and Roland Green and are very attractive. On pp. XV-XVIII of Vol. VI, (Dec. 11, 1917), Edwin Ashley presents a description of a new species.

Mathews, Gregory M.; and Iredale, Tom.

1921. **A manual of the | birds of Australia |** by | Gregory M. Mathews, | F.R.S.E., M.R.A.O.U., | and | Tom Iredale, | Members of the British Ornithologists' Union [*etc.*, *2 lines.*]. | Illustrated with coloured and monochrome plates | by | Lilian Medland. | Volume I. [*all published*] | Orders Casuarii to Columbæ | [*Vignette.*] | H. F. & G. Witherby | 326 High Holborn, London | 1921.

1 vol. 8vo (7¼x9¾), pp. I-XXIV, 1-279, pll. 1-10 (col.), I-XXXVI (on 18 ll.). London. March 9, 1921.

Contains descriptions, synonymies and distributional notes on the species of Australian birds, with the subspecific divisions indicated by brief notes. The genera and higher groups are described and generic characters are illustrated in black-and white plates of exceptional merit. The colored plates are mostly illustrative of nestling plumages. A number of extra-Australian birds are described or renamed in the text. Volume I, alone, has appeared to date.

Matthews, F. Schuyler.

1904. **Field book of | wild birds and | their music |** a description of the character | and music of birds, intended | to assist in the identifica- | tion of species common in the | eastern United States | By F. Schuyler Matthews | author of [*etc.*, *5 lines.*]. | With numerous reproductions of water | color and pen-and-ink studies of birds, | and complete musical notations of bird | songs by the author | [*Blazon.*] | G. P. Putnam's Sons | New York and London | The Knickerbocker Press.

1 vol. cap 8vo (4x6¾), 1 l. (advt.), pp. I-XXXV+1, 1-262, 3 ll. (advt.), frontisp. (col.), 52 pll. (37 col.). New York and London.

A careful study of the songs of the common birds of the eastern United States. The songs, or parts of songs, of each species are transcribed in musical notation, while, in addition, various onomatopes are often suggested. Short accounts of the birds and their habits are added.

Maximilian, Prinz zu Wied.

1825-33. Beiträge | zur | Naturgeschichte | von | Brasilien, | von | Maximilian, Prinzen | zu Wied. | I [-IV]. Band. [| Erste (Zweite) Abtheilung. (*Vols. III and IV.*)] | Mit 3 Kupfertafeln. [Mit 5 Kupfertafeln. (*Vol. II.*); Line omitted (*Vol. III, Pt. I and Vol. IV, Pt. I.*); Mit einer Tafel Abbildungen. (*Vol. III, Pt. II.*); Mit 2 Tafeln Abbildungen. (*Vol. IV, Pt. II.*)] | Weimar, | im Verlage des Gr. H. S. priv. Landes-Industrie-Comptoirs [Im Verlage des Landes-Industrie-Comptoirs (*Vol. IV.*)]. | 1825 [1826; 1830; 1831; 1832; 1833].

4 vols. (6 pts.) in 5, demy 8vo. Vol. I, pp. I-XXII, 1-614, pll. I-III (2 fold.). Vol. II, tit., pp. 1-621, 1 l. (errata), pll. I-V (fold.). Vol. III, Pt. I, 2 pr. ll. (tit. and subtit.), pp. 1-636. Vol. III, Pt. II, tit., pp. III-XII (conts. of Pts. I and II), pp. 637-1277+1, 1 l. (errata), 1 pl. Vol. IV, Pt. I, tit., pp. III-VIII (conts.), 1-442, 1 l. (advt.). Vol. IV, Pt. II, 2 pr. ll. (tit. and subtit.), pp. 443-946, pll. I and II. Weimar.

The entire work, collated above, consists of a descriptive account of the Amphibia, Mammalia and Aves observed by the author on his journey in eastern Brazil in 1815-17. Vols. III and IV (of two parts each) deal with the birds; the three included plates are anatomical. The new species discovered on the journey were described previously in other works by the author.

Maxwell, Aymer.

1911. Partridges and | partridge manors | by | Captain Aymer Maxwell | joint author of 'Grouse and Grouse Moors' | with sixteen illustrations in colour | by | George Rankin | [*Monogram.*] | London | Adam and Charles Black | 1911.

1 vol. post 8vo, pp. I-XII, 1-327, 2 ll. (advt.). 16 pll. (col.), 8 text-figs. London.

A book about partridge rearing and shooting.

Maynard, Charles Johnson.

1870. The | naturalist's guide | in collecting and preserving | objects of natural history, | with | a complete catalogue of the birds | of eastern Massachusetts. | By C. J. Maynard. | With illustrations by E. L. Weeks. | Boston: | Fields, Osgood, & Co. | 1870.

1 vol. crown 8vo, pp. I-IX+1, 1-170, frontisp., pll. I-X (on numbered pp.). Boston.

The first portion of the work is a taxidermist's manual. The second portion, pp. 81-170, contains an annotated list of the birds of eastern Massachusetts, with notes on the distribution and habits of the various species.

Maynard, Charles Johnson.

1881?. **The birds | of | eastern North America; |** with | original descriptions | of all the species which occur | east of the Mississippi River, | between the | Arctic Circle and the Gulf of Mexico, | With Full Notes Upon Their Habits, Etc., | by | C. J. Maynard; | containing | thirty-two plates drawn on stone by the author. | **Revised edition. |** Newtonville, Mass: | C. J. Maynard & Co. | 1881. 1 vol. medium 4to, pp. I-IV, 1-532, pll. I-XXXII. Newtonville.

The present work has a very involved history. In October 1872, the author commenced the publication of a book entitled "The Birds of Florida," issuing Pt. II in 1873 and Pt. III in January 1874. In May 1878, Pt. IV appeared with the title emended to "The Birds of Florida with the Water and Game Birds of Eastern North America." The work was thus continued until March 1879 when Pt. IX was published, carrying the work to p. 232 and pl. XVI, at which point this title and work were abandoned. In 1879 a new edition was begun under the present title which, however, was announced to contain only 30 plates. The Zool. Record states that Pts. I-VIII appeared in 1879 and IX-XIII in 1880, a statement supported by the review in the Auk for July 1880. The Catalogue of the Library of the British Museum (Natural History), confuses the original and the reissued works and catalogues Pts. I-III as having appeared in 1872-74, IV in 1878, IX-XV in 1879 and XVI in 1881, giving pagination and plate numbers for each part but remarking that pll. XXIX and XXX were not issued. The work at hand may constitute a third publication since it bears the inscription "Thirty-two plates . . . Revised edition . . . 1881" and contains the full number of plates. In view of the uncertainty, I have quoted it under the latter date, only. In the author's preface, dated 1879, (probably identical with that of the first reissue whether or not the present work is new), it is stated that the letterpress has been slightly altered from its form as published in "The Birds of Florida" and that the plates are entirely redrawn, but that the pagination remains unchanged from the original. Another revised edition (q.v.) was published in 1889-95.

Maynard, Charles Johnson.

1887. **Illustrations and descriptions | of the | birds of the Bahamas. |** By | Charles J. Maynard. | Boston: | C. J. Maynard and Company. | 1887. 1 vol. (pt.) atlas folio, tit., 1 l. (expl. of pll.), pp. 1-2, pll. I and II (1 col.; II not numbered on pl.). Boston.

Apparently the only part issued of this work. A printed label on the cover is as follows. "Part I. | Illustrations and Descriptions | Birds of Bahama. | Spindalis zena, | Bahama Fruit Finch." The colored plate contains 7 figs. of *Spindalis zena;* the second plate (uncol.) contains 52 figs., mostly anatomical, of various birds. The text (pp. 1 and 2) relates entirely to *Spindalis zena.*

Maynard, Charles Johnson.

1889. **The birds | of | eastern North America; |** with | original descriptions | of all the species which occur | east of the Mississippi

River, | between the | Arctic Circle and the Gulf of Mexico, | With
Full Notes Upon Their Habits, Etc., | by | C. J. Maynard; |
containing | thirty-two plates drawn on stone by the author. |
Revised edition. | Newtonville, Mass.: | C. J. Maynard. | 1889.
1 vol. (pt.) imperial 4to, 2 pr. ll., pp. 1-92, pll. I-VI (col.), text-figs.
1-22 (9 col.). Newtonville.

A revised, enlarged edition of the author's earlier work of the same title (Cf. ed.
1881), with new hand-colored plates, and numerous text-figures, many of which
are also colored. The present copy is incomplete, but the John Crerar Library,
Chicago, possesses a complete copy, dated 1896 on the title-page (see below),
and containing pp. 1-721 with numerous colored plates and colored figures in
the text. The preface to this complete copy advises that the first and second
parts (evidently those collated above), were issued in May 1889 and two or
three more the following year; that publication thereafter was not resumed
until October 1894, while the final portion of the work appeared on December
24, 1895. Neither edition (1889 or 1896) is cited in the Zool. Record nor in
the Auk.

Maynard, Charles Johnson.

1890. Eggs | of | North American Birds | by | Chas. J. Maynard. |
Illustrated | with ten hand-colored plates. | Boston: | De Wolfe,
Fiske & Co. | 1890.
1 vol. 8vo, pp. I-IV, 1-159, pll. I-X (col.). Boston.

An annotated list of North American birds, with short descriptions and measurements of their eggs, notes on distribution and occasional other remarks.

Meeker, D. W.

1907. See Wilcox, Alvin H., A **Pioneer History of Becker County
Minnesota.**

Meisner, Friedrich.

1804. Systematisches | Verzeichniss | der | Vögel | welche die
Schweiz entweder bewohnen, | oder theils zu bestimmten, theils
zu | unbestimmten Zeiten besuchen, | und sich | auf der Gallerie
der Bürger-Bibliothek in Bern | ausgestopft befinden. | Im Nah-
men der Gesellschaft vaterländischer Naturfreunde | in Bern aus-
gearbeitet | von | Friedrich Meisner, | Vorsteher einer Lehranstalt
und Mitglied der genannten | Gesellschaft. | Bern, in der Haller-
schen Buchhandlung. | 1804.
1 vol. 12mo, pp. I-VI, 1-70, 1 l. (errata). Bern. 1804 (post August).

A catalogue of 260 species of birds accredited to Switzerland, with synonymy
and notes on distribution. In 1815, Meisner and Schinz enlarged this catalogue
into a more complete manual which was published under the title, "Die Vögel
der Schweiz" (q.v.). The preface of the present volume is dated August, 1804.

Meisner, Friedrich; and Schinz, Heinrich Rudolf.

1815. Die | Vögel der Schweiz, | systematisch geordnet und beschrieben mit Bemer- | kungen über ihre Lebensart und Aufenthalt, | von | Friedrich Meisner, | Professor der Naturgeschichte in Bern, mehrerer gelehrter | Gesellschaften Mitglied | und | Heinrich Rudolf Schinz, | Med. Dr. Sekretair der Naturforschenden Gesellschaft in Zürich, mehrerer gelehrten Gesellschaften Mit- glied | und Lehrer am medicinisch-chirurgischen Kan- | tonalin- stitut in Zürich. | Zürich, | bey Oredd, Füssli und Comp. | 1815. 1 vol. post 8vo, tit., pp. I-XXVIII, 1-327+1, (frontisp. missing). Zürich.

A descriptive catalogue of Swiss birds, enlarged from the senior author's earlier 'Systematisches Verzeichniss,' 1804 (q.v.). The missing frontispiece is said by the authors, p. 264, to represent *Sterna leucoptera*.

Mellersh, William Lock.

1902. A Treatise | on the | Birds of Gloucestershire | with | a reference list of all the species known | to have appeared in the county | by | W. L. Mellersh, M.A. | Six Illustrations by E. Neale, M.B.O.U., | combining typical birds and views of the county. | Gloucester: | John Bellows, Eastgate. | London: | R. H. Porter, 7 Princes Street, Cavendish Square, W. | 1902. 1 vol. royal 8vo, pp. I-VIII, 1-111+1, frontisp. (map; fold.), 6 pll. London.

A general survey of bird-life in Gloucestershire, England, with a check list of the species.

Ménégaux, Auguste; and Hellmayr, Charles Edward.

1906. Etude | des | especes critiques et des types du groupe | Passeraux Tracheophones | de l'Amerique tropicale | appartenant aux collections du museum | par | MM. A. Menegaux & C.-E. Hellmayr | Autun | Imprimerie et Librairie Dejussieu | 1906. 1 vol. 8vo, pp. 1-86. Autun.

A systematic study of certain forms of the family Dendrocolaptidae. A repaged reprint from the Mem. Soc. d'Hist. Nat. d'Autun, XIX, pp. 43-126, 1906. In effect, this is the second part of an extended paper, the first part of which appeared in the Bull. du Muséum d'histoire naturelle, Vol. XI, No. 6, p. 372, 1905; the third was published in the Bull. de la Société Philomathique de Paris, Ser. 9, Vol. VIII, pp. 24-58, 1906.

Ménégaux, Auguste.

1912. Catalogue | des oiseaux | de la | collection Marmottan | du | Muséum d'Histoire Naturelle de Paris | par | A. Menegaux |

assistant de la chaire de mammalogie et ornithologie | Extrait de
Bulletin de la Société Philomatique de Paris | 1911 et 1912 |
Tours | Imprimerie Deslis Freres et Cie | 6, Rue Gambetta, 6 |
1912.

1 vol. royal 8vo, 3 pr. ll., pp. 1-216. Tours.

A catalogue of the specimens of European birds in the collection of Dr. H. Mar-
mottan, exhibited in the Museum of Natural History of Paris. The work is a
re-paged reprint of three installments published in the Bulletin de la Société
Philomatique (10) **3**, pp. 61-99, and 107-197, 1911; and (10) **4**, pp. 9-78, 1912.

Ménégaux, Auguste.

1913. See Lesson, Réne-Primevère, **Articles d'Ornithologie de R.-P.
Lesson.**

Ménégaux, Auguste.

1918. L'Ami des Oiseaux | Petit manuel de protection | par | A.
Menegaux | Assistant de le chaire de Mammalogie et Ornithologie
[*etc., 5 lines.*] | L'Oiseau est un des facteurs | de la prospérité d'un
pays. | [*Design.*] | Paris Ve | Edition de la Revue Française
d'Ornithologie | 55, Rue de Buffon.

1 vol. (pamphlet, size of post 8vo), cover-tit., pp. 1-35, text-figs. 1-20.
Paris.

A treatise on bird-protection, with designs for nest-boxes, feeding sheds, etc.
Lists of useful and harmful birds of France are appended.

Ménégaux, Auguste; and Rapine, J.

1921(?). Les | noms des oiseaux | trouvés en France | (noms
latins, français, anglais, italiens et allemands) | par | A. Menegaux |
Assistant de la Chaire de Mammalogie et Ornithologie au Mu-
séum | President de la Société ornithologique de France | et | J.
Rapine | Sécretaire générale de la Société ornithologique de France |
Paris (Ve) | Edition de la Revue Française d'Ornithologie | 55
rue de Buffon.

1 vol. 8vo, pp. 1-68. Paris.

A list of the species and subspecies of French birds giving Latin name, authority
and date of publication, one or more French vernacular names, and vernacular
names in English, Italian and German. A prefatory chapter deals with the
principles of nomenclature, being dated November 1, 1921.

Ménégaux, Auguste. (Babault, Guy.)

1923. Voyage de M. Guy Babault | dans | l'Afrique Orientale
Anglaise | et dans l'Ouganda | **Étude | d'une | collection d'ois-
eaux | de | l'Afrique Orientale Anglaise | et de | l'Ouganda** |
par | A. Menegaux | Assistant de la chaire de Mammalogie et

Ornithologie | au Muséum National d'Histoire Naturelle, | Président de la Soctété (*sic*) Ornithologique de France. | Avec notes de route de | M. Guy Babault | Correspondant du Muséum d'Histoire Naturelle de Paris | Paris, 1923 | Tous droits de traduction et de reproduction réservés.

1 vol. medium 4to, pp. 1-157, pll. I-IV (by J. Terrier), 1 map (fold.; col.). Paris.

A catalogue of the birds collected by Babault in British East Africa and Uganda in 1913, with notes on distribution, habitat, relationships, etc. The colors of the soft parts are given in many cases. A description of the various collecting stations is given by Babault on pp. 3-8. The original wrapper cites the title and author as "Voyage dans l'Afrique Oriental Anglaise et dans l'Ouganda 1913 par Guy Babault."

Ménétriés, Eduard.

1832. Catalogue raisonné | des | objets de zoologié | recueillis dans un voyage | au Caucase et jusqu'aux frontières actuelles de la Perse | enterpris par ordre de | S. M. l'Empereur. | par | E. Ménétriés | Conservateur du Musée Zoologique de l'Académie Impériale des sciences de St.-Pétersbourg, | Membre de la Société Impériale des Naturalistes de Moscou. | Présenté a l'Académie Impériale des sciences de St.-Pétersbourg le 1 Février 1832. | St.-Pétersbourg, | de l'imprimerie de l'Académie Impériale des Sciences. | 1832.

1 vol. medium 4to (clipped to 8x10), 2 pr. ll., pp. 1-271+1, I-XXXII +1 (table of geogr. distr. of spp.), I-IV (generic index), 1 l. (errata). St. Petersburg. Sept. 1832.

An annotated list of the species in the zoological collections made by the author in and about Caucasia, with descriptions of many new forms. The ornithological portion of the treatise occupies pp. 26-58. The reverse of the title-page is printed, "Publié par ordre de l'Académie Septembre 1832 Le Secrétaire perpétuel P. H. Fuss." The present copy is inscribed to Prof. Eversmann from the author.

Menzbier, Michel Alexander.

See Menzbīr, Mīkhaīl Aleksandrovīch.

Menzbīr, Mīkhaīl Aleksandrovīch.

1882. Ornīthologhīcheskaya ğheoghrafiya | Evropeīskoī Rossiī. | Mīkhaīla Menzbīra. | Chast' Pervaya. | S' 8-yn khromolīthoghrafīrovannuimī tablītzamī. | Moskva. | V' Unīversītetskoī Tītzoghrafīī (M. Katrov'), | na Strastnom' Bul'varye. | 1882.

1 vol. (?) royal 8vo, 2 pr. ll. (tit. and half-tit.), pp. I-(IV), 5-524, 1 l. (errata), pll. I-VIII (col.; by N. Severtzow). Moscow.

A treatise on the geographical distribution of the birds of European Russia. A second volume is quoted by the Cat. Libr. Brit. Mus. (Nat. Hist.) as published in 1892. The present copy was a presentation by the author to Tschusi zu Schmidhoffen.

Menzbīr, Mīkhaīl Aleksandrovīch.

1888-94. Dr. N. A. Sewertzow. | **Ornithologie du Turkestan | et | des pays adjacents.** | (Partie N.O. de la Mongolie, steppes Kirghiz, contrée Aralo-Caspienne, | partie supérieure du bassin d'Oxus, Pamir). | Par | M. le Docteur M, A. Menzbier, | Professeur a l'Université de Moscou, | Membre de la Société Impériale [*etc.*, *3 lines.*]. | Volume I [Tome deuxième]. | Moscou. | Publiée par l'Auteur | avec le concours de la Société Impériale Géographique de Russie. | 1888 [1888-1893].

6 vols. (pt.), imperial 4to. Vol. I, 2 pr. ll. (tit., ded.), pp. III-VIII. Vol. II, 2 pr. ll. (half-tit. and tit.), pp. I-III+1 (table of conts.), I-II (pref.), 1-391, illustr. tit., pll. I, III-IX, IIa, VIIIa and IXa (col.). Vol. III, (no tit. or text), pll. X and XI (col.). Vol. IV, (no tit. or text), pl. XLIX (col.). Vol. V, (no tit., text or pll.). Vol. VI, (no tit. or text), pl. LXIV (col.). Moscow.

A monograph of the ornithology of Turkestan based on the collections of Aleksyei Nikolaevich Syeverrtzov (= Nicolas Alexius Sewertzow) and notes made by him. The work was planned to occupy six volumes but was never completed. Four livraisons were published as follows. Livr. **I**:- all publ. of Vol. I; pp. 1-112 and pll. III, VI and VII of Vol. II; pl. X of Vol. III = 1888. Livr. **II**:- pp. 113-208 and pll. IV and V of Vol. II; pl. XI of Vol. III = 1889. Livr. **III**:- pp. 209-324 and pll. IIa and VIII of Vol. II; pl. XLIX of Vol. IV; pl. LXIV of Vol. VI = 1891. Livr. **IV**:- pp. 325-391, half-tit. and tit., pp. I-IV and I-II, illustr. tit., pll. I, VIIIa, IX and IXa of Vol. II = 1894 (altered on cover from 1893). The plates are by "Atchouew," "Martinow" and "Menzbier," each plate being accompanied by a guard-sheet containing number and title. Dates and scope of the work have been secured from the fourth page of the original wrappers which are preserved with the work. The copy at hand was presented to Tschusi zu Schmidhoffen by the author.

Merrem, Blasius.

1781. **Vermischte | Abhandlungen | aus der | Thiergeschichte |** von | Blasius Merrem | [*Vignette.*] | Mit Kupfern. | Göttingen, | im Verlag bey Victorinus Bossiegel 1781.

1 vol. demy 4to, 4 pr. ll. (tit., ded. and pref.), pp. 1-172, pll. I-VII (fold.; 5 ornithological). Göttingen.

A collection of several miscellaneous papers on mammals and birds. Three relate to birds:- "Bestimmung der Kennzeichen der Adler und Falken," pp. 76-109; "Weissköpfiger Adler," pp. 110-163, pll. III-VI; "Brauner Falke," pp. 164-168, pl. VII.

Merrem, Blasius.

1786? Beyträge | zur | besondern Geschichte | der Vögel | ge-
sammelt | von | Blasius Merrem. | Erstes [Zweytes] Heft. |
Goettingen. 1784. [Leipzig] | Auf Kosten des Verfassers, und in
Commission in der Vandenhoeckischen, [in der Joh. Gottf. Müller-
schen Buchhandlung] | in Leipzig in der J. F. Müllerschen Buch-
handlung. [1786.].

2 pts. medium folio (11½ x 13). Pt. I, 2 pr. ll. (tit. and pref.), pp.
1-24, pll. I-VI (col.; by C. E. Eberlein). Pt. II, 3 pr. ll. (tit.and
ded.), pp. 25-49+1, pll. VII-XII (col.; by Merrem, Eberlein and
Berkenkamp). Goettingen and Leipzig.

Ornithological contributions, mostly consisting of descriptions of certain species,
several of which are new. Some synonymy is given for a few of the species but
no Latin names are adopted in the text. On the plates, however, both Latin
and German names are used. Copies of Pt. I exist with only German names
on the plates. Where Latin names occur (as in the present copy) the handwriting in which they are engraved is different from that used for the vernacular names in the same part, although it is the same as that used for both Latin
and vernacular names in Pt. II. From these facts Stone (Auk, **37**, p. 468,
1920) concludes that the 1784 edition of Pt. I was without Latin names but
that these were added to the plates in time for a reissue of Pt. I to accompany
Pt. II in 1786. No change was made in the date on the title-page of the reissue,
nor, apparently, in the text. A Latin edition of both parts appeared in 1786.

Merriam, Clinton Hart.

1877. A Review of the Birds of Connecticut, with Remarks on their
Habits. < Trans. Conn. Acad., **4**, Art. 1, pp. 1-150, July - Oct.,
1877.

An annotated catalogue giving full information on the local status of the 291
species of birds recorded from the state. Published in three numbers of the
Transactions of the Connecticut Academy, in July (pp. 1-96), August (pp. 97-
144) and October (pp. 145-150). Coues cites the pagination of this paper as
pp. 1-165, but in a complete copy which I have seen of Vol. 4 of the Transactions, the present paper stops on p. 150, and pp. 151-165 contain the first part
of Art. 2, —an unrelated dissertation. A separate reprint is said (by Coues)
to contain a title-page and pp. 1-166.

Merriam, Clinton Hart.

1889. See American Ornithologists' Union, **Check-list of North
American Birds, Abridged Edition.**

1889. Idem, Supplement to the Code of Nomenclature and Check-
list.

1895. Idem, Check-list of North American Birds, Second Edition.

1910. Idem, Check-list of North American Birds, Third Edition.

Merriam, Florence Augusta.

See (Bailey), Florence A. M.

Mershon, W. B. (Atkinson, George E.; Audubon, John James; Bendire Charles E.; Brewster, William; Cook, Sullivan; Cooper, James Fenimore; Deane, Ruthven; Gibbs, Morris; Martin, E. T.; Pokagon, Simon; Roney, H. B.; Whitman, C. O.)

1907. The | Passenger Pigeon | by | W. B. Mershon | [*Trade-mark.*] | New York | The Outing Publishing Company | 1907.
1 vol. royal 8vo, pp. I-XII, 1 l. (half-tit.), pp. 1-225, 9 pll. (3 col.; by Audubon, A. Brooks and L. A. Fuertes and from photogrs.), 2 text-figs. New York.

A collection of extracts from the works of various authors respecting the life-history and habits of the Passenger Pigeon and the causes of its extinction, with other matter supplied by the author-editor from personal recollections and from correspondence with various observers. The principal authors quoted are as given above.

Le Messurier, Augustus.

1904. Game, shore, and water | birds of India. | With additional references to their | allied species in other parts | of the world. | By | Colonel A. Le Messurier, C.I.E., F.Z.S., F.G.S. | late Royal Engineers. | Author of [*etc.*, *2 lines.*]. | With one hundred and eighty natural size illustrations | from actual specimens. | Fourth edition. | London: | W. Thacker and Co., 2, Creed Lane, E.C. | Calcutta and Simla: Thacker Spink and Co. | 1904. | [All Rights Reserved.].
1 vol. superroyal 8vo, pp. I-XVI, 1-323+1, 4 ll. (advt.), 188 text-figs. London.

A series of detailed descriptions of the game, shore and water birds of India, with short diagnoses of allied species and genera of other countries, and with introductory notes of general ornithological interest. The illustrations are mostly drawings from fresh specimens, illustrative of specific characters. The first edition of the work was printed in 1874 for private circulation; the second was published in 1878 and the third in 1887.

Meyer, Adolph Bernhard.

1878. See Rowley, George D., Ornithological Miscellany, 1875-78.

Meyer, Adolph Bernhard.

1879. Index | zu | L. Reichenbach's | Ornithologischen Werken | zusammengestellt | von | A. B. Meyer. | R. Friedländer & Sohn. | Berlin, | 1879.
1 vol. royal 8vo, pp. I-VII+1, 1-150. Berlin.

An important aid to the consultation of Reichenbach's "Die Vollständigste Natur-geschichte des In- und Auslandes," 1845-63 (q.v.). A preface gives a summary of most of the parts of the work and approximate dates of publication, based on information secured from Reichenbach's son, the publishers of the book in question, and other sources. The text, which is divided into 5 parts, gives indices to the figures on Reichenbach's plates, arranged alphabetically by spe-cies and genera and also listed in sequence according to the numbering of the figures.

Meyer, Adolph Bernhard.

1879-97. Abbildungen | von | Vogel-Skeletten | herausgegeben | mit Unterstützung der Generaldirection der königl. Sammlungen | für Kunst und Wissenschaft in Dresden | von | Dr. A. B. Meyer | Director des k. zoologischen [*etc., 5 lines.*]. | Band I [II] | mit 121 Tafeln (I-CXX) [(CXXI-CXXL)] in Lichtdruck [| (Tafel CCXLA und B mit Röntgenstrahlen aufgenommen)]. | [*Blazon.*] | Dresden [R. Friedländer & Sohn, Berlin] | 1879-1888 [1889-1897]. 2 vols. imperial 4to. Vol. I, pp. I-XIV, 1 l., pp. 1-71, 1 insert-slip (ref. to pl. CI), pll. I-CXX, VIIA and CII(bis) (to replace CI). Vol. II, pp. I-XXI+1, 1-55+1, 55(bis)-120, pll. CXXI-CCXXXIX, CCXLA and CCXLB. Dresden and Berlin.

A series of excellent photogravures of avian osteology, with explanatory text. The work was issued in 24 Lieferungen, arranged as follows, with dates as given on the original wrappers which are bound with the work in the present copy. Lief. **I**, pp. 1-8, pll. I-X and VIIA, 1879; **II-III**, pp. 9-24, pll. XI-XXX, 1881-1882 (publ. in 1882); **IV-V**, pp. 25-40, pll. XXXI-L, 1883; **VI-VII**, pp. 41-48, pll. LI-LXX, 1884; **VIII-IX**, pp. 49-56, pll. LXXI-XC, 1885; **X-XI**, pp. 57-64, pll. XCI-CX, 1886; **XII-XIII**, pp. 65-71+1 and I-XIV (Vol. I), 1-8 (Vol. II), pll. CI (bis), XCI-CXXX, 1888-1889 (publ. in 1889); **XIV-XV**, pp. 9-22, pll. CXXXI-CL, 1890; **XVI-XVIII**, pp. 23-55+1, pll. CLI-CLXXX, 1892; **XIX-XXI**, pp. 55 (bis) -92, pll. CLXXXI-CCX, 1894; **XXII-XXIV**, pp. 93-120, I-XXI+1, pll. CCXI-CCXLB. Lieferungen I-XVIII were published in Dres-den, XIX-XXIV in Berlin. The present copy contains the bookplate of Fred-erick DuCane Godman.

Meyer, Adolf Bernhard.

1887. Unser | Auer-, Rackel- und Birkwild | und seine Abarten | von | Dr. A. B. Meyer | Hofrath, Director [*etc., 4 lines.; 2 lines (Atlas.).*]. | Mit einem Atlas von 17 colorirten Tafeln [Atlas. | (*List of pll., 3 columns, 6 lines.*)]. | Wien | Verlag von Adolph W. Künast | K. K. Hof- und Kammerbuchhändler Sr. K. und K. Hoheit des Durchlauchtigsten Kronprinzen Ehrzherzog Rudolf | 1887. 2 vols. imperial 4to (11x15½) and elephant. Text, pp. I-XII, 1-95. Atlas, 17 pll. (I-XVII on title-p.; col., by G. Mützel). Vienna.

A treatise on the Capercaillie, the Black Grouse and the various hybrids formed between these two and with various other species.

Meyer, Adolf Bernhard; and Wigglesworth, Lionel W.

1898. 598.2(91.2). **The | birds of Celebes | and | the neighboring islands. |** By | A. B. Meyer and L. W. Wigglesworth. | With 45 plates (42 coloured) and 7 coloured maps. | Berlin: | R. Friedländer & Sohn. | 1898. > [*Idem 7 lines.*] | Volume I [II]. | With 17 plates (14 coloured and 7 coloured maps [With 28 coloured plates]. | Berlin: [*etc.*].

2 vols. royal 4to. Vol. I, pp. I-XXXII, 1-392, pll. I-XVII (14 col.; by Geisler), maps I-VII (col.; 2? fold.; I-II missing). Vol. II, 2 ll. (tit. and subt.), pp. 393-962, pll. XVIII-XLV (col.; by Geisler). Berlin.

A monograph of the ornithology of Celebes, with a lengthy discussion of the relationships of the island with adjacent territory and a detailed introduction containing a general discussion, a bibliography, and analyses of the avifaunas of various islands. Most of the work was written by Wigglesworth.

Meyer, Bernhard; and Wolf, Johann.

1810. **Taschenbuch | der | deutschen Vögelkunde |** Oder | kurze | Beschreibung aller Vögel Deutschlands | von | Hofrath Dr. Meyer zu Offenbach | und Professor Dr. Wolf zu Nürnberg | Mitglieder von mehreren gelehrten Gesellschaften. | Erster [Zweiter] Theil | die Landvögel [Sumpf- und Wasservögel] enthaltend. | Mit illuminirten Kupfern. | Frankfurt am Main | verlegt von Friedrich Wilmans. | 1810.

1 vol. (2 pts.), post 8vo, pp. I-XVI+1, 1-310, I-XII (Pt. II.), 311-614, 2 frontisps. (Pts. I and II; col.; by J. M. Hergenroeder), 75 pll. (39 and 36; col.; by G. P. Zwinger). Frankfort on Main.

A manual of the birds of Germany with hand-colored plates illustrating heads and feet. Engelmann quotes 1809 for Pt. 1, possibly from the preface which is dated August 20, 1809. A supplementary volume was issued by Meyer in 1822 under the title of "Zusätze und Berichtigungen zu Meyers und Wolfs Taschenbuch der Deutschen Vögelkunde" (q.v.).

Meyer, Bernhard.

1815. **Kurze | Beschreibung | der Vögel | Liv- und Esthlands |** von | Dr. Bernhard Meyer, | Fürstl. Isenburgischen Hofrathe [*etc., 10 lines.*]. | Mit einer Kupfertafel. | Nürnberg, | bei Johann Leonhard Schrag. | 1815.

1 vol. post 8vo, pp. I-XXIV, 1-292, frontisp. (col.). Nuremberg.

A descriptive catalogue of the birds of Livland and Esthland.

Meyer, Bernhard.

1822. **Zusätze und Berichtigungen | zu | Meyers und Wolfs | Taschenbuch | der | deutschen Vögelkunde, |** nebst kurzer

Beschreibung | derjenigen Vögel, welche ausser Deutschland, in | den übrigen Theilen von Europa vorkommen, | als | dritter Theil jenes Taschenbuchs | von | Hofrath Dr. Bernhard Meyer. | Mit einem vollständigen Register über das ganze Werk. | Frankfurt a. M. 1822. | Gedruckt und verlegt von H. L. Brönner.

1 vol. post 8vo, pp. I-VI, 1-264. Frankfort on Main.

A supplementary and emendatory volume issued as a third part of Meyer and Wolf's "Taschenbuch der Deutschen Vögelkunde," 1810 (q.v.). The three parts of the present copy are bound in one volume.

Meÿer, Henry Leonard.

1841-57. Colored | Illustrations | of | British Birds, | and their Eggs. | by H. L. Meÿer. [| In seven volumes, | containing four hundred and twenty-two coloured plates. (*Vol. VII, only.*) |] Vol. I [-VII]. | Containing sixty plates. [*Line omitted (Vol. VII.).*] | [*Vignette and inscription; inscr. omitted (Vols. II-VII.)*] | London: | G. W. Nickisson, 215, Regent Street, [George Willis, Piazza, Covent Garden. (*Vols. II-V.*); Willis and Sotheran. (*Vols. VI and VII.*)] | successor to the late James Fraser [*Line omitted (Vols. II-VII.).*]. | 1842 [1853; 1854; 1855; 1855; 136, Strand (*N.d., Vol. VI.*); 1857].

7 vols. post 8vo. Vol. I, pp. I-VI, 3-230, pll. 1-45 (col.), 14 pll. (eggs; col.), 6 pll. (uncol.). Vol. II, pp. I-IV, 1-233, pll. 46-90 (col.; pl. 76 wrongly numbered 78), 13 pll. (eggs; col.). Vol. III, pp. I-IV, 1-240, pll. 91-135 (col.), 15 pll. (eggs, col.). Vol. IV, pp. I-IV, 1-215, pll. 136-180 (col.), 15 pll. (eggs; col.). Vol. V, pp. I-IV, 1-192, pll. 181-225 (col.), 15 pll. (eggs; col.). Vol. VI, pp. I-IV, 1-185, pll. 226-270 (col.), 15 pll. (eggs; col.), 1 pl. (uncol.). Vol. VII, pp. I-IV, 1-206, 1 l. (errata), pll. 271-322 (col.), 18 pll. (eggs; col.), 1 pl. (uncol.). London. 1841-42 [-50] and 1852-] 53-57.

The 8vo format of Meÿer's "Illustrations of British Birds," 1835-41 et seq. According to Mullens & Swann and (less explicitly) Carus & Engelmann, there are two editions comprised in the set collated above. The title-page of Vol. I indicates that it belongs to the edition of 1841-50. The remaining volumes belong to the edition of 1852-57 and appeared as indicated on their titles,— Vol. VI probably in 1856, the first volume in 1852. Discrepancies in the number of plates in Vol. I as here represented and as collated by Coues and by Mullens & Swann, indicate a possibility that only the title-page is out of place. Vol. I of the 1841-50 edition is said to have contained 60 pll.; the copy at hand has 65 pll. (59 col.). However, the Cat. Libr. Brit. Mus. (Nat. Hist.) lists a copy of the work under dates of 1842-53—evidently mixed in the same manner as the present set. The original edition was in 4to, and, like the 8vo editions, was issued in parts.

Michelet, Jules. (Adams, William Henry Davenport.)

1870. The bird | by | Jules Michelet. | With 210 illustrations by Giacomelli. | **New Edition, Revised.** | [*Vignette.*] | London: | T. Nelson and Sons, Paternoster Row; | Edinburgh; and New York. | 1870.

1 vol. royal 8vo, pp. I-XII, 1 l., pp. 13-349, 237 text-figs., head- and tail-pieces, borders, etc. London.

A translation, by W. H. D. Adams, of Michelet's sympathetic essay on bird life. The original was published in Paris in 1856 and passed through nine or ten editions in French and others in English, German and Dutch. The present English edition was preceded by one in 1868 and followed by another in 1874 (q.v.).

Michelet, Jules. (Adams, William Henry Davenport.)

1874. The bird | by | Jules Michelet. | With 210 illustrations by Giacomelli. | New Edition, Revised. | [*Vignette.*] | London: | T. Nelson and Sons, Paternoster Row; | Edinburgh; and New York. | 1874.

1 vol. royal 8vo, pp. I-XII, 1 l., pp. 13-349, 237 text-figs., head- and tail-pieces, borders, etc. London.

An exact reprint, except for the omission of the concluding paragraph in the preface, of the edition of 1870 (q.v.).

Middendorff, Alexander Theodore von.

1855. Die Isepiptesen Russlands. | Grundlagen | zur | Erforschung der Zugzeiten und Zugrichtungen | der | Vögel Russlands. | Von | Dr. A. v. Middendorff. | (Aus den Mémoires de l'Académie des Sciences de St.-Pétersbourg. VI Série. Sciences naturelles. | T. VIII, besonders abgedruckt.) | St. Petersburg. | Buchdruckerei der Kaiserlichen Akademie der Wissenschaften. | 1855. | Zu haben bei Eggers und Comp., Commissionaren der Kaiserlichen Akademie der Wissenschaften, und in Leipzig | bei Leopold Voss. | Preis: 1 Rbl. 50 Kop. Silb. = 1 Rthlr. 20 Ngr.

1 vol. medium 4to, pp. 1-143, 2 maps (fold.). St. Petersburg.

A discussion of the migration of Russian birds, with detailed tables showing the dates of appearance of each species at various localities. Although given as an extract from the Mém. Acad. Sci. St. Petersb., it did not appear in that periodical until 1859 when it was published without the maps [Ser. VI, Vol. X, Pt. II, Sci. Nat. VIII (No. 1), 1859].

Mikan, Johann Christian.

1820-25. Delectus | **florae et faunae** | **Brasiliensis** | jussu et auspiciis | Francisci I. | Austriae Imperatoris | investigatae. | Auctore | J. C. Mikan, | M. D. Botanices in Universitate Pragensi |

Professore. | Vindobonae, | Sumtibus Auctoris, typis Antonii
Strauss. | 1820.

1 vol. imperial folio, 3 pr. ll. (tit., ded. and pref.), 24 ll., 24 pll. (col.).
Vienna.

A series of descriptions and plates of new species of plants and animals from Brazil. Five species of birds are described as new, three of them from Natterer's
manuscript. The work was issued in four parts of six plates each, according
to Engelmann, dating 1820-25. Wetmore (Auk, **42**, p. 283, April, 1925) has
given the collation and dates from a copy of the work in the U. S. Department
of Agriculture, which has Pts. I, II and IV in original covers. The date for
Pt. III is quoted from a discovery by Richmond in Flora Regensb. for Nov. **7**,
1823, which announces the appearance of that part. According to Wetmore,
the dates are as follows. Pt. I, including *Lanius undulatus*, 1820; **II**, including
Corvus tricolor, 1822; **III**, including *Oxyrhynchus serratus*, 1823; **IV**, including
Tanagra chalybea and *T. diademata*, 1825.

Millais, John Guille.

1892. Game birds | and | shooting-sketches; | illustrating the |
habits, modes of capture, stages of plumage, | and the | hybrids
and varieties which occur amongst them. | By | John Guille
Millais, F.Z.S. &c. | London: | Henry Sotheran & Co., | 37,
Piccadilly, W. 136, Strand, W.C. | Manchester: 49, Cross Street. |
1892.

1 vol. folio (12x15) (4to by sign.), pp. I-XII, 1-72, frontisp. (portr.),
34 pll. (16 col.; 18 autotype; by the author), 30 text-figs. London
and Manchester.

An account of the habits of the Capercaillie, Blackgame, Grouse and Ptarmigan
of the British Islands.

Millais, John Guille.

1895. A Breath from the Veldt | by | John Guille Millais, F.Z.S.,
etc. | Author of 'Game Birds and Shooting Sketches' | [*Fig.*] |
With illustrations by the author, and frontispiece by | Sir J. E.
Millais, R.A. | London | Henry Sotheran and Co. | 37 Piccadilly,
W., and 140 Strand, W.C. | 1895.

1 vol. 4to (12 x 15), pp. I-X, 1-236, 13 pll. 137 text-figs. (12 full-p.).
London.

The narrative account of the author's hunting experiences in South Africa in
1893, illustrated principally by sketches made by himself. Most of the book
relates to mammals, but there are a great many accounts of the habits of various
birds and excellent illustrations which demonstrate some of their peculiarities
that have rarely, if ever, been described or depicted.

Millais, John Guille.

1902. **The natural history | of the | British | Surface-Feeding Ducks** | by | J. G. Millais, F.Z.S. | Author of 'A Breath from the Veldt' [*etc.*]. | With 6 photogravures, 41 coloured plates, and 25 other illustrations | Longmans, Green, and Co. | 39 Paternoster Row, London | New York and Bombay | 1902 | All rights reserved.

1 vol. 4to (12¼x13½), 3 pr. ll. (edition-no., illustr. tit. and tit.), pp. V-XIV, 1-107, pll. I-XLI (col.; by A. Thorburn and Millais and from photographs), 24 pll. (6 photograv.). London, New York and Bombay.

Descriptions of the habits of the surface-feeding ducks of Great Britain. The present copy is No. 583 of a large paper edition of 600 copies.

Millais, John Guille.

1913. **British | diving ducks** | by | J. G. Millais, F.Z.S., M.B.O.U., Etc. | Author of [*etc.*, *4 lines*.]. | Vol. I [II] | with thirty-two [forty-two] plates (twenty-two [seventeen] of which are coloured) | by Archibald Thorburn, O. Murray Dixon, H. Grönvold | and the author | Longmans, Green and Co. | 39 Paternoster Row, London | New York, Bombay, and Calcutta | 1913 | All rights reserved.

2 vols. 4to (12x16). Vol. I, pp. I-XV+1, 1-141, 32 pll. (22 col.; 8 photograv.; 2 collotype). Vol. II, pp. I-XII, 1-164, 42 pll. (17 col.; 6 photograv.; 19 collotype). London, New York, Bombay and Calcutta.

A detailed monograph, beautifully illustrated.

Miller, John Frederick.

1796. See Shaw, George, **Cimelia Physica.**

Miller, Olive Thorne.

1885. **Bird-ways** | by | Olive Thorne Miller [*Trade-mark.*] | Boston and New York | Houghton, Mifflin and Company | The Riverside Press, Cambridge | 1885.

1 vol. cap 8vo, pp. I-VIII, 1-227+1, 2 ll. (advt.). Boston and New York.

Popular bird-studies and observations.

Miller, Olive Thorne.

1894. **A bird-lover in the | west** | by | Olive Thorne Miller | [*Trade-mark.*] | Boston and New York | Houghton, Mifflin and Company | The Riverside Press, Cambridge | 1894.

1 vol. 8vo, 1 l. (advt.), pp. I-VII+1, 1-278. Boston and New York.

A series of studies in bird life in the middle-western United States. Written in the form of essays, the book contains the results of careful observation clearly expressed.

Miller, Olive Thorne.

1897. Upon the tree-tops | by | Olive Thorne Miller | illustrated by J. Carter Beard | [*Trade-mark.*] | Boston and New York | Houghton, Mifflin and Company | The Riverside Press, Cambridge | 1897.

1 vol. cap 8vo, pp. I-IX+1, 1 l. (illustrs.), pp. 1-245+1, 1 l. (index), 10 pll. Boston and New York.

Popular essays on New England bird-life.

Miller, Olive Thorne.

1904. With the birds | in Maine | by | Olive Thorne Miller | [*Trade-mark.*] | Boston and New York | Houghton, Mifflin and Company | The Riverside Press, Cambridge | 1904.

1 vol. cap 8vo, pp. I-IX+1, 1-300. Boston and New York.

Essays on bird-life, based on the author's observations in Maine.

Milne Edwards, Alphonse.

1867-71. Recherches | anatomiques et paléontologiques | pour servir a l'histoire des | **oiseaux fossiles** | **de la France** | par | M. Alphonse Milne Edwards | Professeur de zoologie [*etc., 5 lines.*]. | Ouvrage qui a obtenu le grand Prix des sciences physiques décerné par l'Académie des sciences en 1866. | Tome premier [Tome second; Atlas | Tome premier | Planches 1 à 96; Atlas | Tome second | Planches 97 à 200] | Paris | Victor Masson et Fils [Libraire de G. Masson (*Vol. II and Atlas, Vol. II.*)] | Place de L'École-de-Médecine | 1867-1868 [1869-1871 (*Vol. II and Atlas, Vol. II.*)].

4 vols. medium 4to. Vol. I, 2 pr. ll. (half-tit. and tit.), pp. 1-474, 1 l. (errata). Vol. II, 2 pr. ll., pp. 1-632. Atlas, Vol. I, 2 pr. ll., 96 ll., pll. 1-96 (monochr.; 4 col.; 7 fold.). Atlas, Vol. II, 2 pr. ll., 104 ll., pll. 97-200 (monochr.; 2 col.). Paris.

A comprehensive account of fossil birds, not entirely restricted to France, developed in conjunction with osteological studies of modern forms. In addition to the descriptions of the new fossil forms, the work presents a mass of information relative to the characteristics and affinities of various taxonomic groups. The work was published in livraisons of which the Zoological Record cites **1-17** in 1867, **18-25** (Vol. I concluding with 22) in 1868; **26-30** in 1869, and the completion of the work in 1871. The issuance of text did not always keep pace with that of the plates so that the two did not appear synchronously in all cases. The copy at hand was presented by the author to A(dolphe Théodore) Brongniart, (Paleobotanist).

Milne Edwards, Alphonse. (Grandidier, Alfred.)

**1874. Recherches | sur la | faune ornithologique éteinte | des |
Iles Mascareignes et de Madagascar** | par | M. Alph. Milne
Edwards | Professeur de zoologie [*etc.*, *2 lines.*]. | Paris | G. Masson
éditeur | Libraire de l'Académie de Médecine | Place de l'École-de-
Médecine | 1866 a 1873.

1 vol. royal 4to, tit., pp. 1-147, pll. 1-33 (3 col.; 24 monochr.; 8 fold.;
6, 11 and 12 num. in Roman). Paris.

Six essays on fossil birds reprinted from the author's papers in the Annales des
Sciences Naturelles, Ser. 5, Zoologie, Vol. VI, pp. 91-111, pll. 2-3, 1866; Vol.
VII, pp. 144-156 and 194-220, pll. 7-8 and 10-13, 1867; Vol. X, pp. 325-346,
pll. 15-18, 1869; Vol. XII, pp. 167-196, pll. 6-16, 1869; Vol. XIX, pp. 167-196,
pll. 11-15, 1874 (all dates according to Zoological Record). As indicated in
the collation, the present reprint is repaged and the plates are renumbered,
in addition to which there are 5 extra plates; possibly there are other alterations. The paper on *Aepyornis* is by Milne Edwards and Grandidier.

Milne Edwards, Alphonse.

1879-82. See Grandidier, Alfred, **Histoire Physique, Naturelle et
Politique de Madagascar; Oiseaux.**

Miner, John Thomas [Jack].

1923(?). Jack Miner | and the Birds | and | some things I know |
about nature | By | Jack Miner | of Kingsville, Ontario, Canada |
Toronto | The Ryerson Press [*Vignette, embracing first three
lines.*].

1 vol. superroyal 8vo, 8 pr. ll., pp. 1-178, frontisp. (portr.), 55 text-figs.
Toronto.

A rambling account of the author's observations on, and experiences with, birds;
illustrated by photographs. Mr. Miner has accomplished some interesting results in the domestication and semi-domestication of wild geese and ducks.
The book was copyrighted 1923; autographed by the author August 21st, 1924.

Minot, Henry Davis. (Brewster, William.)

1895. The | land-birds and game-birds | of | New England | with
descriptions of the birds, their nests | and eggs, their habits and
notes | with illustrations | by | H. D. Minot | **Second edition** |
edited by William Brewster | [*Quot., 4 lines.*] | [*Blazon.*] | Boston
and New York | Houghton, Mifflin and Company | The Riverside
Press, Cambridge | 1895.

1 vol. 8vo, pp. I-XXIV, 1-492, 1 insert-slip (errata), frontisp. (portr.),
pl. I, text-figs. 1-22. Boston and New York.

A series of ornithological biographies based, for the most part, on the author's
personal observations. The book was written when the author was but seven-

teen years of age but was well received because of its general accuracy and originality. The present edition is but little altered from the original except for footnotes supplied by the editor, William Brewster, and for certain changes in nomenclature and style as explained on pp. XIII and XIV. A supplement by Brewster is added to Minot's accounts of the species, on pp. 466-480. The first edition was published in December 1876. The present copy contains the autograph of D. G. Elliot.

Mitchell, Frederick Shaw.

1885.   The | birds of Lancashire. | By | F. S. Mitchell, | Member of the British Ornithologists' Union. | Illustrated by J. G. Keulemans, Victor Prout, | &c. | London: | John Van Voorst, Paternoster Row. | MDCCCLXXXV.

1 vol. post 8vo, pp. 1-12 (tit., list of illustrs. and index), I-XVIII (introd.), 1-224, 3 ll. (list of subscrs.), frontisp. (map; fold.), 2 pll. (col.; by Keulemans), pll. III-XI (uncol.), 3 text-figs. London.

An account of the local occurrence and habits of the species of birds found in Lancashire. A second edition (q.v.) appeared in 1892.

Mitchell, Frederick Shaw.   (Saunders, Howard.)

1892.   The | birds of Lancashire | by | F. S. Mitchell | Member of the British Ornithologists' Union | **Second edition** | revised and annotated by | Howard Saunders, F.L.S., F.Z.S., &c. | With Additions by R. J. Howard, M.B.O.U., | and other Local Authorities | Illustrated by G. E. Lodge, Victor Prout, &c. | [*Blazon.*] | London: | Gurney & Jackson, 1, Paternoster Row. | [Successors to Mr. Van Voorst.] | MDCCCXCII.

1 vol. post 8vo, pp. I-XXVI, 1-271, frontisp. (map; fold.), 6 pll. (on numbered pp.) 6 text-figs. London.

A second edition of the work of the same title (q.v.) of 1885, with additions by the editor, Mr. Saunders. Contributions by R. J. Howard and many others are included in the general discussion and are not set apart as separate articles.

Mivart, St. George.

1896.   A monograph | of the | lories, | or | brush-tongued parrots, | composing the family Loriidæ. | By | St. George Mivart, F.R.S. | London: | R. H. Porter, 7 Princes Street, Cavendish Square, W. | 1896.

1 vol. royal 4to, pp. I-LIII+1, 1-193, pll. I-LXI (col.; by J. G. Keulemans), text-figs. 1-19, maps I-IV (col.). London.

A thorough treatise on the group in question, with excellent, hand-colored plates.

Moehring, Paulus Henricus Gerardus. (Nozeman, Cornelius; Vosmaer, Arnout.)

1906. **Geslachten | der | Vogelen.** | Door | Dr. Paulus Henricus Gerardus Moehring, | Raad en Lyf-Arts [etc., *4 lines.*] | Uit het Latyn vertaald en met Aantekeningen vermeerderd, | door | Cornelius Nozeman, | En naar die Vertaaling uitgegeeven en met eene Voorre- | den, Aantekeningen en Naamlyft der voornaamste | Schryveren die over de Vogelen geschreeven | hebben vermeerderd, door | Arnout Vosmaer | [*Decoration.*] | Te Amsteldam. | By Pieter Meijer. op den Dam | MDCCLVIII. > **Facsimile-Edition.**

1 vol. imperial 8vo (7½x10), tit., 13 ll., pp. 1-97+1+1 l., pll. 20 and 48 (col.). "Amsterdam. 1758" Leipzig. 1906.

A facsimile reproduction of Moehring's treatise on systematic ornithology. The wrapper bears the following inscription. "Facsimile-Edition. Ed.: W. Junk. No. 9. | P. H. G. Moehring | Geslachten der Vogelen | [Avium genera]. | Amsterdam 1758. | Exempl. No. . . . . | [*Vignette.*] | Theodor Oswald Weigel | Leipzig. | 1906." The original "Avium Genera" was published in 1752.

Molina, Giovanni Ignazio.

1782. **Saggio | sulla storia naturale | del Chili** | del Signor Abate | Giovanni Ignazio | Molina. | [*Design.*] | In Bologna MDCCL-XXXII. | Nella Stamperia di S. Tommaso d' Aquino. | Con licenza de' Superiori.

1 vol. demy 8vo, pp. 1-367+1., (1 map, missing). Bologna.

An important, early work on the natural history of Chile. Ornithological matter occupies pp. 232-268 and 343-345. Numerous new species of birds are described and named. There are various translations into English, Spanish, French (Cf. ed. 1789.) and German, and a revised edition in Italian by Molina, dated 1810 (q.v.). The present edition contains, in the colophon, ecclesiastical authorization dated October 12, 1781.

Molina, Giovanni Ignazio. (Gruvel.)

1789. **Essai | sur | l'histoire naturelle | du Chili,** | Par M. l'Abbé Molina; | Traduit de l'Italien, & enrichi de notes, | Par M. Gruvel, D.M. | A Paris, | Chez Née de la Rochelle, Libraire, rue du | Hurepoix, près du pont Saint-Michel, no. 13. | M. DCC. LXXX-IX. | Avec Approbation et Privilège du Roi.

1 vol. crown 8vo, pp. J-XVJ, 1-351+1. Paris.

A French translation of Molina's "Saggio sulla Storia Naturale del Chile," 1782 (q.v.), with a few alterations and occasional notes by the translator, M. Gruvel. The ornithological matter appears to be practically identical in both editions, and in the present one occupies pp. 211-249 and 321-324.

Molina, Giovanni Ignazio.

1810. **Saggio | sulla storia naturale del Chili |** di | Gio: Ignazio Molina | **seconda edizione |** accresciuta e arricchita di una nuova carta geografica | e del ritratto dell' autore. | [*Quot., 5 lines.*] | Bologna 1810. | Tipografia de' Fratelli Masi e Comp.

1 vol. medium 4to, 3 pr. ll. (tit., ded. and ded. address), pp. I-V+1, 1-306, 1 l. (errata), frontisp. (portr.), 1 map (fold.).

A revised edition of the author's work first published in 1782 (q.v.). The text is largely rewritten with many additions and other changes. Ornithological matter occupies pp. 197-226. Catalogo I of the original edition (which contained a summary of the species of animals and plants) has been eliminated but the descriptive notes in the general text have been considerably amplified. Names of a few of the birds have been emended and many species introduced which were not included in the original edition, but none of the species appear to be new. *Trochilus galeritus* of the original is renamed *T. cristatus*.

Mommsen, August. (Krüper, Theobald; Hartlaub, Carl Johann Gustav.)

1875. **> Griechische Jahreszeiten. |** Herausgegeben von | August Mommsen. | **Heft III. |** Inhalt: Zeiten des Gehens und Kommens und des | Brütens der Vögel in Griechenland und Ionien. | Catalog von Dr. Krüper, mit Citaten und Zusätzen | von Dr. Hartlaub.- | Kalendar, vom Herausg.- | Litteratur, von Dr. Hartlaub. | Schleswig. | Julius Vergas. | (Dr. Heiberg's Buch- und Musikalienhandlung. | 1875.

1 vol. post 8vo, 3 pr. ll. (tit., ded. and pref.), pp. 155-330. Schleswig.

A catalogue of the birds of Greece and outlying territory, based on a manuscript catalogue by Dr. Krüper, annotated by Hartlaub, with a migration calendar by Mommsen and a bibliography by Hartlaub. The work as collated is Pt. III of the "Griechische Jahreszeiten" of Mommsen, published (Hefte. I-V) from 1873-77.

Montagu, George.

1802. **Ornithological Dictionary; |** or | Alphabetical Synopsis | of | British birds. | by | George Montagu, F.L.S. | In two volumes. | Vol. I [II]. | London: | printed for J. White, Fleet Street, | by T. Bensley, Bolt Court. | 1802.

2 vols. in 1 vol., post 8vo. Vol. I, tit., pp. I-XL, XLII, 162 ll. (signs. C-I, K-U and X-Y2; unpaged), frontisp. (col.; by Eliza Dorville). Vol. II, tit., 168 ll. (signs. B-I, K-U, X-Y; unpaged), 1 l. (errata to Vols. I and II). London.

An exceedingly useful publication containing a great amount of information about British birds arranged alphabetically under the vernacular names of the species. Volume I contains the introduction, consisting of a general review of avian physiology, and the dictionary from A to L, inclusive. Volume II completes the alphabet and contains, also, a short appendix, a systematic list of British birds, a glossary, a bibliography, and the errata to both volumes. A "Supplement to the Ornithological Dictionary" (q.v.) was issued in 1813, and the work, itself, passed through a number of subsequent editions. The present volume is bound uniformly with a copy of the Supplement, each containing the autograph of J. R. Balston.

Montagu, George.

1813. **Supplement** | **to the** | **Ornithological Dictionary,** | or | synopsis of British birds. | By | George Montagu, Esq. F.L.S. & M.W.S. | Printed by S. Woolmer, Exeter; | and sold by S. Bagster, 81, Strand, T. and A. Arch, | Cornhill, and Thomas Underwood, 32, Fleet-Street, | London; of whom may be had "Testacea Brittanica, | or Synopsis of British Shells, and Supplement,," (*sic*) with | plates coloured or plain. Also, "The Sportsman's | Directory, or Tractate on Gunpowder," by the same | author. | 1813. 1 vol. post 8vo, pp. I-VI, 1 l. (list of pll.), 232 ll. (signs. B-I, K-T, V-Z and Aa-Ff; unpaged), 1 l. (errata), 24 pll. (uncol.; by Eliza Dorville). London.

A supplementary volume, containing additions to the "Ornithological Dictionary," 1802 (q.v.). Signs. Aa8-Ff1 comprise an appendix; Ff2-Ff5, a "Definition of the parts of extraordinary tracheæ" and "Direction for amputating the Wing of a Bird." The remainder of the volume contains the additions and alterations to the systematic catalogue, and the errata. The present copies of the Supplement and the original Dictionary are bound uniformly in two volumes, each containing the autograph of R. J. Balston.

Montbeillard, Philib. Guénau de.

1874-83. See Buffon, **Histoire Naturelle des Oiseaux,** 1770-86.

Moore, John.

1858. See Eaton, John Matthews, **A Treatise on the Art of Breeding and Managing . . . Pigeons.**

Moquin-Tandon, Alfred.

1841. See Webb, Philip Barker; and Berthelot, Sabin, [**Histoire Naturelle des Îles Canaries**] **Ornithologie Canarienne.**

Moquin-Tandon, Alfred.

1857-58. See Bonaparte, Charles Lucien, **Iconographie des Pigeons.**

Morris, Beverley Robinson.

1855. **British** | **game birds** | **and** | **wildfowl.** | By | Beverley R. Morris, Esq., A.B., M.D., T.C.D., | Memb: Wern: Club. | Illustrated with sixty coloured plates. | London: | Groombridge and Sons, Paternoster Row. | 1855.

1 vol. medium 4to, pp. I-IV, 1-252, 60 pll. (col.; by B. Fawcett). London.

Descriptions and accounts of the habits of British game birds and wildfowl. The plates are hand-colored. There are several later editions of the work.

Morris, Francis Orpen.

1866-67. A | natural history | of the | nests and eggs | of | British birds. | By | the Rev. F. O. Morris, B.A., | Member [*etc.*, *2 lines.*] | Vol. I [-III]. | With seventy-eight [seventy-six; seventy-one] coloured plates. | London: | Groombridge and Sons, Paternoster Row. | M DCCC LXVI [M DCCC LXVII (*Vol. III.*)].

3 vols. 4to (6¼x9¾). Vol. I, 2 pr. ll. (tit. and ded.), pp. III-IV, 1-156, 1 insert-slip (regarding missing pll.), pll. I-X, XII-LIV, LVII-LIX, LXI-LXVIII, LXX-LXXXIII (col.). Vol. II, pp. I-IV, 1-148, pll. LXXXIV-XCIII, XCV-CXVIII, CXX-CLXI (col.). Vol. III, pp. I-IV, 1-140, pll. CLXII-CCXXXII (col.). London.

Accounts of the nesting habits of British birds, with colored plates of nests and eggs. The present edition appears to be a reissue of the first one (published in 1853-56), with the addition of pll. XL and XLII which were omitted from the original (as catalogued by Mullens and Swann). The second edition (q.v.) appeared in 1870-71 and was reissued later, while a revised fourth edition (q.v.) was published in 1896.

Morris, Francis Orpen.

1870. A | history | of | British birds. | By | the Rev. F. O. Morris, B.A., | Member of the Ashmolean Society. | **Second edition.** | Volume I [-VI]. | [*Quot.* (*mut. in Vols. V and VI.*)] | London: | Bell and Daldy, York Street, Covent Garden. | M DCCC LXX.

6 vols. 4to (6¾x9⅝). Vol. I, pp. I-XII, 1-303, 60 pll. (col.). Vol. II, pp. I-IV, 1-283, 61 pll. (col.). Vol. III, pp. I-IV, 1-272, 56 pll. (col.). Vol. IV, pp. I-IV, 1-264, 63 pll. (col.). Vol. V, pp. I-IV, 1-247, 65 pll. (col.). Vol. VI, pp. I-IV, 1-225, 60 pll. (col.). London.

A voluminous work of a general nature, containing a mass of information, much of which is from unreliable sources and inaccurate. The plates, which are hand-colored, are fairly good, and the book early obtained considerable popularity on account of its readability and moderate cost. Mullens and Swann record 3 reissues of the first edition, four revised editions, and two cabinet editions. The present copy is of the second (first revised) edition. The first edition appeared in 1851-57, in monthly parts.

Morris, Francis Orpen.

1870-71. A | natural history | of the | nests and eggs | of | British birds. | By | the Rev. F. O. Morris, B.A., | Member of the Ashmolean Society. | **Second edition.** | Volume I [-III]. | London: | Bell and Daldy, York Street, Covent Garden. | M DCCC LXX [M DCCC LXXI (*Vol. III.*)].

3 vols. 4to (6¾x9¾). Vol. I, 2 pr. ll. (tit. and ded.), pp. III-IV, 1-164, pll. I-LXXIX+XVII* (col.). Vol. II, pp. I-IV, 1-164, pll. LXXX-CLVI (col.). Vol. III, pp. I-IV, 1-171, pll. CLVII-CCXXXII (col.). London.

The letterpress of the present edition, except for certain added matter and slight rearrangement, is identical with that of the edition of 1866-67 (q.v.). The pagination, however, is entirely changed.

Morris, Francis Orpen. (Tegetmeier, William Bernhard.)

1896. **A natural history** | **of the** | **nests and eggs** | **of** | **British birds** | **by the** | Rev. F. O. Morris, B.A. | Rector of Nunburnholme, Yorkshire | **Fourth edition** | revised and corrected by | W. B. Tegetmeier, F.Z.S. | Member of the British Ornithologists' Union | with two hundred and forty-eight plates | chiefly coloured by hand | in three volumes | volume the first [-third] | London | John C. Nimmo | 14 King William Street, Strand | MDCCCXCVI.

3 vols. 4to (6¾x10). Vol. I, pp. I-XIX+1, 1-178, pll. I-LXXIX, XVII*, XXVII*, XXXVII*, LVII* and LXXVII* (col.), 5 text-figs Vol. II, pp. I-VIII, 1-155, pll. LXXX-CLVI, LXXXIV*, CXIII*, CXVII*, CXX*, CXLI* and CLV* (col.). Vol. III, pp. I-XI+1, 1-207, pll. CLVII-CCXXXII, CLXXV*, CLXXXV*, CXCI*, CXCII* and CCXXII* (col.). London.

In the present edition the text is much altered from that of the first and second editions, 1866-67 and 1870-71 (q.v.). The numbering of the plates is the same (with interpolations indicated by the figures with asterisks), and the plates are of the same design as the originals although they are executed in a very inferior manner. An introduction (pp. V-XIII) is from the pen of Tegetmeier who is probably responsible for many of the changes in the work.

Morris, Robert O.

1901. The | birds of Springfield | and vicinity | by | Robert O. Morris | Springfield, Mass. | Published by Henry R. Johnson | 1901.

1 vol. 4to (6x8¾), pp. 1-54, frontisp. (map). Springfield.

An annotated list of the species of birds known to have occurred within twenty-five miles of Springfield, Massachusetts. A short bibliography is appended.

Morse, Albert P.

1912. **A pocket list** | of the | **Birds of Eastern Massachusetts** | with special reference to | Essex County | by | Albert P. Morse | Curator [*etc.*, *3 lines.*] | Author of [*etc.*, *3 lines.*] | Published by the | Peabody Academy of Science | Salem, Mass. | 1912.

1 vol. 12mo, pp. 1-92, 8 ll. (seasonal charts), frontisp. Salem.

An annotated list of species, giving the abundance, dates of appearance and habitat of each. The list is printed on but one side of the paper, leaving the opposite pages for manuscript notes.

Morse, Silas R. (Stone, Witmer.)

1909. **Annual Report** | of the | **New Jersey State** | **Museum** | including a report of | the birds of New Jersey | their nests and eggs | And Notes on New Jersey Fishes, Amphibians and Reptiles | 1908 | Trenton, N. J.: | The John L. Murphy Publishing Company, Printers. | 1909. > Part II. | **The birds of New Jersey** | By Witmer Stone, | Curator Academy of Natural Sciences of Philadelphia. | Fellow American Ornithologists' Union.

1 vol. 8vo, pp. 1-432, 1 l. ("Plates"), frontisp., pll. 1-84 (by Audubon, Fuertes, Horsfall and Wilson and from photos.). Trenton.

The ornithological portion of the present report, forming Part II (pp. 11-137 and 409 pt.—419 pt. with pll. 1-84), consists of a descriptive catalogue of the birds of New Jersey. Concise descriptions of each species are followed by notes on distribution, local occurrence, habits, etc. Tables for the determination of species are given under family headings. Part I contains the general annual report and Part III, the notes on fishes, amphibians and reptiles by Henry W. Fowler.

Motley, James; and Dillwyn, Lewis Llewellyn.

1855. Part I. Price 10s. 6d. | **Contributions** | **to the** | **natural history of Labuan,** | and the adjacent | coasts of Borneo. | By | James Motley, of Labuan, | and | Lewis Llewellyn Dillwyn, | F.L.S., etc. | London: | John Van Voorst, 1, Paternoster Row. | July 2nd, 1855. | Woodfall and Kinder, printers, Angel Court, Skinner Street, London. [Cover-title.]

1 vol. royal 8vo, cover-tit., pp. 1-62, 1 l. (advt.), 12 pll. (col.; 5 ornithological by J. Wolf). London. July 2, 1855.

All published of a proposed work on the zoology of Labuan. The present part contains descriptions of mammals, birds and reptiles with colored plates of some of the species. Among the birds, *Copsychus stricklandi* is new. The present copy is from the library of F. D. Godman.

Mudie, Robert. (Martin, W. C. L.)

1854. The | feathered tribes | of | the British Islands. | By | Robert Mudie. | **Fourth edition,** | revised by W. C. L. Martin, Esq. | Late one of the Scientific Officers of the Zoological Society of London. | Illustrated with twenty-eight plates, | containing fifty-two figures of birds, and seven | additional plates of eggs. | In two volumes, Vol. I [II]. | London: | Henry G. Bohn, York Street, Covent Garden. MDCCCLIV.

2 vols. cap 8vo. Vol. I, illum. tit., pp. I-XXIV, 1 l. (list of pll.), pp. 1-422, 10 pll. (col.), vignette (on illum. tit.), pll. 1-4 (eggs: col.), 14 text-figs. Vol. II, illum. tit., tit., pp. 1-440, 9 pll. (col.), vignette (on illum. tit.), pll. 5-7 (eggs; col.), 5 text-figs. London.

A popular account of the habits of British birds, illustrated with colored figures of some of the species. The author's "twenty-eight plates" include text-figures (uncol.) and exclude frontispieces and the title-page vignettes. The first edition was published in 1834; a fourth, in 1853. The illuminated title-pages in the present edition bear the date, 1853; the full title-pages, 1854, as transcribed.

Muirhead, George.

1889-95. The | birds of Berwickshire | with remarks on their local distribution | migration, and habits, and also on the | folk-lore, proverbs, popular rhymes | and sayings connected with them | by | George Muirhead, F.R.S.E., F.Z.S. | Member [etc., 2 lines.]. | In two volumes | [Vignette.] | [Quot., 2 lines.]. | Vol. I [II]. | Edinburgh: David Douglas | 1889 [1895 | (All rights reserved.)].

2 vols. post 8vo. Vol. I, pp. I-XXVI, 1-334, 4 pll., map (col.), 76 text-figs. Vol. II, pp. I-XII, 1-390, 8 pll. (2 charts, 1 col.), 84 text-figs. Edinburgh.

A popular account of the birds of Berwickshire, Scotland.

Mullens, William Herbert; and Swann, Harry Kirke.

1916-17. A bibliography | of | British ornithology | from the earliest times | to the end of 1912 | including | biographical accounts of the principal writers | and bibliographies of their published works | by | W. H. Mullens, M.A., LL.M., F.L.S., M.B.O.U. | and | H. Kirke Swann | [Quot., 4 lines.]. | Macmillan and Co., Limited | St. Martin's Street, London | 1917.

1 vol. 8vo, pp. I-XX, 1-691 (675-691 on one side of paper only). London.

An exceedingly useful and important work containing an enormous amount of information. Only those authors are included who have published separate works on British ornithology, and short notes by these are excluded. The work was published in six parts, issued as follows. Part I, pp. 1-112, June 20, 1916;

II, pp. 113-240, July 25, 1916; III, pp. 241-?, Sept. 19, 1916; IV, pp. ?-
496, Dec. 4, 1916; V, pp. 497-?, Febr. 2, 1917; VI, ?-691, June 29, 1917.
A supplement was issued in 1923 by Swann, under the title of "A Bibliography
of British Ornithology from the Earliest Times; Supplement; A Chronological
List of British Birds" (q.v.). The dates, but not the extent, of the various parts
of the present title are given on the reverse of the title-page. I have secured
the contents of a few parts from the Auk and the Zoological Record.

Mullens, William Herbert; Swann, Harry Kirke; and Jourdain, Francis
Charles Robert.

1919-1920.   A | geographical bibliography | of | British ornithology |
from the earliest times | to the end of 1918 | arranged under
counties | being a record of printed books, published articles, |
notes and records relating to local avifauna | By | W. H. Mullens,
M.A., LLM., F.L.S., M.B.O.U., | H. Kirke Swann, F.Z.S.,
M.B.O.U., and | Rev. F. C. R. Jourdain, M.A., M.B.O.U. |
[*Quot., 6 lines.*]. | Witherby & Co. | 326, High Holborn, London |
1920.

1 vol. 8vo, pp. I-VIII, 1-558. London.

The present volume catalogues "all separate works, articles or notes in periodicals, dealing with local faunas" of British ornithology. The work was issued
in six parts as follows. Part I, pp. 1-96, Nov. 7, 1919; II, pp. 97-192, Jan. 5,
1920; III, pp. 193-288, March 25, 1920; IV, pp. 289-384, May 27, 1920; V,
pp. 385-480, July 1, 1920; VI, pp. 481-558, Sept. 1, 1920. The dates are given
on the reverse of the title-page; the extent of these parts I have ascertained
from the Auk.

Müller, Adolf; and Müller, Karl.

1897.   > Thiere der Heimath. | Deutschlands Säugethiere und
Vögel, | geschildert | von | Adolf und Karl Müller. | Mit Original-
Illustrationen in Farbendruck nach Zeichnungen und Aquarellen |
von | C. F. Deiker und Adolf Müller. | **Zweites Buch.** | Wesen
und Wandel der Vögel. | **Dritte Auflage.** | Cassel 1897. | Verlag
von Theodor Fischer. | Alleinvertrieb: Emil Strauss in Bonn.

1 vol. medium 4to, 4 pr. ll. (tit. and conts.), pp. 1-365, 24 pll. (col.;
by C. F. Deiker and Adolf Müller), 5 text-figs. Cassel.

A popular work on the birds and mammals of Germany, of which the second volume, only, is at hand, containing the birds. Vol. I (not collated) contains the
mammals. The first edition of the work was issued in 1882-3.

Müller, Johannes.

1847.   Über | die bisher unbekannten | typischen Verschiedenheiten
der | Stimmorgane der Passerinen. | Von | J. Müller. | Gelesen
in der Königl. Akademie der Wissenschaften zu Berlin am 26. Juni
1845 | und 14. Mai 1846. | Mit 6 Kupfertafeln. | Berlin. | Ge-

druckt in der Druckerei der Königlichen Akademie der Wissenschaften. | 1847. | [In Commission bei F. Dümmler. (*covered by pasted slip, lettered,-*] Ferd. Dümmler's Buchhandlung.

1 vol. foliopost 4to, tit., pp. 1-71+1, 1 l., pll. I-VI. Berlin.

A separately pages reprint of Müller's paper on the syrinx of the Passeres, first published in the Abhandl. k. Akad. Wiss. Berlin, 1845, Phys, Kl., pp. 321-392 and 405-406 (1845-46). The copy is bound in one volume with Burmeister's "Anatomie der Coracina scutata" and two papers on mammalia. The volume bears the autograph of P. L. Sclater.

Müller, Karl.

1897. See Müller Adolph; and Müller, **Thiere der Heimath.**

Mulsant, Etienne; Verreaux, Jules; and Verreaux, Édouard.

1866? Essai | d'une | classification méthodique | des | trochilidés | ou | oiseaux-mouches, | par | E. Mulsant, | Sous-Bibliothécaire de la ville de Lyon [*etc.*, *2 lines.*], | et | Jules Verreaux, | Attaché au Muséum d'histoire naturelle de Paris, | Edouard Verreaux, | Marchand-naturaliste. | Paris, | F. Savy, Libraire,   Deyrolle, | rue Hautefeuille, 24 rue de la Monnaie, 19, | Verreaux, place Royale, 9.

1 vol. royal 8vo, pp. 1-98. Paris.

A treatise on the classification of the hummingbirds, with descriptions and tables of the sugbenera and higher groups, and lists of the species. The work was originally published in the Mémoires de la Société Impériale des Sciences Naturelles de Cherbourg, XII, 1866, pp. 149-242. It was issued as preliminary to a larger work which appeared in 1873-78 as the "Histoire Naturelle des Oiseaux-Mouches ou Colibris" (q.v.).

Mulsant, Etienne.

1868. Lettres à Julie | sur | l'ornithologie | par | E. Mulsant | sous-bibliothécaire de la ville de Lyon [*etc.*, *5 lines.*]. | Illustrées par Édouard Traviès | de | magnifiques dessins d'après nature, coloriés avec le plus grand soin | Paris | Ancienne Maison Morizot | A. Laplace, Libraire-Éditeur | 3, Rue Séguier, 3 | Tous droits resérvés.

1 vol. superroyal 8vo, pp. I-XII, 1-367+1, 16 pll. (col.; by Traviès). Paris.

A series of fifty-two 'letters' containing an elementary introduction to the study of birds.

Mulsant, Etienne; and Verreaux, Édouard.

1873-78. Histoire naturelle | des | oiseaux-mouches | ou | colibris | constituant la famille des Trochilidés | par | E. Mulsant | Correspondant de l'Institut, | Conservateur de la Bibliothèque de la ville de Lyon, | etc., etc., etc. | et feu | Édouard Verreaux | Tome premier [-quatrième] | Lyon [Lyon-Genève-Bale (*Vols. II and III.*); Paris (*Vol. IV.*)] | Au Bureau de la Société Linnéenne [H. Georg, Libraire-Éditeur (*Vols. II and III.*); Deyrolle, Naturaliste (*Vol. IV.*)] | 2, Place Sathonay [*No address* (*Vols. II and III.*); 19, rue de la Monnaie (*Vol. IV.*)] | et chez tous les libraires et marchands naturalistes de France et de l'étranger [*Vols. I and IV, only.*] | 1874 [1876; 1877; 1877].

4 vols. royal 4to. Vol. I, 3 pr. ll. (half-tit., tit. and ded.), pp. I-V+1 (pref.), 1-343, 18 pll. (col.; by Bevalet). Vol. II, 3 pr. ll., pp. 1-327, 23 pll. (col.). Vol. III, 3 pr. ll., pp. I-III+1 (emend. to Vol. II), 1-303, 16 pll. (col.). Vol. IV, 3 pr. ll., pp. 1-308, 7 pll. (col.). Lyons Geneva, Basel and Paris.

A detailed monograph of the hummingbirds. The work was issued in 16 livraisons as follows. Vol. I, livr. 1, 1873; livr. 2, 1873 (Coues) or 1874 (Ibis); livrs. 3-4, 1874. Vol. II: livrs. 1-2, 1875; livrs. 3-4, 1876. Vol. III: livrs. 1-2, 1876; livrs. 3-4, 1877. Vol. IV: livrs. 1-2, 1877; livrs. 3-4, 1878. The extent of each livraison is indeterminate from the present copy but the Zoologica lrecord lists the various species figured on the plates as they appeared, from which it is possible to get the approximate dates of some of the illustrations. However, it is apparent that plates and text were not synchronous. For example, *Doleromia fallax* is discussed in Vol. I where it is accompanied (in the bound volume) by the plate of this species, but the Zoological Record notes the publication of the figure of this species in Vol. III, Pts. 3-4. A Supplement (q.v.) was published in 1879.

Mulsant, Etienne; and Verreaux, Édouard.

1879. Histoire naturelle | des | oiseaux-mouches | ou | colibris | constituant la famille des Trochilidés | par | E. Mulsant | Correspondant [*etc., 3 lines.*] | et feu | Édouard Verreaux | [*Vignette (col.*).] | **Supplement** | Lyon - Genève - Bale | H. Georg, Libraire-Éditeur | 1877. [*Tit. on original cover.*].

1 vol. royal 4to, (cover-tit.), pp. 1-2, 1 l. (blank), 56 pll. (col.; by Bevalet and Mesplis). Lyons, Geneva and Basel.

A series of plates intended to supplement those in the "Histoire Naturelle des Oiseaux-Mouches ou Colibris," 1873-78 (q.v.). The letterpress consists of a list of the plates (incomplete), with references to the volume and page where each is to be inserted in the general work. Although the cover-title is dated 1877, the supplement appears not to have been issued until 1879, according to the Zoological Record. The addition of these plates to the general work has led, apparently, to the citation of a varying number of plates under the earlier dates. According to a recent advertisement, in which a copy in original covers is offered for sale, the present section of the entire work consists of 7 supplements in 5 parts.

Munn, Philip Winchester.

1905. See Kelsall, John Edward; and Munn, **The Birds of Hampshire and the Isle of Wight.**

Murphy, Robert Cushman.

1925. Bird Islands of Peru | The Record of a Sojourn on the West Coast | By | Robert Cushman Murphy | Assistant Director of the American Museum of Natural History [*etc., 5 lines.*]. | Illustrated from Photographs | by the Author | G. P. Putnam's Sons | New York & London | The Knickerbocker Press | 1925.

1 vol. royal 8vo, pp. I-XX, 1-362, 32 pll. (photographic), 8 text-figs. New York and London.

A narrative and descriptive account of the author's investigations on the western coast of Peru, South America, in 1919-20, with reference to the "oceanic conditions . . . responsible for the abundance of life in Peruvian waters, as well as the interrelationships and distribution of this life." A considerable part of the text and many of the illustrations relate to birds, especially to the important guano producing species of the region.

Murray, James A.

1888-90. The | **avifauna of British India** | and its dependencies. | A systematic account, with descriptions of all the known | species of birds inhabiting British India, | observations on their habits, nidification, &c., | tables of their geographical | distribution in Persia, Beloochistan, | Afghanistan, Sind, Punjab, N. W. provinces, | and the peninsula of India generally, | with | woodcuts, lithographs, and coloured illustrations. | By | James A. Murray, F.S.A.L. | Mem. Nat. Hist. Soc. [*etc., 5 lines; 6 lines (Vol. II.)*]. | [*Vignette.*] | Volume I [II]. | London:-Trübner & Co., Ludgate Hill. | Bombay:-Education Society's Press, Byculla. | 1888 [1890].

2 vols. 4to (6½x9½). Vol. I, tit., pp. I-VI (conts.), 3 ll. (list of illustrs., errata and pref.), pp. I-XXIV (intr.), 1-325, 1 insert-slip, 22 pll. (12 col.; 1 fold.), 38 text-figs. Vol. II, tit., pp. I-VII+1 (pref. and list of illustrs.), I-XVII+1 (conts.), 1-838, 1-42 (distribution table), 2 ll. (addenda, Vol. I), 2 insert-slips (errata), 15 pll. (7 col.), 56 text-figs. London and Bombay.

Title sufficiently explanatory. The work appears to have been issued in 7 parts as follows Vol. I, Pt. I, pp. 1-106, 1887; II, pp. 107-180, 1888 (?); III, pp. 181-325, 1888 Vol. II: Pt. I, pp. 1-128, 1889 (?); II, pp. 129-294, 1889 (?); III, pp. 295-496. 1889; IV, pp. 497-838 and 2 ll. (addenda, Vol. I), 1890. The distribution table at the end of Vol. II probably appeared with Pt. IV; likewise the introductory matter of the second volume. The introductory pages of Vol. I appeared with Pt. III of that volume. The separation of the various parts is marked by differences in the size of paper, signatures with but a single leaf, insertion of errata-slips, etc.; the Zoological Record defines the limits of Vol. II, Pt. IV and gives the date of commencement of the work as 1887. The work is cited but little.

Murray, James A.

1890. The | avifauna of the island | of | Ceylon. | A systematic account, | with descriptions of all the known | species of birds inhabiting the island, also | observations on their habits, nidification, &c., | and tables of their geographical | distribution throughout India. | By | James A. Murray, F.S.A.L., | Mem. of the Natural Hist. and Anthrop. Soc. of Bombay [*etc.*, *9 lines.*] | [*Vignette.*] | London:-Kegan, Paul, Trench, Trübner & Co | Bombay:-Education Society's Press, Byculla. | 1890.

1 vol. 4to (6½x9½), 2 pr. ll. (tit. and pref.), pp. I-XXXIV (introd. and table of conts.), 1 l. (list of illustrs.), pp. 1-382, 4 pll. (2 col.), 39 text-figs. London and Bombay.

A volume composed of extracts from the author's "The Avifauna of British India," 1888-90 (q.v.). The text relating to the species of Indian birds which are found in Ceylon is copied verbatim, the introduction is reprinted, and most of the illustrations are the same as in the larger work.

Museu Paulista. (Ihering, Hermann von; Ihering, Rodolpho von.)

1907. Catalogos | da | Fauna Brazileira | editados pelo | Museu Paulista | S. Paulo - Brazil | Vol. I | As aves do Brazil. | Pelo | Prof. Dr. Hermann von Ihering | Director do Museu Paulista | e | Rodolpho von Ihering | Custos do Museu Paulista | [*Vignette*.]. > As Aves do Brazil [*etc.*] . . . Sao Paulo | Typographia do Diario Official | 1907.

1 vol. 6mo (6¼x9, trimmed), 3 pr. ll., pp. I-XXXVIII, 3-485, maps I-II. Sao Paulo.

An annotated list of the birds of Brazil, with notes on distribution and on the specimens of each species preserved in the Museu Paulista. A new genus and several new species and subspecies are described. The work forms Vol. I of a series of which several other volumes have since been issued, none of which is ornithological.

Myers, Harriet Williams.

1922. Western birds | by | Harriet Williams Myers | Author of "The Birds' Convention" | Vice-President of | "The California Audubon Society" | New York | The Macmillan Company | 1922 | All rights reserved.

1 vol. demy 8vo, pp. I-XII, 1-391, frontisp., 44 pll. (on 22 ll.). New York.

A popular account of the habits of some of the birds of the western coast of the
United States. The scheme adopted for showing the classification of the species is unsatisfactory, and the terms are frequently misspelled, but the general
text is clearly written and contains a variety of interesting notes.

Nachtrieb, Henry F. (Hatch, P. L.)

1892. The Geological and Natural History Survey of | Minnesota. |
First report | of the | **State Zoölogist,** | accompanied with | **notes
on the birds of Minnesota,** By Dr. P. L. Hatch. | Henry F. Nach-
trieb, State Zoölogist. | June, 1892. | Minneapolis: | Harrison &
Smith, Printers. | 1892.

1 vol. 8vo, pp. 1-9+1, 1-487. Minneapolis.

All of the volume, except the first 9 pp., is occupied by the "Notes on the Birds
of Minnesota, with Specific Characters. By P. L. Hatch, M.D." Included in
the latter is "A List of the Principal Popular Synonyms of the Birds of Minnesota" and an index, both of which were prepared by Nachtrieb. The present
copy is from the library of D. G. Elliot.

Nansen, Fridtjof. (Collett, Robert.)

1899. > **The Norwegian** | **North** | **Polar Expedition** | 1893-1896 |
Scientific results | edited by | Fridtjof Nansen | IV. | **An account of
the birds** | by | Robert Collett | and | Fridtjof Nansen | Published
by the Fridtjof Nansen Fund | for the Advancement of Science |

Christiana	London,	Leipzig	
Jacob Dybwad	New York, Bombay	F. A. Brockhaus	1899.
	Longmans, Green, and Co.		

1 vol. medium 4to, tit., pp. 1-53+1, 2 pll. (1 col.). London.

The ornithological observations of the expedition forming Pt. IV of the complete
work. The text is divided into four sections, —The Siberian Coast, The First
Summer in the Ice, The Sledge-journey and Franz Josef Land, and The Last
Two Summers in the Ice.

Nash, C. W.

1900. **Check list** | **of the** | **Birds of Ontario** | and | catalogue of
birds in the biological section | of the | museum. | Department of
Education | Toronto. | Toronto: | Warwick Bro's & Rutter,
Printers, Etc., 68 and 70 Front St. West. | 1900.

1 vol. 8vo, pp. 1-58. Toronto.

An annotated list of species, giving the local status of each and noting those
which are desiderata for the Museum of the Department of Education. A second list (q.v.) was published in 1905.

Nash, C. W.

1905. **Check list** | **of the** | **Vertebrates of Ontario** and Catalogue of |
Specimens in the Biological Section | of the Provincial Museum |

Birds | Department of Education | Toronto | [*Blazon.*] | Toronto | Printed and Published by L. K. Cameron, Printer to the King's Most Excellent Majesty | 1905.

1 vol. royal 8vo, pp. 1-82, (orig. wrapper), 20 text-figs. Toronto. 1905 (post Nov. 15).

An annotated list, giving the local status of each species and some diagnostic peculiarities of the families and orders. An asterisk denotes the species which are desiderata for the Provincial Museum. No reference is made to the author's earlier "Check List of the Birds of Ontario," 1900 (q.v.).

Nash, Joseph.

1824. A | practical treatise | on | British song birds; | in which is given | every information relative to their | Natural History, Incubation, &c. | together with | the method of rearing and managing both | old and young birds. | By Joseph Nash. | Illustrated with Engravings. | London: | Printed for Sherwood, Jones, and Co. | Paternoster-Row; | Sold by Joseph Nash, 39, Great Windmill-Street, | Haymarket. | 1824.

1 vol. 12mo, pp. I-VI, 1 l., pp. 1-102, 6 ll. (advt.), 8 pll. (col.). London.

A book for bird-fanciers, dealing with the rearing of cage-birds. Several later editions were published (Cf. Nash, British Song Birds, 1872.). The preface is dated May 1, 1824.

Nash, Joseph.

1872. British song birds: | A Practical Treatise | on their | habits, nidification, and incubation; | the mode of rearing young birds, | and their treatment in sickness and in health. | By Joseph Nash. | [*Vignette.*] | With Illustrations on Steel by Newton Fielding. | London: William Tegg. | 1872.

1 vol. 12mo, pp. 1-96, 8 pll. (col.), 16 text-figs. London.

A treatise on the rearing of cage-birds. First published in 1824 under the title, "A Practical Treatise on British Song Birds," etc. (q.v.). The present edition is essentially the same as the original; the text is slightly altered in places and the plates are poorly-colored copies.

Naumann, Johann Andreas. (Naumann, Johann Friedrich.)

1795-1817. Naturgeschichte | der | Land- und Wasser-Vögel | des nördlichen | Deutschlands und angränzender Länder, | nach eignen | Erfahrungen entworfen, und nach dem Leben | gezeichnet | von | Johann Andreas Naumann. | [Erster (*Tit. of Vol. I missing.*)] Zweiter [Dritter; (Vierter - *Tit. of Vol. IV missing.*)] Band. | Mit Kupfern. | Köthen, [1797 (*Vol. I.*)] 1799 [1802; (1803 - *Vol. IV.*)]. | Auf Kosten des Verfassers, | und in Kommission bei J. A. Aue. [*No full title for "Nachträge."*].

> Naturgeschichte | der | Land- und Wasser-Vögel | des nörd-
lichen | Deutschlands und angränzender Länder, | nach eignen |
Erfahrungen entworfen, und nach dem Leben | gezeichnet | von |
Johann Andreas Naumann. | Ersten [Erster (*Vol. I, Pt. 6.*);
Zweiter; Dritter; Vierter] Bandes [Band (*Vol. I, Pt. 6; Vols. II,
III and IV, Pts. 1, 3 and 4.*); Band. | (*Vol. IV, Pt. 2.*)] erstes
[(*Vols. I and IV.*); erster (*sic, Vols. II and III.*); zweites (*Vols.
I and III.*); zweiter (*sic. Vol. II.*); | Zweites (*Vol. IV.*); drittes
(*Vols. I, III and IV.*); viertes (*Vols. I and IV.*); vierter (*sic,
Vol. III.*); fünftes (*Vol. I.*); fünfter (*sic, Vol. III.*); sechstes
(*Vol. III.*); siebentes (*Vol. III.*); achtes (*Vol. III.*); (*No subtit.
for Vol. III, Pt.* 9¹.)] Heft. [*No period* (*Vol. IV, Pt. 2.*).] |
Mit 8 Kupfertafeln. | Köthen, 1796² [(*Vol. I, Pts. 1-3.*); 1797
(*Vol. I, Pts. 4-6.*); 1798 (*Vol. II, Pt. 1.*); 1799 (*Vol. II, Pt. 2;
Vol. III, Pts. 1 and 2.*); 1800 (*Vol. III, Pts. 3-5.*); 1801 (*Vol.
III, Pts. 6 and 7*); 1802 (*Vol. III, Pt. 8; Vol. IV, Pt. 1.*); 1803
(*Vol. IV, Pts. 2-4.*)]. | Auf Kosten des Verfassers, | und in Kom-
mission bei J. A. Aue.

> Naturgeschichte [*etc., 9 lines.*] | Johann Andreas Naumann, |
und | Friedrich Naumann, | der Naturforschenden Gesellschaft in
Halle [*etc., 2 lines.* (*Pts. 1 and 2.*); *3 lines.* (*Pt. 3.*); *4 lines.* (*Pts.
4-6.*); *4 lines, mut. mut.* (Pts. 7 and 8.)]. | Nachtrag. [*Period
omitted* (*Pts. 7 and 8.*).] | Erstes [Zweites - Achtes] Heft. [*Period
omitted* (*Pts. 7 and 8.*).] | Mit (mit (*Pts. 7 and 8.*)] 8 Kupfertafeln. |
Köthen, 1804 [1805 (*Pt. 2.*); 1808 (*Pt. 3.*); 1811 (*Pts. 4-6.*); Auf
Kosten der Verfasser (*Pts. 7 and 8.*)]. | Auf Kosten des Verfassers,
[der Verfasser. (*Pts. 4-6.*); Köthen, 1817³. (*Pts. 7 and 8.*)] | und
in Kommission bei J. A. Aue. [und in Kommission der Aueschen
Buchhandlung. (*Pts. 2 and 3.*); *line omitted* (*Pts. 4-8.*).].

> Johann Andreas Naumann's | ausführliche | Beschreibung |
aller | Wald- Feld- und Wasser-Vögel, | welche sich | in den An-
haltischen Fürstenthümern | und | einigen umliegenden Gegenden |
aufhalten und durchziehen. | Ersten [Erster] Band fünftes [sechs-
tes] Heft. | Mit 8 Kupfertafeln. | Köthen, 1797. | Auf Kosten des

¹Leverkühn, Biographisches über die drei Naumanns und Bibliographisches über ihre Werke, 1904 On p. 63, the author concludes that no subtitle for this part ever appeared.

²Leverkühn, l.c., pp. 61 and 62, records the date of 1795 as occurring on the original title-pages of Pts. 1 and 2 of Vol. I, published in Leipzig "in Kommission bei Friedrich Osterloh." With the change in publishers which occurred with Pt. 3, new title-pages were issued for the preceding two parts to agree with the third part, and the remainder followed in accordance. The original title-pages (or, more properly, subtitle-pages) of Pts. 1 and 2 are not preserved with this copy.

³Leverkühn, l.c. p. 65, gives 1811 as the date on the title-page of this part. This may be a typo-graphical error; the date is very clearly 1817 in both copies of this part at hand (Cf. reissue, same date.).

Verfassers, | und in Kommission bei J. A. Aue. [*"Original"*
subtitles.][1].
4 vols. and 8 suppls. in 9 vols., demy 8vo; (plates in demy folio, fold.
and inserted in text). Vol. **I**, (tit. missing), frontisp. (portr.):
Pt. **1**, subtit., 2 ll. (pref.), pp. 1-54, pll. I-VIII (col.); Pt. **2**, subtit.
(=pp. 55-56), pp. 57-78, pll. IX-XVI (col.); Pt. **3**, subtit. (=pp.
79-80), pp. 81-111+1, pll. XVII-XXIV (col.); Pt. **4**, subtit.
(=pp. 113-114), pp. 115-154, 2 ll. (blank), pll. XXV-XXXII
(col.); Pt. **5**, subtit. (=pp. 155-156), orig. subtit. (extra), pp.
157-196, pll. XXXIII-XL (col.); Pt. **6**, subtit., orig. subtit. (extra),
pp. 197-247, 7 pp. (unnum.,- 'Register' and errata), pll. XLI-
XLVIII (col.). Vol. **II**, tit., frontisp. (portr.): Pt. **1**, subtit., 1 l.
(pref.), pp. 1-57+1, pll. I-VIII (col.); Pt. **2**, subtit., pp. 65-106,
1 l. ('Register'), pll. IX-XV and XVII (=XVI, corrected in text)
(col.). Vol. **III**, tit., frontisp. (portr.): Pt. **1**, subtit. (=pp. 1-2),
1 l. (pref.,=pp. 3-4), pp. 5-39+1, pll. I-VIII (col.); Pt. **2**, subtit.
(=pp. 41-42), pp. 43-72, pll. IX-XVI (col.); Pt. **3**, subtit., pp. 72
(*bis*) - 115, 1 l. (blank), pll. XVII-XXIIII (col.); Pt. **4**, subtit.,
pp. 120-169, pll. XXV-XXXII (col.); Pt. **5**, subtit., pp. 173-218,
pll. XXXIII-XXXX (col.); Pt. **6**, subtit., 1 l. ('Nachricht'), pp.
218-298, pll. XLI-XLVIII (col.); Pt. **7**, subtit., pp. 299-350, 1 l.
(advt.), pll. XLVIIII-LVI (col.; originally numbered XLVIII-LV,
but altered by hand to present figures); Pt. **8**, subtit., pp. 353-
401+1, pll. LVII-LXIV (col.; LXII altered by hand from LXI);
(Pt. **9**, no subtit., pp. 403-480, pll. LXV—LXXII,—col.; entire part
missing from this copy). Vol. **IV** (tit. missing), (frontisp. missing):
Pt. **1**, subtit., pp. 1-94, pll. I-VIII (col.); Pt. **2**, subtit., pp. 95-
155+1, (pll. IX-XVI missing,—replaced by 8vo plates of reissue);
Pt. **3**, subtit., pp. 161-220, (pll. XVII-XXIV missing,—replaced by
8vo pll.); Pt. **4**, pp. 223-280, 1 l. ('Nachricht'), (pll. XXV-XXXII
missing,—replaced by 8vo pll.). **Supplement,** (no general title-p.
issued): Pt. **1**, subtit. (=pp. 1-2), pp. 3-56, (pll. I-VIII missing,—
replaced by 8vo pll.); Pt. **2**, subtit., pp. 57-110, (pll. IX-XVI
missing,—replaced by 8vo pll.); Pt. **3**, subtit., pp. 3-72, (pll. XVII-
XXIIII missing,—replaced by 9 8vo pll., pl. XX being replaced by
XX A and XX B); Pt. **4**, subtit., pp. 177-237+1, pll. XXV-XXXII
(col.; 8vo; folio pll. not issued); Pt. **5**, subtit. (=pp. 239-240),

---

[1]Leverkühn, l.c., p. 61, records similar subtitles for all parts of Vol. I and a similar title for the complete volume, but adds that there is no copy of the work which is supplied with a full set of originals and substitutes. Since the region embraced by the "Ausführliche Beschreibung" (Anhaltischen Fürstenthümern) is less extensive than that included in the "Naturgeschichte" (Nördlichen Deutschlands und angränzender Länder), the former is assumed to constitute the original title of the work as first projected while the latter (adopted for the entire work) represents the final title.

pp. 241-286, pll. XXXIII-XL (col.; 8vo; folio pll. not issued; the 'L' of XL is reversed); Pt. **6,** subtit. (=pp. 287-288), pp. 289-342, pll. XLI-XLVIII (col.; 8vo; folio pll. not issued); Pt. **7,** subtit. (=pp. 343-344), pp. 345-406, pll. XLIX-LVI (col.; 8vo; folio pll. not issued); Pt. **8,** subtit. (=pp. 407-408), pp. 409-462, pll. LVII-LXIV (col.; 8vo; folio pll. not issued). Leipzig and Cöthen.

A monumental work on the birds of northern Germany and surrounding country. Begun as a series of descriptions of the birds of the Principalities of Anhalt (now part of Thuringia), Vol. I was issued under the title of "Johann Andreas Naumann's ausfürliche Beschreibung aller Wald- Feld- und Wasser-Vögel," etc. (Cf. above transcription and footnote 4.). Pts. 1 and 2 of this volume were published in Leipzig in 1795 in commission with Friedrich Osterloh. With Pt. 3, the publisher was changed to J. A. Aue and new subtitle-pages were issued for the first two parts to agree with the new arrangement; these new subtitle-pages were also inscribed with the title of "Johann Andreas Naumann's ausführliche Beschreibung," etc., as were the subtitle-pages of Pts. 3-6 of Vol. I and the title-page for the completed volume. With the inception of Vol. II (perhaps beforehand) it apparently was determined to enlarge the scope of the work so as to include the birds of all of northern Germany and outlying regions, and the title was altered, in accordance with this plan, to "Naturgeschichte der Land- und Wasser-Vögel des nördlichen Deutschlands und angränzender Länder." For the sake of uniformity, a new title-page and new subtitle-pages were printed for Vol. I and its six parts, containing the new title, and in this form the work was carried to completion. On account of the various changes just mentioned, two styles of title-page and three of subtitle-page are in existence; the present copy contains one of title and two of subtitle as transcribed above. The final title for the work, however, is "Naturgeschichte der Land- und Wasser-Vögel."

With the early change in publisher, the reissued title-pages for Pts. 1 and 2 were inscribed with the date of the reissue, —the date of Pt. 3, —1796. J. F. Naumann, in the preface (p. VIII) to Vol. I of his "Naturgeschichte der Vögel Deutschlands," 1822-60 (q.v.), gives the inclusive dates of the present work as 1796-1817, but there is no reason to doubt that the first two parts actually appeared in 1795 at Leipzig, as dated on the original subtitle-pages of these parts.

Each part of the work contained 8 plates, drawn and (beginning with pl. XVI of Vol. 1, Pt. 1) engraved by the author's son, Johann Friedrich Naumann (junior author of the supplementary parts). From Pt. 1 of Vol. I to Pt. 3 of the Supplement, the plates were in demy folio (largest example at hand, 10¼x 14¼, trimmed); the remainder were in 8vo, —at least no folio plates are known beyond this point. Somewhere about the date of the first Supplement (1804), the artist commenced the preparation of a series of 8vo plates to take the place of the earlier folio issues, revising the composition and details of every plate and keeping only the original numbers of the plates and figures (with certain corrections) and dividing pl. XX of Suppl., Pt. 3, into two plates, XXA and XXB. This issue of 8vo plates constitutes an insoluble mystery. Various speculations have been advanced regarding the reasons for, and methods of, publication and regarding the consequent disappearance of all but a very limited number of the original folio impressions.

The earliest folio plates undoubtedly were somewhat crude, compared with the later ones or with the 8vo plates, and it is conceivable that the artist may have wished to destroy these earlier examples of his handiwork and to replace them by the later, more perfect drawings, but this motive is by no means proven nor is the method clear by means of which such an object could have been accomplished. There is no printed record of any such transaction requested or fulfilled, and the artist-author later kept silent in the face of published request for information on the early work.

Only three copies of the work are known which have the full number (192) of folio plates and at least one of these copies has been completed from an outside source; nine copies are known which are more or less complete (including the present set, three copies are known in a very fragmentary form,—possibly more which are unrecorded. It seems incredible that the work could have been carried to completion with only fifteen subscribers or with double that number, assuming that half of the original copies have been destroyed; the author was not rich and was not subsidized and he advertised his work for sale at the low price of "1 thl. 16 gr." per part (Vol. III, Pt. 7, advt. leaf). The present set, like others of the imperfect copies, has most of the plates in folio and the remainder in 8vo. Specimens are more common with all of the plates in 8vo; an example of this kind is catalogued below (q.v.).

There are two issues of pl. XXXI of Vol. I, Pt. 4. In one of these the upper figure is looking forward to the left; in the other its body is directed to the right but its head is turned backwards to the left, and there are other differences. The present copy is of the former type.

The preface to Vol. III, Pt. 1 is dated, March 1789. In Suppl., Pt. 4, 1811 (which contains the description of the new genus *Acrocephalus*, p. 199) there is on p. 191 a reference to an occurrence "am 20. Mai dieses Jahres" which may be of assistance in fixing the date of this part. Leverkühn, l.c. (Cf. footn. 1.) gives a very thorough account of the Naumanns and their ornithological works including voluminous details regarding the present title. For further accounts see Lindner, Mitth. ornith. Ver. Wien., 18, pp. 109-111 and 125-128, 1894; Ornith. Monatsb., 21, pp. 47-49 and 52, 1913: Schiller, Ornith. Monatsb., 21, p. 67, 1913.

To recapitulate, the present copy has all of the letterpress except that of Vol. III, Pt. 9, and this gap is filled by the text of the 8vo edition which is identical. The full title-pages of Vols. I and IV, missing here, are also supplied in the 8vo edition. The frontispiece of Vol. IV is missing from both sets. Of the folio plates there are 136 present, including all belonging to Vol. I; Vol. II; Vol. III, Pts. 1-8; and Vol. IV, Pt. 1 (lacking those of Vol. III, Pt. 9; Vol. IV, Pts. 2-4; and Suppl., Pts. 1-3). The 8vo plates (the only ones issued) for Suppl., Pts. 4-8, are all present. Vol. IV, Pts. 2-4 and Suppl., Pts. 1-3 are supplied with 8vo plates instead of the missing folio examples. There are no plates in this set for Vol. III, Pt. 9, but the 8vo plates for that number are in the 8vo set (q.v.).

Naumann, Johann Andreas. (Naumann, Johann Friedrich.)

1795-1817. Naturgeschichte | der | Land- und Wasser-Vögel [*etc.*, *as in original edition collated above, except that full titles to Vols.*

*I and IV are present also, while Supplement Pts. 7 and 8 are missing;
no "original" titles or subtitles for Vol. I in this set.*].

4 vols. and 6 (should be 8) suppls. in 4 vols., demy 8vo; (all plates in
demy 8vo, in separate vol.). Collation otherwise the same as in
first edition except in the degree of completeness of the text and
plates and some alterations in the numbering of the plates, as
follows. Vol. I, title present, frontisp. missing, no 'original' title or
subtitles; Pt. 4, no blank leaves. Vol. II, frontisp. missing. Vol. III,
frontisp. missing; Pt. 3, no blank leaf; Pt. 9 present, complete.
Vol. IV, title present, frontisp. missing. Supplement, Pts. 7 and 8
missing. Atlas of 216 plates in 8vo (col.) (should be 233; pll.
XLIX-LXIV of Suppl., Pts. 7 and 8, missing); all plates correctly
numbered and most of them marked with the volume-number
except the following pll. of Vol. I,—I-VIII, XXXIII, XLIII,
XLIV, XLVI and XLVIII; Suppl., Pt. 3, pll. XX A and XX B
replace pl. XX of the folio series (missing from the set of folio
plates collated above). Leipzig and Cöthen.

The text of the present edition is identical with that which accompanied the folio
plates (collated above), even to the inclusion of the corrigenda which often
have no application here since the required alterations were made in the new
plates. It is evidently the original text, intact. All of the plates, however, are
in 8vo. Those of Suppl., Pts. 4-6 (7 and 8 missing) are the same as in the earlier
issue since no folio plates were published for these parts, but the rest are new.[1]
They are of entirely new designs and are related to the original folio plates
only by reason of representing the same species and by carrying the same numbers for plates and figures (with corrections as necessary and with the substitution of two plates for one, as mentioned in the collation).

These 8vo plates are unquestionably of later issue than the folio plates of
corresponding numbers. A few of them are signed with the date of preparation
and in every such case the date is subsequent to the date of publication of the
original issue. The following examples have been noted. Vol. I, Pt. 3, pl.
XVII, dat. 1804; folio dat. 1796. Vol. I, Pt. 4, pl. XXXI, dat. 1804; folio dat.
1797. Vol. I, Pt. 5, pl. XXXIV, dat. 1805; folio dat. 1797. Vol. I, Pt. 6, pll.
XLI, XLII and XLVIII, dat. 1805; folio dat. 1797. Vol. III, Pt. 1, pl. I, dat.
1806; folio dat. 1799. Vol. III, Pt. 4, pl. XXXI, dat. 1807; folio dat. 1800.
Vol. III, Pt. 9, pl. LXVII, dat. 1807; folio dat. 1802-03?. J. F. Naumann himself (Naturg. Vögel Deutschl., 13, p. 454), referring to pl. XLVI (fig. 105) of
Vol. I, Pt. 6, (folio publ. 1797), says that the 8vo plate of the same species appeared "schon c. 10 Jahr später." Exact dates of publication of any of the
8vo plates, except those which belong to Suppl., Pts. 4-8 as original issues,
are unknown.

The present copy lacks Suppl., Pts. 7 and 8, with the included plates. The
gap is filled by the corresponding parts of the original edition (q.v.) which are
identical with those missing here.

---

[1]The plates in Vol. IV, Pts. 2-4 and Suppl., Pts. 1-3 in the original copy collated above belong to
the present edition, being substitutes for the folio plates which are missing from that copy.
They are duplicated in the present copy.

Immediately after the completion of the present book, J. F. Naumann began the preparation of a work which he considered to be a second edition of the present title but which was so rewritten and improved that it should stand as a distinct production. A copy is collated below under J. F. Naumann, Naturgeschichte der Vögel Deutschlands, 1822-60 (q.v.).

Naumann, Johann Friedrich.

1795-1817. See Naumann, Johann Andreas, **Naturgeschichte der Land- und Wasser-Vögel des nördlichen Deutschlands und angränzender Länder.** (Two issues; same date.)

Naumann, Johann Friedrich. (Blasius, J. H.; Baldamus, Eduard; Sturm, Friedrich.)

1822-60. Johann Andreas Naumann's, | mehrerer gelehrten Gesell-schaften Mitgliede, | **Naturgeschichte** | der | **Vögel Deutschlands,** | nach eigenen | Erfahrungen entworfen. | Durchaus | umgearbeitet, systematisch geordnet, sehr vermehrt, vervollständigt, | und mit getreu nach der Natur eigenhändig gezeichneten und gesto- | chenen Abbildungen aller deutschen Vögel, nebst ihren Hauptver- | schiedenheiten, aufs Neue herausgegeben | von | dessen Sohne | Johann Friedrich Naumann, | der naturforschenden Gesellschaft zu Halle [*etc.*, *6 lines.* (*Vols. I-V.*); *7 lines.* (*Vols. VI-IX.*); *7 lines., altered* (*Vols. X-XI.*); *10 lines.* (*Vol. XII*).] | [*Monogram.*] | Erster [-Zwölfter] Theil. [| Zweiten Bandes erste (zweite) Abtheilung. (*Vols. II and III, only.*)] | Mit 48 colorirten und 2 schwarzen Kupfern [30 colorirten und 1 schwarzen Kupfer (*Vol. II.*); 15 *and* 1 (*III.*); 23 *and* 1 (*IV.*); 28 *and* 1 (*V.*); 23 colorirten Kupfern (*VI.*); 27 *and* 1 (*VII.*); 27 col. (*VIII.*); 28 *and* 1 (*IX.*); 31 col. (*X.*); 29 col. (*XI.*); 32 col. (*XII.*)]. | Leipzig: Ernst Fleischer.[1] | 1822 [(*Vols. I and II.*); 1823 (*III.*); 1824 (*IV.*); 1826 (*V.*); 1833 (*VI.*); 1834 (*VII.*); 1836 (*VIII.*); 1838 (*IX.*); 1840 (*X.*); 1842 (*XI.*); 1844 (*XII.*)].

> J. A. Naumann's | Naturgeschichte | der | Vögel Deutschlands. | Herausgegeben | von | dessen Sohne | J. F. Naumann. | Dreizehnter Theil: | Nachträge, | Zusätze und Verbesserungen. | 13r Theil. 1.

> J. A. Naumann's | Naturgeschichte | der | Vögel Deutschlands. | Fortsetzung der Nachträge, Zusätze | und Verbesserungen | von | Dr. J. H. Blasius, Dr. Ed. Baldamus | und Dr. Fr. Sturm. |

---

[1]The original Vol. I bears the imprint of Gerhard Fleischer and the date 1820. The publishing firm changed to Ernst Fleischer with the issue of Vol. II and new title-pages for Vol. I appear to have been issued to correspond with the later volumes, if, indeed, the entire volume was not reprinted. Cf. Leverkühn's "Biographisches über der drei Naumanns," 1904, p. 37, footn.

Dreizehnter Theil, Schluss. | Stuttgart. | Hoffmann'sche Verlags-Buchhandlung. | 1860.

13 vols. in 15, post 8vo (5½x8¾). Vol. I, pp. I-XXII, 23-516 (516= advt.), frontisp., pll. 1-48 (col.; by Fr. Naumann), 1 pl. (uncol.). Vol. II, 2 ll. (tit. and pref.), pp. I-IV (conts.), 1-508, frontisp., pll. 49-78 (col.). Vol. III, 1 l. (tit.), pp. 509-996+2 inserts (fold.) (no half-tit.), frontisp., pll. 79-93 (col.). Vol. IV, 1 l. (tit.), pp. I-II (conts.), 1-508, frontisp., pll. 94-116 (col.). Vol. V, 1 l. (tit.), pp. I-II (conts.), 1-504, frontisp., pll. 117-144 (col.). Vol. VI, 1 l. (tit.), pp. III-IV (conts.), 1-614, frontisp. (col.), pll. 145-166 (col.). Vol. VII, 1 l. (tit.), pp. III-IV (conts.), 1-554, I-XVI (addenda to *Perdix rubra*), frontisp., pll. 167-193 (col.). Vol. VIII, 1 l. (tit.), pp. III-VIII (pref.; no conts.), 1-560, frontisp. (belongs in Vol. IX), pll. 194-219 (col.), 1 text-fig. Vol. IX, 1 l. (tit.), pp. III-XI+1 (pref.; no conts.; p. IV wrongly printed VI), 1-810, frontisp. (col.; belongs in Vol. VIII), pll. 220-247 (col.). Vol. X, 1 l. (tit.), pp. III-VI (pref. and conts.; V-VI at close of vol.), 1-633, frontisp. (col.), pll. 248-277 (col.). Vol. XI, 1 l. (tit.), pp. III-VIII (pref. and conts.), 1-771, (frontisp., col., is out of place in Vol. XII), pll. 278-306 (col.). Vol. XII, 1 l. (tit.), pp. III-VIII (pref. and conts.), 1-646, 1 l. (errata), pp. 1-64 (index to Vols. I-XII), frontisp. (col.; belongs in Vol. XI; the proper frontisp. is between pll. 337 and 338 in the second volume of the atlas), pll. 307-337 (col.). Vol. XIII (1st part by Naumann), pp. 1-484 (no full title), 1 l. (obit. notice, pll. 338-370 (col.), (conclusion, by Blasius, Baldamus and Sturm), pp. 1-316, pll. 371-391 (col.; by Naumann and Sturm). Leipzig and Stuttgart.

A complete natural history of the birds of Germany. While entitled "J. A. Naumann's Naturgeschichte," etc., the work is quite distinct from J. A. Naumann's work, "Naturgeschichte der Land- und Wasser-Vögel des nördlichen Deutschlands und angränzender Länder" of 1795-1817 (q.v.)., although the earlier book laid the foundations for the later one. A few of the plates are the same but most of them have been remodeled and many of them entirely redrawn while other new ones have been added. The volumes seem to have been issued regularly as indicated by the printed dates on the title-pages, except Vol. XIII. This volume, consisting entirely of supplementary notes and discussions, was begun by Naumann and issued in parts. Interrupted by Naumann's death in 1857, it was then completed by Blasius, Baldamus and Sturm. There is considerable uncertainty about the dates and composition of the earlier parts. Judging from changes in typography, irregularities in signature marks, the appearance of new works in the synonymic references, and such other criteria, the following division seems probable. Part **1**, pp. 1-80; **2**, 81-192; **3**, 193-254; **4**, 255-304; **5**, 305-370; **6**, 371-418; **7**, 419-466; **8**, 467-486; "Fortsetzung der Nachträge," 1-316. Leverkühn (l.c., p. 39) quotes Blasius to the effect that Pts. 1-7, pp. 1-

466, 28 pll., appeared from 1845-54; Carus and Engelmann give 1846-53 for
the same 7 parts, and cite pp. 467-485 and the "Fortsetzung" under date of
1860. Engelmann credits the supplement, with 40 colored plates, to 1847.

Naumann, Johann Friedrich; and Buhle, Christian Adolph.

1818-28. Die Eier | der | Vögel Deutschlands | und | der benach-
barten Länder | in | naturgetreuen Abbildungen und Beschreibung-
en [*Semicolon added (Pts. IV and V.*).] | nebst | einer tabel-
larischen Uebersicht der Naturgeschichte | der hier vorkommenden
Vögel [*Comma added (Pts. IV and V.*).] | von | Johann Friedrich
Naumann und Dr. Christian Adolph Buhle [*Comma added (Pts.
IV and V.*).] | Mitgliedern mehrerer [mehrern (*Pts. IV and V.*)]
gelehrten Gesellschaften [*Period added (Pts. IV and V.*).] | Erstes
[-Fünftes] Heft [*Period added (Pts. IV and V.*).] | mit zwei illu-
minirten Kupfertafeln [*Period added (Pts. IV and V.*).] | Halle |
bei Karl August Kümmel | 1818 [1823; 1826; 1828; 1828].

1 vol. (5 pts.) medium 4to. Pt. I, 2 pr. ll. (tit. and ded.), pp. I-VI,
1-17 1-17+1, pll. I-II (col.). Pt. II, pp. I (tit.)-XII, 1-17, pll.
III-IV (col.). Pt. III, pp. I (tit.)-VIII, 1-17, pll. V-VI (col.).
Pt. IV, pp. I (tit.)-X, III-IX, 1-15, pll. VII-VIII (col.). Pt. V,
1 l. (tit.), pp. 1-17, 1-4, pll. IX-X (col.). Illustr. wrapper with
Pt. I. Halle.

An early work on the nests and eggs of the birds of Germany and neighboring
countries. The pages with Roman numeration contain essays on nests and
nest-building, classification of birds, form and internal anatomy of eggs, embry-
ology, brooding habits, etc. The general text is arranged in six parallel columns containing (1) nomenclature of species; (2) description of species; (3) habitat; (4) food-habits; (5) nidification; (6) description of eggs. The colored plates
of eggs were painted by Naumann. In 1860, a so-called second edition was
published by Fürchtegott Grässner under the title of "Die Vögel Deutschlands
und ihre Eier" (q.v.), but in reality this is a distinct work.

Nehrkorn, Adolph.

1899. Katalog | der | Eiersammlung | nebst Beschreibungen | der
aussereuropäischen Eier | von | Adolph Nehrkorn | Mit 4 Eier-
tafeln in farbigem Steindruck | Braunschweig | Harald Bruhn |
Verlagsbuchhandlung für Naturwissenschaft und Medicin | 1899.

1 vol. royal 8vo, pp. I-VII+1, 1-256, 4 ll. (expl. of pll.), pll. I-IV
(col.). Braunschweig.

An annotated list of 3546 species of extra-European birds represented in the egg
collection of the author. A brief description is given of most of the eggs, the
distribution of the various species is given, and references are made to the
Catalogue of Birds in the British Museum. A second edition appeared in 1910
(q.v.). The present copy was presented to P. L. Sclater by the author.

Nehrkorn, Adolph.

1910. Katalog | der | Eiersammlung | nebst Beschreibungen | der aussereuropäischen Eier | von | Adolph Nehrkorn | II. Auflage | Mit 4 Eiertafeln in farbigem Steindruck | Berlin | Verlag von R. Friedländer & Sohn | 1910.

1 vol. 8vo, pp. I-VII+1, 1-449+1, 4 ll. (expl. of pll.), frontisp. (portr.), pll. I-IV (col.). Berlin.

This is a second edition of the author's earlier work of the same title, 1899 (q.v.), prepared in the same style but cataloguing 5440 species and subspecies. A supplementary volume, "Nachträge zu Nehrkorn's Eierkatalog" (q.v.) appeared in 1914.

Nehrkorn, Adolph.

1914. Nachträge | zu | Nehrkorn's Eierkatalog | von | Adolph Nehrkorn | Mit 2 Eiertafeln in farbigem Steindruck | Berlin | Verlag von R. Friedländer & Sohn | 1914.

1 vol. 8vo, pp. 1-46, 3 ll. (expl. of pll. and errata), pp. 49-128, pll. V and VI (col.; by Georg Krause). Berlin.

A supplement to the author's "Katalog der Eiersammlung," 1910 (q.v.). A supplement, listing 327 additional species, is given, followed by a further supplement cataloguing 13 more species. A systematic list and an index are next in order, followed by the colored plates. The 5780 species and subspecies in the collection are then reviewed in systematic order, after which another additional supplement of 42 species is given, bringing the number of recognized forms represented in the collection to the total of 5822.

Nehrling, Heinrich.

1889-91. Die | Nordamerikanische Vogelwelt. | Von | Heinrich Nehrling, | Kustos des öffentlichen Museums in Milwaukee [etc., 2 lines.]. | Unter künstlerischer Mitwirkung von | Prof. Robert Ridgway vom Smithsonschen Institut und National-Museum | in Washington, Prof. A. Göring in Leipzig, und Akademiemaler | Gustav Mützel in Berlin. | [Vignette.] | Milwaukee, Wis. | Verlag von Geo. Brumder. | 1891.

1 vol. medium 4to, pp. I-XXIX+1, 1-637+1, pll. I-XXXVI (col.; by R. Ridgway, A. Göring and G. Mützel), text-figs. 1-10. Milwaukee.

A popular account of North American birds, of the English edition of which Elliott Coues was most euolgistic in his reviews. The German text (collated above) appeared in 13 parts, of which Pt. 1 appeared in 1889 (reviewed in Auk, July 1889). The Journal für Ornithologie acknowledged the receipt of Pts. 1-6 in the number for Jan. 1890, 7-9 in Jan. 1891, 10-12 in Oct. 1891, and 13 in Oct. 1892, but the final part probably appeared in 1891, the date on the title-page and preface. An edition in English began simultaneously with the German (Pt. 1 is reviewed in the Auk for July, 1889), but it was not completed before 1896. It appeared in two volumes under the title of "Our Native Birds of Song and Beauty," to which it was changed from "North American Birds," under which the first few numbers were issued. It comprised 16 parts, but contained the same matter and the same illustrations as the edition in German.

Nelson, Edward William.

1887. 49th Congress, 1st Session, } Senate. { Mis. Doc. No. 156. }

Report | upon | natural history collections | made in | Alaska | between the years 1877 and 1881 | by Edward W | Nelson. | Edited by Henry W. Henshaw. | Prepared under the direction of the Chief Signal Officer. | No. III. | Arctic Series of Publications issued in connection with the Signal Service, U. S. Army. | With 21 plates. | Washington: | Government Printing Office. | 1887.

1 vol. medium 4to, pp. 1-337, pll. I-XXI (12 col.; by L. and J. R. Ridgway and E. W. Nelson). Washington.

An account of the birds, mammals, fishes and diurnal Lepidoptera, collected by Nelson in Alaska from 1877 to 1881. The introduction (pp. 11-34) contains the narrative of the expedition; the birds are treated on pp. 35-226 and pll. I-XII. Both the introduction and the ornithological portion are by Nelson. The volume forms No. III of the Arctic Series of Publications, of which No. II, "Contributions to the Natural History of Alaska" by L. M. Turner, 1886 (q.v.) is also in the Ayer Ornithological Library.

Nelson, Harry Leverett.

1889. Bird-Songs | about | Worcester. | By | Harry Leverett Nelson, A.M. | Boston | Little, Brown, and Company | 1889.

1 vol. cap 8vo, 3 pr. ll., pp. 3-131. Boston.

A series of pleasantly written essays about birds, with particular notice of the songs of the various species.

Nelson, Thomas Hudson.

1907. The birds | of Yorkshire. | Being a Historical Account of | the Avi-Fauna of the County, | by | T. H. Nelson, M.B.O.U. | with the co-operation of | W. Eagle Clarke, F.R.S.E., F.L.S. | and F. Boyes. | In two volumes. | Vol. I [II]. | London: | A. Brown & Sons, Limited, | 5 Farringdon Avenue, E.C. | And at Hull and York. | 1907.

2 vols. foliopost 4to. Vol. I, pp. I-XVIII, 1 insert-slip (errata), pp. XIX-XLV+1, 1-374, frontisp. (col.), illum. tit. (p. 3), 75 pll., 2 text-figs. Vol. II, pp. I-XII, 375-843, frontisp. (col.), illum. tit. (p. 3), 86 pll. (1 col.), 2 text-figs. London.

A detailed account of the avifauna of Yorkshire, with special reference to the records (published and otherwise) of the local occurrences of the various species.

Many interesting notes are given on methods of hunting, "egging," etc., and on the habits of the birds. The work was originally commenced by W. Eagle Clarke, but under the present title the text was entirely rewritten by Hudson, although acknowledgements are made to Clarke and to F. Boyes for coöperation in the undertaking.

Neumann, J. G.

1828. Allgemeine Uebersicht | der | Lausitz'schen | Haus- Land- und | Wasservögel | von | J. G. Neumann. | Nebst einer illuminir- ten Steintafel. | Görlitz, | in Commission bei C. G. Zobel. | 1828, 1 vol. post 8vo, pp. I-VI, 7-186, frontisp. (col.; by G. Heller). Görlitz.

A review of the birds of the Lausitz region. Schalow, in his "Beiträge zur Vogel- fauna der Mark Brandenburg," p. 64, 1919, collates a copy with a slightly different title-page but of the same date and with similar pagination, etc.

Newton, Alfred.

1862. See Blasius, J. H., A List of the Birds of Europe.

Newton, Alfred.

1864-1907. See Wolley, John, Ootheca Wolleyana.

Newton, Alfred.

1871-82. See Yarrell, William, A History of British Birds, fourth edition, 1871-85.

Newton, Alfred.

1876. See Rowley, George D., Ornithology Miscellany, 1875-78.

Newton, Alfred.

1880. See Desfontaines, René Louiche, The Willughby Society.

Newton, Alfred.

1880. See Tunstall, Marmaduke, [Ornithologia Britannica], The Willughby Society.

Newton, Alfred; and Newton, Edward.

1881. List of the birds of Jamaica | by | Alfred and Edward New- ton. | [Extracted from the Handbook of Jamaica for 1881.] | Jamaica: | Government Printing and Stationery Establishment, 79 Duke Street, Kingston. 1 vol. post 8vo, tit., pp. 103-117. Kingston.

An extract from the Handbook of Jamaica for 1881, supplied with a new title-page but with pagination and general contents unaltered. The paper consists of an annotated list of species, giving vernacular names (as well as the scientific ones) and references to published accounts of local occurrences. A revised list was published in 1910 by P. L. Sclater (q.v.).

Newton, Alfred.

1882. See Scopoli, Giovanni Antonio, [Deliciae Florae et Faunae Insubricae], **The Willughby Society.**

Newton, Alfred.

1883. See Audouin, Jean Victor, [Explication Sommaire des Planches d'Oiseaux de l'Égypte et de la Syrie], **The Willughby Society.**

Newton, Alfred. (Gadow, Hans; Lydekker, Richard; Roy, Charles S.; Shufeldt, Robert W.)

1893-96. > A | dictionary of birds | by | Alfred Newton | assisted by Hans Gadow | with contributions from |
Richard Lydekker   Charles S. Roy | and | Robert W. Shufeldt,
B.A., F.G.S.   M.A., F.R.S. |
M.D. | (late United States' Army) | Part I. (A-GA) [Part II. (GA-MOA); Part III. (MOA-SHEATHBILL); Part IV. (SHEATHBILL-ZYGODACTYLI, | together with index and introduction)] | London | Adam and Charles Black | 1893 [1893; 1894; 1896].

1 vol. 8vo, 3 pr. ll. (half-tit., tit. and ded.; tit. and ded. missing), pp. VII-XII (pref., notanda, etc.; pref. missing), 1-124 (introd.), 1 l. (subtit., Pt. I.), 1 l. (missing), pp. V-VII+1 (note), 1-304, 1 l. (subtit., Pt. II.), pp. 305-576, 1 l. (subtit., Pt. III.), pp. 577-832, 1 l. (subtit., Pt. IV.), pp. 833-1088, 1 map (col.; fold.), 700 text-figs. London.

A volume containing an enormous amount of information relating to various phases of ornithology, conveniently arranged in alphabetical order with copious cross-references. A work of which Coues once wrote (Auk, XIV, p. 236, April 1897), "Far and away the best book ever written about birds." The anatomical paragraphs were written by Gadow and are distinguished by having the titles in Italics. Roy contributed an article on flight; Lydekker, several paragraphs on fossils; and Shufeldt, accounts of several North American birds;—these notes being signed by their respective contributors. Issued in four parts, about as collated above except that the introductory matter up to the first subtitle (pp. I-XII and 1-124, introd.) appeared in the fourth part. The arrangement of pages is taken from the instructions to the binder on the reverse of the subtitle to Pt. IV; the present copy is wrongly assembled and certain pages are lacking. I have quoted the subtitles in the absence of the general title. A second edition, unabridged, was issued in one volume in October 1899.

Newton, Edward.

1881. See Newton, Alfred and Edward, **List of the Birds of Jamaica.**

Nicoll, M. J.

1919. Ministry of Public Works, Egypt. | Zoological Service. | **Handlist** | **of** | **the birds of Egypt,** | by | M. J. Nicoll, F.Z.S., M.B.O.U., | Assistant Director, Zoological Service. | Publication No. 29. | Cairo. | Government Press. | To be obtained either directly or through any Bookseller, | from the Government Publications Office, Old Ismailia Palace, | Sharia Qasr el 'Aini, Cairo. | 1919. | Price: P.T. 15.

1 vol. royal 8vo, pp. I-XII, 1-119, frontisp. (map.; col.; fold.), pll. 1-31 (8 col.; pll. 1-22 on 11 ll.; pll. 24-31 with legends on backs of preceding pll.). Cairo.

A descriptive list of Egyptian birds. References are given, where possible, to Shelley's "A Handbook to the Birds of Egypt," 1872 (q.v.). The uncolored plates are from photographs of skins; the colored ones, from drawings. The introduction is dated October 24, 1919.

Nilsson, Sven.

1817-21. Ornithologia | Svecica. | Auctore | Sv. Nilsson, | Philosophiæ Doctore, | in Academ. Lundensi adjuncto [etc., 2 lines.) in Acad. Lundensi, etc., 4 lines. (Vol. II.)]. | Pars prior [posterior]. | Cum X [II] tabulis æneis pictis. | Havniæ, MDCCCXVII [MDCCCXXI]. | Apud J. H. Schubothium, Aulæ Regiæ Bibliopolam.

2 vols. post 8vo. Vol. I, 4 pr. ll. (tit., ded. and half-tit.), pp. 1-317+1, pll. I-VIII, IX fig. 1 and IX fig. 2 (= 10 pll., col., fold.). Vol. II, pp. I-XIV, 1-277, 1 l. (subtit.), pll. X-XI (col., fold.). Copenhagen.

A descriptive catalogue of Swedish birds. Numerous new names are proposed which are untenable, being antedated by other valid terms. The work appears to have been issued in two parts as collated, but Pt. II contains two subtitle-pages lettered "Fasciculus prior" and "Fasciculus posterior," respectively, which indicate a possible division. "Fasciculus prior" occurs between pp. 112 and 113, on the first leaf of the signature ending on p. 126; "Fasciculis posterior" is on p. 133 (134 blank), at the end of its signature. The texture of the paper on p. 135 and the pages immediately following appears to be slightly different from that of the preceding pages, indicating a possible separation in dates of printing or publication. The preface was signed on Dec. 6, 1830.

Nitsch, Christian Ludwig. (Burmeister, Hermann.)

1840. System | der | Pterylographie | von | Christian Ludwig Nitzsch. | Nach seinen handschriftlich aufbewahrten Untersuchungen | verfasst | von | Hermann Burmeister, | Professor der Zoologie an der Universität zu Halle. | Mit X Kupfertafeln. | Halle, | Eduard Anton | 1840.

1 vol. foliopost 4to, pp. I-XII, 1-228, pll. I-X. Halle.

A dissertation on pterylography, edited by Burmeister from the manuscript of Nitzsch and supplemented by an additional plate (pl. I) with explanation (pp. 227-228) on the structure of the feather, by the editor. The manuscript was prepared by Nitzsch as a revision of his earlier work, only one part of which was published, in 1833, under the title of "Pterylographia avium pars prior."

Nordenskiöld, Nils Adolph Erik von. (Palmén, Johan Axel.)

1887. [**Vega-expeditionens vetenskapliga Iakttagelser** bearbetade af deltagare i resan och andra forskare utgifna af A. E. Nordenskiöld] > **Bidrag | till kännedomen om | Sibiriska Ishafskustens fogelfauna** | enligt | Vega-expeditionens | iakttagelser och samlingar | bearbetade | af | J. A. Palmén. | Bd V. 16.

1 vol. royal 8vo, pp. 241-511, tables 1-8 (fold.), 1 text-fig. (map). Stockholm.

The ornithological portion of Nordenskiöld's report on the voyage of the Vega, published in 5 vols., 1882-87. The present contribution forms part of Vol. V and consists of a detailed report, by Palmén, on the birds of the Arctic coasts of Siberia, not restricted to the material secured by the expedition. Many of the species discussed are commonly found in Arctic North America (some of them are properly Nearctic species) and their distribution in Alaska and northern Canada is, therefore, discussed. A detailed bibliography of the ornithology of all Arctic regions, arranged geographically, and a tabular arrangement of species, showing distribution and records, are important additions to the text. *Larus argentatus Vegae* is described as new.

Norris, J. Parker, Jr.

1899. **Some facts about the consistency | of the chairman of the | A. O. U. Committee on Bird Protection | and an answer to his | "Hints to young students."** | by | J. Parker Norris, Jr. | Philadelphia: | privately printed | 1899.

1 vol. 8vo, pp. 1-10. Philadelphia.

A defense of egg-collecting in large series.

North, Alfred John.

1901-14. Australian Museum, Sydney. | Special Catalogue, No. I. | **Nests and eggs of birds | found breeding | in | Australia and Tasmania,** | by | Alfred J. North, C.M.Z.S., | Colonial Member of the British Ornithologists' Union, Corresponding Fellow of the American | Ornithologists' Union. | Ornithologist, Australian Museum [Ornithologist to the Australian Museum (*Vols. II-IV.*)]. | (Second edition of Catalogue No. XII., entirely re-written | with additions). | Volume I [-IV]. | Printed by order of the Trustees of the Australian Museum. | R. Etheridge, Junr., J. P., Curator. | Sydney. | F. W. White, printer [general printer (*Vols. II-IV.*)],

344 Kent Street. | June, 1901 - July, 1904 [November, 1906, July, 1907, September, 1909 (*Vol. II.*); 1912 (*Vol. III.*); 1913-1914 (*Vol. IV.*)].

4 vols. folio (size of royal 4to). Vol. I, pp. I-VII+1, 1-366, 15 printed guard-sheets, 1 insert-slip (erratum), pll. A1-A8 and B I-B VII, 73 text-figs. Vol. II, pp. I-VII+1, 1-380, 11 printed guard-sheets, 3 insert-slips (ed. notes), pll. A 9-A 13, B VIII-B XIII, 73 text-figs. Vol. III, pp. I-VII+1, 1-362, 7 printed guard-sheets, pll. A 14-A 17, B XIV-B XVI, 59 text-figs. Vol. IV, pp. I-VIII, 1-472; 12 printed guard-sheets, pll. A 18-A 20, B XVII-B XXV, 96 text-figs. Sydney.

A voluminous report, containing descriptions of the plumages, eggs and nesting habits of supposedly all the birds found breeding in Australia and Tasmania; partly original and partly compiled from correspondence, published notes, etc. Unfortunately, many published records were ignored, making the work less complete than it would otherwise have been. H. L. White (Emu, **15**, pp. 57-65, 1915) gives a list of omissions. Plates "A" are of nests; "B" are of eggs.

The work appeared in 17 parts, the dates and contents of which are given in the introductory pages of the various volumes (p. III of Vols. I-III; p. II of Vol. I). These dates are correct but omit to mention the introductory matter of the volumes. In the cases of Vols. II-IV, the introductory matter is dated the same month as that given for the issue of the last part in each of those volumes. In Vol. I, the introduction is dated October, 1904 but the last part of that volume is dated July 11. Possibly the introductory matter formed a final (separate) part; if so it would bring the total number of parts in all volumes to 18.

A supplement was issued in the Records of the Australian Museum, Vol. 1, No. 6, 1891.

Noska, Max. (Tschusi zu Schmidhoffen, Victor Ritter von.)

1895. **Das kaukasische Birkhuhn** | (Tetrao mlokosiewiczi Tacz.) | Eine monographische Studie | von | Max Noska, | weiland Jagd-leiter Sr. kaiserl. Hoheit des Grossfürsten Sergei Michailowitsch, | unter Mitwirkung | von | Victor Ritter von Tschusi zu Schmid-hoffen, | Herausgeber [*etc., 5 lines.*]. | Mit einer colorirten Tafel. | (Separatabdruck aus "Ornith. Jahrb.", VI., 1895) | Hallein 1895. | Druck von Johann L. Bondi & Sohn in Wien, VII., Stiftgasse 3. | Verlag des Ornithologischen Jahrbuches.

1 vol. superroyal 8vo, pp. I-V+1, 1 l., pp. 1-98, frontisp. (col.; by B. Geisler). Hallein.

A monographic study of the Caucasian Black Cock, edited and supplemented by Tschusi zu Schmidhoffen from the manuscript of Noska. The work was originally published in four instalments in the Ornithologischer Jahrbuch, Vol. VI, 1895, Heft 2, pp. 100-125; Heft 3, pp. 129-150; Heft 4, pp. 169-182; and

Heft 5, pp. 209-243, 1 pl. The title-page and table of contents have been added to the present impression and the pagination is altered. The present copy was complimentary to D. G. Elliot from Tschusi zu Schmidhoffen.

Novara, Reise der österreichischen Fregatte—; Vögel.

1865.   See Wüllerstorf-Urbair, B. von.

Nozeman, Cornelius.

1758.   See Moehring, P. H. G., **Geslachten der Vogelen.**

Nozeman, Cornelius. (Houttuyn, Martinus; Sepp, Christian.)

1770-1829. Nederlandsche | Vogelen; | Volgens hunne huishouding, [. . . aard en (*Vol. IV.*)] | aert, en eigenschappen beschreeven [eigenschappen beschreven (*Vol. IV.*); aard, en eigenschappen beschreven (*Vol. V.*)] | door | Cornelius Nozeman, | Leeraer [Leeraar (Vols. IV and V.)] der Remonstranten [*Comma added* (*Vols. II-V.*).] | en Mede-directeur van 't Bataefsch [het Bataafsch (*Vols. IV and V.*)] Genootschap | der proefondervindelyke wys-begeerte [proefondervindelijke wijsbegeerte (*Vols. IV and V.*)] | te Rotterdam. {| en verder, na zyn [zijn (*Vols. IV and V.*)] ed. over-lyden [overlijden (*Vols. IV and V.*)], door | Martinus Houttuyn, | medicinæ Doctor, | lid van de Hollandsche Maatschappy [Maat-schappij (*Vols. IV and V.*) en van het Zeeuwsch | Genootschap der Weetenschappen [Wetenschappen (*Vols. IV and V.*).} | Alle naer 't leven ['t leeven (*Vols. II and III.*); het leven (*Vols. IV and V.*)] geheel nieuw en naeuwkeurig [. . . . . . . naauw-(*Vol. IV.*); . . . . naauwkeurig (Vol. V.)] | geteekend [keurig getekend (*Vol. IV.*); getekend (*Vols. II and III.*)], in 't [het (*Vols. IV and V.*)] koper gebragt, en natuurlyk [*Last two words transferred* (*Vol. IV.*); en natuurlijk (*Vol. V.*)] | gekoleurd [en natuurlyk gekleurd (*Vol. IV.*); gekleurd (*Vol. V.*)] | door, en onder opzicht van | Christian Sepp en Zoon. | [*No vol. no.* (*Vol. I.*); Tweede Deel; Derde Deel; Vierde Deel; Vijfde en laatste Deel]. | Te Amsterdam, | By Jan Christian Sepp, Boekverkoper. [. . . . Boekverkooper. (*Vol. II.*); By J. C. Sepp en Zoon, Boek-verkoopers. (*Vol. III.*); By J. C. Sepp en Zoon, (*Vol. IV.*); By Jan Christian Sepp en Zoon Boekverkoopers. (*Vol. V.*)] | MDCCLXX [MDCCLXXXIX (*Vol. II.*); MDCCXCVII (*Vol. III.*); Boekverkoopers. | MDCCCIX (*Vol. IV.*); MDCCCXXIX (*Vol. V.*)].

5 vols. imperial folio. Vol. I, illum tit., 3 pr. ll. (tit., pref. and conts.), pp. 1-92, 50 pll. (col.; by Sepp; 2 fold.). Vol. II, illum tit. (same as in Vol. I), tit., pp. I-II (pref.), 1 l., pp. 93-194, I-IV (index,

Vols. I and II), 50 pll. (col.). Vol. III, illum. tit. (new), 3 pr. ll. (tit., pref. and conts.), pp. 195-294, 50 pll. (col.). Vol. IV, illum. tit. (same as in Vol. III), 3 pr. ll., pp. 295-394, I-IV (index, Vols. III and IV), 50 pll. (col.). Vol. V, illum. tit. (new), tit., pp. I-VI (pref., corrig. Vols. I-IV, conts.), 395-500, 50 pll. (col.). Amsterdam.

A popular account of the birds of Holland, illustrated by hand-colored plates of all of the species, and of the nests and eggs of some of them. The birds and their habits are described in detail. It appears to be the first comprehensive work on the ornithology of the region. It was begun by Nozeman, who died in 1789, and was taken up by Houttuyn who completed the work. The dates on the title-pages appear to be accurate, but Blaauw, in "Notes from the Leyden Museum," Vol. XV, p. 185, 1893, cites the dates as follows,—1770, 1789, 1812, 1826 and 1829,—a discrepancy of 15 and 17 years, respectively, in Volumes III and IV. No particulars are given and the citations may be in error. The work is sometimes quoted as Nozeman and Sepp.

Nuttall, Thomas.

1832-34. A | manual | of the | ornithology | of the | United States and of Canada. | By | Thomas Nuttall, A.M., F.L.S., &c. ["*&c.*" *omitted*] | The land [water] birds. | Cambridge [Boston]: | Hilliard and Brown, [Hilliard, Gray, and Company.] | booksellers to the university. [*Line omitted.*] | M DCCC XXXII [M DCCC XXXIV].

2 vols. 12mo. "Land birds", pp. I-VIII (I-II, VII-VIII missing), 1-683, 53 woodcuts. "Water birds", pp. I-VII+1, 1-627, 61 woodcuts. Cambridge and Boston.

The original edition of Nuttall's work, one of the early landmarks in the history of American ornithology. Descriptions of the species, including various new ones, and copious notes on their habits, based partly on personal observations and partly on the writings of Wilson, Audubon and others, are united to form an authoritative and readable text. A second edition of Vol. I (q.v.) was issued in 1840. The present copy is from the library of Charles Robert Bree who secured it from that of Rev. John Fleming.

Nuttall, Thomas.

1840. A | manual | of the | ornithology | of the | United States and of Canada. | By | Thomas Nuttall, A.M., F.L.S. &c | Second edition, with additions. | The land birds. | Boston: | Hilliard, Gray, and Company. | MDCCCXL.

1 vol. 12mo, pp. I-VIII, 1-832, 53 woodcuts. Boston.

A revised edition of the first volume of the earlier work of the same title, 1832-34 (q.v.), with "new species and many additional observations........de-rived from my friend Audubon as well as the result of a journey made by my-self and Mr. Townsend across the continent to the coast of the Pacific." Al-though cited by Coues as consisting of two volumes (including the water birds), the present edition appears, properly, to comprise only the single volume on the land birds. The second volume often found associated with this one (as in the present case), either is a copy of the original edition or is printed from the original plates without alteration of any kind, including the date. The present copy is autographed by Capt. George A. McCall.

Nuttall, Thomas. (Chamberlain, Montague.)

1891. A | popular handbook | of the | ornithology | of the | United States and Canada, | Based on Nuttall's Manual. | By Montague Chamberlain. | [*Vignette = ruby-throated hummer (blue-winged teal*).] | Vol. I [II]. | The land birds [game and water birds]. | Boston: | Little, Brown, and Company. | 1891.

2 vols. demy 8vo. Vol. I, pp. I-XLVIII, 1 l., pp. 1-473, frontisp. (col.; by Ernest E. Thompson), 87 woodcuts (+1 headpiece). Vol. II, pp. I-VII+1, 1-431, frontisp. (col.), 86 woodcuts. Boston.

Based on Nuttall's 'Manual' with part of the descriptions rewritten and supplementary notes added to Nuttall's account of habits, distribution, etc. The woodcuts are, in a great many cases, copied from Yarrell's "History of British Birds," 1837-43 (q.v.), and possibly from other sources, but some of them are new. There is a later edition of the same work.

Nuttall, Thomas.

1904. See Weed, Clarence Moores, **Bird Life Stories, Book I.**

Oates, Eugene William.

1883. A handbook | to the | birds of British Burmah, | including those found in the adjoining | state of Karennee. | By | Eugene W. Oates, | Executive Engineer, Public Works Department of India (British Burmah). | Vol. I [II]. | London: | R. H. Porter, 6 Tenterden Street, W., | and | Messrs. Dulau & Co., Soho Square, W. | 1883.

2 vols. royal 8vo. Vol. I, 4 pr. ll. (tit. and conts.), pp. 1-431. Vol. II, pp. I-XXX (incl. ded., pref. and introd.), 1 l. (errata), pp. 1-493, 1 map (col.; fold.). Copy in original covers. London. March and June, 1883.

Detailed descriptions, accounts of distribution and habits, and bibliographic references for 780 species of birds. The dates are from the original wrappers.

Oates, Eugene William.

1889-90. See Hume, Seean O., **The Nests and Eggs of Indian Birds, Second Edition.**

Oates, Eugene William; and Blanford, William Thomas.

1889-98. The fauna of British India, | including | Ceylon and Burma. | Published under the authority of the Secretary of | State for India in Council. | Edited by W. T. Blanford. | **Birds.-**

Vol. I [-IV]. | By | Eugene W. Oates [W. T. Blanford, F.R.S.
(*Vols. III and IV.*)]. | London: | Taylor and Francis, Red Lion
Court, Fleet St. | Calcutta: Bombay: |
Thacker, Spink, & Co. Thacker & Co., Limited. |
Berlin: | R. Friedländer & Sohn, 11 Carlstrasse. | 1889 [1890;
1895; 1898].

4 vols. 8vo. Vol. I, pp. I-XX, 1-556, text-figs. 1-163, 8 text-figs.
(unnum.). Vol. II, pp. I-X, 1-407, text-figs. 1-107. Vol. III,
pp. I-XIV, 1-450, text-figs. 1-102, 4 text-figs. (unnum.). Vol.
IV, pp. I-XXI+1, text-figs. 1-127. London.

The ornithological numbers of a series of eight volumes, including two on fishes,
one on reptiles and batrachians, one on mammals, and the present four on
birds. The first two volumes on birds were written by Oates; the last two by
Blanford who was also the author of the volume on mammals and the editor
of the entire series. The present volumes contain a thorough monograph of the
birds of India, Ceylon and Burma, with descriptions of the various plumages,
measurements, notes on distribution and habits, and detailed synonymies. A
bibliography is included in Vol. IV. A so-called second edition of this work (in
reality an entirely new presentation of the subject) was begun in 1922 and is
still in course of publication (Cf. Baker, E. C. Stuart, The Fauna of British
India—Birds, 1922-date.).

Oates, Eugene William.

**1898-99. A manual | of the | game birds of India. | Part I.-Land
Birds [Part II.-Water Birds]. | By | Eugene William Oates, |
Author of [*etc., 5 lines.*]. | Date of Publication, February 10, 1898
[May 18, 1899]. | Published for the author by | Messrs. A. J.
Combridge & Co., | Bombay, | 1898 [1899].**

2 vols. 16 mo. Vol. I, pp. I-IX+1, 1 l. (conts.), pp. 1-431. Vol. II,
pp. I-VI, 2 ll. (conts. and errata), pp. 1-506. Bombay.

A book intended for the Indian sportsman. It contains brief, simple descriptions
of the game birds of the country, the scientific and vernacular names, and some
account of the habits of each.

Oates, Eugene William.

1901-05. See British Museum, **Catalogue of the Collection of Birds'
Eggs,** 1901-12.

Ober, Frederick Albion. (Lawrence, George Newbold.)

1899. Camps in the Caribbees: | the adventures of a naturalist | in
the Lesser Antilles. | By | Frederick A. Ober. | [*Quot., 2 lines.*] |
Boston | Lee and Shepard Publishers | 1899.

1 vol. crown 8vo, pp. I-XVIII, 1-366, 4 pll., 30 text-figs. Boston.

An interesting narrative of the author's experiences while on an ornithological expedition to the Lesser Antilles in 1876. Notes on the bird-life of the islands are scattered throughout the text, and in the appendix (pp. 347-366) is given a catalogue of all the species noted (from Proc. U. S. Nat. Mus. **1**, pp. 46-69, 185-198, 232-242, 265-278, 349-360 and 449-462) followed by descriptions of the new species (from Ann. New York Acad. Sciences) by Lawrence. The first edition was published in 1880.

Oberholser, Harry C.

1896. See World's Congress on Ornithology, **Papers presented to the—.**

Ogilvie-Grant, William Robert.

1892. See Sharpe, Richard B.; and Ogilvie-Grant, **Catalogue of the Picariae in the Collection of the British Museum.**

See, also, British Museum, **Catalogue of the Birds,** 1874-98, Vol. XVII.

Ogilvie-Grant, William Robert.

1893. Catalogue | of the | game birds | (Pterocletes, Gallinæ, Opisthocomi, Hemipodii) **| in the | collection | of the | British Museum. |** By | W. R. Ogilvie-Grant, | London: | printed by order of the Trustees. | Sold by | Longmans & Co., 39 Paternoster Row; [*etc., 3 lines.*]; | and at the | British Museum (Natural History), Cromwell Road, S.W. | 1893.

See British Museum, **Catalogue of the Birds,** 1874-98, Vol. XXII.

Ogilvie-Grant, William Robert.

1893. See Whitehead, John, **Exploration of Mount Kina Balu, North Borneo.**

Ogilvie-Grant, William Robert.

1895-97. Allen's Naturalist's Library. | Edited by R. Bowdler Sharpe, LL.D., F.L.S., Etc. | **A hand-book | to the | game-birds. |** By | W. R. Ogilvie-Grant, | Zoological Department, British Museum. | Vol. I [II]. | Sand-grouse, Partridges, Pheasants [Pheasants (Continued), Megapodes, Curassows, | Hoatzins, Bustard-quails]. | London: | W. H. Allen & Co., Limited, | 13, Waterloo Place, S.W. | 1895 [1897].

2 vols. crown 8vo. Vol. I, pp. I-XIV, 1 l., pp. 1-304, pll. I-XXI (col.; by J. G. Keulemans and others), 14 text-figs. (variously num.). Vol. II, pp. I-XIV, 1 l., pp. 1-316, 2 ll. (advt.), pll. XXII-XXXIX, XXXA, XXXVA and XXXVIIIA (col.; XXV wrongly numbered XXVI). London.

Based on Vol. XXII of the Catalogue of Birds in the British Museum, by the same author (Cf. British Museum, 1874-98.), the present little work is a concise monograph of all the species of game birds in the world known at the time of publication. The descriptions of the various species are given in non-technical detail, and the habits and distributions are discussed at some length. Two new species are described in the second volume.

Ogilvie-Grant, William Robert.

1898. See Sharpe, Richard Bowdler; and Ogilvie-Grant, **Catalogue of the Plataleae,** etc., **in the Collection of the British Museum.**
See, also, British Museum, **Catalogue of the Birds,** 1874-98, Vol. XXVI.

Ogilvie-Grant, William Robert.

1905. See Annandale, Nelson; and Robinson, Herbert C., **Fasciculi Malayenses.**

Ogilvie-Grant, William Robert. (Wells, Thomas.)

1912. General index | to | **A Hand-list** | of the | **Genera and Species** | of | **Birds.** | [Nomenclator avium tum fossilium | tum viventium.] | Volumes I.-V. | Edited by | W. R. Ogilvie-Grant. | London: | printed by order of the Trustees. | Sold by | Longmans & Co., 39 Paternoster Row, E.C.; [*etc., 3 lines.*]; | and at the | British Museum (Natural History), Cromwell Road, S.W. | 1912. | All rights reserved.

1 vol. post 8vo, pp. I-IV, 1 l. (editor's pref.), pp. 1-199, 1-30 (advt.). London.

A consolidation of the indices in Vols. II-V of Sharpe's "Hand-list," 1899-1909 (q.v.), with corrections of errors noted in the originals. According to the editor's preface, the work was first entrusted to Thomas Wells; the final index was issued under supervision and editorship of Ogilvie-Grant. The editor's preface is dated March 11, 1912.

Ogilvie-Grant, William Robert.

1912. See British Museum, **Catalogue of the Collection of Birds' Eggs,** 1901-12.

Ogilvie-Grant, William Robert.

1916. See British Ornithologists' Union, **Reports on the Collections made by the British Ornithologists' Union Expedition in Dutch New Guinea.**

Oldham, Charles.

1910. See Coward, Thomas A., **The Vertebrate Fauna of Cheshire and Liverpool Bay.**

Oldham, Charles.

1919-24. See Witherby, Harry Forbes, **A Practical Handbook of British Birds.**

Olina, Giovanni Pietro.

1684. Vccelliera | overo discorso | della natvra, | c proprieta di diversi vccelli, | e in particolare di qve'che cantano. | Con il modo di prendergli, | conoscergli, alleurgli, e mantenergli. | E con le Figure cauate dal vero, e diligentemte [*sic*] intagliate | dal Tempesta, e dal Villamena. | Opera di Gio. Pietro Olina | novare se dottor di legge | Dedicata | al Sig. Cavalier dal Pozzo. | In Roma, Presso M. Angelo de Rossi, 1684; [*Title enclosed in broad, figured border.*].

1 vol. foliopost 4to, 5 pr. ll. (pl. on reverse of last), pp. 1-77+1 (1-68 on one side of leaves, with plates on reverse), 6 ll. (index), 69 pll. (by Tempesta and Villamena), 2 tail-pieces and numerous engr. capitals, etc. Rome.

A curious old volume, containing descriptions of numerous birds and of the methods of catching and training them; illustrated by etchings. A former edition was published in 1622.

Olphe-Gaillard, Léon.

1884-91. Contributions | à la | **faune ornithologique** | de | **l'Europe occidentale** | Recueil | comprenant | les espèces d'oiseaux qui se reproduisent dans cette région | ou qui s'y montrent régulièrement de passage | augmenté | de la description des principales espèces exotiques | les plus voisines des indigènes | ou susceptibles d'être confondues avec elles | ainsi que l'énumération des races domestiques | Par Léon Olphe-Gaillard | Bayonne | Imprimerie-Librairie Lasserre | 1884.

40 fascicules+introductory matter (in 4 vols.). Pp. I-XXVIII (tit. and pref.). Fasc. I, pp. 1-116. II, pp. 1-38. III, pp. 1-109, 1 pl. IV, pp. 1-107. V, pp. 1-21. VI, pp. 1-56. VII, pp. 1-31. VIII, pp. 1-46. IX, pp. 1-43. X, pp. 1-110. XI, pp. 1-55. XII, pp. 1-54. XIII, pp. 1-56. XIV, pp. 1-189, 1 pl. XV, pp. 1-129, 1 pl. XVI, pp. 1-74. XVII, pp. 1-62. XVIII, pp. 1-71. XIX, pp. 1-96. XX, pp. 1-69. XXI, pp. 1-88. XXII, pp. 1-110. XXIII, pp. 1-66. XXIV, pp. 1-96. XXV, pp. 1-24. XXVI, pp. 1-82, 1 pl. XXVII, pp. 1-129. XXVIII, pp. 1-82+1 l. (unnum;=pp. *21 bis*+1), XXIX, pp. 1-106. XXX, pp. 1-144. XXXI, pp. 1-59. XXXII, pp. 1-148. XXXIII, pp. 1-34. XXXIV, pp. 1-112. XXXV, pp. 1-38. XXXVI, pp. 1-88. XXXVII, pp. 1-94. XXXVIII,

pp. 1-68. XXXIX, pp. 1-74+8 bis, 1 pl. XL, pp. 1-32, 1-20 (index to entire work). Bayonne.

A review of the birds of western Europe with synonymy, descriptions and critical notes. Numerous extralimital species are discussed. The work appeared in parts as indicated in the collation, but not in the order of present arrangement which is according to the adopted classification. The dates are given on most of the subtitle-pages, as follows. Fasc. **I**, undated (=1884); **II**, June 1887; **III**, May 1888; **IV**, June, 1888; **V**, undated (=March 1885); **VI**, May 1887. **VII**, June 1887; **VIII**, Oct. 1886; **IX**, Oct. 1886; **X**, Oct. 1886; **XI**, Nov. 1886; **XII**, Dec. 1888; **XIII**, Febr. 1890; **XIV**, June 1891; **XV**, April 1891; **XVI**, Oct. 1887; **XVII**, Febr. 1889; **XVIII**, March 1889; **XIX**, May 1889; **XX**, Aug. 1889; **XXI**, Sept. 1889; **XXII**, March 1887; **XXIII**, Jan. 1888; **XXIV**, Aug. 1888; **XXV**, Aug. 1888; **XXVI**, July 1891; **XXVII**, Aug. 1891; **XXVIII**, Sept. 1891; **XXIX**, Nov. 1891; **XXX**, March 1890; **XXXI**, April 1890; **XXXII**, May 1890; **XXXIII**, undated (=June 1885); **XXXIV**, Nov. 1890; **XXXV**, Dec. 1890; **XXXVI**, Jan. 1890; **XXXVII**, Jan. 1886; **XXXVIII**, March 1886; **XXXIX**, May 1886; **XL**, June 1886. The dates of Fascs. I, V and XXXIII are from current reviews in the Ibis. In the present set, Fascs. I-XIII constitute Vol. I; XIV-XXI, Vol. II; XXII-XXX, Vol. III; and XXXI-XL, Vol. IV.

Oort, E. D. van.

See Van Oort, E. D.

Ord, George.

1808-14. See Wilson, Alexander, **American Ornithology.**

1824 (-25). Idem.

1828-29. Idem.

1831. See Wilson, A.; and Bonaparte, **American Ornithology.**

1832. Idem.

1840. See Wilson, **Wilson's American Ornithology.**

1853. Idem.

1876. See Wilson, A.; and Bonaparte, **American Ornithology.**

1877. Idem.

1878. Idem.

Ord, George. (Rhoads, Samuel N.)

**1894. A reprint | of the | North American Zoology, | by | George Ord. | Being an exact reproduction of the part originally compiled | by Mr. Ord for Johnson & Warner, and first | published by them in their | second American edition | of | Guthrie's geography, | in | 1815 | Taken from Mr. Ord's private, annotated copy. | To which is added an appendix on the more important | scientific and historic qestions (*sic*) involved. | By | Samuel N. Rhoads. | Published by the editor. | Haddonfield, New Jersey. | 1894.

1 vol. 8vo, tit., pp. VII-X (introd.), 1 l. (blank), 1 l. (facsim. of tit. of Vol. II of reprinted work), 1 p. (blank), pp. 290-361+1 (orig. pag. of reprinted article), 1-90 (appendix and index). Haddonfield.

A verbatim reprint of the title-page and pp. 290-361 of Vol. II of William Guthrie's "A New Geographical, Historical, and Commercial Grammar; and Present State of the Several Kingdoms of the World.—Second American Edition Improved.—Philadelphia:—1815." The subject matter consists of lists of the mammals, birds, reptiles and amphibians of North America, with biographical sketches of some of these and of a few fishes and insects. The accounts of the birds are taken largely from Wilson. A number of new species are described. The original work is extremely rare. The appendix, by Rhoads, contains annotations relative to the foregoing text.

Osbeck, Pehr.   (Georgi, Johann Gottlieb; Toreen, Olof; Eckeberg, Carl Gustav.)

1765.   Herrn Peter Osbeck | Pastors zu Hasslöf und Wortorp, der Königl. Schwedischen | Akademie zu Stockholm und der Kön. Gesellschaft zu Upsala, | Mitgliedes | Reise | nach Ostindien und China. | Nebst O. Toreens Reise nach Suratte | und | C. G. Ekebergs Nachricht von der Landwirtschaft | der Chineser. | Aus dem Schwedischen übersetzt | von | J. G. Georgi | [*Design.*] | Mit 13 Kupfertafeln. | Rostock, | verlegts Johann Christian Koppe, | 1765.

1 vol. demy 8vo, 3 pr. ll. (tit., ded.), pp. I-XXIV, 1 l. (expl. of pll.), pp. 1-552, 13 ll. (indices), pll. 1-13 (fold.; none of birds). Rostock.

An account of the author's travels in China and the East Indies in 1750-53. The present edition is a translation of the original work which was published in Stockholm in 1757. Voluminous notes on the natural history of the regions traversed are given throughout the volume. Many of these relate to birds, for which binomial names are used. Forster's edition in English was published in 1771.

Osculati, Gaetano.   (Cornalia, Emilio.)

1850.   Esplorazione | delle | regioni equatoriali | lungo il Napo ed el fiume delle Amazzoni | Frammento | di un | viaggio fatto nelle due Americhe | negli anni 1846-1847-1848 | da | Gaetano Osculati | Membro Corrispondante della Societa' Geografica di Parigi | Corredata di 2 Carte topografiche e di 20 Vedute e Costumi | ritratti dal vero dallo stesso Autore. | Milano | Tipografia Bernardoni | dicontro alla Chiesa di S. Tomaso | 1850.

1 vol. superroyal 8vo, pp. 1-320, pll. I-VIII, XI-XII, 1 pl. (unnum. = pl. XIII of text; fold.; by Cornalia), 2 maps (1 fold.). Milan.

Narrative and description of the author's voyage and travels from Panama to Ecuador, across the Andes and down the Amazon, with notes on the zoology of the regions traversed. Pp. 301-315 are occupied by Cornalia's annotated check-list of the collection of vertebrates brought back by Osculati, given under the title of "Vertebratorum synopsis | in Museo Mediolanense extantium | quæ | per novam orbem cajetanus Osculati | collegit | Annis 1846-47-48 | speciebus novis vel minus cognitis adjectis | nec non descriptionibus atque inconibus illustratis | curante | Æmilio Cornalia | Med Doct. Cathed. Histor. Natur. Spec. in Cæs. Reg. Archigym. Ticin. Assist. | Cum tab. lithogr. una." Various new species, not of birds, are described in this paper. A second edition of the volume was published in 1854, including a portrait and pll. IX and X, not given in the first edition.

Oudart, Paul Louis.

1820-21. See Vieillot, L.P.; and Oudart, **La Galerie des Oiseaux,** 1820-26.

Oustalet, Emile.

1882. See Révoil, Georges, **Faune et Flore des Pays Çomalis.**

Oustalet, Emile.

1891. Ministéres de la Marine et de l'Instruction Publique. | **Mission scientifique** | du | **Cap Horn.** | 1882-1883. | **Tome VI.** | Zoologie. | Oiseaux, | par | E. Oustalet. | Paris, | Gauthier-Villars et Fils, Imprimeurs-Libraires | de l'École Polytechnique, du Bureau des Longitudes, | Quai des Grands-Augustins, 55. | 1891.

1 vol. medium 4to, tit. (wrapper), pp. 1-341+1 l., pll. 1-6 (col.; by J. G. Keulemans). Paris.

A report on the birds secured by the French expedition to Cape Horn in 1882-83 (pp. 1-251), followed by an account of species obtained by other investigators in the region but not secured by the expedition (pp. 251-341). Two species are described as new (pp. 98 and 105), but one, *Tinamotis ingoufi,* was previously described by the same author in the Ann. Sci. Nat., Zool., Ser. 7, **9,** p. 18, 1890, under the same name. The present copy is from the library of P. L. Sclater, to whom it was presented by the author.

Over, William H.; and Thoms, Craig S.

1920. South Dakota | Geological and Natural History Survey | Freeman Ward, State Geologist | Bulletin 9 | **Birds** | **of** | **South Dakota** | By | William H. Over and | Craig S. Thoms | Series XXI March 1920 No. 9 | Bulletin | University of South Dakota | Entered as second-class matter [*etc., 2 lines.*].

1 vol. 8vo, 5 pr. ll., pp. 13-142, frontisp. (col.; by Horsfall), 21 pll. (half-tone). Vermilion. March 1920.

An annotated list of 322 species and subspecies of birds recorded from South Dakota. A bibliography is appended.

Owen, Jean A.

1922. See Johns, Charles Alexander, **British Birds in their Haunts.**

Owen, Richard.

1834. See Gould, John, **A Monograph of the Ramphastidae.**

1847. See Gould, John; (Sturm, J. H. C. F.), **J. Gould's Monographie der Ramphastiden,** 1841-47.

1852-54. See Gould, John, **A Monograph of the Ramphastidae, second edition.**

Owen, Richard.

1879. **Memoirs | on the | extinct wingless birds of New Zealand; | with an appendix | on those of | England, Australia, Newfoundland, Mauritius, and Rodriguez. | By | Richard Owen, C.B., F.R.S. | Foreign Associate of the Institute of France, etc. | Vol. I. Text [Vol. II. Plates]. | London: | John Van Voorst, 1 Paternoster Row. | 1879.**

2 vols. royal 4to. Vol. I, pp. I-X, 1-465+1, 1-7+1 (Appendix), 1-48 (Suppls. I-III), frontisp. (fold.; by Gould and Richter), 1 pl., text-figs. 1-2, 1-39, 4 text-figs. (unnum.). Vol. II, pp. I-XIV, pll. I-CXVIII, XXa, XLIa and XLIIa (25 fold.), 1-2, I-V, 1 map. (col.; fold.). London.

A series of 41 articles on the given subject, which is most thoroughly treated.

Paessler, Carl Wilhelm Gottfried.

1855-63. See Baedeker, Fr. W. J., **Die Eier der Europaeischen Voegel.**

Page, Thomas J. (Cassin, John.)

1859. **La Plata, | the | Argentine Confederation, | and | Paraguay. |** Being a narrative of the exploration of the tributaries of the | River La Plata and adjacent countries during the years | 1853, '54, '55, and '56, | under the orders of the United States Government. | By Thomas J. Page, U.S.N., | Commander of the Expedition. | With Map and Numerous Engravings. | New York: | Harper & Brothers, publishers, | Franklin Square. | 1859.

1 vol. 8vo, tit., pp. IX-XXII, 23-632, 3 ll. (advt.), frontisp., 46 text-figs., (map missing). New York.

The narrative of the expedition, with descriptions of the country and localities at many of which zoological specimens were secured. Appendix J, pp. 599-602, gives a list, by Cassin, of the species of birds secured by the expedition, so far as they had been determined at the date of publication, with notes on a few of them. The expedition was primarily nautical, and the collection of natural history specimens was incidental.

Pallas, Peter Simon. (Boddaert, Pieter.)

1767-70. **Dierkundig | mengelwerk, |** in het welke | de nieuwe of nog duistere | zoorten van dieren | Door naauwkeurige Afbeelding-en, Beschryvingen en | Verhandelingen opgehelderd worden. | In het Latyn beschreeven | door den Hooggel. Heer | P. S. Pallas, M.D. | Hoogleeraar in de natuurlyke Historie, [*etc.*, *4 lines.*]. | Vertaald en met Aanmerkingen voorzien | door | P. Boddaert. M.D. | Oudrad der Stad Vlissingen [*etc.*, *2 lines.*]. | VI stukken. | Met Plaaten. | Te Utrecht, | By { Abraham van Paddenburg, en J. van Schoonhoven. } 1770.

1 vol. (6 pts.) foliopost 4to, tit., pp. I-VIII, 1-32 (Pt. I.), 1-38 (Pt. II.), 1-35 (Pt. III.), 1-32 (Pt. IV.), 1-2, (3-4 missing; dedication), 5-30 (Pt. V.), 1-24 (Pt. VI.), 25-28 (bibliogr.), 1 l. (index), pll. A-B (Pt. I.), I-IV (Pt. II.), 4 pll. (Pts. III-VI.) (=10 pll.; col.; 1 of birds). Utrecht.

A series of memoirs on various zoological subjects, translated by Boddaert (with the addition of annotations) from the Latin of Pallas. Each of the six parts has its special subtitle-page differing from the general title-page principally in the indication of serial number and contents, and in the varying dates. The dates, as printed, are as follows. Pt. **I,** 1767 (pref. dated October 4); **II,** 1768; **III,** 1769; **IV,** 1769; **V,** 1770; **VI,** 1770. Part VI, only, contains ornithological matter and is devoted to a discussion of the "Poulpeeintades" and the "Pape-gaaiduikers" (Guinea Fowls and Puffins).

Pallas, Peter Simon.

1776-78. P. S. Pallas, | D.A.D. Professors der Naturgeschichte [*etc.*, *5 lines.*], | **Reise | durch | verschiedene Provinzen | des | Russischen Reichs |** in einem ausführlichen Auszuge. | Erster [-Dritter] Theil [| vom Jahr 1770-1771. (*Vol. II.*); in denen Jahren 1772-1773. (*Vol. III.*)] | mit vielen [22 (*Vol. II.*); 51 (*Vol. III.*)] Kupfern. | Frankfurt und Leipzig, | bey Johann Georg Fleischer, | 1776 [1777; 1778].

3 vols. in 4, cap 8vo and folio (7x9). Vol. I, 4 pr. ll. (tit., pref. and conts.), pp. 1-384, 1-52 (appendix), pll. A-I, K-O and C* (fold.; C** missing?; in atlas). Vol. II, 1 pr. l. (tit.), pp. 1-464, 1-51+1 +2 ll. (appendix, errata and list of pll.), 2 ll. (conts.), pll. I, II, AB, CD, EFGHI, K-Z and T* (all but I fold. and in atlas). Vol. III, 5 pr. ll. (tit., pref. and conts.), pp. 1-488, 1-80 (appendix), 12 ll. (index and list of pll.), pll. I, A-I, K-Z, Aa-Ii, Kk-Nn, G* and Gg* (all but I fold. and in atlas). (Atlas, 76 pll., fold.; 15 from Vol. I, 21 from II and 40 from III, noted under their respective vols.) Frankfurt and Leipzig.

The history of the author's journeys in Russia, with appendices describing the natural history of the region, mostly concerning botany. The birds are discussed in the appendix of Vol. II, pp. 7-18, and figured on pll. CD and EFGHI. Plate C** is listed on p. 52 of the appendix to Vol. I but appears to be missing from the set. Owing to the discrepancy in the size of the plates and text, the plates, except I of Vol. II and I of Vol. III, have been bound in a separate volume without title-page. This is the second edition of the work, the first, in 4to, having been issued in 1771-76.

Pallas, Peter Simon.

1778. P. S. Pallas | Medicinæ Doctoris | **miscellanea** | **zoologica** | Quibus novæ imprimis atque obscuræ | animalium species | describuntur | et observationibus iconibusque | illustrantur. | [*Vignette.*] | [*Quot., 3 lines.*] | Lugduni Batavorum, | Apud Sam. et Joan. Luchtmans, | MDCCLXXVIII.

1 vol. demy 4to, pp. 1-6, VII-XIJ, 1-224, pll. I-XIV (fold.; 1 partly ornithological). Leyden.

A second edition of this work, the first edition of which was published in 1766. The volume consists of detailed descriptions of a variety of animals, including, as the sole ornithological species, "*Grus crepitans* seu *Psophia linnæi*" on pp. 66-71 and pl. I.

Palmén, Johan Axel.

1873. See Wright, Magnus von, **Finlands Foglar**, 1859-1873.

Palmén, Johan Axel.

1876. **Ueber die** | **Zugstrassen der Vögel** | von | J. A. Palmén, | Docent der Zoologie an der Universität Helsingfors. | Mit einer lithographirten Tafel. | Leipzig, | Verlag von Wilhelm Engelmann. | 1876.

1 vol. 8vo, pp. I-VI, 1-292, 1 l. (errata), 1 map (col.; fold.). Leipzig. 1876 (post July).

A detailed study of the migration of Palaearctic birds; partly new, partly translated from the author's "Om Foglarnes Flyttningsvägar" published in Helsingfors in April 1874. The preface of the present work is dated July 1876.

Palmén, Johan Axel.

1887. See Nordenskiöld, Nils Adolph Erik von, **Vega-expeditionens Vetenskapliga Iakttagelser.**

Palmer, William.

1899. **The Avifauna of the Pribilof Islands.**

See [Jordan, David Starr, **The Fur Seals and Fur-Seal Islands of the North Pacific Ocean.**

Paris, Paul.

1906. **Les Oiseaux** | **d'Europe** | Tableaux Synoptiques | par | Paul Paris | Préparateur de Zoologie a la Faculté des Sciences de Dijon | Dessins de Maurice Dessertenne | [*Design.*] | Paris | Lucien Laveur, Éditeur | 13, rue des Saints-Pères | 1906 | Tous droits résérves.

1 vol. 12mo, pp. 1-248, 2 ll. (table and conts.), pll. I-XXV (on num. pp.), text-figs. I-CI. Paris.

Synoptic tables to groups and species or subspecies of 560 European birds. Most of these are illustrated by line drawings of full figure or specific detail. The book appears to be a very useful and compact manual for identification of species. French vernacular names are given, and the species found in France are starred for recognition.

Paris, Paul.

1921. Federation Française des Sociétés de Sciences Naturelles | Office Central de Faunistique | **Faune** | **de France** | **2** | **Oiseaux** | par | P. Paris | Préparateur a la Faculté des Sciences de Dijon | Avec 490 figures | Paris | Paul Lechevalier, 12, Rue de Tournon (VIe) | 1921 | Ouvrage honoré d'une subvention de l'Académie des Sciences de Paris | (fondations R. Bonaparte et Loutreuil).

1 vol. royal 8vo, 2 pr. ll. (half-tit. and tit.), pp. 1-473, text-figs. I-XXX, 1-460. Paris.

A manual of French ornithology, with synoptic tables and full descriptions. The work forms the second volume of an irregular series treating of the various zoological groups of the country.

Parkhurst, H. E.

1897. **Song birds and** | **water fowl** | by | H. E. Parkhurst | Author of the "Birds Calendar" | [*Quot., 2 lines.*] | Illustrated | New York | Charles Scribner's Sons | 1897.

1 vol. crown 8vo, pp. I-VIII, 1-286, 18 pll. (by L. A. Fuertes). New York.

A series of popular essays on bird life.

Parrot, Carl.

1911. See Wytsman, Paul, **Genera Avium,** 1905-14.

Parry, William Edward. (Ross, James Clark.)

1826. Journal | of a | third voyage for the discovery of a | north-west passage | from the Atlantic to the Pacific; | performed in the years 1824-25, | in His Majesty's ships | Hecla and Fury, | under the orders of | Captain William Edward Parry, R.N.,

F.R.S., | and Commander of the Expedition. | Illustrated by numerous plates. | Published by authority of the Lords Commissioners | of the Admiralty. | London: | John Murray, | Publisher to the Admiralty, and Board of Longitude. | MDCCCXXVI.

1 vol. foliopost 4to, pp. I-XXVII+1, 1 l. (dir. to binder and errata), pp. 1-186, 1 l., pp. 1-151 (appendix), 7 pll. (1 fold.), 4 maps (1 fold.), 3 text-figs. London.

The official report on the expedition. The appendix contains (pp. 96-108 of the same) Ross's report on the birds collected or observed by the expedition.

Patten, Charles Joseph.

1906. The | aquatic birds | of   Great Britain and Ireland | by | Charles J. Patten, M.A., M.D., Sc.D. | Professor of Anatomy [*etc., 3 lines.*] | with many illustrations | London | R. H. Porter | 7, Princes Street, Cavendish Square, W. | 1906.

1 vol. post 8vo, pp. I-XXX, 1-590, pll. I-LVI, text-figs. 1-68. London.

A detailed treatment of the subject, with descriptions, measurements, notes on habits and distribution, and references to colored figures of the species in other publications. The plates are mostly half-tones from photographs; some are from drawings by the author.

Patterson, Arthur H.

1903. See Dutt, W. A., **The Norfolk Broads.**

Patterson, Arthur H.

1905. Nature | in | eastern Norfolk | by | Arthur H. Patterson | Associate Member [*etc., 2 lines.*] | with twelve illustrations in colour | by F. Southgate, R.B.A. | Methuen & Co. | 36 Essex Street W.C. | London.

1 vol. crown 8vo, pp. I-VIII, 1-352, 1-40 (advt.), 12 pll. (col.; by Frank Southgate), 1 map. London.

General observations on the fauna of eastern Norfolk, prefaced by an autobiographical introduction, and followed by an annotated catalogue of the birds, fishes, mammals, reptilians, amphibians, stalk-eyed crustaceans and mollusks of the region. The birds are treated in detail on pp. 108-268.

Patterson, Arthur H.

1907. Wild life | on a Norfolk estuary | by | Arthur H. Patterson | Associate Member of the Marine Biological Association | of the United Kingdom | with a prefatory note | by Her Grace the Duchess of Bedford | with forty illustrations | Methuen & Co. | 36 Essex Street W.C. | London.

1 vol. 8vo, pp. I-XV+1, 1-352, 1-47 (advt.), frontisp., 39 text-figs. (14 full-p.). London.

Natural history observations in Norfolk, England, illustrated by the author's sketches. Most of the book is ornithological and contains an abundance of original material on avian habits and characteristics.

Paulsen, J. H.

1846. See Holböll, Carl, **Ornithologischer Beitrag zur Fauna Groenlands.**

Payne-Gallwey, Ralph.

1882. The | fowler in Ireland | or | notes on the haunts and habits | of | wildfowl and seafowl | including | instructions in the art of shooting and capturing | them | by | Sir Ralph Payne-Gallwey, Bart. | With numerous illustrations | London | John Van Voorst, Paternoster Row | MDCCCLXXXII.

1 vol. demy 8vo, 1 l. (tit.), pp. V-XIII+1, 1-503+1, 8 ll. (ruled for keeping a record of birds killed), pll. 1-17, 82 text-cuts. London.

A hunter's account of the game birds of Ireland, and especially of the methods used in shooting and trapping them.

Peabody, William B. O.

1839. See Massachusetts, **Reports on the Fishes Reptiles and Birds of—.**

Pearson, Henry J.

1899. "Beyond Petsora | eastward" | Two summer voyages to | Novaya Zemlya | and the islands of | Barents Sea | by | Henry J. Pearson | with appendices | on the botany and geology | by | Colonel H. W. Feilden | London | R. H. Porter | 7 Princes Street, Cavendish Square, W | 1899.

1 vol. 8vo (7x9¼), pp. I-XIV, 1-335, frontisp. (col.; by Grönvold), pll. 1-88, 2 maps (fold.), 6 figs., figs. 1-5. London.

The diary of two ornithological voyages to the island of Novaya Zemlya and nearby localities. Appendix G, pp. 311-324, contains an annotated list of the species of birds observed by the party; the general text is largely ornithological.

Pearson, Henry J.

1904. **Three summers among | the birds of | Russian Lapland |** by | Henry J. Pearson | Author of "Beyond Petsora Eastward" | with history of | Saint Triphon's monastery | and appendices | London | R. H. Porter | 7 Princes Street, Cavendish Square, W. | 1904.

1 vol. 8vo (6¾x9¼), pp. I-XVI, 1-216, pll. 1-68 (1 fold.), 1 map (col.; fold.). London.

Diaries of three ornithological visits to Russian Lapland. Appendix I, pp. 192-201, contains a tabulated list of birds.

Pearson, T. Gilbert.

1896. See World's Congress on Ornithology, **Papers presented to the—.**

Pearson, T. Gilbert.

1918. Tales from Birdland | [*Vignette.*] | by | T. Gilbert Pearson | Secretary, National Association of Audubon Societies [*etc., 3 lines.*] | [*Blazon.*] | Illustrations by | Charles Livingston Bull | Garden City New York | Doubleday, Page & Company | 1918.

1 vol. crown 8vo, 6 pr. ll., pp. 1-237, frontisp. (col.), 45 text-figs. New York.

A series of ten stories about birds for juvenile readers.

Pearson, T. Gilbert; Brimley, C. S.; and Brimley, H. H.

1919. North Carolina Geological and | Economic Survey | Joseph Hyde Pratt, State Geologist | Volume IV | **Birds of North Carolina** | by | T. Gilbert Pearson, C. S. Brimley, and H. H. Brimley | [*Seal.*] | Raleigh | Edwards & Broughton Printing Co. | State Printers | 1919.

1 vol. superroyal 8vo, pp. I-XXIII+1, 1-380, pll. 1-24 (col.; by Robert Bruce Horsfall and (1) by R. Brasher), A-E, 1 map, text-figs. 1-275. Raleigh.

A descriptive catalogue of the birds of the state, with bibliography, migration tables, etc. Profusely illustrated.

Pearson, T. Gilbert.

1923. The | **bird study book** | by | T. Gilbert Pearson | Secretary, National Association | of Audubon Societies | [*Blazon.*] | Coloured frontispiece | pen and ink drawings by | Will Simmons | and sixteen photographs | Garden City New York | Doubleday, Page & Company | 1923.

1 vol. crown 8vo, pp. I-XV+1, 1-258, frontisp. (col.; by L. A. Fuertes), 16 pll. (photogrs.), 26 text-cuts. Garden City and New York.

A book of general information about birds for beginners in ornithology. Methods of bird study, bird life, migration, economic value, effects of the settlement of the country, bird protection and suggestions for teaching bird study are among the topics interestingly and authoritatively treated.

Peirce, B. K.

1890. Audubon's adventures | or | life in the woods | by B. K. Peirce, D.D. | Eight illustrations | [*Blazon.*] | New York: Hunt & Eaton | Cincinnati: Cranston & Stowe | 1890.

1 vol. cap 8vo, pp. 1-252, frontisp., 7 pll. (num. pp.). New York and Cincinnati.

An account, for juvenile readers, of many of the incidents and adventures in the life of Audubon.

Pelt, Lechner, A. A. van.

See Van Pelt Lechner, A. A.

Pelzeln, August von.

1865. See Wüllerstorf-Urbair, B. von, **Reise der österreichischen Fregatte "Novara," Vögel.**

Pelzeln, August von.

1882. See Holub, Emil; and Pelzeln, **Beiträge zur Ornithologie Südafrikas.**

Pelzeln, August von.

1868-70. Zur | Ornithologie | Brasiliens. | Resultate von Johann Natterers Reisen | in den Jahren 1817 bis 1835. | Dargestellt | von | August von Pelzeln, | Custos [*etc., 3 lines.*]. | Wien. | Druck und Verlag von A. Pichler's Witwe & Sohn, | 1871.

1 vol. post 8vo, 3 pr. ll. (tit. and pref.), pp. 1-462, I-LIX+1 (itinerary and resumé of spp.), 1-18 (addenda and index), 2 maps (col.; 1 fold.). Vienna.

A detailed catalogue of the collection of birds made in Brazil by Johann Natterer during the years 1817 to 1835. The collection consisted of 12,293 bird-skins representing 1238 species. These are arranged and listed and the new forms are described. Pp. 344-390 contain an analysis of the avifauna of Brazil. Pp. 391-462 contain a list of all known Brazilian species, compiled from various sources, comprising a total of 1680 species.

The work appeared in four parts, dates for which are printed on the reverse of the title-page, but these dates as well as that on the title-page are unreliable. Dr. C. E. Hellmayr has kindly furnished me with the list of the contents of each part, obtained from a copy of Pts. I-III in original covers which is preserved in the Museum Heineanum in Halberstadt. The dates on these original covers agree with the dates on the reverse of the title-page of the volume. The following notes are available. Pt. **I** (pp. 1-68, 3 pr. ll., pp. I-XXXI and the route map) bears the date 1868 but the preface is dated September 1867 and the part was noticed in the Journal für Ornithologie for September 1867, although this number of the Journal may not have appeared until 1868; it is likewise mentioned by Sclater and Salvin in a paper read before the Zoological Society of London on January 23, 1868, although this paper was not published until the following year in the Proceedings for 1868, p. 55. Part I, therefore, must remain dated 1868 with a strong probability that it was actually published in 1867. Pt. II (pp. 69-188 and XXXIII-XLIII) is dated 1869 but was presented to the Deutsche Ornith. Gesellschaft at a meeting held on October 6, 1868; furthermore, the publishers have advised Dr. Hellmayr that the part was published in late September of that year. Pt. III (pp. 189-390, XLV-LIX and regional map) is dated 1870 and was presented to the Deutsche Ornith. Gesellschaft at a meeting held on February 1 of that year. Pt. IV (pp. 391-462, 1-18 = addenda and index, and title-page) is dated 1870 and was presented to the Deutsche Ornith. Gesellschaft at a meeting held on Oct. 3 of that year, being reviewed in the Journal für Ornithologie for September.

The work is indispensable to the student of South American ornithology.

Pelzeln, August von; and Madarász, Julius von. (Lorenz, Ludwig von.)

1887. Monographie | der | Pipridæ | oder | Manakin-Vögel | von | August von Pelzeln und Dr Julius von Madarász | unter Mitwirkung von | Dr. Ludwig von Lorenz. | Inhalt der I. Lieferung: | [*List of contents with page and plate references; in two columns.*] | Budapest | 1887. [R. Friedländer & Sohn | Berlin, N.W., Carlstr. 11. (*On pasted slip.*)].

1 vol. demy folio, cover-tit., pp. 1-13+1, pll. I-V (col.; by Julius von Madarász). Budapest.

The first and only part issued of a projected monograph of the manakins.

Penard, Arthur Philip.

1908-10. See Penard, Frederick Paul; and Penard, **De Vogels van Guyana.**

Penard, Frederik Paul; and Penard, Arthur Philip.

1908-10. De vogels van | Guyana | (Suriname, Cayenne en Demerara) | door | Frederik Paul Penard | en | Arthur Philip Penard [| Tweede deel (*Vol. II.*)] | [*Vignette.*] | Uitgave van | Wed. F. P. Penard | Paramaribo ['s-Gravenhage | Martinus Nijhoff | 1910 (*Vol. II, on slip pasted over same imprint as in Vol. I.*)].

2 vols. royal 8vo. Vol. I, 3 pr. ll. (half-tit., tit. and ded.), pp. IX-XLIII+1, 1-587, 1 p. (advt.), 161 text-cuts. Vol. II, 2 pr. ll. (half-tit. and tit.), pp. 1-587, 122 text-cuts. Paramaribo.

A descriptive catalogue of the birds of Guiana, illustrated by half-tones. A statement on the reverse of the title-page of Vol. II gives the dates of publication as follows: I, April 1908; II, May 1910.

Pennant, Thomas.

1761-66-? The | British zoology. | Class I. Quadrupeds. | II. Birds. | Published under the Inspection of the | Cymmrodorion

Society: | instituted for the | Promoting Useful Charities, and the | Knowledge of | Nature, among the Descendants of the | ancient Britons. | Illustrated with | One Hundred and Seven Copper Plates. | London: | Printed by J. and J. March, on Tower-Hill, for the Society: | And Sold for the Benefit of the British Charity-School on | Clerkenwell-Green. M,DCC,LXVI.

1 vol. superroyal folio (14½x21), 7 pr. ll. (tit., ded., pref. review of Class I, and errata), pp. 1-162, 2 ll. (index), 132 pll. (col.; by P. Paillou, Desmoulins, G. Haulner, C. Collins, P. Brown and G. Edwards). London.

A descriptive account of the birds and mammals of Great Britain. Issued in four parts from 1761 to 1766 with the 107 plates (9 of mammals and 92 of birds) as specified on the title-page. To this a fifth part was added later with 25 additional plates (2 of mammals and 23 of birds), making 132 plates in all (11 of mammals and 121 of birds). Most of the plates are by Paillou. This, the original edition, was anonymous; the author's name appeared on the title-page for the first time in the 5th edition (according to Coues), but occurred at the end of the preface in earlier ones (Cf. 4th edition, 1776-77.). The text of the ornithological section of the present work occupies pp. 57-162.

Pennant, Thomas.

1769. > Indian zoology.

1 vol. demy folio, (no tit.), pp. 1-14, pll. I-XII (col.). London.

The first number of a projected work on Indian zoology which, in this form and edition, was abandoned after the issue of the first part, here collated. The plates, including three unpublished ones, were presented to Johann Reinhold Forster who used them in his "Zoologia Indica" or "Indische Zoologie" (Cf. Latham and Davies, Faunula Indica, 1795.). A second edition of the present work (q.v.), including a translation of Forster's additions to it, appeared in 1790. The material for the present work is said to have originated in notes and drawings made in India by John Gideon Loten. Pl. I is mammalogical; the remainder are ornithological. See J. A. Allen, Bull. Am. Mus. Nat. Hist., 24, pp. 111-116, 1908, for a review of this, and the second, edition.

There is no title-page. The title transcribed above is taken from the heading of the pages of text.

Pennant, Thomas.

1776-77. **British zoology.** | Vol. I [-III; *no similar tit. for Vol. IV.*]. | Class I. Quadrupeds [Class II. Division II (*Vol. II.*); Class III. Reptiles (*Vol. III.*)]. | II. Birds [Waterfowl (*Vol. II.*); IV. Fish (*Vol. III.*)]. | **Fourth edition.** [With an | appendix. (*Vol. II.*); *line omitted* (*Vol. III.*)] | Warrington: | printed by William Eyres, | for Benjamin White, at Horace's Head, | Fleet Street [Fleet-Street (*Vols. II and III.*)], London. | MDCCLXXVI. > British zoology. | Vol. IV. | Crustacea. Mollusca. | Testacea. |

[*Quot., 3 lines.*] | [*Vignette, col.*] | London, | Printed for Benj. White, | MDCCLXXVII.

4 vols. post 8vo. Vol. I, illum. subtit., pp. I-XXXIII+1, 1-160, (illum subtit.=pl. XVI), pp. 161-418, pll. I-LIX (58 col.; 1 fold.; by Griffiths, DeSeve, Paillou, etc.). Vol. II, (illum tit.=pl. LX), 2 pr. ll. (tit. and subtit.), pp. 421-786, pll. LX-CIII and App. I-IX (col.), 1 sheet of music (fold.). Vol. III, illum. tit., 2 pr. ll. (tit. and subtit.), pp. 3-425+1, pll. I-LXXIII+XII* (73 col.; 2 fold.), 3 text-figs. Vol. IV, illum. tit. (no printed one), 2 pr. ll. (half-tit. and ded.), pp. III-VIII, 5 ll. (index to pll.), pp. 1-154, 1 l. (corrigenda), pll. I-XCIII+IX A (col.). Warrington and London.

The 8vo issue of the fourth edition (the 4to being entirely different) of Pennant's work (Cf. orig. ed., 1761-66.). The illuminated title-pages and subtitle-pages of Vols. I-III bear a London imprint at variance with the Warrington imprint on the printed title-pages but agreeing with that on the illuminated (and only) title-page of Vol. IV. The second illuminated subtitle-page of Vol. I and the illuminated title-page of Vol. II are numbered as plates; none of the others are so numbered. The regular issue of this edition appears to have uncolored plates. The ornithological matter is contained in Vol. I, pp. 153-418, pll. XV-LIX and Vol. II entire. Only Vol. I is inscribed "Fourth edition." The copy contains the bookplate of W. H. Mullens.

Pennant, Thomas.

1781. Genera | of | Birds | [*Vignette.*] | London. | Printed for B. White | MDCCLXXXI.

1 vol. demy 4to, 3 pr. ll. (engr. tit., author's note, ded.), pp. I-XXV+1 (pref. and expl. of tit.-vign.), 1-68, 1 l. (index), pll. I, II, III-IV (on one pl.), V-XVI (=15 pll.). London.

The second edition. According to the author's note, the work was written in 1772 and presented (for use in classwork) to Dr. Robert Ramsay who published the first edition in 1773, without plates. The work consists of a general discussion of ornithology, followed by diagnoses of 95 genera under English names. The Latin names are given in the synonymy of each genus and in a table of classification (pp. XXII-XXV), to which someone has added, in manuscript, the page-references. It seems to have been the original intention to figure an example of each genus, but the appearance of Latham's "General Synopsis of Birds," 1781-85 (q.v.), discouraged the project, as noted on p. 57.

Pennant, Thomas.

1784-85. Arctic zoology. | Vol. I [II]. | Introduction | Class I. Quadrupeds. [Class II. Birds.] | [*Vignette.*] | [|Pied Duck, No 488 (*Vol. II.*)]| London: | printed by Henry Hughs. | M.DCC.LXXXIV [M.-DCC.LXXXV].

2 vols. demy 4to. Vol. I, tit., pp. I-CC (introd.), 7 ll. (index to introd., pref. and list of pll.), pp. 1-185, frontisp., pll. I-VIII (1 fold.), tit.-vignette. Vol. II, tit. pp. 187-586, 7 ll. (index and errata), pll. IX-XXIII (of birds), tit.-vignette. London.

Originally intended as a sketch of the zoology of North America but later altered to include descriptions of the quadrupeds and birds of the northern parts of Europe and Asia. Vol. I contains the introduction, with its account of the northern regions and incidental mention of birds and other animals, and the detailed discussion of the mammals. Vol. II is entirely ornithological. No binomial names are used, except in the synonymy, but the full descriptions of new (and other) forms formed the basis for Latin names subsequently applied by Gmelin and Latham. In 1787 a supplementary volume was issued, often cited as Vol. III of the complete work. Later editions were published in English and German.

Pennant, Thomas. (Latham, John; Davies, Hugh; Forster, Johann Reinhold.)

1790. Indian Zoology, | **Second Edition.** | [*Vignette*; *col.*] | London. | Printed by Henry Hughs, for Robert Faulder. | MDCCXC.

1 vol. medium 4to, illum. tit., pp. I-VIII, 1-161+1[1] 1 l. (errata), pll. I-XVI (col.; 14 ornithological). London.

A reprint of Pennant's original "Indian Zoology," 1769 (q.v.), with a translation of certain matter which was added by Forster in his Latin-German edition of 1781 (Cf. Latham and Davies, Faunula Indica, 1795.), and a list of oriental and near-oriental animals, entitled, "The Indian Faunula." Pages 1-12 contain a translation of "An Essay on India" by Forster; pp. 13-27, "On the Birds of Paradise and the Phoenix," also by Forster. Pp. 27-56 contain the descriptions of the birds, fishes and the single mammal figured on the sixteen plates. Pll. VII, IX, XIV and XVI are new to this edition of Pennant being taken from Forster. "The Indian Faunula" occupies pp. 57-161 (67-86 ornithological), and is credited by Pennant to Latham (for the portion on insects) and Davies (for the remainder). The names of the mammals and birds are given only in English, but to the remainder of the species Latin binomials are assigned. The "Faunula" was reprinted by Forster, with some additions and with Latin names for the birds and mammals, in his second (1795) edition of his work. The present copy has the plates colored (rare thus), and has the flyleaf inscribed, "To the honorable Sir William Jones this book is presented as a small mark of the esteem in which the character of Sir William is held by his most obedient servant Thomas Pennant London March 27th. 1792."

Petit-Thouars, Abel Aubert du. (Prévost, Florent; Des Murs, M.A.P.O.)

1846-55. > Voyage | autour du monde | sur la frégate | La Vénus | commandée | par Abel du Petit-Thouars | Capitaine de vaisseau, Commandeur de la Légion d'honneur. | **Zoologie** | **Mammifères, Oiseaux, Reptiles et Poissons** | Paris | Gide et J. Baudry, éditeurs | Rue Bonaparte, 5 | 1855.

---

[1]Pp. 59-62, belonging to the copy, are missing but their place has been supplied by pp. 57 (dupl.)-62 from a demy 4to copy of the same work.

> Voyage | autour du monde | sur la frégate | La Vénus, | pendant les années 1836-1839, | publié par ordre du roi, | sous les auspices du Ministre de la Marine, | par | M. Abel du Petit-Thouars, | Capitaine de vaisseau, Grand-Officier de la Légion-d'Honneur. | Atlas de Zoologie. | Paris | Gide et Cie, éditeurs, | Rue des Petits-Augustins, 5, près la Quay Malaquais. | 1846.

2 vols. 8vo (text) and superroyal folio (atlas). Text, 2 pr. ll. (half-tit. and tit.), pp. I-III+1, 1-351. Atlas, 3 ll. (half-tit., tit. and table of pll.), pll. 1-13 (Mammals; 12 col.; by J. C. Werner), 1-10 (Birds; 9 col.; by Oudart), 1-3 (Reptiles; col.; by Oudart), 1-10 (Fishes; col.; by Werner), 1-24, 1(bis), 2(bis), 3(bis) (Mollusks; 26 col.; by Borromée, Oudart, A. Alberti, J. Alberti, V. Gottis and Nouvian), 1-15+15(bis) (Zoophytes; 13 col.; by Borromée and Oudart). Paris.

The entire report of the voyage of the Vénus occupies 11 vols. of text and 4 vols. of plates, and was issued from 1840-64. The ornithological portion of the account of this voyage was written by Prévost and Des Murs and occupies pp. 177-284 of the volume on zoology, collated above. The volume was issued entire in July 1855 as Vol. V, Pt. 1 of the entire "Voyage," but portions of it appeared earlier, that on the birds in 1849 (Cf. Sherborn, Ann. and Mag. Nat. Hist. Ser. 7, Vol. 8, p. 492, 1901.). The plates appeared in 1846 with the list which accompanies them, and as they contain the new scientific names, the latter must be quoted from the plates and not from the text. The two volumes at hand are richly bound with pigskin lining, and contain the bookplate-impression of Henry Arthur Johnstone.

Philippi, Rudolph Amandus.

1860. **Reise | durch | die wueste Atacama** | auf | Befehl der chilenischen Regierung im Sommer 1854-54 | unternommen und beschrieben | von | Doctor Rudolph Amandus Philippi | Professor der Zoologie [etc., 7 lines.] | Nebst einer Karte und XXVII Tafeln. | Halle, | Eduard Anton. | 1860.

1 vol. royal 4to, pp. I-IX+1, 1-192, 1-62 (Florula Atacamensis), pll. I-12 (11 monochr. and col.; 2 fold), I and II (fossils), I-VI and I unnum. (Zool.; col.), I-VI (Botan.), 1 map (fold.), text-figs. 1-4+1 unnum. Halle.

A general account of an expedition to the Desert of Atacama Chile. The birds are treated briefly on pp. 161-165 and pll. (Zool.) III-V, where two new species are described, both of which were published earlier in other places. An edition in Spanish was issued at Halle contemporaneously with the German one collated herewith; the prefaces in both are dated September 3, 1858.

Phillip, Arthur. (Ball, Henry Lidgbird; Watts, John; Latham, John.)

1789. **The | voyage | of | Governor Phillip | to | Botany Bay; |** with an | Account of the Establishment of the Colonies of | Port

Jackson & Norfolk Island; | compiled from Authentic Papers, | which have been obtained from the several Departments. | to which are added, | The Journals of Lieuts. Shortland, Watts, Ball, & Capt. Marshall; | with an Account of their New Discoveries | [*Vignette*.] | embellished with fifty five Copper Plates, | The Maps and Charts taken from Actual Surveys, | & the Plans & Views drawn on the Spot, | by Capt. Hunter, Lieuts. Shortland, Watts, Dawes, Bradley, Capt. Marshall, &c. | London | Printed for John Stockdale, Piccadilly. | MDCCLXXXIX.

1 vol. foliopost 4to, engr. tit., pp. 1-6, 1 l. (errata), pp. I-VIII, 4 ll. (list of subscrs.), 2 ll. (list of pll.), pp. I-X (conts.), 1-298, I-LXXIV (appendix), 1 l. (advt.), 54 pll.+tit.-vignette (31 col.; 7 fold.; 19 col., of birds). London. 1789 (post Nov. 26).

The narrative of the European settlement of Australia under Governor Phillip, compiled from official records and other sources. Incidental remarks are made regarding birds, both in the general account and in the portions of the work taken from the journals of Lieuts. Ball and Watts. Special discussions of various animals of the region are found in Chapters XV and XXII (pp. 144-168 and 267-298), much of which relates to birds. These are usually ascribed to Latham, to whom acknowledgement is made by the editors for unspecified drawings and descriptions. No binomial names are used herein, but Latham included some of the species (many of which are here figured for the first time) in his "Index Ornithologicus," 1790 (q.v.). Second and third editions of the present work were issued in 1790, and German and French editions in 1791. The last plate is dated November 26, 1789; the dedication, November 25, 1789.

Phillips, John C.

1922-25-?. A natural history of | the ducks | by | John C. Phillips | Associate Curator of Birds in the Museum | of Comparative Zoölogy at Harvard College | with plates in color and in black and white | from drawings by | Frank W. Benson, Allan Brooks | and [Louis Agassiz Fuertes] | Louis Agassiz Fuertes [and | Henrik Grönvold] | Volume I [-III] Plectropterinæ, Dendrocygninæ, Anatinæ (in part) [The genus Anas (*Vol. II.*); Anatinæ (concluded) and Fuligulinæ (in part) (*Vol. III.*)] | [*Blazon.*] | Boston and New York | Houghton Mifflin Company | The Riverside Press Cambridge | 1922 [1923; 1925].

3 (-?) vols. royal 4to. Vol. I, pp. I-X, 1 l. (list of maps), pp. 1-264, pll. 1-18 (9 col.), maps 1-27 (1 fold.). Vol. II, pp. I-XII, 1-409, pll. 19-44 (20 col.), maps 28-65 (6 fold.). Vol. III, pp. I-IX+1, 1 l. (list of maps), pp. 1-383, pll. 45-70 (21 col.), maps 66-95 (4 fold.). Boston and New York.

A monographic account of the ducks of the world, containing synonymy, description, distribution, abundance, habits and other characteristics of each of the species. The illustrations are very fine. According to the half-title, the work will be complete in four volumes.

Phillott, D. C.

1908. See Tāymur Mīrzā, **The Bāz-Nāma-yi Nāsirī.**

Pidgeon, Edward.

1827-35. See Cuvier, **The Animal Kingdom.**

Pleske, Theodor Dmītrievīch.

1889-92. Ornithographia | Rossica. | Ornithologhisheskaya fauna Die Vogelfauna | des | Rossiĭskoĭ imperiĭ russischen Reichs | von | T. D. Pleske. Th. Pleske. | Tom' II. Band II. | Sylviinae. | S.-Peterburgh' 1801. - St.-Pétersbourg, 1891. | Commissionaires de

l'Académie Impériale des sciences: à St.-Pétersbourg:
M. Eggers et Cie et J. Glasunof;

à Riga: à Leipzig
M. N. Kymmel;   Voss' Sortiment (G. Haessel).   Prix: 12 Rbl.
35 Kop. = 30 Mark 90 Pf.

1 vol. medium 4to, tit., pp. 1-13+1 (pref. to vol.), I-LIII+1, 1-12 (pref. to Pt. I), 2 ll. (subtit. and pref. to Pt. II), 1-431+1, 431 (*bis*)-665+1, 4 ll. (expl. of pll.), pll. I-IV (col.; by G. Mützel), text-figs. 1-20, (orig. wrapper of Pt. II.). St. Petersburg.

A detailed monograph of the warblers (subfam. Sylviinae) of Russia. The work was issued in 5 parts as follows. Part **I**, pp. I-VIII, 1-154, pl. I, 1889; **II**, 2 ll. (subtit. and pref. of Pt. II), pp. IX-XVIII, 155-320, pl. II, 1889; **III**, pp. XIX-XXXII, 321-431+1, 1890; **IV**, pp, XXXIII-XL, 431 (*bis*)-560, pl. III, 1890; **V**, pp. XLI-LIV, 561-665+1, tit., pp. 1-13+1, 1892. The preface of the entire volume and the imprint on the reverse of the title-page are dated December 1891, but Pt. V appears to have been issued the year afterward. The preface of Pt. I is signed Dec. 18, 1888; the subtit.-p. of Pt. II is dated on the reverse, October 1889, and the preface of that part, September 13, 1889. The duplicated page (p. 431) appears to be a reimpression without change. Although this volume is entitled Vol. II, no Vol. I was issued before or afterward, and an evident intention to publish similar volumes on other groups of Russian birds was never carried out. The present work is printed with the general text in both Russian and German, in parallel columns.

Pocci, Franz Graf von.

1906. Franz Graf v. Pocci. | **Der Fasan in Bayern** | eine historische und zoologische Darstellung | Mit 10 farbigen Tafeln in Autotypie | und zahlreichen Textbildern | München 1906 | Kommissionsverlag von Emil Hirsch.

1 vol. royal 8vo, 8 pr. ll., pp. 1-225, pll. I-X (col.; 1 fold; 1 map, fold.; II-VII by Eugen Rosenfeld), text-cuts 1-47 (num. only in index). Munich.

An account of pheasants and pheasant-rearing in Bavaria.

Pokagon, Simon.

1907. See Mershon, W. B., **The Passenger Pigeon.**

Pollen, François P. L.; and Dam, D. C. van. (Schlegel, Hermann.)

1867-68. Recherches | sur la | fauna de Madagascar | et de | ses dépendances, | d'après les découvertes | de | François P. L. Pollen et D. C. Van Dam. | **2me partie.** | Leyde, | J. K. Steenhoff, Éditeur. | 1868. **Mammifères et oiseaux** | par | H. Schlegel, | Docteur en Philosophie [*etc.*, *2 lines.*] | et | François P. L. Pollen, | Agent Consulaire [*etc.*, *3 lines.*].

1 vol. imperial 4to, pp. I-XIX+1, 1-186, pll. 1-40 (38 col.; by J. G. Keulemans?; 11-40 ornithological). Leyden.

A report on the mammals and birds of Madagascar, based on the collections of Pollen and Dam, but including all known forms whether secured by these investigators or by other workers. Numerous new species are described, but some of these were previously described in other places. The present volume is No. 2 of the series which consists of 5 volumes, all that have been published. Vol. 2 was issued in 4 livraisons, of which **I-III** appeared in 1867 and **IV** in 1868 according to current reviews in the Ibis. Authorship of this volume is by Schlegel and Pollen, but the exact portion attributable to each is uncertain. The ornithology occupies pp. X-XIX and 30-163, 165-166, 168-171, 172 (pt.) 173-174 and portions of the indices. The plates are very good.

Pollard, Hugh B. C.

1924. See Kirkman, Frederick B.; and Hutchinson, **British Sporting Birds.**

Pope, A. (Ingersoll, Ernest.)

1878. Part first. { The Green-winged Teal. The American Snipe. | **Upland game birds** |
and | water fowl $\frac{of}{the}$ | **United States.** | By A Pope Jr | Published by | Charles Scribner's Sons, New York. | Copyright by A. Pope, Jr., 1878. | Chemical Eng. Mandel & Werlitz, Boston. [*Cover-tit.*]

1 vol. elephant, cover-tit. 20 ll., 20 pll. (col.; num. and unnum.) New York. (1877?-) 1878.

A series of chromolithographs accompanied by a brief account of each of the species figured. The text, according to Coues, is by Ernest Ingersoll. The work was issued in ten parts, each with two pll. and the corresponding text. The copy recorded by Coues appears to have the copyright dated 1877 for the first part and 1878 for the remainder; the set at hand has the first part copyrighted in 1878, as collated above. The title on the wrapper of Part First is the only title in the copy.

Portlock, Nathaniel.

1789. A | voyage round the world; | but more particularly to the | north-west coast of America: | performed in 1785, 1786, 1787, and 1788, | in | the King George and Queen Charlotte, | Captains Portlock and Dixon. | Embellished with twenty copper-plates. | Dedicated, by permission, to | His Majesty. | By Captain Nathaniel Portlock. | London: | printed for John Stockdale, opposite Burlington-House, Piccadilly; | and George Goulding, James Street, Covent Garden. | M,DCC,LXXXIX.

1 vol. medium 4to, pp. I-XII, 1-384, I-XL, 14 pll. (5 col.), 6 maps (fold.). London.

An official account of the voyage, interspersed with ornithological and other zoological notes and with five hand-colored plates of birds. Another account of the voyage was published the same year under a nearly identical title, by Captain George Dixon (q.v.), the junior officer of the expedition.

Powys, Thomas Lyttleton.

See Lilford, Lord.

Poynting, Frank.

1895-96. Eggs of British birds, | with an account of their breeding-habits. | Limicolæ. | With 54 coloured plates. | By | Frank Poynting. | London: | R. H. Porter, 7 Princes Street, Cavendish Square, W. | 1895-6.

1 vol. medium 4to, pp. I-VIII, 127 ll. (var. paged), 54 pll. (col.). London.

Compiled accounts of the nesting habits of British shore birds, with excellent plates in color depicting the eggs of the species in considerable individual variation. The work was issued in four parts, with contents and dates as specified on p. XVI of the volume in question. The various accounts are paged separately for each species and the plates are unnumbered, but on pp. III and IV of the introductory matter, the final pagination and numbering of plates are given. The present copy is bound as issued, without reference to this final arrangement.

Praeger, William G.

1896. See World's Congress on Ornithology, **Papers presented to the——**.

Pratt, George B.

1896. See World's Congress on Ornithology, **Papers presented to the—.**

Prentis, Walter.

1894. **Notes | on the | birds of Rainham |** including the | District between Chatham and Sittingbourne | by | Walter Prentis | [*Monogram.*] | London | Gurney & Jackson, I, Paternoster Row | (Successors to Mr. Van Voorst) | MDCCCXCIV.

1 vol. crown 8vo, pp. 1-92. London.

Random notes on various local birds of the region, arranged by species.

Prévost, Florent.

1838-43. See Knip, Madame, **Les Pigeons.**

Prévost, Florent.

1846-55. See Petit-Thouars, **Voyage Autour du Monde sur le Frégate La Vénus.**

Prévost, Florent; and Lemaire, C. L.

1864. **Histoire naturelle | des oiseaux | d'Europe |** par | Florent Prévost, | Aide-Naturaliste de Zoologie au Muséum d'Histoire Naturelle, | Chevalier de la Légion d'Honneur | et | C. L. Lemaire | Docteur en Médecine | avec 80 planches représentant 200 sujets | peintes d'après nature | gravées sur acier par Pauquet | Paris | F. Savy, Libraire-Éditeur | 24, Rue Hautefeuille | Tous droits réservés.

1 vol. 8vo, 2 pr. ll. (half-tit. and tit.), pp. 1-203+1, I-XII (X misprinted XX), illum. tit., pll 1-80 (col.; by Pauquet), 2 pll. (figs. 1-32). Paris.

An account of the birds of Europe, discussed under vernacular names but with some synonymy presented for each species. Only a portion of the avifauna of Europe is discussed, with the apparent intention of adding later volumes, which, however, were never issued. The colored plates are steel engravings, hand-colored. An appendix (pp. I-XII) treats of bird collecting and preservation, illustrated by the uncolored plates. This volume is a revision of Lemaire's earlier (1846) work of the same title forming the third volume (Ser. 2, No. 1) of the second edition of the "Bibliothèque Zoologique." The first edition was published in 1837 (Cf. Lemaire, Bibliothèque Zoologique>Hist. Nat. des Ois. Exotiques, 1836.).

Przheval'skiĭ, Nĭkolaĭ Mĭkhaĭlovĭch.

1877-78. See Rowley, George D., **Ornithological Miscellany,** 1875-78.

Provancher, l'Abbé.

1874.   Les | oiseaux insectivores | et | les arbres d'ornement | et |
forestiers | Par | l'Abbé Provancher. | [*Vignette.*] | Publié sur
demande de l'Hon. P. Fortin, Ministre des Terres de la Couronne. |
Québec: | Atelier Typographique de C. Darveau, | No. 8, Rue
La Montagne, Basse-Ville. | 1874.

1 vol. (pamphlet) 8vo, pp. 1-30+1 l., 4 text-figs. + tit.-fig. Quebec.
1874 (post August 12).

A brief discussion of some beneficial birds of Quebec, with a plea for their protection. The latter part of the pamphlet (pp. 19-30) relates to the planting of
ornamental and other trees and is supplied with a separate title-page.

Pucheran, Jacques.

1853.   See Dumont d'Urville, J., **Voyage au Pole Sud et dans
l'Océanie sur les Corvettes l'Astrolabe et la Zélée, Zoologie,**
1842-54.

Pycraft, William Plane.

1907.   See British Museum, **National Antarctic Expedition 1901-1904;
Natural History Vol. II.**

Pycraft, William Plane.

1910.   See Godman, F. D., **A Monograph of the Petrels,** 1907-10.

Pycraft, William Plane.

1910.   **A history of birds** | by | W. P. Pycraft | Zoological Depart-
ment, British Museum | with an introduction by | Sir Ray
Lankester, K.C.B., F.R.S. | and numerous illustrations and dia-
grams | Methuen and Co. | 36 Essex Street W. C. | London.

1 vol. post 8vo, pp. I-XXXI+1, 1-458, 1 l. (imprint), pp. 1-47 (advt.),
35 pll. (2 col., by G. E. Lodge; 1 fold.), text-figs. 1-50. London.

According to the author's preface, the book is a study of bird life from the point
of view of the evolutionist. There is considerable information and some specu-
lation in the work. A preliminary title-page assigns the book to a place as
Vol. II in "Animal Life | an evolutionary natural history" to be issued in four
volumes.

Pycraft, William Plane.

1910-13.   See Kirkman, Frederick Bernuf Bever, **The British Bird
Book.**

Pycraft, William Plane.

1922.   **Birds in Flight** | by | W. P. Pycraft | Zoological Department
[*etc., 8 lines.*] | Illustrated by | Roland Green, F.Z.S. | London |

Gay & Hancock Limited | 34 Henrietta Street, Covent Garden, W.C.2. | 1922 | All Rights Reserved.

1 vol. 8vo (7¼x9¾), pp. I-X, 1-133, 29 pll. (12 col.; 9 on num. pp.). London.

A popular discussion of the flight of birds and of some of the means of recognizing British species in flight. The illustrations are both accurate and artistic.

Pycraft, William Plane.

1924. See Kirkman, Frederick B.; and Hutchinson, **British Sporting Birds.**

Quarles, E. A.

1916. American Pheasant | Breeding and | Shooting | By | E. A. Quarles | Director, Department of Game Breeding [*etc., 2 lines.*] | With 50 Halftone Illustrations | Hercules Powder Company | Wilmington, Del. | 1916.

1 vol. 8vo, 4 pr. ll., pp. 1-132, 4 ll. (index), frontisp., text-figs 1-21, 1A, 3A-3D, 5A, 5B, 6A, 6B, 7A, 8A, 10A, 11A, 16A and 16B, 14 text-figs. (unnum.). Wilmington.

A treatise on the breeding, shooting, preserving and marketing of the Ring-neck Pheasant.

Quelch, John J.

1896. See World's Congress on Ornithology, **Papers presented to the—.**

Quelch, John J.

1921. See Chubb, Charles, **The Birds of British Guiana,** 1916-1921.

Quoy, Jean René Const.

1824-26. See Freycinet, **Voyage Autour du Monde . . . sur les corvettes . . . l'Uranie et la Physicienne.**

Quoy, Jean René Const.

1830-35. See Dumont D'Urville, Jean, **Voyage de Découvertes de l'Astrolabe.**

Radde, Gustav Ferdinand Richard.

1863. > Reisen | im | Süden von Ost-Siberien | in | den Jahren 1855-1859 incl. | im auftrage der kaiserlichen geographischen Gesellschaft | ausgeführt | von | Gustav Radde. | Band II. | Die Festlands-Ornis des südostlichen Siberiens. | Hierzu 15 chromolithographische Tafeln. | St. Petersburg. | Buchdruckerei von W. Besobrasoff & Co. | 1863.

1 vol. royal 4to, 3 pr. ll. (tit., ded. and half-tit. (expl. of frontisp. on reverse), pp. 1-392, pll. I-XV (col.; by Radde; XI=frontisp.; II duplicated). St. Petersburg.

A report on the ornithology of the expedition. Vol. I of the series, published the preceding year, contained the mammals. The present copy is in the original wrappers.

Radde, Gustav Ferdinand Richard.

1884. **Ornis Caucasica.** | Die Vogelwelt des Kaukasus | systematisch und biologisch-geographisch beschrieben | von | Dr. Gustav Radde | Direktor des Kaukasischen Museums und der öffentlichen Bibliothek | in Tiflis | Mit 26 Tafeln und 1 Karte. | Kassel. | Verlag von Theodor Fischer. | 1884.

1 vol. medium 4to, pp. I-XI+1, 3 ll. (expl. of frontisp., list of subscrs. and conts.), pp. 1-592, frontisp. (col.), pll. I-XXV (col.; by Radde), 1 map (col.; fold.), 6 text-figs. Cassel.

A catalogue of the birds of Caucasia, with systematic and distributional notes on each species and descriptions of several new forms. The work appears to have been issued in four parts, but I am unable to distinguish each part. At the meeting of the Deutsche Ornithologische Gesellschaft on May 5, 1884, the first lieferung (probably with 2 pll.) was presented. At the meeting on September 1, 1884, 2 parts (embracing lieferungen 2 to 16 and 12 pll.) were presented. The Ibis for January 1885 reviews three parts of the work (including pp. 1-480 (?) and pll. I-XVI). The entire work was reviewed by Madarász in the "Zeitschr.f.d.Gesammte Ornith." for January 1885; the preface of the work is dated August 1884 and the title-page, 1884; so the final work probably appeared near the close of the year 1884. Pages 588 and 589 contain a first supplement to the work. The second supplement was published in the "Journ. f. Orn." XXXIII Jahrg., pp. 74-81, 1885. The third and fourth supplements were published in the "Ornis" for 1887, pp. 457-500; and 1890, pp. 400-441, respectively. A reprint of the fourth supplement, paged 1-43, is inserted in the present copy, together with a portrait of Radde extracted from the "Ornithologische Monatschrift, Vol. XII, 1903.

Raine, Walter.

1892. **Bird-nesting** | in | **north-west Canada** | by | Walter Raine. | Illustrated. | Toronto: | printed by Hunter, Rose and Company. | 1892.

1 vol. 8vo, pp. I-VII+1, 1 l., pp. 1-197, 34 pll. (6 col.; 28 monochr.), 6 text-figs. Toronto.

A popular account of an oological excursion to north-western Canada. The illustrations are by the author. The colored plates are of eggs; the monochromes are of birds, mammals and scenery.

Ralfe, Pilcher George.

1906. [*Illustr.*] | **The Birds** | of the | **Isle of Man** | by P. G. Ralfe | Member of the British Ornithologist's (*sic*) Union | Edinburgh. David Douglas. 1905.

1 vol. post 8vo, pp. I-LV+1, 1-321+1, 1 l. (advt.), (photograv. title=p. 3), 47 pll., 2 maps (col.; fold.). Edinburgh.

A popular account of Manx ornithology, giving the distribution, history, vernacular nomenclature and occasional notes on the habits of Manx birds. The introduction is descriptive of the region. The photogravure title-page bears the date 1905, but the Zoological Record, the Ibis, and Mullens & Swann agree in citing 1906 as the date of publication. The present copy is from the library of R. J. Balston who has added occasional marginal notes.

Ramsay, Robert George Wardlaw.

1881. See Hay, Arthur, **The Ornithological Works of Arthur, Ninth Marquis of Tweeddale.**

Ramsay, Robert George Wardlaw.

1923. **Guide to the** | **birds of Europe and** | **North Africa** | by | Colonel R. G. Wardlaw Ramsay | President [*etc.*, *2 lines.*] | with a biographical memoir by | William Eagle Clarke, LL.D. | Gurney and Jackson | London: 33 Paternoster Row | Edinburgh: Tweeddale Court | 1923.

1 vol. crown 8vo, pp. I-XI+1, 1-355+1, 2 ll. (advt.), frontisp. (portr.). London and Edinburgh.

A pocket manual, giving descriptions of all the species and subspecies of European and North African birds and noting their ranges or distribution. Genera and higher groups are characterized in their places.

Rapine, J.

1921. See Ménégaux, A.; and Rapine, **Les Noms des Oiseaux trouvés en France.**

Rastall, R. H.

1911. See [Grouse], **The Grouse in Health and Disease.**

Rathbun, Frank R.

1880-82. **Bright feathers** | or | Some North American | birds of beauty. | By Frank R. Rathbun. | Illustrated with Drawings made from Nature, and carefully | Colored by Hand. | [*Monogram.*] | Auburn, N. Y. | Published by the Author. | 1880.

5 parts royal 4to. Pt. I, pp. I-VII+1, 9-24, 1 pl. (col.), 2 decorations, 1 text-fig. (col.). Pt. II, pp. 25-40, 1 pl. (col.), 1 decoration. Pt. III, pp. 41-56, 1 pl. (col.), 1 text-fig. (col.), 2 decorations. Pt. IV,

pp. 57-72, 1 pl. (col.), text-figs. 1 and 2, 3 decorations. Pt. V, pp. 73-88, 1 pl. (col.), 2 text-figs., 2 decorations (insert,-portrait of author, in each part). Auburn.

All published of a work intended to describe and figure "ten or more species (in as many parts) of such birds as are found in the North-eastern portion of the United States, most attractive for their plumage colorations." Much of the text is quoted from other authors; the remainder is written in attempted literary style but with an inexperienced hand, and is full of poetic fancies and allusions. The species treated are the Purple Finch, Rose-breasted Grosbeak, Goldfinch, Yellow Warbler and Redstart. Part I is dated 1880; II, 1881; III-V, 1882. The original price was $1.00 per part. The present set is in original wrappers.

Rathke, Martin Heinrich.

1833. See Eschscholz, Friedrich, **Zoologischer Atlas,** 1829-33.

Ray, John.

1676. See Willughby, Francis, **Ornithologiae.**

Ray, John.

1678. See Willughby, Francis; and Ray, **The Ornithology of Francis Willughby.**

Ray, John. (Salerne, François.)

1767. **L'Histoire naturelle, | éclaircie | dans une de ses parties principales, | l'ornithologie.** | qui traite | des oiseaux | de terre, de mer et de riviere, | tant de nos climats que des pays étrangers. | Ouvrage traduit du Latin du Synopsis avium de Ray, augmenté d'un | grand nombre de descriptions & de remarques historiques sur le carac- | tere des Oiseaux, leur industrie & leurs ruses. | Par M. Salerne, Docteur en Médecine à Orléans, Correspondant | de l'Académie Royale des Sciences. | Enrichi de trente-une Figures dessinées d'après nature. | [*Design.*] | A Paris, | Chez Debure Pere, Libraire, Quai des Augustins, à l'Image | Saint Paul. | M. DCC. LXVII. | Avec approbation, et privelege du roi.

1 vol. medium 4to, pp. I-XII, 2 ll. ("Approbation" and "Privelege du Roi", errata and dir. for placing pll.), pp. 1-464, pll. 1-31 (figures occasionally in Roman) (by Martinet). (Interleaved, 10 pll. from Buffon, Sonnini ed.; col., by DeSeve). Paris.

This work, according to its own title-page, is a translation of the "Synopsis Methodica Avium" (1713) of John Ray[1] with additions by Salerne, but the additions often far exceed the translations which serve mainly as a basis for

---

[1] "Joannis Raii | Synopsis | methodica | Avium & Piscium; | opus posthumum | —— Londini: | —— MDCCXIII," from copy in Field Museum library; ornithological portion listed also separately under same date by Engelmann.

the extended remarks by Salerne. The book, like Ray's "Synopsis" is post-humous. The subject matter consists of a review of the birds of the world, with brief descriptions, notes on distribution and habits, vernacular names, and other such matter. The volume was intended to form one of a series of which at least one other part (on "La Lithologie, la Conchyliologie et la Zo-omorphose," by Ant. Jos. Dezollier d'Argenville) was issued, in 1742-57. The interleaved plates from the Sonnini edition of Buffon's "Histoire Naturelle," 1800-05 (q.v.) are extraneous.

Rea, Paul Marshall.

1910. See Wayne, Arthur Trezevant, **Birds of South Carolina.**

Reed, Cárlos Samuel.

1907. Ornitolojía económica | **Las Aves Chilenas** | consideradas mui especialmente | desde el punto de vista biolójico | por | Cárlos S. Reed, | Miembro titular [etc., 7 lines.]. | Obra ilustrada con muchos grabados | i precedida de una introduccion del | Prof. Cárlos E. Porter, C.M.Z.S. | Director i Jefe [etc., 6 lines.]. [Vig-niette.] | Concepcion | Lithografia e imprenta "Concepcion" - Soulodre, Juanchuto & Ca, | 1907.

1 vol. 8vo, pp. I-XIV, 15-131+1, frontisp. (portr.; on p. VII), text-figs. 1-30. Concepcion.

Brief accounts of some of the more common Chilean birds.

Reed, Cárlos Samuel.

1916. Museo Educacional de Mendoza | **Las aves** | **de la** | **Provincia de Mendoza** | por | Carlos S. Reed, F.Z.S, | Director Fundador del Museo | de Mendoza | Trabajo presentado a la primera reunión nacional | de la | Sociedad Argentina de Ciencias Naturales | Celebrada en la Ciudad de Tucumán, en la primavera de 1916. [Quot., 2 lines.] | (Parte I, Lista sistematica) | Mendoza | Imprenta de Guillermo Kraft | 1916.

1 pamphlet (7x10½), pp. 1-47, 1 insert-slip (errata). Mendoza.

An annotated check-list of the birds of Mendoza Province, Argentina. References are given to the Catalogue of Birds in the British Museum and to Dabbene's "Catálogo Sistemático y Descriptivo de las Aves Argentinas," with vernacular names and notes on distribution.

Reed, Charles K.; and Reed, Chester A.

1914. Guide to | **taxidermy** | by | Chas. K. Reed | and | Chester A. Reed, B.S. | Author of [etc., 3 lines.]. | Illustrated by | Drawings and Photographs of Mounted Specimens | by the Authors and Mr. N. F. Stone. | **New edition** - Enlarged and Re-written. | Twentieth Thousand | Worcester, Mass., | Chas. K. Reed, | 1914.

1 vol. crown 8vo, pp. 1-304, 2 ll. (index), 45 pll. (on num. pp.), numerous marginal drawings, (col. fig. on cover). Worcester.

A manual of taxidermy, copiously illustrated. On pp. 233-304 there is given a "List of Birds of North America, together with a fair valuation of the eggs, skins and mounted specimens of each."

Reed, Chester Albert.

1904. North American birds eggs | by | Chester A. Reed, B.S. | Author [*etc.*, *2 lines.*] | Illustrating the eggs of nearly every | species of North American birds | [*Col. fig.*] | New York | Doubleday, Page & Company | 1904.

1 vol. 8vo, 5 pr. ll. (tit., pref., list of illustrs., conts. and half-tit.), pp. 1-356, frontisp. (col.), col. fig. on tit., 656 half-tone cuts (84 of nests and eggs; 572 of eggs only), 273 marginal sketches, (col. fig. on cover). New York.

A brief account of the nests and eggs of each of the North American birds, with notes on distribution and a short description of the differentiating characters of the species. Most of the eggs are pictured by an excellent half-tone figure of a typical specimen.

Reed, Chester, Albert.

1911. Camera studies | of | **wild birds** | **in their homes** | by | Chester A. Reed, B.S. | Author of [*etc.*, *2 lines.*]. | With More than 200 Illustrations from Photographs | of Living Wild Birds | 1911 | W. B. Clarke Company | Boston, Mass.

1 vol. demy 8vo, pp. 1-312, frontisp. (col.), 6 pll. (col.; by Reed; on 3 ll.), text-figs. 2-260 (photographic). Boston.

A running account of the author's experiences in photographing and observing birds, and of the habits of the various species discussed; illustrated with a large number of very good photographs of nests and eggs, young and parent birds.

Reed, Chester, Albert.

1912. American | **game birds** | by | Chester A. Reed, S.B. | Author of [*etc.*, *2 lines.*]. | Illustrating more than one hundred species | in natural colors | Charles K. Reed | Worcester, Mass. | 1912.

1 vol. (32mo; 4¾x6⅞), pp. 1-64 (57-64 advt.), frontisp. and 48 pll. (col.; on num. pp.), 12 text-figs. (also col. figs. on front and back cover). Worcester.

A brief account of the habits of each of the North American game birds, illustrated by colored portraits of most of the species. The book is intended for the sportsman.

Reed, Chester Albert.

1912. Wild birds | of | New England | by | Chester A. Reed, S.B. | colored illustrations | Chas. K. Reed, | Worcester, Mass. | 1912.
1 vol. (pamphlet; 5x7), tit., pp. 5-52, 2 ll. (advt.), frontisp. (col.), 41 text-figs. (40 col.). Worcester.

Brief accounts of the habits and characteristics of a number of the common or striking birds of New England. The text is in two distinct parts. On the lower portion of all the pages, running throughout the volume, is a more or less continuous account of various species, not illustrated. The upper part of each page contains the account of a particular species, illustrated by a colored figure taken from one or the other of the author's popular bird guides, "Land Birds" or "Water Birds." A chart of seasonal distribution is given at the close of the volume.

Reed, Chester Albert.

1914. See Reed, Charles K.; and Reed, **Guide to Taxidermy.**

Reed, Chester Albert.

1923. Bird Guide | Land birds east of the Rockies | from parrots to bluebirds | by | Chester A. Reed | Author of | North American Birds' Eggs, [etc., 2 lines.]. | Garden City New York | Doubleday, Page & Company | 1923.
1 vol. 32mo (5½x3¼,-long), pp. 1-228, 6 ll. (advt.), 196 figs. (192 col., by the author). Garden City and New York.

A recent edition of this popular, pocket-sized handbook for the identification, in the field, of the common eastern land birds of North America. The first edition was published in 1906. A colored figure is given of each species, together with a brief discussion of each and with a "field key" at the close of the volume. The colors of most of the figures are less accurate than in the early editions of the work. The volume forms Pt. 2 of the "Bird Guide," being accessory to a similar volume on water birds. A companion volume is found in the author's "Western Bird Guide," 1923 (q.v.).

Reed, Chester Albert.

1923. Western Bird Guide | Birds of the Rockies and West to the Pacific | Illustrations by | Chester A. Reed, B.S.; Harry F. Harvey; R. I. Brasher | [Trade mark.] | Garden City New York | Doubleday, Page & Company | 1923.
1 vol. 32mo (5½x3¼,-long), pp. 1-252, 234 figs. (233 col.). Garden City and New York.

A work similar in construction to the author's "Bird Guide" (Cf. ed. 1923.), to which it forms a companion volume. The figures of the various species are smaller than in the other work, and, consequently, show details less clearly.

Reichenbach, Heinrich Gottlieb Ludwig.

1836-?. > Praktisch-gemeinnützige | Naturgeschichte | der | Vögel | des | In- und Auslandes | von | H. G. L. Reichenbach. | Kupfersammlung, | erster Theil mit 408 Abbildungen der | Schwimmvögel, | nämlich für die Gattung: | [*Double column, 11 lines; list of genera and no. of figs.*] | Leipzig. | Verlag der Wagner'schen Buchhandlung. | 1836. > Das Thierreich. | Zweiter Band. | Vögel. I. Schwimmvögel. > Sumpfvögel oder Stelzvögel.

2 pts. superroyal 8vo. "Schwimmvögel," tit., 7 ll. "Sumpfvögel," 6 ll. Leipzig.

Part of the original work,—precursor of Reichenbach's "Die Vollständigste Naturgeschichte," 1845-63 (q.v.); catalogued by Engelmann as "Der Naturfreund, od. praktisch Gemeinnütz. Naturgesch. des In- und Auslandes," etc., 1834-43. The text at hand consists of a list of the figures on the plates, (1-408, Schwimmvögel; 417-731, Sumpfvögel), with vernacular and scientific names and the habitats of the species. The plates are missing. In general, the numbering of the figures as indicated in the text shows no affinity to that of the figures in the "Vollständigste Naturgeschichte," but in a few cases (Albatrosses and Flamingoes), the numbering agrees and points to a probability that some of the figures of the present work were adapted for use in its successor.

Reichenbach, Heinrich Gottlieb Ludwig.

1845-63. > [Die vollständigste Naturgeschichte des In- und Auslandes, etc. Abtheilung II. Vögel.]

(11 vols.) demy 4to, royal, superroyal and imperial 8vo. 1028 pll. (922 col.).

Under the above title are grouped various parts of a detailed, comprehensive work which was issued under a variety of cover-titles at irregular intervals in a most confusing manner. The entire work is extremely puzzling as to arrangement and method of appearance and I can find no complete and accurate collation of the various components. As nearly as I can decide from available material and references, the history of the work is somewhat as follows.

The book started as "Der Naturfreund, oder praktisch-gemeinnützige Naturgeschichte des In- und Auslandes," 1834-43. Of this early work, two parts are present in the set at hand (Cf. Praktisch-gemeinnütz. Naturg. der Vögel, 1836-?). In 1884, the title was changed and the work continued (or begun anew) as quoted above. Several numbers of plates were issued under subtitles of "Die vollständigste Naturgeschichte der Schwimmvögel [Sumpfvögel], etc., 1845-48 (q.v.), shortly thereafter followed by installments of text. At first, the text consisted merely of a "Synopsis Avium" or list of species containing references to the illustrations. These synopses were continued for five groups of birds, the Natatores to the Gallinaceae, and were considered as Nos. I-III of a series, although I and II are not actually so numbered. They were issued in 1847 and 1848. The series of plates includes many not discussed in the "Synopsis" (apparently being of later issue), and to discuss these, a leaflet called, "Novitiae ad Synopsin Avium", Nos. IV-VII (VI being missing from the present set) was issued from time to time in 1850 and 1851. At the close of each number of this "Novitiae," is a summary of the plates published to date in the respective groups of birds, arranged according to classification, with necessary interpolations.

In the meantime a series of uncolored plates of anatomical details was published in four parts in 1849 and 1850 under the title of "Avium Systema Naturale," without accompanying text. The text appeared in 1853 as Lieferung 3 of the "Handbuch" (mentioned below). In 1851 the plates were continued, beginning with the Alcedineae and running through the Picinae but excluding the Trochilinae. There were five fasciculi of these plates, each of which was accompanied (or shortly followed) by a descriptive text entitled, "Handbuch der Speciellen Ornithologie." The various parts of this text were each prefixed by a list of species, with plate-references, entitled "Incones ad Synopsin Avium," sometimes paged with the text, sometimes unpaged, and numbered VIII-XII in continuation of the "Synopsis" and "Novitiae." The original wrappers of these parts are marked as Lieferungen 1, 2, 4, 5 and 6. Lief. 3 comprised the text of the "Avium Systema Naturele" and 8 is said to have been the first portion of the special text relating to the pigeons (mentioned later); 7 and other numbers subsequent to 8, if any, I can not trace. The five parts properly belonging here are dated from 1851-1854. Following the Picinae, the plates of the Trochilinae appeared from 1855 to 1857, but, instead of the regular text, a revision of a former brief paper by the author was published with the first of the plates in 1855, under the title of "Trochilinarum Enumeratio;" this serves as the only available letterpress for the plates of this group.

The pigeons, already briefly treated in the "Synopsis" and "Novitiae VI" were taken up in detail in a special paper called, "Die vollständigste Naturgeschichte der Tauben," of which the first part was issued in 1861 as Lief. 3 of the "Handbuch." A second part, with 9 new plates, appeared as Lief. 9 and 10 of the "Central Atlas" but it was paged in continuance of the first part. The portions of the first part of the volume which deal with the Curassows and Guans (pp. 129 pt. -160) appear to have been issued also in another form as Lief. 1 and 5 of the "Central Atlas." This "Central Atlas" seems to have been a medium for producing miscellaneous addenda to the earlier parts of the book and contains a number of papers on Mammalia belonging to Abtheilung I of the entire work. Lieferungen 1, 5, 9 and 10 have been mentioned. Lief. 6-8, 11-13 and 17-19 were issued in 1862 and 1863 and contained a descriptive account of "Die Singvögel" (as far as completed) with 51 plates, separately numbered.

Two other titles are sometimes considered as part of the above general work, the "Deutschlands Vögel," 1842, and "Die Vögel Neuhollands," 1845-50. Both seem to have been issued also separately, the former as part of "Deutschland Fauna"; the latter, at least, utilized the plates of the larger work.

In the volume on Natatores examined, there are 8 leaves of text relating to pll. 1-14 as finally arranged, which I am unable to place satisfactorily (Cf. Die vollst. Naturg. der Schwimmvögel.). The plates exhibit a multiplicity of styles of numbering which I have discussed under the separate portions of the work where they appear. Detailed collation of the various sections may be found under the following heads.

1836-? Praktisch-gemeinnützige Naturgeschichte der Vögel.
1845-48. Die Vollständigste Naturgeschichte der Schwimmvögel [*mut. mut.*].
1849-53. Avium Systema Naturale.
1851-54. Handbuch der Speciellen Ornithologie.
1847-48. Synopsis Avium.
1850-51. Novitiae ad Synopsin Avium.
1861-62. Die Vollständigste Naturgeschichte der Tauben.
1848-? [Die Haushühner.]
1862-63. Die Singvögel.
1855-57. Trochilinarum enumeratio.
1862-63. [Central Atlas.]

The species figured are indexed by Adolph Bernhard Meyer in his "Index zu L. Reichenbach's Ornithologischen Werken," 1879 (q.v.).

Reichenbach, Heinrich Gottlieb Ludwig.

1845-48. Die | vollständigste Naturgeschichte | der | Schwimm-vögel: [Sumpfvögel: ; Wasserhühner u. Rallen. ; Tauben | und taubenartigen Vögel. ; Huhnervögel] | Aves Natatores [Aves Grallatores; Fulicariae et Rallariae. ; Columbariae. ; Aves Gallinaceae] | Oiseaux nageurs. [Oiseaux Echassiers. ; Les | Foulques et les Râles ; Les | Pigeons, | les | Pénélopes | et les | Hoccos. | Oiseaux Gallinacées] | von | H. G. L. Reichenbach, | Direct. d. zoolog. Museum [K. zoolog. Museum (*Fulicariae et Rallariae*); K. zoolog. Mus. (*Columbariae*)] in Dresden. | Dresden und Leipzig. [*Engr. border surrounding title.*].

5 vols. in 4 (pt.) imperial 8vo. "Natatores", engr. tit., 8 ll. (expl. of pll. 1-14), pll. 1-111, 111a and 111b (col.). "Grallatores," engr. tit., pll. 112-186 (col.). "Fulicariae et Rallariae," engr. tit., pll. 187-219+197b(=391) (col.). "Columbariae", engr. tit., pll. 220-277, 236b, 240b, 245b, 253b, 257b (col.: Novit. I-VII, 271b, 271c, 272b and 273b incl. in vol.; cf. "Die voll. Naturg. der Tauben," 1861-62.). "Gallinaceae", engr. tit., pll. 281-390 (col.: 321b, 365a-365ag and 365b incl. in vol.; cf. "Die Haushühner" 1848?) Dresden and Leipzig.

The plates of the Natatores to Gallinaceae are found under the above-quoted engraved title-pages. There appear to be several styles of issue represented here. Some of the plates are of full size on heavy paper; others are smaller on a poorer quality of paper, some of these being remounted on larger, heavy paper to agree with the rest of the set. The only text for most of these plates is found in the "Synopsis Avium" and the "Novitiae ad Synopsin Avium," 1847-48 and 1850-51 (q.v.). The Columbariae are further treated in "Die Vollständigste Naturgeschichte der Tauben," 1861-62 (q.v.). A few of the plates of the Gallinaceae seem to belong to a separate issue entitled, "Die Haushühner, 1848? (q.v.).

The numbering of the plates is very confusing. Throughout the entire series (except the plates of "Die Singvögel," the "Avium Systema Naturale" and a few others) each plate bears a serial number in the upper right-hand corner. This serial number runs from I to DCCCLV and seems to indicate, in a measure, the order of preparation of the plates. From the Natatores to the Gallinaceae, it is the number used for reference in the "Synopsis Avium."[1]

Some of the plates carry a "Suppl." number in the middle of the upper margin. This number indicates the position of these plates as they are to be interpolated in the series; the plates marked in this way were probably prepared correspondingly later than most of the regular series, judging by the higher numbers given to the individual figures of birds on them. The "Suppl." number, however, is not used for any reference in the text.

A further set of the plates of the Natatores—Gallinaceae have a third number, prefixed by "Novit." in the upper left-hand corner. These plates are not discussed in the "Synopsis" and appear to have been issued after the publication of the corresponding portions of that pamphlet. On the middle of the upper margin of these plates there is still a different number with a qualifying letter (such as XXXb, XIa, etc.), indicating the position of each plate in the primary series. These plates are discussed (with a few exceptions) in the "Novitiae" where all three of their numbers are used for reference.

In addition to the above enumerations, a table is given at the close of each number of the "Novitiae," showing the final arrangement of all the plates issued to date in the respective portions of the work and assigning an Arabic numeral (sometimes qualified by a letter) to each plate. These Arabic numerals are placed, or it is requested that they be placed, at the bottom of the plates in question, where sometimes they may be found in the series from the Natatores to the Gallinaceae. In the descriptive text to the Columbariae, they are used as reference-numbers. With the exception of the additional plates of "Die Haushühner" and of the Columbariae, they may be checked by the lists in the various numbers of the "Novitiae." With the further exceptions of 111a, 111b and 197b (=391) and lacking 278-280, they are continuous throughout this series.

The dates of the plates are not definitely ascertainable, but as only those of the Natatores which are treated in the first number of the "Synopsis" are named on the plates, most of the dates are unimportant. The work appeared in livraisons of about 10 pll. each as is indicated by notes in some of the numbers of the "Synopsis": Natatores, Grallatores and Fulicariae et Rallariae (I-CXX-IX), 13 livrs.; Columbariae (CXX-CLXXVIII), 5 livrs.; Gallinaceae (CLXXIX -CCLXIII), 12 (?) livrs. Assuming that the plates discussed in the "Novitiae" (but not in the "Synopsis") appeared after the "Synopsis," the inclusive dates may be indicated thus (after data from Meyer's "Index zu L. Reichenbach's Orn. Werken"). Natatores, Febr. 20, 1845- (post) 1848. Grallatores, June 3, 1846- (post) 1848. Fulicariae and Rallariae, Dec. 30, 1846- (post) 1848. Columbariae (pll. 220-277), June 16, 1848. Gallinaceae (pll. 281-390), June 16, 1848.

At the beginning of the volume on Natatores there are 8 leaves of text relating to pll. 1-4 as finally arranged; since certain "Novitiae" plates are included these leaves must date after the "Synopsis I." This text I am unable to place in its proper position as regards publication. The pages are the full size of the

---

[1]Pll. I and III of the original series appear to have been cancelled since those numbers do not agree with the list in the "Synopsis." They were replaced by I and Ia (for I) and CCCXLIV (for III) discussed in the "Novitiae" (Cf. infra.).

plates (8x10¾) and the brochure is entitled, "Die Vögel"—"Ordo Primus"— "Natatores." Each page, after the title-leaf, treats of one plate and gives the name and distribution of the species figured.

Reichenbach, Heinrich Gottlieb Ludwig.

1847-48. Cito continuatur | Lipsiae apud Friedericum Hofmeister. | Synopsis avium | iconibus coloratis hucusque rite cognitarum specierum illustrata | auctore | Ludovico Reichenbach, | Musei Zoologici Dresdensis Directore.

> No. III. Febr. 1848. | Incessament continue. | Leipsic: Frederic Hofmeister. | Synopsis Avium | ornithologie méthodique | concernant | les genres et les espèces des oiseaux de toutes les parties du monde, | réunissant les découvertes les plus récentes, ouvrage orné de plus de cinq mille portraits | exactes et colorées, la plupart après les types originaux vivants ou conservés dans le | Museum Royale de Saxe et dans d'autres musées célèbres, a la suite les détails caracteris- | tiques externes et anatomiques des genres, executés par la main et sous les yeux | de l'auteur | L. Reichenbach, | Direct. du Museum Roy. d'Hist. Nat. de Saxe etc.

3 pts. royal 8vo. Pt. 1 (Natatores, Grallatores, and Rasores - Fulicariae et Rallariae), 4 ll. Pt. II (Columbariae), 2 ll. Pt. III (Gallinaceae), 3 ll. Leipzig. 1848, 1847 and Febr. 1848.

The catalogue of species figured on the original series of plates in Reichenbach's "Die Vollständigste Naturgeschichte de Schwimmvögel [—Huhnervögel]," 1845-48 (q.v.). References are given to the plates by their original numbers (afterwards changed). Additional plates subsequently published for these same groups are catalogued in the "Novitiae ad Synopsin Avium," 1850-51 (q.v.). There are no special title-pages; the above titles head the initial pages in the various parts. Pt. III is from a French edition of the work. The engraved title-page of the Columbariae, which contains 56 numbered figures of domestic pigeons, is treated as a plate and its figures are named in the text.

Reichenbach, Heinrich Gottlieb Ludwig.

1848? [Die Haushühner, vollständigste Darstellung aller bis jetzt bekannten Haupt- und Nebenracen und ihrer ursprünglichen Stammeltern. 185 Abbildgn. auf 15 Taf.]

The above title is quoted from Carus and Engelmann. No text is cited there for this work. The volume of the Gallinaceae in Reichenbach's "Die Vollständigste Naturgeschichte der Schwimmvögel [Huhnervögel]," 1845-48 (q.v.) contains 15 plates of domestic fowls, Nos. 365a-365ag and 366-373, which probably form the illustrations included under the above title. Of these, 366-373 belong to the regular issue of the plates of the Gallinaceae; the remainder are probably of special issue for this present work. No definite date is available.

Reichenbach, Heinrich Gottlieb Ludwig.

1849-53. **Avium systema naturale.** | Das | natürliche System | der | Vögel | mit hundert Tafeln grössentheils Original-Abbildungen der bis jetzt entdeckten | fast zwölfhundert typischen Formen. | Vorläufer | einer | Iconographie der Arten der Vögel aller Welttheile, | welche, | nachdem bereits fast dreitausend Abbildungen erscheinen sind, | ununterbrochen fortgesetzt wird | von | L. Reichenbach, | Director am k. zoolog. Museum in Dresden [*etc.*, *2 lines.*]. | Erscheinen sind: | Taf. I-LI den 1. December 1849. | Taf. LII-LXI[1] den 1. März 1850. | Taf. LXXII-LXXXVI den 1. Juni 1850. | Taf. LXXXVII[2] den 1. August 1850. | Dresden und Leipzig: | Expedition der vollständigsten Naturgeschichte. | Leipzig: | Friedrich Hofmeister. | 1850. [*Title also in French, with imprints of Berlin, Paris, Strasbourg, London, St. Petersburg and Cambridge.*]

1 vol. royal 8vo, 2 pr. ll. (Fr. and Ger. tits.), pp. I-VIII (pref.), 1-36 (gen. text), I-XXXI (synoptic list), 7 engr. subtits., pll. I-C. Dresden and Leipzig.

The descriptive text and plates to the groups from the Alcedineae to the Picinae (excepting the Trochilinae) in the author's "Die vollständigste Naturgeschichte," 1845-63 (q.v.). Each part is prefixed by an "Icones ad Synopsin Avium" consisting of a list of species with references to plates and figures, somewhat similar to the "Synopsis Avium," 1847-48, and "Novitiae ad Synopsin Avium," 1850-51 (of the Grallatores to the Columbariae), and numbered in continuation of those series. The portions collated under this title were issued in 5 Lieferungen under the cover-title of "Handbuch der speciellen Ornithologie." Lief. I contained Icones VIII with text and plates; **2**, Icones IX, etc.; **3**, (original wrapper not present) consisted of the text to the "Avium Systema Naturale," 1849-53 (q.v.), not included under the present title; **4**, contained Icones IX (=X), etc.; **5**, Icones XI, etc.; **6**, Icones XII, etc.[3] The Trochilinae should have begun in Lief. 5 but were deferred until later, being issued eventually without other text than the "Trochilinarum enumeratio," 1855-57 (q.v.). A few of them may have constituted Lief. 7. Lief. 8 appears to have consisted of the first part of "Die Vollständigste Naturgeschichte der Tauben," 1861-62 (q.v.).

The plates in the present series are numbered primarily as shown in the above collation but some of them, which were prepared out of proper sequence, bear an additional number with a qualifying letter indicating their proper place in final arrangement; thus "CCCCIIIb=CCCCLXXVII" or "CCCC-XVIII=CCCCIXb." Some of the plates have been transferred to a very

---

[1]Should be LXII; correctly given in the French title.

[2]Should be "Taf. LXXXVII-C"; correctly given in the French title.

[3]According to A. B. Meyer's "Index zu L. Reichenbach's Orn. Werken," 1879, the plates of the Picinae are dated May 27, and the text, October 1, 1855.

different section of the work. Plates adjacent to the original position of these transferred numbers carry an inscription indicating the consequent hiatus in the continuity of the series at these points.

These plates deal entirely with the details of heads, feet, wings and tails of birds, illustrating the various genera and forming a sort of introduction to the author's "Die Vollständigste Naturgeschichte," 1845-63 (q.v.). They were possibly issued as cited in the titles but are grouped in nine sections, each under a special, engraved subtitle as follows. Natatores, pll. I-X, Grallatores, pll. XI-XVIII; Rasores, pll. XIX-XXXII; Insessores Investigatores, pll. XXXIII-LI; Insessores Trepidatores, pll. LII-LXXI; Insessores Enucleatores, pll. LXXII-LXXXVI; Insessores Raptatores, pll. LXXVII-C. The text, whose preface is dated October 1, 1852, contains a general review of the classification of birds, with a systematic catalogue of genera and typical species, but includes only the Natatores to Gallinaceae; apparently it was never completed. It was issued as Lieferung 3 of the "Handbuch der Speciellen Ornithologie," 1851-54 (q.v.), but is paged separately and has no direct connection with that title except as both are parts of the same general work. Richmond (Proc. U. S. Nat. Mus. **53** p. 615, footn. 1917) regards the actual date of publication as 1853. References are given to the plates and figures in the "Vollständigste Naturgeschichte."

Reichenbach, Heinrich Gottlieb Ludwig.

1850-1851. No. IV [V;VII]. | Dec. 1850 [1. Juli 1851; 1.September 1851]. | **Novitiae** | ad | **synopsin avium.** | Neueste Entdeckungen und Nachträge | zur | Vervollständigung der Classe der Vögel bei Erscheinung des Textes.

3 pts (should be 4) royal 8vo. Pt. IV (Natatores), 3 ll. Pt. V (Grallatores and Rasores), 3 ll. [Pt. VI missing (Columbariae), 1 l.] Pt. VII (Gallinaceae), 2 ll. Leipzig.

The catalogue of the species which are figured on the plates published subsequently to those listed in the "Synopsis Avium," 1847-48 (q.v.). Three numbers are used for reference, all three of which appear on the plates in question,—the original serial number, a "Novitiae" number (so designated), and a number defining the position of the plate in the complete series (Cf. "Die Vollständigste Naturgeschichte der Schwimmvögel," 1845-48.). At the close of each number of the "Novitiae," there is a table of the complete series of plates to date, in the group treated, with an Arabic numeral for each.

Reichenbach, Heinrich Gottlieb Ludwig.

1851-54. Icones ad Synopsin Avium. Cf. Reichenbach, **Handbuch der Speciellen Ornithologie.**

Reichenbach, Heinrich Gottlieb Ludwig.

1851-54. [Handbuch | der| speciellen Ornithologie. | Beschreibender Text zu der vollständigsten Kupfersammlung | der | Vögel aller Welttheile | von | Dr. Ludwig Reichenbach, | Director (*etc., 3 lines.*). | Dresden und Leipzig, | Expedition der vollständigsten

Naturgeschichte. | 1851.] > Continuatio   1 Decembris 1851.
                  No. VIII.   Alcedineae.

{ Continuatio   1 Martii 1852.   Continuatio   1 August 1853.
   No. IX.   Meropinae. ' No. IX (= X?)   Scansoriae. ;
                                        A. Sittinae.

Continuatio   1. Nov. 1853.   Continuatio   1. Oct. 1854 ⎤
  No. XI.   Scansoriae.   No. XII.   Scansoriae. ⎬
           B. Tenuirostres.   C. Picinae ⎦
           a. Dacninae.   ;
           b. Certhiinae.
           (c. Trochilinae.)
           d. Upupinae.

Icones | ad | Synopsin Avium | hucusque rite cognitarum | auctore | Ludovico Reichenbach, | Musei Regii zoolog. Dresdensis Directore.

1 vol. in 4, imperial 8vo. (2 ll.; half-tit. and tit. missing), 3 ll. (subtit., Icones VIII, and ded.), pp. 1-44 (text to Alcedineae), 4 ll. (subtit., ded. and Icones IX), pp. 45-144 (text to Meropinae), 2 ll. (subtit. and ded.), pp. 145-218 (Icones IX=X and text to Sittinae), 2 ll. subtit. and ded.), pp. 219-336+224b+1 p. (Icones XI and text to Tenuirostres, except Trochilinae), 2 ll. (subtit. and ded.), pp. 337-434 (Icones XII and text to Picinae), 5 wrappers, pll. CCCXCII-CCCCLXXI, CCCCLXXVII-DVI, DX-DCLXXXI (DX wrongly num. DC) (col.). Dresden and Leipzig.

Reichenbach, Heinrich Gottlieb Ludwig.

1855-57. Trochilinarum | enumeratio | ex | affinitate naturali re-ciproca primum ducta provisoria | auctore | Ludovico Reichenbach, | Musei Regii Zoologici [etc.]. | Editio post illam in cl. Cabanisii diario ornithologico oblatam | secunda | emendata et aucta. | Lipsiae | apud Friedericum Hofmeister. | 1855.

1 vol, demy 4to, pp. 1-12, pll. DCLXXIX-DCCCLV (col.). Leipzig.

A second, revised edition of the author's "Aufzählung der Colibris," 1854 (issued with Journal für Ornithologie, Vol I), probably published for the purpose of forming a sort of "Synopsis Avium" for this group to accompany the plates in the author's "Die Vollständigste Naturgeschichte," 1845-63. References are given to pll. 679-805 (numbered in Roman on the plates) and a dotted line with "Rchb. t." provides space for the future numbering of the species listed but not yet illustrated. No other text appeared for the hummingbirds. The plates (according to A. B. Meyer's "Index zu L. Reichenbach's Orn. Werken," 1879) appeared from July 18, 1855 to January 12, 1857; the text on July 18, 1855. The plates are numbered consecutively without interruption from DCLXXIX to DCCCLV.

Reichenbach, Heinrich Gottlieb Ludwig.

1861-62. Die | vollständigste Naturgeschichte | der | Tauben | und | taubenartigen Vögel: | Wallnister, Erdtauben, Baumtauben, Hocco's. | Columbariæ | Megapodinæ, Peristerinæ, Columbinæ, Alectorinæ. | Von | H. G. L. Reichenbach. | Mit 461 Abbildungen auf 65 Kupfertafeln, dazu folgen noch 72 Abbildungen | Novitiæ. | Dresden und Leipzig. | Expedition der vollständigsten Naturgeschichte. > [*Idem, 7 lines.*] | in zwei Abtheilungen | mit nunmehr 559 illuminirten Abbildungen. | Zweite Abtheilung: | Neu entdeckte | Taubenvögel | und Nachträge zu den schon beschriebenen. | Hierzu neun neue Tafeln mit 98 Abbildungen. | Von [*etc., 4 lines.*].

1 vol. demy 4to, 2 pr. ll. (tit. and ded.), pp. 1-162, 2 ll. (tit. and ded.), pp. 161-206, [1 l. (engr. tit.)], pll. [220-277, 230b, 236b, 240b, 245b, 253b, 257b] 272b, 273b, "Novit." I-Novit-IX (col.). Dresden and Leipzig.

A complete descriptive text to the pigeons and their allies (as classified by the author). The plates cited above in brackets belong to the original series of "Die Voll. Naturg. der Schwimmvögel [Tauben]", 1845-48 (q.v.), listed in the Synopsis Avium," 1847-48, and the "Novitiae," 1850-51[1]. Pp. 1-128 appear to have been issued regularly in 1861 but regarding the rest of the first part of this volume there is some uncertainty. In footnotes to pp. 3 and 4 of "Die Singvögel," 1862-63 (q.v.), the statements are made that the genus *Penelope* was specially treated in Pt. V of the "Central Atlas" and that Pt. I of the same dealt with the Hoccos (Curassows). In the present volume, the Curassows occupy pp. 129 (pt.)-141 (pt.), and *Penelope* with its allies, pp. 141 (pt.)-160, agreeing with the number of pages for Pts. I and V of the "Central Atlas" as catalogued by the British Museum (Natural History). As exhibited by the copy at hand, however, the letterpress for these two groups is inseparable from the rest of the volume and indivisible on account of overlapping text and signatures, so the same reading matter may have been issued both as part of the present volume and as Pts. I and V of the "Central Atlas." A review in the Ibis for October 1861, p. 405, announces the complete account of the Columbariae, including the family Cracidae, as appearing in the eighth Lieferung of the "Handbuch der speciellen Ornithologie," which would imply that the whole of the first part came out entire. According to a footnote on p. 205 of Pt. II of the present work, pll. 272b and 273b appeared with the "Central Atlas" No. 1, but they are discussed, not in the text on the Curassaos in Pt. I, but in Pt. II. Pt. II, with pll. "Novit." I-VII and VIII-IX (=271b and 271c), appeared later, in 1862, as Nos. IX and X of the "Central-Atlas."

Reichenbach, Heinrich Gottlieb Ludwig.

1861-63. [Central Atlas.]

This section of the author's "Vollständigste Naturgeschichte des In- und Auslandes" appears to have been devoted to miscellaneous portions of various

---

[1] This number of the "Novitiae" is missing from the set at hand; hence there is a little uncertainty about the plates catalogued therein.

other subtitles, including some non-ornithological parts of the complete work. The ornithological portions, in the present copy, have been distributed and will be found collated under the subtitles of their respective heads, as follows:

Pts. I-V.   See Die Vollst. Naturg. der Tauben, 1861-62.
Pts. VI-VIII.   See Les Oiseaux Chanteurs, 1862-63.
Pts. IX-X.   See Die Vollst. Naturg. der Tauben, 1861-62.
Pts. XI-XIII.   See Les Oiseaux Chanteurs, 1862-63.
Pts. XVII-XIX.   See Les Oiseaux Chanteurs, 1862-63.

Reichenbach, Heinrich Gottlieb Ludwig.

1862-63. Les Oiseaux Chanteurs. The Song-Birds. | **Die Singvögel** | als | Fortsetzung der vollstöndigsten Naturgeschichte | und zugleich als | Central-Atlas | fur zoologische Gärten und fur Thierfreunde. | Ein | durch zahlreiche illuminirte Abbildungen | illustrirtes Handbuch | zur | richtigen Bestimmung und Pflege | der Thiere aller Classen. | Herausgegeben | von | H. L. Ludwig Reichenbach | K. Sächsischem Hofrathe [*etc.*, *3 lines.*]. | Dresden und Leipzig: | Expedition der vollständigsten Naturgeschichte | und durch alle Buchhandlungen des In- und Auslandes zu erhalten.

1 vol. superroyal 8vo, 2 pr. ll. (tit. and ded.), pp. 1-43+1, 1 l. (subtit.), pp. 45-70, 71 (subtit.) -90, I-X (list of spp.), pll. I-L and LXI (45 col.). Dresden and Leipzig.

A descriptive text to accompany the plates of "Song-Birds" in the author's "Vollständigste Naturgeschichte" and issued with them. The three parts comprise Nos. VI-VIII, XI-XIII and XVII-XIX of the "Central Atlas." The text is divided, as collated above, by subtitle-dedication leaves ("Fortsetzung der Singvögel" and "Zweite Fortsetzung der Singvögel"). Pt. I, contained pll. I-XV; II, pll. XVI-XXXI; III, pll. XXXII-L and LXI, according to the context; the Catalogue of the Library of the British Museum (Natural History) makes a division at pll. XXX and XXXI. Only Ploceidae (Weaver Finches) are treated in the volume. This marks the end of the ornithology of the "Vollständigste Naturgeschichte" which was never completed or carried beyond this point.

Reichenow, Anton.

1878-83. **Vogelbilder aus fernen Zonen.** | Abbildungen und Beschreibungen | der | Papageien. | Allen Naturfreunden, insbesondere den Liebhabern ausländischer Stubenvögel | und Besuchern zoologischer Gärten | gewidmet von | Dr. Ant. Reichenow. | Aquarelle von G. Mützel. | Kassel, | Verlag von Theodore Fischer. | 1878-1883.

1 vol. medium folio, 5 pr. ll., 33 ll. (gen. text), 4 ll. (suppl.), pll. 1-33 (col.; by G. Mützel). Cassel.

A series of colored plates illustrating the known parrots, accompanied by short descriptions of each and notes on their distribution. The supplement contains descriptions (without figures) of the species discovered after the publication of the other portions of the work. Issued in 11 parts of 3 plates each, as follows. Unless otherwise noted, the dates are those on which copies of the parts were presented to the Deutsche Orn. Gesellschaft. Pt. 1, pll. 1-3, ante Oct. 4, 1878; 2, pll. 4-6, 1878 (Zool. Rec.); 3-4, pll. 7-12, ante Sept. 1, 1879; 5, pll. 13-16, 1880 (Journal für Orn. for July); 6, pll. 16-18, ante Oct. 6, 1880 (noted at meeting); 7, pll. 19-21, ante Febr. 7, 1881; 8-9, pll. 22-29, 1881-82 (so noted in Journ. für Orn. for Jan. 1882); 9, ante March 6, 1882 (noted at meeting); 10, pll. 28-30, 1882 or ante Jan. 8, 1883 (presented on Jan. 8, 1883); 11, pll. 31-33, 1883 (noted Journ. für Orn. for July).

Reichenow, Anton.

1882-84. **Die Vögel | der Zoologischen Gärten. |** Leitfaden zum Studium der Ornithologie | mit besonderer Berücksichtigung der in Gefangenschaft ge- | haltenen Vögel. | Ein Handbuch für Vogel-wirthe. | Von | Dr. Ant. Reichenow. | [*Vignette.*] | In zwei Theil-en. | Leipzig, 1882 [1882-1884]. | Verlag von L. A. Kittler.

2 vols. in 1 vol., post 8vo. Vol. 1 pp. I-XXX, 1-278, 1 text-fig. Vol. II, pp. I-XIX + 1, 1-456. Leipzig.

A descriptive catalogue of birds which are to be found in zoological gardens. The introduction deals with the general classification of birds and shows a genealogical tree for the various families and higher groups. The general text contains short descriptions of 1559 species, with incidental notes on others, giving the distribution and the Latin and German vernacular names of each, and with English and French vernacular names added in most cases. Vol. I contains the "Parkvögel;" Vol. II, the "Stubenvögel." Vol I is noted in the Journae für Ornithologie for April, 1882; Vol. II was presented to the Deutsche Ornithologische Gesellschaft on March 7, 1884.

Reichenow, Anton.

1890. See Heine, Ferdinand; and Reichenow, **Nomenclator Musei Heineani Ornithologici.**

Reichenow, Anton.

1894. **Die Vögel | Deutsch-Ost-Afrikas. |** Von | Dr. Ant. Reiche-now, | Kustos der Ornithologischen Abtheilung der Kgl. Zoolo-gischen Sammlung in Berlin, [*etc., 4 lines.*]. | Mit über 100 in den Text gedruckten, schwarzen und farbigen Abbildungen | nach der Natur gezeichnet von | Anna Held. | 1894. | Geographische Ver-lagshandlung Dietrich Reimer, Berlin. | (Hoefer & Vohsen.).

1 vol. imperial 8vo (trimmed), 2 pr. ll. (tit. and half-tit.), pp. 1-250, 1 l. (errata), text-figs. 1-108 (44 col.). Berlin.

A hand-book of the birds of German East Africa, with brief descriptions of all groups and tables for the determination of the species. A history and bibliog-raphy of the ornithology of the region are prefixed to the general discussion, and the reference to the original description of each species is given in the text. A table to the families is added at the close of the work. Although separately titled and paged, this work forms part of Vol. III of Franz Stuhlmann's "Mit Emin Pascha ins Herz von Africa," this volume being devoted to the vertebrate fauna of "Die Thierwelt-Ost-Afrikas und der Nachbargebiete. Herausgegeben unter Redaktion von – – K. Möbius," etc. Vol. I contained the general narrative, IV the invertebrate fauna, and VII the geography and geology,—all of the work published.

Reichenow, Anton.

1900-05. Die | Vögel Afrikas | von | Ant. Reichenow | Erster Band [-Dritter Band; Atlas] | [Blazon.] | Neudamm | Verlag von J. Neumann | 1900-1901 [1902-1903; 1904-1905; 1902].

4 vols. imperial 8vo. Vol. I, pp. I-CIV, 1-706, frontisp. (portr.), 1 pl. (maps, col.), text-figs. 1-10, 1 text-fig. (unnum.). Vol. II, pp. I-XVI, 1 l. (subtit.), pp. 1-752. Vol. III, pp. I-XXV+1, 1 l. (subtit.), pp. 1-880. Atlas, pp. 1-50, 30 pll. (col.; by Bruno Geisler and T. G. Meisner), maps A-C (col.; fold.), 5 text-figs. Neudamm.

A complete monograph of the birds of Africa. The work was published in 6 parts as follows. Vol. **I**, Pt. **1**, pp. III-XCVI, 1-320, 1900, before Oct. 5[1]. Vol. **I**, Pt. **2**, pp. XCVII-CIV, 321-706, Nov. 1901[2]. Vol. **II**, Pt. **1**, pp. 1-384, 1-46 (Atlas), pll. I, IV, XI, XIV and XV (as numbered in index), Maps. A-C, 1902[3]. Vol. **II**, Pt. **2**, pp. 385-752, (I-XVI ?), pll. II, V, IX, X, XII and XIII, May 1903. Vol. **III**, Pt. **1**, pp. 1-416, pll. III, XVI, XXVII and XXIX, July 1904. Vol. **III**, Pt. **2**, pp. 417-880, I-XXV, 47-50 (Atlas), pll. VI, VII, VIII, XVII, XVIII, XIX, XX, XXI, XXII, XXIII, XXIV, XXV, XXVI, XXVIII and XXX, October 1905. Dates for Vol. II, Pt. 2 and Vol. III are as given on p. 726 of Vol. II and 880 of Vol. III. The Atlas is composed of the maps and plates and their indices which were issued with the various parts of Vols. II and III.

Reichenow, Anton.

1902. Die Kennzeichen | der | Vögel Deutschlands | Schlüssel zum Bestimmen, | deutsche und wissenschaftliche Benennungen, | geographische Verbreitung, Brut- und Zugzeiten | der deutschen Vögel | Von | Prof. Dr. Ant. Reichenow | Kustos der Ornithologischen Abtheilung des Königl. Zoologischen Museums in Berlin | Generalsekretär der Deutschen Ornithologischen Gesellschaft | Mit erläuternden Abbildungen | [Blazon.] | Neudamm | Verlag von J. Neumann | 1902.

1 vol. demy 8vo, pp. I-IV, 1-150, 1 l.+pp. 1-14+1 l. (advt.), pll. I-VIII, text-figs. 1-5, 51, 52, 81, 1 text-fig. (unnum.). Neudamm.

---

[1]Copy laid on table at meeting of Deutsche Orn. Ges. Cf. J. f. O., 1901, p. 105.
[2]Advertised in Ornith. Monatsber. for Nov. 1901, as having been published.
[3]On p. 726 of this volume, the date of publication of the first part is said to have been June 1902, but Hellmayr, in Archiv. für Naturg., II, Heft. 1 p. 117, 1902, says it appeared in August.

A handbook of the birds of Germany, with synoptic tables but no descriptions. Latin names are given, with the date of original publication, and one or more vernacular names are added. Synonymy is restricted to the names adopted in Naumann's "Naturgeschichte der Vögel Deutschlands," 1822-60 (q.v.), and Reichenow's "Systematisches Verzeichniss der Vögel Deutschlands," 1889.

Reid, Philip Savile Grey.

1903-05. See British Museum, **Catalogue of the Collection of Birds' Eggs,** 1901-12.

Reider, Jakob Ernst von; and Hahn, Carl Wilhelm.

1830-35. **Fauna Boica** | oder | gemeinnützige | Naturgeschichte | der | Thiere Bayerns | bearbeitet und herausgegeben | von | Jakob Ernst von Reider, | Landgerichtsassessor und mehrerer gelehrten Gesellschaften | Mitgliede | und | Dr. Carl Wilhelm Hahn, | Naturhistoriker. | Zweite Abtheilung. | Vögel. | Mit 182 fein ausgemalten Tafeln. | Nürnberg, 1835. | In der E. H. Zeh'schen Buchhandlung. > **Deutschlands Vögel** | in | Abbildungen nach der Natur | mit Beschreibungen, | von | Dr. Carl Wilhelm Hahn. | Erste [Zweite] Abtheilung. | Landvögel [Sumpf- und Wasservögel]. | Mit 110 [72] illuminirten Tafeln. | Nürnberg, 1835. | In der E. H. Zeh'schen Buchhandlung.

2 vols. post 8vo (letterpress demy 8vo). Vol. I, 2 pr. ll. (subtit. and tit.), pp. III-LXII, 180 ll., 109 pll. (col.). Vol. II, subtit., 116 ll., 73 pll. (col.). Nuremberg.

The ornithological portion of Reider and Hahn's "Fauna Boica," consisting of Lieferungen 2, 8, 12, 29, 16, 17, 18, 20 and 22-27 [in the order of appearance, according to the Cat. Libr. British Museum (Nat. Hist.)], and forming Part II of the complete work. Under its separate subtitle of "Deutschlands Vögel" it is, itself, divided into Parts I and II. Most of the ornithology is by Hahn whose name appears alone on the subtitle-page. The general text (unpaged) consists of descriptions and discussions of the various species which are figured on the plates. Most of the signatures are signed by Hahn, many are unsigned, and at least one is followed by Reider's name. A general review of the contents is given on the numbered pages in Vol. I, where the plates, themselves unnumbered, are catalogued as if numbered in sequence from 1 to 182. The nomenclature of this review is not consistent with that of the general text nor that of the plates, nor do the text and plates always agree in this respect.

Reiser, Othmar; and Führer, Ludwig von.

1894-1905-date. Materialien | zu einer | **Ornis balcanica.** [| Herausgegeben | vom | Bosnisch-Herzegowinischen Landesmuseum |

in Sarajevo. (*Vols. III and IV.*)] | II [-IV]. |
Bulgarien
(Einschliesslich Ost-Rumeliens und der Dobrudscha).
⎧Griechenland
⎨und die griechischen Inseln (*Vol. III.*); Montenegro. (*Vol. IV.*)⎫
⎩(mit Ausnahme von Kreta).   ⎭
von | Othmar [Otmar (*Vol. III.*)] Reiser, | Custos [Kustos (*Vol.
III.*)] am Bosn.-Herceg. [-Herzeg. (*Vol. III.*)] Landesmuseum.
[| und | Ludwig v. Führer. (*Vol. IV.*)] | Mit drei Tafeln in
Farbendruck und einer Karte [Mit 4 Tafeln in Farbendruck, 5
Abbildungen in Schwarzdruck | und einer Karte (*Vol. III.*);
Mit zwei Tafeln in Farbendruck und einer Karte (*Vol. IV.*)]. |
Wien, 1894 [1905 (*Vol. III.*); 1896 (*Vol. IV.*)]. | In Commission
[Kommission (*Vol. III.*)] bei Carl Gerold's Sohn.

3 vols. (II-IV), imperial 8vo. Vol. II, pp. I-XII, 1 l. (subtit.), pp.
1-204, pll. I-III (col.), 1 map (fold.). Vol. III, pp. I-XIV, 1-589,
1 l. (guard-sheet, expl. of pl. III), pll. I-IV (col.; by Kleinschmidt),
1 map (col.; fold.), 4 text-figs. Vol. IV, pp. I-X, 1 l. (subtit.),
pp. 1-149, pll. I-II (col.), 1 map (col.; fold.). Vienna.

A series of monographs of Balkan birds, including those of Bulgaria, Greece and
Montenegro. Vol. I, not yet published, is planned to contain the birds of
Bosnia and Herzegovina.

Rennie, James.

1831-35. > The library of entertaining knowledge. | The | archi-
tecture | of | birds. | London: | Charles Knight, Pall Mall East; |
Longman, Rees, Orme, Brown, & Green, Paternoster Row; |
Oliver & Boyd, Edinburgh; Atkinson & Co., Glasgow; | Wakeman,
Dublin; Willmer, Liverpool; & Baines & Co. Leeds. | MDCCCXXXI.
> The library of entertaining knowledge. | The | domestic |
habits of birds. | London: | Charles Knight, 22, Ludgate Street,
and | 13, Pall-Mall East; | Longman, Rees [*etc.*, *4 lines.*] |
MDCCCXXXIII.
> The library of entertaining knowledge. | The | faculties of
birds. | London: | Charles Knight, 22, Ludgate Street. | MD-
CCCXXXV.

3 vols. 12mo. (Architecture), pp. I-XII, 1-392, 2 ll. (advt.), 78
text-cuts. (Domestic habits), pp. I-XVI, 1-379, 82 text-cuts.
(Faculties), pp. I-XVI, 1-338, 15 pll., 49 text-cuts. London.

The three volumes, according to the general index in the last one, complete the
subject of ornithology as presented in "The Library of Entertaining Knowledge."
All three works are pure compilations but bring together a large number of

facts and fancies which are presented in a popular manner. The volume on the architecture of birds was reissued under the title of "Bird Architecture" in 1844.

Révoil, Georges. (Oustalet, Emile.)

1882. Georges Révoil | **Faune et flore** | des | **pays Çomalis** | (Afrique Orientale). | [*Vignette.*] | Paris | Challamel Ainé, éditeur, 5, Rue Jacob. | 1882.

1 vol. 8vo, 2 pr. ll. (tit. and ded.), pp. VII-VIII, 1-14 (Mammals), 1-14 (Birds), 1-25 (Reptiles and Batrachians), 1-12 (Fishes), 1-108 (Mollusks), 1-39 (Geology and Paleontology), 1-104 (Insects), 1-70 (Plants), 1-78 (Toxicology), frontisp. (col.), pll. I-II (1 col.; Mammals), I (col.; by J. Terrier; Birds), I-III (Reptiles and Fish), I-IV+2 pll. (unnum.) (Mollusks), I-IV (Paleontology), I (col.; Insects), I-VI (Plants), text-figs. 1-3 (Geology), 1-5 (Toxicology). Paris.

A series of papers dealing with the collections made by Révoil in Somaliland, written by various authors. Oustalet is responsible for the birds and his contribution (pp. 1-14 and pl. I) contains an annotated list of 21 species, one of which (*Merops Revoilii*) is described as new. Pt. I of the entire work, consisting of the Anthropological report, is missing from the set.

Rey, Eugène.

1872. **Synonymik** | der | **Europäischen Brutvögel und Gäste.** | Systematisches Verzeichniss | nebst | Angaben über die geographische Verbreitung der Arten | unter besonderer | Berücksichtigung der Brutverhältnisse | von | Dr. Eugène Rey. | Halle, | G. Schwetschke'scher Verlag. | 1872.

1 vol. post 8vo, pp. I-XVI, 1 l. (subtit.), pp. 1-257. Halle.

A list of 618 species of birds regularly or occasionally found in Europe (including 217 which are visitors from other countries, extinct forms, aberrations, varieties, etc.), with notes on the distribution of each species and with bibliographic references to published accounts and to illustrations of the birds and their eggs.

Rey, Eugène.

1889-1905. **Die Eier** | der | **Vögel Mitteleuropas** | von | Dr. Eugène Rey. | Mit über 1500 farbigen Eierabbildungen auf 128 Tafeln, | nach Originalen der Sammlung des Verfassers. | Band I: Text [II: Tafeln]. | Gera-Untermhaus. | Lithographie, Druck und Verlag von Fr. Eugen Köhler, | 1905.

2 vols. 8vo. Vol. I, tit., pp. 1-681, 1 text-fig. Vol. II, tit., pll. 1-128 (col.; by A. Reichert). Gera-Untermhaus.

A descriptive account of the oology of central Europe, with chromolithographic illustrations of the eggs. The work was issued in 30 Lieferungen, the contents of which have been noted for me by Dr. Hellmayr who reviewed part (1899, 1902, 1903 and 1904) of the work in the Archiv für Naturgeschichte. The dates are not all available. Lief. **1**, pp. 1-24, pll. 1-5, 1899 (Summer; rev. Orn. Monatsb. Aug. 1899); **2**, pp. 25-40, pll. 6-9 and 13, August 1899 (Hellmayr); **3-4**, pp. 41-72, pll. ?, ante Aug. 1900 (rev. Orn. Monatsb.); **5-6**, pp. 73-104, pll. ?, ante Aug. 1900 (rev. Orn. Monatsb.); **7-8**, pp. 105-136, pll. ?, ante Febr. 1901 (rev. Orn. Monatsb.), **9-11**, pp. 137-184, pll. ?,—**9-10** ante July 1901 (rev. Orn. Monatsb.), —**11**, 1901 (Hellmayr); **12-14** and **15-16**, pp. 185-232 and 233-264, pll. 35, 36, 60, 69-77, 79-81,—**12-14** ante Febr. 1903 (rev. Orn. Monatsb.),—**15-16** ante May 1903 (rev. Orn. Monatsb.,—Zool. Rec. reviews Pt. **16** as of 1902); **17-20**, pp. 265-312, pll. 82, 83, 87-95, 97, 98, 100-106, 1903 (Hellmayr); **21-23** and **24-25**, pp. 312-328 and 329-376, pll. 84-86, 96-99, 107-111, 120-123, 125-128, ante July 1904 (rev. Orn. Monatsb.); **26**, pp. 377-408, pll. 53-57, 1904 (Zool. Rec.); **27-30**, pp. 409-681, pll. ?, ante Oct. 1905 (complete work rev. Orn. Monatsb.).

Rhoads, Samuel N.

1894. See Ord, George, **A Reprint of the North American Zoology by George Ord.**

Rich, Walter H.

1907. Feathered Game | of the | Northeast | By | Walter H. Rich | with illustrations by the author | New York | Thomas Y. Crowell & Co. | publishers.

1 vol. 8vo, pp. I-XVI, 1-432, frontisp. (col.), 85 pll. New York.

A popular account of 87 game birds of north-eastern North America, with general descriptions, notes on habits, distribution, methods of hunting, etc. The work is excellently written and accurate, and is illustrated with a profusion of drawings which add to its value. It is intended for the sportsman but is of distinctly broader utility.

Richard, A.

1825-28. See Buffon, George Louis Leclerc, **Oeuvres Complètes de Buffon,** Richard ed.

Richardson, John.

1831. See Wilson, Alexander; and Bonaparte, **American Ornithology.**

Richardson, John. (Swainson, William.)

1832. > **Fauna | Boreali-Americana;** | or the | zoology | of the | northern parts | of | British America: | containing | descriptions of the objects of natural history collected on the late northern land | expeditions under command of Captain Sir John Franklin, R.N. | **Part second, | the birds.** | By | William Swainson, Esq., F.R.S. [*etc., 2 lines.*]. | and | John Richardson, M.D., F.R.S. [*etc., 3 lines.*] | surgeon and naturalist to the expeditions. | Illustrated by numerous plates and woodcuts. | Published under the authority of the Right Honourable the Secretary of State | for Colonial Affairs. | London: | John Murray, Albemarle-Street. | MDCCCXXXI.

1 vol. (2nd of 4 vols.) foliopost 4to, pp. I-LXVI, 1 l. (half-tit.), pp. 1-523+1 (errata), 1 insert-slip, pll. 24-33, (33 dupl., 34 missing), 35, 36, 35 (bis=37), 38-73 (col.; by Swainson), 72 text-figs. London.

An important work on the birds of North America north of the forty-eighth parallel. Detailed descriptions are given, with synonymy and critical remarks, and there are lengthy discussions (by Swainson) on the Quinary System of classification with relation to the species treated or in general. The authorship is divided. In general Swainson is responsible for the classification and synonymy and Richardson for the actual descriptions, with most of Swainson's contributions further identified by his subjoined initial. Some of the new names are by one author, some by the other, and the remainder by both, as stated in each instance. The plates are by Swainson. The work exists, also, with uncolored plates. The date on the title-page is 1831, but Richmond (Auk, 1899, p. 327) gives February, 1832 as the correct date. The work is first mentioned in the Magazine of Natural History for March 1832 (p. 186), as having been published in 1831, and it is reviewed in the same periodical for May, 1832 (pp. 360-364), as having appeared in 1832. Swainson, himself, in his "On the Natural History and Classification of Birds" in Lardner's "Cabinet Cyclopaedia," Vol. I, p. 218, 1836-37 (q.v.), cites the work under date of 1831 as "1 vol. in 2 parts." If the latter statement is not misleading (on account of the entire ornithological volume forming the second part of the "Fauna"), it is possible that a Pt. I of the "Birds" (limits unknown) was issued in 1831, and the remainder in 1832. I can find no confirmation of the statement by Swainson. The work is sometimes quoted as "Northern Zoology." In a portion of Swainson's controversy with Vigors, in a letter written October 1, 1831 and published in the Mag. Nat. Hist. 4, p. 483 (Nov., 1831), Swainson refers the reader to "North. Zoology, vol. ii, p. 315," saying that, "I have there, long ago, spoken," etc. This implies, but does not prove, that p. 483 of the work in question had been published at least by the 1st of October, 1831. Robert Jameson, in his edition of Wilson's "American Ornithology," 1831 (q.v.), 4 pp. 244-362, gives some extracts from the proof sheets of the present work intermixed with selections from other authors and personal remarks of his own. It is possible that these pages from Jameson antedate the publication of the present work.

Richardson, John; and Gray, John Edward. (Gray, George Robert; Sharpe, Richard Bowdler.)

1844-75. The | zoology | of the | voyage of H. M. S. Erebus & Terror, | under the command of Captain Sir James Clark Ross, R.N., F.R.S., | during the years | 1839 to 1843. | By authority of the Lords Commissioners of the Admiralty. | Edited by John Richardson, M.D., F.R.S., &c. | and | John Edward Gray, Esq., Ph.D., F.R.S., &c. | Vol. I [II]. | Mammalia, Birds [Reptiles, Fishes, Crustacea, Insects, Mollusca]. | London: | E. W. Janson, 28, Museum Street, W.C. | M.DCCC.XLIV.-M.DCCC.LXXV.

2 vols. royal 4to. Vol. I, pp. I-XII, 1-12, 12a-12d, 13-53, 1 l. (subtit.),
pp. 1-39, frontisp. (map; col.), pll. I-X, XIV-XVIII, 19-22, 25-29,
1 pl. (unnum.), pll. 1-37+32bis (=63 pll. of mammals; 17 col.),
1-11, 13-21, 23-35, 1*, 11 (*bis*=11*), 20* and XXI* (=37 pll. of
birds; col; by J. Wolf and others). Vol. II, 2 pr. ll. (tit. and conts.),
pp. 1-19+1, 1 l. (subtit.), pp. III-VIII, 1-139+1, 1 l. (subtit.),
pp. 1-51+1, 1 l. (subtit.), pp. 1-7, pll. 1-20 (Reptiles), 1-10, XI-
XII, 13-18, XIX, 20-60 (Fishes), 1-4 (Crustacea), 1-10 (Insects),
1-3+IV (Mollusca). London.

The zoological report of the expedition of the Erebus and Terror to New Zealand
and Antarctic regions. The section on birds (pp. 1-39 of Vol. I) consists of a
report on the birds of New Zealand by G. R. Gray and an appendix to the same
prepared by R. B. Sharpe. Gray's original paper was published in parts (as was
all of the work) at dates which are not all definitely known. Sherborn (Index
Animalium, Sect. 2, Pt. I, p. XLIX, 1922) cites pp. 1-8, 1844; and 9-20, 1845.
To this, Mathews (Birds of Australia, Suppl. 4, Pt. I, p. 61, 1925) adds from
Newton and Pucheran (references not given) the information that pp. 9-12
were issued in Pt. IX in June 1845, and 17-20 with pl. 21 in Oct. 1845. Pp.
21-39 and pll. 1, 7, 20*, 27, 29, 30, 31 and 32 are cited in the Zoological Record
for 1875, being the portion published by Sharpe. A complete list of the plates
issued originally, and those issued with the appendix, is given by Sharpe on pp.
38-39 of the present work, Vol. I. A new title-page, or subtitle, is supplied for
the ornithology (and similarly for most of the other sections of the work). This
differs from the general title-page in the date, here given as "M.DCCC.XLVI.-
M.DCCC.LXXV.", and in lines 13 and 14 of the original which are here re-
placed by the following 6 lines, "Birds. | By | George Robert Gray, F.R.S., &c., |
and | R. Bowdler Sharpe, F.L.S., F.Z.S., &c., | Of the Zoological Department,
British Museum."

Ridgway, Robert.

1874. See Baird, Spencer F.; Brewer; and Ridgway, **A History of
North American Birds, Land Birds.**

Ridgway, Robert.

1877. See King, Clarence, Professional Papers, Engineer Dept.,
U. S. Army, No. 18, **Rept. of the Geol. Explor. Fortieth Parallel.**

Ridgway, Robert.

1881. Department of the Interior: | U. S. National Museum. | 24 |
Bulletin | of the | United States National Museum. | No. 21. |
Published under the direction of the Smithsonian Institution. |
Washington: | Government Printing Office. | 1881. > **Nomen-
clature | of | North American Birds** | chiefly contained in the |
United States National Museum. | By | Robert Ridgway. | Wash-
ington: | Government Printing Office. | 1881.

1 vol. 8vo, pp. 1-94. Washington.

Pp. 11-57 are occupied by a check-list of species and subspecies with vernacular names and a serial number for each. An appendix is given on pp. 59-84 with tabulated lists of species eliminated from former catalogues; added since former catalogues; provisionally included in the check-list; known to be stragglers; supposedly valid but not found since described by Audubon or Wilson; variously restricted in distribution; recently described but untenable; introduced from foreign countries or escaped from confinement; etc. P. 85 contains addenda; pp. 86-87, a table of families showing number of genera and species of each; pp. 87-89, a concordance of the serial numbers of the present check-list with those of Baird's "Catalogue of North American Birds" of 1859 (Cf. same tit., 1858.). The present paper is said by the author to be "a revised edition, very materially modified" of his own former catalogue, published in 1880 on pp. 163-246 of Proc. U. S. Nat. Mus. 3, but not issued separately.

Ridgway, Robert.

1881. A | revised catalogue | of the | birds | Ascertained to Occur in Illinois. | By Robert Ridgway. | Bloomington, Ill.: | Pantagraph Printing Establishment. | 1881. < (*Cover-tit.*) Illinois State Laboratory | of | Natural History | Bulletin No. 4. | A catalogue of the birds of Illinois. | By | Robert Ridgway. | Bloomington, Ill.: | Pantagraph Printing and Binding Establishment. | May, 1881.

1 vol. post 8vo, tit., pp. 163-208, (orig. wrapper). Bloomington. May 1881.

An annotated list of 339 species, prefaced by a bibliography and a discussion of the topography of the state.

Ridgway, Robert.

1883. Great International Fisheries Exhibition. | London, 1883. | United States of America. | C. **Catalogue** | of the | **aquatic and fish-eating birds** | **exhibited by the** | **United States National Museum.** | By | Robert Ridgway, | Curator, Department of Birds, U. S. National Museum. | Washington: | Government Printing Office. | 1883. | 227A - 1.

1 vol. 8vo, pp. 1-46. Washington.

An annotated list of the species of birds exhibited by the. U. S. National Museum at the Exhibition in London, giving the distribution of each species and the data for each specimen. This report occupies pp. 139-184 of Bull. **27**, U. S. Nat. Mus., dated 1884, but, like other papers of its kind, was issued in small numbers, as soon as it was printed,—in this case in 1883. The separate pagination of this advance copy is given in the final issue of the complete bulletin together with the regular pagination of the latter.

Ridgway, Robert.

1884. See Baird, Spencer F.; Brewer; and Ridgway, **The Water Birds of North America.**

Ridgway, Robert.

1886. See American Ornithologists' Union, **The Code of Nomenclature and Check-list of North American Birds.**

Ridgway, Robert.

1887. A | manual | of | North American Birds. | By | Robert Ridgway. | Illustrated by 464 outline drawings of the | generic characters. | Philadelphia: | J. B. Lippincott Company. | 1887.

1 vol. royal 8vo, pp. I-IV, 1 l. (obit.), pp. V-XI+1, 1-631, frontisp., pll. I-CXXIV (on 62 ll.). Philadelphia.

A complete manual of the birds of North America, with full descriptions of the essential characteristics of each species arranged in the form of tables, and with tables for the determination of the higher groups. The work was reviewed by the Auk in October 1887 from advance sheets received August 5, but general distribution was at a later date, since the leaf (pages unnumbered) containing the obituary of Baird is dated August 20. A second edition of the work (q.v.) appeared in 1896.

Ridgway, Robert.

1889. See American Ornithologists' Union, **Check-list of North American Birds, Abridged Edition.**

1889. Idem. **Supplement to the Code of Nomenclature and Check-list.**

Ridgway, Robert.

1889-95. See (Illinois) State Laboratory of Natural History, Natural History Survey of Illinois, **The Ornithology of Illinois.**

Ridgway, Robert.

1892. See American Ornithologists' Union, **The Code of Nomenclature.**

1895. Idem, **Check-list of North American Birds, Second Edition.**

Ridgway, Robert.

1896. A | manual | of | North American Birds. | By | Robert Ridgway. | Illustrated by 464 outline drawings of the | generic characters. | **Second edition.** | Philadelphia: | J. B. Lippincott Company. | 1896.

1 vol. royal 8vo, pp. I-XIII+1, 1-614, frontisp., pll. I-CXXIV (on 62 ll.). Philadelphia.

The second edition of the earlier work of the same title, 1887 (q.v.), with typographical and other corrections. Species added to the North American fauna since the first edition, if they are not included as extralimital forms in the earlier work, are grouped together in the appendix on pp. 583-614.

Ridgway, Robert.

1901-19-date. Smithsonian Institution. | United States National Museum. | Bulletin | of the | United States National Museum. | No. 50. [| Part II (-VII; *this title not printed with Pt. VIII.*).] | [*Seal*] | Washington: | Government Printing Office. | 1901 [1902; 1904; 1907; 1911; 1914; 1916]. > **The birds** | **of** | **North and Middle America:** | a descriptive catalogue | of the | higher groups, genera, species, and subspecies of birds | known to occur in North America, from the | Arctic lands to the Isthmus of Panama, | the West Indies and other islands | of the Caribbean Sea, and the | Galapagos Archipelago. | By | Robert Ridgway, | Curator, Division of Birds. | Part I [-VIII]. | Family Fringillidæ - The Finches [*mut. mut., 1-8 lines, single and double column.*]. | Washington: | Government Printing Office. | 1901 [-1919].

8 vols. (to date), 8vo. Vol. I, pp. I-XXX, 1 l. (errata), pp. 1-715, pll. I-XX. Vol. II, pp. I-XX, 1-834, pll. I-XXII. Vol. III, pp. I-XX, 1-801, pll. I-XIX. Vol. IV, pp. I-XXII, 1-973, pll. I-XXXIV. Vol. V, pp. I-XXIII+1, 1-859, pll. I-XXXIII. Vol. VI, pp. I-XX, 1-882, pll. I-XXXVI. Vol. VII, pll. I-XIII+1, 1-543, pll. I-XXIV. Vol. VIII, (no gen. tit.), pp. I-XVI, 1-852, pll. I-XXXIV (on 17 ll.). Washington.

This monumental work, still in course of publication, is a detailed, taxonomic monograph and the most complete book of its kind ever attempted. It is indispensable to the systematist of North and Middle American ornithology. The actual dates of publication of Vols. I-VII are given in the preface (p. III) of Vol. VIII. The dates are as follows. Vol. **I**, Oct. 24, **1901**; **II**, Oct. 16, **1902**; **III**, Dec. 31, **1904**; **IV**, July 1, **1907**; V, Nov. 29, **1911**; **VI**, April 8, **1914**; **VII**, May 5, **1916**; **VIII**, June 26, **1919** (rev. Auk).

Each volume contains a list of the contents of all volumes to date.

Ridgway, Robert.

1910. See American Ornithologists' Union, **Check-list of North American Birds, Third Edition.**

Ridgway, Robert.

1922. See Gault, Benjamin T., **Check List of the Birds of Illinois.**

Riesenthal, Oskar von.

1876-78. **Die** | **Raubvögel Deutschlands** | und | des angrenzenden Mitteleuropas. | Darstellung und Beschreibung der in Deutschland und den benach- [benachbarten] | barten Ländern von Mitteleuropa vorkommenden Raubvögel. | Allen Naturfreunden | besonders aber | der deutschen Jägerei | gewidmet von | O. v.

Riesenthal, | Oberförster [Oberförster, Mitglied (*etc.*, *2 lines.* | Atlas]. | Cassel. | Verlag [Druck und Verlag] von Theodor Fischer. | 1876 [*No date.*].

2 vols. 8vo and medium folio. Text, pp. I-XXI+1, 1-522, 1 pl. (unnum.), pll. I-V, 1 text-fig. Atlas, tit., pll. I-LX (col.; by the author). Cassel.

A detailed account of the birds of prey of Germany and adjacent parts of Europe. The discussion of each species is divided into sections on description, distribution, life-history and methods of hunting. According to a contemporary review in the Zoological Record, the nomenclature adopted is antiquated even for that date. The chromolithographic plates vary in quality; some of them are very fair. The work was issued in parts of which the Zoological Record for 1876 records the first; the same journal for 1877 records the apparent conclusion of the work with Pts. II-XII of text and II-XIV of plates, but the introduction (p. XVI) is dated 1878.

Riesenthal, Oskar von.

1883. See Robert, Leo Paul; and Riesenthal, **Gefiederte Freunde.**

Rijksmuseum van Naturlijke Historie. (Schlegel, Hermann; Goffin, A.; Jentink, F. A.)

1862-81 (-1907). Muséum | d'histoire naturelle | des | Pays-Bas. | Revue méthodique et critique | des | collections | déposées | dans cet | établissement. | Leyde, | E. J. Brill, | 1862.

> Museum | d'histoire naturelle | des | Pays-Bas, | par | H. Schlegel. | Revue méthodique et critique | des | collections | déposées dans cet | établissement. | Tome VII [VIII]. | Contenant: | Monographie 40 [41]: Simiae [Tinami]. | Leide, E. J. Brill.

> Museum | d'histoire naturelle | des | Pays-Bas | par | H. Schlegel. | Table alphabétique. | (Volumes I-VIII) | par | Dr. F. A. Jentink. | Leide, E. J. Brill. | 1881.

9 vols. (should be 10) in 7, 8vo. Vol. I, pp. I-VIII, 1-22 (Buceros), 1-98 (Buccones), (1 l. "Aves Rapaces. Résumé Général"; belongs in Vol. II), pp. 1-85 (Cuculi), 1-149 (Coraces). Vol. II, (no. tit.), pp. 1-30 (Oti), 1-45 (Striges), 1-36 (Falcones), 1-12 (Circi), 1-57 (Astures), 1-13 (Asturinae), 1-30 (Buteones), 1-24 (Aquilae), 1-12 (Milvi), 1-10 (Pernes), 1-10 (Polybori), 1-12 (Vultures), 1 l. ("Résumé," etc.; bound in Vol. I), 1-156 (Revue de Oiseaux de Proie). Vol. III, (no tit.), pp. 1-166 (Psittaci), 1-14 (Merops), 1-8 (Momotus), 1-52 (Alcedines), 1-47 (Revue des Alcedines), 1-16 (Pitta), 1-19 (Revue des Brèves,-Pitta). Vol. IV, (no tit.), pp. 1-180 (Columbae), 1-14 (Struthiones), 1-80 (Cursores). Vol. V,

(no tit.), pp. 1-112 (Scolopaces), 1-79 (Ralli), 1-26 (Ciconiae), 1-64 (Ardeae), 1-16 (Ibis). Vol. VI, (no tit.), pp. 1-122 (Anseres), 1-40 (Procellariae), 1-52 (Lari), 1-44 (Sternae), 1-44 (Pelecani), 1-52 (Urinatores). Vol. VII, 2 pr. ll. (tit. and pref.), (pp. 3-20; from Vol. IX; index), 1-356 (Simiae). Vol. VIII, tit., pp. 1-86 (Tinami and Megapodii). (Vol. IX), pp. 1-61+1, 1 l. (errata), (pp. 3-20 bound in Vol. VII) (Index to Vols. I-VIII). Leyden.

A critical review and catalogue of the collections of the Rijksmuseum van Natur-lijke Historie. As presented, the work consists of a series of separately paged monographs of different groups. As will be noted, Vol. VII deals with mammals; all the remaining volumes except IX (Index) are ornithological. Numerous new species are described. Vol. IX (Index) is by Jentink and Vol. I, pp. 1-98 (Buccones) is by Goffin; the remainder of the work, as here collated, is by Schlegel. More recently, in 1907, Vol. X has been published, consisting of a catalogue of avian fossils by E. D. van Oort. This volume is not in the series at hand. The work appeared in 14 livraisons (excluding Vol. X). Each mono-graph is dated separately on its initial page but the dates appear to be those of the completion of the manuscript or of printing, not of publication, al-though they sometimes furnish approximate dates for the livraisons in which they appeared. The approximate dates and the contents of the various livraisons are as follows.

Livr. 1, tit. and pref., Buceros, Falcones, Aquilae, Astures, Asturinae and Butsones, 1862 (post Oct. 30—date of pref.). Livr. 2, Milvi, Pernes, Polybori, Vultures, Oti, Striges, Circi, Pitta, Buccones pp. 1-66 and Aves Rapaces-Résumé General, 1863 (antea July—rev. Ibis). Livr. 3, Buccones pp. 67-98, Ardeae, Alcedines and Merops pp. 1-12, 1863 (post June—date of Merops). Livr. 4, Merops pp. 13-14, Momotus, Ibis, Pelecani, Procellariae and Lari, 1863 (post August—date of Lari). Livr. 5, Sternae, Cuculi, Psittaci and Scolo-paces pp. 1-86, 1864 (post November—date of Scolopaces). Livr. 6, Scolopaces pp. 87-102, 1864. Livr. 7, Scolopaces pp. 103-112, Ciconiae, Cursores and Ralli pp. 1-76, 1865 (bet. April and October—date of Ralli and rev. Ibis). Livr. 8, Ralli pp. 77-79 and Anseres pp. 1-108, 1866 (post May—date of An-seres). Livr. 9, Anseres pp. 109-122, Coraces and Urinatores, 1867 (post April—date of Urinatores). Livr. 10, Struthiones, Columbae and Revue des Oiseaux de Proie, 1873 (post July—date of Revue). Livr. 11, Revue des Brèves, Rev. des Perroquets and Rev. des Alcedines, 1874 (post June—date of Rev. des Alcedines). Livr. 12, Simiae, 1876 (dat. March). Livr. 13, Tinami and Megapodii, 1880 (dat. March). (Livr. 14), Index, 1881.

Rives, William C.

1884. List of the birds of Cobham, | Virginia. | By William C. Rives, Jr., M.D. | Newport, R. I.: | Davis & Pitman, Printers. | 1884.

1 vol. 8vo, pp. 1-16. Newport.

An annotated list of 128 species of birds observed by the writer at various times at Cobham, with notes as to abundance, dates of arrival, etc.

Rives, William C.

1890. Proceedings | of | The Newport | Natural History Society, | [*Seal.*] | 1889-90. | Document VII. | **A Catalogue of the Birds of the Virginias,** | by Wm. C. Rives, M.A., M.D. | Newport, R. I.; | printed for the Society by T. T. Pitman, | October, 1890.

1 vol. 8vo, pp. 1-100, 1 map (col.). Newport. October 1890.

An annotated list of 305 species of birds recorded from Virginia and West Virginia, preceded by a chapter on early accounts of the birds of the region, a bibliography of recent literature and a description of topographical and biological features of the area under discussion.

Robbins, Reginald Chauncey.

1901. **Bird-killing as a method** | **in ornithology.** | By | Reginald C. Robbins. | Cambridge, Mass. | Printed by | E. W. Wheeler.

1 vol. 8vo, pp. 1-16. Cambridge. 1901 (post Oct.).

An involved presentation of the author's theories on the subject of ornithology as studied from dead birds.

Robert, Leo Paul; and Riesenthal, O. von.

1883. **Gefiederte Freunde.** | Sechzig Aquarelle | angenehmer und | nützlicher Vögel Mittel-Europas | gemalt von | Leo Paul Robert | geschildert von | O. von Riesenthal. | Leipzig, | Arnoldische Buchhandlung.

> Gefiederte Freunde. | Bilder zur Naturgeschichte | angenehmer und | nützlicher Vögel Mittel-Europas. | Nach der Natur gemalt | von | Leo Paul Robert. | Sechzig chromolithographirte Tafeln in Klein-Folio. | Lithographie von Thurwanger—Farbendruck von Lemercier & Co in Paris. | Mit erläuterndem Text | von | O. von Riesenthal. | Leipzig | Arnoldische Buchhandlung.

2 vols., royal 8vo and medium folio. Text, pp. I-X, 1-162. Atlas, 2 ll. (tit. and conts.), 60 pll. (col.). Leipzig.

A descriptive account of nearly a hundred central European birds, with the majority of the species illustrated by chromo-lithographs. The text is by Riesenthal; the plates are by Robert and form the central feature of the work, according to the title.

Roberts, Thomas S.

1907. See Wilcox, Alvin H., **A Pioneer History of Becker County Minnesota.**

Robinson, E. Kay.

1922-23. See Finn, Frank, **Birds of our Country.**

Robinson, Herbert C.

1905. See Annandale, Nelson; and Robinson, **Fasciculi Malayenses.**

Robinson, Philip Stewart.

1894. Birds of the wave | and woodland | by | Phil Robinson | author of | "Noah's Ark" "The Poets' Birds" etc. | Illustrated by Charles Whymper | and others | London | Isbister and Company Limited | 15 & 16 Tavistock Street Covent Garden | 1894.

1 vol. superroyal 8vo, pp. 1-224, frontisp. (on p. 4), 44 text-figs. (17 full-p.). London.

Popular essays on bird life.

Robson, J. (?) (Edwards, George.)

1776. Some | memoirs | of the | life and works | of | George Edwards, | Fellow of the Royal and Antiquarian Societies. | [*Quot., 4 lines.*] | London: | printed for J. Robson, bookseller, New Bond Street. | MDCCLXXVI.

1 vol. crown folio, tit., pp. 1-38, 4 pll. (3 fold.; by Edwards; 2 ornithological). London.

A sketch of the life of Edwards, apparently by Robson, occupies pp. 1-26. The remainder of the pamphlet consists of reprints of various papers by Edwards extracted from the Philosophical Transactions of the Royal Society of London, and two addenda to certain accounts in his "Gleanings of Natural History," 1758-64 (q.v.). An erratum is given for Linne's "Catalogue of the Birds...... contained in Edwards," (q.v.) published the same year, with a copy of which the present title is united.

Robson was the purchaser (May 1, 1769) of all the remaining copies of Edward's Natural History, the original copper-plates, letter-press and all articles in Edward's possession relative to the same. The unpublished drawings, however, were purchased by the Earl of Bute.

Rodd, Edward Hearle. (Harting, James Edmund; Rodd, F. R.)

1880. The | birds of Cornwall | and | the Scilly Islands | by the late | Edward Hearle Rodd | edited | With an Introduction, Appendix, and Brief Memoir of the Author | by | James Edmund Harting | with portrait and map | London | Trübner & Co., Ludgate Hill | 1880 | [All Rights reserved].

1 vol. 8vo, pp. I-LVI, 1-320, frontisp. (portr.), 1 map (fold.). London.

Miscellaneous ornithological notes made by E. H. Rodd and published, from time to time, in The Zoologist, from 1843 to 1880. These notes, transcribed in chronological sequence, have been rearranged by the editor to bring together the various portions dealing with each species, as begun by the author prior to his death. The appendix, by the editor, contains notes for insertion in the text. Pp. 281-298 contain "A few leaves from the journal of a sportsman and naturalist on the Scilly Islands," by the author's nephew, F. R. Rodd.

Rodd, F. R.

1880. See Rodd, Edward Hearle, **The Birds of Cornwall and the Scilly Islands.**

Rollinat, R.

1914. See Martin, R.; and Rollinat, **Description et Moeurs des Mammifères, Oiseaux, Reptiles, Batraciens et Poissons de la France Centrale.**

Römer, Fritz; and Schaudinn, Fritz. (Schalow, Herman.)

1904. > **Fauna Arctica.** | Eine Zusammenstellung der arktischen Tierformen, mit besonderer Berücksichtigung | des Spitzbergen-Gebietes auf Grund der Ergebnisse der Deutschen Expedition in das | Nördliche Eismeer im Jahre 1898. | Unter Mitwirkung zahl-reicher Fachgenossen herausgegeben von | Dr. Fritz Römer in Frankfurt a.M. | und Dr. Fritz Schaudinn in Berlin | Band IV, Lieferung I. | **Die Vögel der Arktis** | von | Herman Schalow | in Berlin. | Verlag von Gustav Fischer in Jena. | 1904. [*Cover-title.*]

1 vol. imperial 4to, cover-tit., 1 l. (subtit.), pp. 81-288. Jena.

A systematic review of the birds of the Arctic Ice-sea and its islands, with considerable synonymy, some descriptions, and notes on the distribution and time of occurrence of each of the 270 forms of birds included in the discussion. A lengthy bibliography precedes the general text, and distribution-tables and a comparative study of the Arctic and Antarctic avifaunas are appended. The work, entirely by Schalow, forms No. 2 of the first livraison of Vol. IV of the "Fauna Arctica" edited by Römer and Schaudinn and published in five volumes, 1900-10. The title transcribed above is from the original wrapper which bears the date 1904, the year in which the work was reviewed by Hellmayr in the Archiv für Naturgeschichte, although later bibliographers have quoted the date as 1905. The present copy is autographed by Schalow who presented it to Tschusi zu Schmidhoffen.

Roney, H. B.

1907. See Mershon, W. B., **The Passenger Pigeon.**

Rood, E. Irene.

1896. See World's Congress on Ornithology, **Papers presented to the—.**

Roosevelt, Robert B.

1866. **The** | **game-birds** | **of the** | **coasts and lakes of the northern states** | **of America.** | A full account of the sporting along our sea- | shores and inland waters, with a com- | parison of the merits of breech- | loaders and muzzle- | loaders. | By Robert B. Roose-velt, | Author of [*etc.*, *2 lines.*] | New York: | Carleton, Publisher, 413 Broadway. | M DCCC LXVI.

1 vol. 12mo, pp. I-VI, 7-336, 1 text-fig. New York.

A popular account of the ducks and shore birds of the northeastern United States, with descriptions of some of them (taken from Giraud's Birds of Long Island, 1844, q.v.). The text is devoted, principally, to methods of hunting and to various hunting experiences of the author.

Rosenstock, Rudolph.

1895. See Gätke, Heinrich, **Heligoland as an Ornithological Ob-servatory.**

Ross, Alexander Milton.

1872. The | **birds of Canada:** | with descriptions of their | plumage, habits, food, song, nests, eggs, | times of arrival and departure. | By | Alexander Milton Ross, | M.D., M.A., M.R.S.L., Eng. | Member of the Royal Linnæan Society of Belgium [*etc.*, *4 lines.*]. | **Second edition.** | Illustrated. | Toronto: | Roswell and Hutchin-son, | 1872.

1 vol. 16mo, pp. I-XVI, 1-152, 1-6 (advt.), 38 text-figs. Toronto.

An annotated list of species. The descriptions mentioned in the title are mostly lacking in sufficient detail to make them very serviceable. The illustrations are woodcuts,—poor copies (after Audubon and Wilson) or worse originals. The first edition was issued late in 1871.

Ross, James Clark.

1826. See Parry, William Edward, **Journal of a Third Voyage for the Discovery of a North-west Passage.**

Ross, John. (Edwards, John; Beverly, Charles James; Leach, W. E.)

1819. A | **voyage of discovery,** | made under the orders of the admiralty, | in | His Majesty's ships | Isabella and Alexander, | for the purpose of | exploring Baffin's Bay, | and inquiring into the probability of a | north-west passage. | By John Ross, K.S. Captain Royal Navy. | London: | John Murray, Albemarle-Street. | 1819.

1 vol. foliopost 4to, 2 pr. ll. (tit. and ded.), 1 insert-slip (errata), pp. I-XXXIX+1, 1-252, 1 l. (subtit.), pp. I-CXLIV (appendix), frontisp. (chart), 31 pll. and charts (15 col.; 12 fold.; 1 ornithologi-cal), 10 text-figs. London. 1819 (post March 1).

The narrative of the exploring expedition made during the year 1818. Various observations on natural history are noted from time to time in the general text and the complete "Zoological Memoranda" are found in Appendix No. 2, of which pp. XLVIII-LXIV and 1 pl. (col.) relate to birds. Captain Ed-ward Sabine was attached to the expedition for the purpose of assisting in the observation and collection of natural history data and specimens, and was placed in charge of this branch of the work by Captain Ross. On the return of the expedition, Sabine declined to furnish any report on the grounds of lack of ability and knowledge of any branch of natural history except ornithology, yet he published "A Memoir on the Birds of Greenland" (Trans. Linn. Soc. London, 12, pt. 2, pp. 527-559, pl. 30, 1819) based on his notes of the voyage. The zoological report in the present work is accredited by Ross to John Edwards and C. J. Beverly, Surgeon and Assistant Surgeon, respectively. of the Isabella, and to W. E. Leach who revised the paper. Leach and Joseph Sabine, brother of Edward Sabine, previously described the new species of birds in the Trans. Linn. Soc. London, 12, pt. 2, pp. 520-523, pl. 29, 1819 (Sabine) and Thomson's Annals of Philos., 13, pp. 60-61, 1819 (Leach). The final plates in the book are dated as being published March 1, 1819.

Rothschild, Walter.

1893-1900. The | avifauna of Laysan | and the | neighboring islands: | with a complete history to date of the | birds of the Hawaiian possessions. | By | The Hon. Walter Rothschild, Ph.D. | Illustrated with coloured and black plates | by Messrs. Keulemans and Frohawk; | and plates from photographs, showing bird-life and scenery. | London: | R. H. Porter, 7 Princes Street, Cavendish Square, W. | 1893-1900.

1 vol. in 2 vols., imperial 4to, tit., pp. I-XX (pref., bibl., notes on origin and distrib. of Hawaiian birds, list of pll.), I-XIV (introd. notes), 1-320, (Di) 1-(Di) 21, 1 insert-slip (errata; in Pt. I) 83 pll. (55 col., 20 collotype, 6 monochr.), 6 text-figs. London.

A monograph of the birds of Laysan and adjoining regions. The work was issued in three parts as follows. Part I, pp. I-XIV, 1-58, 41 pll., August 1893; II, pp. 59-126, 15 pll., November 1893; III, pp. I-XX (pref., etc.), (Di) 1-(Di) 21, 127-320, 27 pll., December, 1900. In the present copy pp. I-XIV and 1-4 are out of place, being bound between pp. 46 and 47. Part III, except for pp. I-XX (pref., etc.), is bound in a separate volume with original wrapper included. The edition was limited to 250 copies.

Rothschild, Walter.

1898. Das Tierreich. | Eine Zusammenstellung und Kennzeichnung der | rezenten Tierformen. | Herausgegeben | von der | Deutschen Zoologischen Gesellschaft. | Generalredakteur: Franz Eilhard Schulze. | **2. Lieferung.** | Aves. | Redakteur: A. Reichenow. | **Paradiseidae** | bearbeitet von | The Hon. Walter Rothschild. | Mit 15 Abbildungen im Texte. | Ausgegeben im April 1898. | Berlin. | Verlag von R. Friedländer und Sohn. | 1898.

1 vol. (pt.) superroyal 8vo, pp. I-VI, 1-52, text-figs. 1-15. Berlin. April 1898.

A monograph of the Birds of Paradise, with tables for the determination of the species, genera, and higher groups, notes on synonymy, the ranges of the various forms and short descriptions of all groups. See also under "Tierreich."

Rothschild, Walter.

1907. Extinct birds. | An attempt to unite in one volume a short account of | those Birds which have become extinct in historical | times—that is, within the last six or seven | hundred years. To which are | added a few which still | exist, but are on | the verge of | extinction. | By | The Hon. Walter Rothschild, | Ph.D., F.Z.S. | With 45 Coloured Plates, embracing 63 subjects, and | other illustrations. | London. | Hutchinson & Co., Paternoster Row, E. C. | 1907.

1 vol. imperial 4to, pp. I-XXIX+1, 1-244, 1 l., pll. 1-42, 4A, 5A, 24A-24C, 25A, 25B (45 col.; by Keulemans, Lodge, Grönvold, Smit and Frohawk). London.

A detailed account of the subject, with short descriptions, histories of the known facts relating to the species and a good bibliography. The plates are excellent.

Rowley, George Dawson. (Boucard, A; Dresser, H. E.; Finsch, O.; Gurney, J. H., Jr.; Meyer, A. B.; Newton, Alfred; Przheval'skiĭ, Nĭkolaĭ Mĭkhaĭlovĭch; Salvin, Osbert; Sclater, P. L.; Seebohm, Henry; Sharpe, R. B.; Swinhoe, R.; Tweeddale, Arthur (=Hay, Arthur); and Wodzicki, Casimir.)

1875-78. Ornithological miscellany. | Edited by | George Dawson Rowley, M.A., F.Z.S., | Member of the British Ornithologists' Union. | Volume I [-III]. | London: | Trübner and Co., Ludgate Hill, E. C. Bernard Quaritch, 15 Piccadilly. | R. H. Porter, 6 Tenterden Street, Hanover Square, W. | 1876 [1877; 1878]. | [All rights reserved.].

> Ornithological miscellany. | By | George Dawson Rowley, M.A., F.Z.S. | Member of the British Ornithologists' Union. | [*Quot., 4 lines.*] | London: | Trübner and Co., Ludgate Hill, E. C. | Brighton:] Thomas Page, North Street. | 1875. | [All rights reserved.].

3 vols. royal 4to. Vol. I, 10 ll. (half-tit., tit., ded., pref., dates of publ. of Vol. I, conts.=pp. III-IV, illustrs.=pp. V-VI, not. to binder, errata-2 ll.), pp. 1-321, 6 ll. (expl. of maps, orig. tit. and lists of pll. accompanying each part), 66 pll. (41 col., by Keulemans; 22 monochr.), 1 text-fig. Vol. II, 8 ll. (half-tit., tit., dates of publ., conts.=pp. III-IV, illustrs.=pp. V-VI, errata 2 ll., subtit.), pp. 1-477, 7 ll. (lists of pll. issued with each pt. and editor's note), 58 pll. (37 col.; 9 monochr.; 2 fold.), text-figs. 1-3. Vol. III, 7 ll.

(half-tit., tit., dates of publ., conts.=pp. III-IV, illustrs.=pp. V-VI, errata, subtit.), pp. 5-276, 4 ll. (lists of pll. issued with each pt., 36 pll. (26 col., 1 fold.; 1 monochr.), 3 text-figs. London.

A collection of papers of miscellaneous ornithological nature, issued in 14 parts at irregular intervals. The first numbers were written entirely by Rowley, but the work, as it progressed, included contributions by various other authors and partook somewhat of the nature of a periodical. A number of important papers are included in the three volumes, being published in instalments. The dates of each part are given in the containing volume. The original covers, with dates, are bound in with the text in the present copy.

Roy, Charles S.

1893-96. See Newton, Alfred, **A Dictionary of Birds.**

Rudolf, Franz Karl Josef, Crown Prince of Austria. (Danford, C. G., *transl.*)

1889. Notes | on | sport and ornithology | by | His Imperial and Royal Highness the late Crown Prince | Rudolf of Austria. | Translated, with the author's permission, | by | C. G. Danford. | [*Monogram.*] | London: | Gurney and Jackson, 1 Paternoster Row. | (Successors to Mr. Van Voorst.) | 1889.

1 vol. 8vo, pp. I-VIII, 1-648, frontisp. London.

A translation, by C. G. Danford, of Prince Rudolf's "Jagden und Beobachtungen," published in Vienna in 1887. The work consists of hunting and shooting sketches, accounts of travels, and ornithological notes of a more technical nature. The book is replete with valuable field observations, mostly ornithological.

Rüppell, Eduard Wilhelm Peter Simon. (Cretzschmar, Ph. J.)

1826-28. Atlas | zu der Reise im nördlichen Afrika | von | Eduard Rüppell. | Erste Abtheilung | Zoologie. | Herausgegeben | von | der Senkenbergischen naturforschenden Gesellschaft. | Frankfurt am Main | Gedruckt und in Commission bei Heinr. Ludw. Brönner | 1826. > Atlas | zu der Reise im nördlichen Afrika | von | Eduard Rüppell. | Vögel [*mut. mut.*]. | Bearbeitet | von | Dr. Med. Ph. J. Cretzschmar [*mut. mut.*].|Frankfurt am Main. | Gedruckt und in Commission bei Heinr. Ludw. Brönner. | 1826 [*mut. mut.*].

1 vol. demy folio. 3 pr. ll. (tit., ded. and dedic. pref.), pp. I-VI (introd.), 1 l. (subtit.-Säugethiere), pp. 1-78, 1 l. (subtit.-Vögel), pp. 1-55, 1 l. (subtit.-Reptilien), pp. 1-24, 1 l. (subtit.-Wirbellose Thiere), pp. 3-47+1+1 l., 1 l. (subtit.-Fische), pp. 1-141+1+1 l., pll. 1-30 (27 col.), 1-36 (col.; by F. C. Vogel and H. von Kittlitz; ornithological), 1-6 (col.), 1-12 (11 col.), and 1-35 (33 col.; 1 fold.). Frankfort am Main.

The zoology of Rüppell's journey in northern Africa and the district of the Red Sea from 1822-27. According to Engelmann, the work appeared in 20 parts. The ornithological portion was written by Cretzschmar and contains descriptions of the species of birds (some of them new), all of which are illustrated on the 36 colored plates in this section of the work. The subtitle of this section bears the date 1826 but Rüppell, in his "Neue Wirbelthiere," p. 50, quotes pl. 28 of the present work under date of 1827. In the Zoological Journal, IV, p. 385, (for Oct. 1828 to Jan. 1829), Pts. I-VIII of the work are reviewed in detail. The eight numbers are credited with six plates each, including some plates belonging to other non-ornithological sections of the work; their ornithological contents embrace pp. 1-38 and pll. 1-25. A second "Abtheilung" was intended to contain the geography of the expedition, but was never issued as such; the "Reisen in Nubien," etc., 1829, and the "Voyage dans l'Afrique et en Nubie" 1826 et seq., appear to constitute the equivalent. A continuation of the present portions of the work is found in the "Neue Wirbelthiere zu der Fauna von Abyssinien gehörig," 1835-40 (q.v.).

Rüppell, Eduard Wilhelm Peter Simon.

1835-40. **Neue Wirbelthiere** | **zu der** | **Fauna von Abyssinien gehörig,** | entdeckt und beschrieben | von | Dr. Eduard Rüppell. | Frankfurt am Main. | In Commission bei Siegmund Schmerber. | 1835-1840. > [*Idem, 6 lines.*] | Säugethiere [Vögel; Amphibien; Fische des rothen Meeres] Frankfurt am Main. | In Commission bei Siegmund Schmerber. | 1835.

1 vol. medium folio. 2 pr. ll. (tit. and pref.), 2 ll. (subtit.-Säugethiere, ded.), pp. 1-40, 1 l. (subtit.-Vögel), pp. 3-116, 1 l. (subtit.-Amphibien), pp. 1-18, 2 ll. (subtit.-Fische, pref.), pp. 1-148, pll. 1-14 (13 col.), 1-42 (col.; by F. C. Vogel; ornithological), 1-6 (col.), 1-33 (21 col.). Frankfort am Main.

A continuation of Rüppell's "Atlas zu der Reise im nördlichen Afrika," containing descriptions of new mammals, birds, reptiles and fishes. The work appears to have been issued in 13 Lieferungen (according to the preface) during the years 1835 to 1840. A review, in the Magazine of Zoology and Botany, 1, No. III, p. 275, 1846 (after Aug. 25), records 6 parts issued at intervals of three months beginning January 1, 1835. Two ornithological parts are included in this review, embracing pll. 1-12 and pp. 1-32. On p. 109 of the Mag. Zool. Bot. 1, No. 1, 1837, is the statement that each of the first four fasciculi was devoted to a separate section of the subject, so that part 1 of the birds (pp. 1-16 and pll. 1-6) seems to be properly dated 1835. Part 2 of the birds is probably referable to 1836. Page 81 must have been published in or after March 1837[1]; p. 94 in or after 1838[2]; and p. 99 in or after 1839[3]. The preface is dated May 1, 1840. The author's "Systematische Uebersicht der Vögel Nord-Ost-Afrika's," 1845 (q.v.), is supplementary to the present work.

---

[1]Reference given to William Swainson, Birds of West Africa, Vol. I (q.v., 1837).
[2]Reference given to Andrew Smith, Illustr. Zool. S. Africa, Pt. 2 (q.v., 1838-39).
[3]Reference given to Rüppell's monograph of the genus Colius.

Rüppell, Eduard Wilhelm Peter Simon.

1845. Systematische Uebersicht | der | Vögel Nord-Ost-Afrika's | nebst | Abbildung und Beschreibung von fünfzig Theils unbekannten, | Theils noch nicht bildlich dargestellten Arten. | Von | Dr. Eduard Rüppell. | Fortsetzung | der neuen Wirbelthiere, zu der Fauna von Abyssinien gehœrig. | Frankfurt A.M. | In Commission der Schmerber'schen Buchhandlung. | (Nachfolger H. Keller.) | 1845.

1 vol. royal 8vo, pp. I-VII+1, 1-140, pll. 1-50 (col.; by Wolf). Frankfort am Main. 1845 (during or after July).

An ornithological supplement to the author's "Neue Wirbelthiere," 1835-40 (q.v.), containing descriptions of new and recently discovered birds from northeastern Africa. The hand-colored illustrations (backgrounds not colored) are very good, and appear to represent some of the earlier work of the artist. The preface is dated July 1845.

Russ, Karl. (Schultze, Leonora, *transl.*)

1884. The | speaking parrots: | A Scientific Manual. | By Dr. Karl Russ, | Author of [*etc.*, *3 lines.*] | Translated by | Leonora Schultze, | and revised by Dr. Karl Russ. | London: | L. Upcott Gill, 170, Strand, W. C.

1 vol. crown 8vo, pp. I-VIII, 1-296, 9 pll. (8 col.; by A. F. Lydon), figs. 1 and 2. London.

An account of the speaking parrots as cage-birds, with short descriptions of each and with occasional notes on their habits in nature, prefaced by a general discussion of feeding, training, preservation of health, etc. The work is a translation of the author's "Die Sprechenden Papageien" published in 1882.

Russell, Alexander.

1756. The | natural history | of | Aleppo, | and | parts adjacent. | Containing | A Description of the City, and the Principal | Natural Productions in its Neighborhood; | together with | An Account of the Climate, Inhabitants, and Diseases; | particularly of the Plague, with the Methods used by the | Europeans for their Preservation. | By Alex. Russell, M.D. | London: | Printed for A. Millar, in the Strand. | MDCCCLVI (*sic*).

1 vol. medium 4to, pp. I-VIII, 1-266, 5 ll. (index and errata), pll. 1-12, XIII-XVI (col.; fold.; 9-11 ornithological). London.

A general description of Haleb, or Aleppo, Syria, from observations made by the author during his residence there as a physician from 1742 to (at least) 1753. The ornithology of the region is discussed on pp. 63-72, with colored plates of three of the species which are described (but not named) as new.

Russell, William Howard.

1881. See Hay, Arthur, **The Ornithological Works of Arthur, Ninth Marquis of Tweeddale.**

Rüst, Dr.

1897. Katalog | der | systematischen Vogelsammlung | des | Provinzial-Museums | in Hannover. | Hannover. | Druck von Wilh. Riemschneider. | 1897.

1 vol. 8vo, 2 pr. ll. (tit. and pref.), pp. 1-106, (orig. wrapper). Hannover.

A list of the 1376 species and subspecies of birds in the systematic bird-collection of the Provincial Museum of Hannover, with notation of the sex, locality and donor of the various specimens of each form. The local species are further catalogued in a separate paper issued the same year (q.v.). The preface is signed by Dr. Rüst.

? Rüst, Dr.

1897. Katalog | der | Vogelsammlung | aus der | Provinz Hannover. | Hannover. | Druck von Wilh. Riemschneider. | 1897.

1 vol. 8vo, tit., pp. 1-24, (original wrapper). Hannover.

A list of 248 local species of birds in the Provincial Museum of Hannover, with the sex, locality and donor indicated for each specimen. The entire collection, including foreign species and the present series, are treated in a similar paper issued the same year (q.v.). The preface to the larger work is signed by Dr. Rüst, from which it appears probable that the present paper is by the same author.

Sage, John Hall; Bishop, Louis Bennett; and Bliss, Walter Parks.

1913. State of Connecticut | Public Document No. 47 | State Geological and Natural History Survey | Commissioners | [*List of Comm., 5 lines.*] | Superintendent | William North Rice | Bulletin No. 20 | [*Seal*] | Hartford | Printed for the State Geological and Natural History Survey | 1913 > **The Birds of Connecticut** | By | John Hall Sage, M.S. | Secretary of the American Ornithologists' Union | and | Louis Bennett Bishop, M.D. | Fellow of the American Ornithologists' Union | assisted by | Walter Parks Bliss, M.A. | [*Seal*] | Hartford | Printed for the State Geological and Natural History Survey | 1913.

1 vol. 8vo, pp. 1-370. Hartford.

The present work is divided into two parts. Part I contains an annotated list of the species of birds known from Connecticut. Part II (pp. 259-360), by Bishop, alone, contains a discussion of economic ornithology arranged according to the natural groups of birds. A bibliography of Connecticut ornithology is presented with Part I.

Sagra, Ramon de la. (d'Orbigny, Alcide Dessalines.)

1839-40. **> Histoire | physique, politique et naturelle | de | l'ile de Cuba |** par | M. Ramon de la Sagra [par M. Ramon de la Sagra (*Atlas.*)], | Directeur du Jardin Botanique de la Havane, | Correspondant de l'Institut Royal de France, etc. | Mammifères par M. Ramon de la Sagra;

[Ornithologie; Atlas], traduction [par Alcide par M. S. Berthelot.

d'Orbigny. (*Ornith.*); *line omitted* (*Atlas.*)] | [*Design*; *Vignette* (*Atlas.*).] | Paris, | Arthus Bertrand, Éditeur [Libraire-Éditeur (*Atlas.*)], | Libraire de la Société de Géographie | et de la Société Royale des Antiquaires du Nord, | Rue Hautefeuille, 23. | 1840 [1839 (*Ornith.*; *n. d.* (*Atlas.*).].

3 vols. in 2, 8vo, and medium folio. Mammifères, 4 pr. ll. (half-tit., tit., subtit. and conts.), pp. I-XLV+1, 1-18. Ornithologie, pp. I-XXXI+1, 1-336. Atlas, 2 pr. ll. (tit. and conts.), pll. I-VIII (col.; mammals), I-XXXII+XIX bis (col.; by Prêtre and E. Traviès; birds). Paris.

The mammalogy and ornithology of Ramon de la Sagra's history of Cuba. This work was issued, 1839-61, in two editions, Spanish and French,—the former probably the earlier although both bear the same dates on the respective parts. Engelmann divides the publication into 75 livraisons and quotes the mammals and birds in one volume (as above) as well as in two volumes, separately. The ornithological portion, by d'Orbigny, dates from 1839. Probably only 32 plates (I-XXXI and XIX bis) were issued originally; the list of plates in the Atlas tabulates only these and there is evidence that the final plate of eggs (pl. XXXII) was not issued until 1843 (Cf. Sagra, Album d'Oiseaux de Cuba.). The work contains a summary of the knowledge of Cuban birds to date, as well as descriptions of the new forms contained in de la Sagra's collections. The present copy contains the autograph of Wm. Jardine on an original wrapper which is bound in the volume of text.

Sagra, Ramon de la.

1843. **Album | d'oiseaux de Cuba |** réunis pendant le voyage | de | M. Ramon de la Sagra | dédié | a S.M. la Reine Isabelle II. | [*Vignette.*] | Paris | Imprimerie et lithographie de Maulde et Renou, | Rue Bailleul, Nos 9 et 11. | 1843 > Histoire | physique, politique et naturelle | de | l'ile de Cuba | par M. Ramon de la Sagra | Directeur du Jardin Botanique de la Havane, | Correspondant de l'Institut Royal de France, etc. | Atlas | [*Vignette.*] | Paris, | Arthus Bertrand, Libraire-Éditeur, | Libraire de la Société de Géographie, | Rue Hautefeuille, 21.

2 vols. in 1 vol., demy folio and medium folio. Text, pp. 1-16. Atlas, 2 ll. (tit. and conts.), pll. I-VII (col.; mammals), I-XXXII+ XIXbis (col.; by Prêtre, E. Traviès and Hublier; birds). Paris.

The present work is somewhat puzzling. The text appears to consist of a very general discussion of the rich variety of Cuban bird-life, followed by a synoptic list of species supposedly copied from d'Orbigny's arrangement in de la Sagra's "Histoire Physique, Politique et Naturelle de l'Ile de Cuba, Ornithologie," 1839-40 (q.v.). As printed in the present book, the list presents a great number of changes from the original,—most of the changes being alterations in spelling, two of them being changes of genera, but probably all of them being due to errors in copying. The authorship is in doubt, but, presumably, the entire work was arranged by the publishers. In the latter part of the text the announcement is made of the present issue of an album consisting of the ornithological plates from the "Histoire," together with an additional plate of eggs (=pl. XXXII) drawn from specimens received by Baron Delessert from José Ramon de la Paz Morejon. The album in which this letterpress is bound contains plates of both mammals and birds, prefaced by the same list of contents as in the original "Histoire." The title-page is reprinted with certain alterations; the vignette is redrawn; the word, 'Atlas,' is in plain, instead of ornamental, type; a line of print is withdrawn from above the last line on the page, and the address of the publisher is given as "Rue Hautefeuille 21" instead of "23," while general typographical changes are apparent throughout. The plates appear to be from the same copperplates except that the first of both mammals and birds bears the signature, "N Rémond imp. r. Vieille-Estrapade, 15, Paris." instead of "Bougeard imp." as on the originals and on all the remainder in the present issue. The coloration of the plates presents numerous variations from that of the examples of the original at hand.

Saint-Hilaire, Alexandre Bourjot.

See Bourjot Saint-Hilaire, A.

Saint-Hilaire, Isidore Geoffroy.

See Geoffroy Saint-Hilaire, Isidore.

St. John, Claude.

1911. Our canaries | A Thoroughly Practical and Comprehensive Guide to the successful | keeping, breeding and exhibiting of every known | variety of the domesticated Canary | By | Claude St. John | Written in conjunction with C. A. House and G. E. Weston and many | leading present-day authorities on the various breeds | Thirty-two coloured plates | also a large number of Illustrations in wash and line | By H. Norman | Issued from the Offices of | "Cage Birds," 154 Fleet Street | London, E.C.

1 vol. imperial 8vo, tit., pp. I-II, 3-382, 63 pll. (32 col.; by H. Norman), 159 text-cuts. London.

A detailed work as explained by the title, forming an authoritative handbook for the canary-fancier. The plates (colored and uncolored) illustrate the various breeds of these birds.

St. John, H. C.

1880. **Notes and sketches | from the | wild coasts of Nipon |** with chapters on cruising after | pirates in Chinese waters | By Captain H. C. St. John, R.N. | [*Vignette.*] | Edinburgh: David Douglas | MDCCCLXXX.

1 vol. post 8vo, pp. I-XXIII+1, 1-392, 8 pll. (monochr.), 5 maps (col.; 1 fold.), 43 text-figs. (7 ornithological; incl. tit.-vignette). Edinburgh. 1880 (circa November).

Sketches of Japanese life, customs and country, with numerous notes on the bird life of the region scattered through the volume.

Salerne, François.

1767. See Ray, John, L'Histoire Naturelle, Eclaircie dans une de ses Parties Principales, l'Ornithologie.

Salvadori, Tommaso.

1881. See Thomson, C. Wyville, **Reports on the Scientific Results of the Voyage of H. M. S. Challenger; Report on the Birds.**

Salvadori, Tommaso.

1891. **Catalogue | of the | Psittaci,** or parrots, | in the | collection | of the British Museum. | By | T. Salvadori. | London: | printed by order of the Trustees. | Sold by | Longmans & Co., 39 Paternoster Row; [*etc., 3 lines.*]; | and at the | British Museum (Natural History), Cromwell Road, S.W. | 1891.

See British Museum, **Catalogue of the Birds,** 1874-98, Vol. XX.

Salvadori, Tommaso.

1893. **Catalogue | of the | Columbæ,** or pigeons, | in the | collection | of the British Museum. | By | T. Salvadori. | London: | printed by order of the Trustees. | Sold by | Longmans & Co., 39 Paternoster Row; [*etc., 3 lines.*]; | and at the | British Museum (Natural History), Cromwell Road, S.W. | 1893.

See British Museum, **Catalogue of the Birds,** 1874-98, Vol. XXI.

Salvadori, Tommaso.

1895. **Catalogue | of the | Chenomorphæ |** (Palamedeæ, Phoenicopteri, Anseres), | Crypturi, | and | Ratitæ | in the | collection | of the | British Museum. | By | T. Salvadori. | London: | printed by order of the Trustees. | Sold by | Longmans & Co., 39 Paternoster Row; [*etc., 3 lines.*]; | and at the | British Museum (Natural History), Cromwell Road, S.W. | 1895.

See British Museum, **Catalogue of the Birds,** 1874-98, Vol. XXVII.

Salvadori, Tommaso.

1905-10. See Wytsman, Paul, **Genera Avium,** 1905-14.

Salvin, Francis Henry; and Brodrick, William.

1855. Falconry | in | the British Isles. | By | Francis Henry Salvin | and | William Brodrick. | London: | John Van Voorst, Paternoster Row. | MDCCCLV.

1 vol. medium 4to (7½x11¼), pp. I-VI, 1 l., pp. 1-147, pll. I-XXIV (col., by Brodrick; VIII wrongly numbered VII). London.

A complete treatise on the art of falconry, with descriptions and illustrations of the various species of hawks used in England in that sport. A second edition (q.v.) was issued in 1873.

Salvin, Francis Henry; and Brodrick, William.

1873. Falconry | in | the British Isles. | By | Francis Henry Salvin | and William Brodrick, B.A. | **Second edition,** revised and enlarged. | London: | John Van. Voorst, Paternoster Row. | MDCCCLXXIII.

1 vol. foliopost 4to (7½x11), pp. I-VIII, 1 l., pp. 1-171, pll. 1-28 (col.; by Brodrick). London.

A second edition, with some additions to the text, of the work of the same title (q.v.) published in 1855. The plates are all redrawn, owing to the destruction of the original lithographic stones, and several new ones added.

Salvin, Osbert.

1866-69. See Sclater, Philip Lutley; and Salvin, **Exotic Ornithology.**

Salvin, Osbert.

1873. See Sclater, Philip Lutley; and Salvin, **Nomenclator Avium Neotropicalium.**

Salvin, Osbert.

1876. See Rowley, George D., **Ornithological Miscellany,** 1875-78.

Salvin, Osbert; and Godman, Frederick DuCane.

1879-1904. > Biologia | **Centrali-Americana. | Aves. |** Vol. I [-IV]. | (Text.) [(Plates - *Vol. IV.*)] | By | Osbert Salvin, F.R.S., &c., | and | Frederick DuCane Godman, D.C.L., F.R.S., &c. | 1879-1904 [1888-1897; 1897-1904; 1879-1904].

4 vols. royal 4to. Vol. I, pp. I-XLIV, 1-512. Vol. II, 2 pr. ll., pp. 1-598. Vol. III, pp. I-IV, 1-510. Vol. IV, pp. I-VII, pll. 1-79, 15a, 54a, 58a, 58b and 59a (col.; by J. G. Keulemans). London.

A sumptuous monograph of the birds of Central America, forming part of the work treating of the complete natural history of the same region. Of the birds, 1413 species are treated and 149 figured. The present portion appeared in 74 of the 257 parts in which the work was issued. The various signatures are dated so that there is no need to collate the work by parts except as regards the plates. Salvin died in 1898 and Godman completed the work with the assistance of R. B. Sharpe and W. R. Ogilvie-Grant. All portions of Vol. III after p. 184 bear Godman's name, only, on the original wrappers. The plates appeared as follows (according to dates on the original wrappers). Pll. 1-3, Sept. 1879; 4, Nov. '79; 5, Febr. '80; 6 and 7, April '80; 8, Aug. '80; 9 and 10, Febr. '81; 11, Aug. '81; 12, Dec. '81; 13, Febr. '82; 14, March '83; 15, May '83; 15a, 16 and 17, Nov. '83; 18-21, Dec. '83; 22 and 23, Febr. '84; 24, Dec. '84; 25-27, April '86; 28, June '86; 29 and 30, Aug. '86; 31 and 32, Oct. '86; 33-35, April '87; 36, Dec. '88; 37-40, Febr. '89; 41-43, Dec. '90; 44 and 45, July '91; 46-48, Sept. '91; 49-51, Febr. '92; 52 and 53, March '92; 54 and 55, May '92; 54a, 56 and 57, Sept. '92; 58, 58a and 58b, Nov. '94; 59, 59a and 60, Jan. '95; 61 and 62, Nov. '97; 63, Dec. 1900; 64 and 65, Jan. '01; 66, Febr. '01; 67-69, March '02; 70, May '02; 71, Dec. '02; 72 and 73, Febr. '03; 74 and 75, April '03; 76 and 77, May '03; 78 and 79, April '04. A general introductory volume by Godman, contains matter, part of which is of interest ornithologically. Printed by Taylor and Francis, London.

Salvin, Osbert.

1880. See Smith, Andrew, **Sir Andrew Smith's Miscellaneous Ornithological Papers,** The Willughby Society.

Salvin, Osbert.

1881. See Thomson, C. Wyville, **Reports on the Scientific Results of the Voyage of H. M. S. Challenger; Report on the Birds.**

Salvin, Osbert.

1882. **A catalogue | of the | collection of birds | formed by the late | Hugh Edwin Strickland,** M.A. | Fellow of the Royal, Linnean [*etc., 3 lines.*] | by | Osbert Salvin, M.A., F.R.S., &c. | Strickland Curator in the University of Cambridge. | Cambridge: | at the. University Press. | 1882.

1 vol. 8vo, pp. I-XVI, 1-652, 1-31+1 (advt.). Cambridge.

A list of 6006 specimens of birds in the Strickland collection, arranged according to the "Nomenclator Avium Neotropicalum" of Sclater and Salvin, 1873 (q.v.), with references to the original description, to Strickland's writing and to a few other important publications under each species. Date, locality and collector, where these are known, are given for each specimen.

Salvin, Osbert.

1882. See Leach, William Elford, **Systematic Catalogue of the Specimens of the Indigenous Mammalia and Birds that are preserved in the British Museum,** The Willughby Society.

Salvin, Osbert.

1883. See Barton, Benjamin Smith, **Fragments of the Natural History of Pennsylvania,** The Willughby Society.

Salvin Osbert; and Hartert, Ernst.

1892. Catalogue | of the | Picariæ | in the | collection | of the | British Museum. | Upupæ and Trochili, | by | Osbert Salvin. | Coraciæ, | of the families | Cypselidæ, Caprimulgidæ, Podargidæ, and | Steatornithidæ, | by | Ernst Hartert. | London: | printed by order of the Trustees. | Sold by | Longmans & Co., 39 Paternoster Row; [etc., 3 lines.]; | and at the | British Museum (Natural History), Cromwell Road, S.W. | 1892.
See British Museum, **Catalogue of the Birds,** 1874-98, Vol. XVI.

Salvin, Osbert.

1896. See Saunders, Howard; and Salvin, **Catalogue of the Gaviae and Tubinares** in the Collection of the British Museum.
Also, British Museum, **Catalogue of the Birds,** 1874-98, Vol. XXV.

Salvin, Osbert.

1897-98. See Lilford, Lord, **Coloured Figures of the Birds of the British Islands,** 1891-98.

Samuels, Edward Augustus.

1868. **Among the birds:** | a series of sketches for | young folks, | illustrating the | Domestic Life of our Feathered Friends. | By | Edward A. Samuels, | author of [etc., 2 lines.]. | Boston: | Nichols and Noyes. | 1868.
1 vol. cap 8vo, pp. I-VIII, 1-223, 4 pll., 9 text-figs. Boston.

A work for juvenile readers in which the author "has endeavored to weave among the woof of facts regarding our most familiar birds, their habits and peculiarities, a warp of romantic fancy; believing that such will be more attractive than plain . . . . descriptions."

Samuels, Edward Augustus. (Couper, William.)

1869. **Ornithology and oölogy** | of | **New England:** | containing | full descriptions of the birds of New England, and adjoining | states and provinces, arranged by a long-approved | classification and nomenclature; | together with | a complete history of their habits, times of arrival and departure, | their distribution, food, song, time of breeding, and | a careful and accurate description | of their nests and eggs; | with | Illustrations of many Species of the Birds, and accurate Figures | of their Eggs. | By Edward A. Samuels, | Curator of Zoology in the Massachusetts State Cabinet. | Boston: | Nichols and Noyes. | 117, Washington Street. | 1869.

1 vol. 8vo, pp. I-VII+1, 1-587, frontisp. (col.; after Audubon), pll. I-IV (eggs), 23 pll. (after Audubon), 38 text-figs. Boston.

An early edition of a work first published in 1867. It consists of technical descriptions and classification taken from Baird ("Pacific Railroad Surveys," Vol. IX, 1858), and general discussions of the species largely extracted from Wilson, Nuttall and Audubon, with some original matter. William Couper supplied notes on the occurrence and distribution of certain species in Quebec, on pp. 80-81, 368-372, 396, 477-478 and 571-573, as in the first edition (Cf. Coues.). An appendix, not in the original edition, is added on pp. 575-578 to include a few species recorded by various authors but not mentioned in the body of the work. The illustrations are from various sources. Those of the eggs were prepared by M. M. Tidd and Nathan Brown; the frontispiece and most of the unnumbered plates (one of which is an uncolored copy of the frontispiece) are copied from Audubon. The book passed through a number of editions under various titles, at least three of which were issued in 1883. Cf. Samuels, The Birds of New England, 1883, and Our Northern and Eastern Birds, 1883.

Samuels, Edward Augustus. (Couper, William.)

1883. The | Birds of New England | and | adjacent states: | containing descriptions of the birds of New England, and adjoin- | ing states and provinces, arranged by a long-approved | classification and nomenclature; | together with | a history of their habits, times of arrival and departure, their | distribution, food, song, time of breeding, and a | careful and accurate description of | their nests and eggs: | with | Illustrations of many Species of the Birds, and accurate Figures | of their Eggs. | By Edward A. Samuels, | Curator of Zoology in the Massachusetts State Cabinet. | With an appendix containing supplementary notes. | **Tenth edition,** revised and enlarged. | Boston: | Lockwood, Brooks, and Company, | 17 Franklin Street. | 1883.

1 vol. 8vo, pp. I-VII+1, 1-591, frontisp. (col.; after Audubon), pll. I-IV (eggs), 23 pll. (mostly after Audubon), 38 text-figs. Boston.

The present title covers the tenth edition of the author's "Ornithology and Oölogy of New England," 1867, from which it differs only in a new title-page, a different frontispiece and a more extended appendix on pp. 575-583. Couper's contributions are mentioned in the discussion of the edition of 1869 (q.v.). Another edition, under the title of "Our Northern and Eastern Birds" (q.v.) appeared also in 1883.

Samuels, Edward Augustus. (Couper, William.)

1883.   Our | **Northern and Eastern Birds.** | Containing descriptions of the birds of the northern and | eastern states and British provinces; | together with | a history of their habits, times of arrival and departure, | their distribution, food, song, time of breeding, and | a careful and accurate description of | their nests and eggs; | with | illustrations of many species of the birds, | and accurate figures of their eggs. | By Edward A. Samuels. | New York: | R. Worthington, 770 Broadway. | 1883.

1 vol. royal 8vo, pp. I-VII+1, 1-600, frontisp. (col.; after Audubon), 34 pll. (6 col.; by A. Pope and after Audubon), 35 text-figs. New York.

This work, issued the same year as "The Birds of New England and Adjacent States, Tenth Edition" (q.v.), differs from that work in its altered title and title-page, the addition of 5 new colored plates after Audubon, a different frontispiece, 5 new drawings by A. Pope, the omission of several cuts and the revision of a small portion of the text. The Catalogue of the Library of the British Museum (Natural History) records another edition of the same title, date and publisher as the present one, with the addition of a supplement from Hodder's "American Fauna;" this work I have not seen. Couper's contributions are on pp. 80-81, 368-372, 394 (instead of 396 as in the 10th ed.), 477-478 and 571-573.

Sandys, Edwyn; and Van Dyke, T. S.

1902.   **Upland game birds** | by | Edwyn Sandys | and | T. S. Van Dyke | illustrated by L. A. Fuertes, A. B. Frost | J. O. Nugent, and C. L. Bull | [*Vignette.*] | New York | The Macmillan Company | London: Macmillan & Co., Ltd. | 1902 | All rights reserved.

1 vol. post 8vo, pp. I-IX+1, 1 l., pp. 1-429+1, 1 p. (advt.), frontisp., 8 pll. New York.

A popular work forming one of the volumes in The American Sportsman's Library, edited by Caspar Whitney. Concise descriptions of the various species are followed by notes on habits and hunting experiences woven into a very readable narrative which contains a great deal of information. Pages 377-417 (on the quail and grouse of the Pacific Coast) are by Van Dyke; the remainder of the discussions are by Sandys. A companion volume in the same series is Sanford, Bishop and Van Dyke's "The Water-fowl Family," 1903 (q.v.).

Sanford, L. C.; Bishop, L. B.; and Van Dyke, T. S.

1903.   **The water-fowl** | **family** | by | L. C. Sanford, | L. B. Bishop | and | T. S. Van Dyke | [*Vignette.*] New York | The Macmillan Company | London: Macmillan and Co., Ltd. | 1903 | All rights reserved.

1 vol. post 8vo, pp. I-IX+1, 1-598, 1 l. (advt.), 20 pll. (16 bird-portrs., by Fuertes). New York.

A sportsman's reference book, with accounts of the habits of the various species of ducks and geese, rails and shore-birds of North America, prefixed by descriptions and notes on the distribution of each and interspersed with accounts of hunting experiences. The discussion of the waterfowl of the Pacific coast (pp. 503-564) is by Van Dyke, the general account is by Sanford, and a carefully prepared chapter on the diagnoses of families and genera is unaccredited but is ascribed to Bishop (together with other technical matter in the first part of the work) by the reviewer in the Auk **20**, pp. 313-314, July 1903. The work forms one of the volumes in the American Sportsman's Library, in which a companion volume is Sandys and Van Dyke's "Upland Game Birds," 1902 (q.v.).

Sarasin, Fritz; and Roux, Jean.

1913. Fritz Sarasin & Jean Roux | **Nova Caledonia** | Forschungen Recherches scientifiques | in Neu-Caledonien und en Nouvelle Calédonie | auf den Loyalty-Inseln et aux Iles Loyalty | A. Zoologie | Vol. I - L.I | 1. Dr. Fritz Sarasin, **Die Vögel Neu-Caledoniens und der | Loyalty-Inseln** | Mit 3 Tafeln in Lithographie und 6 Abbildungen im Text | Wiesbaden | C. W. Kreidels Verlag | 1913.

1 vol. medium 4to, 4 pr. ll. (tit., subtit., conts. and short subtit.), pp. 1-78, 3 ll. (expl. of pll.), pll. I-III (2 col.; by Frz. Krauss), text-figs. 1-6. Wiesbaden.

A critical list of the birds of New Caledonia and the Loyalty Islands, giving the detailed insular distribution of each, the specimens collected by the Sarasin and Roux expedition, and notes on habits, relationships, etc. Numerous new species and subspecies are described. The work as collated above constitutes the ornithological report by Sarasin, forming part (Vol. I, Lief. I) of a complete report on the expedition to the islands in question, and should be quoted as Sarasin in Sarasin and Roux.

Saunders, Howard.

1881. See Thomson, C. Wyville, **Reports on the Scientific Results of the Voyage of H. M. S. Challenger; Report on the Birds.**

Saunders, Howard.

1882-85. See Yarrell, William, **A History of British Birds, fourth edition,** 1871-85.

Saunders, Howard.

1883. See Vieillot, Louis Jean Pierre, **Analyse d'une Nouvelle Ornithologie Élémentaire,** The Willughby Society.

Saunders, Howard.

1889. **An illustrated manual | of | British birds. |** By | Howard
Saunders, F.L.S., F.Z.S., &c. | Editor of [*etc., 2 lines.*]. | With
illustrations of nearly every species. | [*Monogram.*] | London: |
Gurney and Jackson, 1, Paternoster Row. | (Successors to Mr.
Van Voorst.) | 1889.

1 vol. post 8vo, 2 pr. ll. (half-tit. and tit.), 1 insert-slip (errata), pp.
IV-VI+1, IX-XL, 1-754, 3 maps (col., fold.), 373 text-figs. London.

A handbook of non-technical information relative to British birds, considered
by some reviewers to be the best work of its kind ever published on British
birds. It forms, in effect, a condensed "Yarrell," of the fourth edition of which
(1871-85, q.v.) Saunders was part editor.   Each of 367 species is briefly described and its distribution, breeding habits and claims for recognition as British
are discussed in accounts restricted to two pages.   Most of the species are
figured by woodcuts taken largely from the drawings by E. Neale in Yarrell's
"History of British Birds," 1837-43 (q.v.), with the addition of some new ones
by G. E. Lodge and J. G. Keulemans.   The preface contains the diagnostic
characters of the various genera arranged in the order of classification adopted
in the general text.   An appendix supplies additional notes on certain species
from information secured, apparently, after the work was in press.   The
present copy is from the library, and contains the bookplate of, J. Lewis Bonhote, whose manuscript notes are pencilled through the volume.   There is
added, also, a fragment of a letter, apparently from Mrs. Leverton of Truro,
regarding a certain specimen mentioned in the text (Bartram's Sandpiper).
A second edition (q.v.) was published in 1899.

Saunders, Howard.

1892.   See Mitchell, Frederick Shaw, **The Birds of Lancashire.**

Saunders, Howard; and Salvin, Osbert.

1896. **Catalogue | of the | Gaviæ and Tubinares |** in the | collec-
tion | of the | British Museum. | Gaviæ | (terns, gulls, and
skuas) | by | Howard Saunders. | Tubinares | (petrels and alba-
trosses) | by | Osbert Salvin. | London: | printed by order of the
Trustees. | Sold by | Longmans & Co., 39 Paternoster Row;
[*etc., 3 lines.*]; | and at the | British Museum (Natural History),
Cromwell Road, S.W. | 1896.

See British Museum, **Catalogue of the Birds,** 1874-98, Vol. XXV.

Saunders, Howard.

1899. **An illustrated manual | of | British birds. |** By | Howard
Saunders, F.L.S., F.Z.S., &c. | Editor of [*etc., 2 lines.*]. | With 384
illustrations and 3 coloured maps. | Second edition, revised and
enlarged. | [*Monogram.*] | London: | Gurney and Jackson, 1,
Paternoster Row. | (Successors to Mr. Van Voorst.) | 1899.

1 vol. post 8vo, pp. I-XL, 1-776, 3 maps (col., fold.), 390 text-figs. London.

Of the same general plan as the first edition, 1889 (q.v.), the present work has been largely rewritten to bring the subject matter to date, although still, with a single exception, keeping to the limits of two pages for each species. Numerous species are added, bringing the total to 384, with a consequent increase in the number of woodcuts.

Savi, Adolfo.

1873. See Savi, Paolo, **Ornitologia Italiana,** 1873-76.

Savi, Paolo.

1827-31. **Ornitologia | Toscana** | ossia | descrizione e storia degli uccelli | che trovansi nella Toscana | con l'aggiunta | delle descrizioni di tutti gli altri | proprj al rimanente d'Italia | del Dottore | Paolo Savi | Professore di Storia Naturale [*etc.*, *10 lines* (*Vol. I.*); *11 lines* (*Vol. II.*); *15 lines* (*Vol. III.*).]. | Tomo primo [secondo; terzo] | Pisa | Dalla Tipografia Nistri [Tipografia Nistri E Cc. (*Vol. III.*)] | MDCCCXXVII [MDCCCXXIX; MDCCCXXXI].

3 vols. crown 8vo. Vol. I, pp. I-XLIV, 1-302, text-figs. I-IV, 14 text-figs. (unnum.). Vol. II, 2 pr. ll. (tit. and pref.), pp. 1-383+1, 12 text-figs. Vol. III, 2 pr. ll. (tit. and pref.), pp. 1-296, 1-113 (synoptic tables), 5 text-figs. Pisa.

A descriptive catalogue of the birds of the Department of Tuscany, Italy. Full descriptions of the species, genera and higher groups are given, with some synonymy, vernacular nomenclature in local and foreign terms, dates of occurrence, notes on life-history, etc. Several species are described as new, but the author's "nobis" usually denotes simply a change in generic position of the species. Volume III contains (pp. 237-296) seven indices, to the Latin, Italian, French, English and German names, general subject matter, and errata, respectively; pp. 183-236 contain the appendices to Vols. I and II. The separately paged synoptic tables form a part of Vol. III, according to the signatures, although Engelmann, who lists 4 vols. of the work, may have considered them as forming a separate volume.

Savi, Paolo. (Savi, Adolfo.)

1873-76. **Ornitologia Italiana** | opera postuma | del Prof. Comm. | Paolo Savi | Senatore del Regno. | Volume Primo [Secondo; Terzo] | [*Monogram.*] | Firenze. | Successori Le Monnier. | 1873 [1874; 1876].

3 vols. post 8vo. Vol. I, 3 pr. ll. (half-tit., tit. and pref.), pp. 1-478, text-figs. I-IV, 12 text-figs. (unnum.). Vol. II, pp. 1-485, 14 text-figs. Vol. III, pp. 1-214, 4 text-figs. Florence.

A work on the birds of Italy similar to, and based on, the author's "Ornitologia Toscana," 1827-31 (q.v.). Many species are treated here that are not discussed in the earlier work, but numbers of the descriptions are copied and the text-figures are the same (with the omission of one). An index is given to each volume and Vol. II contains a general index to the three volumes. The appendices, vernacular indices (except the Italian which is embodied in the general index) and synoptic tables are omitted. A short preface is given by Adolfo Savi, the son of the author, since the work was published after the death of the elder Savi.

Savigny, Marie Jules-César Lelorgne de.

1810. Système | des | oiseaux | de l'Égypte et de la Syrie, | présenté a l'assemblée générale de la Commission, | le 29 Août 1808, | Par Jules-César Savigny, | Membre de l'Institut d'Égypte. | [*Design.*] | A Paris, | de l'Imprimerie Impérriale. | M.DCCC.X.

1 vol. 4to (size of demy folio) and double-elephant folio (plates; unbound). Text, pp. 1-54. Atlas, pll. 1-14 (by Barraband). Paris.

A separately paged reprint[1] of the ornithological portion of Vol. I of the Natural History of the "Description de l'Égypte, ou recueil des observations et des recherches qui ont été faites en Égypte pendant l'expédition de l'armée Française [1798-1801]," etc., published in 9 vols. (text) and 10 vols. (Atlas) from 1809-30. The present portion appeared originally in the first livraison (on pp. 63-114) in 1809, according to a footnote on p. 3 of Savigny's "Observations sur le Système des Oiseaux de l'Égypte et de la Syrie," 1811 (q.v.). The "Observations" and the present work are bound in one volume in the copy at hand. The present title embraces the systematic arrangement of some Egyptian and Syrian birds (27 species of birds of prey), with diagnoses of species and groups, and extensive synonymy. The plates are much more comprehensive than the text and of most of them no mention is made by Savigny, although they were destined for inclusion in portions of the work which he was unable to complete through failure of his eyesight. The description of the species figured on the plates was afterwards undertaken by Audoin, who, in 1826, published his "Explication Sommaire des Planches d'Oiseaux de l'Égypte et de la Syrie" (q.v.) in Part 4 of Vol. I of the Hist. Nat. of the "Description de l'Égypte."

Savigny, Marie Jules-César Lelorgne de.

1811. Description | de l'Égypte, | publiée | par les ordres | de | Napoleon-Le-Grand. | Histoire Naturelle. | Supplément | No. 1. Observations | sur | le système des oiseaux | de l'Égypte et de la Syrie, | par Jules-César Savigny, | Membre de l'Institut d'Égypte. A Paris, de l'Imprimerie Impériale. 1811.

1 vol. 4to (size of demy folio), 2 pr. ll. (tit. and subtit.), pp. 1-54. Paris.

---

[1] I am unable to ascertain whether the reprint is a distinct issue or merely an author's separate with distinct pagination and title-page such as is common in many early French publication.

A lengthy dissertation in justification of the author's views expressed in his "Systeme des Oiseaux de l'Égypte et de la Syrie," 1810 (q.v.). Although marked as a supplement to the "Description de l'Égypte," this contribution does not appear to form an integral part of that extensive work and is not included in the collation of it given by the British Museum (Natural History) nor in Sherborn's anaylsis of the dates of publication of the natural history portions of the work (in Proc. Zool. Soc. Lond., 1897, p. 285). It is not mentioned in "A Bibliographic Account and Collation of La Description de l'Égypte" (printed for, but marked as not published by, the London Institution in 1838) nor can I find it in a copy of the complete work in the John Crerar Library, Chicago. The preface is dated December 5, 1810 but the imprint at the bottom of p. 16 is 1811. With the present copy is bound the reprint of the "Système des Oiseaux," collated elsewhere. If the latter is also distinct from the complete "Description de l'Égypte" it may have been issued with the present paper as part of the "Supplément," but I am inclined to think otherwise.

Saxby, Henry Linckmyer. (Saxby, Stephen H., *ed.*)

1874. The | birds of Shetland | with | observations on their habits, migration, | and occasional appearance. | By the late | Henry L. Saxby, M.D., | edited by his brother, | Stephen H. Saxby, M.A., | Vicar of East Clevedon, Somerset. | Edinburgh: | Maclachlan & Stewart, 64 South Bridge. | London: Simpkin, Marshall, & Co. | MDCCCLXXIV.

1 vol. 8vo, pp. I-XV+1, 1 l. (addenda et corrigenda), pp. 1-398, pll. I-VIII (monochr.). Edinburgh.

Detailed notes on the numerous species of birds found in Shetland; based on personal observations. The work was left incomplete at the author's death and was finished by his brother, principally from the author's notebooks, but with occasional inserted remarks. The present copy is from the library of R. J. Balston.

Saxby, Stephen H.

1874. See Saxby, Henry Linckmyer, **The Birds of Shetland.**

Schäffer, Jacob Christian.

1774. Iacobi Christiani Schaeffer | S.S. Theologiae et Philosophiae Doctoris [*etc.*, *8 lines.*] | **Elementa** | **ornithologica** | iconibvs | vivis coloribvs expressis | illvstrata. | [*Vignette.*] | Ratisbonae | Typis Weissianis, MDCCLXXIV.

1 vol. medium 4to, 44 ll., pll. I-LXX (col.; XXXVIII missing). Ratisbon.

The work is divided into four sections as follows. I, "De Avivm Facie et Strvctvra externa," pll. I-IV; II, "De Avivm Classibvs et Ordinibvs," pl. V; III, "Tabvlae Genervm Characteristicae," pll. VI-XVI; IV, "Genera Avivm in Germania praecipve Bavaria et Palatinatv circa Ratisbonam habitantivm, nidificantivm et migrantivm," pll. XVII-LXX. A reissue with altered title-page was published in 1779.

Schalow, Herman.

1904. See Römer, Fritz; and Schaudinn, **Fauna Artica, Die Vögel der Arktis.**

Schalow, Herman.

1919. Beiträge zur Vogelfauna der | Mark Brandenburg | Materialen zu einer Ornithologie | der norddeutschen Tiefebene auf Grund eigener | Beobachtungen und darauf gegründeter Studien | von | Herman Schalow | Mit 1 Photogravure und 13 Lichtdrucktafeln | Berlin | Deutsche Ornithologische Gesellschaft | 1919.

1 vol. superroyal 8vo, pp. I-VI, 1 l. (conts.), pp. 1-601+1, 14 pll. Berlin.

A detailed account of the ornithology of the Province of Brandenburg, Germany. In addition to the faunistic discussion (pp. 159-426), there is a very extensive bibliography, a history of Brandenburg ornithology, a systematic list of species, accounts of provincial ornithological collections (public and private), a section on folk-lore, historical notes, and biographical chapters on various noteworthy, local ornithologists.

Schaudinn, Fritz.

1904. See Römer, Fritz; and Schaudinn, **Fauna Arctica.**

Schilling, Wilhelm.

1822. See Brehm, Christian Ludwig; and Schilling, **Beiträge zur Vögelkunde,** 1820-22.

Schinz, Heinrich Rudolf.

1815. See Meisner, Friedrich; and Schinz, **Die Vögel der Schweiz.**

Schinz, Heinrich Rudolf.

1819-30. Beschreibung und Abbildung | der | künstlichen Nester und Eyer der Vögel, | welche | in der Schweiz, in Deutschland und den angrenzenden Ländern brüten. | Mit illuminirten Kupfern. | Von | H. R. Schinz, Med. Dr. | Mitglied der Wetterauischen Gesellschaft [etc., 4 lines.]. | Zürich, | bey Orell Füssli und Compagnie 1830.

1 vol. (2 parts) royal 4to, 3 pr. ll. (half-tit., tit. and ded.), pp. I-IV (pref.), 1-28, 1-119+1, 1-4 (list of pll.), pll. 1-33 (col.; nests, birds and eggs), 1-40+36a (col.; eggs). Zürich.

A series of popular descriptions of the nests and eggs of the birds of Switzerland, Germany and adjoining countries, accompanied by colored plates. The work appeared in 13 sections, each of which was planned to contain three plates of nests and three of eggs; it is not certain that this plan was followed throughout. The plates in the first part of the work (pp. 1-128 and pll. 1-33) illustrate nests, eggs and birds; those of the second part (pp. 1-119 and pll. 1-40+36a show only the eggs.

Schinz, Heinrich Rudolph.

1821-25. See Cuvier, Georges L. C. F. D., **Das Thierreich.**

Schinz, Heinrich Rudolph.

1837. See Schweizerischen Gesellschaft für die Gesammten Natur-wissenschaften, **Fauna Helvetica, Verzeichniss der in der Schweiz vorkommenden Wirbelthiere,** etc.

Schinz, Heinrich Rudolph.

1840. Europäische Fauna | oder | Verzeichniss der Wirbelthiere | Europa's | von | Dr. Heinrich Schinz, | Professor der Zoologie an der Hochschule in Zürich, [*etc., 8 lines.*]. | Erster [Zweiter] Band. | Säugethiere und Vögel [Reptilien und Fische]. | Stutt-gart. | E. Schweizerbarts Verlagsbuchhandlung. | 1840.

2 vols. post 8vo. Vol. I, pp. I-XXIV, 1-448. Vol. II, pp. I-VIII, 1-535. Stuttgart.

Descriptions of the vertebrates of Europe. The birds occupy pp. 97-425 and 427-440 of Vol. I. A new name is *Sitta saxatilis.*

Schinz, Heinrich Rudolf.

1846-53. Naturgeschichte | **der Vögel.** | Bearbeitet | von | Dr. Hans Rudolf Schinz, | Prof. der Zoologie in Zürich [*etc.*]. | Mit sorgfältig kolorirten Abbildungen | nach der | Natur und der vorzüglichten naturwissenschaftlichen Werken gezeichnet. | **Zweite,** | umgearbeitete und sehr vemehrte **Auflage.** | Zürich, | Verlag von Franz Hanke. | 1854.

1 vol. crown folio and royal 4to, tit., pp. I-XXVII+1, 1 l. (pref. and conts.), pp. 1-253, pll. A-F (4 col.), 1-120 (col.). Zürich.

A general review of the birds of the world with popular descriptions and accounts of the habits of representative species of the various groups. Some synonymy is given and one species (*Pipra iris*) is described as new. The earlier plates are passably good but the less said of the later ones, the better. The work was published in 21 Lieferungen of 6 pll. each with accompanying text. The first three Lieferungen appeared in 1846, (noted by Engelmann), the eighth in 1851 (probably late April or May; see below) and the last in 1853 (noted by Carus and Engelmann), although the title-page bears the date 1854. Lieferungen 1-7 were published by Meyer & Zeller, the remainer by Hanke. The introduc-tion and signatures 1-19 of the general text are in folio, the remainder in 4to, and there is a change in typography from sign. 18 to sign. 19 (from pp. 72 to

73). Bound with the volume are 7 wrappers, but these are all dated 1851, and differ only in the numbers of the included Hefte, which are written by hand. These wrappers contain a prospectus of the work, dated April 1851, in which seven Lieferungen (containing 42 plates) are said to have been published to date while Lieferung 8 is promised for the close of the month.

Schiøler, E. Lehn. (Winge, Herluf.)

1925-date. Danmarks | fugle | med henblik paa de i Grønland, paa Færoerne og i | kongeriget island forekommende arter | Af | E. Lehn Schiøler | Formand for Dansk Ornithologisk Forening [etc., 6 lines.] | [Vignette.] | Bind I [All published to date.] | Indledning og andefugle (Anseriformes) | Gyldendalske Bognandel. Nordisk Forlag. København | Egmont H. Petersens Kgl. Hof-Bogtrykkeri | MCMXXV.

1 vol. (to date) imperial 4to. Vol. I, 6 pr. ll. (half-tit., tit., ded., pref. and conts.), pp. 11-552, pll. I-XCVIII (55 col.), text-figs. 1-159+ 37a (10 col.), 58 text-cuts (unnum.). Copenhagen.

The first volume of an elaborate work on the birds of Denmark, now in course of publication. An extended bibliography is followed by a chapter on avian anatomy and a general discussion of the Danish Avifauna. Herluf Winge contributes (pp. 244-255) a paper on avian remains in the kitchen-middens. The remainder of the volume comprises the detailed discussion of the Anseriformes. The work is profusely illustrated with excellent plates figuring most of the species in series which show variations, etc.

Schlegel, Hermann.

1841-51. Abhandlungen | aus dem | Gebiete | der | Zoologie und vergleichenden Anatomie, | von | H. Schlegel. | 1 Heft. | Leiden, | A. Arnz & Comp. | 1841. | Zu beziehen durch alle solide Buchhandlungen des In- und Auslandes. [Titles to Hefte II and III missing; possibly not published.]

3 pts. in 1 vol., folio (8¼ x 11½). Pt. I, tit., pp. 1-44, 1 l. (expl. of pll.), 1 pl., pll. II-VI (2 col.). Pt. II, pp. 1-12, pll. VII-IX (col., fold.). Pt. III, pp. 1-20, 1 l. (postscript), pll. X-XV (col., of birds). Leiden.

Parts I and II relate to mammals; III, to birds, being devoted to the genus *Falco*. The following are the subtitles of the third part. "Beschreibung einiger neuen grossen Edelfalken, aus Europa und dem nordlichen Afrika," pp. 1-11; "Fortsetzung der Abhandlung über die grossen, langschwanzigen Edelfalken," pp. 12-20. Several new species or subspecies of falcons are described herein, and new names are used for various other forms. According to Engelmann, and Carus and Engelmann, Pt. I appeared in 1841; II and pp. 1-10, pll. X-XI of Pt. III, in 1843; pp. 11-20, pll. XII-XV of Pt. III, in 1851. Hartert (Die Vögel der Paläarktischen Fauna, 1903-22, q.v.) cites all pages of Pt. III as of date "1844-," and Swann ("Synopsis of the Accipitres," 1921-22, q.v.) gives "1844," but the last half of the part could not have been issued before September 1849 since on p. 15 there is a reference to a specimen taken during that month and year. The third edition of the A.O.U. Check-List of North American Birds, under *Falco mexicanus*, cites the date as 1850, but Sherborn (Index Animalium, Sect. 2, Pt. 1, p. CXIII, 1922) gives dates for the whole work as "1841, 1843, 1851," thus agreeing, apparently with Carus and Engelmann.

Schlegel, Hermann.

1844. Kritische Übersicht | der | Europäischen Vögel | von | Dr. H. Schlegel. | Conservator [*etc., 3 lines.*]. | Leiden | bei A. Arnz u.

Comp. | Leipzig | bei Fr. Fleischer. | Paris | bei Roret. | 1844. > Revue critique | des | oiseaux d'Europe [*etc.; dupl. tit. in French.*].

1 vol. 8vo, 5 pr. ll. (half-tit., tit., ded., pref. and subtit., in German and French), pp. I-CXXXV+1 (Pt. I.), 1 l. (subtit.), pp. 1-116 (Pt. II.). Leyden.

The present work is divided into two parts. The first of these contains a catalogue of species with Latin, German and French names, a list of synonyms, and an account of the distribution given in German and French in parallel columns. The second part contains critical notes on certain of the species, including descriptions of new forms, also given in both languages in parallel columns.

See also the note under Siebold, Philipp F. von, "Fauna Japonica," 1844-50.

Schlegel, Hermann.

1844-50. Sie Siebold, Philipp Franz von, **Fauna Japonica.**

Schlegel, Hermann, and Verster de Wulverhorst, A. H.

1844-53. Traité | de | fauconnerie | par | H. Schlegel | et | A. H. Verster de Wulverhorst. | Leiden et Düsseldorf | chez | Arnz & Comp | 1844-1853 | [*Design, occupying entire page.*] | Erfunden u. auf Stein gez. von J. B. Sonderland.

1 vol. double-elephant folio, 3 pr. ll. (lith. tit., ded. and pref.), pp. 1-90, I-VI (bibl.), 1 l. (expl. of pll. and ind.), 16 pll. (14 col., by J. B. Sonderland, Portman, van Wouw, M. Wolf, C. Scheuren and G. Saal), 11 vignettes and 11 misc. figs. (on tit.). Leyden and Düsseldorf.

A general treatise on the art of falconry. Most of the plates contain life-sized portraits of the species of hawks used in falconry; two are of apparatus and two of hawking scenes. The work appears to have been issued in parts and bears the date 1844-53, which is that given by most bibliographers; Engelmann, however, quotes Livraison I as of date 1846.

Schlegel, Hermann. (Susemihl, Johann Conrad; and Susemihl, Erwin Eduard.)

1845. Die | Europäischen Tag-Raubvögel | beschrieben, | von | Dr. H. Schlegel, | Conservator des niederländischen Reichsmuseums (*etc.*, *2 lines.*]. | Mit 44 Tafeln colorirter Stahlstiche | von | Johann, Conrad und Erwin Eduard Susemihl. | Darmstadt, | Verlag der Kunstanstalt von C. Susemihl & Sohn.

1 vol. royal 8vo, tit., pp. 1-100, pll. 1-39, 1a, 3a, 7a, 35a and 38a (col.; by H. Hoffmeister, H. Schlegel and C. Susemihl & Sohn). Darmstadt.

A reprint of pp. 1-100 and the corresponding plates of J. C. and E. E. Susemihl's "Abbildungen der Vögel Europas," 1839-51, the text of which, so far as it was published, was written by Schlegel. The work consists of descriptions of the diurnal birds of prey of Europe, with an account of the distribution treated in detail. The illustrations are engravings, carefully colored by hand.

Schlegel, Hermann.

1850. See Bonaparte, Charles Lucien; and Schlegel, **Monographie des Loxiens.**

Schlegel, Hermann.

1859. De | **vogels van Nederland** | beschreven en afgebeeld | door | H. Schlegel, | Directeur van 's Rijks Museum van Natuurlijke Historie. | Met 362 gekleurde platen. | Te Leyden, bij | D. Noothoven van Goor. | 1860.

2 vols. in 3, crown 8vo. (Vol. I), pp. I-VIII, 1-699+1. (Vol. II), 2 pr. ll. (half-tit. and tit.), 362 pll. (col.; 178 in one vol., 184 in other). Leyden. 1859 (1854-58).

A general work on the birds of Holland, with short descriptions, synonymy and an account of the distribution of each of the species. A systematic list of species follows (pp. 617-642) with references to pages of text and to plates. An index (pp. 643-694), a short bibliography (pp. 695-699) and a list of errata complete the volume. The plates have been bound in two volumes with the half-title inserted in one and the title in the other. The figures are well-drawn and pleasing. The work was originally issued in 45 parts from 1854 to 1858 under the title of "Fauna van Nederlands—Vogels," by H. S. Schlegel and J. H. Herklots, being intended as part of a comprehensive work on the fauna of the country. The plan was discontinued before more than the birds were treated, and the original publisher, Trap, sold the entire edition to van Goor who issued it (according to Carus and Engelmann) in 1859 with a new title-page (as above) and with a preface by Schlegel dated December 24, 1858. The original Pts. **1-7** are acknowledged in the Journ. für Orn. for July 1855; **8-46,** l.c. for March 1860; entire work reviewed, l.c. for Sept. 1862. This work is not to be confused with the author's ornithological volume, also dated 1860, of the "Natuurlijke Historie van Nederland," (q.v.).

Schlegel, Hermann; and Westermann, G. F.

1860.   De toerako's | afgebeeld en beschreven | door | H. Schlegel, | onder medewerking | van | G. F. Westerman. | Opgedragen aan |

B. M. den Koning. | Uitgegeven door | het Koninklijk Zoölogisch Genootschap | Natura Artis Magistra. | Amsterdam. 1860.

1 vol. antiquarian folio (21¾x27¾), pp. 1-24, 1 l. (synopsis), 17 pll. (col.). Amsterdam.

An account of the Touracos (fam. Musophagidae). The general text, in Dutch, contains a description of each species with distribution, synonymy and other notes. The synopsis contains Latin diagnoses of the species. The plates are excellent and suggest the work of Wolf. I am uncertain as to the exact distribution of authorship between Schlegel and Westermann.

Schlegel, Hermann.

1860. > **Natuurlijke historie | van | Nederland.** | De Dieren van Nederland. | Gewervelde dieren, | door | Prof. H. Schlegel. | Haarlem, | A. C. Kruseman. | 1860.

1 vol. post 8vo, 3 pr. ll. (half-tit., tit., subtit.), pp. I-LXXI+1 (introd.), I-II (subtit.), 1-263+1, 54 ll. (subtit. and expl. of pll.), pll. 1-35 (col.), 1-18 (16 col., 2 monochr.). Haarlem.

A rather general account of the birds of Holland; illustrated by a series of excellent plates depicting heads, feet, etc., and a second series (of inferior quality) illustrating various habitats and their occupants. The volume forms part of a more comprehensive series on the natural history of Holland. The date of publication is not unquestioned. Carus and Engelmann list only 2 parts (pp. "VI, XXXII, 128"), while Cabanis (Journal für Orn., April 1860) acknowledges the receipt of 1 part; Taschenberg does not record the remainder of the volume, but, instead, catalogues a second edition of the whole natural history under dates of 1867-69, published by G. L. Funke, Amsterdam. The John Crerar Library, Chicago, has a copy of the volume on birds, published by Funke in 1868, which is evidently of this second edition. Pagination and plates are as in the first edition. I can find no record of the concluding portions of the first edition of the birds, but Snouckaert van Schauburg (Avifauna Neerlandica, 1908, q.v.) cites all portions of the volume as of 1860, which is probably correct. The Cat. Libr. Brit. Mus. (Nat. Hist.) cites a "Tweede Druck" (which must be a third edition, instead) published in Haarlem in 1878. There is also "De Vogels van Nederland" (q.v.) dated, likewise, 1860, but probably published the year before.

Schlegel, Hermann.

1862-81. See Rijksmuseum van Naturlijke Historie, **Muséum d'Histoire Naturelle des Pays-Bas,** 1862-81 (-1907).

Schlegel, Hermann.

1863-66. **De vogels | van | Nederlandsch Indië,** | beschreven en afgebeeld | door | H. Schlegel. | Les oiseaux | des Indes Neêrlandaises, | décrits et figurés. par | H. Schlegel. | Leiden, Amsterdam, | E. J. Brill. G. L. Funke.

1 vol. royal 4to, tit., pp. 1-38, 1 l. (index to pll.), pll. 1-6 (col.) (end of *Pitta*); pp. 1-68, 1 l. (index to pll.), pll. 1-16 (col.) (end of Ijsvogels); pp. 1-79+1, 2 ll. (index to pll.), pll. 1-28 (col.) (end of Valkvogels, Accipitres). Leyden and Amsterdam. 1863, 1864 and 1866.

Three parts comprising all published of a work on the birds of the Dutch East Indies. The descriptive text, including descriptions of several new species, is in both Dutch and French. The plates (some of which, at least, are by J. Smit) have the figures in miniature but are of high quality. Taschenburg quotes "Haarlem, A. C. Kruseman" as well as "Amst., G. L. Funke," as publisher's imprint. The title-page is a subsequent insert. In the present copy, the Alcedinidae or Ijsvogels are bound following the Accipitres. The dates are from reviews in the Zoological Record for 1865 and 1866.

Schlegel, Hermann.

1868. See Pollen, F. P. L.; and Dam, **Recherches sur le Faune de Madagascar.**

Schlegel, Richard.

1925. **Die Vogelwelt des | nordwestlichen | Sachsenlandes |** Versuch einer Avifauna der Leipziger Flachlandsbucht, | zugleich ein Beitrag zur Zoogeographie | des Freistaates Sachsen | von | Richard Schlegel | [*Vignette.*] | Leipzig 1925. Verlag von Max Weg.

1 vol. 8vo, pp. I-V+1, 1 l. (conts.), pp. 1274, 4 pll. (portrs.).

A study of the local distribution and occurrence of the birds of northwestern Saxony, with bibliography and biographies of resident ornithologists. The species and subspecies of birds, herein treated, number 269.

Schley, Frank.

1877. Frank Schley's | **American Partridge | and | pheasant shooting** | written by himself, | describing the | haunts, habits, and methods of hunting and shooting the Ameri- | can partridge; quail. | ruffed grouse; pheasant. | With | directions for handling the gun, hunting the dog, and the art | of shooting on the wing. | Containing | a history of the partridges and grouse inhabiting North | America. | Illustrated. | Frederick, Md.: | Baughman Brothers. | 1877.

1 vol. post 8vo (sign. in 4to), pp. 1-222, 8 pll. Frederick. 1877.

A book intended for the hunter, being devoted principally to methods of hunting. On pp. 9-39 and 125-138 are descriptions of the various species of North American *Tetraonidae* taken from Vol. III of Baird, Brewer and Ridgway's "History of North American Birds, Land Birds," 1874 (q.v.).

Schmarda, Ludwig Karl.

1871-72. **Zoologie |** von | Ludwig K. Schmarda. | Zwei Bände. | I [II]. Band. | Mit 269 [353] Holzschnitten. | Wien, 1871 [1872]. |

Wilhelm Braumüller | K. K. Hof- und Universitätsbuchhändler.
2 vols. 8vo. Vol. I, pp. I-X, 1-372, text-figs. 1-269. Vol. II, pp. I-XII,
1-584, text-figs. 270-622. Vienna.

A text-book of general zoology. The birds are discussed in Vol. II, pp. 399-472.

Schultze, Leonora.

1884. See Russ, Karl, **The Speaking Parrots.**

Schweizerischen Gesellschaft für die Gesammten Naturwissenschaften,
Allgemeinen. (Schinz, Heinrich Rudolph.)

1837. **Fauna Helvetica** | oder | Verzeichniss | aller bis jetzt in der
Schweiz entdeckten Thiere. | Auf Veranstaltung | der allgemeinen |
Schweizerischen Gesellschaft | für die | gesammten Naturwissen-
schaften | entworfen.

> **Verzeichniss** | **der** | **in der Schweiz vorkommenden** | **Wirbel-
thiere,** | von | Professor H. R. Schinz, | als | Erster Theil | der
auf Veranstaltung der allgemeinen Schweizerischen Gesellschaft für
die | gesammten Naturwissenschaften entworfenen | Fauna hel-
vetica. | (Aus dem ersten Bande der "neuen Denkschriften" der
allgemeinen Gesellschaft für die gesammten | Naturwissenschaften
besonders abgedruckt.) | Neuchatel, | in der Buchdruckerei von
Petitpierre. | 1837.

1 vol. demy 4to. pp. 1-165+1, 1 l. (conts.), 1 pl. (col.). Neuchatel.

Pt. I of the Fauna Helvetica (of which 3 parts were published in 1837 and 1840),
consisting of a discussion of the vertebrates of Switzerland. The ornithology
occupies pp. 34-133. One new species, *Anas purpureo-viridis*, is described.
The subject matter of the present volume appeared the same year in Vol. I
of the Neue Denkschriften der allgemeinen Schweizerischen Gesellschaft fur
die gesammten Naturwissenschaften, as indicated on the titles transcribed
above; whether differing in any way from the present impression, I am unable
to say. The pagination appears to be the same.

Schrenck, Leopold von.

1860. [Reisen und Forschungen in Amur-Lande in den Jahren
1854-1856, *etc.*] > Dr. L. v. Schrenck's | Reisen und Forschungen |
im | Amur-Lande. | Band I. | Zweite Lieferung. | **Vögel des
Amur-Landes.** | Mit 7 Tafeln.

1 vol. demy 4to. pp. 1-165+1, 1 l. (conts.), 1 pl. (col.). Neuchatel.
Pape). Berlin.

The ornithological portion of Schrenck's work which was published from 1858-95
(-1900?). The present portion contains a detailed account of the birds observed by the author and by Maack and Maximowicz, including 190 species.
A supplement (pp. 519-565) lists and discusses other species discovered by
various observers or suggested as of probable occurrence in the Amur region

of south-eastern Siberia, which forms the geographical basis of the entire work. One new species and one new subspecies are described, but the former is ante-dated and the name of the latter preoccupied. The reverse of the subtitle-page bears the date of printing as June 1860. The work is reviewed in the Ibis for 1861, pp. 202-8.

Sclater, Philip Lutley.

1853. A | synopsis of the Galbulidæ | by | Philip Lutley Sclater, M.A., F.Z.S.

1 vol. 8vo, pp. 1-10, (orig. wrapper). Edinburgh.

A revised edition of several papers on Galbulidae published by Sclater in Jardine's "Contributions to Ornithology" for 1852. As noted by Coues, the wrapper of this paper supplies some important data with reference to the publication of the "Contributions." The wrapper also bears the date of publiation of the present title and (in the present copy) the inscription, "M. Jules Verreaux fr. the Contributor."

Sclater, Philip Lutley.

1857-58. A | monograph | of | the birds forming | the tanagrine genus Calliste; | illustrated by | coloured plates of all the known species. | By Philip Lutley Sclater, M.A., | Fellow [etc., 5 lines.]. | [Design.] | London: | John Van Voorst, Paternoster Row. | MDCCCLVII.

1 vol. 8vo, pp. I-XVII+1, 1-104, (4 original wrappers), 45 pll. (col.; by Oudart), 1 map (col.). London.

A discussion of all the known species of the tanagers belonging to the genus *Calliste* as then understood. Synonymy, Latin diagnoses and an account of variations, relationships, habits, etc., are given for each species, all but four of which are figured on excellent plates. The work was published in four parts, of the extent and dates of which I am uncertain. The copy at hand contains four original wrappers, but they are all alike, undated and with the part-number inserted by hand. A prospectus of the work announces the publication at short intervals of four parts, each to contain about twelve plates and the corresponding letterpress. The preface is dated December 1, 1857 although Carus and Engelmann give 1858. There is a break suggested between pp. 64 and 84 where signature 'F' contains 10 ll. instead of the ordin-ary 8 ll. Sclater himself, in the Ibis, 1876, p. 407, says he published the work in 1858, but this may refer only to the last part; in the Ibis, 1863, p. 450 he says the work was completed in December 1857, but this may refer only to the manuscript. Additions to the monograph were published by Sclater in the Ibis for 1863, pp. 450-452.

Sclater, Philip Lutley.

1861-62. Catalogue | of | a collection | of | American birds | belonging to | Philip Lutley Sclater, M.A., Ph.D., F.R.S., | Fellow [etc., 3 lines.] | [Vignette.] | [Quot., 3 lines.] | London: | N. Trubner and Co., Paternoster Row. | 1862.

1 vol. post 8vo, pp. I-XIV, 1 l. (list of illustrs. and errata), pp. 1-338, pll. I-XX (col.; by J. Jennens). London.

A catalogue of the author's collection of some 4100 specimens of American birds, representing 2169 species and containing 386 type-specimens. Each specimen is listed and the principal synonyms of each species are given. A number of new species are described. There is a little doubt as to the date or dates of publication. There are 24 signatures, each of which, except the introductory one, bears its date of printing, beginning with May 1, 1861 and closing with May 16, 1862, while the title-page is dated, simply, 1862. Cabanis, in the Journal für Ornithologie acknowledges the receipt of various installments as follows. Signs. **I** and **II** in Journ. für Orn. for May, 1861; **III-VIII**, Sept. 1861; **IX-X** and **XI-XII**, Jan. 1862; **XIII-XVI**, March 1862; and **XVII-XXIII** with introductory matter, Sept. 1862. Coues says, "Some copies of the sheets were distributed as printed." The author, as reviewer for the Ibis, in the Ibis for 1862, p. 379, calls the work a "lately completed 'Catalogue' " and does not give a date. Trübner and Co., on the wrapper of the Ibis for July and October, 1862, advise that "Only 100 copies of the perfect work have been prepared." The evidence seems to point to the issue of signs. I-XII (pp. 1-192) at various dates in 1861, approaching the dates of printing, and of the remainder of the volume at various periods in 1862. Copies without plates are also in existence.

Sclater, Philip Lutley; and Salvin, Osbert.

1866-69. Exotic ornithology, | containing | figures and descriptions of new or rare species | of | American birds, | by | Philip Lutley Sclater, M.A., Ph.D., F.R.S., | Secretary [*etc., 2 lines.*]; | and | Osbert Salvin, M.A., F.L.S., F.Z.S. | London: | Bernard Quaritch, 15 Piccadilly. | 1869.

1 vol. demy folio, pp. I-VI, 1-204, pll. I-C (col.; by J. Smit), 10 text-figs. London.

Descriptions, figures and critical notes, with synonymies, distribution and some biographical account, of 104 species of Neotropical birds. At the end of many of the articles there is given a summary of the congeneric species in America. The hand-colored plates are excellent. The work was planned originally, as may be suggested by the title, to include new and interesting birds from the whole of the world, but was later restricted to America south of the United States. The book was issued in thirteen parts, the dates of which are given by Coues (2nd Inst., p. 286). These dates do not agree, always, with those printed at the close of each article. As given by Coues, they are as follows (with the addition of pagination). Part **I**, pp. 1-16, pll. I-VIII, Oct. 1, 1866; **II**, pp. 17-32, pll. IX-XVI, Feb. 1, 1867; **III**, pp. 33-48, pll. XVII-XXIV, May 1, 1867; **IV**, pp. 49-64, pll. XXV-XXXII, Aug. 1, 1867; **V**, pp. 65-80, pll. XXXIII-XL, Jan. 1, 1868; **VI**, pp. 81-96, pll. XLI-XLVI, April 1, 1868; **VII**, pp. 97-112, pll. XLVII-LVI, July 1, 1868; **VIII**, pp. 113-128, pll. LVII-LXIV, Aug. 1, 1868; **IX**, pp. 129-144, pll. LXV-LXXII, Dec. 1, 1868; **X**, pp. 145-160, pll. LXXIII-LXXX, Jan. 1, 1869; **XI**, pp. 161-176, pll. LXXXI-LXXXVIII, June 1, 1869; **XII**, pp. 177-192, pll. LXXXIX-XCVI, Aug. 1, 1869; **XIII**, pp. 193-204, I-VI, pll. XCVII-C, Nov. 1, 1869.

Sclater, Philip Lutley; and Salvin, Osbert.

1873. **Nomenclator** | **avium neotropicalium** | sive | avium quæ in regione neotropica hucusque repertæ sunt | nomina systematice disposita adjecta sua cuique | speciei patria accedunt generum et | specierum novarum diagnoses. | Auctoribus | Philippo Lutley Sclater, A.M. Phil. Doct. | Soc. Reg. Lond. Socio | Soc. Zool. Lond. Secretario. | et | Osberto Salvin A.M. | Soc. Reg. Lond. Socio. | [*Vignette.*] | Londini: | Sumptibus auctorum. | MDCCC-LXXIII.

I vol. 4to (8½x13½), pp. I-VIII, 1-163. London.

A synoptic list of the species of birds inhabiting America south of the United States, a total of 3,565. The name and Neotropical distribution of each is given. The appendix (pp. 155-163) contains the original descriptions of 9 new genera and 31 new species.

Sclater, Philip Lutley.

1877. See Rowley, George D., **Ornithological Miscellany,** 1875-78.

Sclater, Philip Lutley.

1879-82. **A monograph** | **of the** | **Jacamars and Puff-birds,** | or | Families Galbulidæ and Bucconidæ. | By | P. L. Sclater, M.A., Ph.D., F.R.S., F.G.S., F.R.G.S., &c., | Secretary to the Zoological Society of London. | [*Vignette.*] | Benedicte omnes volucres cæli dominum. | London: | published for the author by | R. H. Porter, 6 Tenterden Street, W.; and | Dulau and Co., Soho Square, W.

I vol. royal 4to, pp. I-LII, I l. (list of subscrs.), pp. 1-171, pll. I-LV (col.; by Keulemans), text-figs. 1-13+vign. on title, (7 orig. wrappers). London.

A complete monograph of the two groups of birds mentioned in the title, with descriptions, synonymies and voluminous notes on the various species. The introductory chapter contains synoptic tables for the determination of genera and species and general remarks on all the groups. A bibliography is supplied on pp. XLV-LII. The hand-colored plates are excellent. The work was published in seven parts the dates and extent of which are given on the original wrappers that are bound with the volume. Part **I,** Oct. 1879, pp. 1-32, pll. I-VIII; **II,** Jan. 1880, pp. 33-60, pll. IX-XVIII; **III,** May 1880, pp. 61-84, pll. XIX-XXVII; **IV,** Nov. 1880, pp. 85-108, pll. XXVIII-XXXV; **V,** July 1881, pp. 109-132, pll. XXXVI-XLIV; **VI,** Nov. 1881, pp. 133-160, pll. XLV-LIV; **VII,** July 1882, pp. 161-171, I- LII, I l., pl. L.

Sclater, Philip Lutley.

1881. See Thomson, C. Wyville, **Reports on the Scientific Results of the Voyage of H. M. S. Challenger; Report on the Birds.**

Sclater, Philip Lutley.

1882. See Forster, John Reinhold, **A Catalogue of the Animals of North America,** The Willughby Society.

Sclater, Philip Lutley.

1884. See Wagler, Johann Georg, **Wagler's six ornithological memoirs from the 'Isis,'** The Willughby Society.

Sclater, Philip Lutley.

1886. Catalogue | of the | **Passeriformes,** | or | perching birds, | in the | collection | of the | British Museum. | **Fringilliformes: Part II.** | Containing the families | Cœrebidæ, Tanagridæ, and Icteridæ. | By | Philip Lutley Sclater. | London: | printed by order of the Trustees. | 1886.
See British Museum, **Catalogue of the Birds,** 1874-98, Vol. XI.

Sclater, Philip Lutley.

1888. Catalogue | of the | **Passeriformes,** | or | perching birds, | in the | collection | of the | British Museum. | **Oligomyodæ,** | or the families | Tyrannidæ, Oxyrhamphidæ, Pipridæ, Cotingidæ, | Phytotomidæ, Philepittidæ, Pittidæ, | Xenicidæ, and Eurylæmidæ. | By | Philip Lutley Sclater. | London: | printed by order of the Trustees. | 1888.
See British Museum, **Catalogue of the Birds,** 1874-98, Vol. XIV.

Sclater, Philip Lutley; and Hudson, William Henry.

1888-89. **Argentine ornithology.** | A | descriptive catalogue | of the | birds of the Argentine Republic. | By | P. L. Sclater, M.A., Ph.D., F.R.S., Etc. | with notes on their habits | by | W. H. Hudson, C.M.Z.S., | late of Buenos Ayres. | [*Vignette.*] | The Cariama [Burmeister's Cariama]. | Volume I [II]. | London: | R. H. Porter, 6 Tenterden Street, W. [18 Princes Street, Cavendish Square, W.] | 1888 [1889].
2 vols. royal 8vo. Vol. I, pp. I-XXIV (XVII-XXIV issued with, and bound with, Vol. II), 1-208, pll. I-X (col.; by Keulemans), 1 fig. (on tit.). Vol. II, pp. I-XVI, 1-251, pll. XI-XX (col.; by Keulemans), 17 text-figs., 1 fig. (on tit.). London.
An account of 434 species of birds from Argentina, with concise descriptions and brief synonymy of each from the pen of Sclater, and with detailed notes on habits by Hudson. Hudson's portion of the work was reprinted in 1920 under the title of "Birds of La Plata by W. H. Hudson" (q.v.). The hand-colored plates in the present work are very fine. The introduction, paged for insertion in Vol. I, was issued with Vol. II. The appendix (pp. 221-232) in Vol. II gives a short bibliography and gazetteer.

Sclater, Philip Lutley.

1890. Catalogue | of the | **Passeriformes,** | or | perching birds, | in the | collection | of the | British Museum. | **Tracheophonæ,** | or the families | Dendrocolaptidæ, Formicariidæ, | Conopophagidæ, and Pteroptochidæ. | By | Philip Lutley Sclater. | London: | printed by order of the Trustees. | 1890.

See British Museum, **Catalogue of the Birds,** 1874-98, Vol. XV.

Sclater, Philip Lutley; and Shelley, George Ernest.

1891. Catalogue | of the | **Picariæ** | in the | collection | of the | British Museum. | Scansores and Coccyges, | containing the families | Rhamphastidæ, Galbulidæ, and Bucconidæ, | by | P. L. Sclater, | and the families | Indicatoridæ, Capitonidæ, Cuculidæ, | and Musophagidæ, | by | G. E. Shelley. | London: | printed by order of the Trustees. | Sold by | Longmans & Co., 39 Paternoster Row; [*etc.*, *3 lines.*]; | and at the | British Museum (Natural History), Cromwell Road, S.W. | 1891.

See British Museum, **Catalogue of the Birds,** 1874-98, Vol. XIX.

Sclater, Philip Lutley.

1892. See James, Harry Berkeley, **A New List of Chilean Birds.**

Sclater, Philip Lutley.

1906-09. See Wytsman, Paul, **Genera Avium,** 1905-14.

Sclater, Philip Lutley.

1910. **Revised list of the** | **birds of Jamaica** | (Based on the List of Alfred and Edward Newton in | the 'Handbook of Jamaica for 1881.') | by | P. L. Sclater, Dr. Sc., F.R.S. | Reprinted from the 'Handbook of Jamaica for 1910.' | Kingston, Jamaica: | The Institute of Jamaica. | Agents in London, H. Sotheran, & Co., 140 Strand W.C., and 28 Piccadilly, W. | 1910.

1 vol. post 8vo, tit., pp. 1-24. Kingston.

A repaged reprint, with separate title, of pp. 596-619 of the Handbook of Jamaica for 1910. The text consists of a revision of Alfred and Edward Newton's "List of the Birds of Jamaica, 1881 (q.v.), with the addition of a statement of the habitat of each species, general notes on the Jamaican avifauna and on each family of birds represented in it, and augmented bibliographic references.

Sclater, William Lutley.

1901-06. See Stark, Arthur Cowell; and Sclater, **The Fauna of South Africa; The Birds of South Africa,** 1900-06.
Birds of South Africa, 1900-06.

Sclater, William Lutley.

1912. A history of | the birds of Colorado | by | William Lutley
Sclater | M.A. (Oxon.) [*etc.*, *2 lines.*] | with seventeen plates and
a map | Witherby & Co. | 326 High Holborn London | 1912.
1 vol. 8vo, pp. I-XXIV, 1-576, frontisp. (portr.), pll. 1-16, 1 map.
London.

A handbook of Colorado ornithology, containing descriptions, references to Colorado records, distribution of species and notes on habits. Much of the work is
complied (of necessity owing to the brevity of the author's residence in Colorado
before undertaking the work) but consequent errors are not numerous. The
contour map (after Rydberg ?) is said by Henderson (Auk, XXIX, p. 429,
1912) to be inaccurate. A bibliography and gazetter are given at the close of
the work.

Sclater, William Lutley.

1912. See Shelley, George Ernest, **The Birds of Africa,** 1896-1912.

Sclater, William Lutley.

1924. **Systema avium | Ethiopicarum.** | A systematic list of the
birds of | the Ethiopian region. | By | William Lutley Sclater,
M.A., M.B.O.U. | Prepared in conjunction with Special Committees
of the | British and American Ornithologists' Unions. | Published
by the | British Ornithologists' Union | and sold by | Wheldon
and Wesley, Ltd., 2-4 Arthur Street, | New Oxford Street, W.C.2. |
1924.
1 vol. (all pub. to date) 8vo, pp. I-IV, 1-304. April 30, 1924.

A carefully prepared check list of all known species and subspecies of Ethiopian
birds, with their accepted scientific and vernacular names, references to original
description, type localities and distribution for each. The wrapper notes this
as Part I of the work and advises of the future publication of the remaining
portions. The current review in the Auk disclaims any participation by the
American Ornithologists' Union in the preparation of the volume to date.

Scopoli, Giovanni Antonio.

1769-72. Ioannis Antonii Scopoli [*Comma added (Vols. IV and
V.*).] | Phil et Med. Doct. [*etc., 8 lines.; omitted (Vols. II and III.*);
S. C. R. & Apost. Maiestatis in Montanisticis, *etc., 6 lines. (Vols.
IV and V.*).] | **Annus I [-V].** | Historico- | naturalis. | Descrip-
tiones avium | musei proprii | earumque rariorum, quas vidit |
in vivario | Augustiss. Imperatoris, | et | in museo Excell. Comi-
tis | Francisci Annib. Turriani [*8 lines., mut. mut. as follows*:
I. Iter Goroziense. | II. Iter Tyrolense. | III. De Cucurbita Pepone
obser- | vationes. | IV. Lichenis Islandici Vires me- | dicæ. (*Vol.
II.*); I. Solutio Questionis, an Medici olim Roma | pulsi, ut ait

Plinius. | II. Luis Bovillæ symptomata, causæ, discri- | mina, remedia, præservativa & cu- | rativa. | III. Observationes aliquæ de Cæruleo Bero- | linensi, aliisque Laccis. | IV. Experimenta de Minera aurifera Na- | gyayensi. (*Vol. III.*); I. Dissertatio de Apibus. | II. Dubia Botanica. | III. Observationes Oeconomicæ. | IV. Fungi quidam rariores in Hungaria | nunc detecti. (*Vol. IV.*); I Emendationes et Additamenta ad Ann. I. II. | III. IV. | II. Tentamen Mineralogicum I. De Minera Ar- | genti alba. | III. Tentamen Mineralogicum II. De Sulphure. | IV. Tentamen Minera- logicum III. De Pseudoga- | lena, Auripigmento, aliisque. | V. Observationes Zoologicae. (*Vol. V.*)] [| *Vignette* (*Vols. II-V.*).] | Lipsiæ, | Sumtib. [Svmtib. (*Vols. II-V.*)] Christ. Gottlob Hil- scheri, | MDCCLXVIIII [MDCCLXIX; MDCCLXIX; MDCC- LXX; MDCCLXXII].

5 vols. in 1, cap 8vo. Vol. I, pp. 1-168. Vol. II, pp. 1-118. Vol. III, 3 pr. ll. (tit., ded., pref.), pp. 6-108, 1 l. (corrigenda). Vol. IV, pp. 1-150, 2 pll., 1 chart (fold.). Vol. V, pp. 1-128. Leipzig.

A series of miscellaneous papers on natural history, as indicated in the lists of contents on the various title-pages. Annus I and Annus V contain all the ornithology. The first is entirely ornithological and is devoted to descriptions of the birds in the author's collection, in the emperor's aviary at Vienna, and in the "Museum Turrianum." Numerous new species and genera are des- cribed. The last volume contains, among other matter, a sort of supplement to the first volume, with discussions of some species not included in the original list. *Falco pannonicus* is new, being, apparently, the earliest name for the bird recently known as *Falco cherrug*.

Scopoli, Giovanni Antonio. (Alfred Newton, *ed.*)

1882. The Willughby Society. | **Scopoli's** | **ornithological papers** | **from his** | **Deliciae** | **Florae et Faunae Insubricae** | (Ticini: 1786 - 1788) | [*Vignette.*] | Edited by | Alfred Newton, M.A., F.R.S., etc. | London: MDCCCLXXXII.

[Deliciae florae et faunae insubricae, seu novae, e minus cognitae species plantarum et animalium, quas in Insubria austriaca, tam spontaneas, quam exoticas vidit, descripsit et aeri incidi curavit. (*Title from Engelmann*)].

1 vol. demy 4to, pp. I-IV, "69-71, 36-37, 84-96, 37" (=1-19), 20. "Pavia. 1786 and 1788." London. 1882.

A verbatim reprint of the ornithological portions of Scopoli's work, reduced in size from the original folio and published by The Willughby Society (q.v.). The original work was published in three volumes,—the first two in 1786 and the last in 1788. The ornithological matter is as follows.
    Observationes zoologicae. De Alaudis nostratibus. Pt. I, 1786, pp. 69-71.
    Falco rufus. Pt. II, 1786, pp. 36 and 37.

Specimen zoologicum exhibens Characteres genericos, & specificos, necnon Nomina trivialia novorum Animalium. Quae Clarissimus Sonnerat in China, & in Indiis orientalibus nuper detexit. Pt. II, 1786, pp. 84-96.

Fringilla alpina. Pt. III, 1788, p. 37.

The first, second and third papers are not of especial importance, but the third contains a discussion of the mammals and birds treated in Sonnerat's "Voyage a la Nouvelle Guinée," 1776 (q.v.), and "Voyage aux Indes Orientales et a la Chine," 1782 (q.v.), with short diagnoses and the first application of binomial names to the species. The preface of the reprint, by the editor, contains an account of the life of the author and some review of the book.

Scott, H. H.

1909. Victoria Museum, Launceston, Tasmania. | **Memoir** | **on** | **The Wedge-Tailed Eagle** | "Uroœtus Audax." | (Latham) | A Study in Avian Osteology. | With the Compliments of | the Museum Committee. | Photographs by F. E. Burbury, Esq., and L. C. Pitfield, Esq.

1 vol. post 8vo, 8 ll., 2 pll., (orig. wrapper). Launceston. 1909 (post Nov. 18).

An osteological study of a specimen of the Wedge-tailed Eagle. The date (of the manuscript) appears on the last page.

Scott, William Earl Dodge.

1898. **Bird studies** | an account of the land birds | of eastern North America | by | William E. D. Scott | with illustrations from original | photographs | New York and London | G. P. Putnam's Sons | The Knickerbocker Press | 1898.

1 vol. 8vo (8x10), 3 pr. ll. (half-tit., tit. and ded.), pp. V-XII, 1-363, 1 l. (advt.), frontisp., 165 text-cuts (many full-p.). New York and London.

An account of the habits and distinguishing characteristics of the land birds of North America "east of the Mississippi River, Lake Winnipeg, and the western borders of Hudson's Bay, together with Greenland and the islands which naturally group themselves with the mainland of the region." Six typical habitats are selected and the birds which occur in each are discussed in sequence. A systematic table of species is given at the close of the volume. The illustrations are from photographs of live birds, mounted specimens, dried skins and freshly-killed examples, with some birds' nests and occasional landscapes.

Scott, William Earl Dodge.

1903. **The** | **story of a bird lover** | by | William Earl Dodge Scott | [*Blazon.*] | New York | The Outlook Company | 1903.

1 vol. post 8vo, pp. I-XI+1, 1-372, frontisp. and cover-fig. New York.

The author's autobiography, dealing with the training and experiences of an ornithologist from his earliest recollections to the date of writing.

Seebohm, Henry.

1876. See Rowley, George D., **Ornithological Miscellany,** 1875-78.

Seebohm, Henry.

1880. **Siberia in Europe:** | a visit to the valley of the Petchora, | in north-east Russia; | with descriptions of the natural history, migration | of birds, etc. | By Henry Seebohm, | F.L.S., F.Z.S., F.R.G.S. | With map and illustrations. | London: | John Murray, Albemarle Street. | 1880. | The right of Translation is reserved.

1 vol. post 8vo, pp. I-XV+1, 1-311+1, 1-24 (advt.), 2 pll. (col.), 1 map (fold.), 48 text-figs. London.

The narrative of the author's journey in company with J. A. Harvie-Brown through parts of Russia in search of the breeding grounds of the Gray Plover, Little Stint, Sanderling, Curlew Sandpiper, Knot and Bewick's Swan. Observations on the bird life of Russia constitute the larger part of the text and are connected by the running account of the journey. The colored plates are taken from the "Ibis" for 1876, pll. V and VII. A companion volume is found in the author's later "Siberia in Asia," 1882 (q.v.). The present copy of the work was presented to Edward Hargitt by the author.

Seebohm, Henry.

1881. Catalogue | of the | **Passeriformes,** | or | perching birds, | in the | collection | of the | British Museum. | **Cichlomorphæ: Part II.** | containing the family | Turdidæ | (Warblers and Thrushes). | By | Henry Seebohm. | London: | printed by order of the Trustees. | 1881.

See British Museum, **Catalogue of the Birds,** 1874-98, Vol. V.

Seebohm, Henry.

1882. **Siberia in Asia:** | a visit to the valley of the Yenesay | in eastern Siberia. | With description of the natural history, migration | of birds, etc. | By Henry Seebohm, | author of 'Siberia in Europe.' | With map and illustrations. | London: | John Murray, Albemarle Street. | 1882. | The right of Translation is reserved.

1 vol. post 8vo, pp. I-XVIII, 1-304, 1-32 (advt.), 1 map (col.; fold.), 68 text-figs. London.

The account of an overland journey through Siberia in 1877 on ornithological and ethnological research. Notes on the bird life of the region are thoroughly interspersed with the narrative and a resumé of the ornithological results of the expedition is given in Chapter XXV, pp. 288-298. The book forms a companion volume to the author's earlier "Siberia in Europe," 1880 (q.v.).

The two volumes were combined, revised and reissued in 1901 as "The Birds of Siberia."

Seebohm, Henry. (Dixon, Charles.)

1882-85. **A history | of | British birds,** | with coloured illustrations | of their | eggs. | By | Henry Seebohm. | Vol. I [Vol. II; Vol. III; Plates]. | London: | published for the author by | R. H. Porter, 6 Tenterden Street, W., | and | Dulau & Co., Soho Square, W. | 1883 [1884; 1885; 1885].

4 vols. royal 8vo. Vol. I, pp. I-XXIII+1, 1-614, 30 text-figs+many decorations. Vol. II, pp. I-XXXIII+1, 1-600, 34 text-figs+decors. Vol. III, pp. I-XXIV, 1-684, 40 text-figs.+decors. Vol. "Plates", tit., pp. 1-18, pll. 1-68 (col.). London.

A debatable work on the life-histories, habits, breeding, distribution, variation and classification of British birds. A considerable amount of first-hand information is given from field observations, and the work is valuable for these, but there are many statements which have been questioned by critics. The classification adopted by the author follows a principle of "auctorum plurimorum" in which priority is disregarded and that name used which has a majority of previous authors behind it. There are numerous caustic remarks, in criticism of antecedent and contemporary authors, which might have been made in more pleasant style. Detailed introductions are given in the three volumes of text; that one in the second volume, "On the Protective Colour of Eggs," was written by Charles Dixon. The work appeared in six parts, two to each of the first three volumes. Part I is usually cited as of 1883, but it is reviewed under date of 1882 in the Ibis for January 1883 (p. 114). Part II appeared in 1883; III (to p. 288, Vol. II) in 1883; IV in July 1884; V and VI in 1885, including the list of plates bound (with all the plates) in a separate volume. The plates, although the title-page to their volume is dated 1885, appeared with the various parts from 1882-1885. A second edition of the entire work appeared in 1896 with plates printed in Paris, and these plates, with occasional notes added, were reissued in 1904.

Seebohm, Henry.

1887. **The | geographical distribution | of the family | Charadriidæ,** | or the | Plovers, Sandpipers, Snipes, | and their allies. | By | Henry Seebohm, | author of [*etc., 2 lines.*] | [*Vignette.*] | London: | Henry Sotheran & Co., | 136, Strand, W.C. and 36, Piccadilly, W.; | Manchester: 49, Cross Street.

1 vol. royal 4to, pp. I-XXIX+1, 1-524, 21 pll. (col.; by Keulemans; nos. I-XXI in index), 247 text-figs, 1 text-map, 17 decorations+fig. on title-p. London and Manchester.

A monograph (in spite of the author's disclaimer on p. 5.) of the shore birds of the world, usually considered as representing several distinct families but united by the author into a single family. The prefatory matter (Chapters I to VIII, pp. 1-65) is devoted to general remarks on classification, evolution, differentiation of species, glacial epochs, migration, "The Paradise of the Charadriidae," zoological regions and subspecific forms. The main body of the text discusses the various species of shore birds in order, with considerable detail. The work met with a varied reception owing to the debatable character of many of the author's views on classification, but it is, nevertheless, a valuable repository of information on the subject. There is no date on the title-page but the back of the cover bears the date 1888. Sharpe, in Seebohm's "Coloured Figures of the Eggs of British Birds," 1896 (q.v.), p. X, gives the date of publication as 1887 on the basis of a copy of the work in his possession bearing the inscription "Christmas, 1887." The work is based on the collections of J. E. Harting, Shelley, and Swinhoe, together with Harting's manuscript notes (which were gathered with the intention of publishing a monograph of the shore birds) to which Seebohm acknowledges free access. The hand-colored plates are excellent.

Seebohm, Henry.

1890. The birds | of the | Japanese Empire. | By | Henry Seebohm, | author of [etc., 5 lines.] | with numerous woodcuts. | London: | R. H. Porter, 18 Princes Street, Cavendish Square. | 1890.

1 vol. royal 8vo, pp. I-XXIV, 1-386, frontisp. (map), 98 text-figs. London.

An attempt to collect the available information respecting Japanese ornithology into a single volume. The work shows extreme carelessness in preparation and much of the information it presents is still half-concealed, owing to the manner of presentation. Synonyms are rarely quoted and then only in the general text; the descriptions of the various species are too brief to be of much service; new names are used without designation as such and sometimes without diagnostic characters; distribution is often erroneously given; species of earlier authors are occasionally dismissed summarily, without adequate reason. In the text the author takes occasion to treat of the general classification of birds, whether Japanese or not, and defines all subclasses, orders and suborders of the class *Aves*, This discussion presents some modifications of the author's views on the same subject which he expressed in his work of a few months' earlier date, the "Classification of Birds," 1890 (q.v.). An annotated bibliography is given in the early part of the volume. A critical review of the work was given by Stejneger in the Auk for January, 1891, pp. 99-101.

Seebohm, Henry.

1890. Classification | of | birds; | an attempt to diagnose the subclasses, orders, suborders, | and some of the families of existing birds. | By | Henry Seebohm. | London: | R. H. Porter, 18 Princes Street, Cavendish Square, W. | 1890.

1 vol. royal 8vo, pp. I-XI+1, 1-53. London.

A treatise on the taxonomy of the higher groups of birds. Fourteen orders and thirty-six suborders are diagnosed and the definitive characters analyzed for all of the suborders, in a tabular form that is easily read. Two arrangements of the orders into subclasses are given,—one with six subclasses, the other with five; the former is used in the body of the work. The author later modified his views in his "The Birds of the Japanese Empire," 1890 (q.v.), and in a "Supplement," 1895, to the present work. However the proposed scheme of classification may be criticised, considerable information is presented in the work.

Seebohm, Henry.

1893. See Whitehead, John, **Exploration of Mount Kina Balu, North Borneo.**

Seebohm, Henry. (Sharpe, Richard Bowdler, *ed.*)

1896. **Coloured figures | of the | eggs | of | British birds,** | with descriptive notices, | by | Henry Seebohm, | author of [*etc.*, 5 *lines.*]. | Edited | (after the author's death) | by | R. Bowdler Sharpe, LL.D., Etc., | Assistant Keeper, Sub-Department of Vertebrata, | British Museum. | Sheffield: | Pawson and Brailsford. | 1896.

1 vol. royal 8vo, pp. I-XXIV, 1-304, frontisp. (portr.), pll. 1-59+58a (col.). Sheffield.

Short accounts of the breeding habits and the occurrence in the British Islands of the birds of the country. The text is modeled after, and is in some cases a condensed reproduction of, that of the author's larger, "History of British Birds," 1882-85 (q.v.). The plates, in chromo-lithograph, represent typical examples of the eggs of the various species and are very good. A memoir of Seebohm, by Sharpe who edited the whole work, is included, fittingly, in the volume.

Seebohm, Henry; and Sharpe, Richard Bowdler.

1898-1902. **A | monograph of the Turdidæ,** | or | family of Thrushes. | By the late | Henry Seebohm, | author of [*etc.*, 4 *lines.*]. | Edited and completed | (after the author's death) | by | R. Bowdler Sharpe, LL.D., F.L.S., etc. | Assistant-Keeper, Sub-Department of Vertebrata, British Museum. | Volume I [II]. | London: | Henry Sotheran & Co., | 37 Piccadilly, W., and 140 Strand, W.C. | 1902.

2 vols. 4to (11½x15). Vol. I, pp. I-XI+1, 1-337, frontisp. (portr.), pll. I-LXXVIII (col.; by Keulemans). Vol. II, pp. I-IX+1, 1-250, pll. LXXIX-CXLIX (col.; by Keulemans). London.

A thorough monograph of a limited section of the family *Turdidae*, comprising the genera *Geocichla*, *Turdus*, *Merula* and *Mimocichla* as recognized by the authors (a group usually further divided by most authors). Synonymy and a brief Latin diagnosis of each species are followed by detailed notes. Several new species are described. The hand-colored plates by Keulemans are excellent. Seebohm had most of the plates prepared but, at his death, left his manuscript unfinished. Sharpe undertook to edit and complete the work, but found that the manuscript in hand covered only the genus *Geocichla*, leaving the much greater portion still to be written; this was done entirely by Sharpe. Seebohm's text occupies pp. 1-91, excluding certain species of *Geocichla* in those pages which were written by Sharpe. The remainder of the work is Sharpe's, whose initials appear at the foot of each article contributed by him. The work was issued in 13 parts, as follows. Part I, pp. 1-40, pll.

I-XII, ante April 1898; **II,**, pp. 41-76, pll. XIII-XXIV, ante July 1898; **III,** pp. 77-114, pll. XXV-XXXVI, ante Oct. 1898; **IV,** pp. 115-212, pll. XXXVII-XLVIII, Oct. 1898; **V,** pp. 213-266, pll. XLIX-LX, ante April 1898; **VI,** pp. 267-312, pll. LXI-LXXII, ante Oct. 1899; **VII,** pp. 313-337 (Vol. I), 1-32 (Vol. II), pll. LXXIII-LXXVIII (Vol. I), LXXIX-LXXXIV (Vol. II), Dec. 1899; **VIII,** pp. 33-70, pll. LXXXVI-XCVII, ante July 1900; **IX,** pp. 71-100, pll. XCVIII-CVIII+LXXXV, 1900; **X,** pp. 101-126, pll. CIX-CXX, 1900; **XI,** pp. 127-156, pll. CXXI-CXXXII, ante July 1901; **XII-XIII** (double no.), pp. 157-250, I-XI+1 (Vol. I), 1-IX+1 (Vol. II), pll. CXXXIII-CXLIX, 1902. Dates are from the reviews in the Zoological Record and the Ibis.

Selby, Prideaux John.

(1821)-1834 (-1839?). **Plates | To | Selby's Illustrations | of British Ornithology** | [*Vignette.*] | Designed & Engraved by W. H. Lizars. | Edinburgh; | published by W. H. Lizars, | and Longman, Rees, Orme, Brown & Green | London.

Plates | To | Selby's Illustrations | of | British Ornithology. | Water birds. | Vol. II. | [*Vignette.*] | MDCCCXXXIV. | Printed for the proprietor, & published by W. H. Lizars, Edinburgh; | Longman, Rees, Orme, Brown, Green & Longman, London; | and W. Curry Junr. & Co. Dublin.

2 vols. double-elephant folio. Vol. (I), engr. tit., pll. I-XXXI, XXXIII-LXV, I*, III*, XII(*bis*), XIII*, XV*, XVII*, XVIII*, XXVI*, XXVII*, XXXIII(*bis = XXXII?*), XXXIV*, XXXVI (*bis*), XLII*, XLIII*, XLV*, XLV**, LIII*, LIII*(*bis*), LVI*, LVIII*, LXIV*, A-D (col.); I-IV (plain) (=93 pll.; col.). Vol. II, engr. tit., pll. I-III, V-VIII, X-XVII, XIX-XXXII, 33, XXXIV-XLIII, XLV-LV, LVII-LIX, LXI-LXIII, LXV-LXXXIV, LXXX-VI, LXXXVIII-CIII, VI*, VII*, VII**, XI*, XXVII*, XXVIII (*bis*), XXX*, XXXIII*, XXXIII**, XXXIX*, XLV(*bis*), XLVII*, XLVIII*, XLVIII**, XLIX*, L(*bis*), LV(*bis*), LVII(*bis*), LVIII*, LVIII**, LXVI*, LXVI**, LXX*, LXXIV(*bis*), LXXVIII(*bis*), LXXXIII(*bis*), LXXXVII*, LXXXIX(*bis*), XCII(*bis*), XCIV*, XCVI*, CI(*bis*), CI*, CII(*bis*), CII* (=129 pll.; 125 col.). Edinburgh.

A series of life-sized, colored plates of British birds. There are numerous editions of the work. According to Engelmann, Coues, Mullens and Swann and the Catalogue of the Library of the British Museum (Natural History), Vol. I, containing the land birds, was issued in 8 parts; Lizars, in the Advertising pages of the early volumes of Jardine's "Naturalist's Library," 1833-43 (q.v.) gives the number of parts as 7, one appearing every six months and each containing 12 pll. Part II, containing the water birds, was issued in similar manner in 11 parts with (according to Lizars) 135 plates. Engelmann cites 228 plates in both volumes. The original edition began in 1821 and was completed in 1834. Volume II, as collated above, belongs to this original set, and has the paper watermarked "1826." Volume I, as collated above, has the paper water-marked "1839" and seems to belong to a later edition which I am unable to trace. The engraved titles of both volumes are uncolored. Mullens and Swann note the issue, with the original plates, of a temporary, explanatory letterpress which is very rare. The full text appeared in 1825-33 under the title of, "Illustrations of British Ornithology" (q.v., 1833). The original cover-title for the plates was also (according to Lizars) "Illustrations of British Ornithology," later altered to that quoted above. In the preface to Vol. I of the text, the author apologizes for a "slight want of regularity in the numbering of the plates."!

Selby, Prideaux, John.

1827-43. See Jardine, William; and Selby, **Illustrations of Ornithology.**

Selby, Prideaux John. (Jardine, William; Chrichton, Andrew.)

1835. The | natural history | of | pigeons. | Illustrated by thirty-two plates, coloured, | and numerous wood-cuts. | By | Prideaux John Selby, Esq. | F.R.S.E. [*etc.*]. | With memoir of Pliny by | Andrew Crichton, | Author of "The History of Arabia," &c. &c. | Edinburgh: | W. H. Lizars, 3 St James' Square | S. Highley, 32 Fleet Street, London; and | W. Curry Jun. & Co. Dublin. | 1835.

1 vol. cap 8vo, 4 pr. ll. (various tits.; 1 illum.), pp. VII-IX+1, XIII-XV+1, 17-228, 2 ll.+pp. 5-20 (advt.), frontisp. (portr.), pll. 1-30 (col.; By E. Lear and Prêtre), 5 text-figs. Edinburgh. 1835 (circa June).

A descriptive account of the various species of pigeons, comprising Vol. V of the Ornithological Series (1st ed.) of Jardine's "The Naturalist's Library," 1833-43 (q.v.); on the serial title page it is called, also, "Gallinaceous birds, Part III." Scientific names, only, are used on the plates, which have the backgrounds partially colored although mostly with little or no scenery added (Cf. reissues, 1844-64, Vol. IX.). The preface is dated June 1835.

Selby, Prideaux John. (Jardine, William; Turner, Rev. Mr.)

1836. The | natural history | of | parrots. | By | Prideaux John Selby, Esq. | F.R.S.E., &c. &c. | Illustrated by thirty-two plates: with memoir and | portrait of Bewick, by the Rev. Mr. Turner, | Newcastle-upon-Tyne. | Edinburgh: | W. H. Lizars, 3 James's Square; | S. Highley, 32 Fleet Street, London; and | W. Curry Jun. & Co. Dublin. | 1836.

1 vol. cap 8vo, 1 l. (list of vols. in series), 4 pr. ll. (titles; 1 illum.), pp. IX-XV+1, 17-187, 1-4+1-4+2 wrappers (advt.), frontisp. (portr.), pll. 1-30 (col.; by E. Lear). Edinburgh.

Vol. VI of the Ornithological Series (1st ed.) of Jardine's "The Naturalist's Library," 1833-43 (q.v.). This volume was reissued later a. Vol. X of the same

A

CATALOGUE

OF THE

GENERIC AND SUB-GENERIC TYPES

OF THE CLASS

AVES, BIRDS,

ARRANGED ACCORDING TO THE NATURAL SYSTEM;

WITH

SEPARATE LISTS,

DISTINGUISHING THE

VARIOUS QUARTERS OF THE GLOBE

IN WHICH

THEY ARE TO BE PROCURED.

—————

NEWCASTLE:

PRINTED BY T. AND J. HODGSON, UNION-STREET.

1840.

TITLE-PAGE OF P. J. SELBY'S "CATALOGUE OF THE GENERIC AND SUB-GENERIC TYPES OF THE CLASS AVES."

See p. 573.

series in later editions (Cf. reissues, 1844-64.). The plates have detailed scenic backgrounds and are lettered with both English and Latin names, but do not give the habitat. The memoir of Bewick occupies pp. 17-51.

Selby, Prideaux John.

1833. Illustrations | of | British ornithology. | By | Prideaux John Selby, Esq. | Fellow of the Royal Society [*etc., 3 lines.*]. | Vol. I [II]. | Land [Water] birds. | Edinburgh: | printed for the proprietor, and published by | W. H. Lizars, Edinburgh; | Longman, Rees, Orme, Brown, Green and Longman, | London; and W. Curry Jun. & Co. Dublin. | MDCCCXXXIII.

2 vols. post 8vo. Vol. I, pp. I-XIII+1, XIII (*bis*) -XXXVII+1, 1 l. (half-tit.), 1-450. Vol. II, pp. I-XII, 1-538. Edinburgh.

A manual of British ornithology, containing accounts of the habits of the various species of birds, with their synonymy, and with descriptions of the genera and higher groups. Reference is made to the colored and other plates in the author's "Plates to Selby's Illustrations," etc., (1821)- 1834 (-1839 ?) (q.v.). Although issued partly in connection with the volume of plates, under the same title (at the time of issue), text and plates were purchasable separately and the publishers (in the advertising pages of Vol. I of Jardine's "Naturalist's Library," 1833-43 (q.v.), express the hope, also voiced by the author in his preface to the present work, that the text will constitute an independent work of reference. Vol. I was issued originally in 1825, with nomenclature according to Temminck. Vol. II was prepared according to the arrangement proposed by Vigors and to make the two volumes uniform, Selby revised Vol. I and reissued it in altered form with the first and only edition of Vol. II. The set, as collated above, consists of the second edition of Vol. I and the only edition of Vol. II.

Selby, Prideaux John.

1840. A | catalogue | of the | generic and sub-generic types | of the class | Aves, birds, | arranged according to the natural system; | with | separate lists, | distinguishing the | various quarters of the globe | in which | they are to be procured. | Newcastle: | printed by T. and J. Hodgson, Union-Street. | 1840.

1 vol. 8vo, 2 pr. ll. (tit. and pref.), pp. 1-70. Newcastle.

A systematic list of the genera and subgenera of birds, indicating the type species of each and its distribution. Pp. 50-70 contain the names of these type species arranged in five lists, according to distribution, as procurable in "Britain and Europe," "America and its dependencies," "Africa," "Asia and its islands" and "Australia and isles of the Pacific." The catalogue contains the new generic names, *Haliastur*, *Mergellus* and *Poliocephalus*. Furthermore, the work is important because of the fixation of the types of a number of genera not mentioned by Gray in his first edition of "A list of the Genera of Birds," 1840 (q.v.). The actual date of publication of the present work is uncertain, but if it should prove to antedate Gray's volume, the modern definitions of a number of genera would have to be altered. Both works were independent of each other and neither is cited by the other, although the second edition of Gray (1841, q.v.) quotes Selby in several instances. It is possible that the current Report of the Natural History Society of Northumberland, Durham and Newcastle-upon-Tyne for which organization the present volume was prepared) might throw some light on the date of publication, but this periodical is inaccessible to me. This work of Selby's is quite rare.

Selby, Prideaux John. (Jardine, William; Turner, Rev. Mr.; Cuvier, G. L. C. F. D.)

1844-64. [The Natural History of Parrots.]

The | naturalist's library. | Edited by | Sir William Jardine, Bart. | F.R.S.E. [etc.]. | Vol. X. | [Design.] | Ornithology. | Parrots. | By Prideaux John Selby, Esq., | F.R.S.E. [etc.]. | London: | Chatto & Windus, Piccadilly.

1 vol. cap 8vo, 3 pr. ll. (various tits.; 1 illum.), pp. 17-207+1, 189-219, frontisp. (portr.), pll. 1-30 (col.; by E. Lear). London. (Date?).

A reprint of Vol. VI, Ornithological Series (1st ed.), of Jardine's "The Naturalist's Library," 1833-43 (q.v.), with some changes. To the memoir of Bewick have been added additional notes on the same topic (pp. 51-72), and at the close of the volume (pp. 189-219) is a memoir of Daubenton, written by Cuvier. This memoir of Daubenton is paged continuously with the first edition of the present volume, but discontinuously with the edition in hand, and is inscribed "(To be placed at the end of the Parrot Volume.)" as though it had been issued primarily with some later volume of the first edition (where however I am unable to place it). The plates differ from those of the first edition in coloration and in the addition of the habitats to the inscriptions. In the copy at hand, the illuminated title-page bears the imprint of Lizars.

Selby, Prideaux John. (Jardine, William; Crichton, Andrew.)

1844-64. [The Natural History of Pigeons.]

The | naturalist's library. | Edited by | Sir William Jardine, Bart., | F.R.S.E. [etc.]. | Vol. IX. | Ornithology. | Pigeons. | By Prideaux John Selby, Esq., | F.R.S.E. [etc.]. | Edinburgh: | W. H. Lizars, 3, St. James' Square. | London: S. Highley, Fleet Street; | T. Nelson, Paternoster Row. Dublin: W. Curry, Jun. & Co. | Manchester: J. Ainsworth, 93, Piccadilly; | and all booksellers.

1 vol. cap 8vo, 6 pr. ll. (various tits., 1 illum.; conts.), pp. 17-252, frontisp. (portr.), pll. 1-30 (col.; by E. Lear and Prêtre), 5 text-figs. Edinburgh. (Date?).

A reprint of Vol. V, Ornithological Series (1st ed.), of Jardine's "The Naturalist's Library," 1833-43 (q.v.), with pp. 229-252 (on the rearing of domestic pigeons) added. The plates contain both Latin and English names and localities, and are embellished by the addition of elaborate scenic backgrounds (uncol.), although the coloring is inferior to that of the plates of the first edition. The illuminated title-page, with Lizars's imprint, is inscribed, "Vol. VI."

Seligmann, Johann Mich.

1772-81. See Edwards, George; and Catesby, **Verzameling van Uit-landsche en Zeldzaame Vogelen.**

Selous, Edmund.

1905. The | bird watcher | in the Shetlands | with some notes on seals | - and digressions | by | Edmund Selous | [*Design.*] | with 10 illustrations | by | J. Smit | London: J. M. Dent & Co. | New York: E. P. Dutton & Co. | 1905.

1 vol. 8vo, pp. I-X, 1 l., pp. 1-388, 10 pll. London.

A series of observations, most of them on bird-life, made in the Shetland Islands and written somewhat in the form of a journal.

Selous, Edmund.

1910-13. See Kirkman, Frederick Bernuf Bever, **The British Bird Book.**

Sepp, Christian.

1770-1829. See Nozeman, Martinus, **Nederlandsche Vogelen.**

Seth-Smith, David.

1902-03. **Parrakeets.** | A handbook to the imported | species. | [*Fig.*] | Photo by G. Seth-Smith. | By | David Seth-Smith, M.B.O.U., F.Z.S. | With twenty coloured plates and other illustrations. | London: | R. H. Porter, | 7, Prince's Street, Cavendish Square, W. | 1903.

1 vol. royal 8vo, pp. I-XVIII, 1 l. (list of illustrs.), pp. 1-281, 20 pll. (col.; by F. W. Frohawk, H. Goodchild, H. Grönvold and W. E. Renaut), 23 text-figs+1 fig. on tit. London.

A description of the habits, in life and in captivity, of about 131 of the smaller species of the parrot groups. An occasional discussion of a family or genus is added. The colored plates are excellent and there are references, in the text, to published colored figures of many of the species not illustrated in the present work. The book was issued in 6 parts at dates given by the author on p. X of the work.

Sharpe, Richard Bowdler.

1868-71. A monograph | of | the Alcedinidæ: | or, family of King-fishers. | By | R. B. Sharpe, F.L.S., &c., | Librarian to the Zoological Society of London, Member of the German Ornithologists' Society, &c., &c. | [*Quot., 3 lines.*] | London: | published by the author. | 1868-71.

1 vol. medium 4to (trimmed to 8¼x11½), 3 pr. ll. (tit., ded. and list of subscrs.), pp. I-II (conts.), I-II (list of pll.), I-LXXI+1 (introd.), 1 l. (subtit.), 152 ll. (text)+1 l. (subtit.), pp. I-XI (index), 121 pll. (120 col.; by Keulemans), 1 map (col.), 2 text-figs. London.

A thorough monograph of the subject, containing all the available information respecting the birds in question and illustrated by fine hand-colored plates. The work appeared in 15 parts, the dates of publication of which are given by Coues as noted below. The contents of each part, secured from the Zoological Record, I have indicated by the number of each plate as given in the index (the plates, themselves, are unnumbered). Part I, pll. 23, 28, 44, 45, 62, 71, 96, 99, July 1, 1868; II, pll. 25, 38, 39, 41, 46, 97, 118, 119, Oct. 1, 1868; III, pll. 37, 40, 55, 56, 58, 104, 116, 117, Jan. 1, 1869; IV, pll. 17, 27, 47, 49, 50, 51, 68, 120, April 1, 1869; V, pll. 7, 9, 10, 24, 48, 53, 66, 69, July 1, 1869; VI, pll. 11, 12, 16, 18, 20, 21, 52, 100, Oct. 6, 1869; VII, pll. 3, 14, 22, 61, 65, 70, 72, 113, Jan. 1, 1870; VIII, pll. 21, 30, 31, 32, 35, 36, 114, 115, April 1, 1870; IX, pll. 2, 8, 29, 57, 60, 63, 76, 106, July 1, 1870; X and XI (double no.), pll. 4, 5, 13, 26, 43, 59, 75, 77, 78, 79, 80, 83, 88, 98, 108, 112, Oct. 1, 1870; XII, pll. 34, 64, 87, 89, 91, 94, 101, 107, Nov. 1, 1870; XIII, pll. 1, 6, 67, 81, 85, 92, 93, 95, Dec. 1, 1870; XIV and XV (double no.), pll. 15, 19, 33, 54, 73, 74, 82, 84, 86, 90, 102, 103, 105, 109, 110, 111, introductory pl. and map, Jan. 1, 1871. The plates not included in this list are of indeterminate position.

The introduction contains a review of the group and presents some emendations of the text, including the definition of a new genus, *Myioceyx*. The text contains the description of a new species, *Tanysiptera emiliae* in Pt. XIV. Several other species, described by the author in the Proceedings of the Zoological Society, are redescribed here with references to the Proceedings without pagination, and the dates of these numbers of the Proceedings and of the parts of the present work are very close, requiring further investigation to determine the priority of reference. The species in question are *Ceyx wallacii*, *Cittura sanghirensis*, *Pelargopsis gouldi*, *P. floresiana* and *P. burmanica*.

Sharpe, Richard Bowdler.

1871. Catalogue | of | African birds | in the | collection | of | R. B. Sharpe, F.L.S. &c., | Librarian to the Zoological Society of London, | Member of the German Ornithologists' Society, etc. | London: | published by the author. | 1871.

1 vol. post 8vo, pp. I-IV, 1-76. London.

A list of 703 species, with some synonymy, bibliographic references, citations of localities from which specimens in the collection had been secured, the number of specimens from each locality and the names of the collectors. The collection embraced only the "Orders *Passeres* and *Picariae*." The introduction is dated January 20, 1871.

Sharpe, Richard Bowdler.

1871. See Dresser, H. E., A History of the Birds of Europe, 1871-82.

Sharpe, Richard Bowdler.

1874. Catalogue | of the | **Accipitres,** | or | diurnal birds of prey, | in the | collection | of the | British Museum. | By | R. Bowdler Sharpe. | London: | printed by order of the Trustees. | 1874.

See British Museum, **Catalogue of the Birds,** 1874-98, Vol. I.

Sharpe, Richard Bowdler.

1875. See Richardson, John; and Gray, John Edward, **The Zoology of the Voyage of H. M. S. Erebus & Terror,** 1844-75.

Sharpe, Richard Bowdler.

1875. Catalogue | of the | **Striges,** | or | nocturnal birds of prey, | in the | collection | of the | British Museum. | By | R. Bowdler Sharpe. | London: | printed by order of the Trustees. | 1875.

See British Museum, **Catalogue of the Birds,** 1874-98, Vol. II.

Sharpe, Richard Bowdler.

1875-78. See Rowley, George D., **Ornithological Miscellany.**

Sharpe, Richard Bowdler.

1875-84. See Layard, **The Birds of South Africa; New Edition.**

Sharpe, Richard Bowdler.

1877. Catalogue | of the | **Passeriformes,** | or | perching birds, | in the | collection | of the | British Museum. | **Coliomorphæ,** | containing the families | Corvidæ, Paradiseidæ, Oriolidæ, Dicruridæ, and | Prionopidæ. | By | R. Bowdler Sharpe. | London: | printed by order of the Trustees. | 1877.

See British Museum, **Catalogue of the Birds,** 1874-98, Vol. III.

Sharpe, Richard Bowdler.

1879. Catalogue | of the | **Passeriformes,** | or | perching birds, | in the | collection | of the | British Museum. | **Cichlomorphæ: Part I.** | Containing the families | Campophagidæ and Muscicapidæ. | By | R. Bowdler Sharpe. | London: | printed by order of the Trustees. | 1879.

See British Museum, **Catalogue of the Birds,** 1874-98, Vol. IV.

Sharpe, Richard Bowdler.

1880-? See Gould, John. **A Monograph of the Pittidae.**

Sharpe, Richard Bowdler.

1881. Catalogue | of the | Passeriformes, | or | perching birds, | in the | collection | of the | British Museum. | **Cichlomorphæ: Part III.** | Containing the first portion of the family | Timeliidæ | (Babbling-Thrushes). | By | R. Bowdler Sharpe. | London: | printed by order of the Trustees. | 1881.

See British Museum, **Catalogue of the Birds,** 1874-98, Vol. VI.

Sharpe, Richard Bowdler.

1881-87. See Gould, John; and Sharpe, **A Monograph of the Tro-chilidae,** 1880-87.

Sharpe, Richard Bowdler.

1882-88. See Gould, John; and Sharpe, Richard Bowdler, **The Birds of New Guinea,** 1875-88.

Sharpe, Richard Bowdler.

1883. Catalogue | of the | Passeriformes, | or | perching birds, | in the | collection | of the | British Museum. | **Cichlomorphæ: Part IV.** | Containing the concluding portion of the family | Timeliidæ | (Babbling Thrushes). | By | R. Bowdler Sharpe. | London: | printed by order of the Trustees. | 1883.

See British Museum, **Catalogue of the Birds,** 1874-98, Vol. VII.

Sharpe, Richard Bowdler.

1885. Catalogue | of the | Passeriformes, | or | perching birds, | in the | collection | of the | British Museum. | **Fringilliformes: Part I.** | Containing the families | Dicæidæ, Hirundinidæ, Ampelidæ, | Mniotiltidæ, and Motacillidæ. | By | R. Bowdler Sharpe. | London: | printed by order of the Trustees. | 1885.

See British Museum, **Catalogue of the Birds,** 1874-98, Vol. X.

Sharpe, Richard Bowdler; and Wyatt, Claude Wilmott.

1885-94. **A monograph** | of the | **Hirundinidæ** | or | family of Swallows. | By | R. Bowdler Sharpe, LL.D., F.L.S., F.Z.S., Etc., | Department of Zoology [*etc., 7 lines.*]: | and | Claude W. Wyatt, | Member of the British Ornithologists' Union. | Volume I [II]. | London: | Henry Sotheran & Co., | 37 Piccadilly, W. 140 Strand, W.C. | 1885-1894.

2 vols. in 1 vol., medium 4to. Vol. I, pp. I-LXX, 173 ll. (num. 1-356 in table of conts.), 54 pll. (col.; by Wyatt), 11 maps (col.; 1 missing) (pll. and maps num. 1-64 in conts.), 1 text-fig. Vol. II, pp. I-VIII,

337 ll. (num. 357-673 in conts.), 50 pll. (col.), 15 maps (col.) (pll. and maps num. 65-129 in conts.), 1 text-fig. London.

A detailed monograph of all the known species of swallows, with fine, hand-colored plates by the junior author. The introductory chapters contain a review of the genera, a discussion of the geographical distribution of the various members of the family, and a bibliography, with a short note on the mythical hibernation of the birds in question. An appendix to each genus, contains supplementary remarks on the various species, added after the publication of the original accounts in earlier numbers of the work. The letterpress for each species is paged separately and the plates are unnumbered, but the tables of contents for the two volumes give a running number to pages and plates, continuous through both volumes. The work was issued in 20 parts (including some double or treble numbers) as follows; the plate-numbers are as given in the tables of contents. Part I, pll. 49, 51, 54, 66, 73, 115, Sept. 1885; II, pll. 1, 4, 17, 53, 70, 74, Dec. 1885; III-IV, pll. 16, 19, 56, 57, 58, 59, or 60, 61, 62, 69, 112, 114, 121, July 1886; V-VI, pll. 12, 18, 21, 22, 48, 92, 100, 103, 107, 108, 109, 118, June 1887; VII-VIII, pll. 5, 60 or 59, 77, 98, 101, 105, 111, 116, 119, 120, 122, 126, map 123 or 124, May 1888; IX-X, pll. 3, 13, 23, 27, 28, 52, 64, 75, 89, 90 91, 97, March 1889; XI-XII, pll. 14, 24, 26, 39, 55, 63, 72, 86, 93, 95, 99, 127, maps 35, 94, 128, 129, Dec. 1889; XIII-XIV, pll. 6, 10, 11, 20, 65, 67, 68, 76, 104, 106, 110, 125, Dec. 1890; XV, pll. 15, 25, 46, 47, 50, 96, Aug. 1892; XVI-XVII, pll. 2, 9, 29, 36, 37, 38, 40, 41, 42, 71, 87, 88, Dec. 1893; XVIII-XX, pl. 117, ? maps 7, 8, 30-34, 43, 44, 45, 78-85, 102, 113, 124 or 123 (these not all unquestioned), Oct. 1894. The text to the following species (without plates) is recorded as having been issued in the parts given. *Hirundo gardoni*, Pt. II; *Petrochelidon timoriensis* and *Cotile anderssoni*, Pt. V-VI; *Progne domestica*, Pt. IX-X; *Hirundo namiyei*, Pt. XV. Some of the letterpress accompanied the corresponding plates, but there are exceptions. *Cotile diluta* and *C. anderssoni* are described as new.

Sharpe, Richard Bowdler.

1888. **Birds in nature** | by | R. Bowdler Sharpe, F.L.S., F.Z.S. | Zoological Department, British Museum, | etc., etc., etc. | With | thirty-nine coloured plates | and other illustrations | by | P. Robert | London | Sampson Low, Marston, Searle, and Rivington | Limited | St. Dunstan's House | Fetter Lane, Fleet Street, E.C. | 1888 | [All rights reserved].

1 vol. medium 4to, 4 pr. ll., pp. 1-78, 39 pll. (col.; by P. Robert), 78 figs. (head and tail pieces, of more or less ornithological interest). London.

A number of popular sketches of European bird-life, treated under the headings of 39 species to which, however, the accounts are not strictly limited. The author acknowledges indebtedness to the writings of Henry Seebohm which are quoted largely, along with those of a few other authors. The colored lithographs are mostly inferior to the line drawings. The edition was limited to 300 copies.

Sharpe, Richard Bowdler.

1888. **Catalogue** | **of the** | **Passeriformes,** | or | perching birds, | in the | collection | of the | British Museum. | **Fringilliformes: Part III.** | Containing the family | Fringillidæ. | By | R. Bowdler Sharpe. | London: | printed by order of the Trustees. | 1888.

See British Museum, **Catalogue of the Birds,** 1874-98, Vol. XII.

Sharpe, Richard Bowdler.

1890. **Catalogue** | **of the** | **Passeriformes,** | or | perching birds, | in the | collection | of the | British Museum. | **Sturniformes,** | containing the families | Artamidæ, Sturnidæ, Ploceidæ, Alaudidæ. | Also the families | **Atrichiidæ** and **Menuridæ.** | By | R. Bowdler Sharpe. | London: | printed by order of the Trustees. | Sold by | Longmans & Co., 39 Paternoster Row; [*etc., 3 lines.*]; | and at the | British Museum (Natural History), Cromwell Road, S.W. | 1890.

See British Museum, **Catalogue of the Birds,** 1874-98, Vol. XIII.

Sharpe, Richard Bowdler.

1890. See Jameson, James Sligo, **The Story of the Rear Column.**

Sharpe, Richard Bowdler.

1891. > **Scientific results** | **of** | **the Second Yarkand Mission;** | based upon the collections and notes | of the late | Ferdinand Stoliczka, Ph.D. | **Aves,** | by | R. Bowdler Sharpe, LL.D., F.L.S., F.Z.S., &c. | Published by Order of the Government of India. | London: | printed by Taylor and Francis, Red Lion Court, Fleet Street. | 1891.

1 vol. imperial 4to and royal 4to, pp. I-XVIII+1, 1-153, pll. (royal 4to) I-XXIV (col.; by Keulemans, Hart and ?J. Smit). London.

A report by Sharpe on the birds collected by Dr. Stoliczka on the Second Yarkand Mission into central Asia, with extracts from Stoliczka's notebook and from that of his companion, Colonel Biddulph, as well as from the published notes of Dr. Henderson (of the First Yarkand Mission) and Dr. Scully. The work thus includes the results of both expeditions to Yarkand. Allan Hume prepared an earlier report on the same material but his manuscript was stolen and destroyed. An appendix to the present book (pp. 149-152) contains descriptions of six species of birds not found in Yarkand, thus serving as an excuse to present plates XVI-XXIV, as explained in the text. The present volume forms Part 5 of the complete report which was published in 14 parts during 1878-91. The present copy is from the library of Tschusi zu Schmidhoffen.

Sharpe, Richard Bowdler.

1891-98. Monograph | of | the Paradiseidæ, | or | Birds of Paradise, | and | Ptilonorhynchidæ, | or | Bower-birds. | By | R. Bowdler Sharpe, LL.D. F.L.S. F.Z.S. etc., | Assistant Keeper, Zoological Department, British Museum [*etc.*, 11 *lines.*]. | In two volumes. | Volume I [II]. | London: | Henry Sotheran & Co., | 37 Piccadilly, W. 140 Strand, W.C. | 1891-1898. | [All rights reserved.].

[2 vols. demy folio. Vol. I, pp. I-XLIII+1, 72 ll., 39 pll. (col.; by J. Gould and W. Hart), figs. 1-6, 1 text-fig. Vol. II, pp. I-V+1, 72 ll., 40 pll. (col.), 8 text-figs. London.]

An excellent monograph of all the known species of these families of birds, illustrated by life-sized, hand-colored plates of many of them. These plates in some cases are printed from the stones used by Gould and Sharpe in the "Birds of New Guinea," 1875-88 (q.v.); some are redrawn and others are entirely new. In the appendix (Vol. I, pp. XXI-XL, the author gives a general review of the species, with the additions necessary to bring the earlier parts up to date. In the introduction, pp. V-XIX, are given tables for the determination of the various groups from families to species. The work appeared in 8 parts as collated below. The present set is still bound in the original board covers which contain a large vignette of *Ptilorhis victoriae*, the title (arranged slightly differently from the title-page), the part-number, a list of contents, the proposed number of parts (originally six but altered in Pt. VI to eight), and the imprint, date and price. The contents and date of each part are as follows. Part **I**, *Lycocorax pyrrhopterus, Parotia lawesi, Cicinnurus regius, Craspedophara magnifica, Epimachus meyeri, Paradisea apoda, Prionodura newtonianu, Xanthomelus aureus, Chlamydodera orientalis* and *Tectornoris dentirostris* 1891. Part **II**, *Ptilorhis paradisea, Craspedophora intercedens, Astrapia nigra, Paradigalla carunculata, Paradisornis rudolphi, Rhipidornis gulielmi tertii, Manucodia chalybeata, Lycocorax obiensis, Amblyornis inornata* and *Aeluroedus stonii,* 1893 (reviewed in Ornithologische Monatsberichte for July, 1893). Part **III**, *Ptilorhis victoriae, Epimachus speciosus, Astrarchia stephaniae, Paradisea augustae-victoriae, Schlegelia respublica, Manucodia comrii, Phonygama purpureo-violacea, Aeluroedus viridis, Chlamydodera occipitalis* and *Amblyornis subalaris,* 1894 (rev. Orn. Monatsb. for Nov. 1894). Part **IV**, *Drepanornis bruijnii, D. cervinicauda, Uranornis rubra, Diphyllodes chrysoptera, Lophorhina superba, Phonygama keraudreni, Cnemophilus macgregorii, Aeluroedus arfakianus, A. melanotis* and *A. buccoides,* 1895 (rev. Orn. Monatsb. for Nov. 1895). Part **V**, *Drepanornis albertisi, Semioptera wallacii, Trichoparadisea gulielmi, Diphyllodes hunsteini, Lophorhina minor, Parotia sexpennis, Sericulus melinus, Aeluroedus maculosus, A. geislerorum* and *Lycocorax morotensis,* 1895 (rev. Orn. Monatsb. as publ. at close of 1895; in no. for Jan. 1897). Part **VI**, *Craspedophora mantoui, Lamprothorax wilhelminae, Epimachus ellioti, Ianthothorax bensbachii, Diphyllodes magnifica, D. seleucides, Paradisea raggiana, Xanthomelus ardens, Loria mariae* and *Ptilonorhynchus violaceus,* 1896 (rev. Orn. Monatsb. for Nov. 1897 as having been published in 1896, but the part contains an insert-slip dated Dec. 30, 1896 and may have been issued in 1897). Part **VII**, *Craspedophora alberti,*

Seleucides nigricans (2 pll.), *Macgregoria pulchra, Paradisea minor* (2 pll.), *Parotia carolae, Phonygama gouldi* (no pl.), *P. jamesi* (no pl.), *Pteridophora alberti, Loboparadisea sericea* and *Aeluroedus melanocephalus,* 1897. Part **VIII,** *Paryphephorus duivenbodii, Drepanornis geisleri* (no pl.), *Epimachus astrapioides* (no pl.), *Astrapia splendidissima, Paradisea novae-guineae* (no pl.), *P. mariae* (no pl.), *P. intermedia, P. decora, P. jobiensis* (no pl.), *P. finschi* (no pl)., *Cicinnurus caccineifrons* (no pl.), *Phonygama hunsteini, Manucodia orientalis* (no pl.), *M. jobiensis* (no pl.), *M. rubiensis* (no pl.), *M. atra, Parotia berlepschi* (no pl.), *P. helenae* (no pl.), *Amblyornis flavifrons, A. inornata, Chlamydodera cerviniventris, C. maculata, C. guttata* (no pl.), *C. nuchalis, C. recondita* (no pl.), *C. lauterbachi* (no pl.), *Aeluroedus jobiensis* (no pl.), title-pages, pref., introd., appendix, conts. (Vols. I and II) and lists of pll. (Vols. I and II), 1898. Two new genera, *Heteroptilorhis* and *Calastrapia,* are described in the introduction where also *Tectornornis,* a new name given in Pt. I for *Scenopoeus* (misspelled in two places '*Scenopaeus*'), is found to be preoccupied by *Scenopoeetes,* and so is relegated to synonymy.

Sharpe, Richard Bowdler; and Ogilvie-Grant, William Robert.

1892. **Catalogue | of the | Picariæ |** in the | collection | of the | British Museum. | **Coraciæ (contin,) and Halcyones,** | with the families | Leptosomatidæ, Coraciidæ, Meropidæ | Alcedinidæ, Momotidæ, Todidæ, and Coliidæ, | by | R. Bowdler Sharpe. | **Bucerotes and Trogones,** | by | W. R. Ogilvie Grant. | London: | printed by order of the Trustees. | Sold by | Longmans & Co., 39 Paternoster Row; [*etc., 3 lines.*]; | and at the | British Museum (Natural History), Cromwell Road, S.W. | 1892.

See British Museum, **Catalogue of the Birds,** 1874-98, Vol. XVII.

Sharpe, Richard Bowdler.

1893. **An | analytical index |** to | **the works of the late | John Gould,** F.R.S. | By | R. Bowdler Sharpe, LL.D., F.L.S., F.Z.S., Etc., | Department of Zoology, British Museum; | Holder of the gold medal [*etc., 7 lines.*] | With a biographical memoir | and portrait. | London: | Henry Sotheran & Co., 37 Piccadilly | (opposite St. James's Church). | 1893.

1 vol. foliopost 4to, pp. I-XLVIII, 1-375, frontisp. (portr.). London.

Contains a biographical memoir of John Gould, a bibliography of his works and an alphabetical index to the generic, specifix and common names of all the species treated in his numerous works. The portrait is of Gould. The present copy is one presented to Dr. Arthur Günther by the author.

Sharpe, Richard Bowdler.

1893. See Whitehead, John, **Exploration of Mount Kina Balu, North Borneo.**

Sharpe, Richard Bowdler.

1894. Catalogue | of the | Fulicariæ | (Rallidæ and Heliornithidæ) | and | Alectorides | (Aramidæ, Eurypygidæ, Mesitidæ, Rhinochetidæ, | Gruidæ, Psophiidæ, and Otididæ) | in the | collection | of the | British Museum. | By | R. Bowdler Sharpe. | London: | printed by order of the Trustees. | Sold by | Longmans & Co., 39 Paternoster Row; [etc., 3 lines.]; | and at the | British Museum (Natural History), Cromwell Road, S.W. | 1894.

See British Museum, **Catalogue of the Birds,** 1874-98, Vol. XXIII.

Sharpe, Richard Bowdler.

1895. **A Chapter on Birds.** | By | R. Bowdler Sharpe, LL.D., F.L.S., etc. | (Zoological Department, British Museum.) | Rare British visitors. | With Eighteen Coloured Plates. | Published under the direction of the General Literature Committee. | Society for Promoting Christian Knowledge. | London: Northumberland Avenue, W.C.; | Brighton: 129, North Street. | New York: E. & J. B. Young & Co. | 1895.

1 vol. crown 8vo, pp. I-IX+1, 1 l. (conts.), pp. 1-124, 18 pll. (col.; by Keulemans). London.

Popular descriptions of the habits, characteristics and distribution of 18 birds which are rare or casual visitors to Great Britain. The illustrations, in chromolithograph, are good and illustrate each species and its egg.

Sharpe, Richard Bowdler.

1896. Catalogue | of the | Limicolæ | in the | collection | of the | British Museum. | By | R. Bowdler Sharpe. | London: | printed by order of the Trustees. | Sold by | Longmans & Co., 39 Paternoster Row; [etc., 3 lines.]; | and at the | British Museum (Natural History), Cromwell Road, S.W.| 1896.

See British Museum, **Catalogue of the Birds,** 1874-98, Vol. XXIV.

Sharpe, Richard Bowdler.

1896. See Seebohm, Henry, **Coloured Figures of the Eggs of British Birds.**

Sharpe, Richard Bowdler.

1896-97. Lloyd's natural history. | Edited by R. Bowdler Sharpe, LL.D., F.L.S., &c. | **A hand-book** | **to the** | **birds** | **of** | **Great Britain.** | By | R. Bowdler Sharpe, LL.D, [LL.D., (Vol. II-IV.)] | Assistant-Keeper, Sub-Department of | Vertebrata, British Museum. | Vol. I [-IV]. | Edward Lloyd, Limited, | 12, Salisbury Square, Fleet Street. | 1896 [1897 (Vol. IV)].

4 vols. crown 8vo. Vol. I, pp. I-XI+1, 1-340, pll. I-XXXI (col.; by Keulemans; XXIX-XXXI of eggs), 3 text-figs. Vol. II, pp. I-XI+1, 1-308, pll. XXXII-LVIII (col.), 13 text-figs. Vol. III, pp. I-XIII, 1 l., pp. 1-338, pll. LIX-XCIII (col.). Vol. IV, pp. I-XVII+1, 1-314, pll. XCIV-CXXIV, CXIa-CXId (col.), 9 text-figs. London.

A compact manual of British ornithology containing synonymies and detailed accounts of the plumages, distribution, habits and nidification of the numerous species of the country. The work was much criticized at the time of its publication on account of the author's strict adherence to certain views on nomenclature which had not received universal approbation in England. The plates are of poor quality. Vol. I first appeared in "Allen's Naturalists' Library" in 1894; Vol. II, in 1895; Vol. III, 1896 in both editions, accompanied by reprints of Vols. I and II of the second (present) issue; and Vol. IV, 1897 in both editions. The pagination of both sets appears to be the same except for the introductory matter in Vol. II (=pp. I-XVIII+2 pp. in ed. I), but I am unaware of any changes in the general text.

Sharpe, Richard Bowdler; and Ogilvie-Grant, William Robert.

1898. Catalogue | of the | Plataleæ, Herodiones, Steganopodes, | Pygopodes, Alcæ, and Impennes | in the | collection | of the | British Museum. | Plataleæ (Ibises and Spoonbills) | and | Herodiones (Herons and Storks), | by | R. Bowdler Sharpe. | Steganopodes (Cormorants, Gannets, Frigate-Birds, Tropic- | Birds, and Pelicans), Pygopodes (Divers and Grebes), Alcæ (Auks), and Impennes (Penguins), | by | W. R. Ogilvie-Grant. | London: | printed by order of the Trustees. | Sold by | Longmans & Co., 39 Paternoster Row, E.C.; [etc., 3 lines.]; | and at the | British Museum (Natural History), Cromwell Road, S.W. | 1898.

See British Museum, **Catalogue of the Birds,** 1874-98, Vol. XXVI.

Sharpe, Richard Bowdler.

1898? Wonders | of the | bird world | by | R. Bowdler Sharpe, LL.D., F.L.S., etc. | late Assistant-keeper, Sub-department of Vertebrata, British Museum | With Illustrations by A. T. Elwes | New York | Frederick A. Stokes Company | 443-449 Fourth Avenue.

1 vol. 8vo (trimmed), pp. I-XVI, 1-399, 106 text-figs. (34 full-p., blank on reverse). New York.

A popular volume in which have been collected notes on the peculiarities and habits of a very large number of the birds of the world, which are especially interesting for one reason or another. The book is composed of matter used by the author in many of his lectures. It is well arranged according to subjects, and, although possibly not designed for purely juvenile consumption, is excellently well adapted for juvenile instruction as well as for the information of older readers. The original edition was published in London in 1898; the present one, printed in Great Britain but published in New York was probably contemporaneous, although I can find no record of the date.

Sharpe, Richard Bowdler.

1898-1902. See Seebohm, Henry; and Sharpe, **A Monograph of the Turdidae.**

Sharpe, Richard Bowdler.

1899-1909. A hand-list | of the | genera and species | of | birds. | [Nomenclator avium tum fossilium tum viventium.] | By | R. Bowdler Sharpe, LL.D., | Assistant Keeper, Department of Zoology, | British Museum. | Volume I [-V]. | London: | printed by order of the Trustees. | Sold by | Longmans & Co., 39 Paternoster Row, E.C.; [etc., *3 lines, mut. mut.*]; | and at the | British Museum (Natural History), Cromwell Road, [*No comma (Vol. II.*).] S.W. | 1899 [1900; 1901; 1903; 1909]. | All rights reserved.

5 vols. post 8vo. Vol. I, pp. I-XXI+1, 1-303, 1 l. (errata; between pp. 204 and 205; issued with Vol. II). Vol. II, pp. I-XV+1, 1-312. Vol. III, pp. I-XII, 1-367. Vol. IV, pp. I-XII, 1-391, 1-24 (advt.). Vol. V, pp. I-XX, 1-694, 1-28 (advt.). London.

Prepared on much the same plan as George Robert Gray's "Hand-list of Genera and Species of Birds," 1869-71 (q.v.), with the subject matter brought up to date and with page-references to the volumes of the British Museum "Catalogue of the Birds," 1874-98 (q.v.). The forms treated are summarized approximately as comprising 2810 genera and 18,939 species. The volumes are composed as follows. Vol. I, Saururae, Palaeognathae and Neognathae,—Galliformes to Strigiformes; II, Psittaciformes to Piciformes; III, Eurylaemiformes to Passeriformes, Acromyodi, Pycnonotidae; Vol. IV, Timeliidae to Certhiidae; Vol. V, Zosteropidae to Streperidae. Vol. II contains an index to Vols. I and II; the remaining volumes each contain an index of their own contents. A "General Index" (q.v.) was prepared by Ogilvie-Grant and published in 1912.

The dates of the present volumes are not all recorded. Vol. **I** was issued in November, 1899 (rev. in Ibis, Jan., 1900); the preface to Vol. **II** is dated June 11, 1900; that of Vol. **III,** July 10, 1901; Vol. **VI** appeared in September, 1903 (rev. Ibis, Jan. 1904); the preface to Vol. **V** is dated Aug. 24, 1909.

The discussion of the Palamedeiformes was omitted, inadvertently, from Vol. I, but was supplied with Vol. II on an insert-slip intended to be attached to its proper place in the preceding number, at p. 205.

Shaw, George. (Miller, John Frederick.)

1796. Cimelia physica. | Figures | of | rare and curious | quadrupeds, birds, &c. | together with | several of the most elegant | plants. | Engraved and coloured from the subjects themselves | by | John Frederick Miller. | With | descriptions | by | George

Shaw, M.D. F.R.S. | &c. &c. &c. | London: | Printed by T. Bensley, | for Benjamin and John White, | Horace's Head, Fleet-Street, | and John Sewell, Cornhill. | 1796.

1 vol. imperial folio (14¼x20¼), tit., pp. 1-106, frontisp. (unnum.;= pl. I), pll. II-LX (col.). London.

A series of descriptions accompanying colored plates of various subjects of natural history. Ornithological matter is illustrated on pll. I-VI, VIII, XII, XIV-XVIII, XXI-XXIV, XXVIII-XXX, XXXIII-XXXVI, XXXVIII, XL-XLII and XLVII-LIX (41 pll.). The present copy is lettered on the back, "Miller's Cimelia Physica," and the Cat. Libr. Brit. Mus. (Nat. Hist.) lists the work as a later edition of Miller's "Various subjects of Natural History wherein are delineated Birds, Animals and many Curious Plants, &c.", 1776-92. The text, however, is the work of Shaw.

Shaw, George; and Stephens, James Francis.

1812-26. > **General zoology.** | Vol. VIII [-XIV].-Part I [II]. [| By | James Francis Stephens, F.L.S. (*Vols. IX-XI.*); *idem*, F.L.S. &c. (*Vols. XII-XIV, Pt. I.*)] | **Birds.** | London. [*Semicolon (Vols. IX-XIV, Pt. I.*).] Printed for George Kearsley, Fleet Street; [for G. Wilkie, *etc., 7 lines (Vols. IX and X.*); for J. Walker, *etc., 6 lines (Vol. XI.*); for J. and A. Arch, *etc., 7 lines (Vols. XII-XIV, Pt. I.*).] | by Thomas Davison, Whitefriars. [*Line omitted (Vols. IX-XIV, Pt. I.*).] | 1811 [1811; 1815; 1815; 1817; 1817; 1819; 1819; 1824; 1824; 1826; 1826; 1826].

> General index | to | the zoology, | by | George Shaw, M.D. &c. | and | James Francis Stephens, J.L.S. &c. | London: | Printed for J. and A. Arch [*etc., 7 lines.*] | 1826.

[*Engr. titles.*] > General Zoology, [*Comma omitted (Vols. IX-XIV, Pt. I.*).] | or | Systematic Natural History | by [commenced by the late (*Vols. IX-XIV, Pt. I.*)] | George Shaw, M.D. F.R.S. &c. | With Plates | from the first authorities and most select specimens. [*Period omitted (Vols. IX-XIV, Pt. I.*).] | Engraved principally by | Mrs. Griffith [Mrs. Griffiths (*Vol. IX.*)]. | [*Vignette (diff. in each Pt.*).] | Vol. VIII [-XIV]. Part I. [II. (*Vol. I.*); I (II). Aves. by J. F. Stephens, F.L.S. (*Vols. IX-XI.*); *idem*, F.L.S. &c. (*Vols. XII-XIV, Pt. I.*)] | Aves. [*Line omitted (Vols. IX-XIV, Pt. I.*).] | London, Printed for Kearsley, Wilkie and Robinson [*etc., 3 lines (Vol. VIII.*); for G. Wilkie, *etc., 4 lines (Vols. IX-X.*); for J. Walker, *etc., 3 lines (Vol. XI.*); for I & A. Arch, *etc., 3 lines (Vols. XII-XIV, Pt. I.*).] | 1812 [1812; 1815; 1815; 1817; 1817; 1819; 1819; 1824 | Fenner sc.; 1824 | Fenner sc.; 1825; 1825; 1826].

7 vols. in 14, royal 8vo, Vol. VIII, Pt. I, engr. tit., pp. I-IX+1, 1-357, pll. 1-45+39* (29 wrongly num. 79). Vol. VIII, Pt. II, engr. tit., pp. I-VI, 1 l. (dir. for pll.), pp. 359-557, pll. 46-84. Vol. IX, Pt. I, engr. tit., 2 ll. (tit. and advt.; half-tit. missing?), pp. VII-XIV, 1 l. (dir. for pll.), pp. 1-227, pll. 1-40+3*, 4*, 35*, 35**, 35***, 35****, 35*****, 35******, 35*******, 36*. Vol. IX, Pt. II, engr. tit., pp. I-XVII+1, 1 l. (dir. for pll. and errata), pp. 229-547, pll. 41-70. Vol. X, Pt. I, engr. tit., pp. I-IX+1, 1-317, pll. 1-29 (29 wrongly num. 30). Vol. X, Pt. II, engr. tit., pp. I-XXXI+1, 319-765+1, pll. 30-60. Vol. XI, Pt. I, engr. tit., pp. I-XIV, 1 l. (dir. for pll.), pp. 1-264, pll. 1-4, (5 not issued), 6-17. Vol. XI, Pt. II, engr. tit., pp. I-XXI+1, 1 l. (dir. for pll. and errata), pp. 265-646, pll. 18-21, (22 not issued), 23-52. Vol. XII, Pt. I, engr. tit., 2 ll. (tit., and dir. for pll. and errata), pp. 1-297, 1 l. (advt.), pll. 1-35. Vol. XII, Pt. II, engr. tit., 2 ll. (tit., dir. for pll. and errata), pp. 1-264, pll. 36-64. Vol. XIII, Pt. I, engr. tit., 2 ll. (tit., dir. for pll. and errata), pp. 1-278, pll. 1-30. Vol. XIII, Pt. II, engr. tit., 2 ll. (tit., dir. for pll. and errata), pp. 1-290, pll. 31-63. Vol. XIV, Pt. I, engr. tit., 2 ll. (tit. and dir. for pll.), pp. 1-385, pll. 1-41. Index (=Vol. XIV, Pt. II.), (no engr. tit.), 2 ll. (half-tit. and tit.), pp. 1-334. London.

Most of the ornithological volumes of a detailed work on zoology, begun by Shaw in 1800 and completed by Stephens after Shaw's death following the publication of Vol. VIII in 1812. The work contains descriptions, synonyms and notes on habits of the various species, illustrated by excellent engravings. There is some discrepancy in the dates as given on the printed and engraved title-pages. Vol. VIII, Pts. I and II, is thus dated 1811 and 1812; an editorial advertisement in Vol. IX, Pt. I, says that Vol. VIII was published in 1812 (agreeing with the engraved title-page). Vol. XIII is similarly dated both 1825 and 1826; I do not know which is correct. Vol. VII, also relating to birds, is absent from the present set.

The index is complete for all branches of the natural history, not only of the birds. The references are not segregated. The volume containing this index is separately titled, as transcribed above, but appears to form the second part of the last volume on birds since its signatures are lettered "V. XIV. P. II."

Shaw, William T.

1908. The China or Denny Pheasant in Oregon | with notes on the | Native Grouse of the Pacific Northwest | written and illustrated | by | William T. Shaw, B.Agr., M.S. | Assistant Professor of Zoology and Curator of the Museum, State College of Washington | [*Design.*] | Philadelphia & London | J. B. Lippincott Company | 1908.

1 vol. (6x9, long), pp. 1-24, 15 printed guard-sheets, 15 pll. (1 col.).
Philadelphia and London.

A brief account of the original introduction of the Chinese Pheasant into Oregon
and some of its subsequent history. Ten of the photographic illustrations are
of birds, three are of nests, and three are of scenery.

Shelley, George Ernest.

1872. **A | handbook | to the | birds of Egypt.** | By | G. E. Shelley,
F.G.S., F.Z.S., etc., | late Captain [*etc.*, *4 lines.*] | London: | John
Van Voorst, Paternoster Row. | MDCCCLXXII.

1 vol. royal 8vo, pp. I-VIII, 1 1. (list of pll.), pp. 1-342, pll. I-XIV
(col.; by Keulemans). London.

A review of the birds previously recorded from Egypt or collected there by the
author, with short descriptions and some account of habits and distribution.
Part I (pp. 1-64) consists of an account of the author's journey in the country,
with occasional notes on the local bird-life. The hand-colored plates are very
good.

Shelley, George Ernest.

1876-80. **A monograph | of | the Nectariniidæ, | or | family of**
Sun-birds. | By | Captain G. E. Shelley, F.Z.S., F.R.G.S., &c. |
Author of [*etc.*] | London: | published by the author, | 6 Tenterden
Street, Hanover Square, W. | 1876-1880.

1 vol. royal 4to, pp. I-CVIII, 197 ll. (pp. 1-393 in table of conts.),
121 pll. (numbered only in table of conts.; col.; by Keulemans).
London.

An excellent monograph of an interesting family of birds, with descriptions in
Latin and English, critical notes, and discussions of habits, etc., from accounts
by many different observers. A total of 138 species of the group are recognized,
of which all but one are figured on excellent, hand-colored plates. Two new
genera (one from Sharpe, *in litt.*) and ten new species are described, and one
previously described form is given a name, which, in a later part of the work
(p. CV), is sunk in synonymy. A detailed review of the classification of the
group, with additions to the text, is given on pp. XV-LII. Tables of geographical distribution follow, on pp. LIII-LVIII, and a very complete bibliography is presented, on pp. LIX-CVIII. There is no pagination or numbering
of plates except in the lists of contents and of plates (pp. V-VIII). The work
appeared in 12 parts from July 28, 1876 to February 1880. Text and plates of
the various species were not always issued synchronously; the author gives a
complete collation of the various parts, with dates of publication, on pp.
XIII-XIV. The original title of the work was, "A Monograph of the Cinny-
ridae," etc., later changed to the wording transcribed above which represents
the final title.

Shelley, George Ernest.

1888. See James, F. L., **The Unknown Horn of Africa.**

Shelley, George Ernest.

1891. See Sclater, Philip Lutley; and Shelley, **Catalogue of the Picariae** in the Collection of the British Museum.
Also, British Museum, **Catalogue of the Birds,** 1874-98, Vol. XIX.

Shelley, George Ernest. (Sclater, William Lutley.)

1896-1912. The | birds of Africa, | comprising all the species which occur | in the | Ethiopian region. | By | G. E. Shelley, F.Z.S., F.R.G.S., &c. | (late Grenadier Guards), | author of [*etc., 1 line*; *2 lines* (*Vols. II-IV.*).]. | Vol. I. List. {Vol. II.; Vol. III.; Vol. IV. Part I. ; Vol. IV. Part II. ; Vol. V. Part I. ; Vol. V. Part II.} [| Completed and edited by | W. L. Sclater, M.A., F.Z.S. (*Vol. V, Pt. II, only,*)] | London: | published for the author by [Henry Sotheran & Co. (*Vol. V, Pt. II.*)]| R. H. Porter, 18 Princes Street, Cavendish Square W. [43 Piccadilly, W., and 140, Strand, W.C. (*Vol. V, Pt. II.*)] | 1896 [1900; 1902; 1905; 1905; 1906; 1912].

5 vols. in 7, imperial 8vo. Vol. I, pp. I-VIII, 1-196. Vol. II, tit., pp. I-VII+1, 1-348, pll. I-XIV (col.; by Grönvold). Vol. III, pp. I-VII+1, 1-276. pll. XV-XXVIII (col.). Vol. IV, Pt. I, pp. I-V+1, 1 l. (list of pll.), pp. 1-287, pll. XXIX-XXXV (col.). Vol. IV, Pt. II, pp. I-IV, 1 l. (list of pll.), pp. 289-511, pll. XXXVI-XLII (col.). Vol. V, Pt. I, 3 pr. ll. (tit., conts. and list of pll.), pp. 1-163, pll. XLIII-XLIX (col.). Vol. V, Pt. II, pp. I-VII+1, 165-502, pll. L-LVII (col.). London.

A review of the birds of Africa and surrounding islands, excepting "those countries bordering on the Mediterranean and eastward of the Red Sea." Volume I comprises a check-list of species. The remainder of the work takes up the various groups systematically, giving descriptions and biographical notes but citing, as synonymy, only references to the Catalogue of Birds in the British Museum and publications not mentioned therein, with further citation of the best published illustration; the original description is omitted unless it falls into the category mentioned and even the authorities for the nomenclature are not necessarily included. Many new genera and species are described. The illustrations are most excellent. The work was published in 8 parts, divided as collated above except that Vol. II appeared in two parts,—the first including pp. 1-160 and the second, the remainder. Vol. I is reviewed in the Ibis for July 1896; **II Pt. I,**, in July 1900; **II Pt. II,** in Jan. 1901 (but publ. in 1900); **III** in Oct. 1902; **IV Pt. I,** in the Auk for April 1905; **IV Pt. II,** in July 1905; **V Pt. I,** in the Ibis for July 1906; and **V Pt. II,** in Jan. 1913 (but publ., probably, in 1912). The various signatures bear varying dates which are evidently those of printing, not of publication. All of the work except Vol. V Pt. II is from the pen of Shelley who died before the work was complete. The final part was prepared by W. L. Sclater from Shelley's manuscript notes and proofs, with some additions of his own. There is an index to each volume except the first, but no general index.

Shepherd, Charles William.

1907. See Balston, Richard J.; Shepherd; and Bartlett, **Notes on the Birds of Kent.**

Shipley, A. E.

1911. See [Grouse], **The Grouse in Health and Disease.**

Short, Ernest. H.

1896. Birds of | Western New York | With Notes. | Ernest H. Short. | Second edition. | 1896. | Frank H. Lattin, Publisher, | Albion, N. Y.

1 vol. 8vo, pp. 1-20. Albion. 1896 (post April 1).

An annotated list of species, giving "A.O.U. numbers," common and Latin names, and brief notes on the status of each species. The present copy has the original front wrapper but lacks the rear one which according to a pencilled note, contains some text. The text, at hand however, does not appear to be interrupted. The first edition from which the present edition is said to differ somewhat, appeared in 1893.

Shriner, Charles A. (Palmer, T. S.; Stone, Witmer.)

1897. The Birds of | New Jersey, | Compiled by | Charles A. Shriner, | State Fish and Game Protector. | By authority of the | Fish and Game Commission | of the State of New Jersey. | Printed for the Commission. | 1897.

1 vol. 8vo, pp. 1-212, 1 l. (note regarding pll.), 31 pll., text-figs. I-VII. Paterson.

An annotated list of New Jersey birds, arranged alphabetically under their English names. Latin nomenclature is purposely omitted. The text consists of simple descriptions, with notes on habits, song, distribution and food, frankly compiled and accredited to Alexander Wilson, Witmer Stone, Frank M. Chapman, D. G. Elliot and others. Stone is thanked for a revision of the work before it went to press. Palmer's "Bird Day in the Schools" (=Circ. 17 U. S. Dept. Agriculture, Biol. Survey) and a chapter on the migration of birds, from "Stone's "The Birds of Eastern Pennsylvania and New Jersey," 1894 (q.v.), are reprinted at the front of the volume. The illustrations are from photographs of mounted birds.

Shufeldt, Robert Wilson.

1887. 1881-1887. | **Contributions to science | and | bibliographical resumé | of the writings | of | R. W. Shufeldt,** M.D., | Captain; Medical Department, U. S. Army, | Member of the Philosophical, the Anthropological, the Biological, [*etc.*, *9 lines.*]. | [By their author.] | Press of L. S. Foster, New York. | 1887.

1 vol. 8vo, pp. 1-20, (orig. wrappers). New York. 1887 (circa Feb. 10).

Title self-explanatory. The list of papers includes those submitted for publication but not issued to date, and also those in course of preparation. The copy at hand is inscribed to Chas. B. Cory under date of Febr. 10, '87.

Shufeldt, Robert Wilson.

1893-96. See Newton, Alfred, A **Dictionary of Birds.**

Shufeldt, Robert Wilson.

1896. See World's Congress on Ornithology, **Papers presented to the—.**

Shufeldt, Robert Wilson.

1909. Education Department Bulletin | Published fortnightly by the University of the State of New York | Entered as second-class matter June 24, 1908, at the Post Office at Albany, N. Y., | under the act of July 16, 1894 | No. 447 Albany, N. Y. May 15, 1909 | New York State Museum | John M. Clarke, Director | Museum bulletin 130 | **Osteology of birds** | by | R. W. Shufeldt | [*Contents, 18 lines, double column.*] | Albany | University of the State of New York | 1909 | M206r-N8-1500.

1 vol. 8vo, cover-tit., 1 l. (letter of transmit.), pp. 5-381+1, 5 ll. (advt.), pll. 1-16, 1-8, 1 and 2, text-figs. 1-65, 1-37, 1-42, 1 and 2. Albany. May 15, 1909.

A very important contribution to the study of avian osteology. The Accipitres, Gallinae and Anseres are treated in detail and a comparison of the Coccyges of the old and new worlds is added, with a bibliography of the author's writings on avian osteology and classification.

Shufeldt, Robert Wilson.

1914. See McIlhenny, Edward A., **The Wild Turkey and its Hunting.**

Shulze, Eliza J.

1879-80. See Jones, Howard E.; and Jones, Mrs. N. E., **Illustrations of the Nests and Eggs of Birds of Ohio,** 1879-86.

Sibree, James.

1915. A naturalist | in Madagascar | A Record of Observation Experiences and | Impressions made during a period of over Fifty Years' | Intimate Association with the Natives and Study of the | Animal & Vegetable Life of the Island | by | James Sibree,

F.R.G.S. | Membre de l'Academie Malgache | Author of "The Great African Island," "Madagascar Ornithology," | &c., &c., &c. | With 52 illustrations & 3 maps | London | Seeley, Service & Co. Limited | 38 Great Russell Street | 1915.

1 vol. 8vo, pp. 1-320, 1-16 (advt.), 39 pll. (on 37 ll.), 1 map (fold.; col.), 6 text-figs. London.

Narrative and description of the author's experiences and impressions in Madagascar, including many observations on natural history, much of which is ornithological. None of the illustrations relate to birds.

Siebold, Philipp Franz von. (Temminck, Coenraad Jacob; Schlegel, Hermann.)

1844-50. > Fauna Japonica | sive | Descriptio animalium, quae in itinere per Japoniam, jussu et auspiciis | superiorum, qui summum in India Batava Imperium tenent, | suscepto, annis 1823-1830 collegit, notis, | observationibus et adumbrationibus illustravit | Ph. Fr. de Siebold. | Conjunctis studiis | C. J. Temminck et H. Schlegel | pro vertebratis | atque | W. de Haan | pro invertebratis | elaborata | regis auspiciis edita. | Lugduni Batavorum. | 1850. | Apud Arnz et Socios. [*Entire page embellished with designs.*].

1 vol. medium folio (11½x15), illustr. tit., pp. 1-141, pll. I-LXXXIX, IB, VB, VIB, VIIB, IXB, XVIIB-E, XXB and C, XXIB-D, XXXIB and C, XXXVIIIB, XXXIXB, LIVB, LVIB, LIXB, LXB-D, LXXVIIIB, LXXXIIB and C, LXXXIIIB, LXXXIVB, (Suppl.) A and B (=120 pll.; col.; by Wolf, ?and others). Leyden.

Descriptions of Japanese birds, new and otherwise, based on collections of Siebold and other visitors to Japan whose specimens were deposited in the London Museum. Some of the new species were based on Japanese drawings, without specimens at hand. No authorities are given for most of the names used, nor is there any indication of which of the names are new. The ornithological text is entirely by Temminck and Schlegel who, alone, are to be quoted in this respect. Plates I-XX are by Wolf; the remainder are unsigned. The work, as collated, consists of the volume on birds only; the entire set is more comprehensive. The ornithological portion was issued in 12 parts, the dates and contents of which are given by Sherborn and Jentink (Proc. Zool. Soc. London, 1895, p. 149) as follows. Part **I**, pp. 1-28, 1844; **II** and **III**, pp. 29-60, 1847; **IV-VIII**, pp. 61-100, 1848; **IX-XI**, pp. 101-124, 1849; **XII**, pp. 125-142, 1850. This work and Schlegel's "Kritische Übersicht der Europäischen Vögel," 1844 (q.v.), appear to be rivals for the honor of constituting the earliest work in which trinomial nomenclature is used in the modern conception for geographic races of species.

Simon, Eugène.

1921. Histoire naturelle | des | Trochilidæ | (Synopsis et Catalogue) | par | Eugène Simon | Correspondant de l'Institut [*etc.*, *3 lines.*] | Paris | Encyclopédie Roret, L. Mulo, Libraire-Éditeur | 12, Rue Hautefeuille, 12 | 1921.

1 vol. imperial 8vo, pp. I-VI, 1-416. Paris. 1921 (before Fcbr. 22)[1].

A very important contribution to the study of the hummingbirds. The work is in two parts. The first of these (pp. 1-244) contains synoptic tables to genera, species and subpsecies in which sufficient detail is used to give complete diagnoses of each. The genera are arranged in 46 groups or series which are given the name of their most characteristic genus and are described, but not arranged, in tabular form. Many new generic and subspecific names are used. The second portion of the volume (pp. 245-407) consists of a catalogue of series, genera, species arïd subspecies, with synonymy, distribution and añ abundance of footnotes. The remainder of the work contains addenda, corrigenda and indices to series and genera. The work is much more comprehensive than the author's "Catalogue des Espèces Actuellement Connues de la Famille des Trochilides" of 1897.

Slater, Henry Horrocks.

1898. See Butler, Arthur G., **British Birds,** 1896-98.

Slater, Henry Horrocks.

1901. Manual | of the | birds of Iceland | by | Henry H. Slater, M.A., F.Z.S. | Member of the British Ornithologists' Union | and Rector of Thornhaugh, Northants | Edinburgh | David Douglas, Castle Street | 1901 | All rights reserved.

1 vol. crown 8vo, pp. I-XXIII+1, 1-150, 1 l. (advt.), 3 pll. (1 by F. W. Frohawk, 2 photos.), 1 map (col.; fold.). Edinburgh.

An annotated list of the species of Icelandic birds, with a bibliography, a copy of the local game-law, and hints for the pronunciation of Icelandic names. The account of each species gives the Latin, English and local names, a discussion of the habits and records of occurrence of each, and field observations by the author.

Smith, Andrew.

1838-49. Illustrations | of the | zoology of South Africa; | consisting chiefly of | figures and descriptions of the objects of natural history | collected during | an expedition into the interior of South Africa, | in the years 1834, 1835, and 1836; fitted out by | "The Cape of Good Hope Association for Exploring Central Africa." | By Andrew Smith, M.D., | Deputy Inspector General of Army Hospitals; |

---

[1] Copy received by C. E. Hellmayr, in Munich, on that date; sent by author immediately upon publication.

Director of the Expedition. | Published under the Authority
of the Lords Commissioners of Her Majesty's Treasury. | Mam-
malia [Aves; Reptilia; Pisces; Invertebratæ]. | London: | Smith,
Elder and Co. 65, Cornhill. | MDCCCXLIX.

5 vols. in 4, royal 4to. Mammalia, tit., pp. I-IV, 63 ll. pll. 1-17 (18
not publ.), 19-36 (37 not publ.), 38-53+8(bis) (52 pll.; 48 col.).
Aves, 132 ll., pll. 1-114 (col.; by Ford). Reptilia, 100 ll., pp. 1-28,
pll. 1-78 (75 col.). Pisces, 42 ll., pll. 1-31 (26 col.). Invertebratae,
2 pr. ll. (tit. and index), pp. 1-75, pll. 1-4 (col.). London.

The title is self-explanatory. The work was issued in 28 parts, the dates and
contents of which are given by Waterhouse in the Proc. Zool. Soc. London, 1880,
pp. 489-91. Ornithological matter occurred in all of these except Pts. III and
XXVIII. Dates, etc. for the birds are as follows. Part I, pll. 1-4, (before Oct.)
1838; II, pll. 5-10, (before Oct.) 1838; IV, pll. 11-17, 1838; V, pll. 18-23, 1839;
VI, pll. 24-26, 1839; VII, pll. 27-32, Sept. 1839; VIII, pll. 33-39, Nov. 1839; IX,
pll. 40-45, Jan. 1840; X, pll. 46-50, March 1840; XI, pll. 51-57, July 1840; XII,
pll. 58-63, Oct. 1840; XIII, pll. 64-66, Jan. 1841; XIV, pll. 67-69, Sept. 1841; XV,
pll. 70 and 71, Febr. 1842; XVI, pll. 72-74, Aug. 1842; XVII, pll. 75-80, Jan. 1843;
XVIII, pll. 81-86, July 1843; XIX, pll. 87-91, Nov. 1843; XX, pll. 92-95, Aug.
1844; XXI, pll. 96-98, Oct. 1844; XXII, pll. 99-102, March 1845; XXIII, 103-105,
Oct. 1845; XXIV, pll. 106 and 107, Dec. 1846; XXV, pll. 108-112, Oct. 1847;
XXVI, pl. 113, Dec. 1847; XXVII, pl. 114, July 1848. Each part contained
matter relating to several volumes, but the numbering of the plates of each
was kept separate and the various matter ultimately was extracted, collected
and bound under the five subjects as collated above. Many new species of
birds are described herein. Others new species secured on the same expedition,
were described previously by Smith in various numbers of "The South African
Quarterly Journal" and in an appendix to the "Report of the Expedition for
Exploring Central Africa from the Cape of Good Hope," etc., 1836. (See
Smith, Andrew, Sir Andrew Smith's miscellaneous ornithological papers, 1880.).

Smith, Andrew. (Verreaux, Jules; Salvin, Osbert, *ed.*)

1880. The Willughby Society. | **Sir Andrew Smith's** | **miscellane-**
ous | **ornithological papers.** | [*Vignette.*] | Edited by |Osbert
Salvin, M.A., F.R.S., Etc. | London: MDCCCLXXX.

1 vol. 4to (size of royal 8vo), pp. I-VI, 1 l. (conts.), pp. 1-127+1
(1-123 with miscellaneous pagination of original papers also given),
2 ll. (advt.). London.

Reprints of 11 papers published in The South African Quarterly Journal and of
the ornithological portion of the author's "Report of the Expedition for Exploring Central Africa," published at Cape Town in 1836. The extracts from the
"Journal" are as follows.
   A Description of the Birds inhabiting the South of Africa. <S. Afr. Quart.
Journ. No. I, Oct. 1829-Jan. 1830 pp. 9-17; l.c., No. II, Jan.-April, 1830, pp.
105-120; l.c., No. III, April-June, 1830, pp. 225-241; l.c., No. IV, July-Sept.,
1830, pp. 380-392.

Contributions to the Natural History of South Africa, &c. <L.c., No. V, Oct. 1831, pp. 5, 11-15.

(Miscellany). <l.c., Second Series, No. 1, Oct.-Dec. 1833, p. 48; (idem, transmitted by Verreaux), l.c., No. 1, p. 80; l.c., No. 2 Jan.-March, 1834, pp. 143-144.

(African Zoology). Part II. Birds. <L.c., No. 3, April-June, 1834, pp. 249-256, 273-288; l.c., No. 4, July-Sept., 1834, pp. 305-320.

These reprints are verbatim from the originals which are extremely scarce, and are published in this form by The Willughby Society (q.v.). All except one are by Andrew Smith. The exception is a single paper by Jules Verreaux which is the only other ornithological article published in The South African Quarterly Journal and which is, therefore, included so as to make the present reprint in effect a copy of all the ornithological matter in that periodical. The editorial preface by the editor gives a sketch of Smith's life and work.

Smith, C. W.; and D'Oyly, C.

1829.   Oriental Ornithology by C. W. Smith Esq. & Sir C. D'Oyly Bart. | C. W. Smith & C. D'Oyly delt. 1st Jan 1829 Behar Lithographic Press.

1 vol. medium folio, illum. tit., 12 pll. (col.). Behar (?).

A series of 12 colored plates of Indian birds, unnamed and without text. The plates are 10x12½, mounted on sheets of the larger size. A printed cover is lettered, "N2 of the Oriental Ornithology, containing 12 subjects."

Smith, Cecil.

1869.   The | birds | of | Somersetshire. | By | Cecil Smith, | of Lydeard House, near Taunton. | London: | John Van Voorst, 1, Paternoster Row. | M.DCCC.LXIX.

1 vol. 12mo, pp. I-X, 1 l. (table of orders and families), pp. 1-643. London.

A "local list" with rather detailed accounts of the various species, including descriptions of the birds and eggs, notes on habits and characteristics and (for which the book is chiefly valuable) considerable information relative to the food of each species.

Smith, Francis.

1872.   The canary | its | varieties, management | and breeding. | With | portraits of the author's own birds. | By | the Rev. Francis Smith, | editor of "Arminius," etc. | **Third edition.** | London: | Groombridge and Sons, | 5 Paternoster Row. | MDCCCLXXII.

1 vol. crown 8vo, pp. I-VIII, 1-146, 12 pll. (col.), 4 text-figs. London.

A popular account of the writer's experience in rearing a number of varieties of canaries, with chapters on diseases, cages, etc.

Smith, H. Hammond.

1911.   See [Grouse], The Grouse in Health and Disease.

Snellman, Joh. F.

1886. See Veth, P. J., **Midden-Sumatra, Natuurlijke Historie, Zoogdieren en Vogels.**

Snouckaert van Schauburg, René Charles E. G. J.

1908. **Avifauna Neerlandica.** | Lijst | der tot dusveere in Nederland in wilden | staat waargenomen Vogelsoorten, | door | Mr. Dr. R. C. E. G. J. Baron Snouckaert van Schauburg, | Voorzitter [*etc.*, *3 lines.*]. | Met 12 Illustratiën, | door | den Heer T. Csörgey, | Adjunktvan het Hongaarsch [*etc.*, *2 lines.*]. | Leeuwarden, | Meijer & Schaafsma. | 1908.

1 vol. superroyal 8vo, pp. 1-160, 1 l. (errata and list of pll.), pll. I-XII (col.; by Csörgey; numbered on guard-sheets). Leeuwarden.

A catalogue of the birds of Holland, enumerating 332 varieties and 14 hybrid forms. Synonymy, bibliographic references, vernacular names and discussions of distribution, breeding ranges, relationships and various local records comprise the text.

Someren, Robert Abraham Logan van; and Someren, Victor Gurnet Logan van.

1911. **Studies | of | birdlife in Uganda** | by | R. A. L. van Someren, M.D., D.P.H., M.B.O.U. | and | V. G. L. van Someren, L.D.S., R.C.S. Ed. | London | John Bale, Sons & Danielsson, Ltd. | Oxford House | 83-91, Great Titchfield Street, Oxford Street, W.| 1911.

1 vol. (portfol.) demy folio, ded. (on inside of cover), pp. 1-22, pll. I-XXV. London.

A series of excellent photographic studies of East African birds, with an account of the habits of each species.

Someren, Victor Gurnet Logan van.

1911. See Someren, Robert A. L.; and Someren, **Studies of Birdlife in Uganda.**

Sonnerat, Pierre.

1776. **Voyage | a la | Nouvelle Guinée,** | Dans lequel on trouve la description des Lieux, des | Observations physiques & morales, & des détails | relatifs à l'Histoire Naturelle dans le Regne Animal | & le Regne Végétal. | Par M. Sonnerat, Sous-Commissaire de la Marine, Naturaliste, | Pensionnaire du Roi, Correspondant de son Cabinet & de l'Académie | Royale des Sciences de Paris, Associé à celles des Sciences, Beaux-Arts & | Belles-Lettres de Lyon. |

Enrichi de cent vingt Figures en taille douce. | [*Design.*] | A Paris, | Chez Ruault, Libraire, rue de la Harpe. | MDCCLXXVI.

1 vol. demy 4to, pp. I-XIJ, 2 ll. (conts.), pp. 1-206, 1 l. (permit to publish), frontisp., pl. II, pll. 3-89, pl. "90 et 91" (combined), pll. 92-120 (by Sonnerat; 6 fold.), many decorations. Paris.

The account of a voyage to New Guinea and the Philippine Islands with the descriptions of many of the plants and animals of these and other places visited en route. The birds are taken up in detail on pp. 51-92, 108-126 and 155-181 and on pll. 20-55, 64-85 and 95-114. Only vernacular names are used but later, 1786-88, the species were discussed and binomial names were applied to them by Scopoli in a paper forming a part of his "Deliciae Florae et Faunae Insubricae " (Cf. reprint by the Willughby Society, 1882.). Many of the localities are erroneous.

Sonnerat, Pierre.

1782. > Voyage | **aux Indes Orientales** | et | a la Chine, | Fait par ordre du Roi, depuis 1774 jusqu'en 1781 : | Dans lequel on traits des Mœurs, de la Religion, des Sciences & des | Arts des Indiens, des Chinois, des Pégouins & des Madégasses; suivi | d'Observations sur le Cap de Bonne-Esperance, les Isles de France & | de Bourbon, les Maldives, Ceylan, Malacca, les Philippines & les | Moluques, & de Recherches sur l'Histoire Naturelle de ces Pays. | Par M. Sonnerat, Commissaire de la Marine, Naturaliste | Pensionnaire du Roi, Correspondant de son Cabinet & de l'Académie | Royale des Sciences de Paris, Membre de celle de Lyon. | **Tome second.** | [*Design.*] | A Paris, |

Chez { l'Auteur, rue Saint-André-des-Arts, vis-à-vis la rue de l' Éperon, maison de M. Ménissier Marchand d'etofes de foies. Froullé, Libraire, pont Notre-Dame, vis-à-vis le quai de Gêvres. Nyon, rue du Jardinet. Barrois, le jeune, rue du Hurepoix.

M. DCC. LXXXII. | Avec approbation et privelege du Roi.

1 vol. (second of two vols.) demy 4to, pp. I-VIIJ, 1-298, pll. 81-140 (by Sonnerat; 5 fold.), numerous decorations. Paris.

The account of the author's observations on the inhabitants of various countries in the Orient, and of the natural history of the same regions. The present volume (II) contains Books 4 and 5, the former devoted to anthropological observations, the latter to natural history, comprising the mammals, birds and plants. The ornithological matter is contained on pp. 148-221 and pll. 94-122. Numerous species are described and figured for the first time, but under French vernacular names only. Later, scientific nomenclature was applied to the species by Sonnerat in a paper forming a part of his "Deliciae Florae et Faunae Insubricae," 1786-88 (C.f. reprint, 1882.).

Sonnini de Manoncour, Charles Nicholas Sigisbert.

1800-05. See Buffon, George L. L., **Histoire Naturelle, Générale et Particuliere.**

Sonnini de Manoncour, Charles Nicholas Sigisbert.

1809. See Azara, Félix de, **Voyage dans l'Amérique Méridionale.**

"Son of the Marshes, A."

1895. See Jordan, Denham.

Sordelli, Ferdinando.

1869? See Bettoni, Eugenio, **Storia Naturale degli Uccelli che Nidificano in Lombardia,** 1865-71.

Souancé, Charles de.

1857-58. **Iconographie | des | perroquets** | non figurés dans les publications de Levaillant et de M. Bourjot Saint-Hilaire | par | M. Charles de Souancé | avec la coopération de S. A. le prince Bonaparte et de M. Émile Blanchard | Histoire naturelle des perroquets | Paris | P. Bertrand, Libraire-Éditeur | Rue de l'Arbre-Sec, 22 | 1857.

1 vol. superroyal folio, 3 pr. ll. (half-tit., tit. and introd.), 48 ll. (unnum.), pll. I-XLVIII[1] (col.; by E. Blanchard and J. Daverne). Paris.

A second supplement to Levaillant's "Hist. Nat. des Perroquets," 1801-05 (q.v.), following the volume by Bourjot Saint-Hilaire,.1837-38 (q.v.) and forming the fourth volume of the series. The work was published in 12 livraisons, dated (by Carus and Engelmann) 1857-58. In the introduction to the "Inconographie," the editor (?) of that work announces a proposed "Histoire Naturelle des Perroquets" in 8vo, to include all the species known to date and treated in the preceding volumes, but this work seems not to have appeared. This proposed work is probably that mentioned by Carus and Engelmann under the "Iconographie" in an ambiguous reference which seems to apply to the latter work but is inconsistent with it as it is known (Cf. Coues, Bull. U. S. Geol. Geog. Surv. Terr. V., p. 738, 1879.). This reference announces a *Hist. Nat.*, 1 vol., 8vo., to be published in 1859 and an *Iconographie*, fol. or 4to, with about 120 pll., to appear in 30 parts, issued monthly.

Souleyet, François Louis Auguste.

1841-52. See Vaillant, Auguste Nicolas, **Voyage autour du Monde sur La Bonite.**

Sousa, Jose Augusto de.

1869. Museu nacional de Lisboa | Secção zoologica | **Catalogo das collecções ornithologicas** | Psittaci - Papagaios. | Accipitres - Aves

---

[1] Plate XLVIII carries a reference to that number in the text, but the figures have been printed over an erasure on the plate. Coues notes the original number as LXXIV.

de Rapina. | Junho de 1869 | [*Blazon.*] | Lisboa | Imprensa Nacional | 1869.

1 vol. royal 8vo, pp. 1-62, (orig. wrapper). Lisbon. June 1869.

A catalogue of the Parrots and Birds of Prey in the National Museum of Lisbon. Coues lists this paper under authorship of Barboza du Bocage who was the Director of the Museum but who was not the author of the catalogue.

Southwell, Thomas.

1890. See Stevenson, Henry; and Southwell, **The Birds of Norfolk,** 1866-90.

Southwell, Thomas.

1896. Memoir | **of** | **the late John Henry Gurney.** | By | Thomas Southwell, F.Z.S. | [Reprinted, with some Revisions, from the 'Transactions of the | Norfolk and Norwich Naturalists' Society,' vol. V. p. 156.] | London: | Taylor and Francis, Red Lion Court, Fleet Street. | 1896. [*Cover-tit.*]

1 vol. (pamphlet, size of post 8vo), cover-tit., pp. 1-12. London.

Sparrman, Andreas.

1786-89. Museum | **Carlsonianum,** | In quo | Novas et Selectas Aves, | Coloribus ad vivum brevique descriptione illustratas, | Suasu et sumtibus Generosissimi Possessoris, | Exhibet | Andreas Sparrman, | M.D. & Profess. Reg. Acad. Scient. Stockholmens. Musei Praefect. Ejusd. Acad. ut et | Societ. Physiograph. Lund. Scient. ac Litt. Gothoburg. Hess. Homburg. Membr. | Fasciculus I [-IV]. | Holmiæ, | Ex Typographia Regia, MDCCLXXXVI [MDCCLXXXVII; MDCCLXXXVIII; MDCCLXXXIX].

1 vol. (4 fascs.) demy folio. Fasc. I, 28 ll., pll. 1-25 (col.). Fasc. II, 28 ll., pll. 26-50 (col.). Fasc. III, 28 ll., pll. 51-75 (col.). Fasc. IV, 28 ll., pll. 76-100 (col.). Stockolm.

Descriptions, with Latin binomials, of new or otherwise interesting species of birds contained in the museum of Gustavus Carlson. Many of the figures and descriptions are unrecognizable but the collection (more or less injured by moths) came eventually, by several routes, to the Rijksmuseum of Sweden where it was studied by Carl. J. Sundevall. In the first part of a "Kritisk Framställning of Fogelarterna uti Äldre Ornithologiska Arbeten" published in the Kon. Vet. Akad. Handl., B. 2, No. 3, 1857, Sundevall identified most of Sparrman's species, listing 9 forms as dubious and 7 as entirely unrecognizable due to the imperfect condition of the skins and to other causes. The "Museum Carlsonianum" is a very rare work and is very important in view of the new species contained therein.

Spencer, Clementina Sinclair.

1918. See Bailey, Bert Heald, Iowa Geological Survey, **The Raptorial Birds of Iowa.**

Spix, Johannes Baptist von.

1811. Geschichte und Beurtheilung | aller Systeme | in der | Zoologie | nach ihrer | Entwicklungsfolge | von Aristoteles | bis | auf die gegenwärtige Zeit, | von | Johannes Spix, | der Weltweisheit und Arzneikunde Doktor [*etc.*, *4 lines.*]. | Nürnberg, | in der Schrag'schen Buchhandlung. | 1811.

1 vol. demy 8vo, pp. I-XXVI, 1-710. Nuremberg.

The history of the development of zoological classification from Aristotle until date. Ornithology occupies pp. 250-312.

Spix, Johannes Baptist von.

1824-25. Avium | species novae, | quas | in itinere per Brasiliam annis MDCCCXVII-MDCCCXX | jussu et auspiciis | Maximiliani Josephi I. | Bavariae Regis | suscepto | collegit et descripsit | Dr. J. B. de Spix, | Ordinis Regii Coronae Bavaricae civilis Eques [*etc.*, *4 lines.*]. | Tabulae XCI [CXVIII] a M. Schmidt [Schmid] Monacensi depictae [sculptae]. [| Tomus II.] | Monachii [*Period added.*] | Typis Franc. Seraph. Hübschmanni. | MDCCCXXIV [MDCCCXXV].

2 vols. imperial 4to. Vol. I, 5 pr. ll. (tit., ded., list of subscrs. and index), pp. 1-90+47(bis; reverse blank; between pp. 48 and 49), pll. I-LXXV, "LXXVI-LXXVII" (combined), LXXVIII-XCI, Ia-Id, IIIa, IVa, VIIIa-VIIIc, IXa, Xa, XIVa, XXXIIa and XXXVIIIa (=104 pll., col.; by M. Schmidt). Vol. II, 3 pr. ll. (tit. and index), pp. 1-85, pll. I-CIX, VIIIa, XXXIa, LXIIa, LXVIIa, LXXVa, LXXVIa-LXXVIc and LXXVIIIa (=118 pll., col.). Munich.

Descriptions of the birds secured by the author during his expedition with von Martius to Brazil in the years 1817-1820; with colored plates of the new species, of which there are a great number. The plates are not always recognizable and are said to vary in coloration in different copies. The descriptions are not sufficiently determinative in every case, but the original specimens (at least many of them) are still in existence and have been studied carefully by Dr. C. E. Hellmayr. The latter author's "Revision der Spix'schen Typen brasilianischer Vögel," published in the Abhandl. der K. Bayer. Akad. Wiss., II Kl., XXII Bd., III Abt., pp. 563-726, pll. I and II, May 20, 1906, gives a full account of the results of these studies. There appears to be a second, revised, edition of Spix edited by von Martius and published in 1840; about this I can find little information [Cf. Cat. Libr. Brit. Mus. (Nat. Hist.).].

Spratt, (Mrs.) G.

1837. The | language of birds | comprising | poetic and prose illustrations | of the | most favourite cage birds. | With twelve highly-coloured plates. | By Mrs. G. Spratt. | [*Quot., 6 lines.*]. | London | Saunders and Otley, Conduit Street. | M DCGC XXXVII.

1 vol. 12mo, 2 pr. ll. (half-tit. and tit.), pp. III-VII+1, 1-342, 1-12 (advt.), pll. 1-12 (col.). London.

A series of brief accounts of various birds, accompanied by extensive poetical quotations relating to the birds in question. The hand-colored illustrations are picturesque rather than accurate portraits of the species they represent.

Stanley, Edward.

1880. A familiar history of | birds. | By the late | Edward Stanley, D.D., F.R.S. | Lord Bishop of Norwich. | [*Vignette.*] | **New edition.** | London: | Longmans, Green, and Co. | 1880.

1 vol. crown 8vo, 3 pr. ll. (half-tit., tit., publishers' note), pp. IX-XII, 1-420, frontisp., 157 text-figs. London.

A general account of bird-life in its various aspects, presenting facts and anecdotes concerning numerous species selected from the entire class, with chapters on classification, structure, flight, etc. The classification is obsolete and many of the statements presented as facts are now known to be inaccurate, but the little book has some value as a juvenile work. Originally published in 1835, the work passed through a number of later editions, of which the present appears to be the 6th.

Stark, Arthur Cowell; and Sclater, William Lutley.

1900-06. The | fauna of South Africa | [*Blazon.*] | edited by | W. L. Sclater, M.A., F.Z.S. | Director of the South African Museum, Cape Town. > The | birds of South Africa | by [commenced by (*Vols. III and IV.*)] | Arthur C. Stark, M.B. [Arthur Stark, M.B. (*Vols. III and IV.*)] [| Completed by W. L. Sclater, M.A., F.Z.S. | Director of the South African Museum, Cape Town (*Vol. II.*)] | Vol. I [-IV]. [| Picarians, parrots, owls and hawks (*Vol. III.*); Game-birds, shore-birds and sea-birds (*Vol. IV.*)] | With a map and illustrations [With a portrait, map and illustrations (*Vol. II.*); With 141 illustrations (*Vol. III.*); With 163 illustrations (*Vol. IV.*)] [| By | W. L. Sclater, M.A., F.Z.S. | Director of the South African Museum, Cape Town (*Vols. III and IV.*)] | London | R. H. Porter | 7, Princes Street, Cavendish Square, W. | 1900 [1901; 1903; 1906].

4 vols. 8vo. Vol. I, pp. I-XXX, 1-322, 1 insert-slip (regarding non-publication of map in Vol. I), 113 text-figs. Vol. II, pp. I-XIV, 1-323, 2 ll. (advt.), frontisp. (portr), 1 map (col.; fold.), figs. 1-83.

Vol. III, pp. I-XVII+1, 1-416, figs. 1-141. Vol. IV, pp. I-XVII+1, 1-545, figs. 1-163. London.

A complete account of the birds of Africa south of the Zambesi and Cunéné rivers. Each species is described, synonymy and distribution are given, and there are copious but concise notes on general habits, food, song and nidification. Tables to families, genera and species are given throughout and a table to the orders is added in Vol. III, pp. VI-VIII. A good bibliography is given in Vol. I. Vols. I and II contain the Passerine forms; the other volumes contain the groups mentioned on their titles. Volume I was written entirely by Stark, who died shortly before its publication. Vol. II was edited by Sclater from Stark's manuscript. Vols. III and IV were written entirely by Sclater with the assistance of Stark's notes. Of the remainder of the series belonging under the general title of "The Fauna of South Africa," only the volumes on the Mammalia, by Sclater, were ever published (1900-01). A "Check-List of the Birds of South Africa," comprising a list of the species contained in the present work, together with such additions as were necessary to bring the work to date, was published in the Annals of the South African Museum, III, Pt. 8, 1905.

Stearns, Winfred A.; and Coues, Elliott.

1881-83. New England Bird Life | being a | manual | of | New England ornithology | revised and edited from the manuscript of | Winfred A. Stearns | Member of the Nuttall Ornithological Club etc. | by | Dr. Elliott Coues U. S. A. [Elliott Coues] | Member of the Academy etc. | Part I.-Oscines [Part II. | Non-oscine Passeres, birds of prey, | game and water birds.] | Boston | Lee and Shepard publishers | New York Charles T. Dillingham | 1881 [1883].

2 vols. post 8vo. Vol. I, 2 pr. ll. (tit. and ded.), pp. 3-324, text-figs. 1-56. Vol. II, 1 l. (advt.), pp. 1-409+1, 1 l. (advt.), text-figs. 1-88. Boston.

According to the editor's preface, the "plan of the work includes brief descriptions of the birds themselves........; the local distribution, migration, and relative abundance of every species; together with as much general information respecting their habits as can conveniently be brought within the compass of a hand-book of New England Ornithology." The original manuscript was written by Stearns, but was revised and partially rewritten by Coues who assumed responsibility for the accurateness and completeness of the work. The text-figures are all taken from Coues's Key, 1st ed., 1872 (q.v.).

Steere, Joseph Beal.

**1890. A list | of the | Birds and Mammals | collected by the |
Steere Expedition to the | Philippines, | With Localities, and with
Brief Preliminary Descriptions of | Supposed New Species, | By
J. B. Steere, Ph. D., | Professor of Zoölogy in the University of**

Michigan. | Ann Arbor, Mich.: | The Courier Office, printers. | July 14, 1890.

1 vol. 8vo, pp. 1-30. Ann Arbor, July 14, 1890.

An annotated list of the 367 species of birds and 22 identified species of mammals collected in 1887-88 by the expedition, giving the insular distribution of each. Descriptions are given of 52 new species of birds and of 3 new mammals.

Stephens, James Francis.

1815-26. See Shaw, George; and Stephens, **General Zoology, Birds,** 1812-26.

Sterland, W. J.

1869. The birds | of | Sherwood Forest. | With notes on their habits, nesting, | migrations, &c. | Being a contribution to the natural history of the county. | By | W. J. Sterland. | Wtih (*sic*) four illustrations by the author. | [*Monogram.*] | London: | L. Reeve & Co., 5, Henrietta Street, Covent Garden. | 1869.

1 vol. crown 8vo, pp. I-IX+1, 1 l.(conts.), pp. 1-244, 1-24 (advt.), pll. I-IV (3 col.; by the author). London.

A series of observations on bird-life, originally published in "The Field" in 1865-67. A clipping from that periodical, dated Nov. 13, 1880, by Sterland, relating to the Tufted Duck, is pasted on p. 220.

Stevenson, Henry; and Southwell, Thomas.

1866-90. The | birds of Norfolk, | with | remarks on their habits, migration, | and local distribution: | by | Henry Stevenson, F.L.S., [*No comma (Vol. III.*).] | Member of the British Ornithologists' Union. [| Continued by | Thomas Southwell, F.Z.S. | Member of the British Ornithologists' Union (*Vol. III, only.*)] | In two [three (*Vols. II and III.*)] volumes. | Vol. I [II; III]. | [*Quot., 3 lines (Vol. I); 5 lines (Vol. II.); 7 lines (Vol. III.*).].| London: | John Van Voorst, 1, Paternoster Row, [Gurney and Jackson, 1, Paternoster Row | (Successors to Mr. VanVoorst). (*Vol. III.*)] | Norwich: | Matchett and Stevenson [Stevenson and Co. (*Vol. II.*); Norfolk Chronicle Co., Limited (*Vol. III.*)]. | 1866 [1870; 1890].

3 vols. post 8vo. Vol. I, pp. I-LXXII, 1-445, 1 insert-slip (errata), frontisp. (monochr.) and pl. II (col.; by J. Wolf). Vol. II, pp. I-X, 1-449, 1 insert-slip (errata), frontisp. (col.; by J. Smit), 2 pll. (monochr.). Vol. III, pp. I-XIII+1, 1-432, pll. I-V (1 monochr.; 1 portr.; 3 col., by J. Wolf and J. Smit). London and Norwich.

An excellent "local" ornithology in which the author presents a mass of accurate information relative to the birds of the County of Norfolk, England, secured from a variety of sources and personally verified where possible. Owing to the painstaking manner in which the work was prepared, it progressed slowly and the author died before it was completed. His portion of the book terminates on p. 160 of Vol. III, at which point the labor was assumed by Southwell who completed the volume and work, quoting largely from Stevenson's notes.

Stone, Witmer.

1894. The | birds of eastern Pennsylvania | and New Jersey | with introductory chapters on | geographical distribution -and migration | prepared under the direction of the | Delaware Valley Ornithological Club | by | Witmer Stone | Conservator Ornithological Section Academy of Natural Sciences of Philadelphia | Philadelphia | Delaware Valley Ornithological Club | 1894.

1 vol. royal 8vo, pp. I-VII+1, 1-185, frontisp., 2 maps (1 col. and fold.), figs. 1 and 2. Philadelphia.

An annotated list of species, giving the breeding range and distribution of each and the evidences of local occurrence of the rarer forms. A bibliography is appended. This main body of the text forms Part II of the work. Part I (to p. 32) contains general remarks on geographical distribution and migration and a discussion of the physical features of the region under consideration.

Stone, Witmer.

1909. See Morse, Silas R., **Annual Report of the New Jersey State Museum,** including a report of the birds of New Jersey.

Stone, Witmer.

1910. See American Ornithologists' Union, **Check-list of North American Birds, Third Edition.**

Stonham, Charles. (Mullens, William Herbert.)

1906-11. The | birds of the | British Islands | by | Charles Stonham | C.M.G., [etc., 4 lines.]. | Illustrated by Lilian M. Medland [Illustrated by Lilian M. Medland, F.Z.S. (*Vols. III-V.*)] | Vol. I [-V] | London | E. Grant Richards [Grant Richards (*Vol. III.*); Grant Richards Ltd. (*Vols. IV and V.*)] | 7 Carlton Street, S.W. | 1906 [1907; 1908; 1910; 1911].

5 vols. royal 4to. Vol. I, pp. I-VII+1, 1-151+1, 1 insert-slip (errata, p. 112), 64 printed guard-sheets, pll. I-LXIV, 2 maps (col.; fold.), 2 text-figs. (full-p.). Vol. II, pp. I-VII+1, 153-323+1, 60 guard-sheets, pll. LXV-CXXIV. Vol. III, pp. I-VII+1, 325-514, 73 guard-sheets, pll. CXXV-CXCVII. Vol. IV, pp. I-VII+1, 515-704, 70 guard-sheets, pll. CXCVIII-CCLXVII. Vol. V, pp. I-VIII, 707-976, 51 guard-sheets, pll. CCLXVIII-CCCXVIII. London.

A popular account of British birds, with common and technical names and their etymology, discussions of habits and characteristics, and descriptions of each species, the latter arranged in convenient, tabular form. The plates, many of which are life-sized, are of variable quality; some of them are excellent but others are not so pleasing. At the end of the work (Vol. V, pp. 941-964) there is a good bibliography compiled by W. H. Mullens. A glossary of vernacular names, technical and English indices, and a list of subscribers are added. The work appeared in 20 parts of about 50 pages and 16 or 17 plates each, as follows (according to Mullens and Swann). I, May 1906; II, Sept. 1906; III, Oct. 1906; IV, Dec. 1906; V, March 1907; VI, June 1907; VII, Sept. 1907; VIII, Dec. 1907; IX, March 1908; X, April 1908; XI, Aug. 1908; XII, Nov. 1908; XIII, March 1909; XIV, May 1909; XV, Sept. 1909; XVI, March 1910; XVII, Oct. 1910; XVIII, March 1911; XIX and XX, July 1911.

Storer, Tracy Irwin.

1918. See Grinnell, Joseph; Bryant; and Storer, **The Game Birds of California.**

Storer, Tracy Irwin.

1924. See Grinnell, Joseph; and Storer, **Animal Life in the Yosemite.**

Strecker, John K. Jr.

1912. Baylor University Bulletin | Volume XV, Number 1 | **The Birds of Texas** | An Annotated Check-List | By John K. Strecker Jr. | Curator Baylor University Museum | [*Seal.*] | Founded in 1845 at Independence | under the Republic of Texas | January, 1912 | Published by the University | Entered as second class matter at the post office at Waco, Texas.

1 vol. demy 4to, pp. 1-69+1. Waco. Jan. 1912.

An annotated list of species, giving the local distribution of each and occasional details regarding the records of occurrence within the state.

Stresemann, Erwin.

1920. **Avifauna Macedonica** | Die ornithologischen Ergebnisse der | Forschungsreisen, unternommen nach Mazedonien | durch | Prof. Dr. Doflein und Prof. L. Müller-Mainz | in den Jahren 1917 und 1918 | von | Dr. Erwin Stresemann | Mit 6 Tafeln | München 1920 | Verlag von Dultz & Co.

1 vol. 8vo, pp. I-XXIV, 1-270, 1 l. (conts.), pll. I-VI (on 3 ll.). Munich. July 1920.

A detailed account of the birds of Macedonia, based on a collection of about 3258 specimens, representing 168 forms, secured by Professor Müller and others during the German occupation of the country, and deposited in the Munich State Museum. Detailed notes on measurement, plumages, etc. are given in tabular form. Part 2 of the book (pp. 247-256) gives a brief account of the Macedonian species not secured by the expedition. Part 3 (pp. 257-260) supplies addenda. Part 4 (pp. 261-268) gives a check-list of all the species, and Part 5 (pp. 269-270) furnishes the explanation of plates. One new sub-species is described and one other new name used. The remaining new species in the collection appear to have been described, previously, by Stresemann in other publications.

Strickland, Hugh Edwin; and Melville, A. G.

1848. **The | dodo and its kindred; | or the | history, affinities, and osteology | of the | dodo, solitaire, | and | other extinct birds | of the islands Mauritius, Rodriguez, and Bourbon. | By | H. E. Strickland, M.A., F.G.S., F.R.G.S., | President of the Ashmolean Society, &c., | and | A. G. Melville, M.D. Edin., M.R.C.S. | [*Vignette.*] | [*Quot.*, *2 lines.*] | London: | Reeve, Benham, and Reeve, 8, King William Street, Strand. | 1848.

1 vol. folio (10x12½), 5 pr. ll., pp. I-IV, 5-141, 1 insert-slip (errata), pp. 1-12 (advt.), pll. I-XV, III* and IV* (2 col., 2 monochr., 1 fold.), 10 text-figs. London.

A detailed account of the subject matter as set forth in the title, with transcriptions and translations from various old works relating to the extinct avifauna of the three islands in question. The work is discussed in the Revue Zoologique for Oct. 1848, p. 306.

Strickland, Hugh Edwin. (Strickland, *Mrs.* H. E.; Jardine, William.)

1855. **Ornithological synonyms.** | By the late | Hugh Edwin Strickland, M.A., | F.R.S., F.R.G.S., F.G.S., | Deputy Reader in Geology in the University of Oxford, etc. | Edited by | Mrs. Hugh E. Strickland | and | Sir W. Jardine, Bart., F.R.S.E., L.S., &c. | Vol. I. | Accipitres. | London: | John Van Voorst, Paternoster Row. | MDCCCLV.

1 vol. 8vo, pp. I-XLVI, 1-222, 2 ll. insert (advt.). London.

A working list of 373 species of birds of prey, giving bibliographic references to the accepted name and the various synonyms of each species. A list of the works quoted in the text is given after the introduction. The book is posthumous and was prepared from Strickland's manuscript by his wife and father-in-law who planned to publish the remaining portions of the work at a later date,— a project never realized although two sheets of the second volume were printed in 1860 or later (Cf. Mathews, Austral Avian Record, **5**, No. 1, pp. 18-19, 1922.). The introduction, dated Sept. 1, 1855, gives a reference to G. R. Gray's "A List" (=Catalogue) "of the Genera and Subgenera of Birds," 1855 (q.v.), which is quoted as already published, but as that work is also of uncertain date, the reference does not aid materially in fixing the date of the present volume.

Strickland, Mrs. Hugh Edwin.

1855. See Strickland, H. E., **Ornithological Synonyms.**

Studer, Jacob Henry.

1874-78. See Jasper, Theodore, **Studer's Popular Ornithology.**
1881. Idem.

Studer, Theophil; and Fatio, Victor. (Burg, Gustav von.)
1889 (-1923)-date. Katalog | der | Schweizerischen Vögel [| von |
Dr. Th. Studer und Dr. V. Fatio (*Pts. V-XII.*)¹] bearbeitet | im
Auftrag des Eidg. Departements für Industrie und Landwirtschaft
[im Auftrag des Eidg. Departements des Innern (*Pts. III-XII.*)] |
(Abtheilung Forstwesen) [(Inspektion für Forstwesen, Jagd und
Fischerei) (*Pts. VII-XII.*)] | von | Dr. Th. Studer und Dr. V.
Fatio [G. von Burg (*Pts. V-XII.*)] | unter Mitwirkung zahl-
reicher Beobachter in verschiedenen [allen (*Pts. V-XII.*)] Kan-
tonen. [*Period omitted* (*Pts. VI and XI.*).] [| Erscheint in jähr-
lichen Lieferungen. (*Pts. VII-XII.*)] | I [III; IV; V]. Lieferung.
[*Semicolon* (*Pts. III-V.*); VI. Lieferung: Calamoherpinæ; VII.
und VIII. Lieferung: Sylviidae, Turdidae, Monticolidae. ; IX.
Lieferung: Ruticillae. ; X. Lieferung: Saxicolinæ, Motacillidæ. ;
XI. Lieferung: Pieper und Lerchen. ; XII. Lieferung: Emberi-
zinae.] | Tagraubvögel [Insessores, Coraces, Scansores, Captores
part (*Pt. III.*); Captores part. fin. (Accentoridae, Troglodytidae,
Cinclidae, | Paridae), Cantores part (*Pt. IV.*) ; Captores (Paridae
fin.). Cantores (Sylvidae part.) (*Pt. V.*); *line omitted* (*Pts. VI-
XII.*).]. | Mit 7 Kartenbeilagen [Mit 2 Kartenbeilagen (*Pt.
III.*); Bearbeitet von Gustav von Burg (*Pt. IV.*); Mit einer far-
bigen Karte (*Pt. IX.*); *line omitted* (*Pts. V-VIII and X-XII.*).]. |
Bern und Genf. [*Period omitted* (*Pts. III-VI.*).] | 1889 [(*1894*);
1901; 1907; 1908; 1909; 1911; 1912; 1913; 1914; 1915]. [*Period
omitted* (*Pts. III-VI.*).].
   > **Die Vögel der Schweiz** | ("Katalog der Schweizerischen
Vögel | von Studer und Fatio") | Von. G. von Burg | unter
Mitwirkung zahlreicher Beobachter in allen Kantonen. | Erscheint
in Lieferungen. [*Period omitted* (*Pt. XIV.*).] | XIII. Lieferung:
Montifringillinae, Passerinae [XIV. Lieferung: Fringillinae, Cocco-
thraustinae, Pyrrhulinae]. | Bern und Genf. | 1918 [1923].
14 pts. in 13 vols., royal 8vo. Pt. I, pp. 1-100, index on inside back
   cover, maps I-VII (col., fold.). Pt. II, pp. 101-192, 1 l. (index),
   maps VIII-XI (col.). Pt. III, pp. I-VIII, 193-418, maps XII-XIII
   (col.). Pt. IV, pp. I-XV+1, 1 insert-slip, pp. 419-601+1, 1 l.
   (index), maps XIV-XV (col.). Pt. V, pp. I-IV, 603-741+1, 1 l.

¹The second Lieferung has no title-page.

(index), map XVI (col.). Pt. VI, pp. I-VII+1, 743-886. Pt. VII
and VIII, pp. I-X, 887-1286, maps XVII-XIX (col.). Pt. IX,
2 pr. ll. (tit. and pref.), pp. 1287-1584, map XX (col.). Pt. X,
pp. I-X, 1585-1800. Pt. XI, pp. I-VI, 1801-2068, map XXI (col.).
Pt. XII, pp. I-VIII, 2069-2306. Pt. XIII, pp. I-XXV+1, 2307-
2512. Pt. XIV, 2 pr. ll. (tit. and pref.), pp. 2513-2710. Bern and
Geneva.

A detailed catalogue of Swiss birds, discussing each species in its place from a
great variety of aspects. It was begun by Studer and Fatio but taken over
by Burg with the 4th part in 1907 and continued by him to date. It is not
yet complete. An edition in French has been issued more or less synchronously
under the title of "Catalogue des Oiseaux de la Suisse," recently changed to
"Les Oiseaux de la Suisse" to conform with the corresponding alteration in the
title of the German edition, as transcribed above.

Sturm, Friedrich.

1860. See Naumann, Johann Friedrich, Johann Andreas Naumann's
mehrerer gelehrten Gesellschaften Mitgliede, **Naturgeschichte der
Vögel Deutschlands,** 1822-1860.

Sturm, Johann Heinrich Christian Friedrich.

1841-47. See Gould, John, **J. Gould's Monographie der Ramphastiden.**

Sturm, Johann Wilhelm.

1841-47. See Gould, John, **J. Gould's Monographie der Ramphastiden.**

Sturtevant, Edward.

1899. See Howe, Reginald Heber; and Sturtevant, **The Birds of
Rhode Island.**

1903. Idem, A **Supplement to The Birds of Rhode Island.**
The Birds of Rhode Island.

Suchetet, André.

1897. **Des | hybrides | a | l'état sauvage |** Règne animal | Premier
volume | **(Classe des Oiseaux) |** par | André Suchetet |[*Quot.,
3 lines.*] | Lille | Imprimerie typographique et lithographique Le
Bigot frères | 68, rue Nationale, et 25, rue Nicolas-Leblanc. | 1896.
1 vol. royal 8vo, pp. I-CLII, 3-1001+1, (original wrapper). Paris.

A detailed treatise on the known hybrids among wild birds. The account is
rearranged from six previous papers by the author, four of which were published in the Mémoires de la Société Zoologique de France in 1890-1893 and

two in book form in 1895-96. The work in its present form appears to be the first volume of a projected treatise intended to include other groups besides birds; Allen (Auk, **12**, p. 384, 1895), in reviewing Pt. 5 of the original papers, notes that the following section is planned to deal with insects and fishes, but I can find no references to the publication of later volumes. The date, 1897, is from the original wrapper which is bound with the present copy.

Sue, P.

1808.   > **Tables** | **analytiques et raisonnées** | des | matières et des auteurs, | **Pour la nouvelle Edition de l'Histoire** | **Naturelle de Buffon,** | rédigée par C. S. Sonnini, | Membre de plusieurs Sociétés savantes. | Ouvrage formant, dans cent vingt-quatre volumes in-8 o. | un Cours Complet d'Histoire Naturelle; les premiers, au | nombre de soixante-quatre, sont consacrés à l'histoire de | la théorie de la Terre, des Minéraux, de l'Homme, des Animaux, des Quadrupèdes et des Oiseaux; les autres sont | partagés ainsi qu'il suit: quatorze pour l'histoire des | Poissons, en y comprenant celle des Cétacées ; six pour celle des Mollusques; huit pour celle des Reptiles; qua- | torze pour celle des Insectes; dix-huit pour celle des Plantes. | Par P. Sue, | Professeur de Medécine légale, à l'ecole de Médecine | de Paris, trésorier de la même Ecole, Membre de | plusieurs Sociétés savantes, nationales et étrangères. | Tome I [-III]. | A.-G. [H.-R. (*Vol. II.*); S.-Z. (*Vol. III.*)] | A Paris,|de l'imprimerie de F. Dufart | 1808.

3 vols. crown 8vo. Vol. I, pp. I-XII, 1-456. Vol. II, 2 pr. ll., pp. 1-464. Vol. III, 2 pr. ll., pp. 1-355+1+1 l. Paris.

A detailed index to the Sonnini edition of Buffon's "Histoire Naturelle," 1800-1805 (q.v.), of which it may be considered to form a part. The volumes are numbered separately, as are all the volumes of the "Suites à Buffon," consisting of the various subjects not included in the original edition of Buffon (1749-1804).

Sulphur, Zoology of the Voyage of. Birds.

1843-44.   See Hinds, Richard Brinsley.

Sundevall, Carl Jacob; and Kinberg, Johan Gustav Hjalmar.

1856-87(?)   **Svenska foglarna** | med text | af | Professor Carl J. Sundevall, | tecknade och lithographierade | af | Peter Åkerlund. | Stockholm, | Tryckt hos J. & A. Riis, 1856.

> Svenska foglarna | av | Professor Carl J. Sundevall | fort-sättning | av | Professor J. G. H. Kinberg | Andra [Tredje; *tit.-p. of Fjerde Bandet missing.*] Bandet | 1883 [*1885*] | Stockholm | F. & G. Beijer | [*Instructions to binder, 1 l.*].

4 vols. in 3. folio and 4to (12½ x 9¼, long) Vol. I, 4 pr. ll. (lith. tit., tit., ded. and pref.), pp. 1-352, 1 l. (expl. of pll.), pll. I-LXXXIV (col.). Vol. II, tit., pp. 363-756. Vol. III, tit., pp. 757-1188. Vol. IV (tit. missing), pp. 1189-1570. Stockholm.

A general descriptive work on the birds of Sweden. Vol. I, with 84 colored lithographs, was published by Sundevall; the remainder of the book, by Kinberg, after Sundevall's death. Vol. I appeared in 22 parts for which the following dates are available from the Journal für Ornithologie and the Zoological Record. Pt. I, pp. 1-8, pll. I-IV, reviewed in Journ. für Orn., July, 1857; II, pp. 9-16, pll. V-VIII, ev. Jan. 1858; III, pp. 17-28, pll. IX, X, XV, XVI, rev. Sept. 1858; IV, pp. 29-32, pll. XI-XIV, rev. July 1859; V, pp. 33-44, pll. XVII, XX, XXII, XXIII, rev. July 1859; VI, pp. 45-52, pll. XXI, XXIV-XXVI, rev. Jan. 1860; VII, pp. 53-60, pll. XVII-XXX, rev. Jan. 1860; VIII, pp. 61-68, pll. XVIII, XIX, XXXI, XXXII, Jan. 1861; IX, pp. 69-84, publ. Aug. 1861; X-XI, pp. 85-124, pll. XXXIII, XXXIV, XXXIX, XL, XLV-XLVII, L, publ. Nov. 1861 and May 1862; XII-XIII, pp. 125-144, pll. XLI, XLII, XLVIII, XLIX, XXXVII, XXXVIII, LI, LII, rev. Jan. 1864; XIV-XV, pp. 145-176, pll. LIII-LV, publ. 1864; XVI-XVII, pp. 177-208, pll. LXI-LXVIII, publ. 1865; XVIII, pp. 209-224, pll. LXIX-LXXI, LXXIX, publ. 1866; XIX, pp. 225-240, pll. LXXII, LXXIII, LXXVII, LXXVIII, rev. July 1867; XX, pp. 241-264, pll. LXXIV-LXXVI, LXXX, publ. 1869; XXI, pp. 265-284, pll. LXXXI-LXXXIV, rev. Jan. 1870; XXII, pp. 285-352, publ. 1871.

Of the remainder of the work, I can find no complete data. Pp. 353-520 are dated (in the signature) 1881; 521-704, 1881-2; 705-916, 1881-3; 917-1060, 1881-4; 1061-1220, 1881-5; 1221-1570, 1881-6. The title-page of Vol. II is dated 1883 but was printed in 1886; that of Vol. III is dated 1885 and was printed that same year; the title-page for the fourth volume is missing. The Zoological Record lists Parts XXIII-XXVIII, pp. 353-755, under date of 1883, and Pts. XXXVI-XL, pp. 1165-1570, under date of 1887. The title-pages of II and III were, evidently, issued out of place, since they are inserts and contain directions to the binder for their insertion. The present copy has pages 757-972 bound in Vol. II, the title-page of Vol. II at p. 973, and all of Vol. IV in Vol. III.

Sundevall, Carl Jacob.

1863. Die | Thierarten des Aristoteles | von den Klassen | der Säugethiere, Vögel, Reptilien | und Insekten | von | Carl J. Sundevall | Custos des Zool. Museums in Stockholm. | Übersetzung | aus dem Schwedischen. | Stockholm, 1863. | Bei Samson & Wallin.

1 vol. post 8vo, pp. 1-242. Stockholm. 1863 (circa March).

A translation, into German, of the author's "Ett försök att bestämma de af Aristoteles omtalade Djurarterna," published in the Kongl. Svenska Vetenskaps-Akad. Handl., Bd. IV, No. 2, 1862,—a study of the natural history in the writings of Aristotle. A prefatory chapter gives a sketch of Aristotle's life and a short review of those of his books which are cited in the following pages. The birds are treated on pp. 92-173. Most of Aristotle's birds are at least partially recognized in this work; a few remain unidentified. A preface (on the reverse of the title-page), signed by the publishers, is dated March 1863.

Sundevall, Carl Jacob.

1866. Conspectus avium Picinarum | edidit | Carolus J. Sundevall | Custos Musei Zool. Stockholmiensis. | Stockholmiæ 1866. | Samson & Wallin.

1 vol. 4to (size of 8vo), pp. I-XIV, 1 l. (blank), pp. 1-116. Stockholm.

A critical revision of the woodpeckers, based on Malherbe's "Monographie des Picidées," 1859-62 (q.v.), an index to which is included. Full descriptions are given of the species, tribes and genera, with the synonymies of the species and notes on their distribution.

Sundevall, Carl Jacob.

1872-73. Methodi naturalis | avium disponendarum | tentamen. | Försök | till | fogelklassens | naturenliga uppställning | av | Carl J. Sundevall. | Stockholm, | Samson & Wallin, | 1872.

1 vol. 4to (size of post 8vo), pp. A-F (pref.), I-LXIX+1 (introd. and transl. of pref. and introd.), 1-187+1, 1*-12* (appendix), 1 pl. Stockholm.

An exposition of the author's system of classification of birds. All groups from families upwards are characterized and the genera frequently are segregated into several groups of subfamily rank which are characterized but not named. Type species are cited for each genus and a certain amount of generic synonymy is given, with types cited for the synonyms. Numerous new genera and one new species are described in the work. The book was issued in two parts, the first of which appeared in 1872 and contained pp. I-XLVIII and 1-72 (Cf. Zool. Record, 1872.); the second completed the volume and appeared in 1873, having been delayed by the illness of the author. Mathews (Birds of Australia, Suppl. 5, p. 130, 1925) cites the date, Aug. 1, 1872, from the back of the original wrapper of Pt. I; he also gives the date of Pt. II as before June 12, 1873, but does not cite the source of this information.

Sundman, Gösta.

1879-88. [Finska Fogelägg, Suomen lintuin munia. Helsingfors. 1879-88.]

1 vol. crown folio, (title and text missing), 25 pll. (col.). Helsingfors.

A series of good chromolithographic plates of the eggs of Finnish birds. The work was issued in 9 parts with 3 pll. in each of Pts. 1-7 and 2 pll. in each of Pts. 8 and 9. The following dates are given by the Zoological Record. Pts. 1 and 2, 1879; 3 and 4, 1881; 5, 1883; 6 and 7, no dates but received by the Library of the British Museum in 1886; 8 and 9, 1888. Text by Johann Axel Palmén was issued with Pts. 1-5, in German and English [according to the Catalogue of the Library of the British Museum (Natural History)] but the Zoological Record quotes only the Swedish title given above. The present copy contains only the plates and has the binding inscribed with the English

title, "Eggs of Finnish Birds | Drawn And Coloured By | G. Sundman."
The figures on the plates are named both in Latin and Swedish vernacular.

Suolahti, Hugo.

1909. Die deutschen Vogelnamen. | Eine wortgeschichtliche Unter-
suchung | von | Hugo Suolahti, Dozent an der Universität Helsing-
fors. | Strassburg | Verlag von Karl J. Trübner | 1909.
1 vol. 8vo, pp. I-XXXIII+1, 1-540. Strassburg.

A study of the derivations of the vernacular names of German birds.

Susemihl, Erwin Eduard.

1845. See Schlegel, Hermann, **Die Europäischen Tag-Raubvögel.**

Susemihl, Johann Conrad.

1845. See Schlegel, Hermann, **Die Europäischen Tag-Raubvögel.**

Swainson, Charles.

1886. The folk lore | and | provincial names | of | British birds | by
the | Rev. Charles Swainson, M.A., | Rector of Old Charlton; |
Author of "A Handbook of Weather Folk Lore." | London: | Pub-
lished for the Folk Lore Society by | Elliot Stock, 62, Paternoster
Row. | 1886.
1 vol. post 8vo, 1 l. (imprint of Society), pp. I-VIII, 1-243. London.

A detailed discussion of the various vernacular names of British birds with respect
to their origin and significance (including foreign terms for the same species)
and of legends and superstitions connected with the various species. The book
in its present form appeared in the "Publications of the Folk-Lore Society
XVII. (1885.)" in 1886 but had been issued the previous year by the Dialect
Society under the title of "Provincial Names and Folk-Lore of British Birds
(Cf. Mullens and Swann.).

Swainson, William.

1820-33. Zoological Illustrations, | or | original figures and descriptions |
of | new, rare, or interesting | animals, | selected chiefly from the classes
of | Ornithology, Entomology, and Conchology, | and arranged on
the principles of | and arranged according to their apparent affinities.
(*Ser. 2.*)] | Cuvier and other modern zoologists. [*Line omitted (Ser.
2.*).] | By | William Swainson, F.R.S.,F.L.S. [Wm. Swainson, Esq.,
F.R.S., F.L.S. (*Ser. 2.*)] | Member of the Wernerian Society of
Edinburgh, etc. [Assistant Commissary General *etc.*, *4 lines (Ser.
2, Vols. I and II.*); *3 lines (Ser. 2, Vol. III.*).]. | Vol. I. [Vol. II.;
Vol. III. ; Vol. I. ; Vol. II. ; Vol. III. } London: |
Second series. Second series. Second series.
printed by R. and A. Taylor, Shoe-Lane: [printed by James Moyes,

Greville Street; (*Vols. II and III.*); printed by R. Havell, Jun.
Newman Street. (*Ser. 2, Vol. I.*); printed by W. J. Sparrow,
Berners Mews, Berners Street. (*Ser. 2, Vol. II.*); printed by
W. J. Sparrow, 3, Edward Street, Hampstead Road. (*Ser. 2,
Vol. III.*)] | for Baldwin, Cradock, and Joy, Paternoster- [for
Baldwin, Cradock, and Joy, Paternoster-Row; (*Vols. II and III.*);
Published by Baldwin and Cradock, (*Ser. 2, Vol. I.*); Published by
Baldwin & Cradock, Paternoster Row, (*Ser. 2, Vols. II and III.*)] |
Row; and W. Wood, Strand [and W. Wood, Strand (*Vols. II and
III.*); Paternoster Row (*Ser. 2, Vol. I.*); and R. Havell, 77, Oxford
Street (*Ser. 2; Vols. II and III.*)]. | 1820-1 [1821-2; 1822-3; 1829;
1831-2; 1832.-1833].

6 vols. 8vo. Vol. I, pp. I-IX+1 (tit., pref. and bibliogr.), 3 ll. (indices
and addenda), 6 ll. (sectional titles and index for each[1]), 66 ll.
(text), pll. 1-66 (col.; 10, 17, 22 and 29 unnum.; 2, 3, 4, 17 and 18
numbered by hand; 14 wrongly numbered 6). Vol. II, 4 pr. ll.
(tit., ded. and indices), 6 ll. (sect. subtits. and indices), 1 l. (addenda), 52 ll. (text), pll. 67-119 (col.). Vol. III, tit., pp. V-X
(pref.), 2 ll. (indices), 6 ll. (sect. subtits and indices), 1 l. (addenda),
62 ll. (text), pll. 120-182 (col.; 126 and 180 wrongly numbered 128
and 179, respectively; 175 unnum.) Ser. 2, Vol. I, pp. I-VII+1
tit., ded. and pref.), 1 l. (index), 6 ll. (sect. tits. and indices[2]), 3 ll.
(list of subscrs., index and bibliogr.), 44 ll. (text), pll. 1-45 (col.;
1-3, 6-8, 11-13, 16-31, 34-35, 37, and 39-45 unnum.). Ser. 2, Vol. II,
5 ll. (tit., ded., pref., and indices), 46 ll. (text), pll. 46-91 (col.;
46-48, 52-56, 64-68, 73, 80, and 91 unnum.; 63, 78 and 81 are wrongly
numbered 65, 79 and 83, respectively). Ser. 2, Vol. III, 5 ll. (tit,
ded., pref. and indices), 45 ll. (text), pll. 92-136 (col.; 101 wrongly
numbered 100). London. 1820-23 and 1829-33.

A series of excellent hand-colored plates, drawn by the author, accompanied by
descriptions of the species and some of the genera and more or less detailed
discussions of the same. Many new names are used. The work appeared in
parts but it is impossible to affix definite dates to these parts or even to give
their exact number or content. Mathews (Austr. Av. Rec. **4**, p. 23, 1920), on
the authority of Sherborn, gives Oct. 1, 1820 as the date of the first number
which contained 6 pll. This seems to have been followed regularly each month
by similar parts, with contents as follows from data given by Sherborn (Index
Anim., Sect. 2, Pt. 1, p. CXX, 1922). Nov. 1820—Aug. 1821, 11 parts (6 pll.
each), pll. 7-66; Sept. 1821, 1 part (5 pll.), pll. 67-71; Oct. 1821—Sept. 1822,

---

[1] Three sectional titles are the same as the title quoted above except for the volume-number which
is replaced by "Vertebrosa. Part I"; "Entomology. Part I"; and "Conchology. Part I."

[2] The sectional titles for the second series, although bound with the first volume, agree in lettering
and date with the title-page of Vol. III from which they differ only in the substitution of "Second
series. The birds."; "Second series. The insects."; and "Second series. The shells." for "Vol.
III. Second series." No sectional subtitles were issued with Vols. II and III of this series.

12 parts (4 pll.), pll. 72-119; Oct. 1822—Sept. 1823, 12 parts (5 pll.), pll. 120-179; Oct. 1823, 1 part (3 pll.), pll. 180-182. Title-pages and indices appeared in the numbers for Sept. 1821 (probably Oct. 1822?), and Oct. 1823. The number of parts (37) thus agrees with a statement by Swainson in a bibliography which is given in Vol. I of the second series.

The second series is even more in doubt than the first. According to Mathews (l.c.) it was announced to begin on February 29, 1829 (is this date possible?); 3 parts were reviewed as early as April but only 6 were published in all in that year, being reviewed in Febr. 1830. Four parts, including one with titles, etc., appeared in 1830, and succeeding parts were issued regularly for the first 8 months in 1831. From Sherborn (Index Animal. Sect. 2, Pt. 1, p. CXX, 1922) and from the indices of Vols. I-III of Ser. 2, which give the number of plates and the parts in which they appeared, the following arrangement appears to be more or less accurate. Pts. 1-6 (5 pll.), pll. 1-30, 1829; Pts. 7-9 (5 pll.), pll. 31-45, 1830; Pt. 10, title-page and index (Vol. I) but no plates, 1830; Pts. 11-18 (5 pll.), pll. 46-85, 1831; Pt. 19 (5 pll.), pll. 86-90, 1832; Pt. 20 (1 pl.), pl. 91 and title-page and index (Vol. II), 1832; Pt. 21 (5 pll.), pll. 92-96, 1832; Pts. 22-29 (5 pll.), pll. 97-136, 1833; Pt. 30, title-page and index (Vol. III) but no plates, 1833. Swainson (Loudon's Mag. Nat. Hist. IV, p. 272, 1831) writing under date of Febr. 1831, says that Pts. 17 and 18 appeared about a month previously.

To complicate matters, it is apparent, from a statement by Swainson in the preface to Vol. III of Ser. 2, that a reissue was made of some of the earlier numbers of the work. An examination of the present copy reveals numerous plates in Ser. 1, Vols. I-III, and Ser. 2, Vol. I, No. 1, which are watermarked 184(0-1 ?; final numeral trimmed off). What changes, if any, may have been made in the reissues, I do not know beyond the fact that certain of the plates in the first series bear a date subsequent to that of their original issue. The following cases have been noted. Vol. I, pl. 49, "21.3.1832." Vol. II, pl. 100, "25.1. 1832"; pl. 115, "17/3/1832." Vol. III, pl. 151, "1829 20 May"; pll. 154, 155 and 156, "1828." On (advertising) p. 34 of Jardine's "Naturalist's Library" Ornithology Vol. II, dated 1833, there is a statement that the second edition of the first series of Swainson's work would be ready that spring. This may represent still another edition than the one in hand.

Of the 318 plates published in the work, 117 are ornithological. Ser. 1, Vol. I contained 24; Vol. II, 20; and Vol. III, 26 plates of birds, and Ser. 2, Vol. I, 24; Vol. II, 15; and Vol. III, 8 plates of birds. A curious error occurs on pl. 97 in Ser. 2, Vol. III, where Swainson, usually a most accurate draughtsman, represents a bird with its feet crossed in an impossible attitude.

Swainson, William.

1829. See Cuvier, G. L. C. F. D., **The Animal Kingdom,** 1827-35.

Swainson, William.

1831. See Wilson, Alexander; and Bonaparte, **American Ornithology.**

Swainson, William.

1832. See Richardson, John, **Fauna Boreali Americana . . . . Birds.**

Swainson, William.

1836-37.   See Lardner, Dionysius, **The Cabinet Cyclopaedia** . . . .
On the Natural History and Classification of Birds.

Swainson, William. (Jardine, William; Crichton, Andrew.)

1837.   **The** | **natural history** | **of the** | **birds of western Africa.** |
By | William Swainson, Esq. | A. C. G. [*etc.*, *2 lines.*]. | Vol. I
[II]. | Illustrated by thirty-four coloured plates, | numerous wood-
cuts, and portrait | of Bruce [Le Vaillant]. | The memoir by |
Andrew Crichton, Esq. | Author of "The History of Arabia,"
&c. &c. | Edinburgh: | W. H. Lizars, 3, St. James' Square; |
S. Highley, 32, Fleet Street, London; and | W. Curry, Jun. and
Co. Dublin. | 1837.

2 vols. cap 8vo. Vol. I, 1 l. (list of vols. in set), 4 pr. ll. (various tits.;
1 illum.), pp. IX-XV+1, 17-286, 1 l. (advt.), frontisp. (portr.),
pll. 1-32 (col.; by Swainson), 9 text-figs. Vol. II, 1 l. (list of vols.
in set), 4 pr. ll. (tits.; 1 illum.), pp. IX-XVI, 17-263, frontisp.
(portr.), pll. 1-32 (col.; by Swainson), 9 text-figs. Edinburgh.

Vols. VII and VIII, Ornithological Series (1st ed.), of Jardine's "The Naturalist's
Library," 1833-43 (q.v.); Vols. XI and XII in subsequent editions. Only
English names appear on the plates, and all of the backgrounds have scenic
details. Richmond (Auk, **17**, p. 179, 1900) gives the date of Vol. I as March
1837.

Swainson, William.

1837.   See Lardner, Dionysius, **The Cabinet Cyclopaedia** . . . . **Animals in Menageries.**

Swainson, William. (Jardine, William.)

1838.   **The** | **natural arrangement** | **and relations of the** | **family of
flycatchers,** | or Muscicapidæ. | By | William Swainson, Esq. |
A.C.G. [*etc.*, *2 lines.*]. | Illustrated by thirty-three coloured plates, |
with portrait and memoir | of Baron Haller. | Edinburgh: | W.
H. Lizars, 3, St. James' Square; | S. Highley, 32, Fleet Street,
London; and | W. Curry, Jun. and Co. Dublin. | 1838.

1 vol. cap 8vo, 1 l. (list of vols.), 4 pr. ll. (tits.; 1 illum.), pp. IX-XIV,
15-256, pll. 1-31 (col.; by Swainson). Edinburgh.

Vol. X Ornithological Series (1st ed.) of Jardine's "The Naturalist's Library,"
1833-43 (q.v.), becoming Vol. XIII in later editions (q.v.). English names
but no localities are given on the plates. Plate 21 is missing. The memoir of
Haller appears to be by the editor.

[Idem.] Another copy, complete.

Swainson, William.

1841.   **A selection of the** | **birds** | **of** | **Brazil and Mexico.** | **The** drawings | by | William Swainson, Esq. A.C.G. | Fellow of the Royal and Linn. Societies of London [*etc.*, *5 lines.*]. | London: | Henry G. Bohn, York Street, Covent Garden. | 1841.

1 vol. 8vo, tit., pp. 1-4, pll. 1-78 (1, 13, 31, 48, 60, 69, 71, 72 and 74-78 num. by hand; 67 and 68 wrongly num. 72 and 73 respectively,- corrected by hand) (col.). London.

A series of 78 hand-colored plates of Neotropical birds, with a list of species prefixed, giving English and Latin names. Most of these names also appear on the plates but pll. 48, 69, 70 and 73-78 have no Latin names on them, the names on pll. 6-8, 40, 41 and 58 have been amended in the list, and the name on pl. 71 has been entirely changed. The work was issued originally in parts from 1834-36? Engelmann cites 7 parts. Pt. 1, containing 13 pll., is reviewed in Loudon's Mag. of Nat. Hist., Vol. VII, p. 183, "March" 1834. Ridgway (Bull. U. S. Nat. Mus., 50, Pt. 2, p. 56; Pt. 3, p. 529; and Pt. 4, pp. 471 and 542) quotes pl. 15 as in Pt. 2, 1834; pl. 37 as in Pt. 3, 1836; pl 48 as in Pt. 4, 1836? and pl. 53 as in Pt. 5, also 1836? Tschudi (Archiv. für Naturg., Jahrg. 11, 1, p. 362, 1845) ascribes pl. 58 to Pt. 5, under date of 1841, but it is possible that Tschudi had a copy of the work similar to the one at hand which seems to be properly dated 1841, throughout. Swainson, in his "Animals in Menageries" (Cf. Lardner, Dionysius, The Cabinet Cyclopaedia, 1837.), mentions pll. 63 and 64 as though they were already published. This note, if accurate, would place Pt. 5 as of December 1837 or before. Coues catalogues a copy containing only 62 plates as comprising Pts. 1-5, Pt. 6 missing, but it is probable that this copy lacked, also, the last three plates of Pt. 5. The conclusion which seems most probable (but which needs confirmation) is that there were 13 plates in each of the six parts as originally issued.

No text appears to have been published with the original edition, which bore as title, "Ornithological Drawings, being Figures of the Rarer and most Interesting Birds of Brazil" (Cf. Engelmann.) or "The Ornithological Drawings of William Swainson - - The Birds of Brazil" (Cf. Coues.). The present edition seems to have appeared as a separate volume with a new title-page and with the addition of a list of plates, while the plates (at least in part) were newly printed. Several kinds of paper are used for the plates; pll. 74-78 are on thin paper which is mounted on some of a heavier quality; pll. 4 and 14 are watermarked "184-" (the final figure lost by trimming the plate). Quotations from the present work may properly be dated 1841. Engelmann catalogues both this edition and the original. Many new names date from the original work.

Swainson, William. (Jardine, William.)

1844-64? [**The Natural Arrangement and Relations of the Family of Flycatchers,** or Muscicapidæ.]

The | naturalist's library. | Edited by | Sir William Jardine, Bart., | F.R.S.E. [*etc.*]. | Vol. XIII. | Ornithology. | Flycatchers. | By W. Swainson, Esq. | A.C.G. [*etc.*]. | Edinburgh: | W. H. Lizars, 3, St. James' Square. | London: | Henry G. Bohn, York St., Covent Garden.

1 vol. cap 8vo, 5 pr. ll. (illum. tit., tit., conts. and subtit.), pp. 17-256, frontisp. (portr.), pll. 1-31 (col.; by Swainson). Edinburgh and London. (Date?).

A reprint of Vol. X, Ornithological Series (1st ed.) of Jardine's "The Naturalist's Library, 1833-43 (q.v.). The plates have lost some of the marginal detail of the backgrounds, some of the legends appear to be re-engraved and localities are frequently added to them. The illuminated title-page bears the single imprint of Henry G. Bohn.

Swainson, William. (Jardine, William; Crichton, Andrew.)

1844-64?   [The Natural History of the Birds of Western Africa.]
The | naturalist's library. | Edited by | Sir William Jardine, Bart., | F.R.S.E. [etc.]. | Vol. XI [XII]. | Ornithology. | Birds of Western Africa - Part I [II]. | By W. Swainson, Esq. | A.C.G·

[etc.]. | Edinburgh: | W. H. Lizars, 3, St. James' Square. | [*Omitted (Vol. II.).*] | London: | Henry G. Bohn, York St., Covent Garden.

2 vols. cap 8vo. Pt. I, 5 pr. ll. (illum. tit., tit. and conts.), pp. 17-286, (frontisp. (portr.), pll. 1-32 (col.; by Swainson), 9 text-figs. Pt. II, 5 pr. ll., pp. 17-263, frontisp. (portr.), pll. 1-32 (col.; by Swainson), 9 text-figs. Edinburgh and London. (Date?).

Reprints of Vols. VII and VIII, Ornithological Series (1st ed.) of Jardine's "The Naturalist's Library," 1833-43 (q.v.). The general typography is the same as in the first edition and the plates differ only in their poorer coloration and in having a slight amount of the background removed. The illuminated title-page of Pt. I bears the imprint of Chatto and Windus; that of Pt. II bears the imprint of Lizars and, furthermore, carries only the subject-title and gives no reference to "The Naturalist's Library."

Swann, Harry Kirke.

1913.   A dictionary | of | English and folk-names | of | British birds | With their History, Meaning and first usage: | and the Folk-lore, Weather-lore, Legends, etc., | relating to the more familiar species. | By | H. Kirke Swann | Witherby & Co. | 326 High Holborn London W.C. | 1913.

1 vol. post 8vo, pp. I-XII, 1-266, 1 l. (advt.), 8 ll. (blank, for memoranda. London.

An alphabetical list of nearly 5000 names including "*book*-names from past authors" and the "*accepted*-names of species" with the "provincial, local and dialect names in use now or formerly in the British Islands." Folk-lore, legends, etc. are added in many cases and a bibliography is prefixed.

Swann, Harry Kirke.

1915-17. See Grönvold, Henrik, **Illustrations of the Game Birds and Water Fowl of South America.**

Swann, Harry Kirke.

1916-17. See Mullens, William Herbert; and Swann, **A Bibliography of British Ornithology.**

Swann, Harry Kirke.

1919-20. **A | synoptical list | of the | Accipitres |** (Diurnal Birds of Prey) | Comprising Species and Subspecies described up to 1919, | with their Characters and Distribution | by | H. Kirke Swann, F.Z.S., M.B.O.U. | Corresponding Fellow of Amer. Orn. Union. | London: | John Wheldon & Co., 38, Great Queen Street, | Kingsway, W.C.2 | 1920.

1 vol. post 8vo, pp. I-VI, 1-164, 2 ll. (add. and corrig.), pp. 15-16 (bis), 4 orig. covers (Pts. I-IV). London.

An annotated list of species, with original references, diagnostic characters and notes on distribution. The work was issued in four parts as follows, according to the dates on the original wrappers which are bound with the work. Part I, pp. 1-38, July 1919; II, pp. 39-74, 15-16 (bis), 1 l. (add. and corrig.), November 7, 1919; III, pp. 75-114, 1 l. (addenda, etc.), January 20, 1920; IV, pp. 115-164, I-VI, March 31, 1920. A second edition (q.v.) appeared in 1921-22.

Swann, Harry Kirke.

1919-20. See Mullens, William Herbert; Swann; and Jourdain, **A Geographical Bibliography of British Ornithology.**

Swann, Harry Kirke.

1921-22. **A | synopsis | of the | Accipitres |** (Diurnal Birds of Prey) | Comprising Species and Subspecies described up to 1920, with | their Characters and Distribution | by | H. Kirke Swann, F.Z.S., M.B.O.U. | Corresponding Fellow, Amer. Orn. Union. | **Second edition** | revised and corrected throughout | London: | Wheldon & Wesley, Ltd., | 38, Great Queen Street, Kingsway, W.C.2, and | 28, Essex Street, Strand, W.C.2. | 1822.

1 vol. 8vo, pp. I-VIII, 1-233, 5 ll. (add. and errata), 4 orig. covers. London.

A revised edition of the "Synoptical List of the Accipitres," 1919-20 (q.v.). Issued in four parts as follows, according to the dates on the original wrappers. Part I, pp. 1-63, Sept. 28, 1921; II, pp. 64-122, January 3, 1922; III, pp. 123-178, 4 ll. (addenda, etc.), February 16, 1922; IV, pp. 179-233, I-VIII, 1 l. (errata, etc.), May 20, 1922. There is also a limited issue of this edition in 4to, under the same date (q.v.).

Swann, Harry Kirke.

1921-22. **A | synopsis | of the | Accipitres |** (Diurnal Birds of Prey) | Comprising Species and Subspecies described up to 1920, with | their Characters and Distribution | by | H. Kirke Swann,

F.Z.S., M.B.O.U. | Corresponding Fellow Amer. Orn. Union |
Second edition | revised and corrected throughout | London |
privately printed for the author.

1 vol. royal 4to, 2 pr. ll. (half-tit. and tit.), pp. III-VIII, 1-233, 5 ll.
(errata, etc.), 1 l. (expl. of pll.), 4 orig. wrappers, 22 pll. (col.).
London.

Identical with the regular second edition in 8vo of the same date (q.v.), except
for the size of the paper and the inclusion of a half-title, the colored plates and
the leaf of explanation of the latter. The copy is No. 7 of 28 copies so issued.
Dates on the wrappers are as in the regular edition.

Swann, Harry Kirke.

1923. **A bibliography** | **of** | **British ornithology** | from the earliest
times | **Supplement** | A chronological list | of British birds | by |
H. Kirke Swann, F.Z.S., M.B.O.U., &c. | Corresponding Fellow
of Amer. Orn. Union | London | Wheldon & Wesley, Ltd. | 2, 3 &
4, Arthur Street, New Oxford Street | 1923.

1 vol. 8vo, pp. I-XVII+1, 1-42. London.

A list of the specific and subspecific names of British birds [based on Hartert,
Jourdain, Ticehurst and Witherby's "Handlist of British Birds," 1912 (q.v.)],
arranged chronologically, with original references. The generic names employed
in the list are catalogued separately in the same manner, and supplementary
lists of discarded generic and specific names are listed with their established
equivalents. The work is intended as a supplement to Mullens and Swann's
"A Bibliography of British Ornithology," 1916-17 (q.v.). The preface is
dated "August 1923."

Swann, Harry Kirke.

1924-date. > Part I [II; III; IV; V] November 15th, 1924 [January
31st, 1925; May 30th, 1925; September 21st, 1925; January 25th,
1926] Price 26s. net | **A** | **monograph** | **of the** | **birds of prey** |
(Order Accipitres) | by | H. Kirke Swann, F.Z.S., M.B.O.U. |
Corresponding Fellow of the Amer. Orn. Union | Illustrated by
Plates reproduced in colour from drawings made expressly for
this | work by H. Gronvold, also Coloured Plates of Eggs, and
Photogravure Plates | London | Wheldon & Wesley, Ltd. | 2, 3 &
4, Arthur Street, New Oxford Street, W.C.2 [*Cover-titles*].

5 parts (all issued to date) royal 4to. Pt. I, (cover tit.), pp. I-XI+1,
1-52, 5 pll. (4 col., 1 of eggs; 1 photograv.). Pt. II, (cover tit.),
pp. 53-124, 5 pll. (3 col.; 2 photograv.). Pt. III, (cover-tit.), pp.
125-196, 5 pll. (3 col., 1 of eggs; 2 photograv.). Pt. IV, (cover-tit.),
pp. 197-276, 5 pll. (4 col., 1 of eggs; 1 photograv.). Pt. V, (cover-
tit.), pp. 277-364, 5 pll. (4 col.; 1 photograv.). London.

The first five numbers of a descriptive and biographical account of all of the diurnal birds of prey, being issued in an edition of 412 copies.

Swann, Harry Kirke.

1925. Two | ornithologists | on the | lower Danube | being a record of a journey to the Dobrogea | and the Danube Delta with a systematic list | of the birds observed | by | H. Kirke Swann, F.Z.S., M.B.O.U. | (Corresponding Fellow American Orn. Union) | illustrated from photographs taken by | J. H. McNeile, M.B.O.U. | London | Wheldon & Wesley, Ltd. | 2, 3 & 4, Arthur Street, New Oxford Street, W.C.2 | 1925.

1 vol. 8vo, 5 pr. ll., pp. 1-67, frontisp., 14 text-figs. London.

A narrative of the experiences of the author and the photographer on a trip through portions of Roumania in April and May, 1925. An annotated list of birds is given on pp. 55-67.

Swaysland, Walter. (Kearton, Richard.)

1883-(88?). Familiar | wild birds. | By | W. Swaysland. | [*Vignette.*] | First [-Fourth] Series. | With coloured plates. | Cassell & Company, Limited: | London, Paris & New York [London, Paris, New York, & Melbourne (*Vols. II-IV.*)]. | [All rights reserved.] | 1883. [*No date (Vols. II-IV.*).].

4 vols. crown 8vo. Vol. I, pp. I-VIII, 1-160, 40 pll. (col.; 36 of birds by Thorburn; 4 of eggs), 74 text-figs. Vol. II, pp. I-VIII, 1-160, 40 pll. (col.; 36 of birds; 4 of eggs), 74 text-figs. Vol. III, pp. I-VIII, 1-160, 40 pll. (col.; 36 of birds; 4 of eggs), 74 text-figs. Vol. IV, pp. I-VIII, 1-176, 40 pll. (col.; 36 of birds; 4 of eggs), 74 text-figs. London.

Popular discussions of the habits of a large number of British birds with 144 chromolithographs of birds by Thorburn and 16 chromolithographs of eggs (some by "A. F. L."). At the close of each volume is a chapter on "Eggs and Egg-Collecting" by R. Kearton. Only Vol. I is dated; I have taken the final date from Mullens and Swann by whom, also it is queried. Later editions are mentioned by Mullens & Swann without date.

Sweet, Robert.

1823-29. The | British warblers, | An | account of the genus | Sylvia; | illustrated by | six beautifully coloured figures, | taken from | Living Specimens in the Author's Collection; | with | directions for their treatment according to the | author's method; | in which is explained, | how the interesting & fine singing birds belonging | to this genus may be managed, | and kept in as good health as any common | birds whatever. | By | Robert Sweet, F.L.S. | Author of [*etc., 2 lines.*]. | The Drawings by E. D. Smith,

Artist for the Geraniaceæ. | London: | published for the author, | by W. Simpkin and R. Marshall, | Stationers'-Hall Court, Ludgate Street. | 1823. | Tilling, Printer, Grosvenor Row, Chelsea.

1 vol. royal 8vo, tit., pp. 1-24, 10 ll. (unnum.), pll. 1-16 (col.). London.

A popular account of certain British warblers, with descriptions and notes on habits, methods of capture, behaviour in captivity, etc. The plates are hand-colored. There is some uncertainty as to dates of publication and manner of issue. Mullens and Swann note the existence of several copies with only six plates (as indicated on the title) and with abbreviated text; these may constitute an original edition. They also quote Neville Wood (Ornith. Text Book, p. 37, 1836) for inclusive dates of 1823 to 1832, and C. T. Wood (Ornith. Guide, 1835) for the statement that the work appeared in 3 numbers. In the Mag. Nat. Hist., I, p. 57, May 1828, Pts. I-III (including pll. 1-11) are reviewed and pll. 12-16 are promised to follow. The next year in the same journal, II, p. 50, March 1829, the work is noted as being complete with 16 pll. To confute this clear statement, pl. 7 of the present copy is on paper watermarked "1829"; this may indicate a re-impression. The work is rather rare.

Sweet, Robert.

1853. See Bechstein, Johann Matthäus, **Cage and Chamber-Birds.**
1900. Idem.

Swenk, Myron Harmon.

1904. See Bruner, Lawrence; Wolcott; and Swenk, A **Preliminary Review of the Birds of Nebraska.**

Swinhoe, Robert.

1877. See Rowley, George D., **Ornithological Miscellany,** 1875-78.

Syme, Patrick.

1823. A | treatise on British | song-birds. | including | observations on their natural habits, man- | ner of incubation, &c. with remarks on | the treatment of the young and | management of the old birds | in a domestic state. | With | fifteen coloured engravings. | John Anderson, Jun. Edinburgh, | 55, North Bridge-Street; | and Simpkin & Marshall, London. | MDCCCXXIII.

1 vol. 8vo, pp. I-VI, 1 l. (advt.), pp. 1-231, 15 pll. (col.). Edinburgh and London.

Account of thirty-three British birds, illustrated by hand-colored plates. The author's name appears at the end of the introduction which is dated July 15, 1823; the advertising leaf is dated October the same year. The book is scarce.

Taczanowski, Ladislas.

1884-86. Ornithologie | du Pérou | Par Ladislas Taczanowski | Tome Premier [-Tome troisième; Tables] | Typographie Oberthur,

a Rennes, Faubourg de Paris [Typographie Oberthur, a Rennes
(*Vols. II and III, and Tables.*)] | 1884 [1884; 1886; 1886].

4 vols. royal 8vo. Vol. I, 4 pr. ll. (half-tit., tit., blank l. and ded.),
pp. III-VII+1, 9-541. Vol. II, 3 pr. ll. (half-tit., tit. and blank
l.), pp. 1-566. Vol. III, 3 pr. ll. (half-tit., tit. and blank l.), pp.
1-522, 1 map (col.; fold.). "Tables", 3 pr. ll. (half-tit., tit. and
blank l.), pp. 1-218. Rennes.

A most important monograph of Peruvian ornithology. Vols. I-III contain
exceedingly detailed descriptions and synonymy, notes on habits from the
field notes of collectors, and accounts of the distribution of each of 1350 species
with the authority for the records. Vol. I (pp. 9-73) also contains topographical
and distributional notes and accounts of localities visited by Stolzmann and
Jelski. The fourth volume consists of synoptic tables to the genera and species
treated in the work, and a Latin index to the first three volumes. The actual
days or months of issue of the four volumes are doubtful; the years appear
to be correctly stated on the title-pages. Vol. I is reviewed in the Ibis for
Oct. 1884; II in April 1885; III in April 1886 and the "Tables" in January
1887. The book is indispensable to the worker in Peruvian ornithology.

Tailor, J.

(Post) 1728? See Ward, Thomas, **The Bird-Fancier's Recreation.**

Tait, William Chaster.

1924. **The | birds of Portugal |** by | William C. Tait | Fellow of
the Zoological Society [*etc.*, *2 lines.*] | H. F. & G. Witherby | 326
High Holborn, W.C. 1 | 1924.

1 vol. post 8vo, pp. I-XII, 1-260, frontisp., 9 pll., 1 map (col.; fold.).
London.

A popular account of the habits of a large number of Portuguese birds, with the
local vernacular names of each, as well as the scientific and English names.
An appendix contains a bibliography and a list of banded birds recovered in
Portugal from 1910 to 1922.

Taverner, Percy A.

1919. Canada | Department of Mines | Hon. Martin Burrell, |
Minister; R. G. McConnell, Deputy Minister. | Geological Sur-
vey | William McInnes, Directing Geologist. | Memoir 104 | No. 3,
Biological Series | **Birds of Eastern Canada** | by | P. A. Taverner |
[*Seal.*] | Ottawa | J. de Labroquerie Taché | Printer to the King's
Most Excellent Majesty | 1919 | No. 1563.

1 vol. royal 8vo, tit., pp. I-III+1, 1-297, pll. I-L (col.; by F. C.
Hennessey; on pp. 223-272), text-figs. 1-68. Ottawa.

A catalogue of the birds occurring in Canada from the Atlantic Ocean to the
"prairies north of the International Boundary." General descriptions, diagnostic characters, field marks, nidification and distribution are given, with

occasional accounts of habits and economic status. French and English vernacular names are cited.

Tāymur Mīrzā. (Phillott, D. C.)

1908. The | Bāz-Nāma-yi Nāsirī | a Persian treatise on falconry | translated by | Lieut.-Colonel D. C. Phillott | Secretary, Board of Examiners, Calcutta [*etc., 5 lines.*] | London | Bernard Quaritch | 1908.

1 vol. royal 8vo, 4 pr. ll., pp. XI-XXIV, 1-195, frontisp. (fig. I), text-figs. II-XXV. London.

A treatise on falconry written in 1868 by Prince Taymur of Persia and translated, in the present edition, by Lieut. Col. Phillott who has added copious notes.

Tegetmeier, William Bernhard.

18(66?-) 67. The | poultry book: | comprising the | breeding and management | of | profitable and ornamental poultry, | their | qualities and characteristics; | to which is added | "The Standard of Excellence in Exhibition Birds," | authorized by the Poultry Club. | By | W. B. Tegetmeier, F.Z.S., | Editor of [*etc., 2 lines.*]. | With | coloured illustrations by Harrison Weir, | and numerous engravings on wood. | London: | George Routledge and Sons, The Broadway, Ludgate. | New York: 416, Broome Street. | 1867.

1 vol. superroyal 8vo, pp. I--IV, 1 insert slip (errata), pp. 1-356, 30 pll. (col.; incl. col. tit.), 53 text-figs. London.

A classic manual for the poultry-keeper. Each of the various breeds of fowls is taken up and discussed in detail. There is a manuscript note on a fly leaf, as follows,—"Issued in 15 numbers, at 1/—each—, Jan: 1866 to March 1867," —a statement which I am unable either to verify or disprove. Later editions of the work are numerous.

Tegetmeier, William Bernhard.

1868. Pigeons: | their | structure, varieties, habits, and management. | By | W. B. Tegetmeier, F.Z.S., | Author of [*etc., 2 lines.*]. | With coloured representations of the different varieties, drawn from life by | Harrison Weir, | and printed in colours by Leighton Brothers. | London: | George Routledge and Sons, | The Broadway, Ludgate. | New York: 416, Broome Street. | 1868.

1 vol. superroyal 8vo, 3 pr. ll. (tit., pref. and conts., and introd.), pp. 3-190, 1 l. (advt.), 16 pll. (col.), text-figs. I-XII, 13 text-figs. (unnum.). London.

A compendium of information relating to the various breeds of domestic pigeons, their origin, care and characteristics.

Tegetmeier, William Bernhard.

1873. Pheasants | for | coverts and aviaries. | By | W. B. Teget-
meier, F.Z.S. | (Member of the British Ornithologists' Union), |
author of [*etc.*, *2 lines.*]. | Illustrated with full-page engravings
drawn from life | by T. W. Wood. | London: | Horace Cox, 346,
Strand, W.C. | 1873. | (All rights reserved.).

1 vol. royal 4to, 3 pr. ll. (tit., pref. and conts.), pp. 1-124, 2 ll. (advt.),
11 pll., 17 text-figs. London.

"A detailed account of the natural history, habits, food, and treatment of the
various species of Pheasants." According to a statement by the author in
his preface, the work appeared in parts. There are several later editions under
the slightly different title,—"Pheasants, their Natural History and Practical
Management," (Cf. ed. 1881.).

Tegetmeier, William Bernhard.

1874. See Boddaert, Petr., **Reprint of Boddaert's Table des Planches
Enluminéez d'Histoire Naturelle.**

Tegetmeier, William Bernhard.

1881. Pheasants: | their | Natural History and Practical Manage-
ment. | By | W. B. Tegetmeier, F.Z.S. | (Member of the British
Ornithologists' Union; General Editor of the Willughby Society.),
Author of [*etc.*, *2 lines.*] | **Second edition,** greatly enlarged. |
[*Monogram.*] | Illustrated with full-page engravings drawn from
life | by T. W. Wood. | London: | Horace Cox, | The Field"
Office, 346, Strand. | 1881. | (All rights reserved.).

1 vol. royal 4to, tit., pp. III-IV, 1 l. (conts.), pp. 1-142, 5 ll. (advt.),
13 pll., 25 text-figs. London.

A second edition, without much change in text, of the author's earlier "Pheasants
for Coverts and Aviaries," 1873 (q.v.). The plates are the same as are most of
the figures, although some of the latter have been omitted and others added.
There are several later editions under the present title.

Tegetmeier, William Bernhard.

1881. See Blyth, Edward; and Tegetmeier, **The Natural History of
the Cranes.**

Tegetmeier, William Bernhard.

1882. See Lichtenstein, Anton August Heinrich, **Catalogus Rerum
Naturalium Rarissimarum,** The Willughby Society.

Tegetmeier, William Bernhard.

1896. See Morris, Francis Orpen, **A Natural History of the Nests
and Eggs of British Birds (Fourth Edition).**

Tegetmeier, William Bernhard.

1897-98. See Butler, Arthur G., **British Birds,** 1896-98.

Temminck, Coenraad Jacob.

1807. Catalogue | systematique | du | cabinet | d'ornithologie | et de la | collection | de | quadrumanes | de | Crd. Jb. Temminck. | Avec une courte description | des oiseaux non-decrits | suivi: | d'une nôte d'oiseaux doubles et de | quelques autres objets d'histoire | naturelle offerts en échange. | à Amsterdam, | Chez C. Sepp Jansz. | MDCCCVII.

1 vol. post 8vo, pp. I-VIII, 1 l. (errata), pp. 1-270, 1-34. Amsterdam.

A catalogue of the author's collection of birds and monkeys with descriptions of new species of birds and a list of the species of birds and mammals for exchange. Pp. 6-196 contain the systematic list of birds, with Latin and vernacular names and references to literature for the known species, and with vernacular names alone for the undescribed species which are not described here but noted, simply, as nondescript. The serial numbers of the author's collection are given throughout. Pp. 197-270 contain the descriptions of the new species, but no Latin names are used. The species were afterwards named by a variety of authors, chief among whom was Vieillot who is said to have copied many of the descriptions of Temminck or to have based his names upon an examination of the same specimens used by the latter. Hartlaub in Jardine's "Contributions to Ornithology" for 1849, published a review of the names given to the birds in this work, as, "A Systematic Index to a series of descriptions of birds, published by C. J. Temminck," etc. The list of birds and mammals for exchange occupies pp. 1-34 at the close of the present volume. The Ayer Ornithological Library is indebted to Dr. Charles W. Richmond for the copy of this rare pamphlet.

Temminck, Coenraad Jacob.

1809-11. See Knip, Madame, **Les Pigeons.**

Temminck, Coenraad Jacob.

1813-15. Histoire naturelle générale | des | pigeons | et des | gallinacés, [*Semicolon added (Vol. III.).*] | par | C. J. Temminck, | Chevalier de l'Ordre Impériale [*etc.*, 5 *lines.* (*Vol. I.*); Chevallier, *etc.*, 5 *lines.* (*Vol. II.*); Directeur de la Société, *etc.*, 4 *lines.* (*Vol. III.*)]. | ouvrage en trois volumes. | accompagné de | planches anatomiques. | Tome premier [-troisième]. | à Amsterdam, | chez J. C. Sepp & Fils, | et à Paris | chez G. Dufour, | 1813 [1813; 1815]. | à l'imprimerie de H. O. Brouwer, heerenmarkt [torensteeg, (*Vols. II and III.*)] | No. 5 [7 (*Vols. II and III.*)]. à Amsterdam.

3 vols. 8vo. Vol. I, pp. 1-16 (half-tit., tit. and pref.), 1-499+1, 1 pl. Vol. II, 2 pr. ll. (half-tit. and tit.), pp. 1-477+1, 1 l. (titles for

cover), pll. I-III. Vol. III, 2 pr. ll. (half-tit. and tit.), pp. 1-757+1, 1 l. (titles for cover), pll. IV-XI. Amsterdam.

A monograph of the pigeons and gallinaceous birds (as construed by the author). Vol. I, besides a preface and general introduction, contains the account of the pigeons,—a reprint of the text which Temminck had prepared for his illustrated folio that was stolen by Madame Knip (Cf. Knip, Les Pigeons, 1807-11.). Vols. II and III relate to the gallinaceous birds and contain an account which Temminck had in preparation for a folio but which he was deterred from publishing in that form by the misfortune he experienced with the volume on pigeons. A detailed statement of the transaction is given on pp. 640-644 of Vol. III. Numerous new names are used.

Temminck, Coenraad Jacob.

1817. C. J. Temminck, | **observations** | **sur la classification métho-dique des** | **oiseaux,** | et remarques sur l'analyse d'une nou- | velle ornithologie élémentaire. | Par | L. P. Vieillot, | Auteur de divers ouvrages d'Ornithologie, | et un des collaborateurs du Nouveau | Dictionnaire d'histoire naturelle. | A Amsterdam, | chez Gabriel Dufour, Libraire sur le Rokin. | Et à Paris, chez le même, rue de Vaugirard, No. 34. | 1817.

1 vol. 8vo, tit., pp. 1-60. Amsterdam.

A general essay on the classification of birds and a criticism of Vieillot's "Analyse d'une nouvelle Ornithologie élémentaire" of 1816 (Cf. reprint, 1883.).

Temminck, Coenraad Jacob; and Laugier de Chartrouse, Meiffren.

1820-39. **Nouveau recueil** | **de planches coloriées** | **d'oiseaux,** | pour servir de suite et de complément aux planches enluminées de Buffon, | édition in-folio et in-40 de l'imprimerie royale, 1770; | publié par | C. J. Temminck, | Chevalier de l'Ordre du Lion Néerlandais [etc., 4 lines.], | et | Le Baron Meiffren Laugier de Chartrouse, | Chevalier de la Légion-d'Honneur, | D'après les Dessins de MM. Huet et Prêtre, Peintres attachés au Muséum d'Histoire naturelle, | et au grand ouvrage de la Commission d'Égypte. | Vol. I [-IV]. | Paris, | G. Levrault, Libraire-Éditeur, Rue de la Harpe, N. 81. | A. Strasbourg, même maison, Rue des Juifs, N. 33. | et a Amsterdam, chez Legras Imbert et Comp., sur le Rockin, N. 139. | M. DCCC. XXXVIII.

5 vols. in 6, demy folio, Vol. I, 3 pr. ll. (half-tit., tit. and ded.), pp. 1-11+1 (prospectus)[1], 1-109+1 (table of plates)[1], 1 l. (post-script)[1], 119 ll., 101 pll. (col.; by Huet and Prêtre). Vol. II, 2 pr. ll. (half-tit. and tit.), 140 ll., 111 pll. (col.). Vol. III, 2 pr. ll., 203 ll.,

---

[1]Prospectus, table of plates and post-script are bound in a separate volume in this set although prospectus and table are included in the contents of Vol. I as given on p. 1 of the table.

134 pll. (col.; 1 fold.). Vol. IV, 2 pr. ll., 151 ll., 123 pll. (col.; 1 fold.). Vol. V, 2 pr. ll., 206 ll., 122 pll. (col.; 3 fold.). Paris.

Intended as a supplement to Buffon's "Planches Enluminées" (Cf. Buffon, Histoire Naturelle des Oiseaux, 1770-86.) which it follows in design and size, having appeared in large folio as well as in its present form. The "Tableau Méthodique," belonging in Vol. I, contains Buffon's species and plates arranged in systematic order with those of the present authors. The work was issued in 102 livraisons, the earlier numbers being published by Dufour and d'Ocagne, the later ones by Levrault, from August 1820 to Jan. 29, 1839. G. R. Crotch (Ibis, 1868, pp. 499-500) published a list of dates for most of the livraisons, extracted from the "Bibliographie Française" (= "Bibliographie de la France" ?). Sherborn (Ibis, 1898, pp. 485-488) revised Crotch's list, and Mathews (Birds of Australia, 7, pp. 468-471) added information secured from the "Bibliographie de la France." Some of the earlier livraisons, recorded in the latter paper, seem to have been supplied to subscribers considerably later than the dates of their original issue, from which fact Mathews deduces a second edition of these numbers. Stresemann (Anzeiger Orn. Ges. Bayern, No. 7, pp. 54-55, Nov. 20, 1922) adds several dates not in the older lists. From the different sources, the earliest dates given for receipt or publication of the various livraisons are as follows.

1- Aug. 1820; 2- Sept. 1820; 3- Oct. 1820; 4- Nov. 1820; 5- Dec. 1820; 6- Jan. 1821; 7- Feb. 1821; 8- March 1821; 9- April 1821; 10- May 1821; 11- June 1821; 12- July 1821; 13- Aug. 1821; 14- Sept. 1821; 15- Oct. 1821; 16- Nov. 1821; 17- Dec. 1821; 18- Jan. 1822; 19- Feb. 1822; 20- March 1822; 21- April 1822; 22- May 1822; 23- June 1822; 24- July 1822; 25- Aug. 22, 1822; 26- Sept. 1822; 27- Oct. 1822; 28- Nov. 1822; 29- Dec. 1822; 30- Jan. 1823; 31- Feb. 1823; 32- March 17, 1823; 33- April 1823; 34- May 1823; 35- June 20, 1823; 36- July 1823; 37- Aug. 30, 1823; 38- Sept. 27, 1823; 39- Oct. 25, 1823; 40- Nov. 1823; 41- Dec. 25, 1823; 42- Jan. 1824; 43- Feb. 28, 1824; 44- March 27, 1824; 45- April 1824; 46- May 22, 1824; 47- June 25, 1824; 48- July 31, 1824; 49- Aug. 28, 1824; 50- Sept. 1824; 51- Oct. 23, 1824; 52- Nov. 27, 1824; 53- Dec. 25, 1824; 54- Jan. 1825; 55- Feb. 26, 1825; 56- March 1825; 57- April 23, 1825; 58- May 28, 1825; 59- June 25, 1825; 60- July 23, 1825; 61- Aug. 27, 1825; 62- Sept. 24, 1825; 63- Oct. 9, 1825; 64- Dec. 21, 1825; 65- May 27, 1826; 66- June 10, 1826; 67- July 12, 1826; 68- Sept. 16, 1826; 69- Oct. 28, 1826; 70- Dec. 27, 1826; 71- Feb. 28, 1827; 72- April 25, 1827; 73- June 30, 1827; 74- Sept. 22, 1827; 75- 1827; 76- March 1, 1828; 77- April 23, 1828; 78- June 1828; 79- Aug. 1, 1829; 80- Sept. 5, 1829; 81- Oct. 1829; 82- Jan. 2, 1830; 83- Feb. 20, 1830; 84- May 8, 1830; 85- July 3, 1830; 86- Sept. 4, 1830; 87- Jan. 22, 1831; 88- May 14, 1831; 89- Feb. 11, 1832; 90- July 28, 1832; 91- Dec. 20, 1832; 92- July 26, 1834; 93 to 99- 1835; 100 to 101- 1836; 102- Jan. 29, 1839.

The publication commenced as a series of plates, and 20 livraisons appeared, without text other than the vernacular names on the plates, but (which is very important) with Latin and vernacular names and the habitats of the species printed on the wrappers (Cf. Vol. I, Prospectus, p. 8; also Sherborn, l.c.). Since there were changes made in parts of the text from time to time, as shown below, and since other irregularities exist, it is desirable to quote, wherever possible to obtain them, the names given on the wrappers. Sherborn pointed out that the text to the first 20 livraisons appeared with that of the 21st livraison and that, thereafter, text and plates were issued together. In some cases, however, the text and the plate of certain species were not in the same livraison. Stresemann offers information tending to show that the first 20 livraisons of text were not issued simultaneously but that they appeared at various dates up to December 1823, but the data which he quotes are rather confusing because of overlapping serial numbers.

The original plan proposed 6 plates for each livraison, and, in most cases, this number seems to have been issued. The 101 livraisons (the 102nd contained only titles, table, etc.) contained only 600 plates, so it is apparent that there was a loss of 6 plates during the course of publication. An analysis of the livraison-numbers on the sheets of text shows a probability that livraisons 27, 63 or 64, 77, 94 and 101 each contained but 5 plates; that 75 or 76 contained 7 plates; and that 82 contained but 4 while 83 contained 6 plates, or that 82 and 83 each contained but 5 plates. There are indeterminate irregularities in the 87th to 89th livraisons, also. Exact calculation is impossible since some of the questionable plates are described in the same pages or paragraphs with other plates of the same species whose numbers are very widely separated, and the text was issued with these other plates.

The following irregularities have been noted in the copy at hand. In Vol. I, the text to pl. 13, livr. 3, and in Vol. III, the discussion of the genus *Pogonias* in livr. 34, were suppressed and substitute sheets were published later which were given the original livraison-numbers. The dates of the reissues are indeterminable as are the Latin name originally given to the subject of pl. 13 and the altered matter of livr. 34. In Vol. IV, livr. 43, the text to pl. 254 was suppressed and replaced by new text in livr. 95, correctly numbered. In Vol. II, the subjects of pl. 21 (livr. 4) and pl. 34 (livr. 6) are described on opposite sides of a leaf in livr. 4; in livr. 17 the text to pl. 98 alters the name first given on the wrapper which accompanied the plate, but the suppressed name is not quoted. The "Tableau Méthodique" of Vol. I, published in livr. 102, suppresses an earlier one published in livr. 87. Many leaves of text, dealing with species figured on two or more plates which are separated by a great interval of numbering, appear to have been issued with the first of the respective plates, but they discuss the other plates which had not then been published; Vol. I, pll. 192 and 224, with text in livr. 33, presents a case in point. Sometimes the first plate came out without text but was discussed with a second plate in a later number. Absolute precision in citing names from the book will be possible only when a set of original wrappers is available for collation.

Minor errors occur in the "Tableau Méthodique" (where plate-numbers are wrongly quoted or placed in the wrong column) and in the numbering in the text and on the plates.

Laugier's share in the work is not clear aside from the fact that many of the specimens described are from his collection. Temminck is to be credited with all nomenclature (Cf. Vol. I, Prospectus, p. 9.). The Prospectus which explains the nature of the work, is from the pen of Cuvier. An unnumbered page of Postscript, issued by Temminck with the 101st livraison, is dated August 30, 1836. A supplement is found in the "Iconographie Ornithologique" of Des Murs, 1845-49 (q.v.).

Temminck, Coenraad Jacob.

1820-40. **Manuel** | **d'ornithologie,** | ou | tableau systématique | des oiseaux qui se trouvent en Europe; | précédé | d'une analyse du système général d'ornithologie, | et suivi | d'une table alphabétique des espèces; [*Comma added* (*Pt. IV.*).] [et | d'une table corrélative des matières contenues dans les quatre | parties de cet ouvrage; (*Pt. IV.*)] | par C. -J. [J. -C. (*Pt. IV.*)] Temminck, | membre de plusieurs académies et sociétés savantes. | **Seconde édition,** | considérablement augmentée et mise au niveau | des découvertes nouvelles.| Première [-Quatrième] partie.| A Paris [Paris (*Pt. IV.*)], chez Gabriel Dufour, Libraire　[chez H. Cousin, Libraire-Éditeur, Quai Voltaire, No. 13.　　　　　Rue Jacob, No. 25.

(*Pt. II.*); chez Edmond D'Ocagne, Éditeur-Libraire, (*Pt. III.*); 12, Rue des Petits-Augustins.

H. Cousin, Rue Jacob, 25.

　　　Amsterdam,

Ve Legras, Imbert et Cie. (*Pt. IV.*)] | Octobre 1820 [1820-1840; Avril 1835; 1840].

4 vols. (pts.) post 8vo. Vol. I, 2 pr. ll. (half-tit. and tit.), pp. I-CXV+1, 1-439+1. Vol. II, 2 pr. ll. (half-tit. and tit.), pp. 440-950. Vol. III, 2 pr. ll. (half-tit. and tit.), pp. I-LXXXIV, 1-305+1, 1-4 (advt.). Vol. IV, 2 pr. ll. (half-tit. and tit.), pp. 307-691+1, 1 l. (errata). Paris.

A manual of European ornithology, forming the second edition of a work of the same title published in 1815 in Amsterdam. In the present edition two parts were issued in 1820; the third part, comprising a supplement to Pt. I, appeared in 1835 and the fourth in 1840,—the latter containing the supplement to Pt. II, a bibliography to Pts. III and IV, and a table correlating the matter of the whole work. Copies exist in which the second part contains a title different from that quoted above and it is possible that the one at hand is of later issue. Probably, only the title-page has been reprinted (publisher, printer and date are more or less in agreement in Pts. II and IV). Pt. I (pp. XLIV-XLVJ) contains a bibliography and (pp. XLVIJ-CXV) a detailed presentation of a general classification of birds. The latter is of considerable importance outside of European ornithology since it is not restricted to the European fauna and since it contains many new names. In Pt. III (p. LXIX) it is announced that illustrations of the species described in the present work are in course of publication by Werner (J. C.). These illustrations were issued in 1848 under the cover title, "Atlas des Oiseaux d'Europe, pour servir de complément au Manuel d'Ornithologie de M. Temninck," changed in a later issue and on the title-page to, "Les Oiseaux d'Europe" by Werner (q.v.). They were sometimes offered for sale in combination with Temminck's "Manuel" as a single work, but, although complementary, the two works are distinct. Engelmann cites the "Manuel" under dates of 1820, '35, '39 and '40; the reason for the "39," I am unable to determine.

Temminck, Coenraad Jacob.

1838-43. See Knip, Madame, **Les Pigeons (2nd ed.).**

Temminck, Coenraad Jacob.

1844-50. See Siebold, Philipp Franz von, **Fauna Japonica.**

Temminck, Coenraad Jacob.

1848. See Werner, Johann Carl, **Les Oiseaux d'Europe.**

Tennessee Ornithological Society.

1917. **Preliminary List | of the | birds of Tennessee |** 1917 **|** Compiled by **|** The Tennessee Ornithological **|** Society **|** Issued by **|** The Department of Game and Fish **|** W. D. Howser, State Warden **|** Nashville, Tenn.

1 vol. 8vo, pp. 1-28, printed covers, 2 text-figs. Nashville.

A preliminary list of the birds of the state, with tabular notes on the local abundance of each.

Thayer, Abbott H.

1909. See Gerald H. Thayer, **Concealing-coloration in the Animal Kingdom.**

Thayer, Gerald H. (Thayer, Abbott H.).

1909. **Concealing-coloration | in the | animal kingdom |** An Exposition of the Laws of Disguise **|** Through Color and Pattern: **|** Being a Summary of **|** Abbott H. Thayer's **|** discoveries **|** By **|** Gerald H. Thayer **|** with an introductory essay by **|** A. H. Thayer **|** illustrated by **|** Abbott H. Thayer   Gerald H. Thayer **|** Richard S. Meryman and others **|** and with photographs **|** New York **|** The Macmillan Co. **|** 1909.

1 vol. 8vo (size of foliopost 4to), 2 pr. ll. (half-tit. and tit.), pp. VII-XIX+1, 1-260, pll. I-XVI (col.; with printed guard-sheets), 58 pll. (uncol. with figs. 1-140), text-figs. A-C. New York.

An exposition of Abbott H. Thayer's views on the theory that almost all animals possess a "coloration that matches the background" and serves as a "device for the *concealment* of its wearer, either throughout the main part of this wearer's life, or under certain peculiarly important circumstances." The illustrations are designed to demonstrate the theory, and the colored plates were prepared by painting birds or other animals against a background in which the colors, or even color-patterns, of the specimens were reproduced. The work has been severely criticised and warmly defended. Among the important papers discussing it may be mentioned the following. F. H. Allen Auk, **39,** pp. 489-507, 1912. J. A. Allen, Auk, **27,** pp. 222-225, 1910. Barbour and Phillips, Auk, **28,** pp. 179-188, 1911. Fuertes, Science, **32** N.S., pp. 466-469, 1910. Roosevelt, Bull. Am. Mus. Nat. Hist., **30**, pp. 119-231, 1911. A. H. Thayer, Auk, **28**, pp. 146-148 and 460-464, 1911; Auk, **30**, p. 471, 1913; Bull. Am. Mus. Nat. Hist., **31**, pp. 313-321, 1912.

Thetis et . . Esperance, Journal de Navigation autour du Globe de, **1837.** See Bougainville.

Thienemann, Friedrich August Ludwig. (Brehm, Christian Ludwig; Thienemann, Georg August Wilhelm.)

1825-38. Systematische Darstellung | der | Fortpflanzung | der Vögel Europa's | mit Abbildung | der Eier | im Vereine | mit | Ludwig Brehm | Pastor in Renthendorf | Georg August Wilhelm Thienemann | Pastor in Droyssig | herausgegeben | von | Friedrich August Ludwig Thienemann | Med. Doct. und Inspector des Königlichen Naturiencabinets zu Dresden. | I - V. Abtheilung. | Mit XXVIII illuminirten Kupfertafeln. | Leipzig, 1838. | Verlag von Iohann Ambrosius Barth.

1 vol. (5 pts.) medium 4to, tit., pp. I-XII, 1-47+1, 1-76, 1-96, 1-54, 1-67, pll. I-XXVIII (col.). Leipzig.

Descriptions of the eggs and nidification of European birds, with hand-colored plates of many of the eggs. At least one new name is used, *Anser brevirostris*, in Pt. V, p. 28. The work appeared in five parts although originally planned for six (Cf. Pref. p. VI.). Each part bears a title-page which is essentially that of the complete volume, with the exception of the number of the part, contents, plates and date which replace ll. 19-20 as follows.

Erste [-Fünfte] Abtheilung | Raubvögel - Krähenarten [Insectenfresser (*Pt. 2.*); Körnerfresser (*Pt. 3.*); Körnerfresser. Sumpfvögel (*Pt. 4.*); Wasservögel. | Vom Herausgeber allein bearbeitet (*Pt. 5.*)]. | Mit IV [(*Pts. 1-3.*); VI (*Pt. 4.*); X (*Pt. 5.*)] Kupfertafeln. | Leipzig, 1825 [1826; 1829; 1830; 1838]. A small original drawing of an egg, signed by L. Thienemann, is pasted on the title-page of Pt. I. As noted, F. A. L. Thienemann claims entire authorship for the fifth part of the work. The other parts are probably to be ascribed to all three authors. The present copy is from the library of William Yarrell and contains the identification of the various figures of eggs written under each in his handwriting. A more elaborate supplementary work by Thienemann is his "Einhundert Tafeln," etc., 1845-56 (q.v.).

Thienemann, Friedrich August Ludwig.

1845-56. Einhundert Tafeln | colorirter Abbildungen von Vogeleiern. | Zur | Fortpflanzungsgeschichte der gesammten Vögel | von | Friedrich August Ludwig Thienemann. | Ausgearbeitet in den Jahren 1845 bis 1854.

2 vols. royal 4to. Text, pp. I-XVII+1, 1 l. (expl. of pl. IC), pp. 1-432. Plates, pll. I-C (89 col.). Leipzig.

A work similar to the author's "Systematische Darstellung," etc., 1825-38 (q.v.), but of wider scope and not confined to European species. It was issued in 10 parts, the dates and contents of which are given as follows by the "Catalogue of the Library of the British Museum (Natural History)." Pt. 1, pp. 1-48, pll. I-X, 1845; 2, pp. 49-96, pll. XI-XX, 1846; 3, pp. 97-144, pll. XXI-XXX, 1848; 4, pp. 145-192, pll. XXXI-XL, 1849; 5, pp. 193-240, pll. XLI-L, 1850; 6, pp. 241-288, pll. LI-LX, 1850; 7, pp. 289-336, pll. LXI-LXX, 1851; 8, pp. 337-376, pll. LXXI-LXXX, 1852; 9, pp. 377-432, pll. LXXXI-XC, 1852; 10, pp. I-XX, pll. XCI-C, 1856. An author's note on p. III, dated October 1856, advises that ill health has interrupted the course of the work and that there are three plates yet unpublished and much of the text unwritten. The text on p. 432 stops in the middle of a sentence and was never completed. The title on the wrappers was "Fortpflanzungsgeschichte der gesammten Vögel nach dem gegenwärtigen Standpunkte der Wissenschaft." There are said to be new names in the book ascribed, erroneously, to other authors; *Todirostrum margaritaceiventer* is renamed *Fluvicola margaritacea* on p. 311.

Thienemann, Georg August Wilhelm.

1825-30. See Thienemann, Friedrich August Ludwig, **Systematische Darstellung der Fortpflanzung der Vögel Europa's,** 1825-1838.

Thompson, W.

1805. See Girton, Daniel, **The New and Complete Pigeon-Fancier.**

Thompson, William.

1849-56. The | natural history | of | Ireland. | Vol. I [-III]. | Birds, | comprising the orders [order (*Vol. III.*)] | Raptores & Insessores [Rasores & Grallatores (*Vol. II.*); Natatores (*Vol. III.*)]. | By | Wm. Thompson, Esq., | President [*etc., 3 lines.*]. | London: | Reeve, Benham, and Reeve, King William Street, Strand [Reeve and Benham, Henrietta Street, Covent Garden (*Vol. III.*)]. | 1849 [1850; 1851].

> The | natural history | of | Ireland. | In four volumes. | Vol. IV. | Mammalia, reptiles, and fishes. | Also | Invertebrata. | By the late | Wm. Thompson, Esq., | President [*etc., 3 lines.*]. | London: | Henry G. Bohn, York Street, Covent Garden. | 1856.

4 vols. post 8vo. Vol. I, pp. I-XX, 1-434. Vol. II, pp. I-XI (*bis*=XII), 1-350. Vol. III, pp. I-VII+1, 1-491+1. Vol. IV, pp. I-XXXII, 1-516, 1 insert-slip (errata), frontisp. (portr.), 9 text-figs. London.

A comprehensive discussion of all the birds of Ireland, with reference to habits and characteristics, is contained in the first three volumes. The author's evident intention was to publish similar volumes on all of the zoological groups, but his death in 1852 put an end to the project. His notes were bequeathed to Robert Patterson and James R. Garrett with the request to edit and publish them, a task which resulted in Vol. IV. The ornithology was completed in the three first volumes and is entirely from the pen of Thompson. The work is highly praised by Coues.

Thoms, Craig L.

1920. See Over, William H.; and Thoms, S. Dak. Geol. and Nat. Hist. Surv. **Birds of South Dakota.**

Thomson, Arthur Landsborough. (Thomson, John Arthur.)

1910. Britain's Birds And | Their Nests: described | by A.Landsborough Thomson | with introduction | By J. Arthur Thomson | Professor of Natural History, Aberdeen University | illustrated with 132 drawings in colour | by | George Rankin | London: 38 Soho Square, W. | W. & R. Chambers, Limited | Edinburgh: 339 High Street | 1910.

1 vol. demy 4to, pp. I-XXVIII, 1-340, pll. 1-132 (col.). Edinburgh.

A popular account of the habits of the birds which nest in the British Isles; published, according to the preface, mainly on account of the plates. Plates 94 and 100 are wrongly labeled and should be transposed. The introduction by J. A. Thomson occupies pp. VII-XXI and is entitled, "The Study of Birds."

Thomson, Arthur Landsborough.

1910-13. See Kirkman, Frederick Bernuf Bever, **The British Bird Book.**

Thomson, Arthur Landsborough.

1924. See Kirkman, Frederick B.; and Hutchinson, **British Sporting Birds.**

Thomson, C. Wyville. (Finsch, Otto; Forbes, William Alexander; Garrod, Alfred H.; Salvadori, Tommaso; Salvin, Osbert; Saunders, Howard; Sclater, Philip Lutley; Tweeddale, Marquis of = Hay, Arthur.)

1881. > (Provisional Title) | **Report | on the | scientific results | of the | voyage of H. M. S. Challenger** | during the years 1873-76 | under the command of | Captain George S. Nares, R.N., F.R.S. | and Captain Frank Turle Thomson, R.N. | Prepared under the superintendence of | Sir C. Wyville Thomson, Knt., F.R.S., &c. | Regius Professor of Natural History [*etc., 2 lines.*] | **Zoology-Vol. II. | Part VIII.- Report on the birds** | Published by Order of Her Majesty's Government | Printed for Her Majesty's Stationery Office | and sold by | London:- Longmans & Co.; John Murray; Macmillan & Co; Simpkin, Marshall, & Co. | Trübner & Co.; E. Stanford; J. D. Potter; and C. Kegan Paul & Co. | Edinburgh:- Adam & Charles Black and Douglas & Foulis | Dublin:- A. Thom & Co. and Hodges, Figgis, & Co. | 1881 | Price Thirty-five Shillings > Report on the Birds collected during the Voyage of H. M. S.

Challenger | in the years 1873-1876. By Philip Lutley Sclater, M.A., P.H.D., | F.R.S., F.L.S., F.G.S., F.R.G.S., Secretary to the Zoological Society | of London.

1 vol. royal 4to, 2 pr. ll. (tit. and ed. note), pp. 1-166, pll. I-XXX (col.; by Smit), text-figs. 1 and 2, 7 text-figs. (unnum.). London.

A series of 13 papers describing the ornithology of the Challenger expedition, under the editorship and partial authorship of Sclater and forming part VIII of Vol. II of the Zoology of the expedition under the general editorship of Thomson. All of the papers, with the exception of Appendix I ("A List of Birds' Eggs Obtained during the Challenger Expedition") were published previously in the Proc. Zool. Soc. London, some changes being made in the present reprints. The authorship of each paper and the reference to its place of previous publication are given for each paper, except in the case of Appendix I. The plates are hand-colored and are very fine.

Thomson, John Arthur.

1910. See Thomson, Arthur Landsborough, **Britain's Birds and Their Nests.**

Thomson, John Arthur.

1923. The biology of | birds | by | J. Arthur Thomson, M.A., LL.D. | Professor of Natural History in the University of Aberdeen | London | Sidgwick & Jackson, Ltd. | 1923.

1 vol. post 8vo, pp. I-XI+1, 1-436, pll. I-IX (1 col.), text-figs. 1-59. London.

An important and authoritative essay on birds as animals; a study of their structure, habits and evolution in the broad relationship to other animal life and applying "such biological concepts as adaptation, struggle, sex, heredity, variation, selection, and behaviour." A short bibliography is appended.

Thorburn, Archibald.

1915-16. British birds | written and illustrated by | A. Thorburn, F.Z.S. | with eighty plates in colour, showing over | four hundred species | in four volumes | Vol. I [-IV] | Longmans, Green and Co. | 39 Paternoster Row, London | Fourth Avenue & 30th Street, New York | Bombay, Calcutta, and Madras | 1915 [(*Vols. I and II.*); 1916 (*Vols. III and IV.*)] | All rights reserved.

4 vols. imperial 4to. Vol. I, pp. I-VIII, 1-142+1, pll. 1-20 (col.). Vol. II, pp. I-VI, 1-71+1, pll. 21-40 (col.). Vol. III, pp. I-VI, 1-86+1, pll. 41-60 (col.). Vol. IV, pp. I-VII+1, 1-106+1, pll. 61-80 (col.). London.

A series of artistic and accurate plates of the various species of British birds, accompanied by short accounts of each. The plates are excellent, although the crowding of many separate figures on some of them detracts a little from their beauty.

Thorburn, Archibald.

1919. A naturalist's | sketch book | by | Archibald Thorburn, F.Z.S. | author of "British Birds" | with sixty plates | twenty-four of which are in colour, | and thirty-six in collotype | Longmans, Green and Co. | 39 Paternoster Row, London | Fourth Avenue & 30th Street, New York | Bombay, Calcutta, and Madras | 1919 | All rights reserved.

1 vol. demy folio, pp. I-VIII, 1-71+1, pll. 1-60 (24 col.). London.

A series of plates containing reproductions of water-color and pencil sketches made by the artist-author over a period of thirty years. The text consists of short explanations of the subjects, most of which are of birds. The work is of unusual value in showing variety of attitude and expression in studies of animal-life. Many of the sketches can be recognized in a more finished form in the various works illustrated by Thorburn.

Thorburn, Archibald.

1923. Game birds and | wild-fowl | of Great Britain and Ireland | written and illustrated by | A. Thorburn, F.Z.S. | containing thirty plates in colour, showing | fifty-eight species | Longmans, Green and Co. | 39 Paternoster Row, London | New York, Toronto, Bombay, Calcutta, and Madras | 1923 | All rights reserved.

1 vol. medium folio, pp. I-VII+1, 1-78+1, pll. 1-30 (col.). London.

A series of splendid plates accompanied by notes on the general habits of the species which are illustrated.

Thrupp, J. Godfrey.

1888. See James, F. L., **The Unknown Horn of Africa.**

Ticehurst, Norman Frederick.

1909. A history | of the | birds of Kent | by | Norman F. Ticehurst, | M.A., F.R.C.S., F.Z.S., M.B.O.U. | With twenty-four plates and a map | Witherby & Co. | 326 High Holborn London | 1909.

1 vol. royal 8vo (6¼ x 8¾), pp. I-LVI, 1-568, 24 pll., 1 map (col., fold.), 1 text-fig. (map). London.

General accounts of each species of bird recorded from the County of Kent (and extralimital portions of Romney Marsh), England, giving biographical notes and distributional details, and with references to published records.

Ticehurst, Norman Frederick.

1912. See Hartert, Ernst; Jourdain; Ticehurst; and Witherby, **A Hand-List of British Birds.**

Ticehurst, Norman Frederick.

1919-24. See Witherby, Harry Forbes, **A Practical Handbook of British Birds.**

"Tierreich, Das" (Finsch, Otto; Hartert, Ernst; Hellmayr, Charles E.; Rothschild, Walter.)

1897-date. Das Tierreich. | Eine Zusammenstellung und Kenn-zeichnung der | rezenten Tierformen. | Herausgegeben | von der | Deutschen Zoologischen Gesellschaft [*mut. mut.*]. | Generalredak-teur: Franz Eilhard Schulze. | 1. Lieferung [*mut. mut.*]. | Aves. | Redakteur: A. Reichenow. | Podargidae, Caprimulgidae | und | Macropterygidae [*mut. mut.*] | bearbeitet von | Ernst Hartert [*mut. mut.*], | Direktor des Zoologischen Museums in Tring (Eng-land) [*mut. mut.*]. | Mit 16 Abbildungen im Texte [*mut. mut.*]. | Berlin. | Verlag von R. Friedländer und Sohn. | 1897 [*mut. mut.*].

A series of monographs issued at irregular intervals and still in course of publica-tion. Five numbers have appeared on birds, Nos. 1, 2, 9, 15 and 18, by Ernst Hartert (1897), Walter Rothschild (1898), Ernst Hartert (1900), Otto Finsch (1901) and Charles E. Hellmayr (1903), respectively. These parts are collected and bound in one volume in the present copy. Owing to separate pagination and various changes in title-pages, I have catalogued each monograph under its author (q.v.). Begun by the Deutschen Zoologischen Gesellschaft, the work was issued latterly by the Königlich Preussischen Akademie der Wissen-schaften zu Berlin. In addition to the title-pages (with alterations) as quoted above, each part bears an additional title-page with the same import but with the general title and the lines relating to editorship, etc., condensed while greater prominence is given to the individual title and author.

Tischler, Friedrich.

1914. Die | Vögel der Provinz Ostpreussen | Von | F. Tischler | Ge-druckt mit Unterstützung durch die Provinz | Ostpreussen und die Physikalisch-Ökonomische | Gesellschaft zu Königsberg i. Pr. | [*Cut.*] | W. Junk | Berlin W 15 | 1914.

1 vol. royal 8vo, pp. 1-331, frontisp. (portrs.). Berlin.

Accounts of the occurrence and distribution of 305 forms of birds found in the Province of Eastern Prussia (as delimited at the date of publication). A check-list of species and a detailed bibliography are prefixed.

Toreen, Olof.

1765. See Osbeck, Peter, **Reise nach Ostindien und China.**

Torrey, Bradford.

1885. Birds in the bush | by | Bradford Torrey | [*Vignette.*] | Boston | Houghton, Mifflin and Company | New York: 11 East Seventeenth Street | The Riverside Press, Cambridge | 1885.

1 vol. 12mo, 3 pr. ll. (tit., quot. and conts.), pp. 1-300, 2 ll. (advt.).
Boston.

Popular essays on ornithological topics, containing much information derived
from close, personal observation.

Torrey, Bradford.

1901. **Everyday birds** | elementary studies | by | Bradford Torrey |
with twelve illustrations in | colors after Audubon, and | two from
photographs | [*Vignette.*] | Boston and New York | Houghton,
Mifflin and Company | The Riverside Press, Cambridge | 1901.

1 vol. post 8vo, 3 pr. ll. (tit., conts. and list of illustrs.), pp. 1-106,
13 pll. (12 col.). Boston and New York.

A series of pleasant, popular sketches of bird life, most of which relate to individual
species. The illustrations are poor.

Townsend, Charles H.

1887. See Healy, Michael A., **Report of the Cruise of the Revenue
Marine Steamer, Corwin.**

Townsend, Charles Wendell.

1905. Memoirs of the Nuttall Ornithological Club. | No. III. | **The
birds of Essex County,** | **Massachusetts.** | By Charles Wendell
Townsend, M.D. | With one plate and map. | Cambridge, Mass. |
Published by the club. | April, 1905.

1 vol. imperial 8vo, pp. 1-352, frontisp., 1 map (fold.). Cambridge.
April 1905.

An annotated list of 321 species and subspecies of birds known from the region in
question (not including one apocryphal species), with detailed notes on local
occurrence, distribution, habits, and other characteristics of the various forms.
A bibliography is appended.

Trevor-Battye, Aubyn.

1895. **Ice-bound on** | **Kolguev** | a chapter in the exploration | of
Arctic Europe to which | is added a record of the | natural history
of the island | by | Aubyn Trevor-Battye | F.L.S., F.Z.S., etc. |
Member of the British Ornithologists' Union | with numerous
illustrations by | J. T. Nettleship, Charles Whymper | and the
author | and three maps | Westminster | Archibald Constable and
Company | publishers to the India Office | 14 Parliament Street,
S.W. | 1895.

1 vol. royal 8vo, pp. I-XXVIII, 1-458, 25 pll. (1 fold.), 3 maps (col.,
fold.), 61 text-cuts. Westminster.

A narrative of experiences and observations on the island of Kolguev. In addition
to many ornithological notes throughout the text, an annotated list of birds

seen or collected is given on pp. 418-440. The present copy is marked, "Third Edition."

Trevor-Battye, Aubyn.

1903. See Lilford, Lord, **Lord Lilford on Birds.**

Trevor-Battye, Aubyn.

1913. **Camping in Crete** | with notes upon the animal | and plant life of the island | by | Aubyn Trevor-Battye | M.A., F.L.S., F.Z.S., F.R.G.S., etc. | Including a Description of certain Caves and their Ancient Deposits | By Dorothea M. A. Bate, M.B.O.U. | With thirty-two plates and a map | Witherby & Co. | 326 High Holborn, London | 1913.

1 vol. 8vo, pp. I-XXI+1, 1-308, 32 pll. (photogrs.), 1 map (col.; fold.), 1 text-fig. London.

A narrative of the author's travels in Crete. Incidental observations on birds are given in the general text, and an annotated list of species is added on pp. 257-263.

Tristram, Henry Baker.

1884. The survey | of | western Palestine. | **The fauna and flora of Palestine.** | By | H. B. Tristram, LL.D., D.D., F.R.S., | Canon of Durham. | Published by | The Cormittee of the Palestine Exploration Fund, | 1, Adam Street, Adelphi, London, W.C. | 1884.

1 vol. medium 4to, 4 pr. ll. (half-tit., tit., conts. and list of pll.), pp. V-XXII (pref.), 1-455, pll. I-XX (13 col., by J. Smit; uncol. by R. Mintern; VII-XIII, col., ornithological). London.

"A catalogue of all the known Vertebrata, Terrestrial and Fluviatile Mollusca, and the Flora of Palestine." The birds are discussed on pp. 30-139 and figured on 7 hand-colored plates (VII-XIII). The present copy is marked, "Special Edition. No. 125."

Tristram, Henry Baker.

1889. **Catalogue** | **of a** | **collection of birds** | **belonging to** | **H. B. Tristram,** D.D., LL.D., F.R.S. | Durham: | printed at the "Advertiser" office, 48, Saddler Street. | 1889.

1 vol. demy 4to, pp. I-XVI, 1-278. Durham.

A catalogue of a collection of over 17,000 specimens of birds in the author's collection, arranged in systematic order, giving the sex, locality, date and collector where known. The collection, increased by several thousand specimens, is now in the Liverpool Museum. Copy presented by the author to Sir Edward Newton.

Trouessart, E. L.

1912. **Catalogue | des | oiseaux d'Europe |** pour servir | de complément et de supplément | a l'Ornithologie Européenne | De Degland et Gerbe (1867) | par | E.-L. Trouessart | Professeur de Zoologie au Muséum National de Paris | Paris | Libraire des Sciences Naturelles | Paul Klincksieck | Léon Lhomme, Successeur | 3, Rue Corneille, 3 | 1912 | Tous droits de reproduction et de traduction réservés pour tous pays.

1 vol. royal 8vo, pp. I-XVIII, 1-545. Paris.

A catalogue of European birds, arranged in two series, on opposite pages. The left-hand series, or page, gives the nomenclature adopted by Degland and Gerbe, "Ornithologie Européenne," 1867 (q.v.), with page-references to that work; species or subspecies subsequently described are indicated but not named. On the opposite page, with corresponding numbers, modern classification is given according to Hartert, "Vögel der Paläarktischen Fauna," 1903-22 (q.v.), with references to original descriptions, to Dresser's "History of the Birds of Europe," 1871-82 (q.v.), and to occasional synonyms, and with marginal notes on distribution; species or subspecies not given by Degland and Gerbe are briefly described or are characterized by a citation of their limited range, etc.

Trumbull, Gurdon.

1888. **Names | and | portraits of birds | which | interest gunners |** with descriptions | In Language Understanded of the People | by | Gurdon Trumbull | New York | Harper & Brothers, Franklin Square | 1888.

1 vol. post 8vo, pp. I-VIII, 1-221+1, 1 l. (advt.), 91 text-figs. New York.

Accounts of 61 species of North American game birds with brief, general descriptions and notes on the various vernacular names applied to the species by hunters.

A second copy is at hand, lacking the date on the title-page and slightly altered in binding; otherwise identical.

Tschudi, Johann Jacob von. (Cabanis, Jean.)

1844-46. **Untersuchungen | über die | Fauna Peruana |** von | J. J. von Tschudi, | Doctor der Philosophie [*etc.*, *2 lines.*] | St. Gallen. | Druck und Verlag von Scheitlin und Zollikofer. | 1844 - 1846.

1 vol. imperial 4to, 3 pr. ll. (tit., ded. and pref.), pp. I-XXX (introd.), 1 l. (subtit. "Therologie"), pp. 1-262, 1-316 (incl. subtit. "Ornithologie"), 1-80 (incl. subtit. "Herpetologie"), 1-35 (incl. subtit. "Ichthyologie"), pll. I-XVIII (col.; Säugethiere; by J. C. Weber, L. Oppenheim, Jos. Dinke., Theodor Fischer, and Schmidt), I-XXXVI (col.; Vögel; by Jos. Dinkel, Schmidt and J. Werner)

I-XII (col.; Amphibien; by J. Werner), I-VI (col.; Fische; by J. Werner). St. Gallen.

A detailed discussion of the vertebrate fauna of Peru based on the author's investigations during five years of travel in that country. The section on birds bears the following subtitle,—"Ornithologie | bearbeitet | von | Dr. J. J. Tschudi | mit Anmerkungen | von | J. Cabanis, | Adjunkt am zoologischen Museum in Berlin | 1845 und 1846." It contains a preface, a systematic list of species (pp. 15-56) and the general text, which includes descriptions of several new species by Cabanis. Most of the new species were described by Tschudi in the Archiv für Naturgeschichte, 10, Hft. 3, pp. 262-317, July 1844 and 11, Hft. 4, 1845. The entire work appeared in 12 Lieferungen, but there is disagreement among bibliographers as to the issue of the ornithological portions. Lafresnaye (Rev. Zool., 1848, p. 5, footn. 1) remarks that the figure of *Scaphorhynchus chrysocephalus* on pl. 8, fig. 1 of Tschudi was not accompanied by the description; this plate is given the date, 1845, on a following page (l.c., p. 7). Dean (Bibliogr. of Fishes, Pt. 2, p. 565, 1917), quoting Sherborn and the Isis, places 12 plates of birds in Pts. 3-5 issued in 1845, and 5 plates and all of the text of birds (including the conclusion of the mammals and all of the reptiles and fishes) in Pts. 6-12 issued in 1846. Sherborn (Index Animalium, Sect. 2, Pt. I, p. CXXIV, 1922) places pp. 1-32 of birds (with the end of mammals) in Pt. 6, 1846, and the rest of the birds (with reptiles and fishes) in Pts. 7-12, 1846. Engelmann includes pll. I-XVIII and pp. 1-32 of birds in Lieferungen 4-6, dated 1844-46, and adds 8 signatures (to p. 96) and 6 pll. (to pl. XXIV) in Lief. 7, dated 1846. Andreas Wagner (Archiv für Naturg., 12, Hft. 2, p. 168, 1846) says that the 6th Lieferung appeared in 1845 and contained all the systematic list (to p. 56). Hartlaub (Archiv für Naturg., 13, Hft. 2, p. 50, 1847) announces the appearance of the remainder of the text in 1846. Schomburgk (Reisen in Britisch-Guiana, Pt. 3, p. 500, footn., 1848) mentions p. 70 of Lief. 7 of Tschudi. It is evident, in any case, that the descriptive text relating to birds all appeared in 1846 with most of the plates. If pll. I-XII appeared in 1845, the fact does not affect nomenclature since all of the species there figured were described in the Archiv für Naturg., 10, Hft. 3, July 1844. The name on pl. I is suppressed on p. 87, footn.

Tschusi zu Schmidhoffen, Victor Ritter von.

1877. **Die Vögel Salzburg's.** | Eine Aufzählung | aller in diesem Lande bisher beobachteten Arten, mit | Bemerkungen und Nachweisen über ihr Vorkommen | von | Viktor Ritter von Tschusi zu Schmidhofen, | Mitglied der allgemein deutschen ornithologischen Gesellschaft [*etc., 5 lines.*] | Salzburg 1877. | Herausgegeben vom Vereine für Vogelkunde u. Vogelschutz in Salzburg. | Selbstverlag des Vereines. | (Preis 1 fl. Oe. W.).

1 vol. post 8vo, pp. I-XXI+1, 1-90, 1 l. (errata). Salzburg.

An account of the birds of Salzburg, revised and enlarged from a series of contributions published the two preceding years in "Der Zoologische Garten," Vols. XVI and XVII.

BIRDS

OF

EAST LOTHIAN

AND A PORTION OF

THE ADJOINING COUNTIES,

FROM

MEMORANDUMS MADE BETWEEN 1845–1850,

BY

WILLIAM P. TURNBULL,

GLADSMUIR,

MEMBER OF THE ACADEMY OF NATURAL SCIENCES OF PHILADELPHIA.

" When snowdrops die, and the green primrose leaves
Announce the coming flower, the MERLE's note,
Mellifluous, rich, deep-toned, fills all the vale,
And charms the ravished ear."

Grahame's Birds of Scotland.

PHILADELPHIA:

CAXTON PRESS OF C. SHERMAN, SON & CO.

TITLE-PAGE OF WILLIAM P. TURNBULL'S OWN COPY (ON VELLUM) OF HIS
"BIRDS OF EAST LOTHIAN."

See p. 641.

Tschusi zu Schmidhoffen, Victor Ritter von.

1895. See Noska, Max, **Das kaukasische Birkhuhn.**

Tschusi zu Schmidhoffen, Victor Ritter von.

1912. See Dombrowski, Robert Ritter von, **Ornis Romaniae.**

Tunstall, Marmaduke.

1771. Ornithologia Britannica: | seu | Avium omnium Britannicarum tam Terrestrium, | quam Aquaticarum | catalogus, | Sermone Latino, Anglico & Gallico redditus: | cui subjicitur appendix, | aves alienigenas, | in Angliam raro advenientes, complectens. | In tenui labor: at tenuis non gloria - Virg. | London: | Printed for the author by J. Dixwell, in St. Martin's Lane. | M.DCC.LXXI.

1 vol. imperial folio (14¾ x 20), tit., pp. 1-4, 1 text-fig. (by P. Brown). London.

A catalogue of British birds, being, simply, a list of species with names in Latin, English and French. Since the vernacular names are identifiable, the Latin names are tenable and various names date from this publication. This original folio is very rare and for that reason was reprinted in 1880 by the Willughby Society (q.v.).

Tunstall, Marmaduke. (Newton, Alfred, *ed.*)

1880. The Willughby Society. | **Tunstall's** | **Ornithologia Britannica** | [*Vignette.*] | Edited by Alfred Newton, M.A., F.R.S., etc. | London: MDCCCLXXX.

[Ornithologia Britannica: | seu | Avium omnium Britannicarum tam Terrestrium, | quam Aquaticarum | catalogus, | Sermone Latino, Anglico & Gallico redditus: | cui subjicitur appendix, | aves alienigenas, | in Angliam raro advenientes, complectens. | In tenui labor: at tenuis non gloria - Virg. | London: | Printed for the author by J. Dixwell, in St. Martin's Lane. | M.DCC.LXXI. | J. Akerman. Photo-lithographer. London.]

1 vol. 8vo, pp. I-IV, "tit., pp. 1-4, 1 text-fig (by P. Brown)", 2 ll. (advt.). London. "1771." 1880.

A reprint published by The Willughby Society (q.v.). It is in facsimile, reduced from the original folio of 1771 (q.v.) by photolithographic process. A preface by the editor gives a few facts relative to the author.

Turnbull, William Patterson.

1863. Birds | **of** | **East Lothian** | and a portion of | the adjoining counties, from | memorandums made between 1845-1850, | by | William P. Turnbull, | Gladsmuir, | Member of the Academy of

Natural Sciences of Philadelphia. | [*Quot., 5 lines.*] | [*Seal.*] | Philadelphia: | Caxton Press of C. Sherman, Son & Co.

1 vol. post 8vo, pp. 1-15+1. Philadelphia.

A list of 201 birds of East Lothian, Scotland, with notes on seasonal distribution, abundance, local records, etc. The book is undated and "1863" is quoted on the authority of Coues and of Taschenberg. The present copy is printed on vellum and contains the following pencilled inscription. "Unique copy. The only copy printed on vellum. The author's own copy, sold by his grandson, 1922. American-printed ornithological works on vellum are almost unknown." A second edition, under the same title (q.v.), was published in Glasgow in 1867.

Turnbull, William Patterson.

1867. The | birds of East Lothian | and a portion of | the adjoining counties | by William P. Turnbull | Gladsmuir | Member of the Academy [*etc., 3 lines.*]. | [*Col. vignette.*] | Glasgow: printed for private circulation | 1867.

1 vol. royal 4to, pp. I-VII+1, 9-48, frontisp. (col.; by Edwin Sheppard), tit.-vign. and 12 text-figs. (col.; by William Sinclair). Glasgow.

A second edition of the author's earlier work of the same title, 1863 (q.v.), with notes on 235 species and with colored illustrations. A note on the reverse of the title-page announces, "The impression has been limited to one hundred and fifty copies 8vo, and fifty 4to—two of the former being on vellum." Mullens and Swann note that all but twelve of the 4to edition (of which the present copy is one) were destroyed by a fire at the publishers.

Turnbull, William Patterson.

1869. The | birds of East Pennsylvania | and New Jersey | by | William P. Turnbull. LL.D. | Author of the "Birds of East Lothian;" [*etc., 4 lines.*] | [*Vignette.*] | Glasgow: printed for private circulation | 1869.

1 vol. 4to (size of royal 8vo), pp. I-X, 1 l. (list of illustrs. and resumé of spp.), pp. 9-62, tit.-vign. and 19 text-figs. (by Alex. Wilson, William Sinclair, Edwin Sheppard, John Faulkner, M. Julliard, William Bartram and Frank Bott). Glasgow.

An annotated list of 342 birds of "Pennsylvania eastward of the Alleghany Mountains, and of New Jersey, including the coast line which extends from Sandy Hook to Cape May." Notes are given on abundance, dates of occurrence, vernacular names, etc. The drawings after Wilson were taken from his portfolio after his death. A note on the reverse of the title-page announces that the edition of this work was limited to 150 copies 8vo (including the present copy which is 8vo in size although 4to in composition) and 50 copies 4to— two of the former being on vellum. There is also an edition of the same date published in Philadelphia (q.v.). A detailed account of the work appeared in "Cassinia," No. XX, pp. 1-6, 1916.

Turnbull, William Patterson.

1869. The | birds of East Pennsylvania | and New Jersey. | By | William P. Turnbull. LL.D. | Author of the "Birds of East Lo-thian;" [*etc., 4 lines.*]. | [*Quot., 4 lines.*]. | **Philadelphia:** | Henry Grambo & Co., Chestnut Street. | 1869.

1 vol. 4to (size of royal 8vo), pp. I-VII+1, 5-50, (orig. wrapper with vignette). Philadelphia.

An American edition of the work published the same year in Glasgow under the same title (q.v.). The two editions differ in various particulars. The title-pages are distinct (as shown in above transcriptions). There are no illustra-tions in the present edition (except on the wrapper) and the portion of the preface referring to the artistic matter is omitted, necessitating some verbal changes in adjacent paragraphs. The space left by the omission of the illus-trations has been partially filled by combining adjacent pages, leaving the "page make-up" of the letterpress unaltered, although the numbering is changed. This was made possible by the arrangement of the cuts, but the spaces still left between sections of the work are very uneven in size. Two changes in nomenclature are to be noted. *Chordeiles Virginianus* and *Ardea cærulea* of the Glasgow edition are changed to *Chordeiles popetue* and *Ardea caerulea*, respectively. Coues is of the opinion that the present edition is the first, but I believe that the Glasgow edition was printed first, although it may not have been issued until later. Both editions were printed in Glasgow and apparently from the same plates, but the typography is rather clearer, and the impression sharper, in the Glasgow edition while the irregular spacing in the present issue points to omission, rather than to insertion of matter.

Turner, Rev. Mr.

1836. See Selby, Prideaux John, The **Natural History of Parrots.**
1844-64? **Idem,** reissue.

Turner, Emma Louisa.

1910-13. See Kirkman, Frederick Bernuf Bever, **The British Bird Book.**

Turner, Lucien M.

1886. 49th Congress, 1st Session. } Senate. { Mis. Doc. No. 155. | **Contributions | to the |** **natural history of Alaska.** | Results of investigations made chiefly in the Yukon | district and the Aleutian Islands; conducted | under the auspices of the Signal Service, | United States Army, extending from | May, 1874, to August, 1881. | Prepared under the direction of | Brig. and Bvt. Maj. Gen. W. B. Hazen. | Chief Signal Officer of the Army, | by | L. M. Turner. | **No II.** | Arctic Series of Pub-lications issued in connection with the Signal Service, U. S. Army. |

With 26 plates. | Washington: | Government Printing Office. | 1886.

1 vol. medium 4to, pp. 1-226, pll. 1-15 (uncol.) and I-XI (col.; by R. and J. L. Ridgway). Washingtcn.

The work contains six parts, dealing with the general description of the region, meteorology, plants, fishes, birds and mammals. Part V, on the birds, occupies pp. 115-196 and pll. I-XI. This report forms No. II of the Arctic Series of Publications" of which No. III, a "Report upon Natural History Collections made in Alaska in 1877-1881" by E. W. Nelson, 1887 (q.v.), is also in the Ayer Ornithological Library.

Turner, William. (Evans, Arthur Humble; Caius, John.)

1903. **Turner on birds:** | a short and succinct history | of the | principal birds noticed by Pliny and Aristotle, | first published by Doctor William Turner, | 1544. | Edited, | with introduction, translation, notes, and appendix, | by | A. H. Evans, M.A. | Clare College, Cambridge. | Cambridge: | at the University Press | 1903.

[Avivm | praecipv | arum, qvarvm | apvd Plinivm et Ari- | stotelem mentio est, | breuis & | succincta historia. | Ex optimis quibusque scripto- | ribus contexta, | scholio illu | strata & aucta. | Adiectis nominibus Græcis, Germanicis & | Britannicis. | Per Dn. Guilielmum Turnerum, artium & Me- | dicinæ Doctorem. | Coloniæ excudebat Ioan. Gymnicus, | Anno M.D.XLIIII.]

1 vol. post 8vo, pp. I-XVIII, 1 l., pp. 1-223. Cambridge.

A reprint of Turner's rare work in Latin with a translation into English opposing the original, both versions annotated; also, in an appendix, extracts from the work of John Caius [=John Kay], "De Rariorum Animalium atque Stirpium Historia" (1570), similarly treated.

Turton, William.

1802. See Linné, Karl von, **A General System of Nature.**

Turton, William.

1807. **British fauna,** | containing | a compendium | of | The zoology | of the | British Islands: | arranged according to the | Linnean system. | By W. Turton, M.D. F.L.S. | Vol. I. | Including the classes | Mammalia, Birds, Amphibia, | Fishes, and Worms. | [*Quot., 4 lines.*]. | Swansea: | printed by J. Evans, Wind-Street. | 1807.

1 vol. 12mo (3 ¾ x 7), pp. 1-230, I-VII+1 (index and errata). Swansea.

A series of brief diagnoses of classes, orders, genera and species of the animals embraced in the title. The birds are treated on pp. 18-77, including 8 orders, 56 genera and 294 species. The work is not highly regarded and was never carried beyond the limits of the present volume, although the author intended to discuss the remaining animals, the vegetables and the minerals in succeeding volumes. The preface is dated January 1, 1807.

Tweeddale, Arthur, Ninth Marquis of.

See Hay, Arthur.

Tyas, Robert.

1854-56? See Cotton, John, **Beautiful Birds.**

Underwood, Cecil F.

1899. Museo Nacional de Costa Rica | **Avifauna Costarriqueña** | (Edición especial) | **Lista revisada** | conforme á las últimas publicaciones | por | Cecilio F. Underwood, | Taxidermista del Museo | 1899 | San José Costa Rica - A.C | Tip. Nacional | MDCCCXCIX.

1 vol. pamphlet (7¼ x 9¾; trimmed), pp. 1-16, (orig. wrapper). San José.

A simple list of 696 species of birds recorded from Costa Rica. The list, apparently, is "revised" from Zeledón's "Catalogo de las Aves de Costa Rica" (Anales Mus. Nac. Costa Rica, I, pp. 103-133, 1887) although Underwood records fewer forms than Zeledón and places the species in fewer families, dropping all of Zeledón's trinomials in favor of obsolescent binomials.

U. S. Exploring Expedition.

1858. See Wilkes, Charles.

U. S. and Mexican Boundary Survey. (Baird, Spencer Fullerton.)

1859. > { 34th Congress, | 1st Session. } House of Representatives. { Ex. Doc. | No. 135 |
Report | on the | **United States and Mexican Boundary Survey** | made under | the direction of the Secretary of the Interior | by William H. Emory. | Major First Cavalry and United States Commissioner. | **Volume II** | Washington: | Cornelius Wendell, printer. | 1859. > **Part II.** | Zoology of the Boundary.] > United States and Mexican | Boundary Survey, | under the order of | Lieut. Col. W. H. Emory, | Major First Cavalry, and United States Commissioner. | **Birds** | **of the boundary,** | by | Spencer F. Baird, | Assistant Secretary of the Smithsonian Institution. | With notes by the naturalists of the survey.

1 vol. medium 4to, pp. 1-32, 1 l., pll. 1, 2, III-XXV (=25 pll., col.). Washington.

The ornithological portion of the report on the U. S. and Mexican Boundary Survey, being the second article of Pt. II of Vol. II. The text consists of a list of the species and specimens of birds collected on the survey, with field

notes; the full report with descriptions, etc., was included in Baird, Cassin
and Lawrence's extended paper in Vol. IX of the Reports of Explorations and
Surveys - - for a railroad from the Mississippi River to the Pacific Ocean,
published the preceding year (Cf. U. S. Pacific Railroad Surveys, 1858.).
The colored plates, for which the present work is chiefly valued, were not
included in the Pacific Railroad Survey report but were utilized, together with
the plates from other parts of that work, to form the atlas accompanying
Baird, Cassin and Lawrence's "The Birds of North America," 1860 (q.v.).

U. S. Pacific Railroad Surveys. (Baird, Spencer Fullerton; Cassin,
John; Lawrence, George Newbold.)

1858. $\left.{>}33\text{d Congress,}\atop\text{2d Session.}\right\}$ Senate. $\left\{{\text{Ex. Doc.}\atop\text{No. 78.}}\right.$ **Reports | of | explora-
tions and surveys,** to | ascertain the most practicable and economi-
cal route **for a railroad | from the | Mississippi River to the Pacific
Ocean.** | Made under the direction of the Secretary of War, in |
1853-6, | according to acts of Congress of March 3, 1853, May 31,
1854 and August 5, 1854. | **Volume IX.** | Washington: | Beverly
Tucker, printer. | 1858. > **Part II.-** General report upon the zoö-
ogy of the Several Pacific Railroad Routes. > Explorations and
surveys for a railroad route from the Mississippi River to the Pacific
Ocean. | War Department. | **Birds:** | by Spencer F. Baird. |
Assistant Secretary Smithsonian Institution. | With the co-opera-
tion of | John Cassin and George N. Lawrence. | Washington,
D. C. | 1858.

1 vol. medium 4to, pp. I-LVI, 1-1005. Washington.

The most important work on North American birds up to its date since Audubon
and Wilson. The work consists of a critical, descriptive account of all the birds
of North America, north of Mexico, and is not restricted to the species collected
by the Pacific Railroad Surveys. Most of it is by Baird, but pp. 4-64, 689-
753 and 900-918 are by Cassin and pp. 820-900 by Lawrence. Pp. XVII-LVI
were reissued, with separate title-page, in 1858 as Baird's "Catalogue of North
American Birds" (q.v.). The entire volume was reprinted in 1860 with few
alterations and issued, together with plates from other volumes of the Pacific
Railroad Survey reports, the U. S. and Mexican Boundary Survey, and other
sources, as Baird, Cassin and Lawrence's "The Birds of North America"
(q.v.)

The present volume also exists as "House of Representatives. Ex. Doc.
No. 91."

U. S. Pacific Railroad Surveys. (Baird, Spencer Fullerton; Heermann,
A. L.; Kennerly, C.B.R.)

1859. $\left.{>}33\text{d Congress,}\atop\text{2d Session.}\right\}$ Senate. $\left\{{\text{Ex. Doc.}\atop\text{No. 78.}}\right.$ **Reports | of | explora-
tions and surveys,** | to | ascertain the most practicable and econ-

omical route **for a railroad | from the Mississippi River to the Pacific Ocean.** | Made under the direction of the Secretary of War, in | 1853-6, | according to acts of Congress of March 3, 1853, May 31, 1854, and August 5, 1854. | **Volume X.** | Washington: | Beverly Tucker, printer. | 1859.

> [Report | of | Lieut. E. G. Beckwith, | Third Artillery, | upon explorations for a railroad route, | near | the 38th and 39th parallels of north latitude | by | Captain J. W. Gunnison | Corps of Topographical Engineers, | and near | the forty-first parallel of north latitude, | by | Lieut. | E. G. Beckwith, Third Artillery. | 1854. > Zoological Report. | Washington, D. C. | 1857.] > No. 2. | **Report on birds collected on the survey.** | By S. F. Baird.

> [Report | of | explorations for a railway route | (near the thirty-fifth parallel of north latitude,) | from the Mississippi River to the Pacific Ocean. | By | Lieutenant J. C. Ives. | Corps of Topographical Engineers. | 1853-'54. > Part VI. | Zoological Report. > Washington, D. C. | 1859.] > No. 3. | **Report on birds collected on the route.** | By C. B. R. Kennerly, M.D.

> [Report | of | explorations for a railroad route | near | the 32d parallel of north latitude, | lying between | Dona Ana, on the Rio Grande, and Pimas villages, on the Gila, | by | Lieutenant John G. Parke, | Corps of Topographical Engineers. | Washington, D. C. | 1855. > Zoological Report. | Washington, D. C. | 1859.] > No. 1. | **Report upon birds collected on the survey.** | By A. L. Heermann, M.D.

> [Report | of | explorations in California for railroad routes | to connect with | the routes near the 35th and 32d parallels of north latitude. | By | Lieutenant R. S. Williamson, | Corps of Topographical Engineers. | 1853. > Part IV. > Zoological Report. | Washington, D. C. | 1859.] > No. 2. | **Report upon birds collected on the survey.** | By A. L. Heermann, M.D.

1 vol. (pt.) medium 4to., tit.; pp. 11-16, pll. XII-XV, XVII, XXXII and XXXV (=7 pll., col.) (Baird); pp. 19-35, pll. XVIII-XX, XXII, XXVII, XXIX-XXXI, XXXIII, XXXVI and XXXVII (=11 pll., col.) (Kennerly); pp. 9-20+1 l., pll. I, IV and VI (=3 pll. (col.) (Heermann, -Parke's survey); pp. 29-80, pll. II, III, V and VII-X (=7 pll., col.) (Heermann, -Williamson's survey). Washington. 1859.

The present volume is composed of the ornithological papers contained in Vol. X of the Pacific Railroad Survey reports, extracted and bound together with the general title to Vol. X. Vol. X was of composite structure, containing miscellaneous matter properly belonging to other antecedent volumes. Thus,

Baird's paper is a part of Gunnison and Beckwith's report in Vol. II; Kennerly's paper belongs to Ives's report in Vol. IV; Heermann's first article belongs with Parke's report in Vol. VII; his second, with Williamson's report in Vol. V. Regardless of the confusing dates on the titles and subtitles of the various reports, all the matter in Vol. X was published in 1859.

The general title also appears as "House of Representatives. Ex. Doc. No. 91."

Uranie et Physicienne, Voyage autour du Monde, . . . Éxecuté sur les corvettes de S. M. l' - .

1824-26. See Freycinet, Louis de.

Ussher, Richard John; and Warren, Robert.

1900. The | **birds of Ireland** | an account of | the distribution, migrations and habits | of birds as observed in Ireland, with | all additions to the Irish list | by | Richard J. Ussher | and | Robert Warren | including | An Introduction and Tables showing the Distribution of | Birds in the Breeding Season | With a Coloured Plate, Maps, and other Illustrations | [*Monogram.*] | London | Gurney and Jackson, I, Paternoster Row | (Successors to Mr. Van Voorst) | 1900.

1 vol. post 8vo, pp. I-XXXI+1, 1-419, frontisp. (col.), 6 pll. (photograv.), 7 text-figs., 2 maps (col.; fold.). London.

A handbook of information relative to the birds of Ireland, containing the records and materials acquired since the publication of William Thompson's "Natural History of Ireland," 1849-56 (q.v.). Numerous collaborators are thanked for contributions, especially R. M. Barrington whose immediate activity in issuing another publication, ? "The Migration of Birds, 1900 (q.v.), alone prevented his name from appearing on the title-page of this one. Most of the text is from the pen of Ussher; several articles are signed by Warren who, however, furnished abundant material for other portions of the work. Mullens and Swann record a large paper edition with portraits of the authors.

Vaillant, Auguste Nicolas. (Eydoux, F.; Souleyet, François Louis Auguste; Blainville, Henri Marie Ducrotay de.)

1841-52. > **Voyage** | **autour du monde** | exécuté pendant les années 1836 et 1837 | **sur la corvette** | **La Bonite** | commandée par M. Vaillant | Capitaine de Vaisseau | Publié par ordre [Ordre (*Atlas.*)] du Roi [du Gouvernement (*Vol. II and Atlas.*)] | sous les auspices du Département de la Marine. [| Histoire Naturelle (*Atlas.*)] | **Zoologie** | par MM. Eydoux et Souleyet, [*No comma (Atlas.*).] | Medécins de l'expédition. [*Period omitted (Vol. II.*)] | Tome premier. [Tome deuxième. | par M. Souleyet (*Vol. II.*); Atlas (*Atlas.*)] | Paris [*Comma added (Atlas.*).] | Arthus Bertrand, Éditeur [*Comma added (Vol. II and Atlas.*).] | Libraire de la

Société de Géographie, rue Hautefeuille, 23. [21. (*Vol. II.*); *no date (Atlas.)*.] | [de l'imprimerie de Crapelet, rue de Vaugirard, 9. (*Atlas, only.*)].

2 vols. royal 8vo (text) and 1 vol. superroyal folio (atlas). Vol. I, 2 pr. ll. (half-tit. and tit.), pp. I-IV (pref.), I-XXXIX+1, 1-334. Vol. II, 2 pr. ll., (half-tit. and tit.), pp. 1-664. Atlas, tit., pp. 1-8, pll. 1-12 (Mammifères; 8 col.); 1-10 (Oiseaux; 9 col.); 1-4 and 9-10 (Reptiles; 6 col.; pll. 5-8 not issued); 1-10 (Poissons; 10 col.); 1-5 (Crustacés; 5 col.); 1-2 (Insectes; 2 col.); 1-45, 15 bis, 23 bis, 24 bis, 24 A-E (Mollusques; 52 col.); 1-2 (Zoophytes; 2 col.); 1 (Vers; 1 col.) (=101 pll.; 95 col.; by Meunier, Werner, Prévost, P. Oudart, Z. Gerbe, Souleyet, Delahaye, Borromée, Riocreux, Vaillant, Lauret, Bevalet and Prêtre). Paris 1841-52 (1840-66).

The zoological portion of the report on the voyage of La Bonite around the world in 1836-37. The entire work (publ. 1840-66) comprises 15 vols. of text (in 11) and 3 vols. of plates, including a separate volume on Zoophytology (published in 1844) which is not included in the present set. The zoology was entrusted to Eydoux and Souleyet who began the preparation of Vol. I (including the birds). The death of Eydoux on July 6, 1841 (Cf. p. II of pref., Vol. I.) necessitated the completion of the project by Souleyet, in which he acknowledges the assistance of P. Gervais. The ornithological matter in Vol. I is contained on pp. 69-132, of which pp. 107-132 were supplied by de Blainville. A few species of birds are mentioned, also, by de Blainville on pp. III-IV in a chapter on "Instructions zoologiques relatives au voyage" and on pp. XIX-XXII in a general survey of the scientific results of the voyage. A number of new species are described by Eydoux and Souleyet. The plates of birds are by Prévost.

Vol. I is divided into two parts bearing the distinguishing signatures, "Partie I" and "Partie II." The first part (as so divided) includes pp. I-IV (pref.), I-XXXIX+1, and 1-132, which just close the ornithological portion of the volume. The second part embraces pp. 133-334. Sherborn (Ann. and Mag. Nat. Hist., **7**, ser. **7**, p. 391, 1901), quoting from the Bibliographie de la France, 18 Dec. 1841, Wiegmann's Archiv, 1842 (Jahrg. 9, 2 Bd.), pp. 16 and 38, and l.c., 1843 p. 156, cites pp. I-XXXIX and 1-106 as of 1841, and 107-328 as of 1842. This division does not accord with the signatures in the volume while, on the other hand, additional evidence seems to point to the publication of pp. 107-132 with "Partie I" where they naturally belong. Wiegmann's Archiv gives no references to pages of the "Voyage," but (in 1842, p. 16) says that that part published includes the mammals and birds, while on pp. 84-85 of the same year an extensive review is given of the paper by de Blainville (on *Chionis*) which occupies the pages in dispute (107-132). In the next year, 1843, p. 156, the reviewer states that he has not seen the remainder of the zoology of the "Voyage" (which is here noted as published) and will have to postpone his review of it, accordingly. Evidently, pp. 107-132 could not have been among the portions included here and must have appeared the year before when it was reviewed. "Partie I" includes the preface (pp. I-IV) which is dated November 1841 and if all of "Partie I" appeared together, it fixes the

date of the ornithology of the voyage as between the first of November and
December 18 of that year. The date on Vol. II is conceded to be correct by
Sherborn (l.c.). The plates may have accompanied the text.

Vallentin, Rupert.

1924. See Boyson, V. F., **The Falkland Islands.**

Valli da Todi, Antonio.

1601. Il canto de gl'avgelli (*sic*), | opera nova | di Antonio Valli | da
Todi, | dove si dichiara la natvra, | di sessanta forte di Vcelli, che
cantano per esperien- | za, e diligenza fatta più volte. | Con le loro
figure, & vinti forte di Caccie, cauate dal naturale | da Antonio
Tempesti. | Con Priuilegio di S. Santità per Anni X. | [*Design.*] | In
Roma, Per gli Heredi di Nicolò Mutij. | Con Licenza de' Superiori.
M.DCI. [*Title surrounded by ornamental border.*].

1 vol. demy 4to (7x9½), 4 pr. ll. (tit., ded., papal privilege, pref.),
50 ll. (numbered 1-50), 4 ll. (unnumbered), 6 inserts (opposite ll.
3, 5, 6, 18, 35 and 37), 60 text-figs.+title-figs. and numerous initials
and tail-pieces. Rome.

A curious old work on song-birds and methods of catching and keeping them.
The illustrations are all woodcuts, most of which are signed, "Iohannes Maivs."
Four illustrations are duplicated on regular leaves and five on inserts, one of
the former being overprinted on a figure which, in turn, is duplicated on one
of the inserts. One of the inserts is not elsewhere printed. These inserts
appear to be proof-sheets since they have no lettering on the reverse (as in the
copies elsewhere in the book) but often are backed by poor impressions of some
other figure; they are pasted on blank sheets. The copy is beautifully bound
in crimson morocco with gold tooling, the binding being signed by "Chambolle-
Duru."

Van Dam, D. C.

See Dam, D. C. van.

Van Dyke, T. S.

1902. See Sandys, Edwyn; and Van Dyke, **Upland Game Birds.**

Van Dyke, T. S.

1903. See Sanford, L. C.; Bishop; and Van Dyke, **The Water-fowl
Family.**

Van Hasselt, J. C.

See Hasselt, J. C. van.

Van Oort, E. D.

1918-date. Ornithologia Neerlandica | De | Vogels | van | **Neder-
land** | door | Prof. Dr. E. D. Van Oort | Directeur van 's Rijks

Museum van Natuurlijke Historie te Leiden | Erste Deel | Colym-
biformes - Procellariiformes - Pelecaniformes - | Ardeiformes -
Anseriformes | Met 87 gekleurde platen | [*Design.*] | 'S Graven-
hage | Martinus Nijhoff | 1922.

27 pts. (work to be complete in 5 vols.) imperial 4to. Vol. I, pp.
I-XII, 1 l. (errata), pp. 1-250, pll. 1-87 (col.; by M. A. Koekkoek),
2 text-figs. Vol. II, pp. 1-96 (more to follow), pll. 88-189 (col.).
Vol. III, (no text yet issued), pll. 190-260 (complete?). Vols. IV
and V, (no text or plates yet issued). The Hague.

A monograph of the birds of Holland with full descriptions of the various plumages
and detailed notes on distribution and habits. The plates are chromolithographic, with large, clear figures and are especially good in showing different plumages. The work is being issued in parts, of which 1-26 have appeared as follows. Pt. **1**, pp. 1-24, pll. 1-10 and Pt. **2**, pp. 25-26, pll. 11-20,
- 1918 (reviewed Orn. Monatsb. Nov.-Dec. 1918); Pts. **3-4**, pp. 57-120, pll.
21-40, - May, 1919 (date given in Auk **37**, p. 147 although included in the Zool.
Record for 1918); Pt. **5**, pp. 121-152, pll. 41-50 and Pt. **6**, pll. 51-60, -(circa
March) 1920 (reviewed Orn. Monatsb., Mar.-April, 1920); Pts. **7-8**, pll. 61-80,
-1921 (reviewed Auk, April 1921); Pt. **9**, pll. 81-87, 91-93, -1921; Pts. **10-12**,
pll. 89, 90, 94, 98-100, 103-105, 107, 109-111, 114, 124-126, 131-133, 138, 144,
167, 168, 170-173, 180 and 183, -1922 (reviewed Auk, July, 1922); Pt. **13**, pll.
88, 101, 112, 113, 118, 123, 134, 135, 140 and 141, and Pt. **14**, pll. 142, 143, 148,
149, 151, 155-158 and 178, - June 1922 (date on slip attached to wrapper);
Pt. **15**, remainder of text of Vol. I, pll. 95-97, 102, 106, 108, 115-117 and 119,
-Nov. 1, 1922 (Cf. Auk, **40**, p. 156, footn., 1923.); Pt. **16**, pll. 120-122, 127-130,
136, 137 and 139, and Pt. **17**, pll. 145-147, 150, 152-154 and 159-161, - Nov.
1922 (date in wrapper); Pts. **18** and **19**, pll. 162-166, 169, 174-177, 179, 181,
182 and 184-189, - Dec. 29, 1922 (date in wrapper); Pts. **20-23**, pll. 190-196,
209, 210, 215-232, 234-236, 238, 248-250, 252-256, 258 and 259, - Nov. 1923
(date in wrapper); Pts. **24-26**, pll. 197-208, 211-214, 233, 237, 239-247, 251,
257 and 260, - Jan. 1924 (date in wrapper). Pt. **27** (? Not numbered.), pp.
1-96 of Vol. II, - Oct. 1925 (date on wrapper).

According to a note on the inside of the rear cover of Pt. 27 (?), Vol. I is
calculated to contain the groups of birds from the Grebes to the Ducks and
Geese; II, Hawks to Snipes; III, Gulls to Woodpeckers; IV, Swallows to Larks;
V, Waxwings to Finches.

Van Pelt Lechner, A. A.

1911-14. "Oologia Neerlandica" | Eggs | of | birds | breeding in
the Netherlands | by | A. A. Van Pelt Lechner | Member of the
Board of the "Nederlandsche Vereeniging" | (Netherland Orni-
thological Society) | With 191 plates containing 667 objects of
which 617 printed in colours and | 50 in collotype, taken from
specimens in the author's collection. | First [Second] volume |
[*Design.*] | The Hague | Martinus Nijhoff | 1910-1913.

2 vols. demy 4to. Vol. I, 3 pr. ll. (half-tit., tit. and conts.), 115 ll., pll. 1-99 (86 col.). Vol. II, 3 pr. ll., 89 ll., 1 insert-slip (errata), pll. 100-191 (89 col.). The Hague.

A work on the eggs of the birds of Holland, of unusual merits. The plates consist of separate figures of single eggs mounted in panels with a very pleasing effect, and the representations are mostly very natural and accurate. The text combines the usual tabulation of nidification-data (placed opposite the respective plates) with a special study of the characteristics of the eggs of the different families (placed at the head of each family). This study embraces the texture, composition and pigmentation of the shell, the dietary and other causes for variation or peculiarity in ground-color or markings, and similar topics not usually discussed in oological handbooks. The work was issued in 7 parts, somewhat as follows. Pt. 1, pll. 1-10, 12, 13, 15, 16, 20, 23, 25, 27-29, 33-35, 37, 39-44, 46, 47, 76, 83 and 84, Sept. 1911 (reviewed Auk, Jan. 1912); II, (40 pll.?), 1911 (Zool. Record); III, 36 pll., 1912 (Auk, July 1912); IV, (20 pll.?), Jan. 1913 (Auk, April 1914); V, (20 pll.?), Aug. 1913 (Auk, April 1914); VI, (20 pll.?), Nov. 1913 (Auk, April 1914); VII, 20 pll., Febr. 1914 (Auk, April 1914). The work was issued in an edition of 250 copies, 100 of which were printed in English (including the present set).

Vega-expeditionens . . . . Bidrag till kännedomen om Sibiriska Ishafskustens fogel-fauna.

See Nondenskiöld, Nils Adolph Erik von.

Vennor, Henry G.

1876. **Our birds of prey,** | or the | eagles, hawks, and owls | of | Canada. | By | Henry G. Vennor, F.G.S. | Of the Geological Survey of Canada. | With 30 Photographic Illustrations by Wm. Notman. | Montreal: | published by Dawson Brothers. | 1876.

1 vol. demy 4to, pp. I-VIII, 1-154, pll. I-XXX+XXVII (bis). Montreal.

Brief descriptions of the species and detailed accounts of their habits, illustrated by photographs of mounted specimens.

Vénus, Voyage autour du Monde sur la fregate La—; Zoologie.

1846-55. See Petit-Thouars, Abel du.

Verreaux, Édouard.

1866. See Mulsant, Etienne; Verreaux; and Verreaux, **Essai d'une Classification Méthodique des Trochilidés ou Oiseaux-Mouches.**

Verreaux, Édouard.

1873-78. See Mulsant, Etienne; and Verreaux, **Histoire Naturelle des Oiseaux-Mouches ou Colibris.**

Verreaux, Édouard.

1879. See Mulsant, Etienne; and Verreaux, **Histoire Naturelle des Oiseaux-Mouches ou Colibris; Supplement.**

Verreaux, Jules.

1866. See Mulsant, Etienne; Verreaux; and Verreaux, **Essai d'une Classification Méthodique des Trochilidés ou Oiseaux-Mouches.**

Verreaux, Jules.

1880. See Smith, Andrew, The Willughby Society, **Sir Andrew Smith's Ornithological papers.**

Verrill, Alpheus Hyatt.

1905. **Addition to the avifauna of Dominica.** | Notes on species hitherto unrecorded with | descriptions of three new species and a | list of all birds now known to occur | on the island. | By A. Hyatt Verrill.

1 vol. post 8vo, 19 ll. (?). Between Aug. 1 and Oct. 24, 1905.

Part I contains a list of birds obtained and observed by the author from Jan. 1, 1904 to Aug. 1, 1905, including only such species as were previously unrecorded from Dominica. Notes are given on the habits or occurrence of each species. Pt. II treats, similarly, those species, also formerly recorded, which were observed during the preceding year, and closes with a list of all species of birds known from the island. A third part, separately (sub)titled and, according to the errata, intended to be separately paged, contains the descriptions of three Dominican birds considered to be new,—*Thalurania belli*, *Buteo* (*latissimus*) *rivierei*, and *Septophaga* (sic) (*ruticilla*) *tropica*.

This pamphlet was privately printed without date or place of publication. The copy is reviewed in the Auk, **23**, p. 236, April 1906, was noted as received Oct. 24, 1905. A more extensive paper on the avifauna of Dominica was published by A. H. and G. E. Verrill in the Trans. Conn. Acad., **8**, pp. 315-359, pll. 1-3, 1892.

Verster de Wulverhorst, A. H.

1844-53. See Schlegel, Hermann; and Wulverhorst, **Traité de Fauconnerie.**

Veth, Pieter Jan. (Snellmann, Joh. F.)

1886. [**Midden-Sumatra.** Reizen en onderzoekingen der Sumatra-Expeditie, mitgerust door het (Aardrijkskundig) Gennotschap, 1877 - 1879, beschreven door de leden der Expeditie, onder tiezicht van . . . . P. J. Veth > Deel IV. Natuurlijke Historie. I. Fauna. Bijdragen tot de Kennis der Fauna van Midden-Sumatra.] > **Natuurlijke historie.** | Eerste afdeeling. | **Zoogdieren en vogels,** | door | Joh. F. Snellman.

1 vol. (pt.) demy 4to, pp. 1-58, 1 pl. (col.; mammal), pll. I-IV (col., by Keulemans; birds). Amsterdam.

The ornithological and mammalogical portion of the Amsterdam Geographical Society's report on central Sumatra, published in 9 vols. from 1881 to 1892. The present portion is part of Section 1 of Vol. IV, and is under the authorship of Snellman. Pages 30-52 are ornithological and contain an annotated list of the birds of the region under consideration.

Vieillot, Louis Jean Pierre.

1800-1802. See Audebert, Jean Baptiste; and Vieillot, **Oiseaux Dorés.**

Vieillot, Louis Jean Pierre.

1805 - ? **Histoire naturelle | des-plus beaux | oiseaux chanteurs | de | la zone torride: | par L. P. Vieillot. | A Paris, | Chez J. E. Gabriel Dufour, Libraire. | M. DCCC. V.**

1 vol. royal folio, 2 pr. ll. (half-tit. and tit.), pp. 1-112, 52* and 52**, pll. 1-70, 28* and 28** (col.; by Prêtre). Paris.

Descriptions and colored plates of a number of tropical weaver-birds, finches, and tanagers. According to Engelmann, the work appeared in 12 livraisons from 1805 onward. The Cat. Libr. Brit. Mus. (Nat. Hist.), quoting the Journ. Gén. Lit. France, credits Pts. 1 and 2 to 1805, 3 and 4 to 1806 and **5** and 6 to 1808, but the limits of the various parts are unknown. On p. 109 there is a reference to p. 239 of Temminck's "Catalogue Systematique du Cabinet d'Ornithologie" (1807 q.v.) which contained a criticism of matter published on p. 58 of the present work; hence it may be inferred that p. 58 was included in Pts. 1-4 and that p. 109 was issued in or after 1807. On p. 110, Temminck is called the author of the "Histoire des Pigeons" (Cf. Knip, Les Pigeons, 1809-11.) the first number of which appeared in 1809; hence the last number of the present work may be supposed to have been issued in 1809 or later.

Vieillot, Louis Jean Pierre.

1807-(1809 ?). **Histoire naturelle | des oiseaux | de | l'Amérique septentrionale, |** contenant un grand nombre d'espèces decrites ou figurées | pour la première fois. | Par M. L. P. Vieillot, | continuateur de l'Histoire des Colibris et des Oiseaux-Mouches; auteur de celle des Jacamars, | des Grimpereaux, des Promerops, des Oiseaux de Paradis, et de la plupart des articles d'Ornithologie | du nouveaux Dictionnaire d'Histoire naturelle, etc. | Tome premier [second]. | A Paris, | chez Desray, Libraire, Rue Hautefeuille, No 4. | M.DCCC.VII. | De l'imprimerie de Crapelet.

2 vols. columbier folio. Vol. I, 2 pr. ll. (half-tit. and tit.), pp. I-IV, 1-90, 28*, 28**, 38* and 38**, pll. 1-57, 2 bis, 3 bis, 10 bis and 14 bis

(col.; by Prêtre). Vol. II, 2 pr. ll., pp. I-II, 1-74, pll. 58-124, 57 bis, 68 bis and 90 bis (col.). Paris.

Descriptions of many North American birds, with hand-colored plates of most of them. Great uncertainty exists as to the dates of appearance of this work. Engelmann notes that it appeared in 22 livraisons of 6 pll. each, dating 1807 and "ann. suiv." Richmond (Auk, 16, p. 327, 1899) gives Dec. 1, 1807 as the date of the first livraison. Sherborn (Index Anim., Sec. 2, Pt. 1, p. CXXVI, 1922) thinks that all of Vol. I should be dated 1807. Owing to the close approximation of dates in Wilson's "American Ornithology," 1808-14 (q.v.), exact determination of the dates of the present work would be very desirable and may necessitate some changes of nomenclature when they are fully known. There is an undated, unsigned manuscript note pasted in the front of the copy at hand, purporting to be from Desray, the editor of the work, advising that 22 livraisons had been published and that he was no longer connected with the work and had no intention to continue it. The note further states that there were two formats, a "Jesus Velin" and a "Columbier, aussi Velin," of which latter there were but 20 copies including the present one. Engelmann catalogues a format with black plates in addition to the two issues here mentioned. As regards the apparent incompleteness of the work, Vol. I, pp. III and IV, contains references to Vols. III and IV which were never published.

Vieillot, Louis Jean Pierre.

1816. **Analyse | d'une nouvelle | ornithologie | élémentaire, |** Par L. P. Vieillot, | auteur de divers ouvrages d'ornithologie, et un des | collaborateurs du Nouveau Dictionnaire d'Histoire | Naturelle. | Paris, | Deterville, Libraire, rue Hautefeuille, no. 8 | De l'imprimerie de A. Berlin. | 1816.

1 vol. demy 8vo, tit., pp. 1-70. Paris.

An essay on the classification of birds, with diagnoses of the genera and higher groups and the nomination of one or more species (usually in vernacular) for each genus. Many of the generic names are new and sixteen new species are described on pp. 68 and 69. The receipt of the work was acknowledged in the Bibliographie de la France on April 14, 1816, according to Mathews (Birds of Australia, 7, p. 472, 1919). The original is quite rare but has been reprinted by the Willughby Society in 1883 (q.v.).

Vieillot, Louis Jean Pierre.

1820-23. See Bonnaterre; and Vieillot, **Tableau Encyclopédique et Méthodique des Trois Règnes de la Nature,** 1790-1823.

Vieillot, Louis Jean Pierre; and Oudart, Paul Louis.

1820-26. **La | galerie des oiseaux, |** Dédiée à Son Altesse Royale | Madame, Duchesse de Berri. | Par M. L. P. Vieillot, | Continuateur de l'Histoire des Oiseaux dorés [etc., 4 lines.]; | et par M. P. Oudart, | peintre en histoire naturelle, [etc.]. | Tome premier [deuxième]. | Premiere et deuxième [Troisième, Quatrième et Cinquième]

Parties. | Paris, | Constant-Chantpie, Éditeur, Rue Sainte-Anne, No 20. | 1825.

2 vols. foliopost 4to. Vol. I, pp. I-V (half-tit., tit. and notice by ed.), 1 l. (ded.), pp. J-IIJ+1 (introd.), pp. 1-56 (Pt. 1), 1-344 (Pt. 2, index to Vol. I and errata), pll. 1-150, 152-198, 23 bis (col.; by Oudart; 2 fold.). Vol. II, 2 pr. ll. (half-tit. and tit.), pp. 1-246, 1 l. (index to Vol. II), pp. 1-8, 1-4, 2 ll. (unpaged), pp. 1-3+1, 1-2, 2 ll. (unpaged), pp. 1-2, 1-2, 1-3+1, 1-3+1, 1-2, 1-2, 1-4, 1-2, 1-3+1, 1-3+1, 1 l. (unpaged) (=29 ll.), pll. 199-301 (col.; 1 fóld.), A-K, M, M(*bis*=L), N-V, X-Z, AA-HH (uncol.), 24 pll. (col.). Paris.

Originally planned to give colored figures of all the birds in the galleries of the Paris Museum, accompanied by brief general accounts of each. Six livraisons were issued thus, with 24 plates by Oudart and with anonymous text which is probably also by Oudart since the dedication is signed by him. This original matter forms the variously paged text and the unnumbered plates at the close of Vol. II. The enormity of this project caused its abandonment and the substitution of a more modest program, with the writing of the text assigned to Vieillot, and livraisons 7-82 carried the work to completion.

Considerable confusion exists as to the composition of the various livraisons, although the date of each is known with fair accuracy from the current numbers of the Bibliographie de la France, quoted by Mathews (Austr. Av. Rec., **2**, No. 7, pp. 153-158, 1913). In general there were 4 colored plates to each livraison, but there were exceptions and the 33 uncolored plates of bills and feet (pll. A-HH in Vol. II) were distributed over the course of the work where their points of occurrence are uncertain. The citations quoted by Mathews give, in most cases, the number of plates to each livraison and sometimes indicate the appearance of a black plate, but the figures fail to agree with other known facts. Livraisons 34, 55 and 58 are said to contain double plates. The three double (or folded) plates of the work are 107, 192 and 204, and these are spaced so as to agree with each other and with the number of plates as given for the intervening livraisons. However, Mathews, quoting the "Bulletin Général et Universel" of Férussac, shows that Livrs. 26-28 contained Pll. 76-87 (in regular order, four to each livraison), and these figures will not permit the occurrence of Pl. 107 in Livr. 34 nor with Pl. 1 in Livr. 7. Livr. 16 is said to be missing from the set reviewed in the Bibl. de la France, so that the number of plates contained in this part remains a matter for conjecture, as does the proper apportionment of some plates in every part thereafter. Furthermore, it is impossible to correlate the number of plates in some of the livraisons with the number discussed in corresponding signatures of text, from which it appears that text and plates were not always synchronous and that a description and name may have preceded the corresponding figure or vice versa.

Irregularities in the bound copy are as follows. Parts I and II (Vol. I) are each paged separately; Pts. III-V (Vol. II) continuously, with the plates numbered consecutively from Pt. I to Pt. V. Plate 151 is omitted and 23 bis added. Pl. 300 occurs between 232 and 233 and 301 between 292 and 293.

Vieillot, Louis Jean Pierre. (Saunders, Howard, *ed.*)

1883. The Willughby Society. | **Vieillot's** | **Analyse** | **d'une** | **Nouvelle Ornithologie Élémentaire.** | [*Vignette.*] | Edited by | Howard Saunders, F.L.S., F.Z.S. | London: MDCCCLXXXIII.

Analyse | d'une nouvelle | ornithologie | élémentaire, | Par L. P. Vieillot, | auteur [*etc., 3 lines.*]. | Paris, | Deterville, Libraire, rue Hautefeuille, no. 8. | De l'imprimerie de A. Belin. | 1816.

1 vol. 8vo, pp. I-IV, "tit., pp. 1-70." "Paris. 1816." London. 1883.

A copy of the original work of 1816 (q.v.), reprinted verbatim, including all typographical errors. The preface, by the editor, contains a brief account of Vieillot.

Vigors, Nicholas Aylward.

1832. See Gould, John, **A Century of Birds from the Himalaya Mountains.**

Vigors, Nicholas Aylward.

1839. See Beechey, Frederick W., **The Zoology of Captain Beechey's Voyage.**

Vines, Stuart.

1899. See Fitz Gerald, Edward A.; and Vines, **The Highest Andes.**

Virey, J. J.

1800-05. See Buffon, George L. L., **Histoire Naturelle, Générele et Particuliere.**

Visger, Mrs. Owen.

See Owen, Jean A.

Voigt, Friedrich Siegfried.

1831-43. See Cuvier, Georges L. C. F. D., **Das Thierreich.**

Vosmaer, Arnout.

1758. See Moehring, P. H. G., **Geslachten der Vogelen.**

Vosmaer, Arnout.

1804. Description | d'un | recueil exquis | d'animaux rares, | Consistant en | quadrupedes, oiseaux et serpents, | des Index orientales, et occidentales. | S'ayant trouvés ci devant vivants aux Ménageries appartenantes à son Altesse | Monseigneur le Prince D'Orange-Nassau. | Par feu Mr. | A. Vosmaer, | De sa vie Conseilleur de S.A.S., Directeur de son Cabinet [*etc., 5 lines.*] | Avec Figures dessinées et enluminées d'après Nature. | A Amsterdam, chez | J. B. Elwe, | MDCCCIV.

1 vol. demy 4to, pp. I-VI, 1 l. (conts.), pp. 1-15+1, 1-8, 1-8, 1-11+1, 1-12, 1-19+1, 1-6, 1-6, 1-6, 1-10, 1-10, 1-6, 1-6, 1-23+1, 1-14 (12 wrongly num. 24), 1-2, 1-13+1, 1-14, 1-11+1, 1-46 (end of Mammals), 1-8, 1-9+1, 1-6, 1-7+1, 1-7+1, 1-7+1, 1-10, 1-8, 1-11+1, 1-8 (end of Birds), 1-20, 1-8, 1-8 (end of Reptiles), illum. tit., pll. I-XXI+1 (Mammals; col.; II-IV unnum.;), I-X (Birds; col.; I-III unnum.), Ia, Ib and II (Reptiles; col.) Plates by A. Schouman, G. Hasbroek, van Noorden, P. C. Haag, G. van den Keurel and C. van Kuik.). Amsterdam.

A posthumous edition of Vosmaer's writings, consisting of 20 papers on mammals 10 on birds and 3 on reptiles, each with separate (original) pagination and title-pages, and provided with a covering title, preface and list of contents. The ornithological matter consists of the following papers. "Trompette Americain" 1768, "Alcyon d'Amerique, à longue queuë," 1768, "Petits Alcyons des Indes Orientales" 1768, "Grive d'Amerique, nommée Quereiva" 1769, "Coqdes-Roches Americain" 1769, "Perroquet des Indes, nommé Lory Rougepourpré" 1769, "Oiseau de Proie, nommé le Sagittaire" 1769, "Pigeon Canelle de Ceilon" 1805, and "Courli Africain" 1805.

Voyages.

Astrolabe. See Dumont D'Urville, Jules Sebastien César, 1830-35.

Astrolabe and Zélée. See Dumont D'Urville, J. S. C., 1842-54.

Beagle, See Darwin, Charles, 1838-44.

Blossom. See Beechey, Frederick William, 1839.

Bonite, La. See Vaillant, Auguste Nicolas, 1841-52.

Challenger. See Thomson, C. Wyville, 1881.

Coquille, La. See Duperrey, Louis Isidore, 1826-30.

Idem. See Lesson, René Primevère, 1839.

Curaçoa. See Brenchley, Julius Lucius, 1873.

Corwin. See Healy, Michael A., 1887.

Erebus and Terror. See Richardson, John; and Gray, John Edward, 1844-75.

Favorite, La. See Laplace, Cyrille Pierre Théodore, 1839.

Hecla and Fury. See Parry, William Edward, 1826.

King George and Queen Charlotte. See Portlock, Nathaniel, 1826.

King George and Queen Charlotte. See Dixon, George, 1826.

Marchesa. See Guillemard, Francis Henry Hill, 1886.

Novara. See Wüllerstorf-Urbair, B. von, 1865.

Sulphur. See Hinds, Richard Brinsley, 1843-44.

Thétis and Espérance. See Bougainville, Louis Antoine, 1837.

Uranie and Physicienne. See Freycinet, Louis de, 1824-26.

Vega. See Nordenskiöld, Nils Adolph Erik von, 1887.

Vénus. See Petit-Thouars, Abel Aubert du, 1846-55.

Voyage dans l'Inde par Victor Jacquemont. See Geoffroy Saint-Hilaire, Isidore, 1842(?)-43.

Wagler, Johann Georg.

1827. Systema avium. | Auctor | Dr. Joannes Wagler. | Pars prima. | Stuttgartiae et Tubingae | Su tibus J. G. Cottae. MDCCCXXVII.

1 vol. cap 8vo, 2 pr. ll. (tit. and ded.), 14 ll. (pref.), 190 ll. Stuttgart and Tubingen.

A descriptive catalogue of genera and species of birds, with synonymies and notes on the distribution of many forms. Numerous new genera and species are described herein. The work was never completed, there is no index, and the various genera with their included species, are not in systematic or alphabetical order. The last three leaves contain addenda.

Wagler, Johann Georg.

1832. Monographia | **Psittacorum.** | Auctor | Wagler.

1 vol. demy 4to, 3 pr. ll. (half-tit., pref.), pp. 469-750 [pll. XXII-XXVII missing; col.]. Munich.

A monograph of the parrots, with descriptions of many new genera and species. The work appeared originally in the Abhandlungen der königl. Bayerischen Akademie der Wissenschaften, Mathematisch-physikal. Classe, 1, 1832. Coues and Engelmann quote the Denkschriften der Königl. Akad. der Wiss. zu München, 1, 1832, but Vol. 1 of that publication appeared in 1808 and the preface to the present work is dated Christmas 1830. The colored plates, missing from the present copy, are listed by Coues. A separate edition is listed by the Catalogue of the Library of the British Museum (Natural History) under date of 1835, apparently separately paged; the copy at hand has the original pagination.

Wagler, Johann Georg. (Sclater, Philip Lutley, *ed.*)

1884. The Willughby Society. | **Wagler's** | **six ornithological memoirs** | **from the 'Isis.'** | [*Vignette.*] | Edited by | P. L. Sclater, M.A., Ph.D., F.R.S., | Secretary to the Zoological Society of London. | London: MDCCCLXXXIV.

1 vol. 4to (size of royal 8vo), pp. I-IV, 1 l. (conts.), pp. 1-137+1 (1-132 with original miscellaneous paging also given), 1 l. (advt.). London.

A reprint (with "corrections of a few very obvious misprints") of six ornithological contributions published by Wagler in the "Isis" from 1829-32, republished by The Willughby Society (q.v.) on account of the rarity of the originals. The six papers are as follows:

Beyträge und Bemerkungen zu dem ersten Bande seines Systema Avium. Isis, 1829, Heft 5, pp. 505-519; idem, Fortsetzung I, l.c., Heft 6, pp. 645-664; idem, Fortsetzung III, l.c., Heft 7, pp. 736-762.

Revisio generis Pipra. L.c., 1830, Heft 9, pp. 928-943.

Revisio generis Penelope. L.c. 1830, Heft 11, pp. 1109-1112.

Einige Mittheilungen über Thiere Mexicos, von Wagler. L.c., 1831, Heft 4, pp. 510-553.

Mittheilungen über einige merkwürdige Thiere von Wagler. L.c. 1832, Heft 3, pp. 275-282.

Neue Sippen und Gattungen der Säugethiere und Vögel, von Wagler. L.c., Heft 11, pp. 1218-1235.

The editor's preface of the reprint contains a short account of the author.

Wagner, Rudolf.

1847. See Gould, John, **J. Gould's Monographie der Ramphastiden,** 1841-47.

Wait, Walter Ernest.

1925. Ceylon Journal of Science | **Manual** | of the | **birds of Ceylon** | by | W. E. Wait, M.A., (Edin), F.Z.S., M.B.O.U. | Ceylon Civil Service | 1925 | Ceylon. | The Director, Colombo Museum. | London. | Dulau & Co., Ltd., 34, Margaret St, Cavendish Sq., W. 1. | Price Rs. 10/- or, in England, 15/-.

1 vol. demy 4to, 3 pr. ll. (half-tit., tit. and conts.), pp. 1-496, 20 printed guard-sheets (expl. of pll.), pll. I-XX, 1 map (fold.), 1 text-fig. Colombo.

A well written manual of the subject, which presents "a classification and nomenclature, as far up to date as possible, of all the birds which have been found in the Island; giving at the same time brief statements of their description, distribution, habits and nidification. Vernacular names are given where known. Artificial keys to the species of the various families, subfamilies or "groups" are supplied, and a glossary of technical terms is added. The plates are half-tone reproductions of drawings, each illustrating three species. The work adopts modern trinomial nomenclature.

Walden, Viscount.

See Hay, Arthur.

Walcott, John.

1789. **Synopsis** | of | **British birds.** | By John Walcott, Esq. | [*Quot., 3 lines.*]. | London: | Printed by W. Justins, Shoemaker Row, Blackfriars, | For the author: | And sold by Mess. White and Son, Fleet Street; | Robson and Clarke, New-Bond Street; | And J. Mathews, Strand. | M,DCC,LXXXIX.

2 vols. in 1 vol., cap 4to. Vol. I, 148 ll., 121 text-figs. Vol. II, 167 ll., 134 text-figs. London.

Descriptions of the appearance and habits of 255 British birds, illustrated by copper-plate engravings of each. One leaf is devoted to each subject, printed on one side only, with text on the lower half of the page and the engraving above. Diagnostic characters of genera and orders are given on interpolated leaves, with the addition of a preface in Vol. I. The title-pages are identical in both volumes. The drawings, with a few exceptions "copied from Brisson, and others", are original, 200 of them from specimens taken by the author, the remainder from specimens in the collections of Parkinson and Latham. The work exists, also, with colored figures.

Walckenaer, Charles Athanese.

1809. See Azara, Félix de, **Voyages dans l'Amérique Méridionale.**

Walker, Margaret Coulson.

1908. **Bird Legend and Life** | by | Margaret Coulson Walker | Author of [*etc., 4 lines.*] | [*Quot., 4 lines.*] | New York | The Baker & Taylor Company | 1908.

1 vol. royal 8vo, pp. I-XVI, 1-229, 34 pll. (on numbered pp.). New York.

A popular work containing a collection of "avian legends and superstitions" from various sources. Illustrated from photographs.

Wallace, Robert L.

1884. **The canary book:** | containing | full directions for the breeding, rearing, and | management of canaries and canary mules; | cage making, &c.; | formation of canary societies; | exhibition canaries, their points, and how to breed | and exhibit them; | and all other matters connected with this fancy. | Illustrated. | By Robert L. Wallace. | **Second edition,** | Enlarged and Revised, with many New Illustrations of Prize | Birds, Cages, &c. | London: | L. Upcott Gill, 170, Strand, W.C.

1 vol. crown 8vo, pp. I-IV, 1-321, 1 p.+1 l.+pp. 1-12+2 ll. (advt.), frontisp. (col.; by A. F. Lydon), 18 pll. (4 col.; by Lydon, T. W. Wood and Ludlow), text-figs. 1-39. London.

A compact handbook for the canary-breeder. The first edition was issued in 1879 and the second in 1884, according to Mullens and Swann.

Walter, Alice Hall.

1901. See Walter, Herbert Eugene; and Walter, A. H., **Wild Birds in City Parks.**

1904. **Idem.**

Walter, Herbert Eugene; and Walter, Alice Hall.

1901. **Wild birds** | in | **city parks** | Being hints on identifying 100 birds, | prepared primarily for the spring | migration in Lincoln

Park, Chicago. | By | Herbert Eugene Walter | and | Alice Hall Walter | Chicago | 1901.

1 vol. (pamphlet; 3½ x 5), pp. 1-48. Chicago.

A list of 100 species giving, for each, the common and scientific names, characteristics for identification in the field, and the names of other species with which the one under discussion might be confused. A chapter of "General Hints" preceds the list, and a table, showing the earliest dates of arrival of the various species in Lincoln Park, Chicago, follows it. The book passed through several later, revised, editions (Cf. second ed., 1904.).

Walter, Herbert Eugene; and Walter, Alice Hall.

1904. Wild Birds in City Parks | Being hints on identifying 145 birds, | prepared primarily for the spring | migration in Lincoln Park, Chicago | by | Herbert Eugene Walter | and | Alice Hall Walter | **Revised and enlarged edition** | with chart and key | Chicago | A. W. Mumford, Publisher | 378 Wabash Avenue | 1904.

1 vol. 16mo, pp. 1-66, 1 l. (advt.), 1 chart (fold.), 1 text-fig. (chart). Chicago.

A revised edition of the authors' work of the same title, 1901 (q.v.). The plan of the present edition is unaltered from that of the original, but various additional species are discussed, a chart is given showing the daily variation in the number of species seen at Lincoln Park, a field-key is added, and a chart for recording migration data is appended.

Ward, Thomas. (Tailor, J.)

(N.d.; post 1728?). The | Bird-Fancier's Recreation: | being curious | remarks | On the Nature of | song-birds, | With proper | instructions | concerning | The Taking, Feeding, Breeding and | Teaching them, and to know the | Cock from the Hen. | Also | The Manner of taken Birds with Lime- | Twigs, and Preparations thereto | with | An Account of the Distempers incident to Song- | Birds, and the Method to Cure them. | **A New Edition.** | London: | Printed for J(. Tailor) ['Ti Morton' *written above almost obliterated name*], and Sold at his House at | the Bird-Cage, the Corner of Silver-Street, in Wood- | Street, near Cripple-gate.

1 vol. 12mo, 2 pr. ll. (tit. and pref.), pp. 7-89+1+2 ll., frontisp. London.

An antiquated manual for the cage-bird fancier. The exact date and authorship are uncertain. Although the publisher's name on the title-page is almost obliterated and another name written above it, on p. 89 the name and address are reprinted, thus ascribing the authorship to J. Tailor. However, Mullens and Swann cite a work of 1728, under the authorship of Thomas Ward, which has a nearly identical title except for minor differences and the absence of the words, "A New Edition." The resemblance appears to be carried into the address of the writer while the pagination of the book is nearly the same. It seems probable, therefore, that the book is a copy of Ward's work and that J. Tailor may have purchased the right to publish it along with the business at The (Bell and) Bird-Cage, all of which may have been transferred later to 'Ti Morton.'

Warren, Benjamin Harry.

1888. **Report | on the | Birds of Pennsylvania.** | With Special Reference to the Food-Habits, based | on over Three Thousand Stomach | Examinations. | By | B. H. Warren, M.D., | Ornithologist of the State Board of Agriculture [*etc., 3 lines.*]. | Illustrated with fifty plates. | Harrisburg: | Edwin K. Meyers, State Printer. | 1888.

1 vol. 8vo, pp. I-XII, 1-260, pll. 1-50 (49 col.; after Audubon). Harrisburg.

An account of the birds of the state, with brief descriptions (from Baird, Coues and Ridgway) and with notes on the habits and the economic importance of each. A check-list of species, with brief annotations, precedes the index at the close of the volume. This work was issued in an edition of 6000 copies which was exhausted almost at once, and a revised and enlarged edition was thereupon prepared and issued in 1890 under the same short title (q.v.). The illustrations consist mostly of figures from Audubon's plates, rearranged and lithographed with more or less departure from the colors of the originals.

Warren, Benjamin Harry. (Barrows, Walter Bradford; Fisher, Albert Kenrick; Wolf, A. G.)

1890. **Report | on the | Birds of Pennsylvania.** | With Special Reference to the Food-Habits, based on over Four | Thousand Stomach Examinations. | By | B. H. Warren, M.D. | Ornithologist, Pennsylvania State Board of Agriculture. | **Second edition.** revised and augmented. | Illustrated by One Hundred Plates. | Published by Authority of the Commonwealth. | Harrisburg: | E. K. Meyers, State Printer. | 1890.

1 vol. 8vo, pp. I-XIV, 1-434, pll. 1-100 (99 col.; after Audubon). Harrisburg.

Enlarged and revised edition of the author's work first published in 1888 (q.v.). Additional matter includes a general account of many of the families and subfamilies and discussions of numerous species not included in the first edition, together with many new plates, copied (like the majority of the remainder) from Audubon. The check-list at the close of the volume is omitted but there is a large appendix (pp. 333-424) containing the following papers. The local game laws and comments on bird-protection by various correspondents; "Food of Hawks and Owls" by A. K. Fisher[1]; "The Food of Crows" by

---

[1]From Ann. Rept. U. S. Dept. Agr. for 1887.

W. B. Barrows[1]; "The English Sparrow" by Barrows[2]; "Some Nocturnal Migrants" by Maj. A. G. Wolf; a bibliography and a glossary.

Warren, Oscar Bird.

1896. See World's Congress on Ornithology, **Papers presented to the—.**

Warren, Robert.

1900. See Ussher, Richard John; and Warren, **The Birds of Ireland.**

Waterhouse, Frederick Herschel.

1885. The | dates of publication | of some of the | zoological works | of the late | **John Gould,** F.R.S. | compiled by | Frederick Herschel Waterhouse, A.L.S., | Librarian to the Zoological Society of London. | London: | R. H. Porter, 6 Tenterden Street, W. | 1885.

1 vol. 8vo, pp. I-XI+1, 1-59. London.

"The Mammals of Australia," "A Monograph of the Macropodidae," "The Birds of Great Britain," "The Birds of Asia," "The Birds of Australia" and supplement, "A Monograph of the Trochilidae" and supplement, parts I-IV (not completed), "A Monograph of the Odontophorinae" and "A Monograph of the Trogonidae" (revised edition) are given a short collation, and the species treated in each are listed alphabetically by genera. Following each specific name are given in tabular form the volume and plate-numbers, the number of the original part, and the year of issue. Since the final arrangement of the plates in Gould's works is without regard to the sequence of issue, the present volume is extremely useful in determining the dates of publication of the various plates.

Waterhouse, Frederick Herschel.

1889. Index generum avium. | A list | of the | genera and subgenera of birds. | By | F. H. Waterhouse, A.L.S., | Librarian to the Zoological Society of London. | London: | R. H. Porter, 18 Princes Street, Cavendish Square. | 1889.

1 vol. 8vo, 3 pr. ll., pp. 1-240. London.

"An alphabetical list of about 7000 terms that have been employed or suggested by various authors, since the date of the twelfth edition of Linnaeus's 'Systema Naturae,' as generic and subgeneric names for Birds, and of references to the places and dates of their publication." Supplementary papers have been published by Richmond in the Proceedings, U. S. National Museum, **24** No. 1267, May 2, 1902, pp. 663-729; **35,** No. 1656, Dec. 16, 1908, pp. 583-655; and **53,** No. 2221, Aug. 16, 1917, pp. 565-636.

---

[1]Idem, 1888.
[2]From Bull. 1, U. S. Dept. Agr., Div. Econ. Orn. and Mammal, 1889.

Waterton, Charles.

1837. An | ornithological | letter | to | **William Swainson,** Esq.
F.R.S. | &c. &c. | By | Charles Waterton, Esq. | Walton-Hall. |
Wakefield: | Richard Nichols, bookseller. | 1837.

1 vol. post 8vo, pp. 1-15. 1837 (circa March 17).

A tirade directed against William Swainson, his beliefs and theories and even his
friend, Audubon, in reply to alleged slights and criticisms by Swainson against
Waterton. This letter was republished in Waterton's "Essays on Natural
History, Second Ser., 1844 (4th ed., pp. 189-204, 1851, q.v.). In the present
form it is a separate publication. The copy at hand was folded and addressed
on the back to John Phillips Esq., Yorkshire Museum, York, and is postmarked
"Wakefield MR 17 1837".

Waterton, Charles.

1851. Essays | on | **natural history,** | chiefly | ornithology [Orni-
thology]. | By | Charles Waterton, Esq. | Author of "Wanderings
in South America." [| Second series:] | With an autobiography of
the author, [with a continuation of] and a view of Walton Hall
[the autobiography of the author]. | Eighth [Fourth] edition. |
London: | Longman, Brown, Green, and Longmans. | 1851.

2 (should be 3) vols. cap 8vo. Vol. I, pp. I-LXXXIII+1, 1-334,
1 l.+pp. 1-32 (advt.), frontisp. Vol. II, pp. I-CXLII, 1 l. (subtit.),
pp. 1-204, 1-4+1-32 (advt.), frontisp. London.

A series of essays on a variety of subjects, many of them ornithological, and many
reprinted from the pages of Loudon's Magazine of Natural History. The
articles are often controversial or contentious, with especial direction against
Waterton's literary adversary, William Swainson. As shown in the transcription of title, the two volumes appear to belong to different editions although
they are dated the same year. Both volumes in their first edition were published somewhat earlier,—the First Series in 1838 and the Second Series in
1844; the Third Series appeared even later than the present reprints, in 1857.
The pagination of the original edition of the present volumes (as given by Mullens and Swann) differs from the reprints at hand, but I think the subject
matter remains unchanged. The present copy contains the autograph of Geo.
N. Lawrence.

Watkins, Morgan George.

1881. Pictures | of | **bird life** | in | **Pen and Pencil.** | By | The
Rev. M. G. Watkins, M.A. | with | Illustrations by Giacomelli. |
Cassell, Petter, Galpin & Co.: | London, Paris & New York. | [All
rights reserved.].

1 vol. imperial 4to (11½x14¾), pp. 1-144, 66 figs. London, Paris
and New York.

Popular essays on a number of common British birds. The cover bears the name
of Giacomelli, only,—the artist for the work.

Watters, John J.

1853. The | natural history | of | the birds of Ireland, | indigenous and migratory, | containing | descriptions of the habits, migrations, occurrence, and | economy, of the 261 species comprised in the fauna. | By | John J. Watters, | Associate Member of the University Zoological Association. | Dublin: | James McGlashan, 50 Upper Sackville-St. | William S. Orr and Co., London. | John Menzies, Edinburgh. | 1853.

1 vol. cap 8vo, pp. I-XV+1, 1-299+1. Dublin.

Accounts of the habits, etc., of the birds of Ireland, without descriptions of plumages. Prepared at the suggestion of William Thompson who regretted the excessive cost of his own "Natural History of Ireland," 1849-56 (q.v.), and expressed a desire to see a cheap work published on the same subject. Many interesting field observations are recorded in this little work.

Watts, John.

1789. See Phillip, Arthur, **The Voyage of Governor Phillip to Botany Bay.**

Wayne, Arthur Trezevant. (Rea, Paul Marshall.)

1910. Contributions from the Charleston Museum | Edited by Paul M. Rea, Director | I | **Birds** | **of** | **South Carolina** | by | Arthur Trezevant Wayne | Honorary Curator of Birds in the Charleston Museum | with an introduction by the editor | Charleston, S. C. | 1910.

1 vol. royal 8vo, pp. I-XXI+1, 1 insert-slip (errata), pp. 1-254, 1 map (fold.). Charleston.

A catalogue of the birds of the state, with extended notes on distribution, habits, local occurrence, etc. The list is constructed on the basis of the coastal region fauna, with additional species from the interior of the state added in a separate section. A hypothetical list follows and a local bibliography is added. The introduction by Rea consists of a short account of the physiography of the region and a history of the ornithology of the state.

Webb, Philip Barker; and Berthelot, Sabin. (Moquin-Tandon, Alfred.)

1841. [Histoire Naturelle des Îles Canaries.] > Ornithologie | Canarienne, | par MM. P. B. Webb, S. Berthelot, | et | M. Alfred Moquin-Tandon, | Docteur Ès-Sciences, | Professeur d'Histoire Naturelle à la Faculté des Sciences de Toulouse, etc. | II. - (2 e partie.) - Zoologie. (Ornithologie.) - 1.

1 vol. imperial 4to, pp. 1-48, pll. 1-4 (col.; by E. Traviés). Paris.

The ornithological portion of Webb and Berthelot's natural history of the Canary Islands, published in the years 1835-50 (Vol. II, Zoology, 1835-44). The present section appears to have been issued as a unit (traces of original ?

wrapper remain), forming a portion of Pt. 2 of Vol. II, and probably dating 1841. Dresser (A History of the Birds of Europe, 1871-82, q.v.) cites 1841, as does Koenig (Journal für Ornithologie, July and Oct., 1890, pp. 398, 404 and 483); a number of references are given in the work itself to publications dated 1840. The paper describes 108 species of birds, 5 of which are new, and gives observations on habits based on the field notes of Webb and Berthelot (Sept. 1828-April 1830) together with other critical discussions. The ornithology has been quoted variously as of Webb and Berthelot, of Moquin-Tandon, and of all three authors, the last being indicated by the subtitle-page transcribed above.

Webber, C. W.

> **1856.** See Adams, Henry Gardiner, **Humming Birds Described and Illustrated.**

Webber, C. W.

> **1858. Wild scenes | and | song-birds. |** By C. W. Webber, | author of [*etc., 2 lines.*]. | With twenty illustrations, printed in colors, | from drawings by | Mrs. C. W. Webber and Alfred J. Miller. | New York: | George P. Putnam & Co., 10 Park Place.
>
> 1 vol. royal 8vo, pp. I-X, 1 l., pp. 1-347, 20 pll. (col.; 13 of birds). New York.
>
> A series of essays on nature, many of them relating to birds.

Weed, Clarence Moores; and Dearborn, Ned.

> **1903. Birds | in their | relations to man |** A Manual of Economic Ornithology for the | United States and Canada | by | Clarence M. Weed, D.Sc. | Professor of Zoology and Entomology, New Hampshire College of Agriculture | and the Mechanic Arts | and | Ned Dearborn, D.Sc. | Assistant Curator, Department of Birds, Field Columbian Museum, Chicago | Illustrated | [*Vignette.*] | Philadelphia and London | J. B. Lippincott Company | 1903.
>
> 1 vol. demy 8vo, pp. I-VIII, 1-380, 19 pll., 96 cuts. Philadelphia.
>
> A thorough discussion of Economic Ornithology with special reference to North American birds.

Weed, Clarence Moores. (Audubon, John James; Bendire, Charles E.; Nuttall, Thomas; Wilson, Alexander.)

> **1904. Bird life | stories |** Compiled from the writings of | Audubon, Bendire, Nuttall, and Wilson | By | Clarence Moores Weed | Professor of Zoölogy [*etc., 3 lines.*] | Book I | Rand, McNally & Company | Chicago New York London.
>
> 1 vol. 8vo (6x7¾), pp. 1-82, 24 pll. (col.). Chicago.

Extracts from the works of Audubon, Bendire, Nuttall and Wilson, modified, giving accounts of 24 species of North American birds. A brief account of the distribution of each species is given by the editor. The illustrations are from photographs of mounted birds and are not very attractive. The book is intended for a school reader in nature study. Book II was published in 1921.

Wells, John Grant.

1886. A | list of the birds | of | **Grenada, West Indies,** | by | John Grant Wells. | Grenada, W.I., 1886. | W. W. C. H. Wells, | St. Andrew's.

1 vol. (sheets not folded; 6 x 8), 2 pr. ll. (tit. and pref.), 12 ll. (num. 1-12, on one side only). Grenada. 1886 (antea June 7; post March).

A check-list of the families, genera and species of the birds of Grenada, with the local vernacular names of the species added. The fly-leaf bears an inscription from the author to Charles B. Cory, dated June 7, 1886; the preface is dated March of the same year.

Wells, Thomas.

1911-13. See Kirkman, Frederick B. B., **The British Bird Book.**

Wells, Thomas.

1912. See Ogilvie-Grant, William R., **General Index to A Hand-list of the Genera and Species of Birds.**

Werner, Johann Carl. (Temminck, Coenraad Jacob.)

1848. Les | oiseaux d'Europe | décrits | Par C.-J. Temminck, | Directeur [etc., 2 lines.]. | Atlas de 530 Planches | dessinées | Par J.-C. Werner, | Peintre au Muséum d'histoire naturelle de Paris. | Tome premier [deuxième]. | A Paris, | chez J.-B. Baillière, | Libraire de l'Académie Nationale de Médecine, | 17, rue de l'École-de-Médecine. | A Londres, chez H. Baillière, 219, Regent-Street. | 1848.

2 vols. post 8vo. Vol. I, 2 pr. ll. (half-tit. and tit.), pp. 1-27, 262 pll. (col.). Vol. II, 2 pr. ll. (half-tit. and tit.), 264 pll. (col.). London.

A series of colored plates illustrating the species of European birds described by C. J. Temminck in the second edition of his "Manuel d'Ornithologie," 1820-40 (q.v.). The only text is the table of species on pp. 1-27 of Vol. I, this being copied, in slightly altered form, from the correlative table in Temminck's "Manuel," Ed. 2, Vol. III pp. 661-691, but containing the same references to the several volumes of that work. This atlas was issued originally in livraisons (Engelmann gives 55) of 10 pll. each (up to livr. 50) under cover-title of "Atlas des Oiseaux d'Europe, pour servir de complément au Manuel d'Ornithologie de M. Temminck" (Cf. the "Manuel," Ed. 2, Vol. III, p. LXX.). This title, apparently, was afterward changed to "Atlas des Oiseaux d'Europe d'après C. J. Temminck" on the title-pages furnished at the completion of the work

[? Cf. Cat. Libr. Brit. Mus. (Nat. Hist.)]. In this original form the work occupies 3 vols. (Brit. Mus.) for which the dates are given by the Cat. Libr. Brit. Mus. (Nat. Hist.) as 1826, 1828 and 1842; the publishers are given by Engelmann as Belin and H. Cousin. The 32nd livraison was on sale at the time of publication of Vol. III of Temminck's "Manuel" in April 1835, according to a statement on p. LXX of that volume. The present copy belongs to a later reissue, possibly consisting of the original plates with new title-pages. The work was sold with or without Temminck's volumes.

Westermann, G. F.

1860. See Schlegel, Hermann; and Westermann, **De Toerako's.**

Wheaton, J. M.

1882. [Report of the Geological Survey of Ohio, Vol. IV, Pt. I. Columbus Ohio. Nevins & Myers, State Printers. 1882.] > Section II. | **Report on the birds of Ohio.** | By J. M. Wheaton, M.D.
1 vol. royal 8vo, pp. 188-628. Columbus.

A concise manual of the birds found in Ohio, with descriptions of species, genera and higher groups, synonymy and distribution of species, and notes on the habits and local occurrence of each. Several synoptic tables are given and an appendix contains a check-list of species with dates of occurrence, a list of birds observed in the author's garden at Columbus, additions and corrections, a bibliography, a reprint of a paper by the author on patterns of coloration, and a glossary of technical terms. The work was long delayed in publication. It was begun in 1873, started through the press in 1879, completed in 1881 and actually published late in 1882 (Cf. Coues, Bull. Nuttall Orn. Club, 8, April 1883, pp. 110-112.). It was revised in 1903 and brought up to date by Lynds Jones in the "Ohio State Acad. Science, Special Papers No. 6, The Birds of Ohio" (q.v.).

Wheeler, George Montague. (Henshaw, Henry Wetherbee.)

1875. {[*Vignette* (*Vol. I, only.*).] | Engineer Department, U. S. [United States (*Vols. III and V.*)] | **Report** | upon | **United States geographical surveys** [geographical and geological | explorations and surveys (*Vols. III and V.*)] | **west of the one hundredth meridian,** | in charge of | Capt. [First Lieut. (*Vols. II, III, IV-VII.*)] Geo. M. Wheeler, | Corps of Engineers, U. S. Army, | under the direction of | the Chief of Engineers [Brig. Gen. A. A. Humphreys, | Chief of Engineers (*Vols. II, III, IV-VII.*); Brig. Gen. H. G. Wright, | Chief of Engineers (*Vol. III Supplement.*)] U. S. Army. | Published by authority of the Honorable the Secretary of War [Hon. Wm. W. Belknap, Secretary of War (*Vol. III.*)], | in accordance with acts of Congress of June 23, 1874, and February 15, 1875. | In seven volumes and one supplement [seven volumes (*Vols. II, III Supplement,* IV, VI, VII.*); six volumes (*Vols. III and V.*)], accompanied by one | topographical and one geologic [accompanied by one topographical and one | geological (*Vols. II-VII.*)] atlas. | Vol. I.-Geographical Report [II.-Astronomy and barometric hypsometry; III.-Geology; III.-Supplement.-Geology; IV.-Paleontology; V.-Zoology; VI.-Botany; VII.-Archaeology]. | Washington: | Government Printing Office. | 1889 [1877 (*Vols. II and IV.*); 1875 (*Vols. III and V.*); 1881 (*Vol. III Supplement.*); 1878 (*Vol. VI.*); 1879 (*Vol. VII.*)].} > [*Chapter III of Vol. V issued separately with title same as for Vol. V but with "Chapter III" in separate line preceding volume-number.*] Chapter III. | **Report** | **upon** | **the ornithological collections** | made in portions of | Nevada, Utah, California, Colorado, New Mexico, and Arizona, | during | the years 1871, 1872, 1873, and 1874, | by | H. W. Henshaw.

[7 vols. and supplement in 8 vols., medium 4to. Washington. 1875-89. Vol. V, pp. 1-1021, 3 ll., pll. I-XLV.] Chapter III (issued separately), 3 ll. (pp. 1, 7 pt., 9 pt.), pp. 13-20, 131-507, pll. I-XV (col.; by Robert Ridgway). Washington. 1875.

A complete report, by H. W. Henshaw, on the birds secured by the Wheeler Surveys in the United States, west of the one hundredth meridian; with descriptions of many species, and with synonymies, tables of measurements and field notes for all the forms treated. The work appeared in Vol. V of the Report of the Survey, including an index to the ornithological section on pp. 977-989 +1 of that volume. The present copy is one of a number issued separately at the same time as the complete Vol. V, but with title-page altered to define the chapter which is included and with the table of contents and list of plates restricted to the references to that chapter; the letter of transmittal and the introductory letter accompanying Vol. V, have the text limited in like manner, and the index is omitted.

Wheeler, H. E.

1925. **The** | **birds of Arkansas** | a preliminary report | H. E. Wheeler | [*Vignette.*] | Published By | State Bureau of Mines, Manufactures | and Agriculture | Jim G. Ferguson, Commissioner | John C. Small, Assistant.

1 vol. 8vo, pp. I-XXV+1, 1-177+1+3 ll., pll. I-X (on numbered pp.), text-figs. 1-113, 1 fig. (unnum.), 96 distribution maps. Little Rock.

An annotated list of the birds of Arkansas, with notes on their habits and local distribution. A check-list of species and a list of permanent and summer residents are prefixed and a bilbiography is appended.

Wheelock, Irene Grosvenor.

1904. Birds of California | an introduction | to more than three hundred common | birds of the state and adjacent | islands | with a supplementary list of rare migrants, accidental | visitants, and hypothetical subspecies | by | Irene Grosvenor Wheelock | author of "Nestlings of Forest and Marsh" | with ten full-page plates and seventy-eight drawings | in the text by Bruce Horsfall | [*Blazon.*] | Chicago | A. C. McClurg & Co. | 1904.

1 vol. crown 8vo, pp. I-XXVIII, 1-578, 1 l. (advt.), frontisp. (monochr.), 9 pll. (by Bruce Horsfall), 77 text-figs. Chicago. Febr. 20, 1904.

A popular hand-book of a selected number of the birds of California, arranged according to habitat and color instead of systematic classification. A brief diagnosis is given of each with notes on its geographical distribution, local breeding range and season and its nidification, while the main text is devoted to an account of its habits, written from personal observations and from the published writings of other observers.

Wheelwright, Horace William. [= "An Old Bushman."]

1871. A | spring and summer | in | Lapland. | By | An Old Bushman, | author of "Ten Years in Sweden." | [*Quot., 6 lines.*]. | **Second Edition,** with Coloured Plates. | London: | Groombridge and Sons, | 5, Paternoster Row. | MDCCCLXXI.

1 vol. crown 8vo, pp. I-VIII, 1-407, 6 pll. (col.; of birds). London.

A narrative of travel and observation in Lapland in 1862. "As the Author's sole object in going up to Lapland was for the purpose of collecting birds and eggs, the present work will be found rather as a guide to the ornithologist than any other class of reader." In addition to miscellaneous notes on birds found elsewhere in the volume, pp. 243-386 and all of the plates are ornithological. The first edition, without colored plates, appeared in 1864.

Whitaker, Joseph I. S.

1905. The | birds of Tunisia | being a history of the birds found in | the regency of Tunis | by | J. I. S. Whitaker | F.Z.S., M.B.O.U., etc. | Vol. I [II]. | London | R. H. Porter | 7, Princes Street, Cavendish Square, W. | 1905.

2 vols. superroyal 8vo. Vol. I, pp. I-XXXII, 1-294, frontisp. (photograv.), 14 pll. (13 col.; by Grönvold), 1 map (col.; fold.). Vol. II, pp. I-XVIII, 1-410, frontisp. (photograv.), 3 pll. (2 col.), 1 map (col.; fold.). London.

A manual of Tunisian ornithology. Synonymy and short descriptions of the species are given, with observations on plumages and other variations and with notes on distribution and habits. A short bibliography is included and the introduction discusses the topography of the area in question. The 15 plates of birds are hand-colored.

White, Adam.

1885. A popular | history of birds | comprising | a familiar account of their classification | and habits. | By | Adam White, | Assistant, Zoological Department, British Museum. | London: | Lovell Reeve, Henrietta Street, Covent Garden. | 1855.

1 vol. 16mo (5x6½), 3 pr. ll. (half-tit., tit. and ded.), pp. V-VIII, 1-347, pll. I-XX (col.). London.

A popular, general account of the entire class of birds, with mention of characteristic or interesting species. The plates are hand-colored but are not very accurate either in color or drawing, although the text appears to be reliable. The preface is dated Nov. 1, 1855.

White, Ernest William.

1881-82. Cameos from the silver-land; | or the | Experiences of a Young Naturalist | in the | Argentine Republic, | by | Ernest William White, F.Z.S. | In two volumes | Vol. I [II]. | With map [*Line omitted.*] | Famam Extendere Factis | London: John Van Voorst, 1 Paternoster Row | MDCCCLXXXI [MDCCCLXXXII]. | (All rights reserved).

2 vols. post 8vo. Vol. I, pp. I-XV+1, 1 l. (errata), pp. 1-436, 1 map (col.; fold.). Vol. II, pp. I-XV+1, 1-527. London.

A general account of the author's travels throughout Argentina, with numerous references to animals and plants, including many notes on the habits of local birds.

White, Gilbert. (Kearton, Richard.)

1924. The Natural History of | Selborne | by | Gilbert White | with notes by | Richard Kearton, F.Z.S. | and 85 photographs | including many taken specially at Selborne | by | Cherry Kearton | and | Richard Kearton | Arrowsmith :: London :: W.C.I.

1 vol. 8vo (7¼ x 9¾), pp. 1-248, frontisp., 78 pll. (on 42 ll.). London.

A recent edition of this classic, which was first published in 1789 and has since been reissued in at least as many editions and reprints as there are years since the date of its first appearance. The first issue by Kearton dates 1902. The illustrations in the present edition are from photographs, many of which are illustrative of Selborne scenery but most of which are of ornithological subjects.

White, John.

1790. Journal | of a | Voyage to new South Wales | with Sixty-five Plates of | Non descript Animals, Birds, Lizards, | Serpents, curious Cones of Trees and other | Natural Productions | By John White Esq.re | Surgeon General to the Settlement. | [*Engraving.*] | View in Port Jackson | I. White Esq delin T. Milton sculp | London | Printed for J. Debrett, Piccadilly | MDCCXC.

1 vol. medium 4to, engr. tit., 8 ll. (ded., advt., list of subscrs., and list of pll.), pp. 1-299+1, 18 ll., 65 pll. (col.; by Stone, Catton, Nodder and others; 29 pll. ornithological). London.

Pages 1-218 contain a general account of the author's voyage to Australia and of his activities after arrival, with incidental mention or brief description of such natural objects as he could identify. Pages 219-297 consist entirely of descriptions of animals, plants and articles of native manufacture with binomial nomenclature employed in many cases, some of the names and descriptions being new. The remainder of the work (unpaged) is devoted to a diary of the winds, weather, temperature, etc. experienced in the outward voyage. The colored plates are taken from specimens which were deposited in the Leverian Museum in London. Mathews (Birds of Australia, **7**, p. 472, 1919) mentions a second edition; judging by his discussion, the present copy belongs to the first edition, since the name *Merops carunculatus* does not appear on p. 240.

Whitehead, John. (Sharpe, Richard Bowdler; Ogilvie-Grant, W. R.; Seebohm, Henry.)

1893. Exploration | of | Mount Kina Balu, North Borneo. | By | John Whitehead. | With coloured plates and original illustrations. | [*Monogram.*] | London: | 1893. | [All rights reserved.].

1 vol. 4to (10 x 14¾), pp. I-X, 1 l. (lists of illustrs.), pp. 1-317, 32 pll. (11 col., 6 of birds; by the author), 21 text-cuts, 1 text-map, 9 decorative initials. London. 1893 (post May 10).

A narrative of the author's travels in Borneo, Java, Palawan and Balabac Islands, especially of his three efforts (the last one successful) to ascend Mt. Kina Balu. The greater part of the work comprises detailed observations on the natural history, especially ornithology, of the regions visited. The appendix, pp. 193-307, "consists of an almost complete description of the zoological collections formed by the Author," reprinted from numerous papers by the author and other workers in various journals, combined, rearranged and augmented so as to make a connected series of catalogues. The ornithological matter occupies pp. 200-263 and comprises three articles; an account of the birds of North Borneo from various articles and descriptions by the author, R. B. Sharpe and Ogilvie-Grant in the Ibis and Proc. Zool. Soc. London; a discussion of the birds of Palawan by the author and Sharpe from the Ibis and the Bull. Brit. Orn. Club; notes on a collection of birds from eastern Java from unpublished field notes, with Seebohm's descriptions of two new species first published in the Bull. Brit. Orn. Club. The introduction is dated May 10.

Whitman, C. O.

1907. See Mershon, W. B., **The Passenger Pigeon.**

Whymper, Charles.

1909. Egyptian | birds | for the most part seen in | the Nile valley | by | Charles Whymper | London | Adam and Charles Black | 1909.

1 vol. 4to (6½x8¾), pp. I-X, 1-221+1, 3 ll. (advt.), 51 pll. (col.;

by Whymper)+51 guard-sheets (printed), text-figs. 1-10, 1 text-fig. (unnum.). London.

A popular work designed "for the wayfaring man who, travelling this ancient Egypt, wishes to learn something of the birds he sees." Succinct descriptions are followed by brief notes on habits, peculiarities, legendary associations, personal experiences of the author and other pertinent facts. The illustrations are interesting and artistic.

Whymper, Edward.

1891. **Supplementary appendix | to | Travels Amongst the Great Andes | of the Equator |** by | Edward Whymper | with contributions by | H. W. Bates, F.R.S. T. G. Bonney, D.Sc., F.R.S. G. A. Boulenger. | Peter Cameron. F. Day, C.I.E., F.L.S., F.Z.S. W. L. Distant, F.Z.S. | A. E. Eaton, M.A. F. D. Godman, F.R.S. H. S. Gorham, F.Z.S. | Martin Jacoby. E. J. Miers, F.L.S., F.Z.S. A. Sidney Olliff. | O. Salvin, F.R.S. David Sharp, M.B., F.R.S. T. R. R. Stebbing, M.A. | Illustrated | [*Quot., 3 lines.*] | London | John Murray, Albemarle Street | 1891 | All rights are reserved.

1 vol. 4to (6¼ x 8¾), pp. I-XXII, 2 ll. (addenda and half-tit.), pp. 1-147, 14 pll., 41 text-cuts. London.

Technical reports on the various collections made by Whymper on the expedition described in his "Travels Amongst the Great Andes of the Equator," 1892 (q.v.). The present copy is "Special Edition Subscribers Copy No. 25," uniform with the two volumes of narrative and maps catalogued under the other title, and forming with them the "Copy No. 25"; for this reason the present title is catalogued here,—it contains no ornithology.

Whymper, Edward.

1892. **Travels | amongst the great Andes | of the equator |** by | Edward Whymper | With maps and illustrations | [*Quot., 8 lines.*] | London | John Murray, Albemarle Street | 1892 | All rights are reserved. [*The second volume has no title-page.*].

2 vols. 4to (6¼ x 8¾). (Vol. I), pp. I-XXIV, 1 l. (subtit.), pp. 1-456, 20 pll., 1 map, 118 text-figs. (Vol. II), 3 maps (fold.). London.

The author's account of his travels in the high mountains of Ecuador, South America. Most of the account is general or with special reference to barometric investigations, but some notes on the avifauna are included. The present copy has imprinted in facsimile handwriting, "Special Edition Subscriber's Copy, No. 25. Edward Whymper." Another edition in 1 vol. was issued in London and New York the same year. A special appendix, containing various reports on collections, was issued in 1891, and a special imprint of this, uniform with the present work, is included in the present set as a third volume (Cf. "Supplementary Appendix, 1891.").

Wied, Prinz zu.

See Maximilian, Prinz zu Wied.

Wigglesworth, Lionel W.

1898. See Meyer, Adolf Bernhard; and Wigglesworth, **The Birds of Celebes and the Neighboring Islands.**

Wilbur, Harriette.

1920. Bird gossip | By | Harriette Wilbur | with twenty-eight | illustrations in color | [*Design.*] | Philadelphia | George W. Jacobs & Company | Publishers.

1 vol. post 8vo, pp. 1-279, 26 pll. (col.; by Horsfall, Brooks and Sawyer)+col. pl. on cover. Philadelphia.

A juvenile work on the habits of a number of North American birds. The illustrations are from the leaflets of the National Association of Audubon Societies.

Wilcox, Alvin H. (Roberts, Thomas S.; Meeker, D. W.)

1907. [A Pioneer History | of | Becker County | Minnesota | including | a brief | Account of its Natural History | as embraced in the Mineral, Vegetable and Animal | Kingdoms, and a History of the early Settlement | of the County; also, including a large Amount of | valuable Historical Information collected by | - | Mrs. Jessie C. West. | - | and numerous Articles written by various early | Pioneers relating to the History of | the Several Townships of | Becker County | - | By Alvin H. Wilcox | - | Pioneer Press Company | St. Paul, Minn | 1907] > Chapter VIII. | **List of birds of Becker County, Minnesota.** | Compiled by Thos. S. Roberts, M.D. | Director Department of Birds, Minn. Nat. Hist. Survey.

1 vol. (pt.), 8vo, 1 l. (transcript of tit. and author's note), pp. 159-190. St. Paul.

Chapter VIII, extracted from the volume in which it appeared. Pp. 159-186 contain an annotated list of 262 species of birds known from Becker County, by Dr. Roberts. The remainder of the chapter consists of an article on "Disappearing Birds and Game Birds" by D. W. Meeker.

Wilkes, Charles. (Cassin, John.)

1858. United States | **Exploring Expedition.** | During the years | 1838, 1839, 1840, 1841, 1842. | Under the command of | Charles Wilkes, U.S.N. | Mammalogy [Atlas.] | and [Mammalogy and Ornithology.] | Ornithology. [*Line omitted.*] | By | John Cassin, | Member of the Academy of Natural Sciences of Philadelphia; [*etc.,* *5 lines.*]. | With a folio atlas. [*Line omitted.*] | Philadelphia: | J. B. Lippincott & Co. | 1858.

2 vols., folio (9½ x 12½) and superroyal folio. Text, tit., pp. V-VIII, 1-466, 18 text-figs. Atlas, 2 pr. ll., pll. 1-11 (col.; mammals), 1-42 (col.; birds, by G. G. White, T. R. Peale, W. E. Hitchcock and E. Sheppard). Philadelphia.

These two volumes together constitute the revised Vol. VIII of the complete report of the Expedition (which visited numerous localities in a voyage around the world). Vol. VIII originally was prepared by Titian Ramsay Peale, the Ornithologist and Mammalogist of the Expedition, and was published in 1848 without plates. Carus and Engelmann cite 15 pll. of mammals and 84 pll. of birds, but Hartlaub, in a critical review of the ornithology of Peale's work (Archiv für Naturg., 18 Jahrg., Bd. 1, pp. 93-138, 1852), although he quotes plate-numbers for the various species, says that he had never seen the plates and that no copy of them had reached Europe. Jardine (Contributions to Ornithology, 1851, p. 113; idem, 1852, pp. 89-90) cites a copy of the work without plates received by the British Museum and notes that the atlas was never completed. Stone (Cassinia, No. 19, pp. 10-11, 1915) states that Peale's report was issued without the plates which he had prepared.

Only 100 copies of the original volume were "printed for distribution amongst foreign governments and by some legislative errors none were printed for distribution at home"; of the number printed, about 90 were distributed, many of them going to countries without scientific establishments, and the remainder were destroyed accidentally in a fire in the Library of Congress. Later, Cassin was commissioned to rewrite the volume, and this new work, with some of Peale's unpublished plates and with various illustrations by other artists, was issued in its present form in 1858 (Stone, l.c., says 1852 in error; the preface is dated May 10, 1858). The original edition is, of course, extremely rare.

In the present edition of the text, pp. 67-416 are occupied by the descriptive account of the birds, 428-452 by the ornithological part (Pt. II) of the catalogue of the collections of mammals and birds made by the expedition, and 453-466 by the general index, including both mammals and birds. Cassin's general text takes no account of many of Peale's newly described species, even omitting certain of his names from the synonymy. However, in the catalogue of the collections, these omitted names are given, together with a transcript of Peale's original descriptions.

Willcox, M. A.

1895. Pocket guide | to the | common land birds | of | New England | by | M. A. Willcox | Professor of Zoölogy, Wellesley College | Lee and Shepard publishers | 10 Milk Street | Boston.

1 vol. 16mo, pp. I-XII, 1-158, 3 ll. (advt.). Boston.

A semi-popular account of 89 common species of New England birds, with artificial keys for determination, based on coloration and size, and with short descriptions of plumage, habitat, nidification and song of each species.

Willughby, Francis. (Ray, John.)

1676. Francisci Willughbeii | De Middleton in agro Warwicensi, Armigeri, | E Regia Societate, | ornithologiæ | libri tres: | In

quibus | Aves omnes hactenus cognitæ in methodum naturis suis | convenientem redactæ accuratè describuntur, | Descriptiones Iconibus elegantissimis & vivarum Avium | simillimis, Æri incisis illustrantur. | Totum opus recognovit, digessit, supplevit | Joannes Raius. | Sumptus in Chalcographos fecit | Illustriss. D. Emma Willughby, Vidua. | [*Blazon.*] | Londini; | Impensis Joannis Martyn, Regiæ Societatis Typographi, ad insigne Campanæ | in Cæmeterio D. Pauli. | MDCLXXVI.

1 vol. 4to (size of crown folio), 6 pr. ll. (notice, tit., pref. and errata), pp. 1-307, 1 p.+2 ll. (index), 2 inserts (at pp. 25 and 199) pll. I-LXXVII, 3 text-figs. London.

The cornerstone of modern systematic ornithology, being the first book on the classification of birds without respect to geographical boundaries. The manuscript was left in an imperfect state by Willughby at his death and was arranged and completed by Ray. The work contains descriptions of all the birds known to the authors or adjudged by them to be sufficiently authenticated by the published accounts of others. It is divided into three parts, the first of which treats of birds in general, the second of land birds, and the third of water birds. The second and third books are divided into several parts, each of which is divided into heads and each of those into articles, each division being characterized by some peculiarity or group of peculiarities. The scheme of classification thus adopted is epitomized on the insert-slips at pp. 25 and 199. An appendix, pp. 297-307, compiled principally from J. E. Nieremberg's Historiae Naturae, Libro Decimo, 1635, discusses a number of birds of doubtful authenticity or of previous, insufficient description. An English translation, with further additions, was issued by Ray in 1678 under the title of "The Ornithology of Francis Willughby" (q.v.).

Willughby, Francis; and Ray, John.

1678. The | ornithology | of | Francis Willughby | of | Middleton in the County of Warwick Esq; | Fellow of the Royal Society. | In Three Books. | Wherein All the | birds | hitherto known, | Being reduced into a Method sutable (*sic*) to their Natures, | are accurately described. | The Descriptions illustrated by most Elegant Figures, nearly resembling | the live Birds, Engraven in LXXVIII Copper Plates. | Translated into English, and enlarged with many Additions | throughout the whole Work. | To which are added, | Three Considerable Discourses, |

I. Of the Art of Fowling: With a Description of several Nets in two large Copper Plates. | By | John Ray,
II. Of the Ordering of Singing Birds.
III. Of Falconry.

Fellow of the Royal Society. | [*Quot., 3 lines.*]. | London: | Printed

by A. C. for John Martyn, Printer to the Royal Society, at the Bell
in | St. Pauls Church-Yard, MDCLXXVIII.

1 vol. 4to (size of crown folio), 6 pr. ll. (tit. and pref.), pp. 1-441+1,
3 ll. (index), 2 insert-ll. (at pp. 55 and 273), pll. I-LXXVIII, 2 pll.
(unnum.), 3 text-figs. London.

A translation of Willughby's "Ornithologiae," 1676 (q.v.), with various corrections and emendations and with the addition of the subjects mentioned in the
title. Article I begins on p. 29, II is inserted at various places in the text under
the species to which it refers, and III begins on p. 397. Three plates are added.
The appendix, pp. 385-396, ascribed in the original edition to Nieremberg, is
here credited to Franc. Hernandez.

Willughby Society for the Reprinting of Scarce Ornithological Works,
The.

1880-84. This society was established on May 7, 1879 for the purpose
of reprinting certain ornithological works interesting for their utility
or rarity. From 1880 to 1884, twelve books or collections of writings
were reprinted *verbatim* et *literatim* or in facsimile. For convenience,
these reprints are here catalogued under their respective authors
(q.v.). The works are as follows. Those preceded by an asterisk
are titles of the reprints only; the others are the original titles of
the works reprinted.

1883. Audouin, Jean Victor. Explication Sommaire des Planches d'Oiseaux de l'Égypte et de la Syrie. 1826. (From Savigny's
"Description de l'Égypte").

1883. Barton, Benjamin Smith. Fragments of the Natural History of Pennsylvania. 1799.

*1880. Desfontaines, René Louiche. Memoire sur quelques
nouvelles especes d'oiseaux des côtes de Barbarie. 1789. (Extract
from "Histoire de l'Académie Royale des Sciences).

*1882. Forster, John Reinhold. An Account of the Birds sent
from Hudson's Bay. 1772. (Extract from Philos. Trans. London).

1882. Forster, John Reinhold. A Catalogue of the Animals of
North America. 1771.

1882. Leach, William Elford. Systematic Catalogue of Indigenous Mammalia and Birds in The British Museum. 1816.

1882. Lichtenstein, Anton August Heinrich. Catalogus Rerum
Naturalium Rarissimarum. (Two reprints, one edited by Sclater
and the other by Tegetmeier.) 1793.

1882. Scopoli, Giovanni Antonio. Deliciae Florae et Faunae
Insubricae. 1786 and 1788 (ornithological portions only).

*1880. Smith, Andrew. (Miscellaneous ornithological papers from The South African Quarterly Journal, including one by Jules Verreaux, and the ornithological portion of the "Report of the Expedition for Exploring Central Africa".) 1829-36.

1880. Tunstall, Marmaduke. Ornithologia Britannica. 1771.

1883. Vieillot, Louis Jean Pierre. Analyse d'une Nouvelle Ornithologie Élémentaire. 1816.

*1884. Wagler, Johann Georg. (Six ornithological memoirs from the 'Isis'). 1829-32.

The above comprise all the papers republished by the society, which dissolved in 1884 owing to lack of support. No copies of the reprints were made for sale, but only for subscribers to the project; consequently the edition was limited.

Wilson, Alexander. (Ord, George.)

1808-14. American ornithology; | or, the natural history | of the | birds of the United States: | illustrated with plates | Engraved and Colored from Original drawings taken from Nature. | By Alexander Wilson. | Vol. I [-IX]. | Philadelphia: | Published by Bradford and Inskeep. | Printed by Robert Carr [R. & W. Carr (*Vols. III-V.*); Robert & William Carr (*Vols. VI-IX.*)]. | 1808 [1810; 1811; 1811; 1812; (1813); (1814); 1814].

7 vols. (VII and VIII of present set belong to revised ed. of 1824, q.v.) folio (size of imperial 4to). Vol. I, pp. I-VI, 1-158, pll. 1-9 (col.). Vol. II, tit., pp. V-XII, 13-167, pll. 10-18 (col.). Vol. III, tit., pp. V-XVI, 17-120, pll. 19-27 (col.). Vol. IV, tit., pp. V-XII, 13-100, pll. 28-36 (col.). Vol. V, tit., pp. V-XII, 13-122, pll. 37-45 (col.; 44 not numbered). Vol. VI, tit., pp. V-XX, 13-102, pll. 46-54 (col.). [Vol. VII, pp. III-XII, 13-132, pll. 55-63 (col.). Vol. VIII, pp. I-XI, 13-146, pll. 64-72 (col.), 2 text-figs.][1]. Vol. IX, tit., pp. V-LVII+1, 1 l. (index to Vol. IX), pp. 61-133+1, 11 ll. (gen. index and list of subscrs.), pll. 73-76 (col.). Philadelphia.

The life-work of "The Father of American Ornithology," of which Coues wrote, "Science would lose little, but, on the contrary, would gain much, if every scrap of pre-Wilsonian writing about United States birds could be annihilated." Vols. I-VII appeared during the author's lifetime; Vol. VIII, edited by Ord, was published the year after his death, and Vol. IX, with four plates left completed by Wilson but with text written by Ord from personal observations and from such meagre notes of Wilson's as he could find, completed the work the same year. The prefaces of the various volumes are dated as follows. Vol. **I,** Sept. 1, 1808; **II,** Jan. 1, 1810; **III,** Febr. 12, 1811; **IV,** Sept. 12, 1811; **V,** Febr. 12, 1812; **VI,** Aug. 12, 1812; **VII,** March 1, 1813; **VIII,** Jan. 19, 1814; **IX,** May 1, 1814.

---

[1]Collation from Coues.

In 1824, Ord published a reissue of Vols. VII and VIII with numerous changes in the nomenclature of the species (Cf. ed. 1824.), and with other alterations in the text; Vol. IX was reissued similarly in 1825. Vols. VII and VIII of the set in hand belong to this reissue. Subsequently, various editions appeared from time to time under different editors. Those at hand for comparison are as follows. Ord edition, 3 vols. and atlas, 1828-9; Jameson ed., 4 vols., 1831; Jardine ed., 3 vols. 1832; Brewer, ed., 1 vol., 1840; Brewer ed., 1 vol., 1853; Jardine ed., 3 vols., 1877; Jardine ed., 3 vols., 1876; "Popular Edition" (Porter & Coates, Philadelphia), 3 vols. in 1, 1878. Charles Lucien Bonaparte, in 1824-25, published (in the Journal of the Academy of Natural Sciences of Philadelphia) a series of articles (five in all) entitled, "Observations on the Nomenclature of Wilson's Ornithology." These form a critical review of Wilson's species so far as they go, although they do not discuss the entire number. Following this series of articles, Bonaparte, from 1825 to 1833, published, in 4 vols., an "American Ornithology; or the Natural History of Birds inhabiting the United States, not given by Wilson" (q.v.), which forms a sort of supplement to Wilson and which is incorporated in the Jameson, Jardine and "Popular" editions of Wilson mentioned above. These editions are all ascribed, on their title-pages, to Wilson and Bonaparte as co-authors.

Wilson, Alexander. (Ord, George.)

1824 (-25). American ornithology; | or, | the natural history | of the | birds of the United States: | illustrated with plates | Engraved and Colored from Original drawings taken from Nature. | By Alexander Wilson. | Vol. VII [VIII]. | Philadelphia: | published by Samuel F. Bradford. | Printed by Thomas H. Palmer. | 1824. 2 vols. (should be 3) folio (size of imperial 4to). Vol. VII, tit., pp. I-XII, 13-138, pll. 55-63 (col.). Vol. VIII, pp. I-XI+1, 13-162, pll. 64-72 (col.), 2 text-figs. Vol. IX missing. Philadelphia.

A revised edition of Wilson's later volumes, prepared by Ord. Verbal alterations are made in the text, original matter is added and the following changes in nomenclature instituted. Vol. VII, *Falco ossifragus* of the original - changed to *F. leucocephalus*, *Charadrius calidris* - *C. arenaria*, *C. rubidus* - *C. arenaria*, *Recurvirostra himantopus* - *Himantopus Mexicanus*, *Tringa hiaticula* - *Charadrius hiaticula*, *Charadrius apricarius* - *Vanellus Helveticus*, *C. pluvialis* - *Vanellus Helveticus*, *Tringa interpres* - *Strepsilas interpres*, *Ardea candidissima* - *A. Carolinensis*, *Scolopax borealis* - *Numenius borealis*, *Tringa cinclus* - *T. Alpina*, *Tringa Bartramia* - *Totanus Bartramius*, *Tringa solitaria* - *Totanus glareolus*, *Tringa macularia* - *Totanus macularius*, *Scolopax vociferus* - *Totanus melanoleucos*, *S. flavipes* - *Totanus flavipes*, *S. semipalmata* - *Totanus semipalmatus*, *S. fedoa* - *Limosa fedoa*, *S. noveboracensis* - *S. grisea*, and *Procellaria pelagica* - *P. Wilsonii;* Vol.VIII, *Ardea Ludoviciana* - *A. leucogaster*, *A. Americana* - *Grus Americanus*, *Tantalus ruber* - *Ibis ruber*, *T. albus* - *I. albus*, *Anas fuligula* - *A. rufitorques*, and *A. rubidus* - *A. Jamaicensis*. Vol. IX was likewise revised, in 1825, but it seems to have been issued under a special title as given below. Jameson, in the preface to his edition of Wilson (Vol. I, p. VII), says that in 1825 Ord was employed to prepare new editions of the seventh, eighth and ninth volumes, which he did with considerable additions; and

Brewer, in his 1840 edition of Wilson, p. 633, footn., says that the revised copy of Vol. IX appeared in 1825 "correcting several mistakes which had appeared in the first." The revised ninth volume, then, is probably the " 'Supplement' by Ord, 'Phila. 1825' " mentioned (but not seen) by Coues and catalogued by Carus and Engelmann under the following title,—"Ord, George, Supplement to the American Ornithology of Alexander Wilson; containing a Sketch of the Author's Life, with a Selection from his Letters; some remarks upon his Writings; and a history of those Birds which were intended to compose part of his Ninth Volume: illustrated with plates engraved from Wilson's original Drawings. Philadelphia, 1825. 4. (298 pag.)." It is, unquestionably the "Mr. Ord's Supplementary Volume" quoted in Ord's edition of Wilson, 1828-9 (q.v.) and it seems probable that the text in that edition, relating to the species discussed in the original Vol. IX of Wilson, is the text of that volume as revised in 1825 (Cf. Ord's ed. for further discussion.). The editorial prefaces to the reprints of VII and VIII are dated, respectively, May 1 and June 1, 1824.

Wilson, Alexander. (Ord, George.)

1828-29. American ornithology; | or | the natural history | of the | birds of the United States. | Illustrated with plates | engraved and coloured from original drawings taken | from nature. | By Alexander Wilson. | With a sketch of the author's life, | by **George Ord,** F.L.S. &c. | In three vols.-Vol. I [-III]. | Published by Collins & Co, [*Period in place of comma (Vol. III.).*] | and | Harrison Hall, Philadelphia. [*Comma in place of period (Vol. III.).*] | 1828 [1829 (*Vol. III.*)].

> American ornithology; | or, | the natural history | of the | birds of the United States. | By Alexander Wilson. | Plates | Engraved and Coloured from Original Drawings taken from Nature. | Published by Collins & Co. New York, | and | Harrison Hall, Philadelphia. | 1829.

4 vols. 4to (size of 8vo) and folio (size of imperial 4to). Vol. I, pp. I-CXCIX, 1-230+1, 2 text-figs. Vol. II, pp. I-VI, 9-456. Vol. III, pp. I-VI, 1-396, 2 text-figs. Atlas, tit., pll. 1-76 (col.). New York and Philadelphia.

The first new edition of Wilson's entire work (1808-14, q.v.), arranged in the systematic sequence of the species, not in the irregular order of the original. The editor states that he "has adhered to the original text, correcting only some erroneous references, and a few verbal inaccuracies, most of which were probably typographical errors." However, considerable new matter is added in the form of footnotes or supplementary remarks; some of the latter are signed G. Ord,—some are not signed. They agree, for the most part, with the additions made by Ord in his revision of Vols. VII and VIII (ed. 1824, q.v.) and appear to comprise the same matter which is added in this way so as to disturb Wilson's text as little as possible. References are frequently made to "Ord's reprint" in this connection. The matter contained in the original Vol. IX is treated in a different manner. Original text and nomenclature of that volume are abandoned and a version given which is credited to "Mr. Ord's Supplementary Volume,"—probably the revision of Vol. IX published in 1825 following the revised editions of VII and VIII. Since the original Vol. IX was written by Ord after Wilson's death, liberties with the original copy were more permissible here than with Wilson's own text. The sketch of Wilson's life, in Vol. I of the present edition, is considerably expanded from that published in the last volume of the original work, although both are from the pen of Ord. Ord is sometimes quoted as the editor of the present edition, but the acknowledgment made in the editorial preface to the "valuable counsel and assistance" of that gentleman, seems to open the question to some doubt. The hand-colored drawings in the Atlas are from the original copper-plates (with the addition of the number added *backwards* to pl. 44; missing in the original), colored anew from fresh or preserved material, with pigments which seem to have been of better quality than those used by Wilson. In the copy at hand, the colors are as bright and fresh as if lately applied, whereas in the copy examined of the original, there are few tints which have not suffered and some which have completely disintegrated. An examination of the clearest of the originals and the copy, shows that there are some differences in coloration of the two, aside from those due to fading.

Wilson, Alexander; and Bonaparte, Charles Lucien. (Ord, George; Jameson, Robert; Audubon, John James; Richardson, John; and Swainson, William; Hetherington, W. H.)

1831. American ornithology; | or the | natural history | of | the birds of the United States. | By Alexander Wilson, and Charles Lucian Bonaparte. | Edited by | **Robert Jameson,** Esq. F.R.S.E. & L. F.L.S. M.W.S. | Regius Professor of Natural History in the University | of Edinburgh, &c. | In four volumes. | Vol. I [-IV]. | Edinburgh: | printed for Constable and Co. Edinburgh; | and Hurst, Chance, and Co. London. | 1831.

4 vols. cap 8vo. Vol. I, pp. I-XCVI, 1-271, frontisp. (portr., by James Craw), 1 pl. (by William Banks). Vol. II, 1 l. (advt.), pp. I-IX+1, 1-334, frontisp. Vol. III, pp. I-VIII, 1-320, frontisp. Vol. IV, 1 l. (advt.), pp. I-X, 1-362, 1 l. (advt), frontisp. Edinburgh.

Vols. I-III are devoted to a reprint of Wilson's work (1808-14, q.v.), rearranged and with occasional editorial notes by Jameson. Reference is given under each species to the number of Wilson's original plate and a notation is made if the species is represented in the Edinburgh College Museum, but the synonymy is transferred to a separate place at the end of Vol. III where it is arranged in the order adopted for the text. A number of Ord's notes and comments are printed with due credit. A sketch of the life of Wilson is given in Vol. I, written by W. M. Hetherington. Vol. IV (pp. 1-217) contains a reprint of the first three volumes of Bonaparte's "American Ornithology," 1825-33 (q.v.), with the synonymy transferred to pp. 219-238. On pp. 241-244 there is a catalogue of the species described and figured by Audubon in his "Ornithological Biography," 1831-39, and "Birds of America," 1827-38 (q.v.). The remainder of the volume consists of extracts made from the proof-sheets of

Richardson and Swainson's "Fauna Boreali-Americana" or "Northern Zoology," 1832, including diagnoses of numerous new species, and with annotations after other authors. As credit is given to Richardson and Swainson for the quotations, authorship should remain with them although the present volume may have appeared in advance of the "Fauna Boreali-Americana." Unfortunately there are a number of typographical errors which may likewise have to be credited to them such as *Larus Rosii* on p. 245 and *Calymbris glacialis* on p. 358 (both nomina nuda). A publishers' note in Vol. I is dated April 1831, and one in Vol. IV, August 1831. The work forms Vols. LXVIII-LXXI of "Constable's Miscellany." Coues notes his copy as without any other illustrations than the portrait of Wilson in Vol. I, but the present set has an engraved plate in each volume in addition to the portrait in the first volume. The publishers' note in Vol. I announces the publication of Part I of Captain Thomas Brown's "Illustrations of American Ornithology" as a companion to the four volumes of letterpress here collated (Cf. Brown, Capt. Thomas, Illustrations of the Game Birds of North America, 1834.). This is announced only in medium folio and elephant folio but there was, apparently, an edition the same size as the letterpress in course of publication at the same time, of which only one or two incomplete copies are known. A discussion of this publication is given by Walter Faxon in the Auk, **20**, pp. 236-241, 1903, and Auk, **36**, pp. 623-626, 1919.

In Vol. III, on p. 98, "*Rubicola* Vieill." is used for the Woodcock. This is evidently a misprint for "*Rusticola* Vieill.," but may be valid since it antedates *Philohela* Gray, 1841. Cf. Ridgway, U. S. Nat. Mus. Bull. **50**, Vol. 8, pp. 155 and 797, 1919; also Oberholser, Auk, **40**, p. 516, July 1923.

Wilson, Alexander; and Bonaparte, Charles Lucien.   (Ord, George; Jardine, William.)

1832. American ornithology; | or, | the natural history | of | the birds of the United States. | By Alexander Wilson; | with a continuation | by Charles Lucian Bonaparte, | Prince of Musignano. | The | illustrative notes, and life of Wilson, | by | **Sir William Jardine,** Bart. F.R.S.E. F.L.S. | Member of the Wernerian Natural History Society, [*etc.*, *4 lines.*]. | In three volumes. | Vol. I [-III]. | MDCCCXXXII. | Whittaker, Treacher, & Arnot, London; | Stirling & Kenney, Edinburgh.

3 vols. 8vo. Vol. I, tit., pp. V-CVII+1, 1-408, frontisp. (portr.), pll. 1-27 (col.; by Wilson). Vol. II, tit., pp. V-VII+1, 1-390, pll. 28-60 (col.; by Wilson). Vol. III, tit., pp. V-VIII, 1-523, pll. 61-76 (col.; by Wilson), 1-21 (col.; by Titian R. Peale and A. Rider), 2 text-figs. London and Edinburgh.

Vols. I, pp. 1-408, Vol. II and Vol. III, to p. 257, contain a reprint of Wilson's original "American Ornithology," 1808-14, including Vol. IX by Ord, with voluminous notes by Jardine; Vol. III, pp. 259-507, contains a reprint of the first three volumes (all then published) of Bonaparte's "American Ornithology," 1825-33, under the subtitle of "Continuation of Wilson's American Ornithology.

By Charles Lucien Bonaparte." The original plates of both authors are re-engraved by Lizars on a reduced scale and hand-colored, except for the backgrounds which are left plain. The coloration usually shows considerable departure from that of the original plates, and the backgrounds are sometimes modified. Vol. I, pp. IX-CVII contains a life of Wilson by Jardine. The editorial notes are detailed and critical and contain references to many contemporary publications, including Richardson and Swainson's "Fauna Boreali Americana," 1832 (q.v.). The synonymy of the various species is brought strictly up to date.

Wilson, Alexander. (Brewer, Thomas Mayo; Jardine, William; Ord, George.)

1840. > **Wilson's | American Ornithology** | with | Additions | Including the Birds | Described by | Audubon, Bonaparte, | Nuttall, | and | Richardson. | Boston, | Otis, Broaders and Company. [*Engr. design on border.*].

1 vol. 12mo (4½x7¼), (tit. missing), engr. tit., pp. III-VIII, 1-746, 25 pll., 2 text-figs. (unnum.), figs. 316-318 and 322. Boston.

Brewer's edition. A reprint of Wilson and Ord's text (Cf. Wilson, 1808-14.) with the footnotes and other matter added from the Jardine edition, 1832 (q.v.). The plates contain the figures from Wilson's drawings, rearranged and combined on a fewer number of plates, very much reduced in size and uncolored; those from pll. 75 and 76 of the original are separated, redrawn and inserted as text-figures. At the close of the volume, pp. 682-746, Brewer gives a "Synopsis of the birds of North America," a list of 491 species with descriptions of those not included by Wilson, synonymy and some biographical notes. This edition was reprinted in cheaper form in 1853 (q.v.). The title-page is missing from the present copy, for which reason I have quoted the engraved title which is somewhat different from the full title as quoted by Coues for this work. The latter is the same as quoted for the reprint of 1853, except for the imprint and date which are as given above in the transcript of the engraved title and the collation.

Wilson, Alexander. (Brewer, Thomas Mayo; Jardine, William; Ord, George.)

1853. **Wilson's | American Ornithology,** | with | notes by Jardine: | to which is added | a synopsis of American birds, | including those described | by | Bonaparte, Audubon, Nuttall, and | Richardson; | By **T. M. Brewer.** | New York: | H. S. Samuels, No. 8 Park Place. | MDCCCLIII.

1 vol. 12mo (5½x9), engr. tit. (col.), pp. I-VIII (incl. tit.), 1-746, 25 pll. (1 col.), 2 text-figs. (unnum.), text-figs. 316-318 and 322. New York.

An exact duplicate of the 1840 issue of Brewer's edition (q.v.) except for the coloring of the frontispiece and engraved title and for the imprint on the title and engraved title. It was printed from the same plates as the original issue although the plates of the illustrations are considerably worn. Coues gives the date of the reissue as 1852 and an examination of the date as printed on the title-page of the present copy shows an irregularity in the last figure which may be due to alteration. The British Museum (Natural History) contains a copy dated 1854.

Wilson, Alexander; and Bonaparte, Charles Lucien. (Jardine, William; Ord, George.)

1876. American ornithology; [*No semicolon (Vol. III.)*] | or, | the natural history | of the | birds of the United States. | By | Alexander Wilson | and | Prince Charles Lucian Bonaparte. | The Illustrative Notes and Life of Wilson | By Sir William Jardine, Bart., F.R.S.E., F.L.S. | [*Design.*] | In three volumes.-Vol. I [-III]. | London: | **Chatto and Windus,** Piccadilly. | 1876.

3 vols. medium 4to. Vol. I, pp. I-CV+1, 1 l. (subtit.), pp. 1-408, frontisp. (portr.), pll. 1-27 (col.; by Wilson). Vol. II, pp. I-VII+1, 1-495, pll. 28-68 (col.; by Wilson). Vol. III, pp. I-VII+1, 1-540, pll. 69-76 (col.; by Wilson), 1-27 (col.; by Titian R. Peale and A. Rider), 2 text-figs. London.

Up to p. 400 of Vol. III, the present edition is a copy of the text of the 1832 Jardine edition of Wilson and Bonaparte; the remainder of the work is a copy of the fourth volume of Bonaparte's "American Ornithology," 1825-33 (without the editorial annotations), which had not been published at the date of the earlier work. The plates are from the same engravings by Lizars as in the 1832 edition, except for pll. 22-27 (belonging to Vol. IV of Bonaparte); the latter are reduced to the same scale as the others but the engraver's name is not given. The plates are hand-colored but the coloring is exaggerated and not a close copy of the original.

Wilson, Alexander; and Bonaparte, Charles Lucien. (Jardine, William; Ord, George.)

1877. American ornithology; | or, | the natural history | of the | birds of the United States. | By | Alexander Wilson | and | Prince Charles Lucian Bonaparte. | The Illustrative Notes and Life of Wilson | By Sir William Jardine, Bart., F.R.S.E., F.L.S. | [*Design.*] | In three volumes.- Vol. I [-III]. | New York: | **J. W. Bouton,** 706 Broadway. | 1877.

3 vols. post 8vo. Vol. I, pp. I-CV+1, 1 l. (subtit.), pp. 1-408, frontisp. (portr.), pll. 1-27 (col.; by Wilson). Vol. II, pp. I-VII+1, 1-495, pll. 28-68 (col.; by Wilson). Vol. III, pp. I-VII+1, 1-540, pll. 69-76 (col.; by Wilson). 1-27 (col.; By Titian R. Peale and A. Rider), 2 text-figs. New York.

The text of the present edition is printed from the same plates as the 4to edition of the previous year. The colored plates are poor chromolithographic reproductions of the engravings by Lizars and others in the same issue.

Wilson, Alexander; and Bonaparte, Charles Lucien. (Ord, George; Baird, Spencer Fullerton.)

1878. **American ornithology;** | or, the | natural history | of the | Birds of the United States. | Illustrated with plates | engraved from drawings from nature. | By | Alexander Wilson | and | Charles Lucian Bonaparte. | **Popular edition.** | Vol. I [-III]. | [*Blazon.*] | Philadelphia: | Porter & Coates, | 822 Chestnut Street.

3 vols. in 1, superroyal 8vo. Vol. I, tit. pp. V-VI (index), IX-CXXXII (biography), I-XVI (Catalogue of N. American birds), 1-214, 28 pll. (relate to all three vols.). Vol. II, tit., pp. V-VIII, 9-390. Vol. III, tit., pp. VII-VIII, 9-426, 2 text-figs. Philadelphia.

A composite reprint, consisting of the Ord (1828-29) edition of Wilson's text, including Ord's biography of the author, and (Vol. III, pp. 135-408) Bonaparte's "American Ornithology," 1825-33, Vols. I-IV, with the prefaces to the first three volumes. A combined index is given at the close of the work. The plates consist of zinc etchings after the original drawings of Wilson's and Bonaparte's works, reduced and slightly modified by the omission of backgrounds and other accessories, and usually combined four to the page. The original numbers are retained for the component drawings, those of Bonaparte being distinguished by the insertion of the letter B. Vol. I, pp. I-XVI, contains a "Catalogue of North American Birds" by Baird, reprinted from the 1859 8vo edition of the original matter first published in Vol. IX of the "Pacific Railroad Surveys" (reprint erroneously credited to October 1858 and original to Vol. IV of the "Surveys," in acknowledgement on p. I). This edition is a reprint of a 5 vol. issue by the same publishers in 1871, 3 vols. text and 2 vols. colored plates. The pagination appears to be the same, although the colored plates have been replaced by the cheaper illustrations. The present issue is reviewed in the Bulletin of the Nuttall Ornithological Club, 4, pp. 53-54, 1879.

Wilson, Alexander.

1904. See Weed, Clarence Moores, **Bird Life Stories, Book I.**

Wilson, Edward Adrian.

1911. See [Grouse], **The Grouse in Health and Disease.**

Wilson, Edward Adrian.

1907. See British Museum, **National Antarctic Expedition 1901-1904; Natural History Vol. II.**

Wilson, Scott Barchard; and Evans, Arthur Humble. (Gadow, Hans.)

1890-99. **Aves Hawaiienses:** | the birds | of the | Sandwich Islands. | By | Scott B. Wilson, F.Z.S., F.R.G.S., | assisted by | A. H. Evans, M.A., F.Z.S. | London: | R. H. Porter, 7 Princes Street, Cavendish Square, W. | 1890-99.

1 vol. royal 4to, 2 pr. ll., pp. IIIa-IIIe+1, V-XXV+1, 1 l., 128 ll. (pp. 1-256 according to index), 71 pll. (64 col., by F. W. Frohawk; I-III by H. Gadow; 3 photogravures; 1 map), 3 text-figs. London.

Published in seven parts beginning in December, 1890 and concluding·in June 1899. The dates and distribution of the subject matter are given in the table of contents on pages IIIa-IIIc. The book is a thorough dissertation on the bird life of this interesting region, with synonymies, descriptions, critical notes and remarks on habits, distribution, native names, etc. The hand-colored illustrations are excellent. Dr. Hans Gadow contributes an article of four leaves (pp. 243-249) entitled, "Further remarks on the relationships of the Drepanididæ" illustrated with three plates (pll. I-III).

Winge, Herluf.

1925-?. See Schiøler, E. Lehn, **Danmarks Fugle.**

Wintle, Ernest D. (Denne, David.)

1896. The | **birds of Montreal** | by | Ernest D. Wintle, | "Associate Member of the American Ornithologists Union." | Birds observed in the vicinity of Montreal, Province of Quebec, | Dominion of Canada, with annotations as to whether they | are "Permanent Residents" or those that are found | regularly throughout the year; "Winter Visitants," | or those that occur only during the winter season, | passing north in the spring; "Transient | Visitants," or those that occur only | during migrations in spring and | autumn; "Summer Residents," or those that are known to | breed, but which depart | southward before winter; and | "Accidental Visitants," or strag- | glers from remote districts; giving | their relative abundance as to whether | they are rare, scarce, common or abundant; | data of nests and eggs when found, and especially | noting the species that breed in the City and Mount | Royal Park; also data of migratory arrivals and de- | partures, and other notes, all of which are deduced | from original observations made during the past fifteen years. | Montreal: | W. Drysdale & Co. | 1896.

1 vol. 8vo, pp. I-XIV, 1-228, 1 l. (subtit.), pp. 229-281, 4 pll., 1 map (frontisp.). Montreal.

An annotated list of 254 species. On pp. 137-214, brief description are given of each of the species. Pages 229-274, with a special title-page, contain a series of "Original sporting sketches compiled by David Denne. 1895." The provincial game-laws complete the volume.

Witchell, Charles A.

1896. The | **evolution of bird-song** | with | observations on the influence of | heredity and imitation | by | Charles A. Witchell |

author of 'The Fauna of Gloucestershire' | London | Adam and
Charles Black | 1896.

1 vol. crown 8vo, pp. I-X, 1-253, 3 ll. (advt.). London.

A detailed study of the voice of birds, beginning with the origin of the voice
and closing with the music of bird-song. Based on personal observations on
British birds and published accounts of other writers. Much of the work is
theoretical but the observations are accurate and the account is interesting.

Witherby, Harry Forbes.

1912. See Hartert, Ernst; Jourdain; Ticehurst; and Witherby, **A
Hand-List of British Birds.**

Witherby, Harry Forbes. (Hartert, Ernst; Jackson, Annie C.; Jourdain,
Francis Charles Robert; Oldham, Charles; Ticehurst, Norman
Frederick.)

1919-24. A | practical handbook | of | British birds | Edited by |
H. F. Witherby, M.B.E., F.Z.S., M.B.O.U. | Editor of "British
Birds" (Mag.) | Authors of the Various Sections: | Ernst Hartert,
Ph.D., M.B.O.U. | Annie C. Jackson, H.M.B.O.U. [(Mrs. Meinertz-
hagen) *(added, Vol. II.)*] | Rev. F. C. R. Jourdain, M.A., M.B.O.U.
[,H.F.A.O.U. *(added, Vol. II.)*] | C. Oldham, F.Z.S., M.B.O.U. |
Norman F. Ticehurst, [O.B.E., *(added, Vol. II.)*] M.A., F.R.C.S.,
M.B.O.U. | and the editor. [*Period omitted (Vol. II.).*] | Volume
I [II]. | With 17 [13] Plates and Numerous Text Figures. [*Period
omitted (Vol. II.).*] | Witherby & Co., [H. F. & G. Witherby] |
326, High Holborn, London. [London, W.C] | 1920. [1924].

2 vols. in 3, post 8vo. Vol. I, pp. I-VIII, *I-*XVI, 1-532, pll. 1-17
(6 col.; by C. G. Davies, F. W. Frohawk and H. Grönvold, and
from photographs), 196 text-figs. Vol. II (Pt. I), pp. I-XII, 1-448,
pll. 1-6 (2 col.; by Grönvold and G. E. Lodge), 122 text-figs.:
(Pt. II), pp. 449-959, pll. 7-13 (col.; by Grönvold), 175 text-figs.
London.

A thorough manual of British ornithology, with descriptions of different plumages,
measurement, field characters, breeding habits, food, distribution, migration
and other such notes systematically arranged. Keys are given throughout;
a glossary of terms and guide for measurement are given in Vol. I while Vol.
II (Pt. II) presents additions and corrections to the entire work and a systematic list of species with a summary of the status of each and a page reference.
The systematic list was published separately in 1924 as "A Check-list of British
Birds" (q.v.). The numerous text-figures are credited to Mrs. Hartert. The
text is by the various authors, each of whom is responsible for certain sections
as outlined in Vol. I, p. *5, deviations from this arrangement being indicated
by the initials attached to the contributions. The work was published in 18
parts from March 3, 1919 to Febr. 26, 1924, dates and contents being published
on p. IV of both volumes.

Witherby, Harry Forbes.

1924. A check-list | of British birds | with a short account of the status of each | compiled from | "A Practical Handbook of British Birds." | By | H. F. Witherby, M.B.E., F.Z.S., M.B.O.U. | H. F. & G. Witherby | 326, High Holborn, London, W.C. | 1924.

1 vol. post 8vo, pp. 1-78. London.

A reprint of pp. 903-936 of Witherby's "A Practical Handbook," etc., 1919-24 (q.v.), here printed on only one side of the paper.

Wodzicki, Casimir.

1878. See Rowley, George D., **Ornithological Miscellany,** 1875-78.

Wood, Casey Albert.

1917. The fundus oculi of birds | especially as viewed by the | microscope | A Study in | Comparative Anatomy and Physiology | by | Casey Albert Wood | Illustrated by 145 drawings in the text; also by sixty-one | colored paintings prepared for this work by | Arthur W. Head, F.Z.S. | London | Chicago | The Lakeside Press | 1917.

1 vol. 8vo (10¼ x 13¼), pp. 1-180, 31 pll. (col.; on num. pp.; containing "pll. I-LXI"), text-figs. 1-145. Chicago.

A most important monograph on the eyes of birds, describing "the conditions found in such birds (especially of living birds) as are most likely to be useful in a study of comparative opthalmology"; a "description of the intraocular appearances and the methods employed in viewing them." In preparing the monograph, the author examined the eyes of some representative of almost all of the different orders of birds, and the descriptions and excellent figures and plates describe and illustrate the results of this comparative study.

Wood, John George.

1866. Homes without hands. | Being a description of | the habitations of animals, classed according to | their principle of construction. | By | The Rev. J. G. Wood, M.A., F.L.S., Etc. | Author of [etc., 2 lines.]. | With new designs by W. F. Keyl and E. Smith. | Engraved by Messrs. Pearson. | New York: | Harper & Brothers, publishers, | Franklin Square. | 1866.

1 vol. 8vo, pp. I-XVIII, 19-651, 1-4 (advt.), 21 pll. (on num. pp.), 110 text-figs. New York.

A popular work containing a vast amount of information of greater or less reliability, considerable of which relates to birds. The first edition was published in London in 1865.

Wood, Theodore.

1921. **Birds | one should know** | beneficial and mischievous | By | The Rev. Canon Theodore Wood | Illustrated by | Roland Green, F.Z.S. | [*Vignette.*] | London: | Gay & Hancock, Limited, | 34, Henrietta Street, Covent Garden, W.C.2. | 1921 | (All Rights Reserved).

1 vol. imperial 8vo (7½x10), pp. I-XI+1, 1-132, 24 pll. (8 col.), 188 text-figs. and decorations. London.

A popular book giving a very brief account of the economic value of 33 species of British birds.

Woodruff, Frank Morley.

1907. The Chicago Academy of Sciences | **The Birds of the Chicago Area** | by | Frank Morley Woodruff | Bulletin No. VI | of | The Natural History Survey | Issued April 15, 1907.

1 vol. royal 8vo, pp. 1-221, frontisp., pll. I-XI (photographic). Chicago. April 15, 1907.

An annotated list of the species of birds known to have occurred in an area embracing Cook and DuPage counties and the nine north townships of Will County, Illinois and the northern portion of Lake County, Indiana. A local bibliography is appended.

Wolcott, Robert Henry.

1904. See Bruner, Lawrence; Wolcott; and Swenk, A **Preliminary Review of the Birds of Nebraska.**

Wolf, A. G.

1890. See Warren, Benjamin H., **Report on the Birds of Pennsylvania, Second Edition.**

Wolf, Johann.

1810. See Meyer, Bernhard; and Wolf, **Taschenbuch der Deutschen Vögelkunde.**

Wolf, Johann.

1816-22. **Abbildungen und Beschreibungen** | merkwürdiger | naturgeschichtlicher Gegenstände | von | Dr. und Professor Johann Wolf, | Kön. Baier'schem Schullehrer [*etc.*, *6 lines.*]. [| II. Band. (*added, in Vol. II.*)] | Mit 36 illuminirten Kupfern. | Nürnberg, | im Verlag des Conrad Tyroff'schen Wappen-, Kunst- und | Commissions-Bureau's. | 1818 [1822].

2 vols. (text 2 vols. in 1; pll. in separate vol.) demy 4to. Vol. I, 2 pr. ll. (tit. and pref.), pp. 1-168, 2 ll. (list of pll., conts. and index),

pll. I-XXXVI (col.; 11 ornithological by Wolf, L. C. Tyroff and A. Gabler). Vol. II, tit., pp. 1-156, 2 ll. (as in Vol. I), pll. I-XXXVI (col.; 9 ornithological by A. Gabler and C. W. Hahn). Nuremberg.

Descriptions and notes on various animals and plants. Nine species of birds are treated in Vol. I and ten in Vol. II. No information is obtainable as to the dates of publication beyond that given by Engelmann and a few references in the text of the work itself. Engelmann notes the inclusive dates, 1816-22, and the division of the work into 27 Hefte of 2 sheets of text and 3 plates each, but these figures do not agree with the totals of 46 signatures and 72 plates. In the text, there is, on p. 86 of Vol. I, a reference to December 1816; on p. 109, a reference to a publication dated 1817; in Vol. II on p. 119, a reference to a publication dated 1820; on p. 133, a reference to one dated 1821; the title-pages are dated as quoted above and the preface to Vol. I is dated June 28, 1815.

Wollaston, Alexander Frederick Richmond.

1916. See British Ornithologists' Union, **Reports on the Collections made by the British Ornithologists' Union Expedition in Dutch New Guinea.**

Wolley, John. (Newton, Alfred.)

1864-1907. Ootheca Wolleyana: | an illustrated catalogue | of | the collection of birds' eggs, | begun by the late | John Wolley, Jun., M.A., F.Z.S., | and continued with additions | by the editor | Alfred Newton. | Volume I [II]. | London: | M.DCCC.LXIV. - M.CM.II [M.CM.V. - M.CM.VII]. | [Sold by R. H. Porter, 7 Prince's Street, Cavendish Square.]. > *Idem* [*4 lines.*] | formed by the late | John Wolley, Jun., M.A., F.Z.S. | edited from the original notes | by | Alfred Newton, M.A., F.L.S., etc. [*No initials (Pts. 2-4.*).] | Part I. Accipitres [Part II. Picariæ-Passeres; Part III. Columbæ - Alcæ; Part IV. Alcæ-Anseres: | with supplement and appendix]. | London: | R. H. Porter, 7 Prince's Street, Cavendish Square. | M.DCCC.LXIV [M.CM.II; M.CM.V; M.CM.VII]. {[| Price £2 2s. net.] (*Pts. II and III.*); [Price £1 5s. net.] (*Pt. IV.*).}

2 vols. (4 pts.) royal 8vo. Vol. I, pp. I-XXXIX+1, 1-531, 1 l. (list of pll. in Pt. I), frontisp. (portr.), pll. I-XIII (col.; by J. T. Balcomb; eggs), A-M (1 col.; by J. Wolf, A.N., J. Wolley, etc.), 1 text-fig. Vol. II, pp. I-VI, 1 l. (blank), pp. 1-665+1, 1-96 (appendices I-LX), pll. XIV-XXI (col.; by H. Grönvold; eggs), N-P (1 col.; by J. Wolf, etc.), 1 map. (col.; fold.), 2 text-figs. London.

An extensively annotated catalogue of the collection of birds' eggs made by John Wolley, with further annotations by the editor, Alfred Newton, and with discussions of numerous specimens added by Newton to the collection after the death of Wolley. Newton's contributions are enclosed in brackets. The work was issued in four parts as follows. Pt. **I**, pp. 1-180, 1 l. (list of pll.), pll. I-IX, A-I; **II**, pp. 181-531, I-XXXIX, frontisp., pll. X-XIII, J-M; **III**, pp. 1-384, pll. XIV-XXI; **IV**, pp. 385-665+1, 1-96, I-VI, pll. N-P, map. The original wrappers, bearing the titles of the four parts, are bound with the set.

Wood, Norman A.

1923. University of Michigan | Museum of Zoology | Miscellaneous Publications No. 10 | **A Preliminary Survey of the Bird** | **Life of North Dakota** | by | Norman A. Wood | Ann Arbor, Michigan | Published by the University | July 2, 1923.

1 vol. superroyal 8vo, pp. 1-96, pll. I-VI (photogrs.), 1 map (fold.). Ann Arbor. July 2, 1923.

An annotated list of 320 species and subspecies of birds found in North Dakota, giving published records and other information relative to each. A bibliography is appended.

Worcester, Dean Conant.

1909-10. See McGregor, Richard C., **A Manual of Philippine Birds.**

World's Congress on Ornithology. (Allen, J. A.; Amery, C. F.; Baskett, James Newton; Bates, Abraham H.; Belding, Lyman; Black, Hortensia; Bowles, J. H.; Butler, A. W.; Cairns, John S.; Chapman, Frank M.; Coombs, Frank B.; Coues, Elliott; Crane, E. H.; Duges, Alfred; Hales, Henry; Hardy, Manly; Holub, Emil; Ingraham, D. P.; Keyser, Leander S.; Leverkuhn, Paul; Oberholser, H. C.; Pearson, T. Gilbert; Praeger, William G.; Pratt, Geo. B.; Quelch, J. J.; Rood, E. Irene; Shufeldt, R. W.; and Warren, Oscar Bird.)

1896. Papers | presented to the | World's Congress | on | Ornithology | edited by | Mrs. E. Irene Rood|Chairman Woman's Committee of the Congress | under the direction of | Dr. Elliott Coues | President of the Congress, Ex-President of the American Ornithologists' Union. | [*Quot.*] | Chicago | Charles H. Sergel Company | 1896.

1 vol. 8vo, pp. 1-208 (135-136 missing). Chicago.

The volume contains 27 of the papers presented at the meeting of the World's Congress on Ornithology, Oct. 18-21, 1893, at the World's Fair in Chicago.

Wright, Lewis.

(Post 1879?). The | practical | pigeon keeper. | By | Lewis Wright, | author of [*etc., 2 lines.*]. | Illustrated. | Tenth thousand. | Cassell & Company, Limited: | London, Paris & Melbourne. | [All rights reserved.].

1 vol. crown 8vo, pp. I-VI, 1 l. (pref.), pp. 1-232, 9 pll. (on num. pp.), text-figs. 1-36, 24 text-figs. (unnum.). London, Paris and Melbourne.

A handbook of information for the pigeon fancier. The first edition was published in London in 1879.

Wright, Mabel Osgood.

1895.   **Birdcraft** | a field book of two hundred song | game, and water birds | by | Mabel Osgood Wright | author of "The Friendship of Nature" | with full-page plates containing 128 birds in the | natural colours, and other illustrations | New York | Macmillan and Co. | and London | 1895 | All rights reserved.

1 vol. 8vo, pp. I-XVI, 1-317, 15 ll. (expl. of pll.), pll. I-XV (double; 10 fold.). New York and London.

An excellent introduction to the field study of a number of the commoner birds of New England. Descriptions, songs, season of occurrence, breeding range and habits, and distributional range are given concisely in tabular form, and notes on habits, mostly from personal observations, follow. Introductory chapters relate to general topics and a key to adult males in spring plumage follows the main text. The plates are after Audubon's "Birds of America," Warren's "Birds of Pennsylvania," De Kay's "Ornithology of the State of New York" and Fisher's "Hawks and Owls of the United States." A second edition, with plates by Fuertes, appeared in 1897.

Wright, Magnus von. (Palmén, Johan Axel.)

1859-73.   **Finlands foglar,** | hufvudsakligen till deras drägter, [*No comma.*] | beskrifna af [beskrifna af] | Magnus von Wright. | Förro Afdelningen [Senare afdelningen, | efter författerens död omarbetad | med särskild hänsyn till arternas utbredning | och utgifven af | Johan Axel Palmén]. | Helsingfors, | Finska Litteratursällskapets Tryckeri, 1859 [Finska Litteratur-Sällskapets tryckeri, 1873].

2 vols. post 8vo. Vol. I, 2 pr. ll. (tit. and ded.), pp. VII-XIV, 1-315+1, 1 l. (errata). Vol. II, tit., pp. I-XVII+1, 1-681+1, 2 ll. (conts.). Helsingfors. 1859 (post Oct. 1) and 1873 (post Sept. 1).

A descriptive and biographical account of the birds of Finland. Vol. I ("Accipitres" to "Columbini") was written by Wright; II ("Gallinae" to "Pygopodes") by Palmén, after Wright's death. The approximate dates are from the prefaces of the two volumes.

Wüllerstorf-Urbair, B. von. (Pelzeln, August von.)

1865.   [Reise der österreichischen Fregatte "Novara" um die Erde, in den Jahren 1857, 1858, 1859, unter den Befehlen des Commodore B. von Wüllerstorf-Urbair. > Zoologischer Theil. I. Bd. Wirbelthiere. > 2.] > **Vögel** | von | August von Pelzeln | Custos-Adjunct am K. K. Zoologischen Cabinete. | Mit 6 Tafeln. | Novara-Expedition. Zoologischer Theil. Bd. I. Pelzeln. Vögel.

1 vol. (pt.), medium 4to, tit., pp. I-IV, 1-176, pll. I-VI (col.; by T. F. Zimmermann). Vienna.

The ornithological portion (Pt. 2 of Vol. II of the Zoological Section) of the report on the voyage of the Novara. It comprises an annotated catalogue of the birds collected by the members of the expedition. The general title is quoted from Taschenberg.

Wyatt, Claude Wilmot.

1885-94. See Sharpe, R. B.; and Wyatt, **A Monograph of the Hirundinidae.**

Wyatt, Claude Wilmot.

1894. **British birds: | being | coloured illustrations | of all the | species of Passerine birds resident in the | British Isles, | with |** some notes in reference to their plumage. | By | Claude W. Wyatt, | Member of the British Ornithologists' Union. | London: | William Wesley & Son, 28 Essex Street, Strand. | 1894.

1 vol. demy folio, 3 pr. ll. (tit., pref. and conts.), ll. 1-25, 25 pll. (col.; by Wyatt). London.

A series of excellent, hand-colored plates illustrating 50 species of resident British birds, with notes relative to individual and other variations which do not appear in the illustrations. A companion volume, with the same short title, was issued in 1899. This second work is designated as Vol. II of the present title, but its full title is different, while a note by the publishers in the present volume describes the forthcoming book as a separate work which was to be sold separately. The second volume is entitled, "British Birds: with Some Notes in Reference to their Plumage" (q.v.).

Wyatt, Claude Wilmot.

1899. **British birds: | with | some notes in reference to their plumage. |** Coloured illustrations. | Vol. II. | By | Claude W. Wyatt, | Member of the British Ornithologists' Union. | London: | William Wesley & Son, 28 Essex Street, Strand. | 1899.

1 vol. demy folio, 3 pr. ll. (tit., pref. and conts.), ll. 1-42, 42 pll. (col.; by Wyatt). London.

A series of fine, hand-colored plates of British birds, including migrant Passeres and resident and migrant "Picariae, Striges, Accipitres and Columbae," excluding occasional visitors. The text is descriptive of variations and differences which do not appear in the illustrations. Although indicated as Vol. II (of the author's "British birds: being Coloured Illustrations of all the Species of Passerine Birds Resident in the British Isles," 1894, q.v.) the present volume was issued and sold separately.

Wyatt, John H.

1924. See Kirkman, Frederick B.; and Hutchinson, **British Sporting Birds.**

Wyman, Luther E.; and Burnell, Elizabeth F.

1925. Field book of birds | of the | southwestern United States | by | Luther E. Wyman, M.S. | Ornithologist, Los Angeles Museum | and | Elizabeth F. Burnell, M.A. | Assistant Supervisor of Nature Study | Los Angeles City Schools | with many illustrations | [*Design.*] | Boston and New York | Houghton Mifflin Company | The Riverside Press Cambridge | 1925.

1 vol. crown 8vo, pp. I-XXIV, 1 l. (explanatory notes), pp. 1-308, frontisp. (col.; by Allan Brooks), 2 maps (col.; fold.), 1 chart (col.), 347 text-figs. Boston and New York.

A descriptive handbook of the birds of one of the most interesting sections of the United States,—a region including Arizona, southern California and Nevada. Each species or subspecies is concisely described and some one of its distinguishing characteristics noted, while on the opposite page the distribution is stated and, in most cases, delineated on a small map accompanied by a pen-and-ink drawing of the bird or some part of it. Most of the drawings are very good although some of them have suffered partial obliteration of detail through too much reduction in size. At the rear of the volume are field color keys to the species of certain families and a check-list of all the forms described in the earlier parts of the work.

Wytsman, Paul. (Brasil, Louis; Dubois, Alphonse; Hartert, Ernst; Hellmayr, Charles Edward; Parrot, Carl; Salvadori, Tommaso; Sclater, Philip Lutley.)

1905-14. 1st [-26th] part Passeres [Picariæ (*Pts. 2, 6, 8, 10, 13, 14.*); Psittaci (*Pts. 3, 4, 5, 11, 12.*); Steganopodes (*Pt. 7.*); Grues (*Pts. 19, 21, 26.*); Casuarii (*Pts. 20, 25.*); Apteryges (*Pt. 22.*)] | **Genera | Avium |** edited by [conducted by (*Pts. 6-26.*)] | P. Wytsman | with contributions by [*etc., mut. mut., 2-3 lines.*] | Passeres [*mut. mut., as in line 1.*] | Fam. Eurylæmidæ [*mut. mut.; see below.*] | by Ernst Hartert [*mut. mut.; see below.*] | with 1 coloured plate [*mut. mut.; see below.*] | 1905 [*mut. mut.; see below.*] | Price 3/9 (Fr. 4.75) [*mut. mut.*] | [*Design.*] | Printed and Published by V. Verteneuil & L. Desmet, Brussels.

[*Mutanda.*]

Pt. 1. Passeres | Fam. Eurylæmidæ | by Ernst Hartert | with 1 coloured plate | 1905.

Pt. 2. Picariæ | Fam. Todidæ | by P. Wytsman | with 1 coloured plate | 1905.

Pt. 3. Psittaci | Fam. Stringopidæ | by T. Salvadori | with 1 coloured plate | 1905.

Pt. 4. Psittaci | Fam. Nestoridæ | by T. Salvadori | with 2 coloured plates | 1905.

Pt. 5. Psittaci | Fam. Cacatuidæ | by T. Salvadori | with 2 coloured plates | 1905.

Pt. 6. Picariæ | Fam. Coliidæ | by P. L. Sclater, Dr. Sc., F.R.S. | with 1 coloured plate | 1906.

Pt. 7. Steganopodes | Fam. Pelecanidæ | by Dr. Alphonse Dubois | with 1 coloured plate | 1907.

Pt. 8. Picariæ | Fam. Musophagidæ | by Dr. Alphonse Dubois | with 2 coloured plates | 1907.

Pt. 9. Passeres | Fam. Pipridæ | by C. E. Hellmayr | with 3 coloured plates | 1910.

Pt. 10. Picariæ | Fam. Galbulidæ | by P. L. Sclater | with 1 coloured plate | 1909.

Pt. 11. Psittaci | Fam. Loriidæ | by T. Salvadori | with 6 coloured plates | 1910.

Pt. 12. Psittaci | Fam. Cyclopsittacidæ | by T. Salvadori | with 2 coloured plates | 1910.

Pt. 13. Picariae | Fam. Bucerotidæ | by Dr. Alphonse Dubois | with 3 coloured plates | 1911.

Pt. 14. Picariæ | Fam. Meropidæ | by Dr. Carl Parrot | with 1 coloured plate | 1911.

Pt. 15. Passeres | Fam. Certhiidæ | by C. E. Hellmayr | with 1 coloured plate | 1911.

Pt. 16. Passeres | Fam. Sittidæ | by C. E. Hellmayr | with 1 coloured plate | 1911.

Pt. 17. Passeres | Fam. Regulidæ | by C. E. Hellmayr | with 1 coloured plate | 1911.

Pt. 18. Passeres | Fam. Paridæ | by C. E. Hellmayr | with 3 coloured plates | 1911.

Pt. 19. Grues | Fam. Gruidæ | by L. Brasil | with 3 coloured plates | 1913.

Pt. 20. Casuarii. Fam. Casuariidæ | by L. Brasil | with 3 coloured plates | 1913.

Pt. 21. Grues | Fam. Rhinochetidæ | by L. Brasil | with 1 coloured plate | 1913.

Pt. 22. Apteryges | Fam. Apterygidæ | by L. Brasil | with 1 coloured plate | 1913.

Pt. 23. Passeres | Fam. Chamæidæ | by C. E. Hellmayr | 1913.

Pt. 24. Passeres | Fam. Hyposittidæ | by C. E. Hellmayr | with 1 coloured plate | 1913.

Pt. 25. Casuarii | Fam. Dromaiidæ | by L. Brasil | with 1 coloured plate | 1914.

Pt. 26. Grues | Fam. Mesitidæ | by L. Brasil | with 1 coloured plate | 1914. .

26 pts. royal 4to. Pt. 1, subtit., pp. 1-8, 1 pl. (col.). Pt. 2, subtit., pp. 1-4, 1 pl. (col.). Pt. 3, subtit., pp. 1-2, 1 pl. (col.). Pt. 4, subtit., pp. 1-3, 1 pl. (col.). Pt. 5, subtit., pp. 1-7, pll. 1-2 (col.). Pt. 6, subtit., pp. 1-6, 1 pl. (col.). Pt. 7, subtit., pp. 1-4, 1 pl. (col.). Pt. 8, subtit., pp. 1-9, pll. 1-2 (col.). Pt. 9, subtit., pp. 1-31, pll. 1-3 (col.). Pt. 10, subtit., pp. 1-7, 1 pl. (col.). Pt. 11, subtit., pp. 1-20, pll. 1-6 (col.). Pt. 12, subtit., pp. 1-6, pll. 1-2 (col.). Pt. 13, subtit., pp. 1-24, pll. 1-3 (col.). Pt. 14, subtit., pp. 1-17, 1 pl. (col.). Pt. 15, subtit., pp. 1-16, 1 pl. (col.). Pt. 16, subtit., pp. 1-18, 1 pl. (col.). Pt. 17, subtit., pp. 1-18, 1 pl. (col.). Pt. 18, subtit., pp. 1-84, pll. 1-3 (col.). Pt. 19, subtit., pp. 1-9, 3 pll. (col.). Pt. 20, subtit., pp. 1-10, 3 pll. (col.). Pt. 21, subtit., pp. 1-3, 1 pl. (col.). Pt. 22, subtit., pp. 1-4, 1 pl. (col.). Pt. 23, subtit., pp. 1-3. Pt. 24, subtit., pp. 1-3, 1 pl. (col.). Pt. 25, subtit., pp. 1-5, 1 pl. (col.). Pt. 26, subtit., pp. 1-3, 1 pl. (col.). [26 original covers.] Brussels.

A series of monographs of various groups of birds, prepared by different workers and issued from time to time. The intention was to have the complete series embrace all avian groups, but, up to date, only those families have been treated which are included in the above list; the death of the editor has probably terminated the project.

The dates on the original wrappers are not reliable. Dr. Hellmayr informs me that he received author's copies of his contributions sent to Munich supposedly as soon as issued, as follows. Pt. 9, dated 1910, recd. Jan. 13, 1910. Pts. 15-18, dated 1911, recd. Febr. 21, 1912. Pt. 23, dated 1913, recd. Dec. 9, 1913.

Yarkand; Scientific Results of the Second Yarkand Mission.

1891. See Sharpe, Richard Bowdler.

Yarrell, William.

1835. See Jenyns, Leonard, **A Manual of British Vertebrate Animals.**

Yarrell, William.

1837-43.· A | history | of | British birds. | By | William Yarrell, F.L.S. V.P.Z.S. | [*Blazon or vignette; different in each vol.*] | Illustrated by 520 wood-engravings. | In three volumes, —Vol. I

[-III]. | London: | John Van Voorst, Paternoster Row. | M. DCCC. XLIII.

> A | history | of | British birds. | By | William Yarrell, F.L.S. F.Z.S. | Illustrated with woodcuts | of each species. | Vol. I [II]. | Containing one hundred and five [nine] birds, | and numerous vignettes. | London: | John Van Voorst, 1, Paternoster Row. | M. DCCC.XXXIX [M.DCCC.XLI]. | [Temporary title-page.] [*Issued only with Vols. I and II.*].

3 vols. royal 8vo. Vol. I, temporary tit., pp. 1-528, 194 figs. Vol. II, temp. tit., pp. 1-672, 209 figs. Vol. III, 2 pr. ll. (half-tit. and tit.), pp. 1-528, 292 figs.; (addenda to Vol. I), pp. I-XXXII (half-tit., tit., pref. and index to 3 vols.), 268*, 269*, 316*, 317*, 420* and 421*, 3 text-figs.; (addenda to Vol. II), 2 ll. (half-tit. and tit.), pp. 232* and 233*, 1 text-fig. London.

For many years a standard work on the natural history of British birds. Prepared on the style of Bewick and Beilby's "History of British Birds," 1797-1804 (q.v.). Issued in 37 parts of three sheets each, at intervals of two months, according to a note in the preface, p. V of Vol. I. The first part was issued in July 1837 and the last in May 1843; probably Pts. 36 and 37 appeared together on the latter date with addenda to Vols. I and II constituting the last part. A second edition appeared in 1845, together with a supplement (q.v.) to the present edition, bringing it up to date; a third edition (q.v.) and second supplement (q.v.) were used in 1856; a fourth edition (q.v.) (edited by Newton and Saunders) was published in 1871-85. "An Illustrated Manual of British Birds" by Saunders, 1889 (q.v.), partakes of the nature of a condensed revision of the present work. The first edition of Yarrell was published also in demy 8vo, 8vo, and imperial 8vo.

The addenda to Vols. I and II, including full title-pages and illustrated discussions of additional species, are paged for insertion in their respective volumes but, in the copy at hand, are bound as issued, at the close of Vol. III. The preface to Vol. I is also included among the addenda and contains some additional remarks on certain species which are discussed in the first two volumes.

Yarrell, William.

1845. **Supplement | to the | history | of | British birds. | By |** William Yarrell, F.L.S. V.P.Z.S. | [*Vignette.*] | Illustrated with wood-engravings. | London: | John Van Voorst, Paternoster Row. | M.DCCC.XLV.

1 vol. royal 8vo, 2 pr. ll. (tit. and pref.), pp. 7-53, 1-4 (advt.), 14 text-figs. London.

Figures and descriptions of the species of birds obtained since the publication of the first edition of the author's "A History of British Birds," 1837-43 (q.v.), but included in the second edition, 1845. The figures of the head of the White Wagtail in summer and winter plumages, are reprinted from the first edition;

the figure of the entire bird is a remodeled copy of that of the Pied Wagtail in the same work. The preface to this supplement is dated October 1845; a publishers' advertisement at the close of the volume is dated December the same year.

Yarrell, William.

1856. A | history | of | British birds. | By | William Yarrell, V.P.L.S. F.Z.S. | [*Vignette; different in each vol.*] Illustrated by 550 wood-engravings. | In three volumes. -Vol. I [-III]. | **Third edition,** with many additions. | London: | John Van Voorst, Paternoster Row. | M.DCCC.LVI.

3 vols. post 8vo. Vol. I, pp. I-XXXV+1, 1-614, 212 text-figs. Vol. II, 2 pr. ll. (half-tit. and tit.), pp. 1-702, 197 text-figs. Vol. III, 2 pr. ll. (half-tit. and tit.), pp. 1-679, 225 text-figs. London.

A third edition of the work of the same title (q.v.), first published in 1837-43. The additions made in the present edition which are not given in the second, were embodied in a "Second Supplement" (q.v.) published the same year, 1856, which brings the second edition (and with the first supplement brings the first edition) up to the date of the third.

Yarrell, William.

1856. Second supplement | to the | history | of | British birds: | being also a | first supplement to the second edition. | By William Yarrell, V.P.L.S. F.Z.S. | [*Blazon.*] | Illustrated with 18 wood-engravings. | London: | John Van Voorst, Paternoster Row. | M.DCCC.LVI.

1 vol. royal 8vo, pp. I-X, 1-71, 18 text-figs. London.

Descriptions and figures of 18 species of birds not included in the second edition of the author's "A History of British Birds." The booklet is designed to bring the second edition up to date with the third edition (q.v.), published the same year, and with the first "Supplement," 1845 (q.v.), to bring the first edition, 1837-43 (q.v.), also up to date.

Yarrell, William. (Newton, Alfred; and Saunders, Howard.)

1871-85. A | history | of | British birds. | By | William Yarrell, V.P.L.S., F.Z.S. | [*Vignette; different in each vol.*] | **Fourth edition,** in four volumes. | Illustrated by 564 wood-engravings. | Volume I [-IV]., revised and enlarged | by | Alfred Newton, M.A., F.R.S., [*etc., 2 lines;* [Howard Saunders, F.L.S., F.Z.S., Etc. (*Vols. III and IV.*)] | London: | John Van Voorst, Paternoster Row. | MDCCCLXXI.-MDCCCLXXIV [MDCCCLXXVI-MDCCCLXXXII; MDCCCLXXXII-MDCCCLXXXIV; MDCCCLXXXIV.-MDCCCLXXXV].

4 vols. 4to (size of post 8vo). Vol. I, pp. I-XII, 1 errata slip, pp. 1-646, 186 text-figs. (some by E. Neale and J. G. Keulemans). Vol. II, pp. I-VII+1, 1-494, 127 text-figs. Vol. III, pp. I-XVI, 1 errata slip, pp. 1-684, 255 text-figs. Vol. IV, pp. I-VIII, 1 errata slip, pp. 1-531, 173 text-figs. London.

The fourth edition of Yarrell's work of 1837-43 (q.v.),—original in three volumes. The first two volumes of the present edition were edited and revised by Newton; the latter two by Saunders. Much material, including a number of new illustrations, are added and the work is thoroughly revised and rewritten. In 1889, Saunders condensed the text and published it, with some of its illustrations, under the title of "An Illustrated Manual of British Birds" (q.v.). The present edition was published in 30 parts, the dates of which are given as follows by Coues and the Zoological Record. Part **I**, pp. 1-80, June 1871; **II**, pp. 81-160, Aug. 1871; **III**, pp. 161-240, 1872; **IV**, pp. 241-320, July 1872; **V**, pp. 321-400, March 1873; **VI**, pp. 401-480, July 1873; **VII**, pp. 481-560, Febr. 1874; **VIII**, pp. 561-646 "with temporary title-page, note, errata and contents" (Coues) (End of **Vol. I.**), Nov. 1874; **IX**, pp. 1-80, Febr. 1876; **X**, pp. 81-160, Nov. 1876; **XI**, pp. 101 and 102 (to replace those in pt. X), 161-238, Sept. 1877; **XII**, pp. 239-318, Oct. 1878; **XIII**, pp. 319-398?, 1880; **XIV** (into Picidae=), pp. 320?-487?, 1881; **XV**, 479?-494 (End of **Vol II**), 1- (genus Tetrao=) 64?, 1882; **XVI-XX**, pp. 65?-456, 1883; **XXI-XXVI**, pp. 457-684 (End of **Vol. III.**), 1-240, 1884; **XXVII-XXX**, 241-531 (End of **Vol. IV.**) errata, title-pages to Vols. I-IV and pref. to Vols. III and IV (dated April 30, 1885), 1885.

Yarrow, H. C.; and Henshaw, Henry W.

1874. Engineer Department, U. S. Army. | **Geographical and Geological Explorations and surveys** | **west of the one hundredth meridian.** | First Lieut. Geo. M. Wheeler, Corps of Engineers, in charge. | **Report** | upon | **ornithological specimens** | **collected in** | **the years 1871, 1872, and 1873.** | Washington: | Government Printing Office. | 1874.

1 vol. 8vo, tit., pp. 1-148. Washington.

A series of separate papers, as follows. "Report upon and list of birds collected by the expedition for explorations west of the one hundredth meridian in 1872," by Yarrow and Henshaw, pp. 5-33; "List of birds collected by Lieut. G. M. Wheeler's expedition, 1871," by Yarrow and Henshaw, pp. 34-38; "An annotated list of the birds of Utah," by Henshaw, pp. 39-54 (reprinted from Annals Lyceum Nat. Hist. New York, 11, pp. 1-14, June 1874, with revisions); "Report upon and list of birds collected by the expedition for geographical and geological explorations and surveys west of the one hundredth meridian in 1873," by Henshaw, pp. 55-148 (in three sections).

Zetterstedt, Johan Wilhelm.

1822. Resa | genom | Sweriges och Norriges | Lappmarker, | Förrättad | Är 1821; | af | Johan Wilhelm Zetterstedt, | Professor

m. m. wid Kongl. Academ. i Lund. | Första Delen, med trenne
illuminerade Kopparstick. [Andra Delen.] | Lund, | Tryckt i Ber-
lingska Boktryckeriet, | 1822.

2 vols. in 1 crown 8vo. Vol. I, pp. I-XV+1, 1-266, pll. I-III (col.:
by B. F. Fries). Vol. II, tit., pp. 1-231. Lund.

An account of the author's travels in Lapland in 1821, with miscellaneous natural
history notes, including the descriptions of two supposed new species of birds,
Emberiza borealis and *Parus lugubris* (pp. 107 and 250), figured on the three
colored plates. A presentation copy from the author to Oken.

Zichy, Jenö. (Horváth, Géza; Madarász, Gyula.)

1901. > **Dritte Asiatische | Forschungsreise** des Grafen Eugen
Zichy. | Band II. | **Zoologische Ergebnisse** | der | dritten asia-
tischen Forschungsreise | des | Grafen Eugen Zichy. | Redigirt
von | Dr. G. Horváth | Ord. Mitglied der Ungarischen Akademie
[*etc., 2 lines.*]. | Mit 28 Tafeln und 22 Textfiguren. | Budapest
1901 Leipzig | Victor Hornyánszky Karl W. Hiersemann. [*Title
also in Hungarian.*]

1 vol. royal 4to, pp. I-XLI+1, 1-470, 1 l. (index and errata), pll. I-
XXVIII (6 col.; 1 ornithological, by Madarász). Budapest and
Leipzig.

The zoological volume of Zichy's report on his expedition from Budapest through
Russia, Siberia and China to Korea in 1898. The volume is edited by Horváth
and the ornithological portion, pp. 21-39, written by Madarász who has given
the first published figure of *Ardeola bacchus* (Bonap.) on Pl. V. No new species
are described except a young, unidentified *Saxicola*.

Zorn, Baron von.

1817. See Frisch, Johann Leonhard, **Vorstellung der Vögel Deutschlands.**

LIST OF PERIODICALS

An asterisk denotes a complete set.

*Abstract of the Proceedings of the Delaware Valley Ornithological Club of Philadelphia. Philadelphia. Nos. 1-4; 1890-1900. Continued as Cassinia (q.v.).

*Alpina. (C. U. Salis and J. R. Steinmüller.) Winterthur. Vols. 1-4; 1806-1809. Continued as Neue Alpina (q.v.).

*Anzeiger der Ornithologischen Gesellschaft in Bayern. Munich. Vols. 1-9; 1919-1925.

*American Ornithology. (Chester A. Reed and Charles K. Reed.) Worcester, Mass. Vols. 1-6; 1901-1906.

Aquila. A Magyar Ornithologiai Központ Folyóirata. Budapest. Vols. 7-19 and 28; 1900-1912 and 1921.

*Ardea. Tijdschrift der Nederlandsche Ornithologische Verseeniging. Leyden. Vols. 1-14; 1912-1925.

Audubon Bulletin, The. (Illinois Audubon Society.) Chicago. Spring 1916, Winter 1916-17, Spring 1917, Winter 1917-18, Spring and Summer 1918, Fall 1920, Spring 1921, Spring 1922, Fall 1922, Spring 1923, Fall 1923, Spring and Summer 1924, Summer 1925.

*Auk, The. (American Ornithologists' Union.) *Variously,*—Boston, New York, Cambridge and Lancaster. Vols. 1-43; 1884-1926. A continuation of the Bulletin of the Nuttall Ornithological Club (q.v.).
An index to Vols. 1-17 (1884-1900) and to the Bull. Nuttall Ornith. Club. 1907.
A ten year index, to Vols. 17-26 (1901-1910). 1915.

*Austral Avian Record, The. (Gregory M. Mathews.) London. Vols. 1-5; 1912-1926.

*Avicultural Magazine, The; being the Journal of The Agricultural Society for the Study of Foreign and British Birds. *Variously,*—Brighton and London. Vols. 1-8; New Series, Vols. 1-7; 3rd Series, Vols. 1-13; 4th Series, Vols. 1-3; 1895-1925.

Berajah, Zoographia infinita. (O. Kleinschmidt.) *Variously,*—Halle and Leipzig. 14 pts. (unnun.) 1905-1923.

*Bird Lore. Official Organ of the Audubon Societies. *Variously,*—Englewood, N. J.; Harrisburg, Pa.; and New York. Vols. 1-28; 1899-1926.

*Birds.
Birds and All Nature. } (A. W. Mumford.) Chicago. Vols. 1-17 (pt.);
Birds and Nature. } 1896-1905.

*British Birds. London. Vols. 1-19; 1907-1926.
Index, Vols. I-XII.

*Bulletin of the British Ornithologists' Club. London. Vols. 1-46; 1893-1926.

*Bulletin of the Cooper Ornithological Club of California. Santa Clara. Vol. I; 1899. Continued as The Condor (q.v.). In a measure supersedes The Nidiologist (q.v.).

Bulletin of the Michigan Ornithological Club. Grand Rapids. Vols. 1-5; 1897-1904.

*Bulletin of the Nuttall Ornithological Club. Cambridge, Mass. Vols. 1-8; 1876-1883. Virtually continued by The Auk (q.v.).
Index to Vols. 1-8 included with index to The Auk, Vols. 1-17.

*Bulletin de la Société Ornithologique Suisse. Geneva and Paris. Vols. 1-2; 1865-1870.

Bull. No.-(1-19); The Wilson Ornithological Chapter of the Agassiz Association. Oberlin, Ohio. Nos. 5-19 (12-19=Vols. 9-10 pt.= New Ser. Vols. 1-5, No. 2); 1895-1898. Thereafter continued as The Wilson Bulletin (q.v.).

*Bulletin Zoologique. (F. E. Guérin-Méneville.) Paris. 1 vol. 1835. Intended as continuation of Férussac's Bulletin des Sciences Naturelles.

*Cassinia. (Delaware Valley Ornithological Club.) Philadelphia. Nos. 5-24; 1901-1921. Nos. 1-4 issued as Abstract of the Proceedings of the Del. Val. Ornith. Club (q.v.).

Comptes Rendus hebdomadaires des séances de l'Académie des Sciences. Paris. Vols. 37-44; July-Dec. 1853- Jan.-June 1857.

*Condor, The. (Cooper Ornithological Club.) *Variously,*—Santa Clara, Hollywood and Berkeley. Vols. 2-27; 1900-1925. Vol. 1 issued as Bulletin of the Cooper Ornith. Club (q.v.).
Index, Vols. 1-10 (1899-1908) issued as Pacific Coast Avifauna, No. 6, 1909.
Index, Vols. 11-20 (1909-1918) issued as Pacific Coast Avifauna, No. 13, 1919.

*Contributions to Ornithology. (Sir William Jardine.) London. 1848-1852.

*Dansk Ornithologisk Forenings Tidsskrift. Copenhagen. Vols. 1-18; 1906-1925.

Emu, The. The official Organ of the Australasian (Royal Australasian; Vols. 10-date) Ornithologists' Union. Melbourne. Vol. 2; 3, Pts. 2 and 3; 4-25; 1902-1926.

*Falco. Unregelmässig im Anschluss an das Werk Berajah erscheinende Zeitschrift. (O. Kleinschmidt.) *Variously,*—Halle and Leipzig. 1905-1921; 1922, Pts. 1 and 2 and Sonderheft 4; 1923, Pts. 1-3 and Sonderheft; 1924, Pt. 1; 1925, Pt. 1.

*Hornero, El. Revista de la Sociedad Ornithologica del Plata. Buenos Aires. Vols. 1-3; 1917-1924.

Ibis, The. (British Ornithologists' Union.) London. Vols. 1-6; Ser. 2, Vols. 2-6; Ser. 3-11, Vols. 1-6, each; Ser. 12, Vol. 1 and Vol. 2, Pt. 1; Jubilee Supplement, 1909; Jubilee Supplement 2, 1915; 1859-1864 and 1866-1926.
Index to the genera and species and to the plates, 1859-76; 77-94; 95-1912 (3 vols.).
General index to Series 1-11, separate or in last vol. of each series.

*Jahresbericht des Ornithologischen Vereins München. Munich. 1897-1902 (publ. 1899-1903). Continued as Verhandlungen der Ornithologischen Gesellschaft in Bayern (q.v.).

*Journal für Ornithologie. (J. Cabanis; continued from 1893 to 1922 by Ant. Reichenow, and from Vol. 70, 1922 by E. Stresemann.) (Organ of Deutsche Ornithologische Gesellschaft.) Berlin. Vols. 1-73; 1853-1925.

Journal of the South African Ornithologists' Union, The. Pretoria. Vols. 1-9; 1905-1913.

*Magasin de Zoologie. (F. E. Guérin-Méneville). Paris. Vols. 1-8; Ser. 2, Vols. 1-7; 1831-1845. Merged with the Revue Zoologique to form the Revue et Magasin de Zoologie (q.v.).

*Mittheilungen des Ornithologischen Vereines in Wien. Vienna. Vols. 1-12; 1877-1888. Continued as Die Schwalbe (q.v.).
Section für Geflügelzucht und Brieftaubenwesen, Nos. 1-2; 1884-1885.

*Naturforscher, Der. (Johann Jacob Gebauer.) Halle. Vols. 1-30; 1774-1804.

*Naumannia. (Edward Baldamus.) (Organ of Deutsche Ornithologische Gesellschaft.) *Variously,*—Stuttgart, Dessau and Leipzig. Vols. 1-8; 1851-1858.

Neue Mannigfaltigkeiten. Berlin. Vol. 4; 1781.

*Neue Alpina. (J. R. Steinmüller.) Winterthur. Vols. 1-2; 1821-1827. Continuation of Alpina (q.v.).

Nidiologist, The. Alameda, Calif. Vols. 1-4; 1893-1897. Official Organ of the Cooper Ornithological Club from Vol. 2, No. 12 onward; continued as the Bull. of the Cooper Ornith. Club (q.v.).

*Nunquam otiosus. Zoologische Mittheilungen. (L. W. Schaufuss.) Dresden. Vols. 1-3; 1870-1882. (For dates see Vol. 1, preliminary leaf; Vol. 2, pp. 241, 280, 320, 260, 400, 440; Vol. 3, pp. XXXII, XXXVIII, 510, 528, 544, 560.

Oologist, The. *Variously,*—Gaines, N. Y.; Albion, N. Y. Vol. 1, No. 6; Vol. 3, No. 1; Vol. 5, Nos. 2-4, 7-9, 12; Vol. 6, No. 1; Vol. 7, No. 10; Vol. 8, Nos. 6-11; Vol. 9, Nos. 1-5, 7, 8, 10, 11; Vol. 9, No. 1 (duplicated numbers dated Jan. 1897; orig. Jan. 1892); Vol. 10, Nos. 1-3, 5, 6, 9, 10, 12; Vol. 11, Nos. 2-4, 6-11; Vol. 12, Nos. 1-12; Vol. 13, Nos. 1, 2, 4, 5; Vol. 14, Nos. 3, 5-8; Vol. 26, No. 7; 1884-1909.

Ornis

oder

das Neueste und Wichtigste
der Vögelkunde

in Verbindung mit mehreren Naturforschern

herausgegeben

von

Chr. L. Brehm,
Pfarrer zu Renthendorf.

I. Heft.

64239

Jena,
Auguſt Schmid.
1824.

TITLE-PAGE OF ONE OF THE EARLIEST ORNITHOLOGICAL PERIODICALS.
See p. 705.

*Ornis oder das Neueste und Wichtigste der Vögelkunde. (Chr. Ludwig Brehm.) Jena. Vols. 1-3; 1824-1827. (See Pl. XI)

*Ornis. Organ des permanenten internationalen ornithologischen Comite's. *Variously*,—Vienna, Braunschweig and London. Vols. 1-13; 1885-1910.

*Ornithologische Centralblatt. Leipzig. Vols. 1-6; 1876-1881.

*Ornithologische Jahrbuch. Hallein. Vols. 2-29; 1891-1919.

*Ornithologische Monatsberichte. (A. Reichenow; continued from and including Vol. 31, 1922 by E. Stresemann.) Berlin. Vols. 1-33; 1893-1925.

Ornithologische Monatschrift des Deutschen Vereins zum Schutze der Vogelwelt. Merseburg, Gera, Leipzig and Halle. Vol. 18; 1893.

Ornithologist and Oologist. *Variously*,—Pawtucket, R. I.; Rockville, Conn.; Norwich, Conn.; Boston, Mass.; Hyde Park, Mass. Vols. 6-10; 17, Nos. 9-12; 18, Nos. 1, 2, 6-10; 1881-1885, 1892 and 1893.

*Osprey, The. Galesburg, Ill. Vols. 1-5; New Series, Vol. 1, Nos. 1-6; 1896-1902.

*Pacific Coast Avifauna (Cooper Ornithological Club of California.) *Variously*,—Santa Clara, Hollywood and Berkeley. Nos. 1-17; 1900-1925.

*Revue Française d'Ornithologie. Paris. Vols. 1-9; 1910-1925.

*Revue et Magasin de Zoologie. (F. E. Guérin-Méneville.) Paris. "2e Série" Vols. 1-23; "3e Série." Vols. 1-7; 1849-1879. The first series appeared under the title of "Revue Zoologique" (q.v.), which was combined with the Magasin de Zoologie to form the present periodical.

Revue Zoologique, par la Société Cuvierienne. Paris. 1838-1879 (number for Dec. 1869 missing).

*Rhea. (F. A. L. Thienemann.) Leipzig. Vols. 1-2; 1846-1849.

Rivista Italiana di Ornitologia. Bologna. Vols. 1-3; 1912-1914.

*Schwalbe, Die; Mittheilungen des Ornithologisches Vereines in Wien. Vienna. Vols. 13-21; 1889-1897. Vols. 1-12 issued, simply, as "Mittheilungen," etc. (q.v.).

Schwalbe, Die. Berichte des Comités für ornithologische Beobachtungs-stationen in Österreich. (Ornithologische Section der K. K. Zoologisch-botanischen Gesellschaft in Wien.) Vienna. Neue Folge 1 and 2 (3, 1913, missing); 1898-1901.

*South Australian Ornithologist, The. (South Australian Ornithological Association.) Adelaide. Vols. 1-8; 1914-1925.

*Stray Feathers. (A. O. Hume.) Calcutta. Vols. 1-11; 1873-1899. Index to Vols. 1-11 = Vol. 12; 1899.

"Tori," The Aves (now simply, Tori): Bulletin of the Ornithological Society of Japan. Tokyo. Nos. 10 (of Vol. 2)-18 (of Vol. 4) and No. 20 (of Vol. 4); 1920-1925.

Transactions of the Zoological Society of London. London. Vols. 1-21, Pt. 1; 1835-1916.

Verhandlungen der Ornithologischen Gesellschaft in Bayern. Munich. Vols. 4-16; 1904-1925. Continued from the Jahresbericht des Ornithologischen Vereins München (q.v.).

Warbler, The. (John Lewis Childs.) Floral Park, N. Y. Second Ser., Vols. 1 and 2; 1905-1906.

*****Wilson Bulletin, The.** (Wilson Ornithological Chapter of the Agassiz Association; later the Wilson Ornithological Club.) Vol. 10 (pt.) =New Ser. Vol. 5, No. 3—Vol. 37=New Ser., Vol. 32; 1898-1925. Continued from the Bulletin No. (1-19) of the Wilson Ornithological Chapter of the Agassiz Association (q.v.).

*****Zeitschrift für die Gesammte Ornithologie.** (Julius von Madarász.) Budapest. Vols. 1-4; 1884-1887.

DICTIONARIES

Drapiez. Dictionnaire Classique des Sciences Naturelles. Brussels. Vols. 1-10 and Atlas; 1837-1845. (19 col. pll. of birds.)

D'Orbigny. Dictionnaire Universel d'Histoire Naturelle. Paris. Vols. 1-12 and Atlas, Vols. 1-3; 1849. 54 pll. of birds; 53 col.

Levrault. Dictionnaire des Sciences Naturelles. Vols. 1-61, 12 vols. Atlas; 1816-1845. 156 pll. of birds; 37 col. Col. pll. duplicated in black and white; not included in total. Birds by Dumont de Sainte-Croix.

NOTE.—In the works catalogued in the foregoing pages, exclusive of the periodicals and the general dictionaries of natural history which are listed separately, there are, approximately, 50,995 plates of birds (39,888 in colors and 11,107 plain), 39,347 text-figures of ornithological subjects (987 in colors and 38,360 plain), and 1,981 plates of birds' eggs (1,914 in colors and 67 plain).

NATURAL SCIENCES IN AMERICA

An Arno Press Collection

Allen, J[oel] A[saph]. **The American Bisons,** Living and Extinct. 1876

Allen, Joel Asaph. **History of the North American Pinnipeds:** A Monograph of the Walruses, Sea-Lions, Sea-Bears and Seals of North America. 1880

American Natural History Studies: The Bairdian Period. 1974

American Ornithological Bibliography. 1974

Anker, Jean. **Bird Books and Bird Art.** 1938

Audubon, John James and John Bachman. **The Quadrupeds of North America.** Three vols. 1854

Baird, Spencer F[ullerton]. **Mammals of North America.** 1859

Baird, S[pencer] F[ullerton], T[homas] M. Brewer and R[obert] Ridgway. **A History of North American Birds:** Land Birds. Three vols., 1874

Baird, Spencer F[ullerton], John Cassin and George N. Lawrence. **The Birds of North America.** 1860. Two vols. in one.

Baird, S[pencer] F[ullerton], T[homas] M. Brewer, and R[obert] Ridgway. **The Water Birds of North America.** 1884. Two vols. in one.

Barton, Benjamin Smith. **Notes on the Animals of North America.** Edited, with an Introduction by Keir B. Sterling. 1792

Bendire, Charles [Emil]. **Life Histories of North American Birds** With Special Reference to Their Breeding Habits and Eggs. 1892/1895. Two vols. in one.

Bonaparte, Charles Lucian [Jules Laurent]. **American Ornithology:** Or The Natural History of Birds Inhabiting the United States, Not Given by Wilson. 1825/1828/1833. Four vols. in one.

Cameron, Jenks. **The Bureau of Biological Survey:** Its History, Activities, and Organization. 1929

Caton, John Dean. **The Antelope and Deer of America:** A Comprehensive Scientific Treatise Upon the Natural History, Including the Characteristics, Habits, Affinities, and Capacity for Domestication of the Antilocapra and Cervidae of North America. 1877

Contributions to American Systematics. 1974

Contributions to the Bibliographical Literature of American Mammals. 1974

Contributions to the History of American Natural History. 1974

Contributions to the History of American Ornithology. 1974

Cooper, J[ames] G[raham]. **Ornithology.** Volume I, Land Birds. 1870

Cope, E[dward] D[rinker]. **The Origin of the Fittest:** Essays on Evolution and **The Primary Factors of Organic Evolution.** 1887/1896. Two vols. in one.

Coues, Elliott. **Birds of the Colorado Valley.** 1878

Coues, Elliott. **Birds of the Northwest.** 1874

Coues, Elliott. **Key To North American Birds.** Two vols. 1903

Early Nineteenth-Century Studies and Surveys. 1974

Emmons, Ebenezer. **American Geology:** Containing a Statement of the Principles of the Science. 1855. Two vols. in one.

Fauna Americana. 1825-1826

Fisher, A[lbert] K[enrick]. **The Hawks and Owls of the United States in Their Relation to Agriculture.** 1893

Godman, John D. **American Natural History:** Part I — Mastology and **Rambles of a Naturalist.** 1826-28/1833. Three vols. in one.

Gregory, William King. **Evolution Emerging:** A Survey of Changing Patterns from Primeval Life to Man. Two vols. 1951

Hay, Oliver Perry. **Bibliography and Catalogue of the Fossil Vertebrata of North America.** 1902

Heilprin, Angelo. **The Geographical and Geological Distribution of Animals.** 1887

Hitchcock, Edward. **A Report on the Sandstone of the Connecticut Valley,** Especially Its Fossil Footmarks. 1858

Hubbs, Carl L., editor. **Zoogeography.** 1958

[Kessel, Edward L., editor]. **A Century of Progress in the Natural Sciences: 1853-1953.** 1955

Leidy, Joseph. **The Extinct Mammalian Fauna of Dakota and Nebraska,** Including an Account of Some Allied Forms from Other Localities, Together with a Synopsis of the Mammalian Remains of North America. 1869

Lyon, Marcus Ward, Jr. **Mammals of Indiana.** 1936

Matthew, W[illiam] D[iller]. **Climate and Evolution.** 1915

Mayr, Ernst, editor. **The Species Problem.** 1957

Mearns, Edgar Alexander. **Mammals of the Mexican Boundary of the United States.** Part I: Families Didelphiidae to Muridae. 1907

Merriam, Clinton Hart. **The Mammals of the Adirondack Region,** Northeastern New York. 1884

Nuttall, Thomas. **A Manual of the Ornithology of the United States and of Canada.** Two vols. 1832-1834

Nuttall Ornithological Club. **Bulletin of the Nuttall Ornithological Club:** A Quarterly Journal of Ornithology. 1876-1883. Eight vols. in three.

[Pennant, Thomas]. **Arctic Zoology.** 1784-1787. Two vols. in one.

Richardson, John. **Fauna Boreali-Americana;** Or the Zoology of the Northern Parts of British America, Containing Descriptions of the Objects of Natural History Collected on the Late Northern Land Expeditions Under Command of Captain Sir John Franklin, R. N. Part I: Quadrupeds. 1829

Richardson, John and William Swainson. **Fauna Boreali-Americana:** Or the Zoology of the Northern Parts of British America, Containing Descriptions of the Objects of Natural History Collected by the Late Northern Land Expeditions Under Command of Captain Sir John Franklin, R. N. Part II: The Birds. 1831

Ridgway, Robert. **Ornithology.** 1877

Selected Works By Eighteenth-Century Naturalists and Travellers. 1974

Selected Works in Nineteenth-Century North American Paleontology. 1974

Selected Works of Clinton Hart Merriam. 1974

Selected Works of Joel Asaph Allen. 1974

Selections From the Literature of American Biogeography. 1974

Seton, Ernest Thompson. **Life-Histories of Northern Animals: An Account of the Mammals of Manitoba.** Two vols. 1909

Sterling, Keir Brooks. **Last of the Naturalists:** The Career of C. Hart Merriam. 1974

Vieillot, L. P. **Histoire Naturelle Des Oiseaux de L'Amerique Septentrionale,** Contenant Un Grand Nombre D'Especes Decrites ou Figurees Pour La Premiere Fois. 1807. Two vols. in one.

Wilson, Scott B., assisted by A. H. Evans. **Aves Hawaiienses:** The Birds of the Sandwich Islands. 1890-99

Wood, Casey A., editor. **An Introduction to the Literature of Vertebrate Zoology.** 1931

Zimmer, John Todd. **Catalogue of the Edward E. Ayer Ornithological Library.** 1926